THE HISTORY OF THE DECLINE
AND FALL OF THE ROMAN EMPIRE

EDWARD GIBBON was born in 1737, in Putney, and was the only child of his parents to survive infancy. Although his education was frequently interrupted by ill health, his knowledge was far-reaching. His brief career as an undergraduate at Magdalen College, Oxford, ended when he joined the Catholic Church. His father sent him to Lausanne, in Switzerland, where, while studying Greek and French for the next five years, he rejoined the Protestant Church. In 1761 he published his *Essai sur l'étude de la littérature*; the English version appeared in 1764. Meanwhile, Gibbon served as a captain in the Hampshire Militia until 1763, when he returned to the Continent. It was while he was in Rome in 1764 that he first conceived the work that was eventually to become *The History of the Decline and Fall of the Roman Empire*. After the death of his father, Gibbon settled in London and in 1774 was elected to Parliament, where he sat for the next eight years, although he never once spoke in the Commons. He also took his place among the literary circles of London. The first volume of his famous *History* was published in 1776; it was highly praised for its learning and style but incurred some censure for its treatment of the early Christians. The second and third volumes appeared in 1781 and the final three, which were written in Lausanne, in 1788. He died while on a visit to his friend Lord Sheffield, who posthumously edited Gibbon's autobiographical papers and published them in 1796.

DAVID WOMERSLEY is a Fellow and Tutor in English Literature at Jesus College, Oxford. His book *The Transformation of The Decline and Fall of the Roman Empire* was published by Cambridge University Press in 1988. He has also edited *Augustan Critical Writing*, a three-volume complete edition of Gibbon's *The History of the Decline and Fall of the Roman Empire* and Edmund Burke's *A Philosophical Enquiry into the Sublime and Beautiful and Other Pre-Revolutionary Writings*, all for Penguin Classics.

EDWARD GIBBON

THE HISTORY OF
THE DECLINE AND FALL
OF THE ROMAN EMPIRE

Abridged Edition

Edited and abridged by
DAVID WOMERSLEY

PENGUIN BOOKS

PENGUIN BOOKS

Published by the Penguin Group
Penguin Books Ltd, 80 Strand, London WC2R 0RL, England
Penguin Putnam Inc., 375 Hudson Street, New York, New York 10014, USA
Penguin Books Australia Ltd, Ringwood, Victoria, Australia
Penguin Books Canada Ltd, 10 Alcorn Avenue, Toronto, Ontario, Canada M4V 3B2
Penguin Books India (P) Ltd, 11 Community Centre, Panchsheel Park, New Delhi – 110 017, India
Penguin Books (NZ) Ltd, Cnr Rosedale and Airborne Roads, Albany, Auckland, New Zealand
Penguin Books (South Africa) (Pty) Ltd, 24 Sturdee Avenue, Rosebank 2196 South Africa

Penguin Books Ltd, Registered Offices: 80 Strand, London WC2R 0RL, England

www.penguin.com

Volumes 1–6 of the full edition first published 1776, 1781 and 1788
This abridged edition published 2000

5

Editorial matter copyright © David Womersley, 2000
All rights reserved

The moral rights of the editor has been asserted

Set in 9.5/12 pt PostScript Monotype Bembo
Typeset by Rowland Phototypesetting Ltd, Bury St Edmunds, Suffolk
Printed in England by Clays Ltd, St Ives plc

CONTENTS

THE HISTORY OF
THE DECLINE AND FALL
OF THE ROMAN EMPIRE

CONTENTS

ABBREVIATIONS

The following abbreviations are used in the references given in the Introduction:

A	J. Murray (ed.), *The Autobiographies of Edward Gibbon* (1896)
ADF	*The History of the Decline and Fall of the Roman Empire*, abridged edition (references are to the pages of the present edition)
DF	*The History of the Decline and Fall of the Roman Empire*, ed. David Womersley, 3 vols (Harmondsworth, 1994)
Journal	D. M. Low (ed.), *Gibbon's Journal to January 28th. 1763* (London, 1929)
L	J. E. Norton (ed.), *The Letters of Edward Gibbon*, 3 vols (London, 1956)
MW	Lord Sheffield (ed.), *The Miscellaneous Works of Edward Gibbon, Eyes,*, 5 vols (1814)
Norton	J. E. Norton, *A Bibliography of the Works of Edward Gibbon* (Oxford, 1940; repr. 1970)
Prothero	R. E. Prothero (ed.), *The Private Letters of Edward Gibbon*, 2 vols (1896)

INTRODUCTION

At the end of his life, Gibbon gratefully acknowledged that *The Decline and Fall* had given him 'a name, a rank, a character, in the world, to which [he] should not otherwise have been entitled' (*A*, p. 346). But at the outset of his literary career, those priorities were necessarily reversed: the book received its character from its author. How did the circumstances of Gibbon's upbringing and early manhood influence his historical vision?

Gibbon's Early Life and Upbringing

Gibbon's great-grandfather had been a linendraper, and his grandfather, the first Edward Gibbon, was a successful man of business. Happily his 'opinions were subordinate to his interest' and accordingly, notwithstanding his Jacobite inclinations, as an army contractor the Continental campaigns of William III had made him a wealthy man (*A*, p. 10). In 1716 he had become a director of the South Sea Company, and inevitably 'his fortune was overwhelmed in the shipwreck of the year twenty, and the labours of thirty years were blasted in a single day' (*A*, p. 11). A fortune of over £100,000 was reduced to £10,000. Yet he was unconquered by adversity: he rebuilt his fortune, and at his death in 1736 he was once more a man of substance.

In 1707 had been born his only son, Edward Gibbon, the father of the historian. Edward Gibbon senior attended Westminster School and Emmanuel College, Cambridge, entering the House of Commons in 1734 as Member for Petersfield, in which neighbourhood the Gibbons owned a considerable estate. On 3 June 1736 he had married Judith, daughter of James Porten, a neighbour of the Gibbons in Putney, and it was from this union ('a marriage of inclination and esteem' – *A*, p. 19) that Edward Gibbon the historian was born on 27 April 1737 OS, some five months after the death of his grandfather. There were six further children, none of whom lived for more than a year, and Mrs Gibbon herself died on 26

December 1747. Gibbon had been largely neglected by his mother, and his father – cast into depression by the death of his wife – was beginning to advance down the path of undramatic yet unremitting dissipation (entertainment, gambling, neglect of business) which was to erode the family wealth and prevent Gibbon's circumstances from ever being truly easy. The sickly child was cared for by his aunt, Catherine Porten, who instilled in him that love of reading which on her death in 1786 Gibbon cited as 'still the pleasure and glory of my life' (*L*, iii. 46). His early education was entrusted initially to a private tutor, the clergyman, minor author and grammarian John Kirkby, and then to the grammar school at Kingston-upon-Thames. In January 1748 he entered Westminster. The shock of arrival at this school, which Gibbon later recalled as 'a cavern of fear and sorrow', was mitigated by the fact that his aunt Porten undertook at the same time to run a boarding-house for the school, and it was with her that Gibbon lodged during his two years at Westminster (*A*, p. 60). In 1750, however, a mysterious nervous illness obliged him to leave off formal schooling and take the waters in Bath. During the next two years the uncertain state of his health inhibited any regular schemes of education. Gibbon's constitution suddenly recovered at the end of 1751, but his father then made two serious errors of judgement which were full of implications for the future life of his son. In the first place, and on the recommendation of his close friends David and Lucy Mallet, he decided to entrust Gibbon's education to the feckless and neglectful Reverend Philip Francis. It was clear within two months that the experiment had been a failure, and in response to this disappointment Edward Gibbon senior thereupon embraced 'a singular and desperate measure' (*A*, p. 56) and made his second great mistake. He resolved to send his son without further ado to Oxford.

Edward Gibbon senior had arranged for his son to proceed to Magdalen College, Oxford, as a Gentleman Commoner, and in April 1752 Gibbon arrived in Oxford 'with a stock of erudition that might have puzzled a Doctor, and a degree of ignorance of which a schoolboy would have been ashamed' (*A*, p. 394). In his *Memoirs* Gibbon drew a damning picture of Oxford, as a university sunk in port and prejudice, and almost completely indifferent to its educational mission. It is a picture which seems now to have been overdrawn. But that the university failed him, there can be no doubt. His first tutor, Dr Waldegrave, was a learned and pious man who seems to have taken his duties seriously, but who was out of his depth when it came to directing the studies of this unusual student. When

Waldegrave departed for a college living in Sussex, Gibbon was transferred 'with the rest of his live stock' to Dr Winchester, who, according to Gibbon, 'well remembered that he had a salary to receive, and only forgot that he had a duty to perform' (*A*, p. 81). Deprived of any regular course of instruction, Gibbon soon fell into habits of indolence and absenteeism, interspersed with bouts of intense but miscellaneous reading – what at the end of his life he was to call the 'blind activity of idleness' (*A*, p. 84).

In the vacancy left by study, Gibbon pursued a course of reading which insensibly disposed him to Roman Catholicism. Accordingly, on 8 June 1753, Gibbon 'abjured the errors of heresy' (*A*, p. 88) and was received into the Romish faith by Baker, one of the chaplains of the Sardinian ambassador. If the 'humanity of the age' (*A*, p. 88) was averse to persecution, there were still in 1753 numerous penal statutes in force against Roman Catholics, and the affair made sufficient stir for Lewis, a Roman Catholic bookseller of Covent Garden who had acted as go-between, to be summoned before the Privy Council and questioned. The crisis elicited from Gibbon's father a characteristic response of contradictory extremity. His first thought was that scepticism was the best antidote to credulity, and so Gibbon was sent to David Mallet, by 'whose philosophy [he] was rather scandalized than reclaimed' (*A*, p. 130). He next sought the advice of his relative Edward Eliot, who recommended a period of residence in Switzerland. Accordingly Gibbon was entrusted to the care of M. Daniel Pavilliard, a Calvinist minister of Lausanne.

Gibbon's first period of residence in Lausanne (1753–8) was one of remarkable development on several fronts. In his *Memoirs* he fully recognized the significance of this episode in his life: 'Whatsoever have been the fruits of my education, they must be ascribed to the fortunate shipwreck which cast me on the shores of the Leman lake' (*A*, p. 239). If it was indeed at Lausanne that, as he was to put it in another draft, 'the statue was discovered in the block of marble' then substantial credit for releasing Gibbon's true identity must rest with Pavilliard, whom his charge would later praise as 'the first father of my mind' (*A*, pp. 152 and 297). His wisdom, tact and kindness were evident immediately in the steps he took to humanize the severe régime which Edward Gibbon senior wished to impose on the son who had displeased him. The first priority was the need to rectify Gibbon's religious opinions. Here Pavilliard found that he was engaged in an intellectual war of attrition, having to despatch each separate perceived error individually. It was only when Gibbon chanced upon what he took to be a decisive argument against transubstantiation that 'the various articles of the Romish creed disappeared like a dream' (A, p. 137). On Christmas Day, 1754, he took communion, returned to Protestantism, and 'suspended [his] Religious enquiries': a form of words compatible with many different shades of both belief and unbelief (A, p. 137).

This indiscretion now behind him, under Pavilliard's guidance Gibbon began a programme of serious and methodical reading in classical and modern literature. In the first place, he began to repair the shortcomings in his reading facility in Latin. Thereafter, he studied mathematics, and the logic of De Crousaz. Although he left off these subjects before his mind was 'hardened by the habit of rigid demonstration, so destructive of the finer feelings of moral evidence', they nevertheless must have reinforced the ability for analysis which gradually began to assert itself in the notes Gibbon kept of his reading (A, p. 142). Gibbon followed the advice of Locke, and 'digested' his reading into a 'large Commonplace-book', although this was a practice concerning which he later had misgivings, agreeing with Johnson that 'what is twice read is commonly better remembered than what is transcribed' (A, pp. 143–4). It was at this time, too, when the possibilities of the life of the mind were becoming vivid to him, and when he may have first suspected the extent of his own abilities, that Gibbon first encountered some of the writers who would most influence his mature work: Pascal, de la Bléterie and Giannone. In due course he became sufficiently emboldened to enter into correspondence on points of classical philology with established scholars such as Crévier, Breitinger and Gesner.

In the autumn of 1755 Gibbon's father gave permission for his son, accompanied by Pavilliard, to undertake a tour of Switzerland. The purpose of the tour was not to imbibe 'the sublime beauties of Nature', but rather to view at first hand the different constitutions of the various cantons, to visit the most substantial towns and cities, and to make the acquaintance of the most eminent persons (A, p. 144). In what may be a foretaste of his mature historical interests, he recalls being particularly struck by the Abbey of Einsidlen, a palace 'erected by the potent magic of Religion' (A, p. 145).

Early in his residence at Lausanne, Gibbon had begun the first of the two important friendships of his life. Georges Deyverdun, a young Swiss of good family but only moderate abilities, became the companion of his studies. Later, in 1757, Gibbon met Suzanne Curchod (who was subsequently to become Mme Necker, and the mother of Mme de Staël):

here he formed a romantic, but ultimately fruitless, attachment which was to founder on the rocks of implacable paternal opposition. Two further connections Gibbon made while at Lausanne throw suggestive light over his intellectual, rather than emotional, life. He became the friend of a local Protestant minister, François-Louis Allamand, with whom he debated Locke's metaphysics: by engaging with Allamand's dissimulated scepticism, Gibbon 'acquired some dexterity in the use of . . . philosophic weapons' (*A*, p. 147). Secondly, when Voltaire took up residence in Lausanne, Gibbon (who was now moving in polite Vaudois society) was occasionally invited to the theatrical performances he gave and the supper parties which followed them. Gibbon later said that as a young man he had 'rated [Voltaire] above his real magnitude' (*A*, p. 148). Certainly in the later volumes of *The Decline and Fall* he permits himself some sharp asides at Voltaire's expense. Nevertheless, the Frenchman's influence is palpable in the first volume of the history, and it is not difficult to imagine the young Englishman being inspired not by Voltaire's scandalous philosophy, to be sure, but rather by the way in which Voltaire embodied literary celebrity. Perhaps uncoincidentally, it was during his last few months at Lausanne that Gibbon began to sketch the outline of and collect the materials for his own first literary work, the *Essai sur l'étude de la littérature* ('Essay on the Study of Literature').

On 8 May 1755 Edward Gibbon senior had married Dorothea Patton, introducing her to his son by letter as the 'Lady that saved your life at Westminster by recommending Dr Ward when you was given over by the regular Physicians' (Prothero, i. 9). Gibbon approached his stepmother with understandable, although happily unnecessary, apprehension. He would soon be able to entrust his journal with the sentiment that 'I love her as a companion, a friend and a mother' (*Journal*, p. 72). On Gibbon's return to England, his father, whose financial difficulties had become pressing, persuaded him to permit the cancelling of the entail on the family estate, so that much-needed money might be raised by a mortgage on the property. In return, Gibbon was to receive an annuity of £300. He thus achieved a measure of independence, but was still in fact very much under his father's control. When Gibbon informed his father that while in Lausanne he had fallen in love with the pretty, but penniless, Suzanne Curchod, his father's opposition to the match was unyielding. This intransigence placed Gibbon in a dilemma between marriage and scholarship, since his annuity was insufficient for him to study and be a husband. In his *Memoirs* Gibbon recorded his capitulation to his father's insistence in a phrase which has done him lasting harm amongst the sentimental: 'I sighed as a lover, I obeyed as a son' (*A*, p. 239).

Between 1758 and 1763 Gibbon's life was divided between the family estate at Buriton and London lodgings in New Bond Street. He frequented the cosmopolitan and philosophic *salon* of the francophile Lady Hervey, and sought relaxation in regular theatre-going. In Hampshire his life was less fashionable but more profitable. For country pursuits he had little relish, although his letters record that he occasionally went hunting and accompanied his father to the local races. It was also out of filial duty that Gibbon became involved in Hampshire politics, where his father continued to be active. But even in the midst of these distractions, he was able to pursue a literary life of sorts. The library at Buriton was acknowledged to be his 'peculiar domain'. It was a mixed collection of books, including 'much trash of the last age . . . much High Church divinity and politics', but also 'some valuable Editions of the Classics and Fathers' (*A*, p. 248). He began to reacquaint himself with 'the purity, the grace, the idiom, of the English style' by studying Swift and Addison, and some of the qualities of his mature prose might be traced to the complementary influences of these writers (*A*, p. 251). At this stage of his life Gibbon also attended church for morning and evening service. He records that the reflections prompted by the lessons drove him to Grotius's *De Veritate Religionis Christianæ*, and thence – he implies for the first time – to a 'regular tryal of the evidence of Christianity'; a telling although silent judgement on the circumstances of his conversion to Roman Catholicism (*A*, p. 249). It was also at this time that he purchased the twenty volumes of the *Mémoires de l'Académie des Inscriptions*; a work which eventually would be of major importance for *The Decline and Fall*.

The main claim on Gibbon's time during these years, however, was the South Hampshire militia, in which he served as captain and his father as major. Their commissions were dated 12 June 1759; the regiment was embodied in May 1760; and it was disembodied on 23 December 1762. At the end of his life Gibbon was willing to credit the militia with bestowing on him a 'larger introduction into the English World'; it was, for instance, through the militia that Gibbon met John Wilkes (*A*, p. 401). Yet, despite leading him into such lively company, even at the time this 'mimic Bellona' was more resented than enjoyed (*A*, p. 299).

It was during his militia service that Gibbon published his first book, and thereby lost (as he put it) his literary maidenhead. In France *philosophes* such as d'Alembert had disparaged as minute and arid the work of the *érudits*, or scholars, especially those associated with the Académie des Inscriptions. The *Essai sur l'étude de la littérature* (1761), which Gibbon had begun in Lausanne, and which he had completed at Buriton, sought to reconcile the *érudits* and the *philosophes* by arguing that 'all the faculties of the mind may be exercised and displayed by [the] study of ancient litterature' (*A*, p. 167). The argument of the *Essai* was a temperate reproach to what Gibbon saw as the intellectual arrogance of the *philosophes*. In 1762 he began also to revolve subjects for a work of biographical or historical narrative, entertaining the possibility of writing on Raleigh, on the history of the liberty of the Swiss, and on the history of Florence under the Medicis. On closer inspection, he rejected all these possibilities; but the very fact of their being weighed was a sign of growing literary ambition. The form which that ambition was to take was determined by the next major event in Gibbon's life. 'According to the law of custom, and perhaps of reason, foreign travel completes the education of an English Gentleman' (*A*, p. 198); Gibbon's father had agreed, after some travailing, to pay for a European tour. Within seven days of the demobilization of the South Hampshire militia, Gibbon was making preparations. He left Dover on 25 January 1763, and arrived in Paris three days later.

Gibbon found Paris thronged with English tourists, but the *Essai* distinguished him to some extent amongst the crowd, and procured for him the reception of a man of letters. He was received by Mme Geoffrin, he engaged in one or two inconsequential flirtations, and mingled (albeit warily) with *philosophes* such as Helvétius and d'Holbach. In May he travelled, by way of Dijon and Besançon, to Lausanne, where he was to remain until the spring of 1764. He resumed his acquaintance with Voltaire, and it was apparently at Ferney that the final rupture with Suzanne Curchod took place. Gibbon's early months in Lausanne were marked by some mildly riotous episodes in which he and some other young Englishmen lodging in the town, too much enlivened by burgundy, created nocturnal disturbances. One of these companions was William Guise, with whom Gibbon would the following year make the tour of Italy. Later they were joined by John Baker Holroyd, afterwards Lord Sheffield. A cavalryman in the regular army, Holroyd initially teased Gibbon over his militia career, and their friendship began slowly, although it was to become the most important relationship of Gibbon's adult life. In the midst of these dissipations Gibbon began to prepare himself for what promised to be the most valuable portion of his tour: he launched himself upon a course of hard study, focusing on the geography of ancient Italy.

The extension of Gibbon's tour to Italy was imperilled at almost the last moment by his father's financial difficulties, but these were temporarily resolved. Gibbon and Guise left Lausanne on 18 April 1764, crossed the Alps, and spent the first summer in Florence. In the autumn they moved on to Rome, and (at least as Gibbon chose later to present it) the conception of his life's work: 'It was at Rome, on the fifteenth of October, 1764, as I sat musing amidst the ruins of the Capitol, while the barefooted fryars were singing Vespers in the temple of Jupiter, that the idea of writing the decline and fall of the City first started to my mind' (*A*, p. 302). From Rome they moved to Naples and Venice, which was not to Gibbon's taste: 'a fine bridge spoilt by two Rows of houses upon it, and a large square decorated with the worst Architecture I ever yet saw' (*L*, i. 193). These final months of Gibbon's tour were marred by the embarrassment of his credit being stopped. It was apparently a misunderstanding, although one symptomatic of the complicated state of the family's finances, which required Gibbon to forget the idea of prolonging his travels in the south of France. He was back in England by late June 1765, but not before he had paused for ten days in Paris to visit Suzanne Curchod, now transformed from a young Swiss woman on the verge of destitution and spinsterhood into the wife of the wealthy financier Jacques Necker.

On his return from the Continent, Gibbon resumed the pattern of life he had formed before his tour. He retained his commission in the militia, rising to the ranks of major and, in 1768, lieutenant-colonel. This involved him in only a month of drilling each year, but he gradually found this connection more irksome and less diverting, and consequently he resigned his commission in 1770. When in London he frequented clubs such as the Cocoa Tree (still in the 1760s the haunt of Tories), the excitingly named, although actually respectable, School of Vice, and the Romans, a weekly gathering of those who had made the tour of Italy. However, Gibbon's ability to enjoy London society was diminished by the worsening state of the family finances, and by the deteriorating state of his father's health. Gibbon devoted much time and energy to attempts at remedying the former, but his father, made petulant and suspicious by illness, frustrated his son's schemes for improvement. Only after Edward Gibbon senior's death could decisive action be taken.

Relief from these difficulties came in the form of friendship, study and writing. In 1765 Georges Deyverdun had come to London, and was to spend the next four summers at Buriton. In due course he obtained a post as clerk in the Northern Department of the office of the Secretary of State, and he and Gibbon began to collaborate on various literary projects. He helped Gibbon by translating for him the German sources for a projected 'History of the Swiss Republics', which Gibbon began to compose in French. Hume (who was then under-secretary in the office where Deyverdun worked) encouraged Gibbon to persevere with this history, advising him only that if he were writing for posterity English was preferable to French. But when in 1767 the work in progress was read to a London literary circle, and was coolly received, Gibbon decided to abandon it. Their next project was a literary periodical, the *Mémoires littéraires de la Grande Bretagne* (1768–9), which was designed to inform Continental readers of developments in English literature. But since it was published in London and not distributed abroad amongst its intended readership, it unsurprisingly failed to achieve its goal. Other works, if not immediately more fruitful, can nevertheless be judged more positively when viewed in the long perspective of Gibbon's literary career, either because they indicate approaches (albeit hesitant) towards the subject matter of *The Decline and Fall*, or because they display the gradual forging of the technical and stylistic resources on which the great history would rely. Gibbon later regretted the *Critical Observations on the Sixth Book of Vergil's Aeneid* (1770), his anonymous attack on Warburton's theory of Virgil as an initiate in the Eleusinian mysteries. But it shows Gibbon beginning to deploy irony for polemical purposes, and refining his understanding of the handling of historical evidence. The unpublished essay on oriental history 'Sur la monarchie des Mèdes' shows Gibbon reflecting on the principles and practice of philosophic history. Other tantalizing hints about Gibbon's scholarly projects in the later 1760s point forwards to *The Decline and Fall*. In particular there was apparently 'an ample dissertation on the miraculous darkness of the passion', which has not survived, but in which Gibbon tells us that he 'privately drew [his] conclusions from the silence of an unbelieving age' (*A*, p. 285).

The Historian of the Roman Empire

Gibbon's father died on 12 November 1770, his constitution undermined by financial anxiety. Guided by Holroyd, who was an efficient and practical man of business, the Gibbon family finances were reorganized and simplified. By the end of 1772, Buriton had been let, Mrs Gibbon had retired to Bath, and Gibbon was elegantly housed in 7 Bentinck Street, Cavendish Square. For the first time he could arrange his life entirely in accordance with his own wishes; and only now did he enjoy 'the first of earthly blessings, independence' (*A*, p. 307). The year 1774 was a notable one: during its course he became a member of Samuel Johnson's Club, 'a large and luminous constellation of British stars' (*A*, p. 307, n. 27); he was admitted as a mason; and in October he was returned as the Member of Parliament for Liskeard, thanks to the influence of his kinsman Edward Eliot. At almost the same time as he was returned to Parliament, Gibbon had been negotiating the contract for *The Decline and Fall* with the eminent firm of Strahan and Cadell. For, during the previous years, Gibbon had 'gradually advanced from the wish to the hope, from the hope to the design, from the design to the execution, of my historical work, of whose nature and limits I had yet a very inadequate notion' (*A*, p. 411). The press was set to work in June 1775, and on 17 February 1776, volume one of *The Decline and Fall* appeared at a price of one guinea, unbound.

The book sold with great rapidity. The first edition of volume one – of which, almost at the last minute, Strahan had presciently ordered the print run to be doubled from five hundred to a thousand copies – was exhausted 'in a few days' (*A*, p. 311; Norton, pp. 36–47). A second edition followed in June 1776, a third in 1777, and the fourth in 1781. Nor does Gibbon seem to have exaggerated when at the end of his life he recalled that 'my book was on every table, and almost on every toilette' (*A*, p. 311). From the chorus of praise, the admiration of Adam Ferguson, Joseph Warton and Horace Walpole must have been deeply gratifying. It was, however, David Hume's letter of congratulation which according to Gibbon 'overpaid the labour of ten years' (*A*, pp. 311–12). But its praise was laced with the warning tones of bitter experience:

When I heard of your undertaking (which was some time ago) I own that I was a little curious to see how you would extricate yourself from the subject of your two last chapters [that is, chapters xv and xvi, on the early Christian church]. I think you have observed a very prudent temperament; but it was impossible to treat the subject so as not to give grounds of suspicion against you, and you may expect that a clamour will arise. (*A*, p. 312, n. 30)

Hume, of all men, would not have claimed to be a prophet. Nevertheless, so it came to pass.

The published attacks on *The Decline and Fall* began with James Chelsum's *Remarks* (1776; second, and significantly enlarged, edition 1778), and continued with – to mention only the most significant – Richard Watson's *Apology for Christianity* (1776), Henry Davis's *Examination* (1778), Joseph Milner's *Gibbon's Account of Christianity Considered* (1781), Joseph Priestley's *History of the Corruptions of Christianity* (1782) and Joseph White's Bampton Lectures (1784); Gibbon had therefore managed to displease all stripes of religious opinion, from High Church dogmatists to dissenters. Their lines of attack resolved into two main charges: first, that Gibbon had merely restated in a fashionable form the familiar arguments levelled by infidels against Christianity since late antiquity; and second, that in order to make his opinions seem less scandalous he had manipulated the historical record, quoting selectively and even with deliberate inaccuracy. Gibbon waited until 1779 to reply to his critics in a pamphlet which was immediately recognized as a classic of literary polemic: his *Vindication of Some Passages in the Fifteenth and Sixteenth Chapters*.

In the *Vindication* Gibbon said that he had been stung to reply to his critics only when, with the publication of Henry Davis's attack on him in 1778, the ground of contention was shifted from his religious to his literary and even moral character. But he seems first to have discussed the possibility of writing a vindication with William Robertson over dinner when Davis's *Examination* was not yet published, and when he had been enraged by the publication of the second edition of Chelsum's *Remarks*. The decision to direct the *Vindication* at Davis must therefore be construed as a tactical choice. Davis had given Gibbon an opportunity to scatter his enemies by engaging them on the terrain of scholarly accuracy and fair-dealing. This was more to his liking than the boggy and equivocal ground of the irreligious tendencies of chapters xv and xvi. More attacks appeared, to which Gibbon did not deign to reply, although in volume two of *The Decline and Fall* some notes vented his irritation at attacks on his scholarly accuracy. The *Vindication* was Gibbon's only public engagement with his detractors, and in the opinion of all but the detractors themselves, his victory was complete. Horace Walpole warmed to its lethal ironies when he praised it as 'the feathered arrow of Cupid, that is more formidable than the club of Hercules' (*MW*, ii. 159).

The success of *The Decline and Fall* smoothed Gibbon's path into fresh areas of society. We find him joining new clubs, such as Almack's, and amusing himself by attending lectures in chemistry and anatomy. In May 1777 he left London to spend six months in Paris, where he found the tribute of flattery much more ample and to his taste than had been the case during his earlier visit in 1763. His political career continued. In a footnote to chapter XXII of *The Decline and Fall*, Gibbon corrected Montesquieu's misapprehension that Jacobite toasts were illegal in England. It was important for him to believe that the political climate of the time was such that party divisions and animosities were obsolete, for only then would politeness be secure. It had therefore pleased him that both supporters of the royal prerogative and Whigs of radical temper had perceived a reflection of their own, widely divergent, political beliefs in the first volume of *The Decline and Fall*. But the war with the American colonists, now in its third year, threatened once more to infect English political life with the curse of party. For the duration of the conflict Gibbon stayed, in respect at least of his actions, if not his sentiments, loyal to Lord North. He even composed a state paper, the *Mémoire justificatif* (1779), criticizing the French for their involvement in the dispute with the colonists. But he was never an enthusiast for the armed struggle, in which he found the issues of right and wrong obscure, the practical consequences appalling. It may be that here we can trace the influence of Burke, and of Charles James Fox, whom Gibbon met from time to time at Almack's, and in whose circle he socialized.

Gibbon had reasons of the most persuasive kind for standing by Lord North. His financial situation was pressing. Because of an amiable tendency to regard luxuries as necessities, his expenditure comfortably exceeded his income. Attempts to sell the Gibbon family estate of Lenborough in Buckinghamshire had come to nothing, and the price of land was now falling because of the war. The alternatives were to abandon his expensive and fashionable life in London, or to acquire a fresh source of income. Gibbon's preferred solution was to receive one of the lucrative sinecures in the gift of government. In July 1779 he received the reward of his silent loyalty to the administration, and was appointed to the Board of Trade and Plantations at a salary of £750. For the time being, his situation was eased.

And throughout all these distractions he had been writing and studying: 'Shall I add that I never found my mind more vigorous or my composition more happy than in the winter hurry of society and Parliament?' (*A*, p. 316). In September 1780, however, Gibbon lost his seat in Parliament when Edward Eliot transferred his loyalty to the opposition, 'and the Electors of Leskeard are commonly of the same opinion as Mr Eliot' (*A*, p. 322). In this interval of Gibbon's senatorial life, volumes two and three of *The Decline and Fall* were published on 1 March 1781.

The public received the second and third volumes of *The Decline and Fall* politely, but (as was only to be expected) without the excitement which Gibbon had found so flattering in 1776. He wisely gave himself a year's holiday after the publication of his second instalment, spending time in Brighton and at Hampton Court, and reading Greek literature. In June 1781 through the influence of Lord North he re-entered the House of Commons as the Member for Lymington. But within the year the Board of Trade was suppressed on grounds of economy, and Gibbon consequently found himself without the salary which made possible his London life. For a while he hung on in the hope of something else (a post in the Customs and a secretaryship at the embassy in Paris were apparently discussed). Against the background of the astonishing political manœuvres of 1782–3, Gibbon resumed work on *The Decline and Fall*, and by 1783 volume four was virtually complete. When it was clear that his political masters were going to do nothing for him, he set about extricating himself from the financial embarrassments which could only become more tightly constricting were he to remain in England.

In May 1783 Gibbon wrote to his friend Georges Deyverdun to explore the possibility of their living together in Switzerland. It was a project they had apparently discussed with enthusiasm on many occasions, and now that Deyverdun had inherited La Grotte, a substantial house in Lausanne, there were no practical obstacles to prevent the realization of this favourite scheme. Despite the misgivings of both Sheffield and his stepmother, Gibbon left Bentinck Street for Lausanne on 1 September 1783. Although all was not quite prepared for his reception, Gibbon soon professed great satisfaction with his new life, which was by some margin less fashionable than that he had led in London, but in the main more wholesome, and more genially sociable. Perhaps as a consequence, the pace of composition now slackened a little, but nevertheless by June 1787 Gibbon had completed the manuscript of the final three volumes of his history, and he embalmed the complex emotion of the moment in a celebrated passage of the *Memoirs*:

It was on the day, or rather the night, of the 27th of June, 1787, between the hours of eleven and twelve, that I wrote the last lines of the last page in a summer-house in my garden. After laying down my pen I took several turns in a *berceau*, or covered walk of Acacias, which commands a prospect of the country, the lake, and the mountains. The air was temperate, the sky was serene, the silver orb of the moon was reflected from the waters, and all Nature was silent. I will not dissemble the first emotions of joy on the recovery of my freedom, and perhaps the establishment of my fame. But my pride was soon humbled, and a sober melancholy was spread over my mind by the idea that I had taken my everlasting leave of an old and agreeable companion, and that, whatsoever might be the future date of my history, the life of the historian must be short and precarious. (*A*, pp. 333–4)

In August he travelled to London with the manuscript, for which he received £4,000 from Strahan and Cadell; for its day, a good price. Social visits to Sheffield Place, to his stepmother in Bath and to friends in London, together with the chaperoning of Wilhelm de Sévery, the son of Swiss friends, occupied Gibbon until, on 8 May 1788, the double festival of his fifty-first birthday and the publication of the third instalment of *The Decline and Fall* could be celebrated with a literary dinner given by Cadell.

Less than a year after Gibbon's return to Lausanne, Deyverdun died, carried away in July 1789 by a series of apoplectic strokes. Deyverdun's will gave Gibbon a life interest in La Grotte, and his financial situation was now more healthy thanks to sales of property in England, so his material circumstances were if anything improved. But Gibbon was profoundly shaken by the death of his friend, and lapsed into a depression from which he only gradually emerged, to resume once more the mild pleasures of society. However, this agreeable life was itself soon to be menaced. Deyverdun had expired almost as the French Revolution was born. Gibbon was at first moderately encouraged by the turn of events in France: the *ancien régime* had needed urgent reform, as he acknowledged. But his sanguine hopes were soon abandoned as the violent character of the Revolution asserted itself. When Sheffield and his family journeyed to Lausanne to visit Gibbon in 1791, they came by way of Paris, and reported gloomily on what they had seen there – sombre news, later to be confirmed by the September massacres of 1792 and the execution of Louis XVI in

1793. The closeness of the historian of decline to the epochal events which began the dismantling of the culture from within which and, to some degree, on behalf of which he had written make these closing years one of the most fascinating periods of Gibbon's life.

The Revolution claimed an unexpected victim when Lady Sheffield died in April 1793; she had fallen sick while caring for *émigrés* at Guy's Hospital. Gibbon set out at once on the potentially dangerous journey across Europe to be with his newly widowed friend. He found Sheffield already reconciled to his loss, and spent a pleasant summer with him in the Sussex countryside. It was soon clear, however, that Gibbon's own health was not sound. For many years he had neglected a swelling in his groin. Its size was now so great – 'almost as big as a small child' was the disconcerting simile on which Gibbon's pen settled (*L*, iii. 359) – that even Gibbon, who had ignored the problem for as long as possible, and who engagingly believed that it had escaped the notice of others, was driven to seek the assistance of the surgeons. It is said that when he first consulted his doctor, he opened the consultation with a joke which mischievously linked his present complaint with his parliamentary career: 'Why is a fat man like a Cornish elector? Because both of them never see their member.' He was tapped three times during the winter of 1793–4, and prodigious quantities of fluid were drawn off. On the third occasion the knife was dirty. Peritonitis set in, and developed swiftly. Three days after his last operation, and only one day after he had pronounced that he was good for a further 'ten, twelve, or perhaps twenty years', at 12.45 p.m. on 16 January 1794, Gibbon died.

The History of the Decline and Fall of the Roman Empire

Reviewing Gibbon's early life, the striking fact emerges that his most effectual education occurred outside England and English institutions. It did not take an English form, and the values which it instilled were not in the first instance English values. And this European conditioning, in which England was but one part of a broader continental grouping of nations (what Gibbon would later call a 'Christian republic'), stayed with Gibbon until the end of his life (*DF*, ii. 433). Although, in the midst of the French Revolution, he would claim to 'glory in the character of an Englishman', his aesthetic judgements (as when for instance he shrewdly described an enthusiasm for Shakespeare as the 'first duty' [*A*, p. 149] of an Englishman) demonstrate his freedom from any narrowly national outlook.

This freedom of mind left a trace even on that most obvious and celebrated feature of his prose, namely his ironic wit:

[The younger Gordian's] manners were less pure, but his character was equally amiable with that of his father. Twenty-two acknowledged concubines, and a library of sixty-two thousand volumes, attested the variety of his inclinations; and from the productions which he left behind him, it appears that the former as well as the latter were designed for use rather than for ostentation. (*ADF*, p. 98–9)

An air of mild indecency often hangs around such moments in *The Decline and Fall*. They recall Richard Porson's comments on Gibbon's lubricity:

Nor does his humanity ever slumber, unless when women are ravished, or the Christians persecuted . . . A less pardonable fault is [a] rage for indecency . . . If the history were anonymous, I should guess that these disgraceful obscenities were written by some debauchee, who having from age, or accident, or excess, survived the practice of lust, still indulged himself in the luxury of speculation.[1]

Gibbon could, we know, offend against English standards of propriety. But Porson is wrong, I think, to see in such passages a simple 'rage for indecency'. Gibbon's neglect of the customary decorums flowed not from the disposition of a libertine, but from the peculiarities of his upbringing, which had not trained his mind to observe the usual boundaries. Although Gibbon eventually moved in the highest circles, in both London and Lausanne, the anecdotes we have about his behaviour in company – his occasionally comic lack of insight into how others perceived him, his carelessness over his personal hygiene – suggest that, beneath or around the edges of his manifest urbanity, he remained oddly unsocialized.

If that disposition to disregard the customary had, in society, some problematic consequences, its effect on Gibbon's historical vision was richly positive. The freedom of character which sometimes caused Gibbon to offend English susceptibilities also ensured that his richly imaginative apprehension of the past was never confined within the boundaries of received opinion. How did that independence of mind show itself? In the first place,

1. Richard Porson, *Letters to Mr Archdeacon Travis* (1790), pp. xxviii–xxxi.

it conditioned what we might call the style of Gibbon's historical thought.

During Gibbon's first period of residence in Switzerland he became, as we have seen, acquainted with Voltaire. This was a point of entry to the world of French Enlightenment philosophy which was later deepened by reading, and broadened by the further personal contacts with other *philosophes* which Gibbon made when visiting Paris in 1763 and 1777. For many of Gibbon's contemporaries – particularly his clerical adversaries – this was enough to make him the 'English Voltaire': a label they used as shorthand for hostility to Christianity and writing 'philosophic' history.[2] Gibbon's attitude to Christianity we shall consider presently. But what was 'philosophic' history, and what did it mean to be a 'philosophic' historian?

Gibbon's first published work, the *Essai sur l'étude de la littérature* (1761), includes the comment that 'if philosophers are not always historians, it were, at any rate, to be wished that historians were always philosophers' (*MW*, iv. 66: my translation). For Gibbon, the philosophic historian was never a mere chronicler, content to trace the fluid surface of the past. Where the naïve would see only randomness, and a believer the workings of divine providence, the philosophic historian saw order and regularity: 'History is to a philosophical mind what play was to the Marquis de Dangeau. He would see a system, relations, connections, where others would pick out only the caprices of Fortune. This science is the science of causes and effects' (*MW*, iv. 63).

But what kind of causes did the philosophic historian perceive? In the first place, philosophic historiography was secular in its focus. Human agency accomplished everything, although not in the way that the actors themselves intended. So the philosophic historian did not offer explanations of the past which depended on a minute and particular divine providence. Secondly, philosophic historiography was not heroic; it would not depict the lives of millions being determined by the masterful will of a single actor. Indeed, in philosophic histories those actors would tend to emerge as deluded and even defeated figures: the instruments of a past they imagined they were directing, the inhabitants of a realm of illusion blinded to the causes ordering their own lives. Thirdly, the sequences of human society would typically appear oxymoronic, as developments arose from the actions

---

2. On Gibbon as the English Voltaire and the clerical hostility to him, see the contributions by Paul Turnbull and Nigel Aston to D. J. Womersley (ed.), *Edward Gibbon: Bicentenary Essays* (Oxford, 1997).

of individuals and the policies of institutions apparently repugnant or antagonistic to them.

So much for the intellectual style of the philosophic historians; what can we say of the content of their historical vision? The historical problems which preoccupied them had, by the time Gibbon composed *The Decline and Fall*, resolved themselves into three. The first concerned civil society. What were the forces which built it up, and what were the forces which undermined it? From these considerations flowed the need to investigate political forms, the effects exerted on society by commerce, the nature of virtue as it related both to individuals and to whole societies. The second concerned barbarism. Was barbarism simply the antagonist of civil society, or were there points of contact and continuity between the two? Was barbarism all of a piece, or could one discern different kinds, or stages, of barbarism? The third concerned religion. What were the social and political consequences of religious belief? To what causes could the rise of any particular religion be ascribed? Which human passions, appetites and faculties were nourished by religious belief, and which did it pervert or stifle? And to which passions, appetites and faculties was it indebted for its origin?

As we shall see, there are good grounds for endorsing Gibbon's reputation as a philosophic historian, in that *The Decline and Fall* broadly conforms to the style and content of the general model I have just described. What makes Gibbon unusual, however, is the simultaneous weakness of his ideological commitments and the strength of his historical instincts. Arnaldo Momigliano, in what may be the most influential single piece of scholarship on Gibbon written in the twentieth century, argues that Gibbon's distinctive contribution to historical method was to unite in his own person the characters of the *philosophe* and the *érudit*, thereby forging an alliance between intellectual sweep and antiquarian precision.[3] On inspection, this seems perhaps to have been less a unification than an endless process of flexible negotiation. Gibbon's intellectual freedom is partly demonstrated through the way his narrative continually checks the general insights of eighteenth-century philosophy against the detail of the historical record.

That freedom and flexibility of judgement is visible most obviously in Gibbon's complex attitude towards the fact of empire. It is often assumed that *The Decline and Fall* is a straightforward lament for departed glory, and

---

3. A. Momigliano, 'Gibbon's Contributions to Historical Method', in *Studies in Historiography* (London, 1966), 40–55.

that the dominant emotional colouring of the work is that of an elegy.[4] But Gibbon was the enemy of empire as a political form, and a friend to the freedom of nations. In 1764, while on the Grand Tour, he wrote to his father from Rome. He had been intoxicated by the vestiges of imperial greatness, he reported, but nevertheless concluded: 'I am convinced there never never [sic] existed such a nation and I hope for the happiness of mankind that there never will again' (L, i. 184).

The views of the young man carried through into the work of his maturity. Chapter III of The Decline and Fall ends with an evocation of the misery of living under the absolute monarchy of the empire:

But the empire of the Romans filled the world, and when that empire fell into the hands of a single person, the world became a safe and dreary prison for his enemies. The slave of Imperial despotism, whether he was condemned to drag his gilded chain in Rome and the senate, or to wear out a life of exile on the barren rock of Seriphus, or the frozen banks of the Danube, expected his fate in silent despair. To resist was fatal, and it was impossible to fly. On every side he was encompassed with a vast extent of sea and land, which he could never hope to traverse without being discovered, seized, and restored to his irritated master. Beyond the frontiers, his anxious view could discover nothing, except the ocean, inhospitable deserts, hostile tribes of barbarians, of fierce manners and unknown language, or dependent kings, who would gladly purchase the emperor's protection by the sacrifice of an obnoxious fugitive. 'Wherever you are,' said Cicero to the exiled Marcellus, 'remember that you are equally within the power of the conqueror.' (ADF, p. 87)

And towards the end of chapter XLIX Gibbon offers this condemnation of the fundamental principle of empire: 'There is nothing perhaps more adverse to nature and reason than to hold in obedience remote countries and foreign nations, in opposition to their inclination and interest' (DF, iii. 142). However much Gibbon may have admired the artistic and cultural achievement of Rome, therefore, he was no admirer of empire as a political system. In this he stands out from his immediate predecessors and near contemporaries in English literature. Pope, Milton, Thomson and Addison had all portrayed the overwhelming of the Roman empire as a catastrophic rupture in the fabric of European history. Gibbon, however, tends to present it as the source of future growth.

4. For such a reading, see H. L. Bond, The Literary Art of Edward Gibbon (Oxford, 1960).

This disenchantment with empire influenced Gibbon's assessment of the barbarians who overran the western provinces of the Roman empire in the fifth century. It was the misfortune of the inhabitants of those western provinces that, at just the moment when it fell to them to be governed by the feeble sons of Theodosius, the Goths, Huns and Vandals along their northern borders came under the sway of a series of effective and resourceful military commanders, such as Attila the Hun. Gibbon's portrait of this leader reflects back tellingly on his understanding of the imperial twilight in western Europe.

Gibbon begins by emphasizing that Attila's military conquests were preceded by a more important victory over the barbaric character of his subjects:

The western world was oppressed by the Goths and Vandals, who fled before the Huns; but the atchievements of the Huns themselves were not adequate to their power and prosperity. Their victorious hords had spread from the Volga to the Danube; but the public force was exhausted by the discord of independent chieftains; their valour was idly consumed in obscure and predatory excursions; and they often degraded their national dignity by condescending, for the hopes of spoil, to enlist under the banners of their fugitive enemies. In the reign of ATTILA, the Huns again became the terror of the world; and I shall now describe the character and actions of that formidable Barbarian; who alternately insulted and invaded the East and the West, and urged the rapid downfal of the Roman empire. (*ADF*, p. 365)

Attila's appearance was indelibly barbaric: 'the portrait of Attila exhibits the genuine deformity of a modern Calmuck'. But in his deeds he transcended the characteristic limitations of barbarism: 'the fame of an adventurous soldier was usefully exchanged for that of a prudent and successful general'. The point is enforced by explicit and implicit comparison with the most accomplished of the Roman emperors, Augustus, whose achievements Attila revived in a barbaric setting. Like Augustus, Attila surpassed his subjects 'in art, rather than in courage', and his use of superstition to support government was the action of a 'magnanimous, or rather [an] artful, prince'. As Gibbon points out in a footnote, the pleasure Attila took in the inability of anyone to support his gaze was a vanity he shared with Augustus (*ADF*, pp. 367, 368, 369, n. 11).

Gibbon's admiration for the barbarians had its limits. He remained convinced that 'the pastoral state of nations' was a condition of intellectual, ethical and material impoverishment. Recounting the atrocities perpetrated by the Thuringian allies of Attila, he distances himself emphatically from the modish cult of the noble savage, promulgated by contemporaries such as Rousseau: 'Such were those savage ancestors, whose imaginary virtues have sometimes excited the praise and envy of civilized ages!' (*ADF*, p. 414). But Gibbon knew that the sequences of human history do not always confirm our ideas of cause and effect, and so he enters a major qualification of the popular understanding of the Huns as purely destructive. Such indeed may have been their intentions, actuated as they were by the 'savage and destructive spirit' (*ADF*, p. 375) typical of their stage of development. But the results of their actions were occasionally at variance with those intentions, as the foundation of the republic of Venice demonstrates: 'It is a saying worthy of the ferocious pride of Attila, that the grass never grew on the spot where his horse had trod. Yet the savage destroyer undesignedly laid the foundations of a republic, which revived, in the feudal state of Europe, the art and spirit of commercial industry' (*ADF*, p. 417).

So it was that the Huns, despite themselves, acted to create a hinge linking barbaric Europe to the civilized republic of commercial states in which the history of that transformation could itself be written. Gibbon discerns in the leaders of the barbarians new paradigms of the human character, in which qualities previously distinct or contrary had met and mingled. Their scavenging of the putrescent corpse of the Western empire contributed in ways which were unintended and unanticipated, yet nevertheless palpable, to the health and vigour of its offspring.

If Gibbon's view of the barbarians is unexpectedly positive, can the same be said for his attitude towards religion? Gibbon is famous for his hostility to Christianity. His ironic treatment of the established church created trouble for him in his own day, and it is probably still his most notorious characteristic as a writer. But Gibbon, although he seems not to have enjoyed any lively Christian faith himself (at least after his brush with Catholicism), nevertheless saw as an historian that the Christian church had played an important role in keeping civil society alive during the collapse of the Roman empire, and had thereby permitted the transferral of precious elements of culture from the ancient world to the modern.

Gibbon devotes chapter XXVIII to two almost simultaneous developments. The end of the fourth century and the beginning of the fifth had seen both the destruction of paganism, and the introduction of the worship of saints and relics among the Christians. At first Gibbon seems to imply that paganism was annihilated: 'The ruin of Paganism, in the age of Theodosius, is perhaps the only example of the total extirpation of any ancient and popular superstition; and may therefore deserve to be considered, as a singular event in the history of the human mind' (*ADF*, p. 334).

However, the apparent extinction of paganism was an illusion. Gibbon describes the state of paganism in the fourth century, and dwells in melancholy over the destruction of its temples ('the fairest structures of antiquity') by 'an army of fanatics', namely the Christians, whom he stigmatizes as '*those* Barbarians, who alone had time and inclination to execute such laborious destruction' (*ADF*, p. 344). This exoneration of the literal barbarians from the guilt of the destruction of the monuments of antiquity accords well with the unexpectedly positive notes in Gibbon's account of the barbarian invasions.

We then move on to the second subject of the chapter, the corruption of Christianity into a religion of superstition:

In the long period of twelve hundred years, which elapsed between the reign of Constantine and the reformation of Luther, the worship of saints and relics corrupted the pure and perfect simplicity of the Christian model; and some symptoms of degeneracy may be observed even in the first generations which adopted and cherished this pernicious innovation. (*ADF*, p.355)

This was, then, a lapse from simplicity into plurality: the unity of the Godhead was divided into the literal fragments which were revered as relics, and the holy and undivided Trinity was refracted into the company of saints. Considered from a purely religious standpoint, the lapse into superstition was indeed degeneracy: 'The sublime and simple theology of the primitive Christians was gradually corrupted; and the MONARCHY of heaven, already clouded by metaphysical subtleties, was degraded by the introduction of a popular mythology, which tended to restore the reign of polytheism' (*ADF*, p. 359). Paganism was thus not annihilated. In Gibbon's view it had been translated into the ceremonies and doctrines of its successor religion, Catholic Christianity, where it persisted in a way which was theologically unfortunate.

But religion can be assessed in terms other than the theological, and Gibbon insinuates at the very end of the chapter how the corruption of

Christianity, considered purely as a religion, might nevertheless be seen in a positive light. For the recurrence of pagan forms in Christianity cannot be attributed to the 'same uniform original spirit of superstition' (*ADF*, p. 360). Gibbon insists that such an hypothesis, however it might save the face of the Catholic church, is not tenable in the face of the stubborn fact of the extraordinary simultaneity of the suppression of paganism and the beginning of Christian superstition. What took place, rather, was a stroke of deliberate and conscious policy, in which theological purity was wisely subordinated to political benefit:

> it must ingenuously be confessed, that the ministers of the Catholic church imitated the profane model, which they were impatient to destroy. The most respectable bishops had persuaded themselves, that the ignorant rustics would more cheerfully renounce the superstitions of Paganism, if they found some resemblance, some compensation, in the bosom of Christianity. The religion of Constantine atchieved, in less than a century, the final conquest of the Roman empire: but the victors themselves were insensibly subdued by the arts of their vanquished rivals. (*ADF*, p. 360)

Gibbon encourages us to view the infection of Christianity by the superstitious temper of paganism in a secular, rather than a theological, light. When we do so, it seems that paganism had innoculated Christianity with superstition. For, as we shall see, Gibbon will go on to suggest that Christianity, corrupted into superstition, exerted a benign and protective influence over the fledgling societies which established themselves on the ruins of the Western empire. To the extent that Christianity became pagan, it acted as a conduit for a civil order which might otherwise have been lost in the gulf between the ancient and the modern worlds. Like barbarian leaders such as Attila, those respectable Catholic bishops were both wiser than they knew, and wiser than, in all probability, they wished to be.

It should be already clear, then, that when Gibbon contemplated late antiquity, he was in part concerned with how the modern world had emerged from it. As many have recognized, *The Decline and Fall* is thus a kind of bridge linking the ancient and modern worlds. One of the aspects of his own world in which Gibbon took the most satisfaction was its organization as a commercial society. But how and where had this commercial principle arisen? Gibbon located its roots in a culture for which most of his contemporaries had only contempt: Byzantium. In conversation

Horace Walpole reproved Gibbon for pitching on 'so disgusting a subject as the Constantinopolitan history.'[5] It was a disgust which Gibbon partially shared, as his comments on what he saw as the derivative and eunuch-like culture of Byzantium and the oriental despotism by which it was governed sufficiently make clear. But his understanding of the Eastern empire was larger than these commonplace attitudes would by themselves suggest.

It is when discussing the emperor Justinian that Gibbon turns his attention to the agriculture and manufactures of the Eastern empire, and expatiates in pleasure on the advances in material prosperity which had accompanied what he recognizes had also been years of military set-back and political corruption:

Justinian reigned over sixty-four provinces, and nine hundred and thirty-five cities; his dominions were blessed by nature with the advantages of soil, situation, and climate: and the improvements of human art had been perpetually diffused along the coast of the Mediterranean and the banks of the Nile, from ancient Troy to the Egyptian Thebes. Abraham had been relieved by the well-known plenty of Egypt; the same country, a small and populous tract, was still capable of exporting, each year, two hundred and sixty thousand quarters of wheat for the use of Constantinople; and the capital of Justinian was supplied with the manufactures of Sidon, fifteen centuries after they had been celebrated in the poems of Homer. The annual powers of vegetation, instead of being exhausted by two thousand harvests, were renewed and invigorated by skilful husbandry, rich manure, and seasonable repose. The breed of domestic animals was infinitely multiplied. Plantations, buildings, and the instruments of labour and luxury, which are more durable than the term of human life, were accumulated by the care of successive generations. Tradition preserved, and experience simplified, the humble practice of the arts: society was enriched by the division of labour and the facility of exchange; and every Roman was lodged, clothed, and subsisted, by the industry of a thousand hands. (*ADF*, pp. 467–8)

This is a passage of exceptional interest, because it indicates very clearly Gibbon's understanding of the cardinal position occupied by Byzantium in the emergence of the modern world from the societies of antiquity. Where we might have expected the hostility of a civic humanist, gloomily

5. *The Yale Edition of Horace Walpole's Correspondence*, ed. W. S. Lewis et al. (New Haven, 1955), xxix. 98.

contemplating the dissipation of strength and energy in the pursuit of luxury, we have instead what is almost a rhapsody on the manifold benefits of commerce. The civilizing effects of trade in strengthening, rather than weakening, the ties which bind society together was a doctrine Gibbon probably learnt from Hume, while his reference to 'the division of labour and the facility of exchange' shows a debt to the writings of another of his friends, Adam Smith. It seems, then, that Gibbon was applying the thought of the Scottish Enlightenment to the phenomenon of Roman decline, with the effect that the Eastern empire during Justinian's reign appeared as a nascent commercial society, rather than a political body akin to the societies of the classical period; it was perhaps somewhere in the plateau of this reign that the frontier between the ancient and the modern might be found. The true heroism of Justinian's reign was thus not military but material. It was to be found in the production and distribution of goods. And when eighteenth-century writers reviled and despised Byzantium and its culture, they were therefore in some sense reviling themselves. It is therefore in these final volumes of *The Decline and Fall*, which critics, commentators and earlier abridgers have in general scanted, but which are given proper representation in this abridgement, that the classic status of the history is most clear, for it is in these volumes that Gibbon's involvement in, but simultaneous independence of, the intellectual currents of his day is most marked.

What of the impact of Gibbon's history, the way it changed historical writing? *The Decline and Fall* did not exert influence in the most obvious way. There was no 'Gibbonian' school which arose after Gibbon's death. From the first, it seems to have been acknowledged that his achievement was unrepeatable, and that his distinctive excellence as an historian was not a question of a particular method which others, less original and gifted, might in their lesser spheres apply. In part, this was surely because a central component of Gibbon's achievement was his prose style which, although mannered, eludes successful imitation, and is in any case too firmly attached to its author to be usable by another. Nevertheless, the most celebrated nineteenth-century historians deferred to Gibbon's greatness. Mommsen, unable to be present at the celebrations to commemorate the centenary of Gibbon's death, sent a written tribute recording his abiding conviction that 'amid all the changes that had come over the study of the Roman Empire . . . no one would in the future be able to read the history of the Roman Empire, unless he read, possibly with a fuller knowledge, but with the broad views, the clear insight, the strong grasp of Edward Gibbon.'[6] But Gibbon's appeal has, from the first publication of *The Decline and Fall*, always been to a broader readership than that of his professional peers. He stands as a monument to the truth that historical excellence need not exist at the expense of literary excellence. In these days of increasingly professionalized scholarship, that is a truth of which we cannot be reminded too often, or too forcibly.

6. *The Times*, 16 November 1894, p. 8.

SELECTED FURTHER READING

1. Bibliography

Craddock, P. B., *Edward Gibbon: A Reference Guide* (Boston, 1987).
Norton, J. E., *A Bibliography of the Works of Edward Gibbon* (Oxford, 1940; repr. 1970).

2. Biography

Craddock, P. B., *Young Edward Gibbon: Gentleman of Letters* (Baltimore, 1982), and *Edward Gibbon, Luminous Historian 1772–1794* (Baltimore, 1989).
Low, D. M., *Edward Gibbon, 1737–1794* (London, 1937).

3. Complete Editions

Gibbon, Edward, *The History of the Decline and Fall of the Roman Empire*, ed. David Womersley, 3 vols (Harmondsworth, 1994).

4. Critical and Scholarly Studies

Bond, H. L., *The Literary Art of Edward Gibbon* (Oxford, 1960).
Bowersock, G. W., et al. (eds), *Edward Gibbon and the Decline and Fall of the Roman Empire* (Harvard, 1977).
Braudy, L., *Narrative Form in History and Fiction* (Princeton, 1970).
Burrow, J. W., *Gibbon* (Oxford, 1985).
Carnochan, W. B., *Gibbon's Solitude: The Inward World of the Historian* (Stanford, 1987).

Craddock, P. B., 'Historical Discovery and Literary Invention in Gibbon's *Decline and Fall*', *Modern Philology*, 85 (1988), 569–87.

Giarrizzo, G., *Edward Gibbon e la Cultura Europea del Settecento* (Naples, 1954).

Gossman, L., *The Empire Unpossess'd: An Essay on Gibbon's Decline and Fall* (Cambridge, 1981).

Jordan, D., *Gibbon and his Roman Empire* (Illinois, 1971).

McKitterick, R. and Quinault, R. (eds), *Edward Gibbon and Empire* (Cambridge, 1997).

Momigliano, A., 'Gibbon's Contributions to Historical Method', in *Studies in Historiography* (London, 1966), 40–55.

Pocock, J. G. A., 'Between Machiavelli and Hume: Gibbon as Civic Humanist and Philosophical Historian', *Daedalus*, 105 (1976), 153–69.

'Gibbon's *Decline and Fall* and the World View of the Late Enlightenment', *Eighteenth-Century Studies*, 10 (1977), 287–303.

'Gibbon and the Shepherds: The Stages of Society in the *Decline and Fall*', *History of European Ideas*, 2 (1981), 193–202.

'Superstition and Enthusiasm in Gibbon's History of Religion', *Eighteenth-Century Life*, 8 (1982), 83–94.

Porter, R., *Edward Gibbon: Making History* (London, 1988).

Womersley, D. J., *The Transformation of The Decline and Fall of the Roman Empire* (Cambridge, 1988).

(ed.), *Edward Gibbon: Bicentenary Essays* (Oxford, 1997).

A NOTE ON THE TEXT

The text for this abridgement has been taken from the Penguin complete edition of *The Decline and Fall*. This was the first edition of the history to offer a text established on a bibliographically secure foundation, as a result of methodical collation of the earliest editions. The present volume thus surpasses other abridgements in respect of accuracy and reliability.

It also differs from them in three further particulars: (a) it includes only whole, complete, chapters; (b) fragments of chapters have therefore not been silently conflated with fragments from other chapters to create heterogeneous monsters unshaped by Gibbon's historical art; (c) the included chapters have been drawn, with a roughly even hand, from all the three instalments of the history. The reasons for this are twofold. In the first place, Gibbon's artistry as an historian included the shaping of individual chapters, and to interfere with or obscure that shaping is to do him a disservice and to mislead the reader. Secondly, Gibbon is no less powerful, imaginative and rewarding an historian in the later, comparatively less-read, chapters of the history, and therefore, if one of the main purposes of an abridgement is to acquaint the reader with an author whom they will feel encouraged on a later occasion to explore in his entirety, these later chapters should be properly represented.

The selected chapters have been linked by bridging passages which summarize, and quote generously from, the chapters which have not been included. The intention is that the reader of this abridgement should nevertheless be able to acquire a general sense of the progress and argument of the whole work. The bridging material is identified in the text by the use of square brackets around chapter headings and around shoulder running-headlines.

CHRONOLOGY

1707 Gibbon's father born.

1734 Gibbon's father becomes MP for Petersfield.

1736 Gibbon's grandfather dies.

1737 Edward Gibbon the historian born on 27 April OS.

1747 Gibbon's mother dies on 26 December.

1748 Gibbon enters Westminster School.

1750 Nervous illness; residence in Bath.

1752 Enters Magdalen College, Oxford, as Gentleman Commoner.

1753 Converts to Roman Catholicism on 8 June.
     Arrives in Lausanne on 30 June at the house of Daniel Pavilliard.

1754 Re-converts to Protestantism on 25 December.

1755 Gibbon's father remarries on 8 May.
     Tour of Switzerland in the company of Pavilliard.

1757 Meets Suzanne Curchod.

1758 Returns to England, arriving in London on 5 May.

1759 Receives commission as captain in the Hampshire Militia.

1761 Publishes the *Essai sur l'étude de la littérature*.

1762 Hampshire Militia disembodied.

1763 Begins Grand Tour, arriving in Paris on 28 January 1763.
     Arrives in Lausanne in May.
     Meets John Baker Holroyd, later Lord Sheffield.

1764 Leaves Lausanne in April.
     Arrives in Rome on 2 October.
     Inspired on 15 October to write on the decline and fall of Rome.

1765 Returns to England in June.

1768–9 Publishes, in conjunction with Georges Deyverdun, the *Mémoires littéraires de la Grande Bretagne*.

1770 Publishes anonymously the *Critical Observations on the Sixth Book of Vergil's Aeneid*.

Gibbon's father dies on 12 November.

1772 Gibbon takes up residence in Cavendish Square, London.

1774 Enters the House of Commons as MP for Liskeard.

1776 Volume one of *The Decline and Fall* published on 17 February.

1777 Spends six months in Paris.

1779 Publishes his reply to his clerical assailants, *A Vindication.*
Publishes the *Mémoire justificatif.*
Appointed to the Board of Trade and Plantations in July.

1780 Loses his seat in Parliament.

1781 Volumes two and three of *The Decline and Fall* published on 1 March.
Re-enters the House of Commons as MP for Lymington in June.

1783 Takes up permanent residence in Lausanne.

1787 Composition of *The Decline and Fall* completed on 27 June.

1788 Volumes four, five and six of *The Decline and Fall* published on 8 May.
Begins composing the *Memoirs of My Life*: six drafts completed by 1793.

1789 Georges Deyverdun dies in July.

1791 Visit of Lord Sheffield and his family to Lausanne.

1793 Death of Lady Sheffield in April.

1794 Gibbon dies of post-operative infection on 16 January.

1796 Sheffield publishes the first edition of Gibbon's *Miscellaneous Works*, including his edition of Gibbon's *Memoirs of My Life.*

THE HISTORY OF
THE DECLINE AND FALL
OF THE ROMAN EMPIRE

GIBBON'S PREFACES

It is not my intention to detain the reader by expatiating on the variety, or the importance of the subject, which I have undertaken to treat; since the merit of the choice would serve to render the weakness of the execution still more apparent, and still less excusable. But as I have presumed to lay before the Public a *first* volume only of the History of the Decline and Fall of the Roman Empire, it will perhaps be expected that I should explain, in a few words, the nature and limits of my general plan.

The memorable series of revolutions, which, in the course of about thirteen centuries, gradually undermined, and at length destroyed, the solid fabric of Roman greatness, may, with some propriety, be divided into the three following periods.

I. The first of these periods may be traced from the age of Trajan and the Antonines, when the Roman monarchy, having attained its full strength and maturity, began to verge towards its decline; and will extend to the subversion of the Western Empire, by the barbarians of Germany and Scythia, the rude ancestors of the most polished nations of modern Europe. This extraordinary revolution, which subjected Rome to the power of a Gothic conqueror, was completed about the beginning of the sixth century.

II. The second period of the Decline and Fall of Rome, may be supposed to commence with the reign of Justinian, who by his laws, as well as by his victories, restored a transient splendour to the Eastern Empire. It will comprehend the invasion of Italy by the Lombards; the conquest of the Asiatic and African provinces by the Arabs, who embraced the religion of Mahomet; the revolt of the Roman people against the feeble princes of Constantinople; and the elevation of Charlemagne, who, in the year eight hundred, established the second, or German Empire of the west.

III. The last and longest of these periods includes about six centuries and a half; from the revival of the Western Empire, till the taking of Constantinople by the Turks, and the extinction of a degenerate race of princes, who continued to assume the titles of Cæsar and Augustus, after their dominions were contracted to the limits of a single city; in which the language, as well as manners, of the ancient Romans, had been long since forgotten. The writer who should undertake to relate the events of this period, would find himself obliged to enter into the general history of the Crusades, as far as they contributed to the ruin of the Greek Empire; and he would scarcely be able to restrain his curiosity from making some inquiry into the state of the city of Rome, during the darkness and confusion of the middle ages.

As I have ventured, perhaps too hastily, to commit to the press, a work, which, in every sense of the word, deserves the epithet of imperfect, I consider myself as contracting an engagement to finish, most probably in a second volume, the first of these memorable periods; and to deliver to the Public, the complete history of the Decline and Fall of Rome, from the age of the Antonines, to the subversion of the Western Empire. With regard to the subsequent periods, though I may entertain some hopes, I dare not presume to give any assurances. The execution of the extensive plan which I have described, would connect the ancient and modern history of the World; but it would require many years of health, of leisure, and of perseverance.

BENTINCK-STREET,
February 1, 1776.

P.S. The entire History, which is now published, of the Decline and Fall of the Roman Empire in the West, abundantly discharges my engagements with the Public. Perhaps their favourable opinion may encourage me to prosecute a work, which, however laborious it may seem, is the most agreeable occupation of my leisure hours.

BENTINCK-STREET
March 1, 1781.

An Author easily persuades himself that the public opinion is still favourable to his labours; and I have now embraced the serious resolution of proceeding to the last period of my original design, and of the Roman Empire, the taking of Constantinople by the Turks, in the year one thousand four hundred and fifty-three. The most patient Reader, who computes that three ponderous volumes have been already employed on the events of four centuries, may, perhaps, be alarmed at the long prospect of nine hundred years. But it is not my intention to expatiate with the same minuteness on the whole series of the Byzantine history. At our entrance into this period, the reign of Justinian, and the conquests of the Mahometans, will deserve and detain our attention, and the last age of Constantinople (the Crusades and the Turks) is connected with the revolutions of Modern Europe. From the seventh to the eleventh century, the obscure interval will be supplied by a concise narrative of such facts, as may still appear either interesting or important.

BENTINCK-STREET,
March 1, 1782.

I now discharge my promise, and complete my design, of writing the History of the Decline and Fall of the Roman Empire, both in the West and the East. The whole period extends from the age of Trajan and the Antonines, to the taking of Constantinople by Mahomet the second; and includes a review of the Crusades and the state of Rome during the middle ages. Since the publication of the first volume, twelve years have elapsed; twelve years, according to my wish, "of health, of leisure, and of perseverance." I may now congratulate my deliverance from a long and laborious service, and my satisfaction will be pure and perfect, if the public favour should be extended to the conclusion of my work.

It was my first intention to have collected under one view, the numerous authors, of every age and language, from whom I have derived the materials of this history; and I am still convinced that the apparent ostentation would be more than compensated by real use. If I have renounced this idea; if I have declined an undertaking which had obtained the approbation of a master-artist,* my excuse may be found in the extreme difficulty of assigning a proper measure to such a catalogue. A naked list of names and editions would not be satisfactory either to myself or my readers: the characters of the principal Authors of the Roman and Byzantine History, have been occasionally connected with the events which they describe; a more copious and critical enquiry might indeed deserve, but it would demand, an elaborate volume, which might swell by degrees into a general library of historical writers. For the present I shall content myself with renewing my serious protestation, that I have always endeavoured to draw from the fountain-head; that my curiosity, as well as a sense of duty, has always urged me to study the originals; and that, if they have sometimes

*See Dr. Robertson's Preface to his History of America.

eluded my search, I have carefully marked the secondary evidence, on whose faith a passage or a fact were reduced to depend.

I shall soon revisit the banks of the lake of Lausanne, a country which I have known and loved from my early youth. Under a mild government, amidst a beauteous landskip, in a life of leisure and independence, and among a people of easy and elegant manners, I have enjoyed, and may again hope to enjoy, the varied pleasures of retirement and society. But I shall ever glory in the name and character of an Englishman: I am proud of my birth in a free and enlightened country; and the approbation of that country is the best and most honourable reward of my labours. Were I ambitious of any other Patron than the public, I would inscribe this work to a Statesman, who, in a long, a stormy, and at length an unfortunate administration, had many political opponents, almost without a personal enemy: who has retained, in his fall from power, many faithful and disinterested friends; and who, under the pressure of severe infirmity, enjoys the lively vigour of his mind, and the felicity of his incomparable temper. LORD NORTH will permit me to express the feelings of friendship in the language of truth: but even truth and friendship should be silent, if he still dispensed the favours of the crown.

In a remote solitude, vanity may still whisper in my ear, that my readers, perhaps, may enquire, whether, in the conclusion of the present work, I am now taking an everlasting farewell. They shall hear all that I know myself, all that I could reveal to the most intimate friend. The motives of action or silence are now equally balanced; nor can I pronounce in my most secret thoughts, on which side the scale will preponderate. I cannot dissemble that six ample quartos must have tried, and may have exhausted, the indulgence of the Public; that, in the repetition of similar attempts, a successful Author has much more to lose, than he can hope to gain; that I am now descending into the vale of years; and that the most respectable of my countrymen, the men whom I aspire to imitate, have resigned the pen of history about the same period of their lives. Yet I consider that the annals of ancient and modern times may afford many rich and interesting subjects; that I am still possessed of health and leisure; that by the practice of writing, some skill and facility must be acquired; and that in the ardent pursuit of truth and knowledge, I am not conscious of decay. To an active mind, indolence is more painful than labour; and the first months of my liberty will be occupied and amused in the excursions of curiosity and taste. By such temptations, I have been sometimes seduced from the rigid duty even of a pleasing and voluntary task: but my time will now be my own; and in the use or abuse of independence, I shall no longer fear my own reproaches or those of my friends. I am fairly entitled to a year of jubilee: next summer and the following winter will rapidly pass away; and experience only can determine whether I shall still prefer the freedom and variety of study to the design and composition of a regular work, which animates, while it confines, the daily application of the Author. Caprice and accident may influence my choice; but the dexterity of self-love will contrive to applaud either active industry, or philosophic repose.

DOWNING-STREET,
May 1, 1788.

P.S. I shall embrace this opportunity of introducing two *verbal* remarks, which have not conveniently offered themselves to my notice. 1. As often as I use the definitions of *beyond* the Alps, the Rhine, the Danube, &c. I generally suppose myself at Rome, and afterwards at Constantinople; without observing whether this relative geography may agree with the local, but variable, situation of the reader, or the historian. 2. In proper names of foreign, and especially of Oriental origin, it should be always our aim to express in our English version, a faithful copy of the original. But this rule, which is founded on a just regard to uniformity and truth, must often be relaxed; and the exceptions will be limited or enlarged by the custom of the language and the taste of the interpreter. Our alphabets may be often defective: a harsh sound, an uncouth spelling, might offend the ear or the eye of our countrymen; and some words, notoriously corrupt, are fixed, and, as it were, naturalised in the vulgar tongue. The prophet *Mohammed* can no longer be stripped of the famous, though improper appellation of Mahomet: the well-known cities of Aleppo, Damascus, and Cairo, would almost be lost in the strange descriptions of *Haleb*, *Demashk*, and *Al Cahira*: the titles and office of the Ottoman empire are fashioned by the practice of three hundred years; and we are pleased to blend the three Chinese monosyllables, *Con-fû-tzee* in the respectable name of Confucius, or even to adopt the Portuguese corruption of Mandarin. But I would vary the use of Zoroaster and *Zerdusht*, as I drew my information from Greece or Persia: since our connection with India, the genuine *Timour* is restored to the throne of Tamerlane: our most correct writers have retrenched the *Al*, the superfluous article, from the Koran; and we escape an ambiguous termination, by adopting *Moslem* instead of Musulman, in the plural number. In these, and in a thousand examples, the shades of distinction are often minute; and I can feel, where I cannot explain, the motives of my choice.

CHAPTER I

The Extent and Military Force of the Empire in the Age of the Antonines.

In the second century of the Christian Æra, the empire of Rome comprehended the fairest part of the earth, and the most civilized portion of mankind. The frontiers of that extensive monarchy were guarded by ancient renown and disciplined valour. The gentle, but powerful influence of laws and manners had gradually cemented the union of the provinces. Their peaceful inhabitants enjoyed and abused the advantages of wealth and luxury. The image of a free constitution was preserved with decent reverence. The Roman senate appeared to possess the sovereign authority, and devolved on the emperors all the executive powers of government. During a happy period of more than fourscore years, the public administration was conducted by the virtue and abilities of Nerva, Trajan, Hadrian, and the two Antonines. It is the design of this, and of the two succeeding chapters, to describe the prosperous condition of their empire; and afterwards, from the death of Marcus Antoninus, to deduce the most important circumstances of its decline and fall; a revolution which will ever be remembered, and is still felt by the nations of the earth.

Introduction.

A.D. 98–180.

The principal conquests of the Romans were atchieved under the republic; and the emperors, for the most part, were satisfied with preserving those dominions which had been acquired by the policy of the senate, the active emulation of the consuls, and the martial enthusiasm of the people. The seven first centuries were filled with a rapid succession of triumphs; but it was reserved for Augustus, to relinquish the ambitious design of subduing the whole earth, and to introduce a spirit of moderation into the public councils. Inclined to peace by his temper and situation, it was easy for him to discover, that Rome, in her present exalted situation, had much less to hope than to fear from the chance of arms; and that, in the prosecution of remote wars, the undertaking became every day more difficult, the event more doubtful, and the possession more precarious, and less beneficial. The experience of Augustus added weight to these

Moderation of Augustus.

salutary reflections, and effectually convinced him, that, by the prudent vigour of his counsels, it would be easy to secure every concession, which the safety or the dignity of Rome might require from the most formidable barbarians. Instead of exposing his person and his legions to the arrows of the Parthians, he obtained, by an honourable treaty, the restitution of the standards and prisoners which had been taken in the defeat of Crassus.[1]

His generals, in the early part of his reign, attempted the reduction of Æthiopia and Arabia Felix. They marched near a thousand miles to the south of the tropic; but the heat of the climate soon repelled the invaders, and protected the unwarlike natives of those sequestered regions.[2] The northern countries of Europe scarcely deserved the expence and labour of conquest. The forests and morasses of Germany were filled with a hardy race of barbarians, who despised life when it was separated from freedom; and though, on the first attack, they seemed to yield to the weight of the Roman power, they soon, by a signal act of despair, regained their independence, and reminded Augustus of the vicissitude of fortune.[3] On the death of that emperor, his testament was publicly read in the senate. He bequeathed, as a valuable legacy to his successors, the advice of confining the empire within those limits which Nature seemed to have placed as its permanent bulwarks and boundaries; on the west the Atlantic ocean; the Rhine and Danube on the north; the Euphrates on the east; and towards the south, the sandy deserts of Arabia and Africa.[4]

Imitated by his successors.
Happily for the repose of mankind, the moderate system recommended by the wisdom of Augustus, was adopted by the fears and vices of his immediate successors. Engaged in the pursuit of pleasure, or in the exercise of tyranny, the first Cæsars seldom shewed

1. Dion Cassius (l. liv. p. 736.), with the annotations of Reymar, who has collected all that Roman vanity has left upon the subject. The marble of Ancyra, on which Augustus recorded his own exploits, asserts that *he compelled* the Parthians to restore the ensigns of Crassus.

2. Strabo (l. xvi. p. 780), Pliny the elder (Hist. Natur. l. vi. c. 32, 35.), and Dion Cassius (l. liii. p. 723, and l. liv. p. 734.), have left us very curious details concerning these wars. The Romans made themselves masters of Mariaba, or Merab, a city of Arabia Felix, well known to the Orientals (see Abulfeda and the Nubian geography, p. 52.). They were arrived within three days journey of the Spice country, the rich object of their invasion.

3. By the slaughter of Varus and his three legions. See the first book of the Annals of Tacitus. Sueton. in August. c. 23. and Velleius Paterculus, l. ii. c. 117, &c. Augustus did not receive the melancholy news with all the temper and firmness that might have been expected from his character.

4. Tacit. Annal. l. ii. Dion Cassius, l. lvi. p. 833, and the speech of Augustus himself, in Julian's Cæsars. It receives great light from the learned notes of his French translator, M. Spanheim.

themselves to the armies, or to the provinces; nor were they disposed to suffer, that those triumphs which *their* indolence neglected, should be usurped by the conduct and valour of their lieutenants. The military fame of a subject was considered as an insolent invasion of the Imperial prerogative; and it became the duty, as well as interest, of every Roman general, to guard the frontiers intrusted to his care, without aspiring to conquests which might have proved no less fatal to himself than to the vanquished barbarians.[5]

The only accession which the Roman empire received, during the first century of the Christian Æra, was the province of Britain. In this single instance the successors of Cæsar and Augustus were persuaded to follow the example of the former, rather than the precept of the latter. The proximity of its *Conquest of Britain was the first exception to it.* situation to the coast of Gaul seemed to invite their arms; the pleasing, though doubtful intelligence of a pearl fishery, attracted their avarice;[6] and as Britain was viewed in the light of a distinct and insulated world, the conquest scarcely formed any exception to the general system of continental measures. After a war of about forty years, undertaken by the most stupid,[7] maintained by the most dissolute, and terminated by the most timid of all the emperors, the far greater part of the island submitted to the Roman yoke.[8] The various tribes of Britons possessed valour without conduct, and the love of freedom without the spirit of union. They took up arms with savage fierceness; they laid them down, or turned them against each other with wild inconstancy; and while they fought singly, they were successively subdued. Neither the fortitude of Caractacus, nor the despair of Boadicea, nor the fanaticism of the Druids, could avert the slavery of their country, or resist the steady progress of the Imperial generals, who maintained the

5. Germanicus, Suetonius Paulinus, and Agricola, were checked and recalled in the course of their victories. Corbulo was put to death. Military merit, as it is admirably expressed by Tacitus, was, in the strictest sense of the word, *imperatoria virtus*.

6. Cæsar himself conceals that ignoble motive; but it is mentioned by Suetonius, c. 47. The British pearls proved, however, of little value, on account of their dark and livid colour. Tacitus observes, with reason (in Agricola, c. 12.), that it was an inherent defect. "Ego facilius crediderim, naturam margaritis

deesse quam nobis avaritiam."

7. Claudius, Nero, and Domitian. A hope is expressed by Pomponius Mela, l. iii. c. 6. (he wrote under Claudius) that, by the success of the Roman arms, the island and its savage inhabitants would soon be better known. It is amusing enough to peruse such passages in the midst of London.

8. See the admirable abridgment given by Tacitus, in the life of Agricola, and copiously, though perhaps not completely, illustrated by our own antiquarians, Camden and Horsley.

national glory, when the throne was disgraced by the weakest, or the most vicious of mankind. At the very time when Domitian, confined to his palace, felt the terrors which he inspired; his legions, under the command of the virtuous Agricola, defeated the collected force of the Caledonians at the foot of the Grampian hills; and his fleets, venturing to explore an unknown and dangerous navigation, displayed the Roman arms round every part of the island. The conquest of Britain was considered as already atchieved; and it was the design of Agricola to complete and ensure his success by the easy reduction of Ireland, for which, in his opinion, one legion and a few auxiliaries were sufficient.[9] The western isle might be improved into a valuable possession, and the Britons would wear their chains with the less reluctance, if the prospect and example of freedom was on every side removed from before their eyes.

But the superior merit of Agricola soon occasioned his removal from the government of Britain; and for ever disappointed this rational, though extensive scheme of conquest. Before his departure, the prudent general had provided for security as well as for dominion. He had observed, that the island is almost divided into two unequal parts by the opposite gulfs, or, as they are now called, the Friths of Scotland. Across the narrow interval of about forty miles, he had drawn a line of military stations, which was afterwards fortified in the reign of Antoninus Pius, by a turf rampart erected on foundations of stone.[10] This wall of Antoninus, at a small distance beyond the modern cities of Edinburgh and Glasgow, was fixed as the limit of the Roman province. The native Caledonians preserved in the northern extremity of the island their wild independence, for which they were not less indebted to their poverty than to their valour. Their incursions were frequently repelled and chastised; but their country was never subdued.[11] The masters of the fairest and most wealthy climates of the globe, turned with contempt from gloomy hills assailed by the winter tempest, from lakes concealed in a blue mist, and from cold and lonely heaths, over which the deer of the forest were chased by a troop of naked barbarians.[12]

9. The Irish writers, jealous of their national honour, are extremely provoked on this occasion, both with Tacitus and with Agricola.

10. See Horsley's Britannia Romana, l. i. c. 10.

11. The poet Buchanan celebrates, with elegance and spirit (see his Sylvæ v.), the

unviolated independence of his native country. But, if the single testimony of Richard of Cirencester was sufficient to create a Roman province of Vespasiana to the north of the wall, that independence would be reduced within very narrow limits.

12. See Appian (in Proæm.) and the uniform

Such was the state of the Roman frontiers, and such the maxims of Imperial policy from the death of Augustus to the accession of Trajan. That virtuous and active prince had received the education of a soldier, and possessed the talents of a general.[13] The peaceful system of his predecessors was interrupted by scenes of war and conquest; and the legions, after a long interval, beheld a military emperor at their head. The first exploits of Trajan were against the Dacians, the most warlike of men, who dwelt beyond the Danube, and who, during the reign of Domitian, had insulted with impunity the Majesty of Rome.[14] To the strength and fierceness of barbarians, they added a contempt for life, which was derived from a warm persuasion of the immortality and transmigration of the soul.[15] Decebalus, the Dacian king, approved himself a rival not unworthy of Trajan; nor did he despair of his own and the public fortune, till, by the confession of his enemies, he had exhausted every resource both of valour and policy.[16] This memorable war, with a very short suspension of hostilities, lasted five years; and as the emperor could exert, without controul, the whole force of the state, it was terminated by an absolute submission of the barbarians.[17] The new province of Dacia, which formed a second exception to the precept of Augustus, was about thirteen hundred miles in circumference. Its natural boundaries were the Niester, the Teyss, or Tibiscus, the Lower Danube, and the Euxine Sea. The vestiges of a military road may still be traced from the banks of the Danube to the neighbourhood of Bender, a place famous in modern history, and the actual frontier of the Turkish and Russian empires.[18]

Conquest of Dacia; the second exception.

Trajan was ambitious of fame; and as long as mankind shall continue to bestow more liberal applause on their destroyers than on their benefactors, the thirst of military glory will ever be the vice of the most exalted characters. The praises of Alexander, transmitted by a succession of poets and historians, had kindled a dangerous

Conquests of Trajan in the east.

---

imagery of Ossian's poems, which, according to every hypothesis, were composed by a native Caledonian.

13. See Pliny's Panegyric, which seems founded on facts.

14. Dion Cassius, l. lxvii.

15. Herodotus, l. iv. c. 94. Julian in the Cæsars, with Spanheim's observations.

16. Plin. Epist. viii. 9.

17. Dion Cassius, l. lxviii. p. 1123. 1131. Julian in Cæsaribus. Eutropius, viii. 2. 6. Aurelius Victor in Epitome.

18. See a Memoir of M. d'Anville, on the Province of Dacia, in the Academie des Inscriptions, tom. xxviii. p. 444–468.

emulation in the mind of Trajan. Like him the Roman emperor undertook an expedition against the nations of the east, but he lamented with a sigh, that his advanced age scarcely left him any hopes of equalling the renown of the son of Philip.[19] Yet the success of Trajan, however transient, was rapid and specious. The degenerate Parthians, broken by intestine discord, fled before his arms. He descended the river Tigris in triumph, from the mountains of Armenia to the Persian gulph. He enjoyed the honour of being the first, as he was the last, of the Roman generals, who ever navigated that remote sea. His fleets ravaged the coasts of Arabia; and Trajan vainly flattered himself that he was approaching towards the confines of India.[20] Every day the astonished senate received the intelligence of new names and new nations, that acknowledged his sway. They were informed that the kings of Bosphorus, Colchos, Iberia, Albania, Osrhoene, and even the Parthian monarch himself, had accepted their diadems from the hands of the emperor; that the independent tribes of the Median and Carduchian hills had implored his protection; and that the rich countries of Armenia, Mesopotamia, and Assyria, were reduced into the state of provinces.[21] But the death of Trajan soon clouded the splendid prospect; and it was justly to be dreaded, that so many distant nations would throw off the unaccustomed yoke, when they were no longer restrained by the powerful hand which had imposed it.

Resigned by his successor Hadrian.   It was an ancient tradition, that when the Capitol was founded by one of the Roman kings, the god Terminus (who presided over boundaries, and was represented according to the fashion of that age by a large stone) alone, among all the inferior deities, refused to yield his place to Jupiter himself. A favourable inference was drawn from his obstinacy, which was interpreted by the augurs, as a sure presage that the boundaries of the Roman power would never recede.[22] During many ages, the prediction, as it is usual, contributed to its own accomplishment. But though Terminus had resisted the majesty of Jupiter, he submitted to the authority of the emperor Hadrian.[23] The resignation

19. Trajan's sentiments are represented in a very just and lively manner in the Cæsars of Julian.
20. Eutropius and Sextus Rufus have endeavoured to perpetuate the illusion. See a very sensible dissertation of M. Freret in the Academie des Inscriptions, tom. xxi. p. 55.
21. Dion Cassius, l. lxviii; and the Abbreviators.

22. Ovid. Fast. l. ii. ver. 667. See Livy, and Dionysius of Halicarnassus, under the reign of Tarquin.
23. St. Augustin is highly delighted with the proof of the weakness of Terminus, and the vanity of the augurs. See De Civitate Dei, iv. 29.

of all the eastern conquests of Trajan was the first measure of his reign. He restored to the Parthians the election of an independent Sovereign, withdrew the Roman garrisons from the provinces of Armenia, Mesopotamia, and Assyria, and, in compliance with the precept of Augustus, once more established the Euphrates as the frontier of the empire.[24] Censure, which arraigns the public actions and the private motives of princes, has ascribed to envy, a conduct, which might be attributed to the prudence and moderation of Hadrian. The various character of that emperor, capable, by turns, of the meanest and the most generous sentiments, may afford some colour to the suspicion. It was, however, scarcely in his power to place the superiority of his predecessor in a more conspicuous light, than by thus confessing himself unequal to the task of defending the conquests of Trajan.

The martial and ambitious spirit of Trajan, formed a very singular contrast with the moderation of his successor. The restless activity of Hadrian was not less remarkable, when compared with the gentle repose of Antoninus Pius. The life of the former was almost a perpetual journey; and as he possessed the various talents *Contrast of Hadrian and Antoninus Pius.* of the soldier, the statesman, and the scholar, he gratified his curiosity in the discharge of his duty. Careless of the difference of seasons and of climates, he marched on foot, and bare-headed, over the snows of Caledonia, and the sultry plains of the Upper Egypt; nor was there a province of the empire, which, in the course of his reign, was not honoured with the presence of the monarch.[25] But the tranquil life of Antoninus Pius was spent in the bosom of Italy; and, during the twenty-three years that he directed the public administration, the longest journies of that amiable prince extended no farther than from his palace in Rome, to the retirement of his Lanuvian Villa.[26]

Notwithstanding this difference in their personal conduct, the general system of Augustus was equally adopted and uniformly pursued by Hadrian and by the two Antonines. They persisted in the design of maintaining the dignity of the empire, without attempting to enlarge its limits. By every honourable expedient *Pacific system of Hadrian and the two Antonines.*

---

24. See the Augustan History, p. 5. Jerome's Chronicle, and all the Epitomisers. It is somewhat surprising, that this memorable event should be omitted by Dion, or rather by Xiphilin.

25. Dion, l. lxix. p. 1158. Hist. August. p. 5 .8.

If all our historians were lost, medals, inscriptions, and other monuments, would be sufficient to record the travels of Hadrian.

26. See the Augustan History and the Epitomes.

they invited the friendship of the barbarians; and endeavoured to convince mankind, that the Roman power, raised above the temptation of conquest, was actuated only by the love of order and justice. During a long period of forty-three years their virtuous labours were crowned with success; and if we except a few slight hostilities that served to exercise the legions of the frontier, the reigns of Hadrian and Antoninus Pius offer the fair prospect of universal peace.[27] The Roman name was revered among the most remote nations of the earth. The fiercest barbarians frequently submitted their differences to the arbitration of the emperor; and we are informed by a cotemporary historian, that he had seen ambassadors who were refused the honour which they came to solicit, of being admitted into the rank of subjects.[28]

Defensive wars of Marcus Antoninus. The terror of the Roman arms added weight and dignity to the moderation of the emperors. They preserved peace by a constant preparation for war; and while justice regulated their conduct, they announced to the nations on their confines, that they were as little disposed to endure, as to offer an injury. The military strength, which it had been sufficient for Hadrian and the elder Antoninus to display, was exerted against the Parthians and the Germans by the emperor Marcus. The hostilities of the barbarians provoked the resentment of that philosophic monarch, and, in the prosecution of a just defence, Marcus and his generals obtained many signal victories, both on the Euphrates, and on the Danube.[29] The military establishment of the Roman empire, which thus assured either its tranquility or success, will now become the proper and important object of our attention.

Military establishment of the Roman emperors. In the purer ages of the commonwealth, the use of arms was reserved for those ranks of citizens who had a country to love, a property to defend, and some share in enacting those laws, which it was their interest, as well as duty, to maintain. But in proportion as the public freedom was lost in extent of conquest, war was

---

27. We must, however, remember, that, in the time of Hadrian, a rebellion of the Jews raged with religious fury, though only in a single province: Pausanias (l. viii. c. 43.) mentions two necessary and successful wars, conducted by the generals of Pius. 1st, Against the wandering Moors, who were driven into the solitudes of Atlas. 2d, Against the Brigantes of Britain, who had invaded the Roman province. Both these wars (with several other

hostilities) are mentioned in the Augustan History, p. 19.
28. Appian of Alexandria, in the preface to his History of the Roman wars.
29. Dion, l. lxxi. Hist. August. in Marco. The Parthian victories gave birth to a crowd of contemptible historians, whose memory has been rescued from oblivion, and exposed to ridicule, in a very lively piece of criticism of Lucian.

gradually improved into an art, and degraded into a trade.[30] The legions themselves, even at the time when they were recruited in the most distant provinces, were supposed to consist of Roman citizens. That distinction was generally considered, either as a legal qualification, or as a proper recompence for the soldier; but a more serious regard was paid to the essential merit of age, strength, and military stature.[31] In all levies, a just preference was given to the climates of the North over those of the South: the race of men born to the exercise of arms, was sought for in the country rather than in cities; and it was very reasonably presumed, that the hardy occupations of smiths, carpenters, and huntsmen, would supply more vigour and resolution, than the sedentary trades which are employed in the service of luxury.[32] After every qualification of property had been laid aside, the armies of the Roman emperors were still commanded, for the most part, by officers of a liberal birth and education; but the common soldiers, like the mercenary troops of modern Europe, were drawn from the meanest, and very frequently from the most profligate, of mankind.

That public virtue which among the ancients was denominated *Discipline.* patriotism, is derived from a strong sense of our own interest in the preservation and prosperity of the free government of which we are members. Such a sentiment, which had rendered the legions of the republic almost invincible, could make but a very feeble impression on the mercenary servants of a despotic prince; and it became necessary to supply that defect by other motives, of a different, but not less forcible nature; honour and religion. The peasant, or mechanic, imbibed the useful prejudice that he was advanced to the more dignified profession of arms, in which his rank and reputation would depend on his own valour: and that, although the prowess of a private soldier must often escape the notice of fame, his own behaviour might sometimes confer glory or disgrace on the company, the legion, or even the army, to whose honours he was associated. On his first entrance into the service, an oath was administered to him, with every circumstance of solemnity. He promised never to desert his standard, to

---

30. The poorest rank of soldiers possessed above forty pounds sterling (Dionys. Halicarn. iv. 17.), a very high qualification, at a time when money was so scarce, that an ounce of silver was equivalent to seventy pound weight of brass. The populace, excluded by the ancient constitution, were indiscriminately admitted by Marius. See Sallust. de Bell. Jugurth. c. 91.

31. Cæsar formed his legion Alauda, of Gauls and strangers; but it was during the licence of civil war; and after the victory, he gave them the freedom of the city for their reward.

32. See Vegetius de Re Militari, l. i. c. 2–7.

submit his own will to the commands of his leaders, and to sacrifice his life for the safety of the emperor and the empire.[33] The attachment of the Roman troops to their standards, was inspired by the united influence of religion and of honour. The golden eagle, which glittered in the front of the legion, was the object of their fondest devotion; nor was it esteemed less impious, than it was ignominious, to abandon that sacred ensign in the hour of danger.[34] These motives, which derived their strength from the imagination, were enforced by fears and hopes of a more substantial kind. Regular pay, occasional donatives, and a stated recompence, after the appointed time of service, alleviated the hardships of the military life,[35] whilst, on the other hand, it was impossible for cowardice or disobedience to escape the severest punishment. The centurions were authorized to chastise with blows, the generals had a right to punish with death; and it was an inflexible maxim of Roman discipline, that a good soldier should dread his officers far more than the enemy. From such laudable arts did the valour of the Imperial troops receive a degree of firmness and docility, unattainable by the impetuous and irregular passions of barbarians.

Exercises.   And yet so sensible were the Romans of the imperfection of valour without skill and practice, that, in their language, the name of an army was borrowed from the word which signified exercise.[36] Military exercises were the important and unremitted object of their discipline. The recruits and young soldiers were constantly trained both in the morning and in the evening, nor was age or knowledge allowed to excuse the veterans from the daily repetition of what they had completely learnt. Large sheds were erected in the winter-quarters of the troops, that their useful labours might not receive any interruption from the most tempestuous

33. The oath of service and fidelity to the emperor, was annually renewed by the troops, on the first of January.

34. Tacitus calls the Roman Eagles, Bellorum Deos. They were placed in a chapel in the camp, and with the other deities received the religious worship of the troops.

35. See Gronovius de Pecunia vetere, l. iii. p. 120, &c. The emperor Domitian raised the annual stipend of the legionaries to twelve pieces of gold, which, in his time, was equivalent to about ten of our guineas. This pay, somewhat higher than our own, had been, and was afterwards, gradually increased, according to the progress of wealth and military government. After twenty years service, the veteran received three thousand denarii (about one hundred pounds sterling), or a proportionable allowance of land. The pay and advantages of the guards were, in general, about double those of the legions.

36. *Exercitus ab exercitando*, Varro de Linguâ Latinâ, l. iv. Cicero in Tusculan. l. ii. 37. There is room for a very interesting work, which should lay open the connexion between the languages and manners of nations.

weather; and it was carefully observed, that the arms destined to this imitation of war, should be of double the weight which was required in real action.[37] It is not the purpose of this work to enter into any minute description of the Roman exercises. We shall only remark, that they comprehended whatever could add strength to the body, activity to the limbs, or grace to the motions. The soldiers were diligently instructed to march, to run, to leap, to swim, to carry heavy burdens, to handle every species of arms that was used either for offence or for defence, either in distant engagement or in a closer onset; to form a variety of evolutions; and to move to the sound of flutes, in the Pyrrhic or martial dance.[38] In the midst of peace, the Roman troops familiarised themselves with the practice of war; and it is prettily remarked by an ancient historian who had fought against them, that the effusion of blood was the only circumstance which distinguished a field of battle from a field of exercise.[39] It was the policy of the ablest generals, and even of the emperors themselves, to encourage these military studies by their presence and example; and we are informed that Hadrian, as well as Trajan, frequently condescended to instruct the unexperienced soldiers, to reward the diligent, and sometimes to dispute with them the prize of superior strength or dexterity.[40] Under the reigns of those princes, the science of tactics was cultivated with success; and as long as the empire retained any vigour, their military instructions were respected as the most perfect model of Roman discipline.

Nine centuries of war had gradually introduced into the service many alterations and improvements. The legions, as they are described by Polybius,[41] in the time of the Punic wars, differed very materially from those which atchieved the victories of Cæsar, *The legions under the emperors.* or defended the monarchy of Hadrian and the Antonines. The constitution of the Imperial legion may be described in a few words.[42] The heavy-armed

---

37. Vegetius, l. ii. and the rest of his first book.

38. The Pyrrhic dance is extremely well illustrated by M. le Beau, in the Academie des Inscriptions, tom. xxxv. p. 262, &c. That learned academician, in a series of memoirs, has collected all the passages of the ancients that relate to the Roman legion.

39. Joseph. de Bell. Judaico, l. iii. c. 5. We are indebted to this Jew for some very curious details of Roman discipline.

40. Plin. Panegyr. c. 13. Life of Hadrian, in the Augustan History.

41. See an admirable digression on the Roman discipline, in the sixth book of his history.

42. Vegetius de Re Militari, l. ii. c. 4, &c. Considerable part of his very perplexed abridgment was taken from the regulations of Trajan and Hadrian; and the legion, as he describes it, cannot suit any other age of the Roman empire.

infantry, which composed its principal strength,[43] was divided into ten cohorts, and fifty-five companies, under the orders of a correspondent number of tribunes and centurions. The first cohort, which always claimed the post of honour and the custody of the eagle, was formed of eleven hundred and five soldiers, the most approved for valour and fidelity. The remaining nine cohorts consisted each of five hundred and fifty-five; and the whole body of legionary infantry amounted to six thousand one hundred men. Their arms were uniform, and admirably adapted to the nature of their service: an open helmet, with a lofty crest; a breast-plate, or coat of mail; greaves on their legs, and an ample buckler on their left arm. The buckler was of an oblong and concave figure, four feet in length, and two and an half in breadth, framed of a light wood, covered with a bull's hide, and strongly guarded with plates of brass. Besides a lighter spear, the legionary soldier grasped in his right hand the formidable *pilum*, a ponderous javelin, whose utmost length was about six feet, and which was terminated by a massy triangular point of steel of eighteen inches.[44] This instrument was indeed much inferior to our modern fire-arms; since it was exhausted by a single discharge, at the distance of only ten or twelve paces. Yet when it was launched by a firm and skilful hand, there was not any cavalry that durst venture within its reach, nor any shield or corslet that could sustain the impetuosity of its weight. As soon as the Roman had darted his *pilum*, he drew his sword, and rushed forwards to close with the enemy. His sword was a short well-tempered Spanish blade, that carried a double edge, and was alike suited to the purpose of striking or of pushing; but the soldier was always instructed to prefer the latter use of his weapon, as his own body remained less exposed, whilst he inflicted a more dangerous wound on his adversary.[45] The legion was usually drawn up eight deep; and the regular distance of three feet was left between the files as well as ranks.[46] A body of troops, habituated to preserve this open order, in a long front and a rapid charge, found themselves prepared

Arms.

---

43. Vegetius de Re Militari, l. ii. c. 1. In the purer age of Cæsar and Cicero, the word *miles* was almost confined to the infantry. Under the lower empire, and in the times of chivalry, it was appropriated almost as exclusively to the men at arms, who fought on horseback.

44. In the time of Polybius and Dionysius of Halicarnassus (l. v. c. 45.), the steel point of the *pilum* seems to have been much longer. In the time of Vegetius, it was reduced to a foot, or even nine inches. I have chosen a medium.

45. For the legionary arms, see Lipsius de Militiâ Romanâ, l. iii. c. 2–7.

46. See the beautiful comparison of Virgil, Georgic. ii. v. 279.

to execute every disposition which the circumstances of war, or the skill of their leader, might suggest. The soldier possessed a free space for his arms and motions, and sufficient intervals were allowed, through which seasonable reinforcements might be introduced to the relief of the exhausted combatants.[47] The tactics of the Greeks and Macedonians were formed on very different principles. The strength of the phalanx depended on sixteen ranks of long pikes, wedged together in the closest array.[48] But it was soon discovered by reflection, as well as by the event, that the strength of the phalanx was unable to contend with the activity of the legion.[49]

The cavalry, without which the force of the legion would have remained imperfect, was divided into ten troops or squadrons; the *Cavalry.* first, as the companion of the first cohort, consisted of an hundred and thirty-two men; whilst each of the other nine amounted only to sixty-six. The entire establishment formed a regiment, if we may use the modern expression, of seven hundred and twenty-six horse, naturally connected with its respective legion, but occasionally separated to act in the line, and to compose a part of the wings of the army.[50] The cavalry of the emperors was no longer composed, like that of the ancient republic, of the noblest youths of Rome and Italy, who, by performing their military service on horseback, prepared themselves for the offices of senator and consul; and solicited, by deeds of valour, the future suffrages of their countrymen.[51] Since the alteration of manners and government, the most wealthy of the equestrian order were engaged in the administration of justice, and of the revenue;[52] and whenever they embraced the profession of arms, they were immediately intrusted with a troop of horse, or a cohort of foot.[53] Trajan and Hadrian formed their cavalry from the same provinces, and the same class of their subjects, which recruited the ranks of the legion. The horses

47. M. Guichardt, Memoires Militaires, tom. i. c. 4. and Nouveaux Memoires, tom. i. p. 293–311, has treated the subject like a scholar and an officer.

48. See Arrian's Tactics. With the true partiality of a Greek, Arrian rather chose to describe the phalanx, of which he had read, than the legions which he had commanded.

49. Polyb. l. xvii.

50. Veget. de Re Militari, l. ii. c. 6. His positive testimony, which might be supported by circumstantial evidence, ought surely to silence those critics who refuse the Imperial legion its proper body of cavalry.

51. See Livy almost throughout, particularly xlii. 61.

52. Plin. Hist. Natur. xxxiii. 2. The true sense of that very curious passage was first discovered and illustrated by M. de Beaufort, Republique Romaine, l. ii. c. 2.

53. As in the instance of Horace and Agricola. This appears to have been a defect in the Roman discipline; which Hadrian endeavoured to remedy, by ascertaining the legal age of a tribune.

were bred, for the most part, in Spain or Cappadocia. The Roman troopers despised the complete armour with which the cavalry of the East was encumbered. *Their* more useful arms consisted in a helmet, an oblong shield, light boots, and a coat of mail. A javelin, and a long broad sword, were their principal weapons of offence. The use of lances and of iron maces they seem to have borrowed from the barbarians.[54]

Auxiliaries.   The safety and honour of the empire was principally intrusted to the legions, but the policy of Rome condescended to adopt every useful instrument of war. Considerable levies were regularly made among the provincials, who had not yet deserved the honourable distinction of Romans. Many dependant princes and communities, dispersed round the frontiers, were permitted, for a while, to hold their freedom and security by the tenure of military service.[55] Even select troops of hostile barbarians were frequently compelled or persuaded to consume their dangerous valour in remote climates, and for the benefit of the state.[56] All these were included under the general name of auxiliaries; and howsoever they might vary according to the difference of times and circumstances, their numbers were seldom much inferior to those of the legions themselves.[57] Among the auxiliaries, the bravest and most faithful bands were placed under the command of præfects and centurions, and severely trained in the arts of Roman discipline; but the far greater part retained those arms, to which the nature of their country, or their early habits of life, more peculiarly adapted them. By this institution each legion, to whom a certain proportion of auxiliaries was allotted, contained within itself every species of lighter troops, and of missile weapons; and was capable of encountering every nation, with the advantages of its respective arms and discipline.[58] Nor was the legion destitute of what, in modern language, would be styled a train

Artillery.   of artillery. It consisted in ten military engines of the largest, and fifty-five of a smaller size; but all of which, either in an oblique or horizontal manner, discharged stones and darts with irresistible violence.[59]

---

54. See Arrian's Tactics.

55. Such, in particular, was the state of the Batavians. Tacit. Germania, c. 29.

56. Marcus Antoninus obliged the vanquished Quadi and Marcomanni to supply him with a large body of troops, which he immediately sent into Britain. Dion Cassius, l. lxxi.

57. Tacit. Annal. iv. 5. Those who fix a regu-

lar proportion of as many foot, and twice as many horse, confound the auxiliaries of the emperors, with the Italian allies of the republic.

58. Vegetius, ii. 2. Arrian, in his order of march and battle against the Alani.

59. The subject of the ancient machines is treated with great knowledge and ingenuity

The camp of a Roman legion presented the appearance of a *Encampment.* fortified city.[60] As soon as the space was marked out, the pioneers carefully levelled the ground, and removed every impediment that might interrupt its perfect regularity. Its form was an exact quadrangle; and we may calculate, that a square of about seven hundred yards was sufficient for the encampment of twenty thousand Romans; though a similar number of our own troops would expose to the enemy a front of more than treble that extent. In the midst of the camp, the prætorium, or general's quarters, rose above the others; the cavalry, the infantry, and the auxiliaries occupied their respective stations; the streets were broad, and perfectly straight, and a vacant space of two hundred feet was left on all sides, between the tents and the rampart. The rampart itself was usually twelve feet high, armed with a line of strong and intricate palisades, and defended by a ditch of twelve feet in depth as well as in breadth. This important labour was performed by the hands of the legionaries themselves; to whom the use of the spade and the pick-axe was no less familiar than that of the sword or *pilum.* Active valour may often be the present of nature; but such patient diligence can be the fruit only of habit and discipline.[61]

Whenever the trumpet gave the signal of departure, the camp was *March.* almost instantly broke up, and the troops fell into their ranks without delay or confusion. Besides their arms, which the legionaries scarcely ·considered as an encumbrance, they were laden with their kitchen furniture, the instruments of fortification, and the provision of many days.[62] Under this weight, which would oppress the delicacy of a modern soldier, they were trained by a regular step to advance, in about six hours, near twenty miles.[63] On the appearance of an enemy, they threw aside their baggage, and by easy and rapid evolutions converted the column of march into an

---

by the Chevalier Folard (Polybe, tom. ii. p. 233–290). He prefers them in many respects to our modern cannon and mortars. We may observe, that the use of them in the field gradually became more prevalent, in proportion as personal valour and military skill declined with the Roman empire. When men were no longer found, their place was supplied by machines. See Vegetius, ii. 25. Arrian.

60. Vegetius finishes his second book, and the description of the legion, with the following emphatic words: "Universa quæ in quoque belli genere necessaria esse creduntur, secum legio debet ubique portare, ut in quovis loco fixerit castra, armatam faciat civitatem."

61. For the Roman Castremetation, see Polybius, l. vi. with Lipsius de Militia Romana, Joseph. de Bel. Jud. l. iii. c. 5. Vegetius, i. 21–25. iii. 9. and Memoires de Guichard, tom. i. c. i.

62. Cicero in Tusculan. ii. 37. – Joseph. de Bell. Jud. l. iii. 5. Frontinus, iv. I.

63. Vegetius, i. 9. See Memoires de l'Academie des Inscriptions, tom. xxv. p. 187.

order of battle.[64] The slingers and archers skirmished in the front; the auxiliaries formed the first line, and were seconded or sustained by the strength of the legions: the cavalry covered the flanks, and the military engines were placed in the rear.

Number and disposition of the legions.   Such were the arts of war, by which the Roman emperors defended their extensive conquests, and preserved a military spirit, at a time when every other virtue was oppressed by luxury and despotism. If, in the consideration of their armies, we pass from their discipline to their numbers, we shall not find it easy to define them with any tolerable accuracy. We may compute, however, that the legion, which was itself a body of six thousand eight hundred and thirty-one Romans, might, with its attendant auxiliaries, amount to about twelve thousand five hundred men. The peace establishment of Hadrian and his successors was composed of no less than thirty of these formidable brigades; and most probably formed a standing force of three hundred and seventy-five thousand men. Instead of being confined within the walls of fortified cities, which the Romans considered as the refuge of weakness or pusillanimity, the legions were encamped on the banks of the great rivers, and along the frontiers of the barbarians. As their stations, for the most part, remained fixed and permanent, we may venture to describe the distribution of the troops. Three legions were sufficient for Britain. The principal strength lay upon the Rhine and Danube, and consisted of sixteen legions, in the following proportions: two in the Lower, and three in the Upper Germany; one in Rhætia, one in Noricum, four in Pannonia, three in Mæsia, and two in Dacia. The defence of the Euphrates was entrusted to eight legions, six of whom were planted in Syria, and the other two in Cappadocia. With regard to Egypt, Africa, and Spain, as they were far removed from any important scene of war, a single legion maintained the domestic tranquillity of each of those great provinces. Even Italy was not left destitute of a military force. Above twenty thousand chosen soldiers, distinguished by the titles of City Cohorts and Prætorian Guards, watched over the safety of the monarch and the capital. As the authors of almost every revolution that distracted the empire, the Prætorians will, very soon, and very loudly, demand our attention; but in their arms and institutions, we cannot find any circumstance which discriminated them from the legions,

64. See those evolutions admirably well explained by M. Guichard, Nouveaux Memoires, tom. i. p. 141–234.

unless it were a more splendid appearance, and a less rigid discipline.[65]

The navy maintained by the emperors might seem inadequate to their greatness; but it was fully sufficient for every useful purpose of *Navy.* government. The ambition of the Romans was confined to the land; nor was that warlike people ever actuated by the enterprising spirit which had prompted the navigators of Tyre, of Carthage, and even of Marseilles, to enlarge the bounds of the world, and to explore the most remote coasts of the ocean. To the Romans the ocean remained an object of terror rather than of curiosity;[66] the whole extent of the Mediterranean, after the destruction of Carthage, and the extirpation of the pirates, was included within their provinces. The policy of the emperors was directed only to preserve the peaceful dominion of that sea, and to protect the commerce of their subjects. With these moderate views, Augustus stationed two permanent fleets in the most convenient ports of Italy, the one at Ravenna, on the Adriatic, the other at Misenum, in the bay of Naples. Experience seems at length to have convinced the ancients, that as soon as their gallies exceeded two, or at the most three ranks of oars, they were suited rather for vain pomp than for real service. Augustus himself, in the victory of Actium, had seen the superiority of his own light frigates (they were called Liburnians) over the lofty but unwieldy castles of his rival.[67] Of these Liburnians he composed the two fleets of Ravenna and Misenum, destined to command, the one the eastern, the other the western division of the Mediterranean; and to each of the squadrons he attached a body of several thousand marines. Besides these two ports, which may be considered as the principal seats of the Roman navy, a very considerable force was stationed at Frejus, on the coast of Provence, and the Euxine was guarded by forty ships, and three thousand soldiers. To all these we add the fleet which preserved the communication between Gaul and Britain, and a great number of vessels constantly maintained on the Rhine and Danube, to harass the country, or to intercept the passage of the barbarians.[68] If we review this general

---

65. Tacitus (Annal. iv. 5.) has given us a state of the legions under Tiberius: and Dion Cassius (l. lv. p. 794.) under Alexander Severus. I have endeavoured to fix on the proper medium between these two periods. See likewise Lipsius de Magnitudine Romanâ, l. i. c. 4, 5.

66. The Romans tried to disguise, by the pretence of religious awe, their ignorance

and terror. See Tacit. Germania, c. 34.

67. Plutarch. in Marc. Anton. And yet, if we may credit Orosius, these monstrous castles were no more than ten feet above the water, vi. 19.

68. See Lipsius, de Magnitud. Rom. l. i. c. 5. The sixteen last chapters of Vegetius relate to naval affairs.

state of the Imperial forces; of the cavalry as well as infantry; of the legions, the auxiliaries, the guards, and the navy; the most liberal computation will not allow us to fix the entire establishment by sea and by land at more

Amount of the whole establishment.

than four hundred and fifty thousand men: a military power, which, however formidable it may seem, was equalled by a monarch of the last century, whose kingdom was confined within a single province of the Roman empire.[69]

View of the provinces of the Roman empire.

We have attempted to explain the spirit which moderated, and the strength which supported, the power of Hadrian and the Antonines. We shall now endeavour, with clearness and precision, to describe the provinces once united under their sway, but, at present, divided into so many independent and hostile states.

Spain.

Spain, the western extremity of the empire, of Europe, and of the ancient world, has, in every age, invariably preserved the same natural limits; the Pyrenæan mountains, the Mediterranean, and the Atlantic Ocean. That great peninsula, at present so unequally divided between two sovereigns, was distributed by Augustus into three provinces, Lusitania, Bætica, and Tarraconensis. The kingdom of Portugal now fills the place of the warlike country of the Lusitanians; and the loss sustained by the former, on the side of the East, is compensated by an accession of territory towards the North. The confines of Grenada and Andalusia correspond with those of ancient Bætica. The remainder of Spain, Gallicia, and the Asturias, Biscay, and Navarre, Leon, and the two Castilles, Murcia, Valencia, Catalonia, and Arragon, all contributed to form the third and most considerable of the Roman governments, which, from the name of its capital, was styled the province of Tarragona.[70] Of the native barbarians, the Celtiberians were the most powerful, as the Cantabrians and Asturians proved the most obstinate. Confident in the strength of their mountains, they were the last who submitted to the arms of Rome, and the first who threw off the yoke of the Arabs.

Gaul.

Ancient Gaul, as it contained the whole country between the Pyrenees, the Alps, the Rhine, and the Ocean, was of greater extent

---

69. Voltaire, Siecle de Louis XIV. c. 29. It must, however, be remembered, that France still feels that extraordinary effort.

70. See Strabo, l. ii. It is natural enough to suppose, that Arragon is derived from Tarraconensis, and several moderns who have written in Latin, use those words as synonymous. It is however certain, that the Arragon, a little stream which falls from the Pyrenees into the Ebro, first gave its name to a country, and gradually to a kingdom. See d'Anville, Geographie du Moyen Age, p. 181.

than modern France. To the dominions of that powerful monarchy, with its recent acquisitions of Alsace and Lorraine, we must add the dutchy of Savoy, the cantons of Switzerland, the four electorates of the Rhine, and the territories of Liege, Luxemburgh, Hainault, Flanders, and Brabant. When Augustus gave laws to the conquests of his father, he introduced a division of Gaul equally adapted to the progress of the legions, to the course of the rivers, and to the principal national distinctions, which had comprehended above an hundred independent states.[71] The sea-coast of the Mediterranean, Languedoc, Provence, and Dauphiné, received their provincial appellation from the colony of Narbonne. The government of Aquitaine was extended from the Pyrenees to the Loire. The country between the Loire and the Seine was styled the Celtic Gaul, and soon borrowed a new denomination from the celebrated colony of Lugdunum, or Lyons. The Belgic lay beyond the Seine, and in more ancient times had been bounded only by the Rhine; but a little before the age of Cæsar, the Germans, abusing their superiority of valour, had occupied a considerable portion of the Belgic territory. The Roman conquerors very eagerly embraced so flattering a circumstance, and the Gallic frontier of the Rhine, from Basil to Leyden, received the pompous names of the Upper and the Lower Germany.[72] Such, under the reign of the Antonines, were the six provinces of Gaul; the Narbonnese, Aquitaine, the Celtic, or Lyonnese, the Belgic, and the two Germanies.

We have already had occasion to mention the conquest of Britain, and to fix the boundary of the Roman province in this island. *Britain.*
It comprehended all England, Wales, and the Lowlands of Scotland, as far as the Friths of Dunbarton and Edinburgh. Before Britain lost her freedom, the country was irregularly divided between thirty tribes of barbarians, of whom the most considerable were the Belgæ in the West, the Brigantes in the North, the Silures in South Wales, and the Iceni in Norfolk and Suffolk.[73] As far as we can either trace or credit the resemblance of manners and language, Spain, Gaul, and Britain were peopled by the same hardy race of savages. Before they yielded to the Roman arms, they often disputed the field, and often renewed the contest. After their

---

71. One hundred and fifteen *cities* appear in the Notitia of Gaul; and it is well known that this appellation was applied not only to the capital town, but to the whole territory of each state. But Plutarch and Appian increase the number of tribes to three or four hundred.

72. D'Anville. Notice de l'Ancienne Gaule.

73. Whitaker's History of Manchester, vol. i. c. 3.

submission they constituted the western division of the European provinces, which extended from the columns of Hercules to the wall of Antoninus, and from the mouth of the Tagus to the sources of the Rhine and Danube.

Italy.

Before the Roman conquest, the country which is now called Lombardy, was not considered as a part of Italy. It had been occupied by a powerful colony of Gauls, who settling themselves along the banks of the Po, from Piedmont to Romagna, carried their arms and diffused their name from the Alps to the Apennine. The Ligurians dwelt on the rocky coast, which now forms the republic of Genoa. Venice was yet unborn; but the territories of that state, which lie to the east of the Adige, were inhabited by the Venetians.[74] The middle part of the peninsula that now composes the dutchy of Tuscany and the ecclesiastical state, was the ancient seat of the Etruscans and Umbrians; to the former of whom Italy was indebted for the first rudiments of civilized life.[75] The Tyber rolled at the foot of the seven hills of Rome, and the country of the Sabines, the Latins, and the Volsci, from that river to the frontiers of Naples, was the theatre of her infant victories. On that celebrated ground the first consuls deserved triumphs; their successors adorned villas, and *their* posterity have erected convents.[76] Capua and Campania possessed the immediate territory of Naples; the rest of the kingdom was inhabited by many warlike nations, the Marsi, the Samnites, the Apulians, and the Lucanians; and the sea-coasts had been covered by the flourishing colonies of the Greeks. We may remark, that when Augustus divided Italy into eleven regions, the little province of Istria was annexed to that seat of Roman sovereignty.[77]

The Danube and Illyrian frontier.

The European provinces of Rome were protected by the course of the Rhine and the Danube. The latter of those mighty streams, which rises at the distance of only thirty miles from the former, flows above thirteen hundred miles, for the most part, to the south-east, collects the tribute of sixty navigable rivers, and is, at length, through six mouths received into the Euxine, which appears scarcely equal to such an accession of waters.[78] The provinces of the Danube soon acquired

---

74. The Italian Veneti, though often confounded with the Gauls, were more probably of Illyrian origin. See M. Freret, Memoires de l'Academie des Inscriptions, tom. xviii.

75. See Maffei Verona illustrata, l. i.

76. The first contrast was observed by the ancients. See Florus, i. ii. The second must strike every modern traveller.

77. Pliny (Hist. Natur. l. iii.) follows the division of Italy, by Augustus.

78. Tournefort, Voyages en Grèce et Asie Mineure, lettre xviii.

the general appellation of Illyricum, or the Illyrian frontier,[79] and were esteemed the most warlike of the empire; but they deserve to be more particularly considered under the names of Rhætia, Noricum, Pannonia, Dalmatia, Dacia, Mæsia, Thrace, Macedonia, and Greece.

The province of Rhætia, which soon extinguished the name of the Vindelicians, extended from the summit of the Alps to the banks *Rhætia.* of the Danube; from its source, as far as its conflux with the Inn. The greatest part of the flat country is subject to the elector of Bavaria; the city of Augsburg is protected by the constitution of the German empire; the Grisons are safe in their mountains, and the country of Tirol is ranked among the numerous provinces of the house of Austria.

The wide extent of territory, which is included between the Inn, the Danube, and the Save; Austria, Styria, Carinthia, *Noricum and* Carniola, the Lower Hungary and Sclavonia, was known to the *Pannonia.* ancients under the names of Noricum and Pannonia. In their original state of independence, their fierce inhabitants were intimately connected. Under the Roman government they were frequently united, and they still remain the patrimony of a single family. They now contain the residence of a German prince, who styles himself Emperor of the Romans, and form the center, as well as strength, of the Austrian power. It may not be improper to observe, that if we except Bohemia, Moravia, the northern skirts of Austria, and a part of Hungary, between the Teyss and the Danube, all the other dominions of the House of Austria were comprised within the limits of the Roman empire.

Dalmatia, to which the name of Illyricum more properly belonged, was a long, but narrow tract, between the Save and the *Dalmatia.* Adriatic. The best part of the sea-coast, which still retains its ancient appellation, is a province of the Venetian state, and the seat of the little republic of Ragusa. The inland parts have assumed the Sclavonian names of Croatia and Bosnia; the former obeys an Austrian governor, the latter a Turkish pasha; but the whole country is still infested by tribes of barbarians, whose savage independence irregularly marks the doubtful limit of the Christian and Mahometan power.[80]

---

79. The name of Illyricum originally belonged to the sea-coast of the Hadriatic, and was gradually extended by the Romans from the Alps to the Euxine Sea. See Severini Pannonia, l. i.c. 3.

80. A Venetian traveller, the Abbate Fortis, has lately given us some account of those very obscure countries. But the geography and antiquities of the western Illyricum can be

Mœsia and Dacia. After the Danube had received the waters of the Teyss and the Save, it acquired, at least, among the Greeks, the name of Ister.[81] It formerly divided Mæsia and Dacia, the latter of which, as we have already seen, was a conquest of Trajan, and the only province beyond the river. If we inquire into the present state of those countries, we shall find that, on the left hand of the Danube, Temeswar and Transylvania have been annexed, after many revolutions, to the crown of Hungary; whilst the principalities of Moldavia and Walachia acknowledge the supremacy of the Ottoman Porte. On the right hand of the Danube, Mæsia, which, during the middle ages, was broken into the barbarian kingdoms of Servia and Bulgaria, is again united in Turkish slavery.

Thrace, Macedonia, and Greece. The appellation of Roumelia, which is still bestowed by the Turks on the extensive countries of Thrace, Macedonia, and Greece, preserves the memory of their ancient state under the Roman empire. In the time of the Antonines, the martial regions of Thrace, from the mountains of Hæmus and Rhodope, to the Bosphorus and the Hellespont, had assumed the form of a province. Notwithstanding the change of masters and of religion, the new city of Rome, founded by Constantine on the banks of the Bosphorus, has ever since remained the capital of a great monarchy. The kingdom of Macedonia, which, under the reign of Alexander, gave laws to Asia, derived more solid advantages from the policy of the two Philips; and with its dependencies of Epirus and Thessaly, extended from the Ægean to the Ionian sea. When we reflect on the fame of Thebes and Argos, of Sparta and Athens, we can scarcely persuade ourselves, that so many immortal republics of ancient Greece were lost in a single province of the Roman empire, which, from the superior influence of the Achæan league, was usually denominated the province of Achaia.

Asia Minor. Such was the state of Europe under the Roman emperors. The provinces of Asia, without excepting the transient conquests of Trajan, are all comprehended within the limits of the Turkish power. But, instead of following the arbitrary divisions of despotism and ignorance, it will be safer for us, as well as more agreeable, to observe the indelible characters of nature. The name of Asia Minor is attributed with some

---

expected only from the munificence of the emperor, its sovereign.

81. The Save rises near the confines of *Istria,*

and was considered by the more early Greeks as the principal stream of the Danube.

propriety to the peninsula, which, confined between the Euxine and the Mediterranean, advances from the Euphrates towards Europe. The most extensive and flourishing district, westward of mount Taurus and the river Halys, was dignified by the Romans with the exclusive title of Asia. The jurisdiction of that province extended over the ancient monarchies of Troy, Lydia, and Phrygia, the maritime countries of the Pamphylians, Lycians, and Carians, and the Grecian colonies of Ionia, which equalled in arts, though not in arms, the glory of their parent. The kingdoms of Bithynia and Pontus possessed the northern side of the peninsula from Constantinople to Trebizond. On the opposite side, the province of Cilicia was terminated by the mountains of Syria: the inland country, separated from the Roman Asia by the river Halys, and from Armenia by the Euphrates, had once formed the independent kingdom of Cappadocia. In this place we may observe, that the northern shores of the Euxine, beyond Trebizond in Asia, and beyond the Danube in Europe, acknowledged the sovereignty of the emperors, and received at their hands, either tributary princes or Roman garrisons. Budzak, Crim Tartary, Circassia, and Mingrelia, are the modern appellations of those savage countries.[82]

Under the successors of Alexander, Syria was the seat of the Seleucidæ, who reigned over Upper Asia, till the successful revolt of the Parthians confined their dominions between the Euphrates and the Mediterranean. When Syria became subject to the Romans, it formed the eastern frontier of their empire; nor did that province, in its utmost latitude, know any other bounds than the mountains of Cappadocia to the north, and towards the south, the confines of Egypt, and the Red Sea. Phœnicia and Palestine were sometimes annexed to, and sometimes separated from, the jurisdiction of Syria. The former of these was a narrow and rocky coast; the latter was a territory scarcely superior to Wales, either in fertility or extent. Yet Phœnicia and Palestine will for ever live in the memory of mankind; since America, as well as Europe, has received letters from the one, and religion from the other.[83] A sandy desert alike destitute of wood and water skirts along the doubtful confine of Syria,

Syria, Phœnicia, and Palestine.

82. See the Periplus of Arrian. He examined the coasts of the Euxine, when he was governor of Cappadocia.

83. The progress of religion is well known. The use of letters was introduced among the savages of Europe about fifteen hundred years before Christ; and the Europeans carried them to America, about fifteen centuries after the Christian æra. But in a period of three thousand years, the Phœnician alphabet received considerable alterations, as it passed through the hands of the Greeks and Romans.

from the Euphrates to the Red Sea. The wandering life of the Arabs was inseparably connected with their independence, and wherever, on some spots less barren than the rest, they ventured to form any settled habitations, they soon became subjects to the Roman empire.[84]

Egypt.   The geographers of antiquity have frequently hesitated to what portion of the globe they should ascribe Egypt.[85] By its situation that celebrated kingdom is included within the immense peninsula of Africa; but it is accessible only on the side of Asia, whose revolutions, in almost every period of history, Egypt has humbly obeyed. A Roman præfect was seated on the splendid throne of the Ptolemies; and the iron sceptre of the Mamalukes is now in the hands of a Turkish pasha. The Nile flows down the country, above five hundred miles from the tropic of Cancer to the Mediterranean, and marks, on either side, the extent of fertility by the measure of its inundations. Cyrene, situate towards the west, and along the sea-coast, was first a Greek colony, afterwards a province of Egypt, and is now lost in the desert of Barca.

Africa.   From Cyrene to the ocean, the coast of Africa extends above fifteen hundred miles; yet so closely is it pressed between the Mediterranean and the Sahara, or sandy desert, that its breadth seldom exceeds fourscore or an hundred miles. The eastern division was considered by the Romans as the more peculiar and proper province of Africa. Till the arrival of the Phœnician colonies, that fertile country was inhabited by the Libyans, the most savage of mankind. Under the immediate jurisdiction of Carthage, it became the center of commerce and empire; but the republic of Carthage is now degenerated into the feeble and disorderly states of Tripoli and Tunis. The military government of Algiers oppresses the wide extent of Numidia, as it was once united under Massinissa and Jugurtha: but in the time of Augustus, the limits of Numidia were contracted; and, at least, two thirds of the country acquiesced in the name of Mauritania, with the epithet of Cæsariensis. The genuine Mauritania, or country of the Moors, which, from the ancient city of Tingi, or Tangier, was distinguished by the appellation of Tingitana, is represented by the modern kingdom of Fez. Sallè, on the Ocean, so infamous at present for its piratical depredations,

---

84. Dion Cassius, lib. lxviii. p. 1131.

85. Ptolemy and Strabo, with the modern geographers, fix the Isthmus of Suez as the boundary of Asia and Africa. Dionysius, Mela, Pliny, Sallust, Hirtius and Solinus, have preferred for that purpose the western branch of the Nile, or even the great Catabathmus, or descent, which last would assign to Asia, not only Egypt, but part of Libya.

was noticed by the Romans, as the extreme object of their power, and almost of their geography. A city of their foundation may still be discovered near Mequinez, the residence of the barbarian whom we condescend to style the Emperor of Morocco; but it does not appear, that his more southern dominions, Morocco itself, and Segelmessa, were ever comprehended within the Roman province. The western parts of Africa are intersected by the branches of mount Atlas, a name so idly celebrated by the fancy of poets;[86] but which is now diffused over the immense ocean that rolls between the ancient and the new continent.[87]

Having now finished the circuit of the Roman empire, we may observe, that Africa is divided from Spain by a narrow strait of about twelve miles, through which the Atlantic flows into the Mediterranean. The columns of Hercules, so famous among the ancients, were two mountains which seemed to have been torn asunder by some convulsion of the elements; and at the foot of the European mountain, the fortress of Gibraltar is now seated. The whole extent of the Mediterranean Sea, its coasts, and its islands, were comprised within the Roman dominion. Of the larger islands, the two Baleares, which derive their names of Majorca and Minorca from their respective size, are subject at present, the former to Spain, the latter to Great Britain. It is easier to deplore the fate, than to describe the actual condition of Corsica. Two Italian sovereigns assume a regal title from Sardinia and Sicily. Crete, or Candia, with Cyprus, and most of the smaller islands of Greece and Asia, have been subdued by the Turkish arms; whilst the little rock of Malta defies their power, and has emerged, under the government of its military Order, into fame and opulence.

The Mediterranean with its islands.

This long enumeration of provinces, whose broken fragments have formed so many powerful kingdoms, might almost induce us to forgive the vanity or ignorance of the ancients. Dazzled with the extensive sway, the irresistible strength, and the real or affected moderation of the emperors, they permitted themselves to despise,

General idea of the Roman empire.

---

86. The long range, moderate height, and gentle declivity of mount Atlas (see Shaw's Travels, p. 5.) are very unlike a solitary mountain which rears its head into the clouds, and seems to support the heavens. The peak of Teneriff, on the contrary, rises a league and a half above the surface of the sea, and as it was frequently visited by the Phœnicians, might engage the notice of the Greek poets. See Buffon, Histoire Naturelle, tom. i. p. 312. Histoire des Voyages, tom. ii.

87. M. de Voltaire, tom. xiv. p. 297. unsupported by either fact or probability, has generously bestowed the Canary Islands on the Roman empire.

and sometimes to forget, the outlying countries which had been left in the enjoyment of a barbarous independence; and they gradually usurped the licence of confounding the Roman monarchy with the globe of the earth.[88] But the temper, as well as knowledge, of a modern historian, require a more sober and accurate language. He may impress a juster image of the greatness of Rome, by observing that the empire was above two thousand miles in breadth, from the wall of Antoninus and the northern limits of Dacia, to mount Atlas and the tropic of Cancer; that it extended, in length, more than three thousand miles from the Western Ocean to the Euphrates; that it was situated in the finest part of the Temperate Zone, between the twenty-fourth and fifty-sixth degrees of northern latitude; and that it was supposed to contain above sixteen hundred thousand square miles, for the most part of fertile and well cultivated land.[89]

88. Bergier, Hist. des Grands Chemins, l. iii. c. 1, 2, 3, 4. a very useful collection.

89. See Templeman's Survey of the Globe: but I distrust both the doctor's learning and his maps.

CHAPTER II

*Of the Union and internal Prosperity of the Roman Empire, in
the Age of the Antonines.*

It is not alone by the rapidity, or extent of conquest, that we should estimate the greatness of Rome. The sovereign of the Russian deserts commands a larger portion of the globe. In the *Principles of government.* seventh summer after his passage of the Hellespont, Alexander erected the Macedonian trophies on the banks of the Hyphasis.[1] Within less than a century, the irresistible Zingis, and the Mogul princes of his race, spread their cruel devastations and transient empire, from the sea of China, to the confines of Egypt and Germany.[2] But the firm edifice of Roman power was raised and preserved by the wisdom of ages. The obedient provinces of Trajan and the Antonines were united by laws, and adorned by arts. They might occasionally suffer from the partial abuse of delegated authority; but the general principle of government was wise, simple, and beneficent. They enjoyed the religion of their ancestors, whilst in civil honours and advantages they were exalted, by just degrees, to an equality with their conquerors.

I. The policy of the emperors and the senate, as far as it concerned religion, was happily seconded by the reflections of *Universal spirit of toleration.* the enlightened, and by the habits of the superstitious, part of their subjects. The various modes of worship, which prevailed in the Roman world, were all considered by the people, as equally true; by the philosopher, as equally false; and by the magistrate, as equally useful. And thus toleration produced not only mutual indulgence, but even religious concord.

The superstition of the people was not embittered by any mixture of theological rancour; nor was it confined by the chains of any *Of the people.* speculative system. The devout polytheist, though fondly attached to

1. They were erected about the midway between Lahor and Dehli. The conquests of Alexander in Hindostan were confined to the Punjab, a country watered by the five great streams of the Indus.
2. See M. de Guignes Histoires des Huns, l. xv, xvi, and xvii.

his national rites, admitted with implicit faith the different religions of the earth.[3] Fear, gratitude, and curiosity, a dream or an omen, a singular disorder, or a distant journey, perpetually disposed him to multiply the articles of his belief, and to enlarge the list of his protectors. The thin texture of the Pagan mythology was interwoven with various, but not discordant materials. As soon as it was allowed that sages and heroes, who had lived, or who had died for the benefit of their country, were exalted to a state of power and immortality, it was universally confessed, that they deserved, if not the adoration, at least the reverence, of all mankind. The deities of a thousand groves and a thousand streams possessed, in peace, their local and respective influence; nor could the Roman who deprecated the wrath of the Tiber, deride the Egyptian who presented his offering to the beneficent genius of the Nile. The visible powers of Nature, the planets, and the elements, were the same throughout the universe. The invisible governors of the moral world were inevitably cast in a similar mould of fiction and allegory. Every virtue, and even vice, acquired its divine representative; every art and profession its patron, whose attributes, in the most distant ages and countries, were uniformly derived from the character of their peculiar votaries. A republic of gods of such opposite tempers and interest required, in every system, the moderating hand of a supreme magistrate, who, by the progress of knowledge and flattery, was gradually invested with the sublime perfections of an Eternal Parent, and an Omnipotent Monarch.[4] Such was the mild spirit of antiquity, that the nations were less attentive to the difference, than to the resemblance, of their religious worship. The Greek, the Roman, and the Barbarian, as they met before their respective altars, easily persuaded themselves, that under various names, and with various ceremonies, they adored the same deities. The elegant mythology of Homer gave a

---

3. There is not any writer who describes in so lively a manner as Herodotus, the true genius of Polytheism. The best commentary may be found in Mr. Hume's Natural History of Religion; and the best contrast in Bossuet's Universal History. Some obscure traces of an intolerant spirit appear in the conduct of the Egyptians (see Juvenal, Sat. xv.); and the Christians as well as Jews, who lived under the Roman empire, formed a very important

exception: so important indeed, that the discussion will require a distinct chapter of this work.

4. The rights, powers, and pretensions of the sovereign of Olympus, are very clearly described in the xvth book of the Iliad: in the Greek original, I mean; for Mr. Pope, without perceiving it, has improved the theology of Homer.

beautiful, and almost a regular form, to the polytheism of the ancient world.[5]

The philosophers of Greece deduced their morals from the nature of man, rather than from that of God. They meditated, *Of philosophers.* however, on the Divine Nature, as a very curious and important speculation; and in the profound inquiry, they displayed the strength and weakness of the human understanding.[6] Of the four most celebrated schools, the Stoics and the Platonists endeavoured to reconcile the jarring interests of reason and piety. They have left us the most sublime proofs of the existence and perfections of the first cause; but, as it was impossible for them to conceive the creation of matter, the workman in the Stoic philosophy was not sufficiently distinguished from the work; whilst, on the contrary, the spiritual God of Plato and his disciples, resembled an idea, rather than a substance. The opinions of the Academics and Epicureans were of a less religious cast; but whilst the modest science of the former induced them to doubt, the positive ignorance of the latter urged them to deny, the providence of a Supreme Ruler. The spirit of inquiry, prompted by emulation, and supported by freedom, had divided the public teachers of philosophy into a variety of contending sects; but the ingenuous youth, who, from every part, resorted to Athens, and the other seats of learning in the Roman empire, were alike instructed in every school to reject and to despise the religion of the multitude. How, indeed, was it possible, that a philosopher should accept, as divine truths, the idle tales of the poets, and the incoherent traditions of antiquity; or, that he should adore, as gods, those imperfect beings whom he must have despised, as men! Against such unworthy adversaries, Cicero condescended to employ the arms of reason and eloquence; but the satire of Lucian was a much more adequate, as well as more efficacious weapon. We may be well assured, that a writer, conversant with the world, would never have ventured to expose the gods of his country to public ridicule, had they not already been the objects of secret contempt among the polished and enlightened orders of society.[7]

5. See for instance, Cæsar de Bell. Gall. vi. 17. Within a century or two the Gauls themselves applied to their gods the names of Mercury, Mars, Apollo, &c.

6. The admirable work of Cicero de Naturâ Deorum, is the best clue we have to guide us through the dark and profound abyss. He represents with candour, and confutes with subtlety, the opinions of the philosophers.

7. I do not pretend to assert, that, in this irreligious age, the natural terrors of superstition, dreams, omens, apparitions, &c. had lost their efficacy.

Notwithstanding the fashionable irreligion which prevailed in the age of the Antonines, both the interest of the priests and the credulity of the people were sufficiently respected. In their writings and conversation, the philosophers of antiquity asserted the independent dignity of reason; but they resigned their actions to the commands of law and of custom. Viewing, with a smile of pity and indulgence, the various errors of the vulgar, they diligently practised the ceremonies of their fathers, devoutly frequented the temples of the gods; and sometimes condescending to act a part on the theatre of superstition, they concealed the sentiments of an Atheist under the sacerdotal robes. Reasoners of such a temper were scarcely inclined to wrangle about their respective modes of faith, or of worship. It was indifferent to them what shape the folly of the multitude might chuse to assume; and they approached, with the same inward contempt, and the same external reverence, the altars of the Lybian, the Olympian, or the Capitoline Jupiter.[8]

Of the magistrate. It is not easy to conceive from what motives a spirit of persecution could introduce itself into the Roman councils. The magistrates could not be actuated by a blind, though honest bigotry, since the magistrates were themselves philosophers; and the schools of Athens had given laws to the senate. They could not be impelled by ambition or avarice, as the temporal and ecclesiastical powers were united in the same hands. The pontiffs were chosen among the most illustrious of the senators; and the office of Supreme Pontiff was constantly exercised by the emperors themselves. They knew and valued the advantages of religion, as it is connected with civil government. They encouraged the public festivals which humanize the manners of the people. They managed the arts of divination, as a convenient instrument of policy; and they respected as the firmest bond of society, the useful persuasion, that, either in this or in a future life, the crime of perjury is most assuredly punished by the avenging gods.[9] But whilst they acknowledged the general advantages of religion, they were convinced, that the various modes of worship contributed alike to the same salutary purposes; and that, in every country, the form of superstition, which had received the sanction of time and experience, was the best adapted to the climate, and to its inhabitants.

8. Socrates, Epicurus, Cicero, and Plutarch, always inculcated a decent reverence for the religion of their own country, and of mankind. The devotion of Epicurus was assiduous and exemplary. Diogen. Laert. x. 10.

9. Polybius, l. vi. c. 53, 54. Juvenal, Sat. xiii. laments, that in his time this apprehension had lost much of its effect.

Avarice and taste very frequently despoiled the vanquished *In the provinces;* nations of the elegant statues of their gods, and the rich orna- ments of their temples:[10] but, in the exercise of the religion which they derived from their ancestors, they uniformly experienced the indulgence, and even protection, of the Roman conquerors. The province of Gaul seems, and indeed only seems, an exception to this universal toleration. Under the specious pretext of abolishing human sacrifices, the emperors Tiberius and Claudius suppressed the dangerous power of the Druids:[11] but the priests themselves, their gods and their altars, subsisted in peaceful obscurity till the final destruction of Paganism.[12]

Rome, the capital of a great monarchy, was incessantly filled with *at Rome.* subjects and strangers from every part of the world,[13] who all introduced and enjoyed the favourite superstitions of their native country.[14] Every city in the empire was justified in maintaining the purity of its ancient ceremonies; and the Roman senate, using the common privilege, sometimes interposed, to check this inundation of foreign rites. The Egyptian super- stition, of all the most contemptible and abject, was frequently prohibited; the temples of Serapis and Isis demolished, and their worshippers banished from Rome and Italy.[15] But the zeal of fanaticism prevailed over the cold and feeble efforts of policy. The exiles returned, the proselytes multiplied, the temples were restored with increasing splendor, and Isis and Serapis at length assumed their place among the Roman deities.[16] Nor was this indulgence a departure from the old maxims of government. In the purest

---

10. See the fate of Syracuse, Tarentum, Ambracia, Corinth, &c. the conduct of Verres, in Cicero (Actio ii. Orat. 4.), and the usual practice of governors, in the viiith Satire of Juvenal.

11. Sueton. in Claud. – Plin. Hist. Nat. xxx. 1.

12. Pelloutier Histoire des Celtes, tom. vi. p. 230–252.

13. Seneca Consolat. ad Helviam, p. 74. Edit. Lips.

14. Dionysius Halicarn. Antiquitat. Roman. l. ii.

15. In the year of Rome 701, the temple of Isis and Serapis was demolished by the order of the senate (Dion Cassius, l. xl. p. 252.), and even by the hands of the consul (Valerius

Maximus, l. 3.). After the death of Cæsar, it was restored at the public expence (Dion, l. xlvii. p. 501.). When Augustus was in Egypt, he revered the majesty of Serapis (Dion, l. li. p. 647.); but in the Pomærium of Rome, and a mile round it, he prohibited the worship of the Egyptian gods (Dion, l. liii. p. 679. l. liv. p. 735.). They remained, however, very fashionable under his reign (Ovid. de Art. Amand. l. i.) and that of his successor, till the justice of Tiberius was provoked to some acts of severity. (See Tacit. Annal. ii. 85. Joseph. Antiquit. l. xviii. c. 3.)

16. Tertullian in Apologetic. c. 6. p. 74. Edit. Havercamp. I am inclined to attribute their establishment to the devotion of the Flavian family.

ages of the commonwealth, Cybele and Æsculapius had been invited by solemn embassies;[17] and it was customary to tempt the protectors of besieged cities, by the promise of more distinguished honours than they possessed in their native country.[18] Rome gradually became the common temple of her subjects; and the freedom of the city was bestowed on all the gods of mankind.[19]

Freedom of Rome.

II. The narrow policy of preserving, without any foreign mixture, the pure blood of the ancient citizens, had checked the fortune, and hastened the ruin, of Athens and Sparta. The aspiring genius of Rome sacrificed vanity to ambition, and deemed it more prudent, as well as honourable, to adopt virtue and merit for her own wheresoever they were found, among slaves or strangers, enemies or barbarians.[20] During the most flourishing æra of the Athenian commonwealth, the number of citizens gradually decreased from about thirty[21] to twenty-one thousand.[22] If, on the contrary, we study the growth of the Roman republic, we may discover, that, notwithstanding the incessant demands of wars and colonies, the citizens, who, in the first census of Servius Tullius, amounted to no more than eighty-three thousand, were multiplied, before the commencement of the social war, to the number of four hundred and sixty-three thousand men, able to bear arms in the service of their country.[23] When the allies of Rome claimed an equal share of honours and privileges, the senate indeed preferred the chance of arms to an ignominious concession. The Samnites and the Lucanians paid the severe penalty of their rashness; but the rest of the Italian states, as they successively returned to their duty, were admitted into the bosom of the republic,[24] and soon contributed to the ruin of public freedom. Under a democratical government, the citizens exercise the powers of sovereignty; and those powers will be first abased, and afterwards lost, if they are committed to an unwieldy multitude. But when the popular

---

17. See Livy, l. xi. and xxix.
18. Macrob. Saturnalia, l. iii. c. 9. He gives us a form of evocation.
19. Minutius Fælix in Octavio, p. 54. Arnobius, l. vi. p. 115.
20. Tacit. Annal. xi. 24. The Orbis Romanus of the learned Spanheim, is a complete history of the progressive admission of Latium, Italy, and the provinces, to the freedom of Rome.
21. Herodotus, v. 97. It should seem, however, that he followed a large and popular estimation.
22. Athenæus Deipnosophist. l. vi. p. 272, Edit. Casaubon. Meursius de Fortunâ Atticâ, c. 4.
23. See a very accurate collection of the numbers of each Lustrum in M. de Beaufort, Republique Romaine, l. iv. c. 4.
24. Appian. de Bell. civil. l. i. Velleius Paterculus, l. ii. c. 15, 16, 17.

assemblies had been suppressed by the administration of the emperors, the conquerors were distinguished from the vanquished nations, only as the first and most honourable order of subjects; and their increase, however rapid, was no longer exposed to the same dangers. Yet the wisest princes, who adopted the maxims of Augustus, guarded with the strictest care the dignity of the Roman name, and diffused the freedom of the city with a prudent liberality.[25]

Till the privileges of Romans had been progressively extended to all the inhabitants of the empire, an important distinction was preserved between Italy and the provinces. The former was esteemed the centre of public unity, and the firm basis of the constitution. Italy claimed the birth, or at least the residence, of the emperors and the senate.[26] The estates of the Italians were exempt from taxes, their persons from the arbitrary jurisdiction of governors. Their municipal corporations, formed after the perfect model of the capital, were intrusted, under the immediate eye of the supreme power, with the execution of the laws. From the foot of the Alps to the extremity of Calabria, all the natives of Italy were born citizens of Rome. Their partial distinctions were obliterated, and they insensibly coalesced into one great nation, united by language, manners, and civil institutions, and equal to the weight of a powerful empire. The republic gloried in her generous policy, and was frequently rewarded by the merit and services of her adopted sons. Had she always confined the distinction of Romans to the ancient families within the walls of the city, that immortal name would have been deprived of some of its noblest ornaments. Virgil was a native of Mantua; Horace was inclined to doubt whether he should call himself an Apulian or a Lucanian: it was in Padua that an historian was found worthy to record the majestic series of Roman victories. The patriot family of the Catos emerged from Tusculum; and the little town of Arpinum claimed the double honour of producing Marius and Cicero, the former of whom deserved, after Romulus and Camillus, to be styled the Third Founder of Rome; and the latter, after saving his country from the

Italy.

25. Mæcenas had advised him to declare by one edict, all his subjects, citizens. But we may justly suspect that the historian Dion was the author of a counsel, so much adapted to the practice of his own age, and so little to that of Augustus.

26. The senators were obliged to have one-third of their own landed property in Italy. See Plin. l. vi. ep. 19. The qualification was reduced by Marcus to one-fourth. Since the reign of Trajan, Italy had sunk nearer to the level of the provinces.

designs of Catiline, enabled her to contend with Athens for the palm of eloquence.[27]

The provinces.   The provinces of the empire (as they have been described in the preceding chapter) were destitute of any public force, or constitutional freedom. In Etruria, in Greece,[28] and in Gaul,[29] it was the first care of the senate to dissolve those dangerous confederacies which taught mankind, that, as the Roman arms prevailed by division, they might be resisted by union. Those princes, whom the ostentation of gratitude or generosity permitted for a while to hold a precarious sceptre, were dismissed from their thrones, as soon as they had performed their appointed task of fashioning to the yoke the vanquished nations. The free states and cities which had embraced the cause of Rome, were rewarded with a nominal alliance, and insensibly sunk into real servitude. The public authority was every where exercised by the ministers of the senate and of the emperors, and that authority was absolute, and without control. But the same salutary maxims of government, which had secured the peace and obedience of Italy, were extended to the most distant conquests. A nation of Romans was gradually formed in the provinces, by the double expedient of introducing colonies, and of admitting the most faithful and deserving of the provincials to the freedom of Rome.

Colonies and municipal towns.   "Wheresoever the Roman conquers, he inhabits," is a very just observation of Seneca,[30] confirmed by history and experience. The natives of Italy, allured by pleasure or by interest, hastened to enjoy the advantages of victory; and we may remark, that, about forty years after the reduction of Asia, eighty thousand Romans were massacred in one day, by the cruel orders of Mithridates.[31] These voluntary exiles were engaged, for the most part, in the occupations of commerce, agriculture, and the farm of the revenue. But after the legions were rendered permanent by the emperors, the provinces were peopled

---

27. The first part of the Verona Illustrata of the Marquis Maffei, gives the clearest and most comprehensive view of the state of Italy under the Cæsars.

28. See Pausanias, l. vii. The Romans condescended to restore the names of those assemblies, when they could no longer be dangerous.

29. They are frequently mentioned by Cæsar. The Abbé Dubos attempts, with very little success, to prove that the assemblies of Gaul were continued under the emperors. Histoire de l'Etablissement de la Monarchie Françoise, l. i. c. 4.

30. Seneca in Consolat. ad Helviam, c. 6.

31. Memnon apud Photium, c. 33. Valer. Maxim. ix. 2. Plutarch and Dion Cassius swell the massacre to 150,000 citizens; but I should esteem the smaller number to be more than sufficient.

by a race of soldiers; and the veterans, whether they received the reward of their service in land or in money, usually settled with their families in the country, where they had honourably spent their youth. Throughout the empire, but more particularly in the western parts, the most fertile districts, and the most convenient situations, were reserved for the establishment of colonies; some of which were of a civil, and others of a military nature. In their manners and internal policy, the colonies formed a perfect representation of their great parent; and as they were soon endeared to the natives by the ties of friendship and alliance, they effectually diffused a reverence for the Roman name, and a desire, which was seldom disappointed, of sharing, in due time, its honours and advantages.[32] The municipal cities insensibly equalled the rank and splendour of the colonies; and in the reign of Hadrian, it was disputed which was the preferable condition, of those societies which had issued from, or those which had been received into, the bosom of Rome.[33] The right of Latium, as it was called, conferred on the cities to which it had been granted, a more partial favour. The magistrates only, at the expiration of their office, assumed the quality of Roman citizens; but as those offices were annual, in a few years they circulated round the principal families.[34] Those of the provincials who were permitted to bear arms in the legions;[35] those who exercised any civil employment; all, in a word, who performed any public service, or displayed any personal talents, were rewarded with a present, whose value was continually diminished by the increasing liberality of the emperors. Yet even, in the age of the Antonines, when the freedom of the city had been bestowed on the greater number of their subjects, it was still accompanied with very solid advantages. The bulk of the people acquired, with that title, the benefit of the Roman laws, particularly in the interesting articles of marriage, testaments, and inheritances; and the road of fortune was open to those whose pretensions were seconded by favour or merit. The grandsons

32. Twenty-five colonies were settled in Spain (see Plin. Hist. Natur. iii. 3, 4. iv. 35.): and nine in Britain, of which London, Colchester, Lincoln, Chester, Gloucester, and Bath, still remain considerable cities (see Richard of Cirencester, p. 36, and Whitaker's History of Manchester, l. i. c. 3.).

33. Aul. Gell. Noctes Atticæ, xvi. 13. The emperor Hadrian expressed his surprise, that the cities of Utica, Gades, and Itatica, which already enjoyed the rights of *Municipia*, should solicit the title of *colonies*. Their example, however, became fashionable, and the empire was filled with honorary colonies. See Spanheim, de Usu Numismatum, Differtat. xiii.

34. Spanheim, Orbis Roman. c. 8. p. 62.

35. Aristid. in Romæ Encomio, tom. i. p. 218. Edit. Jebb.

of the Gauls, who had besieged Julius Cæsar in Alesia, commanded legions, governed provinces, and were admitted into the senate of Rome.[36] Their ambition, instead of disturbing the tranquillity of the state, was intimately connected with its safety and greatness.

Division of the Latin and the Greek provinces.
        So sensible were the Romans of the influence of language over national manners, that it was their most serious care to extend, with the progress of their arms, the use of the Latin tongue.[37] The ancient dialects of Italy, the Sabine, the Etruscan, and the Venetian, sunk into oblivion; but in the provinces, the east was less docile than the west, to the voice of its victorious preceptors. This obvious difference marked the two portions of the empire with a distinction of colours, which, though it was in some degree concealed during the meridian splendor of prosperity, became gradually more visible, as the shades of night descended upon the Roman world. The western countries were civilized by the same hands which subdued them. As soon as the barbarians were reconciled to obedience, their minds were opened to any new impressions of knowledge and politeness. The language of Virgil and Cicero, though with some inevitable mixture of corruption, was so universally adopted in Africa, Spain, Gaul, Britain, and Pannonia,[38] that the faint traces of the Punic or Celtic idioms were preserved only in the mountains, or among the peasants.[39] Education and study insensibly inspired the natives of those countries with the sentiments of Romans; and Italy gave fashions, as well as laws, to her Latin provincials. They solicited with more ardour, and obtained with more facility, the freedom and honours of the state; supported the national dignity in letters[40] and in arms; and, at length, in the person of Trajan, produced an emperor whom the Scipios would not have disowned for their countryman. The situation of the Greeks was very different from that of the barbarians. The former had been long since civilized and corrupted. They had too much taste to

---

36. Tacit. Annal. xi. 23, 24. Hist. iv. 74.

37. See Plin. Hist. Natur. iii. 5. Augustin. de Civitate Dei, xix. 7. Lipsius de pronunciatione Linguæ Latinæ, c. 3.

38. Apuleius and Augustin will answer for Africa; Strabo for Spain and Gaul; Tacitus, in the life of Agricola, for Britain; and Velleius Paterculus, for Pannonia. To them we may add the language of the Inscriptions.

39. The Celtic was preserved in the mountains of Wales, Cornwall, and Armorica. We may observe that Apuleius reproaches an African youth, who lived among the populace, with the use of the Punic; whilst he had almost forgot Greek, and neither could nor would speak Latin (Apolog. p. 596.). The greater part of St. Austin's congregations were strangers to the Punic.

40. Spain alone produced Columella, the Senecas, Lucan, Martial, and Quintilian.

relinquish their language, and too much vanity to adopt any foreign institutions. Still preserving the prejudices, after they had lost the virtues, of their ancestors, they affected to despise the unpolished manners of the Roman conquerors, whilst they were compelled to respect their superior wisdom and power.[41] Nor was the influence of the Grecian language and sentiments confined to the narrow limits of that once celebrated country. Their empire, by the progress of colonies and conquest, had been diffused from the Hadriatic to the Euphrates and the Nile. Asia was covered with Greek cities, and the long reign of the Macedonian kings had introduced a silent revolution into Syria and Egypt. In their pompous courts those princes united the elegance of Athens with the luxury of the East, and the example of the court was imitated, at an humble distance, by the higher ranks of their subjects. Such was the general division of the Roman empire into the Latin and Greek languages. To these we may add a third distinction for the body of the natives in Syria, and especially in Egypt. The use of their ancient dialects, by secluding them from the commerce of mankind, checked the improvements of those barbarians.[42] The slothful effeminacy of the former, exposed them to the contempt; the sullen ferociousness of the latter, excited the aversion of the conquerors.[43] Those nations had submitted to the Roman power, but they seldom desired or deserved the freedom of the city; and it was remarked, that more than two hundred and thirty years elapsed after the ruin of the Ptolemies, before an Egyptian was admitted into the senate of Rome.[44]

It is a just though trite observation, that victorious Rome was herself subdued by the arts of Greece. Those immortal writers who still command the admiration of modern Europe, soon became the favourite object of study and imitation in Italy and the western provinces. But the elegant amusements of the Romans were not suffered to interfere with their sound maxims of policy. Whilst they acknowledged the charms of the Greek, they asserted the dignity of the Latin tongue, and the exclusive use of the latter was inflexibly main-

General use of both languages.

---

41. There is not, I believe, from Dionysius to Libanius, a single Greek critic who mentions Virgil or Horace. They seem ignorant that the Romans had any good writers.

42. The curious reader may see in Dupin (Bibliotheque Ecclesiastique, tom. xix. p. 1. c. 8.) how much the use of the Syriac and

Egyptian languages was still preserved.

43. See Juvenal, Sat. iii. and xv. Ammian. Marcellin. xxii. 16.

44. Dion Cassius, l. lxxvii. p. 1275. The first instance happened under the reign of Septimius Severus.

tained in the administration of civil as well as military government.[45] The two languages exercised at the same time their separate jurisdiction throughout the empire: the former, as the natural idiom of science; the latter, as the legal dialect of public transactions. Those who united letters with business, were equally conversant with both; and it was almost impossible, in any province, to find a Roman subject, of a liberal education, who was at once a stranger to the Greek and to the Latin language.

Slaves.   It was by such institutions that the nations of the empire insensibly melted away into the Roman name and people. But there still remained, in the centre of every province and of every family, an unhappy condition of men who endured the weight, without sharing the benefits, of society. In the free states of antiquity, the domestic slaves were exposed to the wanton rigour of despotism. The perfect settlement of the Roman empire was preceded by ages of violence and rapine. The slaves *Their treatment.*   consisted, for the most part, of barbarian captives, taken in thousands by the chance of war, purchased at a vile price,[46] accustomed to a life of independence, and impatient to break and to revenge their fetters. Against such internal enemies, whose desperate insurrections had more than once reduced the republic to the brink of destruction,[47] the most severe regulations,[48] and the most cruel treatment, seemed almost justified by the great law of self-preservation. But when the principal nations of Europe, Asia, and Africa, were united under the laws of one sovereign, the source of foreign supplies flowed with much less abundance, and the Romans were reduced to the milder but more tedious method of propagation. In their numerous families, and particularly in their country estates, they encouraged the marriage of their slaves. The sentiments of nature, the habits of education, and the possession of a dependent species of property, contributed to alleviate the hardships of servitude.[49] The existence of a slave became an object of greater value, and though his happiness still depended on the temper and circumstances of the master,

---

45. See Valerius Maximus, l. ii. c. 2. n. 2. The emperor Claudius disfranchised an eminent Grecian for not understanding Latin. He was probably in some public office. Suetonius in Claud. c. 16.

46. In the camp of Lucullus, an ox sold for a drachma, and a slave for four drachmæ, or about three shillings. Plutarch. in Lucull. p. 580.

47. Diodorus Siculus in Eclog. Hist. l. xxxiv. and xxxvi. Florus, iii. 19, 20.

48. See a remarkable instance of severity in Cicero in Verrem, v. 3.

49. See in Gruter, and the other collectors, a great number of inscriptions addressed by slaves to their wives, children, fellow-servants, masters, &c. They are all most probably of the Imperial age.

the humanity of the latter, instead of being restrained by fear, was encouraged by the sense of his own interest. The progress of manners was accelerated by the virtue or policy of the emperors; and by the edicts of Hadrian and the Antonines, the protection of the laws was extended to the most abject part of mankind. The jurisdiction of life and death over the slaves, a power long exercised and often abused, was taken out of private hands, and reserved to the magistrates alone. The subterraneous prisons were abolished; and, upon a just complaint of intolerable treatment, the injured slave obtained either his deliverance, or a less cruel master.[50]

Hope, the best comfort of our imperfect condition, was not denied to the Roman slave; and if he had any opportunity *Enfranchisement.* of rendering himself either useful or agreeable, he might very naturally expect that the diligence and fidelity of a few years would be rewarded with the inestimable gift of freedom. The benevolence of the master was so frequently prompted by the meaner suggestions of vanity and avarice, that the laws found it more necessary to restrain than to encourage a profuse and undistinguishing liberality, which might degenerate into a very dangerous abuse.[51] It was a maxim of ancient jurisprudence, that as a slave had not any country of his own, he acquired with his liberty an admission into the political society of which his patron was a member. The consequences of this maxim would have prostituted the privileges of the Roman city to a mean and promiscuous multitude. Some seasonable exceptions were therefore provided; and the honourable distinction was confined to such slaves only, as for just causes, and with the approbation of the magistrate, should receive a solemn and legal manumission. Even these chosen freedmen obtained no more than the private rights of citizens, and were rigorously excluded from civil or military honours. Whatever might be the merit or fortune of their sons, *they* likewise were esteemed unworthy of a seat in the senate; nor were the traces of a servile origin allowed to be completely obliterated till the third or fourth generation.[52] Without destroying the distinction of ranks, a distant prospect of freedom and honours was presented, even to those whom pride and prejudice almost disdained to number among the human species.

---

50. See the Augustan History, and a Dissertation of M. de Burigny, in the xxxvth volume of the Academy of Inscriptions, upon the Roman slaves.

51. See another dissertation of M. de Burigny in the xxxviith volume, on the Roman freedmen.

52. Spanheim, Orbis Roman. l. i. c. 16. p. 124, &c.

Numbers.   It was once proposed to discriminate the slaves by a peculiar
habit; but it was justly apprehended that there might be some danger
in acquainting them with their own numbers.[53] Without interpreting, in
their utmost strictness, the liberal appellations of legions and myriads;[54] we
may venture to pronounce, that the proportion of slaves, who were valued
as property, was more considerable than that of servants, who can be
computed only as an expence.[55] The youths of a promising genius were
instructed in the arts and sciences, and their price was ascertained by the
degree of their skill and talents.[56] Almost every profession, either liberal[57]
or mechanical, might be found in the household of an opulent senator.
The ministers of pomp and sensuality were multiplied beyond the conception of modern luxury.[58] It was more for the interest of the merchant or
manufacturer to purchase, than to hire his workmen; and in the country,
slaves were employed as the cheapest and most laborious instruments
of agriculture. To confirm the general observation, and to display the
multitude of slaves, we might allege a variety of particular instances. It was
discovered, on a very melancholy occasion, that four hundred slaves
were maintained in a single palace of Rome.[59] The same number of four
hundred belonged to an estate which an African widow, of a very private condition, resigned to her son, whilst she reserved for herself a
much larger share of her property.[60] A freedman, under the reign of
Augustus, though his fortune had suffered great losses in the civil wars, left
behind him three thousand six hundred yoke of oxen, two hundred
and fifty thousand head of smaller cattle, and, what was almost included
in the description of cattle, four thousand one hundred and sixteen
slaves.[61]

53. Seneca de Clementiâ, l. i. c. 24. The
original is much stronger, "Quantum periculum immineret si servi nostri numerare nos
cœpissent."

54. See Pliny (Hist. Natur. l. xxxiii.) and
Athenæus (Deipnosophist. l. vi. p. 272.) The
latter boldly asserts, that he knew very many
(παμπολλοι) Romans who possessed, not for
use, but ostentation, ten and even twenty
thousand slaves.

55. In Paris there are not more than 43,700
domestics of every sort, and not a twelfth part
of the inhabitants. Messange Recherches sur
la Population, p. 186.

56. A learned slave sold for many hundred
pounds sterling; Atticus always bred and
taught them himself. Cornel. Nepos in Vit.
c. 13.

57. Many of the Roman physicians were
slaves. See Dr. Middleton's Dissertation and
Defence.

58. Their ranks and offices are very copiously
enumerated by Pignorius de Servis.

59. Tacit. Annal. xiv. 43. They all were
executed for not preventing their master's
murder.

60. Apuleius in Apolog. p. 548. Edit. Delphin.

61. Plin. Hist. Natur. l. xxxiii. 47.

The number of subjects who acknowledged the laws of Rome, of citizens, of provincials, and of slaves, cannot now be fixed with such a degree of accuracy, as the importance of the object would deserve. We are informed, that when the emperor Clau-

Populousness of the Roman empire.

dius exercised the office of censor, he took an account of six millions nine hundred and forty-five thousand Roman citizens, who, with the proportion of women and children, must have amounted to about twenty millions of souls. The multitude of subjects of an inferior rank, was uncertain and fluctuating. But, after weighing with attention every circumstance which could influence the balance, it seems probable, that there existed, in the time of Claudius, about twice as many provincials as there were citizens, of either sex, and of every age; and that the slaves were at least equal in number to the free inhabitants of the Roman world. The total amount of this imperfect calculation would rise to about one hundred and twenty millions of persons: a degree of population which possibly exceeds that of modern Europe,[62] and forms the most numerous society that has ever been united under the same system of government.

Domestic peace and union were the natural consequences of the moderate and comprehensive policy embraced by the Romans. If we turn our eyes towards the monarchies of Asia, we shall behold

Obedience and union.

despotism in the centre, and weakness in the extremities; the collection of the revenue, or the administration of justice, enforced by the presence of an army; hostile barbarians established in the heart of the country, hereditary satraps usurping the dominion of the provinces, and subjects inclined to rebellion, though incapable of freedom. But the obedience of the Roman world was uniform, voluntary, and permanent. The vanquished nations, blended into one great people, resigned the hope, nay even the wish, of resuming their independence, and scarcely considered their own existence as distinct from the existence of Rome. The established authority of the emperors pervaded without an effort the wide extent of their dominions, and was exercised with the same facility on the banks of the Thames, or of the Nile, as on those of the Tyber. The legions were destined to serve

62. Compute twenty millions in France, twenty-two in Germany, four in Hungary, ten in Italy with its islands, eight in Great Britain and Ireland, eight in Spain and Portugal, ten or twelve in the European Russia, six in Poland, six in Greece and Turkey, four in Sweden, three in Denmark and Norway, four in the Low Countries. The whole would amount to one hundred and five, or one hundred and seven millions. See Voltaire, de Histoire Generale.

against the public enemy, and the civil magistrate seldom required the aid of a military force.[63] In this state of general security, the leisure as well as opulence both of the prince and people, were devoted to improve and to adorn the Roman empire.

Roman monuments. Among the innumerable monuments of architecture constructed by the Romans, how many have escaped the notice of history, how few have resisted the ravages of time and barbarism! And yet even the majestic ruins that are still scattered over Italy and the provinces, would be sufficient to prove, that those countries were once the seat of a polite and powerful empire. Their greatness alone, or their beauty, might deserve our attention; but they are rendered more interesting, by two important circumstances, which connect the agreeable history of the arts, with the more useful history of human manners. Many of those works were erected at private expence, and almost all were intended for public benefit.

Many of them erected at private expence. It is natural to suppose that the greatest number, as well as the most considerable of the Roman edifices, were raised by the emperors, who possessed so unbounded a command both of men and money. Augustus was accustomed to boast that he had found his capital of brick, and that he had left it of marble.[64] The strict œconomy of Vespasian was the source of his magnificence. The works of Trajan bear the stamp of his genius. The public monuments with which Hadrian adorned every province of the empire, were executed not only by his orders, but under his immediate inspection. He was himself an artist; and he loved the arts, as they conduced to the glory of the monarch. They were encouraged by the Antonines, as they contributed to the happiness of the people. But if the emperors were the first, they were not the only architects of their dominions. Their example was universally imitated by their principal subjects, who were not afraid of declaring to the world that they had spirit to conceive, and wealth to accomplish, the noblest undertakings. Scarcely had the proud structure of the Coliseum been

63. Joseph. de Bell. Judaico, l. ii. c. 16. The oration of Agrippa, or rather of the historian, is a fine picture of the Roman empire.

64. Sueton. in August. c. 28. Augustus built in Rome the temple and forum of Mars the Avenger; the temple of Jupiter Tonans in the Capitol; that of Apollo Palatine, with public libraries; the portico and basilica of Caius and Lucius, the porticoes of Livia and Octavia, and the theatre of Marcellus. The example of the sovereign was imitated by his ministers and generals; and his friend Agrippa left behind him the immortal monument of the Pantheon.

dedicated at Rome, before the edifices of a smaller scale indeed, but of the same design and materials, were erected for the use, and at the expence, of the cities of Capua and Verona.[65] The inscription of the stupendous bridge of Alcantara, attests that it was thrown over the Tagus by the contribution of a few Lusitanian communities. When Pliny was intrusted with the government of Bithynia and Pontus, provinces by no means the richest or most considerable of the empire, he found the cities within his jurisdiction striving with each other in every useful and ornamental work, that might deserve the curiosity of strangers, or the gratitude of their citizens. It was the duty of the Proconsul to supply their deficiencies, to direct their taste, and sometimes to moderate their emulation.[66] The opulent senators of Rome and the provinces esteemed it an honour, and almost an obligation, to adorn the splendour of their age and country; and the influence of fashion very frequently supplied the want of taste or generosity. Among a crowd of these private benefactors, we may select Herodes Atticus, an Athenian citizen, who lived in the age of the Antonines. Whatever might be the motive of his conduct, his magnificence would have been worthy of the greatest kings.

The family of Herod, at least after it had been favoured by fortune, was lineally descended from Cimon and Miltiades, Theseus and Cecrops, Æacus and Jupiter. But the posterity of *Example of Herodes Atticus.* so many gods and heroes was fallen into the most abject state. His grandfather had suffered by the hands of justice, and Julius Atticus, his father, must have ended his life in poverty and contempt, had he not discovered an immense treasure buried under an old house, the last remains of his patrimony. According to the rigour of law, the emperor might have asserted his claim, and the prudent Atticus prevented, by a frank confession, the officiousness of informers. But the equitable Nerva, who then filled the throne, refused to accept any part of it, and commanded him to use, without scruple, the present of fortune. The cautious Athenian still insisted, that the treasure was too considerable for a subject, and that he knew not how to *use it. Abuse it, then,* replied the monarch, with a good-natured

---

65. See Maffei, Verona illustrata, l. iv. p. 68.

66. See the xth book of Pliny's Epistles. He mentions the following works, carried on at the expence of the cities. At Nicomedia, a new forum, an aqueduct, and a canal, left unfinished by a king; at Nice, a Gymnasium, and a theatre which had already cost near ninety thousand pounds; baths at Prusa and Claudiopolis; and an aqueduct of sixteen miles in length for the use of Sinope.

peevishness; for it is your own.[67] Many will be of opinion, that Atticus literally obeyed the emperor's last instructions; since he expended the greatest part of his fortune, which was much increased by an advantageous marriage, in the service of the Public. He had obtained for his son Herod, the prefecture of the free cities of Asia; and the young magistrate, observing that the town of Troas was indifferently supplied with water, obtained from the munificence of Hadrian, three hundred myriads of drachms (about a hundred thousand pounds) for the construction of a new aqueduct. But in the execution of the work the charge amounted to more than double the estimate, and the officers of the revenue began to murmur, till the generous Atticus silenced their complaints, by requesting that he might be permitted to take upon himself the whole additional expence.[68]

His reputation. The ablest preceptors of Greece and Asia had been invited by liberal rewards to direct the education of young Herod. Their pupil soon became a celebrated orator according to the useless rhetoric of that age, which, confining itself to the schools, disdained to visit either the Forum or the Senate. He was honoured with the consulship at Rome; but the greatest part of his life was spent in a philosophic retirement at Athens, and his adjacent villas; perpetually surrounded by sophists, who acknowledged, without reluctance, the superiority of a rich and generous rival.[69] The monuments of his genius have perished; some considerable ruins still preserve the fame of his taste and munificence: modern travellers have measured the remains of the stadium which he constructed at Athens. It was six hundred feet in length, built entirely of white marble, capable of admitting the whole body of the people, and finished in four years, whilst Herod was president of the Athenian games. To the memory of his wife Regilla, he dedicated a theatre, scarcely to be paralleled in the empire: no wood except cedar, very curiously carved, was employed in any part of the building. The Odeum, designed by Pericles for musical performances, and the rehearsal of new tragedies, had been a trophy of the victory of the arts over Barbaric greatness; as the timbers employed in the construction consisted chiefly of the masts of the Persian vessels. Notwithstanding the repairs bestowed on that ancient edifice by a king of Cappadocia, it was again fallen to decay. Herod restored its ancient

67. Hadrian afterwards made a very equitable regulation, which divided all treasure-trove between the right of property and that of discovery. Hist. August. p. 9.

68. Philostrat. in Vit. Sophist. l. ii. p. 548.
69. Aulus Gellius, in Noct. Attic. i. 2. ix. 2. xviii. 10. xix. 12. Philostrat. p. 564.

beauty and magnificence. Nor was the liberality of that illustrious citizen confined to the walls of Athens. The most splendid ornaments bestowed on the temple of Neptune in the Isthmus, a theatre at Corinth, a stadium at Delphi, a bath at Thermopylæ, and an aqueduct at Canusium in Italy, were insufficient to exhaust his treasures. The people of Epirus, Thessaly, Eubœa, Bœotia, and Peloponnesus, experienced his favours; and many inscriptions of the cities of Greece and Asia gratefully style Herodes Atticus their patron and benefactor.[70]

In the commonwealths of Athens and Rome, the modest simplicity of private houses announced the equal condition of freedom; whilst the sovereignty of the people was represented in the majestic edifices destined to the public use;[71] nor was this republican spirit totally extinguished by the introduction of wealth and monarchy. It was in works of national honour and benefit, that the most virtuous of the emperors affected to display their magnificence. The golden palace of Nero excited a just indignation, but the vast extent of ground which had been usurped by his selfish luxury, was more nobly filled under the succeeding reigns by the Coliseum, the baths of Titus, the Claudian portico, and the temples dedicated to the goddess of Peace, and to the genius of Rome.[72] These monuments of architecture, the property of the Roman people, were adorned with the most beautiful productions of Grecian painting and sculpture; and in the temple of Peace, a very curious library was open to the curiosity of the learned. At a small distance from thence was situated the Forum of Trajan. It was surrounded with a lofty portico, in the form of a quadrangle, into which four triumphal arches opened a noble and spacious entrance: in the centre arose a column of marble, whose height, of one hundred and ten feet, denoted the elevation of the hill that had been cut away. This column, which still subsists in its ancient beauty, exhibited an exact representation of the Dacian victories of its founder.

Most of the Roman monuments for public use; temples, theatres, aqueducts, &c.

70. See Philostrat. l. ii. p. 548. 560. Pausanias, l. i. and vii. 10. The life of Herodes, in the xxxth volume of the Memoirs of the Academy of Inscriptions.

71. It is particularly remarked of Athens by Dicæarchus, de Statu Græciæ, p. 8. inter Geographos Minores, edit. Hudson.

72. Donatus de Roma Vetere, l. iii. c. 4, 5, 6. Nardini Roma Antica, l. iii. 11, 12, 13.

and a MS. description of ancient Rome, by Bernardus Oricellarius, or Rucellai, of which I obtained a copy from the library of the Canon Ricardi at Florence. Two celebrated pictures of Timanthes and of Protogenes are mentioned by Pliny, as in the Temple of Peace; and the Laocoon was found in the baths of Titus.

The veteran soldier contemplated the story of his own campaigns, and by an easy illusion of national vanity, the peaceful citizen associated himself to the honours of the triumph. All the other quarters of the capital, and all the provinces of the empire, were embellished by the same liberal spirit of public magnificence, and were filled with amphitheatres, theatres, temples, porticos, triumphal arches, baths, and aqueducts, all variously conducive to the health, the devotion, and the pleasures of the meanest citizen. The last mentioned of those edifices deserve our peculiar attention. The boldness of the enterprise, the solidity of the execution, and the uses to which they were subservient, rank the aqueducts among the noblest monuments of Roman genius and power. The aqueducts of the capital claim a just pre-eminence; but the curious traveller, who, without the light of history, should examine those of Spoleto, of Metz, or of Segovia, would very naturally conclude, that those provincial towns had formerly been the residence of some potent monarch. The solitudes of Asia and Africa were once covered with flourishing cities, whose populousness, and even whose existence, was derived from such artificial supplies of a perennial stream of fresh water.[73]

Number and greatness of the cities of the empire. We have computed the inhabitants, and contemplated the public works, of the Roman empire. The observation of the number and greatness of its cities will serve to confirm the former, and to multiply the latter. It may not be unpleasing to collect a few scattered instances relative to that subject, without forgetting, however, that from the vanity of nations and the poverty of language, the vague appellation of city has been indifferently bestowed on Rome and upon Laurentum. I. *Ancient* Italy is said to have contained eleven *In Italy.* hundred and ninety-seven cities; and for whatsoever æra of antiquity the expression might be intended,[74] there is not any reason to believe the country less populous in the age of the Antonines, than in that of Romulus. The petty states of Latium were contained within the metropolis of the empire, by whose superior influence they had been attracted. Those parts of Italy which have so long languished under the lazy tyranny of priests and viceroys, had been afflicted only by the more tolerable calamities of war; and the first symptoms of decay, which *they* experienced, were

---

73. Montfaucon l'Antiquité Expliquée, tom. iv. p. 2. l. i. c. 9. Fabretti has composed a very learned treatise on the aqueducts of Rome.

74. Ælian Hist. Var. l. ix. c. 16. He lived in the time of Alexander Severus. See Fabricius, Biblioth. Græca, l. iv. c. 21.

amply compensated by the rapid improvements of the Cisalpine Gaul. The splendor of Verona may be traced in its remains: yet Verona was less celebrated than Aquileia or Padua, Milan or Ravenna. II. The spirit of improvement had passed the Alps, and been felt even in the woods of Britain, which were gradually cleared away to open a free space for convenient and elegant habitations. York was the seat of government; London was already enriched by commerce; and Bath was celebrated for the salutary effects of its medicinal waters. Gaul could boast of her twelve hundred cities;[75] and though, in the northern parts, many of them, without excepting Paris itself, were little more than the rude and imperfect townships of a rising people; the southern provinces imitated the wealth and elegance of Italy.[76] Many were the cities of Gaul, Marseilles, Arles, Nismes, Narbonne, Thoulouse, Bourdeaux, Autun, Vienna, Lyons, Langres, and Treves, whose ancient condition might sustain an equal, and perhaps advantageous comparison with their present state. With regard to Spain, that country flourished as a province, and has declined as a kingdom. Exhausted by the abuse of her strength, by America, and by superstition, her pride might possibly be confounded, if we required such a list of three hundred and sixty cities, as Pliny has exhibited under the reign of Vespasian.[77] III. Three hundred African cities had once acknowledged the authority of Carthage,[78] nor is it likely that their numbers diminished under the administration of the emperors: Carthage itself rose with new splendor from its ashes; and that capital, as well as Capua and Corinth, soon recovered all the advantages which can be separated from independent sovereignty. IV. The provinces of the east present the contrast of Roman magnificence with Turkish barbarism. The ruins of antiquity scattered over uncultivated fields, and ascribed, by ignorance, to the power of magic, scarcely afford a shelter to the oppressed peasant or wandering Arab. Under the reign of the Cæsars, the proper Asia alone contained five hundred populous cities,[79] enriched with all the gifts of nature, and adorned with all the refinements of art. Eleven cities of Asia had once disputed the honour of dedicating a temple to Tiberius, and their respective merits were

Gaul and Spain.

Africa.

Asia.

75. Joseph. de Bell. Jud. ii. 16. The number, however, is mentioned, and should be received with a degree of latitude.

76. Plin. Hist. Natur. iii. 5.

77. Plin. Hist. Natur. iii. 3, 4. iv. 35. The list seems authentic and accurate: the division of

the provinces, and the different condition of the cities, are minutely distinguished.

78. Strabon. Geograph. l. xvii. p. 1189.

79. Joseph. de Bell. Jud. ii. 16. Philostrat. in Vit. Sophist. l. ii. p. 548. Edit. Olear.

examined by the senate.[80] Four of them were immediately rejected as unequal to the burden; and among these was Laodicea, whose splendor is still displayed in its ruins.[81] Laodicea collected a very considerable revenue from its flocks of sheep, celebrated for the fineness of their wool, and had received, a little before the contest, a legacy of above four hundred thousand pounds by the testament of a generous citizen.[82] If such was the poverty of Laodicea, what must have been the wealth of those cities, whose claim appeared preferable, and particularly of Pergamus, of Smyrna, and of Ephesus, who so long disputed with each other the titular primacy of Asia?[83] The capitals of Syria and Egypt held a still superior rank in the empire: Antioch and Alexandria looked down with disdain on a crowd of dependent cities,[84] and yielded, with reluctance, to the majesty of Rome itself.

Roman Roads.   All these cities were connected with each other, and with the capital by the public highways, which issuing from the Forum of Rome, traversed Italy, pervaded the provinces, and were terminated only by the frontiers of the empire. If we carefully trace the distance from the wall of Antoninus to Rome, and from thence to Jerusalem, it will be found that the great chain of communication, from the north-west to the south-east point of the empire, was drawn out to the length of four thousand and eighty Roman miles.[85] The public roads were accurately divided by

80. Tacit. Annal. iv. 55. I have taken some pains in consulting and comparing modern travellers, with regard to the fate of those eleven cities of Asia; seven or eight are totally destroyed, Hypæpe, Tralles, Laodicea, Ilium, Halicarnassus, Miletus, Ephesus, and we may add Sardes. Of the remaining three, Pergamus is a straggling village of two or three thousand inhabitants. Magnesia, under the name of Guzel-hissar, a town of some consequence; and Smyrna, a great city, peopled by an hundred thousand souls. But even at Smyrna, while the Franks have maintained commerce, the Turks have ruined the arts.

81. See a very exact and pleasing description of the ruins of Laodicea, in Chandler's Travels through Asia Minor, p. 225, &c.

82. Strabo, l. xii. p. 866. He had studied at Tralles.

83. See a Dissertation of M. de Boze, Mem.

de l'Academie, tom. xviii. Aristides pronounced an oration which is still extant, to recommend concord to the rival cities.

84. The inhabitants of Egypt, exclusive of Alexandria, amounted to seven millions and a half (Joseph. de Bell. Jud. ii. 16.). Under the military government of the Mamalukes, Syria was supposed to contain sixty thousand villages (Histoire de Timur Bec, l. v. c. 20.).

85. The following Itinerary may serve to convey some idea of the direction of the road, and of the distance between the principal towns. I. From the wall of Antoninus to York, 222 Roman miles. II. London 227. III. Rhutupiæ or Sandwich 67. IV. The navigation to Boulogne 45. V. Rheims 174. VI. Lyons 330. VII. Milan 324. VIII. Rome 426. IX. Brundusium 360. X. The navigation to Dyrrachium 40. XI. Byzantium 711. XII. Ancyra 283. XIII. Tarsus 301. XIV. Antioch 141. XV.

mile-stones, and ran in a direct line from one city to another, with very little respect for the obstacles either of nature or private property. Mountains were perforated, and bold arches thrown over the broadest and most rapid streams.[86] The middle part of the road was raised into a terrace which commanded the adjacent country, consisted of several strata of sand, gravel, and cement, and was paved with large stones, or in some places, near the capital, with granite.[87] Such was the solid construction of the Roman highways, whose firmness has not entirely yielded to the effort of fifteen centuries. They united the subjects of the most distant provinces by an easy and familiar intercourse; but their primary object had been to facilitate the marches of the legions; nor was any country considered as completely subdued, till it had been rendered, in all its parts, pervious to the arms and authority of the conqueror. The advantage of receiving the earliest intelligence, and of conveying their orders with celerity, induced the emperors to establish, throughout their extensive dominions, the regular institution of posts.[88] Houses were every where erected at the distance only of five or six miles; each of them was constantly provided with forty horses, and by the help of these relays, it was easy to travel an hundred miles in a day along the Roman roads.[89] The use of the posts was allowed to those who claimed it by an Imperial mandate; but though originally intended for the public service, it was sometimes indulged to the business or conveniency of private citizens.[90]

Posts.

Nor was the communication of the Roman empire less free and open by sea than it was by land. The provinces surrounded and inclosed the Mediterranean; and Italy, in the shape of an immense

Navigation.

Tyre 252. XVI. Jerusalem 168. In all 4080 Roman, or 3740 English miles. See the Itineraries published by Wesseling, his annotations; Gale and Stukeley for Britain, and M. d'Anville for Gaul and Italy.

86. Montfaucon, l'Antiquité Expliquée, (tom. iv. p. 2. l. i. c. 5.) has described the bridges of Narni, Alcantara, Nismes, &c.

87. Bergier Histoire des grands Chemins de l'Empire Romain, l. ii. c. 1–28.

88. Procopius in Hist. Arcanâ, c. 30. Bergier Hist. des grands Chemins, l. iv. Codex Theodosian. l. viii. tit. v. vol. ii. p. 506–563. with Godefroy's learned commentary.

89. In the time of Theodosius, Cæsarius, a magistrate of high rank, went post from Antioch to Constantinople. He began his journey at night, was in Cappadocia (165 miles from Antioch) the ensuing evening, and arrived at Constantinople the sixth day about noon. The whole distance was 725 Roman, or 665 English miles. See Libanius Orat. xxii. and the Itineraria, p. 572–581.

90. Pliny, though a favourite and a minister, made an apology for granting post-horses to his wife on the most urgent business. Epist. x. 121, 122.

promontory, advanced into the midst of that great lake. The coasts of Italy are, in general, destitute of safe harbours; but human industry had corrected the deficiencies of nature; and the artificial port of Ostia, in particular, situate at the mouth of the Tyber, and formed by the emperor Claudius, was an useful monument of Roman greatness.[91] From this port, which was only sixteen miles from the capital, a favourable breeze frequently carried vessels in seven days to the columns of Hercules, and in nine or ten, to Alexandria in Egypt.[92]

Improvement of agriculture in the western countries of the empire. Whatever evils either reason or declamation have imputed to extensive empire, the power of Rome was attended with some beneficial consequences to mankind; and the same free-dom of intercourse which extended the vices, diffused likewise the improvements, of social life. In the more remote ages of antiquity, the world was unequally divided. The east was in the immemorial possession of arts and luxury; whilst the west was inhabited by rude and warlike barbarians, who either disdained agriculture, or to whom it was totally unknown. Under the protection of an established government, the productions of happier climates, and the industry of more civilized nations, were gradually introduced into the western countries of Europe; and the natives were encouraged, by an open and profitable commerce, to multiply the former, as well as to improve the latter. It would be almost impossible to enumerate all the articles, either of the animal or the vegetable reign, which were successively imported into Europe, from Asia and Egypt;[93] but it will not be unworthy of the dignity, and much less of the utility, of an historical work, slightly to touch on a few of the principal heads.

Introduction of fruits, &c. 1. Almost all the flowers, the herbs, and the fruits, that grow in our European gardens, are of foreign extraction, which, in many cases, is betrayed even by their names: the apple was a native of Italy, and when the Romans had tasted the richer flavour of the apricot, the peach, the pomegranate, the citron, and the orange, they contented themselves with applying to all these new fruits the common denomination of apple, discriminating them from each other by the additional epithet of their country. 2. In the time of Homer, the vine grew wild in the island of Sicily, and most probably in the adjacent continent; but it was not improved by the skill, nor did it afford a liquor grateful to the

The Vine.

---

91. Bergier Hist. des grands Chemins, l. iv. c. 49.
92. Plin. Hist. Natur. xix. 1.
93. It is not improbable that the Greeks and

Phœnicians introduced some new arts and productions into the neighbourhood of Marseilles and Gades.

taste, of the savage inhabitants.[94] A thousand years afterwards, Italy could boast, that of the fourscore most generous and celebrated wines, more than two-thirds were produced from her soil.[95] The blessing was soon communicated to the Narbonnese province of Gaul; but so intense was the cold to the north of the Cevennes, that, in the time of Strabo, it was thought impossible to ripen the grapes in those parts of Gaul.[96] This difficulty, however, was gradually vanquished; and there is some reason to believe, that the vineyards of Burgundy are as old as the age of the Antonines.[97] 3. The olive, in the western world, followed the progress of peace, of which it was considered as the symbol. Two *The olive.* centuries after the foundation of Rome, both Italy and Africa were strangers to that useful plant; it was naturalized in those countries; and at length carried into the heart of Spain and Gaul. The timid errors of the ancients, that it required a certain degree of heat, and could only flourish in the neighbourhood of the sea, were insensibly exploded by industry and experience.[98] 4. The cultivation of flax was transported from Egypt to Gaul, and enriched the whole country, however it might impoverish *Flax.* the particular lands on which it was sown.[99] 5. The use of artificial grasses became familiar to the farmers both of Italy and the provinces, particularly the Lucerne, which derived its name and origin *Artificial grass.* from Media.[100] The assured supply of wholesome and plentiful food for the cattle during winter, multiplied the number of the flocks and herds, which in their turn contributed to the fertility of the soil. To all these improvements may be added an assiduous attention to mines and fisheries, which, by employing a multitude of laborious hands, serve to increase the pleasures of the rich, and the subsistence of the poor. The elegant treatise of Columella describes the advanced state of the Spanish husbandry, *General* under the reign of Tiberius; and it may be observed, that those *plenty.* famines which so frequently afflicted the infant republic, were seldom

94. See Homer Odyss. l. ix. v. 358.
95. Plin. Hist. Natur. l. xiv.
96. Strab. Geograph. l. iv. p. 223. The intense cold of a Gallic winter was almost proverbial among the ancients.
97. In the beginning of the ivth century, the orator Eumenius (Panegyric. Veter. vii. 6. edit. Delphin.) speaks of the vines in the territory of Autun, which were decayed through age, and the first plantation of which was

totally unknown. The Pagus Arebrignus is supposed by M. d'Anville to be the district of Beaune, celebrated, even at present, for one of the first growths of Burgundy.
98. Plin. Hist. Natur. l. xv.
99. Plin. Hist. Natur. l. xix.
100. See the agreeable Essays on Agriculture by Mr. Harte, in which he has collected all that the ancients and moderns have said of lucerne.

or never experienced by the extensive empire of Rome. The accidental scarcity, in any single province, was immediately relieved by the plenty of its more fortunate neighbours.

Arts of luxury.   Agriculture is the foundation of manufactures; since the productions of nature are the materials of art. Under the Roman empire, the labour of an industrious and ingenious people was variously, but incessantly employed, in the service of the rich. In their dress, their table, their houses, and their furniture, the favourites of fortune united every refinement of conveniency, of elegance, and of splendour; whatever could sooth their pride, or gratify their sensuality. Such refinements, under the odious name of luxury, have been severely arraigned by the moralists of every age; and it might perhaps be more conducive to the virtue, as well as happiness, of mankind, if all possessed the necessaries, and none the superfluities, of life. But in the present imperfect condition of society, luxury, though it may proceed from vice or folly, seems to be the only means that can correct the unequal distribution of property. The diligent mechanic, and the skilful artist, who have obtained no share in the division of the earth, receive a voluntary tax from the possessors of land; and the latter are prompted, by a sense of interest, to improve those estates, with whose produce they may purchase additional pleasures. This operation, the particular effects of which are felt in every society, acted with much more diffusive energy in the Roman world. The provinces would soon have been exhausted of their wealth, if the manufactures and commerce of luxury had not insensibly restored to the industrious subjects, the sums which were exacted from them by the arms and authority of Rome. As long as the circulation was confined within the bounds of the empire, it impressed the political machine with a new degree of activity, and its consequences, sometimes beneficial, could never become pernicious.

Foreign trade.   But it is no easy task to confine luxury within the limits of an empire. The most remote countries of the ancient world were ransacked to supply the pomp and delicacy of Rome. The forest of Scythia afforded some valuable furs. Amber was brought over land from the shores of the Baltic to the Danube; and the barbarians were astonished at the price which they received in exchange for so useless a commodity.[101]

---

101. Tacit. Germania, c. 45. Plin. Hist. Natur. xxxviii. II. The latter observed, with some humour, that even fashion had not yet found out the use of amber. Nero sent a Roman knight, to purchase great quantities on the spot, where it was produced; the coast of modern Prussia.

There was a considerable demand for Babylonian carpets, and other manufactures of the East; but the most important and unpopular branch of foreign trade was carried on with Arabia and India. Every year, about the time of the summer solstice, a fleet of an hundred and twenty vessels sailed from Myos-hormos, a port of Egypt, on the Red Sea. By the periodical assistance of the Monsoons, they traversed the ocean in about forty days. The coast of Malabar, or the island of Ceylon,[102] was the usual term of their navigation, and it was in those markets that the merchants from the more remote countries of Asia expected their arrival. The return of the fleet of Egypt was fixed to the months of December or January; and as soon as their rich cargo had been transported on the backs of camels, from the Red Sea to the Nile, and had descended that river as far as Alexandria, it was poured, without delay, into the capital of the empire.[103] The objects of oriental traffic were splendid and trifling: silk, a pound of which was esteemed not inferior in value to a pound of gold;[104] precious stones, among which the pearl claimed the first rank after the diamond;[105] and a variety of aromatics, that were consumed in religious worship and the pomp of funerals. The labour and risk of the voyage was rewarded with almost incredible profit; but the profit was made upon Roman subjects, and a few individuals were enriched at the expence of the Public. As the natives of Arabia and India were contented with the productions and manufactures of their own country, silver, on the side of the Romans, was the principal, if not the only instrument of commerce. It was a complaint worthy of the gravity of the senate, that, in the purchase of female ornaments, the wealth of the state was irrecoverably given away to foreign and hostile nations.[106] The annual loss is computed, by a writer of an inquisitive but censorious temper, at upwards of eight hundred thousand pounds sterling.[107] Such was the style of discontent, brooding over the dark prospect of approaching poverty. And yet, if we compare the proportion between gold

Gold and silver.

102. Called Taprobana by the Romans, and Serendib by the Arabs. It was discovered under the reign of Claudius, and gradually became the principal mart of the East.

103. Plin. Hist. Natur. l. vi. Strabo, l. xvii.

104. Hist. August. p. 224. A silk garment was considered as an ornament to a woman, but as a disgrace to a man.

105. The two great pearl fisheries were the same as at present, Ormuz and Cape Comorin.

As well as we can compare ancient with modern geography, Rome was supplied with diamonds from the mine of Jumelpur, in Bengal, which is described in the Voyages de Tavernier, tom. ii. p. 281.

106. Tacit. Annal. iii. 52. In a speech of Tiberius.

107. Plin. Hist. Natur. xii. 18. In another place he computes half that sum; Quingenties H. S. for India exclusive of Arabia.

and silver, as it stood in the time of Pliny, and as it was fixed in the reign of Constantine, we shall discover within that period a very considerable increase.[108] There is not the least reason to suppose that gold was become more scarce; it is therefore evident that silver was grown more common; that whatever might be the amount of the Indian and Arabian exports, they were far from exhausting the wealth of the Roman world; and that the produce of the mines abundantly supplied the demands of commerce.

General felicity. Notwithstanding the propensity of mankind to exalt the past, and to depreciate the present, the tranquil and prosperous state of the empire was warmly felt, and honestly confessed, by the provincials as well as Romans. "They acknowledged that the true principles of social life, laws, agriculture, and science, which had been first invented by the wisdom of Athens, were now firmly established by the power of Rome, under whose auspicious influence, the fiercest barbarians were united by an equal government and common language. They affirm, that with the improvement of arts, the human species was visibly multiplied. They celebrate the increasing splendour of the cities, the beautiful face of the country, cultivated and adorned like an immense garden; and the long festival of peace, which was enjoyed by so many nations, forgetful of their ancient animosities, and delivered from the apprehension of future danger."[109] Whatever suspicions may be suggested by the air of rhetoric and declamation, which seems to prevail in these passages, the substance of them is perfectly agreeable to historic truth.

Decline of courage; It was scarcely possible that the eyes of contemporaries should discover in the public felicity the latent causes of decay and corruption. This long peace, and the uniform government of the Romans, introduced a slow and secret poison into the vitals of the empire. The minds of men were gradually reduced to the same level, the fire of genius was extinguished, and even the military spirit evaporated. The natives of Europe were brave and robust. Spain, Gaul, Britain, and Illyricum, supplied the legions with excellent soldiers, and constituted the real strength of the monarchy. Their personal valour remained, but they no longer possessed that public courage which is nourished by the love of independence, the sense of national honour, the presence of danger, and the habit of command.

108. The proportion which was 1 to 10, and 12½, rose to 14⅖, the legal regulation of Constantine. See Arbuthnot's Tables of ancient Coins, c. v.

109. Among many other passages, see Pliny (Hist. Natur. iii. 5.), Aristides (de Urbe Româ), and Tertullian (de Animâ, c. 30.).

They received laws and governors from the will of their sovereign, and trusted for their defence to a mercenary army. The posterity of their boldest leaders was contented with the rank of citizens and subjects. The most aspiring spirits resorted to the court or standard of the emperors; and the deserted provinces, deprived of political strength or union, insensibly sunk into the languid indifference of private life.

The love of letters, almost inseparable from peace and refinement, was fashionable among the subjects of Hadrian and the Antonines, *of genius.* who were themselves men of learning and curiosity. It was diffused over the whole extent of their empire; the most northern tribes of Britons had acquired a taste for rhetoric; Homer as well as Virgil were transcribed and studied on the banks of the Rhine and Danube; and the most liberal rewards sought out the faintest glimmerings of literary merit.[110] The sciences of physic and astronomy were successfully cultivated by the Greeks; the observations of Ptolemy and the writings of Galen are studied by those who have improved their discoveries and corrected their errors; but if we except the inimitable Lucian, this age of indolence passed away without having produced a single writer of original genius, or who excelled in the arts of elegant composition. The authority of Plato and Aristotle, of Zeno and Epicurus, still reigned in the schools; and their systems, transmitted with blind deference from one generation of disciples to another, precluded every generous attempt to exercise the powers, or enlarge the limits, of the human mind. The beauties of the poets and orators, instead of kindling a fire like their own, inspired only cold and servile imitations: or if any ventured to deviate from those models, they deviated at the same time from good sense and propriety. On the revival of letters, the youthful vigour of the imagination, after a long repose, national emulation, a new

---

110. Herodes Atticus gave the sophist Polemo above eight thousand pounds for three declamations. See Philostrat. l. i. p. 558. The Antonines founded a school at Athens, in which professors of grammar, rhetoric, politics, and the four great sects of philosophy, were maintained at the public expence for the instruction of youth. The salary of a philosopher was ten thousand drachmæ, between three and four hundred pounds a year. Similar establishments were formed in the other great cities of the empire. See Lucian in Eunuch.

tom. ii. p. 353. edit. Reitz. Philostrat. l. ii. p. 566. Hist. August. p. 21. Dion Cassius, l. lxxi. p. 1195. Juvenal himself, in a morose satire, which in every line betrays his own disappointment and envy, is obliged, however, to say,

——O Juvenes, circumspicit et agitat vos.

Materiamque sibi Ducis indulgentia quærit.

Satir. vii. 20.

religion, new languages, and a new world, called forth the genius of Europe. But the provincials of Rome, trained by a uniform artificial foreign education, were engaged in a very unequal competition with those bold ancients, who, by expressing their genuine feelings in their native tongue, had already occupied every place of honour. The name of Poet was almost forgotten; that of Orator was usurped by the sophists. A cloud of critics, of compilers, of commentators, darkened the face of learning, and the decline of genius was soon followed by the corruption of taste.

Degeneracy.   The sublime Longinus, who in somewhat a later period, and in the court of a Syrian queen, preserved the spirit of ancient Athens, observes and laments this degeneracy of his contemporaries, which debased their sentiments, enervated their courage, and depressed their talents. "In the same manner, says he, as some children always remain pigmies, whose infant limbs have been too closely confined; thus our tender minds, fettered by the prejudices and habits of a just servitude, are unable to expand themselves, or to attain that well-proportioned greatness which we admire in the ancients; who living under a popular government, wrote with the same freedom as they acted."[111] This diminutive stature of mankind, if we pursue the metaphor, was daily sinking below the old standard, and the Roman world was indeed peopled by a race of pygmies; when the fierce giants of the north broke in, and mended the puny breed. They restored a manly spirit of freedom; and after the revolution of ten centuries, freedom became the happy parent of taste and science.

---

111. Longin. de Sublim. c. 43. p. 229. edit. Toll. Here too we may say of Longinus, "his own example strengthens all his laws." Instead of proposing his sentiments with a manly boldness, he insinuates them with the most guarded caution, puts them into the mouth of a friend; and, as far as we can collect from a corrupted text, makes a shew of refuting them himself.

CHAPTER III

Of the Constitution of the Roman Empire, in the Age of the Antonines.

The obvious definition of a monarchy seems to be that of a state, in which a single person, by whatsoever name he may be distinguished, is intrusted with the execution of the laws, the management of the revenue, and the command of the army. But, unless public liberty is protected by intrepid and vigilant guardians, the authority of so formidable a magistrate will soon degenerate into despotism. The influence of the clergy, in an age of superstition, might be usefully employed to assert the rights of mankind; but so intimate is the connexion between the throne and the altar, that the banner of the church has very seldom been seen on the side of the people. A martial nobility and stubborn commons, possessed of arms, tenacious of property, and collected into constitutional assemblies, form the only balance capable of preserving a free constitution against the enterprises of an aspiring prince.

Idea of a monarchy.

Every barrier of the Roman constitution had been levelled by the vast ambition of the dictator; every fence had been extirpated by the cruel hand of the Triumvir. After the victory of Actium, the fate of the Roman world depended on the will of Octavianus, surnamed Cæsar, by his uncle's adoption, and afterwards Augustus, by the flattery of the senate. The conqueror was at the head of forty-four veteran legions,[1] conscious of their own strength, and of the weakness of the constitution, habituated, during twenty years civil war, to every act of blood and violence, and passionately devoted to the house of Cæsar, from whence alone they had received, and expected, the most lavish rewards. The provinces, long oppressed by the ministers of the republic, sighed for the government of a single person, who would be the master, not the accomplice, of those petty tyrants. The people of Rome, viewing, with a secret pleasure, the humiliation of the aristocracy, demanded only bread and public shows; and were supplied with both by the liberal hand of Augustus. The rich and

Situation of Augustus.

1. Orosius, vi. 18.

polite Italians, who had almost universally embraced the philosophy of Epicurus, enjoyed the present blessings of ease and tranquillity, and suffered not the pleasing dream to be interrupted by the memory of their old tumultuous freedom. With its power, the senate had lost its dignity; many of the most noble families were extinct. The republicans of spirit and ability had perished in the field of battle, or in the proscription. The door of the assembly had been designedly left open, for a mixed multitude of more than a thousand persons, who reflected disgrace upon their rank, instead of deriving honour from it.[2]

He reforms the senate.   The reformation of the senate, was one of the first steps in which Augustus laid aside the tyrant, and professed himself the father of his country. He was elected censor; and, in concert with his faithful Agrippa, he examined the list of the senators, expelled a few members, whose vices or whose obstinacy required a public example, persuaded near two hundred to prevent the shame of an expulsion by a voluntary retreat, raised the qualification of a senator to about ten thousand pounds, created a sufficient number of Patrician families, and accepted for himself, the honourable title of Prince of the Senate, which had always been bestowed, by the censors, on the citizen the most eminent for his honours and services.[3] But whilst he thus restored the dignity, he destroyed the independence of the senate. The principles of a free constitution are irrecoverably lost, when the legislative power is nominated by the executive.

Resigns his usurped power.   Before an assembly thus modelled and prepared, Augustus pronounced a studied oration, which displayed his patriotism, and disguised his ambition. "He lamented, yet excused, his past conduct. Filial piety had required at his hands the revenge of his father's murder; the humanity of his own nature had sometimes given way to the stern laws of necessity, and to a forced connexion with two unworthy colleagues: as long as Antony lived, the republic forbad him to abandon her to a degenerate Roman, and a barbarian queen. He was now at liberty to satisfy his duty and his inclination. He solemnly restored the senate and people to all their ancient rights; and wished only to mingle with the crowd of his fellow-citizens, and to share the blessings which he had obtained for his country."[4]

2. Julius Cæsar introduced soldiers, strangers, and half-barbarians, into the senate (Sueton. in Cæsar. c. 77. 80.). The abuse became still more scandalous after his death.

3. Dion Cassius, l. iii. p. 693. Suetonius in August. c. 55.
4. Dion (l. liii. p. 698.) gives us a prolix and bombast speech on this great occasion. I have

It would require the pen of Tacitus (if Tacitus had assisted at this assembly) to describe the various emotions of the senate; those that were suppressed, and those that were affected. It was dangerous to trust the sincerity of Augustus; to seem to distrust it, was still more dangerous. The respective advantages of monarchy and a republic have often divided speculative inquirers; the present greatness of the Roman state, the corruption of manners, and the licence of the soldiers, supplied new arguments to the advocates of monarchy; and these general views of government were again warped by the hopes and fears of each individual. Amidst this confusion of sentiments, the answer of the senate was unanimous and decisive. They refused to accept the resignation of Augustus; they conjured him not to desert the republic, which he had saved. After a decent resistance, the crafty tyrant submitted to the orders of the senate; and consented to receive the government of the provinces, and the general command of the Roman armies, under the well-known names of PROCONSUL and IMPERATOR.[5] But he would receive them only for ten years. Even before the expiration of that period, he hoped that the wounds of civil discord would be completely healed, and that the republic, restored to its pristine health and vigour, would no longer require the dangerous interposition of so extraordinary a magistrate. The memory of this comedy, repeated several times during the life of Augustus, was preserved to the last ages of the empire, by the peculiar pomp with which the perpetual monarchs of Rome always solemnized the tenth years of their reign.[6]

Is prevailed upon to resume it under the title of Emperor or General.

Without any violation of the principles of the constitution, the general of the Roman armies might receive and exercise an authority almost despotic over the soldiers, the enemies, and the subjects of the republic. With regard to the soldiers, the jealousy of freedom had, even from the earliest ages of Rome, given way to the hopes of conquest, and a just sense of military discipline. The dictator, or consul, had a right to command the service of the Roman youth; and to punish an obstinate or cowardly disobedience by the most severe and

Power of the Roman generals.

borrowed from Suetonius and Tacitus the general language of Augustus.

5. *Imperator* (from which we have derived Emperor) signified under the republic no more than *general*, and was emphatically bestowed by the soldiers, when on the field of battle they proclaimed their victorious leader worthy of that title. When the Roman *emperors* assumed it in that sense, they placed it after their name, and marked how often they had taken it.

6. Dion, l. liii. p. 703, &c.

ignominious penalties, by striking the offender out of the list of citizens, by confiscating his property, and by selling his person into slavery.[7] The most sacred rights of freedom, confirmed by the Porcian and Sempronian laws, were suspended by the military engagement. In his camp the general exercised an absolute power of life and death; his jurisdiction was not confined by any forms of trial, or rules of proceeding, and the execution of the sentence was immediate and without appeal.[8] The choice of the enemies of Rome was regularly decided by the legislative authority. The most important resolutions of peace and war were seriously debated in the senate, and solemnly ratified by the people. But when the arms of the legions were carried to a great distance from Italy, the generals assumed the liberty of directing them against whatever people, and in whatever manner, they judged most advantageous for the public service. It was from the success, not from the justice, of their enterprises, that they expected the honours of a triumph. In the use of victory, especially after they were no longer controlled by the commissioners of the senate, they exercised the most unbounded despotism. When Pompey commanded in the east, he rewarded his soldiers and allies, dethroned princes, divided kingdoms, founded colonies, and distributed the treasures of Mithridates. On his return to Rome, he obtained, by a single act of the senate and people, the universal ratification of all his proceedings.[9] Such was the power over the soldiers, and over the enemies of Rome, which was either granted to, or assumed by, the generals of the republic. They were, at the same time, the governors, or rather monarchs, of the conquered provinces, united the civil with the military character, administered justice as well as the finances, and exercised both the executive and legislative power of the state.

Lieutenants of the emperor. From what has been already observed in the first chapter of this work, some notion may be formed of the armies and provinces thus intrusted to the ruling hand of Augustus. But as it was impossible that he could personally command the legions of so many

7. Livy Epitom. l. xiv. Valer. Maxim. vi. 3.
8. See in the viiith book of Livy, the conduct of Manlius Torquatus and Papirius Cursor. They violated the laws of nature and humanity, but they asserted those of military discipline; and the people, who abhorred the action, was obliged to respect the principle.
9. By the lavish but unconstrained suffrages of the people, Pompey had obtained a military

command scarcely inferior to that of Augustus. Among the extraordinary acts of power executed by the former, we may remark the foundation of twenty-nine cities, and the distribution of three or four millions sterling to his troops. The ratification of his acts met with some opposition and delays in the senate. See Plutarch, Appian, Dion Cassius, and the first book of the epistles to Atticus.

distant frontiers, he was indulged by the senate, as Pompey had already been, in the permission of devolving the execution of his great office on a sufficient number of lieutenants. In rank and authority these officers seemed not inferior to the ancient proconsuls; but their station was dependent and precarious. They received and held their commissions at the will of a superior, to whose *auspicious* influence the merit of their action was legally attributed.[10] They were the representatives of the emperor. The emperor alone was the general of the republic, and his jurisdiction, civil as well as military, extended over all the conquests of Rome. It was some satisfaction, however, to the senate, that he always delegated his power to the members of their body. The Imperial lieutenants were of consular or prætorian dignity; the legions were commanded by senators, and the præfecture of Egypt was the only important trust committed to a Roman knight.

Within six days after Augustus had been compelled to accept so very liberal a grant, he resolved to gratify the pride of the senate by an easy sacrifice. He represented to them, that they had enlarged his powers, even beyond that degree which might be required by the melancholy condition of the times. They had not permitted him to refuse the laborious command of the armies *Division of the provinces between the emperor and the senate.* and the frontiers; but he must insist on being allowed to restore the more peaceful and secure provinces, to the mild administration of the civil magistrate. In the division of the provinces, Augustus provided for his own power, and for the dignity of the republic. The proconsuls of the senate, particularly those of Asia, Greece, and Africa, enjoyed a more honourable character than the lieutenants of the emperor, who commanded in Gaul or Syria. The former were attended by lictors, the latter by soldiers. A law was passed, that wherever the emperor was present, his extraordinary commission should supersede the ordinary jurisdiction of the governor, a custom was introduced, that the new conquests belonged to the Imperial portion, and it was soon discovered, that the authority of the *Prince*, the favourite epithet of Augustus, was the same in every part of the empire.

10. Under the commonwealth, a triumph could only be claimed by the general, who was authorised to take the Auspices in the name of the people. By an exact consequence drawn from this principle of policy and religion, the triumph was reserved to the emperor; and his most successful lieutenants were satisfied with some marks of distinction, which, under the name of triumphal honours, were invented in their favour.

The former preserves his military command, and guards in Rome itself.

In return for this imaginary concession, Augustus obtained an important privilege, which rendered him master of Rome and Italy. By a dangerous exception to the ancient maxims, he was authorized to preserve his military command, supported by a numerous body of guards, even in time of peace, and in the heart of the capital. His command, indeed, was confined to those citizens who were engaged in the service by the military oath; but such was the propensity of the Romans to servitude, that the oath was voluntarily taken by the magistrates, the senators, and the equestrian order, till the homage of flattery was insensibly converted into an annual and solemn protestation of fidelity.

Consular and tribunitian powers.

Although Augustus considered a military force as the firmest foundation, he wisely rejected it, as a very odious instrument of government. It was more agreeable to his temper, as well as to his policy, to reign under the venerable names of ancient magistracy, and artfully to collect, in his own person, all the scattered rays of civil jurisdiction. With this view, he permitted the senate to confer upon him, for his life, the powers of the consular[11] and tribunitian offices,[12] which were, in the same manner, continued to all his successors. The consuls had succeeded to the kings of Rome, and represented the dignity of the state. They superintended the ceremonies of religion, levied and commanded the legions, gave audience to foreign ambassadors, and presided in the assemblies both of the senate and people. The general control of the finances was intrusted to their care; and though they seldom had leisure to administer justice in person, they were considered as the supreme guardians of law, equity, and the public peace. Such was their ordinary jurisdiction; but whenever the senate empowered the first magistrate to consult the safety of the commonwealth, he was raised by that degree above the laws, and exercised, in the defence of liberty, a temporary despotism.[13] The character of the tribunes was, in every respect, different from that of the consuls. The appearance of the former was modest and humble; but their persons

---

11. Cicero (de Legibus, iii. 3.) gives the consular office the name of *Regia potestas*: and Polybius (l. vi. c. 3.) observes three powers in the Roman constitution. The monarchical was represented and exercised by the Consuls.

12. As the tribunitian power (distinct from the annual office) was first invented for the dictator Cæsar (Dion, l. xliv. p. 384.), we may

easily conceive, that it was given as a reward for having so nobly asserted, by arms, the sacred rights of the tribunes and people. See his own Commentaries, de Bell. Civil. l. i.

13. Augustus exercised nine annual consulships without interruption. He then most artfully refused that magistracy as well as the dictatorship, absented himself from Rome,

were sacred and inviolable. Their force was suited rather for opposition than for action. They were instituted to defend the oppressed, to pardon offences, to arraign the enemies of the people, and, when they judged it necessary, to stop, by a single word, the whole machine of government. As long as the republic subsisted, the dangerous influence, which either the consul or the tribune might derive from their respective jurisdiction, was diminished by several important restrictions. Their authority expired with the year in which they were elected; the former office was divided between two, the latter among ten persons; and, as both in their private and public interest they were averse to each other, their mutual conflicts contributed, for the most part, to strengthen rather than to destroy the balance of the constitution. But when the consular and tribunitian powers were united, when they were vested for life in a single person, when the general of the army was, at the same time, the minister of the senate and the representative of the Roman people, it was impossible to resist the exercise, nor was it easy to define the limits, of his imperial prerogative.

To these accumulated honours, the policy of Augustus soon added the splendid as well as important dignities of supreme *Imperial prerogatives.* pontiff, and of censor. By the former he acquired the management of the religion, and by the latter a legal inspection over the manners and fortunes of the Roman people. If so many distinct and independent powers did not exactly unite with each other, the complaisance of the senate was prepared to supply every deficiency by the most ample and extraordinary concessions. The emperors, as the first ministers of the republic, were exempted from the obligation and penalty of many inconvenient laws: they were authorized to convoke the senate, to make several motions in the same day, to recommend candidates for the honours of the state, to enlarge the bounds of the city, to employ the revenue at their discretion, to declare peace and war, to ratify treaties; and by a most comprehensive clause, they were empowered to execute whatsoever they should judge advantageous to the empire, and agreeable to the majesty of things private or public, human or divine.[14]

---

and waited till the fatal effects of tumult and faction forced the senate to invest him with a perpetual consulship. Augustus, as well as his successors, affected, however, to conceal so invidious a title.

14. See a fragment of a Decree of the Senate, conferring on the emperor Vespasian, all the powers granted to his predecessors, Augustus, Tiberius, and Claudius. This curious and important monument is published in Gruter's Inscriptions, No. ccxlii.

The magistrates.   When all the various powers of executive government were committed to the *Imperial magistrate*, the ordinary magistrates of the commonwealth languished in obscurity, without vigour, and almost without business. The names and forms of the ancient administration were preserved by Augustus with the most anxious care. The usual number of consuls, prætors, and tribunes,[15] were annually invested with their respective ensigns of office, and continued to discharge some of their least important functions. Those honours still attracted the vain ambition of the Romans; and the emperors themselves, though invested for life with the powers of the consulship, frequently aspired to the title of that annual dignity, which they condescended to share with the most illustrious of their fellow-citizens.[16] In the election of these magistrates, the people, during the reign of Augustus, were permitted to expose all the inconveniences of a wild democracy. That artful prince, instead of discovering the least symptom of impatience, humbly solicited their suffrages for himself or his friends, and scrupulously practised all the duties of an ordinary candidate.[17] But we may venture to ascribe to his councils, the first measure of the succeeding reign, by which the elections were transferred to the senate.[18] The assemblies of the people were for ever abolished, and the emperors were delivered from a dangerous multitude, who, without restoring liberty, might have disturbed, and perhaps endangered, the established government.

The senate.   By declaring themselves the protectors of the people, Marius and Cæsar had subverted the constitution of their country. But as soon as the senate had been humbled and disarmed, such an assembly,

15. Two consuls were created on the Calends of January; but in the course of the year others were substituted in their places, till the annual number seems to have amounted to no less than twelve. The prætors were usually sixteen or eighteen (Lipsius in Excurs. D. ad Tacit. Annal. l. i.). I have not mentioned the Ædiles or Quæstors. Officers of the police or revenue easily adapt themselves to any form of government. In the time of Nero, the tribunes legally possessed the right of *intercession*, though it might be dangerous to exercise it (Tacit. Annal. xvi. 26.). In the time of Trajan, it was doubtful whether the tribuneship was an office or a name (Plin. Epist. i. 23.).

16. The tyrants themselves were ambitious

of the consulship. The virtuous princes were moderate in the pursuit, and exact in the discharge of it. Trajan revived the ancient oath, and swore before the consul's tribunal, that he would observe the laws (Plin. Panegyric. c. 64.).

17. Quoties Magistratuum Comitiis interesset. Tribus cum candidatis suis circuibat: supplicabatque more solemni. Ferebat et ipse suffragium in tribubus, ut unus e populo. Suetonius in August. c. 56.

18. Tum primum Comitia e campo ad patres translata sunt. Tacit. Annal. i. 15. The word *primum* seems to allude to some faint and unsuccessful efforts, which were made towards restoring them to the people.

consisting of five or six hundred persons, was found a much more tractable and useful instrument of dominion. It was on the dignity of the senate, that Augustus and his successors founded their new empire; and they affected, on every occasion, to adopt the language and principles of Patricians. In the administration of their own powers, they frequently consulted the great national council, and *seemed* to refer to its decision the most important concerns of peace and war. Rome, Italy, and the internal provinces were subject to the immediate jurisdiction of the senate. With regard to civil objects, it was the supreme court of appeal; with regard to criminal matters, a tribunal, constituted for the trial of all offences that were committed by men in any public station, or that affected the peace and majesty of the Roman people. The exercise of the judicial power became the most frequent and serious occupation of the senate; and the important causes that were pleaded before them, afforded a last refuge to the spirit of ancient eloquence. As a council of state, and as a court of justice, the senate possessed very considerable prerogatives; but in its legislative capacity, in which it was supposed virtually to represent the people, the rights of sovereignty were acknowledged to reside in that assembly. Every power was derived from their authority, every law was ratified by their sanction. Their regular meetings were held on three stated days in every month, the Calends, the Nones, and the Ides. The debates were conducted with decent freedom; and the emperors themselves, who gloried in the name of senators, sat, voted, and divided with their equals.

To resume, in a few words, the system of the Imperial government; as it was instituted by Augustus, and maintained by those princes who understood their own interest and that of the people, it may be defined an absolute monarchy disguised by the forms of a commonwealth. The masters of the Roman world surrounded their throne with darkness, concealed their irresistible strength, and humbly professed themselves the accountable ministers of the senate, whose supreme decrees they dictated and obeyed.[19]

General idea of the Imperial system.

---

19. Dion Cassius (l. liii. p. 703–714.) has given a very loose and partial sketch of the Imperial system. To illustrate and often to correct him, I have meditated Tacitus, examined Suetonius, and consulted the following moderns: the Abbé de la Bleterie, in the Memoires de l'Academie des Inscriptions, tom. xix. xxi. xxiv. xxv. xxvii. Beaufort Republique Romaine, tom. i. p. 255–275. The Dissertations of Noodt and Gronovius, *de lege Regia*; printed at Leyden, in the year 1731. Gravina de Imperio Romano, p. 479–544 of his Opuscula. Maffei Verona Illustrata, p. i. p. 245, &c.

Court of the emperors.   The face of the court corresponded with the forms of the administration. The emperors, if we except those tyrants whose capricious folly violated every law of nature and decency, disdained that pomp and ceremony which might offend their countrymen, but could add nothing to their real power. In all the offices of life, they affected to confound themselves with their subjects, and maintained with them an equal intercourse of visits and entertainments. Their habit, their palace, their table, were suited only to the rank of an opulent senator. Their family, however numerous or splendid, was composed entirely of their domestic slaves and freedmen.[20] Augustus or Trajan would have blushed at employing the meanest of the Romans in those menial offices, which, in the household and bedchamber of a limited monarch, are so eagerly solicited by the proudest nobles of Britain.

Deification.   The deification of the emperors[21] is the only instance in which they departed from their accustomed prudence and modesty. The Asiatic Greeks were the first inventors, the successors of Alexander the first objects, of this servile and impious mode of adulation. It was easily transferred from the kings to the governors of Asia; and the Roman magistrates very frequently were adored as provincial deities, with the pomp of altars and temples, of festivals and sacrifices.[22] It was natural that the emperors should not refuse what the proconsuls had accepted; and the divine honours which both the one and the other received from the provinces, attested rather the despotism than the servitude of Rome. But the conquerors soon imitated the vanquished nations in the arts of flattery; and the imperious spirit of the first Cæsar too easily consented to assume, during his life-time, a place among the tutelar deities of Rome. The milder temper of his successor declined so dangerous an ambition, which was never afterwards revived, except by the madness of Caligula and Domitian. Augustus permitted indeed some of the provincial cities to erect temples to his honour, on condition that they should associate the worship of Rome with that of the sovereign; he tolerated private superstition, of which he

20. A weak prince will always be governed by his domestics. The power of slaves aggravated the shame of the Romans; and the senate paid court to a Pallas or a Narcissus. There is a chance that a modern favourite may be a gentleman.

21. See a treatise of Vandale de Consecratione Principum. It would be easier for me to copy, than it has been to verify, the quotations of that learned Dutchman.

22. See a dissertation of the Abbé Mongault in the first volume of the Academy of Inscriptions.

might be the object;[23] but he contented himself with being revered by the senate and people in his human character, and wisely left to his successor, the care of his public deification. A regular custom was introduced, that on the decease of every emperor who had neither lived nor died like a tyrant, the senate by a solemn decree should place him in the number of the gods: and the ceremonies of his Apotheosis were blended with those of his funeral. This legal, and as it should seem, injudicious profanation, so abhorrent to our stricter principles, was received with a very faint murmur,[24] by the easy nature of Polytheism; but it was received as an institution, not of religion but of policy. We should disgrace the virtues of the Antonines, by comparing them with the vices of Hercules or Jupiter. Even the character of Cæsar or Augustus were far superior to those of the popular deities. But it was the misfortune of the former to live in an enlightened age, and their actions were too faithfully recorded to admit of such a mixture of fable and mystery, as the devotion of the vulgar requires. As soon as their divinity was established by law, it sunk into oblivion, without contributing either to their own fame, or to the dignity of succeeding princes.

In the consideration of the Imperial government, we have frequently mentioned the artful founder, under his well-known title of Augustus, which was not however conferred upon him, till the edifice was almost completed. The obscure name of *Titles of Augustus and Cæsar.* Octavianus, he derived from a mean family, in the little town of Aricia. It was stained with the blood of the proscription; and he was desirous, had it been possible, to erase all memory of his former life. The illustrious surname of Cæsar, he had assumed, as the adopted son of the dictator; but he had too much good sense, either to hope to be confounded, or to wish to be compared, with that extraordinary man. It was proposed in the senate, to dignify their minister with a new appellation: and after a very serious discussion, that of Augustus was chosen among several others, as being the most expressive of the character of peace and sanctity, which he uniformly affected.[25] *Augustus* was therefore a personal, *Cæsar* a family distinction. The former should naturally have expired with the prince on whom it was

23. Jurandasque tuum per nomen ponimus *aras*, says Horace to the emperor himself, and Horace was well acquainted with the court of Augustus.

24. See Cicero in Philippic. i. 6. Julian in Cæsaribus. Inque Deûm templis jurabit Roma

per umbras, is the indignant expression of Lucan, but it is a patriotic, rather than a devout indignation.

25. Dion Cassius, l. liii. p. 710. with the curious Annotations of Reymar.

bestowed; and however the latter was diffused by adoption and female alliance, Nero was the last prince who could allege any hereditary claim to the honours of the Julian line. But, at the time of his death, the practice of a century had inseparably connected those appellations with the Imperial dignity, and they have been preserved by a long succession of emperors, Romans, Greeks, Franks, and Germans, from the fall of the republic to the present time. A distinction was, however, soon introduced. The sacred title of Augustus was always reserved for the monarch, whilst the name of Cæsar was more freely communicated to his relations; and, from the reign of Hadrian, at least, was appropriated to the second person in the state, who was considered as the presumptive heir of the empire.

Character and policy of Augustus.   The tender respect of Augustus for a free constitution which he had destroyed, can only be explained by an attentive consideration of the character of that subtle tyrant. A cool head, an unfeeling heart, and a cowardly disposition, prompted him, at the age of nineteen, to assume the mask of hypocrisy, which he never afterwards laid aside. With the same hand, and probably with the same temper, he signed the proscription of Cicero, and the pardon of Cinna. His virtues, and even his vices, were artificial; and according to the various dictates of his interest, he was at first the enemy, and at last the father, of the Roman world.[26] When he framed the artful system of the Imperial authority, his moderation was inspired by his fears. He wished to deceive the people by an image of civil liberty, and the armies by an image of civil government.

Image of liberty for the people.   I. The death of Cæsar was ever before his eyes. He had lavished wealth and honours on his adherents; but the most favoured friends of his uncle were in the number of the conspirators. The fidelity of the legions might defend his authority against open rebellion; but their vigilance could not secure his person from the dagger of a determined republican; and the Romans, who revered the memory of Brutus,[27] would applaud the imitation of his virtue. Cæsar had provoked

26. As Octavianus advanced to the banquet of the Cæsars, his colour changed like that of the Camelion; pale at first, then red, afterwards black, he at last assumed the mild livery of Venus and the Graces (Cæsars, p. 309.). This image employed by Julian, in his ingenious fiction, is just and elegant; but when he considers this change of character as real, and ascribes it to the power of philosophy, he does too much honour to philosophy, and to Octavianus.

27. Two centuries after the establishment of monarchy, the emperor Marcus Antoninus recommends the character of Brutus as a perfect model of Roman virtue.

his fate, as much by the ostentation of his power, as by his power itself. The consul or the tribune might have reigned in peace. The title of king had armed the Romans against his life. Augustus was sensible that mankind is governed by names; nor was he deceived in his expectation, that the senate and people would submit to slavery, provided they were respectfully assured, that they still enjoyed their ancient freedom. A feeble senate and enervated people cheerfully acquiesced in the pleasing illusion, as long as it was supported by the virtue, or by even the prudence, of the successors of Augustus. It was a motive of self-preservation, not a principle of liberty, that animated the conspirators against Caligula, Nero, and Domitian. They attacked the person of the tyrant, without aiming their blow at the authority of the emperor.

There appears, indeed, *one* memorable occasion, in which the senate, after seventy years of patience, made an ineffectual attempt to reassume its long forgotten rights. When the throne was vacant by the murder of Caligula, the consuls convoked that assembly in the Capitol, condemned the memory of the *Attempt of the senate after the death of Caligula.* Cæsars, gave the watch-word *liberty* to the few cohorts who faintly adhered to their standard, and during eight and forty hours acted as the independent chiefs of a free commonwealth. But while they deliberated, the Prætorian guards had resolved. The stupid Claudius, brother of Germanicus, was already in their camp, invested with the Imperial purple, and prepared to support his election by arms. The dream of liberty was at an end; and the senate awoke to all the horrors of inevitable servitude. Deserted by the people, and threatened by a military force, that feeble assembly was compelled to ratify the choice of the Prætorians, and to embrace the benefit of an amnesty, which Claudius had the prudence to offer, and the generosity to observe.[28]

II. The insolence of the armies inspired Augustus with fears of a still more alarming nature. The despair of the citizens could only attempt, what the power of the soldiers was, at any time, able to execute. How precarious was his own authority over *Image of government for the armies.* men whom he had taught to violate every social duty! He had heard their seditious clamours; he dreaded their calmer moments of reflection. One revolution had been purchased by immense rewards; but a second revolution

28. It is much to be regretted, that we have lost the part of Tacitus, which treated of that transaction. We are forced to content ourselves with the popular rumours of Josephus, and the imperfect hints of Dion and Suetonius.

might double those rewards. The troops professed the fondest attachment to the house of Cæsar; but the attachments of the multitude are capricious and inconstant. Augustus summoned to his aid, whatever remained in those fierce minds, of Roman prejudices; enforced the rigour of discipline by the sanction of law; and interposing the majesty of the senate, between the emperor and the army, boldly claimed their allegiance, as the first magistrate of the republic.[29]

Their obedience. During a long period of two hundred and twenty years, from the establishment of this artful system to the death of Commodus, the dangers inherent to a military government were, in a great measure, suspended. The soldiers were seldom roused to that fatal sense of their own strength, and of the weakness of the civil authority, which was, before and afterwards, productive of such dreadful calamities. Caligula and Domitian were assassinated in their palace by their own domestics: the convulsions which agitated Rome on the death of the former, were confined to the walls of the city. But Nero involved the whole empire in his ruin. In the space of eighteen months, four princes perished by the sword; and the Roman world was shaken by the fury of the contending armies. Excepting only this short, though violent, eruption of military licence, the two centuries from Augustus to Commodus passed away unstained with civil blood, and undisturbed by revolutions. The emperor was elected by *the authority of the senate*, and *the consent of the soldiers*.[30] The legions respected their oath of fidelity; and it requires a minute inspection of the Roman annals to discover three inconsiderable rebellions, which were all suppressed in a few months, and without even the hazard of a battle.[31]

Designation of a successor. In elective monarchies, the vacancy of the throne is a moment big with danger and mischief. The Roman emperors, desirous to spare the legions that interval of suspense, and the

---

29. Augustus restored the ancient severity of discipline. After the civil wars, he dropped the endearing name of Fellow-Soldiers, and called them only Soldiers (Sueton. in August. c. 25.). See the use Tiberius made of the senate in the mutiny of the Pannonian legions (Tacit. Annal. i.).

30. These words seem to have been the constitutional language. See Tacit. Annal. xiii. 4.

31. The first was Camillus Scribonianus, who took up arms in Dalmatia against Claudius,

and was deserted by his own troops in five days. The second, L. Antonius, in Germany, who rebelled against Domitian; and the third, Avidius Cassius, in the reign of M. Antoninus. The two last reigned but a few months, and were cut off by their own adherents. We may observe, that both Camillus and Cassius coloured their ambition with the design of restoring the republic; a task, said Cassius, peculiarly reserved for his name and family.

temptation of an irregular choice, invested their designed successor with
so large a share of present power, as should enable him, after their decease,
to assume the remainder, without suffering the empire to perceive   *Of Tiberius.*
the change of masters. Thus Augustus, after all his fairer prospects
had been snatched from him by untimely deaths, rested his last hopes on
Tiberius, obtained for his adopted son the censorial and tribunitian powers,
and dictated a law, by which the future prince was invested with an
authority equal to his own, over the provinces and the armies.[32] Thus
Vespasian subdued the generous mind of his eldest son. Titus was   *Of Titus.*
adored by the eastern legions, which, under his command, had
recently atchieved the conquest of Judæa. His power was dreaded, and, as
his virtues were clouded by the intemperance of youth, his designs were
suspected. Instead of listening to such unworthy suspicions, the prudent
monarch associated Titus to the full powers of the Imperial dignity; and
the grateful son ever approved himself the humble and faithful minister of
so indulgent a father.[33]

The good sense of Vespasian engaged him indeed to em-   *The race of the*
brace every measure that might confirm his recent and precari-   *Cæsars and the*
ous elevation. The military oath, and the fidelity of the troops,   *Flavian family.*
had been consecrated, by the habits of an hundred years, to the
name and family of the Cæsars: and although that family had been continued
only by the fictitious rite of adoption, the Romans still revered, in the
person of Nero, the grandson of Germanicus, and the lineal successor of
Augustus. It was not without reluctance and remorse, that the Prætorian
guards had been persuaded to abandon the cause of the tyrant.[34] The rapid
downfal of Galba, Otho, and Vitellius, taught the armies to consider the
emperors as the creatures of *their* will, and the instruments of *their* licence.
The birth of Vespasian was mean; his grandfather had been a private soldier,
his father a petty officer of the revenue;[35] his own merit had raised him, in
an advanced age, to the empire; but his merit was rather useful than shining,
and his virtues were disgraced by a strict and even sordid parsimony. Such
a prince consulted his true interest by the association of a son, whose more

---

32. Velleius Paterculus, l. ii. c. 121. Sueton.
in Tiber. c. 20.

33. Sueton. in Tit. c. 6. Plin. in Præfat. Hist.
Natur.

34. This idea is frequently and strongly inculcated by Tacitus. See Hist. i. 5.16. ii. 76.

35. The emperor Vespasian, with his usual
good sense, laughed at the Genealogists, who
deduced his family from Flavius, the founder
of Reate (his native country), and one of the
companions of Hercules. Suet. in Vespasian.
c. 12.

splendid and amiable character might turn the public attention, from the obscure origin, to the future glories of the Flavian house. Under the mild administration of Titus, the Roman world enjoyed a transient felicity, and his beloved memory served to protect, above fifteen years, the vices of his brother Domitian.

A.D. 96.
Adoption
and character
of Trajan.

Nerva had scarcely accepted the purple from the assassins of Domitian, before he discovered that his feeble age was unable to stem the torrent of public disorders, which had multiplied under the long tyranny of his predecessor. His mild disposition was respected by the good; but the degenerate Romans required a more vigorous character, whose justice should strike terror into the guilty. Though he had several relations, he fixed his choice on a stranger. He adopted Trajan, then about forty years of age, and who commanded a powerful army in the Lower Germany; and immediately, by a decree of the senate, declared him his colleague and successor in the empire.[36]

A.D. 98.

It is sincerely to be lamented, that whilst we are fatigued with the disgustful relation of Nero's crimes and follies, we are reduced to collect the actions of Trajan from the glimmerings of an abridgment, or the doubtful light of a panegyric. There remains, however, one panegyric far removed beyond the suspicion of flattery. Above two hundred and fifty years after the death of Trajan, the senate, in pouring out the customary acclamations on the accession of a new emperor, wished that he might surpass the felicity of Augustus, and the virtue of Trajan.[37]

We may readily believe, that the father of his country hesitated whether he ought to intrust the various and doubtful character of his kinsman

A.D. 117.
Of Hadrian.

Hadrian with sovereign power. In his last moments, the arts of the empress Plotina either fixed the irresolution of Trajan, or boldly supposed a fictitious adoption;[38] the truth of which could not be safely disputed, and Hadrian was peaceably acknowledged as his lawful successor. Under his reign, as has been already mentioned, the empire flourished in peace and prosperity. He encouraged the arts, reformed the laws, asserted military discipline, and visited all his provinces in person.

---

36. Dion, l. lxviii. p. 1121. Plin. Secund. in Panegyric.

37. Felicior Augusto, MELIOR TRAJANO. Eutrop. viii. 5.

38. Dion (l. lxix. p. 1249.) affirms the whole to have been a fiction, on the authority of his father, who being governor of the province where Trajan died, had very good opportunities of sifting this mysterious transaction. Yet Dodwell (Prælect. Camden. xvii.) has maintained, that Hadrian was called to the certain hope of the empire, during the lifetime of Trajan.

His vast and active genius was equally suited to the most enlarged views, and the minute details of civil policy. But the ruling passions of his soul were curiosity and vanity. As they prevailed, and as they were attracted by different objects, Hadrian was, by turns, an excellent prince, a ridiculous sophist, and a jealous tyrant. The general tenor of his conduct deserved praise for its equity and moderation. Yet in the first days of his reign, he put to death four consular senators, his personal enemies, and men who had been judged worthy of empire; and the tediousness of a painful illness rendered him, at last, peevish and cruel. The senate doubted whether they should pronounce him a god or a tyrant; and the honours decreed to his memory were granted to the prayers of the pious Antoninus.[39]

The caprice of Hadrian influenced his choice of a successor. After revolving in his mind several men of distinguished merit, whom he esteemed and hated, he adopted Ælius Verus, a gay and voluptuous nobleman, recommended by uncommon beauty to the lover of Antinous.[40] But whilst Hadrian was delighting *Adoption of the elder and younger Verus.* himself with his own applause, and the acclamations of the soldiers, whose consent had been secured by an immense donative, the new Cæsar[41] was ravished from his embraces by an untimely death. He left only one son. Hadrian commended the boy to the gratitude of the Antonines. He was adopted by Pius; and, on the accession of Marcus, was invested with an equal share of sovereign power. Among the many vices of this younger Verus, he possessed one virtue; a dutiful reverence for his wiser colleague, to whom he willingly abandoned the ruder cares of empire. The philosophic emperor dissembled his follies, lamented his early death, and cast a decent veil over his memory.

As soon as Hadrian's passion was either gratified or disappointed, he resolved to deserve the thanks of posterity, by placing the most exalted merit on the Roman throne. His *Adoption of the two Antonines.* discerning eye easily discovered a senator about fifty years of age, blameless in all the offices of life, and a youth of about seventeen, whose riper years opened the fair prospect of every virtue: the elder of these was declared

---

39. Dion (l. lxx. p. 1171). Aurel. Victor.

40. The deification of Antinous, his medals, statues, temples, city, oracles, and constellation, are well known, and still dishonour the memory of Hadrian. Yet we may remark, that of the first fifteen emperors, Claudius was the only one whose taste in love was entirely correct. For the honours of Antinous, see Spanheim, Commentaire sur les Cæsars de Julien, p. 80.

41. Hist. August. p. 13. Aurelius Victor in Epitom.

the son and successor of Hadrian, on condition, however, that he himself
should immediately adopt the younger. The two Antonines
A.D. 138–180.   (for it is of them that we are now speaking) governed the
Roman world forty-two years, with the same invariable spirit of wisdom
and virtue. Although Pius had two sons,[42] he preferred the welfare of Rome
to the interest of his family, gave his daughter Faustina in marriage to young
Marcus, obtained from the senate the tribunitian and proconsular powers,
and with a noble disdain, or rather ignorance of jealousy, associated him
to all the labours of government. Marcus, on the other hand, revered the
character of his benefactor, loved him as a parent, obeyed him as his
sovereign,[43] and, after he was no more, regulated his own administration
by the example and maxims of his predecessor. Their united reigns are
possibly the only period of history in which the happiness of a great people
was the sole object of government.

*Character
and reign of
Pius.*
        Titus Antoninus Pius has been justly denominated a second
Numa. The same love of religion, justice, and peace, was the
distinguishing characteristic of both princes. But the situation of
the latter opened a much larger field for the exercise of those virtues.
Numa could only prevent a few neighbouring villages from plundering each
other's harvests. Antoninus diffused order and tranquillity over the greatest
part of the earth. His reign is marked by the rare advantage of furnishing
very few materials for history; which is, indeed, little more than the register
of the crimes, follies, and misfortunes of mankind. In private life, he was
an amiable, as well as a good man. The native simplicity of his virtue was
a stranger to vanity or affectation. He enjoyed, with moderation, the con-
veniencies of his fortune, and the innocent pleasures of society;[44] and the
benevolence of his soul displayed itself in a cheerful serenity of temper.

Of Marcus.
        The virtue of Marcus Aurelius Antoninus was of a severer and
more laborious kind.[45] It was the well-earned harvest of many a
learned conference, of many a patient lecture, and many a midnight

42. Without the help of medals and inscriptions, we should be ignorant of this fact, so
honourable to the memory of Pius.
43. During the twenty-three years of Pius's
reign, Marcus was only two nights absent
from the palace, and even those were at
different times. Hist. August. p. 25.
44. He was fond of the theatre, and not insensible to the charms of the fair sex. Marcus

Antoninus, i. 16. Hist. August. p. 20, 21. Julian
in Cæsar.
45. The enemies of Marcus charged him with
hypocrisy, and with a want of that simplicity
which distinguished Pius and even Verus
(Hist. Aug. 6. 34.). This suspicion, unjust as
it was, may serve to account for the superior
applause bestowed upon personal qualifications, in preference to the social virtues. Even

lucubration. At the age of twelve years he embraced the rigid system of
the Stoics, which taught him to submit his body to his mind, his passions
to his reason; to consider virtue as the only good, vice as the only evil, all
things external, as things indifferent.[46] His meditations, composed in the
tumult of a camp, are still extant; and he even condescended to give lessons
of philosophy, in a more public manner, than was perhaps consistent with
the modesty of a sage, or the dignity of an emperor.[47] But his life was the
noblest commentary on the precepts of Zeno. He was severe to himself,
indulgent to the imperfection of others, just and beneficent to all mankind.
He regretted that Avidius Cassius, who excited a rebellion in Syria, had
disappointed him, by a voluntary death, of the pleasure of converting an
enemy into a friend; and he justified the sincerity of that sentiment, by
moderating the zeal of the senate against the adherents of the traitor.[48] War
he detested, as the disgrace and calamity of human nature; but when the
necessity of a just defence called upon him to take up arms, he readily
exposed his person to eight winter campaigns, on the frozen banks of the
Danube, the severity of which was at last fatal to the weakness of his
constitution. His memory was revered by a grateful posterity, and above a
century after his death, many persons preserved the image of Marcus
Antoninus among those of their household gods.[49]

If a man were called to fix the period in the history of the
world, during which the condition of the human race was most *Happiness of*
happy and prosperous, he would, without hesitation, name that *the Romans.*
which elapsed from the death of Domitian to the accession of Commodus.
The vast extent of the Roman empire was governed by absolute power,
under the guidance of virtue and wisdom. The armies were restrained by
the firm but gentle hand of four successive emperors, whose characters
and authority commanded involuntary respect. The forms of the civil

Marcus Antoninus has been called a hypocrite;
but the wildest scepticism never insinuated
that Cæsar might possibly be a coward, or
Tully a fool. Wit and valour are qualifications
more easily ascertained, than humanity or the
love of justice.

46. Tacitus has characterized, in a few words,
the principles of the portico: Doctores sapien-
tiæ secutus est, qui sola bona quæ honesta,
mala tantum quæ turpia; potentiam, nobili-
tatem, cæteraque extra animum, neque bonis

neque malis adnumerant. Tacit. Hist. iv. 5.

47. Before he went on the second expedition
against the Germans, he read lectures of philosophy to the Roman people, during three
days. He had already done the same in the
cities of Greece and Asia. Hist. August. in
Cassio, c. 3.

48. Dion. l. lxxi. p. 1190. Hist. August. in
Avid. Cassio.

49. Hist. August. in Marc. Antonin. c. 18.

administration were carefully preserved by Nerva, Trajan, Hadrian, and the Antonines, who delighted in the image of liberty, and were pleased with considering themselves as the accountable ministers of the laws. Such princes deserved the honour of restoring the republic, had the Romans of their days been capable of enjoying a rational freedom.

Its precarious nature. The labours of these monarchs were over-paid by the immense reward that inseparably waited on their success; by the honest pride of virtue, and by the exquisite delight of beholding the general happiness of which they were the authors. A just, but melancholy reflection embittered, however, the noblest of human enjoyments. They must often have recollected the instability of a happiness which depended on the character of a single man. The fatal moment was perhaps approaching, when some licentious youth, or some jealous tyrant, would abuse, to the destruction, that absolute power, which they had exerted for the benefit of their people. The ideal restraints of the senate and the laws might serve to display the virtues, but could never correct the vices, of the emperor. The military force was a blind and irresistible instrument of oppression; and the corruption of Roman manners would always supply flatterers eager to applaud, and ministers prepared to serve, the fear or the avarice, the lust or the cruelty, of their masters.

Memory of Tiberius, Caligula, Nero, and Domitian. These gloomy apprehensions had been already justified by the experience of the Romans. The annals of the emperors exhibit a strong and various picture of human nature, which we should vainly seek among the mixed and doubtful characters of modern history. In the conduct of those monarchs we may trace the utmost lines of vice and virtue; the most exalted perfection, and the meanest degeneracy of our own species. The golden age of Trajan and the Antonines had been preceded by an age of iron. It is almost superfluous to enumerate the unworthy successors of Augustus. Their unparalleled vices, and the splendid theatre on which they were acted, have saved them from oblivion. The dark unrelenting Tiberius, the furious Caligula, the feeble Claudius, the profligate and cruel Nero, the beastly Vitellius,[50] and the timid inhuman Domitian, are condemned to everlasting infamy.

---

50. Vitellius consumed in mere eating, at least six millions of our money, in about seven months. It is not easy to express his vices with dignity, or even decency. Tacitus fairly calls him a hog; but it is by substituting to a coarse word a very fine image. "At Vitellius, umbraculis hortorum abditus, ut *ignava animalia*, quibus si cibum suggeras jacent torpentque, præterita, instantia, futura, pari oblivione dimiserat. Atque illum nemore

During fourscore years (excepting only the short and doubtful respite of Vespasian's reign[51]) Rome groaned beneath an unremitting tyranny, which exterminated the ancient families of the republic, and was fatal to almost every virtue, and every talent, that arose in that unhappy period.

Under the reign of these monsters, the slavery of the Romans was accompanied with two peculiar circumstances, the one occasioned by their former liberty, the other by their extensive conquests, which rendered their condition more completely wretched than that of the victims of tyranny in any other age *Peculiar misery of the Romans under their tyrants.* or country. From these causes were derived, 1. The exquisite sensibility of the sufferers; and, 2. the impossibility of escaping from the hand of the oppressor.

I. When Persia was governed by the descendants of Sefi, a race of princes, whose wanton cruelty often stained their divan, their table, and their bed, with the blood of their favourites, *Insensibility of the Orientals.* there is a saying recorded of a young nobleman. That he never departed from the sultan's presence, without satisfying himself whether his head was still on his shoulders. The experience of every day might almost justify the scepticism of Rustan.[52] Yet the fatal sword suspended above him by a single thread, seems not to have disturbed the slumbers, or interrupted the tranquillity, of the Persian. The monarch's frown, he well knew, could level him with the dust; but the stroke of lightning or apoplexy might be equally fatal; and it was the part of a wise man, to forget the inevitable calamities of human life in the enjoyment of the fleeting hour. He was dignified with the appellation of the king's slave; had, perhaps, been purchased from obscure parents, in a country which he had never known; and was trained up from his infancy in the severe discipline of the seraglio.[53] His name, his wealth, his honours, were the gift of a master, who might, without injustice, resume what he had bestowed. Rustan's knowledge, if he possessed any, could only serve to confirm his habits by prejudices. His language afforded not words for any form of government, except absolute monarchy. The history of the east informed him, that such

---

Aricino, desidem et marcentem, &c." Tacit. Hist. iii. 36. ii. 95. Sueton. in Vitell. c. 13. Dion Cassius, l. lxv. p. 1062.

51. The execution of Helvidius Priscus, and of the virtuous Eponina, disgraced the reign of Vespasian.

52. Voyage de Chardin en Perse, vol. iii. p. 293.
53. The practice of raising slaves to the great offices of state is still more common among the Turks than among the Persians. The miserable countries of Georgia and Circassia supply rulers to the greatest part of the east.

had ever been the condition of mankind.[54] The Koran, and the interpreters of that divine book, inculcated to him, that the sultan was the descendant of the prophet, and the vicegerent of heaven; that patience was the first virtue of a Mussulman, and unlimited obedience the great duty of a subject.

Knowledge and free spirit of the Romans.

The minds of the Romans were very differently prepared for slavery. Oppressed beneath the weight of their own corruption and of military violence, they for a long while preserved the sentiments, or at least the ideas, of their freeborn ancestors. The education of Helvidius and Thrasea, of Tacitus and Pliny, was the same as that of Cato and Cicero. From Grecian philosophy, they had imbibed the justest and most liberal notions of the dignity of human nature, and the origin of civil society. The history of their own country had taught them to revere a free, a virtuous, and a victorious commonwealth; to abhor the successful crimes of Cæsar and Augustus; and inwardly to despise those tyrants whom they adored with the most abject flattery. As magistrates and senators, they were admitted into the great council, which had once dictated laws to the earth, whose name still gave a sanction to the acts of the monarch, and whose authority was so often prostituted to the vilest purposes of tyranny. Tiberius, and those emperors who adopted his maxims, attempted to disguise their murders by the formalities of justice, and perhaps enjoyed a secret pleasure in rendering the senate their accomplice as well as their victim. By this assembly, the last of the Romans were condemned for imaginary crimes and real virtues. Their infamous accusers assumed the language of independent patriots, who arraigned a dangerous citizen before the tribunal of his country; and the public service, was rewarded by riches and honours.[55] The servile judges professed to assert the majesty of the commonwealth, violated in the person of its first magistrate,[56] whose clemency they most applauded when they trembled the most at his

54. Chardin says, that European travellers have diffused among the Persians some ideas of the freedom and mildness of our governments. They have done them a very ill office.

55. They alleged the example of Scipio and Cato (Tacit. Annal. iii. 66.). Marcellus Eprius and Crispus Vibius had acquired two millions and a half under Nero. Their wealth, which aggravated their crimes, protected them under Vespasian. See Tacit. Hist. iv. 43. Dialog. de Orator. c. 8. For one accusation, Regulus, the just object of Pliny's satire, received from the senate the consular ornaments, and a present of sixty-thousand pounds.

56. The crime of *majesty* was formerly a treasonable offence against the Roman people. As tribunes of the people, Augustus and Tiberius applied it to their own persons, and extended it to an infinite latitude.

inexorable and impending cruelty.[57] The tyrant beheld their baseness with just contempt, and encountered their secret sentiments of detestation with sincere and avowed hatred for the whole body of the senate.

II. The division of Europe into a number of independent states, connected, however, with each other, by the general resemblance of religion, language, and manners, is productive of the most beneficial consequences to the liberty of mankind. A modern tyrant, who should find no resistance either in his *Extent of their empire left them no place of refuge.* own breast, or in his people, would soon experience a gentle restraint from the example of his equals, the dread of present censure, the advice of his allies, and the apprehension of his enemies. The object of his displeasure, escaping from the narrow limits of his dominions, would easily obtain, in a happier climate, a secure refuge, a new fortune adequate to his merit, the freedom of complaint, and perhaps the means of revenge. But the empire of the Romans filled the world, and when that empire fell into the hands of a single person, the world became a safe and dreary prison for his enemies. The slave of Imperial despotism, whether he was condemned to drag his gilded chain in Rome and the senate, or to wear out a life of exile on the barren rock of Seriphus, or the frozen banks of the Danube, expected his fate in silent despair.[58] To resist was fatal, and it was impossible to fly. On every side he was encompassed with a vast extent of sea and land, which he could never hope to traverse without being discovered, seized, and restored to his irritated master. Beyond the frontiers, his anxious view could discover nothing, except the ocean, inhospitable deserts, hostile tribes of barbarians, of fierce manners and unknown language, or dependent kings, who would gladly purchase the emperor's protection by the sacrifice of an obnoxious fugitive.[59] "Wherever you are," said Cicero to the exiled Marcellus, "remember that you are equally within the power of the conqueror."[60]

57. After the virtuous and unfortunate widow of Germanicus had been put to death, Tiberius received the thanks of the senate for his clemency. She had not been publicly strangled; nor was the body drawn with a hook to the Gemoniæ, where those of common malefactors were exposed. See Tacit. Annal. vi. 25. Sueton. in Tiberio, c. 53.

58. Seriphus was a small rocky island in the Ægean Sea, the inhabitants of which were despised for their ignorance and obscurity. The place of Ovid's exile is well known, by

his just, but unmanly lamentations. It should seem, that he only received an order to leave Rome in so many days, and to transport himself to Tomi. Guards and gaolers were unnecessary.

59. Under Tiberius, a Roman knight attempted to fly to the Parthians. He was stopt in the Streights of Sicily; but so little danger did there appear in the example, that the most jealous of tyrants disdained to punish it. Tacit. Annal. vi. 14.

60. Cicero ad Familiares, iv. 7.

[CHAPTERS IV—VI]

After chapter III Gibbon moves into his circumstantial narrative of the gradual undermining of the political and social health of the empire. His main theme in chapters IV to VI is the collapse of the Antonine régime into excess, and the advent of a pernicious remedy for that excess in the form of the conversion of the principate into the military monarchy of Severus:

The victory over the senate was easy and inglorious. Every eye and every passion were directed to the supreme magistrate, who possessed the arms and treasure of the state; whilst the senate, neither elected by the people, nor guarded by military force, nor animated by public spirit, rested its declining authority on the frail and crumbling basis of ancient opinion. The fine theory of a republic insensibly vanished, and made way for the more natural and substantial feelings of monarchy. As the freedom and honours of Rome were successively communicated to the provinces, in which the old government had been either unknown, or was remembered with abhorrence, the tradition of republican maxims was gradually obliter-ated. The Greek historians of the age of the Antonines observe, with a malicious pleasure, that although the sovereign of Rome, in compliance with an obsolete prejudice, abstained from the name of king, he possessed the full measure of regal power. In the reign of Severus, the senate was filled with polished and eloquent slaves from the eastern provinces, who justified personal flattery by speculative principles of servitude. These new advocates of prerogative were heard with pleasure by the court, and with patience by the people, when they inculcated the duty of passive obedi-ence, and descanted on the inevitable mischiefs of freedom. The lawyers and the historians concurred in teaching, that the Imperial authority was held, not by the delegated commission, but by the irrevocable resignation of the senate; that the emperor was freed from the restraint of civil laws, could command by his arbitrary will the lives and fortunes of his subjects, and might dispose of the empire as of his private patrimony. The most eminent of the civil lawyers, and particularly Papinian, Paulus, and Ulpian, flourished under the house of Severus; and the Roman jurisprudence having closely united itself with the system of monarchy, was supposed to have attained its full maturity and perfection.

The contemporaries of Severus, in the enjoyment of the peace and glory of his reign, forgave the cruelties by which it had been introduced. Posterity, who experienced the fatal effects of his maxims and example, justly considered him as the principal author of the decline of the Roman empire. (*DF*, i. 147–8)

The sentiments which undergird monarchy may be 'natural and substantial', but nevertheless not all forms of monarchy are benign. It was the institution of this new form of government which enabled the rise to power of the tyrant Maximin, the dramatic and lurid figure around whom Gibbon constructs chapter VII.

CHAPTER VII

The Elevation and Tyranny of Maximin. – Rebellion in Africa and Italy, under the Authority of the Senate. – Civil Wars and Seditions. – Violent Deaths of Maximin and his Son, of Maximus and Balbinus, and of the three Gordians. – Usurpation and secular Games of Philip.

The apparent ridicule

Of the various forms of government, which have prevailed in the world, an hereditary monarchy seems to present the fairest scope for ridicule. Is it possible to relate, without an indignant smile, that, on the father's decease, the property of a nation, like that of a drove of oxen, descends to his infant son, as yet unknown to mankind and to himself; and that the bravest warriors and the wisest statesmen, relinquishing their natural right to empire, approach the royal cradle with bended knees and protestations of inviolable fidelity? Satire and declamation may paint these obvious topics in the most dazzling colours, but our more serious thoughts will respect a useful prejudice, that establishes a rule of succession, independent of the passions of mankind; and we shall cheerfully acquiesce in any expedient which deprives the multitude of the dangerous, and indeed the ideal, power of giving themselves a master.

and solid advantages of hereditary succession.

In the cool shade of retirement, we may easily devise imaginary forms of government, in which the sceptre shall be constantly bestowed on the most worthy, by the free and incorrupt suffrage of the whole community. Experience overturns these airy fabrics, and teaches us, that, in a large society, the election of a monarch can never devolve to the wisest, or to the most numerous, part of the people. The army is the only order of men sufficiently united to concur in the same sentiments, and powerful enough to impose them on the rest of their fellow-citizens: but the temper of soldiers, habituated at once to violence and to slavery, renders them very unfit guardians of a legal, or even a civil constitution. Justice, humanity, or political wisdom, are qualities they are too little acquainted with in themselves, to appreciate them in others. Valour will acquire their esteem, and liberality will purchase their suffrage; but the first of these merits is often lodged in the most savage breasts; the latter can only exert itself at the expence of the public; and both may be turned against the possessor of the throne, by the ambition of a daring rival.

The superior prerogative of birth, when it has obtained the sanction of time and popular opinion, is the plainest and least invidious of all distinctions among mankind. The acknow-ledged right extinguishes the hopes of faction, and the conscious security disarms the cruelty of the monarch. To the firm establishment of this idea, we owe the peaceful succession, and mild administration, of European monarchies. To the defect *Want of it in the Roman empire productive of the greatest calamities.*

of it, we must attribute the frequent civil wars, through which an Asiatic Despot is obliged to cut his way to the throne of his fathers. Yet, even in the East, the sphere of contention is usually limited to the princes of the reigning house, and as soon as the more fortunate competitor has removed his brethren, by the sword and the bow-string, he no longer entertains any jealousy of his meaner subjects. But the Roman empire, after the authority of the senate had sunk into contempt, was a vast scene of confusion. The royal, and even noble, families of the provinces, had long since been led in triumph before the car of the haughty republicans. The ancient families of Rome had successively fallen beneath the tyranny of the Cæsars; and whilst those princes were shackled by the forms of a commonwealth, and disappointed by the repeated failure of their posterity,[1] it was impossible that any idea of hereditary succession should have taken root in the minds of their subjects. The right to the throne, which none could claim from birth, every one assumed from merit. The daring hopes of ambition were set loose from the salutary restraints of law and prejudice; and the meanest of mankind might, without folly, entertain a hope of being raised by valour and fortune to a rank in the army, in which a single crime would enable him to wrest the sceptre of the world from his feeble and unpopular master. After the murder of Alexander Severus, and the elevation of Maximin, no emperor could think himself safe upon the throne, and every barbarian peasant of the frontier might aspire to that august, but dangerous station.

1. There had been no example of three successive generations on the throne; only three instances of sons who succeeded their fathers. The marriages of the Cæsars (not- withstanding the permission, and the fre-quent practice of divorces) were generally unfruitful.

Birth and fortunes of Maximin.

About thirty-two years before that event, the emperor Severus, returning from an eastern expedition, halted in Thrace, to celebrate, with military games, the birth-day of his younger son, Geta. The country flocked in crowds to behold their sovereign, and a young barbarian of gigantic stature earnestly solicited, in his rude dialect, that he might be allowed to contend for the prize of wrestling. As the pride of discipline would have been disgraced in the overthrow of a Roman soldier by a Thracian peasant, he was matched with the stoutest followers of the camp, sixteen of whom he successively laid on the ground. His victory was rewarded by some trifling gifts, and a permission to inlist in the troops. The next day, the happy barbarian was distinguished above a crowd of recruits, dancing and exulting after the fashion of his country. As soon as he perceived that he had attracted the emperor's notice, he instantly ran up to his horse, and followed him on foot, without the least appearance of fatigue, in a long and rapid career. "Thracian," said Severus, with astonishment, "art thou disposed to wrestle after thy race?" Most willingly, Sir, replied the unwearied youth, and, almost in a breath, overthrew seven of the strongest soldiers in the army. A gold collar was the prize of his matchless vigour and activity, and he was immediately appointed to serve in the horse-guards who always attended on the person of the sovereign.[2]

His military service and honours.

Maximin, for that was his name, though born on the territories of the empire, descended from a mixed race of barbarians. His father was a Goth, and his mother, of the nation of the Alani. He displayed, on every occasion, a valour equal to his strength; and his native fierceness was soon tempered or disguised by the knowledge of the world. Under the reign of Severus and his son, he obtained the rank of centurion, with the favour and esteem of both those princes, the former of whom was an excellent judge of merit. Gratitude forbade Maximin to serve under the assassin of Caracalla. Honour taught him to decline the effeminate insults of Elagabalus. On the accession of Alexander he returned to court, and was placed by that prince in a station useful to the service, and honourable to himself. The fourth legion, to which he was appointed tribune, soon became, under his care, the best disciplined of the whole army. With the general applause of the soldiers, who bestowed on their favourite hero the names of Ajax and Hercules, he was successively pro-

2. Hist. August. p. 138.

moted to the first military command;[3] and had not he still retained too much of his savage origin, the emperor might perhaps have given his own sister in marriage to the son of Maximin.[4]

Instead of securing his fidelity, these favours served only to inflame the ambition of the Thracian peasant, who deemed his fortune inadequate to his merit, as long as he was constrained to acknowledge a superior. Though a stranger to real wisdom, he was not devoid of a selfish cunning, which shewed him, that the emperor had lost the affection of the army, and taught him to improve their discontent to his own advantage. It is easy for faction and calumny to shed their poison on the administration of the best of princes, and to accuse even their virtues, by artfully confounding them with those vices to which they bear the nearest affinity. The troops listened with pleasure to the emissaries of Maximin. They blushed at their own ignominious patience, which, during thirteen years, had supported the vexatious discipline imposed by an effeminate Syrian, the timid slave of his mother and of the senate. It was time, they cried, to cast away that useless phantom of the civil power, and to elect for their prince and general a real soldier, educated in camps, exercised in war, who would assert the glory, and distribute among his companions the treasures, of the empire. A great army was at that time assembled on the banks of the Rhine, under the command of the emperor himself, who, almost immediately after his return from the Persian war, had been obliged to march against the barbarians of Germany. The important care of training and reviewing the new levies was intrusted to Maximin. One day as he entered the field of exercise, the troops, either from a sudden impulse or a formed conspiracy, saluted him emperor, silenced by their loud acclamations his obstinate refusal, and hastened to consummate their rebellion by the murder of Alexander Severus.

Conspiracy of Maximin.

A.D. 235. March 19.

The circumstances of his death are variously related. The writers, who suppose that he died in ignorance of the ingratitude and ambition of Maximin, affirm, that, after taking a frugal repast in the sight of the army, he retired to sleep, and that, about the seventh

Murder of Alexander Severus.

---

3. Hist. August. p. 140. Herodian, l. vi. p. 223. Aurelius Victor. By comparing these authors, it should seem, that Maximin had the particular command of the Triballian horse, with the general commission of disciplining the recruits of the whole army. His Biographer ought to have marked, with more care, his exploits, and the successive steps of his military promotions.

4. See the original letter of Alexander Severus, Hist. August. p. 149.

hour of the day, a part of his own guards broke into the Imperial tent, and, with many wounds, assassinated their virtuous and unsuspecting prince.[5] If we credit another, and indeed a more probable account, Maximin was invested with the purple by a numerous detachment, at the distance of several miles from the headquarters; and he trusted for success rather to the secret wishes than to the public declarations of the great army. Alexander had sufficient time to awaken a faint sense of loyalty among his troops; but their reluctant professions of fidelity quickly vanished on the appearance of Maximin, who declared himself the friend and advocate of the military order, and was unanimously acknowledged emperor of the Romans by the applauding legions. The son of Mamæa, betrayed and deserted, withdrew into his tent, desirous at least to conceal his approaching fate from the insults of the multitude. He was soon followed by a tribune and some centurions, the ministers of death; but, instead of receiving with manly resolution the inevitable stroke, his unavailing cries and entreaties disgraced the last moments of his life, and converted into contempt some portion of the just pity which his innocence and misfortunes must inspire. His mother Mamæa, whose pride and avarice he loudly accused as the cause of his ruin, perished with her son. The most faithful of his friends were sacrificed to the first fury of the soldiers. Others were reserved for the more deliberate cruelty of the usurper; and those who experienced the mildest treatment, were stripped of their employments, and ignominiously driven from the court and army.[6]

Tyranny of Maximin.

The former tyrants, Caligula and Nero, Commodus and Caracalla, were all dissolute and unexperienced youths,[7] educated in the purple, and corrupted by the pride of empire, the luxury of Rome, and the perfidious voice of flattery. The cruelty of Maximin was derived from a different source, the fear of contempt. Though he depended on the attachment of the soldiers, who loved him for virtues like their own, he was conscious that his mean and barbarian origin, his savage appearance, and his total ignorance of the arts and institutions of civil

5. Hist. August. p. 135. I have softened some of the most improbable circumstances of this wretched biographer. From this ill-worded narration, it should seem, that the prince's buffoon having accidentally entered the tent, and awakened the slumbering monarch, the fear of punishment urged him to persuade the disaffected soldiers to commit the murder.

6. Herodian, l. vi. p. 223–227.

7. Caligula, the eldest of the four, was only twenty-five years of age when he ascended the throne; Caracalla was twenty-three, Commodus nineteen, and Nero no more than seventeen.

life,[8] formed a very unfavourable contrast with the amiable manners of the unhappy Alexander. He remembered, that, in his humbler fortune, he had often waited before the door of the haughty nobles of Rome, and had been denied admittance by the insolence of their slaves. He recollected too the friendship of a few who had relieved his poverty, and assisted his rising hopes. But those who had spurned, and those who had protected the Thracian, were guilty of the same crime, the knowledge of his original obscurity. For this crime many were put to death; and by the execution of several of his benefactors, Maximin published, in characters of blood, the indelible history of his baseness and ingratitude.[9]

The dark and sanguinary soul of the tyrant, was open to every suspicion against those among his subjects who were the most distinguished by their birth or merit. Whenever he was alarmed with the sound of treason, his cruelty was unbounded and unrelenting. A conspiracy against his life was either discovered or imagined, and Magnus, a consular senator, was named as the principal author of it. Without a witness, without a trial, and without an opportunity of defence, Magnus, with four thousand of his supposed accomplices, were put to death; Italy and the whole empire were infested with innumerable spies and informers. On the slightest accusation, the first of the Roman nobles, who had governed provinces, commanded armies, and been adorned with the consular and triumphal ornaments, were chained on the public carriages, and hurried away to the emperor's presence. Confiscation, exile, or simple death, were esteemed uncommon instances of his lenity. Some of the unfortunate sufferers he ordered to be sewed up in the hides of slaughtered animals, others to be exposed to wild beasts, others again to be beaten to death with clubs. During the three years of his reign, he disdained to visit either Rome or Italy. His camp, occasionally removed from the banks of the Rhine to those of the Danube, was the seat of his stern despotism, which trampled on every principle of law and justice, and was supported by the avowed power of the sword.[10] No man

---

8. It appears that he was totally ignorant of the Greek language; which, from its universal use in conversation and letters, was an essential part of every liberal education.

9. Hist. August. p. 141. Herodian, l. vii. p. 237. The latter of these historians has been most unjustly censured for sparing the vices of Maximin.

10. The wife of Maximin, by insinuating wise counsels with female gentleness, sometimes brought back the tyrant to the way of truth and humanity. See Ammianus Marcellinus, l. xiv. c. 1. where he alludes to the fact which he had more fully related under the reign of the Gordians. We may collect from the medals, that Paullina was the name of this

of noble birth, elegant accomplishments, or knowledge of civil business, was suffered near his person; and the court of a Roman emperor revived the idea of those ancient chiefs of slaves and gladiators, whose savage power had left a deep impression of terror and detestation.[11]

Oppression of the provinces. As long as the cruelty of Maximin was confined to the illustrious senators, or even to the bold adventurers, who in the court or army expose themselves to the caprice of fortune, the body of the people viewed their sufferings with indifference, or perhaps with pleasure. But the tyrant's avarice, stimulated by the insatiate desires of the soldiers, at length attacked the public property. Every city of the empire was possessed of an independent revenue, destined to purchase corn for the multitude, and to supply the expences of the games and entertainments. By a single act of authority, the whole mass of wealth was at once confiscated for the use of the Imperial treasury. The temples were stripped of their most valuable offerings of gold and silver, and the statues of gods, heroes, and emperors were melted down and coined into money. These impious orders could not be executed without tumults and massacres, as in many places the people chose rather to die in the defence of their altars, than to behold in the midst of peace their cities exposed to the rapine and cruelty of war. The soldiers themselves, among whom this sacrilegious plunder was distributed, received it with a blush; and, hardened as they were in acts of violence, they dreaded the just reproaches of their friends and relations. Throughout the Roman world a general cry of indignation was heard, imploring vengeance on the common enemy of human kind; and at length, by an act of private oppression, a peaceful and unarmed province was driven into rebellion against him.[12]

Revolt in Africa. A.D. 237. April. The procurator of Africa was a servant worthy of such a master, who considered the fines and confiscations of the rich as one of the most fruitful branches of the Imperial revenue. An iniquitous sentence had been pronounced against some opulent youths of that country, the execution of which would have stripped them of far the greater part of their patrimony. In this extremity, a resolution that must either complete or prevent their ruin, was dictated by despair. A respite of

---

benevolent empress; and from the title of *Diva*, that she died before Maximin. (Valesius ad loc. cit. Ammian.) Spanheim de U. et P. N. tom. ii. p. 300.

11. He was compared to Spartacus and Athenio. Hist. August. p. 141.

12. Herodian, l. vii. p. 238. Zosim. l. i. p. 15.

three days, obtained with difficulty from the rapacious treasurer, was employed in collecting from their estates a great number of slaves and peasants, blindly devoted to the commands of their lords, and armed with the rustic weapons of clubs and axes. The leaders of the conspiracy, as they were admitted to the audience of the procurator, stabbed him with the daggers concealed under their garments, and, by the assistance of their tumultuary train, seized on the little town of Thysdrus,[13] and erected the standard of rebellion against the sovereign of the Roman empire. They rested their hopes on the hatred of mankind against Maximin, and they judiciously resolved to oppose to that detested tyrant, an emperor whose mild virtues had already acquired the love and esteem of the Romans, and whose authority over the province would give weight and stability to the enterprise. Gordianus, their proconsul, and the object of their choice, refused, with unfeigned reluctance, the dangerous honour, and begged with tears that they would suffer him to terminate in peace a long and innocent life, without staining his feeble age with civil blood. Their menaces compelled him to accept the Imperial purple, his only refuge indeed against the jealous cruelty of Maximin; since, according to the reasoning of tyrants, those who have been esteemed worthy of the throne deserve death, and those who deliberate have already rebelled.[14]

The family of Gordianus was one of the most illustrious of the Roman senate. On the father's side, he was descended from the Gracchi; on his mother's, from the emperor Trajan. A great estate enabled him to support the dignity of his birth, and, in the enjoyment of it, he displayed an elegant taste and beneficent disposition. *Character and elevation of the two Gordians.* The palace in Rome, formerly inhabited by the great Pompey, had been, during several generations, in the possession of Gordian's family.[15] It was distinguished by ancient trophies of naval victories, and decorated with the works of modern painting. His villa on the road to Præneste, was

---

13. In the fertile territory of Byzacium, one hundred and fifty miles to the south of Carthage. This city was decorated, probably by the Gordians, with the title of colony, and with a fine amphitheatre, which is still in a very perfect state. See Itinerar. Wesseling, p. 59. and Shaw's Travels, p. 117.

14. Herodian, l. vii. p. 239. Hist. August. p. 153.

15. Hist. August. p. 152. The celebrated house of Pompey *in carinis*, was usurped by Marc Antony, and consequently became, after the Triumvir's death, a part of the Imperial domain. The emperor Trajan allowed and even encouraged the rich senators to purchase those magnificent and useless palaces (Plin. Panegyric. c. 50.): and it may seem probable, that, on this occasion, Pompey's house came into the possession of Gordian's great-grandfather.

celebrated for baths of singular beauty and extent, for three stately rooms of an hundred feet in length, and for a magnificent portico, supported by two hundred columns of the four most curious and costly sorts of marble.[16] The public shows exhibited at his expence, and in which the people were entertained with many hundreds of wild beasts and gladiators,[17] seem to surpass the fortune of a subject; and whilst the liberality of other magistrates was confined to a few solemn festivals in Rome, the magnificence of Gordian was repeated, when he was ædile, every month in the year, and extended, during his consulship, to the principal cities of Italy. He was twice elevated to the last mentioned dignity, by Caracalla and by Alexander; for he possessed the uncommon talent of acquiring the esteem of virtuous princes, without alarming the jealousy of tyrants. His long life was innocently spent in the study of letters and the peaceful honours of Rome; and, till he was named proconsul of Africa by the voice of the senate and the approbation of Alexander,[18] he appears prudently to have declined the command of armies and the government of provinces. As long as that emperor lived, Africa was happy under the administration of his worthy representative; after the barbarous Maximin had usurped the throne, Gordianus alleviated the miseries which he was unable to prevent. When he reluctantly accepted the purple, he was above fourscore years old; a last and valuable remains of the happy age of the Antonines, whose virtues he revived in his own conduct, and celebrated in an elegant poem of thirty books. With the venerable proconsul, his son, who had accompanied him into Africa as his lieutenant, was likewise declared emperor. His manners were less pure, but his character was equally amiable with that of his father. Twenty-two acknowledged concubines, and a library of sixty-two thousand volumes, attested the variety of his inclinations; and from the productions which he left behind him, it appears that the former as well as the latter

---

16. The Claudian, the Numidian, the Carystian, and the Synnadian. The colours of Roman marbles have been faintly described and imperfectly distinguished. It appears, however, that the Carystian was a sea green, and that the marble of Synnada was white mixed with oval spots of purple. See Salmasius ad Hist. August. p. 164.

17. Hist. August. p. 151, 152. He sometimes gave five hundred pair of Gladiators, never less than one hundred and fifty. He once gave for the use of the Circus one hundred Sicilian, and as many Cappadocian horses. The animals designed for hunting, were chiefly bears, boars, bulls, stags, elks, wild asses, &c. Elephants and lions seem to have been appropriated to Imperial magnificence.

18. See the original letter, in the Augustan History, p. 152, which at once shews Alexander's respect for the authority of the senate, and his esteem for the proconsul appointed by that assembly.

were designed for use rather than for ostentation.[19] The Roman people acknowledged in the features of the younger Gordian the resemblance of Scipio Africanus, recollected with pleasure that his mother was the grand-daughter of Antoninus Pius, and rested the public hope on those latent virtues which had hitherto, as they fondly imagined, lain concealed in the luxurious indolence of a private life.

As soon as the Gordians had appeased the first tumult of a popular election, they removed their court to Carthage. They were received with the acclamations of the Africans, who honoured their virtues, and who, since the visit of Hadrian, had *They solicit the confirmation of their authority.* never beheld the majesty of a Roman emperor. But these vain acclamations neither strengthened nor confirmed the title of the Gordians. They were induced by principle, as well as interest, to solicit the approbation of the senate; and a deputation of the noblest provincials was sent, without delay, to Rome, to relate and justify the conduct of their countrymen, who, having long suffered with patience, were at length resolved to act with vigour. The letters of the new princes were modest and respectful, excusing the necessity which had obliged them to accept the Imperial title; but submitting their election and their fate to the supreme judgment of the senate.[20]

The inclinations of the senate were neither doubtful nor divided. The birth and noble alliances of the Gordians had intimately connected them with the most illustrious houses of Rome. Their fortune had created many dependants in that assembly, their merit had acquired many friends. Their mild administration opened the *The senate ratifies their election of the Gordians;* flattering prospect of the restoration, not only of the civil but even of the republican government. The terror of military violence, which had first obliged the senate to forget the murder of Alexander, and to ratify the election of a barbarian peasant,[21] now produced a contrary effect, and provoked them to assert the injured rights of freedom and humanity. The hatred of Maximin towards the senate was declared and implacable; the tamest submission had not appeased his fury, the most cautious innocence would not remove his suspicions; and even the care of their own safety urged them to share the fortune of an enterprise, of which (if unsuccessful)

---

19. By each of his concubines, the younger Gordian left three or four children. His literary productions, though less numerous, were by no means contemptible.

20. Herodian, l. vii. p. 243. Hist. August. p. 144.
21. Quod tamen patres dum periculosum existimant; inermes armato resistere approbaverunt. *Aurelius Victor.*

they were sure to be the first victims. These considerations, and perhaps others of a more private nature, were debated in a previous conference of the consuls and the magistrates. As soon as their resolution was decided, they convoked in the temple of Castor the whole body of the senate, according to an ancient form of secrecy,[22] calculated to awaken their attention, and to conceal their decrees. "Conscript fathers," said the consul Syllanus, "the two Gordians, both of consular dignity, the one your proconsul, the other your lieutenant, have been declared emperors by the general consent of Africa. Let us return thanks," he boldly continued, "to the youth of Thysdrus; let us return thanks to the faithful people of Carthage, our generous deliverers from an horrid monster – Why do you hear me thus coolly, thus timidly? Why do you cast those anxious looks on each other? why hesitate? Maximin is a public enemy! may his enmity soon expire with him, and may we long enjoy the prudence and felicity of Gordian the father, the valour and constancy of Gordian the son!"[23] The noble ardour of the consul revived the languid spirit of the senate. By an unanimous decree the election of the Gordians was ratified, Maximin,

and declares Maximin a public enemy. his son, and his adherents, were pronounced enemies of their country, and liberal rewards were offered to whosoever had the courage and good fortune to destroy them.

Assumes the command of Rome and Italy, During the emperor's absence, a detachment of the Prætorian guards remained at Rome, to protect, or rather to command the capital. The Præfect Vitalianus had signalized his fidelity to Maximin, by the alacrity with which he had obeyed, and even prevented, the cruel mandates of the tyrant. His death alone could rescue the authority of the senate and the lives of the senators, from a state of danger and suspence. Before their resolves had transpired, a quæstor and some tribunes were commissioned to take his devoted life. They executed the order with equal boldness and success; and, with their bloody daggers in their hands, ran through the streets, proclaiming to the people and the soldiers, the news of the happy revolution. The enthusiasm of liberty was seconded by the promise of a large donative, in lands and money; the statues of Maximin were thrown down; the capital of the empire

22. Even the servants of the house, the scribes, &c. were excluded, and their office was filled by the senators themselves. We are obliged to the Augustan History, p. 159, for preserving this curious example of the old discipline of the commonwealth.

23. This spirited speech, translated from the Augustan historian, p. 156, seems transcribed by him from the original registers of the senate.

acknowledged, with transport, the authority of the two Gordians and the senate;[24] and the example of Rome was followed by the rest of Italy.

A new spirit had arisen in that assembly, whose long patience had been insulted by wanton despotism and military licence. The senate assumed the reins of government, and, with a calm intrepidity, prepared to vindicate by arms the cause of freedom. *and prepares for a civil war.* Among the consular senators recommended by their merit and services to the favour of the emperor Alexander, it was easy to select twenty, not unequal to the command of an army, and the conduct of a war. To these was the defence of Italy intrusted. Each was appointed to act in his respective department, authorized to enrol and discipline the Italian youth; and instructed to fortify the ports and highways, against the impending invasion of Maximin. A number of deputies, chosen from the most illustrious of the senatorian and equestrian orders, were dispatched at the same time to the governors of the several provinces, earnestly conjuring them to fly to the assistance of their country, and to remind the nations of their ancient ties of friendship with the Roman senate and people. The general respect with which these deputies were received, and the zeal of Italy and the provinces in favour of the senate, sufficiently prove that the subjects of Maximin were reduced to that uncommon distress, in which the body of the people has more to fear from oppression than from resistance. The consciousness of that melancholy truth, inspires a degree of persevering fury, seldom to be found in those civil wars which are artificially supported for the benefit of a few factious and designing leaders.[25]

For while the cause of the Gordians was embraced with such diffusive ardour, the Gordians themselves were no more. The feeble court of Carthage was alarmed with the rapid approach of Capelianus, governor of Mauritania, who, with a small band of veterans, and a fierce host of barbarians, attacked a faithful, but unwarlike province. The younger Gordian sallied out to *Defeat and death of the two Gordians. A.D. 237. 3d July.* meet the enemy at the head of a few guards, and a numerous undisciplined multitude, educated in the peaceful luxury of Carthage. His useless valour served only to procure him an honourable death, in the field of battle. His aged father, whose reign had not exceeded thirty-six days, put an end to his life on the first news of the defeat. Carthage, destitute of defence,

24. Herodian, l. vii. p. 244.
25. Herodian, l. vii. p. 247. l. viii. p. 277.
Hist. August. p. 156–158.

opened her gates to the conqueror, and Africa was exposed to the rapacious cruelty of a slave, obliged to satisfy his unrelenting master with a large account of blood and treasure.[26]

Election of Maximus and Balbinus by the senate.

9th July.

The fate of the Gordians filled Rome with just, but unexpected terror. The senate convoked in the temple of Concord, affected to transact the common business of the day; and seemed to decline, with trembling anxiety, the consideration of their own, and the public danger. A silent consternation prevailed on the assembly, till a senator, of the name and family of Trajan, awakened his brethren from their fatal lethargy. He represented to them, that the choice of cautious dilatory measures had been long since out of their power; that Maximin, implacable by nature, and exasperated by injuries, was advancing towards Italy, at the head of the military force of the empire; and that their only remaining alternative, was either to meet him bravely in the field, or tamely to expect the tortures and ignominious death reserved for unsuccessful rebellion. "We have lost, continued he, two excellent princes; but unless we desert ourselves, the hopes of the republic have not perished with the Gordians. Many are the senators, whose virtues have deserved, and whose abilities would sustain, the Imperial dignity. Let us elect two emperors, one of whom may conduct the war against the public enemy, whilst his colleague remains at Rome to direct the civil administration. I cheerfully expose myself to the danger and envy of the nomination, and give my vote in favour of Maximus and Balbinus. Ratify my choice, conscript fathers, or appoint in their place, others more worthy of the empire." The general apprehension silenced the whispers of jealousy; the merit of the candidates was universally acknowledged; and the house resounded with the sincere acclamations, of "long life and victory to the emperors Maximus and Balbinus. You are happy in the judgment of the senate; may the republic be happy under your administration!"[27]

Their characters.

The virtues and the reputation of the new emperors justified the most sanguine hopes of the Romans. The various nature

---

26. Herodian, l. vii. p. 254. Hist. August. p. 150–160. We may observe, that one month and six days, for the reign of Gordian, is a just correction of Casaubon and Panvinius, instead of the absurd reading of one year and six months. See Commentar. p. 193. Zosimus relates, l. i. p. 17. that the two Gordians

perished by a tempest in the midst of their navigation. A strange ignorance of history, or a strange abuse of metaphors!

27. See the Augustan History, p. 166, from the registers of the senate; the date is confessedly faulty, but the coincidence of the Apollinarian games enables us to correct it.

of their talents seemed to appropriate to each his peculiar department of peace and war, without leaving room for jealous emulation. Balbinus was an admired orator, a poet of distinguished fame, and a wise magistrate, who had exercised with innocence and applause the civil jurisdiction in almost all the interior provinces of the empire. His birth was noble,[28] his fortune affluent, his manners liberal and affable. In him, the love of pleasure was corrected by a sense of dignity, nor had the habits of ease deprived him of a capacity for business. The mind of Maximus was formed in a rougher mould. By his valour and abilities he had raised himself from the meanest origin to the first employments of the state and army. His victories over the Sarmatians and the Germans, the austerity of his life, and the rigid impartiality of his justice, whilst he was Præfect of the city, commanded the esteem of a people, whose affections were engaged in favour of the more amiable Balbinus. The two colleagues had both been consuls (Balbinus had twice enjoyed that honourable office), both had been named among the twenty lieutenants of the senate; and since the one was sixty and the other seventy-four years old,[29] they had both attained the full maturity of age and experience.

After the senate had conferred on Maximus and Balbinus an equal portion of the consular and tribunitian powers, the title of Fathers of their country, and the joint office of Supreme Pontiff, they ascended to the Capitol, to return thanks to the gods, protectors of Rome.[30] The solemn rites of sacrifice were disturbed by a sedition of the people. The licentious multitude neither loved the rigid Maximus, nor did they sufficiently fear the mild and humane Balbinus. Their increasing numbers surrounded the temple of Jupiter; with

Tumult at Rome. The younger Gordian is declared Cæsar.

---

28. He was descended from Cornelius Balbus, a noble Spaniard, and the adopted son of Theophanes the Greek historian. Balbus obtained the freedom of Rome by the favour of Pompey, and preserved it by the eloquence of Cicero (see Orat. pro Cornel. Balbo). The friendship of Cæsar (to whom he rendered the most important secret services in the civil war) raised him to the consulship and the pontificate, honours never yet possessed by a stranger. The nephew of this Balbus triumphed over the Garamantes. See Dictionnaire de Bayle, au mot *Balbus*, where he distinguishes the several persons of that name,

and rectifies, with his usual accuracy, the mistakes of former writers concerning them.

29. Zonaras, l. xii. p. 622. But little dependence is to be had on the authority of a modern Greek, so grossly ignorant of the history of the third century, that he creates several imaginary emperors, and confounds those who really existed.

30. Herodian, l. vii. p. 256, supposes that the senate was at first convoked in the Capitol, and is very eloquent on the occasion. The Augustan History, p. 116, seems much more authentic.

obstinate clamours they asserted their inherent right of consenting to the election of their sovereign; and demanded, with an apparent moderation, that, besides the two emperors chosen by the senate, a third should be added of the family of the Gordians, as a just return of gratitude to those princes who had sacrificed their lives for the republic. At the head of the city-guards, and the youth of the equestrian order, Maximus and Balbinus attempted to cut their way through the seditious multitude. The multitude, armed with sticks and stones, drove them back into the Capitol. It is prudent to yield when the contest, whatever may be the issue of it, must be fatal to both parties. A boy, only thirteen years of age, the grandson of the elder, and nephew of the younger, Gordian, was produced to the people, invested with the ornaments and title of Cæsar. The tumult was appeased by this easy condescension; and the two emperors, as soon as they had been peaceably acknowledged in Rome, prepared to defend Italy against the common enemy.

Maximin prepares to attack the senate and their emperors.

Whilst in Rome and Africa revolutions succeeded each other with such amazing rapidity, the mind of Maximin was agitated by the most furious passions. He is said to have received the news of the rebellion of the Gordians, and of the decree of the senate against him, not with the temper of a man, but the rage of a wild beast; which, as it could not discharge itself on the distant senate, threatened the life of his son, of his friends, and of all who ventured to approach his person. The grateful intelligence of the death of the Gordians, was quickly followed by the assurance that the senate, laying aside all hopes of pardon or accommodation, had substituted in their room two emperors, with whose merit he could not be unacquainted. Revenge was the only consolation left to Maximin, and revenge could only be obtained by arms. The strength of the legions had been assembled by Alexander from all parts of the empire. Three successful campaigns against the Germans and the Sarmatians, had raised their fame, confirmed their discipline, and even increased their numbers, by filling the ranks with the flower of the barbarian youth. The life of Maximin had been spent in war, and the candid severity of history cannot refuse him the valour of a soldier, or even the abilities of an experienced general.[31] It might naturally be

31. In Herodian, l. vii. p. 249, and in the Augustan History, we have three several orations of Maximin to his army, on the rebellion of Africa and Rome: M. de Tillemont has very justly observed, that they neither agree with each other, nor with truth. Histoire des Empereurs, tom. iii. p. 799.

expected, that a prince of such a character, instead of suffering the rebellion to gain stability by delay, should immediately have marched from the banks of the Danube to those of the Tyber, and that his victorious army, instigated by contempt for the senate, and eager to gather the spoils of Italy, should have burned with impatience to finish the easy and lucrative conquest. Yet as far as we can trust to the obscure chronology of that period,[32] it appears that the operations of some foreign war deferred the Italian expedition till the ensuing spring. From the prudent conduct of Maximin, we may learn that the savage features of his character have been exaggerated by the pencil of party, that his passions, however impetuous, submitted to the force of reason, and that the barbarian possessed something of the generous spirit of Sylla, who subdued the enemies of Rome, before he suffered himself to revenge his private injuries.[33]

When the troops of Maximin, advancing in excellent order, arrived at the foot of the Julian Alps, they were terrified by the silence and desolation that reigned on the frontiers of Italy. The villages and open towns had been abandoned on their approach by the inhabitants, the cattle was driven away, the provisions removed, or destroyed, the bridges broke down, nor was any thing left which could afford either shelter or subsistence to an invader. Such had been the wise orders of the generals of the senate; whose design was to protract the war, to ruin the army of Maximin by the slow operation of famine, and to consume his strength in the sieges of the principal cities of Italy, which they had plentifully stored with men and provisions from the deserted country. Aquileia received and withstood the first shock of the invasion. The streams that issue from the head of the

Marches into Italy. A.D. 238. February.

Siege of Aquileia.

---

32. The carelessness of the writers of that age leaves us in a singular perplexity. 1. We know that Maximus and Balbinus were killed during the Capitoline games. Herodian, l. viii. p. 285. The authority of Censorinus (de Die Natali, c. 18.) enables us to fix those games with certainty to the year 238, but leaves us in ignorance of the month or day. 2. The election of Gordian by the senate, is fixed, with equal certainty, to the 27th of May; but we are at a loss to discover, whether it was in the same or the preceding year. Tillemont and Muratori, who maintain the two opposite opinions, bring into the field a desultory troop of authorities, conjectures and probabilities. The one seems to draw out, the other to contract the series of events, between those periods, more than can be well reconciled to reason and history. Yet it is necessary to chuse between them.

33. Velleius Paterculus, l. ii. c. 24. The president de Montesquieu (in his dialogue between Sylla and Eucrates) expresses the sentiments of the dictator, in a spirited and even a sublime manner.

Hadriatic gulf, swelled by the melting of the winter snows,[34] opposed an unexpected obstacle to the arms of Maximin. At length, on a singular bridge, constructed with art and difficulty, of large hogsheads, he transported his army to the opposite bank, rooted up the beautiful vineyards in the neighbourhood of Aquileia, demolished the suburbs, and employed the timber of the buildings in the engines and towers, with which on every side he attacked the city. The walls, fallen to decay during the security of a long peace, had been hastily repaired on this sudden emergency; but the firmest defence of Aquileia consisted in the constancy of the citizens; all ranks of whom, instead of being dismayed, were animated by the extreme danger, and their knowledge of the tyrant's unrelenting temper. Their courage was supported and directed by Crispinus and Menophilus, two of the twenty lieutenants of the senate, who, with a small body of regular troops, had thrown themselves into the besieged place. The army of Maximin was repulsed in repeated attacks, his machines destroyed by showers of artificial fire; and the generous enthusiasm of the Aquileians was exalted into a confidence of success, by the opinion, that Belenus, their tutelar deity, combated in person in the defence of his distressed worshippers.[35]

Conduct of Maximus. The emperor Maximus, who had advanced as far as Ravenna, to secure that important place, and to hasten the military preparations, beheld the event of the war in the more faithful mirror of reason and policy. He was too sensible, that a single town could not resist the persevering efforts of a great army; and he dreaded, lest the enemy, tired with the obstinate resistance of Aquileia, should on a sudden relinquish the fruitless siege, and march directly towards Rome. The fate of the empire and the cause of freedom must then be committed to the chance of a battle;

---

34. Muratori (Annali d'Italia, tom. ii. p. 294.) thinks the melting of the snows suits better with the months of June or July, than with those of February. The opinion of a man who passed his life between the Alps and the Apennines, is undoubtedly of great weight; yet I observe, 1. That the long winter, of which Muratori takes advantage, is to be found only in the Latin version, and not in the Greek text of Herodian. 2. That the vicissitude of suns and rains, to which the soldiers of Maximin were exposed (Herodian, l. viii. p. 277.), denotes the spring rather than the summer. We may observe likewise, that these several streams, as they melted into one, composed the Timavus, so poetically (in every sense of the word) described by Virgil. They are about twelve miles to the east of Aquileia. See Cluver. Italia Antiqua, tom. i. p. 189, &c.

35. Herodian, l. viii. p. 272. The Celtic deity was supposed to be Apollo, and received under that name the thanks of the senate. A temple was likewise built to Venus the bald, in honour of the women of Aquileia, who had given up their hair to make ropes for the military engines.

and what arms could he oppose to the veteran legions of the Rhine and Danube? Some troops newly levied among the generous but enervated youth of Italy; and a body of German auxiliaries, on whose firmness, in the hour of trial, it was dangerous to depend. In the midst of these just alarms, the stroke of domestic conspiracy punished the crimes of Maximin, and delivered Rome and the senate from the calamities that would surely have attended the victory of an enraged barbarian.

The people of Aquileia had scarcely experienced any of the common miseries of a siege, their magazines were plentifully supplied, and several fountains within the walls assured them of an inexhaustible resource of fresh water. The soldiers of Maximin were, on the contrary, exposed to the inclemency of the season, the contagion of disease, and the horrors of famine. The open *Murder of Maximin and his son. A.D. 238. April.* country was ruined, the rivers filled with the slain, and polluted with blood. A spirit of despair and disaffection began to diffuse itself among the troops; and as they were cut off from all intelligence, they easily believed that the whole empire had embraced the cause of the senate, and that they were left as devoted victims to perish under the impregnable walls of Aquileia. The fierce temper of the tyrant was exasperated by disappointments, which he imputed to the cowardice of his army; and his wanton and ill-timed cruelty, instead of striking terror, inspired hatred and a just desire of revenge. A party of Prætorian guards, who trembled for their wives and children in the camp of Alba, near Rome, executed the sentence of the senate. Maximin, abandoned by his guards, was slain in his tent, with his son (whom he had associated to the honours of the purple), Anulinus the præfect, and the principal ministers of his tyranny.[36] The sight of their heads, borne on the point of spears, convinced the citizens of Aquileia, that the siege was at an end; the gates of the city were thrown open, a liberal market was provided for the hungry troops of Maximin, and the whole army joined in solemn protestations of fidelity to the senate and the people of Rome, and to their lawful emperors Maximus and Balbinus. Such was the deserved *His portrait.* fate of a brutal savage, destitute, as he has generally been represented, of every sentiment that distinguishes a civilized, or even a human being. The body was suited to the soul. The stature of Maximin exceeded

---

36. Herodian, l. viii. p. 279. Hist. August. p. 146. The duration of Maximin's reign has not been defined with much accuracy, except by Eutropius, who allows him three years and a few days (l. ix. 1.); we may depend on the integrity of the text, as the Latin original is checked by the Greek version of Pæanius.

the measure of eight feet, and circumstances almost incredible are related of his matchless strength and appetite.[37] Had he lived in a less enlightened age, tradition and poetry might well have described him as one of those monstrous giants, whose supernatural power was constantly exerted for the destruction of mankind.

Joy of the Roman world.   It is easier to conceive than to describe the universal joy of the Roman world on the fall of the tyrant, the news of which is said to have been carried in four days from Aquileia to Rome. The return of Maximus was a triumphal procession, his colleague and young Gordian went out to meet him, and the three princes made their entry into the capital, attended by the ambassadors of almost all the cities of Italy, saluted with the splendid offerings of gratitude and superstition, and received with the unfeigned acclamations of the senate and people, who persuaded themselves that a golden age would succeed to an age of iron.[38] The conduct of the two emperors corresponded with these expectations. They administered justice in person; and the rigour of the one was tempered by the other's clemency. The oppressive taxes with which Maximin had loaded the rights of inheritance and succession, were repealed, or at least moderated. Discipline was revived, and with the advice of the senate many wise laws were enacted by their imperial ministers, who endeavoured to restore a civil constitution on the ruins of military tyranny. "What reward may we expect for delivering Rome from a monster?" was the question asked by Maximus, in a moment of freedom and confidence. Balbinus answered it without hesitation, "The love of the senate, of the people, and of all mankind." "Alas!" replied his more penetrating colleague, "Alas! I dread the hatred of the soldiers, and the fatal effects of their resentment."[39] His apprehensions were but too well justified by the event.

Sedition at Rome.   Whilst Maximus was preparing to defend Italy against the common foe, Balbinus, who remained at Rome, had been engaged in scenes of blood and intestine discord. Distrust and jealousy reigned in the senate; and even in the temples where they assembled,

---

37. Eight Roman feet and one third, which are equal to above eight English feet, as the two measures are to each other in the proportion of 967 to 1000. See Greaves's discourse on the Roman foot. We are told that Maximin could drink in a day an amphora (or about seven gallons of wine), and eat thirty or forty pounds of meat. He could move a

loaded waggon, break a horse's leg with his fist, crumble stones in his hand, and tear up small trees by the roots. See his life in the Augustan History.

38. See the congratulatory letter of Claudius Julianus the consul, to the two emperors, in the Augustan History.

39. Hist. August. p. 171.

every senator carried either open or concealed arms. In the midst of their deliberations, two veterans of the guards, actuated either by curiosity or a sinister motive, audaciously thrust themselves into the house, and advanced by degrees beyond the altar of Victory. Gallicanus, a consular, and Mæcenas, a Prætorian senator, viewed with indignation their insolent intrusion: drawing their daggers, they laid the spies, for such they deemed them, dead at the foot of the altar, and then advancing to the door of the senate, imprudently exhorted the multitude to massacre the Prætorians, as the secret adherents of the tyrant. Those who escaped the first fury of the tumult took refuge in the camp, which they defended with superior advantage against the reiterated attacks of the people, assisted by the numerous bands of gladiators, the property of opulent nobles. The civil war lasted many days, with infinite loss and confusion on both sides. When the pipes were broken that supplied the camp with water, the Prætorians were reduced to intolerable distress; but in their turn they made desperate sallies into the city, set fire to a great number of houses, and filled the streets with the blood of the inhabitants. The emperor Balbinus attempted, by ineffectual edicts and precarious truces, to reconcile the factions at Rome. But their animosity, though smothered for a while, burnt with redoubled violence. The soldiers, detesting the senate and the people, despised the weakness of a prince who wanted either the spirit or the power to command the obedience of his subjects.[40]

After the tyrant's death, his formidable army had acknowledged, from necessity rather than from choice, the authority of Maximus, who transported himself without delay to the camp before Aquileia. As soon as he had received their oath of fidelity, *Discontent of the Prætorian guards.* he addressed them in terms full of mildness and moderation; lamented, rather than arraigned, the wild disorders of the times, and assured the soldiers, that of all their past conduct, the senate would remember only their generous desertion of the tyrant, and their voluntary return to their duty. Maximus enforced his exhortations by a liberal donative, purified the camp by a solemn sacrifice of expiation, and then dismissed the legions to their several provinces, impressed, as he hoped, with a lively sense of gratitude and obedience.[41] But nothing could reconcile the haughty spirit of the Prætorians. They attended the emperors on the memorable day of

40. Herodian, l. viii. p. 258.
41. Herodian, l. viii. p. 213.

their public entry into Rome; but amidst the general acclamations, the sullen dejected countenance of the guards, sufficiently declared that they considered themselves as the object, rather than the partners, of the triumph. When the whole body was united in their camp, those who had served under Maximin, and those who had remained at Rome, insensibly communicated to each other their complaints and apprehensions. The emperors chosen by the army had perished with ignominy; those elected by the senate were seated on the throne.[42] The long discord between the civil and military powers was decided by a war, in which the former had obtained a complete victory. The soldiers must now learn a new doctrine of submission to the senate; and whatever clemency was affected by that politic assembly, they dreaded a slow revenge, coloured by the name of discipline, and justified by fair pretences of the public good. But their fate was still in their own hands; and if they had courage to despise the vain terrors of an impotent republic, it was easy to convince the world, that those who were masters of the arms, were masters of the authority, of the state.

Massacre of Maximus and Balbinus. When the senate elected two princes, it is probable that, besides the declared reason of providing for the various emergencies of peace and war, they were actuated by the secret desire of weakening by division the despotism of the supreme magistrate. Their policy was effectual, but it proved fatal both to their emperors and to themselves. The jealousy of power was soon exasperated by the difference of character. Maximus despised Balbinus as a luxurious noble, and was in his turn disdained by his colleague as an obscure soldier. Their silent discord was understood rather than seen;[43] but the mutual consciousness prevented them from uniting in any vigorous measures of defence against their common enemies of the Prætorian camp. The whole city was employed in the Capitoline games, and the emperors were left almost alone in the palace. On a sudden they were alarmed by the approach of a troop of desperate assassins. Ignorant of each other's situation or designs, for they already occupied very distant apartments, afraid to give or to receive assistance, they wasted the important moments in idle debates and fruitless recriminations. The arrival of the guards put an end to the

A.D. 238. July 15.

---

42. The observation had been made imprudently enough in the acclamations of the senate, and with regard to the soldiers it carried the appearance of a wanton insult. Hist. August. p. 170.

43. Discordiæ tacitæ, et quæ intelligerentur potius quam viderentur. Hist. August. p. 170. This well-chosen expression is probably stolen from some better writer.

vain strife. They seized on these emperors of the senate, for such they called them with malicious contempt, stripped them of their garments, and dragged them in insolent triumph through the streets of Rome, with a design of inflicting a slow and cruel death on these unfortunate princes. The fear of a rescue from the faithful Germans of the Imperial guards, shortened their tortures; and their bodies, mangled with a thousand wounds, were left exposed to the insults or to the pity of the populace.[44]

In the space of a few months, six princes had been cut off by the sword. Gordian, who had already received the title of Cæsar, was the only person that occurred to the soldiers as proper to fill the vacant throne.[45] They carried him to the *The third Gordian remains sole emperor.* camp, and unanimously saluted him Augustus and Emperor. His name was dear to the senate and people; his tender age promised a long impunity of military licence; and the submission of Rome and the provinces to the choice of the Prætorian guards, saved the republic, at the expence indeed of its freedom and dignity, from the horrors of a new civil war in the heart of the capital.[46]

As the third Gordian was only nineteen years of age at the time of his death, the history of his life, were it known to us with greater accuracy than it really is, would contain little more than the account of his education, and the conduct of the ministers, who by turns *Innocence and virtues of Gordian.* abused or guided the simplicity of his unexperienced youth. Immediately after his accession, he fell into the hands of his mother's eunuchs, that pernicious vermin of the East, who, since the days of Elagabalus, had infested the Roman palace. By the artful conspiracy of these wretches, an impenetrable veil was drawn between an innocent prince and his oppressed subjects, the virtuous disposition of Gordian was deceived, and the honours of the empire sold without his knowledge, though in a very public manner, to the most worthless of mankind. We are ignorant by what fortunate accident the emperor escaped from this ignominious slavery, and

44. Herodian, l. viii. p. 287, 288.
45. Quia non alius erat in præsenti, is the expression of the Augustan History.
46. Quintus Curtius (l. x. c. 9.) pays an elegant compliment to the emperor of the day, for having, by his happy accession, extinguished so many firebrands, sheathed so many swords, and put an end to the evils of a divided government. After weighing with attention every word of the passage, I am of opinion, that it suits better with the elevation of Gordian, than with any other period of the Roman History. In that case, it may serve to decide the age of Quintus Curtius. Those who place him under the first Cæsars, argue from the purity of his style, but are embarrassed by the silence of Quintilian, in his accurate list of Roman historians.

devolved his confidence on a minister, whose wise councils had no object

A.D. 240.
Administration
of Misitheus.

except the glory of his sovereign, and the happiness of the people. It should seem that love and learning introduced Misitheus to the favour of Gordian. The young prince married the daughter of his master of rhetoric, and promoted his father-in-law to the first offices of the empire. Two admirable letters that passed between them, are still extant. The minister, with the conscious dignity of virtue, congratulates Gordian that he is delivered from the tyranny of the eunuchs,[47] and still more that he is sensible of his deliverance. The emperor acknowledges, with an amiable confusion, the errors of his past conduct; and laments, with singular propriety, the misfortune of a monarch, from whom a venal tribe of courtiers perpetually labour to conceal the truth.[48]

The Persian
war. A.D. 242.

The life of Misitheus had been spent in the profession of letters, not of arms; yet such was the versatile genius of that great man, that, when he was appointed Prætorian Præfect, he discharged the military duties of his place with vigour and ability. The Persians had invaded Mesopotamia, and threatened Antioch. By the persuasion of his father-in-law, the young emperor quitted the luxury of Rome, opened, for the last time recorded in history, the temple of Janus, and marched in person into the East. On his approach with a great army, the Persians withdrew their garrisons from the cities which they had already taken, and retired from the Euphrates to the Tigris. Gordian enjoyed the pleasure of announcing to the senate the first success of his arms, which he ascribed with a becoming modesty and gratitude to the wisdom of his father and Præfect. During the whole expedition, Misitheus watched over the safety and discipline of the army; whilst he prevented their dangerous murmurs by maintaining a regular plenty in the camp, and by establishing ample magazines of vinegar, bacon, straw, barley, and wheat, in all the cities of the frontier.[49] But the prosperity of Gordian expired with

---

47. Hist. August. p. 161. From some hints in the two letters, I should expect that the eunuchs were not expelled the palace, without some degree of gentle violence, and that young Gordian rather approved of, than consented to, their disgrace.

48. Duxit uxorem filiam Misithei, quem causâ eloquentiæ dignum parentela suâ putavit; et

præfectum statim fecit; post quod, non puerile jam et contemptibile videbatur imperium.

49. Hist. August. p. 162. Aurelius Victor. Porphyrius in Vit. Plotin. ap. Fabricium Biblioth. Græc. l. iv. c. 36. The philosopher Plotinus accompanied the army, prompted by the love of knowledge, and by the hope of penetrating as far as India.

Misitheus, who died of a flux, not without very strong suspicions of poison. Philip, his successor in the præfecture, was an Arab by birth, and consequently, in the earlier part of his life, a robber by profession. His rise from so obscure a station to the first dignities of the empire, seems to prove that he was a bold and able leader.

A.D. 243.
Arts of
Philip.

But his boldness prompted him to aspire to the throne, and his abilities were employed to supplant, not to serve, his indulgent master. The minds of the soldiers were irritated by an artificial scarcity, created by his contrivance in the camp; and the distress of the army was attributed to the youth and incapacity of the prince. It is not in our power to trace the successive steps of the secret conspiracy and open sedition, which were at length fatal to Gordian. A sepulchral monument was erected to his memory on the spot[50] where he was killed, near the conflux of the Euphrates with the little river Aboras.[51] The fortunate Philip, raised to the empire by the votes of the soldiers, found a ready obedience from the senate and the provinces.[52]

Murder of
Gordian.
A.D. 244.
March.

We cannot forbear transcribing the ingenious, though somewhat fanciful description, which a celebrated writer of our own times has traced of the military government of the Roman empire. "What in that age was called the Roman empire, was only an irregular republic, not unlike the Aristocracy[53] of Algiers,[54] where the militia, possessed of the sovereignty, creates and deposes a magistrate, who is styled a Dey. Perhaps, indeed, it may be laid down as a general rule, that a military government is, in some respects, more republican than monarchical. Nor can it be said that the soldiers only partook of the government by their disobedience and rebellions. The speeches made to them by the emperors, were they not at length of the same nature as those

Form of a
military republic.

50. About twenty miles from the little town of Circesium, on the frontier of the two empires.

51. The inscription (which contained a very singular pun) was erased by the order of Licinius, who claimed some degree of relationship to Philip (Hist. August. p. 165.); but the *tumulus* or mound of earth which formed the sepulchre, still subsisted in the time of Julian. See Ammian. Marcellin. xxiii. 5.

52. Aurelius Victor. Eutrop. ix. 2. Orosius, vii. 20. Ammianus Marcellinus, xxiii. 5. Zosimus,

l. i. p. 19. Philip, who was a native of Bostra, was about forty years of age.

53. Can the epithet of *Aristocracy* be applied, with any propriety, to the government of Algiers? Every military government floats between the extremes of absolute monarchy and wild democracy.

54. The military republic of the Mamalukes in Egypt, would have afforded M. de Montesquieu (see Considerations sur la Grandeur et la Decadence des Romains, c. 16.) a juster and more noble parallel.

formerly pronounced to the people by the consuls and the tribunes? And although the armies had no regular place or forms of assembly; though their debates were short, their action sudden, and their resolves seldom the result of cool reflection, did they not dispose, with absolute sway, of the public fortune? What was the emperor, except the minister of a violent government elected for the private benefit of the soldiers?

"When the army had elected Philip, who was Prætorian præfect to the third Gordian; the latter demanded, that he might remain sole emperor; he was unable to obtain it. He requested, that the power might be equally divided between them; the army would not listen to his speech. He consented to be degraded to the rank of Cæsar; the favour was refused him. He desired, at least, he might be appointed Prætorian præfect; his prayer was rejected. Finally, he pleaded for his life. The army, in these several judgments, exercised the supreme magistracy." According to the historian, whose doubtful narrative the president De Montesquieu has adopted, Philip, who, during the whole transaction, had preserved a sullen silence, was inclined to spare the innocent life of his benefactor; till, recollecting that his innocence might excite a dangerous compassion in the Roman world; he commanded, without regard to his suppliant cries, that he should be seized, stript, and led away to instant death. After a moment's pause the inhuman sentence was executed.[55]

Reign of Philip.   On his return from the east to Rome, Philip, desirous of obliterating the memory of his crimes, and of captivating the affections of the people, solemnized the secular games with infinite pomp and magnificence. Since their institution or revival by Augustus,[56] they had been celebrated by Claudius, by Domitian, and by Severus, and were now renewed the fifth time, on the accomplishment of the full period of a thousand years from the foundation of Rome. Every circumstance of the

---

55. The Augustan History (p. 163, 164.) cannot, in this instance, be reconciled with itself or with probability. How could Philip condemn his predecessor, and yet consecrate his memory? How could he order his public execution, and yet, in his letters to the senate, exculpate himself from the guilt of his death? Philip, though an ambitious usurper, was by no means a mad tyrant. Some chronological difficulties have likewise been discovered by the nice eyes of Tillemont and Muratori, in

this supposed association of Philip to the empire.

56. The account of the last supposed celebration, though in an enlightened period of history, was so very doubtful and obscure, that the alternative seems not doubtful. When the popish jubilees, the copy of the secular games, were invented by Boniface VIII. the crafty pope pretended, that he only revived an ancient institution. See M. le Chais Lettres sur les Jubilés.

secular games was skilfully adapted to inspire the superstitious mind with deep and solemn reverence. The long interval between them[57] exceeded the term of human life; and as none of the spectators had already seen them, none could flatter themselves with the expectation of beholding them a second time. The mystic sacrifices were performed, during three nights, on the banks of the Tyber; and the Campus Martius resounded with music and dances, and was illuminated with innumerable lamps and torches. Slaves and strangers were excluded from any participation in these national ceremonies. A chorus of twenty-seven youths, and as many virgins, of noble families, and whose parents were both alive, implored the propitious gods in favour of the present, and for the hope of the rising generation; requesting, in religious hymns, that, according to the faith of their ancient oracles, they would still maintain the virtue, the felicity, and the empire of the Roman people.[58] The magnificence of Philip's shows and entertainments dazzled the eyes of the multitude. The devout were employed in the rites of superstition, whilst the reflecting few revolved in their anxious minds the past history and the future fate of the empire.

Secular games. A.D. 248. April 21.

Since Romulus, with a small band of shepherds and outlaws, fortified himself on the hills near the Tiber, ten centuries had already elapsed.[59] During the four first ages, the Romans, in the laborious school of poverty, had acquired the virtues of war and government. By the vigorous exertion of those virtues, and by the assistance of fortune, they had obtained, in the course of the three succeeding centuries, an absolute empire over many countries of Europe, Asia, and Africa. The last three hundred years had been consumed in apparent prosperity and internal decline. The nation of soldiers, magistrates, and legislators, who composed the thirty-five tribes of the Roman people, was dissolved into the common mass of mankind, and confounded with the millions of servile provincials, who had received the name, without adopting the spirit of Romans. A

Decline of the Roman empire.

---

57. Either of a hundred, or a hundred and ten years. Varro and Livy adopted the former opinion, but the infallible authority of the Sibyl consecrated the latter (Censorinus de Die Natal. c. 17.). The emperors Claudius and Philip, however, did not treat the oracle with implicit respect.

58. The idea of the secular games is best understood from the poem of Horace, and

the description of Zosimus, l. ii. p. 167, &c.

59. The received calculation of Varro assigns to the foundation of Rome, an æra that corresponds with the 754th year before Christ. But so little is the chronology of Rome to be depended on, in the more early ages, that Sir Isaac Newton has brought the same event as low as the year 627.

mercenary army, levied among the subjects and barbarians of the frontier, was the only order of men who preserved and abused their independence. By their tumultuary election, a Syrian, a Goth, or an Arab, was exalted to the throne of Rome, and invested with despotic power over the conquests and over the country of the Scipios.

The limits of the Roman empire still extended from the Western Ocean to the Tigris, and from Mount Atlas to the Rhine and the Danube. To the undiscerning eye of the vulgar, Philip appeared a monarch no less powerful than Hadrian or Augustus had formerly been. The form was still the same, but the animating health and vigour were fled. The industry of the people was discouraged and exhausted by a long series of oppression. The discipline of the legions, which alone, after the extinction of every other virtue, had propped the greatness of the state, was corrupted by the ambition, or relaxed by the weakness, of the emperors. The strength of the frontiers, which had always consisted in arms rather than in fortifications, was insensibly undermined; and the fairest provinces were left exposed to the rapaciousness or ambition of the barbarians, who soon discovered the decline of the Roman empire.

[CHAPTERS VIII–XIV]

Chapters VIII and IX are really two concise essays on, respectively, the Persian and Germanic barbarians pressing on the empire's eastern and northern borders. The tendency of Gibbon's analysis is to diminish the gravity of the barbarian threat to the empire, as the last paragraph of chapter IX makes explicit:

Wars, and the administration of public affairs, are the principal subjects of history; but the number of persons interested in these busy scenes, is very different, according to the different condition of mankind. In great monarchies, millions of obedient subjects pursue their useful occupations in peace and obscurity. The attention of the Writer, as well as of the Reader, is solely confined to a court, a capital, a regular army, and the districts which happen to be the occasional scene of military operations. But a state of freedom and barbarism, the season of civil commotions, or the situation of petty republics, raises almost every member of the community into action, and consequently into notice. The irregular divisions, and the restless motions, of the people of Germany, dazzle our imagination, and seem to multiply their numbers. The profuse enumeration of kings and warriors, of armies and nations, inclines us to forget that the same objects are continually repeated under a variety of appellations, and that the most splendid appellations have been frequently lavished on the most inconsiderable objects. (*DF*, i. 252)

The irruption of the Goths therefore conforms to what is already becoming a recognizable paradigm in *The Decline and Fall*: internal weakness invites calamities for which the remedies are themselves harmful. In this case, the malign palliative is the Illyrian monarchy established by Diocletian. It contained the barbarian threat, but in return it exacted a heavy toll on the manners of the Romans:

From the time of Augustus to that of Diocletian, the Roman princes, conversing in a familiar manner among their fellow-citizens, were saluted only with the same respect that was usually paid to senators and magistrates. Their principal distinction was the Imperial or military robe of purple; whilst the senatorial garment was marked by a broad, and the equestrian by a narrow, band or stripe of the same honourable colour. The pride, or rather the policy, of Diocletian, engaged that artful prince to introduce the stately magnificence of the court of Persia. He ventured to assume the diadem, an ornament detested by the Romans as the odious ensign of royalty, and the use of which had been considered as the most desperate act of the madness of Caligula. It was no more than a broad white fillet set with pearls, which encircled the emperor's head. The sumptuous robes of Diocletian and his successors were of silk and gold; and it is remarked with indignation, that even their shoes were studded with the most precious gems. The access to their sacred person was every day rendered more difficult, by the institution of new forms and ceremonies. The avenues of the palace were strictly guarded by the various *schools*, as they began to be called, of domestic officers. The interior apartments were intrusted to the jealous vigilance of the eunuchs; the increase of whose numbers and influence was the most infallible symptom of the progress of despotism. When a subject was at length admitted to the Imperial presence, he was obliged, whatever might be his rank, to fall prostrate on the ground, and to adore, according to the eastern fashion, the divinity of his lord and master. Diocletian was a man of sense, who, in the course of private as well as public life, had formed a just estimate both of himself and of mankind: nor is it easy to conceive, that in substituting the manners of Persia to those of Rome, he was seriously actuated by so mean a principle as that of vanity. He flattered himself, that an ostentation of splendour and luxury would subdue the imagination of the multitude; that the monarch would be less exposed to the rude licence of the people and the soldiers, as his person was secluded from the public view; and that habits of submission would insensibly be productive of sentiments of veneration. Like the modesty affected by Augustus, the state maintained by Diocletian was a theatrical representation; but it must be confessed, that of the two comedies, the former was of a much more liberal and manly character than the latter. It was the aim of the one to disguise, and the object of the other to display, the unbounded power which the emperors possessed over the Roman world.

Ostentation was the first principle of the new system instituted by

Diocletian. The second was division. He divided the empire, the provinces, and every branch of the civil as well as military administration. He multiplied the wheels of the machine of government, and rendered its operations less rapid but more secure. Whatever advantages, and whatever defects might attend these innovations, they must be ascribed in a very great degree to the first inventor; but as the new frame of policy was gradually improved and completed by the succeeding princes, it will be more satisfactory to delay the consideration of it till the season of its full maturity and perfection. Reserving, therefore, for the reign of Constantine a more exact picture of the new empire, we shall content ourselves with describing the principal and decisive outline, as it was traced by the hand of Diocletian. He had associated three colleagues in the exercise of the supreme power; and as he was convinced that the abilities of a single man were inadequate to the public defence, he considered the joint administration of four princes not as a temporary expedient, but as a fundamental law of the constitution. It was his intention, that the two elder princes should be distinguished by the use of the diadem, and the title of *Augusti*: that, as affection or esteem might direct their choice, they should regularly call to their assistance two subordinate colleagues; and that the *Cæsars*, rising in their turn to the first rank, should supply an uninterrupted succession of emperors. The empire was divided into four parts. The East and Italy were the most honourable, the Danube and the Rhine the most laborious stations. The former claimed the presence of the *Augusti*, the latter were intrusted to the administration of the *Cæsars*. The strength of the legions was in the hands of the four partners of sovereignty, and the despair of successively vanquishing four formidable rivals, might intimidate the ambition of an aspiring general. In their civil government, the emperors were supposed to exercise the undivided power of the monarch, and their edicts, inscribed with their joint names, were received in all the provinces, as promulgated by their mutual councils and authority. Notwithstanding these precautions, the political union of the Roman world was gradually dissolved, and a principle of division was introduced, which, in the course of a few years, occasioned the perpetual separation of the eastern and western empires. (*DF*, i. 388–90)

As Gibbon indicates, it was with the reign of Constantine that the system of Diocletian attained (for either good or ill) its 'full maturity and perfection'. At the end of chapter XIV the narrative of *The Decline and Fall* deposits us on the threshold of that reign, to consider the rise and growth of the new faith which Constantine would eventually introduce as the established religion of the empire.

CHAPTER XV

The Progress of the Christian Religion, and the Sentiments, Manners, Numbers, and Condition, of the primitive Christians.

A candid but rational inquiry into the progress and establishment of Christianity, may be considered as a very essential part of the history of the Roman empire. While that great body was invaded *Importance of the inquiry.* by open violence, or undermined by slow decay, a pure and humble religion gently insinuated itself into the minds of men, grew up in silence and obscurity, derived new vigour from opposition, and finally erected the triumphant banner of the cross on the ruins of the Capitol. Nor was the influence of Christianity confined to the period or to the limits of the Roman empire. After a revolution of thirteen or fourteen centuries, that religion is still professed by the nations of Europe, the most distinguished portion of human kind in arts and learning as well as in arms. By the industry and zeal of the Europeans, it has been widely diffused to the most distant shores of Asia and Africa; and by the means of their colonies has been firmly established from Canada to Chili, in a world unknown to the ancients.

But this inquiry, however useful or entertaining, is attended with two peculiar difficulties. The scanty and suspicious materials *Its difficulties.* of ecclesiastical history seldom enable us to dispel the dark cloud that hangs over the first age of the church. The great law of impartiality too often obliges us to reveal the imperfections of the uninspired teachers and believers of the gospel; and, to a careless observer, *their* faults may seem to cast a shade on the faith which they professed. But the scandal of the pious Christian, and the fallacious triumph of the Infidel, should cease as soon as they recollect not only *by whom*, but likewise *to whom*, the Divine Revelation was given. The theologian may indulge the pleasing task of describing Religion as she descended from Heaven, arrayed in her native purity. A more melancholy duty is imposed on the historian. He must discover the inevitable mixture of error and corruption, which she contracted in a long residence upon earth, among a weak and degenerate race of beings.

Five causes of the growth of Christianity.

Our curiosity is naturally prompted to inquire by what means the Christian faith obtained so remarkable a victory over the established religions of the earth. To this inquiry, an obvious but satisfactory answer may be returned; that it was owing to the convincing evidence of the doctrine itself, and to the ruling providence of its great Author. But as truth and reason seldom find so favourable a reception in the world, and as the wisdom of Providence frequently condescends to use the passions of the human heart, and the general circumstances of mankind, as instruments to execute its purpose; we may still be permitted, though with becoming submission, to ask, not indeed what were the first, but what were the secondary causes of the rapid growth of the Christian church. It will, perhaps, appear, that it was most effectually favoured and assisted by the five following causes: I. The inflexible, and, if we may use the expression, the intolerant zeal of the Christians, derived, it is true, from the Jewish religion, but purified from the narrow and unsocial spirit, which, instead of inviting, had deterred the Gentiles from embracing the law of Moses. II. The doctrine of a future life, improved by every additional circumstance which could give weight and efficacy to that important truth. III. The miraculous powers ascribed to the primitive church. IV. The pure and austere morals of the Christians. V. The union and discipline of the Christian republic, which gradually formed an independent and increasing state in the heart of the Roman empire.

THE FIRST CAUSE. Zeal of the Jews.

I. We have already described the religious harmony of the ancient world, and the facility with which the most different and even hostile nations embraced, or at least respected, each other's superstitions. A single people refused to join in the common intercourse of mankind. The Jews, who, under the Assyrian and Persian monarchies, had languished for many ages the most despised portion of their slaves,[1] emerged from obscurity under the successors of Alexander; and as they multiplied to a surprising degree in the East, and afterwards in the West, they soon excited the curiosity and wonder of other nations.[2] The sullen obstinacy with which they maintained their

---

1. Dum Assyrios penes, Medosque, et Persas Oriens fuit, despectissima pars servientium. Tacit. Hist. v. 8. Herodotus, who visited Asia whilst it obeyed the last of those empires, slightly mentions the Syrians of Palestine, who, according to their own confession, had received from Egypt the rite of circumcision. See l. ii.c. 104.

2. Diodorus Siculus, l. xl. Dion Cassius, l. xxxvii. p. 121. Tacit. Hist. v. 1–9. Justin, xxxvi. 2, 3.

peculiar rites and unsocial manners, seemed to mark them out a distinct species of men, who boldly professed, or who faintly disguised, their implacable hatred to the rest of human-kind.[3] Neither the violence of Antiochus, nor the arts of Herod, nor the example of the circumjacent nations, could ever persuade the Jews to associate with the institutions of Moses the elegant mythology of the Greeks.[4] According to the maxims of universal toleration, the Romans protected a superstition which they despised.[5] The polite Augustus condescended to give orders, that sacrifices should be offered for his prosperity in the temple of Jerusalem;[6] while the meanest of the posterity of Abraham, who should have paid the same homage to the Jupiter of the Capitol, would have been an object of abhorrence to himself and to his brethren. But the moderation of the conquerors was insufficient to appease the jealous prejudices of their subjects, who were alarmed and scandalized at the ensigns of paganism, which necessarily introduced themselves into a Roman province.[7] The mad attempt of Caligula to place his own statue in the temple of Jerusalem, was defeated by the unanimous resolution of a people who dreaded death much less than such an idolatrous profanation.[8] Their attachment to the law of Moses was equal to their detestation of foreign religions. The current of zeal and devotion, as it was contracted into a narrow channel, ran with the strength, and sometimes with the fury, of a torrent.

[3.]
Tradidit arcano quæcunque volumine Moses,

Non monstrare vias eadem nisi sacra colenti,

Quæsitos ad fontes solos deducere verpas.

The letter of this law is not to be found in the present volume of Moses. But the wise, the humane Maimonides openly teaches, that if an idolater fall into the water, a Jew ought not to save him from instant death. See Basnage, Histoire des Juifs, l. vi. c. 28.

[4.] A Jewish sect, which indulged themselves in a sort of occasional conformity, derived from Herod, by whose example and authority they had been seduced, the name of Herodians. But their numbers were so inconsiderable, and their duration so short, that Josephus has not thought them worthy of his notice.

See Prideaux's Connection, vol. ii. p. 285.

[5.] Cicero pro Flacco, c. 28.

[6.] Philo de Legatione. Augustus left a foundation for a perpetual sacrifice. Yet he approved of the neglect which his grandson Caius expressed towards the temple of Jerusalem. See Sueton. in August. c. 93. and Casaubon's notes on that passage.

[7.] See, in particular, Joseph. Antiquitat. xvii. 6. xviii. 3. and de Bel. Judaic. i. 33. and ii. 9. Edit. Havercamp.

[8.] Jussi a Caio Cæsare, effigiem ejus in templo locare arma potius sumpsere. Tacit. Hist. v. 9. Philo and Josephus gave a very circumstantial, but a very rhetorical, account of this transaction, which exceedingly perplexed the governor of Syria. At the first mention of this idolatrous proposal, King Agrippa fainted away; and did not recover his senses till the third day.

Its gradual increase.

This inflexible perseverance, which appeared so odious or so ridiculous to the ancient world, assumes a more awful character, since Providence has deigned to reveal to us the mysterious history of the chosen people. But the devout and even scrupulous attachment to the Mosaic religion, so conspicuous among the Jews who lived under the second temple, becomes still more surprising, if it is compared with the stubborn incredulity of their forefathers. When the law was given in thunder from Mount Sinai; when the tides of the ocean, and the course of the planets were suspended for the convenience of the Israelites; and when temporal rewards and punishments were the immediate consequences of their piety or disobedience, they perpetually relapsed into rebellion against the visible majesty of their Divine King, placed the idols of the nations in the sanctuary of Jehovah, and imitated every fantastic ceremony that was practised in the tents of the Arabs, or in the cities of Phœnicia.[9] As the protection of Heaven was deservedly withdrawn from the ungrateful race, their faith acquired a proportionable degree of vigour and purity. The contemporaries of Moses and Joshua had beheld with careless indifference the most amazing miracles. Under the pressure of every calamity, the belief of those miracles has preserved the Jews of a later period from the universal contagion of idolatry; and in contradiction to every known principle of the human mind, that singular people seems to have yielded a stronger and more ready assent to the traditions of their remote ancestors, than to the evidence of their own senses.[10]

Their religion better suited to defence than to conquest.

The Jewish religion was admirably fitted for defence, but it was never designed for conquest; and it seems probable that the number of proselytes was never much superior to that of apostates. The divine promises were originally made, and the distinguishing rite of circumcision was enjoined to a single family. When the posterity of Abraham had multiplied like the sands of the sea, the Deity, from whose mouth they received a system of laws and ceremonies, declared himself the proper and as it were the national God

---

9. For the enumeration of the Syrian and Arabian deities, it may be observed, that Milton has comprised in one hundred and thirty very beautiful lines, the two large and learned syntagmas, which Selden had composed on that abstruse subject.

10. "How long will this people provoke me? and how long will it be ere they *believe* me, for all the *signs* which I have shewn among them?" (Numbers xiv. 11.) It would be easy, but it would be unbecoming, to justify the complaint of the Deity from the whole tenor of the Mosaic history.

of Israel; and with the most jealous care separated his favourite people from the rest of mankind. The conquest of the land of Canaan was accompanied with so many wonderful and with so many bloody circumstances, that the victorious Jews were left in a state of irreconcilable hostility with all their neighbours. They had been commanded to extirpate some of the most idolatrous tribes, and the execution of the Divine will had seldom been retarded by the weakness of humanity. With the other nations they were forbidden to contract any marriages or alliances, and the prohibition of receiving them into the congregation, which in some cases was perpetual, almost always extended to the third, to the seventh, or even to the tenth generation. The obligation of preaching to the Gentiles the faith of Moses, had never been inculcated as a precept of the law, nor were the Jews inclined to impose it on themselves as a voluntary duty. In the admission of new citizens, that unsocial people was actuated by the selfish vanity of the Greeks, rather than by the generous policy of Rome. The descendants of Abraham were flattered by the opinion, that they alone were the heirs of the covenant, and they were apprehensive of diminishing the value of their inheritance, by sharing it too easily with the strangers of the earth. A larger acquaintance with mankind, extended their knowledge without correcting their prejudices; and whenever the God of Israel acquired any new votaries, he was much more indebted to the inconstant humour of polytheism than to the active zeal of his own missionaries.[11] The religion of Moses seems to be instituted for a particular country as well as for a single nation; and if a strict obedience had been paid to the order, that every male, three times in the year, should present himself before the Lord Jehovah, it would have been impossible that the Jews could ever have spread themselves beyond the narrow limits of the promised land.[12] That obstacle was indeed removed by the destruction of the temple of Jerusalem; but the most considerable part of the Jewish religion was involved in its destruction; and the pagans, who had long wondered at the strange report of an empty sanctuary,[13] were at a loss to discover what could be the object,

11. All that relates to the Jewish proselytes has been very ably treated by Basnage, Hist. des Juifs, l. vi. c. 6, 7.

12. See Exod. xxiv. 23. Deut. xvi. 16. the commentators, and a very sensible note in the Universal History, vol. i. p. 603. edit. fol.

13. When Pompey, using or abusing the right of conquest, entered into the Holy of Holies, it was observed with amazement, "Nullâ intus Deûm effigie, vacuam sedem et inania arcana." Tacit. Hist. v. 9. It was a popular saying, with regard to the Jews,

Nil præter nubes et cœli numen adorant.

or what could be the instruments, of a worship which was destitute of temples and of altars, of priests and of sacrifices. Yet even in their fallen state, the Jews, still asserting their lofty and exclusive privileges, shunned, instead of courting, the society of strangers. They still insisted with inflexible rigour on those parts of the law which it was in their power to practise. Their peculiar distinctions of days, of meats, and a variety of trivial though burdensome observances, were so many objects of disgust and aversion for the other nations, to whose habits and prejudices they were diametrically opposite. The painful and even dangerous rite of circumcision was alone capable of repelling a willing proselyte from the door of the synagogue.[14]

More liberal zeal of Christianity.   Under these circumstances, Christianity offered itself to the world, armed with the strength of the Mosaic law, and delivered from the weight of its fetters. An exclusive zeal for the truth of religion, and the unity of God, was as carefully inculcated in the new as in the ancient system: and whatever was now revealed to mankind concerning the nature and designs of the Supreme Being, was fitted to increase their reverence for that mysterious doctrine. The divine authority of Moses and the prophets was admitted, and even established, as the firmest basis of Christianity. From the beginning of the world, an uninterrupted series of predictions had announced and prepared the long expected coming of the Messiah, who, in compliance with the gross apprehensions of the Jews, had been more frequently represented under the character of a King and Conqueror, than under that of a Prophet, a Martyr, and the Son of God. By his expiatory sacrifice, the imperfect sacrifices of the temple were at once consummated and abolished. The ceremonial law, which consisted only of types and figures, was succeeded by a pure and spiritual worship, equally adapted to all climates as well as to every condition of mankind; and to the initiation of blood, was substituted a more harmless initiation of water. The promise of divine favour, instead of being partially confined to the posterity of Abraham, was universally proposed to the freeman and the slave, to the Greek and to the barbarian, to the Jew and to the Gentile. Every privilege that could raise the proselyte from earth to Heaven, that could exalt his devotion, secure his happiness, or even gratify that secret pride, which, under the semblance of devotion, insinuates itself into the human heart, was still reserved for the members of the Christian church;

14. A second kind of circumcision was inflicted on a Samaritan or Egyptian proselyte. The sullen indifference of the Talmudists, with respect to the conversion of strangers, may be seen in Basnage, Histoire des Juifs, l. vi. c. 6.

but at the same time all mankind was permitted, and even solicited, to accept the glorious distinction, which was not only proffered as a favour, but imposed as an obligation. It became the most sacred duty of a new convert to diffuse among his friends and relations the inestimable blessing which he had received, and to warn them against a refusal that would be severely punished as a criminal disobedience to the will of a benevolent but all-powerful deity.

The enfranchisement of the church from the bonds of the synagogue, was a work however of some time and of some difficulty. The Jewish converts, who acknowledged Jesus in the character of the Messiah foretold by their ancient oracles, *Obstinacy and reasons of the believing Jews.* respected him as a prophetic teacher of virtue and religion; but they obstinately adhered to the ceremonies of their ancestors, and were desirous of imposing them on the Gentiles, who continually augmented the number of believers. These Judaising Christians seem to have argued with some degree of plausibility from the divine origin of the Mosaic law, and from the immutable perfections of its great Author. They affirmed, *that* if the Being, who is the same through all eternity, had designed to abolish those sacred rites which had served to distinguish his chosen people, the repeal of them would have been no less clear and solemn than their first promulgation: *that*, instead of those frequent declarations, which either suppose or assert the perpetuity of the Mosaic religion, it would have been represented as a provisionary scheme intended to last only till the coming of the Messiah, who should instruct mankind in a more perfect mode of faith and of worship:[15] *that* the Messiah himself, and his disciples who conversed with him on earth, instead of authorizing by their example the most minute observances of the Mosaic law,[16] would have published to the world the abolition of those useless and obsolete ceremonies, without suffering Christianity to remain during so many years obscurely confounded among the sects of the Jewish church. Arguments like these appear to have been used in the defence of the expiring cause of the Mosaic law; but the industry

15. These arguments were urged with great ingenuity by the Jew Orobio, and refuted with equal ingenuity and candour by the Christian Limborch. See the Amica Collatio (it well deserves that name), or account of the dispute between them.

16. Jesus . . . circumcisus erat; cibis utebatur Judaicis; vestitû simili; purgatos scabie mitte-

bat ad sacerdotes; Paschata et alios dies festos religiose observabat: Si quos sanavit sabatho, ostendit non tantum ex lege, sed et exceptis sententiis talia opera sabatho non interdicta. Grotius de Veritate Religionis Christianæ, l. v. c. 7. A little afterwards (c. 12.), he expatiates on the condescension of the apostles.

of our learned divines has abundantly explained the ambiguous language of the Old Testament, and the ambiguous conduct of the apostolic teachers. It was proper gradually to unfold the system of the Gospel, and to pronounce, with the utmost caution and tenderness, a sentence of condemnation so repugnant to the inclination and prejudices of the believing Jews.

The Nazarene church of Jerusalem. The history of the church of Jerusalem affords a lively proof of the necessity of those precautions, and of the deep impression which the Jewish religion had made on the minds of its sectaries. The first fifteen bishops of Jerusalem were all circumcised Jews; and the congregation over which they presided, united the law of Moses with the doctrine of Christ.[17] It was natural that the primitive tradition of a church which was founded only forty days after the death of Christ, and was governed almost as many years under the immediate inspection of his apostles, should be received as the standard of orthodoxy.[18] The distant churches very frequently appealed to the authority of their venerable Parent, and relieved her distresses by a liberal contribution of alms. But when numerous and opulent societies were established in the great cities of the empire, in Antioch, Alexandria, Ephesus, Corinth, and Rome, the reverence which Jerusalem had inspired to all the Christian colonies insensibly diminished. The Jewish converts, or, as they were afterwards called, the Nazarenes, who had laid the foundations of the church, soon found themselves overwhelmed by the increasing multitudes, that from all the various religions of polytheism inlisted under the banner of Christ: and the Gentiles, who, with the approbation of their peculiar apostle, had rejected the intolerable weight of Mosaic ceremonies, at length refused to their more scrupulous brethren the same toleration which at first they had humbly solicited for their own practice. The ruin of the temple, of the city, and of the public religion of the Jews, was severely felt by the Nazarenes; as in their manners, though not in their faith, they maintained so intimate a connexion with their impious countrymen, whose misfortunes were attributed by the Pagans to the contempt, and more justly ascribed by the Christians to the wrath, of the Supreme Deity. The Nazarenes retired from

17. Pæne omnes Christum Deum sub legis observatione credebant. Sulpicius Severus, ii. 31. See Eusebius, Hist. Ecclesiast. l. iv. c. 5.
18. Mosheim de Rebus Christianis ante Constantinum Magnum, p. 153. In this masterly performance, which I shall often have occasion to quote, he enters much more fully into the state of the primitive church, than he has an opportunity of doing in his General History.

the ruins of Jerusalem to the little town of Pella beyond the Jordan, where that ancient church languished above sixty years in solitude and obscurity.[19] They still enjoyed the comfort of making frequent and devout visits to the *Holy City*, and the hope of being one day restored to those seats which both nature and religion taught them to love as well as to revere. But at length, under the reign of Hadrian, the desperate fanaticism of the Jews filled up the measure of their calamities; and the Romans, exasperated by their repeated rebellions, exercised the rights of victory with unusual rigour. The emperor founded, under the name of Ælia Capitolina, a new city on Mount Sion,[20] to which he gave the privileges of a colony; and denouncing the severest penalties against any of the Jewish people who should dare to approach its precincts, he fixed a vigilant garrison of a Roman cohort to enforce the execution of his orders. The Nazarenes had only one way left to escape the common proscription, and the force of truth was on this occasion assisted by the influence of temporal advantages. They elected Marcus for their bishop, a prelate of the race of the Gentiles, and most probably a native either of Italy or of some of the Latin provinces. At his persuasion, the most considerable part of the congregation renounced the Mosaic law, in the practice of which they had persevered above a century. By this sacrifice of their habits and prejudices, they purchased a free admission into the colony of Hadrian, and more firmly cemented their union with the Catholic church.[21]

When the name and honours of the church of Jerusalem had been restored to Mount Sion, the crimes of heresy and schism   *The Ebionites.* were imputed to the obscure remnant of the Nazarenes, which refused to accompany their Latin bishop. They still preserved their former habitation of Pella, spread themselves into the villages adjacent to Damascus, and formed an inconsiderable church in the city of Bœrea, or, as it is now

---

19. Eusebius, l. iii. c. 5. Le Clerc, Hist. Ecclesiast. p. 605. During this occasional absence, the bishop and church of Pella still retained the title of Jerusalem. In the same manner, the Roman pontiffs resided seventy years at Avignon; and the patriarchs of Alexandria have long since transferred their episcopal seat to Cairo.

20. Dion Cassius, l. lxix. The exile of the Jewish nation from Jerusalem is attested by Aristo of Pella (apud Euseb. l. iv. c. 6.), and

is mentioned by several ecclesiastical writers; though some of them too hastily extend this interdiction to the whole country of Palestine.

21. Eusebius, l. iv. c. 6. Sulpicius Severus, ii. 31. By comparing their unsatisfactory accounts, Mosheim (p. 327, &c.) has drawn out a very distinct representation of the circumstances and motives of this revolution.

called, of Aleppo, in Syria.[22] The name of Nazarenes was deemed too honourable for those Christian Jews, and they soon received from the supposed poverty of their understanding, as well as of their condition, the contemptuous epithet of Ebionites.[23] In a few years after the return of the church of Jerusalem, it became a matter of doubt and controversy, whether a man who sincerely acknowledged Jesus as the Messiah, but who still continued to observe the law of Moses, could possibly hope for salvation. The humane temper of Justin Martyr inclined him to answer this question in the affirmative; and though he expressed himself with the most guarded diffidence, he ventured to determine in favour of such an imperfect Christian, if he were content to practise the Mosaic ceremonies, without pretending to assert their general use or necessity. But when Justin was pressed to declare the sentiment of the church, he confessed that there were very many among the orthodox Christians, who not only excluded their Judaising brethren from the hope of salvation, but who declined any intercourse with them in the common offices of friendship, hospitality, and social life.[24] The more rigorous opinion prevailed, as it was natural to expect, over the milder; and an eternal bar of separation was fixed between the disciples of Moses and those of Christ. The unfortunate Ebionites, rejected from one religion as apostates, and from the other as heretics, found themselves compelled to assume a more decided character; and although some traces of that obsolete sect may be discovered as late as the fourth century, they insensibly melted away either into the church or the synagogue.[25]

---

22. Le Clerc (Hist. Ecclesiast. p. 477. 535.) seems to have collected from Eusebius, Jerome, Epiphanius, and other writers, all the principal circumstances that relate to the Nazarenes or Ebionites. The nature of their opinions soon divided them into a stricter and a milder sect; and there is some reason to conjecture, that the family of Jesus Christ remained members, at least, of the latter and more moderate party.

23. Some writers have been pleased to create an Ebion, the imaginary author of their sect and name. But we can more safely rely on the learned Eusebius than on the vehement Tertullian, or the credulous Epiphanius. According to Le Clerc, the Hebrew word

Ebjonim may be translated into Latin by that of *Pauperes*. See Hist. Ecclesiast. p. 477.

24. See the very curious Dialogue of Justin Martyr with the Jew Tryphon. The conference between them was held at Ephesus, in the reign of Antoninus Pius, and about twenty years after the return of the church of Pella to Jerusalem. For this date consult the accurate note of Tillemont, Memoires Ecclesiastiques, tom. ii. p. 511.

25. Of all the systems of Christianity, that of Abyssinia is the only one which still adheres to the Mosaic rites (Geddes's Church History of Æthiopia, and Dissertations de le Grand sur la Relation du P. Lobo). The eunuch of the queen Candace might suggest some

While the orthodox church preserved a just medium between *The Gnostics.* excessive veneration and improper contempt for the law of Moses, the various heretics deviated into equal but opposite extremes of error and extravagance. From the acknowledged truth of the Jewish religion, the Ebionites had concluded that it could never be abolished. From its supposed imperfections the Gnostics as hastily inferred that it never was instituted by the wisdom of the Deity. There are some objections against the authority of Moses and the prophets, which too readily present themselves to the sceptical mind; though they can only be derived from our ignorance of remote antiquity, and from our incapacity to form an adequate judgment of the divine œconomy. These objections were eagerly embraced and as petulantly urged by the vain science of the Gnostics.[26] As those heretics were, for the most part, averse to the pleasures of sense, they morosely arraigned the polygamy of the patriarchs, the galantries of David, and the seraglio of Solomon. The conquest of the land of Canaan, and the extirpation of the unsuspecting natives, they were at a loss how to reconcile with the common notions of humanity and justice. But when they recollected the sanguinary list of murders, of executions, and of massacres, which stain almost every page of the Jewish annals, they acknowledged that the barbarians of Palestine had exercised as much compassion towards their idolatrous enemies, as they had ever shewn to their friends or countrymen.[27] Passing from the sectaries of the law to the law itself, they asserted that it was impossible that a religion which consisted only of bloody sacrifices and trifling ceremonies, and whose rewards as well as punishments were all of a carnal and temporal nature, could inspire the love of virtue, or restrain the impetuosity of passion. The Mosaic account of the creation and fall of man was treated with profane derision by the Gnostics, who would not listen with patience to the repose of the Deity after six days labour, to the

suspicions; but as we are assured (Socrates, i. 19. Sozomen, ii. 24. Ludolphus, p. 281.), that the Æthiopians were not converted till the fourth century; it is more reasonable to believe, that they respected the Sabbath, and distinguished the forbidden meats, in imitation of the Jews, who, in a very early period, were seated on both sides of the Red Sea. Circumcision had been practised by the most ancient Æthiopians, from motives of health and cleanliness, which seem to be explained

in the Recherches Philosophiques sur les Americains, tom. ii. p. 117.

26. Beausobre, Histoire du Manicheisme, l. i. c. 3. has stated their objections, particularly those of Faustus, the adversary of Augustin, with the most learned impartiality.

27. Apud ipsos fides obstinata, misericordia in promptû: adversus omnes alios hostile odium. Tacit. Hist. v. 4. Surely Tacitus had seen the Jews with too favourable an eye. The perusal of Josephus must have destroyed the antithesis.

rib of Adam, the garden of Eden, the trees of life and of knowledge, the speaking serpent, the forbidden fruit, and the condemnation pronounced against human kind for the venial offence of their first progenitors.[28] The God of Israel was impiously represented by the Gnostics, as a being liable to passion and to error, capricious in his favour, implacable in his resentment, meanly jealous of his superstitious worship, and confining his partial providence to a single people, and to this transitory life. In such a character they could discover none of the features of the wise and omnipotent father of the universe.[29] They allowed that the religion of the Jews was somewhat less criminal than the idolatry of the Gentiles; but it was their fundamental doctrine, that the Christ whom they adored as the first and brightest emanation of the Deity, appeared upon earth to rescue mankind from their various errors, and to reveal a *new* system of truth and perfection. The most learned of the fathers, by a very singular condescension, have imprudently admitted the sophistry of the Gnostics. Acknowledging that the literal sense is repugnant to every principle of faith as well as reason, they deem themselves secure and invulnerable behind the ample veil of allegory, which they carefully spread over every tender part of the Mosaic dispensation.[30]

Their sects, progress, and influence.   It has been remarked with more ingenuity than truth, that the virgin purity of the church was never violated by schism or heresy before the reign of Trajan or Hadrian, about one hundred years after the death of Christ.[31] We may observe with much more propriety, that, during that period, the disciples of the Messiah were indulged in a freer latitude both of faith and practice, than has ever been allowed in succeeding ages. As the terms of communion were insensibly narrowed, and the spiritual authority of the prevailing party was exercised with increasing severity, many of its most respectable adherents, who were called upon to renounce, were provoked to assert their private opinions, to pursue the consequences of their mistaken principles, and openly to erect the standard of rebellion against the unity of the church. The Gnostics were distinguished as the most polite, the most learned, and the most

---

28. Dr. Burnet (Archæologia, l. ii. c. 7.) has discussed the first chapters of Genesis with too much wit and freedom.

29. The milder Gnostics considered Jehovah, the Creator, as a Being of a mixed nature between God and the Dæmon. Others confounded him with the evil principle. Consult the second century of the general history of Mosheim, which gives a very distinct, though concise, account of their strange opinions on this subject.

30. See Beausobre, Hist. du Manicheisme, l. i. c. 4. Origen and St. Augustin were among the Allegorists.

31. Hegesippus, ap. Euseb. l. iii. 32. iv. 22. Clemens Alexandrin. Stromat. vii. 17.

wealthy of the Christian name, and that general appellation which expressed a superiority of knowledge, was either assumed by their own pride, or ironically bestowed by the envy of their adversaries. They were almost without exception of the race of the Gentiles, and their principal founders seem to have been natives of Syria or Egypt, where the warmth of the climate disposes both the mind and the body to indolent and contemplative devotion. The Gnostics blended with the faith of Christ many sublime but obscure tenets, which they derived from oriental philosophy, and even from the religion of Zoroaster, concerning the eternity of matter, the existence of two principles, and the mysterious hierarchy of the invisible world.[32] As soon as they launched out into that vast abyss, they delivered themselves to the guidance of a disordered imagination; and as the paths of error are various and infinite, the Gnostics were imperceptibly divided into more than fifty particular sects,[33] of whom the most celebrated appear to have been the Basilidians, the Valentinians, the Marcionites, and, in a still later period, the Manichæans. Each of these sects could boast of its bishops and congregations, of its doctors and martyrs,[34] and, instead of the four gospels adopted by the church, the heretics produced a multitude of histories, in which the actions and discourses of Christ and of his apostles were adapted to their respective tenets.[35] The success of the Gnostics was rapid and extensive.[36] They covered Asia and Egypt, established themselves

32. In the account of the Gnostics of the second and third centuries, Mosheim is ingenious and candid; Le Clerc dull, but exact; Beausobre almost always an apologist; and it is much to be feared, that the primitive fathers are very frequently calumniators.

33. See the catalogues of Irenæus and Epiphanius. It must indeed be allowed, that those writers were inclined to multiply the number of sects which opposed the *unity* of the church.

34. Eusebius, l. iv. c. 15. Sozomen. l. ii. c. 32. See in Bayle, in the article of *Marcion*, a curious detail of a dispute on that subject. It should seem that some of the Gnostics (the Basilidians) declined, and even refused, the honour of martyrdom. Their reasons were singular and abstruse. See Mosheim, p. 359.

35. See a very remarkable passage of Origen (Proem. ad Lucan.). That indefatigable writer, who had consumed his life in the study of the scriptures, relies for their authenticity on the inspired authority of the church. It was impossible that the Gnostics could receive our present gospels, many parts of which (particularly in the resurrection of Christ) are directly, and as it might seem designedly, pointed against their favourite tenets. It is therefore somewhat singular that Ignatius (Epist. ad Smyrn. Patr. Apostol. tom. ii. p. 34.) should chuse to employ a vague and doubtful tradition, instead of quoting the certain testimony of the evangelists.

36. Faciunt favos et vespæ; faciunt ecclesias et Marcionitæ, is the strong expression of Tertullian, which I am obliged to quote from memory. In the time of Epiphanius (advers. Hæreses, p. 302.) the Marcionites were very numerous in Italy, Syria, Egypt, Arabia, and Persia.

in Rome, and sometimes penetrated into the provinces of the West. For the most part they arose in the second century, flourished during the third, and were suppressed in the fourth or fifth, by the prevalence of more fashionable controversies, and by the superior ascendant of the reigning power. Though they constantly disturbed the peace, and frequently disgraced the name, of religion, they contributed to assist rather than to retard the progress of Christianity. The Gentile converts, whose strongest objections and prejudices were directed against the law of Moses, could find admission into many Christian societies, which required not from their untutored mind any belief of an antecedent revelation. Their faith was insensibly fortified and enlarged, and the church was ultimately benefited by the conquests of its most inveterate enemies.[37]

The dæmons considered as the gods of antiquity.   But whatever difference of opinion might subsist between the Orthodox, the Ebionites, and the Gnostics, concerning the divinity or the obligation of the Mosaic law, they were all equally animated by the same exclusive zeal, and by the same abhorrence for idolatry which had distinguished the Jews from the other nations of the ancient world. The philosopher, who considered the system of polytheism as a composition of human fraud and error, could disguise a smile of contempt under the mask of devotion, without apprehending that either the mockery, or the compliance, would expose him to the resentment of any invisible, or, as he conceived them, imaginary powers. But the established religions of Paganism were seen by the primitive Christians in a much more odious and formidable light. It was the universal sentiment both of the church and of heretics, that the dæmons were the authors, the patrons, and the objects of idolatry.[38] Those rebellious spirits who had been degraded from the rank of angels, and cast down into the infernal pit, were still permitted to roam upon earth, to torment the bodies, and to seduce the minds, of sinful men. The dæmons soon discovered and abused the natural propensity of the human heart towards devotion, and, artfully withdrawing the adoration of mankind from their Creator, they usurped the place and honours of the Supreme Deity. By the success of their malicious contrivances, they at once gratified their own vanity and revenge,

---

37. Augustin is a memorable instance of this gradual progress from reason to faith. He was, during several years, engaged in the Manichæan sect.

38. The unanimous sentiment of the primitive church is very clearly explained by Justin Martyr. Apolog. Major, by Athenagoras Legat. c. 22, &c. and by Lactantius, Institut. Divin. ii. 14-19.

and obtained the only comfort of which they were yet susceptible, the hope of involving the human species in the participation of their guilt and misery. It was confessed, or at least it was imagined, that they had distributed among themselves the most important characters of polytheism, one dæmon assuming the name and attributes of Jupiter, another of Æsculapius, a third of Venus, and a fourth perhaps of Apollo;[39] and that, by the advantage of their long experience and aërial nature, they were enabled to execute, with sufficient skill and dignity, the parts which they had undertaken. They lurked in the temples, instituted festivals and sacrifices, invented fables, pronounced oracles, and were frequently allowed to perform miracles. The Christians, who, by the interposition of evil spirits, could so readily explain every præternatural appearance, were disposed and even desirous to admit the most extravagant fictions of the Pagan mythology. But the belief of the Christian was accompanied with horror. The most trifling mark of respect to the national worship he considered as a direct homage yielded to the dæmon, and as an act of rebellion against the majesty of God.

In consequence of this opinion, it was the first but arduous duty of a Christian to preserve himself pure and undefiled by the practice of idolatry. The religion of the nations was not merely a speculative doctrine professed in the schools or preached in the temples. *Abhorrence of the Christians for idolatry.* The innumerable deities and rites of polytheism were closely interwoven with every circumstance of business or pleasure, of public or of private life; and it seemed impossible to escape the observance of them, without, at the same time, renouncing the commerce of mankind, and all the offices and amusements of society.[40] The important transactions of peace and war were prepared or concluded by solemn sacrifices, in which the magistrate, the senator, and the soldier, were obliged to preside or to participate.[41] *Ceremonies.* The public spectacles were an essential part of the cheerful devotion of the Pagans, and the gods were supposed to accept, as the most grateful offering, the games that the

---

39. Tertullian (Apolog. c. 23.) alleges the confession of the Dæmons themselves as often as they were tormented by the Christian exorcists.
40. Tertullian has written a most severe treatise against idolatry, to caution his brethren against the hourly danger of incurring that guilt.

Recogita sylvam, et quantæ latitant spinæ. De Coronâ Militis, c. 10.
41. The Roman senate was always held in a temple or consecrated place (Aulus Gellius, xiv. 7.). Before they entered on business, every senator dropt some wine and frankincense on the altar. Sueton. in August. c. 35.

prince and people celebrated in honour of their peculiar festivals.[42] The Christian, who with pious horror avoided the abomination of the circus or the theatre, found himself encompassed with infernal snares in every convivial entertainment, as often as his friends, invoking the hospitable deities, poured out libations to each other's happiness.[43] When the bride, struggling with well-affected reluctance, was forced in hymenæal pomp over the threshold of her new habitation,[44] or when the sad procession of the dead slowly moved towards the funeral pile;[45] the Christian, on these interesting occasions, was compelled to desert the persons who were the dearest to him, rather than contract the guilt inherent to those impious ceremonies. Every art and every trade that was in the least concerned in the framing or adorning of idols was polluted by the stain of idolatry;[46] a severe sentence, since it devoted to eternal misery the far greater part of the community, which is employed in the exercise of liberal or mechanic professions. If we cast our eyes over the numerous remains of antiquity, we shall perceive, that besides the immediate representations of the Gods, and the holy instruments of their worship, the elegant forms and agreeable fictions consecrated by the imagination of the Greeks, were introduced as the richest ornaments of the houses, the dress, and the furniture, of the Pagans.[47] Even the arts of music and painting, of eloquence and poetry, flowed from the same impure origin. In the style of the fathers, Apollo and the Muses were the organs of the infernal spirit, Homer and Virgil were the most eminent of his servants, and the beautiful mythology which pervades and animates the compositions of their genius, is destined to

Arts.

42. See Tertullian, De Spectaculis. This severe reformer shews no more indulgence to a tragedy of Euripides, than to a combat of gladiators. The dress of the actors particularly offends him. By the use of the lofty buskin, they impiously strive to add a cubit to their stature, c. 23.

43. The ancient practice of concluding the entertainment with libations, may be found in every classic. Socrates and Seneca, in their last moments, made a noble application of this custom. Postquam stagnum calidæ aquæ introiit, respergens proximos servorum, additâ voce, libare se liquorem illum Jovi Liberatori. Tacit. Annal. xv. 64.

44. See the elegant but idolatrous hymn of Catullus, on the nuptials of Manlius and Julia. O Hymen, Hymenæe Iö! Quis huic Deo compararier ausit?

45. The ancient funerals (in those of Misenus and Pallas) are no less accurately described by Virgil, than they are illustrated by his commentator Servius. The pile itself was an altar, the flames were fed with the blood of victims, and all the assistants were sprinkled with lustral water.

46. Tertullian de Idololatria, c. 11.

47. See every part of Montfaucon's Antiquities. Even the reverses of the Greek and Roman coins were frequently of an idolatrous nature. Here indeed the scruples of the Christian were suspended by a stronger passion.

celebrate the glory of the dæmons. Even the common language of Greece and Rome abounded with familiar but impious expressions, which the imprudent Christian might too carelessly utter, or too patiently hear.[48]

The dangerous temptations which on every side lurked in ambush to surprise the unguarded believer, assailed him with redoubled violence on the days of solemn festivals. So artfully were they framed and disposed throughout the year, that superstition always wore the appearance of pleasure, and often of virtue.[49] Some of the most sacred festivals in the Roman ritual were destined to salute the new calends of January with vows of public and private felicity, to indulge the pious remembrance of the dead and living, to ascertain the inviolable bounds of property, to hail, on the return of spring, the genial powers of fecundity, to perpetuate the two memorable æras of Rome, the foundation of the city, and that of the republic, and to restore, during the humane license of the Saturnalia, the primitive equality of mankind. Some idea may be conceived of the abhorrence of the Christians for such impious ceremonies, by the scrupulous delicacy which they displayed on a much less alarming occasion. On days of general festivity, it was the custom of the ancients to adorn their doors with lamps and with branches of laurel, and to crown their heads with a garland of flowers. This innocent and elegant practice might perhaps have been tolerated as a mere civil institution. But it most unluckily happened that the doors were under the protection of the household gods, that the laurel was sacred to the lover of Daphne, and that garlands of flowers, though frequently worn as a symbol either of joy or mourning, had been dedicated in their first origin to the service of superstition. The trembling Christians, who were persuaded in this instance to comply with the fashion of their country, and the commands of the magistrate, laboured under the most gloomy apprehensions, from the reproaches of their own conscience, the censures of the church, and the denunciations of divine vengeance.[50]

Festivals.

---

48. Tertullian de Idololatria, c. 20, 21, 22. If a Pagan friend (on the occasion perhaps of sneezing) used the familiar expression of "Jupiter bless you," the Christian was obliged to protest against the divinity of Jupiter.

49. Consult the most laboured work of Ovid, his imperfect *Fasti*. He finished no more than the first six months of the year. The compilation of Macrobius is called the *Saturnalia*,

but it is only a small part of the first book that bears any relation to the title.

50. Tertullian has composed a defence, or rather panegyric, of the rash action of a Christian soldier, who, by throwing away his crown of laurel, had exposed himself and his brethren to the most imminent danger. By the mention of the *emperors* (Severus and Cara-calla) it is evident, notwithstanding the wishes

Zeal for Christianity.   Such was the anxious diligence which was required to guard the chastity of the gospel from the infectious breath of idolatry. The superstitious observances of public or private rites were carelessly practised, from education and habit, by the followers of the established religion. But as often as they occurred, they afforded the Christians an opportunity of declaring and confirming their zealous opposition. By these frequent protestations their attachment to the faith was continually fortified, and in proportion to the increase of zeal, they combated with the more ardour and success in the holy war, which they had undertaken against the empire of the dæmons.

THE SECOND CAUSE. The doctrine of the immortality of the soul among the philosophers;   II. The writings of Cicero[51] represent in the most lively colours the ignorance, the errors, and the uncertainty of the ancient philosophers with regard to the immortality of the soul. When they are desirous of arming their disciples against the fear of death, they inculcate, as an obvious, though melancholy position, that the fatal stroke of our dissolution releases us from the calamities of life; and that those can no longer suffer who no longer exist. Yet there were a few sages of Greece and Rome who had conceived a more exalted, and, in some respects, a juster idea of human nature; though it must be confessed, that, in the sublime inquiry, their reason had been often guided by their imagination, and that their imagination had been prompted by their vanity. When they viewed with complacency the extent of their own mental powers, when they exercised the various faculties of memory, of fancy, and of judgment, in the most profound speculations, or the most important labours, and when they reflected on the desire of fame, which transported them into future ages, far beyond the bounds of death and of the grave; they were unwilling to confound themselves with the beasts of the field, or to suppose, that a being, for whose dignity they entertained the most sincere admiration, could be limited to a spot of earth, and to a few years of duration. With this favourable prepossession they summoned to their aid the science, or rather the language, of Metaphysics. They soon discovered, that as none

---

of M. de Tillemont, that Tertullian composed his treatise De Coronâ, long before he was engaged in the errors of the Montanists. See Memoires Ecclesiastiques, tom. iii. p. 384. 51. In particular, the first book of the Tusculan Questions, and the treatise De Senectute; and the Somnium Scipionis, contain, in the most beautiful language, every thing that Grecian philosophy, or Roman good sense, could possibly suggest on this dark but important object.

of the properties of matter will apply to the operations of the mind, the human soul must consequently be a substance distinct from the body, pure, simple, and spiritual, incapable of dissolution, and susceptible of a much higher degree of virtue and happiness after the release from its corporeal prison. From these specious and noble principles, the philosophers who trod in the footsteps of Plato, deduced a very unjustifiable conclusion, since they asserted, not only the future immortality, but the past eternity of the human soul, which they were too apt to consider as a portion of the infinite and self-existing spirit, which pervades and sustains the universe.[52] A doctrine thus removed beyond the senses and the experience of mankind, might serve to amuse the leisure of a philosophic mind; or, in the silence of solitude, it might sometimes impart a ray of comfort to desponding virtue; but the faint impression which had been received in the schools, was soon obliterated by the commerce and business of active life. We are sufficiently acquainted with the eminent persons who flourished in the age of Cicero, and of the first Cæsars, with their actions, their characters, and their motives, to be assured that their conduct in this life was never regulated by any serious conviction of the rewards or punishments of a future state. At the bar and in the senate of Rome the ablest orators were not apprehensive of giving offence to their hearers, by exposing that doctrine as an idle and extravagant opinion, which was rejected with contempt by every man of a liberal education and understanding.[53]

Since therefore the most sublime efforts of philosophy can extend no farther than feebly to point out the desire, the hope, or, at most, the probability, of a future state, there is nothing, except a divine revelation, that can ascertain the existence, and describe the condition of the invisible country which is destined *among the Pagans of Greece and Rome;* to receive the souls of men after their separation from the body. But we may perceive several defects inherent to the popular religions of Greece and Rome, which rendered them very unequal to so arduous a task. 1. The general system of their mythology was unsupported by any solid

---

52. The pre-existence of human souls, so far at least as that doctrine is compatible with religion, was adopted by many of the Greek and Latin fathers. See Beausobre, Hist. du Manicheisme, l. vi. c. 4.

53. See Cicero pro Cluent. c. 61. Cæsar ap. Sallust. de Bell. Catilin. c. 50. Juvenal. Satir. ii. 149.

Esse aliquos manes, et subterranea regna,
   .   .   .   .   .

Nec pueri credunt, nisi qui nondum ære lavantur.

proofs; and the wisest among the Pagans had already disclaimed its usurped authority. 2. The description of the infernal regions had been abandoned to the fancy of painters and of poets, who peopled them with so many phantoms and monsters, who dispensed their rewards and punishments with so little equity, that a solemn truth, the most congenial to the human heart, was oppressed and disgraced by the absurd mixture of the wildest fictions.[54] 3. The doctrine of a future state was scarcely considered among the devout polytheists of Greece and Rome as a fundamental article of faith. The providence of the gods, as it related to public communities rather than to private individuals, was principally displayed on the visible theatre of the present world. The petitions which were offered on the altars of Jupiter or Apollo, expressed the anxiety of their worshippers for temporal happiness, and their ignorance or indifference concerning a future life.[55] The important truth of the immortality of the soul was inculcated with more diligence as well as success in India, in Assyria, in Egypt, and in Gaul; and since we cannot attribute such a difference to the superior knowledge

among the barbarians; of the barbarians, we must ascribe it to the influence of an established priesthood, which employed the motives of virtue as the instrument of ambition.[56]

among the Jews; We might naturally expect, that a principle so essential to religion, would have been revealed in the clearest terms to the chosen people of Palestine, and that it might safely have been intrusted to the hereditary priesthood of Aaron. It is incumbent on us to adore the mysterious dispensations of Providence,[57] when we discover, that the doctrine of

---

54. The xith book of the Odyssey gives a very dreary and incoherent account of the infernal shades. Pindar and Virgil have embellished the picture; but even those poets, though more correct than their great model, are guilty of very strange inconsistencies. See Bayle, Responses aux Questions d'un Provincial, part iii. c. 22.

55. See the xvith epistle of the first book of Horace, the xiiith Satire of Juvenal, and the iid Satire of Persius: these popular discourses express the sentiment and language of the multitude.

56. If we confine ourselves to the Gauls, we may observe, that they intrusted, not only their lives, but even their money, to the secur-

ity of another world. Vetus ille mos Gallorum occurrit (says Valerius Maximus, l. ii. c. 6. p. 10.), quos memoria proditur est, pecunias mutuas, quæ his apud inferos redderentur, dare solitos. The same custom is more darkly insinuated by Mela, l. iii. c. 2. It is almost needless to add, that the profits of trade hold a just proportion to the credit of the merchant, and that the Druids derived from their holy profession a character of responsibility, which could scarcely be claimed by any other order of men.

57. The right reverend author of the Divine Legation of Moses assigns a very curious reason for the omission, and most ingeniously retorts it on the unbelievers.

the immortality of the soul is omitted in the law of Moses; it is darkly insinuated by the prophets, and during the long period which elapsed between the Egyptian and the Babylonian servitudes, the hopes as well as fears of the Jews appear to have been confined within the narrow compass of the present life.[58] After Cyrus had permitted the exiled nation to return into the promised land, and after Ezra had restored the ancient records of their religion, two celebrated sects, the Sadducees and the Pharisees, insensibly arose at Jerusalem.[59] The former selected from the more opulent and distinguished ranks of society, were strictly attached to the literal sense of the Mosaic law, and they piously rejected the immortality of the soul, as an opinion that received no countenance from the divine book, which they revered as the only rule of their faith. To the authority of scripture the Pharisees added that of tradition, and they accepted, under the name of traditions, several speculative tenets from the philosophy or religion of the eastern nations. The doctrines of fate or predestination, of angels and spirits, and of a future state of rewards and punishments, were in the number of these new articles of belief; and as the Pharisees, by the austerity of their manners, had drawn into their party the body of the Jewish people, the immortality of the soul became the prevailing sentiment of the synagogue, under the reign of the Asmonæan princes and pontiffs. The temper of the Jews was incapable of contenting itself with such a cold and languid assent as might satisfy the mind of a Polytheist; and as soon as they admitted the idea of a future state, they embraced it with the zeal which has always formed the characteristic of the nation. Their zeal, however, added nothing to its evidence, or even probability: and it was still necessary, that the doctrine of life and immortality, which had been dictated by nature, approved by reason, and received by superstition, should obtain the sanction of divine truth from the authority and example of Christ.

When the promise of eternal happiness was proposed to mankind, on condition of adopting the faith, and of observing the precepts of the gospel, it is no wonder that so advantageous an offer *among the Christians.*

---

58. See Le Clerc (Prolegomena ad Hist. Ecclesiast. sect. 1. c. 8.). His authority seems to carry the greater weight, as he has written a learned and judicious commentary on the books of the Old Testament.

59. Joseph. Antiquitat. l. xiii. c. 10. De Bell. Jud. ii. 8. According to the most natural interpretation of his words, the Sadducees admitted only the Pentateuch; but it has pleased some modern critics to add the prophets to their creed, and to suppose, that they contented themselves with rejecting the traditions of the Pharisees. Dr. Jortin has argued that point in his Remarks on Ecclesiastical History, vol. ii. p. 103.

should have been accepted by great numbers of every religion, of every rank, and of every province in the Roman empire. The ancient Christians were animated by a contempt for their present existence, and by a just confidence of immortality, of which the doubtful and imperfect faith of modern ages cannot give us any adequate notion. In the primitive

Approaching end of the world.

church, the influence of truth was very powerfully strengthened by an opinion, which, however it may deserve respect for its usefulness and antiquity, has not been found agreeable to experience. It was universally believed, that the end of the world, and the kingdom of Heaven, were at hand. The near approach of this wonderful event had been predicted by the apostles; the tradition of it was preserved by their earliest disciples, and those who understood in their literal sense the discourses of Christ himself, were obliged to expect the second and glorious coming of the Son of Man in the clouds, before that generation was totally extinguished, which had beheld his humble condition upon earth, and which might still be witness of the calamities of the Jews under Vespasian or Hadrian. The revolution of seventeen centuries has instructed us not to press too closely the mysterious language of prophecy and revelation; but as long as, for wise purposes, this error was permitted to subsist in the church, it was productive of the most salutary effects on the faith and practice of Christians, who lived in the awful expectation of that moment when the globe itself, and all the various race of mankind, should tremble at the appearance of their divine judge.[60]

Doctrine of the Millennium.

The ancient and popular doctrine of the Millennium was intimately connected with the second coming of Christ. As the works of the creation had been finished in six days, their duration in their present state, according to a tradition which was attributed to the prophet Elijah, was fixed to six thousand years.[61] By the same analogy it was inferred, that this long period of labour and contention, which was now almost elapsed,[62] would be succeeded by a joyful Sabbath of a thousand

60. This expectation was countenanced by the twenty-fourth chapter of St. Matthew, and by the first epistle of St. Paul to the Thessalonians. Erasmus removes the difficulty by the help of allegory and metaphor; and the learned Grotius ventures to insinuate, that, for wise purposes, the pious deception was permitted to take place.

61. See Burnet's Sacred Theory, part iii. c. 5.

This tradition may be traced as high as the author of the Epistle of Barnabas, who wrote in the first century, and who seems to have been half a Jew.

62. The primitive church of Antioch computed almost 6000 years from the creation of the world to the birth of Christ. Africanus, Lactantius, and the Greek church, have reduced that number to 5500, and Eusebius

years; and that Christ, with the triumphant band of the saints and the elect who had escaped death, or who had been miraculously revived, would reign upon earth till the time appointed for the last and general resurrection. So pleasing was this hope to the mind of believers, that the *New Jerusalem*, the seat of this blissful kingdom, was quickly adorned with all the gayest colours of the imagination. A felicity consisting only of pure and spiritual pleasure, would have appeared too refined for its inhabitants, who were still supposed to possess their human nature and senses. A garden of Eden, with the amusements of the pastoral life, was no longer suited to the advanced state of society which prevailed under the Roman empire. A city was therefore erected of gold and precious stones, and a supernatural plenty of corn and wine was bestowed on the adjacent territory; in the free enjoyment of whose spontaneous productions, the happy and benevolent people was never to be restrained by any jealous laws of exclusive property.[63] The assurance of such a Millennium, was carefully inculcated by a succession of fathers from Justin Martyr[64] and Irenæus, who conversed with the immediate disciples of the apostles, down to Lactantius, who was preceptor to the son of Constantine.[65] Though it might not be universally received, it appears to have been the reigning sentiment of the orthodox believers; and it seems so well adapted to the desires and apprehensions of mankind, that it must have contributed in a very considerable degree to the progress of the Christian faith. But when the edifice of the church was almost completed, the temporary support was laid aside. The doctrine of Christ's reign upon earth, was at first treated as a profound allegory, was considered

---

has contented himself with 5200 years. These calculations were formed on the Septuagint, which was universally received during the six first centuries. The authority of the Vulgate and of the Hebrew text has determined the moderns, Protestants as well as Catholics, to prefer a period of about 4000 years; though, in the study of profane antiquity, they often find themselves streightened by those narrow limits.

63. Most of these pictures were borrowed from a misinterpretation of Isaiah, Daniel, and the Apocalypse. One of the grossest images may be found in Irenæus (l. v. p. 455.), the disciple of Papias, who had seen the apostle St. John.

64. See the second dialogue of Justin with Tryphon, and the seventh book of Lactantius. It is unnecessary to allege all the intermediate fathers, as the fact is not disputed. Yet the curious reader may consult Daillè de Usu Patrum, l. ii. c. 4.

65. The testimony of Justin, of his own faith and that of his orthodox brethren, in the doctrine of a Millennium, is delivered in the clearest and most solemn manner (Dialog. cum Tryphonte Jud. p. 177, 178. Edit. Benedictin.). If in the beginning of this important passage there is any thing like an inconsistency, we may impute it, as we think proper, either to the author or to his transcribers.

by degrees as a doubtful and useless opinion, and was at length rejected as the absurd invention of heresy and fanaticism.[66] A mysterious prophecy, which still forms a part of the sacred canon, but which was thought to favour the exploded sentiment, has very narrowly escaped the proscription of the church.[67]

Conflagration of Rome and of the world.   Whilst the happiness and glory of a temporal reign were promised to the disciples of Christ, the most dreadful calamities were denounced against an unbelieving world. The edification of the new Jerusalem was to advance by equal steps with the destruction of the mystic Babylon; and as long as the emperors who reigned before Constantine persisted in the profession of idolatry, the epithet of Babylon was applied to the city and to the empire of Rome. A regular series was prepared of all the moral and physical evils which can afflict a flourishing nation; intestine discord, and the invasion of the fiercest barbarians from the unknown regions of the North; pestilence and famine, comets and eclipses, earthquakes and inundations.[68] All these were only so many preparatory and alarming signs of the great catastrophe of Rome, when the country of the Scipios and Cæsars should be consumed by a flame from Heaven, and the city of the seven hills, with her palaces, her temples, and her triumphal arches, should be buried in a vast lake of fire and brimstone. It might, however, afford some consolation to Roman vanity, that the period of their empire would be that of the world itself; which, as it had once perished by the element of water, was destined to

66. Dupin, Bibliothéque Ecclesiastique, tom. i. p. 223. tom. ii. p. 366. and Mosheim, p. 720; though the latter of these learned divines is not altogether candid on this occasion.

67. In the council of Laodicea (about the year 360) the Apocalypse was tacitly excluded from the sacred canon, by the same churches of Asia to which it is addressed; and we may learn from the complaint of Sulpicius Severus, that their sentence had been ratified by the greater number of Christians of his time. From what causes then is the Apocalypse at present so generally received by the Greek, the Roman, and the Protestant churches? The following ones may be assigned. I. The Greeks were subdued by the authority of an impostor, who, in the sixth century, assumed the character of Dionysius the Areopagite. 2. A just apprehension, that the grammarians might become more important than the theologians, engaged the council of Trent to fix the seal of their infallibility on all the books of Scripture, contained in the Latin Vulgate, in the number of which the Apocalypse was fortunately included. (Fra Paolo, Istoria del Concilio Tridentino, l. ii.) 3. The advantage of turning those mysterious prophecies against the See of Rome, inspired the protestants with uncommon veneration for so useful an ally. See the ingenious and elegant discourses of the present bishop of Litchfield on that unpromising subject.

68. Lactantius (Institut. Divin. vii. 15, &c.) relates the dismal tale of futurity with great spirit and eloquence.

experience a second and a speedy destruction from the element of fire. In the opinion of a general conflagration, the faith of the Christian very happily coincided with the tradition of the East, the philosophy of the Stoics, and the analogy of Nature; and even the country, which, from religious motives, had been chosen for the origin and principal scene of the conflagration, was the best adapted for that purpose by natural and physical causes; by its deep caverns, beds of sulphur, and numerous volcanoes, of which those of Ætna, of Vesuvius, and of Lipari, exhibit a very imperfect representation. The calmest and most intrepid sceptic could not refuse to acknowledge, that the destruction of the present system of the world by fire, was in itself extremely probable. The Christian, who founded his belief much less on the fallacious arguments of reason than on the authority of tradition and the interpretation of scripture, expected it with terror and confidence as a certain and approaching event; and as his mind was perpetually filled with the solemn idea, he considered every disaster that happened to the empire as an infallible symptom of an expiring world.[69]

The condemnation of the wisest and most virtuous of the Pagans, on account of their ignorance or disbelief of the divine truth, seems to offend the reason and the humanity of the present age.[70] But the primitive church, whose faith was of a much firmer consistence, delivered over, without hesitation, to eternal torture, *The Pagans devoted to eternal punishment.* the far greater part of the human species. A charitable hope might perhaps be indulged in favour of Socrates, or some other sages of antiquity, who had consulted the light of reason before that of the gospel had arisen.[71] But it was unanimously affirmed, that those who, since the birth or the death of Christ, had obstinately persisted in the worship of the dæmons, neither

69. On this subject every reader of taste will be entertained with the third part of Burnet's Sacred Theory. He blends philosophy, scripture, and tradition, into one magnificent system; in the description of which, he displays a strength of fancy not inferior to that of Milton himself.

70. And yet whatever may be the language of individuals, it is still the public doctrine of all the Christian churches; nor can even our own refuse to admit the conclusions which must be drawn from the viiith and the xviiith of her Articles. The Jansenists, who have so diligently studied the works of the fathers, maintain this sentiment with distinguished zeal, and the learned M. de Tillemont never dismisses a virtuous emperor without pronouncing his damnation. Zuinglius is perhaps the only leader of a party who has ever adopted the milder sentiment, and he gave no less offence to the Lutherans than to the Catholics. See Bossuet, Histoire des Variations des Eglises Protestantes, l. ii. c. 19–22.

71. Justin and Clemens of Alexandria allow that some of the philosophers were instructed by the Logos; confounding its double signification, of the human reason, and of the Divine Word.

deserved nor could expect a pardon from the irritated justice of the Deity. These rigid sentiments, which had been unknown to the ancient world, appear to have infused a spirit of bitterness into a system of love and harmony. The ties of blood and friendship were frequently torn asunder by the difference of religious faith; and the Christians, who, in this world, found themselves oppressed by the power of the Pagans, were sometimes seduced by resentment and spiritual pride to delight in the prospect of their future triumph. "You are fond of spectacles," exclaims the stern Tertullian, "expect the greatest of all spectacles, the last and eternal judgment of the universe. How shall I admire, how laugh, how rejoice, how exult, when I behold so many proud monarchs, and fancied gods, groaning in the lowest abyss of darkness; so many magistrates who persecuted the name of the Lord, liquefying in fiercer fires than they ever kindled against the Christians; so many sage philosophers blushing in red hot flames with their deluded scholars; so many celebrated poets trembling before the tribunal, not of Minos, but of Christ; so many tragedians, more tuneful in the expression of their own sufferings; so many dancers – " But the humanity of the reader will permit me to draw a veil over the rest of this infernal description, which the zealous African pursues in a long variety of affected and unfeeling witticisms.[72]

Were often converted by their fears.   Doubtless there were many among the primitive Christians of a temper more suitable to the meekness and charity of their profession. There were many who felt a sincere compassion for the danger of their friends and countrymen, and who exerted the most benevolent zeal to save them from the impending destruction. The careless Polytheist, assailed by new and unexpected terrors, against which neither his priests nor his philosophers could afford him any certain protection, was very frequently terrified and subdued by the menace of eternal tortures. His fears might assist the progress of his faith and reason; and if he could once persuade himself to suspect that the Christian religion might possibly be true, it became an easy task to convince him that it was the safest and most prudent party that he could possibly embrace.

---

72. Tertullian, De Spectaculis, c. 30. In order to ascertain the degree of authority which the zealous African had acquired, it may be sufficient to allege the testimony of Cyprian, the doctor and guide of all the western churches. (See Prudent. Hymn. xiii. 100.) As often as he applied himself to his daily study of the writings of Tertullian, he was accustomed to say, "*Da mihi magistrum*; Give me my master." (Hieronym. de Viris Illustribus, tom. i. p. 284.)

III. The supernatural gifts, which even in this life were ascribed to the Christians above the rest of mankind, must have conduced to their own comfort, and very frequently to the conviction of infidels. Besides the occasional prodigies, which might sometimes be effected by the immediate interposition of the Deity when he suspended the laws of Nature for the service of religion, the Christian church, from the time of the apostles and their first disciples,[73] has claimed an uninterrupted succession of miraculous powers, the gift of tongues, of vision and of prophecy, the power of expelling dæmons, of healing the sick, and of raising the dead. The knowledge of foreign languages was frequently communicated to the contemporaries of Irenæus, though Irenæus himself was left to struggle with the difficulties of a barbarous dialect whilst he preached the gospel to the natives of Gaul.[74] The divine inspiration, whether it was conveyed in the form of a waking or of a sleeping vision, is described as a favour very liberally bestowed on all ranks of the faithful, on women as on elders, on boys as well as upon bishops. When their devout minds were sufficiently prepared by a course of prayer, of fasting, and of vigils, to receive the extraordinary impulse, they were transported out of their senses, and delivered in extasy what was inspired, being mere organs of the holy spirit, just as a pipe or flute is of him who blows into it.[75] We may add, that the design of these visions was, for the most part, either to disclose the future history, or to guide the present administration of the church. The expulsion of the dæmons from the bodies of those unhappy persons whom they had been permitted to torment, was considered as a signal though ordinary triumph of religion, and is repeatedly alleged by the ancient apologists, as the most convincing evidence of the truth of Christianity. The awful ceremony was usually performed in a public manner, and in the presence of a great number of spectators; the patient was relieved by the power or skill of the exorcist, and the vanquished dæmon was heard to confess, that he was one of the

THE THIRD CAUSE. Miraculous powers of the primitive church.

73. Notwithstanding the evasions of Dr. Middleton, it is impossible to overlook the clear traces of visions and inspiration, which may be found in the apostolic fathers.

74. Irenæus adv. Hæres. Proem. p. 3. Dr. Middleton (Free Inquiry, p. 96, &c.) observes, that as this pretension of all others was the most difficult to support by art, it was the soonest given up. The observation suits his hypothesis.

75. Athenagoras in Legatione. Justin Martyr, Cohort. ad Gentes. Tertullian advers. Marcionit. l. iv. These descriptions are not very unlike the prophetic fury, for which Cicero (de Divinat. ii. 54.) expresses so little reverence.

fabled gods of antiquity, who had impiously usurped the adoration of mankind.[76] But the miraculous cure of diseases of the most inveterate or even preternatural kind, can no longer occasion any surprise, when we recollect, that in the days of Irenæus, about the end of the second century, the resurrection of the dead was very far from being esteemed an uncommon event; that the miracle was frequently performed on necessary occasions, by great fasting and the joint supplication of the church of the place, and that the persons thus restored to their prayers, had lived afterwards among them many years.[77] At such a period, when faith could boast of so many wonderful victories over death, it seems difficult to account for the scepticism of those philosophers, who still rejected and derided the doctrine of the resurrection. A noble Grecian had rested on this important ground the whole controversy, and promised Theophilus, bishop of Antioch, that if he could be gratified with the sight of a single person who had been actually raised from the dead, he would immediately embrace the Christian religion. It is somewhat remarkable, that the prelate of the first eastern church, however anxious for the conversion of his friend, thought proper to decline this fair and reasonable challenge.[78]

Their truth contested. The miracles of the primitive church, after obtaining the sanction of ages, have been lately attacked in a very free and ingenious inquiry;[79] which, though it has met with the most favourable reception from the Public, appears to have excited a general scandal among the divines of our own as well as of the other protestant churches of Europe.[80] Our different sentiments on this subject will be much less influenced by any particular arguments, than by our habits of study and reflection; and above all, by the degree of the evidence which we have accustomed ourselves to require for the proof of a miraculous event. The duty of an historian does not call upon him to interpose his private

76. Tertullian (Apolog. c. 23.) throws out a bold defiance to the Pagan magistrates. Of the primitive miracles, the power of exorcising, is the only one which has been assumed by Protestants.

77. Irenæus adv. Hæreses, l. ii. 56, 57. l. v. c. 6. Mr. Dodwell (Dissert. ad Irenæum, ii. 42.) concludes, that the second century was still more fertile in miracles than the first.

78. Theophilus ad Autolycum, l. i. p. 345. Edit. Benedictin. Paris, 1742.

79. Dr. Middleton sent out his Introduction in the year 1747, published his Free Inquiry in 1749, and before his death, which happened in 1750, he had prepared a vindication of it against his numerous adversaries.

80. The university of Oxford conferred degrees on his opponents. From the indignation of Mosheim (p. 221.), we may discover the sentiments of the Lutheran divines.

judgment in this nice and important controversy; but he ought
not to dissemble the difficulty of adopting such a theory as may
reconcile the interest of religion with that of reason, of making
a proper application of that theory, and of defining with precision
the limits of that happy period exempt from error and from

*Our perplexity
in defining
the miraculous
period.*

deceit, to which we might be disposed to extend the gift of supernatural
powers. From the first of the fathers to the last of the popes, a succession
of bishops, of saints, of martyrs, and of miracles, is continued without
interruption, and the progress of superstition was so gradual and almost
imperceptible, that we know not in what particular link we should break
the chain of tradition. Every age bears testimony to the wonderful events
by which it was distinguished, and its testimony appears no less weighty
and respectable than that of the preceding generation, till we are insensibly
led on to accuse our own inconsistency, if in the eighth or in the twelfth
century we deny to the venerable Bede, or to the holy Bernard, the same
degree of confidence which, in the second century, we had so liberally
granted to Justin or to Irenæus.[81] If the truth of any of those miracles is
appreciated by their apparent use and propriety, every age had unbelievers
to convince, heretics to confute, and idolatrous nations to convert; and
sufficient motives might always be produced to justify the interposition of
Heaven. And yet since every friend to revelation is persuaded of the reality,
and every reasonable man is convinced of the cessation, of miraculous
powers, it is evident that there must have been *some period* in which they
were either suddenly or gradually withdrawn from the Christian church.
Whatever æra is chosen for that purpose, the death of the apostles, the
conversion of the Roman empire, or the extinction of the Arian heresy,[82]
the insensibility of the Christians who lived at that time will equally afford
a just matter of surprise. They still supported their pretensions after they
had lost their power. Credulity performed the office of faith; fanaticism
was permitted to assume the language of inspiration, and the effects of

---

81. It may seem somewhat remarkable, that
Bernard of Clairvaux, who records so many
miracles of his friend St. Malachi, never
takes any notice of his own, which, in their
turn, however, are carefully related by his
companions and disciples. In the long series
of ecclesiastical history, does there exist a
single instance of a saint asserting that he

himself possessed the gift of miracles?
82. The conversion of Constantine is the æra
which is most usually fixed by protestants.
The more rational divines are unwilling to
admit the miracles of the ivth, whilst the more
credulous are unwilling to reject those of the
vth century.

accident or contrivance were ascribed to supernatural causes. The recent experience of genuine miracles should have instructed the Christian world in the ways of providence, and habituated their eye (if we may use a very inadequate expression) to the style of the divine artist. Should the most skilful painter of modern Italy presume to decorate his feeble imitations with the name of Raphael or of Correggio, the insolent fraud would be soon discovered and indignantly rejected.

Use of the primitive miracles.   Whatever opinion may be entertained of the miracles of the primitive church since the time of the apostles, this unresisting softness of temper, so conspicuous among the believers of the second and third centuries, proved of some accidental benefit to the cause of truth and religion. In modern times, a latent and even involuntary scepticism adheres to the most pious dispositions. Their admission of supernatural truths is much less an active consent, than a cold and passive acquiescence. Accustomed long since to observe and to respect the invariable order of Nature, our reason, or at least our imagination, is not sufficiently prepared to sustain the visible action of the Deity. But, in the first ages of Christianity, the situation of mankind was extremely different. The most curious, or the most credulous, among the Pagans, were often persuaded to enter into a society, which asserted an actual claim of miraculous powers. The primitive Christians perpetually trod on mystic ground, and their minds were exercised by the habits of believing the most extraordinary events. They felt, or they fancied, that on every side they were incessantly assaulted by dæmons, comforted by visions, instructed by prophecy, and surprisingly delivered from danger, sickness, and from death itself, by the supplications of the church. The real or imaginary prodigies, of which they so frequently conceived themselves to be the objects, the instruments, or the spectators, very happily disposed them to adopt with the same ease, but with far greater justice, the authentic wonders of the evangelic history; and thus miracles that exceeded not the measure of their own experience, inspired them with the most lively assurance of mysteries which were acknowledged to surpass the limits of their understanding. It is this deep impression of supernatural truths, which has been so much celebrated under the name of faith; a state of mind described as the surest pledge of the divine favour and of future felicity, and recommended as the first or perhaps the only merit of a Christian. According to the more rigid doctors, the moral virtues, which may be equally practised by infidels, are destitute of any value or efficacy in the work of our justification.

IV. But the primitive Christian demonstrated his faith by his virtues; and it was very justly supposed that the divine persuasion which enlightened or subdued the understanding, must, at the same time, purify the heart and direct the actions of the believer. The first apologists of Christianity who justify the innocence *THE FOURTH CAUSE. Virtues of the first Christians.* of their brethren, and the writers of a later period who celebrate the sanctity of their ancestors, display, in the most lively colours, the reformation of manners which was introduced into the world by the preaching of the gospel. As it is my intention to remark only such human causes as were permitted to second the influence of revelation, I shall slightly mention two motives which might naturally render the lives of the primitive Christians much purer and more austere than those of their Pagan contemporaries, or their degenerate successors; repentance for their past sins, and the laudable desire of supporting the reputation of the society in which they were engaged.

It is a very ancient reproach, suggested by the ignorance or the malice of infidelity, that the Christians allured into their party the most atrocious criminals, who, as soon as they were *Effects of their repentance.* touched by a sense of remorse, were easily persuaded to wash away, in the water of baptism, the guilt of their past conduct, for which the temples of the gods refused to grant them any expiation. But this reproach, when it is cleared from misrepresentation, contributes as much to the honour as it did to the increase of the church.[83] The friends of Christianity may acknowledge without a blush, that many of the most eminent saints had been before their baptism the most abandoned sinners. Those persons, who in the world had followed, though in an imperfect manner, the dictates of benevolence and propriety, derived such a calm satisfaction from the opinion of their own rectitude, as rendered them much less susceptible of the sudden emotions of shame, of grief, and of terror, which have given birth to so many wonderful conversions. After the example of their Divine Master, the missionaries of the gospel disdained not the society of men, and especially of women, oppressed by the consciousness, and very often by the effects, of their vices. As they emerged from sin and superstition to the glorious hope of immortality, they resolved to devote themselves to a life, not only of virtue, but of penitence. The desire of perfection became

---

83. The imputations of Celsus and Julian, with the defence of the fathers, are very fairly stated by Spanheim, Commentaire sur les Cesars de Julian, p. 468.

the ruling passion of their soul; and it is well known, that while reason embraces a cold mediocrity, our passions hurry us, with rapid violence, over the space which lies between the most opposite extremes.

Care of their reputation.

When the new converts had been enrolled in the number of the faithful, and were admitted to the sacraments of the church, they found themselves restrained from relapsing into their past disorders by another consideration of a less spiritual, but of a very innocent and respectable nature. Any particular society that has departed from the great body of the nation, or the religion to which it belonged, immediately becomes the object of universal as well as invidious observation. In proportion to the smallness of its numbers, the character of the society may be affected by the virtue and vices of the persons who compose it; and every member is engaged to watch with the most vigilant attention over his own behaviour, and over that of his brethren, since, as he must expect to incur a part of the common disgrace, he may hope to enjoy a share of the common reputation. When the Christians of Bithynia were brought before the tribunal of the younger Pliny, they assured the proconsul, that, far from being engaged in any unlawful conspiracy, they were bound by a solemn obligation to abstain from the commission of those crimes which disturb the private or public peace of society, from theft, robbery, adultery, perjury, and fraud.[84] Near a century afterwards, Tertullian, with an honest pride, could boast, that very few Christians had suffered by the hand of the executioner, except on account of their religion.[85] Their serious and sequestered life, averse to the gay luxury of the age, inured them to chastity, temperance, œconomy, and all the sober and domestic virtues. As the greater number were of some trade or profession, it was incumbent on them, by the strictest integrity and the fairest dealing, to remove the suspicions which the profane are too apt to conceive against the appearances of sanctity. The contempt of the world exercised them in the habits of humility, meekness, and patience. The more they were persecuted, the more closely they adhered to each other. Their mutual charity and unsuspecting confidence has been remarked by infidels, and was too often abused by perfidious friends.[86]

84. Plin. Epistol. x. 97.

85. Tertullian, Apolog. c. 44. He adds, however, with some degree of hesitation, "Aut si aliud, jam non Christianus."

86. The philosopher Peregrinus (of whose life and death Lucian has left us so entertaining an account) imposed, for a long time, on the credulous simplicity of the Christians of Asia.

It is a very honourable circumstance for the morals of the primitive Christians, that even their faults, or rather errors, were derived from an excess of virtue. The bishops and doctors of the church, whose evidence attests, and whose authority might influence, the professions, the principles, and even the practice, of their contemporaries, had studied the scriptures with less skill than devotion, and they often received, in the most literal sense, those rigid precepts of Christ and the apostles, to which the prudence of succeeding commentators has applied a looser and more figurative mode of interpretation. Ambitious to exalt the perfection of the gospel above the wisdom of philosophy, the zealous fathers have carried the duties of self-mortification, of purity, and of patience, to a height which it is scarcely possible to attain, and much less to preserve, in our present state of weakness and corruption. A doctrine so extraordinary and so sublime must inevitably command the veneration of the people; but it was ill calculated to obtain the suffrage of those worldly philosophers, who, in the conduct of this transitory life, consult only the feelings of nature and the interest of society.[87]

Morality of the fathers.

There are two very natural propensities which we may distinguish in the most virtuous and liberal dispositions, the love of pleasure and the love of action. If the former is refined by art and learning, improved by the charms of social intercourse, and corrected by a just regard to œconomy, to health, and to reputation, it is productive of the greatest part of the happiness of private life. The love of action is a principle of a much stronger and more doubtful nature. It often leads to anger, to ambition, and to revenge; but when it is guided by the sense of propriety and benevolence, it becomes the parent of every virtue; and if those virtues are accompanied with equal abilities, a family, a state, or an empire, may be indebted for their safety and prosperity to the undaunted courage of a single man. To the love of pleasure we may therefore ascribe most of the agreeable, to the love of action we may attribute most of the useful and respectable, qualifications. The character in which both the one and the other should be united and harmonised, would seem to constitute the most perfect idea of human nature. The insensible and inactive disposition, which should be supposed alike destitute of both, would be rejected, by the common consent of mankind, as utterly incapable of procuring any

Principles of human nature.

---

87. See a very judicious treatise of Barbeyrac
sur la Morale des Peres.

happiness to the individual, or any public benefit to the world. But it was not in *this* world that the primitive Christians were desirous of making themselves either agreeable or useful.

The primitive Christians condemn pleasure and luxury.

The acquisition of knowledge, the exercise of our reason or fancy, and the cheerful flow of unguarded conversation, may employ the leisure of a liberal mind. Such amusements, however, were rejected with abhorrence, or admitted with the utmost caution, by the severity of the fathers, who despised all knowledge that was not useful to salvation, and who considered all levity of discourse as a criminal abuse of the gift of speech. In our present state of existence, the body is so inseparably connected with the soul, that it seems to be our interest to taste, with innocence and moderation, the enjoyments of which that faithful companion is susceptible. Very different was the reasoning of our devout predecessors; vainly aspiring to imitate the perfection of angels, they disdained, or they affected to disdain, every earthly and corporeal delight.[88] Some of our senses indeed are necessary for our preservation, others for our subsistence, and others again for our information, and thus far it was impossible to reject the use of them. The first sensation of pleasure was marked as the first moment of their abuse. The unfeeling candidate for Heaven was instructed, not only to resist the grosser allurements of the taste or smell, but even to shut his ears against the profane harmony of sounds, and to view with indifference the most finished productions of human art. Gay apparel, magnificent houses, and elegant furniture, were supposed to unite the double guilt of pride and of sensuality: a simple and mortified appearance was more suitable to the Christian who was certain of his sins and doubtful of his salvation. In their censures of luxury, the fathers are extremely minute and circumstantial;[89] and among the various articles which excite their pious indignation, we may enumerate false hair, garments of any colour except white, instruments of music, vases of gold or silver, downy pillows (as Jacob reposed his head on a stone), white bread, foreign wines, public salutations, the use of warm baths, and the practice of shaving the beard, which, according to the expression of Tertullian, is a lie against our own faces, and an impious attempt to improve the works of the Creator.[90] When Christianity was introduced among the

---

88. Lactant. Institut. Divin. l. vi. c. 20, 21, 22.

89. Consult a work of Clemens of Alexandria, intitled the Pædagogue, which contains the rudiments of ethics, as they were taught in the most celebrated of the Christian schools.

90. Tertullian, de Spectaculis, c. 23. Clemens Alexandrin. Pædagog. l. iii. c. 8.

rich and the polite, the observation of these singular laws was left, as it would be at present, to the few who were ambitious of superior sanctity. But it is always easy, as well as agreeable, for the inferior ranks of mankind to claim a merit from the contempt of that pomp and pleasure, which fortune has placed beyond their reach. The virtue of the primitive Christians, like that of the first Romans, was very frequently guarded by poverty and ignorance.

The chaste severity of the fathers, in whatever related to the commerce of the two sexes, flowed from the same principle; their abhorrence of every enjoyment, which might gratify the sensual, and degrade the spiritual, nature of man. It was their favourite opinion, that if Adam had preserved his obedience *Their sentiments concerning marriage and chastity.* to the Creator, he would have lived for ever in a state of virgin purity, and that some harmless mode of vegetation might have peopled paradise with a race of innocent and immortal beings.[91] The use of marriage was permitted only to his fallen posterity, as a necessary expedient to continue the human species, and as a restraint, however imperfect, on the natural licentiousness of desire. The hesitation of the orthodox casuists on this interesting subject, betrays the perplexity of men, unwilling to approve an institution, which they were compelled to tolerate.[92] The enumeration of the very whimsical laws, which they most circumstantially imposed on the marriage-bed, would force a smile from the young, and a blush from the fair. It was their unanimous sentiment, that a first marriage was adequate to all the purposes of nature and of society. The sensual connexion was refined into a resemblance of the mystic union of Christ with his church, and was pronounced to be indissoluble either by divorce or by death. The practice of second nuptials was branded with the name of a legal adultery; and the persons who were guilty of so scandalous an offence against Christian purity, were soon excluded from the honours, and even from the alms, of the church.[93] Since desire was imputed as a crime, and marriage was tolerated as a defect, it was consistent with the same principles to consider a state of celibacy as the nearest approach to the Divine perfection. It was with the utmost difficulty that ancient Rome could support the institution of six

91. Beausobre, Hist. Critique du Manicheisme, l. vii. c. 3. Justin, Gregory of Nyssa, Augustin, &c. strongly inclined to this opinion.

92. Some of the Gnostic heretics were more consistent; they rejected the use of marriage.

93. See a chain of tradition, from Justin Martyr to Jerome, in the Morale des Peres; c. iv. 6–26.

vestals;[94] but the primitive church was filled with a great number of persons of either sex, who had devoted themselves to the profession of perpetual chastity.[95] A few of these, among whom we may reckon the learned Origen, judged it the most prudent to disarm the tempter.[96] Some were insensible and some were invincible against the assaults of the flesh. Disdaining an ignominious flight, the virgins of the warm climate of Africa encountered the enemy in the closest engagement; they permitted priests and deacons to share their bed, and gloried amidst the flames in their unsullied purity. But insulted Nature sometimes vindicated her rights, and this new species of martyrdom served only to introduce a new scandal into the church.[97] Among the Christian ascetics, however (a name which they soon acquired from their painful exercise), many, as they were less presumptuous, were probably more successful. The loss of sensual pleasure was supplied and compensated by spiritual pride. Even the multitude of Pagans were inclined to estimate the merit of the sacrifice by its apparent difficulty; and it was in the praise of these chaste spouses of Christ that the fathers have poured forth the troubled stream of their eloquence.[98] Such are the early traces of monastic principles and institutions, which, in a subsequent age, have counterbalanced all the temporal advantages of Christianity.[99]

Their aversion to the business of war and government.

The Christians were not less averse to the business than to the pleasures of this world. The defence of our persons and property they knew not how to reconcile with the patient doctrine which enjoined an unlimited forgiveness of

---

94. See a very curious Dissertation on the Vestals, in the Memoires de l'Academie des Inscriptions, tom. iv. p. 161–227. Notwithstanding the honours and rewards which were bestowed on those virgins, it was difficult to procure a sufficient number; nor could the dread of the most horrible death always restrain their incontinence.

95. Cupiditatem procreandi aut unam scimus aut nullam. Minucius Fælix, c. 31. Justin. Apolog. Major. Athenagoras in Legat. c. 28. Tertullian de Cultu Fœmin. l. ii.

96. Eusebius, l. vi. 8. Before the fame of Origen had excited envy and persecution, this extraordinary action was rather admired than censured. As it was his general practice to allegorize scripture; it seems unfortunate that,

in this instance only, he should have adopted the literal sense.

97. Cyprian. Epistol. 4. and Dodwell Dissertat. Cyprianic. iii. Something like this rash attempt was long afterwards imputed to the founder of the order of Fontevrault. Bayle has amused himself and his readers on that very delicate subject.

98. Dupin (Bibliothéque Ecclesiastique, tom. i. p. 195.) gives a particular account of the dialogue of the ten virgins, as it was composed by Methodius, bishop of Tyre. The praises of virginity are excessive.

99. The Ascetics (as early as the second century) made a public profession of mortifying their bodies, and of abstaining from the use of flesh and wine. Mosheim, p. 310.

past injuries, and commanded them to invite the repetition of fresh insults. Their simplicity was offended by the use of oaths, by the pomp of magistracy, and by the active contention of public life, nor could their humane ignorance be convinced, that it was lawful on any occasion to shed the blood of our fellow-creatures, either by the sword of justice, or by that of war; even though their criminal or hostile attempts should threaten the peace and safety of the whole community.[100] It was acknowledged, that, under a less perfect law, the powers of the Jewish constitution had been exercised, with the approbation of Heaven, by inspired prophets and by anointed kings. The Christians felt and confessed, that such institutions might be necessary for the present system of the world, and they cheerfully submitted to the authority of their Pagan governors. But while they inculcated the maxims of passive obedience, they refused to take any active part in the civil administration or the military defence of the empire. Some indulgence might perhaps be allowed to those persons who, before their conversion, were already engaged in such violent and sanguinary occupations;[101] but it was impossible that the Christians, without renouncing a more sacred duty, could assume the character of soldiers, of magistrates, or of princes.[102] This indolent, or even criminal disregard to the public welfare, exposed them to the contempt and reproaches of the Pagans, who very frequently asked, what must be the fate of the empire, attacked on every side by the barbarians, if all mankind should adopt the pusillanimous sentiments of the new sect?[103] To this insulting question the Christian apologists returned obscure and ambiguous answers, as they were unwilling to reveal the secret cause of their security; the expectation that, before the conversion of mankind was accomplished, war, government, the Roman empire, and the world itself, would be no more. It may be observed, that, in this instance likewise, the situation of the first Christians coincided very happily

---

100. See the Morale des Peres. The same patient principles have been revived since the Reformation by the Socinians, the modern Anabaptists, and the Quakers. Barclay, the apologist of the Quakers, has protected his brethren, by the authority of the primitive Christians, p. 542–549.

101. Tertullian, Apolog. c. 21. De Idololatriâ, c. 17, 18. Origen contra Celsum, l. v. p. 253. l. vii. p. 348. l. viii. p. 423–428.

102. Tertullian (de Corona Militis, c. 11.) suggests to them the expedient of deserting; a counsel, which, if it had been generally known, was not very proper to conciliate the favour of the emperors towards the Christian sect.

103. As well as we can judge from the mutilated representation of Origen (l. viii. p. 423.), his adversary, Celsus, had urged his objection with great force and candour.

with their religious scruples, and that their aversion to an active life contributed rather to excuse them from the service, than to exclude them from the honours, of the state and army.

THE FIFTH CAUSE.
The Christians active in the government of the church.

V. But the human character, however it may be exalted or depressed by a temporary enthusiasm, will return by degrees to its proper and natural level, and will resume those passions that seem the most adapted to its present condition. The primitive Christians were dead to the business and pleasures of the world; but their love of action, which could never be entirely extinguished, soon revived, and found a new occupation in the government of the church. A separate society, which attacked the established religion of the empire, was obliged to adopt some form of internal policy, and to appoint a sufficient number of ministers, intrusted not only with the spiritual functions, but even with the temporal direction of the Christian commonwealth. The safety of that society, its honour, its aggrandisement, were productive, even in the most pious minds, of a spirit of patriotism, such as the first of the Romans had felt for the republic, and sometimes, of a similar indifference, in the use of whatever means might probably conduce to so desirable an end. The ambition of raising themselves or their friends to the honours and offices of the church, was disguised by the laudable intention of devoting to the public benefit, the power and consideration, which, for that purpose only, it became their duty to solicit. In the exercise of their functions, they were frequently called upon to detect the errors of heresy, or the arts of faction, to oppose the designs of perfidious brethren, to stigmatize their characters with deserved infamy, and to expel them from the bosom of a society, whose peace and happiness they had attempted to disturb. The ecclesiastical governors of the Christians were taught to unite the wisdom of the serpent with the innocence of the dove; but as the former was refined, so the latter was insensibly corrupted, by the habits of government. In the church as well as in the world, the persons who were placed in any public station rendered themselves considerable by their eloquence and firmness, by their knowledge of mankind, and by their dexterity in business, and while they concealed from others, and perhaps from themselves, the secret motives of their conduct, they too frequently relapsed into all the turbulent passions of active life, which were tinctured with an additional degree of bitterness and obstinacy from the infusion of spiritual zeal.

The government of the church has often been the subject as well as the prize of religious contention. The hostile disputants of Rome, of Paris, of Oxford, and of Geneva, have alike struggled to reduce the primitive and apostolic model,[104] to the respective standards of their own policy. The few who have pursued this inquiry with more candour and impartiality, are of opinion,[105] that the apostles declined the office of legislation, and rather chose to endure some partial scandals and divisions, than to exclude the Christians of a future age from the liberty of varying their forms of ecclesiastical government according to the changes of times and circumstances. The scheme of policy, which, under their approbation, was adopted for the use of the first century, may be discovered from the practice of Jerusalem, of Ephesus, or of Corinth. The societies which were instituted in the cities of the Roman empire, were united only by the ties of faith and charity. Independence and equality formed the basis of their internal constitution. The want of discipline and human learning was supplied by the occasional assistance of the *prophets*,[106] who were called to that function without distinction of age, of sex, or of natural abilities, and who, as often as they felt the divine impulse, poured forth the effusions of the spirit in the assembly of the faithful. But these extraordinary gifts were frequently abused or misapplied by the prophetic teachers. They displayed them at an improper season, presumptuously disturbed the service of the assembly, and by their pride or mistaken zeal they introduced, particularly into the apostolic church of Corinth, a long and melancholy train of disorders.[107] As the institution of prophets became useless, and even pernicious, their powers were withdrawn, and their office abolished. The public functions of religion were solely intrusted to the established ministers of the church, the *bishops* and the *presbyters*; two appellations which, in their first origin, appear to have distinguished the same office and the same order of persons. The name of Presbyter was expressive of their age, or rather of their gravity and wisdom. The title of Bishop denoted their in-spection over the faith and manners of the Christians who were committed

Its primitive freedom and equality.

104. The Aristocratical party, in France, as well as in England, has strenuously maintained the divine origin of bishops. But the Calvinist-ical presbyters were impatient of a superior; and the Roman Pontiff refused to acknow-ledge an equal. See Fra Paolo.

105. In the history of the Christian hierarchy,

I have, for the most part, followed the learned and candid Mosheim.

106. For the prophets of the primitive church, see Mosheim, Dissertationes ad Hist. Eccles. pertinentes, tom. ii. p. 132–208.

107. See the epistles of St. Paul, and of Clemens, to the Corinthians.

to their pastoral care. In proportion to the respective numbers of the faithful, a larger or smaller number of these *episcopal presbyters* guided each infant congregation with equal authority, and with united counsels.[108]

Institution of bishops as presidents of the college of presbyters.

But the most perfect equality of freedom requires the directing hand of a superior magistrate; and the order of public deliberations soon introduces the office of a president, invested at least with the authority of collecting the sentiments, and of executing the resolutions, of the assembly. A regard for the public tranquillity, which would so frequently have been interrupted by annual or by occasional elections, induced the primitive Christians to constitute an honourable and perpetual magistracy, and to choose one of the wisest and most holy among their presbyters to execute, during his life, the duties of their ecclesiastical governor. It was under these circumstances that the lofty title of Bishop began to raise itself above the humble appellation of presbyter; and while the latter remained the most natural distinction for the members of every Christian senate, the former was appropriated to the dignity of its new president.[109] The advantages of this episcopal form of government, which appears to have been introduced before the end of the first century,[110] were so obvious, and so important for the future greatness, as well as the present peace, of Christianity, that it was adopted without delay by all the societies which were already scattered over the empire, had acquired in a very early period the sanction of antiquity,[111] and is still revered by the most powerful churches, both of the East and of the West, as a primitive and even as a divine establishment.[112] It is needless to observe, that the pious and humble presbyters, who were first dignified with the episcopal title, could not possess, and would probably have rejected, the

---

108. Hooker's Ecclesiastical Polity, l. vii.

109. See Jerome ad Titum, c. 1. and Epistol. 85. (in the Benedictine edition, 101.) and the elaborate apology of Blondel, pro sententia Hieronymi. The ancient state, as it is described by Jerome, of the bishop and presbyters of Alexandria, receives a remarkable confirmation from the patriarch Eutichius (Annal. tom. i. p. 330. Vers. Pocock); whose testimony I know not how to reject; in spite of all the objections of the learned Pearson, in his Vindiciæ Ignatianæ, part i. c. 11.

110. See the introduction to the Apocalypse. Bishops, under the name of angels, were

already instituted in seven cities of Asia. And yet the epistle of Clemens (which is probably of as ancient a date) does not lead us to discover any traces of episcopacy either at Corinth or Rome.

111. Nulla Ecclesia sine Episcopo, has been a fact as well as a maxim since the time of Tertullian and Irenæus.

112. After we have passed the difficulties of the first century, we find the episcopal government universally established, till it was interrupted by the republican genius of the Swiss and German reformers.

power and pomp which now encircles the tiara of the Roman pontiff, or the mitre of a German prelate. But we may define, in a few words, the narrow limits of their original jurisdiction, which was chiefly of a spiritual, though in some instances of a temporal, nature.[113] It consisted in the administration of the sacraments and discipline of the church, the superintendency of religious ceremonies, which imperceptibly increased in number and variety, the consecration of ecclesiastical ministers, to whom the bishop assigned their respective functions, the management of the public fund, and the determination of all such differences as the faithful were unwilling to expose before the tribunal of an idolatrous judge. These powers, during a short period, were exercised according to the advice of the presbyteral college, and with the consent and approbation of the assembly of Christians. The primitive bishops were considered only as the first of their equals, and the honourable servants of a free people. Whenever the episcopal chair became vacant by death, a new president was chosen among the presbyters by the suffrage of the whole congregation, every member of which supposed himself invested with a sacred and sacerdotal character.[114]

Such was the mild and equal constitution by which the Christians were governed more than an hundred years after the death of the apostles. Every society formed within itself a separate and *Provincial councils.* independent republic: and although the most distant of these little states maintained a mutual as well as friendly intercourse of letters and deputations, the Christian world was not yet connected by any supreme authority or legislative assembly. As the numbers of the faithful were gradually multiplied, they discovered the advantages that might result from a closer union of their interest and designs. Towards the end of the second century, the churches of Greece and Asia adopted the useful institutions of provincial synods, and they may justly be supposed to have borrowed the model of a representative council from the celebrated examples of their own country, the Amphictyons, the Achæan league, or the assemblies of the Ionian cities. It was soon established as a custom and as a law, that the

113. See Mosheim in the first and second centuries. Ignatius (ad Smyrnæos, c. 3, &c.) is fond of exalting the episcopal dignity. Le Clerc (Hist. Ecclesiast. p. 569.) very bluntly censures his conduct. Mosheim, with a more critical judgment (p. 161.), suspects the purity even of the smaller epistles.

114. Nonne et Laici sacerdotes sumus? Tertullian, Exhort. ad Castitat. c. 7. As the human heart is still the same, several of the observations which Mr. Hume has made on Enthusiasm (Essays, vol. i. p. 76, quarto edit.), may be applied even to real inspiration.

bishops of the independent churches should meet in the capital of the province at the stated periods of spring and autumn. Their deliberations were assisted by the advice of a few distinguished presbyters, and moderated by the presence of a listening multitude.[115] Their decrees, which were styled Canons, regulated every important controversy of faith and discipline; and it was natural to believe that a liberal effusion of the holy spirit would be poured on the united assembly of the delegates of the Christian people. The institution of synods was so well suited to private *Union of the* ambition and to public interest, that in the space of a few years *church.* it was received throughout the whole empire. A regular correspondence was established between the provincial councils, which mutually communicated and approved their respective proceedings; and the catholic church soon assumed the form, and acquired the strength, of a great fœderative republic.[116]

Progress of As the legislative authority of the particular churches was insen-
episcopal sibly superseded by the use of councils, the bishops obtained by
authority. their alliance a much larger share of executive and arbitrary power;
and as soon as they were connected by a sense of their common interest, they were enabled to attack, with united vigour, the original rights of their clergy and people. The prelates of the third century imperceptibly changed the language of exhortation into that of command, scattered the seeds of future usurpations, and supplied, by scripture allegories and declamatory rhetoric, their deficiency of force and of reason. They exalted the unity and power of the church, as it was represented in the EPISCOPAL OFFICE, of which every bishop enjoyed an equal and undivided portion.[117] Princes and magistrates, it was often repeated, might boast an earthly claim to a transitory dominion: it was the episcopal authority alone which was derived from the deity, and extended itself over this and over another world. The bishops were the vicegerents of Christ, the successors of the apostles, and the mystic substitutes of the high priest of the Mosaic law. Their exclusive privilege of conferring the sacerdotal character, invaded

115. Acta Concil. Carthag. apud Cyprian. Edit. Fell, p. 158. This council was composed of eighty-seven bishops from the provinces of Mauritania, Numidia, and Africa; some presbyters and deacons assisted at the assembly; præsente plebis maximâ parte.
116. Aguntur præterea per Græcias illas, certis in locis concilia, &c. Tertullian de Jejuniis, c. 13. The African mentions it as a recent and foreign institution. The coalition of the Christian churches is very ably explained by Mosheim, p. 164–170.
117. Cyprian, in his admired treatise De Unitate Ecclesiæ, p. 75–86.

the freedom both of clerical and of popular elections; and if, in the administration of the church, they still consulted the judgment of the presbyters, or the inclination of the people, they most carefully inculcated the merit of such a voluntary condescension. The bishops acknowledged the supreme authority which resided in the assembly of their brethren; but in the government of his peculiar diocese, each of them exacted from his *flock* the same implicit obedience as if that favourite metaphor had been literally just, and as if the shepherd had been of a more exalted nature than that of his sheep.[118] This obedience, however, was not imposed without some efforts on one side, and some resistance on the other. The democratical part of the constitution was, in many places, very warmly supported by the zealous or interested opposition of the inferior clergy. But their patriotism received the ignominious epithets of faction and schism; and the episcopal cause was indebted for its rapid progress to the labours of many active prelates, who, like Cyprian of Carthage, could reconcile the arts of the most ambitious statesman with the Christian virtues which seem adapted to the character of a saint and martyr.[119]

The same causes which at first had destroyed the equality of the presbyters, introduced among the bishops a pre-eminence of rank, and from thence a superiority of jurisdiction. As often as in the spring and autumn they met in provincial synod, the difference of personal merit and reputation was very sensibly felt

Pre-eminence of the metropolitan churches.

among the members of the assembly, and the multitude was governed by the wisdom and eloquence of the few. But the order of public proceedings required a more regular and less invidious distinction; the office of perpetual presidents in the councils of each province, was conferred on the bishops of the principal city, and these aspiring prelates, who soon acquired the lofty titles of Metropolitans and Primates, secretly prepared themselves to usurp over their episcopal brethren the same authority which the bishops had so lately assumed above the college of presbyters.[120] Nor was it long

---

118. We may appeal to the whole tenor of Cyprian's conduct, of his doctrine, and of his Epistles. Le Clerc, in a short life of Cyprian (Bibliothéque Universelle, tom. xii. p. 207-378.), has laid him open with great freedom and accuracy.

119. If Novatus, Felicissimus, &c. whom the bishop of Carthage expelled from his church,

and from Africa, were not the most detestable monsters of wickedness, the zeal of Cyprian must occasionally have prevailed over his veracity. For a very just account of these obscure quarrels, see Mosheim, p. 497-512.

120. Mosheim, p. 269. 574. Dupin, Antiquæ Eccles. Disciplin. p. 19, 20.

before an emulation of pre-eminence and power prevailed among the metropolitans themselves, each of them affecting to display, in the most pompous terms, the temporal honours and advantages of the city over which he presided; the numbers and opulence of the Christians, who were subject to their pastoral care; the saints and martyrs who had arisen among them, and the purity with which they preserved the tradition of the faith, as it had been transmitted through a series of orthodox bishops from the apostle of the apostolic disciple, to whom the foundation of their church was ascribed.[121] From every cause either of a civil or of an ecclesiastical nature, it was easy to foresee that Rome must enjoy the respect, and would

Ambition of the Roman pontiff.

soon claim the obedience, of the provinces. The society of the faithful bore a just proportion to the capital of the empire; and the Roman church was the greatest, the most numerous, and, in regard to the West, the most ancient of all the Christian establishments, many of which had received their religion from the pious labours of her missionaries. Instead of *one* apostolic founder, the utmost boast of Antioch, of Ephesus, or of Corinth, the banks of the Tyber were supposed to have been honoured with the preaching and martyrdom of the *two* most eminent among the apostles;[122] and the bishops of Rome very prudently claimed the inheritance of whatsoever prerogatives were attributed either to the person or to the office of St. Peter.[123] The bishops of Italy and of the provinces were disposed to allow them a primacy of order and association (such was their very accurate expression) in the Christian aristocracy.[124] But the power of a monarch was rejected with abhorrence, and the aspiring genius of Rome experienced from the nations of Asia and Africa, a more vigorous resistance to her spiritual, than she had formerly done to

---

121. Tertullian, in a distinct treatise, has pleaded against the heretics, the right of prescription, as it was held by the apostolic churches.

122. The journey of St. Peter to Rome is mentioned by most of the ancients (see Eusebius, ii. 25.), maintained by all the catholics, allowed by some protestants (see Pearson and Dodwell de Success. Episcop. Roman.), but has been vigorously attacked by Spanheim (Miscellanea Sacra, iii. 3.). According to father Hardouin, the monks of the thirteenth century, who composed the Æneid, represented St. Peter under the al-

legorical character of the Trojan hero.

123. It is in French only, that the famous allusion to St. Peter's name is exact. Tu es *Pierre* et sur cette *pierre*. – The same is imperfect in Greek, Latin, Italian, &c. and totally unintelligible in our Teutonic languages.

124. Irenæus adv. Hæreses, iii. 3. Tertullian de Præscription. c. 36, and Cyprian Epistol. 27. 55. 71. 75. Le Clerc (Hist. Eccles. p. 764.) and Mosheim (p. 258. 578.) labour in the interpretation of these passages. But the loose and rhetorical style of the fathers often appears favourable to the pretensions of Rome.

her temporal, dominion. The patriotic Cyprian, who ruled with the most absolute sway the church of Carthage and the provincial synods, opposed with resolution and success the ambition of the Roman pontiff, artfully connected his own cause with that of the eastern bishops, and, like Hannibal, sought out new allies in the heart of Asia.[125] If this Punic war was carried on without any effusion of blood, it was owing much less to the moderation than to the weakness of the contending prelates. Invectives and excommunications were *their* only weapons; and these, during the progress of the whole controversy, they hurled against each other with equal fury and devotion. The hard necessity of censuring either a pope, or a saint and martyr, distresses the modern catholics, whenever they are obliged to relate the particulars of a dispute, in which the champions of religion indulged such passions as seem much more adapted to the senate or to the camp.[126]

The progress of the ecclesiastical authority gave birth to the memorable distinction of the laity and of the clergy, which had been unknown to the Greeks and Romans.[127] The former of these *Laity and clergy.* appellations comprehend the body of the Christian people; the latter, according to the signification of the word, was appropriated to the chosen portion that had been set apart for the service of religion; a celebrated order of men which has furnished the most important, though not always the most edifying, subjects for modern history. Their mutual hostilities sometimes disturbed the peace of the infant church, but their zeal and activity were united in the common cause, and the love of power, which (under the most artful disguises) could insinuate itself into the breasts of bishops and martyrs, animated them to increase the number of their subjects, and to enlarge the limits of the Christian empire. They were destitute of any temporal force, and they were for a long time discouraged and oppressed, rather than assisted, by the civil magistrate; but they had acquired, and they employed within their own society, the two most efficacious instruments of government, rewards and punishments; the former derived from the pious liberality, the latter from the devout apprehensions, of the faithful.

125. See the sharp epistle from Firmilianus bishop of Cæsarea, to Stephen bishop of Rome, ap. Cyprian. Epistol. 75.

126. Concerning this dispute of the rebaptism of heretics; see the epistles of Cyprian, and the seventh book of Eusebius.

127. For the origin of these words, see Mosheim, p. 141. Spanheim, Hist. Ecclesiast. p. 633. The distinction of *Clerus* and *Laicus* was established before the time of Tertullian.

Oblations and revenue of the church.

I. The community of goods, which had so agreeably amused the imagination of Plato,[128] and which subsisted in some degree among the austere sect of the Essenians,[129] was adopted for a short time in the primitive church. The fervour of the first proselytes prompted them to sell those worldly possessions, which they despised, to lay the price of them at the feet of the apostles, and to content themselves with receiving an equal share out of the general distribution.[130] The progress of the Christian religion relaxed, and gradually abolished this generous institution, which, in hands less pure than those of the apostles, would too soon have been corrupted and abused by the returning selfishness of human nature; and the converts who embraced the new religion were permitted to retain the possession of their patrimony, to receive legacies and inheritances, and to increase their separate property by all the lawful means of trade and industry. Instead of an absolute sacrifice, a moderate proportion was accepted by the ministers of the gospel; and in their weekly or monthly assemblies, every believer, according to the exigency of the occasion, and the measure of his wealth and piety, presented his voluntary offering for the use of the common fund.[131] Nothing, however inconsiderable, was refused; but it was diligently inculcated, that, in the article of Tythes, the Mosaic law was still of divine obligation; and that since the Jews, under a less perfect discipline, had been commanded to pay a tenth part of all that they possessed, it would become the disciples of Christ to distinguish themselves by a superior degree of liberality,[132] and to acquire some merit by resigning a superfluous treasure, which must so soon be annihilated with the world itself.[133] It is almost unnecessary to observe, that

---

128. The community instituted by Plato, is more perfect than that which Sir Thomas More had imagined for his Utopia. The community of women, and that of temporal goods, may be considered as inseparable parts of the same system.

129. Joseph. Antiquitat. xviii. 2. Philo, de Vit. Contemplativ.

130. See the Acts of the Apostles, c. 2. 4, 5. with Grotius's Commentary. Mosheim, in a particular dissertation, attacks the common opinion with very inconclusive arguments.

131. Justin Martyr, Apolog. Major, c. 89. Tertullian, Apolog. c. 39.

132. Irenæus ad Hæres. l. iv. c. 27. 34. Origen in Num. Hom. ii. Cyprian de Unitat. Eccles. Constitut. Apostol. l. ii. c. 34, 35. with the notes of Cotelerius. The constitutions introduce this divine precept, by declaring that priests are as much above kings, as the soul is above the body. Among the tythable articles, they enumerate corn, wine, oil, and wool. On this interesting subject, consult Prideaux's History of Tythes, and Fra-Paolo delle Materie Beneficiarie; two writers of a very different character.

133. The same opinion which prevailed about the year one thousand, was productive of the

the revenue of each particular church, which was of so uncertain and fluctuating a nature, must have varied with the poverty or the opulence of the faithful, as they were dispersed in obscure villages, or collected in the great cities of the empire. In the time of the emperor Decius, it was the opinion of the magistrates, that the Christians of Rome were possessed of very considerable wealth; that vessels of gold and silver were used in their religious worship, and that many among their proselytes had sold their lands and houses to increase the public riches of the sect, at the expence, indeed, of their unfortunate children, who found themselves beggars, because their parents had been saints.[134] We should listen with distrust to the suspicions of strangers and enemies: on this occasion, however, they receive a very specious and probable colour from the two following circumstances, the only ones that have reached our knowledge, which define any precise sums, or convey any distinct idea. Almost at the same period, the bishop of Carthage, from a society less opulent than that of Rome, collected an hundred thousand sesterces (above eight hundred and fifty pounds sterling) on a sudden call of charity to redeem the brethren of Numidia, who had been carried away captives by the barbarians of the desert.[135] About an hundred years before the reign of Decius, the Roman church had received, in a single donation, the sum of two hundred thousand sesterces from a stranger of Pontus, who proposed to fix his residence in the capital.[136] These oblations, for the most part, were made in money; nor was the society of Christians either desirous or capable of acquiring, to any considerable degree, the incumbrance of landed property. It had been provided by several laws, which were enacted with the same design as our

---

same effects. Most of the Donations express their motive, "appropinquante mundi fine." See Mosheim's General History of the Church, vol. i. p. 457.

134.
　　Tum summa cura est fratribus
　　(Ut sermo testatur loquax.)
　　Offerre, fundis venditis
　　Sestertiorum millia.
　　Addicta avorum prædia
　　Fœdis sub auctionibus,
　　Successor exheres gemit
　　Sanctis egens Parentibus.
　　Hæc occuluntur abditis
　　Ecclesiarum in Angulis:

Et summa pietas creditur
Nudare dulces liberos.
　　Prudent. περι στεφανων. Hymn. 2.

The subsequent conduct of the deacon Laurence, only proves how proper a use was made of the wealth of the Roman church; it was undoubtedly very considerable; but Fra-Paolo (c. 3.) appears to exaggerate, when he supposes, that the successors of Commodus were urged to persecute the Christians by their own avarice, or that of their Prætorian præfects.

135. Cyprian. Epistol. 62.
136. Tertullian de Prescriptione, c. 30.

statutes of mortmain, that no real estates should be given or bequeathed to any corporate body, without either a special privilege or a particular dispensation from the emperor or from the senate;[137] who were seldom disposed to grant them in favour of a sect, at first the object of their contempt, and at last of their fears and jealousy. A transaction however is related under the reign of Alexander Severus, which discovers that the restraint was sometimes eluded or suspended, and that the Christians were permitted to claim and to possess lands within the limits of Rome itself.[138] The progress of Christianity, and the civil confusion of the empire, contributed to relax the severity of the laws, and before the close of the third century many considerable estates were bestowed on the opulent churches of Rome, Milan, Carthage, Antioch, Alexandria, and the other great cities of Italy and the provinces.

Distribution of the revenue.   The bishop was the natural steward of the church; the public stock was intrusted to his care without account or controul; the presbyters were confined to their spiritual functions, and the more dependent order of deacons was solely employed in the management and distribution of the ecclesiastical revenue.[139] If we may give credit to the vehement declamations of Cyprian, there were too many among his African brethren, who, in the execution of their charge, violated every precept, not only of evangelic perfection, but even of moral virtue. By some of these unfaithful stewards the riches of the church were lavished in sensual pleasures, by others they were perverted to the purposes of private gain, of fraudulent purchases, and of rapacious usury.[140] But as long as the contributions of the Christian people were free and unconstrained, the abuse of their confidence could not be very frequent, and the general uses to which their liberality was applied, reflected honour on the religious society. A decent portion was reserved for the maintenance of the bishop and his clergy; a sufficient sum was allotted for the expences of the public worship, of which the feasts of love, the *agapæ*, as they were called,

137. Diocletian gave a rescript, which is only a declaration of the old law; "Collegium, si nullo speciali privilegio subnixum sit, hæreditatem capere non posse, dubium non est." Fra-Paolo (c. 4.) thinks that these regulations had been much neglected since the reign of Valerian.

138. Hist. August. p. 131. The ground had been public; and was now disputed between the society of Christians, and that of butchers.

139. Constitut. Apostol. ii. 35.

140. Cyprian de Lapsis, p. 89. Epistol. 65. The charge is confirmed by the 19th and 20th canon of the council of Illiberis.

constituted a very pleasing part. The whole remainder was the sacred patrimony of the poor. According to the discretion of the bishop, it was distributed to support widows and orphans, the lame, the sick, and the aged of the community; to comfort strangers and pilgrims, and to alleviate the misfortunes of prisoners and captives, more especially when their sufferings had been occasioned by their firm attachment to the cause of religion.[141] A generous intercourse of charity united the most distant provinces, and the smaller congregations were cheerfully assisted by the alms of their more opulent brethren.[142] Such an institution, which paid less regard to the merit than to the distress of the object, very materially conduced to the progress of Christianity. The Pagans, who were actuated by a sense of humanity, while they derided the doctrines, acknowledged the benevolence of the new sect.[143] The prospect of immediate relief and of future protection allured into its hospitable bosom many of those unhappy persons whom the neglect of the world would have abandoned to the miseries of want, of sickness, and of old age. There is some reason likewise to believe, that great numbers of infants, who, according to the inhuman practice of the times, had been exposed by their parents, were frequently rescued from death, baptised, educated, and maintained by the piety of the Christians, and at the expence of the public treasure.[144]

II. It is the undoubted right of every society to exclude from its communion and benefits, such among its members *Excommunication.* as reject or violate those regulations which have been established by general consent. In the exercise of this power, the censures of the Christian church were chiefly directed against scandalous sinners, and particularly those who were guilty of murder, of fraud, or of incontinence; against the authors, or the followers of any heretical opinions which had been condemned by the judgment of the episcopal order; and against those unhappy persons, who, whether from choice or from compulsion, had polluted themselves after

---

141. See the apologies of Justin, Tertullian, &c.

142. The wealth and liberality of the Romans to their most distant brethren, is gratefully celebrated by Dionysius of Corinth, ap. Euseb. l. iv. c. 23.

143. See Lucian in Peregrin. Julian (Epist. 49.) seems mortified, that the Christian charity maintains not only their own, but like-wise the heathen poor.

144. Such, at least, has been the laudable conduct of more modern missionaries, under the same circumstances. Above three thousand new-born infants are annually exposed in the streets of Pekin. See Le Comte Memoires sur la Chine, and the Recherches sur les Chinois et les Egyptiens, tom. i. p. 61.

their baptism by any act of idolatrous worship. The consequences of excommunication were of a temporal as well as a spiritual nature. The Christian against whom it was pronounced, was deprived of any part in the oblations of the faithful. The ties both of religious and of private friendship were dissolved: he found himself a profane object of abhorrence to the persons whom he the most esteemed, or by whom he had been the most tenderly beloved; and as far as an expulsion from a respectable society could imprint on his character a mark of disgrace, he was shunned or suspected by the generality of mankind. The situation of these unfortunate exiles was in itself very painful and melancholy; but, as it usually happens, their apprehensions far exceeded their sufferings. The benefits of the Christian communion were those of eternal life, nor could they erase from their minds the awful opinion, that to those ecclesiastical governors by whom they were condemned, the Deity had committed the keys of Hell and of Paradise. The heretics, indeed, who might be supported by the consciousness of their intentions, and by the flattering hope that they alone had discovered the true path of salvation, endeavoured to regain, in their separate assemblies, those comforts, temporal as well as spiritual, which they no longer derived from the great society of Christians. But almost all those who had reluctantly yielded to the power of vice or idolatry, were sensible of their fallen condition, and anxiously desirous of being restored to the benefits of the Christian communion.

With regard to the treatment of these penitents two opposite opinions, the one of justice, the other of mercy, divided the primitive church. The more rigid and inflexible casuists refused them for ever, and without exception, the meanest place in the holy community, which they had disgraced or deserted, and leaving them to the remorse of a guilty conscience, indulged them only with a faint ray of hope, that the contrition of their life and death might possibly be accepted by the Supreme Being.[145] A milder sentiment was embraced in practice as well as in theory, by the purest and most respectable of the Christian churches.[146] The gates of reconciliation and of Heaven were seldom shut against the returning penitent; but a severe and solemn form of discipline was instituted, which, while it served to expiate his crime, might powerfully deter the spectators

145. The Montanists and the Novatians, who adhered to this opinion with the greatest rigour and obstinacy, found *themselves* at last in the number of excommunicated heretics.

See the learned and copious Mosheim, Secul. ii. and iii.

146. Dionysius ap. Euseb. iv. 23. Cyprian, de Lapsis.

from the imitation of his example. Humbled by a public confession, emaciated by fasting, and clothed in sackcloth, the penitent lay prostrate at the door of the assembly, imploring with tears the pardon of his offences, and soliciting the prayers of the faithful.[147] If the fault was of a very heinous nature, whole years of penance were esteemed an inadequate satisfaction to the Divine Justice; and it was always by slow and painful gradations that the sinner, the heretic, or the apostate, was re-admitted into the bosom of the church. A sentence of perpetual excommunication was, however, reserved for some crimes of an extraordinary magnitude, and particularly for the inexcusable relapses of those penitents who had already experienced and abused the clemency of their ecclesiastical superiors. According to the circumstances or the number of the guilty, the exercise of the Christian discipline was varied by the discretion of the bishops. The councils of Ancyra and Illiberis were held about the same time, the one in Galatia, the other in Spain; but their respective canons, which are still extant, seem to breathe a very different spirit. The Galatian, who after his baptism had repeatedly sacrificed to idols, might obtain his pardon by a penance of seven years, and if he had seduced others to imitate his example, only three years more were added to the term of his exile. But the unhappy Spaniard, who had committed the same offence, was deprived of the hope of reconciliation, even in the article of death; and his idolatry was placed at the head of a list of seventeen other crimes, against which a sentence no less terrible was pronounced. Among these we may distinguish the inexpiable guilt of calumniating a bishop, a presbyter, or even a deacon.[148]

Public penance.

The well-tempered mixture of liberality and rigour, the judicious dispensation of rewards and punishments, according to the maxims of policy as well as justice, constituted the *human* strength of the church. The bishops, whose paternal care extended itself to the government of both worlds, were sensible of the importance of these prerogatives, and covering their ambition with the fair pretence of the love

The dignity of episcopal government.

---

147. Cave's Primitive Christianity, part iii. c. 5. The admirers of antiquity regret the loss of this public penance.

148. See in Dupin, Bibliothèque Ecclesiastique, tom. ii. p. 304–313, a short but rational exposition of the canons of those councils, which were assembled in the first

moments of tranquillity, after the persecution of Diocletian. This persecution had been much less severely felt in Spain than in Galatia; a difference which may, in some measure, account for the contrast of their regulations.

of order, they were jealous of any rival in the exercise of a discipline so necessary to prevent the desertion of those troops which had inlisted themselves under the banner of the cross, and whose numbers every day became more considerable. From the imperious declamations of Cyprian, we should naturally conclude, that the doctrines of excommunication and penance formed the most essential part of religion; and that it was much less dangerous for the disciples of Christ to neglect the observance of the moral duties, than to despise the censures and authority of their bishops. Sometimes we might imagine that we were listening to the voice of Moses, when he commanded the earth to open, and to swallow up, in consuming flames, the rebellious race which refused obedience to the priesthood of Aaron; and we should sometimes suppose that we heard a Roman consul asserting the majesty of the republic, and declaring his inflexible resolution to enforce the rigour of the laws. "If such irregularities are suffered with impunity (it is thus that the bishop of Carthage chides the lenity of his colleague), if such irregularities are suffered, there is an end of EPISCOPAL VIGOUR;[149] an end of the sublime and divine power of governing the church, an end of Christianity itself." Cyprian had renounced those temporal honours, which it is probable he would never have obtained; but the acquisition of such absolute command over the consciences and understanding of a congregation, however obscure or despised by the world, is more truly grateful to the pride of the human heart, than the possession of the most despotic power, imposed by arms and conquest on a reluctant people.

Recapitulation of the five causes. In the course of this important, though perhaps tedious, inquiry, I have attempted to display the secondary causes which so efficaciously assisted the truth of the Christian religion. If among these causes we have discovered any artificial ornaments, any accidental circumstances, or any mixture of error and passion, it cannot appear surprising that mankind should be the most sensibly affected by such motives as were suited to their imperfect nature. It was by the aid of these causes, exclusive zeal, the immediate expectation of another world, the claim of miracles, the practice of rigid virtue, and the constitution of the primitive church, that Christianity spread itself with so much success in the Roman empire. To the first of these the Christians were indebted for their invincible valour, which disdained to capitulate with the enemy whom they were resolved to vanquish. The three succeeding causes supplied

149. Cyprian. Epist. 69.

their valour with the most formidable arms. The last of these causes united their courage, directed their arms, and gave their efforts that irresistible weight, which even a small band of well-trained and intrepid volunteers has so often possessed over an undisciplined multitude, ignorant of the subject, and careless of the event of the war. In the various religions of Polytheism, some wandering fanatics of Egypt and Syria, who addressed themselves to the credulous superstition of *Weakness of polytheism.* the populace, were perhaps the only order of priests[150] that derived their whole support and credit from their sacerdotal profession, and were very deeply affected by a personal concern for the safety or prosperity of their tutelar deities. The ministers of polytheism, both in Rome and in the provinces, were, for the most part, men of a noble birth, and of an affluent fortune, who received, as an honourable distinction, the care of a celebrated temple, or of a public sacrifice, exhibited, very frequently at their own expence, the sacred games,[151] and with cold indifference performed the ancient rites, according to the laws and fashion of their country. As they were engaged in the ordinary occupations of life, their zeal and devotion were seldom animated by a sense of interest, or by the habits of an ecclesiastical character. Confined to their respective temples and cities, they remained without any connexion of discipline or government; and whilst they acknowledged the supreme jurisdiction of the senate, of the college of pontiffs, and of the emperor, those civil magistrates contented themselves with the easy task of maintaining, in peace and dignity, the general worship of mankind. We have already seen how various, how loose, and how uncertain were the religious sentiments of Polytheists. They were abandoned, almost without controul, to the natural workings of a superstitious fancy. The accidental circumstances of their life and situation determined the object as well as the degree of their devotion; and as long as their adoration was successively prostituted to a thousand deities, it was scarcely possible that their hearts could be susceptible of a very sincere or lively passion for any of them.

150. The arts, the manners, and the vices of the priests of the Syrian goddess, are very humourously described by Apuleius, in the eighth book of his Metamorphoses.

151. The office of Asiarch was of this nature, and it is frequently mentioned in Aristides, the Inscriptions, &c. It was annual and elective. None but the vainest citizens could

desire the honour; none but the most wealthy could support the expence. See in the Patres Apostol. tom. ii. p. 200. with how much indifference Philip the Asiarch conducted himself in the martyrdom of Polycarp. There were likewise Bithyniarchs, Lyciarchs, &c.

The scepticism of the Pagan world proved favourable to the new religion,

When Christianity appeared in the world, even these faint and imperfect impressions had lost much of their original power. Human reason, which by its unassisted strength is incapable of perceiving the mysteries of faith, had already obtained an easy triumph over the folly of Paganism; and when Tertullian or Lactantius employ their labours in exposing its falsehood and extravagance, they are obliged to transcribe the eloquence of Cicero or the wit of Lucian. The contagion of these sceptical writings had been diffused far beyond the number of their readers. The fashion of incredulity was communicated from the philosopher to the man of pleasure or business, from the noble to the plebeian, and from the master to the menial slave who waited at his table, and who eagerly listened to the freedom of his conversation. On public occasions the philosophic part of mankind affected to treat with respect and decency the religious institutions of their country; but their secret contempt penetrated through the thin and awkward disguise, and even the people, when they discovered that their deities were rejected and derided by those whose rank or understanding they were accustomed to reverence, were filled with doubts and apprehensions concerning the truth of those doctrines, to which they had yielded the most implicit belief. The decline of ancient prejudice exposed a very numerous portion of human kind to the danger of a painful and comfortless situation. A state of scepticism and suspense may amuse a few inquisitive minds. But the practice of superstition is so congenial to the multitude, that if they are forcibly awakened, they still regret the loss of their pleasing vision. Their love of the marvellous and supernatural, their curiosity with regard to future events, and their strong propensity to extend their hopes and fears beyond the limits of the visible world, were the principal causes which favoured the establishment of Polytheism. So urgent on the vulgar is the necessity of believing, that the fall of any system of mythology will most probably be succeeded by the introduction of some other mode of superstition. Some deities of a more recent and fashionable cast might soon have occupied the deserted temples of Jupiter and Apollo, if, in the decisive moment, the wisdom of Providence had not interposed a genuine revelation, fitted to inspire the most rational esteem and conviction, whilst, at the same time, it was adorned with all that could attract the curiosity, the wonder, and the veneration of the people. In their actual disposition, as many were almost disengaged from their artificial prejudices, but equally susceptible and desirous of a devout attachment; an object much less deserving would have been sufficient to fill the vacant place in their hearts, and to gratify the uncertain eagerness of their passions. Those who are inclined to pursue this reflection, instead of viewing with astonishment the rapid progress of Christianity, will perhaps be surprised that its success was not still more rapid and still more universal.

It has been observed, with truth as well as propriety, that the conquests of Rome prepared and facilitated those of Christianity. In the second chapter of this work we have attempted to explain in what manner the most civilized provinces of Europe, Asia, and Africa, were united under the dominion of one *as well as the peace and union of the Roman empire.* sovereign, and gradually connected by the most intimate ties of laws, of manners, and of language. The Jews of Palestine, who had fondly expected a temporal deliverer, gave so cold a reception to the miracles of the divine prophet, that it was found unnecessary to publish, or at least to preserve, any Hebrew gospel.[152] The authentic histories of the actions of Christ were composed in the Greek language, at a considerable distance from Jerusalem, and after the Gentile converts were grown extremely numerous.[153] As soon as those histories were translated into the Latin tongue, they were perfectly intelligible to all the subjects of Rome, excepting only to the peasants of Syria and Egypt, for whose benefit particular versions were afterwards made. The public highways, which had been constructed for the use of the legions, opened an easy passage for the Christian missionaries from Damascus to Corinth, and from Italy to the extremity of Spain or Britain; nor did those spiritual conquerors encounter any of the obstacles which usually retard or prevent the introduction of a foreign religion into a distant country. There is the strongest reason to believe, that before the reigns of Diocletian and Constantine, the faith of Christ had been preached in every province, and in all the great cities of the empire; but the foundation of the several congregations, the numbers of the faithful who composed them, and their proportion to the unbelieving multitude, are now buried in obscurity, or disguised by *Historical view of the progress of Christianity* fiction and declamation. Such imperfect circumstances, however, as have

---

152. The modern critics are not disposed to believe what the fathers almost unanimously assert, that St. Matthew composed a Hebrew gospel, of which only the Greek translation is extant. It seems, however, dangerous to reject their testimony.

153. Under the reigns of Nero and Domitian, and in the cities of Alexandria, Antioch, Rome, and Ephesus. See Mill. Prolegomena ad Nov. Testament. and Dr. Lardner's fair and extensive collection, vol. xv.

reached our knowledge concerning the increase of the Christian name in Asia and Greece, in Egypt, in Italy, and in the West, we shall now proceed to relate, without neglecting the real or imaginary acquisitions which lay beyond the frontiers of the Roman empire.

in the East.   The rich provinces that extend from the Euphrates to the Ionian sea, were the principal theatre on which the apostle of the Gentiles displayed his zeal and piety. The seeds of the gospel, which he had scattered in a fertile soil, were diligently cultivated by his disciples; and it should seem that, during the two first centuries, the most considerable body of Christians was contained within those limits. Among the societies which were instituted in Syria, none were more ancient or more illustrious than those of Damascus, of Berea or Aleppo, and of Antioch. The prophetic introduction of the Apocalypse has described and immortalised the seven churches of Asia; Ephesus, Smyrna, Pergamus, Thyatira,[154] Sardes, Laodicea, and Philadelphia; and their colonies were soon diffused over that populous country. In a very early period, the islands of Cyprus and Crete, the provinces of Thrace and Macedonia, gave a favourable reception to the new religion; and Christian republics were soon founded in the cities of Corinth, of Sparta, and of Athens.[155] The antiquity of the Greek and Asiatic churches allowed a sufficient space of time for their increase and multiplication, and even the swarms of Gnostics and other heretics serve to display the flourishing condition of the orthodox church, since the appellation of heretics has always been applied to the less numerous party. To these domestic testimonies we may add the confession, the complaints, and the apprehensions of the Gentiles themselves. From the writings of Lucian, a philosopher who had studied mankind, and who describes their manners in the most lively colours, we may learn, that, under the reign of Commodus, his native country of Pontus was filled with Epicureans and *Christians*.[156] Within fourscore years after the death of

154. The Alogians (Epiphanius de Hæres. 51.) disputed the genuineness of the Apocalypse, because the church of Thyatira was not yet founded. Epiphanius, who allows the fact, extricates himself from the difficulty, by ingeniously supposing, that St. John wrote in the spirit of prophecy. See Abauzit Discours sur l'Apocalypse.

155. The epistles of Ignatius and Dionysius (ap. Euseb. iv. 23.) point out many churches in Asia and Greece. That of Athens seems to have been one of the least flourishing.

156. Lucian in Alexandro, c. 25. Christianity however must have been very unequally diffused over Pontus; since in the middle of the third century there were no more than seventeen believers in the extensive diocese of Neo-Cæsarea. See M. de Tillemont,

Christ,[157] the humane Pliny laments the magnitude of the evil which he vainly attempted to eradicate. In his very curious epistle to the emperor Trajan, he affirms, that the temples were almost deserted, that the sacred victims scarcely found any purchasers, and that the superstition had not only infected the cities, but had even spread itself into the villages and the open country of Pontus and Bithynia.[158]

The church of Antioch.

Without descending into a minute scrutiny of the expressions, or of the motives of those writers who either celebrate or lament the progress of Christianity in the East, it may in general be observed, that none of them have left us any grounds from whence a just estimate might be formed of the real numbers of the faithful in those provinces. One circumstance, however, has been fortunately preserved, which seems to cast a more distinct light on this obscure but interesting subject. Under the reign of Theodosius, after Christianity had enjoyed, during more than sixty years, the sunshine of Imperial favour, the ancient and illustrious church of Antioch consisted of one hundred thousand persons, three thousand of whom were supported out of the public oblations.[159] The splendour and dignity of the queen of the East, the acknowledged populousness of Cæsarea, Seleucia, and Alexandria, and the destruction of two hundred and fifty thousand souls in the earthquake which afflicted Antioch under the elder Justin,[160] are so many convincing proofs that the whole number of its inhabitants was not less than half a million, and that the Christians, however multiplied by zeal and power, did not exceed a fifth part of that great city. How different a proportion must we adopt when we compare the persecuted with the triumphant church, the West with the East, remote villages with populous towns, and countries recently converted to the faith, with the place where the believers first received the appellation of Christians! It must not, however, be dissembled, that, in another passage, Chrysostom, to whom we are indebted for this useful information, computes the multitude of the faithful as even

Memoires Ecclesiast. tom. iv. p. 675. from Basil and Gregory of Nyssa, who were themselves natives of Cappadocia.

157. According to the ancients, Jesus Christ suffered under the consulship of the two Gemini, in the year 29 of our present æra. Pliny was sent into Bithynia (according to Pagi) in the year 110.

158. Plin. Epist. x. 97.

159. Chrysostom. Opera. tom. vii. p. 658, 810.

160. John Malela, tom. ii. p. 144. He draws the same conclusion with regard to the populousness of Antioch.

superior to that of the Jews and Pagans.[161] But the solution of this apparent difficulty is easy and obvious. The eloquent preacher draws a parallel between the civil and the ecclesiastical constitution of Antioch; between the list of Christians who had acquired Heaven by baptism, and the list of citizens who had a right to share the public liberality. Slaves, strangers, and infants were comprised in the former; they were excluded from the latter.

In Egypt.   The extensive commerce of Alexandria, and its proximity to Palestine, gave an easy entrance to the new religion. It was at first embraced by great numbers of the Therapeutæ, or Essenians of the lake Mareotis, a Jewish sect which had abated much of its reverence for the Mosaic ceremonies. The austere life of the Essenians, their fasts and excommunications, the community of goods, the love of celibacy, their zeal for martyrdom, and the warmth though not the purity of their faith, already offered a very lively image of the primitive discipline.[162] It was in the school of Alexandria that the Christian theology appears to have assumed a regular and scientifical form; and when Hadrian visited Egypt, he found a church composed of Jews and of Greeks, sufficiently important to attract the notice of that inquisitive prince.[163] But the progress of Christianity was for a long time confined within the limits of a single city, which was itself a foreign colony, and till the close of the second century the predecessors of Demetrius were the only prelates of the Egyptian church. Three bishops were consecrated by the hands of Demetrius, and the number was increased to twenty by his successor Heraclas.[164] The body of the natives, a people distinguished by a sullen inflexibility of temper,[165] entertained the new doctrine with coldness and reluctance: and even in the time of Origen, it

161. Chrysostom. tom. i. p. 592. I am indebted for these passages, though not for my inference, to the learned Dr. Lardner. Credibility of the Gospel History, vol. xii. p. 370.

162. Basnage, Histoire des Juifs, l. 2. c. 20, 21, 22, 23. has examined, with the most critical accuracy, the curious treatise of Philo, which describes the Therapeutæ. By proving that it was composed as early as the time of Augustus, Basnage has demonstrated, in spite of Eusebius (l. ii. c. 17.), and a crowd of modern Catholics, that the Therapeutæ were neither Christians nor monks. It still remains probable that they changed their name, preserved their manners, adopted some new articles of faith, and gradually became the fathers of the Egyptian Ascetics.

163. See a letter of Hadrian, in the Augustan History, p. 245.

164. For the succession of Alexandrian bishops, consult Renaudot's History, p. 24, &c. This curious fact is preserved by the patriarch Eutychius (Annal. tom. i. p. 334. Vers. Pocock), and its internal evidence would alone be a sufficient answer to all the objections which Bishop Pearson has urged in the Vindiciæ Ignatianæ.

165. Ammian. Marcellin. xxii. 16.

was rare to meet with an Egyptian who had surmounted his early prejudices in favour of the sacred animals of his country.[166] As soon, indeed, as Christianity ascended the throne, the zeal of those barbarians obeyed the prevailing impulsion; the cities of Egypt were filled with bishops, and the deserts of Thebais swarmed with hermits.

A perpetual stream of strangers and provincials flowed into the capacious bosom of Rome. Whatever was strange or odious, who-*In Rome.* ever was guilty or suspected, might hope, in the obscurity of that immense capital, to elude the vigilance of the law. In such a various conflux of nations, every teacher, either of truth or of falsehood, every founder, whether of a virtuous or a criminal association, might easily multiply his disciples or accomplices. The Christians of Rome, at the time of the accidental persecution of Nero, are represented by Tacitus as already amounting to a very great multitude,[167] and the language of that great historian is almost similar to the style employed by Livy, when he relates the introduction and the suppression of the rites of Bacchus. After the Bacchanals had awakened the severity of the senate, it was likewise apprehended that a very great multitude, as it were *another people*, had been initiated into those abhorred mysteries. A more careful inquiry soon demonstrated, that the offenders did not exceed seven thousand; a number indeed sufficiently alarming, when considered as the object of public justice.[168] It is with the same candid allowance that we should interpret the vague expressions of Tacitus, and in a former instance of Pliny, when they exaggerate the crowds of deluded fanatics who had forsaken the established worship of the gods. The church of Rome was undoubtedly the first and most populous of the empire; and we are possessed of an authentic record which attests the state of religion in that city about the middle of the third century, and after a peace of thirty-eight years. The clergy, at that time, consisted of a bishop, forty-six presbyters, seven deacons, as many sub-deacons, forty-two acolythes, and fifty readers, exorcists, and porters. The number of widows, of the infirm, and of the poor, who were maintained by the oblations of the faithful, amounted to fifteen hundred.[169]

---

166. Origen contra Celsum, l. i. p. 40.
167. Ingens multitudo is the expression of Tacitus, xv. 44.
168. T. Liv. xxxix. 13. 15, 16, 17. Nothing could exceed the horror and consternation of the senate on the discovery of the

Bacchanalians, whose depravity is described, and perhaps exaggerated, by Livy.
169. Eusebius, l. vi. c. 43. The Latin translator (M. de Valois) has thought proper to reduce the number of presbyters to forty-four.

From reason, as well as from the analogy of Antioch, we may venture to estimate the Christians of Rome at about fifty thousand. The populousness of that great capital cannot perhaps be exactly ascertained; but the most modest calculation will not surely reduce it lower than a million of inhabitants, of whom the Christians might constitute at the most a twentieth part.[170]

In Africa and the western provinces.   The western provincials appeared to have derived the knowledge of Christianity from the same source which had diffused among them the language, the sentiments, and the manners of Rome. In this more important circumstance, Africa, as well as Gaul, was gradually fashioned to the imitation of the capital. Yet notwithstanding the many favourable occasions which might invite the Roman missionaries to visit their Latin provinces, it was late before they passed either the sea or the Alps;[171] nor can we discover in those great countries any assured traces either of faith or of persecution that ascend higher than the reign of the Antonines.[172] The slow progress of the gospel in the cold climate of Gaul, was extremely different from the eagerness with which it seems to have been received on the burning sands of Africa. The African Christians soon formed one of the principal members of the primitive church. The practice introduced into that province, of appointing bishops to the most inconsiderable towns, and very frequently to the most obscure villages, contributed to multiply the splendour and importance of their religious societies, which during the course of the third century were animated by the zeal of Tertullian, directed by the abilities of Cyprian, and adorned by the eloquence of Lactantius. But if, on the contrary, we turn our eyes towards Gaul, we must content ourselves with discovering, in the time of Marcus Antoninus, the feeble and united congregations of Lyons

170. This proportion of the presbyters and of the poor, to the rest of the people, was originally fixed by Burnet (Travels into Italy, p. 168.), and is approved by Moyle (vol. ii. p. 151.). They were both unacquainted with the passage of Chrysostom, which converts their conjecture almost into a fact.

171. Serius trans Alpes, religione Dei susceptâ. Sulpicius Severus, l. ii. These were the celebrated martyrs of Lyons. See Eusebius, v. 1. Tillemont, Mem. Ecclesiast. tom. ii. p. 316. According to the Donatists, whose asser-

tion is confirmed by the tacit acknowledgment of Augustin, Africa was the last of the provinces which received the gospel. Tillemont, Mem. Ecclesiast. tom. i. p. 754.

172. Tum primum intra Gallias martyria visa. Sulp. Severus, l. ii. With regard to Africa, see Tertullian ad Scapulam, c. 3. It is imagined, that the Scyllitan martyrs were the first (Acta Sincera Ruinart. p. 34.). One of the adversaries of Apuleius seems to have been a Christian. Apolog. p. 496, 497. edit. Delphin.

and Vienna; and even as late as the reign of Decius, we are assured, that in a few cities only, Arles, Narbonne, Thoulouse, Limoges, Clermont, Tours, and Paris, some scattered churches were supported by the devotion of a small number of Christians.[173] Silence is indeed very consistent with devotion, but as it is seldom compatible with zeal, we may perceive and lament the languid state of Christianity in those provinces which had exchanged the Celtic for the Latin tongue; since they did not, during the three first centuries, give birth to a single ecclesiastical writer. From Gaul, which claimed a just pre-eminence of learning and authority over all the countries on this side of the Alps, the light of the gospel was more faintly reflected on the remote provinces of Spain and Britain; and if we may credit the vehement assertions of Tertullian, they had already received the first rays of the faith, when he addressed his apology to the magistrates of the emperor Severus.[174] But the obscure and imperfect origin of the western churches of Europe has been so negligently recorded, that if we would relate the time and manner of their foundation, we must supply the silence of antiquity by those legends which avarice or superstition long afterwards dictated to the monks in the lazy gloom of their convents.[175] Of these holy romances, that of the apostle St. James can alone, by its singular extravagance, deserve to be mentioned. From a peaceful fisherman of the lake of Gennesareth, he was transformed into a valorous knight, who charged at the head of the Spanish chivalry in their battles against the Moors. The gravest historians have celebrated his exploits; the miraculous shrine of Compostella displayed his power; and the sword of a military order, assisted by the terrors of the Inquisition, was sufficient to remove every objection of profane criticism.[176]

173. Raræ in aliquibus civitatibus ecclesiæ, paucorum Christianorum devotione, resurgerent. Acta Sincera, p. 130. Gregory of Tours, l. i. c. 28. Mosheim, p. 207. 449. There is some reason to believe, that, in the beginning of the fourth century, the extensive dioceses of Liege, of Treves, and of Cologne, composed a single bishopric, which had been very recently founded. See Memoires de Tillemont, tom. vi. part i. p. 43. 411.

174. The date of Tertullian's Apology is fixed, in a dissertation of Mosheim, to the year 198.

175. In the fifteenth century, there were few who had either inclination or courage to question whether Joseph of Arimathea founded the monastery of Glastenbury, and whether Dionysius the Areopagite preferred the residence of Paris to that of Athens.

176. The stupendous metamorphosis was performed in the ninth century. See Mariana (Hist. Hispan. l. vii. c. 13. tom. i. p. 285. edit. Hag. Com. 1733), who in every sense, imitates Livy, and the honest detection of the legend of St. James by Dr. Geddes, Miscellanies, vol. ii. p. 221.

Beyond the limits of the Roman empire.   The progress of Christianity was not confined to the Roman empire; and according to the primitive fathers, who interpret facts by prophecy, the new religion, within a century after the death of its divine author, had already visited every part of the globe. "There exists not," says Justin Martyr, "a people, whether Greek or Barbarian, of any other race of men, by whatsoever appellation or manners they may be distinguished, however ignorant of arts or agriculture, whether they dwell under tents, or wander about in covered waggons, among whom prayers are not offered up in the name of a crucified Jesus to the Father and Creator of all things."[177] But this splendid exaggeration, which even at present it would be extremely difficult to reconcile with the real state of mankind, can be considered only as the rash sally of a devout but careless writer, the measure of whose belief was regulated by that of his wishes. But neither the belief, nor the wishes of the fathers, can alter the truth of history. It will still remain an undoubted fact, that the barbarians of Scythia and Germany, who afterwards subverted the Roman monarchy, were involved in the darkness of paganism; and that even the conversion of Iberia, of Armenia, or of Æthiopia, was not attempted with any degree of success till the sceptre was in the hands of an orthodox emperor.[178] Before that time, the various accidents of war and commerce might indeed diffuse an imperfect knowledge of the gospel among the tribes of Caledonia,[179] and among the borderers of the Rhine, the Danube, and the Euphrates.[180] Beyond the last-mentioned river, Edessa was distinguished by a firm and early adherence to the faith.[181] From Edessa, the principles

---

177. Justin Martyr, Dialog. cum Tryphon, p. 341. Irenæus adv. Hæres. l. i. c. 10. Tertullian adv. Jud. c. 7. See Mosheim, p. 203.

178. See the fourth century of Mosheim's History of the Church. Many, though very confused circumstances, that relate to the conversion of Iberia and Armenia, may be found in Moses of Chorene, l. ii. c. 78–89.

179. According to Tertullian, the Christian faith had penetrated into parts of Britain inaccessible to the Roman arms. About a century afterwards, Ossian, the son of Fingal, is *said* to have disputed, in his extreme old age, with one of the foreign missionaries, and the dispute is still extant, in verse, and in the Erse language. See Mr. Macpherson's

Dissertation on the Antiquity of Ossian's Poems, p. 10.

180. The Goths, who ravaged Asia in the reign of Gallienus, carried away great numbers of captives; some of whom were Christians, and became missionaries. See Tillemont, Memoires Ecclesiast. tom. iv. p. 44.

181. The Legend of Abgarus, fabulous as it is, affords a decisive proof, that many years before Eusebius wrote his history, the greatest part of the inhabitants of Edessa had embraced Christianity. Their rivals, the citizens of Carrhæ, adhered, on the contrary, to the cause of Paganism, as late as the sixth century.

of Christianity were easily introduced into the Greek and Syrian cities which obeyed the successors of Artaxerxes; but they do not appear to have made any deep impression on the minds of the Persians, whose religious system, by the labours of a well-disciplined order of priests, had been constructed with much more art and solidity than the uncertain mythology of Greece and Rome.[182]

From this impartial though imperfect survey of the progress of Christianity, it may perhaps seem probable, that the number of its proselytes has been excessively magnified by fear on the one side, and by devotion on the other. According to the irreproachable testimony of Origen,[183] the proportion of the faithful was very

General proportion of Christians and Pagans.

inconsiderable when compared with the multitude of an unbelieving world; but, as we are left without any distinct information, it is impossible to determine, and it is difficult even to conjecture, the real numbers of the primitive Christians. The most favourable calculation, however, that can be deduced from the examples of Antioch and of Rome, will not permit us to imagine that more than a twentieth part of the subjects of the Empire had enlisted themselves under the banner of the cross before the important conversion of Constantine. But their habits of faith, of zeal, and of union, seemed to multiply their numbers; and the same causes which contributed to their future increase, served to render their actual strength more apparent and more formidable.

Such is the constitution of civil society, that whilst a few persons are distinguished by riches, by honours, and by knowledge, the body of the people is condemned to obscurity, ignorance, and poverty. The Christian religion, which addressed itself to the whole human race, must consequently collect a far

Whether the first Christians were mean and ignorant.

greater number of proselytes from the lower than from the superior ranks of life. This innocent and natural circumstance has been improved into a very odious imputation, which seems to be less strenuously denied by the apologists, than it is urged by the adversaries, of the faith; that the new sect of Christians was almost entirely composed of the dregs of the populace, of peasants and mechanics, of boys and women, of beggars and slaves, the

---

182. According to Bardesanes (ap. Euseb. Præpar. Evangel.) there were some Christians in Persia before the end of the second century. In the time of Constantine (see his Epistle to Sapor, Vit. l. iv. c. 13.) they composed a flourishing church. Consult Beausobre, Hist. Critique du Manicheisme, tom. i. p. 180. and the Bibliotheca Orientalis of Assemani.

183. Origen contra Celsum, l. viii. p. 424.

last of whom might sometimes introduce the missionaries into the rich and noble families to which they belonged. These obscure teachers (such was the charge of malice and infidelity) are as mute in public as they are loquacious and dogmatical in private. Whilst they cautiously avoid the dangerous encounter of philosophers, they mingle with the rude and illiterate crowd, and insinuate themselves into those minds, whom their age, their sex, or their education, has the best disposed to receive the impression of superstitious terrors.[184]

Some exceptions with regard to learning;

This unfavourable picture, though not devoid of a faint resemblance, betrays, by its dark colouring and distorted features, the pencil of an enemy. As the humble faith of Christ diffused itself through the world, it was embraced by several persons who derived some consequence from the advantages of nature or fortune. Aristides, who presented an eloquent apology to the emperor Hadrian, was an Athenian philosopher.[185] Justin Martyr had sought divine knowledge in the schools of Zeno, of Aristotle, of Pythagoras, and of Plato, before he fortunately was accosted by the old man, or rather the angel, who turned his attention to the study of the Jewish prophets.[186] Clemens of Alexandria had acquired much various reading in the Greek, and Tertullian in the Latin, language. Julius Africanus and Origen possessed a very considerable share of the learning of their times; and although the style of Cyprian is very different from that of Lactantius, we might almost discover that both those writers had been public teachers of rhetoric. Even the study of philosophy was at length introduced among the Christians, but it was not always productive of the most salutary effects; knowledge was as often the parent of heresy as of devotion, and the description which was designed for the followers of Artemon, may, with equal propriety, be applied to the various sects that resisted the successors of the apostles. "They presume to alter the holy scriptures, to abandon the ancient rule of faith, and to form their opinions according to the subtile precepts of logic. The science of the church is neglected for the study of geometry, and they lose sight of Heaven while they are employed in measuring the earth. Euclid is perpetually in their hands. Aristotle and Theophrastus are the objects of their

---

184. Minucius Fœlix, c. 8. with Wowerus's notes. Celsus ap. Origen. l. iii. p. 138. 142. Julian ap. Cyril. l. vi. p. 206. edit. Spanheim. 185. Euseb. Hist. Eccles. iv. 3. Hieronym. Epist. 83.

186. The story is prettily told in Justin's Dialogues. Tillemont (Mem. Ecclesiast. tom. ii. p. 334.), who relates it after him, is sure that the old man was a disguised angel.

admiration; and they express an uncommon reverence for the works of Galen. Their errors are derived from the abuse of the arts and sciences of the infidels, and they corrupt the simplicity of the gospel by the refinements of human reason."[187]

    Nor can it be affirmed with truth, that the advantages of birth and fortune were always separated from the profession of Christianity. Several Roman citizens were brought before the tribunal of Pliny, and he soon discovered, that a great number of *with regard to rank and fortune.* persons of *every order* of men in Bithynia had deserted the religion of their ancestors.[188] His unsuspected testimony may, in this instance, obtain more credit than the bold challenge of Tertullian, when he addresses himself to the fears as well as to the humanity of the proconsul of Africa, by assuring him, that if he persists in his cruel intentions, he must decimate Carthage, and that he will find among the guilty many persons of his own rank, senators and matrons of noblest extraction, and the friends or relations of his most intimate friends.[189] It appears, however, that about forty years afterwards the emperor Valerian was persuaded of the truth of this assertion, since in one of his rescripts he evidently supposes, that senators, Roman knights, and ladies of quality, were engaged in the Christian sect.[190] The church still continued to encrease its outward splendour as it lost its internal purity; and, in the reign of Diocletian, the palace, the courts of justice, and even the army, concealed a multitude of Christians, who endeavoured to reconcile the interests of the present, with those of a future, life.

    And yet these exceptions are either too few in number, or too recent in time, entirely to remove the imputation of ignorance and obscurity which has been so arrogantly cast on the first proselytes of Christianity. Instead of employing in our defence the fictions of later ages, it will be more prudent to *Christianity most favourably received by the poor and simple.* convert the occasion of scandal into a subject of edification. Our serious thoughts will suggest to us, that the apostles themselves were chosen by providence among the fishermen of Galilee, and that the lower we depress

---

187. Eusebius, v. 28. It may be hoped, that none, except the heretics, gave occasion to the complaint of Celsus (ap. Origen. l. ii. p. 77.), that the Christians were perpetually correcting and altering their Gospels.

188. Plin. Epist. x. 97. Fuerunt alii similis amentiæ, cives Romani ... Multi enim

omnis ætatis, *omnis ordinis*, utriusque sexûs, etiam vocantur in periculum et vocabuntur.

189. Tertullian ad Scapulam. Yet even his rhetoric rises no higher than to claim a *tenth* part of Carthage.

190. Cyprian. Epist. 79.

the temporal condition of the first Christians, the more reason we shall find to admire their merit and success. It is incumbent on us diligently to remember, that the kingdom of Heaven was promised to the poor in spirit, and that minds afflicted by calamity and the contempt of mankind, cheerfully listen to the divine promise of future happiness; while, on the contrary, the fortunate are satisfied with the possession of this world; and the wise abuse in doubt and dispute their vain superiority of reason and knowledge.

Rejected by some eminent men of the first and second centuries.

We stand in need of such reflections to comfort us for the loss of some illustrious characters, which in our eyes might have seemed the most worthy of the heavenly present. The names of Seneca, of the elder and the younger Pliny, of Tacitus, of Plutarch, of Galen, of the slave Epictetus, and of the emperor Marcus Antoninus, adorn the age in which they flourished, and exalt the dignity of human nature. They filled with glory their respective stations, either in active or contemplative life; their excellent understandings were improved by study; Philosophy had purified their minds from the prejudices of the popular superstition; and their days were spent in the pursuit of truth and the practice of virtue. Yet all these sages (it is no less an object of surprise than of concern) overlooked or rejected the perfection of the Christian system. Their language or their silence equally discover their contempt for the growing sect, which in their time had diffused itself over the Roman empire. Those among them who condescend to mention the Christians, consider them only as obstinate and perverse enthusiasts, who exacted an implicit submission to their mysterious doctrines, without being able to produce a single argument that could engage the attention of men of sense and learning.[191]

Their neglect of prophecy

It is at least doubtful whether any of these philosophers perused the apologies which the primitive Christians repeatedly published in behalf of themselves and of their religion; but it is much to be lamented that such a cause was not defended by abler advocates. They expose with superfluous wit and eloquence, the extravagance of Polytheism. They interest our compassion by displaying the innocence and sufferings of their injured brethren. But when they would demonstrate

---

191. Dr. Lardner, in his first and second volume of Jewish and Christian testimonies, collects and illustrates those of Pliny the younger, of Tacitus, of Galen, of Marcus Antoninus, and perhaps of Epictetus (for it is doubt- ful whether that philosopher means to speak of the Christians). The new sect is totally unnoticed by Seneca, the elder Pliny, and Plutarch.

the divine origin of Christianity, they insist much more strongly on the predictions which announced, than on the miracles which accompanied, the appearance of the Messiah. Their favourite argument might serve to edify a Christian or to convert a Jew, since both the one and the other acknowledge the authority of those prophecies, and both are obliged, with devout reverence, to search for their sense and their accomplishment. But this mode of persuasion loses much of its weight and influence, when it is addressed to those who neither understand nor respect the Mosaic dispensation and the prophetic style.[192] In the unskilful hands of Justin and of the succeeding apologists, the sublime meaning of the Hebrew oracles evaporates in distant types, affected conceits, and cold allegories; and even their authenticity was rendered suspicious to an unenlightened Gentile, by the mixture of pious forgeries, which, under the names of Orpheus, Hermes, and the Sibyls,[193] were obtruded on him as of equal value with the genuine inspirations of Heaven. The adoption of fraud and sophistry in the defence of revelation, too often reminds us of the injudicious conduct of those poets who load their *invulnerable* heroes with a useless weight of cumbersome and brittle armour.

But how shall we excuse the supine inattention of the Pagan and philosophic world, to those evidences which were pre- *and of miracles.* sented by the hand of Omnipotence, not to their reason, but to their senses? During the age of Christ, of his apostles, and of their first disciples, the doctrine which they preached was confirmed by innumerable prodigies. The lame walked, the blind saw, the sick were healed, the dead were raised, dæmons were expelled, and the laws of Nature *General silence* were frequently suspended for the benefit of the church. But *concerning the* the sages of Greece and Rome turned aside from the awful *darkness of the* spectacle, and pursuing the ordinary occupations of life and *Passion.*

---

192. If the famous prophecy of the Seventy Weeks had been alleged to a Roman philosopher, would he not have replied in the words of Cicero, "Quæ tandem ista auguratio est, annorum potius quam aut mensium aut dierum?" De Divinatione, ii. 30. Observe with what irreverence Lucian (in Alexandro, c. 13.) and his friend Celsus ap. Origen, (l. vii. p. 327.) express themselves concerning the Hebrew prophets.

193. The Philosophers, who derided the more ancient predictions of the Sibyls, would easily have detected the Jewish and Christian forgeries, which have been so triumphantly quoted by the fathers from Justin Martyr to Lactantius. When the Sibylline verses had performed their appointed task, they, like the system of the millennium, were quietly laid aside. The Christian Sibyl had unluckily fixed the ruin of Rome for the year 195, A.U.C. 948.

study, appeared unconscious of any alterations in the moral or physical government of the world. Under the reign of Tiberius, the whole earth,[194] or at least a celebrated province of the Roman empire,[195] was involved in a præternatural darkness of three hours. Even this miraculous event, which ought to have excited the wonder, the curiosity, and the devotion of mankind, passed without notice in an age of science and history.[196] It happened during the lifetime of Seneca and the elder Pliny, who must have experienced the immediate effects, or received the earliest intelligence, of the prodigy. Each of these philosophers, in a laborious work, has recorded all the great phenomena of Nature, earthquakes, meteors, comets, and eclipses, which his indefatigable curiosity could collect.[197] Both the one and the other have omitted to mention the greatest phenomenon to which the mortal eye has been witness since the creation of the globe. A distinct chapter of Pliny[198] is designed for eclipses of an extraordinary nature and unusual duration; but he contents himself with describing the singular defect of light which followed the murder of Cæsar, when, during the greatest part of a year, the orb of the sun appeared pale and without splendour. This season of obscurity, which cannot surely be compared with the præternatural darkness of the Passion, had been already celebrated by most of the poets[199] and historians of that memorable age.[200]

194. The fathers, as they are drawn out in battle array by Dom Calmet (Dissertations sur la Bible, tom. iii. p. 295–308.), seem to cover the whole earth with darkness, in which they are followed by most of the moderns.

195. Origen ad Matth. c. 27. and a few modern critics, Beza, Le Clerc, Lardner, &c. are desirous of confining it to the land of Judea.

196. The celebrated passage of Phlegon is now wisely abandoned. When Tertullian assures the Pagans, that the mention of the prodigy is found in Arcanis (not Archivis) vestris (see his Apology, c. 21.), he probably appeals to the Sibylline verses, which relate it exactly in the words of the Gospel.

197. Seneca Quæst. Natur. i. l.15. vi. l. vii. 17. Plin. Hist. Natur. l. ii.

198. Plin. Hist. Natur. ii. 30.

199. Virgil Georgic. i. 466. Tibullus, l. i. Eleg. v. ver. 75. Ovid Metamorph. xv. 782. Lucan. Pharsal. i. 540. The last of these poets places this prodigy before the civil war.

200. See a public epistle of M. Antony in Joseph. Antiquit. xiv. 12. Plutarch in Cæsar. p. 471. Appian, Bell. Civil. l. iv. Dion Cassius, l. xlv. p. 431. Julius Obsequens, c. 128. His little treatise is an abstract of Livy's prodigies.

[CHAPTERS XVI–XXI]

Chapter XVI sustains the polemical drive of the preceding chapter. The claims of Christian apologists concerning the extent and severity of the persecutions inflicted on the new faith by the Roman state are dispassionately examined and coolly recalculated:

In this general view of the persecution, which was first authorized by the edicts of Diocletian, I have purposely refrained from describing the particular sufferings and deaths of the Christian martyrs. It would have been an easy task, from the history of Eusebius, from the declamations of Lactantius, and from the most ancient acts, to collect a long series of horrid and disgustful pictures, and to fill many pages with racks and scourges, with iron hooks, and red hot beds, and with all the variety of tortures which fire and steel, savage beasts and more savage executioners, could inflict on the human body. These melancholy scenes might be enlivened by a crowd of visions and miracles destined either to delay the death, to celebrate the triumph, or to discover the relics, of those canonized saints who suffered for the name of Christ. But I cannot determine what I ought to transcribe, till I am satisfied how much I ought to believe. The gravest of the ecclesiastical historians, Eusebius himself, indirectly confesses, that he has related whatever might redound to the glory, and that he has suppressed all that could tend to the disgrace, of religion. Such an acknowledgment will naturally excite a suspicion, that a writer who has so openly violated one of the fundamental laws of history, has not paid a very strict regard to the observance of the other: and the suspicion will derive additional credit from the character of Eusebius, which was less tinctured with credulity, and more practised in the arts of courts, than that of almost any of his contemporaries. On some particular occasions, when the magistrates were exasperated by some personal motives of interest or resentment, when the zeal of the martyrs urged them to forget the rules of prudence, and perhaps of decency, to overturn the altars, to pour out imprecations against the emperors, or to strike the judge as he sat on his tribunal, it may be presumed that every mode of torture, which cruelty could invent or constancy could endure, was exhausted on those devoted victims. Two circumstances, however, have been unwarily mentioned, which insinuate that the general treatment of the Christians, who had been apprehended by the officers of justice, was less intolerable than it is usually imagined to have been. 1. The confessors who were condemned to work in the mines, were permitted, by the humanity or the negligence of their keepers, to build chapels, and freely to profess their religion in the midst of those dreary habitations. 2. The bishops were obliged to check and to censure the forward zeal of the Christians, who voluntarily threw themselves into the hands of the magistrates. Some of these were persons oppressed by poverty and debts, who blindly sought to terminate a miserable existence by a glorious death. Others were allured by the hope, that a short confinement would expiate the sins of a whole life; and others again were actuated by the less honourable motive of deriving a plentiful subsistence, and perhaps a considerable profit, from the alms which the charity of the faithful bestowed on the prisoners. After the church had triumphed over all her enemies, the interest as well as vanity of the captives prompted them to magnify the merit of their respective suffering. A convenient distance of time or place gave an ample scope to the progress of fiction; and the frequent instances which might be alleged of holy martyrs, whose wounds had been instantly healed, whose strength had been renewed, and whose lost members had miraculously been restored, were extremely convenient for the purpose of removing every difficulty, and of silencing every objection. The most extravagant legends, as they conduced to the honour of the church, were applauded by the credulous multitude, countenanced by the power of the clergy, and attested by the suspicious evidence of ecclesiastical history.

The vague descriptions of exile and imprisonment, of pain and torture, are so easily exaggerated or softened by the pencil of an artful orator, that we are naturally induced to inquire into a fact of a more distinct and stubborn kind; the number of persons who suffered death in consequence of the edicts published by Diocletian, his associates, and his successors. The recent legendaries record whole armies and cities, which were at once swept away by the undistinguishing rage of persecution. The more ancient writers content themselves with pouring out a liberal effusion of loose and tragical invectives, without condescending to ascertain the precise number of those persons who were permitted to seal with their blood their belief of the gospel. From the history of Eusebius, it may however be collected, that only nine bishops were punished with death; and we are assured, by his particular enumeration of the martyrs of Palestine, that no more than ninety-two Christians were entitled to that honourable appellation. As we are unacquainted with the degree of episcopal zeal and courage which prevailed at that time, it is not in our power to draw any useful inference from the former of these facts: but the latter may serve to justify a very important and probable conclusion. According to the distribution of Roman provinces, Palestine may be considered as the sixteenth part of the Eastern empire; and since there were some governors, who from a real or affected clemency had preserved their hands unstained with the blood of the faithful, it is reasonable to believe, that the country which had given birth to Christianity produced at least the sixteenth part of the martyrs who suffered death within the dominions of Galerius and Maximin; the whole might consequently amount to about fifteen hundred, a number which, if it is equally divided between the ten years of the persecution, will allow an annual consumption of one hundred and fifty martyrs. Allotting the same proportion to the provinces of Italy, Africa, and perhaps Spain, where, at the end of two or three years, the rigour of the penal laws was either suspended or abolished, the multitude of Christians in the Roman empire, on whom a capital punishment was inflicted by a judicial sentence, will be reduced to somewhat less than two thousand persons. Since it cannot be doubted that the Christians were more numerous, and their enemies more exasperated, in the time of Diocletian than they had ever been in any former persecution, this probable and moderate computation may teach us to estimate the number of primitive saints and martyrs who sacrificed their lives for the important purpose of introducing Christianity into the world.

We shall conclude this chapter by a melancholy truth, which obtrudes itself on the reluctant mind; that even admitting, without hesitation or enquiry, all that history has recorded, or devotion has feigned, on the subject of martyrdoms, it must still be acknowledged, that the Christians, in the course of their intestine dissentions, have inflicted far greater severities on each other, than they had experienced from the zeal of infidels. During the ages of ignorance which followed the subversion of the Roman empire in the West, the bishops of the Imperial city extended their dominion over the laity as well as clergy of the Latin church. The fabric of superstition which they had erected, and which might long have defied the feeble efforts of reason, was at length assaulted by a crowd of daring fanatics, who, from the twelfth to the sixteenth century, assumed the popular character of reformers. The church of Rome defended by violence the empire which she had acquired by fraud; a system of peace and benevolence was soon disgraced by proscriptions, wars, massacres, and the institution of the holy office. And as the reformers were animated by the love of civil, as well as of religious freedom, the Catholic princes connected their own interest with that of the clergy, and enforced by fire and the sword the terrors of spiritual censures. In the Netherlands alone, more than one hundred thousand of the subjects of Charles the Fifth are said to have suffered by the hand of the executioner; and this extraordinary number is attested by Grotius, a man of genius and learning, who preserved his moderation amidst the fury of contending sects, and who composed the annals of his own age and country, at a time when the invention of printing had facilitated the means of intelligence, and increased the danger of detection. If we are obliged to submit our belief to the authority of Grotius, it must be allowed, that the number of Protestants, who were executed in a single province and a single reign, far exceeded that of the primitive martyrs in the space of three centuries, and of the Roman empire. But if the improbability of the fact itself should prevail over the weight of evidence; if Grotius should be convicted of exaggerating the merit and sufferings of the Reformers; we shall be naturally led to inquire, what confidence can be placed in the doubtful and imperfect monuments of ancient credulity; what degree of credit can be assigned to a courtly bishop, and a passionate declaimer, who, under the protection of Constantine, enjoyed the exclusive privilege of recording the persecutions inflicted on the Christians by the vanquished rivals or disregarded predecessors of their gracious sovereign. (*DF*, i. 576–81)

With this firm, but melancholy, reflection on the comparative vigour of fanaticism and reason, and on the vulnerability of historiography to passion, the first volume and therefore also the first, 1776, instalment of *The Decline and Fall* is concluded. The second instalment, published five years later in 1781 and comprising the second and third volumes, picks up the thread left hanging at the end of chapter XIV and begins by describing the reign of Constantine (including a remarkable account of the founding and situation of Constantinople, in which Gibbon's very up-to-date understanding of the utility of analytical geography to the historian is plainly at work). In judging the Illyrian monarchy, he judiciously balances what was lost against what was preserved:

A people elated by pride, or soured by discontent, is seldom qualified to form a just estimate of their actual situation. The subjects of Constantine were incapable of discerning the decline of genius and manly virtue, which so far degraded them below the dignity of their ancestors; but they could feel and lament the rage of tyranny, the relaxation of discipline, and the encrease of taxes. The impartial historian, who acknowledges the justice of their complaints, will observe some favourable circumstances which tended to alleviate the misery of their condition. The threatening tempest of Barbarians, which so soon subverted the foundations of Roman greatness, was still repelled, or suspended, on the frontiers. The arts of luxury and literature were cultivated, and the elegant pleasures of society were enjoyed by the inhabitants of a considerable portion of the globe. The forms, the pomp, and the expence of the civil administration contributed to restrain the irregular licence of the soldiers; and although the laws were violated by power, or perverted by subtlety, the sage principles of the Roman jurisprudence preserved a sense of order and equity, unknown to the despotic governments of the east. The rights of mankind might derive some protection from religion and philosophy; and the name of freedom, which could no longer alarm, might sometimes admonish, the successors of Augustus, that they did not reign over a nation of Slaves or Barbarians. (*DF*, i. 641–2)

However, in chapters XVIII to XXI Gibbon carefully substantiates the implicit view that the virtues which in previous centuries had upheld the empire were now finding new outlets. The insight crystallizes around the figure of the early church father Athanasius:

We have seldom an opportunity of observing, either in active or speculative life, what effect may be produced, or what obstacles may be surmounted, by the force of a single mind, when it is inflexibly applied to the pursuit of a single object. The immortal name of Athanasius will never be separated from the Catholic doctrine of the Trinity, to whose defence he consecrated every moment and every faculty of his being. Educated in the family of Alexander, he had vigorously opposed the early progress of the Arian heresy: he exercised the important functions of secretary under the aged prelate; and the fathers of the Nicene council beheld with surprise and respect, the rising virtues of the young deacon. In a time of public danger, the dull claims of age and of rank are sometimes superseded; and within five months after his return from Nice, the deacon Athanasius was seated on the archiepiscopal throne of Egypt. He filled that eminent station above forty-six years, and his long administration was spent in a perpetual combat against the powers of Arianism. Five times was Athanasius expelled from his throne; twenty years he passed as an exile or a fugitive; and almost every province of the Roman empire was successively witness to his merit, and his sufferings in the cause of the Homoousion, which he considered as the sole pleasure and business, as the duty, and as the glory, of his life. Amidst the storms of persecution, the archbishop of Alexandria was patient of labour, jealous of fame, careless of safety; and although his mind was tainted by the contagion of fanaticism, Athanasius displayed a superiority of character and abilities, which would have qualified him, far better than the degenerate sons of Constantine, for the government of a great monarchy. (*DF*, i. 796)

Gibbon's understanding of the way in which the social distribution of the practical virtues was changing prepares his reader to embark with already elegiac spirits on the narrative of the ultimately unsuccessful pagan *revanche* undertaken by Julian the Apostate.

CHAPTER XXII

Julian is declared Emperor by the Legions of Gaul. – His March and Success. –
The Death of Constantius. – Civil Administration of Julian.

While the Romans languished under the ignominious tyranny
of enunchs and bishops, the praises of Julian were repeated with
transport in every part of the empire, except in the palace of
Constantius. The Barbarians of Germany had felt, and still
dreaded, the arms of the young Cæsar; his soldiers were the companions
of his victory; the grateful provincials enjoyed the blessings of his reign;
but the favourites, who had opposed his elevation, were offended by his
virtues; and they justly considered the friend of the people as the enemy
of the court. As long as the fame of Julian was doubtful, the buffoons of
the palace, who were skilled in the language of satire, tried the efficacy of
those arts which they had so often practised with success. They easily
discovered, that his simplicity was not exempt from affectation: the ridiculous epithets of an hairy savage, of an ape invested with the purple, were
applied to the dress and person of the philosophic warrior; and his modest
dispatches were stigmatized as the vain and elaborate fictions of a loquacious
Greek, a speculative soldier, who had studied the art of war amidst the
groves of the academy.[1] The voice of malicious folly was at length silenced
by the shouts of victory; the conqueror of the Franks and Alemanni could
no longer be painted as an object of contempt; and the monarch himself
was meanly ambitious of stealing from his lieutenant the honourable reward
of his labours. In the letters crowned with laurel, which, according to
ancient custom, were addressed to the provinces, the name of Julian was

The jealousy
of Constantius
against Julian.

---

1. Omnes qui plus poterant in palatio, adul-
andi professores jam docti, recte consulta, pro-
spereque completa vertebant in deridiculum:
talia sine modo strepentes insulse; in odium
venit cum victoriis suis; capella, non homo; ut
hirsutum Julianum carpentes, appellantesque
loquacem talpam, et purpuratam simiam, et
litterionem Græcum: et his congruentia plur-
ima atque vernacula principi resonantes,
audire hæc taliaque gestienti, virtutes ejus
obruere verbis impudentibus conabantur, ut
segnem incessentes et timidum et umbratilem,
gestaque secus verbis comptioribus exornan-
tem. Ammianus, xvii. 11.

omitted. "Constantius had made his dispositions in person; *he* had signalized his valour in the foremost ranks; *his* military conduct had secured the victory; and the captive king of the Barbarians was presented to *him* on the field of battle," from which he was at that time distant above forty days journey.[2] So extravagant a fable was incapable, however, of deceiving the public credulity, or even of satisfying the pride of the emperor himself. Secretly conscious that the applause and favour of the Romans accompanied the rising fortunes of Julian, his discontented mind was prepared to receive the subtle poison of those artful sycophants, who coloured their mischievous designs with the fairest appearances of truth and candour.[3] Instead of depreciating the merits of Julian, they acknowledged, and even exaggerated, his popular fame, superior talents, and important services. But they darkly insinuated, that the virtues of the Cæsar might instantly be converted into the most dangerous crimes; if the inconstant multitude should prefer their inclinations to their duty; or if the general of a victorious army should be tempted from his allegiance by the hopes of revenge, and independent greatness. The personal fears of Constantius were interpreted by his council as laudable anxiety for the public safety; whilst in private, and perhaps in his own breast, he disguised, under the less odious appellation of fear, the sentiments of hatred and envy, which he had secretly conceived for the inimitable virtues of Julian.

Fears and envy of Constantius.

The legions of Gaul are ordered to march into the East, A.D. 360, April.

The apparent tranquillity of Gaul, and the imminent danger of the eastern provinces, offered a specious pretence for the design which was artfully concerted by the Imperial ministers. They resolved to disarm the Cæsar; to recall those faithful troops who guarded his person and dignity; and to employ in a distant war against the Persian monarch, the hardy veterans who had vanquished, on the banks of the Rhine, the fiercest nations of Germany. While Julian used the laborious hours of his winter-quarters at Paris in the administration of power, which, in his hands, was the exercise

---

2. Ammian. xvi. 12. The orator Themistius (iv. p. 56, 57.) believed whatever was contained in the Imperial letters, which were addressed to the senate of Constantinople. Aurelius Victor, who published his Abridgment in the last year of Constantius, ascribes the German victories to the *wisdom* of the emperor, and the *fortune* of the Cæsar. Yet the historian, soon afterwards, was indebted to the favour or esteem of Julian for the honour of a brass statue; and the important offices of consular of the second Pannonia, and præfect of the city. Ammian. xxi. 10.

3. Callido nocendi artificio, accusatoriam diritatem laudum titulis peragebant . . . Hæ voces fuerunt ad inflammanda odia probris omnibus potentiores. See Mamertin. in Actione Gratiarum in Vet. Panegyr. xi. 5. 6.

of virtue, he was surprised by the hasty arrival of a tribune and a notary; with positive orders from the emperor, which *they* were directed to execute, and *he* was commanded not to oppose. Constantius signified his pleasure, that four entire legions, the Celtæ, and Petulants, the Heruli, and the Batavians, should be separated from the standard of Julian, under which they had acquired their fame and discipline; that in each of the remaining bands, three hundred of the bravest youths should be selected; and that this numerous detachment, the strength of the Gallic army, should instantly begin their march, and exert their utmost diligence to arrive, before the opening of the campaign, on the frontiers of Persia.[4] The Cæsar foresaw, and lamented, the consequences of this fatal mandate. Most of the auxiliaries, who engaged their voluntary service, had stipulated, that they should never be obliged to pass the Alps. The public faith of Rome, and the personal honour of Julian, had been pledged for the observance of this condition. Such an act of treachery and oppression would destroy the confidence, and excite the resentment, of the independent warriors of Germany, who considered truth as the noblest of their virtues, and freedom as the most valuable of their possessions. The legionaries, who enjoyed the title and privileges of Romans, were enlisted for the general defence of the republic; but those mercenary troops heard with cold indifference the antiquated names of the republic and of Rome. Attached, either from birth or long habit, to the climate and manners of Gaul, they loved and admired Julian; they despised, and perhaps hated, the emperor; they dreaded the laborious march, the Persian arrows, and the burning deserts of Asia. They claimed, as their own, the country which they had saved; and excused their want of spirit, by pleading the sacred and more immediate duty of protecting their families and friends. The apprehensions of the Gauls were derived from the knowledge of the impending and inevitable danger. As soon as the provinces were exhausted of their military strength, the Germans would violate a treaty which had been imposed on their fears; and notwithstanding the abilities and valour of Julian, the general of a nominal army, to whom the public calamities would be imputed, must find himself, after a vain resistance, either a prisoner in the camp of the Barbarians, or a criminal in

---

4. The minute interval, which may be interposed between the *hyeme adultâ* and the *primo vere* of Ammianus (xx. 1.4.), instead of allowing a sufficient space for a march of three thousand miles, would render the orders of Constantius as extravagant as they were unjust. The troops of Gaul could not have reached Syria till the end of autumn. The memory of Ammianus must have been inaccurate, and his language incorrect.

the palace of Constantius. If Julian complied with the orders which he had received, he subscribed his own destruction, and that of a people who deserved his affection. But a positive refusal was an act of rebellion, and a declaration of war. The inexorable jealousy of the emperor, the peremptory, and perhaps insidious, nature of his commands, left not any room for a fair apology, or candid interpretation; and the dependent station of the Cæsar scarcely allowed him to pause or to deliberate. Solitude encreased the perplexity of Julian; he could no longer apply to the faithful counsels of Sallust, who had been removed from his office by the judicious malice of the eunuchs: he could not even enforce his representations by the concurrence of the ministers, who would have been afraid, or ashamed, to approve the ruin of Gaul. The moment had been chosen, when Lupicinus,[5] the general of the cavalry, was dispatched into Britain, to repulse the inroads of the Scots and Picts; and Florentius was occupied at Vienna by the assessment of the tribute. The latter, a crafty and corrupt statesman, declining to assume a responsible part on this dangerous occasion, eluded the pressing and repeated invitations of Julian, who represented to him, that in every important measure, the presence of the præfect was indispensable in the council of the prince. In the mean while the Cæsar was oppressed by the rude and importunate solicitations of the Imperial messengers, who presumed to suggest, that if he expected the return of his ministers, he would charge himself with the guilt of the delay, and reserve for them the merit of the execution. Unable to resist, unwilling to comply, Julian expressed, in the most serious terms, his wish, and even his intention, of resigning the purple, which he could not preserve with honour, but which he could not abdicate with safety.

Their discontents.   After a painful conflict, Julian was compelled to acknowledge, that obedience was the virtue of the most eminent subject, and that the sovereign alone was entitled to judge of the public welfare. He issued the necessary orders for carrying into execution the commands of Constantius; a part of the troops began their march for the Alps; and the detachments from the several garrisons moved towards their respective places of assembly. They advanced with difficulty through the trembling

5. Ammianus, xx. 1. The valour of Lupicinus, and his military skill, are acknowledged by the historian, who, in his affected language, accuses the general of exalting the horns of his pride, bellowing in a tragic tone, and exciting a doubt, whether he was more cruel or avaricious. The danger from the Scots and Picts was so serious, that Julian himself had some thoughts of passing over into the island.

and affrighted crowds of provincials; who attempted to excite their pity by silent despair, or loud lamentations; while the wives of the soldiers, holding their infants in their arms, accused the desertion of their husbands in the mixed language of grief, of tenderness, and of indignation. This scene of general distress afflicted the humanity of the Cæsar; he granted a sufficient number of post-waggons to transport the wives and families of the soldiers,[6] endeavoured to alleviate the hardships which he was constrained to inflict, and encreased, by the most laudable arts, his own popularity, and the discontent of the exiled troops. The grief of an armed multitude is soon converted into rage; their licentious murmurs, which every hour were communicated from tent to tent with more boldness and effect, prepared their minds for the most daring acts of sedition; and by the connivance of their tribunes, a seasonable libel was secretly dispersed, which painted, in lively colours, the disgrace of the Cæsar, the oppression of the Gallic army, and the feeble vices of the tyrant of Asia. The servants of Constantius were astonished and alarmed by the progress of this dangerous spirit. They pressed the Cæsar to hasten the departure of the troops; but they imprudently rejected the honest and judicious advice of Julian; who proposed that they should not march through Paris, and suggested the danger and temptation of a last interview.

As soon as the approach of the troops was announced, the Cæsar went out to meet them, and ascended his tribunal, which had been erected in a plain before the gates of the city. After *They proclaim Julian emperor.* distinguishing the officers and soldiers, who by their rank or merit deserved a peculiar attention, Julian addressed himself in a studied oration to the surrounding multitude: he celebrated their exploits with grateful applause; encouraged them to accept, with alacrity, the honour of serving under the eyes of a powerful and liberal monarch; and admonished them, that the commands of Augustus required an instant and cheerful obedience. The soldiers, who were apprehensive of offending their general by an indecent clamour, or of belying their sentiments by false and venal acclamations, maintained an obstinate silence; and, after a short pause, were dismissed to their quarters. The principal officers were entertained by the Cæsar, who professed, in the warmest language of friendship, his desire and his inability to reward, according to their deserts, the brave companions of his victories.

---

6. He granted them the permission of the *cursus clavularis*, or *clabularis*. These post-waggons are often mentioned in the Code, and were supposed to carry fifteen hundred pounds weight. See Vales. ad Ammian. xx. 4.

They retired from the feast, full of grief and perplexity; and lamented the hardship of their fate, which tore them from their beloved general and their native country. The only expedient which could prevent their separation was boldly agitated and approved; the popular resentment was insensibly moulded into a regular conspiracy; their just reasons of complaint were heightened by passion, and their passions were inflamed by wine; as on the eve of their departure, the troops were indulged in licentious festivity. At the hour of midnight, the impetuous multitude, with swords, and bowls, and torches, in their hands, rushed into the suburbs; encompassed the palace;[7] and, careless of future dangers, pronounced the fatal and irrevocable words, JULIAN AUGUSTUS! The prince, whose anxious suspence was interrupted by their disorderly acclamations, secured the doors against their intrusion; and, as long as it was in his power, secluded his person and dignity from the accidents of a nocturnal tumult. At the dawn of day, the soldiers, whose zeal was irritated by opposition, forcibly entered the palace, seized, with respectful violence, the object of their choice, guarded Julian with drawn swords through the streets of Paris, placed him on the tribunal, and with repeated shouts saluted him as their emperor. Prudence, as well as loyalty, inculcated the propriety of resisting their treasonable designs; and of preparing for his oppressed virtue, the excuse of violence. Addressing himself by turns to the multitude and to individuals, he sometimes implored their mercy, and sometimes expressed his indignation; conjured them not to sully the fame of their immortal victories; and ventured to promise, that if they would immediately return to their allegiance, he would undertake to obtain from the emperor, not only a free and gracious pardon, but even

---

7. Most probably the palace of the baths *(Thermarum)*, of which a solid and lofty hall still subsists in the *rue de la Harpe*. The buildings covered a considerable space of the modern quarter of the university; and the gardens, under the Merovingian kings, communicated with the abbey of St. Germain des Prez. By the injuries of time and the Normans, this ancient palace was reduced, in the twelfth century, to a maze of ruins; whose dark recesses were the scene of licentious love.

   Explicat aula sinus montemque
     amplectitur alis;
   Multiplici latebrâ scelerum tersura
     ruborem.

—— pereuntis sæpe pudoris
Celatura nefas, Venerisque accommoda
   furtis.

(These lines are quoted from the Architrenius, l. iv. c. 8., a poetical work of John de Hauteville, or Hanville, a Monk of St. Albans, about the year 1190. See Warton's History of English Poetry, vol. i. dissert. ii.) Yet such *thefts* might be less pernicious to mankind, than the theological disputes of the Sorbonne, which have been since agitated on the same ground. Bonamy, Mem. de l'Academie, tom. xv. p. 678–682.

the revocation of the orders which had excited their resentment. But the soldiers, who were conscious of their guilt, chose rather to depend on the gratitude of Julian, than on the clemency of the emperor. Their zeal was insensibly turned into impatience, and their impatience into rage. The inflexible Cæsar sustained till the third hour of the day, their prayers, their reproaches, and their menaces; nor did he yield, till he had been repeatedly assured, that if he wished to live, he must consent to reign. He was exalted on a shield in the presence, and amidst the unanimous acclamations, of the troops; a rich military collar, which was offered by chance, supplied the want of a diadem;[8] the ceremony was concluded by the promise of a moderate donative;[9] and the new emperor, overwhelmed with real or affected grief, retired into the most secret recesses of his apartment.[10]

The grief of Julian could proceed only from his innocence; but his innocence must appear extremely doubtful[11] in the eyes of those who have learned to suspect the motives and the professions of princes. His lively and active mind was susceptible of the various impressions of hope and fear, of gratitude and revenge, of duty and of ambition, of the love of fame and of the fear of reproach. But it is impossible for us to calculate the respective weight and operation of these sentiments; or to ascertain the principles of action, which might escape the observation, while they guided, or rather impelled, the steps of Julian himself. The discontent of the troops was produced by the malice of his enemies; their tumult was the natural effect of interest and of passion; and if Julian had tried to conceal a deep design under the appearances of chance,

His protestations of innocence.

---

8. Even in this tumultuous moment, Julian attended to the forms of superstitious ceremony; and obstinately refused the inauspicious use of a female necklace, or a horse-collar, which the impatient soldiers would have employed in the room of a diadem.

9. An equal proportion of gold and silver, five pieces of the former, one pound of the latter; the whole amounting to about five pounds ten shillings of our money.

10. For the whole narrative of this revolt, we may appeal to authentic and original materials; Julian himself (ad S.P.Q. Atheniensem, p. 282, 283, 284.), Libanius (Orat. Parental. c. 44–

48. in Fabricius Bibliot. Græc. tom. vii. p. 269–273.), Ammianus (xx. 4), and Zosimus (l. iii. p. 151, 152, 153.), who in the reign of Julian, appears to follow the more respectable authority of Eunapius. With such guides, we *might* neglect the abbreviators and ecclesiastical historians.

11. Eutropius, a respectable witness, uses a doubtful expression, "consensu militum" (x. 15.). Gregory Nazianzen, whose ignorance might excuse his fanaticism, directly charges the apostate with presumption, madness, and impious rebellion, $\alpha\nu\theta\alpha\delta\epsilon\iota\alpha$, $\alpha\pi\sigma\nuο\iota\alpha$, $\alpha\sigma\epsilon\beta\epsilon\iota\alpha$. Orat. iii. p. 67.

he must have employed the most consummate artifice without necessity, and probably without success. He solemnly declares, in the presence of Jupiter, of the Sun, of Mars, of Minerva, and of all the other deities, that, till the close of the evening which preceded his elevation, he was utterly ignorant of the designs of the soldiers;[12] and it may seem ungenerous to distrust the honour of a hero, and the truth of a philosopher. Yet the superstitious confidence that Constantius was the enemy, and that he himself was the favourite, of the gods, might prompt him to desire, to solicit, and even to hasten the auspicious moment of his reign, which was predestined to restore the ancient religion of mankind. When Julian had received the intelligence of the conspiracy, he resigned himself to a short slumber; and afterwards related to his friends, that he had seen the Genius of the empire waiting with some impatience at his door, pressing for admittance, and reproaching his want of spirit and ambition.[13] Astonished and perplexed, he addressed his prayers to the great Jupiter; who immediately signified, by a clear and manifest omen, that he should submit to the will of heaven and of the army. The conduct which disclaims the ordinary maxims of reason, excites our suspicion and eludes our enquiry. Whenever the spirit of fanaticism, at once so credulous and so crafty, has insinuated itself into a noble mind, it insensibly corrodes the vital principles of virtue and veracity.

His embassy to Constantius. To moderate the zeal of his party, to protect the persons of his enemies,[14] to defeat and to despise the secret enterprises which were formed against his life and dignity, were the cares which employed the first days of the reign of the new Emperor. Although he was firmly resolved to maintain the station which he had assumed, he was still desirous of saving his country from the calamities of civil war, of declining a contest with the superior forces of Constantius, and of preserving his own character from the reproach of perfidy and ingratitude. Adorned

12. Julian. ad S.P.Q. Athen. p. 284. The *devout* Abbé de la Bleterie (Vie de Julien, p. 159.) is almost inclined to respect the *devout* protestations of a Pagan.

13. Ammian. xx. 5. with the note of Lindenbrogius on the Genius of the empire. Julian himself, in a confidential letter to his friend and physician, Oribasius (Epist. xvii. p. 384.), mentions another dream, to which, before the event, he gave credit; of a stately

tree thrown to the ground, of a small plant striking a deep root into the earth. Even in his sleep, the mind of the Cæsar must have been agitated by the hopes and fears of his fortune. Zosimus (l. iii. p. 155.) relates a subsequent dream.

14. The difficult situation of the prince of a rebellious army is finely described by Tacitus (Hist. 1. 80–85.). But Otho had much more guilt, and much less abilities, than Julian.

with the ensigns of military and Imperial pomp, Julian shewed himself in the field of Mars to the soldiers, who glowed with ardent enthusiasm in the cause of their pupil, their leader, and their friend. He recapitulated their victories, lamented their sufferings, applauded their resolution, animated their hopes, and checked their impetuosity; nor did he dismiss the assembly, till he had obtained a solemn promise from the troops, that if the emperor of the East would subscribe an equitable treaty, they would renounce any views of conquest, and satisfy themselves with the tranquil possession of the Gallic provinces. On this foundation he composed, in his own name, and in that of the army, a specious and moderate epistle,[15] which was delivered to Pentadius, his master of the offices, and to his chamberlain Eutherius; two ambassadors whom he appointed to receive the answer, and observe the dispositions of Constantius. This epistle is inscribed with the modest appellation of Cæsar; but Julian solicits in a peremptory, though respectful manner, the confirmation of the title of Augustus. He acknowledges the irregularity of his own election, while he justifies, in some measure, the resentment and violence of the troops which had extorted his reluctant consent. He allows the supremacy of his brother Constantius; and engages to send him an annual present of Spanish horses, to recruit his army with a select number of Barbarian youths, and to accept from his choice a Prætorian præfect of approved discretion and fidelity. But he reserves for himself the nomination of his other civil and military officers, with the troops, the revenue, and the sovereignty of the provinces beyond the Alps. He admonishes the emperor to consult the dictates of justice; to distrust the arts of those venal flatterers, who subsist only by the discord of princes; and to embrace the offer of a fair and honourable treaty, equally advantageous to the republic, and to the house of Constantine. In this negociation Julian claimed no more than he already possessed. The delegated authority which he had long exercised over the provinces of Gaul, Spain, and Britain, was still obeyed under a name more independent and august. The soldiers and the people rejoiced in a revolution which was not stained even with the blood of the guilty. Florentius was a fugitive; Lupicinus a prisoner. The persons who were disaffected to the new government were disarmed and secured; and the vacant offices were distributed, according

---

15. To this ostensible epistle he added, says Ammianus, private letters, objurgatorias et mordaces, which the historian had not seen, and would not have published. Perhaps they never existed.

to the recommendation of merit, by a prince, who despised the intrigues of the palace, and the clamours of the soldiers.[16]

His fourth and fifth expeditions beyond the Rhine, A.D. 360, 361.

The negociations of peace were accompanied and supported by the most vigorous preparations for war. The army, which Julian held in readiness for immediate action, was recruited and augmented by the disorders of the times. The cruel persecution of the faction of Magnentius had filled Gaul with numerous bands of outlaws and robbers. They cheerfully accepted the offer of a general pardon from a prince whom they could trust, submitted to the restraints of military discipline, and retained only their implacable hatred to the person and government of Constantius.[17] As soon as the season of the year permitted Julian to take the field, he appeared at the head of his legions; threw a bridge over the Rhine in the neighbourhood of Cleves; and prepared to chastise the perfidy of the Attuarii, a tribe of Franks, who presumed that they might ravage, with impunity, the frontiers of a divided empire. The difficulty, as well as glory, of this enterprize, consisted in a laborious march; and Julian had conquered, as soon as he could penetrate into a country, which former princes had considered as inaccessible. After he had given peace to the Barbarians, the emperor carefully visited the fortifications along the Rhine from Cleves to Basil; surveyed, with peculiar attention, the territories which he had recovered from the hands of the Alemanni, passed through Besançon,[18] which had severely suffered from their fury, and fixed his headquarters at Vienna for the ensuing winter. The barrier of Gaul was improved and strengthened with additional fortifications; and Julian entertained some hopes, that the Germans, whom he had so often vanquished, might, in his absence, be restrained, by the terror of his name. Vadomair[19] was the only prince of

16. See the first transactions of his reign, in Julian ad S.P.Q. Athen. p. 285, 286. Ammianus, xx. 5. 8. Liban. Orat. Parent. c. 49, 50. p. 273–275.

17. Liban. Orat. Parent. c. 50. p. 275, 276. A strange disorder, since it continued above seven years. In the factions of the Greek republics, the exiles amounted to 20,000 persons; and Isocrates assures Philip, that it would be easier to raise an army from the vagabonds than from the cities. See Hume's Essays, tom. i. p. 426, 427.

18. Julian (Epist. xxxviii. p. 414.) gives a short description of Vesontio, or Besançon: a rocky peninsula almost encircled by the river Doux; once a magnificent city, filled with temples, &c. now reduced to a small town, emerging however from its ruins.

19. Vadomair entered into the Roman service, and was promoted from a Barbarian kingdom to the military rank of duke of Phænicia. He still retained the same artful character (Ammian. xxi. 4.); but, under the reign of Valens, he signalised his valour in the Armenian war (xxix. 1.).

the Alemanni, whom he esteemed or feared; and while the subtle Barbarian affected to observe the faith of treaties, the progress of his arms threatened the state with an unseasonable and dangerous war. The policy of Julian condescended to surprise the prince of the Alemanni by his own arts; and Vadomair, who, in the character of a friend, had incautiously accepted an invitation from the Roman governors, was seized in the midst of the entertainment, and sent away prisoner into the heart of Spain. Before the Barbarians were recovered from their amazement, the emperor appeared in arms on the banks of the Rhine, and, once more crossing the river, renewed the deep impressions of terror and respect which had been already made by four preceding expeditions.[20]

The ambassadors of Julian had been instructed to execute, with the utmost diligence, their important commission. But, in their passage through Italy and Illyricum, they were detained by the tedious and affected delays of the provincial governors; they were conducted by slow journies from Constantinople to Cæsarea in Cappadocia; and when at length they were admitted to the presence of Constantius, they found that he had already conceived, from the dispatches of his own officers, the most unfavourable opinion of the conduct of Julian, and of the Gallic army. The letters were heard with impatience; the trembling messengers were dismissed with indignation and contempt; and the looks, the gestures, the furious language of the monarch, expressed the disorder of his soul. The domestic connection, which might have reconciled the brother and the husband of Helena, was recently dissolved by the death of that princess, whose pregnancy had been several times fruitless, and was at last fatal to herself.[21] The empress Eusebia had preserved to the last moment of her life the warm, and even jealous, affection which she had conceived for Julian; and her mild influence might have moderated the resentment of a prince, who, since her death, was abandoned to his own passions, and to the arts of his eunuchs. But the terror of a foreign

Fruitless treaty and declaration of war, A.D. 361.

20. Ammian, xx. 10. xxi. 3, 4. Zosimus, l. iii. p. 155.

21. Her remains were sent to Rome, and interred near those of her sister Constantina, in the suburb of the *Via Nomentana.* Ammian. xxi. 1. Libanius has composed a very weak apology to justify his hero from a very absurd charge; of poisoning his wife, and rewarding her physician with his mother's jewels. (See the seventh of seventeen new orations, published at Venice 1754, from a MS. in St. Mark's library, p. 117–127.) Elpidius, the Prætorian præfect of the East, to whose evidence the accuser of Julian appeals, is arraigned by Libanius, as *effeminate* and ungrateful; yet the religion of Elpidius is praised by Jerom (tom. i. p. 243.), and his humanity by Ammianus (xxi. 6.).

invasion obliged him to suspend the punishment of a private enemy; he continued his march towards the confines of Persia, and thought it sufficient to signify the conditions which might entitle Julian and his guilty followers to the clemency of their offended sovereign. He required, that the presumptuous Cæsar should expressly renounce the appellation and rank of Augustus, which he had accepted from the rebels; that he should descend to his former station of a limited and dependent minister; that he should vest the powers of the state and army in the hands of those officers who were appointed by the Imperial court; and that he should trust his safety to the assurances of pardon, which were announced by Epictetus, a Gallic bishop, and one of the Arian favourites of Constantius. Several months were ineffectually consumed in a treaty which was negociated at the distance of three thousand miles between Paris and Antioch; and, as soon as Julian perceived that his moderate and respectful behaviour served only to irritate the pride of an implacable adversary, he boldly resolved to commit his life and fortune to the chance of a civil war. He gave a public and military audience to the quæstor Leonas: the haughty epistle of Constantius was read to the attentive multitude; and Julian protested, with the most flattering deference, that he was ready to resign the title of Augustus, if he could obtain the consent of those whom he acknowledged as the authors of his elevation. The faint proposal was impetuously silenced; and the acclamations of "Julian Augustus, continue to reign, by the authority of the army, of the people, of the republic, which you have saved," thundered at once from every part of the field, and terrified the pale ambassador of Constantius. A part of the letter was afterwards read, in which the emperor arraigned the ingratitude of Julian, whom he had invested with the honours of the purple; whom he had educated with so much care and tenderness; whom he had preserved in his infancy, when he was left a helpless orphan; "an orphan!" interrupted Julian, who justified his cause by indulging his passions: "Does the assassin of my family reproach me that I was left an orphan? He urges me to revenge those injuries, which I have long studied to forget." The assembly was dismissed; and Leonas, who, with some difficulty, had been protected from the popular fury, was sent back to his master, with an epistle, in which Julian expressed, in a strain of the most vehement eloquence, the sentiments of contempt, of hatred, and of resentment, which had been suppressed and embittered by the dissimulation of twenty years. After this message, which might be considered as a signal of irreconcilable war, Julian, who, some weeks before, had celebrated the Christian festival of the Epiphany,[22] made a public declaration that he committed the care of his safety to the IMMORTAL GODS; and thus publicly renounced the religion, as well as the friendship, of Constantius.[23]

The situation of Julian required a vigorous and immediate resolution. He had discovered, from intercepted letters, that his adversary, sacrificing the interest of the state to that of the monarch, had again excited the Barbarians to invade the provinces of the West. The position of two magazines, one of them collected on the banks of the lake of Constance, the other formed at the foot of the Cottian Alps, seemed to indicate the march of two armies; and the size of those magazines, each of which consisted of six hundred thousand quarters of wheat, or rather flour,[24] was a threatening evidence of the strength and numbers of the enemy, who prepared to surround him. But the Imperial legions were still in their distant quarters of Asia; the Danube was feebly guarded; and if Julian could occupy, by a sudden incursion, the important provinces of Illyricum, he might expect that a people of soldiers would resort to his standard, and that the rich mines of gold and silver would contribute to the expences of the civil war. He proposed this bold enterprise to the assembly of the soldiers; inspired them with a just confidence in their general, and in themselves; and exhorted them to maintain their reputation, of being terrible to the enemy, moderate to their fellow-citizens, and obedient to their officers. His spirited discourse was received with the loudest acclamations, and the same troops which had taken up

Julian prepares to attack Constantius.

22. Feriarum die quem celebrantes mense Januario, Christiani *Epiphania* dictitant, progressus in eorum ecclesiam, solemniter numine orato discessit. Ammian. xxi. 2. Zonaras observes, that it was on Christmas-day, and his assertion is not inconsistent; since the churches of Egypt, Asia, and perhaps Gaul, celebrated on the same day (the sixth of January), the nativity and the baptism of their Saviour. The Romans, as ignorant as their brethren of the real date of his birth, fixed the solemn festival to the 25th of December, the *Brumalia*, or winter solstice, when the Pagans annually celebrated the birth of the Sun. See Bingham's Antiquities of the Christian Church, l. xx. c. 4. and Beausobre Hist. Critique du Manicheisme, tom. ii. p. 690–700.

23. The public and secret negociations between Constantius and Julian, must be extracted, with some caution, from Julian himself (Orat. ad S.P.Q. Athen. p. 286.), Libanius (Orat. Parent. c. 51. p. 276.), Ammianus (xx. 9.), Zosimus (l. iii. p. 154.), and even Zonaras (tom. ii. l. xiii. p. 20, 21, 22.), who, on this occasion, appears to have possessed and used some valuable materials.

24. Three hundred myriads, or three millions of *medimni*, a corn-measure familiar to the Athenians, and which contained six Roman *modii*. Julian explains, like a soldier and a statesman, the danger of his situation, and the necessity and advantages of an offensive war (ad S.P.Q. Athen. p. 286, 287.).

arms against Constantius, when he summoned them to leave Gaul, now declared with alacrity, that they would follow Julian to the farthest extremities of Europe or Asia. The oath of fidelity was administered; and the soldiers, clashing their shields, and pointing their drawn swords to their throats, devoted themselves, with horrid imprecations, to the service of a leader whom they celebrated as the deliverer of Gaul, and the conqueror of the Germans.[25] This solemn engagement, which seemed to be dictated by affection, rather than by duty, was singly opposed by Nebridius, who had been admitted to the office of Prætorian præfect. That faithful minister, alone and unassisted, asserted the rights of Constantius in the midst of an armed and angry multitude, to whose fury he had almost fallen an honourable, but useless, sacrifice. After losing one of his hands by the stroke of a sword, he embraced the knees of the prince whom he had offended. Julian covered the præfect with his Imperial mantle, and protecting him from the zeal of his followers, dismissed him to his own house, with less respect than was perhaps due to the virtue of an enemy.[26] The high office of Nebridius was bestowed on Sallust; and the provinces of Gaul, which were now delivered from the intolerable oppression of taxes, enjoyed the mild and equitable administration of the friend of Julian, who was permitted to practise those virtues which he had instilled into the mind of his pupil.[27]

His march from the Rhine into Illyricum. The hopes of Julian depended much less on the number of his troops, than on the celerity of his motions. In the execution of a daring enterprise, he availed himself of every precaution, as far as prudence could suggest; and where prudence could no longer accompany his steps, he trusted the event to valour and to fortune. In the neighbourhood of Basil he assembled and divided his army.[28] One body, which consisted of ten thousand men, was directed, under the command of Nevitta, general of the cavalry, to advance through the midland parts of Rhætia and Noricum. A similar division of troops, under the orders

---

25. See his oration, and the behaviour of the troops, in Ammian. xxi. 5.

26. He sternly refused his hand to the suppliant præfect, whom he sent into Tuscany (Ammian. xxi. 5.). Libanius, with savage fury, insults Nebridius, applauds the soldiers, and almost censures the humanity of Julian (Orat. Parent. c. 53. p. 278.).

27. Ammian. xxi. 8. In this promotion, Julian obeyed the law which he publicly imposed

on himself. Neque civilis quisquam judex nec militaris rector, alio quodam præter merita suffragante, ad potiorum veniat gradum (Ammian. xx. 5.). Absence did not weaken his regard for Sallust, with whose name (A.D. 363.) he honoured the consulship.

28. Ammianus (xxi. 8.) ascribes the same practice, and the same motive, to Alexander the Great, and other skilful generals.

of Jovius and Jovinus, prepared to follow the oblique course of the highways, through the Alps and the northern confines of Italy. The instructions to the generals were conceived with energy and precision: to hasten their march in close and compact columns, which, according to the disposition of the ground, might readily be changed into any order of battle; to secure themselves against the surprises of the night by strong posts and vigilant guards; to prevent resistance by their unexpected arrival; to elude examination by their sudden departure; to spread the opinion of their strength, and the terror of his name; and to join their sovereign under the walls of Sirmium. For himself, Julian had reserved a more difficult and extraordinary part. He selected three thousand brave and active volunteers, resolved, like their leader, to cast behind them every hope of a retreat: at the head of this faithful band, he fearlessly plunged into the recesses of the Marcian, or black forest, which conceals the sources of the Danube;[29] and, for many days, the fate of Julian was unknown to the world. The secrecy of his march, his diligence, and vigour, surmounted every obstacle; he forced his way over mountains and morasses, occupied the bridges or swam the rivers, pursued his direct course,[30] without reflecting whether he traversed the territory of the Romans or of the Barbarians, and at length emerged, between Ratisbon and Vienna, at the place where he designed to embark his troops on the Danube. By a well-concerted stratagem, he seized a fleet of light brigantines,[31] as it lay at anchor; secured a supply of coarse provisions sufficient to satisfy the indelicate, but voracious, appetite of a Gallic army; and boldly committed himself to the stream of the Danube. The labours of his mariners, who plied their oars with incessant diligence, and the steady continuance of a favourable wind, carried his fleet above seven hundred

---

29. This wood was a part of the great Hercynian forest, which, in the time of Cæsar, stretched away from the country of the Rauraci (Basil) into the boundless regions of the North. See Cluver. Germania Antiqua, l. iii. c. 47.

30. Compare Libanius, Orat. Parent. c. 53. p. 278, 279, with Gregory Nazianzen, Orat. iii. p. 68. Even the saint admires the speed and secrecy of this march. A modern divine might apply to the progress of Julian, the lines which were originally designed for another apostate:

——So eagerly the fiend,
O'er bog, or steep, through strait,
    rough, dense, or rare,
With head, hands, wings, or feet,
    pursues his way,
And swims, or sinks, or wades, or
    creeps, or flies.

31. In that interval the *Notitia* places two or three fleets, the Lauriacensis (at Lauriacum, or Lorch), the Arlapensis, the Maginensis; and mentions five legions, or cohorts, of Liburnarii, who should be a sort of marines. Sect. lviii. edit. Labb.

miles in eleven days;[32] and he had already disembarked his troops at Bononia, only nineteen miles from Sirmium, before his enemies could receive any certain intelligence that he had left the banks of the Rhine. In the course of this long and rapid navigation, the mind of Julian was fixed on the object of his enterprise; and though he accepted the deputations of some cities, which hastened to claim the merit of an early submission, he passed before the hostile stations, which were placed along the river, without indulging the temptation of signalizing an useless and ill-timed valour. The banks of the Danube were crowded on either side with spectators, who gazed on the military pomp, anticipated the importance of the event, and diffused through the adjacent country the fame of a young hero, who advanced with more than mortal speed at the head of the innumerable forces of the West. Lucilian, who, with the rank of general of the cavalry, commanded the military powers of Illyricum, was alarmed and perplexed by the doubtful reports, which he could neither reject nor believe. He had taken some slow and irresolute measures for the purpose of collecting his troops; when he was surprised by Dagalaiphus, an active officer, whom Julian, as soon as he landed at Bononia, had pushed forwards with some light infantry. The captive general, uncertain of his life or death, was hastily thrown upon a horse, and conducted to the presence of Julian; who kindly raised him from the ground, and dispelled the terror and amazement which seemed to stupify his faculties. But Lucilian had no sooner recovered his spirits, than he betrayed his want of his discretion, by presuming to admonish his conqueror, that he had rashly ventured, with a handful of men, to expose his person in the midst of his enemies. "Reserve for your master Constantius these timid remonstrances," replied Julian, with a smile of contempt; "when I gave you my purple to kiss, I received you not as a counsellor, but as a suppliant." Conscious that success alone could justify his attempt, and that boldness only could command success, he instantly advanced, at the head of three thousand soldiers, to attack the strongest and most populous city of the Illyrian provinces. As he entered the long suburb of Sirmium, he was received by the joyful acclamations of the army and people; who, crowned with flowers, and holding lighted tapers in their hands, conducted their acknowledged sovereign to his Imperial residence. Two days were

32. Zosimus alone (l. iii. p. 156.) has specified this interesting circumstance. Mamertinus (in Panegyr. Vet. xi. 6, 7, 8.), who accompanied Julian, as count of the sacred largesses, describes this voyage in a florid and picturesque manner, challenges Triptolemus and the Argonauts of Greece, &c.

devoted to the public joy, which was celebrated by the games of the Circus; but, early on the morning of the third day, Julian marched to occupy the narrow pass of Succi, in the defiles of Mount Hæmus; which, almost in the mid-way between Sirmium and Constantinople, separates the provinces of Thrace and Dacia, by an abrupt descent towards the former, and a gentle declivity on the side of the latter.[33] The defence of this important post was entrusted to the brave Nevitta; who, as well as the generals of the Italian division, successfully executed the plan of the march and junction which their master had so ably conceived.[34]

The homage which Julian obtained, from the fears or the inclination of the people, extended far beyond the immediate effect of his arms.[35] The præfectures of Italy and Illyricum were *He justifies his cause.* administered by Taurus and Florentius, who united that important office with the vain honours of the consulship; and as those magistrates had retired with precipitation to the court of Asia, Julian, who could not always restrain the levity of his temper, stigmatized their flight by adding, in all the Acts of the Year, the epithet of *fugitive* to the names of the two consuls. The provinces which had been deserted by their first magistrates acknowledged the authority of an emperor, who, conciliating the qualities of a soldier with those of a philosopher, was equally admired in the camps of the Danube, and in the cities of Greece. From his palace, or, more properly, from his headquarters of Sirmium and Naissus, he distributed to the principal cities of the empire, a laboured apology for his own conduct; published the secret dispatches of Constantius; and solicited the judgment of mankind between two competitors, the one of whom had expelled, and the other had invited, the Barbarians.[36] Julian, whose mind was deeply wounded by

33. The description of Ammianus, which might be supported by collateral evidence, ascertains the precise situation of the *Angustiæ Succarum*, or passes of *Succi*. M. d'Anville, from the trifling resemblance of names, has placed them between Sardica and Naissus. For my own justification, I am obliged to mention the *only* error which I have discovered in the maps or writings of that admirable geographer.

34. Whatever circumstances we may borrow elsewhere, Ammianus (xxi. 8, 9, 10.) still supplies the series of the narrative.

35. Ammian. xxi. 9, 10. Libanius, Orat.

Parent. c. 54. p. 279, 280. Zosimus, l. iii. p. 156, 157.

36. Julian (ad S.P.Q. Athen. p. 286.) positively asserts, that he intercepted the letters of Constantius to the Barbarians: and Libanius as positively affirms, that he read them on his march to the troops and the cities. Yet Ammianus (xxi. 4.) expresses himself with cool and candid hesitation, *si famæ solius admittenda est fides*. He specifies, however, an intercepted letter from Vadomair to Constantius, which supposes an intimate correspondence between them: "Cæsar tuus disciplinam non habet."

the reproach of ingratitude, aspired to maintain, by argument as well as by arms, the superior merits of his cause; and to excel, not only in the arts of war, but in those of composition. His epistle to the senate and people of Athens[37] seems to have been dictated by an elegant enthusiasm; which prompted him to submit his actions and his motives to the degenerate Athenians of his own times, with the same humble deference, as if he had been pleading, in the days of Aristides, before the tribunal of the Areopagus. His application to the senate of Rome, which was still permitted to bestow the titles of Imperial power, was agreeable to the forms of the expiring republic. An assembly was summoned by Tertullus, præfect of the city; the epistle of Julian was read; and as he appeared to be master of Italy, his claims were admitted without a dissenting voice. His oblique censure of the innovations of Constantine, and his passionate invective against the vices of Constantius, were heard with less satisfaction; and the senate, as if Julian had been present, unanimously exclaimed, "Respect, we beseech you, the author of your own fortune."[38] An artful expression, which, according to the chance of war, might be differently explained; as a manly reproof of the ingratitude of the usurper, or as a flattering confession, that a single act of such benefit to the state ought to atone for all the failings of Constantius.

Hostile preparations   The intelligence of the march and rapid progress of Julian was speedily transmitted to his rival, who, by the retreat of Sapor, had obtained some respite from the Persian war. Disguising the anguish of his soul under the semblance of contempt, Constantius professed his intention of returning into Europe, and of giving chace to Julian; for he never spoke of this military expedition in any other light than that of a hunting party.[39] In the camp of Hierapolis, in Syria, he communicated this design to his army; slightly mentioned the guilt and rashness of the Cæsar; and ventured to assure them, that if the mutineers of Gaul presumed to meet them in the field, they would be unable to sustain the fire of their

---

37. Zosimus mentions his epistles to the Athenians, the Corinthians, and the Lacedæmonians. The substance was probably the same, though the address was properly varied. The epistle to the Athenians is still extant (p. 268–287.), and has afforded much valuable information. It deserves the praises of the Abbé de la Bleterie (Pref. à l'Histoire de Jovien, p. 24, 25.), and is one of the best

manifestoes to be found in any language.
38. *Auctori tuo reverentiam rogamus.* Ammian. xxi. 10. It is amusing enough to observe the secret conflicts of the senate between flattery and fear. See Tacit. Hist. i. 85.
39. Tanquam venaticiam prædam caperet: hoc enim ad leniendum suorum metum subinde prædicabat. Ammian. xxi. 7.

eyes, and the irresistible weight of their shout of onset. The speech of the emperor was received with military applause, and Theodotus, the president of the council of Hierapolis, requested, with tears of adulation, that *his* city might be adorned with the head of the vanquished rebel.[40] A chosen detachment was dispatched away in post-waggons, to secure, if it were yet possible, the pass of Succi; the recruits, the horses, the arms, and the magazines which had been prepared against Sapor, were appropriated to the service of the civil war; and the domestic victories of Constantius inspired his partisans with the most sanguine assurances of success. The notary Gaudentius had occupied in his name the provinces of Africa; the subsistence of Rome was intercepted; and the distress of Julian was increased, by an unexpected event, which might have been productive of fatal consequences. Julian had received the submission of two legions and a cohort of archers, who were stationed at Sirmium; but he suspected, with reason, the fidelity of those troops, which had been distinguished by the emperor; and it was thought expedient, under the pretence of the exposed state of the Gallic frontier, to dismiss them from the most important scene of action. They advanced, with reluctance, as far as the confines of Italy; but as they dreaded the length of the way, and the savage fierceness of the Germans, they resolved, by the instigation of one of their tribunes, to halt at Aquileia, and to erect the banners of Constantius on the walls of that impregnable city. The vigilance of Julian perceived at once the extent of the mischief, and the necessity of applying an immediate remedy. By his order, Jovinus led back a part of the army into Italy; and the siege of Aquileia was formed with diligence, and prosecuted with vigour. But the legionaries, who seemed to have rejected the yoke of discipline, conducted the defence of the place with skill and perseverance; invited the rest of Italy to imitate the example of their courage and loyalty; and threatened the retreat of Julian, if he should be forced to yield to the superior numbers of the armies of the East.[41]

---

40. See the speech and preparations in Ammianus, xxi. 13. The vile Theodotus afterwards implored and obtained his pardon from the merciful conqueror, who signified his wish of diminishing his enemies, and increasing the number of his friends (xxii. 14.).

41. Ammian, xxi. 7. 11, 12. He seems to describe, with superfluous labour, the operations of the siege of Aquileia, which, on this occasion, maintained its impregnable fame. Gregory Nazianzen (Orat. iii. p. 68.) ascribes this accidental revolt to the wisdom of Constantius, whose assured victory he announces with some appearance of truth. Constantio quem credebat proculdubio fore victorem: nemo enim omnium tunc ab hac constanti sententia discrepebat. Ammian. xxi. 7.

and death of
Constantius,
A.D. 361,
November 30.

But the humanity of Julian was preserved from the cruel alternative, which he pathetically laments, of destroying, or of being himself destroyed: and the seasonable death of Constantius delivered the Roman empire from the calamities of civil war. The approach of winter could not detain the monarch at Antioch; and his favourites durst not oppose his impatient desire of revenge. A slight fever, which was perhaps occasioned by the agitation of his spirits, was encreased by the fatigues of the journey; and Constantius was obliged to halt at the little town of Mopsucrene, twelve miles beyond Tarsus, where he expired, after a short illness, in the forty-fifth year of his age, and the twenty-fourth of his reign.[42] His genuine character, which was composed of pride and weakness, of superstition and cruelty, has been fully displayed in the preceding narrative of civil and ecclesiastical events. The long abuse of power rendered him a considerable object in the eyes of his contemporaries; but as personal merit can alone deserve the notice of posterity, the last of the sons of Constantine may be dismissed from the world with the remark, that he inherited the defects, without the abilities, of his father. Before Constantius expired, he is said to have named Julian for his successor; nor does it seem improbable, that his anxious concern for the fate of a young and tender wife, whom he left with child, may have prevailed, in his last moments, over the harsher passions of hatred and revenge. Eusebius, and his guilty associates, made a faint attempt to prolong the reign of the eunuchs, by the election of another emperor: but their intrigues were rejected with disdain by an army which now abhorred the thought of civil discord; and two officers of rank were instantly dispatched, to assure Julian, that every sword in the empire would be drawn for his service. The military designs of that prince, who had formed three different attacks against Thrace, were prevented by this fortunate event. Without shedding the blood of his fellow-citizens, he escaped the dangers of a doubtful conflict, and acquired the advantages of a complete victory. Impatient to visit the place of his birth, and the new capital of the empire, he advanced from Naissus through the mountains of Hæmus, and the

---

42. His death and character are faithfully delineated by Ammianus (xxi. 14, 15, 16.); and we are authorised to despise and detest the foolish calumny of Gregory (Orat. iii. p. 68.), who accuses Julian of contriving the death of his benefactor. The private repentance of the emperor, that he had spared and promoted Julian (p. 69. and Orat. xxi. p. 389.), is not improbable in itself, nor incompatible with the public verbal testament, which prudential considerations might dictate in the last moments of his life.

cities of Thrace. When he reached Heraclea, at the distance of sixty miles, all Constantinople was poured forth to receive him; and he made his triumphal entry, amidst the dutiful acclamations of the soldiers, the people, and the senate. An innumerable multitude pressed around him with eager respect; and were perhaps disappointed when they beheld the small stature, and simple garb, of a hero, whose unexperienced youth had vanquished the Barbarians of Germany, and who had now traversed, in a successful career, the whole continent of Europe, from the shores of the Atlantic to those of the Bosphorus.[43] A few days afterwards, when the remains of the deceased emperor were landed in the harbour, the subjects of Julian applauded the real or affected humanity of their sovereign. On foot, without his diadem, and clothed in a mourning habit, he accompanied the funeral as far as the church of the Holy Apostles, where the body was deposited: and if these marks of respect may be interpreted as a selfish tribute to the birth and dignity of his Imperial kinsman, the tears of Julian professed to the world, that he had forgot the injuries, and remembered only the obligations, which he had received from Constantius.[44] As soon as the legions of Aquileia were assured of the death of the emperor, they opened the gates of the city, and, by the sacrifice of their guilty leaders, obtained an easy pardon from the prudence or lenity of Julian; who, in the thirty-second year of his age, acquired the undisputed possession of the Roman empire.[45]

Julian enters Constantinople, December 11,

and is acknowledged by the whole empire.

Philosophy had instructed Julian to compare the advantages of action and retirement; but the elevation of his birth, and the accidents of his life, never allowed him the freedom of choice. He might perhaps sincerely have preferred the groves of the academy, and the society of Athens; but he was constrained, at first by the

His civil government and private life.

---

43. In describing the triumph of Julian, Ammianus (xxii. 1, 2.) assumes the lofty tone of an orator or poet; while Libanius (Orat. Parent. c. 56. p. 281.) sinks to the grave simplicity of an historian.

44. The funeral of Constantius is described by Ammianus (xxi. 16.), Gregory Nazianzen (Orat. iv. p. 119.), Mamertinus (in Panegyr. Vet. xi. 27.), Libanius (Orat. Parent. c. lvi. p. 283.), and Philostorgius (l. vi. c. 6. with Godefroy's Dissertations, p. 265.). These

writers, and their followers, Pagans, Catholics, Arians, beheld with very different eyes both the dead and the living emperor.

45. The day and year of the birth of Julian are not perfectly ascertained. The day is probably the sixth of November, and the year must be either 331 or 332. Tillemont, Hist. des Empereurs, tom. iv. p. 693. Ducange, Fam. Byzantin. p. 50. I have preferred the earlier date.

will, and afterwards by the injustice, of Constantius, to expose his person and fame to the dangers of Imperial greatness; and to make himself accountable to the world, and to posterity, for the happiness of millions.[46] Julian recollected with terror the observation of his master Plato,[47] that the government of our flocks and herds is always committed to beings of a superior species; and that the conduct of nations requires and deserves the celestial powers of the Gods or of the Genii. From this principle he justly concluded, that the man who presumes to reign, should aspire to the perfection of the divine nature; that he should purify his soul from her mortal and terrestrial part; that he should extinguish his appetites, enlighten his understanding, regulate his passions, and subdue the wild beast, which, according to the lively metaphor of Aristotle,[48] seldom fails to ascend the throne of a despot. The throne of Julian, which the death of Constantius fixed on an independent basis, was the seat of reason, of virtue, and perhaps of vanity. He despised the honours, renounced the pleasures, and discharged with incessant diligence the duties, of his exalted station; and there were few among his subjects who would have consented to relieve him from the weight of the diadem, had they been obliged to submit their time and their actions to the rigorous laws which their philosophic emperor imposed on himself. One of his most intimate friends,[49] who had often shared the frugal simplicity of his table, has remarked, that his light and sparing diet (which was usually of the vegetable kind) left his mind and body always free and active, for the various and important business of an author, a pontiff, a magistrate, a general, and a prince. In one and the same day, he gave audience to several ambassadors, and wrote, or dictated, a great number of letters to his generals, his civil magistrates, his private friends, and the different cities of his dominions. He listened to the memorials which had

---

46. Julian himself (p. 253–267.) has expressed these philosophical ideas, with much eloquence, and some affectation, in a very elaborate epistle to Themistius. The Abbé de la Bleterie (tom. ii. p. 146–193.), who has given an elegant translation, is inclined to believe that it was the celebrated Themistius, whose orations are still extant.

47. Julian ad Themist. p. 258. Petavius (not. p. 95.) observes, that this passage is taken from the fourth book de Legibus; but either Julian quoted from memory, or his MSS. were different from ours. Xenophon opens the

Cyropædia with a similar reflection.

48. Ο δε ανθρωπον κελευων αρχειν, προστιθησι και θηριον. Aristot. ap Julian. p. 261. The MS. of Vossius, unsatisfied with a single beast, affords the stronger reading of θηρια, which the experience of despotism may warrant.

49. Libanius (Orat. Parentalis, c. lxxxiv. lxxxv. p. 310, 311, 312.) has given this interesting detail of the private life of Julian. He himself (in Misopogon, p. 350.) mentions his vegetable diet, and upbraids the gross and sensual appetite of the people of Antioch.

been received, considered the subject of the petitions, and signified his intentions more rapidly than they could be taken in short-hand by the diligence of his secretaries. He possessed such flexibility of thought, and such firmness of attention, that he could employ his hand to write, his ear to listen, and his voice to dictate; and pursue at once three several trains of ideas, without hesitation, and without error. While his ministers reposed, the prince flew with agility from one labour to another, and, after a hasty dinner, retired into his library, till the public business, which he had appointed for the evening, summoned him to interrupt the prosecution of his studies. The supper of the emperor was still less substantial than the former meal; his sleep was never clouded by the fumes of indigestion; and, except in the short interval of a marriage, which was the effect of policy rather than love, the chaste Julian never shared his bed with a female companion.[50] He was soon awakened by the entrance of fresh secretaries, who had slept the preceding day; and his servants were obliged to wait alternately, while their indefatigable master allowed himself scarcely any other refreshment than the change of occupations. The predecessors of Julian, his uncle, his brother, and his cousin, indulged their puerile taste for the games of the circus, under the specious pretence of complying with the inclinations of the people; and they frequently remained the greatest part of the day, as idle spectators, and as a part of the splendid spectacle, till the ordinary round of twenty-four races[51] was completely finished. On solemn festivals, Julian, who felt and professed an unfashionable dislike to these frivolous amusements, condescended to appear in the circus; and

50. Lectulus . . . Vestalium toris purior, is the praise which Mamertinus (Panegyr. Vet. xi. 13.) addresses to Julian himself. Libanius affirms, in sober peremptory language, that Julian never knew a woman before his marriage, or after the death of his wife (Orat. Parent. c. lxxxviii. p. 313.). The chastity of Julian is confirmed by the impartial testimony of Ammianus (xxv. 4.), and the partial silence of the Christians. Yet Julian ironically urges the reproach of the people of Antioch, that he *almost always* (ως επιπαν, in Misopogon. p. 345.) lay alone. This suspicious expression is explained by the Abbé de la Bleterie (Hist. de Jovien. tom. ii. p. 103–109.) with candour and ingenuity.

51. See Salmasius ad Sueton. in Claud. c. xxi. A twenty-fifth race, or *missus*, was added, to complete the number of one hundred chariots, four of which, the four colours, started each heat.

Centum quadrijugos agitabo ad flumina currus.

It appears, that they ran five or seven times round the *Meta* (Sueton. in Domitian. c. 4.); and (from the measure of the Circus Maximus at Rome, the Hippodrome at Constantinople, &c.) it might be about a four-mile course.

after bestowing a careless glance on five or six of the races, he hastily withdrew, with the impatience of a philosopher, who considered every moment as lost, that was not devoted to the advantage of the public, or the improvement of his own mind.[52] By this avarice of time, he seemed to protract the short duration of his reign; and if the dates were less securely ascertained, we should refuse to believe, that only sixteen months elapsed between the death of Constantius and the departure of his successor for the Persian war. The actions of Julian can only be preserved by the care of the historian; but the portion of his voluminous writings, which is still extant, remains as a monument of the application, as well as of the genius, of the emperor. The Misopogon, the Cæsars, several of his orations, and his elaborate work against the Christian religion, were composed in the long nights of the two winters, the former of which he passed at Constantinople, and the latter at Antioch.

December,
A.D. 361.

March,
A.D. 363.

Reformation
of the palace.

The reformation of the Imperial court was one of the first and most necessary acts of the government of Julian.[53] Soon after his entrance into the palace of Constantinople, he had occasion for the service of a barber. An officer, magnificently dressed, immediately presented himself. "It is a barber," exclaimed the prince, with affected surprise, "that I want, and not a receiver-general of the finances."[54] He questioned the man concerning the profits of his employment; and was informed, that besides a large salary, and some valuable perquisites, he enjoyed a daily allowance for twenty servants, and as many horses. A thousand barbers, a thousand cup-bearers, a thousand cooks, were distributed in the several offices of luxury; and the number of eunuchs could be compared only with the insects of a summer's day.[55] The monarch who resigned to his subjects the superiority of merit and virtue, was distinguished

---

52. Julian. in Misopogon, p. 340. Julius Cæsar had offended the Roman people by reading his dispatches during the actual race. Augustus indulged their taste, or his own, by his constant attention to the important business of the circus, for which he professed the warmest inclination. Sueton. in August. c. xlv.

53. The reformation of the palace is described by Ammianus (xxii. 4.), Libanius (Orat. Parent. c. lxii. p. 288, &c.), Mamertinus (in Panegyr. Vet. xi. 11.), Socrates (l. iii. c. 1.), and Zonaras (tom. ii. l. xiii. p. 24.).

54. Ego non *rationalem* jussi sed tonsorem acciri. Zonaras uses the less natural image of a *senator*. Yet an officer of the finances, who was satiated with wealth, might desire and obtain the honours of the senate.

55. Μαγειρους μεν χιλιους, κουρεας δε ουκ ελαττους, οινοχοους δε πλειους, σμηνη τραπεζοποιων, ευνουχους υπερ τας μυιας παρα τοις ποιμεσι εν ηρι, are the original words of Libanius, which I have faithfully quoted, lest I should be suspected of magnifying the abuses of the royal household.

by the oppressive magnificence of his dress, his table, his buildings, and his train. The stately palaces erected by Constantine and his sons, were decorated with many coloured marbles, and ornaments of massy gold. The most exquisite dainties were procured, to gratify their pride, rather than their taste; birds of the most distant climates, fish from the most remote seas, fruits out of their natural season, winter roses, and summer snows.[56] The domestic crowd of the palace surpassed the expence of the legions; yet the smallest part of this costly multitude was subservient to the use, or even to the splendor, of the throne. The monarch was disgraced, and the people was injured, by the creation and sale of an infinite number of obscure, and even titular employments; and the most worthless of mankind might purchase the privilege of being maintained, without the necessity of labour, from the public revenue. The waste of an enormous household, the encrease of fees and perquisites, which were soon claimed as a lawful debt, and the bribes which they extorted from those who feared their enmity, or solicited their favour, suddenly enriched these haughty menials. They abused their fortune, without considering their past, or their future, condition; and their rapine and venality could be equalled only by the extravagance of their dissipations. Their silken robes were embroidered with gold, their tables were served with delicacy and profusion; the houses which they built for their own use, would have covered the farm of an ancient consul; and the most honourable citizens were obliged to dismount from their horses, and respectfully to salute an eunuch whom they met on the public highway. The luxury of the palace excited the contempt and indignation of Julian, who usually slept on the ground, who yielded with reluctance to the indispensable calls of nature; and who placed his vanity, not in emulating, but in despising, the pomp of royalty. By the total extirpation of a mischief which was magnified even beyond its real extent, he was impatient to relieve the distress, and to appease the murmurs, of the people; who support with less uneasiness the weight of taxes, if they are convinced that the fruits of their industry are appropriated to the service of the state. But in the execution of this salutary work, Julian is accused of proceeding with too much haste and inconsiderate severity. By a single edict, he reduced the palace of Constantinople to an immense desert, and

---

56. The expressions of Mamertinus are lively and forcible. Quin etiam prandiorum et cænarum laboratas magnitudines Romanus populus sensit; cum quæsitissimæ dapes non gustu sed difficultatibus æstimarentur; miracula avium, longinqui maris pisces, alieni temporis poma, æstivæ nives, hybernæ rosæ.

dismissed with ignominy the whole train of slaves and dependents,[57] without providing any just, or at least benevolent, exceptions, for the age, the services, or the poverty, of the faithful domestics of the Imperial family. Such indeed was the temper of Julian, who seldom recollected the fundamental maxim of Aristotle, that true virtue is placed at an equal distance between the opposite vices. The splendid and effeminate dress of the Asiatics, the curls and paint, the collars and bracelets, which had appeared so ridiculous in the person of Constantine, were consistently rejected by his philosophic successor. But with the fopperies, Julian affected to renounce the decencies, of dress; and seemed to value himself for his neglect of the laws of cleanliness. In a satirical performance, which was designed for the public eye, the emperor descants with pleasure, and even with pride, on the length of his nails, and the inky blackness of his hands; protests, that although the greatest part of his body was covered with hair, the use of the razor was confined to his head alone; and celebrates, with visible complacency, the shaggy and *populous*[58] beard, which he fondly cherished, after the example of the philosophers of Greece. Had Julian consulted the simple dictates of reason, the first magistrate of the Romans would have scorned the affectation of Diogenes, as well as that of Darius.

Chamber of justice.   But the work of public reformation would have remained imperfect, if Julian had only corrected the abuses, without punishing the crimes, of his predecessor's reign. "We are now delivered," says he, in a familiar letter to one of his intimate friends, "we are now surprisingly delivered from the voracious jaws of the Hydra.[59] I do not mean to apply that epithet to my brother Constantius. He is no more; may the earth lie light on his head! But his artful and cruel favourites studied to deceive and exasperate a prince, whose natural mildness cannot

---

57. Yet Julian himself was accused of bestowing whole towns on the eunuchs (Orat. vii. against Polyclet. p. 117–127.). Libanius contents himself with a cold but positive denial of the fact, which seems indeed to belong more properly to Constantius. This charge, however, may allude to some unknown circumstance.

58. In the Misopogon (p. 338, 339.) he draws a very singular picture of himself, and the following words are strangely characteristic; αυτος προσεθεικα τον βαθυν τουτονι πωγωνα ... ταυτα τοι διαθεοντων

ανεχομαι των φθειρων οσπερ εν λοχμη των θηρων. The friends of the Abbé de la Bleterie adjured him, in the name of the French nation, not to translate this passage, so offensive to their delicacy. (Hist. de Jovien, tom. ii. p. 94.). Like him, I have contented myself with a transient allusion; but the little animal, which Julian *names*, is a beast familiar to man, and signifies love.

59. Julian, epist. xxiii. p. 389. He uses the words πολυκεφαλον υδραν, in writing to his friend Hermogenes, who, like himself, was conversant with the Greek poets.

be praised without some efforts of adulation. It is not, however, my intention, that even those men should be oppressed: they are accused, and they shall enjoy the benefit of a fair and impartial trial." To conduct this enquiry, Julian named six judges of the highest rank in the state and army; and as he wished to escape the reproach of condemning his personal enemies, he fixed this extraordinary tribunal at Chalcedon, on the Asiatic side of the Bosphorus; and transferred to the commissioners an absolute power to pronounce and execute their final sentence, without delay, and without appeal. The office of president was exercised by the venerable præfect of the East, a *second* Sallust,[60] whose virtues conciliated the esteem of Greek sophists, and of Christian bishops. He was assisted by the eloquent Mamertinus,[61] one of the consuls elect, whose merit is loudly celebrated by the doubtful evidence of his own applause. But the civil wisdom of two magistrates was overbalanced by the ferocious violence of four generals, Nevitta, Agilo, Jovinus, and Arbetio. Arbetio, whom the public would have seen with less surprise at the bar than on the bench, was supposed to possess the secret of the commission; the armed and angry leaders of the Jovian and Herculian bands encompassed the tribunal; and the judges were alternately swayed by the laws of justice, and by the clamours of faction.[62]

The chamberlain Eusebius, who had so long abused the favour of Constantius, expiated, by an ignominious death, the insolence, the corruption, and cruelty of his servile reign. The executions of Paul and Apodemius (the former of whom was burnt alive) *Punishment of the innocent and the guilty.* were accepted as an inadequate atonement by the widows and orphans of so many hundred Romans, whom those legal tyrants had betrayed and murdered. But Justice herself (if we may use the pathetic expression of Ammianus[63]) appeared to weep over the fate of Ursulus, the treasurer of

---

60. The two Sallusts, the præfect of Gaul, and the præfect of the East, must be carefully distinguished (Hist. des Empereurs, tom. iv. p. 696.). I have used the surname of *Secundus*, as a convenient epithet. The second Sallust extorted the esteem of the Christians themselves; and Gregory Nazianzen, who condemned his religion, has celebrated his virtues (Orat. iii. p. 90). See a curious note of the Abbé de la Bleterie, Vie de Julien, p. 363.

61. Mamertinus praises the emperor (ix. 1.) for bestowing the offices of Treasurer and

Præfect on a man of wisdom, firmness, integrity, &c. like himself. Yet Ammianus ranks him (xxi. 1.) among the ministers of Julian, quorum merita nôrat et fidem.

62. The proceedings of this chamber of justice are related by Ammianus (xxii. 3.), and praised by Libanius (Orat. Parent. c. 74. p. 299, 300).

63. Ursuli vero necem ipsa mihi videtur flêsse justitia. Libanius, who imputes his death to the soldiers, attempts to criminate the count of the largesses.

the empire; and his blood accused the ingratitude of Julian, whose distress had been seasonably relieved by the intrepid liberality of that honest minister. The rage of the soldiers, whom he had provoked by his indiscretion, was the cause and the excuse of his death; and the emperor, deeply wounded by his own reproaches and those of the public, offered some consolation to the family of Ursulus, by the restitution of his confiscated fortunes. Before the end of the year in which they had been adorned with the ensigns of the prefecture and consulship,[64] Taurus and Florentius were reduced to implore the clemency of the inexorable tribunal of Chalcedon. The former was banished to Vercellæ in Italy, and a sentence of death was pronounced against the latter. A wise prince should have rewarded the crime of Taurus: the faithful minister, when he was no longer able to oppose the progress of a rebel, had taken refuge in the court of his benefactor and his lawful sovereign. But the guilt of Florentius justified the severity of the judges; and his escape served to display the magnanimity of Julian; who nobly checked the interested diligence of an informer, and refused to learn what place concealed the wretched fugitive from his just resentment.[65] Some months after the tribunal of Chalcedon had been dissolved, the prætorian vicegerent of Africa, the notary Gaudentius, and Artemius[66] duke of Egypt, were executed at Antioch. Artemius had reigned the cruel and corrupt tyrant of a great province; Gaudentius had long practised the arts of calumny against the innocent, the virtuous, and even the person of Julian himself. Yet the circumstances of their trial and condemnation were so unskilfully managed, that these wicked men obtained, in the public opinion, the glory of suffering for the obstinate loyalty with which they had supported the cause of Constantius. The rest of his servants were protected by a general act of oblivion; and they were left to enjoy with impunity the bribes which they had accepted, either to defend the oppressed, or to oppress the friendless. This measure, which, on the soundest principles of policy, may

---

64. Such respect was still entertained for the venerable names of the commonwealth, that the public was surprised and scandalized to hear Taurus summoned as a criminal under the consulship of Taurus. The summons of his colleague Florentius was probably delayed till the commencement of the ensuing year.
65. Ammian. xx. 7.
66. For the guilt and punishment of Artemius, see Julian (Epist. x. p. 379.), and Ammianus

(xxii. 6. and Vales. ad loc.). The merit of Artemius, who demolished temples, and was put to death by an apostate, has tempted the Greek and Latin churches to honour him as a martyr. But as ecclesiastical history attests, that he was not only a tyrant, but an Arian, it is not altogether easy to justify this indiscreet promotion. Tillemont, Mem. Eccles. tom. vii. p. 1319.

deserve our approbation, was executed in a manner which seemed to degrade the majesty of the throne. Julian was tormented by the importunities of a multitude, particularly of Egyptians, who loudly redemanded the gifts which they had imprudently or illegally bestowed; he foresaw the endless prosecution of vexatious suits; and he engaged a promise, which ought always to have been sacred, that if they would repair to Chalcedon, he would meet them in person, to hear and determine their complaints. But as soon as they were landed, he issued an absolute order, which prohibited the watermen from transporting any Egyptian to Constantinople; and thus detained his disappointed clients on the Asiatic shore, till their patience and money being utterly exhausted, they were obliged to return with indignant murmurs to their native country.[67]

The numerous army of spies, of agents, and informers, enlisted by Constantius to secure the repose of one man, and to interrupt that of millions, was immediately disbanded by his generous successor. Julian was slow in his suspicions, and gentle in his punishments; and his contempt of treason was the result of judgment, of vanity, and of courage. Conscious of superior merit, he was persuaded that few among his subjects would dare, to meet him in the field, to attempt his life, or even to seat themselves on his vacant throne. The philosopher could excuse the hasty sallies of discontent; and the hero could despise the ambitious projects, which surpassed the fortune or the abilities of the rash conspirators. A citizen of Ancyra had prepared for his own use a purple garment; and this indiscreet action, which, under the reign of Constantius, would have been considered as a capital offence,[68] was reported to Julian by the officious importunity of a private enemy. The monarch, after making some inquiry into the rank and character of his rival, dispatched the informer with a present of a pair of purple slippers, to complete the magnificence of his Imperial habit. A more dangerous conspiracy was formed by ten of the domestic guards, who had resolved to assassinate Julian in the field of exercise near Antioch. Their intemperance revealed their guilt; and they

Clemency of Julian.

---

67. See Ammian. xxii. 6. and Vales. ad locum; and the Codex Theodosianus, l. ii. tit. xxxix. leg. 1.; and Godefroy's Commentary, tom. i. p. 218, ad locum.

68. The president Montesquieu (Considerations sur la Grandeur, &c. des Romains, c. xiv. in his works, tom. iii. p. 448, 449.) excuses this minute and absurd tyranny, by supposing,

that actions the most indifferent in our eyes might excite, in a Roman mind, the idea of guilt and danger. This strange apology is supported by a strange misapprehension of the English laws, 'chez une nation . . . où il est defendû de boire à la santé d'une certaine personne.'

were conducted in chains to the presence of their injured sovereign, who, after a lively representation of the wickedness and folly of their enterprise, instead of a death of torture, which they deserved and expected, pronounced a sentence of exile against the two principal offenders. The only instance in which Julian seemed to depart from his accustomed clemency, was the execution of a rash youth, who with a feeble hand had aspired to seize the reins of empire. But that youth was the son of Marcellus, the general of cavalry, who, in the first campaign of the Gallic war, had deserted the standard of the Cæsar, and the republic. Without appearing to indulge his personal resentment, Julian might easily confound the crime of the son and of the father; but he was reconciled by the distress of Marcellus, and the liberality of the emperor endeavoured to heal the wound which had been inflicted by the hand of justice.[69]

His love of freedom, and the republic.

Julian was not insensible of the advantages of freedom.[70] From his studies he had imbibed the spirit of ancient sages and heroes: his life and fortunes had depended on the caprice of a tyrant; and when he ascended the throne, his pride was sometimes mortified by the reflection, that the slaves who would not dare to censure his defects, were not worthy to applaud his virtues.[71] He sincerely abhorred the system of Oriental despotism, which Diocletian, Constantine, and the patient habits of fourscore years, had established in the empire. A motive of superstition prevented the execution of the design which Julian had frequently meditated, of relieving his head from the weight of a costly diadem:[72] but he absolutely refused the title of *Dominus*, or *Lord*,[73] a word

69. The clemency of Julian, and the conspiracy which was formed against his life at Antioch, are described by Ammianus (xxii. 9, 10. and Vales. ad loc.), and Libanius (Orat. Parent. c. 99. p. 323.).

70. According to some, says Aristotle (as he is quoted by Julian ad Themist. p. 261.), the form of absolute government, the παμβασιλεια, is contrary to nature. Both the prince and the philosopher chuse, however, to involve this eternal truth in artful and laboured obscurity.

71. That sentiment is expressed almost in the words of Julian himself. Ammian. xxii. 10.

72. Libanius (Orat. Parent. c. 95. p. 320.), who mentions the wish and design of Julian,

insinuates, in mysterious language (θεων οντω γνοντων . . . αλλ' ην αμεινων ὁ κωλυων), that the emperor was restrained by some particular revelation.

73. Julian in Misopogon, p. 343. As he never abolished, by any public law, the proud appellations of *Despot*, or *Dominus*, they are still extant on his medals (Ducange, Fam. Byzantin. p. 38, 39.): and the private displeasure which he affected to express, only gave a different tone to the servility of the court. The Abbé de la Bleterie (Hist. de Jovien, tom. ii. p. 99–102.) has curiously traced the origin and progress of the word *Dominus* under the Imperial government.

which was grown so familiar to the ears of the Romans, that they no longer remembered its servile and humiliating origin. The office, or rather the name, of consul, was cherished by a prince who contemplated with reverence the ruins of the republic; and the same behaviour which had been assumed by the prudence of Augustus, was adopted by Julian from choice and inclination. On the calends of January, at break of day, the new consuls, Mamertinus and Nevitta, hastened to the palace to salute the emperor. As soon as he was informed of their approach, he leaped from his throne, eagerly advanced to meet them, and compelled the blushing magistrates to receive the demonstrations of his affected humility. From the palace they proceeded to the senate. The emperor, on foot, marched before their litters; and the gazing multitude admired the image of ancient times, or secretly blamed a conduct, which, in their eyes, degraded the majesty of the purple.[74] But the behaviour of Julian was uniformly supported. During the games of the Circus, he had, imprudently or designedly, performed the manumission of a slave in the presence of the consul. The moment he was reminded that he had trespassed on the jurisdiction of *another* magistrate, he condemned himself to pay a fine of ten pounds of gold; and embraced this public occasion of declaring to the world, that he was subject, like the rest of his fellow-citizens, to the laws,[75] and even to the forms, of the republic. The spirit of his administration, and his regard for the place of his nativity, induced Julian to confer on the senate of Constantinople, the same honours, privileges, and authority, which were still enjoyed by the senate of ancient Rome.[76] A legal fiction was introduced, and gradually established, that one half of the national council had migrated into the East: and the despotic successors of Julian, accepting the title of Senators, acknowledged themselves the members of a respectable body, which was permitted to represent the majesty of the

A.D. 363, January 1.

---

74. Ammian. xxii. 7. The consul Mamertinus (in Panegyr. Vet. xi. 28, 29, 30.) celebrates the auspicious day, like an eloquent slave, astonished and intoxicated by the condescension of his master.

75. Personal satire was condemned by the laws of the twelve tables:

  Si male condiderit in quem quis
    carmina, jus est,
  Judiciumque. ——

Julian (in Misopogon, p. 337.) owns himself subject to the law; and the Abbé de la Bleterie (Hist. de Jovien, tom. ii. p. 92.) has eagerly embraced a declaration so agreeable to his own system, and indeed to the true spirit, of the Imperial constitution.

76. Zosimus, l. iii. p. 158.

Roman name. From Constantinople, the attention of the monarch was extended to the municipal senates of the provinces. He abolished, by repeated edicts, the unjust and pernicious exemptions, which had withdrawn so many idle citizens from the service of their country; and by imposing an equal distribution of public duties, he restored the strength, the splendour, or, according to the glowing expression of Libanius,[77] the soul of the expiring cities of his empire. The venerable age of Greece excited the most tender compassion in the mind of Julian; which kindled into rapture when he recollected the gods; the heroes; and the men, superior to heroes and to gods; who had bequeathed to the latest posterity the monuments of their genius, or the example of their virtues. He relieved the distress, and restored the beauty, of the cities of Epirus and Peloponnesus.[78] Athens acknowledged him for her benefactor; Argos, for her deliverer. The pride of Corinth, again rising from her ruins with the honours of a Roman colony, exacted a tribute from the adjacent republics, for the purpose of defraying the games of the Isthmus, which were celebrated in the amphitheatre with the hunting of bears and panthers. From this tribute the cities of Elis, of Delphi, and of Argos, which had inherited from their remote ancestors the sacred office of perpetuating the Olympic, the Pythian, and the Nemean games, claimed a just exemption. The immunity of Elis and Delphi was respected by the Corinthians; but the poverty of Argos tempted the insolence of oppression; and the feeble complaints of its deputies were silenced by the decree of a provincial magistrate, who seems to have consulted only the interest of the capital, in which he resided. Seven years after this sentence, Julian[79] allowed the cause to be referred to a superior tribunal; and his eloquence was interposed, most probably with success, in the defence of a city, which had

His care of the Grecian cities.

---

77. ἡ τῆς βουλῆς ισχυς ψυχη πολεως εστιν. See Libanius (Orat. Parent. c. 71. p. 296), Ammianus (xxii. 9.), and the Theodosian Code (l. xii. tit. i. leg. 50–55), with Godefroy's Commentary (tom. iv. p. 390–402.). Yet the whole subject of the *Curiæ*, notwithstanding very ample materials, still remains the most obscure in the legal history of the empire.

78. Quæ paulo ante arida et siti anhelantia visebantur, ea nunc perlui, mundari, madere; Fora, Deambulacra, Gymnasia, lætis et gaudentibus populis frequentari; dies festos, et celebrari veteres, et novos in honorem principis consecrari (Mamertin. xi. 9.). He particularly restored the city of Nicopolis, and the Actiac games, which had been instituted by Augustus.

79. Julian. Epist. xxxv. p. 407–411. This epistle, which illustrates the declining age of Greece, is omitted by the Abbé de la Bleterie; and strangely disfigured by the Latin translator, who, by rendering ατελεια, *tributum*, and ιδιωται, *populus*, directly contradicts the sense of the original.

been the royal seat of Agamemnon,[80] and had given to Macedonia a race of kings and conquerors.[81]

The laborious administration of military and civil affairs, which were multiplied in proportion to the extent of the empire, exercised the abilities of Julian; but he frequently assumed the two characters of Orator[82] and of Judge,[83] which are almost unknown to the modern sovereigns of Europe. The arts of persuasion, so diligently cultivated by the first Cæsars, were neglected by the military ignorance and Asiatic pride of their successors; and if they condescended to harangue the soldiers, whom they feared, they treated with silent disdain the senators, whom they despised. The assemblies of the senate, which Constantius had avoided, were considered by Julian as the place where he could exhibit, with the most propriety, the maxims of a republican, and the talents of a rhetorician. He alternately practised, as in a school of declamation, the several modes of praise, of censure, of exhortation; and his friend Libanius has remarked, that the study of Homer taught him to imitate the simple, concise style of Menelaus, the copiousness of Nestor, whose words descended like the flakes of a winter's snow, or the pathetic and forcible eloquence of Ulysses. The functions of a judge, which are sometimes incompatible with those of a prince, were exercised by Julian, not only as a duty, but as an amusement; and although he might have trusted the integrity and discernment of his Prætorian præfects, he often placed himself

Julian, an orator and a judge.

---

80. He reigned in Mycenæ, at the distance of fifty stadia, or six miles, from Argos: but those cities which alternately flourished, are confounded by the Greek poets. Strabo, l. viii. p. 579. edit. Amstel. 1707.

81. Marsham, Canon. Chron. p. 421. This pedigree from Temenus and Hercules may be suspicious; yet it was allowed, after a strict enquiry by the judges of the Olympic games (Herodot. l. v. c. 22.), at a time when the Macedonian kings were obscure and unpopular in Greece. When the Achæan league declared against Philip, it was thought decent that the deputies of Argos should retire (T. Liv. xxxii. 22.).

82. His eloquence is celebrated by Libanius (Orat. Parent. c. 75, 76. p. 300, 301.), who distinctly mentions the orators of Homer. Socrates (l. iii. c. 1.) has rashly asserted that

Julian was the only prince, since Julius Cæsar, who harangued the senate. All the predecessors of Nero (Tacit. Annal. xiii. 3.), and many of his successors, possessed the faculty of speaking in public; and it might be proved by various examples, that they frequently exercised it in the senate.

83. Ammianus (xxii. 10.) has impartially stated the merits and defects of his judicial proceedings. Libanius (Orat. Parent. c. 90, 91. p. 315, &c.) has seen only the fair side, and his picture, if it flatters the person, expresses at least the duties, of the Judge. Gregory Nazianzen (Orat. iv. p. 120.), who suppresses the virtues, and exaggerates even the venial faults, of the apostate; triumphantly asks, Whether such a judge was fit to be seated between Minos and Rhadamanthus, in the Elysian fields?

by their side on the seat of judgment. The acute penetration of his mind was agreeably occupied in detecting and defeating the chicanery of the advocates, who laboured to disguise the truth of facts, and to pervert the sense of the laws. He sometimes forgot the gravity of his station, asked indiscreet or unseasonable questions, and betrayed, by the loudness of his voice, and the agitation of his body, the earnest vehemence with which he maintained his opinion against the judges, the advocates, and their clients. But his knowledge of his own temper prompted him to encourage, and even to solicit, the reproof of his friends and ministers; and whenever they ventured to oppose the irregular sallies of his passions, the spectators could observe the shame, as well as the gratitude, of their monarch. The decrees of Julian were almost always founded on the principles of justice; and he had the firmness to resist the two most dangerous temptations, which assault the tribunal of a sovereign, under the specious forms of compassion and equity. He decided the merits of the cause without weighing the circumstances of the parties; and the poor, whom he wished to relieve, were condemned to satisfy the just demands of a noble and wealthy adversary. He carefully distinguished the judge from the legislator;[84] and though he meditated a necessary reformation of the Roman jurisprudence, he pronounced sentence according to the strict and literal interpretation of those laws, which the magistrates were bound to execute, and the subjects to obey.

His character.   The generality of princes, if they were stripped of their purple, and cast naked into the world, would immediately sink to the lowest rank of society, without a hope of emerging from their obscurity. But the personal merit of Julian was, in some measure, independent of his fortune. Whatever had been his choice of life; by the force of intrepid courage, lively wit, and intense application, he would have obtained, or at least he would have deserved, the highest honours of his profession; and Julian might have raised himself to the rank of minister, or general, of the state in which he was born a private citizen. If the jealous caprice of power had disappointed his expectations; if he had prudently declined the paths of greatness, the employment of the same talents in studious solitude, would have placed, beyond the reach of kings, his present happiness and his

---

84. Of the laws which Julian enacted in a reign of sixteen months, fifty-four have been admitted into the Codes of Theodosius and Justinian. (Gothofred. Chron. Legum, p. 64–

67.) The Abbé de la Bleterie (tom. ii. p. 329–336.) has chosen one of these laws to give an idea of Julian's Latin style, which is forcible and elaborate, but less pure than his Greek.

immortal fame. When we inspect, with minute, or perhaps malevolent attention, the portrait of Julian, something seems wanting to the grace and perfection of the whole figure. His genius was less powerful and sublime than that of Cæsar; nor did he possess the consummate prudence of Augustus. The virtues of Trajan appear more steady and natural, and the philosophy of Marcus is more simple and consistent. Yet Julian sustained adversity with firmness, and prosperity with moderation. After an interval of one hundred and twenty years from the death of Alexander Severus, the Romans beheld an emperor who made no distinction between his duties and his pleasures; who laboured to relieve the distress, and to revive the spirit, of his subjects; and who endeavoured always to connect authority with merit, and happiness with virtue. Even faction, and religious faction, was constrained to acknowledge the superiority of his genius, in peace as well as in war; and to confess, with a sigh, that the apostate Julian was a lover of his country, and that he deserved the empire of the world.[85]

85. —— Ductor fortissimus armis;
    Conditor et legum celeberrimus; ore manûque
    Consultor patriæ; sed non consultor habendæ
    Religionis; amans tercentûm millia Divûm.

Perfidus ille Deo, sed non et perfidus orbi.
                    Prudent. Apotheosis, 450, &c.

The consciousness of a generous sentiment seems to have raised the Christian poet above his usual mediocrity.

CHAPTER XXIII

The Religion of Julian. – Universal Toleration. – He attempts to restore and reform the Pagan Worship – to rebuild the Temple of Jerusalem. – His artful Persecution of the Christians. – Mutual Zeal and Injustice.

Religion of Julian. The character of Apostate has injured the reputation of Julian; and the enthusiasm which clouded his virtues, has exaggerated the real and apparent magnitude of his faults. Our partial ignorance may represent him as a philosophic monarch, who studied to protect, with an equal hand, the religious factions of the empire; and to allay the theological fever which had inflamed the minds of the people, from the edicts of Diocletian to the exile of Athanasius. A more accurate view of the character and conduct of Julian, will remove this favourable prepossession for a prince who did not escape the general contagion of the times. We enjoy the singular advantage of comparing the pictures which have been delineated by his fondest admirers, and his implacable enemies. The actions of Julian are faithfully related by a judicious and candid historian, the impartial spectator of his life and death. The unanimous evidence of his contemporaries is confirmed by the public and private declarations of the emperor himself; and his various writings express the uniform tenor of his religious sentiments, which policy would have prompted him to dissemble rather than to affect. A devout and sincere attachment for the gods of Athens and Rome, constituted the ruling passion of Julian;[1] the powers of an enlightened understanding were betrayed and corrupted by the influence of superstitious prejudice; and the phantoms which existed only in the mind of the emperor, had a real and pernicious effect on the government of the empire. The vehement zeal of the Christians, who

---

1. I shall transcribe some of his own expressions from a short religious discourse which the Imperial pontiff composed to censure the bold impiety of a Cynic: Αλλ' ομως ουτω δη τι τους θεους πεφρικα, και φιλω, μαι σεβω, και αζομαι, και πανθ' απλως τα τοιαυτα πασχω, οσπερ αν τις και οια προς αγαθους δεσποτας, προς διδασκαλους, προς πατερας, προς κηδεμονας. Orat. vii. p. 212. The variety and copiousness of the Greek tongue seems inadequate to the fervour of his devotion.

despised the worship, and overturned the altars, of those fabulous deities, engaged their votary in a state of irreconcilable hostility with a very numerous party of his subjects; and he was sometimes tempted, by the desire of victory, or the shame of a repulse, to violate the laws of prudence, and even of justice. The triumph of the party, which he deserted and opposed, has fixed a stain of infamy on the name of Julian; and the unsuccessful apostate has been overwhelmed with a torrent of pious invectives, of which the signal was given by the sonorous trumpet[2] of Gregory Nazianzen.[3] The interesting nature of the events which were crowded into the short reign of this active emperor, deserve a just and circumstantial narrative. His motives, his counsels, and his actions, as far as they are connected with the history of religion, will be the subject of the present chapter.

The cause of his strange and fatal apostacy, may be derived from the early period of his life, when he was left an orphan in the hands of the murderers of his family. The names of Christ *His education and apostacy.* and of Constantius, the ideas of slavery and of religion, were soon associated in a youthful imagination, which was susceptible of the most lively impressions. The care of his infancy was entrusted to Eusebius, bishop of Nicomedia,[4] who was related to him on the side of his mother; and till Julian reached the twentieth year of his age, he received from his Christian preceptors, the education not of a hero, but of a saint. The emperor, less jealous of a heavenly, than of an earthly crown, contented himself with the imperfect character of a catechumen, while he bestowed the advantages

---

2. The orator, with some eloquence, much enthusiasm, and more vanity, addresses his discourse to heaven and earth, to men and angels, to the living and the dead; and above all, to the great Constantius (ει τις αισθησις, an odd Pagan expression). He concludes with a bold assurance, that he has erected a monument not less durable, and much more portable, than the columns of Hercules. See Greg. Nazianzen, Orat. iii. p. 50. iv. p. 134.

3. See this long invective, which has been injudiciously divided into two orations, in Gregory's Works, tom. i. p. 49–134. Paris, 1630. It was published by Gregory and his friend Basil (iv. p. 133.), about six months

after the death of Julian, when his remains had been carried to Tarsus (iv. p. 120.); but while Jovian was still on the throne (iii. p. 54. iv. p. 117.). I have derived much assistance from a French version and remarks, printed at Lyons 1735.

4. Nicomediæ ab Eusebio educatus Episcopo, quem genere longius contingebat. (Ammian. xxii. 9.) Julian never expresses any gratitude towards that Arian prelate; but he celebrates his preceptor, the eunuch Mardonius, and describes his mode of education, which inspired his pupil with a passionate admiration for the genius, and perhaps the religion, of Homer. Misopogon. p. 351, 352.

of baptism[5] on the nephews of Constantine.[6] They were even admitted to the inferior offices of the ecclesiastical order; and Julian publicly read the Holy Scriptures in the church of Nicomedia. The study of religion, which they assiduously cultivated, appeared to produce the fairest fruits of faith and devotion.[7] They prayed, they fasted, they distributed alms to the poor, gifts to the clergy, and oblations to the tombs of the martyrs; and the splendid monument of St. Mamas, at Cæsarea, was erected, or at least was undertaken, by the joint labour of Gallus and Julian.[8] They respectfully conversed with the bishops who were eminent for superior sanctity, and solicited the benediction of the monks and hermits, who had introduced into Cappadocia the voluntary hardships of the ascetic life.[9] As the two princes advanced towards the years of manhood, they discovered, in their religious sentiments, the difference of their characters. The dull and obstinate understanding of Gallus embraced, with implicit zeal, the doctrines of Christianity; which never influenced his conduct, or moderated his passions. The mild disposition of the younger brother was less repugnant to the precepts of the Gospel; and his active curiosity might have been gratified by a theological system, which explains the mysterious essence of the Deity; and opens the boundless prospect of invisible and future worlds. But the independent spirit of Julian refused to yield the passive and unresisting obedience which was required, in the name of religion, by the haughty ministers of the church. Their speculative opinions were imposed as positive laws, and guarded by the terrors of eternal punishments; but while they prescribed the rigid formulary of the thoughts, the words, and

5. Greg. Naz. iii. p. 70. He laboured to efface that holy mark in the blood, perhaps, of a Taurobolium. Baron. Annal. Eccles. A.D. 361. N° 3, 4.

6. Julian himself (Epist. li. p. 454.) assures the Alexandrians that he had been a Christian (he must mean a sincere one) till the twentieth year of his age.

7. See his Christian, and even ecclesiastical education, in Gregory (iii. p. 58.), Socrates (l. iii. c. 1.), and Sozomen, (l. v. c. 2.). He escaped very narrowly from being a bishop, and perhaps a saint.

8. The share of the work which had been allotted to Gallus, was prosecuted with vigour and success; but the earth obstinately rejected and subverted the structures which were imposed by the sacrilegious hand of Julian. Greg. iii. p. 59, 60, 61. Such a partial earthquake, attested by many living spectators, would form one of the clearest miracles in ecclesiastical story.

9. The *philosopher* (Fragment, p. 288.) ridicules the iron-chains, &c. of these solitary fanatics (see Tillemont, Mem. Eccles. tom. ix. p. 661, 662.), who had forgot that man is by nature a gentle and social animal, ανθρωπον φυσει πολιτικον ζωον και ημερον. The *Pagan* supposes, that because they had renounced the gods, they were possessed and tormented by evil dæmons.

the actions of the young prince; whilst they silenced his objections, and severely checked the freedom of his enquiries, they secretly provoked his impatient genius to disclaim the authority of his ecclesiastical guides. He was educated in the Lesser Asia, amidst the scandals of the Arian controversy.[10] The fierce contests of the Eastern bishops, the incessant alterations of their creeds, and the profane motives which appeared to actuate their conduct, insensibly strengthened the prejudice of Julian, that they neither understood nor believed the religion for which they so fiercely contended. Instead of listening to the proofs of Christianity with that favourable attention which adds weight to the most respectable evidence, he heard with suspicion, and disputed with obstinacy and acuteness, the doctrines for which he already entertained an invincible aversion. Whenever the young princes were directed to compose declamations on the subject of the prevailing controversies, Julian always declared himself the advocate of Paganism; under the specious excuse that, in the defence of the weaker cause, his learning and ingenuity might be more advantageously exercised and displayed.

As soon as Gallus was invested with the honours of the purple, Julian was permitted to breathe the air of freedom, of literature, and of Paganism.[11] The crowd of sophists, who were attracted by the taste and liberality of their royal pupil, had formed a strict *He embraces the mythology of Paganism.* alliance between the learning and the religion of Greece; and the poems of Homer, instead of being admired as the original productions of human genius, were seriously ascribed to the heavenly inspiration of Apollo and the muses. The deities of Olympus, as they are painted by the immortal bard, imprint themselves on the minds which are the least addicted to superstitious credulity. Our familiar knowledge of their names and characters, their forms and attributes, *seems* to bestow on those airy beings a real and substantial existence; and the pleasing enchantment produces an imperfect and momentary assent of the imagination to those fables, which are the most repugnant to our reason and experience. In the age of Julian, every circumstance contributed to prolong and fortify the illusion; the

---

10. See Julian apud Cyril. l. vi. p. 206. l. viii. p. 253. 262. "You persecute," says he, "those heretics who do not mourn the dead man precisely in the way which you approve." He shews himself a tolerable theologian; but he maintains that the Christian Trinity is not derived from the doctrine of Paul, of Jesus, or of Moses.

11. Libanius, Orat. Parentalis, c. 9, 10. p. 232, &c. Greg. Nazianzen, Orat. iii. p. 61. Eunap. Vit. Sophist. in Maximo, p. 68, 69, 70. Edit. Commelin.

magnificent temples of Greece and Asia; the works of those artists who had expressed, in painting or in sculpture, the divine conceptions of the poet; the pomp of festivals and sacrifices; the successful arts of divination; the popular traditions of oracles and prodigies; and the ancient practice of two thousand years. The weakness of polytheism was, in some measure, excused by the moderation of its claims; and the devotion of the Pagans was not incompatible with the most licentious scepticism.[12] Instead of an indivisible and regular system, which occupies the whole extent of the believing mind, the mythology of the Greeks was composed of a thousand loose and flexible parts, and the servant of the gods was at liberty to define the degree and measure of his religious faith. The creed which Julian adopted for his own use, was of the largest dimensions; and, by a strange contradiction, he disdained the salutary yoke of the Gospel, whilst he made a voluntary offering of his reason on the altars of Jupiter and Apollo. One of the orations of Julian is consecrated to the honour of Cybele, the mother of the gods, who required from her effeminate priests the bloody sacrifice, so rashly performed by the madness of the Phrygian boy. The pious emperor condescends to relate, without a blush, and without a smile, the voyage of the goddess from the shores of Pergamus to the mouth of the Tyber; and the stupendous miracle, which convinced the senate and people of Rome that the lump of clay, which their ambassadors had transported over the seas, was endowed with life, and sentiment, and divine power.[13] For the truth of this prodigy, he appeals to the public monuments of the city; and censures, with some acrimony, the sickly and affected taste of those men, who impertinently derided the sacred traditions of their ancestors.[14]

---

12. A modern philosopher has ingeniously compared the different operation of theism and polytheism, with regard to the doubt or conviction which they produce in the human mind. See Hume's Essays, vol. ii. p. 444–457. in 8vo edit. 1777.

13. The Idæan mother landed in Italy about the end of the second Punic war. The miracle of Claudia, either virgin or matron, who cleared her fame by disgracing the graver modesty of the Roman ladies, is attested by a cloud of witnesses. Their evidence is collected by Drakenborch (ad Silium Italicum, xvii. 33.): but we may observe that Livy (xxix.

14.) slides over the transaction with discreet ambiguity.

14. I cannot refrain from transcribing the emphatical words of Julian: εμοι δε δοκει ταις πολεσι πιστευειν μαλλον τα τοιαυτα, ἡ τουτοισι τοις κομψοις, ὧν το ψυχαριον δριμυ μεν, ὑλιες δε ουδε ἑν βλεπει. Orat. v. p. 161. Julian likewise declares his firm belief in the ancilia, the holy shields, which dropt from heaven on the Quirinal hill; and pities the strange blindness of the Christians, who preferred the *cross* to these celestial trophies. Apud Cyril. l. vi. p. 194.

But the devout philosopher, who sincerely embraced, and warmly encouraged, the superstition of the people, reserved for himself the privilege of a liberal interpretation; and silently withdrew from the foot of the altars into the sanctuary of the temple. The extravagance of the Grecian mythology proclaimed with a clear and audible voice, that the pious enquirer, instead of being scandalized or satisfied with the literal sense, should diligently explore the occult wisdom, which had been disguised, by the prudence of antiquity, under the mask of folly and of fable.[15] The philosophers of the Platonic school,[16] Plotinus, Porphyry, and the divine Iamblichus, were admired as the most skilful masters of this allegorical science, which laboured to soften and harmonize the deformed features of paganism. Julian himself, who was directed in the mysterious pursuit by Ædesius, the venerable successor of Iamblichus, aspired to the possession of a treasure, which he esteemed, if we may credit his solemn asseverations, far above the empire of the world.[17] It was indeed a treasure, which derived its value only from opinion; and every artist, who flattered himself that he had extracted the precious ore from the surrounding dross, claimed an equal right of stamping the name and figure the most agreeable to his peculiar fancy. The fable of Atys and Cybele had been already explained by Porphyry; but his labours served only to animate the pious industry of Julian, who invented and published his own allegory of that ancient and mystic tale. This freedom of interpretation, which might gratify the pride of the Platonists, exposed the vanity of their art. Without a tedious detail, the modern reader could not form a just idea of the strange allusions, the forced etymologies, the solemn trifling, and the impenetrable obscurity of these sages, who professed to reveal the system of the universe. As the traditions of pagan mythology were variously related, the sacred interpreters were at liberty to select the most convenient circumstances; and as they translated an arbitrary cypher, they could extract from *any* fable *any* sense which was adapted to their favourite system of religion and philosophy.

The allegories.

15. See the principles of allegory, in Julian (Orat. vii. p. 216. 222.). His reasoning is less absurd than that of some modern theologians, who assert that an extravagant or contradictory doctrine *must* be divine; since no man alive could have thought of inventing it.

16. Eunapius has made these sophists the subject of a partial and fanatical history: and the learned Brucker (Hist. Philosoph. tom. ii. p. 217–303.) has employed much labour to illustrate their obscure lives, and incomprehensible doctrines.

17. Julian, Orat. vii. p. 222. He swears with the most fervent and enthusiastic devotion; and trembles, lest he should betray too much of these holy mysteries, which the profane might deride with an impious Sardonic laugh.

The lascivious form of a naked Venus was tortured into the discovery of some moral precept, or some physical truth; and the castration of Atys explained the revolution of the sun between the tropics, or the separation of the human soul from vice and error.[18]

Theological system of Julian.   The theological system of Julian appears to have contained the sublime and important principles of natural religion. But as the faith, which is not founded on revelation, must remain destitute of any firm assurance, the disciple of Plato imprudently relapsed into the habits of vulgar superstition; and the popular and philosophic notion of the Deity seems to have been confounded in the practice, the writings, and even in the mind of Julian.[19] The pious emperor acknowledged and adored the Eternal Cause of the universe, to whom he ascribed all the perfections of an infinite nature, invisible to the eyes, and inaccessible to the understanding, of feeble mortals. The Supreme God had created, or rather, in the Platonic language, had generated, the gradual succession of dependent spirits, of gods, of dæmons, of heroes, and of men; and every being which derived its existence immediately from the First Cause, received the inherent gift of immortality. That so precious an advantage might not be lavished upon unworthy objects, the Creator had entrusted to the skill and power of the inferior gods, the office of forming the human body, and of arranging the beautiful harmony of the animal, the vegetable, and the mineral kingdoms. To the conduct of these divine ministers he delegated the temporal government of this lower world; but their imperfect administration is not exempt from discord or error. The earth, and its inhabitants, are divided among them, and the characters of Mars or Minerva, of Mercury or Venus, may be distinctly traced in the laws and manners of their peculiar votaries. As long as our immortal souls are confined in a mortal prison, it is our interest, as well as our duty, to solicit the favour, and to deprecate the wrath, of the powers of heaven; whose pride is gratified by the devotion of mankind; and whose grosser parts may be supposed to derive some

---

18. See the fifth oration of Julian. But all the allegories which ever issued from the Platonic school, are not worth the short poem of Catullus on the same extraordinary subject. The transition of Atys, from the wildest enthusiasm to sober pathetic complaint, for his irretrievable loss, must inspire a man with pity, an eunuch with despair.

19. The true religion of Julian may be deduced from the Cæsars, p. 308. with Spanheim's notes and illustrations, from the fragments in Cyril, l. ii. p. 57, 58. and especially from the theological oration in Solem Regem, p. 130–158. addressed, in the confidence of friendship, to the præfect Sallust.

nourishment from the fumes of sacrifice.[20] The inferior gods might some-times condescend to animate the statues, and to inhabit the temples, which were dedicated to their honour. They might occasionally visit the earth, but the heavens were the proper throne and symbol of their glory. The invariable order of the sun, moon, and stars, was hastily admitted by Julian, as a proof of their *eternal* duration; and their eternity was a sufficient evidence that they were the workmanship, not of an inferior deity, but of the Omnipotent King. In the system of the Platonists, the visible, was a type of the invisible, world. The celestial bodies, as they were informed by a divine spirit, might be considered as the objects the most worthy of religious worship. The SUN, whose genial influence pervades and sustains the universe, justly claimed the adoration of mankind, as the bright representa-tive of the LOGOS, the lively, the rational, the beneficent image of the intellectual Father.[21]

In every age, the absence of genuine inspiration is supplied by the strong illusions of enthusiasm, and the mimic arts of imposture. If, in the time of Julian, these arts had been practised only by the pagan priests, for the support of an expiring cause, some indulgence might perhaps be allowed to the interest and habits of the sacerdotal character. But it may appear a subject of surprise and scandal, that the philosophers themselves should have contributed to abuse the superstitious credulity of mankind,[22] and that the Grecian mysteries should have been supported by the magic or theurgy of the modern Platonists. They arrogantly pretended to controul the order of nature, to explore the secrets of futurity, to command the service of the inferior dæmons, to

Fanaticism of the philosophers.

---

20. Julian adopts this gross conception, by ascribing it to his favourite Marcus Antoninus (Cæsares, p. 333.). The Stoics and Platonists hesitated between the analogy of bodies, and the purity of spirits; yet the gravest philo-sophers inclined to the whimsical fancy of Aristophanes and Lucian, that an unbelieving age might starve the immortal gods. See Observations de Spanheim, p. 284. 444, &c.

21. Ἡλιον λεγω, το ζων αγαλμα και εμψυχον, και εννουν, και αγαθοεργον του νοητου πατρος. Julian, epist. xli. In another place (apud Cyril. l. ii. p. 69), he calls the Sun, God, and the throne of God. Julian believed the Platonician Trinity; and only blames the Christians for preferring a mortal, to an immortal, *Logos*.

22. The sophists of Eunapius perform as many miracles as the saints of the desert; and the only circumstance in their favour is, that they are of a less gloomy complexion. Instead of devils with horns and tails, Iamblichus evoked the genii of love, Eros and Anteros, from two adjacent fountains. Two beautiful boys issued from the water, fondly embraced him as their father, and retired at his com-mand. P. 26, 27.

enjoy the view and conversation of the superior gods, and, by disengaging the soul from her material bands, to reunite that immortal particle with the Infinite and Divine Spirit.

Initiation and fanaticism of Julian.

The devout and fearless curiosity of Julian tempted the philosophers with the hopes of an easy conquest; which, from the situation of their young proselyte, might be productive of the most important consequences.[23] Julian imbibed the first rudiments of the Platonic doctrines from the mouth of Ædesius, who had fixed at Pergamus his wandering and persecuted school. But as the declining strength of that venerable sage was unequal to the ardour, the diligence, the rapid conception of his pupil, two of his most learned disciples, Chrysanthes and Eusebius, supplied, at his own desire, the place of their aged master. These philosophers seem to have prepared and distributed their respective parts; and they artfully contrived, by dark hints, and affected disputes, to excite the impatient hopes of the *aspirant*, till they delivered him into the hands of their associate Maximus, the boldest and most skilful master of the Theurgic science. By his hands, Julian was secretly initiated at Ephesus, in the twentieth year of his age. His residence at Athens confirmed this unnatural alliance of philosophy and superstition. He obtained the privilege of a solemn initiation into the mysteries of Eleusis, which, amidst the general decay of the Grecian worship, still retained some vestiges of their primæval sanctity; and such was the zeal of Julian, that he afterwards invited the Eleusinian pontiff to the court of Gaul, for the sole purpose of consummating, by mystic rites and sacrifices, the great work of his sanctification. As these ceremonies were performed in the depth of caverns, and in the silence of the night; and as the inviolable secret of the mysteries was preserved by the discretion of the initiated, I shall not presume to describe the horrid sounds, and fiery apparitions, which were presented to the senses, or the imagination, of the credulous aspirant,[24] till the visions of comfort and knowledge broke upon him in a blaze of celestial

---

23. The dexterous management of these sophists, who played their credulous pupil into each other's hands, is fairly told by Eunapius (p. 69–76.), with unsuspecting simplicity. The Abbé de la Bleterie understands, and neatly describes, the whole comedy (Vie de Julien, p. 61–67.).

24. When Julian, in a momentary panic, made

the sign of the cross, the dæmons instantly disappeared (Greg. Naz. Orat. iii. p. 71.). Gregory supposes that they were frightened, but the priests declared that they were indignant. The reader, according to the measure of his faith, will determine this profound question.

light.[25] In the caverns of Ephesus and Eleusis, the mind of Julian was penetrated with sincere, deep, and unalterable enthusiasm; though he might sometimes exhibit the vicissitudes of pious fraud and hypocrisy, which may be observed, or at least suspected, in the characters of the most conscientious fanatics. From that moment he consecrated his life to the service of the gods; and while the occupations of war, of government, and of study, seemed to claim the whole measure of his time, a stated portion of the hours of the night was invariably reserved for the exercise of private devotion. The temperance which adorned the severe manners of the soldier and the philosopher, was connected with some strict and frivolous rules of religious abstinence; and it was in honour of Pan or Mercury, of Hecate or Isis, that Julian, on particular days, denied himself the use of some particular food, which might have been offensive to his tutelar deities. By these voluntary fasts, he prepared his senses and his understanding for the frequent and familiar visits with which he was honoured by the celestial powers. Notwithstanding the modest silence of Julian himself, we may learn from his faithful friend, the orator Libanius, that he lived in a perpetual intercourse with the gods and goddesses; that they descended upon earth, to enjoy the conversation of their favourite hero; that they gently interrupted his slumbers, by touching his hand or his hair; that they warned him of every impending danger, and conducted him, by their infallible wisdom, in every action of his life; and that he had acquired such an intimate knowledge of his heavenly guests, as readily to distinguish the voice of Jupiter from that of Minerva, and the form of Apollo from the figure of Hercules.[26] These sleeping or waking visions, the ordinary effects of abstinence and fanaticism, would almost degrade the emperor to the level of an Egyptian monk. But the useless lives of Antony or Pachomius were consumed in these vain occupations. Julian could break from the dream of superstition to arm himself for battle; and after vanquishing in the field the enemies of Rome, he calmly retired into his tent, to dictate the wise and salutary laws of an empire, or to indulge his genius in the elegant pursuits of literature and philosophy.

25. A dark and distant view of the terrors and joys of initiation is shewn by Dion Chrysostom, Themistius, Proclus, and Stobæus. The learned author of the Divine Legation has exhibited their words (vol. i. p. 239. 247, 248. 280. edit. 1765.), which he dexterously or forcibly applies to his own hypothesis.

26. Julian's modesty confined him to obscure and occasional hints; but Libanius expatiates with pleasure on the fasts and visions of the religious hero (Legat. ad Julian. p. 157. and Orat. Parental. c. lxxxiii. p. 309, 310.).

His religious dissimulation.

The important secret of the apostacy of Julian was entrusted to the fidelity of the *initiated*, with whom he was united by the sacred ties of friendship and religion.[27] The pleasing rumour was cautiously circulated among the adherents of the ancient worship; and his future greatness became the object of the hopes, the prayers, and the predictions of the pagans, in every province of the empire. From the zeal and virtues of their royal proselyte, they fondly expected the cure of every evil, and the restoration of every blessing; and instead of disapproving of the ardour of their pious wishes, Julian ingenuously confessed, that he was ambitious to attain a situation, in which he might be useful to his country, and to his religion. But this religion was viewed with an hostile eye by the successor of Constantine, whose capricious passions alternately saved and threatened the life of Julian. The arts of magic and divination were strictly prohibited under a despotic government, which condescended to fear them; and if the pagans were reluctantly indulged in the exercise of their superstition, the rank of Julian would have excepted him from the general toleration. The apostate soon became the presumptive heir of the monarchy, and his death could alone have appeased the just apprehensions of the Christians.[28] But the young prince, who aspired to the glory of a hero rather than of a martyr, consulted his safety by dissembling his religion; and the easy temper of polytheism permitted him to join in the public worship of a sect which he inwardly despised. Libanius has considered the hypocrisy of his friend as a subject, not of censure, but of praise. "As the statues of the gods," says that orator, "which have been defiled with filth, are again placed in a magnificent temple; so the beauty of truth was seated in the mind of Julian, after it had been purified from the errors and follies of his education. His sentiments were changed; but as it would have been dangerous to have avowed his sentiments, his conduct still continued the same. Very different from the ass in Æsop, who disguised himself with a lion's hide, our lion was obliged to conceal himself under the skin of an ass; and, while he embraced the dictates of reason, to obey

---

27. Libanius, Orat. Parent. c. x. p. 233, 234. Gallus had some reason to suspect the secret apostacy of his brother; and in a letter, which may be received as genuine, he exhorts Julian to adhere to the religion of their *ancestors*; an argument, which, as it should seem, was not yet perfectly ripe. See Julian. Op. p. 454. and Hist. de Jovien, tom. ii. p. 141.

28. Gregory (iii. p. 50.), with inhuman zeal, censures Constantius for sparing the infant apostate (κακῶς σωθέντα). His French translator (p. 265.) cautiously observes, that such expressions must not be prises à la lettre.

the laws of prudence and necessity."[29] The dissimulation of Julian lasted above ten years, from his secret initiation at Ephesus, to the beginning of the civil war; when he declared himself at once the implacable enemy of Christ and of Constantius. This state of constraint might contribute to strengthen his devotion; and as soon as he had satisfied the obligation of assisting, on solemn festivals, at the assemblies of the Christians, Julian returned, with the impatience of a lover, to burn his free and voluntary incense on the domestic chapels of Jupiter and Mercury. But as every act of dissimulation must be painful to an ingenuous spirit, the profession of Christianity encreased the aversion of Julian for a religion, which oppressed the freedom of his mind, and compelled him to hold a conduct repugnant to the noblest attributes of human nature, sincerity and courage.

The inclination of Julian might prefer the gods of Homer, and of the Scipios, to the new faith, which his uncle had estab- *He writes* lished in the Roman empire; and in which he himself had been *against* sanctified by the sacrament of baptism. But as a philosopher, it *Christianity.* was incumbent on him to justify his dissent from Christianity, which was supported by the number of its converts, by the chain of prophecy, the splendor of miracles, and the weight of evidence. The elaborate work,[30] which he composed amidst the preparations of the Persian war, contained the substance of those arguments which he had long revolved in his mind. Some fragments have been transcribed and preserved, by his adversary, the vehement Cyril of Alexandria;[31] and they exhibit a very singular mixture of wit and learning, of sophistry and fanaticism. The elegance of the style, and the rank of the author, recommended his writings to the public attention;[32] and in the impious list of the enemies of Christianity,

---

29. Libanius, Orat. Parental. c. ix. p. 233.

30. Fabricius (Bibliot. Græc. l. v. c. viii. p. 88–90.) and Lardner (Heathen Testimonies, vol. iv. p. 44–47.) have accurately compiled all that can now be discovered of Julian's work against the Christians.

31. About seventy years after the death of Julian, he executed a task which had been feebly attempted by Philip of Side, a prolix and contemptible writer. Even the work of Cyril has not entirely satisfied the most favourable judges: and the Abbé de la Bleterie

(Preface à l'Hist. de Jovien, p. 30. 32.) wishes that some *theologien philosophe* (a strange centaur) would undertake the refutation of Julian.

32. Libanius (Orat. Parental. c. lxxxvii. p. 313.), who has been suspected of assisting his friend, prefers this divine vindication (Orat. ix. in necem Julian, p. 255. edit. Morel.) to the writings of Porphyry. His judgment may be arraigned (Socrates, l. iii. c. 23), but Libanius cannot be accused of flattery to a dead prince.

the celebrated name of Porphyry was effaced by the superior merit or reputation of Julian. The minds of the faithful were either seduced, or scandalized, or alarmed; and the pagans, who sometimes presumed to engage in the unequal dispute, derived, from the popular work of their Imperial missionary, an inexhaustible supply of fallacious objections. But in the assiduous prosecution of these theological studies, the emperor of the Romans imbibed the illiberal prejudices and passions of a polemic divine. He contracted an irrevocable obligation, to maintain and propagate his religious opinions; and whilst he secretly applauded the strength and dexterity with which he wielded the weapons of controversy, he was tempted to distrust the sincerity, or to despise the understandings, of his antagonists, who could obstinately resist the force of reason and eloquence.

Universal toleration.   The Christians, who beheld with horror and indignation the apostacy of Julian, had much more to fear from his power than from his arguments. The pagans, who were conscious of his fervent zeal, expected, perhaps with impatience, that the flames of persecution should be immediately kindled against the enemies of the gods; and that the ingenious malice of Julian would invent some cruel refinements of death and torture, which had been unknown to the rude and inexperienced fury of his predecessors. But the hopes, as well as the fears, of the religious factions were apparently disappointed, by the prudent humanity of a prince,[33] who was careful of his own fame, of the public peace, and of the rights of mankind. Instructed by history and reflection, Julian was persuaded, that if the diseases of the body may sometimes be cured by salutary violence, neither steel nor fire can eradicate the erroneous opinions of the mind. The reluctant victim may be dragged to the foot of the altar; but the heart still abhors and disclaims the sacrilegious act of the hand. Religious obstinacy is hardened and exasperated by oppression; and, as soon as the persecution subsides, those who have yielded, are restored as penitents, and those who have resisted, are honoured as saints and martyrs. If Julian adopted the unsuccessful cruelty of Diocletian and his colleagues, he was sensible that he should stain his memory with the name of tyrant, and add new glories to the Catholic church, which had derived strength and encrease from

---

33. Libanius (Orat. Parent. c. lviii. p. 283, 284.) has eloquently explained the tolerating principles and conduct of his Imperial friend. In a very remarkable epistle to the people of Bostra, Julian himself (epist. lii.) professes his moderation, and betrays his zeal; which is acknowledged by Ammianus, and exposed by Gregory (Orat. iii. p. 72.).

the severity of the pagan magistrates. Actuated by these motives, and apprehensive of disturbing the repose of an unsettled reign, Julian surprised the world by an edict, which was not unworthy of a statesman, or a philosopher. He extended to all the inhabitants of the Roman world, the benefits of a free and equal toleration; and the only hardship which he inflicted on the Christians, was to deprive them of the power of tormenting their fellow-subjects, whom they stigmatised with the odious titles of idolaters and heretics. The Pagans received a gracious permission, or rather an express order, to open ALL their temples;[34] and they were at once delivered from the oppressive laws, and arbitrary vexations, which they had sustained under the reign of Constantine, and of his sons. At the same time, the bishops and clergy, who had been banished by the Arian monarch, were recalled from exile, and restored to their respective churches; the Donatists, the Novations, the Macedonians, the Eunomians, and those who, with a more prosperous fortune, adhered to the doctrine of the council of Nice. Julian, who understood and derided their theological disputes, invited to the palace the leaders of the hostile sects, that he might enjoy the agreeable spectacle of their furious encounters. The clamour of controversy sometimes provoked the emperor to exclaim, "Hear me! the Franks have heard me, and the Alemanni;" but he soon discovered that he was now engaged with more obstinate and implacable enemies; and though he exerted the powers of oratory to persuade them to live in concord, or at least in peace, he was perfectly satisfied, before he dismissed them from his presence, that he had nothing to dread from the union of the Christians. The impartial Ammianus has ascribed this affected clemency to the desire of fomenting the intestine divisions of the church; and the insidious design of undermining the foundations of Christianity, was inseparably connected with the zeal, which Julian professed, to restore the ancient religion of the empire.[35]

---

34. In Greece, the temples of Minerva were opened by his express command, before the death of Constantius (Liban. Orat. Parent. c. 55. p. 280.); and Julian declares himself a pagan in his public manifesto to the Athenians. This unquestionable evidence may correct the hasty assertion of Ammianus, who seems to suppose Constantinople to be the place where he discovered his attachment to the gods.

35. Ammianus, xxii. 5. Sozomen, l. v. c. 5. Bestia moritur, tranquillitas redit . . . omnes episcopi qui de propriis sedibus fuerant exterminati per indulgentiam novi principis ad ecclesias redeunt. Jerom. adversus Luciferianos, tom. ii. p. 143. Optatus accuses the Donatists for owing their safety to an apostate (l. ii. c. 16. p. 36, 37. edit. Dupin).

Zeal and devotion of Julian in the restoration of paganism.

As soon as he ascended the throne, he assumed, according to the custom of his predecessors, the character of supreme pontiff; not only as the most honourable title of Imperial greatness, but as a sacred and important office; the duties of which he was resolved to execute with pious diligence. As the business of the state prevented the emperor from joining every day in the public devotion of his subjects, he dedicated a domestic chapel to his tutelar deity the Sun; his gardens were filled with statues and altars of the gods; and each apartment of the palace displayed the appearance of a magnificent temple. Every morning he saluted the parent of light with a sacrifice; the blood of another victim was shed at the moment when the Sun sunk below the horizon; and the Moon, the Stars, and the Genii of the night received their respective and seasonable honours from the indefatigable devotion of Julian. On solemn festivals, he regularly visited the temple of the god or goddess to whom the day was peculiarly consecrated, and endeavoured to excite the religion of the magistrates and people by the example of his own zeal. Instead of maintaining the lofty state of a monarch, distinguished by the splendor of his purple, and encompassed by the golden shields of his guards, Julian solicited, with respectful eagerness, the meanest offices which contributed to the worship of the gods. Amidst the sacred but licentious crowd of priests, of inferior ministers, and of female dancers, who were dedicated to the service of the temple, it was the business of the emperor to bring the wood, to blow the fire, to handle the knife, to slaughter the victim, and thrusting his bloody hands into the bowels of the expiring animal, to draw forth the heart or liver, and to read, with the consummate skill of an haruspex, the imaginary signs of future events. The wisest of the pagans censured this extravagant superstition, which affected to despise the restraints of prudence and decency. Under the reign of a prince, who practised the rigid maxims of œconomy, the expence of religious worship consumed a very large portion of the revenue; a constant supply of the scarcest and most beautiful birds was transported from distant climates, to bleed on the altars of the gods; an hundred oxen were frequently sacrificed by Julian on one and the same day; and it soon became a popular jest, that if he should return with conquest from the Persian war, the breed of horned cattle must infallibly be extinguished. Yet this expence may appear inconsiderable, when it is compared with the splendid presents which were offered, either by the hand, or by order, of the emperor, to all the celebrated places of devotion in the Roman world; and with the sums allotted to repair and decorate the ancient temples, which had suffered the silent decay of time, or the recent injuries of Christian rapine. Encouraged by the example, the exhortations, the liberality, of their pious sovereign, the cities and families resumed the practice of their neglected ceremonies. "Every part of the world," exclaims Libanius, with devout transport, "displayed the triumph of religion; and the grateful prospect of flaming altars, bleeding victims, the smoke of incense, and a solemn train of priests and prophets, without fear and without danger. The sound of prayer and of music was heard on the tops of the highest mountains; and the same ox afforded a sacrifice for the gods, and a supper for their joyous votaries."[36]

But the genius and power of Julian were unequal to the enterprise of restoring a religion, which was destitute of theological principles, of moral precepts, and of ecclesiastical discipline; which rapidly hastened to decay and dissolution, and was not susceptible of any solid or consistent reformation. The jurisdiction of the supreme pontiff, more especially after that office had been united with the Imperial dignity, comprehended the whole extent of the Roman empire. Julian named for his vicars, in the several provinces, the priests and philosophers, whom he esteemed the best qualified to co-operate in the execution of his great design; and his pastoral letters,[37] if we may use that name, still represent a very curious sketch of his wishes and intentions. He directs, that in every city the sacerdotal order should be composed, without any distinction of birth or fortune, of those persons who were the most conspicuous for their love of the gods, and of men. "If they are guilty," continues he, "of any scandalous offence, they should be censured or degraded by the superior pontiff; but, as long as they retain their rank, they are entitled to the respect of the magistrates and people. Their humility may be shewn in the plainness of their domestic garb; their dignity, in the pomp of holy vestments. When they are summoned in their turn to officiate before the altar, they ought

Reformation of Paganism.

36. The restoration of the Pagan worship is described by Julian (Misopogon, p. 346.), Libanius (Orat. Parent. c. 60, p. 286, 287. and Orat. Consular. ad Julian. p. 245, 246. edit. Morel.), Ammianus (xxii. 12.), and Gregory Nazianzen (Orat. iv. p. 121.). These writers agree in the essential, and even minute, facts: but the different lights in which they view the extreme devotion of Julian, are expressive of the gradations of self-applause, passionate admiration, mild reproof, and partial invective.

37. See Julian. Epistol. xlix. lxii, lxiii. and a long and curious fragment, without beginning or end (p. 288–305.). The supreme pontiff derides the Mosaic history, and the Christian discipline, prefers the Greek poets to the Hebrew prophets, and palliates, with the skill of a Jesuit, the *relative* worship of images.

not, during the appointed number of days, to depart from the precincts of the temple; nor should a single day be suffered to elapse, without the prayers and the sacrifice, which they are obliged to offer for the prosperity of the state, and of individuals. The exercise of their sacred functions requires an immaculate purity, both of mind and body; and even when they are dismissed from the temple to the occupations of common life, it is incumbent on them to excel in decency and virtue the rest of their fellow-citizens. The priest of the gods should never be seen in theatres or taverns. His conversation should be chaste, his diet temperate, his friends of honourable reputation; and, if he sometimes visits the Forum or the Palace, he should appear only as the advocate of those who have vainly solicited either justice or mercy. His studies should be suited to the sanctity of his profession. Licentious tales, or comedies, or satires, must be banished from his library; which ought solely to consist of historical and philosophical writings; of history which is founded in truth, and of philosophy which is connected with religion. The impious opinions of the Epicureans and Sceptics deserve his abhorrence and contempt;[38] but he should diligently study the systems of Pythagoras, of Plato, and of the Stoics, which unanimously teach that there *are* gods; that the world is governed by their providence; that their goodness is the source of every temporal blessing; and that they have prepared for the human soul a future state of reward or punishment." The Imperial pontiff inculcates, in the most persuasive language, the duties of benevolence and hospitality; exhorts his inferior clergy to recommend the universal practice of those virtues; promises to assist their indigence from the public treasury; and declares his resolution of establishing hospitals in every city, where the poor should be received without any invidious distinction of country or of religion. Julian beheld with envy the wise and humane regulations of the church; and he very frankly confesses his intention to deprive the Christians of the applause, as well as advantage, which they had acquired by the exclusive practice of charity and beneficence.[39] The same spirit of imitation might dispose the

---

38. The exultation of Julian (p. 301.), that these impious sects, and even their writings, are extinguished, may be consistent enough with the sacerdotal character: but it is unworthy of a philosopher to wish that any opinions and arguments the most repugnant to his own should be concealed from the knowledge of mankind.

39. Yet he insinuates, that the Christians, under the pretence of charity, inveigled children from their religion and parents, conveyed them on shipboard, and devoted those victims to a life of poverty or servitude in a remote country (p. 305.). Had the charge been proved, it was his duty, not to complain, but to punish.

emperor to adopt several ecclesiastical institutions, the use and importance of which were approved by the success of his enemies. But if these imaginary plans of reformation had been realized, the forced and imperfect copy would have been less beneficial to Paganism, than honourable to Christianity.[40] The Gentiles, who peaceably followed the customs of their ancestors, were rather surprised than pleased with the introduction of foreign manners; and, in the short period of his reign, Julian had frequent occasions to complain of the want of fervour of his own party.[41]

The enthusiasm of Julian prompted him to embrace the friends of Jupiter as his personal friends and brethren; and though he partially overlooked the merit of Christian constancy, he admired *The philosophers.* and rewarded the noble perseverance of those Gentiles who had preferred the favour of the gods to that of the emperor.[42] If they cultivated the literature, as well as the religion, of the Greeks, they acquired an additional claim to the friendship of Julian, who ranked the Muses in the number of his tutelar deities. In the religion which he had adopted, piety and learning were almost synonimous;[43] and a crowd of poets, of rhetoricians, and of philosophers, hastened to the Imperial court, to occupy the vacant places of the bishops, who had seduced the credulity of Constantius. His successor esteemed the ties of common initiation as far more sacred than those of consanguinity: he chose his favourites among the sages, who were deeply skilled in the occult sciences of magic and divination; and every impostor, who pretended to reveal the secrets of futurity, was assured of enjoying the present hour in honour and affluence.[44] Among the philosophers, Maximus obtained the most eminent rank in the friendship of his royal disciple, who communicated, with unreserved confidence, his actions, his sentiments, and his religious designs, during the anxious suspense of the

---

40. Gregory Nazianzen is facetious, ingenious, and argumentative (Orat. iii. p. 101, 102, &c.). He ridicules the folly of such vain imitation; and amuses himself with inquiring, what lessons, moral or theological, could be extracted from the Grecian fables.

41. He accuses one of his pontiffs of a secret confederacy with the Christian bishops and presbyters (Epist. lxii.). Οϱων ουν πολλην μεν ολιγωϱιαν ουσαν ημιν πϱος τους θεους; and again, ημας δε ουτω ϱαθυμως, &c. Epist. lxiii.

42. He praises the fidelity of Callixene, priestess of Ceres, who had been twice as constant

as Penelope, and rewards her with the priesthood of the Phrygian goddess at Pessinus (Julian. Epist. xxi.). He applauds the firmness of Sopater of Hierapolis, who had been repeatedly pressed by Constantius and Gallus to *apostatize* (Epist. xxvii. p. 401.).

43. Ο δε νομιζων αδελφα λογους τε και θεων ιεϱα. Orat. parent. c. 77. p. 302. The same sentiment is frequently inculcated by Julian, Libanius, and the rest of their party.

44. The curiosity and credulity of the emperor, who tried every mode of divination, are fairly exposed by Ammianus, xxii. 12.

civil war.[45] As soon as Julian had taken possession of the palace of Constantinople, he dispatched an honourable and pressing invitation to Maximus; who then resided at Sardes in Lydia, with Chrysanthius, the associate of his art and studies. The prudent and superstitious Chrysanthius refused to undertake a journey which shewed itself, according to the rules of divination, with the most threatening and malignant aspect: but his companion, whose fanaticism was of a bolder cast, persisted in his interrogations, till he had extorted from the gods a seeming consent to his own wishes, and those of the emperor. The journey of Maximus through the cities of Asia, displayed the triumph of philosophic vanity; and the magistrates vied with each other in the honourable reception which they prepared for the friend of their sovereign. Julian was pronouncing an oration before the senate, when he was informed of the arrival of Maximus. The emperor immediately interrupted his discourse, advanced to meet him, and, after a tender embrace, conducted him by the hand into the midst of the assembly: where he publicly acknowledged the benefits which he had derived from the instructions of the philosopher. Maximus,[46] who soon acquired the confidence, and influenced the councils, of Julian, was insensibly corrupted by the temptations of a court. His dress became more splendid, his demeanour more lofty, and he was exposed, under a succeeding reign, to a disgraceful inquiry into the means by which the disciple of Plato had accumulated, in the short duration of his favour, a very scandalous proportion of wealth. Of the other philosophers and sophists, who were invited to the Imperial residence by the choice of Julian, or by the success of Maximus, few were able to preserve their innocence, or their reputation.[47] The liberal gifts of money, lands, and houses, were insufficient to satiate their rapacious avarice; and the indignation of the people was justly excited by the remembrance of their abject poverty and disinterested professions. The penetration of Julian could not always be deceived: but he was unwilling to despise the characters

45. Julian. Epist. xxxviii. Three other epistles (xv, xvi. xxxix.) in the same style of friendship and confidence, are addressed to the philosopher Maximus.

46. Eunapius (in Maximo, p. 77, 78, 79, and in Chrysanthio, p. 147, 148.) has minutely related these anecdotes, which he conceives to be the most important events of the age. Yet he fairly confesses the frailty of Maximus. His reception at Constantinople is described by Libanius (Orat. Parent. c. 86. p. 301.) and Ammianus (xxii. 7.).

47. Chrysanthius, who had refused to quit Lydia, was created high-priest of the province. His cautious and temperate use of power secured him after the revolution; and he lived in peace; while Maximus, Priscus, &c. were persecuted by the Christian ministers. See the adventures of those fanatic sophists, collected by Brucker, tom. ii. p. 281-293.

of those men whose talents deserved his esteem; he desired to escape the double reproach of imprudence and inconstancy; and he was apprehensive of degrading, in the eyes of the profane, the honour of letters and of religion.[48]

The favour of Julian was almost equally divided between the Pagans, who had firmly adhered to the worship of their ancestors, *Conversions.* and the Christians, who prudently embraced the religion of their sovereign. The acquisition of new proselytes[49] gratified the ruling passions of his soul, superstition and vanity; and he was heard to declare, with the enthusiasm of a missionary, that if he could render each individual richer than Midas, and every city greater than Babylon, he should not esteem himself the benefactor of mankind, unless, at the same time, he could reclaim his subjects from their impious revolt against the immortal gods.[50] A prince, who had studied human nature, and who possessed the treasures of the Roman empire, could adapt his arguments, his promises, and his rewards, to every order of Christians;[51] and the merit of a seasonable conversion was allowed to supply the defects of a candidate, or even to expiate the guilt of a criminal. As the army is the most forcible engine of absolute power, Julian applied himself, with peculiar diligence, to corrupt the religion of his troops, without whose hearty concurrence every measure must be dangerous and unsuccessful; and the natural temper of soldiers made this conquest as easy as it was important. The legions of Gaul devoted themselves to the faith, as well as to the fortunes, of their victorious leader; and even before the death of Constantius, he had the satisfaction of announcing to his friends, that they assisted with fervent devotion, and voracious appetite, at the sacrifices, which were repeatedly offered in his camp, of whole

---

48. See Libanius (Orat. Parent. c. 101, 102. p. 324, 325, 326.) and Eunapius (Vit. Sophist. in Proæresio, p. 126.). Some students, whose expectations perhaps were groundless, or extravagant, retired in disgust (Greg. Naz. Orat. iv. p. 120.). It is strange that we should not be able to contradict the title of one of Tillemont's chapters (Hist. des Empereurs, tom. iv. p. 960.), "La Cour de Julien est pleine de philosophes et de gens perdûs."

49. Under the reign of Lewis XIV. his subjects of every rank aspired to the glorious title of *Convertisseur*, expressive of their zeal and success in making proselytes. The word and the idea are growing obsolete in France; may they never be introduced into England!

50. See the strong expressions of Libanius, which were probably those of Julian himself (Orat. Parent. c. 59. p. 285.).

51. When Gregory Nazianzen (Orat. x. p. 167.) is desirous to magnify the Christian firmness of his brother Cæsarius, physician to the Imperial court, he owns that Cæsarius disputed with a formidable adversary, πολυν εν οπλοις, και μεγαν εν λογων διενοτητι. In his invectives, he scarcely allows any share of wit or courage to the apostate.

hecatombs of fat oxen.[52] The armies of the East, which had been trained under the standard of the cross, and of Constantius, required a more artful and expensive mode of persuasion. On the days of solemn and public festivals, the emperor received the homage, and rewarded the merit, of the troops. His throne of state was encircled with the military ensigns of Rome and the republic; the holy name of Christ was erazed from the *Labarum*; and the symbols of war, of majesty, and of pagan superstition, were so dexterously blended, that the faithful subject incurred the guilt of idolatry, when he respectfully saluted the person or image of his sovereign. The soldiers passed successively in review; and each of them, before he received from the hand of Julian a liberal donative, proportioned to his rank and services, was required to cast a few grains of incense into the flame which burnt upon the altar. Some Christian confessors might resist, and others might repent; but the far greater number, allured by the prospect of gold, and awed by the presence of the emperor, contracted the criminal engagement; and their future perseverance in the worship of the gods was enforced by every consideration of duty and of interest. By the frequent repetition of these arts, and at the expence of sums which would have purchased the service of half the nations of Scythia, Julian gradually ac-quired for his troops the imaginary protection of the gods, and for himself the firm and effectual support of the Roman legions.[53] It is indeed more than probable, that the restoration and encouragement of Paganism revealed a multitude of pretended Christians, who, from motives of temporal advan-tage, had acquiesced in the religion of the former reign; and who afterwards returned, with the same flexibility of conscience, to the faith which was professed by the successors of Julian.

The Jews.   While the devout monarch incessantly laboured to restore and propagate the religion of his ancestors, he embraced the extraordinary design of rebuilding the temple of Jerusalem. In a public

---

52. Julian. Epist. xxxviii. Ammianus, xxii. 12. Adeo ut in dies pæne singulos milites carnis distentiore sagina victitantes incultius, potusque aviditate corrupti, humeris impositi transeuntium per plateas, ex publicis ædibus . . . ad sua diversoria portarentur. The devout prince and the indignant historian describe the same scene; and in Illyricum or Antioch,

similar causes must have produced similar effects.

53. Gregory (Orat. iii. p. 74, 75. 83–86.) and Libanius (Orat. Parent. c. lxxxi. lxxxii. p. 307, 308.) περι ταυτην την σπουδην, ουκ αρνου-μαι πλουτον ανηλωσθαι μεγαν. The sophist owns and justifies the expence of these mili-tary conversions.

epistle[54] to the nation or community of the Jews, dispersed through the provinces, he pities their misfortunes, condemns their oppressors, praises their constancy, declares himself their gracious protector, and expresses a pious hope, that after his return from the Persian war, he may be permitted to pay his grateful vows to the Almighty in his holy city of Jerusalem. The blind superstition, and abject slavery, of those unfortunate exiles, must excite the contempt of a philosophic emperor; but they deserved the friendship of Julian, by their implacable hatred of the Christian name. The barren synagogue abhorred and envied the fecundity of the rebellious church: the power of the Jews was not equal to their malice; but their gravest rabbis approved the private murder of an apostate;[55] and their seditious clamours had often awakened the indolence of the pagan magistrates. Under the reign of Constantine, the Jews became the subjects of their revolted children, nor was it long before they experienced the bitterness of domestic tyranny. The civil immunities which had been granted, or confirmed, by Severus, were gradually repealed by the Christian princes; and a rash tumult, excited by the Jews of Palestine,[56] seemed to justify the lucrative modes of oppression, which were invented by the bishops and eunuchs of the court of Constantius. The Jewish patriarch, who was still permitted to exercise a precarious jurisdiction, held his residence at Tiberias;[57] and the neighbouring cities of Palestine were filled with the remains of a people, who fondly adhered to the promised land. But the edict of Hadrian was renewed and enforced; and they viewed from afar the walls of the holy city, which were profaned in their eyes by the triumph of the cross, and the devotion of the Christians.[58]

---

54. Julian's epistle (xxv.) is addressed to the community of the Jews. Aldus (Venet. 1499.) has branded it with an ει γνησιος; but this stigma is justly removed by the subsequent editors, Petavius and Spanheim. The epistle is mentioned by Sozomen (l. v. c. 22.), and the purport of it is confirmed by Gregory (Orat. iv. p. 111.), and by Julian himself, Fragment. p. 295.

55. The Misnah denounced death against those who abandoned the foundation. The judgment of zeal is explained by Marsham (Canon. Chron. p. 161, 162. edit. fol. London, 1672.) and Basnage (Hist. des Juifs, tom. viii. p. 120.). Constantine made a law to protect Christian converts from Judaism. Cod. Theod. l. xvi. tit. viii. leg. 1. Godefroy, tom. vi. p. 215.

56. Et interea (during the civil war of Magnentius) Judæorum seditio, qui Patricium nefarie in regni speciem sustulerunt, oppressa. Aurelius Victor, in Constantio, c. xlii. See Tillemont, Hist. des Empereurs, tom. iv. p. 379, in 4to.

57. The city and synagogue of Tiberias are curiously described by Reland. Palestin. tom. ii. p. 1036–1042.

58. Basnage has fully illustrated the state of the Jews under Constantine and his successors (tom. viii. c. iv. p. 111–153.).

Jerusalem.   In the midst of a rocky and barren country, the walls of Jerusalem[59] inclosed the two mountains of Sion and Acra, within an
oval figure of about three English miles.[60] Towards the south, the upper
town, and the fortress of David, were erected on the lofty ascent of
Mount Sion: on the north side, the buildings of the lower town covered
the spacious summit of Mount Acra; and a part of the hill, distinguished
by the name of Moriah, and levelled by human industry, was crowned
with the stately temple of the Jewish nation. After the final destruction
of the temple, by the arms of Titus and Hadrian, a ploughshare was
drawn over the consecrated ground, as a sign of perpetual interdiction.
Sion was deserted: and the vacant space of the lower city was filled with
the public and private edifices of the Ælian colony, which spread themselves over the adjacent hill of Calvary. The holy places were polluted
with monuments of idolatry; and, either from design or accident, a chapel
was dedicated to Venus, on the spot which had been sanctified by the
death and resurrection of Christ.[61] Almost three hundred years after those
stupendous events, the profane chapel of Venus was demolished by the
order of Constantine; and the removal of the earth and stones revealed the
holy sepulchre to the eyes of mankind. A magnificent church was erected
on that mystic ground, by the first Christian emperor; and the effects of
his pious munificence were extended to every spot, which had been
consecrated by the footsteps of patriarchs, of prophets, and of the Son of
God.[62]

Pilgrimages.   The passionate desire of contemplating the original monuments
of their redemption, attracted to Jerusalem a successive crowd of
pilgrims, from the shores of the Atlantic ocean, and the most distant

---

59. Reland (Palestin. l. i. p. 309. 390. l. iii.
p. 838.) describes, with learning and perspi-
cuity, Jerusalem, and the face of the adjacent
country.

60. I have consulted a rare and curious treatise
of M. d'Anville (sur l'ancienne Jerusalem,
Paris, 1747. p. 75.). The circumference of the
ancient city (Euseb. Præparat. Evangel. l. ix.
c. 36.) was twenty-seven stadia, or 2550 *toises*.
A plan, taken on the spot, assigns no more
than 1980 for the modern town. The circuit
is defined by natural land-marks, which cannot be mistaken, or removed.

61. See two curious passages in Jerom (tom.
i. p. 102. tom. vi. p. 315.), and the ample
details of Tillemont (Hist. des Empereurs,
tom. i. p. 569. tom. ii. p. 289. 294. 4to edition).

62. Eusebius, in Vit. Constantin. l. iii. c. 25–
47. 51–53. The emperor likewise built
churches at Bethlem, the Mount of Olives,
and the oak of Mambre. The holy sepulchre
is described by Sandys (Travels, p. 125–133.),
and curiously delineated by Le Bruyn (Voyage
au Levant, p. 288–296.).

countries of the East;[63] and their piety was authorised by the example of the empress Helena; who appears to have united the credulity of age with the warm feelings of a recent conversion. Sages and heroes, who have visited the memorable scenes of ancient wisdom or glory, have confessed the inspiration of the genius of the place,[64] and the Christian, who knelt before the holy sepulchre, ascribed his lively faith, and his fervent devotion, to the more immediate influence of the Divine spirit. The zeal, perhaps the avarice, of the clergy of Jerusalem, cherished and multiplied these beneficial visits. They fixed, by unquestionable tradition, the scene of each memorable event. They exhibited the instruments which had been used in the passion of Christ; the nails and the lance that had pierced his hands, his feet, and his side; the crown of thorns that was planted on his head; the pillar at which he was scourged: and, above all they shewed the cross on which he suffered, and which was dug out of the earth in the reign of those princes, who inserted the symbol of Christianity in the banners of the Roman legions.[65] Such miracles, as seemed necessary to account for its extraordinary preservation, and seasonable discovery, were gradually propagated without opposition. The custody of the *true cross*, which on Easter Sunday was solemnly exposed to the people, was entrusted to the bishop of Jerusalem; and he alone might gratify the curious devotion of the pilgrims, by the gift of small pieces, which they enchased in gold or gems, and carried away in triumph to their respective countries. But as this gainful branch of commerce must soon have been annihilated, it was found convenient to suppose, that the marvellous wood possessed a secret power of vegetation; and that its substance, though continually diminished, still remained entire and unimpaired.[66] It might perhaps have been expected,

63. The Itinerary from Bourdeaux to Jerusalem, was composed in the year 333, for the use of pilgrims; among whom Jerom (tom. i. p. 126.) mentions the Britons and the Indians. The causes of this superstitious fashion are discussed in the learned and judicious preface of Wesseling (Itinerar. p. 537–545.).

64. Cicero (de Finibus, v. 1.) has beautifully expressed the common sense of mankind.

65. Baronius, (Annal. Eccles. A.D. 326. N° 42–50.) and Tillemont (Mem. Eccles. tom. vii. p. 8–16.) are the historians and champions of the miraculous *invention* of the cross,

under the reign of Constantine. Their oldest witnesses are Paulinus, Sulpicius Severus, Rufinus, Ambrose, and perhaps Cyril of Jerusalem. The silence of Eusebius, and the Bourdeaux pilgrim, which satisfies those who think, perplexes those who believe. See Jortin's sensible remarks, vol. ii. p. 238–248.

66. This multiplication is asserted by Paulinus, (epist. xxxvi. See Dupin, Bibliot. Eccles. tom. iii. p. 149.), who seems to have improved a rhetorical flourish of Cyril into a real fact. The same supernatural privilege must have been communicated to the Virgin's

that the influence of the place, and the belief of a perpetual miracle, should have produced some salutary effects on the morals, as well as on the faith, of the people. Yet the most respectable of the ecclesiastical writers have been obliged to confess, not only that the streets of Jerusalem were filled with the incessant tumult of business and pleasure,[67] but that every species of vice; adultery, theft, idolatry, poisoning, murder, was familiar to the inhabitants of the holy city.[68] The wealth and pre-eminence of the church of Jerusalem excited the ambition of Arian, as well as orthodox, candidates; and the virtues of Cyril, who, since his death, has been honoured with the title of Saint, were displayed in the exercise, rather than in the acquisition, of his episcopal dignity.[69]

Julian attempts to rebuild the temple.

The vain and ambitious mind of Julian might aspire to restore the ancient glory of the temple of Jerusalem.[70] As the Christians were firmly persuaded that a sentence of everlasting destruction had been pronounced against the whole fabric of the Mosaic law, the Imperial sophist would have converted the success of his undertaking into a specious argument against the faith of prophecy, and the truth of revelation.[71] He was displeased with the spiritual worship of the synagogue; but he approved the institutions of Moses, who had not disdained

---

milk (Erasmi Opera, tom. i. p. 778. Lugd. Batav. 1703. in Colloq. de Peregrinat. Religionis ergo), saints heads, &c. and other relics, which are repeated in so many different churches.

67. Jerom (tom. i. p. 103.), who resided in the neighbouring village of Bethlem, describes the vices of Jerusalem from his personal experience.

68. Gregor. Nyssen, apud Wesseling, p. 539. The whole epistle, which condemns either the use or the abuse of religious pilgrimage, is painful to the Catholic divines; while it is dear and familiar to our Protestant polemics.

69. He renounced his orthodox ordination, officiated as a deacon, and was reordained by the hands of the Arians. But Cyril afterwards changed with the times, and prudently conformed to the Nicene faith. Tillemont (Mem. Eccles. tom. viii.), who treats his memory with tenderness and respect, has thrown his

virtues into the text, and his faults into the notes, in decent obscurity, at the end of the volume.

70. Imperii sui memoriam magnitudine operum gestiens propagare. Ammian. xxiii. 1. The temple of Jerusalem had been famous even among the Gentiles. *They* had many temples in each city (at Sichem five, at Gaza eight, at Rome four hundred and twenty-four); but the wealth and religion of the Jewish nation was centered in one spot.

71. The secret intentions of Julian are revealed by the late bishop of Gloucester, the learned and dogmatic Warburton; who, with the authority of a theologian, prescribes the motives and conduct of the Supreme Being. The discourse entitled *Julian* (2d edition, London, 1751), is strongly marked with all the peculiarities which are imputed to the Warburtonian school.

to adopt many of the rites and ceremonies of Egypt.[72] The local and national deity of the Jews was sincerely adored by a polytheist, who desired only to multiply the number of the gods;[73] and such was the appetite of Julian for bloody sacrifice, that his emulation might be excited by the piety of Solomon, who had offered, at the feast of the dedication, twenty-two thousand oxen, and one hundred and twenty thousand sheep.[74] These considerations might influence his designs; but the prospect of an immediate and important advantage, would not suffer the impatient monarch to expect the remote and uncertain event of the Persian war. He resolved to erect, without delay, on the commanding eminence of Moriah, a stately temple, which might eclipse the splendor of the church of the Resurrection on the adjacent hill of Calvary; to establish an order of priests, whose interested zeal would detect the arts, and resist the ambition, of their Christian rivals; and to invite a numerous colony of Jews, whose stern fanaticism would be always prepared to second, and even to anticipate, the hostile measures of the pagan government. Among the friends of the emperor (if the names of emperor, and of friend, are not incompatible) the first place was assigned, by Julian himself, to the virtuous and learned Alypius.[75] The humanity of Alypius was tempered by severe justice, and manly fortitude; and while he exercised his abilities in the civil administration of Britain, he imitated, in his poetical compositions, the harmony and softness of the odes of Sappho. This minister, to whom Julian communicated, without reserve, his most careless levities, and his most serious counsels, received an extraordinary commission to restore, in its pristine beauty, the temple of Jerusalem; and the diligence of Alypius required and obtained the strenuous support of the governor of Palestine. At the call of their great deliverer, the Jews, from all the provinces of

72. I shelter myself behind Maimonides, Marsham, Spencer, Le Clerc, Warburton, &c. who have fairly derided the fears, the folly, and the falsehood, of some superstitious divines. See Divine Legation, vol. iv. p. 25, &c.

73. Julian (Fragment, p. 295.) respectfully styles him μεγας θεος, and mentions him elsewhere (epist. lxiii.) with still higher reverence. He doubly condemns the Christians: for believing, and for renouncing, the religion of the Jews. Their Deity was a *true*, but not

the *only*, God. Apud Cyril, l. ix. p. 305, 306.

74. 1 Kings viii. 63. 2 Chronicles vii. 5. Joseph. Antiquitat. Judaic. l. viii. c. 4. p. 431. edit. Havercamp. As the blood and smoke of so many hecatombs might be inconvenient, Lightfoot, the Christian rabbi, removes them by a miracle. Le Clerc (ad loca) is bold enough to suspect the fidelity of the numbers.

75. Julian, epist. xxix. xxx. La Bleterie has neglected to translate the second of these epistles.

the empire, assembled on the holy mountain of their fathers; and their insolent triumph alarmed and exasperated the Christian inhabitants of Jerusalem. The desire of rebuilding the temple has, in every age, been the ruling passion of the children of Israel. In this propitious moment the men forgot their avarice, and the women their delicacy; spades and pickaxes of silver were provided by the vanity of the rich, and the rubbish was transported in mantles of silk and purple. Every purse was opened in liberal contributions, every hand claimed a share in the pious labour; and the commands of a great monarch were executed by the enthusiasm of a whole people.[76]

The enterprize is defeated, Yet, on this occasion, the joint efforts of power and enthusiasm were unsuccessful; and the ground of the Jewish temple, which is now covered by a Mahometan mosque,[77] still continued to exhibit the same edifying spectacle of ruin and desolation. Perhaps the absence and death of the emperor, and the new maxims of a Christian reign, might explain the interruption of an arduous work, which was attempted only in the last six months of the life of Julian.[78] But the Christians entertained a natural and pious expectation, that, in this memorable contest, the honour of religion would be vindicated by some signal miracle. An earthquake, a whirlwind, and a fiery eruption, which overturned and scattered the new foundations of the temple, are attested, with some variations, by contemporary and respectable evidence.[79] This public event is described by Ambrose,[80] bishop of Milan, in an epistle to the emperor Theodosius, which must provoke the severe animadversion of the Jews;

76. See the zeal and impatience of the Jews in Gregory Nazianzen (Orat. iv. p. 111.) and Theodoret (l. iii. c. 20.).

77. Built by Omar, the second Khalif, who died A.D. 644. This great mosque covers the whole consecrated ground of the Jewish temple, and constitutes almost a square of 760 *toises*, or one Roman mile in circumference. See d'Anville Jerusalem, p. 45.

78. Ammianus records the consuls of the year 363, before he proceeds to mention the *thoughts* of Julian. Templum . . . instaurare sumptibus *cogitabat* immodicis. Warburton has a secret wish to anticipate the design; but he must have understood, from former examples, that the execution of such a

work would have demanded many years.

79. The subsequent witnesses, Socrates, Sozomen, Theodoret, Philostorgius, &c. add contradictions, rather than authority. Compare the objections of Basnage (Hist. des Juifs, tom. viii. p. 157–168) with Warburton's answers (Julian, p. 174–258.). The bishop has ingeniously explained the miraculous crosses which appeared on the garments of the spectators by a similar instance, and the natural effects of lightning.

80. Ambros. tom. ii. epist. xl. p. 946. edit. Benedictin. He composed this fanatic epistle (A.D. 388.) to justify a bishop, who had been condemned by the civil magistrate for burning a synagogue.

by the eloquent Chrysostom,[81] who might appeal to the memory of the elder part of his congregation at Antioch; and by Gregory Nazianzen,[82] who published his account of the miracle before the expiration of the same year. The last of these writers has boldly declared, that this præternatural event was not disputed by the infidels; and his assertion, strange as it may seem, is confirmed by the unexceptionable testimony of Ammianus Marcellinus.[83] The philosophic soldier, who loved the virtues, without adopting the prejudices, of his master, has recorded, in his judicious and candid history of his own times, the extraordinary obstacles which interrupted the restoration of the temple of Jerusalem. "Whilst Alypius, assisted by the governor of the province, urged, with vigour and diligence, the execution of the work, horrible balls of fire breaking out near the foundations, with frequent and reiterated attacks, rendered the place, from time to time, inaccessible to the scorched and blasted workmen; and the victorious element continuing in this manner obstinately and resolutely bent, as it were, to drive them to a distance, the undertaking was abandoned." Such authority should satisfy a believing, and must astonish an incredulous, mind. Yet a philosopher may still require the original evidence of impartial and intelligent spectators. At this important crisis, any singular accident of nature would assume the appearance, and produce the effects, of a real prodigy. This glorious deliverance would be speedily improved and magnified by the pious art of the clergy of Jerusalem, and the active credulity of the Christian world; and, at the distance of twenty years, a Roman historian, careless of theological disputes, might adorn his work with the specious and splendid miracle.[84]

perhaps by a præternatural event.

81. Chrysostom, tom. i. p. 580. advers. Judæos et Gentes, tom. ii. p. 574. de S[to]. Babylâ, edit. Montfaucon. I have followed the common and natural supposition; but the learned Benedictine, who dates the composition of these sermons in the year 383, is confident they were never pronounced from the pulpit.

82. Greg. Nazianzen, Orat. iv. p. 110–113. Το δε ουν περιβοητον πασι θαυμα, και ουδε τοις αθεοις αυτοις απιστουμενον λεξων ερχομαι.

83. Ammian. xxiii. 1. Cum itaque rei fortiter instaret Alypius, juvaretque provinciæ rector, metuendi globi flammarum prope funda-menta crebris assultibus erumpentes fecere locum exustis aliquoties operantibus inaccessum: hocque modo elemento destinatius repellente, cessavit inceptum. Warburton labours (p. 60–90.) to extort a confession of the miracle from the mouths of Julian and Libanius, and to employ the evidence of a rabbi, who lived in the fifteenth century. Such witnesses can only be received by a very favourable judge.

84. Dr. Lardner, perhaps alone of the Christian critics, presumes to doubt the truth of this famous miracle (Jewish and Heathen Testimonies, vol. iv. p. 47–71.). The silence

Partiality of
Julian.

The restoration of the Jewish temple was secretly connected with the ruin of the Christian church. Julian still continued to maintain the freedom of religious worship, without distinguishing, whether this universal toleration proceeded from his justice, or his clemency. He affected to pity the unhappy Christians, who were mistaken in the most important object of their lives; but his pity was degraded by contempt, his contempt was embittered by hatred; and the sentiments of Julian were expressed in a style of sarcastic wit, which inflicts a deep and deadly wound, whenever it issues from the mouth of a sovereign. As he was sensible that the Christians gloried in the name of their Redeemer, he countenanced, and perhaps enjoined, the use of the less honourable appellation of GALILÆANS.[85] He declared, that, by the folly of the Galilæans, whom he describes as a sect of fanatics, contemptible to men, and odious to the gods, the empire had been reduced to the brink of destruction; and he insinuates in a public edict, that a frantic patient might sometimes be cured by salutary violence.[86] An ungenerous distinction was admitted into the mind and counsels of Julian, that, according to the difference of their religious sentiments, one part of his subjects deserved his favour and friendship, while the other was entitled only to the common benefits, that his justice could not refuse to an obedient people.[87] According to a principle, pregnant with mischief and oppression, the emperor transferred, to the pontiffs of his own religion, the management of the liberal allowances from the public revenue, which had been granted to the church by the piety of Constantine and his sons. The proud system of clerical honours and immunities, which had been constructed with so much art and labour, was

---

of Jerom would lead to a suspicion, that the same story, which was celebrated at a distance, might be despised on the spot.

85. Greg. Naz. Orat. iii. p. 81. And this law was confirmed by the invariable practice of Julian himself. Warburton has justly observed (p. 35.), that the Platonists believed in the mysterious virtue of words; and Julian's dislike for the name of Christ might proceed from superstition, as well as from contempt.

86. Fragment. Julian. p. 288. He derides the μορια Γαλιλαιων (epist. vii.), and so far loses sight of the principles of toleration, as to wish (epist. xlii.) ακοντας ιασθαι.

87.
Ου γαρ μοι θεμις εστι κομιζεμεν η
     ελεαιρειν
Ανδρας, οι κε θεοισιν απεχθωντ'
     αθανατοισιν.

These two lines, which Julian has changed and perverted in the true spirit of a bigot (Epist. xlix.), are taken from the speech of Æolus, when he refuses to grant Ulysses a fresh supply of winds (Odyss. x. 73). Libanius (Orat. Parent. c. 59. p. 286.) attempts to justify this partial behaviour, by an apology, in which persecution peeps through the mask of candour.

levelled to the ground; the hopes of testamentary donations were intercepted by the rigour of the laws; and the priests of the Christian sect were confounded with the last and most ignominious class of the people. Such of these regulations as appeared necessary to check the ambition and avarice of the ecclesiastics, were soon afterwards imitated by the wisdom of an orthodox prince. The peculiar distinctions which policy has bestowed, or superstition has lavished, on the sacerdotal order, *must* be confined to those priests who profess the religion of the state. But the will of the legislator was not exempt from prejudice and passion; and it was the object of the insidious policy of Julian, to deprive the Christians of all the temporal honours and advantages which rendered them respectable in the eyes of the world.[88]

A just and severe censure has been inflicted on the law which prohibited the Christians from teaching the arts of grammar and rhetoric.[89] The motives alleged by the emperor to justify this partial and oppressive measure, might command, during his life-time, the silence of slaves and the applause of flatterers. Julian

He prohibits the Christians from teaching schools.

abuses the ambiguous meaning of a word which might be indifferently applied to the language and the religion of the GREEKS: he contemptuously observes, that the men who exalt the merit of implicit faith are unfit to claim or to enjoy the advantages of science; and he vainly contends, that if they refuse to adore the gods of Homer and Demosthenes, they ought to content themselves with expounding Luke and Matthew in the churches of the Galilæans.[90] In all the cities of the Roman world, the education of the youth was entrusted to masters of grammar and rhetoric; who were elected by the magistrates, maintained at the public expence, and distin-guished by many lucrative and honourable privileges. The edict of Julian appears to have included the physicians, and professors of all the liberal arts; and the emperor, who reserved to himself the approbation of the

88. These laws which affected the clergy, may be found in the slight hints of Julian himself (Epist. lii.), in the vague declamations of Gregory (Orat. iii. p. 86, 87.), and in the positive assertions of Sozomen (l. v. c. 5.).
89. Inclemens ... perenni obruendum silentio. Ammian. xxii. 10. xxv. 5.
90. The edict itself, which is still extant among the epistles of Julian (xlii.), may be compared

with the loose invectives of Gregory (Orat. iii. p. 96.). Tillemont (Mem. Eccles. tom. vii. p. 1291–1294.) has collected the seeming differences of ancients and moderns. They may be easily reconciled. The Christians were *directly* forbid to teach, they were *indirectly* forbid to learn; since they would not frequent the schools of the Pagans.

candidates, was authorised by the laws to corrupt, or to punish, the religious constancy of the most learned of the Christians.[91] As soon as the resignation of the more obstinate[92] teachers had established the unrivalled dominion of the Pagan sophists, Julian invited the rising generation to resort with freedom to the public schools, in a just confidence, that their tender minds would receive the impressions of literature and idolatry. If the greatest part of the Christian youth should be deterred by their own scruples, or by those of their parents, from accepting this dangerous mode of instruction, they must, at the same time, relinquish the benefits of a liberal education. Julian had reason to expect that, in the space of a few years, the church would relapse into its primæval simplicity, and that the theologians, who possessed an adequate share of the learning and eloquence of the age, would be succeeded by a generation of blind and ignorant fanatics, incapable of defending the truth of their own principles, or of exposing the various follies of Polytheism.[93]

Disgrace and oppression of the Christians. It was undoubtedly the wish and the design of Julian to deprive the Christians of the advantages of wealth, of knowledge, and of power; but the injustice of excluding them from all offices of trust and profit, seems to have been the result of his general policy, rather than the immediate consequence of any positive law.[94] Superior merit might deserve, and obtain, some extraordinary exceptions; but the greater part of the Christian officers were gradually removed from their employments in the state, the army, and the provinces. The hopes of future candidates were extinguished by the declared partiality of a prince, who maliciously reminded them, that it was unlawful for a

---

91. Codex Theodos. l. xiii. tit. iii. de medicis et professoribus, leg. 5. (published the 17th of June, received, at Spoleto in Italy, the 29th of July, A.D. 363.) with Godefroy's Illustrations, tom. v. p. 31.

92. Orosius celebrates their disinterested resolution, Sicut a majoribus nostris compertum habemus, omnes ubique propemodum . . . officium quam fidem deserere maluerunt, vii. 30. Proæresius, a Christian sophist, refused to accept the partial favour of the emperor. Hieronym. in Chron. p. 185. Edit. Scaliger. Eunapius in Proæresio, p. 126.

93. They had recourse to the expedient of composing books for their own schools. Within a few months Apollinaris produced his Christian imitations of Homer (a sacred history in xxiv. books), Pindar, Euripides, and Menander; and Sozomen is satisfied, that they equalled, or excelled, the originals.

94. It was the instruction of Julian to his magistrates (Epist. vii.) προτιμασθαι μεν τοι τους θεοσεβεις και πανυ φημι δειν. Sozomen (l. v. c. 18.) and Socrates (l. iii. c. 13.) must be reduced to the standard of Gregory (Orat. iii. p. 95.), not less prone to exaggeration, but more restrained by the actual knowledge of his contemporary readers.

Christian to use the sword, either, of justice, or, of war: and who studiously guarded the camp and the tribunals with the ensigns of idolatry. The powers of government were entrusted to the Pagans, who professed an ardent zeal for the religion of their ancestors; and as the choice of the emperor was often directed by the rules of divination, the favourites whom he preferred as the most agreeable to the gods, did not always obtain the approbation of mankind.[95] Under the administration of their enemies, the Christians had much to suffer, and more to apprehend. The temper of Julian was averse to cruelty; and the care of his reputation, which was exposed to the eyes of the universe, restrained the philosophic monarch from violating the laws of justice and toleration, which he himself had so recently established. But the provincial ministers of his authority were placed in a less conspicuous station. In the exercise of arbitrary power, they consulted the wishes, rather than the commands, of their sovereign; and ventured to exercise a secret and vexatious tyranny against the sectaries, on whom they were not permitted to confer the honours of martyrdom. The emperor, who dissembled, as long as possible, his knowledge of the injustice that was exercised in his name, expressed his real sense of the conduct of his officers, by gentle reproofs and substantial rewards.[96]

The most effectual instrument of oppression, with which they were armed, was the law that obliged the Christians to make full and ample satisfaction for the temples which they had destroyed under the preceding reign. The zeal of the triumphant church had not always expected the sanction of the public *They are condemned to restore the Pagan temples.* authority; and the bishops, who were secure of impunity, had often marched, at the head of their congregations, to attack and demolish the fortresses of the prince of darkness. The consecrated lands, which had encreased the patrimony of the sovereign or of the clergy, were clearly defined, and easily restored. But on these lands, and on the ruins of Pagan superstition, the Christians had frequently erected their own religious edifices: and as it was necessary to remove the church before the temple could be rebuilt, the justice and piety of the emperor were applauded by one party, while the other deplored and execrated his sacrilegious violence.[97]

---

95. Ψηφω θεων και διδους και μη διδους. Libanius, Orat. Parent. c. 88. p. 314.

96. Greg. Naz. Orat. iii. p. 74. 91, 92. Socrates, l. iii. c. 14. Theodoret, l. iii. c. 6. Some drawback may however be allowed for the violence of *their* zeal, not less partial than the zeal of Julian.

97. If we compare the gentle language of Libanius (Orat. Parent. c. 60. p. 286.) with the passionate exclamations of Gregory (Orat.

After the ground was cleared, the restitution of those stately structures, which had been levelled with the dust; and of the precious ornaments, which had been converted to Christian uses; swelled into a very large account of damages and debt. The authors of the injury had neither the ability nor the inclination to discharge this accumulated demand: and the impartial wisdom of a legislator would have been displayed in balancing the adverse claims and complaints, by an equitable and temperate arbitration. But the whole empire, and particularly the East, was thrown into confusion by the rash edicts of Julian; and the Pagan magistrates, inflamed by zeal and revenge, abused the rigorous privilege of the Roman law; which substitutes, in the place of his inadequate property, the person of the insolvent debtor. Under the preceding reign, Mark, bishop of Arethusa,[98] had laboured in the conversion of his people with arms more effectual than those of persuasion.[99] The magistrates required the full value of a temple which had been destroyed by his intolerant zeal: but as they were satisfied of his poverty, they desired only to bend his inflexible spirit to the promise of the slightest compensation. They apprehended the aged prelate, they inhumanly scourged him, they tore his beard; and his naked body, anointed with honey, was suspended, in a net, between heaven and earth, and exposed to the stings of insects and the rays of a Syrian sun.[100] From this lofty station, Mark still persisted to glory in his crime, and to insult the impotent rage of his persecutors. He was at length rescued from their hands, and dismissed to enjoy the honour of his divine triumph. The Arians

iii. p. 86, 87.), we may find it difficult to persuade ourselves, that the two orators are really describing the same events.

98. Restan or Arethusa, at the equal distance of sixteen miles between Emesa (*Hems*), and Epiphania (*Hamath*), was founded, or at least named, by Seleucus Nicator. Its peculiar æra dates from the year of Rome 685; according to the medals of the city. In the decline of the Seleucides, Emesa and Arethusa were usurped by the Arab Sampsiceramus, whose posterity, the vassals of Rome, were not extinguished in the reign of Vespasian. See d'Anville's Maps and Geographie Ancienne, tom. ii. p. 134. Wesseling. Itineraria, p. 188. and Noris. Epoch. Syro-Macedon. p. 80, 481, 482.

99. Sozomen, l. v. c. 10. It is surprising, that Gregory and Theodoret should suppress a circumstance, which, in their eyes, must have enhanced the religious merit of the confessor.

100. The sufferings and constancy of Mark, which Gregory has so tragically painted (Orat. iii. p. 88–91.), are confirmed by the unexceptionable and reluctant evidence of Libanius. Μαρκος εκεινος κρεμαμενος, και παστιγουμενος, και του πωγωνος αυτω τιλλομενου, παντα ενεγκων ανδρειως νυν ισοθεος εστι ταις τιμαις, καν φανη που, περιμαχητος ευθυς. Epist. 730. p. 350, 351. Edit. Wolf. Amstel. 1738.

celebrated the virtue of their pious confessor; the catholics ambitiously claimed his alliance;[101] and the Pagans, who might be susceptible of shame or remorse, were deterred from the repetition of such unavailing cruelty.[102] Julian spared his life: but if the bishop of Arethusa had saved the infancy of Julian,[103] posterity will condemn the ingratitude, instead of praising the clemency, of the emperor.

At the distance of five miles from Antioch, the Macedonian kings of Syria had consecrated to Apollo one of the most elegant places of devotion in the Pagan world.[104] A magnificent temple rose in honour of the god of light; and his Colossal figure[105] almost filled the capacious sanctuary, which was enriched with gold and gems, and adorned by the skill of the Grecian artists. The deity was represented in a bending attitude, with a golden cup in his hand, pouring out a libation on the earth; as if he supplicated the venerable mother to give to his arms the cold and beauteous DAPHNE: for the spot was ennobled by fiction; and the fancy of the Syrian poets had transported the amorous tale from the banks of the Peneus to those of the Orontes. The ancient rites of Greece were imitated by the royal colony of Antioch. A stream of prophecy, which rivalled the truth and reputation of the Delphic oracle, flowed from the *Castalian* fountain of Daphne.[106] In the adjacent fields a

The temple and sacred grove of Daphne.

---

101. Περιμαχητός, certatim eum sibi (Christiani) vindicant. It is thus that La Croze and Wolfius (ad loc.) have explained a Greek word, whose true signification had been mistaken by former interpreters, and even by le Clerc (Bibliotheque Ancienne et Moderne, tom. iii. p. 371.). Yet Tillemont is strangely puzzled to understand (Mem. Eccles. tom. vii. p. 1309.) *how* Gregory and Theodoret could mistake a Semi-Arian bishop for a saint.

102. See the probable advice of Sallust (Greg. Nazianzen, Orat. iii. 90, 91.). Libanius intercedes for a similar offender, lest they should find many *Marks*; yet he allows, that if Orion had secreted the consecrated wealth, he deserved to suffer the punishment of Marsyas; to be flayed alive (Epist. 730. p. 349–351.).

103. Gregory (Orat. iii. p. 90.) is satisfied, that by saving the apostate, Mark had deserved still more than he had suffered.

104. The grove and temple of Daphne are described by Strabo (l. xvi. p. 1089, 1090. edit. Amstel. 1707.), Libanius (Nænia, p. 185–188. Antiochic. Orat. xi. p. 380, 381.), and Sozomen (l. v. c. 19.). Wesseling (Itinerar. p. 581.), and Casaubon (ad Hist. August. p. 64.) illustrate this curious subject.

105. Simulacrum in eo Olympiaci Jovis imitamenti æquiparans magnitudinem. Ammian. xxii. 13. The Olympic Jupiter was sixty feet high, and his bulk was consequently equal to that of a thousand men. See a curious *Memoire* of the Abbé Gedoyn (Academie des Inscriptions, tom. ix. p. 198.).

106. Hadrian read the history of his future fortunes on a leaf dipped in the Castalian stream; a trick, which, according to the physician Vandale (de Oraculis, p. 281, 282.), might be easily performed by chymical preparations. The emperor stopped the source of such dangerous knowledge; which was again opened by the devout curiosity of Julian.

stadium was built by a special privilege,[107] which had been purchased from
Elis; the Olympic games were celebrated at the expence of the city; and a
revenue of thirty thousand pounds sterling was annually applied to the
public pleasures.[108] The perpetual resort of pilgrims and spectators insensibly
formed, in the neighbourhood of the temple, the stately and populous
village of Daphne, which emulated the splendor, without acquiring the
title, of a provincial city. The temple and the village were deeply bosomed
in a thick grove of laurels and cypresses, which reached as far as a circumference of ten miles, and formed in the most sultry summers a cool and
impenetrable shade. A thousand streams of the purest water, issuing from
every hill, preserved the verdure of the earth, and the temperature of the
air; the senses were gratified with harmonious sounds and aromatic odours;
and the peaceful grove was consecrated to health and joy, to luxury and
love. The vigorous youth pursued, like Apollo, the object of his desires;
and the blushing maid was warned, by the fate of Daphne, to shun the
folly of unseasonable coyness. The soldier and the philosopher wisely
avoided the temptation of this sensual paradise;[109] where pleasure, assuming
the character of religion, imperceptibly dissolved the firmness of manly
virtue. But the groves of Daphne continued for many ages to enjoy the
veneration of natives and strangers; the privileges of the holy ground were
enlarged by the munificence of succeeding emperors; and every generation
added new ornaments to the splendor of the temple.[110]

Neglect and profanation of Daphne.   When Julian, on the day of the annual festival, hastened to
adore the Apollo of Daphne, his devotion was raised to the
highest pitch of eagerness and impatience. His lively imagination
anticipated the grateful pomp of victims, of libations, and of

107. It was purchased, A.D. 44, in the year
92 of the æra of Antioch (Noris. Epoch. Syro-
Maced. p. 139–174.) for the term of ninety
Olympiads. But the Olympic games of
Antioch were not regularly celebrated till the
reign of Commodus. See the curious details
in the Chronicle of John Malala (tom. i.
p. 290. 320. 372–381.), a writer whose merit
and authority are confined within the limits
of his native city.

108. Fifteen talents of gold, bequeathed by
Sosibius, who died in the reign of Augustus.
The theatrical merits of the Syrian cities, in
the age of Constantine, are compared in

the Expositio totius Mundi, p. 6. (Hudson,
Geograph. Minor, tom. iii.).

109. Avidio Cassio Syriacos legiones dedi lux-
uriâ diffluentes et *Daphnicis* moribus. These
are the words of the emperor Marcus Antoninus in an original letter preserved by his
biographer in Hist. August. p. 41. Cassius
dismissed or punished every soldier who was
seen at Daphne.

110. Aliquantum agrorum Daphnensibus
dedit (*Pompey*), quo lucus ibi spatiosior fieret;
delectatus amœnitate loci et aquarum abund-
antiâ. Eutropius, vi. 14. Sextus Rufus, de Provinciis, c. 16.

incense; a long procession of youths and virgins, clothed in white robes, the symbol of their innocence; and the tumultuous concourse of an innumerable people. But the zeal of Antioch was diverted, since the reign of Christianity, into a different channel. Instead of hecatombs of fat oxen sacrificed by the tribes of a wealthy city, to their tutelar deity, the emperor complains that he found only a single goose, provided at the expence of a priest, the pale and solitary inhabitant of this decayed temple.[111] The altar was deserted, the oracle had been reduced to silence, and the holy ground was profaned by the introduction of Christian and funereal rites. After Babylas[112] (a bishop of Antioch, who died in prison in the persecution of Decius) had rested near a century in his grave, his body, by the order of the Cæsar Gallus, was transported into the midst of the grove of Daphne. A magnificent church was erected over his remains; a portion of the sacred lands was usurped for the maintenance of the clergy, and for the burial of the Christians of Antioch, who were ambitious of lying at the feet of their bishop; and the priests of Apollo retired, with their affrighted and indignant votaries. As soon as another revolution seemed to restore the fortune of Paganism, the church of St. Babylas was demolished, and new buildings were added to the mouldering edifice which had been raised by the piety of Syrian kings. But the first and most serious care of Julian was to deliver his oppressed deity from the odious presence of the dead and living Christians, who had so effectually suppressed the voice of fraud or enthusiasm.[113] The scene of infection was purified, according to the forms of ancient rituals; the bodies were decently removed; and the ministers of the church were permitted to convey the remains of St. Babylas to their former habitation within the walls of Antioch. The modest behaviour which might have assuaged the jealousy of an hostile government, was neglected on this

Removal of the dead bodies, and conflagration of the temple.

---

111. Julian (Misopogon, p. 361, 362.) discovers his own character with that *naïveté*, that unconscious simplicity, which always constitutes genuine humour.

112. Babylas is named by Eusebius in the succession of the bishops of Antioch (Hist. Eccles. l. vi. c. 29. 39.). His triumph over two emperors (the first fabulous, the second historical) is diffusely celebrated by Chrysostom (tom. ii. p. 536–579. edit. Montfaucon.). Tillemont (Mem. Eccles. tom. iii. part ii.

p. 287–302. 459–465.) becomes almost a sceptic.

113. Ecclesiastical critics, particularly those who love relics, exult in the confession of Julian (Misopogon, p. 361.) and Libanius (Nænia, p. 185.), that Apollo was disturbed by the vicinity of *one* dead man. Yet Ammianus (xxii. 12) clears and purifies the whole ground, according to the rites which the Athenians formerly practised in the isle of Delos.

occasion by the zeal of the Christians. The lofty car, that transported the relics of Babylas, was followed, and accompanied, and received, by an innumerable multitude; who chanted, with thundering acclamations, the Psalms of David the most expressive of their contempt for idols and idolaters. The return of the saint was a triumph; and the triumph was an insult on the religion of the emperor, who exerted his pride to dissemble his resentment. During the night which terminated this indiscreet procession, the temple of Daphne was in flames; the statue of Apollo was consumed; and the walls of the edifice were left a naked and awful monument of ruin. The Christians of Antioch asserted, with religious confidence, that the powerful intercession of St. Babylas had pointed the lightnings of heaven against the devoted roof: but as Julian was reduced to the alternative, of believing either a crime or a miracle, he chose, without hesitation, without evidence, but with some colour of probability, to impute the fire of Daphne to the revenge of the Galilæans.[114]

Julian shuts the cathedral of Antioch. Their offence, had it been sufficiently proved, might have justified the retaliation, which was immediately executed by the order of Julian, of shutting the doors, and confiscating the wealth, of the cathedral of Antioch. To discover the criminals who were guilty of the tumult, of the fire, or of secreting the riches of the church, several ecclesiastics were tortured;[115] and a presbyter, of the name of Theodoret, was beheaded by the sentence of the Count of the East. But this hasty act was blamed by the emperor; who lamented, with real or affected concern, that the imprudent zeal of his ministers would tarnish his reign with the disgrace of persecution.[116]

The zeal of the ministers of Julian was instantly checked by the frown of their sovereign; but when the father of his country declares himself the leader of a faction, the licence of popular fury cannot easily be restrained,

---

114. Julian (in Misopogon, p. 361.) rather insinuates, than affirms, their guilt. Ammianus (xxii. 13.) treats the imputation as *levissimus rumor*, and relates the story with extraordinary candour.

115. Quo tam atroci casû repente consumpto, ad id usque imperatoris ira provexit, ut quæstiones agitare juberet solito acriores (yet Julian blames the lenity of the magistrats of Antioch), et majorem ecclesiam Antiochiæ claudi. This interdiction was performed with some circumstances of indignity and profanation: and the seasonable death of the principal actor, Julian's uncle, is related with much superstitious complacency by the Abbé de la Bleterie. Vie de Julien, p. 362–369.

116. Besides the ecclesiastical historians, who are more or less to be suspected, we may allege the passion of St. Theodore, in the Acta Sincera of Ruinart, p. 591. The complaint of Julian gives it an original and authentic air.

nor consistently punished. Julian, in a public composition, applauds the devotion and loyalty of the holy cities of Syria, whose pious inhabitants had destroyed, at the first signal, the sepulchres of the Galilæans; and faintly complains, that they had revenged the injuries of the gods with less moderation than he should have recommended.[117] This imperfect and reluctant confession may appear to confirm the ecclesiastical narratives; that in the cities of Gaza, Ascalon, Cæsarea, Heliopolis, &c. the Pagans abused, without prudence or remorse, the moment of their prosperity. That the unhappy objects of their cruelty were released from torture only by death; that as their mangled bodies were dragged through the streets, they were pierced (such was the universal rage) by the spits of cooks, and the distaffs of enraged women; and that the entrails of Christian priests and virgins, after they had been tasted by those bloody fanatics, were mixed with barley, and contemptuously thrown to the unclean animals of the city.[118] Such scenes of religious madness exhibit the most contemptible and odious picture of human nature; but the massacre of Alexandria attracts still more attention, from the certainty of the fact, the rank of the victims, and the splendour of the capital of Egypt.

George,[119] from his parents or his education, surnamed the Cappadocian, was born at Epiphania in Cilicia, in a fuller's shop. From this obscure and servile origin he raised himself by the talents of a parasite: and the patrons, whom he assiduously flattered, procured for their worthless dependent a lucrative commission, or contract, to supply the army with bacon. His employment was mean: he rendered it infamous. He accumulated wealth by the basest arts of fraud and corruption; but his malversations were so notorious, that George was compelled to escape from the pursuits of justice. After this disgrace, in which he appears to have saved his fortune at the expence of his honour, he embraced, with real or affected zeal, the profession of Arianism. From the love, or

George of Cappadocia

117. Julian. Misopogon, p. 361.

118. See Gregory Nazianzen (Orat. iii. p. 87.). Sozomen (l. v. c. 9.) may be considered as an original, though not impartial, witness. He was a native of Gaza, and had conversed with the confessor Zeno, who, as bishop of Maiuma, lived to the age of an hundred (l. vii. c. 28.). Philostorgius (l. vii. c. 4. with Godefroy's Dissertations, p. 284.) adds some tragic circumstances, of Christians, who were *liter-*

ally sacrificed at the altars of the gods, &c.

119. The life and death of George of Cappadocia are described by Ammianus (xxii. 11.), Gregory Nazianzen (Orat. xxi. p. 382. 385. 389, 390.), and Epiphanius (Hæres. lxxvi.). The invectives of the two saints might not deserve much credit, unless they were confirmed by the testimony of the cool and impartial infidel.

the ostentation, of learning, he collected a valuable library of history, rhetoric, philosophy, and theology;[120] and the choice of the prevailing faction promoted George of Cappadocia to the throne of Athanasius. The entrance of the new archbishop was that of a Barbarian conqueror; and each moment of his reign was polluted by cruelty and avarice. The Catholics of Alexandria and Egypt were abandoned to a tyrant, qualified, by nature and education, to exercise the office of persecution; but he *oppresses Alexandria and Egypt.* oppressed with an impartial hand the various inhabitants of his extensive diocese. The primate of Egypt assumed the pomp and insolence of his lofty station; but he still betrayed the vices of his base and servile extraction. The merchants of Alexandria were impoverished by the unjust, and almost universal, monopoly, which he acquired, of nitre, salt, paper, funerals, &c.: and the spiritual father of a great people condescended to practise the vile and pernicious arts of an informer. The Alexandrians could never forget, nor forgive, the tax, which he suggested, on all the houses of the city; under an obsolete claim, that the royal founder had conveyed to his successors, the Ptolemies and the Cæsars, the perpetual property of the soil. The Pagans, who had been flattered with the hopes of freedom and toleration, excited his devout avarice; and the rich temples of Alexandria were either pillaged or insulted by the haughty prelate, who exclaimed, in a loud and threatening tone, "How long will these sepulchres be permitted to stand?" Under the reign of Constantius, he was expelled by the fury, or rather by the justice, of the people; and it was not without a violent struggle, that the civil and military powers of the state could restore his authority, and gratify his revenge. The messenger who proclaimed at Alexandria the accession of Julian, announced the downfal of the archbishop. George, with two of his obsequious ministers, count Diodorus, and Dracontius, master of the mint, were ignominiously dragged in chains to the public prison. At the end of twenty-four days, the prison was forced open by the rage of a superstitious multitude,

A.D. 361, November 30.

He is massacred by the people,

December 24,

---

120. After the massacre of George, the emperor Julian repeatedly sent orders to preserve the library for his own use, and to torture the slaves who might be suspected of secreting any books. He praises the merit of the collection, from whence he had borrowed and transcribed several manuscripts while he pursued his studies in Cappadocia. He could wish indeed that the works of the Galilæans might perish; but he requires an exact account even of those theological volumes, lest other treaties more valuable should be confounded in their loss. Julian. Epist. ix. xxxvi.

impatient of the tedious forms of judicial proceedings. The enemies of gods and men expired under their cruel insults; the lifeless bodies of the archbishop and his associates were carried in triumph through the streets on the back of a camel; and the inactivity of the Athanasian party[121] was esteemed a shining example of evangelical patience. The remains of these guilty wretches were thrown into the sea; and the popular leaders of the tumult declared their resolution to disappoint the devotion of the Christians, and to intercept the future honours of these *martyrs*, who had been punished, like their predecessors, by the enemies of their religion.[122] The fears of the Pagans were just, and their precautions ineffectual. The meritorious death of the archbishop obliterated the memory of his life. The rival of Athanasius was dear and sacred to the Arians, and the seeming conversion of those sectaries introduced his worship into the bosom of the Catholic church.[123] The odious stranger, disguising every circumstance of time and place, assumed the mask of a martyr, a saint, and a Christian hero;[124] and the infamous George of Cappadocia has been transformed[125] into the renowned *and worshipped as a saint and martyr.* St George of England, the patron of arms, of chivalry, and of the garter.[126]

About the same time that Julian was informed of the tumult of Alexandria,

---

121. Philostorgius, with cautious malice, insinuates their guilt, και τον Αθανασιον γνωμην στρατηγησαι της πραξεως, l. vii. c. 2. Godefroy, p. 267.

122. Cineres projecit in mare, id metuens ut clamabat, ne, collectis supremis, ædes illis exstruerent; ut reliquis, qui deviare a religione compulsi, pertulere cruciabiles pœnas, adusque gloriosam mortem intemeratâ fide progressi, et nunc MARTYRES appellantur. Ammian. xxii. 11. Epiphanius proves to the Arians, that George was not a martyr.

123. Some Donatists (Optatus Milev. p. 60. 303. edit. Dupin; and Tillemont, Mem. Eccles. tom. vi. p. 713. in 4to) and Priscillianists (Tillemont, Mem. Eccles. tom. viii. p. 517. in 4to) have in like manner usurped the honours of Catholic saints and martyrs.

124. The saints of Cappadocia, Basil and the Gregories, were ignorant of their holy companion. Pope Gelasius (A.D. 494.), the first Catholic who acknowledges St. George, places him among the martyrs, "qui Deo magis quam hominibus noti sunt." He rejects his Acts as the composition of heretics. Some, perhaps not the oldest, of the spurious Acts, are still extant; and, through a cloud of fiction, we may yet distinguish the combat which St. George of Cappadocia sustained, in the presence of Queen *Alexandra*, against the *magician Athanasius*.

125. This transformation is not given as absolutely certain, but as *extremely* probable. See the Longueruana, tom. i. p. 194.

126. A curious history of the worship of St. George, from the sixth century (when he was already revered in Palestine, in Armenia, at Rome, and at Treves in Gaul), might be extracted from Dr. Heylin (History of St. George, 2d edition, London 1633, in 4to, p. 429.), and the Bollandists (Act. SS. Mens. April. tom. iii. p. 100–163.). His fame and popularity in Europe, and especially in England, proceeded from the Crusades.

he received intelligence from Edessa, that the proud and wealthy faction of the Arians had insulted the weakness of the Valentinians; and committed such disorders, as ought not to be suffered with impunity in a well-regulated state. Without expecting the slow forms of justice, the exasperated prince directed his mandate to the magistrates of Edessa,[127] by which he confiscated the whole property of the church: the money was distributed among the soldiers; the lands were added to the domain; and this act of oppression was aggravated by the most ungenerous irony. "I shew myself," says Julian, "the true friend of the Galilæans. Their *admirable* law has promised the kingdom of heaven to the poor; and they will advance with more diligence in the paths of virtue and salvation, when they are relieved by my assistance from the load of temporal possessions. Take care," pursued the monarch, in a more serious tone, "take care how you provoke my patience and humanity. If these disorders continue, I will revenge on the magistrates the crimes of the people; and you will have reason to dread, not only confiscation and exile, but fire and the sword." The tumults of Alexandria were doubtless of a more bloody and dangerous nature: but a Christian bishop had fallen by the hands of the Pagans; and the public epistle of Julian affords a very lively proof of the partial spirit of his administration. His reproaches to the citizens of Alexandria are mingled with expressions of esteem and tenderness; and he laments, that, on this occasion, they should have departed from the gentle and generous manners which attested their Grecian extraction. He gravely censures the offence which they had committed against the laws of justice and humanity; but he recapitulates, with visible complacency, the intolerable provocations which they had so long endured from the impious tyranny of George of Cappadocia. Julian admits the principle, that a wise and vigorous government should chastise the insolence of the people: yet, in consideration of their founder Alexander, and of Serapis their tutelar deity, he grants a free and gracious pardon to the guilty city, for which he again feels the affection of a brother.[128]

Restoration of Athanasius, A.D. 362, February 21. After the tumult of Alexandria had subsided, Athanasius, amidst the public acclamations, seated himself on the throne from whence his unworthy competitor had been precipitated: and as the zeal of the archbishop was tempered with discretion, the exercise of his authority tended not to inflame, but to

127. Julian. Epist. xliii.
128. Julian. Epist. x. He allowed his friends to assuage his anger. Ammian. xxii. 11.

reconcile, the minds of the people. His pastoral labours were not confined to the narrow limits of Egypt. The state of the Christian world was present to his active and capacious mind; and the age, the merit, the reputation of Athanasius, enabled him to assume, in a moment of danger, the office of Ecclesiastical Dictator.[129] Three years were not yet elapsed since the majority of the bishops of the West had ignorantly, or reluctantly, subscribed, the Confession of Rimini. They repented, they believed, but they dreaded the unseasonable rigour of their orthodox brethren; and if their pride was stronger than their faith, they might throw themselves into the arms of the Arians, to escape the indignity of a public penance, which must degrade them to the condition of obscure laymen. At the same time, the domestic differences concerning the union and distinction of the divine persons, were agitated with some heat among the Catholic doctors; and the progress of this metaphysical controversy seemed to threaten a public and lasting division of the Greek and Latin churches. By the wisdom of a select synod, to which the name and presence of Athanasius gave the authority of a general council, the bishops, who had unwarily deviated into error, were admitted to the communion of the church, on the easy condition of subscribing the Nicene Creed; without any formal acknowledgment of their past fault, or any minute definition of their scholastic opinions. The advice of the primate of Egypt had already prepared the clergy of Gaul and Spain, of Italy and Greece, for the reception of this salutary measure; and, notwithstanding the opposition of some ardent spirits,[130] the fear of the common enemy promoted the peace and harmony of the Christians.[131]

The skill and diligence of the primate of Egypt had improved the season of tranquillity, before it was interrupted by the hostile edicts of the emperor.[132] Julian, who despised the Christians, honoured Athanasius with his sincere and peculiar hatred. For his sake alone, he introduced an arbitrary

He is persecuted and expelled by Julian, A.D. 362, October 23.

---

129. See Athanas. ad Rufin. tom. ii. p. 40, 41.; and Greg. Nazianzen, Orat. iii. p. 395, 396, who justly states the temperate zeal of the primate, as much more meritorious than his prayers, his fasts, his persecutions, &c.

130. I have not leisure to follow the blind obstinacy of Lucifer of Cagliari. See his adventures in Tillemont (Mem. Eccles. tom. vii. p. 900–926.); and observe how the colour of the narrative insensibly changes, as the confessor becomes a schismatic.

131. Assensus est huic sententiæ Occidens, et, per tam necessarium concilium, Satanæ faucibus mundus ereptus. The lively and artful Dialogue of Jerom against the Luciferians (tom. ii. p. 135–155.) exhibits an original picture of the ecclesiastical policy of the times.

132. Tillemont, who supposes that George was massacred in August, crowds the actions of Athanasius into a narrow space (Mem.

distinction, repugnant, at least to the spirit, of his former declarations. He maintained, that the Galilæans, whom he had recalled from exile, were not restored, by that general indulgence, to the possession of their respective churches: and he expressed his astonishment, that a criminal, who had been repeatedly condemned by the judgment of the emperors, should dare to insult the majesty of the laws, and insolently usurp the archiepiscopal throne of Alexandria, without expecting the orders of his sovereign. As a punishment for the imaginary offence, he again banished Athanasius from the city; and he was pleased to suppose, that this act of justice would be highly agreeable to his pious subjects. The pressing solicitations of the people soon convinced him, that the majority of the Alexandrians were Christians; and that the greatest part of the Christians were firmly attached to the cause of their oppressed primate. But the knowledge of their sentiments, instead of persuading him to recall his decree, provoked him to extend to all Egypt the term of the exile of Athanasius. The zeal of the multitude rendered Julian still more inexorable: he was alarmed by the danger of leaving at the head of a tumultuous city, a daring and popular leader; and the language of his resentment discovers the opinion which he entertained of the courage and abilities of Athanasius. The execution of the sentence was still delayed, by the caution or negligence of Ecdicius, præfect of Egypt, who was at length awakened from his lethargy by a severe reprimand. "Though you neglect," says Julian, "to write to me on any other subject, at least it is your duty to inform me of your conduct towards Athanasius, the enemy of the gods. My intentions have been long since communicated to you. I swear by the great Serapis, that unless, on the calends of December, Athanasius has departed from Alexandria, nay from Egypt, the officers of your government shall pay a fine of one hundred pounds of gold. You know my temper: I am slow to condemn, but I am still slower to forgive." This epistle was enforced by a short postscript, written with the emperor's own hand. "The contempt that is shewn for all the gods fills me with grief and indignation. There is nothing that I should see, nothing that I should hear, with more pleasure, than the expulsion of Athanasius from all Egypt. The abominable wretch! Under my reign, the baptism of several Grecian ladies of the highest rank has been

---

Eccles. tom. viii. p. 360.). An original fragment, published by the marquis Maffei from the old Chapter-library of Verona (Osserva-

zioni Letterarie, tom. iii. p. 60–92.) affords many important dates, which are authenticated by the computation of Egyptian months.

the effect of his persecutions."[133] The death of Athanasius was not *expressly* commanded; but the præfect of Egypt understood, that it was safer for him to exceed, than to neglect, the orders of an irritated master. The archbishop prudently retired to the monasteries of the Desert: eluded, with his usual dexterity, the snares of the enemy; and lived to triumph over the ashes of a prince, who, in words of formidable import, had declared his wish that the whole venom of the Galilæan school were contained in the single person of Athanasius.[134]

I have endeavoured faithfully to represent the artful system by which Julian proposed to obtain the effects, without incurring the guilt, or reproach, of persecution. But if the deadly spirit of fanaticism perverted the heart and understanding of a virtuous *Zeal and imprudence of the Christians.* prince, it must, at the same time, be confessed, that the *real* sufferings of the Christians were inflamed and magnified by human passions and religious enthusiasm. The meekness and resignation which had distinguished the primitive disciples of the gospel, was the object of the applause, rather than of the imitation, of their successors. The Christians, who had now possessed above forty years the civil and ecclesiastical government of the empire, had contracted the insolent vices of prosperity,[135] and the habit of believing, that the saints alone were entitled to reign over the earth. As soon as the enmity of Julian deprived the clergy of the privileges which had been conferred by the favour of Constantine, they complained of the most cruel oppression; and the free toleration of idolaters and heretics was a subject of grief and scandal to the orthodox party.[136] The acts of violence, which were no longer countenanced by the magistrates, were still committed by the zeal of the people. At Pessinus, the altar of Cybele was overturned almost in the presence of the emperor; and in the city of Cæsarea in Cappadocia, the temple of Fortune, the sole place of worship which had been left to the Pagans, was destroyed by the rage of a popular tumult. On

133. *Τον μιαρον, ος ετολμησεν Ελληνιδας, επ' εμου, γυναικας των επισημων βαπτισαι διωκεσθαι.* I have preserved the ambiguous sense of the last word, the ambiguity of a tyrant who wished to find, or to create, guilt. 134. The three Epistles of Julian, which explain his intentions and conduct with regard to Athanasius, should be disposed in the following chronological order, xxvi, x, vi. See likewise Greg. Nazianzen, xxi p. 393.

Sozomen, l. v. c. 15. Socrates, l. iii. c. 14. Theodoret, l. iii. c. 9, and Tillemont, Mem. Eccles. tom. viii. p. 361–368, who has used some materials prepared by the Bollandists. 135. See the fair confession of Gregory (Orat. iii. p. 61, 62.). 136. Hear the furious and absurd complaint of Optatus (de Schismat. Donatist. l. ii. c. 16, 17.).

these occasions, a prince, who felt for the honour of the gods, was not disposed to interrupt the course of justice; and his mind was still more deeply exasperated, when he found, that the fanatics, who had deserved and suffered the punishment of incendiaries, were rewarded with the honours of martyrdom.[137] The Christian subjects of Julian were assured of the hostile designs of their sovereign; and, to their jealous apprehension, every circumstance of his government might afford some grounds of discontent and suspicion. In the ordinary administration of the laws, the Christians, who formed so large a part of the people, must frequently be condemned: but their indulgent brethren, without examining the merits of the cause, presumed their innocence, allowed their claims, and imputed the severity of their judge to the partial malice of religious persecution.[138] These present hardships, intolerable as they might appear, were represented as a slight prelude of the impending calamities. The Christians considered Julian as a cruel and crafty tyrant; who suspended the execution of his revenge, till he should return victorious from the Persian war. They expected, that as soon as he had triumphed over the foreign enemies of Rome, he would lay aside the irksome mask of dissimulation; that the amphitheatres would stream with the blood of hermits and bishops; and that the Christians, who still persevered in the profession of the faith, would be deprived of the common benefits of nature and society.[139] Every calumny[140] that could wound the reputation of the Apostate, was credulously embraced by the fears and hatred of his adversaries; and their indiscreet clamours provoked the temper of a sovereign, whom it was their duty to

137. Greg. Nazianzen, Orat. iii. p. 91. iv. p. 133. He praises the rioters of Cæsarea, τουτων δε των μεγαλοφυων και θερμων εισ Ευσεβειαν. See Sozomen, l. v. 4. 11. Tillemont (Mem. Eccles. tom. vii. p. 649, 650.) owns, that their behaviour was not, dans l'ordre commun; but he is perfectly satisfied, as the great St. Basil always celebrated the festival of these blessed martyrs.

138. Julian determined a law-suit against the new Christian city at Maiuma, the port of Gaza; and his sentence, though it might be imputed to bigotry, was never reversed by his successors. Sozomen, l. v. c. 3. Reland. Palestin. tom. ii. p. 791.

139. Gregory (Orat. iii. p. 93, 94, 95. Orat.

iv. p. 114.) pretends to speak from the information of Julian's confidents, whom Orosius (vii. 30.) could not have seen.

140. Gregory (Orat. iii. p. 91.) charges the Apostate with secret sacrifices of boys and girls; and positively affirms, that the dead bodies were thrown into the Orontes. See Theodoret, l. iii. c. 26, 27.; and the equivocal candour of the Abbé de la Bleterie, Vie de Julien, p. 351, 352. Yet *contemporary* malice could not impute to Julian the troops of martyrs, more especially in the West, which Baronius so greedily swallows, and Tillemont so faintly rejects (Mem. Eccles. tom. vii. p. 1295–1315.).

respect, and their interest to flatter. They still protested, that prayers and tears were their only weapons against the impious tyrant, whose head they devoted to the justice of offended Heaven. But they insinuated, with sullen resolution, that their submission was no longer the effect of weakness; and that, in the imperfect state of human virtue, the patience, which is founded on principle, may be exhausted by persecution. It is impossible to determine how far the zeal of Julian would have prevailed over his good sense and humanity: but, if we seriously reflect on the strength and spirit of the church, we shall be convinced, that, before the emperor could have extinguished the religion of Christ, he must have involved his country in the horrors of a civil war.[141]

141. The resignation of Gregory is truly edifying (Orat. iv. p. 123, 124.). Yet, when an officer of Julian attempted to seize the church of Nazianzus, he would have lost his life, if he had not yielded to the zeal of the bishop and people (Orat. xix. p. 308.). See the reflections of Chrysostom, as they are alleged by Tillemont (Mem. Eccles. tom. vii. p. 575.).

CHAPTER XXIV

Residence of Julian at Antioch. – His successful Expedition against the Persians. – Passage of the Tigris. – The Retreat and Death of Julian. – Election of Jovian. – He saves the Roman Army by a disgraceful Treaty.

The Cæsars of Julian.

The philosophical fable which Julian composed under the name of the CÆSARS,[1] is one of the most agreeable and instructive productions of ancient wit.[2] During the freedom and equality of the days of the Saturnalia, Romulus prepared a feast for the deities of Olympus, who had adopted him as a worthy associate, and for the Roman princes, who had reigned over his martial people, and the vanquished nations of the earth. The immortals were placed in just order on their thrones of state, and the table of the Cæsars was spread below the Moon, in the upper region of the air. The tyrants, who would have disgraced the society of gods and men, were thrown headlong, by the inexorable Nemesis, into the Tartarean abyss. The rest of the Cæsars successively advanced to their seats; and, as they passed, the vices, the defects, the blemishes of their respective characters, were maliciously noticed by old Silenus, a laughing moralist, who disguised the wisdom of a philosopher under the mask of a Bacchanal.[3] As soon as the feast was ended, the voice of Mercury proclaimed the will of Jupiter, that a celestial crown should be the reward of superior merit. Julius Cæsar, Augustus, Trajan, and Marcus Antoninus, were selected

1. See this fable or satire, p. 306–336. of the Leipsig edition of Julian's works. The French version of the learned Ezekiel Spanheim (Paris, 1683.) is coarse, languid, and correct; and his notes, proofs, illustrations, &c. are piled on each other till they form a mass of 557 close-printed quarto pages. The Abbé de la Bleterie (Vie de Jovien, tom. i. p. 241–393.) has more happily expressed the spirit, as well as the sense, of the original, which he illustrates with some concise and curious notes.

2. Spanheim (in his preface) has most learnedly discussed the etymology, origin, resemblance, and disagreement of the Greek *satyrs*, a dramatic piece, which was acted after the tragedy; and the Latin *satires* (from *Satura*), a *miscellaneous* composition, either in prose or verse. But the Cæsars of Julian are of such an original cast, that the critic is perplexed to which class he should ascribe them.

3. This mixed character of Silenus is finely painted in the sixth eclogue of Virgil.

as the most illustrious candidates; the effeminate Constantine[4] was not excluded from this honourable competition, and the great Alexander was invited to dispute the prize of glory with the Roman heroes. Each of the candidates was allowed to display the merit of his own exploits; but, in the judgment of the gods, the modest silence of Marcus pleaded more powerfully than the elaborate orations of his haughty rivals. When the judges of this awful contest proceeded to examine the heart, and to scrutinize the springs of action; the superiority of the Imperial Stoic appeared still more decisive and conspicuous.[5] Alexander and Cæsar, Augustus, Trajan, and Constantine, acknowledged with a blush, that fame, or power, or pleasure, had been the important object of *their* labours: but the gods themselves beheld, with reverence and love, a virtuous mortal, who had practised on the throne the lessons of philosophy; and who, in a state of human imperfection, had aspired to imitate the moral attributes of the Deity. The value of this agreeable composition (the Cæsars of Julian) is enhanced by the rank of the author. A prince, who delineates with freedom the vices and virtues of his predecessors, subscribes, in every line, the censure or approbation of his own conduct.

In the cool moments of reflection, Julian preferred the useful and benevolent virtues of Antoninus: but his ambitious spirit was inflamed by the glory of Alexander; and he solicited, with equal ardour, the esteem of the wise, and the applause of the multitude. In the season of life, when the powers of the mind and body enjoy the most active vigour, the emperor, who was instructed by the experience, and animated by the success, of the German war, resolved to signalize his reign by some more splendid and memorable atchievement. The ambassadors of the East, from the continent of India, and the isle of Ceylon,[6] had respectfully saluted the Roman

He resolves to march against the Persians, A.D. 362.

---

4. Every impartial reader must perceive and condemn the partiality of Julian against his uncle Constantine, and the Christian religion. On this occasion, the interpreters are compelled, by a more sacred interest, to renounce their allegiance, and to desert the cause of their author.

5. Julian was secretly inclined to prefer a Greek to a Roman. But when he seriously compared a hero with a philosopher, he was sensible that mankind had much greater obligations

to Socrates than to Alexander (Orat. ad Themistium, p. 264.).

6. Inde nationibus Indicis certatim cum donis optimates mittentibus . . . ab usque Divis et *Serendivis*. Ammian. xx. 7. This island, to which the names of Taprobana, Serendib, and Ceylon, have been successively applied, manifests how imperfectly the seas and lands, to the east of cape Comorin, were known to the Romans. 1. Under the reign of Claudius, a freedman, who farmed the customs of the

purple.[7] The nations of the West esteemed and dreaded the personal virtues of Julian, both in peace and war. He despised the trophies of a Gothic victory,[8] and was satisfied that the rapacious Barbarians of the Danube would be restrained from any future violation of the faith of treaties, by the terror of his name, and the additional fortifications, with which he strengthened the Thracian and Illyrian frontiers. The successor of Cyrus and Artaxerxes was the only rival whom he deemed worthy of his arms; and he resolved, by the final conquest of Persia, to chastise the haughty nation, which had so long resisted and insulted the majesty of Rome.[9] As soon as the Persian monarch was informed that the throne of Constantius was filled by a prince of a very different character, he condescended to make some artful, or perhaps sincere, overtures, towards a negociation of peace. But the pride of Sapor was astonished by the firmness of Julian; who sternly declared, that he would never consent to hold a peaceful conference among the flames and ruins of the cities of Mesopotamia; and who added, with a smile of contempt, that it was needless to treat by ambassadors, as he himself had determined to visit speedily the court of Persia. The impatience of the emperor urged the diligence of the military preparations. The generals were named; a formidable army was destined for this important service; and Julian, marching from Constantinople through the provinces of Asia Minor, arrived at Antioch about eight months after the death of his predecessor. His ardent desire to march into the heart of Persia, was checked by the indispensable duty of regulating the state of the empire; by his zeal to revive the worship of the gods; and by the advice of his

Julian proceeds from Constantinople to Antioch, August.

Red Sea, was accidentally driven by the winds upon this strange and undiscovered coast: he conversed six months with the natives; and the king of Ceylon, who heard, for the first time, of the power and justice of Rome, was persuaded to send an embassy to the emperor (Plin. Hist. Nat. vi. 24.). 2. The geographers (and even Ptolemy) have magnified, above fifteen times, the real size of this new world, which they extended as far as the equator, and the neighbourhood of China.

7. These embassies had been sent to Constantius. Ammianus, who unwarily deviates into gross flattery, must have forgotten the length of the way, and the short

duration of the reign of Julian.

8. Gothos sæpe fallaces et perfidos; hostes quærere se meliores aiebat: illis enim sufficere mercatores Galatas per quos ubique sine conditionis discrimine venumdantur. Within less than fifteen years, these Gothic slaves threatened and subdued their masters.

9. Alexander reminds his rival Cæsar, who depreciated the fame and merit of an Asiatic victory, that Crassus and Antony had felt the Persian arrows; and that the Romans, in a war of three hundred years, had not yet subdued the single province of Mesopotamia or Assyria (Cæsares, p. 324.).

wisest friends; who represented the necessity of allowing the salutary interval of winter-quarters, to restore, the exhausted strength of the legions of Gaul, and the discipline and spirit of the Eastern troops. Julian was persuaded to fix, till the ensuing spring, his residence at Antioch, among a people maliciously disposed to deride the haste, and to censure the delays, of their sovereign.[10]

If Julian had flattered himself, that his personal connection with the capital of the East would be productive of mutual satisfaction to the prince and people, he made a very false estimate of his own character, and of the manners of Antioch.[11] The warmth of the climate disposed the natives to the most intemperate enjoyment *Licentious manners of the people of Antioch.* of tranquillity and opulence; and the lively licentiousness of the Greeks was blended with the hereditary softness of the Syrians. Fashion was the only law, pleasure the only pursuit, and the splendour of dress and furniture was the only distinction of the citizens of Antioch. The arts of luxury were honoured; the serious and manly virtues were the subject of ridicule; and the contempt for female modesty, and reverent age, announced the universal corruption of the capital of the East. The love of spectacles was the taste, or rather passion, of the Syrians: the most skilful artists were procured from the adjacent cities;[12] a considerable share of the revenue was devoted to the public amusements; and the magnificence of the games of the theatre and circus was considered as the happiness, and as the glory, of Antioch. The rustic manners of a prince who disdained such glory, and was insensible of such happiness, soon disgusted the delicacy of his subjects; and the effeminate Orientals could neither imitate, nor admire, the severe simplicity which Julian always maintained, and sometimes affected. The days of festivity, consecrated, by ancient custom, to the honour of the gods, were the only occasions in which Julian relaxed his philosophic severity; and those festivals were the only days in which the Syrians of Antioch could reject the allurements of pleasure. The majority of the people supported the glory of the Christian name, which had been first invented by their

10. The design of the Persian war is declared by Ammianus (xxii. 7. 12.), Libanius (Orat. Parent. c. 79, 80. p. 305, 306.), Zosimus (l. iii. p. 158.), and Socrates (l. iii. c. 19.).

11. The Satire of Julian, and the Homilies of St. Chrysostom, exhibit the same picture of Antioch. The miniature which the Abbé de la Bleterie has copied from thence (Vie de Julien, p. 332.), is elegant and correct.

12. Laodicea furnished charioteers; Tyre and Berytus, comedians; Cæsarea, pantomimes; Heliopolis, singers; Gaza, gladiators; Ascalon, wrestlers; and Castabala, rope-dancers. See the Expositio totius Mundi, p. 6. in the third tome of Hudson's Minor Geographers.

ancestors:[13] they contented themselves with disobeying the moral precepts, but they were scrupulously attached to the speculative doctrines, of their religion. The church of Antioch was distracted by heresy and schism; but the Arians and the Athanasians, the followers of Meletius and those of Paulinus,[14] were actuated by the same pious hatred of their common adversary.

Their aversion to Julian.

The strongest prejudice was entertained against the character of an apostate, the enemy and successor of a prince who had engaged the affections of a very numerous sect; and the removal of St. Babylas excited an implacable opposition to the person of Julian. His subjects complained, with superstitious indignation, that famine had pursued the emperor's steps from Constantinople to Antioch: and the discontent of a hungry people was exasperated by the injudicious attempt to relieve their distress. The inclemency of the season had affected the harvests of Syria; and the price of bread,[15] in the markets of Antioch, had naturally risen in proportion to the scarcity of corn.

Scarcity of corn, and public discontent.

But the fair and reasonable proportion was soon violated by the rapacious arts of monopoly. In this unequal contest, in which the produce of the land is claimed by one party, as his exclusive property; is used by another as a lucrative object of trade; and is required by a third, for the daily and necessary support of life; all the profits of the intermediate agents are accumulated on the head of the defenceless consumers. The hardships of their situation were exaggerated and encreased by their own impatience and anxiety; and the apprehension of a scarcity gradually produced the appearances of a famine. When the luxurious citizens of Antioch

13. Χριστον δε αγαπωντες, εχετε πολιουχον αντι τον Διος. The people of Antioch ingeniously professed their attachment to the *Chi* (Christ) and the *Kappa* (Constantius), Julian in Misopogon, p. 357.

14. The schism of Antioch, which lasted eighty-five years (A.D. 330–415.), was inflamed, while Julian resided in that city, by the indiscreet ordination of Paulinus. See Tillemont, Mem. Eccles. tom. vii. p. 803. of the quarto edition (Paris, 1701, &c.), which henceforward I shall quote.

15. Julian states three different proportions of five, ten, or fifteen *modii* of wheat, for one piece of gold, according to the degrees of plenty and scarcity (in Misopogon, p. 369.). From this fact, and from some collateral examples, I conclude, that under the successors of Constantine, the moderate price of wheat was about thirty-two shillings the English quarter, which is equal to the average price of the sixty-four first years of the present century. See Arbuthnot's Tables of Coins, Weights, and Measures, p. 88, 89. Plin. Hist. Natur. xviii. 12. Mem. de l'Academie des Inscriptions, tom. xxviii. p. 718–721. Smith's Inquiry into the Nature and Causes of the Wealth of Nations, vol. i. p. 246. This last I am proud to quote, as the work of a sage and a friend.

complained of the high price of poultry and fish, Julian publicly declared, that a frugal city ought to be satisfied with a regular supply of wine, oil, and bread; but he acknowledged that it was the duty of a sovereign to provide for the subsistence of his people. With this salutary view, the emperor ventured on a very dangerous and doubtful step, of fixing, by legal authority, the value of corn. He enacted, that in a time of scarcity, it should be sold at a price which had seldom been known in the most plentiful years; and that his own example might strengthen his laws, he sent into the market four hundred and twenty-two thousand *modii*, or measures, which were drawn, by his order, from the granaries of Hierapolis, of Chalcis, and even of Egypt. The consequences might have been foreseen, and were soon felt. The Imperial wheat was purchased by the rich merchants; the proprietors of land, or of corn, withheld from the city the accustomed supply; and the small quantities that appeared in the market, were secretly sold at an advanced and illegal price. Julian still continued to applaud his own policy, treated the complaints of the people as a vain and ungrateful murmur, and convinced Antioch, that he had inherited the obstinacy, though not the cruelty, of his brother Gallus.[16] The remonstrances of the municipal senate served only to exasperate his inflexible mind. He was persuaded, perhaps with truth, that the senators of Antioch who possessed lands, or were concerned in trade, had themselves contributed to the calamities of their country; and he imputed the disrespectful boldness which they assumed, to the sense, not of public duty, but of private interest. The whole body, consisting of two hundred of the most noble and wealthy citizens, were sent, under a guard, from the palace to the prison; and though they were permitted, before the close of evening, to return to their respective houses,[17] the emperor himself could not obtain the forgiveness which he had so easily granted. The same grievances were still the subject of the same complaints, which were industriously circulated by the wit and levity of the Syrian Greeks. During the licentious days of the Saturnalia, the streets of the city resounded with insolent songs, which derided the laws, the religion, the personal conduct, and even the *beard* of the emperor; and

---

16. Nunquam a proposito declinabat, Galli similis fratris, licet incruentus. Ammian. xxii. 14. The ignorance of the most enlightened princes may claim some excuse; but we cannot be satisfied with Julian's own defence (in Misopogon, p. 368, 369), or the elaborate

apology of Libanius (Orat. Parental. c. xcvii. p. 321.).

17. Their short and easy confinement is gently touched by Libanius (Orat. Parental. c. xcviii. p. 322, 323.).

the spirit of Antioch was manifested by the connivance of the magistrates, and the applause of the multitude.[18] The disciple of Socrates was too deeply affected by these popular insults; but the monarch, endowed with quick sensibility, and possessed of absolute power, refused his passions the gratification of revenge. A tyrant might have proscribed, without distinction, the lives and fortunes of the citizens of Antioch; and the unwarlike Syrians must have patiently submitted to the lust, the rapaciousness, and the cruelty of the faithful legions of Gaul. A milder sentence might have deprived the capital of the East of its honours and privileges; and the courtiers, perhaps the subjects, of Julian, would have applauded an act of justice, which asserted the dignity of the supreme magistrate of the republic.[19] But instead of abusing, or exerting, the authority of the state, to revenge his personal injuries, Julian contented himself with an inoffensive mode of retaliation, which it would be in the power of few princes to employ. He had been insulted by satires and libels; in his turn he composed, under the title of the *Enemy of the Beard*, an ironical confession of his own faults, and a severe satire of the licentious and effeminate manners of Antioch. This Imperial reply was publicly exposed before the gates of the palace; and the MISOPOGON[20] still remains a singular monument of the resentment, the wit, the humanity, and the indiscretion of Julian. Though he affected to laugh, he could not forgive.[21] His contempt was expressed, and his revenge might be gratified, by the nomination of a governor[22] worthy only of such subjects: and the

Julian composes a satire against Antioch.

---

18. Libanius (ad Antiochenos de Imperatoris ira, c. 17, 18, 19. in Fabricius, Bibliot. Græc. tom. vii. p. 221–223.), like a skilful advocate, severely censures the folly of the people, who suffered for the crime of a few obscure and drunken wretches.

19. Libanius (ad Antiochen. c. vii. p. 213.) reminds Antioch of the recent chastisement of Cæsarea: and even Julian (in Misopogon, p. 355.) insinuates how severely Tarentum had expiated the insult to the Roman ambassadors.

20. On the subject of the Misopogon, see Ammianus (xxii. 14.), Libanius (Orat. Parentalis, c. xcix. p. 323.), Gregory Nazianzen (Orat. iv. p. 133.), and the Chronicle of Antioch, by John Malela, (tom. ii. p. 15, 16.). I have essential obligations to the translation

and notes of the Abbé de la Bleterie (Vie de Jovien, tom. ii. p. 1–138.).

21. Ammianus very justly remarks, Coactus dissimulare pro tempore irâ sufflabatur internâ. The elaborate irony of Julian at length bursts forth into serious and direct invective.

22. Ipse autem Antiochiam egressurus, Heliopoliten quendam Alexandrum Syriacæ jurisdictioni præfecit, turbulentum et sævum; dicebatque non illum meruisse, sed Antiochensibus avaris et contumeliosis hujusmodi judicem convenire. Ammian. xxiii. 2. Libanius (Epist. 722. p. 346, 347.), who confesses to Julian himself, that he had shared the general discontent, pretends that Alexander was an useful, though harsh, reformer of the manners and religion of Antioch.

emperor, for ever renouncing the ungrateful city, proclaimed his resolution to pass the ensuing winter at Tarsus in Cilicia.[23]

Yet Antioch possessed one citizen, whose genius and virtues might atone, in the opinion of Julian, for the vice and folly of his country. The sophist Libanius was born in the capital of the East; he publicly professed the arts of rhetoric and declamation at Nice, Nicomedia, Constantinople, Athens, and, during the remainder of his life, at Antioch. His school was assiduously frequented by the Grecian youth; his disciples, who sometimes exceeded the number of eighty, celebrated their incomparable master; and the jealousy of his rivals, who persecuted him from one city to another, confirmed the favourable opinion which Libanius ostentatiously displayed of his superior merit. The præceptors of Julian had extorted a rash but solemn assurance, that he would never attend the lectures of their adversary: the curiosity of the royal youth was checked and inflamed: he secretly procured the writings of this dangerous sophist, and gradually surpassed, in the perfect imitation of his style, the most laborious of his domestic pupils.[24] When Julian ascended the throne, he declared his impatience to embrace and reward the Syrian sophist, who had preserved, in a degenerate age, the Grecian purity of taste, of manners, and of religion. The emperor's prepossession was encreased and justified by the discreet pride of his favourite. Instead of pressing, with the foremost of the crowd, into the palace of Constantinople, Libanius calmly expected his arrival at Antioch; withdrew from court on the first symptoms of coldness and indifference; required a formal invitation for each visit; and taught his sovereign an important lesson, that he might command the obedience of a subject, but that he must deserve the attachment of a friend. The sophists of every age, despising, or affecting to despise, the accidental distinctions of birth and fortune,[25] reserve their esteem for the superior qualities of the mind, with which they themselves are so plentifully endowed. Julian might disdain the acclamations of a venal court, who adored the Imperial purple; but he was deeply flattered by the praise, the admonition, the freedom, and the envy of an independent philosopher,

The sophist Libanius. A.D. 314– 390, &c.

---

23. Julian, in Misopogon, p. 364. Ammian. xxiii. 2. and Valesius ad loc. Libanius, in a professed oration, invites him to return to his loyal and penitent city of Antioch.

24. Libanius, Orat. Parent. c. vii. p. 230, 231.

25. Eunapius reports, that Libanius refused the honorary rank of Prætorian præfect, as less illustrious than the title of Sophist (in Vit. Sophist. p. 135.). The critics have observed a similar sentiment in one of the epistles (xviii. edit. Wolf.) of Libanius himself.

who refused his favours, loved his person, celebrated his fame, and protected his memory. The voluminous writings of Libanius still exist; for the most part, they are the vain and idle compositions of an orator, who cultivated the science of words; the productions of a recluse student, whose mind, regardless of his contemporaries, was incessantly fixed on the Trojan war, and the Athenian commonwealth. Yet the sophist of Antioch sometimes descended from this imaginary elevation; he entertained a various and elaborate correspondence;[26] he praised the virtues of his own times; he boldly arraigned the abuses of public and private life; and he eloquently pleaded the cause of Antioch against the just resentment of Julian and Theodosius. It is the common calamity of old age,[27] to lose whatever might have rendered it desirable; but Libanius experienced the peculiar misfortune of surviving the religion and the sciences, to which he had consecrated his genius. The friend of Julian was an indignant spectator of the triumph of Christianity; and his bigotry, which darkened the prospect of the visible world, did not inspire Libanius with any lively hopes of celestial glory and happiness.[28]

March of Julian to the Euphrates, A.D. 363, March 5. The martial impatience of Julian urged him to take the field in the beginning of the spring; and he dismissed, with contempt and reproach, the senate of Antioch, who accompanied the emperor beyond the limits of their own territory, to which he was resolved never to return. After a laborious march of two days,[29] he halted on the third, at Beræa, or Aleppo, where he had the

---

26. Near two thousand of his letters, a mode of composition in which Libanius was thought to excel, are still extant, and already published. The critics may praise their subtle and elegant brevity; yet Dr. Bentley (Dissertation upon Phalaris, p. 487.) might justly, though quaintly, observe, that "you feel by the emptiness and deadness of them, that you converse with some dreaming pedant, with his elbow on his desk."

27. His birth is assigned to the year 314. He mentions the seventy-sixth year of his age (A.D. 390), and seems to allude to some events of a still later date.

28. Libanius has composed the vain, prolix, but curious narrative of his own life (tom. ii. p. 1–84. edit. Morell.), of which Eunapius

(p. 130–135.) has left a concise and unfavourable account. Among the moderns, Tillemont (Hist. des Empereurs, tom. iv. p. 571–576.), Fabricius (Bibliot. Græc. tom. vii. p. 378–414.), and Lardner (Heathen Testimonies, tom. iv. p. 127–163.), have illustrated the character and writings of this famous sophist.

29. From Antioch to Litarbe, on the territory of Chalcis, the road, over hills and through morasses, was extremely bad; and the loose stones were cemented only with sand (Julian, epist. xxvii.). It is singular enough, that the Romans should have neglected the great communication between Antioch and the Euphrates. See Wesseling. Itinerar. p. 190. Bergier, Hist. des Grands Chemins, tom. ii. p. 100.

mortification of finding a senate almost entirely Christian; who received with cold and formal demonstrations of respect, the eloquent sermon of the apostle of paganism. The son of one of the most illustrious citizens of Beræa, who had embraced, either from interest or conscience, the religion of the emperor, was disinherited by his angry parent. The father and the son were invited to the Imperial table. Julian, placing himself between them, attempted, without success, to inculcate the lesson and example of toleration; supported, with affected calmness, the indiscreet zeal of the aged Christian, who seemed to forget the sentiments of nature, and the duty of a subject; and, at length turning towards the afflicted youth, "Since you have lost a father," said he, "for my sake, it is incumbent on me to supply his place."[30] The emperor was received in a manner much more agreeable to his wishes at Batnæ, a small town pleasantly seated in a grove of cypresses, about twenty miles from the city of Hierapolis. The solemn rites of sacrifice were decently prepared by the inhabitants of Batnæ, who seemed attached to the worship of their tutelar deities, Apollo and Jupiter; but the serious piety of Julian was offended by the tumult of their applause; and he too clearly discerned, that the smoke which arose from their altars was the incense of flattery, rather than of devotion. The ancient and magnificent temple, which had sanctified, for so many ages, the city of Hierapolis,[31] no longer subsisted; and the consecrated wealth, which afforded a liberal maintenance to more than three hundred priests, might hasten its downfall. Yet Julian enjoyed the satisfaction of embracing a philosopher and a friend, whose religious firmness had withstood the pressing and repeated solicitations of Constantius and Gallus, as often as those princes lodged at his house, in their passage through Hierapolis. In the hurry of military preparation, and the careless confidence of a familiar correspondence, the zeal of Julian appears to have been lively and uniform. He had now undertaken an important and difficult war; and the anxiety of the event rendered him still more attentive to observe and register the most trifling presages, from which, according to the rules of divination, any knowledge

---

30. Julian alludes to this incident (epist. xxvii.), which is more distinctly related by Theodoret (l. iii. c. 22.). The intolerant spirit of the father is applauded by Tillemont (Hist. des Empereurs, tom. iv. p. 534.), and even by La Bleterie (Vie de Julien, p. 413.).

31. See the curious treatise de Deâ Syriâ, inserted among the works of Lucian (tom. iii. p. 451-490. edit. Reitz.). The singular appellation of *Ninus vetus* (Ammian. xiv. 8.) might induce a suspicion, that Hierapolis had been the royal seat of the Assyrians.

of futurity could be derived.[32] He informed Libanius of his progress as far as Hierapolis, by an elegant epistle,[33] which displays the facility of his genius, and his tender friendship for the sophist of Antioch.

His design of invading Persia.
Hierapolis, situate almost on the banks of the Euphrates,[34] had been appointed for the general rendezvous of the Roman troops, who immediately passed the great river on a bridge of boats, which was previously constructed.[35] If the inclinations of Julian had been similar to those of his predecessor, he might have wasted the active and important season of the year in the circus of Samosata, or in the churches of Edessa. But as the warlike emperor, instead of Constantius, had chosen Alexander for his model, he advanced without delay to Carrhæ,[36] a very ancient city of Mesopotamia, at the distance of fourscore miles from Hierapolis. The temple of the Moon attracted the devotion of Julian; but the halt of a few days was principally employed in completing the immense preparations of the Persian war. The secret of the expedition had hitherto remained in his own breast; but as Carrhæ is the point of separation of the two great roads, he could no longer conceal, whether it was his design to attack the dominions of Sapor on the side of the Tigris, or on that of the Euphrates. The emperor detached an army of thirty thousand men, under the command of his kinsman Procopius, and of Sebastian, who had been duke of Egypt. They were ordered to direct their march towards Nisibis, and to secure the frontier from the desultory incursions of the enemy, before they attempted the passage of the Tigris. Their subsequent operations were left to the discretion of the generals; but Julian expected, that after wasting with fire and sword the fertile districts of Media and Adiabene, they might arrive under the walls of Ctesiphon about the same time, that he himself, advancing with equal steps along

32. Julian (epist. xxviii.) kept a regular account of all the fortunate omens; but he suppresses the inauspicious signs, which Ammianus (xxiii. 2.) has carefully recorded.

33. Julian, epist. xxvii. p. 399–402.

34. I take the earliest opportunity of acknowledging my obligations to M. d'Anville, for his recent geography of the Euphrates and Tigris (Paris, 1780, in 4to.), which particularly illustrates the expedition of Julian.

35. There are three passages within a few miles of each other; 1. Zeugma, celebrated

by the ancients; 2. Bir, frequented by the moderns; and, 3. The bridge of Menbigz, or Hierapolis, at the distance of four parasangs from the city.

36. Haran, or Carrhæ, was the ancient residence of the Sabæans, and of Abraham. See the Index Geographicus of Schultens (ad calcem Vit. Saladin.), a work from which I have obtained much *Oriental* knowledge, concerning the ancient and modern geography of Syria and the adjacent countries.

the banks of the Euphrates, should besiege the capital of the Persian monarchy. The success of this well-concerted plan depended, in a great measure, on the powerful and ready assistance of the king of Armenia, who, without exposing the safety of his own dominions, might detach an army of four thousand horse, and twenty thousand foot, to the assistance of the Romans.[37] But the feeble Arsaces Tiranus,[38] king of Armenia, had degenerated still more shamefully than his father Chosroes, from the manly virtues of the great Tiridates; and as the pusillanimous monarch was averse to any enterprize of danger and glory, he could disguise his timid indolence by the more decent excuses of religion and gratitude. He expressed a pious attachment to the memory of Constantius, from whose hands he had received in marriage Olympias, the daughter of the præfect Ablavius; and the alliance of a female, who had been educated as the destined wife of the emperor Constans, exalted the dignity of a Barbarian king.[39] Tiranus professed the Christian religion; he reigned over a nation of Christians; and he was restrained, by every principle of conscience and interest, from contributing to the victory, which would consummate the ruin of the church. The alienated mind of Tiranus was exasperated by the indiscretion of Julian, who treated the king of Armenia as *his* slave, and as the enemy of the gods. The haughty and threatening style of the Imperial mandates[40] awakened the secret indignation of a prince, who, in the humiliating state of dependence, was still conscious of his royal descent from the Arsacides, the lords of the East, and the rivals of the Roman power.

Disaffection of the king of Armenia.

The military dispositions of Julian were skilfully contrived to deceive the spies, and to divert the attention, of Sapor. The legions appeared to direct their march towards Nisibis and the Tigris. On a sudden they wheeled to the right; traversed the level and

Military preparations.

---

37. See Xenophon. Cyropœd. l. iii. p. 189. edit. Hutchinson. Artavasdes might have supplied Marc Antony with 16,000 horse, armed and disciplined after the Parthian manner (Plutarch, in M. Antonio, tom. v. p. 117.).

38. Moses of Chorene (Hist. Armeniac. l. iii. c. 11. p. 242.) fixes his accession (A.D. 354.) to the 17th year of Constantius.

39. Ammian. xx. 11. Athanasius (tom. i. p. 856.) says, in general terms, that Constantius gave his brother's widow τοις βαρβαροις, an

expression more suitable to a Roman than a Christian.

40. Ammianus (xxiii. 2.) uses a word much too soft for the occasion, *monuerat*. Muratori (Fabricius, Bibliothec. Græc. tom. vii. p. 86.) has published an epistle from Julian to the satrap Arsaces; fierce, vulgar, and (though it might deceive Sozomen, l. vi. c. 5.), most probably spurious. La Bleterie (Hist. de Jovien, tom. ii. p. 339.) translates and rejects it.

naked plain of Carrhæ; and reached, on the third day, the banks of the Euphrates, where the strong town of Nicephorium, or Callinicum, had been founded by the Macedonian kings. From thence the emperor pursued his march, above ninety miles, along the winding stream of the Euphrates, till, at length, about one month after his departure from Antioch, he discovered the towers of Circesium, the extreme limit of the Roman dominions. The army of Julian, the most numerous that any of the Cæsars had ever led against Persia, consisted of sixty-five thousand effective and well-disciplined soldiers. The veteran bands of cavalry and infantry, of Romans and Barbarians, had been selected from the different provinces; and a just pre-eminence of loyalty and valour was claimed by the hardy Gauls, who guarded the throne and person of their beloved prince. A formidable body of Scythian auxiliaries had been transported from another climate, and almost from another world, to invade a distant country, of whose name and situation they were ignorant. The love of rapine and war allured to the Imperial standard several tribes of Saracens, or roving Arabs, whose service Julian had commanded, while he sternly refused the payment of the accustomed subsidies. The broad channel of the Euphrates[41] was crowded by a fleet of eleven hundred ships, destined to attend the motions, and to satisfy the wants, of the Roman army. The military strength of the fleet was composed of fifty armed gallies; and these were accompanied by an equal number of flat-bottomed boats, which might occasionally be connected into the form of temporary bridges. The rest of the ships, partly constructed of timber, and partly covered with raw hides, were laden with an almost inexhaustible supply of arms and engines, of utensils and provisions. The vigilant humanity of Julian had embarked a very large magazine of vinegar and biscuit for the use of the soldiers, but he prohibited the indulgence of wine; and rigorously stopped a long string of superfluous camels that attempted to follow the rear of the army. The river Chaboras falls into the Euphrates at Circesium;[42] and as soon as the trumpet gave the signal of march, the

Julian enters the Persian territories, April 7th.

---

41. Latissimum flumen Euphraten artabat. Ammian. xxiii. 3. Somewhat higher, at the fords of Thapsacus, the river is four stadia, or 800 yards, almost half an English mile, broad (Xenophon Anabasis, l. i. p. 41. edit. Hutchinson, with Foster's Observations, p. 29, &c. in the 2d volume of Spelman's translation). If the breadth of the Euphrates at Bir and Zeugma is no more than 130 yards (Voyages de Niebuhr, tom. ii. p. 335.), the enormous difference must chiefly arise from the depth of the channel. 42. Monumentum tutissimum et fabrè politum, cujus mœnia Abora (the Orientals aspire Chaboras or Chabour) et Euphrates ambiunt flumina, velut spatium insulare fingentes. Ammian. xxiii. 5.

Romans passed the little stream which separated two mighty and hostile empires. The custom of ancient discipline required a military oration; and Julian embraced every opportunity of displaying his eloquence. He animated the impatient and attentive legions by the example of the inflexible courage and glorious triumphs of their ancestors. He excited their resentment by a lively picture of the insolence of the Persians; and he exhorted them to imitate his firm resolution, either to extirpate that perfidious nation, or to devote his life in the cause of the republic. The eloquence of Julian was enforced by a donative of one hundred and thirty pieces of silver to every soldier; and the bridge of the Chaboras was instantly cut away, to convince the troops that they must place their hopes of safety in the success of their arms. Yet the prudence of the emperor induced him to secure a remote frontier, perpetually exposed to the inroads of the hostile Arabs. A detachment of four thousand men was left at Circesium, which completed, to the number of ten thousand, the regular garrison of that important fortress.[43]

From the moment that the Romans entered the enemy's country,[44] the country of an active and artful enemy, the order of march was disposed in three columns.[45] The strength of the infantry, and consequently of the whole army, was placed in *His march over the desert of Mesopotamia.* the centre, under the peculiar command of their master-general Victor. On the right, the brave Nevitta led a column of several legions along the banks of the Euphrates, and almost always in sight of the fleet. The left flank of the army was protected by the column of cavalry. Hormisdas and Arinthæus were appointed generals of the horse; and the singular adventures of Hormisdas[46] are not undeserving of our notice. He was a Persian prince, of the royal race of the Sassanides, who, in the troubles of the minority of Sapor, had escaped from prison to the hospitable court of the great

---

43. The enterprise and armament of Julian are described by himself (Epist. xxvii.), Ammianus Marcellinus (xxiii. 3, 4, 5.), Libanius (Orat. Parent. c. 108, 109. p. 332, 333.), Zosimus (l. iii. p. 160, 161, 162.), Sozomen (l. vi. c. 1.), and John Malela (tom. ii. p. 17.).

44. Before he enters Persia, Ammianus copiously describes (xxiii. 6. p. 396–419. edit. Gronov. in 4to.) the eighteen great satrapies, or provinces (as far as the Seric, or Chinese frontiers), which were subject to the Sassanides.

45. Ammianus (xxiv. 1.) and Zosimus (l. iii. p. 162, 163.) have accurately expressed the order of march.

46. The adventures of Hormisdas are related with some mixture of fable (Zosimus, l. ii. p. 100–102; Tillemont, Hist. des Empereurs, tom. iv. p. 198.). It is almost impossible that he should be the brother (frater germanus) of an *eldest* and *posthumous* child: nor do I recollect that Ammianus ever gives him that title.

Constantine. Hormisdas, at first, excited the compassion, and, at length, acquired the esteem, of his new masters; his valour and fidelity raised him to the military honours of the Roman service; and, though a Christian, he might indulge the secret satisfaction of convincing his ungrateful country, that an oppressed subject may prove the most dangerous enemy. Such was the disposition of the three principal columns. The front and flanks of the army were covered by Lucillianus with a flying detachment of fifteen hundred light-armed soldiers, whose active vigilance observed the most distant signs, and conveyed the earliest notice, of any hostile approach. Dagalaiphus, and Secundinus duke of Osrhoene, conducted the troops of the rear-guard; the baggage, securely, proceeded in the intervals of the columns; and the ranks, from a motive either of use or ostentation, were formed in such open order, that the whole line of march extended almost ten miles. The ordinary post of Julian was at the head of the centre column; but as he preferred the duties of a general to the state of a monarch, he rapidly moved, with a small escort of light cavalry, to the front, the rear, the flanks, wherever his presence could animate or protect the march of the Roman army. The country which they traversed from the Chaboras, to the cultivated lands of Assyria, may be considered as a part of the desert of Arabia, a dry and barren waste, which could never be improved by the most powerful arts of human industry. Julian marched over the same ground which had been trod above seven hundred years before by the footsteps of the younger Cyrus, and which is described by one of the companions of his expedition, the sage and heroic Xenophon.[47] "The country was a plain throughout, as even as the sea, and full of wormwood; and if any other kind of shrubs or reeds grew there, they had all an aromatic smell; but no trees could be seen. Bustards and ostriches, antelopes and wild asses,[48] appeared to be the only inhabitants of the desert; and the fatigues of the march were alleviated by the amusements of the chace." The loose sand of the desert was frequently raised by the wind into clouds of dust: and a great number of the soldiers of Julian, with their tents, were suddenly thrown to the ground by the violence of an unexpected hurricane.

---

47. See the first book of the Anabasis, p. 45, 46. This pleasing work is original and authentic. Yet Xenophon's memory, perhaps many years after the expedition, has sometimes betrayed him; and the distances which he marks are often larger than either a soldier or a geographer will allow.

48. Mr. Spelman, the English translator of the Anabasis (vol. i. p. 51.), confounds the antelope with the roe-buck, and the wildass with the zebra.

The sandy plains of Mesopotamia were abandoned to the ante-
lopes and wild asses of the desert; but a variety of populous towns *His success.*
and villages were pleasantly situated on the banks of the Euphrates, and in
the islands which are occasionally formed by that river. The city of Annah,
or Anatho,[49] the actual residence of an Arabian Emir, is composed of two
long streets, which inclose within a natural fortification, a small island in
the midst, and two fruitful spots on either side, of the Euphrates. The
warlike inhabitants of Anatho shewed a disposition to stop the march of a
Roman emperor; till they were diverted from such fatal presumption by
the mild exhortations of prince Hormisdas, and the approaching terrors of
the fleet and army. They implored, and experienced, the clemency of
Julian; who transplanted the people to an advantageous settlement, near
Chalcis in Syria, and admitted Pusæus, the governor, to an honourable
rank in his service and friendship. But the impregnable fortress of Thilutha
could scorn the menace of a siege; and the emperor was obliged to content
himself with an insulting promise, that when he had subdued the interior
provinces of Persia, Thilutha would no longer refuse to grace the triumph
of the conqueror. The inhabitants of the open towns, unable to resist, and
unwilling to yield, fled with precipitation; and their houses, filled with
spoil and provisions, were occupied by the soldiers of Julian, who massacred,
without remorse, and without punishment, some defenceless women.
During the march, the Surenas, or Persian general, and Malek Rodosaces,
the renowned Emir of the tribe of Gassan,[50] incessantly hovered round the
army: every straggler was intercepted; every detachment was attacked; and
the valiant Hormisdas escaped with some difficulty from their hands. But
the Barbarians were finally repulsed: the country became every day less
favourable to the operations of cavalry; and when the Romans arrived
at Macepracta, they perceived the ruins of the wall, which had been
constructed by the ancient kings of Assyria, to secure their dominions
from the incursions of the Medes. These preliminaries of the expedition

49. See Voyages de Tavernier, part i. l. iii.
p. 316. and more especially Viaggi di Pietro
della Valle, tom. i. lett. xvii. p. 671, &c. He
was ignorant of the old name and condition
of Annah. Our blind travellers *seldom* possess
any previous knowledge of the countries
which they visit. Shaw and Tournefort
deserve an honourable exception.
50. Famosi nominis latro, says Ammianus; an

high encomium for an Arab. The tribe of
Gassan had settled on the edge of Syria, and
reigned some time in Damascus, under a dynasty of thirty-one kings, or emirs, from the
time of Pompey to that of the Khalif Omar.
D'Herbelot, Bibliothéque Orientale, p. 360.
Pocock, Specimen Hist. Arabicæ, p. 75–78.
The name of Rodosaces does not appear in
the list.

of Julian appear to have employed about fifteen days; and we may compute near three hundred miles from the fortress of Circesium to the wall of Macepracta.[51]

Description of Assyria. The fertile province of Assyria,[52] which stretched beyond the Tigris, as far as the mountains of Media,[53] extended about four hundred miles from the ancient wall of Macepracta to the territory of Basra, where the united streams of the Euphrates and Tigris discharge themselves into the Persian Gulf.[54] The whole country might have claimed the peculiar name of Mesopotamia; as the two rivers, which are never more distant than fifty, approach, between Bagdad and Babylon, within twenty-five, miles of each other. A multitude of artificial canals, dug without much labour in a soft and yielding soil, connected the rivers, and intersected the plain, of Assyria. The uses of these artificial canals were various and important. They served to discharge the superfluous waters from one river into the other, at the season of their respective inundations. Subdividing themselves into smaller and smaller branches, they refreshed the dry lands, and supplied the deficiency of rain. They facilitated the intercourse of peace and commerce; and, as the dams could be speedily broke down, they armed the despair of the Assyrians with the means of opposing a sudden deluge to the progress of an invading army. To the soil and climate of Assyria, nature had denied some of her choicest gifts, the vine, the olive, and the fig-tree; but the food which supports the life of man, and particularly wheat and barley, were produced with inexhaustible fertility; and the husbandman, who committed his seed to the earth, was frequently rewarded with an encrease of two, or even of three, hundred.

51. See Ammianus (xxiv. 1, 2.), Libanius (Orat. Parental. c. 110, 111. p. 334.), Zosimus (l. iii. p. 164-168.).

52. The description of Assyria is furnished by Herodotus (l. i. c. 192, &c.), who sometimes writes for children, and sometimes for philosophers; by Strabo (l. xvi. p. 1070-1082.), and by Ammianus (l. xxiii. c. 6.). The most useful of the modern travellers are Tavernier (part i. l. ii. p. 226-258.), Otter (tom. ii. p. 35-69. and 189-224.), and Niebuhr (tom. ii. p. 172-288.). Yet I much regret that the *Irak Arabi* of Abulfeda has not been translated.

53. Ammianus remarks, that the primitive Assyria, which comprehended Ninus

(Niniveh) and Arbela, had assumed the more recent and peculiar appellation of Adiabene: and he seems to fix Teredon, Vologesia, and Apollonia, as the *extreme* cities of the actual province of Assyria.

54. The two rivers unite at Apamea, or Corna (one hundred miles from the Persian Gulf), into the broad stream of the Pasitigris, or Shat-ul-Arab. The Euphrates formerly reached the sea by a separate channel, which was obstructed and diverted by the citizens of Orchoe, about twenty miles to the south-east of modern Basra (d'Anville, in the Memoires de l'Acad. des Inscriptions, tom. xxx. p. 170-191.).

The face of the country was interspersed with groves of innumerable palm-trees;[55] and the diligent natives celebrated, either in verse or prose, the three hundred and sixty uses to which the trunk, the branches, the leaves, the juice, and the fruit, were skilfully applied. Several manufactures, especially those of leather and linen, employed the industry of a numerous people, and afforded valuable materials for foreign trade; which appears, however, to have been conducted by the hands of strangers. Babylon had been converted into a royal park; but near the ruins of the ancient capital, new cities had successively arisen, and the populousness of the country was displayed in the multitude of towns and villages, which were built of bricks, dried in the sun, and strongly cemented with bitumen; the natural and peculiar production of the Babylonian soil. While the successors of Cyrus reigned over Asia, the province of Assyria alone maintained, during a third part of the year, the luxurious plenty of the table and household of the Great King. Four considerable villages were assigned for the subsistence of his Indian dogs; eight hundred stallions, and sixteen thousand mares, were constantly kept, at the expence of the country, for the royal stables: and as the daily tribute, which was paid to the satrap, amounted to one English bushel of silver, we may compute the annual revenue of Assyria at more than twelve hundred thousand pounds sterling.[56]

The fields of Assyria were devoted by Julian to the calamities of war; and the philosopher retaliated on a guiltless people the acts of rapine and cruelty, which had been committed by their haughty master in the Roman provinces. The trembling *Invasion of Assyria. A.D. 363. May.* Assyrians summoned the rivers to their assistance; and completed, with their own hands, the ruin of their country. The roads were rendered impracticable; a flood of waters was poured into the camp; and, during several days, the troops of Julian were obliged to contend with the most

---

55. The learned Kæmpfer, as a botanist, an antiquary, and a traveller, has exhausted (Amœnitat. Exoticæ, Fascicul. iv. p. 660–764.) the whole subject of palm-trees.
56. Assyria yielded to the Persian satrap, an *Artaba* of silver each day. The well-known proportion of weights and measures (see Bishop Hooper's elaborate Inquiry), the specific gravity of water and silver, and the value of that metal, will afford, after a short process, the annual revenue which I have stated.

Yet the Great King received no more than 1000 Euboic, or Tyrian, talents (252,000l.) from Assyria. The comparison of two passages in Herodotus (l. i. c. 192. l. iii. c. 89–96.) reveals an important difference between the *gross*, and the *net*, revenue of Persia; the sums paid by the province, and the gold or silver deposited in the royal treasure. The monarch might annually save three millions six hundred thousand pounds, of the seventeen or eighteen millions raised upon the people.

discouraging hardships. But every obstacle was surmounted by the perseverance of the legionaries, who were inured to toil as well as to danger, and who felt themselves animated by the spirit of their leader. The damage was gradually repaired; the waters were restored to their proper channels; whole groves of palm-trees were cut down, and placed along the broken parts of the road; and the army passed over the broad and deeper canals, on bridges of floating rafts which were supported by the help of bladders. Two cities of Assyria presumed to resist the arms of a Roman emperor: and they both paid the severe penalty of their rashness. At the distance of fifty miles from the royal residence of Ctesiphon, Perisabor, or Anbar, held the second rank in the province: a city, large, populous, and well fortified, surrounded with a double wall, almost encompassed by a branch of the Euphrates, and defended by the valour of a numerous garrison. The exhortations of Hormisdas were repulsed with contempt; and the ears of the Persian prince were wounded by a just reproach, that, unmindful of his royal birth, he conducted an army of strangers against his king and country. The Assyrians maintained their loyalty by a skilful, as well as vigorous, defence; till the lucky stroke of a battering-ram having opened a large breach, by shattering one of the angles of the wall, they hastily retired into the fortifications of the interior citadel. The soldiers of Julian rushed impetuously into the town, and, after the full gratification of every military appetite, Perisabor was reduced to ashes; and the engines which assaulted the citadel were planted on the ruins of the smoking houses. The contest was continued by an incessant and mutual discharge of missile weapons; and the superiority which the Romans might derive from the mechanical powers of their balistæ and catapultæ was counterbalanced by the advantage of the ground on the side of the besieged. But as soon as an *Helepolis* had been constructed, which could engage on equal terms with the loftiest ramparts; the tremendous aspect of a moving turret, that would leave no hope of resistance or of mercy, terrified the defenders of the citadel into an humble submission; and the place was surrendered only two days after Julian first appeared under the walls of Perisabor. Two thousand five hundred persons, of both sexes, the feeble remnant of a flourishing people, were permitted to retire: the plentiful magazines of corn, of arms, and of splendid furniture, were partly distributed among the troops, and partly reserved for the public service: the useless stores were destroyed by fire, or thrown into the stream of the Euphrates; and the fate of Amida was revenged by the total ruin of Perisabor.

Siege of Perisabor,

The city, or rather fortress, of Maogamalcha, which was defended by sixteen large towers, a deep ditch, and two strong *of Maogamalcha.* and solid walls of brick and bitumen, appears to have been constructed at the distance of eleven miles, as the safeguard of the capital of Persia. The emperor, apprehensive of leaving such an important fortress in his rear, immediately formed the siege of Maogamalcha; and the Roman army was distributed, for that purpose, into three divisions. Victor, at the head of the cavalry, and of a detachment of heavy-armed foot, was ordered to clear the country, as far as the banks of the Tigris, and the suburbs of Ctesiphon. The conduct of the attack was assumed by Julian himself, who seemed to place his whole dependence in the military engines which he erected against the walls; while he secretly contrived a more efficacious method of introducing his troops into the heart of the city. Under the direction of Nevitta and Dagalaiphus, the trenches were opened at a considerable distance, and gradually prolonged as far as the edge of the ditch. The ditch was speedily filled with earth; and, by the incessant labour of the troops, a mine was carried under the foundations of the walls, and sustained, at sufficient intervals, by props of timber. Three chosen cohorts, advancing in a single file, silently explored the dark and dangerous passage; till their intrepid leader whispered back the intelligence, that he was ready to issue from his confinement into the streets of the hostile city. Julian checked their ardour, that he might ensure their success; and immediately diverted the attention of the garrison, by the tumult and clamour of a general assault. The Persians, who, from their walls, contemptuously beheld the progress of an impotent attack, celebrated, with songs of triumph, the glory of Sapor; and ventured to assure the emperor, that he might ascend the starry mansion of Ormusd, before he could hope to take the impregnable city of Maogamalcha. The city was already taken. History has recorded the name of a private soldier, the first who ascended from the mine into a deserted tower. The passage was widened by his companions, who pressed forwards with impatient valour. Fifteen hundred enemies were already in the midst of the city. The astonished garrison abandoned the walls, and their only hope of safety; the gates were instantly burst open; and the revenge of the soldier, unless it were suspended by lust or avarice, was satiated by an undistinguishing massacre. The governor, who had yielded on a promise of mercy, was burnt alive, a few days afterwards, on a charge of having uttered some disrespectful words against the honour of Prince Hormisdas. The fortifications were razed to the ground; and not a vestige was left, that

the city of Maogamàlcha had ever existed. The neighbourhood of the
capital of Persia was adorned with three stately palaces, laboriously enriched
with every production that could gratify the luxury and pride of an Eastern
monarch. The pleasant situation of the gardens along the banks of the
Tigris, was improved, according to the Persian taste, by the symmetry of
flowers, fountains, and shady walks: and spacious parks were inclosed for
the reception of the bears, lions, and wild boars, which were maintained
at a considerable expence for the pleasure of the royal chace. The park-walls
were broke down, the savage game was abandoned to the darts of the
soldiers, and the palaces of Sapor were reduced to ashes, by the command
of the Roman emperor. Julian, on this occasion, shewed himself ignorant,
or careless, of the laws of civility, which the prudence and refinement of
polished ages have established between hostile princes. Yet these wanton
ravages need not excite in our breasts any vehement emotions of pity or
resentment. A simple, naked, statue, finished by the hand of a Grecian
artist, is of more genuine value than all these rude and costly monuments
of Barbaric labour: and, if we are more deeply affected by the ruin of a
palace, than by the conflagration of a cottage, our humanity must have
formed a very erroneous estimate of the miseries of human life.[57]

Personal behaviour of Julian.   Julian was an object of terror and hatred to the Persians: and the
painters of that nation represented the invader of their country
under the emblem of a furious lion, who vomited from his mouth
a consuming fire.[58] To his friends and soldiers, the philosophic
hero appeared in a more amiable light; and his virtues were never more
conspicuously displayed, than in the last, and most active, period of his life.
He practised, without effort, and almost without merit, the habitual qualities
of temperance and sobriety. According to the dictates of that artificial
wisdom, which assumes an absolute dominion over the mind and body,
he sternly refused himself the indulgence of the most natural appetites.[59]
In the warm climate of Assyria, which solicited a luxurious people to the
gratification of every sensual desire,[60] a youthful conqueror preserved his

---

57. The operations of the Assyrian war are
circumstantially related by Ammianus (xxiv.
2, 3, 4, 5.), Libanius (Orat. Parent. c. 112–
123. p. 335–347.), Zosimus (l. iii. p. 168–
180.), and Gregory Nazianzen (Orat. iv.
p. 113. 144.). The *military* criticisms of the
saint are devoutly copied by Tillemont, his
faithful slave.

58. Libanius de ulciscendâ Juliani nece, c. 13.
p. 162.

59. The famous examples of Cyrus, Alexander, and Scipio, were acts of justice. Julian's
chastity was voluntary, and, in his opinion,
meritorious.

60. Sallust (ap. Vet. Scholiast. Juvenal. Satir. i.
104.) observes, that nihil corruptius moribus.

chastity pure and inviolate: nor was Julian ever tempted, even by a motive of curiosity, to visit his female captives of exquisite beauty,[61] who, instead of resisting his power, would have disputed with each other the honour of his embraces. With the same firmness that he resisted the allurements of love, he sustained the hardships of war. When the Romans marched through the flat and flooded country, their sovereign, on foot, at the head of his legions, shared their fatigues, and animated their diligence. In every useful labour, the hand of Julian was prompt and strenuous; and the Imperial purple was wet and dirty, as the coarse garment of the meanest soldier. The two sieges allowed him some remarkable opportunities of signalising his personal valour, which, in the improved state of the military art, can seldom be exerted by a prudent general. The emperor stood before the citadel of Perisabor, insensible of his extreme danger, and encouraged his troops to burst open the gates of iron, till he was almost overwhelmed under a cloud of missile weapons, and huge stones, that were directed against his person. As he examined the exterior fortifications of Maogamalcha, two Persians, devoting themselves for their country, suddenly rushed upon him with drawn scimitars: the emperor dexterously received their blows on his uplifted shield; and, with a steady and well-aimed thrust, laid one of his adversaries dead at his feet. The esteem of a prince who possesses the virtues which he approves, is the noblest recompence of a deserving subject; and the authority which Julian derived from his personal merit, enabled him to revive and enforce the rigour of ancient discipline. He punished with death, or ignominy, the misbehaviour of three troops of horse, who, in a skirmish with the Surenas, had lost their honour, and one of their standards: and he distinguished with *obsidional*[62] crowns the valour of the foremost soldiers, who had ascended into the city of Maogamalcha. After the siege of Perisabor, the firmness of the emperor was exercised by the insolent

---

The matrons and virgins of Babylon freely mingled with the men, in licentious banquets: and as they felt the intoxication of wine and love, they gradually, and almost completely, threw aside the incumbrance of dress; ad ultimum ima corporum velamenta projiciunt. Q. Curtius, v. 1.

61. Ex virginibus autem, quæ speciosæ sunt captæ, et in Perside, ubi fœminarum pulchritudo excellit, nec contrectare aliquam voluit nec videre. Ammian. xxiv. 4. The native race

of Persians is small and ugly: but it has been improved, by the perpetual mixture of Circassian blood (Herodot. l. iii. c. 97. Buffon, Hist. Naturelle, tom. iii. p. 420.).

62. Obsidionalibus coronis donati. Ammian. xxiv. 4. Either Julian or his historian were unskilful antiquaries. He should have given *mural* crowns. The *obsidional* were the reward of a general who had delivered a besieged city (Aulus Gellius, Noct. Attic. v. 6.).

avarice of the army, who loudly complained, that their services were rewarded by a trifling donative of one hundred pieces of silver. His just indignation was expressed in the grave and manly language of a Roman. "Riches are the object of your desires? those riches are in the hands of the Persians; and the spoils of this fruitful country are proposed as the prize of your valour and discipline. Believe me," added Julian, "the Roman republic, which formerly possessed such immense treasures, is now reduced to want and wretchedness; since our princes have been persuaded, by weak and interested ministers, to purchase with gold the tranquillity of the Barbarians. The revenue is exhausted; the cities are ruined; the provinces are dispeopled. For myself, the only inheritance that I have received from my royal ancestors, is a soul incapable of fear; and as long as I am convinced that every real advantage is seated in the mind, I shall not blush to acknowledge an honourable poverty, which, in the days of ancient virtue, was considered as the glory of Fabricius. That glory, and that virtue, may be your own, if you will listen to the voice of Heaven, and of your leader. But if you will rashly persist, if you are determined to renew the shameful and mischievous examples of old seditions, proceed – As it becomes an emperor who has filled the first rank among men, I am prepared to die, standing; and to despise a precarious life, which, every hour, may depend on an accidental fever. If I have been found unworthy of the command, there are now among you (I speak it with pride and pleasure), there are many chiefs, whose merit and experience are equal to the conduct of the most important war. Such has been the temper of my reign, that I can retire, without regret, and without apprehension, to the obscurity of a private station."[63] The modest resolution of Julian was answered by the unanimous applause and cheerful obedience of the Romans; who declared their confidence of victory, while they fought under the banners of their heroic prince. Their courage was kindled by his frequent and familiar asseverations (for such wishes were the oaths of Julian), "So may I reduce the Persians under the yoke!" "Thus may I restore the strength and splendour of the republic!" The love of fame was the ardent passion of his soul: but it was not before he trampled on the ruins of Maogamalcha, that he allowed himself to say, "We have now provided some materials for the sophist of Antioch."[64]

63. I give this speech as original and genuine. Ammianus might hear, could transcribe, and was incapable of inventing, it. I have used some slight freedoms, and conclude with the most forcible sentence.

64. Ammian. xxiv. 3. Libanius, Orat. Parent. c. 122. p. 346.

The successful valour of Julian had triumphed over all the obstacles that opposed his march to the gates of Ctesiphon. But the reduction, or even the siege, of the capital of Persia, was still at a distance: nor can the military conduct of the emperor be clearly apprehended, without a knowledge of the country which was the theatre of his bold and skilful operations.[65] Twenty miles to the south of Bagdad, and on the eastern bank of the Tigris, the curiosity of travellers has observed some ruins of the palaces of Ctesiphon, which, in the time of Julian, was a great and populous city. The name and glory of the adjacent Seleucia were for ever extinguished; and the only remaining quarter of that Greek colony had resumed, with the Assyrian language and manners, the primitive appellation of Coche. Coche was situate on the western side of the Tigris; but it was naturally considered as a suburb of Ctesiphon, with which we may suppose it to have been connected by a permanent bridge of boats. The united parts contributed to form the common epithet of Al Modain, THE CITIES, which the Orientals have bestowed on the winter residence of the Sassanides; and the whole circumference of the Persian capital was strongly fortified by the waters of the river, by lofty walls, and by impracticable morasses. Near the ruins of Seleucia, the camp of Julian was fixed; and secured, by a ditch and rampart, against the sallies of the numerous and enterprising garrison of Coche. In this fruitful and pleasant country, the Romans were plentifully supplied with water and forage: and several forts, which might have embarrassed the motions of the army, submitted, after some resistance, to the efforts of their valour. The fleet passed from the Euphrates into an artificial derivation of that river, which pours a copious and navigable stream into the Tigris, at a small distance *below* the great city. If they had followed this royal canal, which bore the name of Nahar-Malcha,[66] the intermediate situation of Coche would have separated the fleet and army of Julian; and the rash attempt of steering against the current of the Tigris, and forcing their way through the midst of a hostile capital, must have been attended with the

He transports his fleet from the Euphrates to the Tigris.

65. M. d'Anville (Mem. de l'Academie des Inscriptions, tom. xxviii. p. 246–259.) has ascertained the true position and distance of Babylon, Seleucia, Ctesiphon, Bagdad, &c. The Roman traveller, Pietro della Valle (tom. i. lett. xvii. p. 650–780.), seems to be the most intelligent spectator of that famous province. He is a gentleman and a scholar,

but intolerably vain and prolix.

66. The Royal Canal (*Nahar-Malcha*) might be successively restored, altered, divided, &c. (Cellarius, Geograph. Antiq. tom. ii. p. 453.): and these changes may serve to explain the seeming contradictions of antiquity. In the time of Julian, it must have fallen into the Euphrates *below* Ctesiphon.

total destruction of the Roman navy. The prudence of the emperor foresaw the danger, and provided the remedy. As he had minutely studied the operations of Trajan in the same country, he soon recollected, that his warlike predecessor had dug a new and navigable canal, which, leaving Coche on the right-hand, conveyed the waters of the Nahar-Malcha into the river Tigris, at some distance *above* the cities. From the information of the peasants, Julian ascertained the vestiges of this ancient work, which were almost obliterated by design or accident. By the indefatigable labour of the soldiers, a broad and deep channel was speedily prepared for the reception of the Euphrates. A strong dike was constructed to interrupt the ordinary current of the Nahar-Malcha: a flood of waters rushed impetuously into their new bed; and the Roman fleet, steering their triumphant course into the Tigris, derided the vain and ineffectual barriers which the Persians of Ctesiphon had erected to oppose their passage.

Passage of the Tigris, and victory of the Romans.

As it became necessary to transport the Roman army over the Tigris, another labour presented itself, of less toil, but of more danger, than the preceding expedition. The stream was broad and rapid; the ascent steep and difficult; and the intrenchments which had been formed on the ridge of the opposite bank, were lined with a numerous army of heavy cuirassiers, dexterous archers, and huge elephants; who (according to the extravagant hyperbole of Libanius) could trample, with the same ease, a field of corn, or a legion of Romans.[67] In the presence of such an enemy, the construction of a bridge was impracticable; and the intrepid prince, who instantly seized the only possible expedient, concealed his design, till the moment of execution, from the knowledge of the Barbarians, of his own troops, and even of his generals themselves. Under the specious pretence of examining the state of the magazines, fourscore vessels were gradually unladen; and a select detachment, apparently destined for some secret expedition, was ordered to stand to their arms on the first signal. Julian disguised the silent anxiety of his own mind with smiles of confidence and joy; and amused the hostile nations with the spectacle of military games, which he insultingly celebrated under the walls of Coche. The day was consecrated to pleasure; but, as soon as the hour of supper was past, the emperor summoned the generals to his tent; and acquainted them, that he had fixed that night for

---

67. Καιμεγεθεσιν ελεφαντων, οις ισον εργον δια σταχυων ελθειν, και φαλαγγος. Rien n'est beau que le vrai; a maxim which should be inscribed on the desk of every rhetorician.

the passage of the Tigris. They stood in silent and respectful astonishment; but, when the venerable Sallust assumed the privilege of his age and experience, the rest of the chiefs supported with freedom the weight of his prudent remonstrances.[68] Julian contented himself with observing, that conquest and safety depended on the attempt; that, instead of diminishing, the number of their enemies would be increased, by successive reinforcements; and that a longer delay would neither contract the breadth of the stream, nor level the height of the bank. The signal was instantly given, and obeyed: the most impatient of the legionaries leaped into five vessels that lay nearest to the bank; and, as they plied their oars with intrepid diligence, they were lost, after a few moments, in the darkness of the night. A flame arose on the opposite side; and Julian, who too clearly understood that his foremost vessels, in attempting to land, had been fired by the enemy, dexterously converted their extreme danger into a presage of victory. "Our fellow-soldiers," he eagerly exclaimed, "are already masters of the bank; see – they make the appointed signal: let us hasten to emulate and assist their courage." The united and rapid motion of a great fleet broke the violence of the current, and they reached the eastern shore of the Tigris with sufficient speed to extinguish the flames, and rescue their adventurous companions. The difficulties of a steep and lofty ascent were increased by the weight of armour, and the darkness of the night. A shower of stones, darts, and fire, was incessantly discharged on the heads of the assailants; who, after an arduous struggle, climbed the bank, and stood victorious upon the rampart. As soon as they possessed a more equal field, Julian, who, with his light-infantry, had led the attack,[69] darted through the ranks a skilful and experienced eye: his bravest soldiers, according to the precepts of Homer,[70] were distributed in the front and rear; and all the trumpets of the Imperial army sounded to battle. The Romans, after sending up a military shout, advanced in measured steps to the animating notes of martial music; launched their formidable javelins; and rushed forwards with drawn swords, to deprive the Barbarians, by a closer onset, of the advantage

---

68. Libanius alludes to the most powerful of the generals. I have ventured to name *Sallust*. Ammianus says, of all the leaders, quôd acri metû territi duces concordi precatû fieri prohibere tentarent.

69. Hinc Imperator ... (says Ammianus) ipse cum levis armaturæ auxiliis per prima postremaque discurrens, &c. Yet Zosimus, his friend, does not allow him to pass the river till two days after the battle.

70. Secundum Homericam dispositionem. A similar disposition is ascribed to the wise Nestor, in the fourth book of the Iliad: and Homer was never absent from the mind of Julian.

of their missile weapons. The whole engagement lasted above twelve hours; till the gradual retreat of the Persians was changed into a disorderly flight, of which the shameful example was given by the principal leaders, and the Surenas himself. They were pursued to the gates of Ctesiphon; and the conquerors might have entered the dismayed city,[71] if their general Victor, who was dangerously wounded with an arrow, had not conjured them to desist from a rash attempt, which must be fatal, if it were not successful. On *their* side, the Romans acknowledged the loss of only seventy-five men; while they affirmed, that the Barbarians had left on the field of battle two thousand five hundred, or even six thousand, of their bravest soldiers. The spoil was such as might be expected from the riches and luxury of an Oriental camp; large quantities of silver and gold, splendid arms and trappings, and beds and tables of massy silver. The victorious emperor distributed, as the rewards of valour, some honourable gifts, civic, and mural, and naval, crowns; which he, and perhaps he alone, esteemed more precious than the wealth of Asia. A solemn sacrifice was offered to the god of war, but the appearances of the victims threatened the most inauspicious events; and Julian soon discovered, by less ambiguous signs, that he had now reached the term of his prosperity.[72]

Situation and obstinacy of Julian, A.D. 363. June.   On the second day after the battle, the domestic guards, the Jovians and Herculians, and the remaining troops, which composed near two-thirds of the whole army, were securely wafted over the Tigris.[73] While the Persians beheld from the walls of Ctesiphon the desolation of the adjacent country, Julian cast many an anxious look towards the North, in full expectation, that as he himself had victoriously penetrated to the capital of Sapor, the march and junction of his lieutenants, Sebastian and Procopius, would be

---

71. Persas terrore subito miscuerunt, versisque agminibus totius gentis, apertas Ctesiphontis portas victor miles intrâsset, ni major prædarum occasio fuisset, quam cura victoriæ (Sextus Rufus de Provinciis, c. 28.). Their avarice might dispose them to hear the advice of Victor.

72. The labour of the canal, the passage of the Tigris, and the victory, are described by Ammianus (xxiv. 5, 6.), Libanius (Orat. Parent. c. 124–128. p. 347–353.), Greg. Nazianzen (Orat. iv. p. 115.), Zosimus (l. iii.

p. 181–183.), and Sextus Rufus (de Provinciis, c. 28.).

73. The fleet and army were formed in three divisions, of which the first only had passed during the night (Ammian. xxiv. 6.). The πασῃ δορυφορια, whom Zosimus transports on the third day (l. iii. p. 183.), might consist of the protectors, among whom the historian Ammianus, and the future emperor Jovian, actually served; some *schools* of the *domestics*, and perhaps the Jovians and Herculians, who often did duty as guards.

executed with the same courage and diligence. His expectations were disappointed by the treachery of the Armenian king, who permitted, and most probably directed, the desertion of his auxiliary troops from the camp of the Romans;[74] and by the dissentions of the two generals, who were incapable of forming or executing any plan for the public service. When the emperor had relinquished the hope of this important reinforcement, he condescended to hold a council of war, and approved, after a full debate, the sentiment of those generals, who dissuaded the siege of Ctesiphon, as a fruitless and pernicious undertaking. It is not easy for us to conceive, by what arts of fortification, a city thrice besieged and taken by the predecessors of Julian, could be rendered impregnable against an army of sixty thousand Romans, commanded by a brave and experienced general, and abundantly supplied with ships, provisions, battering engines, and military stores. But we may rest assured, from the love of glory, and contempt of danger, which formed the character of Julian, that he was not discouraged by any trivial or imaginary obstacles.[75] At the very time when he declined the siege of Ctesiphon, he rejected, with obstinacy and disdain, the most flattering offers of a negociation of peace. Sapor, who had been so long accustomed to the tardy ostentation of Constantius, was surprised by the intrepid diligence of his successor. As far as the confines of India and Scythia, the satraps of the distant provinces were ordered to assemble their troops, and to march, without delay, to the assistance of their monarch. But their preparations were dilatory, their motions slow; and before Sapor could lead an army into the field, he received the melancholy intelligence of the devastation of Assyria, the ruin of his palaces, and the slaughter of his bravest troops, who defended the passage of the Tigris. The pride of royalty was humbled in the dust; he took his repasts on the ground; and the disorder of his hair expressed the grief and anxiety of his mind. Perhaps he would not have refused to purchase, with one half of his kingdom, the safety of the remainder; and he would have gladly subscribed himself, in a treaty of peace, the faithful and dependent ally of the Roman conqueror. Under

---

74. Moses of Chorene (Hist. Armen. l. iii. c. 15. p. 246.) supplies us with a national tradition, and a spurious letter. I have borrowed only the leading circumstance, which is consistent with truth, probability, and Libanius (Orat. Parent. c. 131. p. 355.).

75. Civitas inexpugnabilis, facinus audax et importunum. Ammianus, xxiv. 7. His fellow-soldier, Eutropius, turns aside from the difficulty, Assyriamque populatus, castra apud Ctesiphontem stativa aliquandiu habuit: remeansque victor, &c. x. 16. Zosimus is artful or ignorant, and Socrates inaccurate.

the pretence of private business, a minister of rank and confidence was secretly dispatched to embrace the knees of Hormisdas, and to request, in the language of a suppliant, that he might be introduced into the presence of the emperor. The Sassanian prince, whether he listened to the voice of pride or humanity, whether he consulted the sentiments of his birth, or the duties of his situation, was equally inclined to promote a salutary measure, which would terminate the calamities of Persia, and secure the triumph of Rome. He was astonished by the inflexible firmness of a hero, who remembered, most unfortunately for himself, and for his country, that Alexander had uniformly rejected the propositions of Darius. But as Julian was sensible, that the hope of a safe and honourable peace might cool the ardour of his troops; he earnestly requested, that Hormisdas would privately dismiss the minister of Sapor, and conceal this dangerous temptation from the knowledge of the camp.[76]

He burns his fleet,   The honour, as well as interest, of Julian, forbade him to consume his time under the impregnable walls of Ctesiphon; and as often as he defied the Barbarians, who defended the city, to meet him on the open plain, they prudently replied, that if he desired to exercise his valour, he might seek the army of the Great King. He felt the insult, and he accepted the advice. Instead of confining his servile march to the banks of the Euphrates and Tigris, he resolved to imitate the adventurous spirit of Alexander, and boldly to advance into the inland provinces, till he forced his rival to contend with him, perhaps in the plains of Arbela, for the empire of Asia. The magnanimity of Julian was applauded and betrayed, by the arts of a noble Persian, who, in the cause of his country, had generously submitted to act a part full of danger, of falsehood, and of shame.[77] With a train of faithful followers, he deserted to the Imperial camp; exposed, in a specious tale, the injuries which he had sustained; exaggerated the cruelty of Sapor, the discontent of the people, and the weakness of the monarchy, and confidently offered himself as the hostage and guide of the Roman march. The most rational grounds of suspicion

76. Libanius, Orat. Parent. c. 130. p. 354. c. 139. p. 361. Socrates, l. iii. c. 21. The ecclesiastical historian imputes the refusal of peace to the advice of Maximus. Such advice was unworthy of a philosopher; but the philosopher was likewise a magician, who flattered the hopes and passions of his master.
77. The arts of this new Zopyrus (Greg. Nazi-anzen, Orat. iv. p. 115, 116.) may derive some credit from the testimony of two abbreviators (Sextus Rufus and Victor), and the casual hints of Libanius (Orat. Parent. c. 134. p. 357.) and Ammianus (xxiv. 7.). The course of genuine history is interrupted by a most unseasonable chasm in the text of Ammianus.

were urged, without effect, by the wisdom and experience of Hormisdas; and the credulous Julian, receiving the traitor into his bosom, was persuaded to issue an hasty order, which, in the opinion of mankind, appeared to arraign his prudence, and to endanger his safety. He destroyed, in a single hour, the whole navy, which had been transported above five hundred miles, at so great an expence of toil, of treasure, and of blood. Twelve, or, at the most, twenty-two, small vessels were saved, to accompany, on carriages, the march of the army, and to form occasional bridges for the passage of the rivers. A supply of twenty days provisions was reserved for the use of the soldiers; and the rest of the magazines, with a fleet of eleven hundred vessels, which rode at anchor in the Tigris, were abandoned to the flames, by the absolute command of the emperor. The Christian bishops, Gregory and Augustin, insult the madness of the apostate, who executed, with his own hands, the sentence of divine justice. Their authority, of less weight, perhaps, in a military question, is confirmed by the cool judgment of an experienced soldier, who was himself spectator of the conflagration, and who could not disapprove the reluctant murmurs of the troops.[78] Yet there are not wanting some specious, and perhaps solid, reasons, which might justify the resolution of Julian. The navigation of the Euphrates never ascended above Babylon, nor that of the Tigris above Opis.[79] The distance of the last-mentioned city from the Roman camp was not very considerable; and Julian must soon have renounced the vain and impracticable attempt of forcing upwards a great fleet against the stream of a rapid river,[80] which in several places was embarrassed by natural or artificial cataracts.[81] The power of sails and oars was insufficient; it became necessary to tow the ships against the current of the river; the strength of twenty thousand soldiers was exhausted in this tedious and servile labour; and if the Romans continued to march along the banks of the Tigris, they could

78. See Ammianus (xxiv. 7.), Libanius (Orat. Parentalis, c. 132, 133. p. 356, 357.), Zosimus (l. iii, p. 183.), Zonaras (tom. ii. l. xiii. p. 26.), Gregory (Orat. iv. p. 116.), Augustin de Civitate Dei, l. iv. c. 29. l. v. c. 21.). Of these, Libanius alone attempts a faint apology for his hero; who, according to Ammianus, pronounced his own condemnation, by a tardy and ineffectual attempt to extinguish the flames.

79. Consult Herodotus (l. i. c. 194.), Strabo

(l. xvi. p. 1074.), and Tavernier (p. i. l. ii. p. 152.).

80. A celeritate Tigris incipit vocari, ita appellant Medi sagittam. Plin. Hist. Natur. vi. 31.

81. One of these dykes, which produces an artificial cascade or cataract, is described by Tavernier (part i. l. ii. p. 226.) and Thevenot (part ii. l. i. p. 193.). The Persians, or Assyrians, laboured to interrupt the navigation of the river (Strabo, l. xv. p. 1075. D'Anville, l'Euphrate et le Tigre, p. 98, 99.).

only expect to return home without atchieving any enterprize worthy of the genius or fortune of their leader. If, on the contrary, it was advisable to advance into the inland country, the destruction of the fleet and magazines was the only measure which could save that valuable prize from the hands of the numerous and active troops which might suddenly be poured from the gates of Ctesiphon. Had the arms of Julian been victorious, we should now admire the conduct, as well as the courage, of a hero, who, by depriving his soldiers of the hopes of a retreat, left them only the alternative of death or conquest.[82]

and marches against Sapor. The cumbersome train of artillery and waggons, which retards the operations of a modern army, were in a great measure unknown in the camps of the Romans.[83] Yet, in every age, the subsistence of sixty thousand men must have been one of the most important cares of a prudent general; and that subsistence could only be drawn from his own or from the enemy's country. Had it been possible for Julian to maintain a bridge of communication on the Tigris, and to preserve the conquered places of Assyria, a desolated province could not afford any large or regular supplies, in a season of the year when the lands were covered by the inundation of the Euphrates,[84] and the unwholesome air was darkened with swarms of innumerable insects.[85] The appearance of the hostile country was far more inviting. The extensive region that lies between the river Tigris and the mountains of Media, was filled with villages and towns; and the fertile soil, for the most part, was in a very improved state of cultivation. Julian might expect, that a conqueror, who possessed the two forcible instruments of persuasion, steel and gold, would easily procure a plentiful subsistence from the fears or avarice of the natives. But, on the approach of the Romans, this rich and smiling prospect was instantly blasted. Wher-

82. Recollect the successful and applauded rashness of Agathocles and Cortez, who burnt their ships on the coast of Africa and Mexico.

83. See the judicious reflections of the author of the Essai sur la Tactique, tom. ii. p. 287–353, and the learned remarks of M. Guichardt, Nouveaux Memoires Militaires, tom. i. p. 351–382. on the baggage and subsistence of the Roman armies.

84. The Tigris rises to the south, the Euphrates to the north, of the Armenian mountains. The former overflows in March, the latter in July. These circumstances are well explained in the Geographical Dissertation of Foster, inserted in Spelman's Expedition of Cyrus, vol. ii. p. 26.

85. Ammianus (xxiv. 8.) describes, as he had felt, the inconveniency of the flood, the heat, and the insects. The lands of Assyria, oppressed by the Turks, and ravaged by the Curds, or Arabs, yield an increase of ten, fifteen, and twenty fold, for the seed which is cast into the ground by the wretched and unskilful husbandman. Voyages de Niebuhr, tom. ii. p. 279. 285.

ever they moved, the inhabitants deserted the open villages, and took shelter in the fortified towns; the cattle was driven away; the grass and ripe corn were consumed with fire; and, as soon as the flames had subsided which interrupted the march of Julian, he beheld the melancholy face of a smoking and naked desert. This desperate but effectual method of defence, can only be executed by the enthusiasm of a people who prefer their independence to their property; or by the rigour of an arbitrary government, which consults the public safety without submitting to their inclinations the liberty of choice. On the present occasion, the zeal and obedience of the Persians seconded the commands of Sapor; and the emperor was soon reduced to the scanty stock of provisions, which continually wasted in his hands. Before they were entirely consumed he might still have reached the wealthy and unwarlike cities of Ecbatana, or Susa, by the effort of a rapid and well-directed march;[86] but he was deprived of this last resource by his ignorance of the roads, and by the perfidy of his guides. The Romans wandered several days in the country to the eastward of Bagdad: the Persian deserter, who had artfully led them into the snare, escaped from their resentment: and his followers, as soon as they were put to the torture, confessed the secret of the conspiracy. The visionary conquests of Hyrcania and India, which had so long amused, now tormented, the mind of Julian. Conscious that his own imprudence was the cause of the public distress, he anxiously balanced the hopes of safety or success, without obtaining a satisfactory answer either from gods or men. At length, as the only practicable measure, he embraced the resolution of directing his steps towards the banks of the Tigris, with the design of saving the army by a hasty march to the confines of Corduene; a fertile and friendly province, which acknowledged the sovereignty of Rome. The desponding troops obeyed the signal of the retreat, only seventy days after they had passed the Chaboras, with the sanguine expectation of subverting the throne of Persia.[87]

June 16.

---

86. Isidore of Charax (Mansion. Parthic. p. 5, 6. in Hudson, Geograph. Minor. tom. ii.) reckons 129 schæni from Seleucia, and Thevenot (part i. l. i. ii. p. 209–245.), 128 hours of march from Bagdad to Ecbatana, or Hamadan. These measures cannot exceed an ordinary parasang, or three Roman miles.

87. The march of Julian from Ctesiphon, is circumstantially, but not clearly, described by Ammianus (xxiv. 7, 8.), Libanius (Orat. Parent. c. 134. p. 357.), and Zosimus (l. iii. p. 183.). The two last seem ignorant that their conqueror was retreating; and Libanius absurdly confines him to the banks of the Tigris.

Retreat and distress of the Roman army. As long as the Romans seemed to advance into the country, their march was observed and insulted from a distance, by several bodies of Persian cavalry; who shewing themselves, sometimes in loose, and sometimes in closer, order, faintly skirmished with the advanced guards. These detachments were, however, supported by a much greater force; and the heads of the columns were no sooner pointed towards the Tigris, than a cloud of dust arose on the plain. The Romans, who now aspired only to the permission of a safe and speedy retreat, endeavoured to persuade themselves, that this formidable appearance was occasioned by a troop of wild asses, or perhaps by the approach of some friendly Arabs. They halted, pitched their tents, fortified their camp, passed the whole night in continual alarms; and discovered, at the dawn of day, that they were surrounded by an army of Persians. This army, which might be considered only as the van of the Barbarians, was soon followed by the main body of cuirassiers, archers, and elephants, commanded by Meranes, a general of rank and reputation. He was accompanied by two of the king's sons, and many of the principal satraps; and fame and expectation exaggerated the strength of the remaining powers, which slowly advanced under the conduct of Sapor himself. As the Romans continued their march, their long array, which was forced to bend or divide, according to the varieties of the ground, afforded frequent and favourable opportunities to their vigilant enemies. The Persians repeatedly charged with fury; they were repeatedly repulsed with firmness; and the action at Maronga, which almost deserved the name of a battle, was marked by a considerable loss of satraps and elephants, perhaps of equal value in the eyes of their monarch. These splendid advantages were not obtained without an adequate slaughter on the side of the Romans: several officers of distinction were either killed or wounded; and the emperor himself, who, on all occasions of danger, inspired and guided the valour of his troops, was obliged to expose his person, and exert his abilities. The weight of offensive and defensive arms, which still constituted the strength and safety of the Romans, disabled them from making any long or effectual pursuit; and as the horsemen of the East were trained to dart their javelins, and shoot their arrows, at full speed, and in every possible direction,[88] the cavalry of Persia was never more formidable

---

88. Chardin, the most judicious of modern travellers, describes (tom. iii. p. 57, 58, &c. edit. in 4to.) the education and dexterity of the Persian horsemen. Brissonius (de Regno Persico, p. 650. 661, &c.) has collected the testimonies of antiquity.

than in the moment of a rapid and disorderly flight. But the most certain and irreparable loss of the Romans, was that of time. The hardy veterans, accustomed to the cold climate of Gaul and Germany, fainted under the sultry heat of an Assyrian summer; their vigour was exhausted by the incessant repetition of march and combat; and the progress of the army was suspended by the precautions of a slow and dangerous retreat, in the presence of an active enemy. Every day, every hour, as the supply diminished, the value and price of subsistence increased in the Roman camp.[89] Julian, who always contented himself with such food as a hungry soldier would have disdained, distributed, for the use of the troops, the provisions of the Imperial household, and whatever could be spared from the sumpter-horses of the tribunes and generals. But this feeble relief served only to aggravate the sense of the public distress; and the Romans began to entertain the most gloomy apprehensions, that before they could reach the frontiers of the empire, they should all perish, either by famine, or by the sword of the Barbarians.[90]

While Julian struggled with the almost insuperable difficulties of his situation, the silent hours of the night were still devoted to study and contemplation. Whenever he closed his eyes in short and interrupted slumbers, his mind was agitated with painful anxiety; nor can it be thought surprising, that the Genius of the empire should once more appear before him, covering with a funereal veil, his head, and his horn of abundance, and slowly retiring from the Imperial tent. The monarch started from his couch, and stepping forth, to refresh his wearied spirits with the coolness of the midnight air, he beheld a fiery meteor, which shot athwart the sky, and suddenly vanished. Julian was convinced that he had seen the menacing countenance of the god of war;[91] the council which he

Julian is mortally wounded.

---

89. In Mark Antony's retreat, an Attic chænix sold for fifty drachmæ, or, in other words, a pound of flour for twelve or fourteen shillings: barley-bread was sold for its weight in silver. It is impossible to peruse the interesting narrative of Plutarch (tom. v. p. 102–116.), without perceiving that Mark Antony and Julian were pursued by the same enemies, and involved in the same distress.

90. Ammian. xxiv. 8. xxv. 1. Zosimus. l. iii. p. 184, 185, 186. Libanius, Orat. Parent. c. 134, 135. p. 357, 358, 359. The sophist of Antioch appears ignorant that the troops were hungry.

91. Ammian. xxv. 2. Julian had sworn in a passion, nunquam se Marti sacra facturum (xxiv. 6.). Such whimsical quarrels were not uncommon between the gods and their insolent votaries; and even the prudent Augustus, after his fleet had been twice shipwrecked, excluded Neptune from the honours of public professions. See Hume's Philosophical Reflections. Essays, vol. ii. p. 418.

summoned, of Tuscan Haruspices,[92] unanimously pronounced that he should abstain from action: but on this occasion, necessity and reason were more prevalent than superstition; and the trumpets sounded at the break of day. The army marched through a hilly country; and the hills had been secretly occupied by the Persians. Julian led the van, with the skill and attention of a consummate general; he was alarmed by the intelligence that his rear was suddenly attacked. The heat of the weather had tempted him to lay aside his cuirass; but he snatched a shield from one of his attendants, and hastened, with a sufficient reinforcement, to the relief of the rear-guard. A similar danger recalled the intrepid prince to the defence of the front; and as he galloped between the columns, the centre of the left was attacked, and almost overpowered, by a furious charge of the Persian cavalry and elephants. This huge body was soon defeated, by the well-timed evolution of the light-infantry, who aimed their weapons, with dexterity and effect, against the backs of the horsemen, and the legs of the elephants. The Barbarians fled; and Julian, who was foremost in every danger, animated the pursuit with his voice and gestures. His trembling guards, scattered and oppressed by the disorderly throng of friends and enemies, reminded their fearless sovereign that he was without armour; and conjured him to decline the fall of the impending ruin. As they exclaimed,[93] a cloud of darts and arrows was discharged from the flying squadrons; and a javelin, after razing the skin of his arm, transpierced the ribs, and fixed in the inferior part of the liver. Julian attempted to draw the deadly weapon from his side; but his fingers were cut by the sharpness of the steel, and he fell senseless from his horse. His guards flew to his relief; and the wounded emperor was gently raised from the ground, and conveyed out of the tumult of the battle into an adjacent tent. The report of the melancholy event passed from rank to rank; but the grief of the Romans inspired them with invincible valour, and the desire of revenge. The bloody and obstinate conflict was maintained by the two armies till they were separated by the total darkness of the night. The Persians derived some honour from the advantage which they obtained against the left wing, where Anatolius, master of the offices, was slain, and

---

92. They still retained the monopoly of the vain, but lucrative, science, which had been invented in Hetruria, and professed to derive their knowledge of signs and omens, from the ancient books of Tarquitius, a Tuscan sage.

93. Clamabant hinc inde *candidati* (see the note of Valesius) quos disjecerat terror, ut fugientium molem tanquam ruinam male compositi culminis declinaret. Ammian. xxv. 3.

the præfect Sallust very narrowly escaped. But the event of the day was adverse to the Barbarians. They abandoned the field; their two generals, Meranes, and Nohordates,[94] fifty nobles or satraps, and a multitude of their bravest soldiers: and the success of the Romans, if Julian had survived, might have been improved into a decisive and useful victory.

The first words that Julian uttered, after his recovery from the fainting fit, into which he had been thrown by loss of blood, were expressive of his martial spirit. He called for his horse and arms, and was impatient to rush into the battle. His remaining strength was exhausted by the painful effort; and the surgeons, *The death of Julian, A.D. 363. June 26.* who examined his wound, discovered the symptoms of approaching death. He employed the awful moments with the firm temper of a hero and a sage; the philosophers who had accompanied him in this fatal expedition, compared the tent of Julian with the prison of Socrates; and the spectators, whom duty, or friendship, or curiosity, had assembled round his couch, listened with respectful grief to the funeral oration of their dying emperor.[95] "Friends and fellow-soldiers, the seasonable period of my departure is now arrived, and I discharge, with the cheerfulness of a ready debtor, the demands of nature. I have learned from philosophy, how much the soul is more excellent than the body; and that the separation of the nobler substance, should be the subject of joy, rather than of affliction. I have learned from religion, that an early death has often been the reward of piety;[96] and I accept, as a favour of the gods, the mortal stroke, that secures me from the danger of disgracing a character, which has hitherto been supported by virtue and fortitude. I die without remorse, as I have lived without guilt. I am pleased to reflect on the innocence of my private life; and I can affirm with confidence, that the supreme authority, that emanation of the Divine Power, has been preserved in my hands pure and immaculate. Detesting the corrupt and destructive maxims of despotism, I have considered the

94. Sapor himself declared to the Romans, that it was his practice, to comfort the families of his deceased satraps, by sending them, as a present, the heads of the guards and officers who had not fallen by their master's side. Libanius, de nece Julian. ulcis. c. xiii. p. 163.
95. The character and situation of Julian might countenance the suspicion, that he had previously composed the elaborate oration, which Ammianus heard, and has transcribed.

The version of the Abbé de la Bleterie is faithful and elegant. I have followed him in expressing the Platonic idea of emanations, which is darkly insinuated in the original.
96. Herodotus (l. i. c. 31.) has displayed that doctrine in an agreeable tale. Yet the Jupiter (in the 16th book of the Iliad), who laments with tears of blood the death of Sarpedon his son, had a very imperfect notion of happiness or glory beyond the grave.

happiness of the people as the end of government. Submitting my actions to the laws of prudence, of justice, and of moderation, I have trusted the event to the care of Providence. Peace was the object of my counsels, as long as peace was consistent with the public welfare; but when the imperious voice of my country summoned me to arms, I exposed my person to the dangers of war, with the clear fore-knowledge (which I had acquired from the art of divination) that I was destined to fall by the sword. I now offer my tribute of gratitude to the Eternal Being, who has not suffered me to perish by the cruelty of a tyrant, by the secret dagger of conspiracy, or by the slow tortures of lingering disease. He has given me, in the midst of an honourable career, a splendid and glorious departure from this world; and I hold it equally absurd, equally base, to solicit, or to decline, the stroke of fate. – Thus much I have attempted to say; but my strength fails me, and I feel the approach of death. – I shall cautiously refrain from any word that may tend to influence your suffrages in the election of an emperor. My choice might be imprudent, or injudicious; and if it should not be ratified by the consent of the army, it might be fatal to the person whom I should recommend. I shall only, as a good citizen, express my hopes, that the Romans may be blessed with the government of a virtuous sovereign." After this discourse, which Julian pronounced in a firm and gentle tone of voice, he distributed, by a military testament,[97] the remains of his private fortune; and making some enquiry why Anatolius was not present, he understood, from the answer of Sallust, that Anatolius was killed; and bewailed, with amiable inconsistency, the loss of his friend. At the same time he reproved the immoderate grief of the spectators; and conjured them not to disgrace, by unmanly tears, the fate of a prince, who in a few moments would be united with heaven, and with the stars.[98] The spectators were silent; and Julian entered into a metaphysical argument with the philosophers Priscus and Maximus, on the nature of the soul. The efforts which he made, of mind, as well as body, most probably hastened his death. His wound began to bleed with fresh violence; his respiration was

---

97. The soldiers who made their verbal, or nuncupatory, testaments upon actual service (in procinctû) were exempted from the formalities of the Roman law. See Heineccius (Antiquit. Jur. Roman. tom. i. p. 504.) and Montesquieu (Esprit des Loix, l. xxvii.).
98. This union of the human soul with the divine ætherial substance of the universe, is the ancient doctrine of Pythagoras and Plato; but it seems to exclude any personal or conscious immortality. See Warburton's learned and rational observations. Divine Legation, vol. ii. p. 199–216.

embarrassed by the swelling of the veins: he called for a draught of cold water, and, as soon as he had drank it, expired without pain, about the hour of midnight. Such was the end of that extraordinary man, in the thirty-second year of his age, after a reign of one year and about eight months, from the death of Constantius. In his last moments he displayed, perhaps with some ostentation, the love of virtue and of fame, which had been the ruling passions of his life.[99]

The triumph of Christianity, and the calamities of the empire, may, in some measure, be ascribed to Julian himself, who had neglected to secure the future execution of his designs, by the timely and judicious nomination of an associate and successor. But the royal race of Constantius Chlorus was reduced to his own person, and if he entertained any serious thoughts of investing *Election of the emperor Jovian, A.D. 363, June 27.* with the purple the most worthy among the Romans, he was diverted from his resolution by the difficulty of the choice, the jealousy of power, the fear of ingratitude, and the natural presumption of health, of youth, and of prosperity. His unexpected death left the empire without a master, and without an heir, in a state of perplexity and danger, which, in the space of fourscore years, had never been experienced, since the election of Diocletian. In a government, which had almost forgotten the distinction of pure and noble blood, the superiority of birth was of little moment; the claims of official rank were accidental and precarious; and the candidates, who might aspire to ascend the vacant throne, could be supported only by the consciousness of personal merit, or by the hopes of popular favour. But the situation of a famished army, encompassed on all sides by an host of Barbarians, shortened the moments of grief and deliberation. In this scene of terror and distress, the body of the deceased prince, according to his own directions, was decently embalmed; and, at the dawn of day, the generals convened a military senate, at which the commanders of the legions, and the officers, both of cavalry and infantry, were invited to assist. Three or four hours of the night had not passed away without some secret cabals; and when the election of an emperor was proposed, the spirit of faction began to agitate the assembly. Victor and Arinthæus collected the remains of the court of Constantius; the friends of Julian attached

---

99. The whole relation of the death of Julian is given by Ammianus (xxv. 3.), an intelligent spectator. Libanius, who turns with horror from the scene, has supplied some circum- stances (Orat. Parental. c. 136–140. p. 359– 362.). The calumnies of Gregory, and the legends of more recent saints, may now be *silently* despised.

themselves to the Gallic chiefs, Dagalaiphus and Nevitta; and the most fatal consequences might be apprehended from the discord of two factions, so opposite in their character and interest, in their maxims of government, and perhaps in their religious principles. The superior virtues of Sallust could alone reconcile their divisions, and unite their suffrages; and the venerable præfect would immediately have been declared the successor of Julian, if he himself, with sincere and modest firmness, had not alleged his age and infirmities, so unequal to the weight of the diadem. The generals, who were surprised and perplexed by his refusal, shewed some disposition to adopt the salutary advice of an inferior officer,[100] that they should act as they would have acted in the absence of the emperor; that they should exert their abilities to extricate the army from the present distress; and, if they were fortunate enough to reach the confines of Mesopotamia, they should proceed with united and deliberate counsels in the election of a lawful sovereign. While they debated, a few voices saluted Jovian, who was no more than *first*[101] of the domestics, with the names of Emperor and Augustus. The tumultuary acclamation was instantly repeated by the guards who surrounded the tent, and passed, in a few minutes, to the extremities of the line. The new prince, astonished with his own fortune, was hastily invested with the Imperial ornaments, and received an oath of fidelity from the generals, whose favour and protection he so lately solicited. The strongest recommendation of Jovian was the merit of his father, Count Varronian, who enjoyed, in honourable retirement, the fruit of his long services. In the obscure freedom of a private station, the son indulged his taste for wine and women; yet he supported, with credit, the character of a Christian[102] and a soldier. Without being conspicuous for any of the ambitious qualifications which excite the admiration and envy of mankind, the comely person of Jovian, his cheerful temper, and familiar wit, had

---

100. Honoratior aliquis miles; perhaps Ammianus himself. The modest and judicious historian describes the scene of the election, at which he was undoubtedly present (xxv. 5.).

101. The *primus*, or *primicerius*, enjoyed the dignity of a senator; and though only a tribune, he ranked with the military dukes. Cod. Theodosian. l. vi. tit. xxiv. These privileges are perhaps more recent than the time of Jovian.

102. The ecclesiastical historians, Socrates

(l. iii. c. 22.), Sozomen (l. vi. c. 3.), and Theodoret (l. iv. c. 1.), ascribe to Jovian the merit of a confessor under the preceding reign; and piously suppose, that he refused the purple, till the whole army unanimously exclaimed that they were Christians. Ammianus, calmly pursuing his narrative, overthrows the legend by a single sentence. Hostiis pro Joviano extisque inspectis, pronuntiatum est, &c. xxv. 6.

gained the affection of his fellow-soldiers; and the generals of both parties acquiesced in a popular election, which had not been conducted by the arts of their enemies. The pride of this unexpected elevation was moderated by the just apprehension, that the same day might terminate the life and reign of the new emperor. The pressing voice of necessity was obeyed without delay; and the first orders issued by Jovian, a few hours after his predecessor had expired, were to prosecute a march, which could alone extricate the Romans from their actual distress.[103]

The esteem of an enemy is most sincerely expressed by his fears; and the degree of fear may be accurately measured by the joy with which he celebrates his deliverance. The welcome news of the death of Julian, which a deserter revealed to the camp of Sapor, inspired the desponding monarch with a sudden confidence of victory. He immediately detached the royal cavalry, perhaps the ten thousand *Immortals*,[104] to second and support the pursuit; and discharged the whole weight of his united forces on the rear-guard of the Romans. The rear-guard was thrown into disorder; the renowned legions, which derived their titles from Diocletian, and his warlike colleague, were broke and trampled down by the elephants; and three tribunes lost their lives in attempting to stop the flight of their soldiers. The battle was at length restored by the persevering valour of the Romans; the Persians were repulsed with a great slaughter of men and elephants; and the army, after marching and fighting a long summer's day, arrived, in the evening, at Samara on the banks of the Tigris, about one hundred miles above Ctesiphon.[105] On the ensuing day, the Barbarians, instead of harassing the march, attacked the camp, of Jovian; which had been seated in a deep and sequestered valley. From the hills, the archers of Persia insulted and annoyed

Danger and difficulty of the retreat.

June 27th – July 1st.

103. Ammianus (xxv. 10.) has drawn from the life an impartial portrait of Jovian: to which the younger Victor has added some remarkable strokes. The Abbé de la Bleterie (Histoire de Jovien, tom. i. p. 1–238.) has composed an elaborate history of his short reign; a work remarkably distinguished by elegance of style, critical disquisition, and religious prejudice.
104. Regius equitatus. It appears from Procopius, that the Immortals, so famous under Cyrus and his successors, were revived, if we may use that improper word, by the Sassan-

ides. Brisson de Regno Persico, p. 268, &c.
105. The obscure villages of the inland country are irrecoverably lost, nor can we name the field of battle where Julian fell: but M. d'Anville has demonstrated the precise situation of Sumere, Carche, and Dura, along the banks of the Tigris (Geographie Ancienne, tom. ii. p. 248. l'Euphrate et le Tigre, p. 95. 97.). In the ninth century, Sumere, or Samara, became, with a slight change of name, the royal residence of the Khalifs of the house of Abbas.

the wearied legionaries; and a body of cavalry, which had penetrated with desperate courage through the Prætorian gate, was cut in pieces, after a doubtful conflict, near the Imperial tent. In the succeeding night, the camp of Carche was protected by the lofty dykes of the river; and the Roman army, though incessantly exposed to the vexatious pursuit of the Saracens, pitched their tents near the city of Dura,[106] four days after the death of Julian. The Tigris was still on their left; their hopes and provisions were almost consumed; and the impatient soldiers, who had fondly persuaded themselves, that the frontiers of the empire were not far distant, requested their new sovereign, that they might be permitted to hazard the passage of the river. With the assistance of his wisest officers, Jovian endeavoured to check their rashness; by representing, that if they possessed sufficient skill and vigour to stem the torrent of a deep and rapid stream, they would only deliver themselves naked and defenceless to the Barbarians, who had occupied the opposite banks. Yielding at length to their clamorous importunities, he consented, with reluctance, that five hundred Gauls and Germans, accustomed from their infancy to the waters of the Rhine and Danube, should attempt the bold adventure, which might serve either as an encouragement, or as a warning, for the rest of the army. In the silence of the night, they swam the Tigris, surprised an unguarded post of the enemy, and displayed at the dawn of day the signal of their resolution and fortune. The success of this trial disposed the emperor to listen to the promises of his architects, who proposed to construct a floating bridge of the inflated skins of sheep, oxen, and goats, covered with a floor of earth and fascines.[107] Two important days were spent in the ineffectual labour; and the Romans, who already endured the miseries of famine, cast a look of despair on the Tigris, and upon the Barbarians; whose numbers and obstinacy increased with the distress of the Imperial army.[108]

---

106. Dura was a fortified place in the wars of Antiochus against the rebels of Media and Persia (Polybius, l. v. c. 48. 52. p. 548. 552. edit. Casaubon, in 8vo.).

107. A similar expedient was proposed to the leaders of the ten thousand, and wisely rejected. Xenophon, Anabasis, l. iii. p. 255, 256, 257. It appears, from our modern travellers, that rafts floating on bladders perform the trade and navigation of the Tigris.

108. The first military acts of the reign of Jovian are related by Ammianus (xxv. 6.), Libanius (Orat. Parent. c. 146. p. 364.), and Zosimus (l. iii. p. 189, 190, 191.). Though we may distrust the fairness of Libanius, the ocular testimony of Eutropius (uno a Persis atque altero prœlio victus, x. 17.) must incline us to suspect, that Ammianus has been too jealous of the honour of the Roman arms.

In this hopeless situation, the fainting spirits of the Romans were revived by the sound of peace. The transient presumption of Sapor had vanished: he observed, with serious concern, that, in the repetition of doubtful combats, he had lost his most faithful and intrepid nobles, his bravest troops, and the greatest part of his train of elephants: and the experienced monarch feared to provoke the resistance of despair, the vicissitudes of fortune, and the unexhausted powers of the Roman empire; which might soon advance to relieve, or to revenge, the successor of Julian. The Surenas himself, accompanied by another satrap, appeared in the camp of Jovian;[109] and declared, that the clemency of his sovereign was not averse to signify the conditions, on which he would consent to spare and to dismiss the Cæsar, with the relics of his captive army. The hopes of safety subdued the firmness of the Romans; the emperor was compelled, by the advice of his council, and the cries of the soldiers, to embrace the offer of peace; and the præfect Sallust was immediately sent, with the general Arinthæus, to understand the pleasure of the Great King. The crafty Persian delayed, under various pretences, the conclusion of the agreement; started difficulties, required explanations, suggested expedients, receded from his concessions, encreased his demands, and wasted four days in the arts of negociation, till he had consumed the stock of provisions which yet remained in the camp of the Romans. Had Jovian been capable of executing a bold and prudent measure, he would have continued his march with unremitting diligence; the progress of the treaty would have suspended the attacks of the Barbarians; and, before the expiration of the fourth day, he might have safely reached the fruitful province of Corduene, at the distance only of one hundred miles.[110] The irresolute emperor, instead of breaking through the toils of the enemy, expected his fate with patient resignation; and accepted the humiliating conditions of peace, which it was no longer in his power to refuse. The five provinces beyond the Tigris, which had been ceded by the grandfather of Sapor, were restored to the Persian monarchy. He acquired, by a single article, the impregnable city of Nisibis; which had sustained, in three

Negotiation and treaty of peace.

July.

---

109. Sextus Rufus (de Provinciis, c. 29.) embraces a poor subterfuge of national vanity. Tanta reverentia nominis Romani fuit, ut a Persis *primus* de pace sermo haberetur.

110. It is presumptuous to controvert the opinion of Ammianus, a soldier and a spectator. Yet it is difficult to understand, *how* the mountains of Corduene could extend over the plain of Assyria, as low as the conflux of the Tigris and the great Zab: or *how* an army of sixty thousand men could march one hundred miles in four days.

successive sieges, the effort of his arms. Singara, and the castle of the Moors one of the strongest places of Mesopotamia, were likewise dismembered from the empire. It was considered as an indulgence, that the inhabitants of those fortresses were permitted to retire with their effects; but the conqueror rigorously insisted, that the Romans should for ever abandon the king and kingdom of Armenia. A peace, or rather a long truce, of thirty years, was stipulated between the hostile nations; the faith of the treaty was ratified by solemn oaths, and religious ceremonies; and hostages of distinguished rank were reciprocally delivered to secure the performance of the conditions.[111]

The weakness and disgrace of Jovian.

The sophist of Antioch, who saw with indignation the sceptre of his hero in the feeble hand of a Christian successor, professes to admire the moderation of Sapor, in contenting himself with so small a portion of the Roman empire. If he had stretched as far as the Euphrates the claims of his ambition, he might have been secure, says Libanius, of not meeting with a refusal. If he had fixed, as the boundary of Persia, the Orontes, the Cydnus, the Sangarius, or even the Thracian Bosphorus, flatterers would not have been wanting in the court of Jovian to convince the timid monarch, that his remaining provinces would still afford the most ample gratifications of power and luxury.[112] Without adopting in its full force this malicious insinuation, we must acknowledge, that the conclusion of so ignominious a treaty was facilitated by the private ambition of Jovian. The obscure domestic, exalted to the throne by fortune, rather than by merit, was impatient to escape from the hands of the Persians; that he might prevent the designs of Procopius, who commanded the army of Mesopotamia, and establish his doubtful reign over the legions and provinces, which were still ignorant of the hasty and tumultuous choice of the camp beyond the Tigris.[113] In the neighbourhood of the same river, at no very considerable distance from the fatal station of

---

111. The treaty of Dura is recorded with grief or indignation by Ammianus (xxv. 7.), Libanius (Orat. Parent. c. 142, p. 364), Zosimus (l. iii. p. 190, 191.), Gregory Nazianzen (Orat. iv. p. 117, 118, who imputes the distress to Julian, the deliverance to Jovian); and Eutropius (x. 17.). The last mentioned writer, who was present in a military station, styles this peace necessariam quidem sed ignobilem.

112. Libanius, Orat. Parent. c. 143. p. 364, 365.
113. Conditionibus . . . dispendiosis Romanæ reipublicæ impositis . . . quibus cupidior regni quam gloriæ Jovianus imperio rudis adquievit. Sextus Rufus de Provinciis, c. 29. La Bleterie has expressed, in a long direct oration, these specious considerations of public and private interest (Hist. de Jovien, tom. i. p. 39, &c.).

Dura,[114] the ten thousand Greeks, without generals, or guides, or provisions, were abandoned, above twelve hundred miles from their native country, to the resentment of a victorious monarch. The difference of *their* conduct and success depended much more on their character than on their situation. Instead of tamely resigning themselves to the secret deliberations and private views of a single person, the united councils of the Greeks were inspired by the generous enthusiasm of a popular assembly: where the mind of each citizen is filled with the love of glory, the pride of freedom, and the contempt of death. Conscious of their superiority over the Barbarians in arms and discipline, they disdained to yield, they refused to capitulate; every obstacle was surmounted by their patience, courage, and military skill; and the memorable retreat of the ten thousand exposed and insulted the weakness of the Persian monarchy.[115]

As the price of his disgraceful concessions, the emperor might perhaps have stipulated, that the camp of the hungry Romans should be plentifully supplied;[116] and that they should be permitted to pass the Tigris on the bridge which was constructed by the hands of the Persians. But, if Jovian presumed to solicit those equitable terms, they were sternly refused by the haughty tyrant of the East; whose clemency had pardoned the invaders of his country. The Saracens sometimes intercepted the stragglers of the march; but the generals and troops of Sapor respected the cessation of arms; and Jovian was suffered to explore the most convenient place for the passage of the river. The small vessels, which had been saved from the conflagration of the fleet, performed the most essential service. They first conveyed the emperor and his favourites; and afterwards transported, in many successive voyages, a great part of the army. But, as every man was anxious for his personal safety, and apprehensive of being left on the hostile shore, the soldiers, who were too impatient to wait the slow returns of the boats, boldly ventured themselves on light hurdles, or

He continues his retreat to Nisibis.

---

114. The generals were murdered on the banks of the Zabatus (Anabasis, l. ii. p. 156. l. iii. p. 226.), or great Zab, a river of Assyria, 400 feet broad, which falls into the Tigris fourteen hours below Mosul. The error of the Greeks bestowed on the great and lesser Zab the names of the *Wolf* (Lycus), and the *Goat* (Capros). They created these animals to attend the *Tyger* of the East.

115. The *Cyropædia* is vague and languid: the

Anabasis circumstantial and animated. Such is the eternal difference between fiction and truth.

116. According to Rufinus, an immediate supply of provisions was stipulated by the treaty; and Theodoret affirms, that the obligation was faithfully discharged by the Persians. Such a fact is probable, but undoubtedly false. See Tillemont, Hist. des Empereurs, tom. iv. p. 702.

inflated skins; and, drawing after them their horses, attempted, with various success, to swim across the river. Many of these daring adventurers were swallowed by the waves; many others, who were carried along by the violence of the stream, fell an easy prey to the avarice, or cruelty, of the wild Arabs: and the loss which the army sustained in the passage of the Tigris, was not inferior to the carnage of a day of battle. As soon as the Romans had landed on the western bank, they were delivered from the hostile pursuit of the Barbarians; but, in a laborious march of two hundred miles over the plains of Mesopotamia, they endured the last extremities of thirst and hunger. They were obliged to traverse a sandy desert, which, in the extent of seventy miles, did not afford a single blade of sweet grass, nor a single spring of fresh water; and the rest of the inhospitable waste was untrod by the footsteps either of friends or enemies. Whenever a small measure of flour could be discovered in the camp, two pounds weight were greedily purchased with ten pieces of gold;[117] beasts of burden were slaughtered and devoured; and the desert was strew with the arms and baggage of the Roman soldiers, whose tattered garme and meagre countenances displayed their past sufferings, and actual mis A small convoy of provisions advanced to meet the army as far as the ca of Ur; and the supply was the more grateful, since it declared the fide of Sebastian and Procopius. At Thilsaphata,[118] the emperor most graciou received the generals of Mesopotamia; and the remains of a once flourish army at length reposed themselves under the walls of Nisibis. The messeng of Jovian had already proclaimed, in the language of flattery, his electi his treaty, and his return; and the new prince had taken the most effectual measures to secure the allegiance of the armies and provinces of Europe; by placing the military command in the hands of those officers, who, from

---

117. We may recollect some lines of Lucan (Pharsal. iv. 95.), who describes a similar distress of Cæsar's army in Spain:

Sæva fames aderat——
Miles eget: toto censû non prodigus emit
Exiguam Cererem. Proh lucri pallida tabes!
Non deest prolato jejunus venditor auro.

See Guichardt (Nouveaux Memoires Milit-aires, tom. i. p. 379–382.). His Analysis of the two Campaigns in Spain and Africa, is the noblest monument that has ever been raised to the fame of Cæsar.

118. M. d'Anville (see his Maps, and l'Euphrate et le Tigre, p. 92, 93.) traces their march, and assigns the true position of Hatra, Ur, and Thilsaphata, which Ammianus has mentioned. He does not complain of the Samiel, the deadly hot wind, which Thevenot (Voyages, part ii. l. i. p. 192.) so much dreaded.

motives of interest, or inclination, would firmly support the cause of their benefactor.[119]

The friends of Julian had confidently announced the success of his expedition. They entertained a fond persuasion, that the temples of the gods would be enriched with the spoils of the East; that Persia would be reduced to the humble state of a tributary province, governed by the laws and magistrates of Rome; that the Barbarians would adopt the dress, and manners, and language, *Universal clamour against the treaty of peace.* of their conquerors; and that the youth of Ecbatana and Susa would study the art of rhetoric under Grecian masters.[120] The progress of the arms of Julian interrupted his communication with the empire; and, from the moment that he passed the Tigris, his affectionate subjects were ignorant of the fate and fortunes of their prince. Their contemplation of fancied triumphs was disturbed by the melancholy rumour of his death; and they persisted to doubt, after they could no longer deny, the truth of that fatal event.[121] The messengers of Jovian promulgated the specious tale of a prudent and necessary peace: the voice of fame, louder and more sincere, revealed the disgrace of the emperor, and the conditions of the ignominious treaty. The minds of the people were filled with astonishment and grief, with indignation and terror, when they were informed, that the unworthy successor of Julian relinquished the five provinces, which had been acquired by the victory of Galerius; and that he shamefully surrendered to the Barbarians the important city of Nisibis, the firmest bulwark of the provinces of the East.[122] The deep and dangerous question, how far the public faith should be observed, when it becomes incompatible with the public safety, was freely agitated in popular conversation; and some hopes were entertained, that the emperor would redeem his pusillanimous behaviour by a splendid act of patriotic perfidy. The inflexible spirit of the Roman

119. The retreat of Jovian is described by Ammianus (xxv. 9.), Libanius (Orat. Parent. c. 143. p. 365.), and Zosimus (l. iii. p. 194.).
120. Libanius, Orat. Parent. c. 145. p. 366. Such were the natural hopes and wishes of a rhetorician.
121. The people of Carrhæ, a city devoted to Paganism, buried the inauspicious messenger under a pile of stones (Zosimus, l. iii. p. 196.). Libanius, when he received the fatal intelligence, cast his eye on his sword: but he

recollected that Plato had condemned suicide, and that he must live to compose the panegyric of Julian (Libanius de Vitâ suâ, tom. ii. p. 45, 46.).
122. Ammianus and Eutropius may be admitted as fair and credible witnesses of the public language and opinions. The people of Antioch reviled an ignominious peace, which exposed them to the Persians, on a naked and defenceless frontier (Excerpt. Valesiana, p. 845. ex Joanne Antiocheno.).

senate had always disclaimed the unequal conditions which were extorted from the distress of her captive armies; and, if it were necessary to satisfy the national honour, by delivering the guilty general into the hands of the Barbarians, the greatest part of the subjects of Jovian would have cheerfully acquiesced in the precedent of ancient times.[123]

Jovian evacuates Nisibis, and restores the five provinces to the Persians.

August.

But the emperor, whatever might be the limits of his constitutional authority, was the absolute master of the laws and arms of the state; and the same motives which had forced him to subscribe, now pressed him to execute, the treaty of peace. He was impatient to secure an empire at the expence of a few provinces; and the respectable names of religion and honour concealed the personal fears and the ambition of Jovian. Notwithstanding the dutiful solicitations of the inhabitants, decency, as well as prudence, forbade the emperor to lodge in the palace of Nisibis; but, the next morning after his arrival, Bineses, the ambassador of Persia, entered the place, displayed from the citadel the standard of the Great King, and proclaimed, in his name, the cruel alternative of exile or servitude. The principal citizens of Nisibis, who, till that fatal moment, had confided in the protection of their sovereign, threw themselves at his feet. They conjured him not to abandon, or, at least, not to deliver, a faithful colony to the rage of a Barbarian tyrant, exasperated by the three successive defeats, which he had experienced under the walls of Nisibis. They still possessed arms and courage to repel the invaders of their country: they requested only the permission of using them in their own defence; and, as soon as they had asserted their independence, they should implore the favour of being again admitted into the rank of his subjects. Their arguments, their eloquence, their tears were ineffectual. Jovian alleged, with some confusion, the sanctity of oaths; and, as the reluctance with which he accepted the present of a crown of gold, convinced the citizens of their hopeless condition, the advocate Sylvanus was provoked to exclaim, "O Emperor! may you thus be crowned by all the cities of your dominions!" Jovian, who, in a few weeks had assumed the habits of a prince,[124] was displeased with

123. The Abbé de la Bleterie (Hist. de Jovien, tom. i. p. 212–227.), though a severe casuist, has pronounced that Jovian was not bound to execute his promise; since he *could not* dismember the empire, nor alienate, without

their consent, the allegiance of his people. I have never found much delight or instruction in such political metaphysics.

124. At Nisibis he performed a *royal* act. A brave officer, his namesake, who had been

freedom, and offended with truth: and as he reasonably supposed, that the discontent of the people might incline them to submit to the Persian government, he published an edict, under pain of death, that they should leave the city within the term of three days. Ammianus has delineated in lively colours the scene of universal despair which he seems to have viewed with an eye of compassion.[125] The martial youth deserted, with indignant grief, the walls which they had so gloriously defended: the disconsolate mourner dropt a last tear over the tomb of a son or husband, which must soon be profaned by the rude hand of a Barbarian master; and the aged citizen kissed the threshold, and clung to the doors, of the house, where he had passed the cheerful and careless hours of infancy. The highways were crowded with a trembling multitude: the distinctions of rank, and sex, and age, were lost in the general calamity. Every one strove to bear away some fragment from the wreck of his fortunes; and as they could not command the immediate service of an adequate number of horses or waggons, they were obliged to leave behind them the greatest part of their valuable effects. The savage insensibility of Jovian appears to have aggravated the hardships of these unhappy fugitives. They were seated, however, in a new-built quarter of Amida; and that rising city, with the reinforcement of a very considerable colony, soon recovered its former splendour, and became the capital of Mesopotamia.[126] Similar orders were dispatched by the emperor for the evacuation of Singara and the castle of the Moors; and for the restitution of the five provinces beyond the Tigris. Sapor enjoyed the glory and the fruits of his victory; and this ignominious peace has justly been considered as a memorable æra in the decline and fall of the Roman empire. The predecessors of Jovian had sometimes relinquished the dominion of distant and unprofitable provinces: but, since the foundation of the city, the genius of Rome, the god Terminus, who guarded the boundaries of the republic, had never retired before the sword of a victorious enemy.[127]

---

thought worthy of the purple, was dragged from death, thrown into a well, and stoned to death, without any form of trial or evidence of guilt. Ammian. xxv. 8.

125. See xxv. 9. and Zosimus, l. iii. p. 194, 195.

126. Chron. Paschal, p. 300. The Ecclesiastical Notitiæ may be consulted.

127. Zosimus, l. iii. p. 192, 193. Sextus Rufus de Provinciis, c. 29. Augustin de Civitat. Dei, l. iv. c. 29. This general position must be applied and interpreted with some caution.

Reflections on the death,

After Jovian had performed those engagements, which the voice of his people might have tempted him to violate, he hastened away from the scene of his disgrace, and proceeded with his whole court to enjoy the luxury of Antioch.[128] Without consulting the dictates of religious zeal, he was prompted by humanity and gratitude, to bestow the last honours on the remains of his deceased sovereign:[129] and Procopius, who sincerely bewailed the loss of his kinsman, was removed from the command of the army, under the decent pretence of conducting the funeral. The corpse of Julian was transported from Nisibis to Tarsus, in a slow march of fifteen days; and, as it passed through the cities of the East, was saluted by the hostile factions, with mournful lamentations and clamorous insults. The Pagans already placed their beloved hero in the rank of those gods whose worship he had restored; while the invectives of the Christians pursued the soul of the apostate to hell, and his body to the grave.[130] One party lamented the approaching ruin of their altars; the other celebrated the marvellous deliverance of the church. The Christians applauded, in lofty and ambiguous strains, the stroke of divine vengeance, which had been so long suspended over the guilty head of Julian. They acknowledged, that the death of the tyrant, at the instant he expired beyond the Tigris, was *revealed* to the saints of Egypt, Syria, and Cappadocia;[131] and, instead of suffering him to fall by the Persian darts, their indiscretion ascribed the heroic deed to the obscure hand of some mortal or immortal champion of the faith.[132] Such imprudent declarations were eagerly adopted by the malice, or credulity, of their adversaries;[133] who darkly insinuated,

128. Ammianus, xxv. 9. Zosimus, l. iii. p. 196. He might be edax, et vino Venerique indulgens. But I agree with La Bleterie (tom. i. p. 148–154.), in rejecting the foolish report of a Bacchanalian riot (ap. Suidam) celebrated at Antioch, by the emperor, his *wife*, and a troop of concubines.

129. The Abbé de la Bleterie (tom. i. p. 156. 209.) handsomely exposes the brutal bigotry of Baronius, who would have thrown Julian to the dogs, ne cespititiâ quidem sepulturâ dignus.

130. Compare the sophist and the saint (Libanius, Monod. tom. ii. p. 251. and Orat. Parent. c. 145. p. 367. c. 156. p. 377. with Gregory Nazianzen, Orat. iv. p. 125–132.). The Chris-

tian orator faintly mutters some exhortations to modesty and forgiveness: but he is well satisfied, that the real sufferings of Julian will far exceed the fabulous torments of Ixion or Tantalus.

131. Tillemont (Hist. des Empereurs, tom. iv. p. 549.) has collected these visions. Some saint or angel was observed to be absent in the night on a secret expedition, &c.

132. Sozomen (l. vi. 2.) applauds the Greek doctrine of *tyrannicide*; but the whole passage, which a Jesuit might have translated, is prudently suppressed by the president Cousin.

133. Immediately after the death of Julian, an uncertain rumour was scattered, telo cecidisse Romano. It was carried, by some deserters,

or confidently asserted, that the governors of the church had instigated and directed the fanaticism of a domestic assassin.[134] Above sixteen years after the death of Julian, the charge was solemnly and vehemently urged, in a public oration, addressed by Libanius to the emperor Theodosius. His suspicions are unsupported by fact or argument; and we can only esteem the generous zeal of the sophist of Antioch, for the cold and neglected ashes of his friend.[135]

It was an ancient custom in the funerals, as well as in the triumphs, of the Romans, that the voice of praise should be corrected by that of satire and ridicule; and, that in the midst of *and funeral of Julian.* the splendid pageants, which displayed the glory of the living or of the dead, their imperfections should not be concealed from the eyes of the world.[136] This custom was practised in the funeral of Julian. The comedians, who resented his contempt and aversion for the theatre, exhibited, with the applause of a Christian audience, the lively and exaggerated representation of the faults and follies of the deceased emperor. His various character and singular manners afforded an ample scope for pleasantry and ridicule.[137] In the exercise of his uncommon talents, he often descended below the majesty of his rank. Alexander was transformed into Diogenes; the philosopher was degraded into a priest. The purity of his virtue was sullied by excessive vanity; his superstition disturbed the peace, and endangered the safety, of a mighty empire; and his irregular sallies were the

---

to the Persian camp; and the Romans were reproached as the assassins of the emperor by Sapor and his subjects (Ammian. xxv. 6. Libanius de ulciscendâ Juliani nece, c. xiii. p. 162, 163.). It was urged, as a decisive proof, that no Persian had appeared to claim the promised reward (Liban. Orat. Parent. c. 141. p. 363.). But the flying horseman, who darted the fatal javelin, might be ignorant of its effect; or he might be slain in the same action. Ammianus neither feels nor inspires a suspicion.

134. Ὅς τις εντολην πληρων τω σφων αυτων αρχοντι. This dark and ambiguous expression may point to Athanasius, the first, without a rival, of the Christian clergy (Libanius de ulcis. Jul. nece, c. 5. p. 149. La Bleterie, Hist. de Jovien, tom. i. p. 179.).

135. The Orator (Fabricius, Bibliot. Græc. tom. vii. p. 145–179.) scatters suspicions, demands an inquiry, and insinuates, that proofs might still be obtained. He ascribes the success of the Huns to the criminal neglect of revenging Julian's death.

136. At the funeral of Vespasian, the comedian who personated that frugal emperor, anxiously inquired how much it cost – Fourscore thousand pounds (centies) – Give me the tenth part of the sum, and throw my body into the Tyber. Sueton. in Vespasian. c. 19. with the notes of Casaubon and Gronovius.

137. Gregory (Orat. iv. p. 119, 120.) compares this supposed ignominy and ridicule to the funeral honours of Constantius, whose body was chaunted over mount Taurus by a choir of angels.

less intitled to indulgence, as they appeared to be the laborious efforts of art, or even of affectation. The remains of Julian were interred at Tarsus in Cilicia; but his stately tomb, which arose in that city, on the banks of the cold and limpid Cydnus,[138] was displeasing to the faithful friends, who loved and revered the memory of that extraordinary man. The philosopher expressed a very reasonable wish, that the disciple of Plato might have reposed amidst the groves of the academy:[139] while the soldier exclaimed in bolder accents, that the ashes of Julian should have been mingled with those of Cæsar, in the field of Mars, and among the antient monuments of Roman virtue.[140] The history of princes does not very frequently renew the example of a similar competition.

138. Quintus Curtius, l. iii. c. 4. The luxuriancy of his descriptions has been often censured. Yet it was almost the duty of the historian to describe a river, whose waters had nearly proved fatal to Alexander.

139. Libanius, Orat. Parent. c. 156. p. 377. Yet he acknowledges with gratitude the liberality of the two royal brothers in decorating the tomb of Julian (de ulcis. Jul. nece, c. 7. p. 152.).

140. Cujus suprema et cineres, si qui tunc justè consuleret, non Cydnus videre deberet, quamvis gratissimus amnis et liquidus: sed ad perpetuandam gloriam recte factorum præterlambere Tiberis, intersecans urbem æternam, divorumque veterum monumenta præstringens. Ammian. xxv. 10.

[CHAPTERS XXV—XXVII]

There follow three chapters in which Roman lassitude is contrasted with barbarian energy. The fatal principle of division, introduced by Diocletian, reaches its logical conclusion in the separation of the Eastern and Western empires by the emperor Valentinian:

Before Valentinian divided the provinces, he reformed the administration of the empire. All ranks of subjects, who had been injured or oppressed under the reign of Julian, were invited to support their public accusations. The silence of mankind attested the spotless integrity of the præfect Sallust; and his own pressing solicitations, that he might be permitted to retire from the business of the state, were rejected by Valentinian with the most honourable expressions of friendship and esteem. But among the favourites of the late emperor, there were many who had abused his credulity or superstition; and who could no longer hope to be protected either by favour or justice. The greater part of the ministers of the palace, and the governors of the provinces, were removed from their respective stations; yet the eminent merit of some officers was distinguished from the obnoxious crowd; and, notwithstanding the opposite clamours of zeal and resentment, the whole proceedings of this delicate enquiry appear to have been conducted with a reasonable share of wisdom and moderation. The festivity of a new reign received a short and suspicious interruption, from the sudden illness of the two princes: but as soon as their health was restored, they left Constantinople in the beginning of the spring. In the castle or palace of Mediana, only three miles from Naissus, they executed the solemn and final division of the Roman empire. Valentinian bestowed on his brother the rich præfecture of the *East*, from the Lower Danube to the confines of Persia; whilst he reserved for his immediate government the warlike præfectures of *Illyricum*, *Italy*, and *Gaul*, from the extremity of Greece to the Caledonian rampart; and from the rampart of Caledonia, to the foot of Mount Atlas. The provincial administration remained on its former basis; but a double supply of generals and magistrates was required for two councils, and two courts: the division was made with a just regard to their peculiar merit and situation, and seven master-generals were soon created, either of the cavalry or infantry. When this important business had been amicably transacted, Valentinian and Valens embraced for the last time. The emperor of the West established his temporary residence at Milan; and the emperor of the East returned to Constantinople, to assume the dominion of fifty provinces, of whose language he was totally ignorant. (*DF*, i. 968–9)

In chapter XXVI Gibbon explores how the westward movements of the Huns, following reverses at the hands of the Chinese emperor Vouti, exerted pressure on the Goths and drove them into intensified conflict with the Roman empire. Gibbon's sensitivity to the largest, most wavelike, rhythms of the past does not, however, drive out his alertness to the most minute hinges around which the destiny of nations may turn, as is shown by the acute focus in his account of the outbreak of hostilities that took place once corrupt officials had allowed the assembled Gothic tribes to cross the Danube:

Lupicinus had invited the Gothic chiefs to a splendid entertainment; and their martial train remained under arms at the entrance of the palace. But the gates of the city were strictly guarded; and the Barbarians were sternly excluded from the use of a plentiful market, to which they asserted their equal claim of subjects and allies. Their humble prayers were rejected with insolence and derision; and as their patience was now exhausted, the townsmen, the soldiers, and the Goths, were soon involved in a conflict of passionate altercation and angry reproaches. A blow was imprudently given; a sword was hastily drawn; and the first blood that was spilt in this accidental quarrel, became the signal of a long and destructive war. In the midst of noise and brutal intemperance, Lupicinus was informed, by a secret messenger, that many of his soldiers were slain, and despoiled of their arms; and as he was already inflamed by wine, and oppressed by sleep, he issued a rash command, that their death should be revenged by the massacre of the guards of Fritigern and Alavivus. The clamorous shouts and dying groans apprised Fritigern of his extreme danger: and, as he possessed the calm and intrepid spirit of a hero, he saw that he was lost if he allowed a moment of deliberation to the man who had so deeply injured him. "A trifling dispute, said the Gothic leader, with a firm but gentle tone of voice, appears to have arisen between the two nations; but it may be productive of the most dangerous consequences, unless the tumult is immediately pacified by the assurance of our safety, and the authority of our presence." At these words, Fritigern and his companions drew their swords, opened their passage through the unresisting crowd, which filled the palace, the streets, and the gates, of Marcianopolis, and, mounting their horses, hastily vanished from the eyes of the astonished Romans. The generals of the Goths were saluted by the fierce and joyful acclamations of the camp: war was instantly resolved, and the resolution was executed without delay: the banners of the nation were displayed according to the custom of their ancestors; and the air resounded with the harsh and mournful music of the Barbarian trumpet. The weak and guilty Lupicinus, who had dared to provoke, who had neglected to destroy, and who still presumed to despise, his formidable enemy, marched against the Goths, at the head of such a military force as could be collected on this sudden emergency. The Barbarians expected his approach about nine miles from Marcianopolis; and on this occasion the talents of the general were found to be of more prevailing efficacy than the weapons and discipline of the troops. The valour of the Goths was so ably directed by the genius of Fritigern, that they broke, by a close and vigorous attack, the ranks of the Roman legions. Lupicinus left his arms and standards, his tribunes and his bravest soldiers, on the field of battle; and their useless courage served only to protect the ignominious flight of their leader. "That successful day put an end to the distress of the Barbarians, and the security of the Romans: from that day, the Goths, renouncing the precarious condition of strangers and exiles, assumed the character of citizens and masters, claimed an absolute dominion over the possessors of land, and held, in their own right, the northern provinces of the empire, which are bounded by the Danube." Such are the words of the Gothic historian, who celebrates, with rude eloquence, the glory of his countrymen. But the dominion of the Barbarians was exercised only for the purposes of rapine and destruction. As they had been deprived, by the ministers of the emperor, of the common benefits of nature, and the fair intercourse of social life, they retaliated the injustice on the subjects of the empire; and the crimes of Lupicinus were expiated by the ruin of the peaceful husbandmen of Thrace, the conflagration of their villages, and the massacre, or captivity, of their innocent families. The report of the Gothic victory was soon diffused over the adjacent country; and while it filled the minds of the Romans with terror and dismay, their own hasty imprudence contributed to increase the forces of Fritigern, and the calamities of the province. Some time before the great emigration, a numerous body of Goths, under the command of Suerid and Colias, had been received into the protection and service of the empire. They were encamped under the walls of Hadrianople: but the ministers of Valens were anxious to remove them beyond the Hellespont, at a distance from the dangerous temptation which might so easily be communicated by the neighbourhood, and the success, of their countrymen. The respectful submission with which they yielded to the order of their march, might be considered as a proof of their fidelity; and their moderate request of a sufficient allowance of provisions, and of a delay of only two days, was expressed in the most dutiful terms. But the first magistrate of Hadrianople, incensed by some disorders which had been committed at his country-house, refused this indulgence; and arming against them the inhabitants and manufacturers of a populous city, he urged, with hostile threats, their instant departure. The Barbarians stood silent and amazed, till they were exasperated by the insulting clamours, and missile weapons, of the populace: but when patience or contempt was fatigued, they crushed the undisciplined multitude, inflicted many a shameful wound on the backs of their flying enemies, and despoiled them of the splendid armour, which they were unworthy to bear. The resemblance of their sufferings and their actions soon united this victorious detachment to the nation of the Visigoths; the troops of Colias and Suerid expected the approach of the great Fritigern, ranged themselves under his standard, and signalised their ardour in the siege of Hadrianople. But the resistance of the garrison informed the Barbarians, that, in the attack of regular fortifications, the efforts of unskilful courage are seldom effectual. Their general acknowledged his error, raised the siege, declared that, "he was at peace with stone walls," and revenged his disappointment on the adjacent country. He accepted, with pleasure, the useful reinforcement of hardy workmen, who laboured in the gold mines of Thrace, for the emolument, and under the lash, of an unfeeling master: and these new associates conducted the Barbarians, through the secret paths, to the most sequestered places, which had been chosen to secure the inhabitants, the cattle, and the magazines of corn. With the assistance of such guides, nothing could remain impervious, or inaccessible: resistance was fatal; flight was impracticable; and the patient submission of helpless innocence seldom found mercy from the Barbarian conqueror. In the course of these depredations, a great number of the children of the Goths, who had been sold into captivity, were restored to the embraces of their afflicted parents;

but these tender interviews, which might have revived and cherished in their minds some sentiments of humanity, tended only to stimulate their native fierceness by the desire of revenge. They listened, with eager attention, to the complaints of their captive children, who had suffered the most cruel indignities from the lustful or angry passions of their masters; and the same cruelties, the same indignities, were severely retaliated on the sons and daughters of the Romans. (*DF*, i. 1052–5)

That focus on minute causation ('*A* blow was imprudently given; *a* sword was hastily drawn . . .') shows that Gibbon was no prisoner of the more advanced, fashionably philosophical, historiography of his own times, which – at least as represented by a figure such as Montesquieu – had tended to disdain such immediate historical triggers, and to search instead for a more general and impersonal causation.

But where the historical record offered support to the work of those he admired, such as David Hume and Adam Smith, who had both argued against the commonly held view that material luxury led to moral and political decadence, then Gibbon sets out the evidence with care, as here in his thoughtful comments on the moral corruption of the reign of Theodosius:

In the faithful picture of the virtues of Theodosius, his imperfections have not been dissembled; the act of cruelty, and the habits of indolence, which tarnished the glory of one of the greatest of the Roman princes. An historian, perpetually adverse to the fame of Theodosius, has exaggerated his vices, and their pernicious effects; he boldly asserts, that every rank of subjects imitated the effeminate manners of their sovereign; that every species of corruption polluted the course of public and private life; and that the feeble restraints of order and decency were insufficient to resist the progress of that degenerate spirit, which sacrifices, without a blush, the consideration of duty and interest to the base indulgence of sloth and appetite. The complaints of contemporary writers, who deplore the increase of luxury, and depravation of manners, are commonly expressive of their peculiar temper and situation. There are few observers, who possess a clear and comprehensive view of the revolutions of society; and who are capable of discovering the nice and secret springs of action, which impel, in the same uniform direction, the blind and capricious passions of a multitude of individuals. If it can be affirmed, with any degree of truth, that the luxury of the Romans was more shameless and dissolute in the reign of Theodosius than in the age of Constantine, perhaps, or of Augustus, the alteration cannot be ascribed to any beneficial improvements, which had gradually increased the stock of national riches. A long period of calamity or decay must have checked the industry, and diminished the wealth, of the people; and their profuse luxury must have been the result of that indolent despair, which enjoys the present hour, and declines the thoughts of futurity. The uncertain condition of their property discouraged the subjects of Theodosius from engaging in those useful and laborious undertakings, which require an immediate expence, and promise a slow and distant advantage. The frequent examples of ruin and desolation tempted them not to spare the remains of a patrimony, which might, every hour, become the prey of the rapacious Goth. And the mad prodigality which prevails in the confusion of a shipwreck, or a siege, may serve to explain the progress of luxury amidst the misfortunes and terrors of a sinking nation.

The effeminate luxury, which infected the manners of courts and cities, had instilled a secret and destructive poison into the camps of the legions: and their degeneracy has been marked by the pen of a military writer, who had accurately studied the genuine and ancient principles of Roman discipline. It is the just and important observation of Vegetius, that the infantry was invariably covered with defensive armour, from the foundation of the city, to the reign of the emperor Gratian. The relaxation of discipline, and the disuse of exercise, rendered the soldiers less able, and less willing, to support the fatigues of the service; they complained of the weight of the armour, which they seldom wore; and they successively obtained the permission of laying aside both their cuirasses and their helmets. The heavy weapons of their ancestors, the short sword, and the formidable *pilum*, which had subdued the world, insensibly dropped from their feeble hands. As the use of the shield is incompatible with that of the bow, they reluctantly marched into the field; condemned to suffer, either the pain of wounds, or the ignominy of flight, and always disposed to prefer the more shameful alternative. The cavalry of the Goths, the Huns, and the Alani, had felt the benefits, and adopted the use, of defensive armour; and, as they excelled in the management of missile weapons, they easily overwhelmed the naked and trembling legions, whose heads and breasts were exposed, without defence, to the arrows of the Barbarians. The loss of armies, the destruction of cities, and the dishonour of the Roman name, ineffectually solicited the successors of Gratian to restore the helmets and cuirasses of the infantry. The enervated soldiers abandoned their own, and the public, defence; and their pusillanimous indolence may be considered as the immediate cause of the downfal of the empire. (*DF*, ii. 69–70)

Such is the crooked timber of humanity that luxury may just as easily be a consequence as a cause of decline. In chapter XXVIII, in which Gibbon juxtaposes the eradication of paganism and the establishment of superstitious forms of Christianity, he explores further this atmosphere of moral paradox.

CHAPTER XXVIII

Final Destruction of Paganism – Introduction of the Worship of Saints, and Relics, among the Christians.

The destruction of the Pagan religion, A.D. 378–395. The ruin of Paganism, in the age of Theodosius, is perhaps the only example of the total extirpation of any ancient and popular superstition; and may therefore deserve to be considered, as a singular event in the history of the human mind. The Christians, more especially the clergy, had impatiently supported the prudent delays of Constantine, and the equal toleration of the elder Valentinian; nor could they deem their conquest perfect or secure, as long as their adversaries were permitted to exist. The influence, which Ambrose and his brethren had acquired over the youth of Gratian, and the piety of Theodosius, was employed to infuse the maxims of persecution into the breasts of their Imperial proselytes. Two specious principles of religious jurisprudence were established, from whence they deduced a direct and rigorous conclusion, against the subjects of the empire, who still adhered to the ceremonies of their ancestors: *that*, the magistrate is, in some measure, guilty of the crimes which he neglects to prohibit, or to punish; and, *that* the idolatrous worship of fabulous deities, and real dæmons, is the most abominable crime against the supreme majesty of the Creator. The laws of Moses, and the examples of Jewish history,[1] were hastily, perhaps erroneously, applied, by the clergy, to the mild and universal reign of Christianity.[2] The zeal of the emperors was excited to vindicate their own honour, and that of the Deity: and the temples of the Roman world were subverted, about sixty years after the conversion of Constantine.

---

1. St. Ambrose (tom. ii. de Obit. Theodos. p. 1208.) expressly praises and recommends the zeal of Josiah in the destruction of idolatry. The language of Julius Firmicus Maternus on the same subject (de Errore Profan. Relig. p. 467, edit. Gronov.) is piously inhuman. Nec filio jubet (the Mosaic Law) parci, nec

fratri, et per amatam conjugem gladium vindicem ducit, &c.
2. Bayle (tom. ii. p. 406, in his Commentaire Philosophique) justifies, and limits, these intolerant laws by the temporal reign of Jehovah over the Jews. The attempt is laudable.

From the age of Numa, to the reign of Gratian, the Romans preserved the regular succession of the several colleges of the sacerdotal order.[3] Fifteen PONTIFFS exercised their supreme jurisdiction over all things, and persons, that were consecrated to the service of the gods; and the various questions which perpetually arose in a loose and traditionary system, were submitted to the judgment of their holy tribunal. Fifteen grave and learned AUGURS observed the face of the heavens, and prescribed the actions of heroes, according to the flight of birds. Fifteen keepers of the Sybilline books (their name of QUINDECEMVIRS was derived from their number) occasionally consulted the history of future, and, as it should seem, of contingent, events. Six VESTALS devoted their virginity to the guard of the sacred fire, and of the unknown pledges of the duration of Rome; which no mortal had been suffered to behold with impunity.[4] Seven EPULOS prepared the table of the gods, conducted the solemn procession, and regulated the ceremonies of the annual festival. The three FLAMENS of Jupiter, of Mars, and of Quirinus, were considered as the peculiar ministers of the three most powerful deities, who watched over the fate of Rome and of the universe. The KING of the SACRIFICES represented the person of Numa, and of his successors, in the religious functions, which could be performed only by royal hands. The confraternities of the SALIANS, the LUPERCALS, &c. practised such rites, as might extort a smile of contempt from every reasonable man, with a lively confidence of recommending themselves to the favour of the immortal gods. The authority, which the Roman priests had formerly obtained in the counsels of the republic, was gradually abolished by the establishment of monarchy, and the removal of the seat of empire. But the dignity of their sacred character was still protected by the laws and manners of their country; and they still continued, more especially the college of pontiffs, to exercise in the capital, and sometimes in the provinces, the rights of their ecclesiastical and civil jurisdiction. Their robes of purple, chariots of

State of Paganism at Rome.

3. See the outlines of the Roman hierarchy in Cicero (de Legibus, ii. 7, 8.), Livy (i. 20.), Dionysius Halicarnassensis (l. ii. p. 119–129. edit. Hudson), Beaufort (Republique Romaine, tom. i. p. 1–90.), and Moyle (vol. i. p. 10–5.). The last is the work of an English Whig, as well as of a Roman antiquary.
4. These mystic, and perhaps imaginary, symbols have given birth to various fables and conjectures. It seems probable, that the Palladium was a small statue (three cubits and a half high) of Minerva, with a lance and distaff; that it was usually inclosed in a *seria*, or barrel; and that a similar barrel was placed by its side, to disconcert curiosity, or sacrilege. See Mezeriac (Comment. sur les Epitres d'Ovide, tom. i. p. 60–66.), and Lipsius (tom. iii. p. 610. de Vesta, &c. c. 10.).

state, and sumptuous entertainments, attracted the admiration of the people; and they received, from the consecrated lands, and the public revenue, an ample stipend, which liberally supported the splendour of the priesthood, and all the expences of the religious worship of the state. As the service of the altar was not incompatible with the command of armies, the Romans, after their consulships and triumphs, aspired to the place of pontiff, or of augur; the seats of Cicero[5] and Pompey were filled, in the fourth century, by the most illustrious members of the senate; and the dignity of their birth reflected additional splendour on their sacerdotal character. The fifteen priests, who composed the college of pontiffs, enjoyed a more distinguished rank as the companions of their sovereign; and the Christian emperors condescended to accept the robe and ensigns, which were appropriated to the office of supreme pontiff. But when Gratian ascended the throne, more scrupulous, or more enlightened, he sternly rejected those prophane symbols;[6] applied to the service of the state, or of the church, the revenues of the priests and vestals; abolished their honours and immunities; and dissolved the ancient fabric of Roman superstition, which was supported by the opinions, and habits, of eleven hundred years. Paganism was still the constitutional religion of the senate. The hall, or temple, in which they assembled, was adorned by the statue and altar of victory;[7] a majestic female standing on a globe, with flowing garments, expanded wings, and a crown of laurel in her out-stretched hand.[8] The senators were sworn on the altar of the goddess, to observe the laws of the emperor and of the empire; and a solemn offering of wine and incense was the ordinary prelude of their public deliberations.[9] The removal of this ancient monument was the only injury which Constantius had offered to the superstition of the Romans. The altar of Victory was again restored by Julian, tolerated by Valentinian, and once more banished from the senate by the zeal of Gratian.[10] But the

---

5. Cicero, frankly (ad Atticum, l. ii. epist. 5.), or indirectly (ad Familiar. l. xv. epist. 4.), confesses, that the *Augurate* is the supreme object of his wishes. Pliny is proud to tread in the footsteps of Cicero (l. iv. epist. 8.), and the chain of tradition might be continued from history, and marbles.

6. Zosimus, l. iv. p. 249, 250. I have suppressed the foolish pun about *Pontifex* and *Maximus*.

7. This statue was transported from Tarentum to Rome, placed in the *Curia Julia* by Cæsar, and decorated by Augustus with the spoils of Egypt.

8. Prudentius (l. ii. in initio) has drawn a very awkward portrait of Victory: but the curious reader will obtain more satisfaction from Montfaucon's Antiquities (tom. i. p. 341.).

9. See Suetonius (in August. c. 35.), and the Exordium of Pliny's Panegyric.

10. These facts are mutually allowed by the two advocates, Symmachus and Ambrose.

emperor yet spared the statues of the gods which were exposed to the public veneration: four hundred and twenty-four temples, or chapels, still remained to satisfy the devotion of the people; and in every quarter of Rome, the delicacy of the Christians was offended by the fumes of idolatrous sacrifice.[11]

But the Christians formed the least numerous party in the senate of Rome;[12] and it was only by their absence, that they could express their dissent from the legal, though profane, acts of a Pagan majority. In that assembly, the dying embers of freedom were, for a moment, revived and inflamed by the breath of fanaticism. Four respectable deputations were successively voted to the Imperial court,[13] to represent the grievances of the priesthood and the senate; and to solicit the restoration of the altar of Victory. The conduct of this important business was entrusted to the eloquent Symmachus,[14] a wealthy and noble senator, who united the sacred characters of pontiff and augur, with the civil dignities of proconsul of Africa, and præfect of the city. The breast of Symmachus was animated by the warmest zeal for the cause of expiring Paganism; and his religious antagonists lamented the abuse of his genius, and the inefficacy of his moral virtues.[15] The orator, whose petition is extant to the emperor Valentinian, was conscious of the difficulty and danger of the office which he had assumed. He cautiously avoids every topic which might appear to reflect on the religion of his sovereign; humbly declares, that prayers and entreaties are his only arms; and artfully draws his arguments from the schools of rhetoric, rather than from those of philosophy. Symmachus endeavours to seduce the imagination of a young

Petition of the senate for the altar of Victory. A.D. 384.

11. The *Notitia Urbis*, more recent than Constantine, does not find one Christian church worthy to be named among the edifices of the city. Ambrose (tom. ii. epist. xvii. p. 825.) deplores the public scandals of Rome, which continually offended the eyes, the ears, and the nostrils of the faithful.

12. Ambrose repeatedly affirms, in contradiction to common sense (Moyle's Works, vol. ii. p. 147.), that the Christians had a majority in the senate.

13. The *first* (A.D. 382.) to Gratian, who refused them audience. The *second* (A.D. 384.) to Valentinian, when the field was disputed by Symmachus and Ambrose. The *third* (A.D.

388.) to Theodosius; and the *fourth* (A.D. 392.) to Valentinian. Lardner (Heathen Testimonies, vol. iv. p. 372–399.) fairly represents the whole transaction.

14. Symmachus, who was invested with all the civil and sacerdotal honours, represented the emperor under the two characters of *Pontifex Maximus*, and *Princeps Senatûs*. See the proud inscription at the head of his works.

15. As if any one, says Prudentius (in Symmach. i. 639.), should dig in the mud with an instrument of gold and ivory. Even saints, and polemic saints, treat this adversary with respect and civility.

prince, by displaying the attributes of the goddess of victory; he insinuates, that the confiscation of the revenues, which were consecrated to the service of the gods, was a measure unworthy of his liberal and disinterested character; and he maintains, that the Roman sacrifices would be deprived of their force and energy, if they were no longer celebrated at the expence, as well as in the name, of the republic. Even scepticism is made to supply an apology for superstition. The great and incomprehensible *secret* of the universe eludes the enquiry of man. Where reason cannot instruct, custom may be permitted to guide; and every nation seems to consult the dictates of prudence, by a faithful attachment to those rites, and opinions, which have received the sanction of ages. If those ages have been crowned with glory and prosperity, if the devout people has frequently obtained the blessings which they have solicited at the altars of the gods, it must appear still more advisable to persist in the same salutary practice; and not to risk the unknown perils that may attend any rash innovations. The test of antiquity and success was applied with singular advantage to the religion of Numa; and ROME herself, the cælestial genius that presided over the fates of the city, is introduced by the orator to plead her own cause before the tribunal of the emperors. "Most excellent princes," says the venerable matron, "fathers of your country! pity and respect my age, which has hitherto flowed in an uninterrupted course of piety. Since I do not repent, permit me to continue in the practice of my ancient rites. Since I am born free, allow me to enjoy my domestic institutions. This religion has reduced the world under my laws. These rites have repelled Hannibal from the city, and the Gauls from the capitol. Were my gray hairs reserved for such intolerable disgrace? I am ignorant of the new system, that I am required to adopt; but I am well assured, that the correction of old age is always an ungrateful and ignominious office."[16] The fears of the people supplied what the discretion of the orator had suppressed; and the calamities, which afflicted, or threatened, the declining empire, were unanimously imputed, by the Pagans, to the new religion of Christ and of Constantine.

---

16. See the fifty-fourth epistle of the tenth book of Symmachus. In the form and disposition of his ten books of epistles, he imitated the younger Pliny; whose rich and florid style he was supposed, by his friends, to equal or excel (Macrob. Saturnal l. v. c. 1.). But the luxuriancy of Symmachus consists of barren leaves, without fruits, and even without flowers. Few facts, and few sentiments, can be extracted from his verbose correspondence.

But the hopes of Symmachus were repeatedly baffled by the firm and dexterous opposition of the archbishop of Milan; who fortified the emperors against the fallacious eloquence of the advocate of Rome. In this controversy, Ambrose condescends to speak the language of a philosopher, and to ask, with some contempt, why it should be thought necessary to introduce an imaginary and invisible power, as the cause of those victories, which were sufficiently explained by the valour and discipline of the legions. He justly derides the absurd reverence for antiquity, which could only tend to discourage the improvements of art, and to replunge the human race into their original barbarism. From thence gradually rising to a more lofty and theological tone, he pronounces, that Christianity alone is the doctrine of truth and salvation; and that every mode of Polytheism conducts its deluded votaries, through the paths of error, to the abyss of eternal perdition.[17] Arguments like these, when they were suggested by a favourite bishop, had power to prevent the restoration of the altar of Victory; but the same arguments fell, with much more energy and effect, from the mouth of a conqueror; and the gods of antiquity were dragged in triumph at the chariot-wheels of Theodosius.[18] In a full meeting of the senate, the emperor proposed, according to the forms of the republic, the important question, Whether the worship of Jupiter, or that of Christ, should be the religion of the Romans. The liberty of suffrages, which he affected to allow, was destroyed by the hopes and fears, that his presence inspired; and the arbitrary exile of Symmachus was a recent admonition, that it might be dangerous to oppose the wishes of the monarch. On a regular division of the senate, Jupiter was condemned and degraded by the sense of a very large majority; and it is rather surprising, that any members should be found bold enough to declare, by their speeches and votes, that they were still attached

Conversion of Rome, A.D. 388, &c.

17. See Ambrose (tom. ii. epist. xvii, xviii, p. 825–833.). The former of these epistles is a short caution; the latter is a formal reply to the petition or *libel* of Symmachus. The same ideas are more copiously expressed in the poetry, if it may deserve that name, of Prudentius; who composed his two books against Symmachus (A.D. 404.) while that senator was still alive. It is whimsical enough, that Montesquieu (Considerations, &c. c. xix. tom. iii. p. 487.) should overlook the two professed antagonists of Symmachus; and amuse himself with descanting on the more remote and indirect confutations of Orosius, St. Augustin, and Salvian.

18. See Prudentius (in Symmach. l. i. 545, &c.). The Christian agrees with the Pagan Zosimus (l. iv. p. 283.), in placing this visit of Theodosius after the *second* civil war, gemini bis victor cæde Tyranni (l. i. 410.). But the time and circumstances are better suited to his first triumph.

to the interest of an abdicated deity.[19] The hasty conversion of the senate must be attributed either to supernatural or to sordid motives; and many of these reluctant proselytes betrayed, on every favourable occasion, their secret disposition to throw aside the mask of odious dissimulation. But they were gradually fixed in the new religion, as the cause of the ancient became more hopeless; they yielded to the authority of the emperor, to the fashion of the times, and to the entreaties of their wives and children,[20] who were instigated and governed by the clergy of Rome and the monks of the East. The edifying example of the Anician family was soon imitated by the rest of the nobility: the Bassi, the Paullini, the Gracchi, embraced the Christian religion; and "the luminaries of the world, the venerable assembly of Catos (such are the high-flown expressions of Prudentius), were impatient to strip themselves of their pontifical garment; to cast the skin of the old serpent; to assume the snowy robes of baptismal innocence; and to humble the pride of the consular fasces before the tombs of the martyrs.'[21] The citizens, who subsisted by their own industry, and the populace, who were supported by the public liberality, filled the churches of the Lateran, and Vatican, with an incessant throng of devout proselytes. The decrees of the senate, which proscribed the worship of idols, were ratified by the general consent of the Romans;[22] the splendour

---

19. Prudentius, after proving that the sense of the senate is declared by a legal majority, proceeds to say (609, &c.).

> Adspice quam pleno subsellia nostra
>   Senatû
> Decernant infame Jovis pulvinar, et
>   omne
> Idolium longe purgatâ ab urbe
>   fugandum.
> Qua vocat egregii sententia Principis,
>   illuc
> Libera, cum pedibus, tum corde,
>   frequentia transit.

Zosimus ascribes to the conscript fathers an heathenish courage, which few of them are found to possess.

20. Jerom specifies the pontiff Albinus, who was surrounded with such a believing family of children, and grand-children, as would have been sufficient to convert even Jupiter

himself; an extraordinary proselyte! (tom. i. ad Lætam, p. 54.)

21.
> Exsultare Patres videas, pulcherrima
>   mundi
> Lumina; conciliumque senûm gestire
>   Catonum
> Candidiore togâ niveum pietatis
>   amictum
> Sumere; et exuvias deponere
>   pontificales.

The fancy of Prudentius is warmed and elevated by victory.

22. Prudentius, after he has described the conversion of the senate and people, asks, with some truth and confidence,

> Et dubitamus adhuc Romam, tibi,
>   Christe, dicatam
> In leges transîsse tuas?

of the capitol was defaced, and the solitary temples were abandoned to ruin and contempt.[23] Rome submitted to the yoke of the Gospel; and the vanquished provinces had not yet lost their reverence for the name and authority of Rome.

The filial piety of the emperors themselves engaged them to proceed, with some caution and tenderness, in the reformation of the eternal city. Those absolute monarchs acted with less regard to the prejudices of the provincials. The pious labour which had been suspended near twenty years since the death of Constantius,[24] was vigorously resumed, and finally, accomplished, by the zeal of Theodosius. Whilst that warlike prince yet struggled with the Goths, not for the glory, but for the safety, of the republic; he ventured to offend a considerable party of his subjects, by some acts which might perhaps secure the protection of Heaven, but which must seem rash and unseasonable in the eye of human prudence. The success of his first experiments against the Pagans, encouraged the pious emperor to reiterate and enforce his edicts of proscription: the same laws which had been originally published in the provinces of the East, were applied, after the defeat of Maximus, to the whole extent of the Western empire; and every victory of the orthodox Theodosius contributed to the triumph of the Christian and Catholic faith.[25] He attacked superstition in her most vital part, by prohibiting the use of sacrifices, which he declared to be criminal, as well as infamous: and if the terms of his edicts more strictly condemned the impious curiosity which examined the entrails of the victims,[26] every subsequent explanation tended to involve, in the same guilt, the general practice of *immolation*, which essentially constituted the religion of the Pagans. As the temples had been erected for the purpose of sacrifice, it was the duty of a benevolent prince to remove from his subjects the dangerous temptation, of offending against the laws which he had enacted. A special

Destruction of the temples in the provinces. A.D. 381, &c.

23. Jerom exults in the desolation of the capitol, and the other temples of Rome (tom. i. p. 54. tom. ii. p. 95.).

24. Libanius (Orat. pro Templis, p. 10. Genev. 1634, published by James Godefroy, and now extremely scarce) accuses Valentinian and Valens of prohibiting sacrifices. Some partial order may have been issued by the Eastern emperor; but the idea of any general law is contradicted by the silence of the Code, and

the evidence of ecclesiastical history.

25. See his laws in the Theodosian Code, l. xvi. tit. x. leg. 7–11.

26. Homer's sacrifices are not accompanied with any inquisition of entrails (see Feithius, Antiquitat. Homer. l. i. c. 10. 16.). The Tuscans, who produced the first *Haruspices*, subdued both the Greeks and the Romans (Cicero de Divinatione, ii. 23.).

commission was granted to Cynegius, the Prætorian præfect of the East, and afterwards to the counts Jovius and Gaudentius, two officers of distinguished rank in the West; by which they were directed to shut the temples, to seize or destroy the instruments of idolatry, to abolish the privileges of the priests, and to confiscate the consecrated property for the benefit of the emperor, of the church, or of the army.[27] Here the desolation might have stopped: and the naked edifices, which were no longer employed in the service of idolatry, might have been protected from the destructive rage of fanaticism. Many of those temples were the most splendid and beautiful monuments of Grecian architecture: and the emperor himself was interested not to deface the splendour of his own cities, or to diminish the value of his own possessions. Those stately edifices might be suffered to remain, as so many lasting trophies of the victory of Christ. In the decline of the arts, they might be usefully converted into magazines, manufactures, or places of public assembly: and perhaps, when the walls of the temple had been sufficiently purified by holy rites, the worship of the true Deity might be allowed to expiate the ancient guilt of idolatry. But as long as they subsisted, the Pagans fondly cherished the secret hope, that an auspicious revolution, a second Julian, might again restore the altars of the gods; and the earnestness with which they addressed their unavailing prayers to the throne,[28] increased the zeal of the Christian reformers to extirpate, without mercy, the root of superstition. The laws of the emperors exhibit some symptoms of a milder disposition:[29] but their cold and languid efforts were insufficient to stem the torrent of enthusiasm and rapine, which was conducted, or rather impelled, by the spiritual rulers of the church. In Gaul, the holy Martin, bishop of Tours,[30] marched at the head of his faithful monks to destroy the idols, the temples, and the consecrated trees of his extensive diocese; and,

---

27. Zosimus, l. iv. p. 245. 249. Theodoret, l. v. c. 21. Idatius in Chron. Prosper. Aquitan. l. iii. c. 38. apud Baronium, Annal. Eccles. A.D. 389. N° 52. Libanius (pro Templis, p. 10.) labours to prove, that the commands of Theodosius were not direct and positive.

28. Cod. Theodos. l. xvi. tit. x. leg. 8. 18. There is room to believe, that this temple of Edessa, which Theodosius wished to save for civil uses, was soon afterwards a heap of ruins (Libanius pro Templis, p. 26, 27. and Godefroy's notes, p. 59.).

29. See this curious oration of Libanius pro Templis, pronounced, or rather composed, about the year 390. I have consulted, with advantage, Dr. Lardner's version and remarks (Heathen Testimonies, vol. iv. p. 135–163.).

30. See the life of Martin, by Sulpicius Severus, c. 9–14. The saint once mistook (as Don Quixote might have done) an harmless funeral for an idolatrous procession, and imprudently committed a miracle.

in the execution of this arduous task, the prudent reader will judge whether Martin was supported by the aid of miraculous powers, or of carnal weapons. In Syria, the divine and excellent Marcellus,[31] as he is stiled by Theodoret, a bishop animated with apostolic fervour, resolved to level with the ground the stately temples within the diocese of Apamea. His attack was resisted, by the skill and solidity, with which the temple of Jupiter had been constructed. The building was seated on an eminence: on each of the four sides, the lofty roof was supported by fifteen massy columns, sixteen feet in circumference; and the large stones of which they were composed, were firmly cemented with lead and iron. The force of the strongest and sharpest tools had been tried without effect. It was found necessary to undermine the foundations of the columns, which fell down as soon as the temporary wooden props had been consumed with fire; and the difficulties of the enterprise are described under the allegory of a black dæmon, who retarded, though he could not defeat, the operations of the Christian engineers. Elated with victory, Marcellus took the field in person against the powers of darkness; a numerous troop of soldiers and gladiators marched under the episcopal banner, and he successively attacked the villages and country temples of the diocese of Apamea. Whenever any resistance or danger was apprehended, the champion of the faith, whose lameness would not allow him either to fight or fly, placed himself at a convenient distance, beyond the reach of darts. But this prudence was the occasion of his death: he was surprised and slain by a body of exasperated rustics; and the synod of the province pronounced, without hesitation, that the holy Marcellus had sacrificed his life in the cause of God. In the support of this cause, the monks, who rushed, with tumultuous fury, from the desert, distinguished themselves by their zeal and diligence. They deserved the enmity of the Pagans; and some of them might deserve the reproaches of avarice and intemperance; of avarice, which they gratified with holy plunder, and of intemperance, which they indulged at the expence of the people, who foolishly admired their tattered garments, loud psalmody, and artificial paleness.[32] A small number of temples was protected by the fears, the venality, the taste, or the prudence, of the civil and ecclesiastical governors. The temple of the celestial Venus at Carthage, whose sacred precincts

---

31. Compare Sozomen (l. vii. c. 15.) with Theodoret (l. v. c. 21). Between them, they relate the crusade and death of Marcellus.
32. Libanius pro Templis, p. 10–13. He rails at these black-garbed men, the Christian Monks, who eat more than elephants. Poor elephants! *they* are temperate animals.

formed a circumference of two miles, was judiciously converted into a Christian church;[33] and a similar consecration has preserved inviolate the majestic dome of the Pantheon at Rome.[34] But in almost every province of the Roman world, an army of fanatics, without authority, and without discipline, invaded the peaceful inhabitants; and the ruin of the fairest structures of antiquity still displays the ravages of *those* Barbarians, who alone had time and inclination to execute such laborious destruction.

The temple of Serapis at Alexandria.

In this wide and various prospect of devastation, the spectator may distinguish the ruins of the temple of Serapis, at Alexandria.[35] Serapis does not appear to have been one of the native gods, or monsters, who sprung from the fruitful soil of superstitious Egypt.[36] The first of the Ptolemies had been commanded, by a dream, to import the mysterious stranger from the coast of Pontus, where he had been long adored by the inhabitants of Sinope; but his attributes and his reign were so imperfectly understood, that it became a subject of dispute, whether he represented the bright orb of day, or the gloomy monarch of the subterraneous regions.[37] The Egyptians, who were obstinately devoted to the religion of their fathers, refused to admit this foreign deity within the walls of their cities.[38] But the obsequious priests, who were seduced by the liberality of the Ptolemies, submitted, without resistance, to the power of the god of Pontus: an honourable and domestic genealogy was provided; and this fortunate usurper was introduced into the throne and bed of Osiris,[39] the husband of Isis, and the celestial monarch of Egypt. Alexandria,

33. Prosper. Aquitan. l. iii. c. 38. apud Baronium; Annal. Eccles. A.D. 389. Nº 58, &c. The temple had been shut some time, and the access to it was overgrown with brambles.

34. Donatus, Roma Antiqua et Nova, l. iv. c. 4. p. 468. This consecration was performed by pope Boniface IV. I am ignorant of the favourable circumstances which had preserved the Pantheon above two hundred years after the reign of Theodosius.

35. Sophronius composed a recent and separate history (Jerom, in Script. Eccles. tom. i. p. 303.), which has furnished materials to Socrates (l. v. c. 16.), Theodoret (l. v. c. 22.), and Rufinus (l. ii. c. 22.). Yet the last, who had been at Alexandria, before, and after, the event, may deserve the credit of an original witness.

36. Gerard Vossius (Opera, tom. v. p. 80. & de Idololatria, l. i. c. 29.) strives to support the strange notion of the Fathers; that the patriarch Joseph was adored in Egypt, as the bull Apis, and the god Serapis.

37. Origo dei nondum nostris celebrata. Ægyptiorum antistites *sic* memorant, &c. Tacit. Hist. iv. 83. The Greeks, who had travelled into Egypt, were alike ignorant of this new deity.

38. Macrobius, Saturnal. l. 1. c. 7. Such a living fact decisively proves his foreign extraction.

39. At Rome, Isis and Serapis were united in the same temple. The precedency which the queen assumed, may seem to betray her unequal alliance with the stranger of Pontus. But the superiority of the female sex was established in Egypt as a civil and religious

which claimed his peculiar protection, gloried in the name of the city of Serapis. His temple,[40] which rivalled the pride and magnificence of the capitol, was erected on the spacious summit of an artificial mount, raised one hundred steps above the level of the adjacent parts of the city; and the interior cavity was strongly supported by arches, and distributed into vaults and subterraneous apartments. The consecrated buildings were surrounded by a quadrangular portico; the stately halls and exquisite statues, displayed the triumph of the arts; and the treasures of ancient learning were preserved in the famous Alexandrian library, which had arisen with new splendour from its ashes.[41] After the edicts of Theodosius had severely prohibited the sacrifices of the Pagans, they were still tolerated in the city and temple of Serapis; and this singular indulgence was imprudently ascribed to the superstitious terrors of the Christians themselves: as if they had feared to abolish those ancient rites, which could alone secure the inundations of the Nile, the harvests of Egypt, and the subsistence of Constantinople.[42]

At that time[43] the archiepiscopal throne of Alexandria was filled by Theophilus,[44] the perpetual enemy of peace and virtue; a bold, bad man, whose hands were alternately polluted with gold, and with blood. His pious indignation was excited by the honours of Serapis; and the insults which he offered to an ancient chapel of Bacchus, convinced the Pagans that he meditated a more important and dangerous enterprise. In the tumultuous capital of Egypt, the slightest provocation was sufficient to inflame a civil war. The votaries of Serapis, whose strength and numbers were much inferior to those of their antagonists, rose in arms

Its final destruction, A.D. 389.

institution (Diodor. Sicul. tom. i. l. i. p. 31. edit. Wesseling), and the same order is observed in Plutarch's Treatise of Isis and Osiris, whom he identifies with Serapis.

40. Ammianus (xxii. 16.). The Expositio totius Mundi (p. 8. in Hudson's Geograph. Minor, tom. iii.), and Rufinus (l. ii. c. 22.), celebrate the *Serapeum*, as one of the wonders of the world.

41. See Memoires de l'Acad. des Inscriptions, tom. ix. p. 397–416. The *old* library of the Ptolemies was *totally* consumed in Cæsar's Alexandrian war. Marc Antony gave the whole collection of Pergamus (200,000 volumes) to Cleopatra, as the foundation

of the *new* library of Alexandria.

42. Libanius (pro Templis, p. 21.) indiscreetly provokes his Christian masters by this insulting remark.

43. We may chuse between the date of Marcellinus (A.D. 389.) or that of Prosper (A.D. 391.). Tillemont (Hist. des Emp. tom. v. p. 310. 756.) prefers the former and Pagi the latter.

44. Tillemont, Mem. Eccles. tom. xi. p. 441–500. The ambiguous situation of Theophilus, a *saint*, as the friend of Jerom; a *devil*, as the enemy of Chrysostom; produce a fort of impartiality: yet, upon the whole, the balance is justly inclined against him.

at the instigation of the philosopher Olympius,[45] who exhorted them to die in the defence of the altars of the gods. These Pagan fanatics fortified themselves in the temple, or rather fortress, of Serapis; repelled the besiegers by daring sallies, and a resolute defence; and, by the inhuman cruelties which they exercised on their Christian prisoners, obtained the last consolation of despair. The efforts of the prudent magistrate were usefully exerted for the establishment of a truce, till the answer of Theodosius should determine the fate of Serapis. The two parties assembled, without arms, in the principal square; and the Imperial rescript was publicly read. But when a sentence of destruction against the idols of Alexandria was pronounced, the Christians sent up a shout of joy and exultation, whilst the unfortunate Pagans, whose fury had given way to consternation, retired with hasty and silent steps, and eluded, by their flight or obscurity, the resentment of their enemies. Theophilus proceeded to demolish the temple of Serapis, without any other difficulties, than those which he found in the weight and solidity of the materials; but these obstacles proved so insuperable, that he was obliged to leave the foundations; and to content himself with reducing the edifice itself to a heap of rubbish, a part of which was soon afterwards cleared away, to make room for a church, erected in honour of the Christian martyrs. The valuable library of Alexandria was pillaged or destroyed; and, near twenty years afterwards, the appearance of the empty shelves excited the regret and indignation of every spectator, whose mind was not totally darkened by religious prejudice.[46] The compositions of ancient genius, so many of which have irretrievably perished, might surely have been excepted from the wreck of idolatry, for the amusement and instruction of succeeding ages; and either the zeal or the avarice of the archbishop,[47] might have been satiated with the rich spoils, which were the reward of his victory. While the images and vases of gold and silver were carefully melted, and those of a less valuable metal were contemptuously broken, and cast into the streets, Theophilus laboured to expose the frauds and vices of the

---

45. Lardner (Heathen Testimonies, vol. iv. p. 411.) has alleged a beautiful passage from Suidas, or rather, from Damascius, which shews the devout and virtuous Olympius not in the light of a warrior, but of a prophet.

46. Nos vidimus armaria librorum, quibus direptis, exinanita ea a nostris hominibus, nostris temporibus memorent. Orosius. l. vi. c. 15. p. 421. edit. Havercamp. Though a bigot, and a controversial writer, Orosius seems to blush.

47. Eunapius, in the lives of Antoninus and Ædesius, execrates the sacrilegious rapine of Theophilus. Tillemont (Mem. Eccles. tom. xiii. p. 453.) quotes an epistle of Isidore of Pelusium, which reproaches the primate with the *idolatrous* worship of gold, the auri *sacra* fames.

ministers of the idols; their dexterity in the management of the loadstone; their secret methods of introducing an human actor into a hollow statue; and their scandalous abuse of the confidence of devout husbands, and unsuspecting females.[48] Charges like these may seem to deserve some degree of credit, as they are not repugnant to the crafty and interested spirit of superstition. But the same spirit is equally prone to the base practice of insulting and calumniating a fallen enemy; and our belief is naturally checked by the reflection, that it is much less difficult to invent a fictitious story, than to support a practical fraud. The colossal statue of Serapis[49] was involved in the ruin of his temple and religion. A great number of plates of different metals, artificially joined together, composed the majestic figure of the Deity, who touched on either side the walls of the sanctuary. The aspect of Serapis, his sitting posture, and the sceptre, which he bore in his left hand, were extremely similar to the ordinary representations of Jupiter. He was distinguished from Jupiter by the basket, or bushel, which was placed on his head; and by the emblematic monster, which he held in his right hand: the head and body of a serpent branching into three tails, which were again terminated by the triple heads of a dog, a lion, and a wolf. It was confidently affirmed, that if any impious hand should dare to violate the majesty of the god, the heavens and the earth would instantly return to their original chaos. An intrepid soldier, animated by zeal, and armed with a weighty battle-axe, ascended the ladder; and even the Christian multitude expected, with some anxiety, the event of the combat.[50] He aimed a vigorous stroke against the cheek of Serapis; the cheek fell to the ground; the thunder was still silent, and both the heavens and the earth

---

48. Rufinus names the priest of Saturn who, in the character of the god, familiarly conversed with many pious ladies of quality; till he betrayed himself, in a moment of transport, when he could not disguise the tone of his voice. The authentic and impartial narrative of Æschines (see Bayle, Dictionnaire Critique, SCAMANDRE), and the adventure of Mundus (Joseph. Antiquitat. Judaic. l. xviii. c. 3. p. 877. edit. Havercamp.), may prove that such amorous frauds have been practised with success.

49. See the images of Serapis, in Montfaucon (tom. ii. p. 297.): but the description of Macrobius (Saturnal. l. i. c. 20.) is much more picturesque and satisfactory.

50.
Sed fortes tremuere manus, motique
     verendâ
Majestate loci, si robora sacra ferirent
In sua credebant reditturas membra
     secures.

(Lucan. iii. 429.) "Is it true (said Augustus to a veteran of Italy, at whose house he supped), that the man, who gave the first blow to the golden statue of Anaitis, was instantly deprived of his eyes, and of his life?" "I was that man (replied the clear-sighted veteran), and you now sup on one of the legs of the goddess." (Plin. Hist. Natur. xxxiii. 24.)

continued to preserve their accustomed order and tranquillity. The victorious soldier repeated his blows: the huge idol was overthrown, and broken in pieces; and the limbs of Serapis were ignominiously dragged through the streets of Alexandria. His mangled carcase was burnt in the Amphitheatre, amidst the shouts of the populace; and many persons attributed their conversion to this discovery of the impotence of their tutelar deity. The popular modes of religion, that propose any visible and material objects of worship, have the advantage of adapting and familiarising themselves to the senses of mankind: but this advantage is counterbalanced by the various and inevitable accidents to which the faith of the idolater is exposed. It is scarcely possible, that, in every disposition of mind, he should preserve his implicit reverence for the idols, or the relics, which the naked eye, and the profane hand, are unable to distinguish from the most common productions of art, or nature; and if, in the hour of danger, their secret and miraculous virtue does not operate for their own preservation, he scorns the vain apologies of his priests, and justly derides the object, and the folly, of his superstitious attachment.[51] After the fall of Serapis, some hopes were still entertained by the Pagans, that the Nile would refuse his annual supply to the impious masters of Egypt; and the extraordinary delay of the inundation seemed to announce the displeasure of the river-god. But this delay was soon compensated by the rapid swell of the waters. They suddenly rose to such an unusual height, as to comfort the discontented party with the pleasing expectation of a deluge; till the peaceful river again subsided to the well-known and fertilising level of sixteen cubits, or about thirty English feet.[52]

The Pagan religion is prohibited, A.D. 390. The temples of the Roman empire were deserted, or destroyed; but the ingenious superstition of the Pagans still attempted to elude the laws of Theodosius, by which all sacrifices had been severely prohibited. The inhabitants of the country, whose conduct was less exposed to the eye of malicious curiosity, disguised their *religious*, under the appearance of *convivial*, meetings. On the days of solemn festivals, they assembled in great numbers under the spreading shade of some con-

---

51. The History of the Reformation affords frequent examples of the sudden change from superstition to contempt.

52. Sozomen, l. vii. c. 20. I have supplied the measure. The same standard, of the inundation, and consequently of the cubit, has uniformly subsisted since the time of Herodotus. See Freret, in the Mem. de l'Academie des Inscriptions, tom. xvi. p. 344–353. Greaves's Miscellaneous Works, vol. i. p. 233. The Egyptian cubit is about twenty-two inches of the English measure.

secrated trees; sheep and oxen were slaughtered and roasted; and this rural entertainment was sanctified by the use of incense, and by the hymns, which were sung in honour of the gods. But it was alleged, that, as no part of the animal was made a burnt-offering, as no altar was provided to receive the blood, and as the previous oblation of salt cakes, and the concluding ceremony of libations, were carefully omitted, these festal meetings did not involve the guests in the guilt, or penalty, of an illegal sacrifice.[53] Whatever might be the truth of the facts, or the merit of the distinction,[54] these vain pretences were swept away by the last edict of Theodosius; which inflicted a deadly wound on the superstition of the Pagans.[55] This prohibitory law is expressed in the most absolute and comprehensive terms. "It is our will and pleasure," says the emperor, "that none of our subjects, whether magistrates or private citizens, however exalted, or however humble may be their rank and condition, shall presume, in any city, or in any place, to worship an inanimate idol, by the sacrifice of a guiltless victim." The act of sacrificing, and the practice of divination by the entrails of the victim, are declared (without any regard to the object of the enquiry) a crime of high-treason against the state; which can be expiated only by the death of the guilty. The rites of Pagan superstition, which might seem less bloody and atrocious, are abolished, as highly injurious to the truth and honour of religion, luminaries, garlands, frankincense, and libations of wine, are specially enumerated and condemned; and the harmless claims of the domestic genius, of the household gods, are included in this rigorous proscription. The use of any of these profane and illegal ceremonies, subjects the offender to the forfeiture of the house, or estate, where they have been performed; and if he has artfully chosen the property of another for the scene of his impiety, he is compelled to discharge, without delay, a heavy fine of twenty-five pounds of gold, or more than one thousand pounds sterling. A fine, not less considerable, is imposed on the connivance of the secret enemies of religion, who shall neglect the duty of their respective

---

53. Libanius (pro Templis, p. 15, 16, 17.) pleads their cause with gentle and insinuating rhetoric. From the earliest age, such feasts had enlivened the country; and those of Bacchus (Georgic ii. 380.) had produced the theatre of Athens. See Godefroy, ad loc. Liban. and Codex Theodos. tom. vi. p. 284.

54. Honorius tolerated these rustic festivals (A.D. 399,). "Absque ullo sacrificio, atque ullâ superstitione damnabili." But nine years afterwards he found it necessary to reiterate and enforce the same proviso (Codex Theodos. l. xvi. tit. x. leg. 17. 19.).

55. Cod. Theodos. l. xvi. tit. x. leg. 12. Jortin (Remarks on Eccles. History, vol. iv. p. 134.) censures, with becoming asperity, the style and sentiments of this intolerant law.

stations, either to reveal, or to punish, the guilt of idolatry. Such was the persecuting spirit of the laws of Theodosius, which were repeatedly enforced by his sons and grandsons, with the loud and unanimous applause of the Christian world.[56]

Oppressed,   In the cruel reigns of Decius and Diocletian, Christianity had been proscribed, as a revolt from the ancient and hereditary religion of the empire; and the unjust suspicions which were entertained of a dark and dangerous faction, were, in some measure, countenanced by the inseparable union, and rapid conquests, of the Catholic church. But the same excuses of fear and ignorance cannot be applied to the Christian emperors, who violated the precepts of humanity and of the gospel. The experience of ages had betrayed the weakness, as well as folly, of Paganism; the light of reason and of faith had already exposed, to the greatest part of mankind, the vanity of idols; and the declining sect, which still adhered to their worship, might have been permitted to enjoy, in peace and obscurity, the religious customs of their ancestors. Had the Pagans been animated by the undaunted zeal, which possessed the minds of the primitive believers, the triumph of the church must have been stained with blood; and the martyrs of Jupiter and Apollo might have embraced the glorious opportunity of devoting their lives and fortunes at the foot of their altars. But such obstinate zeal was not congenial to the loose and careless temper of polytheism. The violent and repeated strokes of the orthodox princes, were broken by the soft and yielding substance against which they were directed; and the ready obedience of the Pagans protected them from the pains and penalties of the Theodosian Code.[57] Instead of asserting, that the authority of the gods was superior to that of the emperor, they desisted, with a plaintive murmur, from the use of those sacred rites which their sovereign had condemned. If they were sometimes tempted, by a sally of passion, or by the hopes of concealment, to indulge their favourite superstition; their humble repentance disarmed the severity of the Christian magistrate, and

56. Such a charge should not be lightly made; but it may surely be justified by the authority of St. Augustin, who thus addresses the Donatists. "Quis nostrûm, quis vestrûm non laudat leges ab Imperatoribus datas adversus sacrificia Paganorum? Et certe longe ibi pœna severior constituta est; illius quippe impietatis capitale supplicium est." Epist. xciii. Nº 10. quoted by Le Clerc (Bibliotheque Choisie,

tom. viii. p. 277.), who adds some judicious reflections on the intolerance of the victorious Christians.

57. Orosius, l. vii. c. 28. p. 537. Augustin (Enarrat. in Psalm cxl. apud Lardner, Heathen Testimonies, vol. iv. p. 458.) insults their cowardice. "Quis eorum comprehensus est in sacrificio (cum his legibus ista prohiberentur) et non negavit?"

they seldom refused to atone for their rashness, by submitting, with some secret reluctance, to the yoke of the Gospel. The churches were filled with the increasing multitude of these unworthy proselytes, who had conformed from temporal motives, to the reigning religion; and whilst they devoutly imitated the postures, and recited the prayers, of the faithful, they satisfied their conscience by the silent and sincere invocation of the gods of antiquity.[58] If the Pagans wanted patience to suffer, they wanted spirit to resist; and the scattered myriads, who deplored the ruin of the temples, yielded, without a contest, to the fortune of their adversaries. The disorderly opposition[59] of the peasants of Syria, and the populace of Alexandria, to the rage of private fanaticism, was silenced by the name and authority of the emperor. The Pagans of the West, without contributing to the elevation of Eugenius, disgraced, by their partial attachment, the cause and character of the usurper. The clergy vehemently exclaimed, that he aggravated the crime of rebellion by the guilt of apostasy; that, by his permission, the altar of Victory was again restored; and that the idolatrous symbols of Jupiter and Hercules were displayed in the field, against the invincible standard of the cross. But the vain hopes of the Pagans were soon annihilated by the defeat of Eugenius; and they were left exposed to the resentment of the conqueror, who laboured to deserve the favour of Heaven by the extirpation of idolatry.[60]

A nation of slaves is always prepared to applaud the clemency of their master, who, in the abuse of absolute power, does not proceed to the last extremes of injustice and oppression. Theodosius might undoubtedly have proposed to his Pagan subjects the alternative of baptism or of death; and the eloquent Libanius has praised the moderation of a prince, who never enacted, by any positive law, that all his subjects should immediately embrace and practise the religion of their sovereign.[61] The profession of Christianity was not made an essential qualification for the enjoyment of the civil rights of society,

and finally extinguished, A.D. 390– 420, &c.

---

58. Libanius (pro Templis, p. 17, 18.) mentions, without censure, the occasional conformity, and as it were theatrical play, of these hypocrites.
59. Libanius concludes his apology (p. 32.), by declaring to the emperor, that unless he expressly warrants the destruction of the temples, ισθι τους των αγρων δεσποτας, και αυτοις, και τω νομω βοηθησοντας, the

proprietors will defend themselves and the laws.
60. Paulinus, in Vit. Ambros. c. 26. Augustin de Civitat. Dei, l. v. c. 26. Theodoret, l. v. c. 24.
61. Libanius suggests the form of a persecuting edict, which Theodosius might enact (pro Templis, p. 32.); a rash joke, and a dangerous experiment. Some princes would have taken his advice.

nor were any peculiar hardships imposed on the sectaries, who credulously received the fables of Ovid, and obstinately rejected the miracles of the Gospel. The palace, the schools, the army, and the senate, were filled with declared and devout Pagans; they obtained, without distinction, the civil and military honours of the empire. Theodosius distinguished his liberal regard for virtue and genius by the consular dignity, which he bestowed on Symmachus;[62] and by the personal friendship which he expressed to Libanius;[63] and the two eloquent apologists of Paganism were never required either to change, or to dissemble, their religious opinions. The Pagans were indulged in the most licentious freedom of speech and writing; the historical and philosophic remains of Eunapius, Zosimus,[64] and the fanatic teachers of the school of Plato, betray the most furious animosity, and contain the sharpest invectives against the sentiments and conduct of their victorious adversaries. If these audacious libels were publicly known, we must applaud the good sense of the Christian princes, who viewed, with a smile of contempt, the last struggles of superstition and despair.[65] But the Imperial laws, which prohibited the sacrifices and ceremonies of Paganism, were rigidly executed; and every hour contributed to destroy the influence of a religion, which was supported by custom, rather than by argument. The devotion of the poet, or the philosopher, may be secretly nourished by prayer, meditation, and study; but the exercise of public worship appears to be the only solid foundation of the religious sentiments of the people, which derive their force from imitation and habit. The interruption of that public exercise may consummate, in the period of a few years, the important work of a national revolution. The memory of theological opinions cannot

62.
　　Denique pro meritis terrestribus æque
　　　　rependens
　　Munera, sacricolis summos impertit
　　　　honores.
　　　　　　　　.　　　　　．
　　Ipse magistratum tibi consulis, ipse
　　　　tribunal
　　Contulit.
　　　　　　　　Prudent. in Symmach. i. 617, &c.

63. Libanius (pro Templis, p. 32.) is proud that Theodosius should thus distinguish a man, who even in his *presence* would swear by Jupiter. Yet this presence seems to be no more than a figure of rhetoric.

64. Zosimus, who styles himself Count and Ex-advocate of the Treasury, reviles, with partial and indecent bigotry, the Christian princes, and even the father of his sovereign. His work must have been privately circulated, since it escaped the invectives of the ecclesiastical historians prior to Evagrius (l. iii. c. 40–42.), who lived towards the end of the sixth century.

65. Yet the Pagans of Africa complained, that the times would not allow them to answer with freedom the City of God: nor does St. Augustin (v. 26.) deny the charge.

long be preserved, without the artificial helps of priests, of temples, and of books.[66] The ignorant vulgar, whose minds are still agitated by the blind hopes and terrors of superstition, will be soon persuaded by their superiors, to direct their vows to the reigning deities of the age; and will insensibly imbibe an ardent zeal for the support and propagation of the new doctrine, which spiritual hunger at first compelled them to accept. The generation that arose in the world after the promulgation of the Imperial laws, was attracted within the pale of the Catholic church: and so rapid, yet so gentle, was the fall of Paganism, that only twenty-eight years after the death of Theodosius, the faint and minute vestiges were no longer visible to the eye of the legislator.[67]

The ruin of the Pagan religion is described by the sophists, as a dreadful and amazing prodigy, which covered the earth with darkness, and restored the ancient dominion of chaos and of night. They relate, into solemn and pathetic strains, that the

The worship of the Christian martyrs.

temples were converted into sepulchres, and that the holy places, which had been adorned by the statues of the gods, were basely polluted by the relics of Christian martyrs. "The monks" (a race of filthy animals, to whom Eunapius is tempted to refuse the name of men) "are the authors of the new worship, which, in the place of those deities, who are conceived by the understanding, has substituted the meanest and most contemptible slaves. The heads, salted and pickled, of those infamous malefactors, who for the multitude of their crimes have suffered a just and ignominious death; their bodies, still marked by the impression of the lash, and the scars of those tortures which were inflicted by the sentence of the magistrate; such" (continues Eunapius) "are the gods which the earth produces in our days; such are the martyrs, the supreme arbitrators of our prayers and petitions to the Deity, whose tombs are now consecrated as the objects of the veneration of the people."[68] Without approving the malice, it is natural enough to share the surprise, of the Sophist, the spectator of a revolution, which raised those obscure victims of the laws of Rome, to the rank of

66. The Moors of Spain, who secretly preserved the Mahometan religion, above a century, under the tyranny of the Inquisition, possessed the Koran, with the peculiar use of the Arabic tongue. See the curious and honest story of their expulsion in Geddes (Miscellanies, vol. i. p. 1–198.).
67. Paganos qui supersunt, quanquam jam

nullos esse credamus, &c. Cod. Theodos. l. xvi. tit. x. leg. 22. A.D. 423. The younger Theodosius was afterwards satisfied, that his judgment had been somewhat premature.
68. See Eunapius, in the life of the sophist Ædesius; in that of Eustathius he foretels the ruin of Paganism, καὶ τι μυθῶδες, καὶ ἀειδὲς σκότος τυραννήσει τὰ ἐπι γῆς κάλλιστα.

celestial and invisible protectors of the Roman empire. The grateful respect of the Christians for the martyrs of the faith, was exalted, by time and victory, into religious adoration; and the most illustrious of the saints and prophets were deservedly associated to the honours of the martyrs. One hundred and fifty years after the glorious deaths of St. Peter and St. Paul, the Vatican and the Ostian road were distinguished by the tombs, or rather by the trophies, of those spiritual heroes.[69] In the age which followed the conversion of Constantine, the emperors, the consuls, and the generals of armies devoutly visited the sepulchres of a tent-maker and a fisherman;[70] and their venerable bones were deposited under the altars of Christ, on which the bishops of the royal city continually offered the unbloody sacrifice.[71] The new capital of the eastern world, unable to produce any ancient and domestic trophies, was enriched by the spoils of dependent provinces. The bodies of St. Andrew, St. Luke, and St. Timothy, had reposed, near three hundred years, in the obscure graves, from whence they were transported, in solemn pomp, to the church of the Apostles, which the magnificence of Constantine had founded on the banks of the Thracian Bosphorus.[72] About fifty years afterwards, the same banks were honoured by the presence of Samuel, the judge and prophet of the people of Israel. His ashes, deposited in a golden vase, and covered with a silken veil, were delivered by the bishops into each others hands. The relics of Samuel were received by the people, with the same joy and reverence which they would have shewn to the living prophet; the highways, from Palestine to the gates of Constantinople, were filled with an uninterrupted procession; and the emperor Arcadius himself, at the head of the most illustrious members of the clergy and senate, advanced to meet his extraordi-

69. Caius (apud Euseb. Hist. Eccles. l. ii. c. 25.), a Roman presbyter, who lived in the time of Zephyrinus (A.D. 202–219.), is an early witness of this superstitious practice.

70. Chrysostom. Quod Christus sit Deus. Tom. i. nov. edit. Nº 9. I am indebted for this quotation to Benedict the XIVth's pastoral letter on the jubilee of the year 1750. See the curious and entertaining letters of M. Chais, tom. iii.

71. Male facit ergo Romanus episcopus? qui, super mortuorum hominum, Petri & Pauli, secundum nos, ossa veneranda ... offert

Domino sacrificia, et tumulos eorum, Christi arbitratur altaria. Jerom. tom. ii. advers. Vigilant. p. 153.

72. Jerom (tom. ii. p. 122.) bears witness to these translations, which are neglected by the ecclesiastical historians. The passion of St. Andrew at Patræ, is described in an epistle from the clergy of Achaia, which Baronius (Annual. Eccles. A.D. 60. Nº 34.) wishes to believe, and Tillemont is forced to reject. St. Andrew was adopted as the spiritual founder of Constantinople (Mem. Eccles. tom. i. p. 317–323. 588–594.).

nary guest, who had always deserved and claimed the homage of kings.[73] The example of Rome and Constantinople confirmed the faith and discipline of the Catholic world. The honours of the saints and martyrs, after a feeble and ineffectual murmur of profane reason,[74] were universally established; and in the age of Ambrose and Jerom, something was still deemed wanting to the sanctity of a Christian church, till it had been consecrated by some portion of holy relics, which fixed and inflamed the devotion of the faithful.

In the long period of twelve hundred years, which elapsed between the reign of Constantine and the reformation of Luther, the worship of saints and relics corrupted the pure and perfect simplicity of the Christian model; and some symptoms of degeneracy may be observed even in the first generations which adopted and cherished this pernicious innovation.

General reflections.

I. The satisfactory experience, that the relics of saints were more valuable than gold or precious stones,[75] stimulated the clergy to multiply the treasures of the church. Without much regard for truth or probability, they invented names for skeletons, and actions for names. The fame of the apostles, and of the holy men who had imitated their virtues, was darkened by religious fiction. To the invincible band of genuine and primitive martyrs, they added myriads of imaginary heroes, who had never existed, except in the fancy of crafty or credulous legendaries; and there is reason to suspect, that Tours might not be the only diocese in which the bones of a malefactor were adored, instead of those of a saint.[76] A superstitious practice, which tended to increase the temptations of fraud, and credulity, insensibly extinguished the light of history, and of reason, in the Christian world.

I. Fabulous martyrs and relics.

---

73. Jerom (tom. ii. p. 122.) pompously describes the translation of Samuel, which is noticed in all the chronicles of the times.

74. The presbyter Vigilantius, the protestant of his age, firmly, though ineffectually, withstood the superstition of monks, relics, saints, fasts, &c. for which Jerom compares him to the Hydra, Cerberus, the Centaurs, &c. and considers him only as the organ of the Dæmon (tom. ii. p. 120–126.). Whoever will peruse the controversy of St. Jerom and Vigilantius, and St. Augustin's account of the miracles of St. Stephen, may speedily gain some idea of

the spirit of the Fathers.

75. M. de Beausobre (Hist. du Manicheisme, tom. ii. p. 648.) has applied a worldly sense to the pious observation of the clergy of Smyrna, who carefully preserved the relics of St. Polycarp the martyr.

76. Martin of Tours (See his life, c. 8. by Sulpicius Severus) extorted this confession from the mouth of the dead man. The error is allowed to be natural; the discovery is supposed to be miraculous. Which of the two was likely to happen most frequently?

II. Miracles. II. But the progress of superstition would have been much less rapid and victorious, if the faith of the people had not been assisted by the seasonable aid of visions and miracles, to ascertain the authenticity and virtue of the most suspicious relics. In the reign of the younger Theodosius, Lucian,[77] a presbyter of Jerusalem, and the ecclesiastical minister of the village of Caphargamala, about twenty miles from the city, related a very singular dream, which, to remove his doubts, had been repeated on three successive Saturdays. A venerable figure stood before him, in the silence of the night, with a long beard, a white robe, and a gold rod; announced himself by the name of Gamaliel, and revealed to the astonished presbyter, that his own corpse, with the bodies of his son Abibas, his friend Nicodemus, and the illustrious Stephen, the first martyr of the Christian faith, were secretly buried in the adjacent field. He added, with some impatience, that it was time to release himself, and his companions, from their obscure prison; that their appearance would be salutary to a distressed world; and that they had made choice of Lucian to inform the bishop of Jerusalem of their situation, and their wishes. The doubts and difficulties which still retarded this important discovery, were successively removed by new visions: and the ground was opened by the bishop, in the presence of an innumerable multitude. The coffins of Gamaliel, of his son, and of his friend, were found in regular order; but when the fourth coffin, which contained the remains of Stephen, was shewn to the light, the earth trembled, and an odour, such as that of paradise, was smelt, which instantly cured the various diseases of seventy-three of the assistants. The companions of Stephen were left in their peaceful residence of Caphargamala: but the relics of the first martyr were transported, in solemn procession, to a church constructed in their honour on Mount Sion; and the minute particles of those relics, a drop of blood,[78] or the scrapings of a bone, were acknowledged, in almost every province of the Roman world, to possess a divine and miraculous virtue. The grave and learned Augustin,[79] whose understanding

77. Lucian composed in Greek his original narrative, which has been translated by Avitus, and published by Baronius (Annal. Eccles. A.D. 415. Nº 7–16.). The Benedictine editors of St. Augustin have given (at the end of the work De Civitate Dei) two several copies, with many various readings. It is the character of falsehood to be loose and inconsistent. The most incredible parts of the legend are smoothed and softened by Tillemont (Mem. Eccles. tom. ii. p. 9, &c.).

78. A phial of St. Stephen's blood was annually liquefied at Naples, till he was superseded by St. Januarius (Ruinart. Hist. Persecut. Vandal. p. 529.).

79. Augustin composed the two-and-twenty books de Civitate Dei in the space of thirteen years, A.D. 413–426 (Tillemont, Mem.

scarcely admits the excuse of credulity, has attested the innumerable prodigies which were performed in Africa, by the relics of St. Stephen; and this
marvellous narrative is inserted in the elaborate work of the City of God,
which the bishop of Hippo designed as a solid and immortal proof of the
truth of Christianity. Augustin solemnly declares, that he has selected those
miracles only which were publicly certified by the persons, who were
either the objects, or the spectators, of the power of the martyr. Many
prodigies were omitted, or forgotten; and Hippo had been less favourably
treated than the other cities of the province. And yet the bishop enumerates
above seventy miracles, of which three were resurrections from the dead,
in the space of two years, and within the limits of his own diocese.[80] If we
enlarge our view to all the dioceses, and all the saints, of the Christian
world, it will not be easy to calculate the fables, and the errors, which
issued from this inexhaustible source. But we may surely be allowed to
observe, that a miracle, in that age of superstition and credulity, lost its
name and its merit, since it could scarcely be considered as a deviation
from the ordinary, and established, laws of nature.

III. The innumerable miracles, of which the tombs of the
martyrs were the perpetual theatre, revealed to the pious believer   *III. Revival of*
the actual state and constitution of the invisible world; and his   *polytheism.*
religious speculations appeared to be founded on the firm basis of fact and
experience. Whatever might be the condition of vulgar souls, in the long
interval between the dissolution and the resurrection of their bodies, it was
evident that the superior spirits of the saints and martyrs did not consume
that portion of their existence in silent and inglorious sleep.[81] It was evident
(without presuming to determine the place of their habitation, or the nature
of their felicity) that they enjoyed the lively and active consciousness of
their happiness, their virtue, and their powers; and that they had already
secured the possession of their eternal reward. The enlargement of their

---

Eccles. tom. xiv. p. 608, &c.). His learning is
too often borrowed, and his arguments are
too often his own; but the whole work claims
the merit of a magnificent design, vigorously,
and not unskilfully, executed.

80. See Augustin de Civitat. Dei, l. xxii. c. 22.
and the Appendix, which contains two books
of St. Stephen's miracles, by Evodius, bishop
of Uzalis. Freculphus (apud Basnage, Hist. des
Juifs, tom. viii. p. 249.) has preserved a Gallic

or Spanish proverb, "Whoever pretends to
have read all the miracles of St. Stephen, he
lies."

81. Burnet (de Statû Mortuorum, p. 56–84.)
collects the opinions of the Fathers, as far as
they assert the sleep, or repose, of human souls
till the day of judgment. He afterwards exposes
(p. 91, &c.) the inconveniencies which must
arise, if they possessed a more active and sensible existence.

intellectual faculties, surpassed the measure of the human imagination; since it was proved by *experience*, that they were capable of hearing and understanding the various petitions of their numerous votaries; who in the same moment of time, but in the most distant parts of the world, invoked the name and assistance of Stephen or of Martin.[82] The confidence of their petitioners was founded on the persuasion, that the saints, who reigned with Christ, cast an eye of pity upon earth; that they were warmly interested in the prosperity of the Catholic church; and that the individuals, who imitated the example of their faith and piety, were the peculiar and favourite objects of their most tender regard. Sometimes, indeed, their friendship might be influenced by considerations of a less exalted kind: they viewed, with partial affection, the places which had been consecrated by their birth, their residence, their death, their burial, or the possession of their relics. The meaner passions of pride, avarice, and revenge, may be deemed unworthy of a celestial breast; yet the saints themselves condescended to testify their grateful approbation of the liberality of their votaries: and the sharpest bolts of punishment were hurled against those impious wretches, who violated their magnificent shrines, or disbelieved their supernatural power.[83] Atrocious, indeed, must have been the guilt, and strange would have been the scepticism, of those men, if they had obstinately resisted the proofs of a divine agency, which the elements, the whole range of the animal creation, and even the subtle and invisible operations of the human mind, were compelled to obey.[84] The immediate, and almost instantaneous, effects, that were supposed to follow the prayer, or the offence, satisfied the Christians, of the ample measure of favour and authority, which the saints enjoyed in the presence of the Supreme God; and it seemed almost superfluous to enquire, whether they were continually obliged to intercede

---

82. Vigilantius placed the souls of the prophets and martyrs, either in the bosom of Abraham (in loco refrigerii), or else under the altar of God. Nec posse suis tumulis et ubi voluerunt adesse præsentes. But Jerom (tom. ii. p. 122.) sternly refuses this *blasphemy*. Tu Deo leges pones? Tu apostolis vincula injicies, ut usque ad diem judicii teneantur custodiâ, nec sint cum Domino suo; de quibus scriptum est, Sequuntur Agnum quocunque vadit. Si Agnus ubique, ergo, et hi, qui cum Agno sunt, ubique esse credendi sunt. Et cum diabolus

et dæmones toto vagentur in orbe, &c.

83. Fleury, Discours sur l'Hist. Ecclesiastique, iii. p. 80.

84. At Minorca, the relics of St. Stephen converted, in eight days, 540 Jews; with the help, indeed, of some wholesome severities, such as burning the synagogue, driving the obstinate infidels to starve among the rocks, &c. See the original letter of Severus bishop of Minorca (ad calcem St. Augustin. de. Civ. Dei), and the judicious remarks of Basnage (tom. viii. p. 245–251.).

before the throne of grace; or whether they might not be permitted to exercise, according to the dictates of their benevolence and justice, the delegated powers of their subordinate ministry. The imagination, which had been raised by a painful effort to the contemplation and worship of the Universal Cause, eagerly embraced such inferior objects of adoration, as were more proportioned to its gross conceptions and imperfect faculties. The sublime and simple theology of the primitive Christians was gradually corrupted; and the MONARCHY of heaven, already clouded by metaphysical subtleties, was degraded by the introduction of a popular mythology, which tended to restore the reign of polytheism.[85]

IV. As the objects of religion were gradually reduced to the standard of the imagination, the rites and ceremonies were introduced that seemed most powerfully to affect the senses of the vulgar. If, in the beginning of the fifth century,[86] Tertullian, or Lactantius,[87] had been suddenly raised from the dead, to assist at the festival of some popular saint, or martyr;[88] they would have gazed with astonishment, and indignation, on the profane spectacle, which had succeeded to the pure and spiritual worship of a Christian congregation. As soon as the doors of the church were thrown open, they must have been offended by the smoke of incense, the perfume of flowers, and the glare of lamps and tapers, which diffused, at noonday, a gawdy, superfluous, and, in their opinion, a sacrilegious light. If they approached the balustrade of the altar, they made their way through the prostrate crowd, consisting, for the most part, of strangers and pilgrims, who resorted to the city on the vigil of the feast; and who already felt the strong intoxication of fanaticism, and, perhaps, of wine. Their devout kisses were imprinted on the walls and pavement of the sacred edifice; and their fervent prayers were

IV. Introduction of Pagan ceremonies.

---

85. Mr. Hume (Essays, vol. ii. p. 434.) observes, like a philosopher, the natural flux and reflux of polytheism and theism.

86. D'Aubigné (See his own Memoires, p. 156–160.) frankly offered, with the consent of the Huguenot ministers, to allow the first 400 years as the rule of faith. The cardinal du Perron haggled for forty years more, which were indiscreetly given. Yet neither party would have found their account in this foolish bargain.

87. The worship practised and inculcated by Tertullian, Lactantius, Arnobius, &c. is so *extremely* pure and spiritual, that their declamations against the Pagan, sometimes glance against the Jewish, ceremonies.

88. Faustus the Manichæan accuses the Catholics of idolatry. Vertitis idola in martyres . . . quos votis similibus colitis. M. de Beausobre (Hist. Critique du Manicheisme, tom. ii. p. 629–700.), a Protestant, but a philosopher, has represented, with candour and learning, the introduction of *Christian idolatry* in the fourth and fifth centuries.

directed, whatever might be the language of their church, to the bones, the blood, or the ashes of the saint, which were usually concealed, by a linen or silken veil, from the eyes of the vulgar. The Christians frequented the tombs of the martyrs, in the hope of obtaining, from their powerful intercession, every sort of spiritual, but more especially of temporal, blessings. They implored the preservation of their health, or the cure of their infirmities; the fruitfulness of their barren wives, or the safety and happiness of their children. Whenever they undertook any distant or dangerous journey, they requested, that the holy martyrs would be their guides and protectors on the road; and if they returned, without having experienced any misfortune, they again hastened to the tombs of the martyrs, to celebrate, with grateful thanksgivings, their obligations to the memory and relics of those heavenly patrons. The walls were hung round with symbols of the favours, which they had received; eyes, and hands, and feet, of gold and silver: and edifying pictures, which could not long escape the abuse of indiscreet or idolatrous devotion, represented the image, the attributes, and the miracles of the tutelar saint. The same uniform original spirit of superstition might suggest, in the most distant ages and countries, the same methods of deceiving the credulity, and of affecting the senses of mankind:[89] but it must ingenuously be confessed, that the ministers of the Catholic church imitated the profane model, which they were impatient to destroy. The most respectable bishops had persuaded themselves, that the ignorant rustics would more cheerfully renounce the superstitions of Paganism, if they found some resemblance, some compensation, in the bosom of Christianity. The religion of Constantine atchieved, in less than a century, the final conquest of the Roman empire: but the victors themselves were insensibly subdued by the arts of their vanquished rivals.[90]

89. The resemblance of superstition, which could not be imitated, might be traced from Japan to Mexico. Warburton has seized this idea, which he distorts, by rendering it too general and absolute (Divine Legation, vol. iv. p. 126, &c.).

90. The imitation of Paganism is the subject of Dr. Middleton's agreeable letter from Rome. Warburton's animadversions obliged him to connect (vol. iii. p. 120–132.) the history of the two religions; and to prove the antiquity of the Christian copy.

[CHAPTERS XXIX–XXXIII]

The central event of chapters XXIX to XXXIII is the sack of Rome by Alaric, the king of the Goths, on 24 August 410. Once again, Gibbon seizes the opportunity to challenge the casual assumptions and prejudices of his readership, in particular their likely assumptions about the relation of the recent and more distant past:

There exists in human nature a strong propensity to depreciate the advantages, and to magnify the evils, of the present times. Yet, when the first emotions had subsided, and a fair estimate was made of the real damage, the more learned and judicious contemporaries were forced to confess, that infant Rome had formerly received more essential injury from the Gauls, than she had now sustained from the Goths in her declining age. The experience of eleven centuries has enabled posterity to produce a much more singular parallel; and to affirm with confidence, that the ravages of the Barbarians, whom Alaric had led from the banks of the Danube, were less destructive, than the hostilities exercised by the troops of Charles the Fifth, a Catholic prince, who styled himself Emperor of the Romans. The Goths evacuated the city at the end of six days, but Rome remained above nine months in the possession of the Imperialists; and every hour was stained by some atrocious act of cruelty, lust, and rapine. The authority of Alaric preserved some order and moderation among the ferocious multitude, which acknowledged him for their leader and king: but the constable of Bourbon had gloriously fallen in the attack of the walls; and the death of the general removed every restraint of discipline, from an army which consisted of three independent nations, the Italians, the Spaniards, and the Germans. In the beginning of the sixteenth century, the manners of Italy exhibited a remarkable scene of the depravity of mankind. They united the sanguinary crimes that prevail in an unsettled state of society, with the polished vices which spring from the abuse of art and luxury: and the loose adventurers, who had violated every prejudice of patriotism and superstition to assault the palace of the Roman pontiff, must deserve to be considered as the most profligate of the *Italians*. At the same æra, the

Spaniards were the terror both of the Old and New World: but their high-spirited valour was disgraced by gloomy pride, rapacious avarice, and unrelenting cruelty. Indefatigable in the pursuit of fame and riches, they had improved, by repeated practice, the most exquisite and effectual methods of torturing their prisoners: many of the Castillans, who pillaged Rome, were familiars of the holy inquisition; and some volunteers, perhaps, were lately returned from the conquest of Mexico. The *Germans* were less corrupt than the Italians, less cruel than the Spaniards; and the rustic, or even savage, aspect of those *Tramontane* warriors, often disguised a simple and merciful disposition. But they had imbibed, in the first fervour of the reformation, the spirit, as well as the principles, of Luther. It was their favourite amusement to insult, or destroy, the consecrated objects of Catholic superstition: they indulged, without pity, or remorse, a devout hatred against the clergy of every denomination and degree, who form so considerable a part of the inhabitants of modern Rome; and their fanatic zeal might aspire to subvert the throne of Antichrist, to purify, with blood and fire, the abominations of the spiritual Babylon. (*DF*, ii. 207–9)

The historian's understanding of the relation between different areas of the past needs always to be as flexible and undogmatic as possible; and Gibbon clearly considered that confronting his readership with vivid and imaginative evocations of time's lapse was no small portion of the historian's art. It is for this reason that he preserves, but ingeniously redeploys, a Christian fable of the fifth century:

Among the insipid legends of ecclesiastical history, I am tempted to distinguish the memorable fable of the SEVEN SLEEPERS: whose imaginary date corresponds with the reign of the younger Theodosius, and the conquest of Africa by the Vandals. When the emperor Decius persecuted the Christians, seven noble youths of Ephesus concealed themselves in a spacious cavern in the side of an adjacent mountain; where they were doomed to perish by the tyrant, who gave orders that the entrance should be firmly secured with a pile of huge stones. They immediately fell into a deep slumber, which was miraculously prolonged, without injuring the powers of life, during a period of one hundred and eighty-seven years. At the end of that time, the slaves of Adolius, to whom the inheritance of the mountain had descended, removed the stones, to supply materials for some rustic edifice: the light of the sun darted into the cavern, and the seven sleepers were permitted to awake. After a slumber, as they thought of a few hours, they were pressed by the calls of hunger; and resolved that Jamblichus, one of their number, should secretly return to the city, to purchase bread for the use of his companions. The youth (if we may still employ that appellation) could no longer recognise the once familiar aspect of his native country; and his surprise was increased by the appearance of a large cross, triumphantly erected over the principal gate of Ephesus. His singular dress, and obsolete language, confounded the baker, to whom he offered an ancient medal of Decius as the current coin of the empire; and Jamblichus, on the suspicion of a secret treasure, was dragged before the judge. Their mutual enquiries produced the amazing discovery, that two centuries were almost elapsed since Jamblichus, and his friends, had escaped from the rage of a Pagan tyrant. The bishop of Ephesus, the clergy, the magistrates, the people, and as it is said the emperor Theodosius himself, hastened to visit the cavern of the Seven Sleepers; who bestowed their benediction, related their story, and at the same instant peaceably expired. The origin of this marvellous fable cannot be ascribed to the pious fraud and credulity of the *modern* Greeks, since the authentic tradition may be traced within half a century of the supposed miracle. James of Sarug, a Syrian bishop, who was born only two years after the death of the younger Theodosius, has devoted one of his two hundred and thirty homilies to the praise of the young men of Ephesus. Their legend, before the end of the sixth century, was translated from the Syriac, into the Latin, language, by the care of Gregory of Tours. The hostile communions of the East preserve their memory with equal reverence; and their names are honourably inscribed in the Roman, the Habyssinian, and the Russian calendar. Nor has their reputation been confined to the Christian world. This popular tale, which Mahomet might learn when he drove his camels to the fairs of Syria, is introduced, as a divine revelation, into the Koran. The story of the Seven Sleepers has been adopted, and adorned by the nations, from Bengal to Africa, who profess the Mahometan religion; and some vestiges of a similar tradition have been discovered in the remote extremities of Scandinavia. This easy and universal belief, so expressive of the sense of mankind, may be ascribed to the genuine merit of the fable itself. We imperceptibly advance from youth to age, without observing the gradual, but incessant, change of human affairs; and even in our larger experience of history, the imagination is accustomed, by a perpetual series of causes and effects, to unite the most distant revolutions. But if the interval between two memorable æras could be instantly annihilated; if it were possible, after a momentary slumber of two hundred years, to display the *new* world to the eyes of a spectator, who still retained a lively and recent impression of the *old*, his surprise and his reflections would furnish the pleasing subject of a philosophical romance. The scene could not be more advantageously placed, than in the two centuries which elapsed between the reigns of Decius and of Theodosius the Younger. During this period, the seat of government had been transported from Rome to a new city on the banks of the Thracian Bosphorus; and the abuse of military spirit had been suppressed, by an artificial system of tame and ceremonious servitude. The throne of the persecuting Decius was filled by a succession of Christian and orthodox princes, who had extirpated the fabulous gods of antiquity: and the public devotion of the age was impatient to exalt the saints and martyrs of the Catholic church, on the altars of Diana and Hercules. The union of the Roman empire was dissolved: its genius was humbled in the dust; and armies of unknown Barbarians, issuing from the frozen regions of the North, had established their victorious reign over the fairest provinces of Europe and Africa. (*DF*, ii. 291–3)

It is in such passages, which combine human insight, historical vision and philosophical reach, that Gibbon's range and power as an historian are most vividly displayed.

CHAPTER XXXIV

The Character, Conquests, and Court of Attila, King of the Huns. – Death of Theodosius the Younger. – Elevation of Marcian to the Empire of the East.

The western world was oppressed by the Goths and Vandals, who fled before the Huns; but the atchievements of the Huns themselves were not adequate to their power and prosperity. *The Huns, A.D. 376–433.* Their victorious hords had spread from the Volga to the Danube; but the public force was exhausted by the discord of independent chieftains; their valour was idly consumed in obscure and predatory excursions; and they often degraded their national dignity by condescending, for the hopes of spoil, to enlist under the banners of their fugitive enemies. In the reign of ATTILA,[1] the Huns again became the terror of the world; and I shall now describe the character and actions of that formidable Barbarian; who alternately insulted and invaded the East and the West, and urged the rapid downfal of the Roman empire.

In the tide of emigration, which impetuously rolled from the confines of China to those of Germany, the most powerful and populous tribes may commonly be found on the verge of the Roman provinces. The accumulated weight was sustained for a while by artificial barriers; and the easy condescension of the *Their establishment in modern Hungary.* emperors invited, without satisfying, the insolent demands of the Barbarians, who had acquired an eager appetite for the luxuries of civilized life. The Hungarians, who ambitiously insert the name of Attila among their native kings, may affirm with truth, that the hords, which were subject to his

---

1. The authentic materials for the history of Attila may be found in Jornandes (de Rebus Geticis, c. 34–50. p. 600–688. edit. Grot.) and Priscus (Excerpta de Legationibus, p. 33–76. Paris, 1648.). I have not seen the lives of Attila, composed by Juvencus Cælius Calanus Dalmatinus, in the twelfth century, or by Nicolas Olahus, archbishop of Gran, in the sixteenth. See Mascou's History of the Germans, ix. 23. and Maffei Osservazioni Litterarie, tom. i. p. 88, 89. Whatever the modern Hungarians have added, must be fabulous; and they do not seem to have excelled in the art of fiction. They suppose, that when Attila invaded Gaul and Italy, married innumerable wives, &c. he was one hundred and twenty years of age. Thwrocz Chron. p. i. c. 22. in Script. Hungar. tom. i. p. 76.

uncle Roas, or Rugilas, had formed their encampments within the limits of modern Hungary,[2] in a fertile country, which liberally supplied the wants of a nation of hunters and shepherds. In this advantageous situation, Rugilas, and his valiant brothers, who continually added to their power and reputation, commanded the alternative of peace or war with the two empires. His alliance with the Romans of the West was cemented by his personal friendship for the great Ætius; who was always secure of finding, in the Barbarian camp, a hospitable reception, and a powerful support. At his solicitation, and in the name of John the usurper, sixty thousand Huns advanced to the confines of Italy; their march and their retreat were alike expensive to the state; and the grateful policy of Ætius abandoned the possession of Pannonia to his faithful confederates. The Romans of the East were not less apprehensive of the arms of Rugilas, which threatened the provinces, or even the capital. Some ecclesiastical historians have destroyed the Barbarians with lightning and pestilence;[3] but Theodosius was reduced to the more humble expedient of stipulating an annual payment of three hundred and fifty pounds of gold, and of disguising this dishonourable tribute by the title of general, which the king of the Huns condescended to accept. The public tranquillity was frequently interrupted by the fierce impatience of the Barbarians, and the perfidious intrigues of the Byzantine court. Four dependent nations, among whom we may distinguish the Bavarians, disclaimed the sovereignty of the Huns; and their revolt was encouraged and protected by a Roman alliance; till the just claims, and formidable power, of Rugilas, were effectually urged by the voice of Eslaw his ambassador. Peace was the unanimous wish of the senate: their decree was ratified by the emperor; and two ambassadors were named, Plinthas, a general of Scythian extraction, but of consular rank; and the quæstor Epigenes, a wise and experienced statesman, who was recommended to that office by his ambitious colleague.

---

2. Hungary has been successively occupied by three Scythian colonies. 1. The Huns of Attila; 2. the Abares, in the sixth century; and, 3. the Turks or Magiars, A.D. 889.; the immediate and genuine ancestors of the modern Hungarians, whose connection with the two former is extremely faint and remote. The *Prodromus* and *Notitia* of Matthew Belius, appear to contain a rich fund of information concerning ancient and modern Hungary. I have seen the extracts in Bibliotheque Ancienne et Moderne, tom. xxii. p. 1–51. and Bibliotheque Raisonnée, tom. xvi. p. 127–175.

3. Socrates, l. vii. c. 43. Theodoret, l. v. c. 36. Tillemont, who always depends on the faith of his ecclesiastical authors, strenuously contends (Hist. des Emp. tom. vi. p. 136. 607.), that the wars and personages were not the same.

The death of Rugilas suspended the progress of the treaty. *Reign of Attila,* His two nephews, Attila and Bleda, who succeeded to the *A.D. 433–453.* throne of their uncle, consented to a personal interview with the ambassadors of Constantinople; but as they proudly refused to dismount, the business was transacted on horseback, in a spacious plain near the city of Margus, in the Upper Mæsia. The kings of the Huns assumed the solid benefits, as well as the vain honours, of the negociation. They dictated the conditions of peace, and each condition was an insult on the majesty of the empire. Besides the freedom of a safe and plentiful market on the banks of the Danube, they required that the annual contribution should be augmented from three hundred and fifty, to seven hundred, pounds of gold; that a fine, or ransom, of eight pieces of gold, should be paid for every Roman captive, who had escaped from his Barbarian master; that the emperor should renounce all treaties and engagements with the enemies of the Huns; and that all the fugitives, who had taken refuge in the court, or provinces, of Theodosius, should be delivered to the justice of their offended sovereign. This justice was rigorously inflicted on some unfortunate youths of a royal race. They were crucified on the territories of the empire, by the command of Attila: and, as soon as the king of the Huns had impressed the Romans with the terror of his name, he indulged them in a short and arbitrary respite, whilst he subdued the rebellious or independent nations of Scythia and Germany.[4]

Attila, the son of Mundzuk, deduced his noble, perhaps his regal, descent[5] from the ancient Huns, who had formerly *His figure and* contended with the monarchs of China. His features, according *character;* to the observation of a Gothic historian, bore the stamp of his national origin; and the portrait of Attila exhibits the genuine deformity of a modern Calmuck;[6] a large head, a swarthy complexion, small deep-seated eyes, a flat nose, a few hairs in the place of a beard, broad shoulders, and a short square body, of nervous strength, though of a disproportioned form. The haughty step and demeanour of the king of the Huns expressed the

4. See Priscus, p. 47, 48. and Hist. des Peuples de l'Europe, tom. vii. c. xii, xiii, xiv, xv.
5. Priscus, p. 39. The modern Hungarians have deduced his genealogy, which ascends, in the thirty-fifth degree, to Ham the son of Noah; yet they are ignorant of his father's real name (de Guignes, Hist. des Huns, tom. ii. p. 297.).

6. Compare Jornandes (c. 35. p. 661.) with Buffon, Hist. Naturelle, tom. iii. p. 380. The former had a right to observe, originis suæ signa restituens. The character and portrait of Attila are probably transcribed from Cassiodorius.

consciousness of his superiority above the rest of mankind; and he had a custom of fiercely rolling his eyes, as if he wished to enjoy the terror which he inspired. Yet this savage hero was not inaccessible to pity: his suppliant enemies might confide in the assurance of peace or pardon; and Attila was considered by his subjects as a just and indulgent master. He delighted in war; but, after he had ascended the throne in a mature age, his head, rather than his hand, atchieved the conquest of the North; and the fame of an adventurous soldier was usefully exchanged for that of a prudent and successful general. The effects of personal valour are so inconsiderable, except in poetry or romance, that victory, even among Barbarians, must depend on the degree of skill, with which the passions of the multitude are combined and guided for the service of a single man. The Scythian conquerors, Attila and Zingis, surpassed their rude countrymen in art, rather than in courage; and it may be observed, that the monarchies, both of the Huns, and of the Moguls, were erected by their founders on the basis of popular superstition. The miraculous conception, which fraud and credulity ascribed to the virgin-mother of Zingis, raised him above the level of human nature; and the naked prophet, who, in the name of the Deity, invested him with the empire of the earth, pointed the valour of the Moguls with irresistible enthusiasm.[7] The religious arts of Attila were not less skilfully adapted to the character of his age and country. It was natural enough, that the Scythians should adore, with peculiar devotion, the god of war; but as they were incapable of forming either an abstract idea, or a corporeal representation, they worshipped their tutelage deity under the symbol of an iron cimeter.[8] One of the shepherds of the Huns perceived, that a heifer, who was grazing, had wounded herself in the foot, and curiously followed the track of the blood, till he discovered, among the long grass, the point of an ancient sword; which he dug out of the ground, and presented to Attila. That magnanimous, or rather that artful, prince accepted, with pious

he discovers the sword of Mars,

---

7. Abulpharag. Dynast. vers. Pocock, p. 281. Genealogical History of the Tartars, by Abulghazi Bahader Khan, part iii. c. 15. part iv. c. 3. Vie de Gengiscan, par Petit de la Croix, l. i. c. 1. 6. The relations of the missionaries, who visited Tartary in the thirteenth century (see the seventh volume of the Histoire des Voyages), express the popular language and opinions; Zingis is styled the Son of God, &c. &c.

8. Nec templum apud eos visitur, aut delubrum, ne tugurium quidem culmo tectum cerni usquam potest; sed *gladius* Barbarico ritû humi figitur nudus, eumque ut Martem regionum quas circumcircant præsulem verecundius colunt. Ammian. Marcellin. xxxi. 2. and the learned Notes of Lindenbrogius and Valesius.

gratitude, this celestial favour; and, as the rightful possessor of the *sword of Mars*, asserted his divine and indefeasible claim to the dominion of the earth.[9] If the rites of Scythia were practised on this solemn occasion, a lofty altar, or rather pile of faggots, three hundred yards in length and in breadth, was raised in a spacious plain; and the sword of Mars was placed erect on the summit of this rustic altar, which was annually consecrated by the blood of sheep, horses, and of the hundredth captive.[10] Whether human sacrifices formed any part of the worship of Attila, or whether he propitiated the god of war with the victims which he continually offered in the field of battle, the favourite of Mars soon acquired a sacred character, which rendered his conquests more easy, and more permanent; and the Barbarian princes confessed, in the language of devotion or flattery, that they could not presume to gaze, with a steady eye, on the divine majesty of the king of the Huns.[11] His brother Bleda, who reigned over a considerable part of the nation, was compelled to resign his sceptre, and his life. Yet even this cruel act was attributed to a supernatural impulse; and the vigour with which Attila wielded the sword of Mars, convinced the world that it had been reserved alone for his invincible arm.[12] But the extent of his empire affords the only remaining evidence of the number, and importance, of his victories; and the Scythian monarch, however ignorant of the value of science and philosophy, might, perhaps, lament, that his illiterate subjects were destitute of the art which could perpetuate the memory of his exploits.

If a line of separation were drawn between the civilized and the savage climates of the globe; between the inhabitants of cities, who cultivated the earth, and the hunters and shepherds, who dwelt in tents, Attila might aspire to the title of supreme

and acquires the empire of Scythia and Germany.

---

9. Priscus relates this remarkable story, both in his own text (p. 65.), and in the quotation made by Jornandes (c. 35. p. 662). He might have explained the tradition, or fable, which characterised this famous sword, and the name, as well as attributes, of the Scythian deity, whom he has translated into the Mars of the Greeks and Romans.

10. Herodot. l. iv. c. 62. For the sake of œconomy, I have calculated by the smallest stadium. In the human sacrifices, they cut off the shoulder and arm of the victim, which they threw up into the air, and drew omens and presages from the manner of their falling on the pile.

11. Priscus, p. 55. A more civilized hero, Augustus himself, was pleased, if the person on whom he fixed his eyes seemed unable to support their divine lustre. Sueton. in August. c. 79.

12. The count de Buat (Hist. des Peuples de l'Europe, tom. vii. p. 428, 429.) attempts to clear Attila from the murder of his brother; and is almost inclined to reject the concurrent testimony of Jornandes, and the contemporary Chronicles.

and sole monarch of the Barbarians.[13] He alone, among the conquerors of ancient and modern times, united the two mighty kingdoms of Germany and Scythia; and those vague appellations, when they are applied to his reign, may be understood with an ample latitude. Thuringia, which stretched beyond its actual limits, as far as the Danube, was in the number of his provinces: he interposed, with the weight of a powerful neighbour, in the domestic affairs of the Franks; and one of his lieutenants chastised, and almost exterminated, the Burgundians of the Rhine. He subdued the islands of the ocean, the kingdoms of Scandinavia, encompassed and divided by the waters of the Baltic; and the Huns might derive a tribute of furs from that northern region, which has been protected from all other conquerors by the severity of the climate, and the courage of the natives. Towards the East, it is difficult to circumscribe the dominion of Attila over the Scythian deserts; yet we may be assured, that he reigned on the banks of the Volga; that the king of the Huns was dreaded, not only as a warrior, but as a magician;[14] that he insulted and vanquished the Khan of the formidable Geougen; and that he sent ambassadors to negociate an equal alliance with the empire of China. In the proud review of the nations who acknowledged the sovereignty of Attila, and who never entertained, during his lifetime, the thought of a revolt, the Gepidæ and the Ostrogoths were distinguished by their numbers, their bravery, and the personal merit of their chiefs. The renowned Ardaric, king of the Gepidæ, was the faithful and sagacious counsellor of the monarch; who esteemed his intrepid genius, whilst he loved the mild and discreet virtues of the noble Walamir, king of the Ostrogoths. The crowd of vulgar kings, the leaders of so many martial tribes, who served under the standard of Attila, were ranged in the submissive order of guards and domestics, round the person of their master. They watched his nod; they trembled at his frown; and, at the first signal of his will, they executed, without murmur or hesitation, his stern and absolute commands. In time of peace, the dependent princes, with their national troops, attended the royal camp in regular succession; but when

13. Fortissimarum gentium dominus, qui inauditâ ante se potentiâ, solus Scythica et Germanica regna possedit. Jornandes, c. 49. p. 684. Priscus, p. 64, 65. M. de Guignes, by his knowledge of the Chinese, has acquired (tom. ii. p. 295–301.) an adequate idea of the empire of Attila:

14. See Hist. des Huns, tom. ii. p. 296. The Geougen believed, that the Huns could excite at pleasure, storms of wind and rain. This phænomenon was produced by the stone *Gezi*; to whose magic power the loss of a battle was ascribed by the Mahometan Tartars of the fourteenth century. See Cherefeddin Ali, Hist. de Timur Bec, tom. i. p. 82, 83.

Attila collected his military force, he was able to bring into the field an army of five, or, according to another account, of seven hundred thousand Barbarians.[15]

The ambassadors of the Huns might awaken the attention of Theodosius, by reminding him, that they were his neighbours both in Europe and Asia; since they touched the Danube on one hand, and reached, with the other, as far as the Tanais. *The Huns invade Persia, A.D. 430–440.* In the reign of his father Arcadius, a band of adventurous Huns had ravaged the provinces of the East; from whence they brought away rich spoils and innumerable captives.[16] They advanced, by a secret path, along the shores of the Caspian sea; traversed the snowy mountains of Armenia; passed the Tigris, the Euphrates, and the Halys; recruited their weary cavalry with the generous breed of Cappadocian horses; occupied the hilly country of Cilicia, and disturbed the festal songs, and dances, of the citizens of Antioch. Egypt trembled at their approach; and the monks and pilgrims of the Holy Land prepared to escape their fury by a speedy embarkation. The memory of this invasion was still recent in the minds of the Orientals. The subjects of Attila might execute, with superior forces, the design which these adventurers had so boldly attempted; and it soon became the subject of anxious conjecture, whether the tempest would fall on the dominions of Rome, or of Persia. Some of the great vassals of the king of the Huns, who were themselves in the rank of powerful princes, had been sent to ratify

15. Jornandes, c. 35. p. 661. c. 37. p. 667. See Tillemont, Hist. des Empereurs, tom. vi. p. 129. 138. Corneille has represented the pride of Attila to his subject kings; and his tragedy opens with these two ridiculous lines:

> Ils ne sont pas venus, nos deux rois!
>   qu'on leur die
> Qu'ils se font trop attendre, et qu'Attila
>   s'ennuie.

The two kings of the Gepidæ and the Ostrogoths are profound politicians and sentimental lovers; and the whole piece exhibits the defects, without the genius, of the poet.

16. —— alii per Caspia claustra
    Armeniasque nives, inopino tramite
    ducti.

Invadunt Orientis opes: jam pascua
    fumant
Cappadocum, volucrumque parens
    Argæus equorum.
Jam rubet altus Halys, nec se defendit
    iniquo
Monte Cilix; Syriæ tractus vastantur
    amæni;
Assuetumque choris et lætâ plebe
    canorum
Proterit imbellem sonipes hostilis
    Orontem.
            Claudian, in Rufin. l. ii. 28–35.

See, likewise, in Eutrop. l. i. 243–251. and the strong description of Jerom, who wrote from his feelings, tom. i. p. 26. ad Heliodor. p. 200. ad Ocean. Philostorgius (l. ix. c. 8.) mentions this irruption.

an alliance and society of arms with the emperor, or rather with the general, of the West. They related, during their residence at Rome, the circumstances of an expedition, which they had lately made into the East. After passing a desert and a morass, supposed by the Romans to be the lake Mæotis, they penetrated through the mountains, and arrived, at the end of fifteen days march, on the confines of Media; where they advanced as far as the unknown cities of Basic and Cursic. They encountered the Persian army in the plains of Media; and the air, according to their own expression, was darkened by a cloud of arrows. But the Huns were obliged to retire, before the numbers of the enemy. Their laborious retreat was effected by a different road; they lost the greatest part of their booty; and at length returned to the royal camp, with some knowledge of the country, and an impatient desire of revenge. In the free conversation of the Imperial ambassadors, who discussed, at the court of Attila, the character and designs of their formidable enemy, the ministers of Constantinople expressed their hope, that his strength might be diverted and employed in a long and doubtful contest with the princes of the house of Sassan. The more sagacious Italians admonished their Eastern brethren of the folly and danger of such a hope; and convinced them, *that* the Medes and Persians were incapable of resisting the arms of the Huns; and, *that* the easy and important acquisition would exalt the pride, as well as power, of the conqueror. Instead of contenting himself with a moderate contribution, and a military title, which equalled him only to the generals of Theodosius, Attila would proceed to impose a disgraceful and intolerable yoke on the necks of the prostrate and captive Romans, who would then be encompassed, on all sides, by the empire of the Huns.[17]

They attack the Eastern empire, A.D. 441, &c. While the powers of Europe and Asia were solicitous to avert the impending danger, the alliance of Attila maintained the Vandals in the possession of Africa. An enterprise had been concerted between the courts of Ravenna and Constantinople, for the recovery of that valuable province; and the ports of Sicily were already filled with the military and naval forces of Theodosius. But the subtle Genseric, who spread his negociations round the world, prevented their designs, by exciting the king of the Huns to invade the Eastern empire; and a trifling incident soon became the motive, or pretence,

17. See the original conversation in Priscus, p. 64, 65.

of a destructive war.[18] Under the faith of the treaty of Margus, a free market was held on the northern side of the Danube, which was protected by a Roman fortress, surnamed Constantia. A troop of Barbarians violated the commercial security: killed, or dispersed, the unsuspecting traders; and levelled the fortress with the ground. The Huns justified this outrage as an act of reprisal; alleged, that the bishop of Margus had entered their territories, to discover and steal a secret treasure of their kings; and sternly demanded the guilty prelate, the sacrilegious spoil, and the fugitive subjects, who had escaped from the justice of Attila. The refusal of the Byzantine court was the signal of war; and the Mæsians at first applauded the generous firmness of their sovereign. But they were soon intimidated by the destruction of Viminiacum and the adjacent towns; and the people was persuaded to adopt the convenient maxim, that a private citizen, however innocent or respectable, may be justly sacrificed to the safety of his country. The bishop of Margus, who did not possess the spirit of a martyr, resolved to prevent the designs which he suspected. He boldly treated with the princes of the Huns; secured, by solemn oaths, his pardon and reward; posted a numerous detachment of Barbarians, in silent ambush, on the banks of the Danube; and, at the appointed hour, opened, with his own hand, the gates of his episcopal city. This advantage, which had been obtained by treachery, served as a prelude to more honourable and decisive victories. The Illyrian frontier was covered by a line of castles and fortresses; and though the greatest part of them consisted only of a single tower, with a small garrison, they were commonly sufficient to repel, or to intercept, the inroads of an enemy, who was ignorant of the art, and impatient of the delay, of a regular siege. But these slight obstacles were instantly swept away by the inundation of the Huns.[19] They destroyed, with fire and sword, the populous cities of Sirmium and Singidunum, of Ratiaria and Marcianapolis, of

---

18. Priscus, p. 331. His history contained a copious and elegant account of the war (Evagrius, l. i. c. 17.); but the extracts which relate to the embassies are the only parts that have reached our times. The original work was accessible, however, to the writers, from whom we borrow our imperfect knowledge, Jornandes, Theophanes, Count Marcellinus, Prosper-Tyro, and the author of the Alexandrian, or Paschal, Chronicle. M de Buat (Hist. des Peuples de l'Europe, tom. vii. c. xv.) has examined the cause, the circumstances, and the duration, of this war; and will not allow it to extend beyond the year four hundred and forty-four.

19. Procopius, de Edificiis, l. iv.c. 5. These fortresses were afterwards restored, strengthened, and enlarged by the emperor Justinian; but they were soon destroyed by the Abares, who succeeded to the power and possessions of the Huns.

Naissus and Sardica; where every circumstance, in the discipline of the people, and the construction of the buildings, had been gradually adapted to the sole purpose of defence. The whole breadth of Europe, as it extends above five hundred miles from the Euxine to the Hadriatic, was at once invaded, and occupied, and desolated, by the myriads of Barbarians whom Attila led into the field.

and ravage Europe, as far as Constantinople.

The public danger and distress could not, however, provoke Theodosius to interrupt his amusements and devotion, or to appear in person at the head of the Roman legions. But the troops, which had been sent against Genseric, were hastily recalled from Sicily; the garrisons, on the side of Persia, were exhausted; and a military force was collected in Europe, formidable by their arms and numbers, if the generals had understood the science of command, and their soldiers the duty of obedience. The armies of the Eastern empire were vanquished in three successive engagements; and the progress of Attila may be traced by the fields of battle. The two former, on the banks of the Utus, and under the walls of Marcianapolis, were fought in the extensive plains between the Danube and Mount Hæmus. As the Romans were pressed by a victorious enemy, they gradually, and unskilfully, retired towards the Chersonesus of Thrace; and that narrow peninsula, the last extremity of the land, was marked by their third, and irreparable, defeat. By the destruction of this army, Attila acquired the indisputable possession of the field. From the Hellespont to Thermopylæ, and the suburbs of Constantinople, he ravaged, without resistance, and without mercy, the provinces of Thrace and Macedonia. Heraclea and Hadrianople might, perhaps, escape this dreadful irruption of the Huns; but the words, the most expressive of total extirpation and erasure, are applied to the calamities which they inflicted on seventy cities of the Eastern empire.[20] Theodosius, his court and the unwarlike people, were protected by the walls of Constantinople; but those walls had been shaken by a recent earthquake, and the fall of fifty-eight towers had opened a large and tremendous breach. The damage indeed was speedily repaired; but this accident was aggravated by a superstitious fear, that Heaven itself had delivered the Imperial city to the shepherds of Scythia, who were strangers to the laws, the language, and the religion, of the Romans.[21]

---

20. Septuaginta civitates (says Prosper-Tyro) deprædatione vastatæ. The language of count Marcellinus is still more forcible. Pene totam Europam, invasis *excisisque* civitatibus atque castellis, *conrasit.*

21. Tillemont (Hist. des Empereurs, tom. vi.

In all their invasions of the civilized empires of the South, the Scythian shepherds have been uniformly actuated by a savage and destructive spirit. The laws of war, that restrain the exercise of national rapine and murder, are founded on two principles of substantial interest: the knowledge of the permanent benefits which may be obtained by a moderate use of conquest; and a just apprehension, lest the desolation which we inflict on the enemy's country, may be retaliated on our own. But these considerations of hope and fear are almost unknown in the pastoral state of nations. The Huns of Attila may, without injustice, be compared to the Moguls and Tartars, before their primitive manners were changed by religion and luxury; and the evidence of Oriental history may reflect some light on the short and imperfect annals of Rome. After the Moguls had subdued the northern provinces of China, it was seriously proposed, not in the hour of victory and passion, but in calm deliberate council, to exterminate all the inhabitants of that populous country, that the vacant land might be converted to the pasture of cattle. The firmness of a Chinese mandarin,[22] who insinuated some principles of rational policy into the mind of Zingis, diverted him from the execution of this horrid design. But in the cities of Asia, which yielded to the Moguls, the inhuman abuse of the rights of war was exercised, with a regular form of discipline, which may, with equal reason, though not with equal authority, be imputed to the victorious Huns. The inhabitants, who had submitted to their discretion, were ordered to evacuate their houses, and to assemble in some plain adjacent to the city; where a division was made of the vanquished into three parts. The first class consisted of the soldiers of the garrison, and of the young men capable of bearing arms; and their fate was instantly decided: they were either inlisted among the Moguls, or they were massacred on the spot by the troops, who, with pointed spears and bended bows, had formed a circle round the captive multitude. The second class, composed

The Scythian, or Tartar, wars.

---

p. 106, 107.) has paid great attention to this memorable earthquake; which was felt as far from Constantinople as Antioch and Alexandria, and is celebrated by all the ecclesiastical writers. In the hands of a popular preacher, an earthquake is an engine of admirable effect.
22. He represented, to the emperor of the Moguls, that the four provinces (Petcheli, Chantong, Chansi, and Leaotong) which he already possessed, might annually produce, under a mild administration, 500,000 ounces of silver, 400,000 measures of rice, and 800,000 pieces of silk. Gaubil. Hist. de la Dynastie des Mongous, p. 58, 59. Yelutchousay (such was the name of the mandarin) was a wise and virtuous minister, who saved his country, and civilized the conquerors. See p. 102, 103.

of the young and beautiful women, of the artificers of every rank and profession, and of the more wealthy or honourable citizens, from whom a private ransom might be expected, was distributed in equal or proportionable lots. The remainder, whose life or death was alike useless to the conquerors, were permitted to return to the city; which, in the mean while, had been stripped of its valuable furniture; and a tax was imposed on those wretched inhabitants for the indulgence of breathing their native air. Such was the behaviour of the Moguls, when they were not conscious of any extraordinary rigour.[23] But the most casual provocation, the slightest motive, of caprice or convenience, often provoked them to involve a whole people in an indiscriminate massacre: and the ruin of some flourishing cities was executed with such unrelenting perseverance, that, according to their own expression, horses might run, without stumbling, over the ground where they had once stood. The three great capitals of Khorasan, Maru, Neisabour, and Herat, were destroyed by the armies of Zingis; and the exact account, which was taken of the slain, amounted to four millions three hundred and forty-seven thousand persons.[24] Timur, or Tamerlane, was educated in a less barbarous age; and in the profession of the Mahometan religion: yet, if Attila equalled the hostile ravages of Tamerlane,[25] either the Tartar or the Hun might deserve the epithet of the SCOURGE OF GOD.[26]

State of the captives. It may be affirmed, with bolder assurance, that the Huns depopulated the provinces of the empire, by the number of Roman subjects whom they led away into captivity. In the hands

---

23. Particular instances would be endless; but the curious reader may consult the life of Gengiscan, by Petit de la Croix, the Histoire des Mongous, and the fifteenth book of the History of the Huns.

24. At Maru, 1,300,000; at Herat, 1,600,000; at Neisabour, 1,747,000. D'Herbelot, Bibliotheque Orientale, p. 380, 381. I use the orthography of d'Anville's maps. It must however be allowed, that the Persians were disposed to exaggerate their losses, and the Moguls, to magnify their exploits.

25. Cherefeddin Ali, his servile panegyrist, would afford us many horrid examples. In his camp before Delhi, Timur massacred 100,000 Indian prisoners who had *smiled* when the army of their countrymen appeared in sight

(Hist. de Timur Bec, tom. iii. p. 90.). The people of Ispahan supplied 70,000 human sculls for the structure of several lofty towers (Id. tom. i. p. 434.). A similar tax was levied on the revolt of Bagdad (tom. iii. p. 370.); and the exact account, which Cherefeddin was not able to procure from the proper officers, is stated by another historian (Ahmed Arabsiada, tom. ii. p. 175. vers. Manger) at 90,000 heads.

26. The ancients, Jornandes, Priscus, &c. are ignorant of this epithet. The modern Hungarians have imagined, that it was applied, by a hermit of Gaul, to Attila, who was pleased to insert it among the titles of his royal dignity. Mascou, ix. 23. and Tillemont, Hist. des Empereurs, tom. vi. p. 143.

of a wise legislator, such an industrious colony might have contributed to diffuse, through the deserts of Scythia, the rudiments of the useful and ornamental arts; but these captives, who had been taken in war, were accidentally dispersed among the hords, that obeyed the empire of Attila. The estimate of their respective value was formed by the simple judgment of unenlightened, and unprejudiced, Barbarians. Perhaps they might not understand the merit of a theologian, profoundly skilled in the controversies of the Trinity and the Incarnation: yet they respected the ministers of every religion; and the active zeal of the Christian missionaries, without approaching the person, or the palace, of the monarch, successfully laboured in the propagation of the gospel.[27] The pastoral tribes, who were ignorant of the distinction of landed property, must have disregarded the use, as well as the abuse, of civil jurisprudence; and the skill of an eloquent lawyer could excite only their contempt, or their abhorrence.[28] The perpetual intercourse of the Huns and the Goths had communicated the familiar knowledge of the two national dialects; and the Barbarians were ambitious of conversing in Latin, the military idiom, even of the Eastern empire.[29] But they disdained the language, and the sciences, of the Greeks; and the vain sophist, or grave philosopher, who had enjoyed the flattering applause of the schools, was mortified to find, that his robust servant was a captive of more value and importance than himself. The mechanic arts were encouraged and esteemed, as they tended to satisfy the wants of the Huns. An architect, in the service of Onegesius, one of the favourites of Attila, was employed to construct a bath; but this work was a rare example of private luxury; and the trades of the smith, the carpenter, the armourer, were much more adapted to supply a wandering people with the useful instruments of peace and war. But the merit of the physician was received with universal favour and respect; the Barbarians, who despised death,

---

27. The missionaries of St. Chrysostom had converted great numbers of the Scythians, who dwelt, beyond the Danube, in tents and waggons. Theodoret, l. v. c. 31. Photius, p. 1517. The Mahometans, the Nestorians, and the Latin Christians, thought themselves secure of gaining the sons and grandsons of Zingis, who treated the rival missionaries with impartial favour.

28. The Germans, who exterminated Varus and his legions, had been particularly offended with the Roman laws and lawyers. One of the Barbarians, after the effectual precautions of cutting out the tongue of an advocate, and sewing up his mouth, observed with much satisfaction, that the viper could no longer hiss. Florus, iv. 12.

29. Priscus, p. 59. It should seem, that the Huns preferred the Gothic and Latin languages to their own; which was probably a harsh and barren idiom.

might be apprehensive of disease; and the haughty conqueror trembled in the presence of a captive, to whom he ascribed, perhaps, an imaginary power, of prolonging, or preserving, his life.[30] The Huns might be provoked to insult the misery of their slaves, over whom they exercised a despotic command;[31] but their manners were not susceptible of a refined system of oppression; and the efforts of courage and diligence were often recompensed by the gift of freedom. The historian Priscus, whose embassy is a source of curious instruction, was accosted, in the camp of Attila, by a stranger, who saluted him in the Greek language, but whose dress and figure displayed the appearance of a wealthy Scythian. In the siege of Viminiacum, he had lost, according to his own account, his fortune and liberty: he became the slave of Onegesius; but his faithful services, against the Romans and the Acatzires, had gradually raised him to the rank of the native Huns; to whom he was attached by the domestic pledges of a new wife and several children. The spoils of war had restored and improved his private property; he was admitted to the table of his former lord; and the apostate Greek blessed the hour of his captivity, since it had been the introduction to an happy and independent state; which he held by the honourable tenure of military service. This reflection naturally produced a dispute on the advantages, and defects, of the Roman government, which was severely arraigned by the apostate, and defended by Priscus in a prolix and feeble declamation. The freedman of Onegesius exposed, in true and lively colours, the vices of a declining empire, of which he had so long been the victim; the cruel absurdity of the Roman princes, unable to protect their subjects against the public enemy, unwilling to trust them with arms for their own defence; the intolerable weight of taxes, rendered still more oppressive by the intricate or arbitrary modes of collection; the obscurity of numerous and contradictory laws; the tedious and expensive forms of judicial proceedings; the partial administration of justice; and the universal corruption, which increased the influence of the rich, and aggravated the misfortunes of the poor. A sentiment of patriotic sympathy was at length revived in the breast

---

30. Philip de Comines, in his admirable picture of the last moments of Lewis XI. (Memoires, l. vi. c. 12.) represents the insolence of his physician, who, in five months, extorted 54,000 crowns, and a rich bishopric, from the stern avaricious tyrant.

31. Priscus (p. 61.) extols the equity of the Roman laws, which protected the life of a slave. Occidere solent (says Tacitus of the Germans) non disciplinâ et severitate, sed impetu et irâ, ut unimicum, nisi quòd impune. De Moribus Germ. c. 25. The Heruli, who were the subjects of Attila, claimed, and exercised, the power of life and death over their slaves. See a remarkable instance in the second book of Agathias.

of the fortunate exile; and he lamented, with a flood of tears, the guilt or weakness of those magistrates, who had perverted the wisest and most salutary institutions.[32]

The timid, or selfish, policy of the western Romans had abandoned the Eastern empire to the Huns.[33] The loss of armies, and the want of discipline, or virtue, were not supplied by the personal character of the monarch. Theodosius might still affect the style, as well as the title, of *Invincible Augustus*; but he was reduced to solicit the clemency of Attila, who imperiously dictated these harsh and humiliating conditions of peace. I. The emperor of the East resigned, by an express or tacit convention, an extensive and important territory, which stretched along the southern banks of the Danube, from Singidunum or Belgrade, as far as Novæ, in the diocese of Thrace. The breadth was defined by the vague computation of fifteen days journey; but, from the proposal of Attila, to remove the situation of the national market, it soon appeared, that he comprehended the ruined city of Naissus within the limits of his dominions. II. The king of the Huns required, and obtained, that his tribute or subsidy should be augmented from seven hundred pounds of gold to the annual sum of two thousand one hundred; and he stipulated the immediate payment of six thousand pounds of gold to defray the expences, or to expiate the guilt, of the war. One might imagine, that such a demand, which scarcely equalled the measure of private wealth, would have been readily discharged by the opulent empire of the East; and the public distress affords a remarkable proof of the impoverished, or at least of the disorderly, state of the finances. A large proportion of the taxes, extorted from the people, was detained and intercepted in their passage, through the foulest channels, to the treasury of Constantinople. The revenue was dissipated by Theodosius, and his favourites, in wasteful and profuse luxury; which was disguised by the names of Imperial magnificence, or Christian charity. The immediate supplies had been exhausted by the unforeseen necessity of military preparations. A personal contribution, rigorously, but capriciously, imposed on the members of the senatorian order, was the only expedient that could disarm, without loss of time, the impatient avarice of Attila: and the poverty

Treaty of peace between Attila and the Eastern empire, A.D. 446.

32. See the whole conversation in Priscus, p. 59–62.
33. Nova iterum Orienti assurgit ruina ... quum nulla ab Occidentalibus ferrentur auxilia. Prosper-Tyro composed his Chronicle in the West; and his observation implies a censure.

379

of the nobles compelled them to adopt the scandalous resource of exposing to public auction the jewels of their wives, and the hereditary ornaments of their palaces.[34] III. The king of the Huns appears to have established, as a principle of national jurisprudence, that he could never lose the property, which he had once acquired, in the persons, who had yielded either a voluntary, or reluctant, submission to his authority. From this principle he concluded, and the conclusions of Attila were irrevocable laws, that the Huns, who had been taken prisoners in war, should be released without delay, and without ransom; that every Roman captive, who had presumed to escape, should purchase his right to freedom at the price of twelve pieces of gold; and that all the Barbarians, who had deserted the standard of Attila, should be restored, without any promise, or stipulation, of pardon. In the execution of this cruel and ignominious treaty, the Imperial officers were forced to massacre several loyal and noble deserters, who refused to devote themselves to certain death; and the Romans forfeited all reasonable claims to the friendship of any Scythian people, by this public confession, that they were destitute either of faith, or power, to protect the suppliants, who had embraced the throne of Theodosius.[35]

Spirit of the Azimuntines. The firmness of a single town, so obscure, that, except on this occasion, it has never been mentioned by any historian or geographer, exposed the disgrace of the emperor and empire. Azimus, or Azimuntium, a small city of Thrace on the Illyrian borders,[36] had been distinguished by the martial spirit of its youth, the skill and reputation of the leaders whom they had chosen, and their daring exploits against the innumerable host of the Barbarians. Instead of tamely expecting their approach, the Azimuntines attacked, in frequent and successful sallies,

---

34. According to the description, or rather invective, of Chrysostom, an auction of Byzantine luxury must have been very productive. Every wealthy house possessed a semicircular table of massy silver, such as two men could scarcely lift, a vase of solid gold of the weight of forty pounds, cups, dishes of the same metal, &c.

35. The articles of the treaty, expressed without much order or precision, may be found in Priscus (p. 34, 35, 36, 37. 53, &c.). Count Marcellinus dispenses some comfort, by observing, 1st, *That* Attila himself solicited the peace and presents, which he had for-

merly refused; and 2dly, *That*, about the same time, the ambassadors of India presented a fine large tame tyger to the emperor Theodosius. 36. Priscus, p. 35, 36. Among the hundred and eighty-two forts, or castles, of Thrace, enumerated by Procopius (de Edificiis, l. iv. c. xi. tom. ii. p. 92. edit. Paris), there is one of the name of *Esimontou*, whose position is doubtfully marked, in the neighbourhood of Anchialus, and the Euxine Sea. The name and walls of Azimuntium might subsist till the reign of Justinian; but the race of its brave defenders had been carefully extirpated by the jealousy of the Roman princes.

the troops of the Huns, who gradually declined the dangerous neighbour-hood; rescued from their hands the spoil and the captives, and recruited their domestic force by the voluntary association of fugitives and deserters. After the conclusion of the treaty, Attila still menaced the empire with implacable war, unless the Azimuntines were persuaded, or compelled, to comply with the conditions which their sovereign had accepted. The ministers of Theodosius confessed with shame, and with truth, that they no longer possessed any authority over a society of men, who so bravely asserted their natural independence; and the king of the Huns condescended to negociate an equal exchange with the citizens of Azimus. They demanded the restitution of some shepherds, who, with their cattle, had been accident-ally surprised. A strict, though fruitless, inquiry was allowed: but the Huns were obliged to swear, that they did not detain any prisoners belonging to the city, before they could recover two surviving countrymen, whom the Azimuntines had reserved as pledges for the safety of their lost companions. Attila, on his side, was satisfied, and deceived, by their solemn asseveration, that the rest of the captives had been put to the sword; and that it was their constant practice, immediately to dismiss the Romans and the deserters, who had obtained the security of the public faith. This prudent and officious dissimulation may be condemned, or excused, by the casuists, as they incline to the rigid decree of St. Augustin, or to the milder sentiment of St. Jerom and St. Chrysostom: but every soldier, every statesman, must acknowledge, that, if the race of the Azimuntines had been encouraged and multiplied, the Barbarians would have ceased to trample on the majesty of the empire.[37]

It would have been strange, indeed, if Theodosius had purchased, by the loss of honour, a secure and solid tranquillity; or if his tameness had not invited the repetition of injuries. The Byzantine court was insulted by five or six successive embassies;[38] and the ministers of Attila were uniformly instructed to press the tardy or imperfect execution of the last treaty; to produce the names

Embassies from Attila to Constantinople.

---

37. The peevish dispute of St. Jerom and St. Augustin, who laboured, by different expedients, to reconcile the *seeming* quarrel of the two apostles St. Peter and St. Paul, depends on the solution of an important question (Middleton's Works, vol. ii. p. 5–10.), which has been frequently agitated by Catholic and Protestant divines, and even by lawyers and philosophers of every age.

38. Montesquieu (Considerations sur la Gran-deur, &c. c. xix.) has delineated, with a bold and easy pencil, some of the most striking circumstances of the pride of Attila, and the disgrace of the Romans. He deserves the praise of having read the Fragments of Priscus, which have been too much disregarded.

of fugitives and deserters, who were still protected by the empire; and to declare, with seeming moderation, that unless their sovereign obtained complete and immediate satisfaction, it would be impossible for him, were it even his wish, to check the resentment of his warlike tribes. Besides the motives of pride and interest, which might prompt the king of the Huns to continue this train of negociation, he was influenced by the less honourable view of enriching his favourites at the expence of his enemies. The Imperial treasury was exhausted, to procure the friendly offices of the ambassadors, and their principal attendant, whose favourable report might conduce to the maintenance of peace. The Barbarian monarch was flattered by the liberal reception of his ministers; he computed with pleasure the value and splendour of their gifts, rigorously exacted the performance of every promise, which would contribute to their private emolument, and treated as an important business of state, the marriage of his secretary Constantius.[39] That Gallic adventurer, who was recommended by Ætius to the king of the Huns, had engaged his service to the ministers of Constantinople, for the stipulated reward of a wealthy and noble wife; and the daughter of count Saturninus was chosen to discharge the obligations of her country. The reluctance of the victim, some domestic troubles, and the unjust confiscation of her fortune, cooled the ardour of her interested lover; but he still demanded, in the name of Attila, an equivalent alliance; and, after many ambiguous delays and excuses, the Byzantine court was compelled to sacrifice to this insolent stranger the widow of Armatius, whose birth, opulence, and beauty, placed her in the most illustrious rank of the Roman matrons. For these importunate and oppressive embassies, Attila claimed a suitable return: he weighed, with suspicious pride, the character and station of the Imperial envoys; but he condescended to promise, that he would advance as far as Sardica, to receive any ministers who had been invested with the consular dignity. The council of Theodosius eluded this proposal, by representing the desolate and ruined condition of Sardica; and even ventured to insinuate, that every officer of the army or household was qualified to treat with the most powerful princes of Scythia. Maximin,[40] a respectable courtier, whose abilities had been

39. See Priscus, p. 69. 71, 72, &c. I would fain believe, that this adventurer was afterwards crucified by the order of Attila, on a suspicion of treasonable practices: but Priscus (p. 57.) has too plainly distinguished *two* persons of the name of Constantius, who, from the similar events of their lives, might have been easily confounded.

40. In the Persian treaty concluded in the year 422, the wise and eloquent Maximin

long exercised in civil and military employments, accepted with reluctance the troublesome, and, perhaps, dangerous commission, of reconciling the angry spirit of the king of the Huns. His friend, the historian Priscus,[41] embraced the opportunity of observing the Barbarian hero in the peaceful and domestic scenes of life: but the secret of the embassy, a fatal and guilty secret, was entrusted only to the interpreter Vigilius. The two last ambassadors of the Huns, Orestes, a noble subject of the Pannonian province, and Edecon, a valiant chieftain of the tribe of the Scyrri, returned at the same time from Constantinople to the royal camp. Their obscure names were afterwards illustrated by the extraordinary fortune and the contrast of their sons: the two servants of Attila became the fathers of the last Roman emperor of the West, and of the first Barbarian king of Italy.

The ambassadors, who were followed by a numerous train of men and horses, made their first halt at Sardica, at the distance of three hundred and fifty miles, or thirteen days journey, from Constantinople. As the remains of Sardica were still included within the limits of the empire, it was incumbent on the Romans to exercise the duties of hospitality. They provided, with the assistance of the provincials, a sufficient number of sheep and oxen; and invited the Huns to a splendid, or at least a plentiful, supper. But the harmony of the entertainment was soon disturbed by mutual prejudice and indiscretion. The greatness of the emperor and the empire was warmly maintained by their ministers; the Huns, with equal ardour, asserted the superiority of their victorious monarch: the dispute was inflamed by the rash and unseasonable flattery of Vigilius, who passionately rejected the comparison of a mere mortal with the divine Theodosius; and it was with extreme difficulty that Maximin and Priscus were able to divert the conversation, or to soothe the angry minds of the Barbarians. When they rose from table, the Imperial ambassador presented Edecon and Orestes with rich gifts of silk robes and

The embassy of Maximin to Attila, A.D. 448.

---

had been the assessor of Ardaburius (Socrates, l. vii. c. 20.). When Marcian ascended the throne, the office of Great Chamberlain was bestowed on Maximin, who is ranked, in a public edict, among the four principal ministers of state (Novell. ad. Calc. Cod. Theod. p. 31.). He executed a civil and military commission in the Eastern provinces; and his death was lamented by the savages of Æthiopia, whose incursions he had repressed. See Priscus, p. 40, 41.

41. Priscus was a native of Panium in Thrace, and deserved, by his eloquence, an honourable place among the sophists of the age. His Byzantine history, which related to his own times, was comprised in seven books. See Fabricius, Bibliot. Græc. tom. vi. p. 235, 236. Notwithstanding the charitable judgment of the critics, I suspect that Priscus was a Pagan.

Indian pearls, which they thankfully accepted. Yet Orestes could not forbear insinuating, that *he* had not always been treated with such respect and liberality: and the offensive distinction, which was implied, between his civil office and the hereditary rank of his colleague, seems to have made Edecon a doubtful friend, and Orestes an irreconcileable enemy. After this entertainment, they travelled about one hundred miles from Sardica to Naissus. That flourishing city, which had given birth to the great Constantine, was levelled with the ground: the inhabitants were destroyed, or dispersed; and the appearance of some sick persons, who were still permitted to exist among the ruins of the churches, served only to increase the horror of the prospect. The surface of the country was covered with the bones of the slain; and the ambassadors, who directed their course to the north-west, were obliged to pass the hills of modern Servia, before they descended into the flat and marshy grounds, which are terminated by the Danube. The Huns were masters of the great river: their navigation was performed in large canoes, hollowed out of the trunk of a single tree; the ministers of Theodosius were safely landed on the opposite bank; and their Barbarian associates immediately hastened to the camp of Attila, which was equally prepared for the amusements of hunting, or of war. No sooner had Maximin advanced about two miles from the Danube, than he began to experience the fastidious insolence of the conqueror. He was sternly forbid to pitch his tents in a pleasant valley, lest he should infringe the distant awe that was due to the royal mansion. The ministers of Attila pressed him to communicate the business, and the instructions, which he reserved for the ear of their sovereign. When Maximin temperately urged the contrary practice of nations, he was still more confounded to find, that the resolutions of the Sacred Consistory, those secrets (says Priscus) which should not be revealed to the gods themselves, had been treacherously disclosed to the public enemy. On his refusal to comply with such ignominious terms, the Imperial envoy was commanded instantly to depart: the order was recalled; it was again repeated; and the Huns renewed their ineffectual attempts to subdue the patient firmness of Maximin. At length, by the intercession of Scotta, the brother of Onegesius, whose friendship had been purchased by a liberal gift, he was admitted to the royal presence; but, instead of obtaining a decisive answer, he was compelled to undertake a remote journey towards the North, that Attila might enjoy the proud satisfaction of receiving, in the same camp, the ambassadors of the Eastern and Western empires. His journey was regulated by the guides, who obliged him to halt, to hasten his march, or to deviate from the common road, as it best suited the convenience of the King. The Romans who traversed the plains of Hungary, suppose that they passed *several* navigable rivers, either in canoes or portable boats; but there is reason to suspect, that the winding stream of the Teyss, or Tibiscus, might present itself in different places, under different names. From the contiguous villages they received a plentiful and regular supply of provisions; mead instead of wine, millet in the place of bread, and a certain liquor named *camus*, which, according to the report of Priscus, was distilled from barley.[42] Such fare might appear coarse and indelicate to men who had tasted the luxury of Constantinople: but, in their accidental distress, they were relieved by the gentleness and hospitality of the same Barbarians, so terrible and so merciless in war. The ambassadors had encamped on the edge of a large morass. A violent tempest of wind and rain, of thunder and lightning, overturned their tents, immersed their baggage and furniture in the water, and scattered their retinue, who wandered in the darkness of the night, uncertain of their road, and apprehensive of some unknown danger, till they awakened by their cries the inhabitants of a neighbouring village, the property of the widow of Bleda. A bright illumination, and, in a few moments, a comfortable fire of reeds, was kindled by their officious benevolence: the wants, and even the desires, of the Romans were liberally satisfied; and they seem to have been embarrassed by the singular politeness of Bleda's widow, who added to her other favours the gift, or at least the loan, of a sufficient number of beautiful and obsequious damsels. The sunshine of the succeeding day was dedicated to repose; to collect and dry the baggage, and to the refreshment of the men and horses: but, in the evening, before they pursued their journey, the ambassadors expressed their gratitude to the bounteous lady of the village, by a very acceptable present of silver cups, red fleeces, dried fruits, and Indian pepper. Soon after this adventure, they rejoined the march of Attila, from whom they had been separated about six days; and slowly proceeded to the capital of an empire, which did not contain, in the space of several thousand miles, a single city.

---

42. The Huns themselves still continued to despise the labours of agriculture: they abused the privilege of a victorious nation; and the Goths, their industrious subjects who cultivated the earth, dreaded their neighbourhood, like that of so many ravenous wolves (Priscus, p. 45.). In the same manner the Sarts and Tadgics provide for their own subsistence, and for that of the Usbec Tartars, their lazy and rapacious sovereigns. See Genealogical History of the Tartars, p. 423. 455, &c.

The royal village and palace.

As far as we may ascertain the vague and obscure geography of Priscus, this capital appears to have been seated between the Danube, the Teyss, and the Carpathian hills, in the plains of Upper Hungary, and most probably in the neighbourhood of Jazberin, Agria, or Tokay.[43] In its origin it could be no more than an accidental camp, which, by the long and frequent residence of Attila, had insensibly swelled into a huge village, for the reception of his court, of the troops who followed his person, and of the various multitude of idle or industrious slaves and retainers.[44] The baths, constructed by Onegesius, were the only edifice of stone; the materials had been transported from Pannonia; and since the adjacent country was destitute even of large timber, it may be presumed, that the meaner habitations of the royal village consisted of straw, of mud, or of canvas. The wooden houses of the more illustrious Huns, were built and adorned with rude magnificence, according to the rank, the fortune, or the taste of the proprietors. They seem to have been distributed with some degree of order and symmetry; and each spot became more honourable, as it approached the person of the sovereign. The palace of Attila, which surpassed all other houses in his dominions, was built entirely of wood, and covered an ample space of ground. The outward enclosure was a lofty wall, or pallisade, of smooth square timber, intersected with high towers, but intended rather for ornament than defence. This wall, which seems to have encircled the declivity of a hill, comprehended a great variety of wooden edifices, adapted to the uses of royalty. A separate house was assigned to each of the numerous wives of Attila; and, instead of the rigid and illiberal confinement imposed by Asiatic jealousy, they politely admitted the Roman ambassadors to their presence, their table, and even to the freedom of an innocent embrace. When Maximin offered his presents to Cerca, the principal queen, he admired

43. It is evident, that Priscus passed the Danube and the Teyss, and that he did not reach the foot of the Carpathian hills. Agria, Tokay, and Jazberin, are situate in the plains circumscribed by this definition. M. de Buat (Histoire des Peuples, &c. tom. vii. p. 461.) has chosen Tokay; Otrokosci (p. 180. apud Mascou, ix, 23.), a learned Hungarian, has preferred Jazberin, a place about thirty-six miles westward of Buda and the Danube.

44. The royal village of Attila may be com-

pared to the city of Karacorum, the residence of the successors of Zingis; which, though it appears to have been a more stable habitation, did not equal the size or splendor of the town and abbey of St. Denys, in the 13th century (see Rubruquis, in the Histoire Generale des Voyages, tom. vii. p. 286.). The camp of Aurengzebe, as it is so agreeably described by Bernier (tom. ii. p. 217–235.), blended the manners of Scythia with the magnificence and luxury of Hindostan.

the singular architecture of her mansion, the height of the round columns, the size and beauty of the wood, which was curiously shaped or turned, or polished, or carved; and his attentive eye was able to discover some taste in the ornaments, and some regularity in the proportions. After passing through the guards, who watched before the gate, the ambassadors were introduced into the private apartment of Cerca. The wife of Attila received their visit sitting, or rather lying, on a soft couch; the floor was covered with a carpet; the domestics formed a circle round the queen; and her damsels, seated on the ground, were employed in working the variegated embroidery which adorned the dress of the Barbaric warriors. The Huns were ambitious of displaying those riches which were the fruit and evidence of their victories: the trappings of their horses, their swords, and even their shoes, were studded with gold and precious stones; and their tables were profusely spread with plates, and goblets, and vases of gold and silver, which had been fashioned by the labour of Grecian artists. The monarch alone assumed the superior pride of still adhering to the simplicity of his Scythian ancestors.[45] The dress of Attila, his arms, and the furniture of his horse, were plain, without ornament, and of a single colour. The royal table was served in wooden cups and platters; flesh was his only food; and the conqueror of the North never tasted the luxury of bread.

When Attila first gave audience to the Roman ambassadors on the banks of the Danube, his tent was encompassed with a formidable guard. The monarch himself was seated in a wooden chair. His stern countenance, angry gestures, and impatient tone, astonished the firmness of Maximin; but Vigilius had more *The behaviour of Attila to the Roman ambassadors.* reason to tremble, since he distinctly understood the menace, that if Attila did not respect the law of nations, he would nail the deceitful interpreter to a cross, and leave his body to the vultures. The Barbarian condescended, by producing an accurate list, to expose the bold falsehood of Vigilius, who had affirmed that no more than seventeen deserters could be found. But he arrogantly declared, that he apprehended only the disgrace of contending with his fugitive slaves; since he despised their impotent efforts to defend the provinces which Theodosius had entrusted to their arms: "For what fortress" (added Attila), "what city, in the wide extent of the Roman

---

45. When the Moguls displayed the spoils of Asia, in the diet of Toncat, the throne of Zingis was still covered with the original black felt carpet, on which he had been seated, when he was raised to the command of his warlike countrymen. See Vie de Gengiscan, l. iv. c. 9.

empire, can hope to exist, secure and impregnable, if it is our pleasure that it should be erazed from the earth?" He dismissed, however, the interpreter, who returned to Constantinople with his peremptory demand of more complete restitution, and a more splendid embassy. His anger gradually subsided, and his domestic satisfaction, in a marriage which he celebrated on the road with the daughter of Eslam, might perhaps contribute to mollify the native fierceness of his temper. The entrance of Attila into the royal village, was marked by a very singular ceremony. A numerous troop of women came out to meet their hero, and their king. They marched before him, distributed into long and regular files: the intervals between the files were filled by white veils of thin linen, which the women on either side bore aloft in their hands, and which formed a canopy for a chorus of young virgins, who chanted hymns and songs in the Scythian language. The wife of his favourite Onegesius, with a train of female attendants, saluted Attila at the door of her own house, on his way to the palace; and offered, according to the custom of the country, her respectful homage, by intreating him to taste the wine and meat, which she had prepared for his reception. As soon as the monarch had graciously accepted her hospitable gift, his domestics lifted a small silver table to a convenient height, as he sat on horseback; and Attila, when he had touched the goblet with his lips, again saluted the wife of Onegesius, and continued his march. During his residence at the seat of empire, his hours were not wasted in the recluse idleness of a seraglio; and the king of the Huns could maintain his superior dignity, without concealing his person from the public view. He frequently assembled his council, and gave audience to the ambassadors of the nations; and his people might appeal to the supreme tribunal, which he held at stated times, and, according to the eastern custom, before the principal gate of his wooden palace. The Romans both of the East and of the West, were twice invited to the banquets, where Attila feasted with the princes and nobles of Scythia. Maximin and his colleagues were stopped on the threshold, till they had made a devout libation to the health and prosperity of the king of the Huns; and were conducted, after this ceremony, to their respective seats in a spacious hall. The royal table and couch, covered with carpets and fine linen, was raised by several steps in the midst of the hall; and a son, an uncle, or perhaps a favourite king, were admitted to share the simple and homely repast of Attila. Two lines of small tables, each of which contained three or four guests, were ranged in order on either hand; the right was esteemed the

The royal feast.

most honourable, but the Romans ingenuously confess, that they were placed on the left; and that Beric, an unknown chieftain, most probably of the Gothic race, preceded the representatives of Theodosius and Valentinian. The Barbarian monarch received from his cup bearer a goblet filled with wine, and courteously drank to the health of the most distinguished guest; who rose from his seat, and expressed, in the same manner, his loyal and respectful vows. This ceremony was successively performed for all, or at least for the illustrious persons of the assembly; and a considerable time must have been consumed, since it was thrice repeated, as each course or service was placed on the table. But the wine still remained after the meat had been removed; and the Huns continued to indulge their intemperance long after the sober and decent ambassadors of the two empires had withdrawn themselves from the nocturnal banquet. Yet before they retired, they enjoyed a singular opportunity of observing the manners of the nation in their convivial amusements. Two Scythians stood before the couch of Attila, and recited the verses which they had composed, to celebrate his valour and his victories. A profound silence prevailed in the hall; and the attention of the guests was captivated by the vocal harmony, which revived and perpetuated the memory of their own exploits: a martial ardour flashed from the eyes of the warriors, who were impatient for battle; and the tears of the old men expressed their generous despair, that they could no longer partake the danger and glory of the field.[46] This entertainment, which might be considered as a school of military virtue, was succeeded by a farce, that debased the dignity of human nature. A Moorish and a Scythian buffoon successively excited the mirth of the rude spectators, by their deformed figure, ridiculous dress, antic gestures, absurd speeches, and the strange unintelligible confusion of the Latin, the Gothic, and the Hunnic languages; and the hall resounded with loud and licentious peals of laughter. In the midst of this intemperate riot, Attila alone, without a change of countenance, maintained his steadfast and inflexible gravity; which was never relaxed, except on the entrance of Irnac, the youngest of his sons: he embraced the boy with a smile of paternal tenderness, gently pinched him by the cheek, and betrayed a partial affection, which was justified by the assurance of his prophets, that Irnac would be the future support of his family and empire. Two days afterwards, the

---

46. If we believe Plutarch (in Demetrio, tom. v. p. 24.), it was the custom of the Scythians, when they indulged in the pleasures of the table, to awaken their languid courage by the martial harmony of twanging their bow-strings.

ambassadors received a second invitation; and they had reason to praise the politeness, as well as the hospitality, of Attila. The king of the Huns held a long and familiar conversation with Maximin; but his civility was interrupted by rude expressions, and haughty reproaches; and he was provoked, by a motive of interest, to support with unbecoming zeal, the private claims of his secretary Constantius. "The emperor" (said Attila) "has long promised him a rich wife: Constantius must not be disappointed; nor should a Roman emperor deserve the name of liar." On the third day, the ambassadors were dismissed; the freedom of several captives was granted, for a moderate ransom, to their pressing entreaties; and, besides the royal presents, they were permitted to accept from each of the Scythian nobles, the honourable and useful gift of a horse. Maximin returned, by the same road, to Constantinople; and though he was involved in an accidental dispute with Beric, the new ambassador of Attila, he flattered himself that he had contributed, by the laborious journey, to confirm the peace and alliance of the two nations.[47]

Conspiracy of the Romans against the life of Attila.   But the Roman ambassador was ignorant of the treacherous design, which had been concealed under the mask of the public faith. The surprise and satisfaction of Edecon, when he contemplated the splendour of Constantinople, had encouraged the interpreter Vigilius to procure for him a secret interview with the eunuch Chrysaphius,[48] who governed the emperor and the empire. After some previous conversation, and a mutual oath of secrecy, the eunuch, who had not, from his own feelings or experience, imbibed any exalted notions of ministerial virtue, ventured to propose the death of Attila, as an important service, by which Edecon might deserve a liberal share of the wealth and luxury which he admired. The ambassador of the Huns listened to the tempting offer; and professed, with apparent zeal, his ability, as well as readiness, to execute the bloody deed: the design was communicated to

---

47. The curious narrative of this embassy, which required few observations, and was not susceptible of any collateral evidence, may be found in Priscus, p. 49–70. But I have not confined myself to the same order; and I had previously extracted the historical circumstances, which were less intimately connected with the journey, and business, of the Roman ambassadors.

48. M. de Tillemont has very properly given the succession of Chamberlains, who reigned in the name of Theodosius. Chrysaphius was the last, and, according to the unanimous evidence of history, the worst of these favourites (see Hist. des Empereurs, tom. vi. p. 117–119. Mem Eccles. tom. xv. p. 438.). His partiality for his godfather, the heresiarch Eutyches, engaged him to persecute the orthodox party.

the master of the offices, and the devout Theodosius consented to the assassination of his invincible enemy. But this perfidious conspiracy was defeated by the dissimulation, or the repentance, of Edecon; and, though he might exaggerate his inward abhorrence for the treason, which he seemed to approve, he dexterously assumed the merit of an early and voluntary confession. If we *now* review the embassy of Maximin, and the behaviour of Attila, we must applaud the Barbarian, who respected the laws of hospitality, and generously entertained and dismissed the minister of a prince, who had conspired against his life. But the rashness of Vigilius will appear still more extraordinary, since he returned, conscious of his guilt and danger, to the royal camp; accompanied by his son, and carrying with him a weighty purse of gold, which the favourite eunuch had furnished, to satisfy the demands of Edecon, and to corrupt the fidelity of the guards. The interpreter was instantly seized, and dragged before the tribunal of Attila, where he asserted his innocence with specious firmness, till the threat of inflicting instant death on his son, extorted from him a sincere discovery of the criminal transaction. Under the name of ransom, or confiscation, the rapacious king of the Huns accepted two hundred pounds of gold for the life of a traitor, whom he disdained to punish.

He pointed his just indignation against a nobler object. His ambassadors Eslaw and Orestes were immediately dispatched to Constantinople, with a peremptory instruction, which it was *He reprimands and forgives the Emperor.* much safer for them to execute than to disobey. They boldly entered the Imperial presence, with the fatal purse hanging down from the neck of Orestes; who interrogated the eunuch Chrysaphius, as he stood beside the throne, whether he recognised the evidence of his guilt. But the office of reproof was reserved for the superior dignity of his colleague Eslaw, who gravely addressed the Emperor of the East in the following words: "Theodosius is the son of an illustrious and respectable parent: Attila likewise is descended from a noble race; and *he* has supported, by his actions, the dignity which he inherited from his father Mundzuk. But Theodosius has forfeited his paternal honours, and, by consenting to pay tribute, has degraded himself to the condition of a slave. It is therefore just, that he should reverence the man whom fortune and merit have placed above him; instead of attempting, like a wicked slave, clandestinely to conspire against his master." The son of Arcadius, who was accustomed only to the voice of flattery, heard with astonishment the severe language of truth: he blushed and trembled; nor did he presume directly to refuse the head of Chrysaphius, which Eslaw and Orestes were instructed to demand. A solemn embassy, armed with full powers and magnificent gifts, was hastily sent to deprecate the wrath of Attila; and his pride was gratified by the choice of Nomius and Anatolius, two ministers of consular or patrician rank, of whom the one was great treasurer, and the other was master-general of the armies of the East. He condescended to meet these ambassadors on the banks of the river Drenco; and though he at first affected a stern and haughty demeanour, his anger was insensibly mollified by their eloquence and liberality. He condescended to pardon the emperor, the eunuch, and the interpreter; bound himself by an oath to observe the conditions of peace; released a great number of captives; abandoned the fugitives and deserters to their fate; and resigned a large territory to the south of the Danube, which he had already exhausted of its wealth and inhabitants. But this treaty was purchased at an expence which might have supported a vigorous and successful war; and the subjects of Theodosius were compelled to redeem the safety of a worthless favourite by oppressive taxes, which they would more cheerfully have paid for his destruction.[49]

Theodosius the Younger dies, A.D. 450. July 28.

The emperor Theodosius did not long survive the most humiliating circumstance of an inglorious life. As he was riding, or hunting, in the neighbourhood of Constantinople, he was thrown from his horse into the river Lycus: the spine of the back was injured by the fall; and he expired some days afterwards, in the fiftieth year of his age, and the forty-third of his reign.[50] His sister Pulcheria, whose authority had been controuled both in civil and ecclesiastical affairs by the pernicious influence of the eunuchs, was unanimously proclaimed Empress of the East; and the Romans, for the first time, submitted to a female reign. No sooner had Pulcheria ascended the throne, than she indulged her own, and the public resentment, by an act of popular justice. Without any legal trial, the eunuch Chrysaphius was executed before the gates of the city; and the immense riches which had

49. This secret conspiracy, and its important consequences, may be traced in the fragments of Priscus, p. 37, 38, 39. 54. 70, 71, 72. The chronology of that historian is not fixed by any precise date; but the series of negociations between Attila and the Eastern empire, must be included within the three or four years, which are terminated, A.D. 450, by the death of Theodosius.

50. Theodorus the Reader (see Vales. Hist. Eccles. tom. iii. p. 563.), and the Paschal Chronicle, mention the fall, without specifying the injury: but the consequence was so likely to happen, and so unlikely to be invented, that we may safely give credit to Nicephorus Callistus, a Greek of the fourteenth century.

been accumulated by the rapacious favourite, served only to hasten and justify his punishment.[51] Amidst the general acclamations of the clergy and people, the empress did not forget the prejudice and disadvantage to which her sex was exposed; and she wisely resolved to prevent their murmurs by the choice of a colleague, who would always respect the superior rank and virgin chastity of his wife. She gave her hand to Marcian, a senator, about sixty years of age, and the nominal husband of Pulcheria was solemnly invested with the Imperial purple. The zeal which he displayed for the orthodox creed,

and is succeeded by Marcian, August 25.

as it was established by the council of Chalcedon, would alone have inspired the grateful eloquence of the Catholics. But the behaviour of Marcian in a private life, and afterwards on the throne, may support a more rational belief, that he was qualified to restore and invigorate an empire, which had been almost dissolved by the successive weakness of two hereditary monarchs. He was born in Thrace, and educated to the profession of arms; but Marcian's youth had been severely exercised by poverty and misfortune, since his only resource, when he first arrived at Constantinople, consisted in two hundred pieces of gold, which he had borrowed of a friend. He passed nineteen years in the domestic and military service of Aspar, and his son Ardaburius; followed those powerful generals to the Persian and African wars; and obtained, by their influence, the honourable rank of tribune and senator. His mild disposition, and useful talents, without alarming the jealousy, recommended Marcian to the esteem and favour, of his patrons; he had seen, perhaps he had felt, the abuses of a venal and oppressive administration; and his own example gave weight and energy to the laws, which he promulgated for the reformation of manners.[52]

---

51. Pulcheriæ nutû (says Count Marcellinus) suâ cum avaritiâ interemptus est. She abandoned the eunuch to the pious revenge of a son, whose father had suffered at his instigation.

52. Procopius, de Bell. Vandal, l. i. c. 4. Evag-

rius, l. ii. c. 1. Theophanes, p. 90. 91. Novell. ad Calcem Cod. Theod. tom. vi. p. 30. The praises which St. Leo, and the Catholics, have bestowed on Marcian, are diligently transcribed by Baronius, as an encouragement for future princes.

CHAPTER XXXV

Invasion of Gaul by Attila. – He is repulsed by Ætius and the Visigoths. – Attila invades and evacuates Italy. – The Deaths of Attila, Ætius, and Valentinian the Third.

Attila threatens both empires, and prepares to invade Gaul, A.D. 450.

It was the opinion of Marcian, that war should be avoided, as long as it is possible to preserve a secure and honourable peace; but it was likewise his opinion, that peace cannot be honourable or secure, if the sovereign betrays a pusillanimous aversion to war. This temperate courage dictated his reply to the demands of Attila, who insolently pressed the payment of the annual tribute. The emperor signified to the Barbarians, that they must no longer insult the majesty of Rome, by the mention of a tribute; that he was disposed to reward, with becoming liberality, the faithful friendship of his allies; but that, if they presumed to violate the public peace, they should feel that he possessed troops, and arms, and resolution, to repel their attacks. The same language, even in the camp of the Huns, was used by his ambassador Apollonius, whose bold refusal to deliver the presents, till he had been admitted to a personal interview, displayed a sense of dignity, and a contempt of danger, which Attila was not prepared to expect from the degenerate Romans.[1] He threatened to chastise the rash successor of Theodosius; but he hesitated, whether he should first direct his invincible arms against the Eastern or the Western empire. While mankind awaited his decision with awful suspense, he sent an equal defiance to the courts of Ravenna and Constantinople; and his ministers saluted the two emperors with the same haughty declaration. "Attila, *my* lord, and *thy* lord, commands thee to provide a palace for his immediate reception."[2] But as the Barbarian despised, or affected to despise, the Romans of the East, whom he had so often vanquished, he soon declared his resolution of

1. See Priscus, p. 39. 72.
2. The Alexandrian or Paschal Chronicle, which introduces this haughty message, during the lifetime of Theodosius, may have anticipated the date; but the dull annalist was incapable of inventing the original and genuine style of Attila.

suspending the easy conquest, till he had atchieved a more glorious and important enterprise. In the memorable invasions of Gaul and Italy, the Huns were naturally attracted by the wealth and fertility of those provinces; but the particular motives and provocations of Attila, can only be explained by the state of the Western empire under the reign of Valentinian, or, to speak more correctly, under the administration of Ætius.[3]

After the death of his rival Boniface, Ætius had prudently retired to the tents of the Huns; and he was indebted to their alliance for his safety and his restoration. Instead of the suppliant language of a guilty exile, he solicited his pardon at the head of sixty thousand Barbarians; and the empress Placidia confessed, by a feeble resistance, that the condescension, which might have been ascribed to clemency, was the effect of weakness or fear. She delivered herself, her son Valentinian, and the Western empire, into the hands of an insolent subject; nor could Placidia protect the son-in-law of Boniface, the virtuous and faithful Sebastian,[4] from the implacable persecution, which urged him from one kingdom to another, till he miserably perished in the service of the Vandals. The fortunate Ætius, who was immediately promoted to the rank of patrician, and thrice invested with the honours of the consulship, assumed, with the title of master of the cavalry and infantry, the whole military power of the state; and he is sometimes styled, by contemporary writers, the Duke, or General, of the Romans of the West. His prudence, rather than his virtue, engaged him to leave the grandson of Theodosius in the possession of the purple; and Valentinian was permitted to enjoy the peace and luxury of Italy, while the patrician appeared in the glorious light of a hero and a patriot, who supported near twenty years the ruins of the Western empire. The Gothic historian ingenuously confesses, that Ætius was born for the salvation of the Roman republic;[5] and the

Character and administration of Ætius, A.D. 433–454.

---

3. The second book of the Histoire Critique de l'Etablissement de la Monarchie Françoise, tom. i. p. 189–424, throws great light on the state of Gaul, when it was invaded by Attila; but the ingenious author, the Abbé Dubos, too often bewilders himself in system and conjecture.

4. Victor Vitensis (de Persecut. Vandal. l. i. c. 6. p. 8. edit. Ruinart) calls him, acer consilio et strenuus in bello: but his courage, when he became unfortunate, was censured as desperate rashness; and Sebastian deserved, or obtained, the epithet of *præceps* (Sidon. Apollinar. Carmen ix. 181.). His adventures at Constantinople, in Sicily, Gaul, Spain, and Africa, are faintly marked in the Chronicles of Marcellinus and Idatius. In his distress he was always followed by a numerous train; since he could ravage the Hellespont and Propontis, and seize the city of Barcelona.

5. Reipublicæ Romanæ singulariter natus, qui superbiam Suevorum, Francorumque

following portrait, though it is drawn in the fairest colours, must be allowed to contain a much larger proportion of truth than of flattery. "His mother was a wealthy and noble Italian, and his father Gaudentius, who held a distinguished rank in the province of Scythia, gradually rose from the station of a military *domestic*, to the dignity of master of the cavalry. Their son, who was enrolled almost in his infancy in the guards, was given as a hostage, first to Alaric, and afterwards to the Huns; and he successively obtained the civil and military honours of the palace, for which he was equally qualified by superior merit. The graceful figure of Ætius was not above the middle stature; but his manly limbs were admirably formed for strength, beauty, and agility; and he excelled in the martial exercises of managing a horse, drawing the bow, and darting the javelin. He could patiently endure the want of food or of sleep; and his mind and body were alike capable of the most laborious efforts. He possessed the genuine courage, that can despise not only dangers but injuries; and it was impossible either to corrupt, or deceive, or intimidate, the firm integrity of his soul."[6] The Barbarians, who had seated themselves in the Western provinces, were insensibly taught to respect the faith and valour of the patrician Ætius. He soothed their passions, consulted their prejudices, balanced their interests, and checked their ambition. A seasonable treaty, which he concluded with Genseric, protected Italy from the depredations of the Vandals; the independent Britons implored and acknowledged his salutary aid; the Imperial authority was restored and maintained in Gaul and Spain; and he compelled the Franks and the Suevi, whom he had vanquished in the field, to become the useful confederates of the republic.

His connection with the Huns and Alani.

From a principle of interest, as well as gratitude, Ætius assiduously cultivated the alliance of the Huns. While he resided in their tents as a hostage, or an exile, he had familiarly conversed with Attila himself, the nephew of his benefactor; and the two famous antagonists appear to have been connected by a personal and military friendship, which they afterwards confirmed by mutual gifts, frequent embassies, and the education of Carpilio, the son of Ætius, in the camp of

---

barbariem immensis cædibus servīre Imperio Romano coegisset. Jornandes de Rebus Geticis, c. 34. p. 660.

6. This portrait is drawn by Renatus Profuturus Frigeridus, a contemporary historian, known only by some extracts, which are preserved by Gregory of Tours (l. ii. c. 8. in tom. ii. p. 163.). It was probably the duty, or at least the interest, of Renatus, to magnify the virtues of Ætius; but he would have shewn more dexterity, if he had not insisted on his patient, *forgiving* disposition.

Attila. By the specious professions of gratitude and voluntary attachment, the patrician might disguise his apprehensions of the Scythian conqueror, who pressed the two empires with his innumerable armies. His demands were obeyed or eluded. When he claimed the spoils of a vanquished city, some vases of gold, which had been fraudulently embezzled; the civil and military governors of Noricum were immediately dispatched to satisfy his complaints:[7] and it is evident, from their conversation with Maximin and Priscus, in the royal village, that the valour and prudence of Ætius had not saved the Western Romans from the common ignominy of tribute. Yet his dexterous policy prolonged the advantages of a salutary peace; and a numerous army of Huns and Alani, whom he had attached to his person, was employed in the defence of Gaul. Two colonies of these Barbarians were judiciously fixed in the territories of Valance and Orleans:[8] and their active cavalry secured the important passages of the Rhône and of the Loire. These savage allies were not indeed less formidable to the subjects than to the enemies of Rome. Their original settlement was enforced with the licentious violence of conquest; and the province through which they marched, was exposed to all the calamities of an hostile invasion.[9] Strangers to the emperor or the republic, the Alani of Gaul were devoted to the ambition of Ætius; and though he might suspect, that, in a contest with Attila himself, they would revolt to the standard of their national king,

7. The embassy consisted of Count Romulus; of Promotus, president of Noricum; and of Romanus, the military duke. They were accompanied by Tatullus, an illustrious citizen of Petovio, in the same province, and father of Orestes, who had married the daughter of Count Romulus. See Priscus, p. 57. 65. Cassiodorius (Variar. i. 4.) mentions another embassy, which was executed by his father and Carpilio, the son of Ætius; and as Attila was no more, he could safely boast of their manly intrepid behaviour in his presence.

8. Deserta Valentinæ urbis rura Alanis partienda traduntur. Prosper. Tyronis Chron. in Historiens de France, tom. i. p. 639. A few lines afterwards, Prosper observes, that lands in the *ulterior* Gaul were assigned to the Alani. Without admitting the correction of Dubos (tom. i. p. 300.); the reasonable supposition of *two* colonies or garrisons of Alani, will

confirm his arguments, and remove his objections.

9. See Prosper. Tyro, p. 639. Sidonius (Panegyr. Avit. 246.) complains, in the name of Auvergne, his native country,

Litorius Scythicos equites tunc forte
    subacto
Celsus Aremorico, Geticum rapiebat in
    agmen
Per terras, Arverne, tuas, qui proxima
    quæque
Discursu, flammis, ferro, feritate,
    rapinis,
Delebant; pacis fallentes nomen inane.

Another poet, Paulinus of Perigord, confirms the complaint:

Nam socium vix ferre queas, qui durior
    hoste.
                    See Dubos, tom. i. p. 330.

the patrician laboured to restrain, rather than to excite, their zeal and resentment against the Goths, the Burgundians, and the Franks.

The Visigoths in Gaul under the reign of Theodoric, A.D. 419–451. The kingdom established by the Visigoths in the southern provinces of Gaul, had gradually acquired strength and maturity; and the conduct of those ambitious Barbarians, either in peace or war, engaged the perpetual vigilance of Ætius. After the death of Wallia, the Gothic sceptre devolved to Theodoric, the son of the great Alaric;[10] and his prosperous reign, of more than thirty years, over a turbulent people, may be allowed to prove, that his prudence was supported by uncommon vigour, both of mind and body. Impatient of his narrow limits, Theodoric aspired to the possession of Arles, the wealthy seat of government and commerce; but the city was saved by the timely approach of Ætius; and the Gothic king, who had raised the siege with some loss and disgrace, was persuaded, for an adequate subsidy, to divert the martial valour of his subjects in a Spanish war. Yet Theodoric still watched, and eagerly seized, the favourable moment of renewing his hostile attempts. The Goths besieged

A.D. 435–439. Narbonne, while the Belgic provinces were invaded by the Burgundians; and the public safety was threatened on every side by the apparent union of the enemies of Rome. On every side, the activity of Ætius, and his Scythian cavalry, opposed a firm and successful resistance. Twenty thousand Burgundians were slain in battle; and the remains of the nation humbly accepted a dependent seat in the mountains of Savoy.[11] The walls of Narbonne had been shaken by the battering engines, and the inhabitants had endured the last extremities of famine, when count Litorius, approaching in silence, and directing each horseman to carry behind him two sacks of flour, cut his way through the intrenchments of the besiegers. The siege was immediately raised; and the more decisive victory, which is

---

10. Theodoric II. the son of Theodoric I., declares to Avitus his resolution of repairing, or expiating, the fault which his *grandfather* had committed.

> Quæ *noster* peccavit *avus*, quem fuscat id unum,
> Quod te, Roma, capit. ——
>   Sidon. Panegyr. Avit. 505.

This character, applicable only to the great Alaric, establishes the genealogy of the Gothic kings, which has hitherto been unnoticed.

11. The name of *Sapaudia*, the origin of *Savoy*, is first mentioned by Ammianus Marcellinus; and two military posts are ascertained, by the Notitia, within the limits of that province; a cohort was stationed at Grenoble in Dauphiné; and Ebredunum, or Iverdun, sheltered a fleet of small vessels, which commanded the lake of Neufchâtel. See Valesius, Notit. Galliarum, p. 503. D'Anville, Notice de l'Ancienne Gaule, p. 284. 579.

ascribed to the personal conduct of Ætius himself, was marked with the blood of eight thousand Goths. But in the absence of the patrician, who was hastily summoned to Italy by some public or private interest, count Litorius succeeded to the command; and his presumption soon discovered, that far different talents are required to lead a wing of cavalry, or to direct the operations of an important war. At the head of an army of Huns, he rashly advanced to the gates of Thoulouse, full of careless contempt for an enemy, whom his misfortunes had rendered prudent, and his situation made desperate. The predictions of the Augurs had inspired Litorius with the profane confidence, that he should enter the Gothic capital in triumph; and the trust which he reposed in his Pagan allies, encouraged him to reject the fair conditions of peace, which were repeatedly proposed by the bishops in the name of Theodoric. The king of the Goths exhibited in his distress the edifying contrast of Christian piety and moderation; nor did he lay aside his sackcloth and ashes till he was prepared to arm for the combat. His soldiers, animated with martial and religious enthusiasm, assaulted the camp of Litorius. The conflict was obstinate; the slaughter was mutual. The Roman general, after a total defeat, which could be imputed only to his unskilful rashness, was actually led through the streets of Thoulouse, not in his own, but in a hostile, triumph; and the misery which he experienced, in a long and ignominious captivity, excited the compassion of the Barbarians themselves.[12] Such a loss, in a country whose spirit and finances were long since exhausted, could not easily be repaired; and the Goths, assuming, in their turn, the sentiments of ambition and revenge, would have planted their victorious standards on the banks of the Rhône, if the presence of Ætius had not restored strength and discipline to the Romans.[13] The two armies expected the signal of a decisive action; but

12. Salvian has attempted to explain the moral government of the Deity; a task which may be readily performed by supposing, that the calamities of the wicked are, *judgments*, and those of the righteous, *trials*.

13. —— Capto terrarum damna patebant
Litorio, in Rhodanum proprios
    producere fines,
Theudoridæ fixum; nec erat pugnare
    necesse,
Sed migrare Getis; rabidam trux asperat
    iram

Victor; quòd sensit Scythicum sub
    mœnibus hostem
Imputat, et nihil est gravius, si forsitan
    unquam
Vincere contingat, trepido. ——
                    Panegyr. Avit. 300, &c.

Sidonius then proceeds, according to the duty of a panegyrist, to transfer the whole merit from Ætius, to his minister Avitus.

the generals, who were conscious of each other's force, and doubtful of their own superiority, prudently sheathed their swords in the field of battle; and their reconciliation was permanent and sincere. Theodoric, king of the Visigoths, appears to have deserved the love of his subjects, the confidence of his allies, and the esteem of mankind. His throne was surrounded by six valiant sons, who were educated with equal care in the exercises of the Barbarian camp, and in those of the Gallic schools: from the study of the Roman jurisprudence, they acquired the theory, at least, of law and justice; and the harmonious sense of Virgil contributed to soften the asperity of their native manners.[14] The two daughters of the Gothic king were given in marriage to the eldest sons of the kings of the Suevi and of the Vandals, who reigned in Spain and Africa; but these illustrious alliances were pregnant with guilt and discord. The queen of the Suevi bewailed the death of an husband, inhumanly massacred by her brother. The princess of the Vandals was the victim of a jealous tyrant, whom she called her father. The cruel Genseric suspected, that his son's wife had conspired to poison him; the supposed crime was punished by the amputation of her nose and ears; and the unhappy daughter of Theodoric was ignominiously returned to the court of Thoulouse in that deformed and mutilated condition. This horrid act, which must seem incredible to a civilized age, drew tears from every spectator; but Theodoric was urged, by the feelings of a parent and a king, to revenge such irreparable injuries. The Imperial ministers, who always cherished the discord of the Barbarians, would have supplied the Goths with arms, and ships, and treasures, for the African war; and the cruelty of Genseric might have been fatal to himself, if the artful Vandal had not armed, in his cause, the formidable power of the Huns. His rich gifts and pressing solicitations inflamed the ambition of Attila; and the designs of Ætius and Theodoric were prevented by the invasion of Gaul.[15]

14. Theodoric II. revered, in the person of Avitus, the character of his preceptor.

—— Mihi Romula dudum
Per te jura placent: parvumque ediscere
    jussit
Ad tua verba pater, docili quo prisca
    Maronis
Carmine molliret Scythicos mihi pagina
    mores.

    Sidon. Panegyr. Avit. 495, &c.

15. Our authorities for the reign of Theodoric I. are, Jornandes de Rebus Geticis, c. 34. 36. and the Chronicles of Idatius, and the two Prospers, inserted in the Historians of France, tom. i. p. 612–640. To these we may add Salvian de Gubernatione Dei, l. vii. p. 243, 244, 245. and the Panegyric of Avitus, by Sidonius.

The Franks, whose monarchy was still confined to the neighbourhood of the Lower Rhine, had wisely established the right of hereditary succession in the noble family of the Merovingians.[16] These princes were elevated on a buckler, the symbol of military command;[17] and the royal fashion of long hair was the ensign of their birth and dignity. Their flaxen locks, which they combed and dressed with singular care, hung down in flowing ringlets on their back and shoulders; while the rest of the nation were obliged, either by law or custom, to shave the hinder part of their head; to comb their hair over the forehead, and to content themselves with the ornament of two small whiskers.[18] The lofty stature of the Franks, and their blue eyes, denoted a Germanic origin; their close apparel accurately expressed the figure of their limbs; a weighty sword was suspended from a broad belt; their bodies were protected by a large shield: and these warlike Barbarians were trained, from their earliest youth, to run, to leap, to swim; to dart the javelin, or battle-axe, with unerring aim; to advance, without hesitation, against a superior enemy; and to maintain, either in life or death, the invincible reputation of their ancestors.[19] Clodion, the first of their long-haired kings, whose name and actions are mentioned in authentic history, held his residence at

The Franks in Gaul, under the Merovingian kings, A.D. 420–451.

16. Reges *Crinitos* se creavisse de primâ, et ut ita dicam nobiliori suorum familiâ (Greg. Turon. l. ii. c. 9. p. 166, of the second volume of the Historians of France). Gregory himself does not mention the *Merovingian* name, which may be traced, however, to the beginning of the seventh century, as the distinctive appellation of the royal family, and even of the French monarchy. An ingenious critic has deduced the Merovingians from the great Maroboduus; and he has clearly proved, that the prince, who gave his name to the first race, was more ancient than the father of Childeric. See Memoires de l'Academie des Inscriptions, tom. xx. p. 52–90. tom. xxx. p. 557–587.

17. This German custom, which may be traced from Tacitus to Gregory of Tours, was at length adopted by the emperors of Constantinople. From a MS. of the tenth century, Montfaucon has delineated the rep-

resentation of a similar ceremony, which the ignorance of the age had applied to king David. See Monuments de la Monarchie Françoise, tom. i. Discourse Preliminaire.

18. Cæsaries prolixa . . . crinium flagellis per terga dimissis, &c. See the Preface to third volume of the Historians of France, and the Abbé Le Bœuf (Dissertat. tom. iii. p. 47–79.). This peculiar fashion of the Merovingians has been remarked by natives and strangers; by Priscus (tom. i. p. 608.), by Agathias (tom. ii. p. 49.), and by Gregory of Tours, l. iii. 18. vi. 24. viii. 10. tom. ii. p. 196. 278. 316.

19. See an original picture of the figure, dress, arms, and temper of the ancient Franks in Sidonius Apollinaris (Panegyr. Majorian, 238–254.); and such pictures, though coarsely drawn, have a real and intrinsic value. Father Daniel (Hist. de la Milice Françoise, tom. i. p. 2–7.) has illustrated the description.

Dispargum,[20] a village, or fortress, whose place may be assigned between Louvain and Brussels. From the report of his spies, the king of the Franks was informed, that the defenceless state of the second Belgic must yield, on the slightest attack, to the valour of his subjects. He boldly penetrated through the thickets and morasses of the Carbonarian forest;[21] occupied Tournay and Cambray, the only cities which existed in the fifth century, and extended his conquests as far as the river Somme, over a desolate country, whose cultivation and populousness are the effects of more recent industry.[22] While Clodion lay encamped in the plains of Artois,[23] and celebrated, with vain and ostentatious security, the marriage, perhaps, of his son, the nuptial feast was interrupted by the unexpected and unwelcome presence of Ætius, who had passed the Somme at the head of his light cavalry. The tables, which had been spread under the shelter of a hill, along the banks of a pleasant stream, were rudely overturned; the Franks were oppressed before they could recover their arms, or their ranks; and their unavailing valour was fatal only to themselves. The loaded waggons which had followed their march, afforded a rich booty; and the virgin-bride, with her female attendants, submitted to the new lovers, who were imposed on them by the chance of war. This advantage, which had been obtained by the skill and activity of Ætius, might reflect some disgrace on the military prudence of Clodion; but the king of the Franks soon regained his strength and reputation, and still maintained the possession of his Gallic kingdom from the Rhine to the Somme.[24] Under his reign, and most probably from the enterprising spirit of his subjects, the three capitals, Mentz, Treves, and

20. Dubos, Hist. Critique, &c. tom. i. p. 271, 272. Some geographers have placed Dispargum on the German side of the Rhine. See a note of the Benedictine Editors to the Historians of France, tom. ii. p. 166.

21. The Carbonarian wood, was that part of the great forest of the Ardennes, which lay between the Escaut, or Scheld, and the Meuse. Vales. Notit. Gall. p. 126.

22. Gregor. Turon. l. ii. c. 9. in tom. ii. p. 166, 167. Fredegar. Epitom. c. 9. p. 395. Gesta Reg. Francor. c. 5. in tom. ii. p. 544. Vit. St. Remig. ab Hincmar, in tom. iii. p. 373.

23. —— Francus quâ Cloio patentes
    Atrebatum terras pervaserat. ——
            Panegyr. Majorian. 212.

The precise spot was a town, or village, called Vicus *Helena*; and both the name and the place are discovered by modern geographers at Lens. See Vales. Notit. Gall. p. 246. Longuerue, Description de la France, tom. ii. p. 88.

24. See a vague account of the action in Sidonius. Panegyr. Majorian. 212–230. The French critics, impatient to establish their monarchy in Gaul, have drawn a strong argument from the silence of Sidonius, who dares not insinuate, that the vanquished Franks were compelled to repass the Rhine. Dubos, tom. i. p. 322.

Cologne, experienced the effects of hostile cruelty and avarice. The distress of Cologne was prolonged by the perpetual dominion of the same Barbarians, who evacuated the ruins of Treves; and Treves, which, in the space of forty years, had been four times besieged and pillaged, was disposed to lose the memory of her afflictions in the vain amusements of the circus.[25] The death of Clodion, after a reign of twenty years, exposed his kingdom to the discord and ambition of his two sons. Meroveus, the younger,[26] was persuaded to implore the protection of Rome; he was received at the Imperial court, as the ally of Valentinian, and the adopted son of the patrician Ætius; and dismissed, to his native country, with splendid gifts, and the strongest assurances of friendship and support. During his absence, his elder brother had solicited, with equal ardour, the formidable aid of Attila; and the king of the Huns embraced an alliance, which facilitated the passage of the Rhine, and justified, by a specious and honourable pretence, the invasion of Gaul.[27]

When Attila declared his resolution of supporting the cause of his allies, the Vandals and the Franks, at the same time, and almost in the spirit of romantic chivalry, the savage monarch professed himself the lover and the champion of the princess Honoria. The sister of Valentinian was educated in the palace of Ravenna; and as her marriage might be productive of some danger to the state, she was raised, by the title of *Augusta*,[28] above the hopes of the most presumptuous subject. But the fair Honoria had no sooner attained the sixteenth year of her age, than she detested the importunate greatness, which must for ever

The adventures of the princess Honoria.

---

25. Salvian (de Gubernat. Dei, l. vi.) has expressed, in vague and declamatory language, the misfortunes of these three cities, which are distinctly ascertained by the learned Mascou, Hist. of the Ancient Germans, ix. 21.

26. Priscus, in relating the contest, does not name the two brothers; the second of whom he had seen at Rome, a beardless youth, with long flowing hair (Historians of France, tom. i. p. 607, 608.). The Benedictine Editors are inclined to believe, that they were the sons of some unknown king of the Franks, who reigned on the banks of the Necker: but the arguments of M. de Foncemagne (Mem. de l'Academie, tom. viii. p. 464.) seem to prove,

that the succession of Clodion was disputed by his two sons, and that the younger was Meroveus, the father of Childeric.

27. Under the Merovingian race, the throne was hereditary: but all the sons of the deceased monarch were equally intitled to their share of his treasures and territories. See the Dissertations of M. de Foncemagne in the sixth and eighth volumes of the Memoires de l'Academie.

28. A medal is still extant, which exhibits the pleasing countenance of Honoria, with the title of Augusta; and on the reverse, the improper legend of *Salus Reipublicæ* round the monagram of Christ. See Ducange, Famil. Byzantin. p. 67. 73.

exclude her from the comforts of honourable love: in the midst of vain and unsatisfactory pomp, Honoria sighed, yielded to the impulse of nature, and threw herself into the arms of chamberlain Eugenius. Her guilt and shame (such is the absurd language of imperious man) were soon betrayed by the appearances of pregnancy: but the disgrace of the royal family was published to the world by the imprudence of the empress Placidia; who dismissed her daughter, after a strict and shameful confinement, to a remote exile at Constantinople. The unhappy princess passed twelve or fourteen years in the irksome society of the sisters of Theodosius, and their chosen virgins; to whose *crown* Honoria could no longer aspire, and whose monastic assiduity of prayer, fasting, and vigils, she reluctantly imitated. Her impatience of long and hopeless celibacy, urged her to embrace a strange and desperate resolution. The name of Attila was familiar and formidable at Constantinople; and his frequent embassies entertained a perpetual intercourse between his camp and the Imperial palace. In the pursuit of love, or rather of revenge, the daughter of Placidia sacrificed every duty, and every prejudice; and offered to deliver her person into the arms of a Barbarian, of whose language she was ignorant, whose figure was scarcely human, and whose religion and manners she abhorred. By the ministry of a faithful eunuch, she transmitted to Attila a ring, the pledge of her affection; and earnestly conjured him to claim her as a lawful spouse, to whom he had been secretly betrothed. These indecent advances were received, however, with coldness and disdain; and the king of the Huns continued to multiply the number of his wives, till his love was awakened by the more forcible passions of ambition and avarice. The invasion of Gaul was preceded, and justified, by a formal demand of the princess Honoria, with a just and equal share of the Imperial patrimony. His predecessors, the ancient Tanjous, had often addressed, in the same hostile and peremptory manner, the daughters of China; and the pretensions of Attila were not less offensive to the majesty of Rome. A firm, but temperate, refusal was communicated to his ambassadors. The right of female succession, though it might derive a specious argument from the recent examples of Placidia and Pulcheria, was strenuously denied; and the indissoluble engagements of Honoria were opposed to the claims of her Scythian lover.[29] On the discovery of her connection with the king of the Huns, the guilty

29. See Priscus, p. 39. 40. It might be fairly alleged, that if females could succeed to the throne, Valentinian himself, who had married the daughter and heiress of the younger Theodosius, would have asserted his right to the eastern empire.

princess had been sent away, as an object of horror, from Constantinople to Italy: her life was spared; but the ceremony of her marriage was performed with some obscure and nominal husband, before she was immured in a perpetual prison, to bewail those crimes and misfortunes, which Honoria might have escaped, had she not been born the daughter of an emperor.[30]

A native of Gaul, and a contemporary, the learned and eloquent Sidonius, who was afterwards bishop of Clermont, had made a promise to one of his friends, that he would compose a regular history of the war of Attila. If the modesty of Sidonius had not discouraged him from the prosecution of this interesting work,[31] the historian would have related, with the simplicity of truth, those memorable events, to which the poet, in vague and doubtful metaphors, has concisely alluded.[32] The kings and nations of Germany and Scythia, from the Volga perhaps to the Danube, obeyed the warlike summons of Attila. From the royal village, in the plains of Hungary, his standard moved towards the West; and, after a march of seven or eight hundred miles, he reached the conflux of the Rhine and the Necker; where he was joined by the Franks, who adhered to his ally, the elder of the sons of Clodion. A troop of light Barbarians, who roamed in quest of plunder, might chuse the winter for the convenience of passing the river on the ice; but the innumerable cavalry of the Huns required such plenty of forage and provisions, as could be procured only in a milder season; the Hercynian forest supplied materials for a bridge of boats; and the hostile myriads were poured, with resistless violence, into the Belgic

Attila invades Gaul, and besieges Orleans, A.D. 451.

---

30. The adventures of Honoria are imperfectly related by Jornandes, de Successione Regn. c. 97. and de Reb. Get. c. 42. p. 674.; and in the Chronicles of Prosper, and Marcellinus; but they cannot be made consistent, or probable, unless we separate, by an interval of time and place, her intrigue with Eugenius, and her invitation of Attila.

31. Exegeras mihi, ut promitterem tibi, Attilæ bellum stylo me posteris intimaturum . . . cœperam scribere, sed operis arrepti fasce perspecto, tæduit inchoasse. Sidon. Apoll. l. viii. epist. 15. p. 246.

32. —— Subito cum rupta tumultu
Barbaries totas in te transfuderat Arctos,
Gallia. Pugnacem Rugum comitante
    Gelono
Gepida trux sequitur; Scyrum
    Burgundio cogit:
Chunus, Bellonotus, Neurus, Basterna,
    Toringus
Bructerus, ulvosâ vel quem Nicer abluit
    unda
Prorumpit Francus. Cecidit cito secta
    bipenni
Hercynia in lintres, et Rhenum texuit
    alno.
Et jam terrificis diffuderat Attila turmis
In campos se Belga tuos. ——
                    Panegyr. Avit. 319, &c.

provinces.[33] The consternation of Gaul was universal; and the various fortunes of its cities have been adorned by tradition with martyrdoms and miracles.[34] Troyes was saved by the merits of St. Lupus; St. Servatius was removed from the world, that he might not behold the ruin of Tongres; and the prayers of St. Genevieve diverted the march of Attila from the neighbourhood of Paris. But as the greatest part of the Gallic cities were alike destitute of saints and soldiers, they were besieged and stormed by the Huns; who practised, in the example of Metz,[35] their customary maxims of war. They involved, in a promiscuous massacre, the priests who served at the altar, and the infants, who, in the hour of danger, had been providently baptized by the bishop; the flourishing city was delivered to the flames, and a solitary chapel of St. Stephen marked the place where it formerly stood. From the Rhine and Moselle, Attila advanced into the heart of Gaul; crossed the Seine at Auxerre; and, after a long and laborious march, fixed his camp under the walls of Orleans. He was desirous of securing his conquests by the possession of an advantageous post, which commanded the passage of the Loire; and he depended on the secret invitation of Sangiban, king of the Alani, who had promised to betray the city, and to revolt from the service of the empire. But this treacherous conspiracy was detected and disappointed: Orleans had been strengthened with recent fortifications; and the assaults of the Huns were vigorously

33. The most authentic and circumstantial account of this war, is contained in Jornandes (de Reb. Geticis, c. 36–41, p. 662–672.), who has sometimes abridged, and sometimes transcribed, the larger history of Cassiodorius. Jornandes, a quotation which it would be superfluous to repeat, may be corrected and illustrated by Gregory of Tours, l. 2. c. 5, 6, 7. and the Chronicles of Idatius, Isidore, and the two Prospers. All the ancient testimonies are collected and inserted in the Historians of France; but the reader should be cautioned against a supposed extract from the Chronicle of Idatius (among the fragments of Fredegarius, tom. ii. p. 462.), which often contradicts the genuine text of the Gallician bishop.

34. The *ancient* legendaries deserve some regard, as they are obliged to connect their fables with the real history of their own times. See the lives of St. Lupus, St. Anianus, the bishops of Metz, Ste. Genevieve, &c. in the Historians of France, tom. i. p. 644, 645. 649. tom. iii. p. 369.

35. The scepticism of the count de Buat (Hist. des Peuples, tom. vii. p. 539, 540.) cannot be reconciled with any principles of reason or criticism. Is not Gregory of Tours precise and positive in his account of the destruction of Metz? At the distance of no more than an hundred years, could he be ignorant, could the people be ignorant, of the fate of a city, the actual residence of his sovereigns, the kings of Austrasia? The learned Count, who seems to have undertaken the apology of Attila, and the Barbarians, appeals to the false Idatius, *parcens* civitatibus Germaniæ et Galliæ, and forgets, that the true Idatius had explicitly affirmed, plurimæ civitates *effractæ*, among which he enumerates Metz.

repelled by the faithful valour of the soldiers, or citizens, who defended the place. The pastoral diligence of Anianus, a bishop of primitive sanctity and consummate prudence, exhausted every art of religious policy to support their courage, till the arrival of the expected succours. After an obstinate siege, the walls were shaken by the battering rams; the Huns had already occupied the suburbs; and the people, who were incapable of bearing arms, lay prostrate in prayer. Anianus, who anxiously counted the days and hours, dispatched a trusty messenger to observe, from the rampart, the face of the distant country. He returned twice, without any intelligence, that could inspire hope or comfort; but in his third report, he mentioned a small cloud, which he had faintly descried at the extremity of the horizon. "It is the aid of God," exclaimed the bishop, in a tone of pious confidence; and the whole multitude repeated after him, "It is the aid of God." The remote object, on which every eye was fixed, became each moment larger, and more distinct; the Roman and Gothic banners were gradually perceived; and a favourable wind blowing aside the dust, discovered, in deep array, the impatient squadrons of Ætius and Theodoric, who pressed forwards to the relief of Orleans.

The facility with which Attila had penetrated into the heart of Gaul, may be ascribed to his insidious policy, as well as to the terror of his arms. His public declarations were skilfully mitigated by his private assurances; he alternately soothed and threatened the Romans and the Goths; and the courts of Ravenna and Thoulouse, mutually suspicious of each other's intentions, beheld, with supine indifference, the approach of their common enemy. Ætius was the sole guardian of the public safety; but his wisest measures were embarrassed by a faction, which, since the death of Placidia, infested the Imperial palace: the youth of Italy trembled at the sound of the trumpet; and the Barbarians, who, from fear or affection, were inclined to the cause of Attila, awaited, with doubtful and venal faith, the event of the war. The patrician passed the Alps at the head of some troops, whose strength and numbers scarcely deserved the name of an army.[36] But on his arrival at Arles, or Lyons, he was confounded by the intelligence, that the Visigoths, refusing to embrace

Alliance of the Romans and Visigoths.

---

36. — Vix liquerat Alpes
   Aetius, tenue, et rarum sine milite ducens
   Robur, in auxiliis Geticum male credulus agmen

Incassum propriis præsumens adfore castris.

   Panegyr. Avit. 328, &c.

the defence of Gaul, had determined to expect, within their own territories, the formidable invader, whom they professed to despise. The senator Avitus, who, after the honourable exercise of the prætorian Præfecture, had retired to his estate in Auvergne, was persuaded to accept the important embassy, which he executed with ability and success. He represented to Theodoric, that an ambitious conqueror, who aspired to the dominion of the earth, could be resisted only by the firm and unanimous alliance of the powers whom he laboured to oppress. The lively eloquence of Avitus inflamed the Gothic warriors, by the description of the injuries which their ancestors had suffered from the Huns; whose implacable fury still pursued them from the Danube to the foot of the Pyrenees. He strenuously urged, that it was the duty of every Christian to save, from sacrilegious violation, the churches of God, and the relics of the saints: that it was the interest of every Barbarian, who had acquired a settlement in Gaul, to defend the fields and vineyards, which were cultivated for his use, against the desolation of the Scythian shepherds. Theodoric yielded to the evidence of truth; adopted the measure at once the most prudent and the most honourable; and declared, that, as the faithful ally of Ætius and the Romans, he was ready to expose his life and kingdom for the common safety of Gaul.[37] The Visigoths, who, at that time, were in the mature vigour of their fame and power, obeyed with alacrity the signal of war; prepared their arms and horses, and assembled under the standard of their aged king, who was resolved, with his two eldest sons, Torismond and Theodoric, to command in person his numerous and valiant people. The example of the Goths determined several tribes or nations, that seemed to fluctuate between the Huns and the Romans. The indefatigable diligence of the patrician gradually collected the troops of Gaul and Germany, who had formerly acknowledged themselves the subjects, or soldiers, of the republic, but who now claimed the rewards of voluntary service, and the rank of independent allies; the Læti, the Armoricans, the Breones, the Saxons, the Burgundians, the Sarmatians, or Alani, the Ripuarians, and the Franks who followed Mero-veus as their lawful prince. Such was the various army, which, under the

---

37. The policy of Attila, of Ætius, and of the Visigoths, is imperfectly described in the Panegyric of Avitus, and the thirty-sixth chapter of Jornandes. The poet and the historian were both biassed by personal or national prejudices. The former exalts the merit and importance of Avitus; orbis, Avite, salus, &c.! The latter is anxious to shew the Goths in the most favourable light. Yet their agreement, when they are fairly interpreted, is a proof of their veracity.

conduct of Ætius and Theodoric, advanced, by rapid marches, to relieve Orleans, and to give battle to the innumerable host of Attila.[38]

On their approach, the king of the Huns immediately raised the siege, and sounded a retreat to recal the foremost of his troops from the pillage of a city which they had already entered.[39] The valour of Attila was always guided by his prudence; and as he foresaw the fatal consequences of a defeat in the heart of Gaul, he repassed the Seine, and expected the enemy in the plains of Châlons, whose smooth and level surface was adapted to the operations of his Scythian cavalry. But in this tumultuary retreat, the vanguard of the Romans, and their allies, continually pressed, and sometimes engaged, the troops whom Attila had posted in the rear; the hostile columns, in the darkness of night, and the perplexity of the roads, might encounter each other without design; and the bloody conflict of the Franks and Gepidæ, in which fifteen thousand[40] Barbarians were slain, was a prelude to a more general and decisive action. The Catalaunian fields[41] spread themselves round Châlons, and extend, according to the vague measurement of Jornandes, to the length of one hundred and fifty, and the breadth of one hundred, miles, over the whole province, which is intitled to the appellation of a *champaign* country.[42] This spacious plain was distinguished, however, by some inequalities of ground; and the importance of an height, which commanded the camp of Attila, was understood, and disputed, by the two generals. The young and valiant Torismond first occupied the summit; the Goths rushed

Attila retires to the plains of Champagne.

---

38. The review of the army of Ætius is made by Jornandes, c. 36. p. 664. edit. Grot. tom. ii. p. 23. of the Historians of France, with the notes of the Benedictine Editor. The *Læti* were a promiscuous race of Barbarians, born or naturalized in Gaul; and the Riparii, or *Ripuarii*, derived their name from their posts on the three rivers, the Rhine, the Meuse, and the Moselle; the *Armoricans* possessed the independent cities between the Seine and the Loire. A colony of *Saxons* had been planted in the diocese of Bayeux; the *Burgundians* were settled in Savoy; and the *Breones* were a warlike tribe of Rhætians, to the east of the lake of Constance.

39. Aurelianensis urbis obsidio, oppugnatio, irruptio, nec direptio, l. v. Sidon. Apollin. l. viii. epist. 15. p. 246. The preservation of Orleans might easily be turned into a miracle, obtained, and foretold, by the holy bishop.

40. The common editions read xcm; but there is some authority of manuscripts (and almost any authority is sufficient) for the more reasonable number of xvm.

41. Châlons, or Duro-Catalaunum, afterwards *Catalauni*, had formerly made a part of the territory of Rheims, from whence it is distant only twenty-seven miles. See Vales. Notit. Gall. p. 136. D'Anville, Notice de l'Ancienne Gaule, p. 212. 279.

42. The name of Campania, or Champagne, is frequently mentioned by Gregory of Tours; and that great province, of which Rheims was the capital, obeyed the command of a duke. Vales. Notit. p. 120–123.

with irresistible weight on the Huns, who laboured to ascend from the opposite side; and the possession of this advantageous post inspired both the troops and their leaders with a fair assurance of victory. The anxiety of Attila prompted him to consult his priests and haruspices. It was reported, that, after scrutinizing the entrails of victims, and scraping their bones, they revealed, in mysterious language, his own defeat, with the death of his principal adversary; and that the Barbarian, by accepting the equivalent, expressed his involuntary esteem for the superior merit of Ætius. But the unusual despondency, which seemed to prevail among the Huns, engaged Attila to use the expedient, so familiar to the generals of antiquity, of animating his troops by a military oration; and his language was that of a king, who had often fought and conquered at their head.[43] He pressed them to consider their past glory, their actual danger, and their future hopes. The same fortune, which opened the deserts and morasses of Scythia to their unarmed valour, which had laid so many warlike nations prostrate at their feet, had reserved the *joys* of this memorable field for the consummation of their victories. The cautious steps of their enemies, their strict alliance, and their advantageous posts he artfully represented as the effects, not of prudence, but of fear. The Visigoths alone were the strength and nerves of the opposite army; and the Huns might securely trample on the degenerate Romans, whose close and compact order betrayed their apprehensions, and who were equally incapable of supporting the dangers, or the fatigues, of a day of battle. The doctrine of predestination, so favourable to martial virtue, was carefully inculcated by the king of the Huns; who assured his subjects, that the warriors, protected by Heaven, were safe and invulnerable amidst the darts of the enemy; but that the unerring Fates would strike their victims in the bosom of inglorious peace. "I myself," continued Attila, "will throw the first javelin, and the wretch who refuses to imitate the example of his sovereign, is devoted to inevitable death." The spirit of the Barbarians was rekindled by the presence, the voice, and the example of their intrepid leader; and Attila, yielding to their impatience, immediately formed his order of battle. At the head of his brave and faithful Huns, he occupied, in person, the centre of the line. The nations, subject to his empire, the Rugians, the Heruli, the Thuringians,

---

43. I am sensible that these military orations are usually composed by the historian; yet the old Ostrogoths, who had served under Attila, might repeat his discourse to Cassiodorius: the ideas, and even the expressions, have an original Scythian cast; and I doubt, whether an Italian of the sixth century, would have thought of the, hujus certaminis *gaudia.*

the Franks, the Burgundians, were extended, on either hand, over the ample space of the Catalaunian fields; the right wing was commanded by Ardaric, king of the Gepidæ; and the three valiant brothers, who reigned over the Ostrogoths, were posted on the left to oppose the kindred tribes of the Visigoths. The disposition of the allies was regulated by a different principle. Sangiban, the faithless king of the Alani, was placed in the centre; where his motions might be strictly watched, and his treachery might be instantly punished. Ætius assumed the command of the left, and Theodoric of the right, wing; while Torismond still continued to occupy the heights which appear to have stretched on the flank, and perhaps the rear, of the Scythian army. The nations from the Volga to the Atlantic were assembled on the plain of Châlons; but many of these nations had been divided by faction, or conquest, or emigration; and the appearance of similar arms and ensigns, which threatened each other, presented the image of a civil war.

The discipline and tactics of the Greeks and Romans form an interesting part of their national manners. The attentive study of the *Battle of* military operations of Xenophon, or Cæsar, or Frederic, when they *Châlons.* are described by the same genius which conceived and executed them, may tend to improve (if such improvement can be wished) the art of destroying the human species. But the battle of Châlons can only excite our curiosity, by the magnitude of the object; since it was decided by the blind impetuosity of Barbarians, and has been related by partial writers, whose civil or ecclesiastical profession secluded them from the knowledge of military affairs. Cassiodorius, however, had familiarly conversed with many Gothic warriors, who served in that memorable engagement; "a conflict," as they informed him, "fierce, various, obstinate, and bloody; such as could not be paralleled, either in the present, or in past ages." The number of the slain amounted to one hundred and sixty-two thousand, or, according to another account, three hundred thousand persons;[44] and these incredible exaggerations suppose a real and effective loss, sufficient to justify the historian's remark, that whole generations may be swept away,

---

44. The expressions of Jornandes, or rather of Cassiodorius, are extremely strong. Bellum atrox, multiplex, immane, pertinax, cui simili nulla usquam narrat antiquitas: ubi talia gesta referuntur, ut nihil esset quod in vità suâ conspicere potuisset egregius, qui hujus miraculi privaretur aspectû. Dubos (Hist. Critique, tom. i. p. 392, 393.) attempts to reconcile the 162,000 of Jornandes, with the 300,000 of Idatius and Isidore; by supposing, that the larger number included the total destruction of the war, the effects of disease, the slaughter of the unarmed people, &c.

by the madness of kings, in the space of a single hour. After the mutual and repeated discharge of missile weapons, in which the archers of Scythia might signalize their superior dexterity, the cavalry and infantry of the two armies were furiously mingled in closer combat. The Huns, who fought under the eyes of their king, pierced through the feeble and doubtful centre of the allies, separated their wings from each other, and wheeling, with a rapid effort, to the left, directed their whole force against the Visigoths. As Theodoric rode along the ranks, to animate his troops, he received a mortal stroke from the javelin of Andages, a noble Ostrogoth, and immediately fell from his horse. The wounded king was oppressed in the general disorder, and trampled under the feet of his own cavalry; and this important death served to explain the ambiguous prophecy of the Haruspices. Attila already exulted in the confidence of victory, when the valiant Torismond descended from the hills, and verified the remainder of the prediction. The Visigoths, who had been thrown into confusion by the flight, or defection, of the Alani, gradually restored their order of battle; and the Huns were undoubtedly vanquished, since Attila was compelled to retreat. He had exposed his person with the rashness of a private soldier; but the intrepid troops of the centre had pushed forwards beyond the rest of the line: their attack was faintly supported; their flanks were unguarded; and the conquerors of Scythia and Germany were saved by the approach of the night from a total defeat. They retired within the circle of waggons that fortified their camp; and the dismounted squadrons prepared themselves for a defence, to which neither their arms, nor their temper, were adapted. The event was doubtful: but Attila had secured a last and honourable resource. The saddles and rich furniture of the cavalry were collected, by his order, into a funeral pile; and the magnanimous Barbarian had resolved, if his intrenchments should be forced, to rush headlong into the flames, and to deprive his enemies of the glory which they might have acquired, by the death or captivity of Attila.[45]

Retreat of Attila.

But his enemies had passed the night in equal disorder and anxiety. The inconsiderate courage of Torismond was tempted to urge the pursuit, till he unexpectedly found himself, with a few followers, in the midst of the Scythian waggons. In the confusion of a

45. The count de Buat (Hist. des Peuples, &c. tom. vii. p. 554–573.), still depending on the *false*, and again rejecting the *true* Idatius, has divided the defeat of Attila into two great battles; the former near Orleans, the latter in Champagne: in the one, Theodoric was slain, in the other, he was revenged.

nocturnal combat, he was thrown from his horse; and the Gothic prince must have perished like his father, if his youthful strength, and the intrepid zeal of his companions, had not rescued him from this dangerous situation. In the same manner, but on the left of the line, Ætius himself, separated from his allies, ignorant of their victory, and anxious for their fate, encountered and escaped the hostile troops, that were scattered over the plains of Châlons; and at length reached the camp of the Goths, which he could only fortify with a slight rampart of shields, till the dawn of day. The Imperial general was soon satisfied of the defeat of Attila, who still remained inactive within his intrenchments; and when he contemplated the bloody scene, he observed, with secret satisfaction, that the loss had principally fallen on the Barbarians. The body of Theodoric, pierced with honourable wounds, was discovered under a heap of the slain: his subjects bewailed the death of their king and father; but their tears were mingled with songs and acclamations, and his funeral rites were performed in the face of a vanquished enemy. The Goths, clashing their arms, elevated on a buckler his eldest son Torismond, to whom they justly ascribed the glory of their success; and the new king accepted the obligation of revenge, as a sacred portion of his paternal inheritance. Yet the Goths themselves were astonished by the fierce and undaunted aspect of their formidable antagonist; and their historian has compared Attila to a lion encompassed in his den, and threatening his hunters with redoubled fury. The kings and nations, who might have deserted his standard in the hour of distress, were made sensible, that the displeasure of their monarch was the most imminent and inevitable danger. All his instruments of martial music incessantly sounded a loud and animating strain of defiance; and the foremost troops who advanced to the assault, were checked, or destroyed, by showers of arrows from every side of the intrenchments. It was determined in a general council of war, to besiege the king of the Huns in his camp, to intercept his provisions, and to reduce him to the alternative of a disgraceful treaty, or an unequal combat. But the impatience of the Barbarians soon disdained these cautious and dilatory measures: and the mature policy of Ætius was apprehensive, that, after the extirpation of the Huns, the republic would be oppressed by the pride and power of the Gothic nation. The patrician exerted the superior ascendant of authority and reason, to calm the passions, which the son of Theodoric considered as a duty; represented, with seeming affection, and real truth, the dangers of absence and delay; and persuaded Torismond to disappoint, by his speedy return, the ambitious designs of his brothers, who might occupy the throne and treasures of Thoulouse.[46] After the departure of the Goths, and the separation of the allied army, Attila was surprised at the vast silence that reigned over the plains of Châlons: the suspicion of some hostile stratagem detained him several days within the circle of his waggons; and his retreat beyond the Rhine confessed the last victory which was atchieved in the name of the Western empire. Meroveus and his Franks, observing a prudent distance, and magnifying the opinion of their strength, by the numerous fires which they kindled every night, continued to follow the rear of the Huns, till they reached the confines of Thuringia. The Thuringians served in the army of Attila: they traversed, both in their march and in their return, the territories of the Franks; and it was perhaps in this war that they exercised the cruelties, which, about fourscore years afterwards, were revenged by the son of Clovis. They massacred their hostages, as well as their captives: two hundred young maidens were tortured with exquisite and unrelenting rage; their bodies were torn asunder by wild horses, or their bones were crushed under the weight of rolling waggons; and their unburied limbs were abandoned on the public roads, as a prey to dogs and vultures. Such were those savage ancestors, whose imaginary virtues have sometimes excited the praise and envy of civilized ages![47]

Invasion of Italy by Attila, A.D. 452.   Neither the spirit, nor the forces, nor the reputation, of Attila, were impaired by the failure of the Gallic expedition. In the ensuing spring, he repeated his demand, of the princess Honoria, and her patrimonial treasures. The demand was again rejected, or eluded; and the indignant lover immediately took the field, passed the Alps, invaded Italy, and besieged Aquileia with an innumerable host of Barbarians. Those Barbarians were unskilled in the methods of

---

46. Jornandes de Rebus Geticis, c. 41. p. 671. The policy of Ætius, and the behaviour of Torismond, are extremely natural; and the patrician, according to Gregory of Tours (l. ii. c. 7. p. 163.), dismissed the prince of the Franks, by suggesting to him a similar apprehension. The false Idatius ridiculously pretends, that Ætius paid a clandestine, nocturnal, visit to the kings of the Huns and of the Visigoths; from each of whom he obtained a bribe of ten thousand pieces of gold, as the price of an undisturbed retreat.

47. These cruelties, which are passionately deplored by Theodoric the son of Clovis (Gregory of Tours, l. iii. c. 10. p. 190.), suit the time and circumstances of the invasion of Attila. His residence in Thuringia was long attested by popular tradition; and he is supposed to have assembled a *couroultai*, or diet, in the territory of Eisenach. See Mascou, ix. 30. who settles with nice accuracy the extent of ancient Thuringia, and derives its name from the Gothic tribe of the Thervingi.

conducting a regular siege, which, even among the ancients, required some knowledge, or at least some practice, of the mechanic arts. But the labour of many thousand provincials and captives, whose lives were sacrificed without pity, might execute the most painful and dangerous work. The skill of the Roman artists might be corrupted to the destruction of their country. The walls of Aquileia were assaulted by a formidable train of battering rams, moveable turrets, and engines, that threw stones, darts, and fire;[48] and the monarch of the Huns employed the forcible impulse of hope, fear, emulation, and interest, to subvert the only barrier which delayed the conquest of Italy. Aquileia was at that period one of the richest, the most populous, and the strongest of the maritime cities of the Hadriatic coast. The Gothic auxiliaries, who appear to have served under their native princes Alaric and Antala, communicated their intrepid spirit; and the citizens still remembered the glorious and successful resistance, which their ancestors had opposed to a fierce, inexorable Barbarian, who disgraced the majesty of the Roman purple. Three months were consumed without effect in the siege of Aquileia; till the want of provisions, and the clamours of his army, compelled Attila to relinquish the enterprise; and reluctantly to issue his orders, that the troops should strike their tents the next morning, and begin their retreat. But as he rode round the walls, pensive, angry, and disappointed, he observed a stork, preparing to leave her nest, in one of the towers, and to fly with her infant family towards the country. He seized, with the ready penetration of a statesman, this trifling incident, which chance had offered to superstition; and exclaimed, in a loud and cheerful tone, that such a domestic bird, so constantly attached to human society, would never have abandoned her ancient seats, unless those towers had been devoted to impending ruin and solitude.[49] The favourable omen inspired an assurance of victory; the siege was renewed, and prosecuted with fresh vigour; a large breach was made in the part of the wall from

---

48. Machinis constructis, omnibusque tormentorum generibus adhibitis. Jornandes, c. 42. p. 673. In the thirteenth century, the Moguls battered the cities of China with large engines, constructed by the Mahometans or Christians in their service, which threw stones from 150 to 300 pounds weight. In the defence of their country, the Chinese used gunpowder, and even bombs, above an hundred years before they were known in Europe; yet

even those celestial, or infernal, arms were insufficient to protect a pusillanimous nation. See Gaubil. Hist. des Mongous, p. 70, 71. 155. 157, &c.

49. The same story is told by Jornandes, and by Procopius (de Bell. Vandal. l. i. c. 4. p. 187, 188.): nor is it easy to decide, which is the original. But the Greek historian is guilty of an inexcuseable mistake, in placing the siege of Aquileia *after* the death of Ætius.

whence the stork had taken her flight; the Huns mounted to the assault with irresistible fury; and the succeeding generation could scarcely discover the ruins of Aquileia.[50] After this dreadful chastisement, Attila pursued his march; and as he passed, the cities of Altinum, Concordia, and Padua, were reduced into heaps of stones and ashes. The inland towns, Vicenza, Verona, and Bergamo, were exposed to the rapacious cruelty of the Huns. Milan and Pavia submitted, without resistance, to the loss of their wealth; and applauded the unusual clemency, which preserved from the flames the public, as well as private, buildings; and spared the lives of the captive multitude. The popular traditions of Comum, Turin, or Modena, may justly be suspected; yet they concur with more authentic evidence to prove, that Attila spread his ravages over the rich plains of modern Lombardy; which are divided by the Po, and bounded by the Alps and Apennine.[51] When he took possession of the royal palace of Milan, he was surprised, and offended, at the sight of a picture, which represented the Cæsars seated on their throne, and the princes of Scythia prostrate at their feet. The revenge which Attila inflicted on this monument of Roman vanity, was harmless and ingenious. He commanded a painter to reverse the figures, and the attitudes; and the emperors were delineated on the same canvas, approaching in a suppliant posture to empty their bags of tributary gold before the throne of the Scythian monarch.[52] The spectators must have confessed the truth and propriety of the alteration; and were perhaps tempted to apply, on this singular occasion, the well-known fable of the dispute between the lion and the man.[53]

50. Jornandes, about an hundred years afterwards, affirms, that Aquileia was so completely ruined, ita ut vix ejus vestigia, ut appareant, reliquerint. See Jornandes de Reb. Geticis, c. 42. p. 673. Paul. Diacon. l. ii. c. 14. p. 785. Liutprand Hist. l. iii. c. 2. The name of Aquileia was sometimes applied to Forum Julii (Cividad del Friuli), the more recent capital of the Venetian province.

51. In describing this war of Attila, a war so famous, but so imperfectly known, I have taken for my guides two learned Italians, who considered the subject with some peculiar advantages; Sigonius, de Imperio Occidentali, l. xiii. in his works tom. i. p. 495–502.; and Muratori, Annali d'Italia, tom. iv.

p. 229–236, 8vo edition.

52. This anecdote may be found under two different articles (μεδιολανον and κορυκος) of the miscellaneous compilation of Suidas.

53.

Leo respondit, humanâ hoc pictum manû:

Videres hominem dejectum, si pingere Leones scirent.

Appendix ad Phædrum, Fab. xxv.

The lion in Phædrus very foolishly appeals from pictures to the amphitheatre: and I am glad to observe, that the native taste of La Fontaine (l. iii. fable x.) has omitted this most lame and impotent conclusion.

It is a saying worthy of the ferocious pride of Attila, that the grass never grew on the spot where his horse had trod. Yet the savage destroyer undesignedly laid the foundations of a republic, which revived, in the feudal state of Europe, the art and spirit of commercial industry. The celebrated name of Venice, or Venetia,[54] was formerly diffused over a large and fertile province of Italy, from the confines of Pannonia to the river Addua, and from the Po to the Rhætian and Julian Alps. Before the irruption of the Barbarians, fifty Venetian cities flourished in peace and prosperity: Aquileia was placed in the most conspicuous station: but the ancient dignity of Padua was supported by agriculture and manufactures; and the property of five hundred citizens, who were entitled to the equestrian rank, must have amounted, at the strictest computation, to one million seven hundred thousand pounds. Many families of Aquileia, Padua, and the adjacent towns, who fled from the sword of the Huns, found a safe, though obscure, refuge in the neighbouring islands.[55] At the extremity of the Gulf, where the Hadriatic feebly imitates the tides of the ocean, near an hundred small islands are separated by shallow water from the continent, and protected from the waves by several long slips of land, which admit the entrance of vessels through some secret and narrow channels.[56] Till the middle of the fifth century, these remote and sequestered spots remained without cultivation, with few inhabitants, and almost without a name. But the manners of the Venetian fugitives, their arts and their government, were gradually formed by their new situation; and one of the epistles of Cassiodorius,[57] which

Foundation of the republic of Venice.

54. Paul the Deacon (de Gestis Langobard. l. ii. c. 14. p. 784.) describes the provinces of Italy about the end of the eighth century. *Venetia non solum in paucis insulis quas nunc Venetias dicimus, constat; sed ejus terminus a Pannoniae finibus usque Adduam fluvium protelatur.* The history of that province till the age of Charlemagne forms the first and most interesting part of the Verona Illustrata (p. 1–388.), in which the marquis Scipio Maffei has shewn himself equally capable of enlarged views and minute disquisitions.

55. This emigration is not attested by any contemporary evidence; but the fact is proved by the event, and the circumstances might be preserved by tradition. The citizens of

Aquileia retired to the Isle of Gradus, those of Padua to Rivus Altus, or Rialto, where the city of Venice was afterwards built, &c.

56. The topography and antiquities of the Venetian islands, from Gradus to Clodia, or Chioggia, are accurately stated in the Dissertatio Chorographica de Italiâ Medii Ævi, p. 151–155.

57. Cassiodor. Variar. l. xii. epist. 24. Maffei (Verona Illustrata, part i. p. 240–254.) has translated and explained this curious letter, in the spirit of a learned antiquarian and a faithful subject, who considered Venice as the only legitimate offspring of the Roman republic. He fixes the date of the epistle, and consequently the præfecture, of Cassiodorius, A.D.

describes their condition about seventy years afterwards, may be considered as the primitive monument of the republic. The minister of Theodoric compares them, in his quaint declamatory style, to water-fowl, who had fixed their nests on the bosom of the waves; and though he allows, that the Venetian provinces had formerly contained many noble families, he insinuates, that they were now reduced by misfortune to the same level of humble poverty. Fish was the common, and almost the universal, food of every rank: their only treasure consisted in the plenty of salt, which they extracted from the sea: and the exchange of that commodity, so essential to human life, was substituted in the neighbouring markets to the currency of gold and silver. A people, whose habitations might be doubtfully assigned to the earth or water, soon became alike familiar with the two elements; and the demands of avarice succeeded to those of necessity. The islanders, who, from Grado to Chiozza, were intimately connected with each other, penetrated into the heart of Italy, by the secure, though laborious, navigation of the rivers and inland canals. Their vessels, which were continually increasing in size and number, visited all the harbours of the Gulf; and the marriage, which Venice annually celebrates with the Hadriatic, was contracted in her early infancy. The epistle of Cassiodorius, the Prætorian præfect, is addressed to the maritime tribunes: and he exhorts them, in a mild tone of authority, to animate the zeal of their countrymen for the public service, which required their assistance to transport the magazines of wine and oil from the province of Istria to the royal city of Ravenna. The ambiguous office of these magistrates is explained by the tradition, that, in the twelve principal islands, twelve tribunes, or judges, were created by an annual and popular election. The existence of the Venetian republic under the Gothic kingdom of Italy, is attested by the same authentic record, which annihilates their lofty claim of original and perpetual independence.[58]

523; and the marquis's authority has the more weight, as he had prepared an edition of his works, and actually published a Dissertation on the true orthography of his name. See Osservazioni Letterarie, tom. ii. p. 290–339.

58. See, in the second volume of Amelot de la Houssaie Histoire du Gouvernement de Venise, a translation of the famous *Squittinio*. This book, which has been exalted far above its merits, is stained, in every line, with the disingenuous malevolence of party: but the principal evidence, genuine and apocryphal, is brought together, and the reader will easily chuse the fair medium.

The Italians, who had long since renounced the exercise of arms, were surprised, after forty years peace, by the approach of a formidable Barbarian, whom they abhorred, as the enemy of their religion, as well as of their republic. Amidst the general consternation, Ætius alone was incapable of fear; but it was impossible that he should atchieve, alone, and unassisted, any military exploits worthy of his former renown. The Barbarians who had defended Gaul, refused to march to the relief of Italy; and the succours promised by the Eastern emperor were distant and doubtful. Since Ætius, at the head of his domestic troops, still maintained the field, and harassed or retarded the march of Attila, he never shewed himself more truly great, than at the time when his conduct was blamed by an ignorant and ungrateful people.[59] If the mind of Valentinian had been susceptible of any generous sentiments, he would have chosen such a general for his example and his guide. But the timid grandson of Theodosius, instead of sharing the dangers, escaped from the sound of war; and his hasty retreat from Ravenna to Rome, from an impregnable fortress to an open capital, betrayed his secret intention of abandoning Italy, as soon as the danger should approach his Imperial person. This shameful abdication was suspended, however, by the spirit of doubt and delay, which commonly adheres to pusillanimous counsels, and sometimes corrects their pernicious tendency. The Western emperor, with the senate and people of Rome, embraced the more salutary resolution of deprecating, by a solemn and suppliant embassy, the wrath of Attila. This important commission was accepted by Avienus, who, from his birth and riches, his consular dignity, the numerous train of his clients, and his personal abilities, held the first rank in the Roman senate. The specious and artful character of Avienus,[60] was admirably qualified to conduct a negociation, either of public or private interest: his colleague Trigetius had exercised the Prætorian præfecture of Italy; and Leo, bishop of Rome, consented to expose his life

Attila gives peace to the Romans.

59. Sirmond (Not. ad Sidon. Apollin. p. 19.) has published a curious passage from the Chronicle of Prosper. Attila redintegratis viribus, quas in Gallia amiserat, Italiam ingredi per Pannonias intendit; nihil duce nostro Ætio secundum prioris belli opera prospiciente, &c. He reproaches Ætius with neglecting to guard the Alps, and with a design to abandon Italy: but this rash censure may at least be counter-balanced by the favourable testimonies of Idatius and Isidore.

60. See the original portraits of Avienus, and his rival Basilius, delineated and contrasted in the epistles (i. 9. p. 22) of Sidonius. He had studied the characters of the two chiefs of the senate; but he attached himself to Basilius, as the more solid and disinterested friend.

for the safety of his flock. The genius of Leo[61] was exercised and displayed in the public misfortunes; and he has deserved the appellation of *Great*, by the successful zeal, with which he laboured to establish his opinions, and his authority, under the venerable names of orthodox faith, and ecclesiastical discipline. The Roman ambassadors were introduced to the tent of Attila, as he lay encamped at the place where the slow-winding Mincius is lost in the foaming waves of the lake Benacus,[62] and trampled with his Scythian cavalry the farms of Catullus and Virgil.[63] The Barbarian monarch listened with favourable, and even respectful, attention; and the deliverance of Italy was purchased by the immense ransom, or dowry, of the princess Honoria. The state of his army might facilitate the treaty, and hasten his retreat. Their martial spirit was relaxed by the wealth and indolence of a warm climate. The shepherds of the North, whose ordinary food consisted of milk and raw flesh, indulged themselves too freely in the use of bread, of wine, and of meat, prepared and seasoned by the arts of cookery; and the progress of disease revenged in some measure the injuries of the Italian.[64] When Attila declared his resolution of carrying his victorious arms to the gates of Rome, he was admonished by his friends, as well as by his enemies, that Alaric had not long survived the conquest of the eternal city. His mind, superior to real danger, was assaulted by imaginary terrors; nor could he escape the influence of superstition, which had so often been subservient

---

61. The character and principles of Leo, may be traced in one hundred and forty-one original epistles, which illustrate the ecclesiastical history of his long and busy pontificate, from A.D. 440, to 461. See Dupin, Bibliotheque Ecclesiastique, tom. iii. part ii. p. 120–165.

62.
—— tardis ingens ubi flexibus errat
Mincius, et tenerâ prætexit arundine
ripas

.   .   .   .

Anne lacus tantos, te Lari maxime,
teque
Fluctibus, et fremitu assurgens *Benace*
marino.

63. The Marquis Maffei (Verona Illustrata, part i. p. 95. 129. 221. part ii. p. ii. 6.) has illustrated with taste and learning this interesting topography. He places the interview of

Attila and St. Leo near Ariolica, or Ardelica, now Peschiera, at the conflux of the lake and river; ascertains the villa of Catullus, in the delightful peninsula of Sarmio, and discovers the Andes of Virgil, in the village of Bandes, precisely situate, quâ se subducere colles incipiunt, where the Veronese hills imperceptibly slope down into the plain of Mantua.

64. Si statim infesto agmine urbem petiissent, grande discrimen esset: sed in Venetiâ quo fere tractu Italia mollissima est, ipsâ soli cœlique clementiâ robur elanguit. Adhoc panis usû carnisque coctæ, et dulcedine vini mitigatos, &c. This passage of Florus (iii. 3.) is still more applicable to the Huns than to the Cimbri, and it may serve as a commentary on the *celestial* plague, with which Idatius and Isidore have afflicted the troops of Attila.

to his designs.[65] The pressing eloquence of Leo, his majestic aspect, and sacerdotal robes, excited the veneration of Attila for the spiritual father of the Christians. The apparition of the two apostles, St. Peter and St. Paul, who menaced the Barbarian with instant death, if he rejected the prayer of their successor, is one of the noblest legends of ecclesiastical tradition. The safety of Rome might deserve the interposition of celestial beings; and some indulgence is due to a fable, which has been represented by the pencil of Raphael, and the chissel of Algardi.[66]

Before the king of the Huns evacuated Italy, he threatened to return more dreadful, and more implacable, if his bride, the princess Honoria, were not delivered to his ambassadors within the term stipulated by the treaty. Yet, in the mean while, Attila relieved *The death of Attila, A.D. 453.* his tender anxiety, by adding a beautiful maid, whose name was Ildico, to the list of his innumerable wives.[67] Their marriage was celebrated with barbaric pomp and festivity, at his wooden palace beyond the Danube; and the monarch, oppressed with wine and sleep, retired, at a late hour, from the banquet to the nuptial bed. His attendants continued to respect his pleasures, or his repose, the greatest part of the ensuing day, till the unusual silence alarmed their fears and suspicions; and, after attempting to awaken Attila by loud and repeated cries, they at length broke into the royal apartment. They found the trembling bride sitting by the bedside, hiding her face with her veil, and lamenting her own danger, as well as the death of the king, who had expired during the night.[68] An artery had suddenly burst; and as Attila lay in a supine posture, he was suffocated by

65. The historian Priscus had positively mentioned the effect which this example produced on the mind of Attila. Jornandes, c. 42. p. 673.
66. The picture of Raphael is in the Vatican; the basso (or perhaps the alto) relievo of Algardi, on one of the altars of St. Peter's (see Dubos, Reflexions sur la Poesie et sur la Peinture, tom. i. p. 519, 520.). Baronius (Annal. Eccles. A.D. 452. N° 57, 58.) bravely sustains the truth of the apparition; which is rejected, however, by the most learned and pious Catholics.
67. Attila, ut Priscus historicus refert, extinctionis suæ tempore, puellam Ildico nomine, decoram valde, sibi matrimonium post innumerabiles uxores . . . socians. Jornandes,

c. 49. p. 683, 684. He afterwards adds (c. 50. p. 686.), Filii Attilæ, quorum per licentiam libidinis pœne populus fuit. Polygamy has been established among the Tartars of every age. The rank of plebeian wives is regulated only by their personal charms; and the faded matron prepares, without a murmur, the bed which is destined for her blooming rival. But in royal families, the daughters of Khans communicate to their sons a prior right of inheritance. See Genealogical History, p. 406, 407, 408.
68. The report of her *guilt* reached Constantinople, where it obtained a very different name; and Marcellinus observes, that the tyrant of Europe was slain in the night by

a torrent of blood, which, instead of finding a passage through the nostrils, regurgitated into the lungs and stomach. His body was solemnly exposed in the midst of the plain, under a silken pavilion; and the chosen squadrons of the Huns, wheeling round in measured evolutions, chaunted a funeral song to the memory of a hero, glorious in his life, invincible in his death, the father of his people, the scourge of his enemies, and the terror of the world. According to their national custom, the Barbarians cut off a part of their hair, gashed their faces with unseemly wounds, and bewailed their valiant leader as he deserved, not with the tears of women, but with the blood of warriors. The remains of Attila were inclosed within three coffins, of gold, of silver, and of iron, and privately buried in the night: the spoils of nations were thrown into his grave; the captives who had opened the ground were inhumanly massacred; and the same Huns, who had indulged such excessive grief, feasted, with dissolute and intemperate mirth, about the recent sepulchre of their king. It was reported at Constantinople, that on the fortunate night in which he expired, Marcian beheld in a dream the bow of Attila broken asunder: and the report may be allowed to prove, how seldom the image of that formidable Barbarian was absent from the mind of a Roman emperor.[69]

Destruction of his empire. The revolution which subverted the empire of the Huns, established the fame of Attila, whose genius alone had sustained the huge and disjointed fabric. After his death, the boldest chieftains aspired to the rank of kings; the most powerful kings refused to acknowledge a superior; and the numerous sons, whom so many various mothers bore to the deceased monarch, divided and disputed, like a private inheritance, the sovereign command of the nations of Germany and Scythia. The bold Ardaric felt and represented the disgrace of this servile partition; and his subjects, the warlike Gepidæ, with the Ostrogoths, under the conduct of three valiant brothers, encouraged their allies to vindicate the rights of freedom and royalty. In a bloody and decisive conflict on the banks of the river Netad, in Pannonia, the lance of the Gepidæ, the sword

---

the hand, and the knife, of a woman. Corneille, who has adapted the genuine account to his tragedy, describes the irruption of blood in forty bombast lines, and Attila exclaims, with ridiculous fury,

——— S'il ne veut s'arreter *(his blood),*

(Dit-il) on me payera ce qui m'en va couter.

69. The curious circumstances of the death and funeral of Attila, are related by Jornandes (c. 49. p. 683, 684, 685.), and were probably transcribed from Priscus.

of the Goths, the arrows of the Huns, the Suevic infantry, the light arms of the Heruli, and the heavy weapons of the Alani, encountered or supported each other; and the victory of Ardaric was accompanied with the slaughter of thirty thousand of his enemies. Ellac, the eldest son of Attila, lost his life and crown in the memorable battle of Netad: his early valour had raised him to the throne of the Acatzires, a Scythian people, whom he subdued; and his father, who loved the superior merit, would have envied the death, of Ellac.[70] His brother Dengisich, with an army of Huns, still formidable in their flight and ruin, maintained his ground above fifteen years on the banks of the Danube. The palace of Attila, with the old country of Dacia, from the Carpathian hills to the Euxine, became the seat of a new power, which was erected by Ardaric, king of the Gepidæ. The Pannonian conquests, from Vienna to Sirmium, were occupied by the Ostrogoths; and the settlements of the tribes, who had so bravely asserted their native freedom, were irregularly distributed, according to the measure of their respective strength. Surrounded and oppressed by the multitude of his father's slaves, the kingdom of Dengisich was confined to the circle of his waggons; his desperate courage urged him to invade the Eastern empire; he fell in battle; and his head, ignominiously exposed in the Hippodrome, exhibited a grateful spectacle to the people of Constantinople. Attila had fondly or superstitiously believed, that Irnac, the youngest of his sons, was destined to perpetuate the glories of his race. The character of that prince, who attempted to moderate the rashness of his brother Dengisich, was more suitable to the declining condition of the Huns; and Irnac, with his subject hords, retired into the heart of the Lesser Scythia. They were soon overwhelmed by a torrent of new Barbarians, who followed the same road which their own ancestors had formerly discovered. The *Geougen*, or Avares, whose residence is assigned by the Greek writers to the shores of the ocean, impelled the adjacent tribes; till at length the Igours of the North, issuing from the cold Siberian regions, which produce the most valuable furs, spread themselves over the desert,

---

70. See Jornandes, de Rebus Geticis, c. 50. p. 685, 686, 687, 688. His distinction of the national arms is curious and important. Nam ibi admirandum reor fuisse spectaculum, ubi cernere erat cunctis, pugnantem Gothum ense furentem, Gepidam in vulnere suorum cuncta tela frangentem, Suevum pede, Hunnum sagittâ præsumere, Alanum gravi, Herulum levi, armaturâ, aciem instruere. I am not precisely informed of the situation of the river Netad.

as far as the Boristhenes and the Caspian gates; and finally extinguished the empire of the Huns.[71]

Valentinian murders the patrician Ætius, A.D. 454.

Such an event might contribute to the safety of the Eastern empire, under the reign of a prince, who conciliated the friendship, without forfeiting the esteem, of the Barbarians. But the emperor of the West, the feeble and dissolute Valentinian, who had reached his thirty-fifth year, without attaining the age of reason or courage, abused this apparent security, to undermine the foundations of his own throne, by the murder of the patrician Ætius. From the instinct of a base and jealous mind, he hated the man, who was universally celebrated as the terror of the Barbarians, and the support of the republic; and his new favourite, the eunuch Heraclius, awakened the emperor from the supine lethargy, which might be disguised, during the life of Placidia,[72] by the excuse of filial piety. The fame of Ætius, his wealth and dignity, the numerous and martial train of Barbarian followers, his powerful dependents, who filled the civil offices of the state, and the hopes of his son Gaudentius, who was already contracted to Eudoxia, the emperor's daughter, had raised him above the rank of a subject. The ambitious designs, of which he was secretly accused, excited the fears, as well as the resentment, of Valentinian. Ætius himself, supported by the consciousness of his merit, his services, and perhaps his innocence, seems to have maintained a haughty and indiscreet behaviour. The patrician offended his sovereign by an hostile declaration; he aggravated the offence, by compelling him to ratify, with a solemn oath, a treaty of reconciliation and alliance; he proclaimed his suspicions; he neglected his safety; and from a vain confidence that the enemy, whom he despised, was incapable even of a manly crime, he rashly ventured his person in the palace of Rome. Whilst he urged, perhaps with intemperate vehemence, the marriage of his son; Valentinian, drawing his sword, the first sword he had ever drawn, plunged it in the breast of a general who had saved his empire: his courtiers and

71. Two modern historians have thrown much new light on the ruin and division of the empire of Attila. M. de Buat, by his laborious and minute diligence (tom. viii. p. 3-31. 68-94); and M. de Guignes, by his extraordinary knowledge of the Chinese language and writers. See Hist. des Huns, tom. ii. p. 315-319.

72. Placidia died at Rome, November 27,

A.D. 450. She was buried at Ravenna, where her sepulchre, and even her corpse, seated in a chair of cypress wood, were preserved for ages. The empress received many compliments from the orthodox clergy; and St. Peter Chrysologus assured her, that her zeal for the Trinity had been recompensed by an august trinity of children. See Tillemont, Hist. des Emp. tom. vi. p. 240.

eunuchs ambitiously struggled to imitate their master; and Ætius, pierced with an hundred wounds, fell dead in the royal presence. Boethius, the Prætorian præfect, was killed at the same moment; and before the event could be divulged, the principal friends of the patrician were summoned to the palace, and separately murdered. The horrid deed, palliated by the specious names of justice and necessity, was immediately communicated by the emperor to his soldiers, his subjects, and his allies. The nations, who were strangers or enemies to Ætius, generously deplored the unworthy fate of a hero: the Barbarians, who had been attached to his service, dissembled their grief and resentment; and the public contempt, which had been so long entertained for Valentinian, was at once converted into deep and universal abhorrence. Such sentiments seldom pervade the walls of a palace; yet the emperor was confounded by the honest reply of a Roman, whose approbation he had not disdained to solicit. "I am ignorant, Sir, of your motives or provocations; I only know, that you have acted like a man who cuts off his right hand with his left."[73]

The luxury of Rome seems to have attracted the long and frequent visits of Valentinian; who was consequently more despised at Rome than in any other part of his dominions. A republican spirit was insensibly revived in the senate, as their *and ravishes the wife of Maximus.* authority, and even their supplies, became necessary for the support of his feeble government. The stately demeanour of an hereditary monarch offended their pride; and the pleasures of Valentinian were injurious to the peace and honour of noble families. The birth of the empress Eudoxia was equal to his own, and her charms and tender affection deserved those testimonies of love, which her inconstant husband dissipated in vague and unlawful amours. Petronius Maximus, a wealthy senator of the Anician family, who had been twice consul, was possessed of a chaste and beauti-ful wife: her obstinate resistance served only to irritate the desires of Valentinian; and he resolved to accomplish them either by stratagem or force. Deep gaming was one of the vices of the court: the emperor, who, by chance or contrivance, had gained from Maximus a considerable sum, uncourteously exacted his ring as a security for the debt; and sent it by a trusty messenger to his wife, with an order, in her husband's name, that she should immediately attend the empress Eudoxia. The unsuspecting

---

73. Aetium Placidus mactavit semivir amens, is the expression of Sidonius (Panegyr. Avit. 359.). The poet knew the world, and was not inclined to flatter a minister who had injured or disgraced Avitus and Majorian, the success-ive heroes of his song.

wife of Maximus was conveyed in her litter to the Imperial palace; the emissaries of her impatient lover conducted her to a remote and silent bed-chamber; and Valentinian violated, without remorse, the laws of hospitality. Her tears, when she returned home; her deep affliction; and her bitter reproaches against a husband, whom she considered as the accomplice of his own shame, excited Maximus to a just revenge; the desire of revenge was stimulated by ambition; and he might reasonably aspire, by the free suffrage of the Roman senate, to the throne of a detested and despicable rival. Valentinian, who supposed that every human breast was devoid, like his own, of friendship and gratitude, had imprudently admitted among his guards several domestics and followers of Ætius. Two of these, of Barbarian race, were persuaded to execute a sacred and honourable duty, by punishing with death the assassin of their patron; and their intrepid courage did not long expect a favourable moment. Whilst Valentinian amused himself in the field of Mars with the spectacle of

Death of Valentinian, A.D. 455, March 16. some military sports, they suddenly rushed upon him with drawn weapons, dispatched the guilty Heraclius, and stabbed the emperor to the heart, without the least opposition from his numerous train, who seemed to rejoice in the tyrant's death. Such was the fate of Valentinian the Third,[74] the last Roman emperor of the family of Theodosius. He faithfully imitated the hereditary weakness of his cousin and his two uncles, without inheriting the gentleness, the purity, the innocence, which alleviate in their characters the want of spirit and ability. Valentinian was less excusable, since he had passions, without virtues: even his religion was questionable; and though he never deviated into the paths of heresy, he scandalized the pious Christians by his attachment to the profane arts of magic and divination.

Symptoms of decay and ruin. As early as the time of Cicero and Varro, it was the opinion of the Roman augurs, that the *twelve vultures*, which Romulus had seen, represented the *twelve centuries*, assigned for the fatal

---

74. With regard to the cause and circumstances of the deaths of Ætius and Valentinian, our information is dark and imperfect. Procopius (de Bell. Vandal. l. i. c. 4. p. 186, 187, 188.) is a fabulous writer for the events which precede his own memory. His narrative must therefore be supplied and corrected by five or six Chronicles, none of which were composed in Rome or Italy; and which can only express, in broken sentences, the popular rumours, as they were conveyed to Gaul, Spain, Africa, Constantinople, or Alexandria.

period of his city.[75] This prophecy, disregarded perhaps in the season of health and prosperity, inspired the people with gloomy apprehensions, when the twelfth century, clouded with disgrace and misfortune, was almost elapsed;[76] and even posterity must acknowledge with some surprise, that the arbitrary interpretation of an accidental or fabulous circumstance, has been seriously verified in the downfall of the Western empire. But its fall was announced by a clearer omen than the flight of vultures: the Roman government appeared every day less formidable to its enemies, more odious and oppressive to its subjects.[77] The taxes were multiplied with the public distress; œconomy was neglected in proportion as it became necessary; and the injustice of the rich shifted the unequal burden from themselves to the people, whom they defrauded of the *indulgencies* that might sometimes have alleviated their misery. The severe inquisition, which confiscated their goods, and tortured their persons, compelled the subjects of Valentinian to prefer the more simple tyranny of the Barbarians, to fly to the woods and mountains, or to embrace the vile and abject condition of mercenary servants. They abjured and abhorred the name of Roman citizens, which had formerly excited the ambition of mankind. The Armorican provinces of Gaul, and the greatest part of Spain, were thrown into a state of disorderly independence, by the confederations of the Bagaudæ; and the Imperial ministers pursued with proscriptive laws, and ineffectual arms, the rebels whom they had made.[78] If all the Barbarian conquerors had been annihilated in the same hour, their

75. This interpretation of Vettius, a celebrated augur, was quoted by Varro, in the xviiith book of his Antiquities. Censorinus, de Die Natali, c. 17. p. 90, 91. edit. Havercamp.

76. According to Varro, the twelfth century would expire A.D. 447, but the uncertainty of the true æra of Rome might allow some latitude of anticipation or delay. The poets of the age, Claudian (de Bell. Getico, 265.) and Sidonius (in Panegyr. Avit. 357.), may be admitted as fair witnesses of the popular opinion.

> Jam reputant annos, interceptoque volatû
> Vulturis, incidunt properatis sæcula metis.

Jam prope fata tui bissenas Vulturis alas Implebant; scis namque tuos, scis,
    Roma, labores.

See Dubos, Hist. Critique, tom. i. p. 340–346.

77. The fifth book of Salvian is filled with pathetic lamentations, and vehement invectives. His immoderate freedom serves to prove the weakness, as well as the corruption, of the Roman government. His book was published after the loss of Africa (A.D. 439.), and before Attila's war (A.D. 451.).

78. The Bagaudæ of Spain, who fought pitched battles with the Roman troops, are repeatedly mentioned in the Chronicle of Idatius. Salvian has described their distress and rebellion in very forcible language. Itaque

total destruction would not have restored the empire of the West: and if Rome still survived, she survived the loss of freedom, of virtue, and of honour.

---

nomen civium Romanorum . . . nunc ultro repudiatur ac fugitur, nec vile tamen sed etiam abominabile pœne habetur. . . . Et hinc est ut etiam hi qui ad Barbaros non confugiunt, Barbari tamen esse coguntur, scilicet ut est pars magna Hispanorum, et non minima Gallorum. . . . De Bagaudis nunc mihi sermo est, qui per malos judices et cruentos spoliati, afflicti, necati postquam jus Romanæ libertatis amiserant, etiam honorem Romani nominis perdiderunt . . . Vocamus rebelles, vocamus perditos quos esse compulimus criminosos. De Gubernat. Dei, l. v. p. 158, 159.

[CHAPTERS XXXVI–XXXVIII]

The collapse of Roman dominion in the West brings the second instalment, and third volume, of *The Decline and Fall* to a close. In describing the final spasm of the Western empire under its last emperor, Augustulus, Gibbon indicates the moral poisons responsible for its destruction:

The unfortunate Augustulus was made the instrument of his own disgrace: he signified his resignation to the senate; and that assembly, in their last act of obedience to a Roman prince, still affected the spirit of freedom, and the forms of the constitution. An epistle was addressed, by their unanimous decree, to the emperor Zeno, the son-in-law and successor of Leo; who had lately been restored, after a short rebellion, to the Byzantine throne. They solemnly "disclaim the necessity, or even the wish, of continuing any longer the Imperial succession in Italy; since, in their opinion, the majesty of a sole monarch is sufficient to pervade and protect, at the same time, both the East and the West. In their own name, and in the name of the people, they consent that the seat of universal empire shall be transferred from Rome to Constantinople; and they basely renounce the right of chusing their master, the only vestige that yet remained of the authority which had given laws to the world. The republic (they repeat that name without a blush) might safely confide in the civil and military virtues of Odoacer; and they humbly request, that the emperor would invest him with the title of Patrician, and the administration of the *diocese* of Italy." The deputies of the senate were received at Constantinople with some marks of displeasure and indignation; and when they were admitted to the audience of Zeno, he sternly reproached them with their treatment of the two emperors, Anthemius and Nepos, whom the East had successively granted to the prayers of Italy. "The first" (continued he) "you have murdered; the second you have expelled: but the second is still alive, and whilst he lives he is your lawful sovereign." But the prudent Zeno soon deserted the hopeless cause of his abdicated colleague. His vanity was gratified by the title of sole emperor, and by the statues erected to his honour in the several quarters of Rome; he entertained a friendly, though ambiguous, correspondence with the *patrician* Odoacer; and he gratefully accepted the Imperial ensigns, the sacred ornaments of the throne and palace, which the Barbarian was not unwilling to remove from the sight of the people. (*DF*, ii. 404–5)

At this point Gibbon pauses to consider, in chapter XXXVII, two developments in religious culture: the prevalence of monasticism, and the conversion of the barbarians to Christianity. The choice of subjects in this chapter, and the treatment they receive, reveal very clearly the complexity of Gibbon's thinking on religion, and how misleading it is to see him as merely an implacable foe of Christianity. The credulity and fanaticism inherent in the monastic way of life of course did little to recommend it to Gibbon's esteem:

The monastic saints, who excite only the contempt and pity of a philosopher, were respected, and almost adored, by the prince and people. Successive crowds of pilgrims from Gaul and India saluted the divine pillar of Simeon: the tribes of Saracens disputed in arms the honour of his benediction; the queens of Arabia and Persia gratefully confessed his supernatural virtue; and the angelic Hermit was consulted by the younger Theodosius, in the most important concerns of the church and state. His remains were transported from the mountain of Telenissa, by a solemn procession of the patriarch, the master-general of the East, six bishops, twenty-one counts or tribunes, and six thousand soldiers; and Antioch revered his bones, as her glorious ornament and impregnable defence. The fame of the apostles and martyrs was gradually eclipsed by these recent and popular Anachorets; the Christian world fell prostrate before their shrines; and the miracles ascribed to their relics exceeded, at least in number and duration, the spiritual exploits of their lives. But the golden legend of their lives was embellished by the artful credulity of their interested brethren; and a believing age was easily persuaded, that the slightest caprice of an Egyptian or a Syrian monk, had been sufficient to interrupt the eternal laws of the universe. The favourites of Heaven were accustomed to cure inveterate diseases with a touch, a word, or a distant message; and to expel the most obstinate dæmons from the souls, or bodies, which they possessed. They familiarly accosted, or imperiously commanded, the lions and serpents of the desert; infused vegetation into a sapless trunk; suspended iron on the surface of the water; passed the Nile on the back of a crocodile, and refreshed themselves in a fiery furnace. These extravagant tales, which display the fiction, without the genius, of poetry, have seriously affected the reason, the faith, and the morals, of the Christians. Their credulity debased and vitiated the faculties of the mind: they corrupted the evidence of history; and superstition gradually extinguished the hostile light of philosophy and science. Every mode of religious worship which had been practised by the saints, every mysterious doctrine which they believed, was fortified by the sanction of divine revelation, and all the manly virtues were oppressed by the servile and pusillanimous reign of the monks. If it be possible to measure the interval, between the philosophic writings of Cicero and the sacred legend of Theodoret, between the character of Cato and that of Simeon, we may appreciate the memorable revolution which was accomplished in the Roman empire within a period of five hundred years. (*DF*, ii. 428–9)

But the conversion of the barbarians was a very different matter. Here the subtle and far-reaching influence of a milder form of Christianity bestowed real benefits:

The different motives which influenced the reason, or the passions, of the Barbarian converts, cannot easily be ascertained. They were often capricious and accidental; a dream, an omen, the report of a miracle, the example of some priest, or hero, the charms of a believing wife, and above all, the fortunate event of a prayer, or vow, which, in a moment of danger, they had addressed to the God of the Christians. The early prejudices of education were insensibly erased by the habits of frequent and familiar society; the moral precepts of the Gospel were protected by the extravagant virtues of the monks; and a spiritual theology was supported by the visible power of relics, and the pomp of religious worship. But the rational and ingenious mode of persuasion, which a Saxon bishop suggested to a popular saint, might sometimes be employed by the missionaries, who laboured for the conversion of infidels. "Admit," says the sagacious disputant, "whatever they are pleased to assert of the fabulous, and carnal, genealogy of their gods and goddesses, who are propagated from each other. From this principle deduce their imperfect nature, and human infirmities, the assurance they were *born*, and the probability that they will *die*. At what time, by what means, from what cause, were the eldest of the gods or goddesses produced? Do they still continue, or have they ceased, to propagate? If they have ceased, summon your antagonists to declare the reason of this strange alteration. If they still continue, the number of the gods must become infinite; and shall we not risk, by the indiscreet worship of some impotent deity, to excite the resentment of his jealous superior? The visible heavens and earth, the whole system of the universe, which may be conceived by the mind, is it created or eternal? If created, how, or where, could the gods themselves exist before the creation? If eternal, how could they assume the empire of an independent and pre-existing world? Urge these arguments with temper and moderation; insinuate, at seasonable intervals, the truth, and beauty, of the Christian revelation; and endeavour to make the unbelievers ashamed, without making them angry." This metaphysical reasoning, too refined perhaps for the Barbarians of Germany, was fortified by the grosser weight of authority and popular consent. The advantage of temporal prosperity had deserted the Pagan cause, and passed over to the service of Christianity. The Romans themselves, the most powerful and enlightened nation of the globe, had renounced their ancient superstition; and, if the ruin of their empire seemed to accuse the efficacy of the new faith, the disgrace was already retrieved by the conversion of the victorious Goths. The valiant and fortunate Barbarians, who subdued the provinces of the West, successively received, and reflected, the same edifying example. Before the age of Charlemagne, the Christian nations of Europe might exult in the exclusive possession of the temperate climates, of the fertile lands, which produced corn, wine, and oil; while the savage idolaters, and their helpless idols, were confined to the extremities of the earth, the dark and frozen regions of the North.

Christianity, which opened the gates of Heaven to the Barbarians, introduced an important change in their moral and political condition. They received, at the same time, the use of letters, so essential to a religion whose doctrines are contained in a sacred book; and while they studied the divine truth, their minds were insensibly enlarged by the distant view of history, of nature, of the arts, and of society. The version of the Scriptures into their native tongue, which had facilitated their conversion, must excite, among their clergy, some curiosity to read the original text, to understand the sacred liturgy of the church, and to examine, in the writings of the fathers, the chain of ecclesiastical tradition. These spiritual gifts were preserved in the Greek and Latin languages, which concealed the inestimable monuments of ancient learning. The immortal productions of Virgil, Cicero, and Livy, which were accessible to the Christian Barbarians, maintained a silent intercourse between the reign of Augustus, and the times of Clovis and Charlemagne. The emulation of mankind was encouraged by the remembrance of a more perfect state; and the flame of science was secretly kept alive, to warm and enlighten the mature age of the Western world. In the most corrupt state of Christianity, the Barbarians might learn justice from the *law*, and mercy from the *gospel*: and if the knowledge of their duty was insufficient to guide their actions, or to regulate their passions; they were sometimes restrained by conscience, and frequently punished by remorse. But the direct authority of religion was less effectual, than the holy communion which united them with their Christian brethren in spiritual friendship. The influence of these sentiments contributed to secure their fidelity in the service, or the alliance, of the Romans, to alleviate the horrors of war, to moderate the insolence of conquest, and to preserve, in the downfall of the empire, a permanent respect for the name and institutions of Rome. In the days of Paganism, the priests of Gaul and Germany reigned over the people, and controuled the jurisdiction of the magistrates; and the zealous proselytes transferred an equal, or more ample, measure of devout obedience, to the pontiffs of the Christian faith. The sacred character of the bishops was supported by their temporal possessions; they obtained an honourable seat in the legislative assemblies of soldiers and freemen; and it was their interest, as well as their duty, to mollify, by peaceful counsels, the fierce spirit of the Barbarians. The perpetual correspondence of the Latin clergy, the frequent pilgrimages to Rome and Jerusalem, and the growing authority of the Popes, cemented the union of the Christian republic: and gradually produced the similar manners, and common juris-prudence, which have distinguished, from the rest of mankind, the inde-pendent, and even hostile, nations of modern Europe. (*DF*, ii. 431–3)

In his *Memoirs* Gibbon tells us that the 'General Observations on the Fall of the Roman Empire in the West', which serves as a coda to the third volume of *The Decline and Fall*, was written before the accession of Louis XVI in 1774 (*A*, p. 324). But if so, it was surely also revised to reflect some of the finer shades of fact which Gibbon had glimpsed and grasped in the intervening years of study and composition.

General Observations on the Fall of the Roman Empire in the West

The Greeks, after their country had been reduced into a province, imputed the triumphs of Rome, not to the merit, but to the FORTUNE, of the republic. The inconstant goddess, who so blindly distributes and resumes her favours, had *now* consented (such was the language of envious flattery) to resign her wings, to descend from her globe, and to fix her firm and immutable throne on the banks of the Tyber.[1] A wiser Greek, who has composed, with a philosophic spirit, the memorable history of his own times, deprived his countrymen of this vain and delusive comfort, by opening to their view the deep foundations of the greatness of Rome.[2] The fidelity of the citizens to each other, and to the state, was confirmed by the habits of education, and the prejudices of religion. Honour, as well as virtue, was the principle of the republic; the ambitious citizens laboured to deserve the solemn glories of a triumph; and the ardour of the Roman youth was kindled into active emulation, as often as they beheld the domestic images of their ancestors.[3] The temperate struggles of the patricians and plebeians had finally established the firm and equal balance of the constitution; which united the freedom of popular assemblies, with the authority and wisdom of a senate, and the executive powers of a regal magistrate. When the consul displayed the standard of the republic, each citizen bound himself, by the obligation of an oath, to draw his sword in

1. Such are the figurative expressions of Plutarch (Opera, tom. ii. p. 318. edit. Wechel), to whom, on the faith of his son Lamprias (Fabricius, Bibliot. Græc. tom. iii. p. 341.), I shall boldly impute the malicious declamation, περι της Ρωμαιων τυχης. The same opinions had prevailed among the Greeks one hundred and fifty years before Plutarch; and to confute them is the professed intention of Polybius (Hist. l. i. p. 90. edit. Gronov. Amstel. 1670.).

2. See the inestimable remains of the sixth book of Polybius, and many other parts of his general history, particularly a digression in the seventeenth book, in which he compares the phalanx and the legion.

3. Sallust *heard* the generous professions of P. Scipio and Q. Maximus (de Bell. Jugurthin. c. 4.); yet these noble brothers were dead many years before the birth of Sallust. But the Latin historian had read, and most probably transcribes, Polybius, their contemporary and friend.

the cause of his country, till he had discharged the sacred duty by a military service of ten years. This wise institution continually poured into the field the rising generations of freemen and soldiers; and their numbers were reinforced by the warlike and populous states of Italy, who, after a brave resistance, had yielded to the valour, and embraced the alliance, of the Romans. The sage historian, who excited the virtue of the younger Scipio, and beheld the ruin of Carthage,[4] has accurately described their military system; their levies, arms, exercises, subordination, marches, encampments; and the invincible legion, superior in active strength to the Macedonian phalanx of Philip and Alexander. From these institutions of peace and war, Polybius has deduced the spirit and success of a people, incapable of fear, and impatient of repose. The ambitious design of conquest, which might have been defeated by the seasonable conspiracy of mankind, was attempted and atchieved; and the perpetual violation of justice was maintained by the political virtues of prudence and courage. The arms of the republic, sometimes vanquished in battle, always victorious in war, advanced with rapid steps to the Euphrates, the Danube, the Rhine, and the Ocean; and the images of gold, or silver, or brass, that might serve to represent the nations and their kings, were successively broken by the *iron* monarchy of Rome.[5]

The rise of a city, which swelled into an empire, may deserve, as a singular prodigy, the reflection of a philosophic mind. But the decline of Rome was the natural and inevitable effect of immoderate greatness. Prosperity ripened the principle of decay; the causes of destruction multiplied with the extent of conquest; and as soon as time or accident had removed the artificial supports, the stupendous fabric yielded to the pressure of its own weight. The story of its ruin is simple and obvious; and instead of inquiring *why* the Roman empire was destroyed, we should rather be

---

4. While Carthage was in flames, Scipio repeated two lines of the Iliad, which express the destruction of Troy, acknowledging to Polybius, his friend and preceptor (Polyb. in Excerpt. de Virtut. et Vit. tom. ii. p. 1455–1465), that while he recollected the vicissitudes of human affairs, he inwardly applied them to the future calamities of Rome (Appian. in Libycis, p. 136. edit. Toll.).

5. See Daniel ii. 31–40. "And the fourth kingdom shall be strong as *iron*; forasmuch

as iron breaketh in pieces, and subdueth all things." The remainder of the prophecy (the mixture of iron and *clay*) was accomplished, according to St. Jerom, in his own time. Sicut enim in principio nihil Romano Imperio fortius et durius, ita in fine rerum nihil imbecillius: quum et in bellis civilibus et adversus diversas nationes, aliarum gentium barbararum auxilio indigemus (Opera, tom. v. p. 572.).

surprised that it had subsisted so long. The victorious legions, who, in distant wars acquired the vices of strangers and mercenaries, first oppressed the freedom of the republic, and afterwards violated the majesty of the Purple. The emperors, anxious for their personal safety and the public peace, were reduced to the base expedient of corrupting the discipline which rendered them alike formidable to their sovereign and to the enemy; the vigour of the military government was relaxed, and finally dissolved, by the partial institutions of Constantine; and the Roman world was overwhelmed by a deluge of Barbarians.

The decay of Rome has been frequently ascribed to the translation of the seat of empire; but this history has already shewn, that the powers of government were *divided*, rather than *removed*. The throne of Constantinople was erected in the East; while the West was still possessed by a series of emperors who held their residence in Italy, and claimed their equal inheritance of the legions and provinces. This dangerous novelty impaired the strength, and fomented the vices, of a double reign: the instruments of an oppressive and arbitrary system were multiplied; and a vain emulation of luxury, not of merit, was introduced and supported between the degenerate successors of Theodosius. Extreme distress, which unites the virtue of a free people, embitters the factions of a declining monarchy. The hostile favourites of Arcadius and Honorius betrayed the republic to its common enemies; and the Byzantine court beheld with indifference, perhaps with pleasure, the disgrace of Rome, the misfortunes of Italy, and the loss of the West. Under the succeeding reigns, the alliance of the two empires was restored; but the aid of the Oriental Romans was tardy, doubtful, and ineffectual; and the national schism of the Greeks and Latins was enlarged by the perpetual difference of language and manners, of interest, and even of religion. Yet the salutary event approved in some measure the judgment of Constantine. During a long period of decay, his impregnable city repelled the victorious armies of Barbarians, protected the wealth of Asia, and commanded, both in peace and war, the important streights which connect the Euxine and Mediterranean seas. The foundation of Constantinople more essentially contributed to the preservation of the East, than to the ruin of the West.

As the happiness of a *future* life is the great object of religion, we may hear without surprise or scandal, that the introduction, or at least the abuse, of Christianity, had some influence on the decline and fall of the Roman empire. The clergy successfully preached the doctrines of patience and pusillanimity; the active virtues of society were discouraged; and the last remains of military spirit were buried in the cloyster: a large portion of public and private wealth was consecrated to the specious demands of charity and devotion; and the soldiers pay was lavished on the useless multitudes of both sexes, who could only plead the merits of abstinence and chastity. Faith, zeal, curiosity, and the more earthly passions of malice and ambition, kindled the flame of theological discord; the church, and even the state, were distracted by religious factions, whose conflicts were sometimes bloody, and always implacable; the attention of the emperors was diverted from camps to synods; the Roman world was oppressed by a new species of tyranny; and the persecuted sects became the secret enemies of their country. Yet party-spirit, however pernicious or absurd, is a principle of union as well as of dissention. The bishops, from eighteen hundred pulpits, inculcated the duty of passive obedience to a lawful and orthodox sovereign; their frequent assemblies, and perpetual correspondence, maintained the communion of distant churches; and the benevolent temper of the gospel was strengthened, though confined, by the spiritual alliance of the Catholics. The sacred indolence of the monks was devoutly embraced by a servile and effeminate age; but if superstition had not afforded a decent retreat, the same vices would have tempted the unworthy Romans to desert, from baser motives, the standard of the republic. Religious precepts are easily obeyed, which indulge and sanctify the natural inclinations of their votaries; but the pure and genuine influence of Christianity may be traced in its beneficial, though imperfect, effects on the Barbarian proselytes of the North. If the decline of the Roman empire was hastened by the conversion of Constantine, his victorious religion broke the violence of the fall, and mollified the ferocious temper of the conquerors.

This awful revolution may be usefully applied to the instruction of the present age. It is the duty of a patriot to prefer and promote the exclusive interest and glory of his native country: but a philosopher may be permitted to enlarge his views, and to consider Europe as one great republic, whose various inhabitants have attained almost the same level of politeness and cultivation. The balance of power will continue to fluctuate, and the prosperity of our own, or the neighbouring kingdoms, may be alternately exalted or depressed; but these partial events cannot essentially injure our general state of happiness, the system of arts, and laws, and manners, which so advantageously distinguish, above the rest of mankind, the Europeans and their colonies. The savage nations of the globe are the common enemies of civilised society; and we may enquire with anxious curiosity, whether Europe is still threatened with a repetition of those calamities, which formerly oppressed the arms and institutions of Rome. Perhaps the same reflections will illustrate the fall of that mighty empire, and explain the probable causes of our actual security.

I. The Romans were ignorant of the extent of their danger, and the number of their enemies. Beyond the Rhine and Danube, the northern countries of Europe and Asia were filled with innumerable tribes of hunters and shepherds, poor, voracious, and turbulent; bold in arms, and impatient to ravish the fruits of industry. The Barbarian world was agitated by the rapid impulse of war; and the peace of Gaul or Italy was shaken by the distant revolutions of China. The Huns, who fled before a victorious enemy, directed their march towards the West; and the torrent was swelled by the gradual accession of captives and allies. The flying tribes who yielded to the Huns, assumed in *their* turn the spirit of conquest; the endless column of Barbarians pressed on the Roman empire with accumulated weight; and, if the foremost were destroyed, the vacant space was instantly replenished by new assailants. Such formidable emigrations no longer issue from the North; and the long repose, which has been imputed to the decrease of population, is the happy consequence of the progress of arts and agriculture. Instead of some rude villages, thinly scattered among its woods and morasses, Germany now produces a list of two thousand three hundred walled towns: the Christian kingdoms of Denmark, Sweden, and Poland have been successively established; and the Hanse merchants, with the Teutonic knights, have extended their colonies along the coast of the Baltic, as far as the Gulf of Finland. From the Gulf of Finland to the Eastern Ocean, Russia now assumes the form of a powerful and civilised empire. The plough, the loom, and the forge are introduced on the banks of the Volga, the Oby, and the Lena; and the fiercest of the Tartar hords have been taught to tremble and obey. The reign of independent Barbarism is now contracted to a narrow span; and the remnant of Calmucks or Uzbeks, whose forces may be almost numbered, cannot seriously excite the apprehensions of the great republic of Europe.[6] Yet this apparent security should not tempt us to forget, that

---

6. The French and English editors of the Genealogical History of the Tartars have subjoined a curious, though imperfect, descrip- tion of their present state. We might question the independence of the Calmucks, or Eluths, since they have been recently vanquished by

new enemies, and unknown dangers, may *possibly* arise from some obscure people, scarcely visible in the map of the world. The Arabs or Saracens, who spread their conquests from India to Spain, had languished in poverty and contempt, till Mahomet breathed into those savage bodies the soul of enthusiasm.

II. The empire of Rome was firmly established by the singular and perfect coalition of its members. The subject nations, resigning the hope, and even the wish, of independence, embraced the character of Roman citizens; and the provinces of the West were reluctantly torn by the Barbarians from the bosom of their mother-country.[7] But this union was purchased by the loss of national freedom and military spirit; and the servile provinces, destitute of life and motion, expected their safety from the mercenary troops and governors, who were directed by the orders of a distant court. The happiness of an hundred millions depended on the personal merit of one, or two, men, perhaps children, whose minds were corrupted by education, luxury, and despotic power. The deepest wounds were inflicted on the empire during the minorities of the sons and grandsons of Theodosius; and, after those incapable princes seemed to attain the age of manhood, they abandoned the church to the bishops, the state to the eunuchs, and the provinces to the Barbarians. Europe is now divided into twelve powerful, though unequal, kingdoms, three respectable commonwealths, and a variety of smaller, though independent, states: the chances of royal and ministerial talents are multiplied, at least, with the number of its rulers; and a Julian, or Semiramis, may reign in the North, while Arcadius and Honorius slumber on the thrones of the house of Bourbon. The abuses of tyranny are restrained by the mutual influence of fear and shame; republics have acquired order and stability; monarchies have imbibed the principles of freedom, or, at least, of moderation; and some sense of honour and justice is introduced into the most defective constitutions by the general manners of the times. In peace, the progress of knowledge and industry is

---

the Chinese, who, in the year 1759, subdued the lesser Bucharia, and advanced into the country of Badakshan, near the sources of the Oxus (Memoires sur les Chinois, tom. i. p. 325–400.). But these conquests are precarious, nor will I venture to ensure the safety of the Chinese empire.

7. The prudent reader will determine how far this general proposition is weakened by the revolt of the Isaurians, the independence of Britain and Armorica, the Moorish tribes, or the Bagaudæ of Gaul and Spain (vol. i. p. 293. vol. ii. p. 231. 281. 356.).

accelerated by the emulation of so many active rivals: in war, the European forces are exercised by temperate and undecisive contests. If a savage conqueror should issue from the deserts of Tartary, he must repeatedly vanquish the robust peasants of Russia, the numerous armies of Germany, the gallant nobles of France, and the intrepid freemen of Britain; who, perhaps, might confederate for their common defence. Should the victorious Barbarians carry slavery and desolation as far as the Atlantic Ocean, ten thousand vessels would transport beyond their pursuit the remains of civilised society; and Europe would revive and flourish in the American world, which is already filled with her colonies, and institutions.[8]

III. Cold, poverty, and a life of danger and fatigue, fortify the strength and courage of Barbarians. In every age they have oppressed the polite and peaceful nations of China, India, and Persia, who neglected, and still neglect, to counterbalance these natural powers by the resources of military art. The warlike states of antiquity, Greece, Macedonia, and Rome, educated a race of soldiers; exercised their bodies, disciplined their courage, multiplied their forces by regular evolutions, and converted the iron, which they possessed, into strong and serviceable weapons. But this superiority insensibly declined with their laws and manners; and the feeble policy of Constantine and his successors armed and instructed, for the ruin of the empire, the rude valour of the Barbarian mercenaries. The military art has been changed by the invention of gunpowder; which enables man to command the two most powerful agents of nature, air and fire. Mathematics, chymistry, mechanics, architecture, have been applied to the service of war; and the adverse parties oppose to each other the most elaborate modes of attack and of defence. Historians may indignantly observe, that the preparations of a siege would found and maintain a flourishing colony;[9] yet we cannot be displeased, that the subversion of a city should be a work

8. America now contains about six millions of European blood and descent; and their numbers, at least in the North, are continually increasing. Whatever may be the changes of their political situation, they must preserve the manners of Europe; and we may reflect with some pleasure, that the English language will probably be diffused over an immense and populous continent.

9. On avoit fait venir (for the siege of Turin)

140 pieces de canon; et il est à remarquer que chaque gros canon monté revient à environ 2000 ecus: il y avoit 110,000 boulets; 106,000 cartouches d'une façon, et 300,000 d'une autre; 21,000 bombes; 27,700 grenades, 15,000 sacs à terre, 30,000 instrumens pour le pionnage; 1,200,000 livres de poudre. Ajoutez à ces munitions, le plomb, le fer, et le ferblanc, les cordages, tout ce qui sert aux mineurs, le souphre, le salpêtre, les outils de toute

of cost and difficulty; or that an industrious people should be protected by those arts, which survive and supply the decay of military virtue. Cannon and fortifications now form an impregnable barrier against the Tartar horse; and Europe is secure from any future irruption of Barbarians; since, before they can conquer, they must cease to be barbarous. Their gradual advances in the science of war would always be accompanied, as we may learn from the example of Russia, with a proportionable improvement in the arts of peace and civil policy; and they themselves must deserve a place among the polished nations whom they subdue.

Should these speculations be found doubtful or fallacious, there still remains a more humble source of comfort and hope. The discoveries of ancient and modern navigators, and the domestic history, or tradition, of the most enlightened nations, represent the *human savage*, naked both in mind and body, and destitute of laws, of arts, of ideas, and almost of language.[10] From this abject condition, perhaps the primitive and universal state of man he has gradually arisen to command the animals, to fertilise the earth, to traverse the ocean, and to measure the heavens. His progress in the improvement and exercise of his mental and corporeal faculties[11] has been irregular and various; infinitely slow in the beginning, and increasing by degrees with redoubled velocity: ages of laborious ascent have been followed by a moment of rapid downfal; and the several climates of the globe have felt the vicissitudes of light and darkness. Yet the experience of four thousand years should enlarge our hopes, and diminish our apprehensions: we cannot determine to what height the human species may aspire in their advances towards perfection; but it may safely be presumed, that

---

espece. Il est certain que les frais de tous ces préparatifs de destruction suffiroient pour fonder et pour faire fleurir la plus nombreuse colonie. Voltaire, Siécle de Louis XIV. c. xx. in his Works, tom, xi. p. 391.

10. It would be an easy, though tedious task, to produce the authorities of poets, philosophers, and historians. I shall therefore content myself with appealing to the decisive and authentic testimony of Diodorus Siculus (tom. i. l. i. p. 11, 12. l. iii. p. 184, &c. edit. Wesseling.). The Icthyophagi, who in his time wandered along the shores of the Red Sea, can only be

compared to the natives of New Holland (Dampier's Voyages, vol. i. p. 464–469.). Fancy, or perhaps reason, may still suppose an extreme and absolute state of nature far below the level of these savages, who had acquired some arts and instruments.

11. See the learned and rational work of the President Goguet, de l'Origine des Loix, des Arts et des Sciences. He traces from facts, or conjectures (tom. i. p. 147–337, edit. 12mo.), the first and most difficult steps of human invention.

no people, unless the face of nature is changed, will relapse into their original barbarism. The improvements of society may be viewed under a threefold aspect. 1. The poet or philosopher illustrates his age and country by the efforts of a *single* mind; but these superior powers of reason or fancy are rare and spontaneous productions; and the genius of Homer, or Cicero, or Newton, would excite less admiration, if they could be created by the will of a prince, or the lessons of a preceptor. 2. The benefits of law and policy, of trade and manufactures, of arts and sciences, are more solid and permanent; and *many* individuals may be qualified, by education and discipline, to promote, in their respective stations, the interest of the community. But this general order is the effect of skill and labour; and the complex machinery may be decayed by time, or injured by violence. 3. Fortunately for mankind, the most useful, or, at least, more necessary arts, can be performed without superior talents, or national subordination; without the powers of *one*, or the union of *many*. Each village, each family, each individual, must always possess both ability and inclination, to perpetuate the use of fire[12] and of metals; the propagation and service of domestic animals; the methods of hunting and fishing; the rudiments of navigation; the imperfect cultivation of corn, or other nutritive grain; and the simple practice of the mechanic trades. Private genius and public industry may be extirpated; but these hardy plants survive the tempest, and strike an everlasting root into the most unfavourable soil. The splendid days of Augustus and Trajan were eclipsed by a cloud of ignorance; and the Barbarians subverted the laws and palaces of Rome. But the scythe, the invention or emblem of Saturn,[13] still continued annually to mow the harvests of Italy; and the human feasts of the Læstrigons[14] have never been renewed on the coast of Campania.

Since the first discovery of the arts, war, commerce, and religious zeal have diffused, among the savages of the Old and New World, these

12. It is certain, however strange, that many nations have been ignorant of the use of fire. Even the ingenious natives of Otaheite, who are destitute of metals, have not invented any earthen vessels capable of sustaining the action of fire, and of communicating the heat to the liquids which they contain.

13. Plutarch. Quæst. Rom in tom. ii. p. 275. Macrob. Saturnal. l. i. c. 8. p. 152. edit.

London. The arrival of Saturn (of his religious worship) in a ship, may indicate, that the savage coast of Latium was first discovered and civilised by the Phœnicians.

14. In the ninth and tenth books of the Odyssey, Homer has embellished the tales of fearful and credulous sailors, who transformed the cannibals of Italy and Sicily into monstrous giants.

inestimable gifts: they have been successively propagated; they can never be lost. We may therefore acquiesce in the pleasing conclusion, that every age of the world has increased, and still increases, the real wealth, the happiness, the knowledge, and perhaps the virtue, of the human race.[15]

15. The merit of discovery has too often been stained with avarice, cruelty, and fanaticism; and the intercourse of nations has produced the communication of disease and prejudice. A singular exception is due to the virtue of our own times and country. The five great voyages successively undertaken by the command of his present Majesty, were inspired by the pure and generous love of science and of mankind. The same prince, adapting his benefactions to the different stages of society, has founded a school of painting in his capital; and has introduced into the islands of the South Sea, the vegetables and animals most useful to human life.

[CHAPTER XXXIX]

In his account of the Gothic kingdom of Italy, Gibbon's undoctrinaire subtlety in respect of the barbarians is again on display:

As the patron of the republic, it was the interest and duty of the Gothic king to cultivate the affections of the senate and people. The nobles of Rome were flattered by sonorous epithets and formal professions of respect, which had been more justly applied to the merit and authority of their ancestors. The people enjoyed, without fear or danger, the three blessings of a capital, order, plenty, and public amusements. A visible diminution of their numbers may be found even in the measure of liberality; yet Apulia, Calabria, and Sicily, poured their tribute of corn into the granaries of Rome; an allowance of bread and meat was distributed to the indigent citizens; and every office was deemed honourable which was consecrated to the care of their health and happiness. (*DF*, ii. 542)

Yet Theodoric was not above persecution, and his weakness is commemorated in the figure of Boethius:

From the earth, Boethius ascended to heaven in search of the SUPREME GOOD; explored the metaphysical labyrinth of chance and destiny, of prescience and free-will, of time and eternity; and generously attempted to reconcile the perfect attributes of the Deity, with the apparent disorders of his moral and physical government. Such topics of consolation, so obvious, so vague, or so abstruse, are ineffectual to subdue the feelings of human nature. Yet the sense of misfortune may be diverted by the labour of thought; and the sage who could artfully combine in the same work, the various riches of philosophy, poetry, and eloquence, must already have possessed the intrepid calmness, which he affected to seek. (*DF*, ii. 553–4)

Gibbon avoids the common topics of praise and blame even when dealing with as celebrated a figure as Boethius. That same freshness of approach is evident when he considers Justinian and Belisarius in chapters XL and XLI.

CHAPTER XL

Elevation of Justin the Elder. – Reign of Justinian: – I. The Empress Theodora. – II. Factions of the Circus, and Sedition of Constantinople. – III. Trade and Manufacture of Silk. – IV. Finances and Taxes. – V. Edifices of Justinian. – Church of St. Sophia. – Fortifications and Frontiers of the Eastern Empire. – Abolition of the Schools of Athens, and the Consulship of Rome.

Birth of the emperor Justinian, A.D. 482, May 5 – or A.D. 483, May 11.

The emperor Justinian was born[1] near the ruins of Sardica (the modern Sophia), of an obscure race[2] of Barbarians,[3] the inhabitants of a wild and desolate country, to which the names of Dardania, of Dacia, and of Bulgaria, have been successively applied. His elevation was prepared by the adventurous spirit of his uncle Justin, who, with two other peasants of the same village, deserted, for the profession of arms, the more useful employment of husbandmen or shepherds.[4] On foot, with a scanty provision of biscuit in their knapsacks, the three youths followed the high-road of Constantinople, and were soon enrolled, for their strength and stature, among the guards of the emperor Leo. Under the two succeeding reigns, the fortunate peasant emerged to wealth and honours; and his escape from some dangers which threatened his life, was afterwards ascribed to the guardian angel who watches over the fate of kings. His long and laudable service in the Isaurian and Persian wars, would not have preserved from

---

1. There is some difficulty in the date of his birth (Ludewig in Vit. Justiniani, p. 125.); none in the place – the district Bederiana – the village Tauresium, which he afterwards decorated with his name and splendour (D'Anville, Hist. de l'Acad. &c. tom. xxxi. p. 287–292.).

2. The names of these Dardanian peasants are Gothic, and almost English: *Justinian* is a translation of *uprauda* (*upright*); his father *Sabatius* (in Græco-barbarous language *stipes*) was styled in his village *Istock* (*Stock*); his mother Bigleniza was softened into Vigilantia.

3. Ludewig (p. 127–135.) attempts to justify the Anician name of Justinian and Theodora, and to connect them with a family from which the house of Austria has been derived.

4. See the Anecdotes of Procopius (c. 6.), with the notes of N. Alemannus. The satirist would not have sunk, in the vague and decent appellation of γεωργος the βουκολος and συφορβος of Zonaras. Yet why are those names disgraceful? – and what German baron would not be proud to descend from the Eumæus of the Odyssey?

oblivion the name of Justin; yet they might warrant the military promotion, which in the course of fifty years he gradually obtained; the rank
of tribune, of count, and of general, the dignity of senator, and the command
of the guards, who obeyed him as their chief, at the important crisis when
the emperor Anastasius was removed from the world. The powerful kinsmen whom he had raised and enriched, were excluded from the
throne; and the eunuch Amantius, who reigned in the palace, had secretly
resolved to fix the diadem on the head of the most obsequious of his
creatures. A liberal donative, to conciliate the suffrage of the guards, was
entrusted for that purpose in the hands of their commander. But these
weighty arguments were treacherously employed by Justin in his own
favour; and as no competitor presumed to appear, the Dacian
peasant was invested with the purple, by the unanimous consent
of the soldiers who knew him to be brave and gentle, of the
clergy and people who believed him to be orthodox, and of the
provincials who yielded a blind and implicit submission to the
will of the capital. The elder Justin, as he is distinguished from
another emperor of the same family and name, ascended the
Byzantine throne at the age of sixty-eight years; and, had he

*Elevation and
reign of his
uncle Justin I.
A.D. 518, July
10; A.D., 527,
April 1 – or
August 1.*

been left to his own guidance, every moment of a nine years reign must
have exposed to his subjects the impropriety of their choice. His ignorance
was similar to that of Theodoric; and it is remarkable, that in an age not
destitute of learning, two contemporary monarchs had never been instructed
in the knowledge of the alphabet. But the genius of Justin was far inferior
to that of the Gothic king: the experience of a soldier had not qualified
him for the government of an empire; and, though personally brave, the
consciousness of his own weakness was naturally attended with doubt,
distrust, and political apprehension. But the official business of the state
was diligently and faithfully transacted by the quæstor Proclus;[5] and the
aged emperor adopted the talents and ambition of his nephew Justinian,
an aspiring youth, whom his uncle had drawn from the rustic solitude of
Dacia, and educated at Constantinople, as the heir of his private fortune
and at length of the Eastern empire.

---

5. His virtues are praised by Procopius (Persic.
l. i. c. 11). The quæstor Proclus was the friend
of Justinian, and the enemy of every other
adoption.

Since the eunuch Amantius had been defrauded of his money, it became necessary to deprive him of his life. The task was easily accomplished by the charge of a real or fictitious conspiracy; and the judges were informed, as an accumulation of guilt, that he was secretly addicted to the Manichæan heresy.[6] Amantius lost his head; three of his companions, the first domestics of the palace, were punished either with death or exile; and their unfortunate candidate for the purple was cast into a deep dungeon, overwhelmed with stones, and ignominiously thrown, without burial, into the sea. The ruin of Vitalian was a work of more difficulty and danger. That Gothic chief had rendered himself popular by the civil war which he boldly waged against Anastasius for the defence of the orthodox faith, and after the conclusion of an advantageous treaty, he still remained in the neighbourhood of Constantinople at the head of a formidable and victorious army of Barbarians. By the frail security of oaths, he was tempted to relinquish this advantageous situation, and to trust his person within the walls of a city, whose inhabitants, particularly the *blue* faction, were artfully incensed against him by the remembrance even of his pious hostilities. The emperor and his nephew embraced him as the faithful and worthy champion of the church and state; and gratefully adorned their favourite with the titles of consul and general; but in the seventh month of his consulship, Vitalian was stabbed with seventeen wounds at the royal banquet;[7] and Justinian, who inherited the spoil, was accused as the assassin of a spiritual brother, to whom he had recently pledged his faith in the participation of the Christian mysteries.[8] After the fall of his rival, he was promoted, without any claim of military service, to the office of master-general of the Eastern armies, whom it was his duty to lead into the field against the public enemy. But, in the pursuit of fame, Justinian might have lost his present dominion

---

6. Manichæan signifies Eutychian. Hear the furious acclamations of Constantinople and Tyre, the former no more than six days after the decease of Anastasius. *They* produced, the latter applauded, the eunuch's death (Baronius, A.D. 518. P. ii. Nº 15. Fleury, Hist. Eccles. tom. vii. p. 200. 205. from the Councils, tom. v. p. 182. 207.).

7. His power, character, and intentions, are perfectly explained by the Count de Buat (tom. ix. p. 54–81.). He was great-grandson

of Aspar, hereditary prince in the Lesser Scythia, and count of the Gothic *fœderati* of Thrace. The Bessi, whom he could influence, are the minor Goths of Jornandes (c. 51.).

8. Justiniani patricii factione dicitur interfectus fuisse (Victor Tununenis, Chron. in Thesaur. Temp. Scaliger, P. ii. p. 7.). Procopius (Anecdot. c. 7.) styles him a tyrant, but acknowledges the αδελφοπιστια, which is well explained by Alemannus.

over the age and weakness of his uncle; and, instead of acquiring by Scythian or Persian trophies the applause of his countrymen,[9] the prudent warrior solicited their favour in the churches, the circus, and the senate, of Constantinople. The Catholics were attached to the nephew of Justin, who, between the Nestorian and Eutychian heresies, trod the narrow path of inflexible and intolerant orthodoxy.[10] In the first days of the new reign, he prompted and gratified the popular enthusiasm against the memory of the deceased emperor. After a schism of thirty-four years, he reconciled the proud and angry spirit of the Roman pontiff, and spread among the Latins a favourable report of his pious respect for the apostolic see. The thrones of the East were filled with Catholic bishops devoted to his interest, the clergy and the monks were gained by his liberality, and the people were taught to pray for their future sovereign, the hope and pillar of the true religion. The magnificence of Justinian was displayed in the superior pomp of his public spectacles, an object not less sacred and important in the eyes of the multitude, than the creed of Nice or Chalcedon: the expence of his consulship was esteemed at two hundred and eighty-eight thousand pieces of gold; twenty lions, and thirty leopards, were produced at the same time in the amphitheatre, and a numerous train of horses, with their rich trappings, was bestowed as an extraordinary gift on the victorious charioteers of the circus. While he indulged the people of Constantinople, and received the addresses of foreign kings, the nephew of Justin assiduously cultivated the friendship of the senate. That venerable name seemed to qualify its members to declare the sense of the nation, and to regulate the succession of the Imperial throne: the feeble Anastasius had permitted the vigour of government to degenerate into the form or substance of an aristocracy; and the military officers who had obtained the senatorial rank, were followed by their domestic guards, a band of veterans, whose arms or acclamations might fix in a tumultuous moment the diadem of the East. The treasures of the state were lavished to procure the voices of the senators, and their unanimous wish, that he would be pleased to adopt Justinian for his colleague, was communicated to the emperor. But this request, which

---

9. In his earliest youth (plane adolescens) he had passed some time as an hostage with Theodoric. For this curious fact, Alemannus (ad Procop. Anecdot. c. 9. p. 34. of the first edition) quotes a MS. history of Justinian, by his preceptor Theophilus. Ludewig (p. 143.)

wishes to make him a soldier.

10. The ecclesiastical history of Justinian will be shewn hereafter. See Baronius, A.D. 518– 521. and the copious article *Justinianus* in the index to the viith volume of his Annals.

too clearly admonished him of his approaching end, was unwelcome to the jealous temper of an aged monarch, desirous to retain the power which he was incapable of exercising; and Justin, holding his purple with both his hands, advised them to prefer, since an election was so profitable, some older candidate. Notwithstanding this reproach, the senate proceeded to decorate Justinian with the royal epithet of *nobilissimus*; and their decree was ratified by the affection or the fears of his uncle. After some time the languor of mind and body, to which he was reduced by an incurable wound in his thigh, indispensably required the aid of a guardian. He summoned the patriarch and senators; and in their presence solemnly placed the diadem on the head of his nephew, who was conducted from the palace to the circus, and saluted by the loud and joyful applause of the people. The life of Justin was prolonged about four months, but from the instant of this ceremony, he was considered as dead to the empire, which acknowledged Justinian, in the forty-fifth year of his age, for the lawful sovereign of the East.[11]

The reign of Justinian, A.D. 527, April 1– A.D. 565, Nov. 14.

From his elevation to his death, Justinian governed the Roman empire thirty-eight years, seven months, and thirteen days. The events of his reign, which excite our curious attention by their number, variety, and importance, are diligently related by the secretary of Belisarius, a rhetorician, whom eloquence had promoted to the rank of senator and præfect of Constantinople. According to the vicissitudes of courage or servitude, of favour or disgrace, Procopius[12] successively composed the *history*, the *panegyric*, and the *satire* of his own times. The eight books of the Persian, Vandalic, and Gothic wars,[13] which are continued in the five books of Agathias, deserve our esteem as a laborious and successful imitation of the Attic, or at least of the Asiatic writers of

Character and histories of Procopius.

11. The reign of the elder Justin may be found in the three Chronicles of Marcellinus, Victor, and John Malala (tom. ii. p. 130–150.), the last of whom (in spite of Hody, Prolegom Nº 14. 39. edit. Oxon.) lived soon after Justinian (Jortin's Remarks, &c. vol. iv. p. 383,): in the Ecclesiastical History of Evagrius (l. iv. c. 1, 2, 3. 9.), and the Excerpta of Theodorus (Lector, Nº 37.), and in Cedrenus (p. 362–366.) and Zonaras (l. xiv. p. 58–61.), who may pass for an original.

12. See the characters of Procopius and Agathias in La Mothe le Vayer (tom. viii. p. 144–174.), Vossius (de Historicis Græcis, l. ii. c. 22.), and Fabricius (Bibliot. Græc. l. v. c. 5. tom. vi. p. 248–278.). Their religion, an honourable problem, betrays occasional conformity, with a secret attachment to Paganism and philosophy.

13. In the seven first books, two Persic, two Vandalic, and three Gothic, Procopius has borrowed from Appian the division of

ancient Greece. His facts are collected from the personal experience and free conversation of a soldier, a statesman, and a traveller; his style continually aspires, and often attains, to the merit of strength and elegance; his reflections, more especially in the speeches, which he too frequently inserts, contain a rich fund of political knowledge; and the historian, excited by the generous ambition of pleasing and instructing posterity, appears to disdain the prejudices of the people, and the flattery of courts. The writings of Procopius[14] were read and applauded by his contemporaries;[15] but, although he respectfully laid them at the foot of the throne, the pride of Justinian must have been wounded by the praise of an hero, who perpetually eclipses the glory of his inactive sovereign. The conscious dignity of independence was subdued by the hopes and fears of a slave; and the secretary of Belisarius laboured for pardon and reward in the six books of the imperial *edifices*. He had dextrously chosen a subject of apparent splendour, in which he could loudly celebrate the genius, the magnificence, and the piety of a prince, who, both as a conqueror and legislator, had surpassed the puerile virtues of Themistocles and Cyrus.[16] Disappointment might urge the flatterer to secret revenge; and the first glance of favour might again tempt him to suspend and suppress a libel,[17] in which the

---

provinces and wars: the viiith book, though it bears the name of Gothic, is a miscellaneous and general supplement down to the spring of the year 553, from whence it is continued by Agathias till 559 (Pagi, Critica, A.D. 579. Nº 5.).

14. The literary fate of Procopius has been somewhat unlucky. 1. His books de Bello Gothico were stolen by Leonard Aretin, and published (Fulginii, 1470. Venet. 1471 apud Janson. Mattaire, Annal. Typograph. tom. i. edit. posterior, p. 290. 304. 279. 299.) in his own name (See Vossius de Hist. Lat. l. iii. c. 5. and the feeble defence of the Venice Giornale de Letterati, tom. xix. p. 207.). 2. His works were mutilated by the first Latin translators, Christopher Persona (Giornale, tom, xix. p. 340–348.) and Raphael de Volaterra (Huet de Claris. Interpretibus, p. 166.), who did not even consult the MS. of the Vatican library, of which they were præfects (Aleman. in Præfat. Anecdot.). 3. The Greek

text was not printed till 1607, by Hoeschelius of Augsburgh (Dictionaire de Bayle, tom. ii. p. 782.). 4. The Paris edition was imperfectly executed by Claude Maltret, a Jesuit of Tholouse (in 1663), far distant from the Louvre press and the Vatican MS. from which, however, he obtained some supplements. His promised commentaries, &c. have never appeared. The Agathias of Leyden (1594) has been wisely reprinted by the Paris editor, with the Latin version of Bonaventura Vulcanius, a learned interpreter (Huet, p. 176).

15. Agathias in Præfat. p. 7, 8. l. iv. p. 137. Evagrius (l. iv. c. 12.). See likewise Photius, cod. lxiii. p. 65.

16. *Κυρου παιδεια* (says he, Præfat. ad l. de Edificiis *περι κτισματων*) is no more than *Κυρου παιδια* – a pun! In these five books, Procopius affects a Christian, as well as a courtly style.

17. Procopius discloses himself (Præfat. ad Anecdot, c. 1. 2. 5)., and the anecdotes are

Roman Cyrus is degraded into an odious and contemptible tyrant, in which both the emperor and his consort Theodora are seriously represented as two dæmons, who had assumed an human form for the destruction of mankind.[18] Such base inconsistency must doubtless sully the reputation, and detract from the credit, of Procopius: yet, after the venom of his malignity has been suffered to exhale, the residue of the *anecdotes*, even the most disgraceful facts, some of which had been tenderly hinted in his public history, are established by their internal evidence, or the authentic monuments of the times.[19] From these various materials, I shall now proceed to describe the reign of Justinian, which will deserve and occupy an ample space. The present chapter will explain the elevation and character of Theodora, the factions of the circus, and the peaceful administration of the sovereign of the East. In the three succeeding chapters, I shall relate the wars of Justinian which atchieved the conquest of Africa and Italy; and I shall follow the victories of Belisarius and Narses, without disguising the vanity of their triumphs, or the hostile virtue of the Persian and Gothic heroes. The series of this volume will embrace the jurisprudence and theology of the emperor; the controversies and sects which still divide the oriental church; the reformation of the Roman law, which is obeyed or respected by the nations of modern Europe.

Division of the reign of Justinian.

I. In the exercise of supreme power, the first act of Justinian was to divide it with the woman whom he loved, the famous Theodora,[20] whose strange elevation cannot be applauded as the triumph of female virtue. Under the reign of Anastasius,

Birth and vices of the empress Theodora.

---

reckoned as the ixth book by Suidas (tom. iii. p. 186. edit. Kuster). The silence of Evagrius is a poor objection. Baronius (A.D. 548. N° 24.) regrets the loss of this secret history: it was then in the Vatican library, in his own custody, and was first published sixteen years after his death, with the learned, but partial, notes of Nicholas Alemannus (Lugd. 1623.).
18. Justinian an ass – the perfect likeness of Domitian (Anecdot. c. 8.) – Theodora's lovers driven from her bed by rival dæmons – her marriage foretold with a great dæmon – a monk saw the prince of the dæmons, instead of Justinian, on the throne – the servants who watched, beheld a face without

features, a body walking without an head, &c. &c. Procopius declares his own and his friends belief in these diabolical stories (c. 12.).
19. Montesquieu (Considerations sur la Grandeur et la Decadence des Romains, c. xx.) gives credit to these anecdotes, as connected, 1. with the weakness of the empire, and, 2. with the instability of Justinian's laws.
20. For the life and manners of the empress Theodora, see the Anecdotes; more especially c. 1–5. 9, 10–15, 16, 17. with the learned notes of Alemannus – a reference which is always implied.

the care of the wild beasts maintained by the green faction at Constantinople, was entrusted to Acacius a native of the isle of Cyprus, who, from
his employment, was surnamed the master of the bears. This honourable
office was given after his death to another candidate, notwithstanding
the diligence of his widow, who had already provided a husband and a
successor. Acacius had left three daughters, Comito,[21] THEODORA, and
Anastasia, the eldest of whom did not then exceed the age of seven years.
On a solemn festival, these helpless orphans were sent by their distressed
and indignant mother, in the garb of suppliants, into the midst of the
theatre: the green faction received them with contempt, the blues with
compassion; and this difference, which sunk deep into the mind of Theodora, was felt long afterwards in the administration of the empire. As they
improved in age and beauty, the three sisters were successively devoted to
the public and private pleasures of the Byzantine people; and Theodora,
after following Comito on the stage, in the dress of a slave, with a stool on
her head, was at length permitted to exercise her independent talents. She
neither danced, nor sung, nor played on the flute; her skill was confined
to the pantomime arts; she excelled in buffoon characters, and as often as
the comedian swelled her cheeks, and complained with a ridiculous tone
and gesture of the blows that were inflicted, the whole theatre of Constantinople resounded with laughter and applause. The beauty of Theodora[22]
was the subject of more flattering praise, and the source of more exquisite
delight. Her features were delicate and regular; her complexion, though
somewhat pale, was tinged with a natural colour; every sensation was
instantly expressed by the vivacity of her eyes; her easy motions displayed
the graces of a small but elegant figure; and either love or adulation might
proclaim, that painting and poetry were incapable of delineating
the matchless excellence of her form. But this form was degraded by the
facility with which it was exposed to the public eye, and prostituted to
licentious desire. Her venal charms were abandoned to a promiscuous
crowd of citizens and strangers, of every rank, and of every profession: the
fortunate lover who had been promised a night of enjoyment, was often

---

21. Comito was afterwards married to Sittas
duke of Armenia, the father perhaps, at least
she might be the mother, of the empress
Sophia. Two nephews of Theodora may be
the sons of Anastasia (Aleman. p. 30, 31.).
22. Her statue was raised at Constantinople,

on a porphyry column. See Procopius (de
Edif. l. i. c. 11.), who gives her portrait in the
Anecdotes (c. 10.). Aleman. (p. 47.) produces
one from a Mosaic at Ravenna, loaded with
pearls and jewels, and yet handsome.

driven from her bed by a stronger or more wealthy favourite; and when she passed through the streets, her presence was avoided by all who wished to escape either the scandal or the temptation. The satirical historian has not blushed[23] to describe the naked scenes which Theodora was not ashamed to exhibit in the theatre.[24] After exhausting the arts of sensual pleasure,[25] she most ungratefully murmured against the parsimony of Nature;[26] but her murmurs, her pleasures, and her arts, must be veiled in the obscurity of a learned language. After reigning for some time, the delight and contempt of the capital, she condescended to accompany Ecebolus, a native of Tyre, who had obtained the government of the African Pentapolis. But this union was frail and transient; Ecebolus soon rejected an expensive or faithless concubine; she was reduced at Alexandria to extreme distress; and in her laborious return to Constantinople, every city of the East admired and enjoyed the fair Cyprian, whose merit appeared to justify her descent from the peculiar island of Venus. The vague commerce of Theodora, and the most detestable precautions, preserved her from the danger which she feared; yet once, and once only, she became a mother. The infant was saved and educated in Arabia, by his father, who imparted to him on his death-bed, that he was the son of an empress. Filled with ambitious hopes, the unsuspecting youth immediately hastened to the palace of Constantinople, and was admitted to the presence of his mother. As he was never more seen, even after the decease of Theodora, she deserves

23. A fragment of the Anecdotes (c. 9.), somewhat too naked, was suppressed by Alemannus, though extant in the Vatican MS.; nor has the defect been supplied in the Paris or Venice editions. La Mothe le Vayer (tom. viii. p. 155.) gave the first hint of this curious and genuine passage (Jortin's Remarks, vol. iv. p. 366.), which he had received from Rome, and it has been since published in the Menagiana (tom. iii. p. 254–259.), with a Latin version.

24. After the mention of a narrow girdle (as none could appear stark-naked in the theatre), Procopius thus proceeds: αναπεπτοκυια τε εν τω εδαφει υπτια εκειτο. Θητες δε τινες ... κριθας αυτη υπερθεν των αιδοιων εριπτον ἁς δε ὁι χηνες, δι ες τουτο παρεσχευασμενοι εντυγχανον τοις στομασιν ενθενδε κατα μιαν ανελομενοι εισθιον. I have heard

that a learned prelate, now deceased, was fond of quoting this passage in conversation.

25. Theodora surpassed the Crispa of Ausonius (Epigram lxxi.) who imitated the capitalis luxus of the females of Nola. See Quintilian Institut. viii. 6. and Torrentius ad Horat. Sermon. l. i. sat. 2. v. 101. At a memorable supper, thirty slaves waited round the table; ten young men feasted with Theodora. Her charity was *universal*.

Et lassata viris, necdum satiata, recessit.

26. Ἡδε κακ' τριων τρυπηματων εργαζομενη ενεκαλει τη φυσει δυσφορουμενη ὁτι δε μη και τιτθους αυτη ευρυτερον η νυν εισι τρυπωη, οπως δυνατη ειη και εκεινη εργαζεσθαι. She wished for a *fourth* altar, on which she might pour libations to the god of love.

the foul imputation of extinguishing with his life a secret so offensive to
her Imperial virtue.

In the most abject state of her fortune and reputation, some
vision, either of sleep or of fancy, had whispered to Theodora
the pleasing assurance that she was destined to become the
spouse of a potent monarch. Conscious of her approaching greatness, she
returned from Paphlagonia to Constantinople; assumed, like a skilful actress,
a more decent character; relieved her poverty by the laudable industry of
spinning wool; and affected a life of chastity and solitude in a small house,
which she afterwards changed into a magnificent temple.[27] Her beauty,
assisted by art or accident, soon attracted, captivated, and fixed, the patrician
Justinian, who already reigned with absolute sway under the name of his
uncle. Perhaps she contrived to enhance the value of a gift which she had
so often lavished on the meanest of mankind: perhaps she inflamed, at first
by modest delays, and at last by sensual allurements, the desires of a lover,
who from nature or devotion was addicted to long vigils and abstemious
diet. When his first transports had subsided, she still maintained the same
ascendant over his mind, by the more solid merit of temper and understanding. Justinian delighted to ennoble and enrich the object of his affection;
the treasures of the East were poured at her feet, and the nephew of Justin
was determined, perhaps by religious scruples, to bestow on his concubine
the sacred and legal character of a wife. But the laws of Rome expressly
prohibited the marriage of a senator with any female, who had been
dishonoured by a servile origin or theatrical profession: the empress Lupi-
cina, or Euphemia, a Barbarian of rustic manners, but of irreproachable
virtue, refused to accept a prostitute for her niece; and even Vigilantia the
superstitious mother of Justinian, though she acknowledged the wit and
beauty of Theodora, was seriously apprehensive, lest the levity and arrogance
of that artful paramour might corrupt the piety and happiness of her son.
These obstacles were removed by the inflexible constancy of Justinian. He
patiently expected the death of the empress; he despised the tears of his
mother, who soon sunk under the weight of her affliction; and a law was
promulgated in the name of the emperor Justin, which abolished the rigid
jurisprudence of antiquity. A glorious repentance (the words of the edict)
was left open for the unhappy females who had prostituted their persons

*Her marriage
with Justinian.*

27. Anonym. de Antiquitat. C. P. l. iii. 132.
in Banduri Imperium Orient. tom. i. p. 48.
Ludewig (p. 154.) argues sensibly that
Theodora would not have immortalised a
brothel: but I apply this fact to her second
and chaster residence at Constantinople.

on the theatre, and they were permitted to contract a legal union with the most illustrious of the Romans.[28] This indulgence was speedily followed by the solemn nuptials of Justinian and Theodora; her dignity was gradually exalted with that of her lover; and, as soon as Justin had invested his nephew with the purple, the patriarch of Constantinople placed the diadem on the heads of the emperor and empress of the East. But the usual honours which the severity of Roman manners had allowed to the wives of princes, could not satisfy either the ambition of Theodora or the fondness of Justinian. He seated her on the throne as an equal and independent colleague in the sovereignty of the empire, and an oath of allegiance was imposed on the governors of the provinces in the joint names of Justinian and Theodora.[29] The Eastern world fell prostrate before the genius and fortune of the daughter of Acacius. The prostitute who, in the presence of innumerable spectators, had polluted the theatre of Constantinople, was adored as a queen in the same city, by grave magistrates, orthodox bishops, victorious generals, and captive monarchs.[30]

Her tyranny.   Those who believe that the female mind is totally depraved by the loss of chastity, will eagerly listen to all the invectives of private envy or popular resentment, which have dissembled the virtues of Theodora, exaggerated her vices, and condemned with rigour the venal or voluntary sins of the youthful harlot. From a motive of shame or contempt, she often declined the servile homage of the multitude, escaped from the odious light of the capital, and passed the greatest part of the year in the palaces and gardens which were pleasantly seated on the sea-coast of the Propontis and the Bosphorus. Her private hours were devoted to the prudent as well as grateful care of her beauty, the luxury of the bath and table, and the long slumber of the evening and the morning. Her secret

28. See the old law in Justinian's Code (l. v. tit. v. leg. 7. tit. xxvii. leg. 1.) under the years 336 and 454. The new edict (about the year 521 or 522. Aleman. p. 38. 96.) very awkwardly repeals no more than the clause of mulieres *scenicæ*, libertinæ tabernariæ. See the novels 89 and 117. and a Greek rescript from Justinian to the bishops (Aleman. p. 41.).

29. I swear by the Father, &c. by the Virgin Mary, by the four Gospels, quæ in manibus teneo, and by the holy Archangels Michael and Gabriel, puram conscientiam germanumque servitium me servaturum, sacratissimis

DDNN. Justiniano et Theodoræ conjugi ejus (Novell. viii. tit. 3.). Would the oath have been binding in favour of the widow? Communes tituli et triumphi, &c. (Aleman. p. 47, 48.).

30. "Let greatness own her, and she's mean no more," &c.

Without Warburton's critical telescope, I should never have seen, in this general picture of triumphant vice, any personal allusion to Theodora.

apartments were occupied by the favourite women and eunuchs, whose interests and passions she indulged at the expence of justice; the most illustrious personages of the state were crowded into a dark and sultry antichamber, and when at last, after tedious attendance, they were admitted to kiss the feet of Theodora, they experienced, as her humour might suggest, the silent arrogance of an empress, or the capricious levity of a comedian. Her rapacious avarice to accumulate an immense treasure, may be excused by the apprehension of her husband's death, which could leave no alternative between ruin and the throne; and fear as well as ambition might exasperate Theodora against two generals, who, during a malady of the emperor, had rashly declared that they were not disposed to acquiesce in the choice of the capital. But the reproach of cruelty, so repugnant even to her softer vices, has left an indelible stain on the memory of Theodora. Her numerous spies observed, and zealously reported, every action, or word, or look, injurious to their royal mistress. Whomsoever they accused were cast into her peculiar prisons,[31] inaccessible to the enquiries of justice; and it was rumoured, that the torture of the rack, or scourge, had been inflicted in the presence of a female tyrant, insensible to the voice of prayer or of pity.[32] Some of these unhappy victims perished in deep unwholesome dungeons, while others were permitted, after the loss of their limbs, their reason, or their fortune, to appear in the world the living monuments of her vengeance, which was commonly extended to the children of those whom she had suspected or injured. The senator or bishop, whose death or exile Theodora had pronounced, was delivered to a trusty messenger, and his diligence was quickened by a menace from her own mouth. "If you fail in the execution of my commands, I swear by him who liveth for ever, that your skin shall be flayed from your body."[33]

If the creed of Theodora had not been tainted with heresy, her exemplary devotion might have atoned, in the opinion of *Her virtues,* her contemporaries, for pride, avarice, and cruelty. But, if she employed her influence to assuage the intolerant fury of the emperor, the present age will allow some merit to her religion, and much indulgence to her

---

31. Her prisons, a labyrinth, a Tartarus (Anecdot. c. 4.), were under the palace. Darkness is propitious to cruelty, but it is likewise favourable to calumny and fiction.
32. A more jocular whipping was inflicted on Saturninus, for presuming to say that his wife, a favourite of the empress, had not been found ατρητος (Anecdot. c. 17.).
33. Per viventem in sæcula excoriari te faciam. Anastasius de Vitis Pont. Roman. in Vigilio, p. 40.

speculative errors.[34] The name of Theodora was introduced, with equal honour, in all the pious and charitable foundations of Justinian; and the most benevolent institution of his reign may be ascribed to the sympathy of the empress for her less fortunate sisters, who had been seduced or compelled to embrace the trade of prostitution. A palace, on the Asiatic side of the Bosphorus, was converted into a stately and spacious monastery, and a liberal maintenance was assigned to five hundred women, who had been collected from the streets and brothels of Constantinople. In this safe and holy retreat, they were devoted to perpetual confinement; and the despair of some, who threw themselves headlong into the sea, was lost in the gratitude of the penitents, who had been delivered from sin and misery by their generous benefactress.[35] The prudence of Theodora is celebrated by Justinian himself; and his laws are attributed to the sage counsels of his most reverend wife, whom he had received as the gift of the Deity.[36] Her courage was displayed amidst the tumult of the people and the terrors of the court. Her chastity, from the moment of her union with Justinian, is founded on the silence of her implacable enemies; and, although the daughter of Acacius might be satiated with love, yet some applause is due to the firmness of a mind which could sacrifice pleasure and habit to the stronger sense either of duty or interest. The wishes and prayers of Theodora could never obtain the blessing of a lawful son, and she buried an infant daughter, the sole offspring of her marriage.[37] Notwithstanding this disappointment, her dominion was permanent and absolute; she preserved, by art or merit, the affections of Justinian; and their seeming dissensions were always fatal to the courtiers who believed them to be sincere. Perhaps her health had been impaired by the licentiousness of her youth; but it was always delicate, and she was directed by her physicians to use the Pythian warm baths. In this journey, the empress was followed by the prætorian præfect, the great treasurer, several counts and patricians, and a splendid train of four thousand attendants: the highways

---

34. Ludewig, p. 161–166. I give him credit for the charitable attempt, although *he* hath not much charity in his temper.

35. Compare the Anecdotes (c. 17.) with the Edifices (l. i. c. 9.) – how differently may the same fact be stated! John Malala (tom. ii. p. 174, 175.) observes, that on this, or a similar occasion, she released and clothed the girls whom she had purchased from the

stews at five aurei a-piece.

36. Novell. viii 1. An allusion to Theodora. Her enemies read the name Dæmonodora (Aleman. p. 66.).

37. St. Sabas refused to pray for a son of Theodora, lest he should prove an heretic worse than Anastasius himself (Cyril in Vit. St. Sabæ, apud Aleman. p. 70. 109.).

were repaired at her approach; a palace was erected for her reception; and as she passed through Bithynia, she distributed liberal alms, to the churches, the monasteries, and the hospitals, that they might implore heaven for the restoration of her health.[38] At length, in the twenty-fourth year of her marriage, and the twenty-second of her reign, she was consumed by a cancer;[39] and the irreparable loss was deplored by her husband, who, in the room of a theatrical prostitute, might have selected the purest and most noble virgin of the East.[40]

and death, A.D. 548, June 11.

II. A material difference may be observed in the games of antiquity: the most eminent of the Greeks were actors, the Romans were merely spectators. The Olympic stadium was open to wealth, merit, and ambition; and if the candidates could depend on their personal skill and activity, they might pursue the footsteps of Diomede and Menelaus, and conduct their own horses in the rapid career.[41] Ten, twenty, forty chariots, were allowed to start at the same instant; a crown of leaves was the reward of the victor; and his fame, with that of his family and country, was chaunted in lyric strains more durable than monuments of brass and marble. But a senator, or even a citizen, conscious of his dignity, would have blushed to expose his person or his horses in the circus of Rome. The games were exhibited at the expence of the republic, the magistrates, or the emperors: but the reins were abandoned to servile hands, and if the profits of a favourite charioteer sometimes exceeded those of an advocate, they must be considered as the effects of popular extravagance, and the high wages of a disgraceful profession. The race, in its first institution, was a simple contest of two chariots, whose drivers were distinguished by *white* and *red* liveries; two additional colours, a light *green*, and a cærulean *blue*, were afterwards introduced; and, as the

The factions of the circus,

---

38. See John Malala, tom. ii. p. 174. Theophanes, p. 158. Procopius de Edific. l. v. c. 3.
39. Theodora Chalcedonensis synodi inimica canceris plagâ toto corpore perfusa vitam prodigiose finivit (Victor Tununensis in Chron.). On such occasions, an orthodox mind is steeled against pity. Alemannus (p. 12, 13.) understands the ευσεβως εκοιμηθη of Theophanes as civil language, which does not imply either piety or repentance; yet two years after her death, St. Theodora is celebrated by Paul Silentiarius (in Proem. v. 58–62.).
40. As she persecuted the Popes, and rejected

a council, Baronius exhausts the names of Eve, Dalila, Herodias, &c.; after which he has recourse to his infernal dictionary: civis inferni – alumna dæmonum – satanico agitata spiritû – æstro percita diabolico, &c. &c. (A.D. 548. Nº 24.).
41. Read and feel the xxiiid book of the Iliad, a living picture of manners, passions, and the whole form and spirit of the chariot race. West's Dissertation on the Olympic Games (sect. xii-xvii.) affords much curious and authentic information.

races were repeated twenty-five times, one hundred chariots contributed in the same day to the pomp of the circus. The four *factions* soon acquired a legal establishment, and a mysterious origin, and their fanciful colours were derived from the various appearances of nature in the four seasons of the year; the red dog-star of summer, the snows of winter, the deep shades of autumn, and the cheerful verdure of the spring.[42] Another interpretation preferred the elements to the seasons, and the struggle of the green and blue was supposed to represent the conflict of the earth and sea. Their respective victories announced either a plentiful harvest or a prosperous navigation, and the hostility of the husbandmen and mariners was some-what less absurd than the blind ardour of the Roman people, who devoted their lives and fortunes to the colour which they had espoused. Such folly was disdained and indulged by the wisest princes; but the names of Caligula, Nero, Vitellius, Verus, Commodus, Caracalla, and Elagabalus, were enrolled in the blue or green factions of the circus: they frequented their stables, applauded their favourites, chastised their antagonists, and deserved the esteem of the populace, by the natural or affected imitation of their manners. The bloody and tumultuous contest continued to disturb the public festivity, till the last age of the spectacles of Rome; and Theodoric, from a motive of justice or affection, inter-posed his authority to protect the greens against the violence of a consul and a patrician, who were passionately addicted to the blue faction of the circus.[43]

at Rome.

They distract Constantinople and the East.

Constantinople adopted the follies, though not the virtues, of ancient Rome; and the same factions which had agitated the circus, raged with redoubled fury in the hippodrome. Under the reign of Anastasius, this popular frenzy was inflamed by religious zeal; and the greens, who had treacherously concealed stones and daggers under baskets of fruit, massacred at a solemn festival, three thousand of their blue adversaries.[44] From the capital, this pestilence was diffused

---

42. The four colours, *albati, russati, prasini, veneti,* represent the four seasons, according to Cassiodorius (Var. iii. 51.), who lavishes much wit and eloquence on this theatrical mystery. Of these colours, the three first may be fairly translated *white, red,* and *green. Venetus* is explained by *cæruleus,* a word various and vague: it is properly the sky reflected in the sea; but custom and convenience may allow

blue as an equivalent (Robert. Stephan. sub voce. Spence's Polymetis, p. 228.).

43. See Onuphrius Panvinius de Ludis Circensibus, l. i. c. 10, 11.; the xviith Annotation on Mascou's History of the Germans; and Aleman. ad c. vii.

44. Marcellin. in Chron. p. 47. Instead of the vulgar word *veneta,* he uses the more exquisite terms of *cærulea* and *cærealis.* Baronius (A.D.

into the provinces and cities of the East, and the sportive distinction of two colours produced two strong and irreconcileable factions, which shook the foundations of a feeble government.[45] The popular dissensions, founded on the most serious interest, or holy pretence, have scarcely equalled the obstinacy of this wanton discord, which invaded the peace of families, divided friends and brothers, and tempted the female sex, though seldom seen in the circus, to espouse the inclinations of their lovers, or to contradict the wishes of their husbands. Every law, either human or divine, was trampled under foot, and as long as the party was successful, its deluded followers appeared careless of private distress or public calamity. The licence, without the freedom of democracy, was revived at Antioch and Constantinople, and the support of a faction became necessary to every candidate for civil or ecclesiastical honours. A secret attachment to the family or sect of Anastasius, was imputed to the greens; the blues were zealously devoted to the cause of orthodoxy and Justinian,[46] and their grateful patron, protected, above five years, the disorders of a faction, whose seasonable tumults overawed the palace, the senate, and the capitals of the East. Insolent with royal favour, the blues affected to strike terror by a peculiar and Barbaric dress, the long hair of the Huns, their close sleeves and ample garments, a lofty step, and a sonorous voice. In the day they concealed their two-edged ponyards, but in the night they boldly assembled in arms, and in numerous bands, prepared for every act of violence and rapine. Their adversaries of the green faction, or even inoffensive citizens, were stripped and often murdered by these nocturnal robbers, and it became dangerous to wear any gold buttons or girdles, or to appear at a late hour in the streets of a peaceful capital. A daring spirit, rising with impunity, proceeded to violate the safeguard of private houses; and fire was employed to facilitate the attack, or to conceal the crimes of these factious rioters. No place was safe or sacred from their depredations; to gratify either avarice or revenge, they profusely spilt the

Justinian favours the blues.

---

501. Nº 4, 5, 6.) is satisfied that the blues were orthodox; but Tillemont is angry at the supposition, and will not allow any martyrs in a playhouse (Hist. des Emp. tom. vi. p. 554.).

45. See Procopius (Persic. l. i. c. 24.). In describing the vices of the factions and of the government, the *public*, is not more favourable than the *secret*, historian. Aleman. (p. 26.) has

quoted a fine passage from Gregory Nazianzen, which proves the inveteracy of the evil.

46. The partiality of Justinian for the blues (Anecdot. c. 7.) is attested by Evagrius (Hist. Eccles. l. iv. c. 32.); John Malala (tom. ii. p. 138, 139.), especially for Antioch; and Theophanes (p. 142.).

blood of the innocent; churches and altars were polluted by atrocious murders, and it was the boast of the assassins, that their dexterity could always inflict a mortal wound with a single stroke of their dagger. The dissolute youth of Constantinople adopted the blue livery of disorder; the laws were silent, and the bonds of society were relaxed: creditors were compelled to resign their obligations; judges to reserve their sentence; masters to enfranchise their slaves; fathers to supply the extravagance of their children; noble matrons were prostituted to the lust of their servants; beautiful boys were torn from the arms of their parents; and wives, unless they preferred a voluntary death, were ravished in the presence of their husbands.[47] The despair of the greens, who were persecuted by their enemies, and deserted by the magistrate, assumed the privilege of defence, perhaps of retaliation: but those who survived the combat, were dragged to execution, and the unhappy fugitives escaping to woods and caverns, preyed without mercy on the society from whence they were expelled. Those ministers of justice who had courage to punish the crimes, and to brave the resentment of the blues, became the victims of their indiscreet zeal: a præfect of Constantinople fled for refuge to the holy sepulchre, a count of the East was ignominiously whipped, and a governor of Cilicia was hanged by the order of Theodora. on the tomb of two assassins whom he had condemned for the murder of his groom, and a daring attack upon his own life.[48] An aspiring candidate may be tempted to build his greatness on the public confusion, but it is the interest as well as duty of a sovereign to maintain the authority of the laws. The first edict of Justinian, which was often repeated, and sometimes executed, announced his firm resolution to support the innocent, and to chastise the guilty of every denomination and *colour*. Yet the balance of justice was still inclined in favour of the blue faction, by the secret affection, the habits, and the fears of the emperor; his equity, after an apparent struggle, submitted, without reluctance, to the implacable passions of Theodora, and the empress never forgot or forgave the injuries of the comedian. At the accession of the younger Justin, the proclamation of equal and rigorous justice indirectly

47. A wife (says Procopius) who was seized and almost ravished by a blue-coat, threw herself into the Bosphorus. The bishops of the second Syria (Aleman. p. 26.) deplore a similar suicide, the guilt or glory of female chastity, and name the heroine.

48. The doubtful credit of Procopius (Anecdot. c. 17.) is supported by the less partial Evagrius, who confirms the fact, and specifies the names. The tragic fate of the præfect of Constantinople is related by John Malala (tom. ii. p. 139.).

condemned the partiality of the former reign. "Ye blues, Justinian is no more! ye greens, he is still alive!"[49]

A sedition, which almost laid Constantinople in ashes, was excited by the mutual hatred and momentary reconciliation of the two factions. In the fifth year of his reign, Justinian celebrated the festival of the ides of January: the games were incessantly disturbed by the clamorous discontent of the greens; till the twenty-second race, the emperor maintained his silent gravity; at length, yielding to his impatience, he condescended to hold, in abrupt sentences, and by the voice of a cryer, the most singular dialogue[50] that ever passed between a prince and his subjects. Their first complaints were respectful and modest; they accused the subordinate ministers of oppression, and proclaimed their wishes for the long life and victory of the emperor. "Be patient and attentive, ye insolent railers," exclaimed Justinian; "be mute, ye Jews, Samaritans, and Manichæans." The greens still attempted to awaken his compassion. "We are poor, we are innocent, we are injured, we dare not pass through the streets: a general persecution is exercised against our name and colour. Let us die, O emperor, but let us die by your command, and for your service!" But the repetition of partial and passionate invectives degraded, in their eyes, the majesty of the purple; they renounced allegiance to the prince who refused justice to his people; lamented that the father of Justinian had been born; and branded his son with the opprobrious names of an homicide, an ass, and a perjured tyrant. "Do you despise your lives?" cried the indignant monarch: the blues rose with fury from their seats; their hostile clamours thundered in the hippodrome; and their adversaries, deserting the unequal contest, spread terror and despair through the streets of Constantinople. At this dangerous moment, seven notorious assassins of both factions, who had been condemned by the præfect, were carried round the city, and afterwards transported to the place of execution in the suburb of Pera. Four were immediately beheaded; a fifth was hanged: but when the same punishment

Sedition of Constantinople, surnamed Nika, *A.D. 532, January.*

---

49. See John Malala (tom. ii. p. 147.); yet he owns that Justinian was attached to the blues. The seeming discord of the emperor and Theodora, is perhaps viewed with too much jealousy and refinement by Procopius (Anecdot. c. 10.). See Aleman. Præfat. p. 6.

50. This dialogue, which Theophanes has preserved, exhibits the popular language, as well as the manners, of Constantinople in the vith century. Their Greek is mingled with many strange and barbarous words, for which Ducange cannot always find a meaning or etymology.

was inflicted on the remaining two, the rope broke, they fell alive to the ground, the populace applauded their escape, and the monks of St. Conon, issuing from the neighbouring convent, conveyed them in a boat to the sanctuary of the church.[51] As one of these criminals was of the blue, and the other of the green livery, the two factions were equally provoked by the cruelty of their oppressor, or the ingratitude of their patron; and a short truce was concluded till they had delivered their prisoners and satisfied their revenge. The palace of the præfect, who withstood the seditious torrent, was instantly burnt, his officers and guards were massacred, the prisons were forced open, and freedom was restored to those who could only use it for the public destruction. A military force, which had been dispatched to the aid of the civil magistrate, was fiercely encountered by an armed multitude, whose numbers and boldness continually encreased; and the Heruli, the wildest Barbarians in the service of the empire, over-turned the priests and their relics, which, from a pious motive, had been rashly interposed to separate the bloody conflict. The tumult was exas-perated by this sacrilege, the people fought with enthusiasm in the cause of God; the women, from the roofs and windows, showered stones on the heads of the soldiers, who darted firebrands against the houses; and the various flames, which had been kindled by the hands of citizens and strangers, spread without controul over the face of the city. The conflag-ration involved the cathedral of St. Sophia, the baths of Zeuxippus, a part of the palace, from the first entrance to the altar of Mars, and the long portico from the palace to the forum of Constantine; a large hospital, with the sick patients, was consumed; many churches and stately edifices were destroyed, and an immense treasure of gold and silver was either melted or lost. From such scenes of horror and distress, the wise and wealthy citizens escaped over the Bosphorus to the Asiatic side; and during five days Constantinople was abandoned to the factions, whose watch-word, NIKA, *vanquish!* has given a name to this memorable sedition.[52]

The distress of Justinian.

As long as the factions were divided, the triumphant blues, and desponding greens, appeared to behold with the same indifference the disorders of the state. They agreed to censure

51. See this church and monastery in Ducange, C. P. Christiana, l. iv. p. 182.
52. The history of the *Nika* sedition is extracted from Marcellinus (in Chron.), Procopius (Persic. l. i. c. 26.), John Malala

(tom. ii. p. 213–218.), Chron. Paschal. (p. 336–340.), Theophanes (Chronograph. p. 154–158.), and Zonaras (l. xiv. p. 61–63.).

the corrupt management of justice and the finances; and the two responsible ministers, the artful Tribonian, and the rapacious John of Cappadocia, were loudly arraigned as the authors of the public misery. The
peaceful murmurs of the people would have been disregarded: they were
heard with respect when the city was in flames; the quæstor, and the
præfect, were instantly removed, and their offices were filled by two senators
of blameless integrity. After this popular concession, Justinian proceeded
to the hippodrome to confess his own errors, and to accept the repentance
of his grateful subjects; but they distrusted his assurances, though solemnly
pronounced in the presence of the holy gospels; and the emperor, alarmed
by their distrust, retreated with precipitation to the strong fortress of the
palace. The obstinacy of the tumult was now imputed to a secret and
ambitious conspiracy; and a suspicion was entertained, that the insurgents,
more especially the green faction, had been supplied with arms and money
by Hypatius and Pompey, two patricians, who could neither forget with
honour, nor remember with safety, that they were the nephews of the
emperor Anastasius. Capriciously trusted, disgraced, and pardoned, by the
jealous levity of the monarch, they had appeared as loyal servants before
the throne; and, during five days of the tumult, they were detained as
important hostages; till at length, the fears of Justinian prevailing over his
prudence, he viewed the two brothers in the light of spies, perhaps of
assassins, and sternly commanded them to depart from the palace. After a
fruitless representation, that obedience might lead to involuntary treason,
they retired to their houses, and in the morning of the sixth day Hypatius
was surrounded and seized by the people, who, regardless of his virtuous
resistance, and the tears of his wife, transported their favourite to the forum
of Constantine, and instead of a diadem, placed a rich collar on his head.
If the usurper, who afterwards pleaded the merit of his delay, had complied
with the advice of his senate, and urged the fury of the multitude, their
first irresistible effort might have oppressed or expelled his trembling
competitor. The Byzantine palace enjoyed a free communication with the
sea; vessels lay ready at the garden-stairs; and a secret resolution was already
formed, to convey the emperor with his family and treasures to a safe
retreat, at some distance from the capital.

Justinian was lost, if the prostitute whom he raised from the
theatre had not renounced the timidity, as well as the virtues, of   *Firmness of*
her sex. In the midst of a council, where Belisarius was present,   *Theodora.*
Theodora alone displayed the spirit of an hero; and she alone, without

apprehending his future hatred, could save the emperor from the imminent danger, and his unworthy fears. "If flight," said the consort of Justinian, "were the only means of safety, yet I should disdain to fly. Death is the condition of our birth; but they who have reigned should never survive the loss of dignity and dominion. I implore heaven, that I may never be seen, not a day, without my diadem and purple; that I may no longer behold the light, when I cease to be saluted with the name of queen. If you resolve, O Cæsar, to fly, you have treasures; behold the sea, you have ships; but tremble lest the desire of life should expose you to wretched exile and ignominious death. For my own part, I adhere to the maxim of antiquity, that the throne is a glorious sepulchre." The firmness of a woman restored the courage to deliberate and act, and courage soon discovers the resources of the most desperate situation. It was an easy and a decisive measure to revive the animosity of the factions; the blue were astonished at their own guilt and folly, that a trifling injury should provoke them to conspire with their implacable enemies against a gracious and liberal benefactor; they again proclaimed the majesty of Justinian, and the greens, with their upstart emperor, were left alone in the hippodrome. The fidelity of the guards was doubtful; but the military force of Justinian consisted in three thousand veterans, who had been trained to valour and discipline in the Persian and Illyrian wars. Under the command of Belisarius and Mundus, they silently marched in two divisions from the palace, forced their obscure way through narrow passages, expiring flames, and falling edifices, and burst open at the same moment the two opposite gates of the hippodrome. In this narrow space, the disorderly and affrighted crowd was incapable of resisting on either side a firm and regular attack; the blues signalized the fury of their repentance; and it is computed, that above thirty thousand persons were slain in the merciless and promiscuous carnage of the day. Hypatius was dragged from his throne, and conducted with his brother Pompey to the feet of the emperor: they implored his clemency; but their crime was manifest, their innocence uncertain, and Justinian had been too much terrified to forgive. The next morning the two nephews of Anastasius, with eighteen *illustrious* accomplices, of patrician or consular rank, were privately executed by the soldiers; their bodies were thrown into the sea, their palaces razed, and their fortunes confiscated. The hippodrome itself was condemned, during several years, to a mournful silence: with the restoration of the games, the same disorders revived; and the blue and green factions continued to

The sedition is suppressed.

afflict the reign of Justinian, and to disturb the tranquillity of the Eastern empire.[53]

III. That empire, after Rome was barbarous, still embraced the nations whom she had conquered beyond the Hadriatic, and as far as the frontiers of Æthiopia and Persia. Justinian reigned over sixty-four provinces, and nine hundred and thirty-five cities;[54] his dominions were blessed by nature with the advantages of soil, situation, and climate: and the improvements of human art had been perpetually diffused along the coast of the Mediterranean and the banks of the Nile, from ancient Troy to the Egyptian Thebes. Abraham[55] had been relieved by the well-known plenty of Egypt; the same country, a small and populous tract, was still capable of exporting, each year, two hundred and sixty thousand quarters of wheat for the use of Constantinople;[56] and the capital of Justinian was supplied with the manufactures of Sidon, fifteen centuries after they had been celebrated in the poems of Homer.[57] The annual powers of vegetation, instead of being exhausted by two thousand harvests, were renewed and invigorated by skilful husbandry, rich manure, and seasonable repose. The breed of domestic animals was infinitely multiplied. Plantations, buildings, and the instruments of labour and luxury, which are more durable than the term of human life, were accumulated by the care of successive generations. Tradition preserved, and experience simplified, the humble practice of the arts: society was enriched by the division of labour and the facility of exchange; and every Roman was lodged, clothed, and subsisted, by the industry of a thousand

Agriculture and manufactures of the Eastern empire.

---

53. Marcellinus says in general terms, innumeris populis in circo trucidatis. Procopius numbers 30,000 victims; and the 35,000 of Theophanes are swelled to 40,000 by the more recent Zonaras. Such is the usual progress of exaggeration.

54. Hierocles, a contemporary of Justinian, composed his Συνδεχμος (Itineraria, p. 631.), or review, of the eastern provinces and cities before the year 535 (Wesseling in Præfat. and Not. ad p. 623, &c.).

55. See the book of Genesis (xii. 10.), and the administration of Joseph. The annals of the Greeks and Hebrews agree in the early arts and plenty of Egypt: but this antiquity supposes a long series of improvement; and Warburton,

who is almost stifled by the Hebrew, calls aloud for the Samaritan, chronology (Divine Legation, vol. iii. p. 29. &c.).

56. Eight millions of Roman modii, besides a contribution of 80,000 aurei for the expences of water-carriage, from which the subject was graciously excused. See the xiiith Edict of Justinian: the numbers are checked and verified by the agreement of the Greek and Latin texts.

57. Homer's Iliad, vi. 289. These veils, πεπλοι παμποικιλοι, were the work of the Sidonian women. But this passage is more honourable to the manufactures than to the navigation of Phœnicia, from whence they had been imported to Troy in Phrygian bottoms.

hands. The invention of the loom and distaff has been piously ascribed to the gods. In every age, a variety of animal and vegetable productions, hair, skins, wool, flax, cotton, and at length *silk*, have been skilfully manufactured to hide or adorn the human body; they were stained with an infusion of permanent colours; and the pencil was successfully employed to improve the labours of the loom. In the choice of those colours[58] which imitate the beauties of nature, the freedom of taste and fashion was indulged; but the deep purple[59] which the Phœnicians extracted from a shell-fish, was restrained to the sacred person and palace of the emperor; and the penalties of treason were denounced against the ambitious subjects, who dared to usurp the prerogative of the throne.[60]

The use of silk by the Romans.

I need not explain that *silk*[61] is originally spun from the bowels of a caterpillar, and that it composes the golden tomb from whence a worm emerges in the form of a butterfly. Till the reign of Justinian, the silk-worms who feed on the leaves of the white mulberry-tree, were confined to China; those of the pine, the oak, and the ash, were common in the forests both of Asia and Europe; but as their education is more difficult, and their produce more uncertain, they were generally neglected, except in the little island of Ceos, near the coast of Attica. A thin gauze was procured from their webs, and this Cean manufacture, the invention of a woman, for female use, was long admired both in the East and at Rome. Whatever suspicions may be raised by the garments of the Medes and Assyrians, Virgil is the most ancient writer, who expressly

58. See in Ovid (de Arte Amandi, iii. 269, &c.) a poetical list of twelve colours borrowed from flowers, the elements, &c. But it is almost impossible to discriminate by words all the nice and various shades both of art and nature. **59**. By the discovery of cochineal, &c. we far surpass the colours of antiquity. Their royal purple had a strong smell, and a dark cast as deep as bull's blood – obscuritas rubens (says Cassiodorius, Var. 1, 2.) nigredo sanguinea. The president Goguet (Origine des Loix et des Arts, part ii. l. ii. c. 2. p. 184–215.) will amuse and satisfy the reader. I doubt whether his book, especially in England, is as well known as it deserves to be.

60. Historical proofs of this jealousy have been occasionally introduced, and many more might have been added: but the arbitrary acts of despotism were justified by the sober and general declarations of law (Codex Theodosian. l. x. tit. 21. leg. 3. Codex Justinian. l. xi. tit. 8. leg. 5.). An inglorious permission, and necessary restriction, was applied to the *mimæ*, the female dancers (Cod. Theodos. l. xv. tit. 7. leg. 11.).

61. In the history of insects (far more wonderful than Ovid's Metamorphoses) the silk-worm holds a conspicuous place. The bombyx of the isle of Ceos, as described by Pliny (Hist. Natur. xi. 26, 27. with the notes of the two learned Jesuits, Hardouin and Brotier), may be illustrated by a similar species in China (Memoires sur les Chinois, tom. ii. p. 575–598.): but our silk-worm, as well as the white mulberry-tree, were unknown to Theophrastus and Pliny.

mentions the soft wool which was combed from the trees of the Seres or Chinese;[62] and this natural error, less marvellous than the truth, was slowly corrected by the knowledge of a valuable insect, the first artificer of the luxury of nations. That rare and elegant luxury was censured, in the reign of Tiberius, by the gravest of the Romans; and Pliny, in affected though forcible language, has condemned the thirst of gain, which explored the last confines of the earth, for the pernicious purpose of exposing to the public eye naked draperies and transparent matrons.[63] A dress which shewed the turn of the limbs, and colour of the skin, might gratify vanity, or provoke desire; the silks which had been closely woven in China, were sometimes unravelled by the Phœnician women, and the precious materials were multiplied by a looser texture, and the intermixture of linen threads.[64] Two hundred years after the age of Pliny, the use of pure or even of mixed silks was confined to the female sex, till the opulent citizens of Rome and the provinces were insensibly familiarised with the example of Elagabalus, the first who, by this effeminate habit, had sullied the dignity of an emperor and a man. Aurelian complained, that a pound of silk was sold at Rome for twelve ounces of gold: but the supply encreased with the demand, and the price diminished with the supply. If accident or monopoly sometimes raised the value even above the standard of Aurelian, the manufacturers of Tyre and Berytus were sometimes compelled by the operation of the same causes to content themselves with a ninth part of that extravagant rate.[65] A law was thought necessary to discriminate the dress of comedians from that of senators, and of the silk exported from its native country the far greater part was consumed by the subjects of Justinian. They were still more

62. Georgic ii. 121. Serica quando venerint in usum planissime non scio: suspicor tamen in Julii Cæsaris ævo, nam ante non invenio, says Justus Lipsius (Excursus i. ad Tacit. Annal. ii. 32.). See Dion Cassius (l. xliii. p. 358. edit. Reimar), and Pausanias (l. vi. p. 519.), the first who describes, however strangely, the Seric insect.

63. Tam longinquo orbe petitur, ut in publico matrona transluceat . . . ut denudet fœminas vestis (Plin. vi. 20. xi. 21.). Varro and Publius Syrus had already played on the Toga vitrea, ventus textilis, and nebula linea (Horat. Sermon. i. 2. 101. with the notes of Torrentius and Dacier).

64. On the texture, colours, names, and use of the silk, half silk, and linen garments of antiquity, see the profound, diffuse, and obscure researches of the great Salmasius (in Hist. August. p. 127. 309, 310. 339. 341, 342. 344. 388—391. 395. 513.), who was ignorant of the most common trades of Dijon or Leyden.

65. Flavius Vopiscus in Aurelian. c. 45. in Hist. August. p. 224. See Salmasius ad Hist. Aug. p. 392. and Plinian. Exercitat. in Solinum, p. 694, 695. The Anecdotes of Procopius (c. 25.) state a partial and imperfect rate of the price of silk in the time of Justinian.

intimately acquainted with a shell-fish of the Mediterranean, surnamed the silk-worm of the sea: the fine wool or hair by which the mother-of-pearl affixes itself to the rock, is now manufactured for curiosity rather than use; and a robe obtained from the same singular materials, was the gift of the Roman emperor to the satraps of Armenia.[66]

Importation from China by land and sea.   A valuable merchandize of small bulk is capable of defraying the expence of land carriage; and the caravans traversed the whole latitude of Asia in two hundred and forty-three days from the Chinese ocean to the sea-coast of Syria. Silk was immediately delivered to the Romans by the Persian merchants,[67] who frequented the fairs of Armenia and Nisibis: but this trade, which in the intervals of truce was oppressed by avarice and jealousy, was totally interrupted by the long wars of the rival monarchies. The great king might proudly number Sogdiana, and even *Serica*, among the provinces of his empire, but his real dominion was bounded by the Oxus; and his useful intercourse with the Sogdoites, beyond the river, depended on the pleasure of their conquerors, the white Huns, and the Turks, who successively reigned over that industrious people. Yet the most savage dominion has not extirpated the seeds of agriculture and commerce, in a region which is celebrated as one of the four gardens of Asia; the cities of Samarcand and Bochara are advantageously seated for the exchange of its various productions; and their merchants purchased from the Chinese[68] the raw or manufactured silk which they transported into Persia for the use of the Roman empire. In the vain capital of China, the Sogdian caravans were entertained as the suppliant embassies of tributary kingdoms, and if they

---

66. Procopius de Edis. l. iii. c. 1. These *pinnes de mer* are found near Smyrna, Sicily, Corsica, and Minorca; and a pair of gloves of their silk was presented to Pope Benedict XIV.

67. Procopius, Persic. l. i. c. 20. l. ii. c. 25. Gothic. l. iv. c. 17. Menander in Excerpt. Legat. p. 107. Of the Parthian or Persian empire, Isidore of Charax (in Stathmis Parthicis, p. 7, 8. in Hudson, Geograph. Minor. tom. ii.) has marked the roads, and Ammianus Marcellinus (l. xxiii. c. 6. p. 400.) has enumerated the provinces.

68. The blind admiration of the Jesuits confounds the different periods of the Chinese history. They are more critically distinguished by M. de Guignes (Hist. des Huns, tom. i. part i. in the Tables, part ii. in the Geography. Memoires de l'Academie des Inscriptions, tom. xxxii. xxxvi. xlii, xliii.), who discovers the gradual progress of the truth of the annals and the extent of the monarchy, till the Christian æra. He has searched, with a curious eye, the connections of the Chinese with the nations of the West: but these connections are slight, casual, and obscure; nor did the Romans entertain a suspicion that the Seres or Sinæ possessed an empire not inferior to their own.

returned in safety, the bold adventure was rewarded with exorbitant gain. But the difficult and perilous march from Samarcand to the first town of Shensi, could not be performed in less than sixty, eighty, or one hundred days: as soon as they had passed the Jaxartes they entered the desert; and the wandering hords, unless they are restrained by armies and garrisons, have always considered the citizen and the traveller as the objects of lawful rapine. To escape the Tartar robbers, and the tyrants of Persia, the silk-caravans explored a more southern road; they traversed the mountains of Thibet, descended the streams of the Ganges or the Indus, and patiently expected, in the ports of Guzerat and Malabar, the annual fleets of the West.[69] But the dangers of the desert were found less intolerable than toil, hunger, and the loss of time; the attempt was seldom renewed, and the only European who has passed that unfrequented way, applauds his own diligence, that, in nine months after his departure from Pekin, he reached the mouth of the Indus. The ocean, however, was open to the free communication of mankind. From the great river to the tropic of Cancer, the provinces of China were subdued and civilized by the emperors of the North; they were filled about the time of the Christian æra with cities and men, mulberry-trees and their precious inhabitants; and if the Chinese, with the knowledge of the compass, had possessed the genius of the Greeks or Phœnicians, they might have spread their discoveries over the southern hemisphere. I am not qualified to examine, and I am not disposed to believe, their distant voyages to the Persian gulf or the Cape of Good Hope: but their ancestors might equal the labours and success of the present race, and the sphere of their navigation might extend from the isles of Japan to the streights of Malacca, the pillars, if we may apply that name, of an Oriental Hercules.[70] Without losing sight of land they might sail along the coast to the extreme promontory of Achin, which is annually visited by ten or twelve ships laden with the productions, the manufactures, and even the artificers, of China; the island of Sumatra and the opposite peninsula,

---

69. The roads from China to Persia and Hindostan may be investigated in the relations of Hackluyt and Thevenot (the ambassadors of Sharokh, Anthony Jenkinson, the Pere Greuber, &c. See likewise Hanway's Travels, vol. i. p. 345–357.). A communication through Thibet has been lately explored by the English sovereigns of Bengal.

70. For the Chinese navigation to Malacca and Achin, perhaps to Ceylon, see Renaudot (on the two Mahometan Travellers, p. 8–11. 13–17. 141–157.), Dampier (vol. ii. p. 136.), the Hist. Philosophique des deux Indes (tom. i. p. 98.), and the Hist. Generale des Voyages (tom. vi. p. 201.).

are faintly delineated[71] as the regions of gold and silver; and the trading cities named in the geography of Ptolemy, may indicate, that this wealth was not solely derived from the mines. The direct interval between Sumatra and Ceylon is about three hundred leagues; the Chinese and Indian navigators were conducted by the flight of birds and periodical winds, and the ocean might be securely traversed in square-built ships, which, instead of iron, were sewed together with the strong thread of the cocoa-nut. Ceylon, Serendib, or Taprobana, was divided between two hostile princes; one of whom possessed the mountains, the elephants, and the luminous carbuncle, and the other enjoyed the more solid riches of domestic industry, foreign trade, and the capacious harbour of Trinquemale, which received and dismissed the fleets of the East and West. In this hospitable isle, at an equal distance (as it was computed) from their respective countries, the silk merchants of China, who had collected in their voyages aloes, cloves, nutmeg, and santal wood, maintained a free and beneficial commerce with the inhabitants of the Persian gulf. The subjects of the great king exalted, without a rival, his power and magnificence; and the Roman, who confounded their vanity by comparing his paltry coin with a gold medal of the emperor Anastatius, had sailed to Ceylon, in an Æthiopian ship, as a simple passenger.[72]

Introduction of silk-worms into Greece. As silk became of indispensable use, the emperor Justinian saw, with concern, that the Persians had occupied by land and sea the monopoly of this important supply, and that the wealth of his subjects was continually drained by a nation of enemies and idolaters. An active government would have restored the trade of Egypt and the navigation of the Red Sea, which had decayed with the prosperity of the empire; and the Roman vessels might have sailed, for the purchase of silk, to the ports of Ceylon, of Malacca, or even of China. Justinian

---

71. The knowledge, or rather ignorance, of Strabo, Pliny, Ptolemy, Arrian, Marcian, &c. of the countries eastward of Cape Comorin, is finely illustrated by d'Anville (Antiquité Geographique de l'Inde, especially p. 161–198.). Our geography of India is improved by commerce and conquest; and has been illustrated by the excellent maps and memoirs of major Rennel. If he extends the sphere of his enquiries with the same critical knowledge and sagacity, he will succeed, and may surpass the first of modern geographers.

72. The Taprobane of Pliny (vi. 24.), Solinus (c. 53.), and Salmas. Plinianæ Exercitat. (p. 781, 782.), and most of the ancients, who often confound the islands of Ceylon and Sumatra, is more clearly described by Cosmas Indicopleustes; yet even the Christian topographer has exaggerated its dimensions. His information on the Indian and Chinese trade is rare and curious (l. ii. p. 138. l. xi. p. 337, 338. edit. Montfaucon).

embraced a more humble expedient, and solicited the aid of his Christian allies, the Æthiopians of Abyssinia, who had recently acquired the arts of navigation, the spirit of trade, and the sea-port of Adulis,[73] still decorated with the trophies of a Grecian conqueror. Along the African coast, they penetrated to the equator in search of gold, emeralds, and aromatics; but they wisely declined an unequal competition, in which they must be always prevented by the vicinity of the Persians to the markets of India; and the emperor submitted to the disappointment, till his wishes were gratified by an unexpected event. The gospel had been preached to the Indians: a bishop already governed the Christians of St. Thomas on the pepper-coast of Malabar; a church was planted in Ceylon, and the missionaries pursued the footsteps of commerce to the extremities of Asia.[74] Two Persian monks had long resided in China, perhaps in the royal city of Nankin, the seat of a monarch addicted to foreign superstitions, and who actually received an embassy from the isle of Ceylon. Amidst their pious occupations, they viewed with a curious eye the common dress of the Chinese, the manufactures of silk, and the myriads of silk-worms, whose education (either on trees or in houses) had once been considered as the labour of queens.[75] They soon discovered that it was impracticable to transport the short-lived insect, but that in the eggs a numerous progeny might be preserved and multiplied in a distant climate. Religion or interest had more power over the Persian monks than the love of their country: after a long journey, they arrived at Constantinople, imparted their project to the emperor, and were liberally encouraged by the gifts and promises of Justinian. To the historians of that prince, a campaign at the foot of mount Caucasus has seemed more deserving of a minute relation than the labours of these missionaries of commerce, who again entered China, deceived a jealous people by concealing the eggs of the silk-worm in a hollow cane, and returned in triumph with the spoils of the East. Under their direction, the eggs were hatched at the proper season by the artificial heat of dung; the worms were fed with

73. See Procopius, Persic. (l. ii. c. 20.). Cosmas affords some interesting knowledge of the port and inscription of Adulis (Topograph. Christ. l. ii. p. 138. 140–143.), and of the trade of the Axumites along the African coast of Barbaria or Zingi (p. 138, 139.), and as far as Taprobane (l. xi. p. 339.).

74. See the Christian missions in India, in Cosmas (l. iii. p. 178, 179. l. xi. p. 337.), and consult Asseman. Bibliot. Orient. (tom. iv. p. 413–548.).

75. The invention, manufacture, and general use of silk in China, may be seen in Duhalde (Description Generale de la Chine, tom. ii. p. 165. 205–223.). The province of Chekian is the most renowned both for quantity and quality.

mulberry leaves; they lived and laboured in a foreign climate; a sufficient number of butterflies was saved to propagate the race, and trees were planted to supply the nourishment of the rising generations. Experience and reflection corrected the errors of a new attempt, and the Sogdoite ambassadors acknowledged, in the succeeding reign, that the Romans were not inferior to the natives of China in the education of the insects, and the manufactures of silk,[76] in which both China and Constantinople have been surpassed by the industry of modern Europe. I am not insensible of the benefits of elegant luxury; yet I reflect with some pain, that if the importers of silk had introduced the art of printing, already practised by the Chinese, the comedies of Menander and the entire decads of Livy would have been perpetuated in the editions of the sixth century. A larger view of the globe might at least have promoted the improvement of speculative science, but the Christian geography was forcibly extracted from texts of scripture, and the study of nature was the surest symptom of an unbelieving mind. The orthodox faith confined the habitable world to *one* temperate zone, and represented the earth as an oblong surface, four hundred days journey in length, two hundred in breadth, encompassed by the ocean, and covered by the solid crystal of the firmament.[77]

State of the revenue.   IV. The subjects of Justinian were dissatisfied with the times, and with the government. Europe was over-run by the Barbarians, and Asia by the monks: the poverty of the West discouraged the trade and manufactures of the East; the produce of labour was consumed by the unprofitable servants of the church, the state, and the army; and a rapid decrease was felt in the fixed and circulating capitals which constitute

---

76. Procopius (l. viii. Gothic. iv. c. 17. Theophanes, Byzant. apud Phot. Cod. lxxxiv. p. 38. Zonaras, tom. ii. l. xiv. p. 69.). Pagi (tom. ii. p. 602.) assigns to the year 552 this memorable importation. Menander (in Excerpt. Legat. p. 107.) mentions the admiration of the Sogdoites; and Theophylact Simocatta (l. vii. c. 9.) darkly represents the two rival kingdoms in *(China)* the country of silk.

77. Cosmas, surnamed Indicopleustes, or the Indian navigator, performed his voyage about the year 522, and composed at Alexandria, between 535 and 547, Christian Topography (Montfaucon, Præfat. c. 1.), in which he refutes the impious opinion, that the earth is a globe; and Photius had read this work (Cod. xxxvi. p. 9, 10.), which displays the prejudices of a monk, with the knowledge of a merchant: the most valuable part has been given in French and in Greek by Melchisedec Thevenot (Relations Curieuses, part i.), and the whole is since published in a splendid edition by the Pere Montfaucon (Nova Collectio Patrum, Paris, 1707. 2 vols. in fol. tom. ii. p. 113–346.). But the editor, a theologian, might blush at not discovering the Nestorian heresy of Cosmas, which has been detected by la Croze (Christianisme des Indes, tom. i. p. 40–56.).

the national wealth. The public distress had been alleviated by the œconomy of Anastasius, and that prudent emperor accumulated an immense treasure while he delivered his people from the most odious or oppressive taxes. Their gratitude universally applauded the abolition of the *gold of affliction*, a personal tribute on the industry of the poor,[78] but more intolerable, as it should seem, in the form than in the substance, since the flourishing city of Edessa paid only one hundred and forty pounds of gold, which was collected in four years from ten thousand artificers.[79] Yet such was the parsimony which supported this liberal disposition, that in a reign of twenty-seven years, Anastasius saved, from his annual revenue, the enormous sum of thirteen millions sterling, or three hundred and twenty thousand pounds of gold.[80] His example was neglected, and his treasure was abused, by the nephew of Justin. The riches of Justinian were speedily exhausted by alms and buildings, by ambitious wars, and ignominious treaties. His revenues were found inadequate to his expences. Every art was tried to extort from the people the gold and silver which he scattered with a lavish hand from Persia to France:[81] his reign was marked by the vicissitudes, or rather by the combat, of rapaciousness and avarice, of splendour and poverty; he lived with the reputation of hidden treasures,[82] and bequeathed to his successor the payment of his debts.[83] Such a character has been justly accused by the voice of the people and of posterity: but public discontent

Avarice and profusion of Justinian.

---

78. Evagrius (l. iii. c. 39, 40.) is minute and grateful, but angry with Zosimus for calumniating the great Constantine. In collecting all the bonds and records of the tax, the humanity of Anastasius was diligent and artful: fathers were sometimes compelled to prostitute their daughters (Zosim. Hist. l. ii. c. 38. p. 165, 166. Lipsiæ, 1784.). Timotheus of Gaza chose such an event for the subject of a tragedy (Suidas, tom. iii. p. 475.), which contributed to the abolition of the tax (Cedrenus, p. 35.) – an happy instance (if it be true) of the use of the theatre.

79. See Josua Stylites, in the Bibliotheca Orientalis of Asseman (tom. i. p. 268.). This capitation tax is slightly mentioned in the Chronicle of Edessa.

80. Procopius (Anecdot. c. 19) fixes this sum from the report of the treasurers themselves.

Tiberius had *vicies ter millies*; but far different was his empire from that of Anastasius.

81. Evagrius (l. iv. c. 30.), in the next generation, was moderate and well informed; and Zonaras (l. xiv. c. 61.), in the xiith century, had read with care, and thought without prejudice: yet their colours are almost as black as those of the Anecdotes.

82. Procopius (Anecdot. c. 30.) relates the idle conjectures of the times. The death of Justinian, says the secret historian, will expose his wealth or poverty.

83. See Corippus de Laudibus Justini Aug. l. ii. 260, &c. 384, &c.

> "Plurima sunt vivo nimium neglecta
>   parenti,
> Unde tot exhaustus contraxit debita
>   fiscus."

is credulous; private malice is bold; and a lover of truth will peruse with a suspicious eye the instructive anecdotes of Procopius. The secret historian represents only the vices of Justinian, and those vices are darkened by his malevolent pencil. Ambiguous actions are imputed to the worst motives: error is confounded with guilt, accident with design, and laws with abuses: the partial injustice of a moment is dextrously applied as the general maxim of a reign of thirty-two years: the emperor alone is made responsible for the faults of his officers, the disorders of the times, and the corruption of his subjects; and even the calamities of nature, plagues, earthquakes, and inundations, are imputed to the prince of the dæmons, who had mischievously assumed the form of Justinian.[84]

Pernicious savings. After this precaution, I shall briefly relate the anecdotes of avarice and rapine, under the following heads: I. Justinian was so profuse that he could not be liberal. The civil and military officers, when they were admitted into the service of the palace, obtained an humble rank and a moderate stipend; they ascended by seniority to a station of affluence and repose; the annual pensions, of which the most honourable class was abolished by Justinian, amounted to four hundred thousand pounds; and this domestic œconomy was deplored by the venal or indigent courtiers as the last outrage on the majesty of the empire. The posts, the salaries of physicians, and the nocturnal illuminations, were objects of more general concern; and the cities might justly complain, that he usurped the municipal revenues which had been appropriated to these useful institutions. Even the soldiers were injured; and such was the decay of military spirit, that they were injured with impunity. The emperor refused, at the return of each fifth year, the customary donative of five pieces of gold, reduced his veterans to beg their bread, and suffered unpaid armies to melt away in the wars of Italy and Persia. II. The humanity of his predecessors *Remittances.* had always remitted, in some auspicious circumstance of their reign, the arrears of the public tribute; and they dextrously assumed the merit of resigning those claims which it was impracticable to enforce. "Justinian, in the space of thirty-two years, has never granted a similar indulgence; and many of his subjects have renounced the possession of those lands whose value is insufficient to satisfy the demands of the treasury.

Centenaries of gold were brought by strong arms into the hippodrome:

"Debita genitoris persolvit, cauta recepit."

84. The Anecdotes (c. 11–14. 18. 20–30.) supply many facts and more complaints.

To the cities which had suffered by hostile inroads, Anastasius promised a general exemption of seven years: the provinces of Justinian have been ravaged by the Persians and Arabs, the Huns and Sclavonians; but his vain and ridiculous dispensation of a single year has been confined to those places which were actually taken by the enemy." Such is the language of the secret historian, who expressly denies that *any* indulgence was granted to Palestine after the revolt of the Samaritans; a false and odious charge, confuted by the authentic record, which attests a relief of thirteen centenaries of gold (fifty-two thousand pounds) obtained for that desolate province by the intercession of St. Sabas.[85] III. Procopius has not condescended to explain the system of taxation, which fell like a hail-storm upon the land, like a devouring pestilence on its inhabitants: but we should become the accomplices of his malignity, if we imputed to Justinian alone the ancient though rigorous principle, that a whole district should be condemned to sustain the partial loss of the persons or property of individuals. The *Anona*, or supply of corn for the use of the army and capital, was a grievous and arbitrary exaction, which exceeded, perhaps in a tenfold proportion, the ability of the farmer; and his distress was aggravated by the partial injustice of weights and measures, and the expence and labour of distant carriage. In a time of scarcity, an extraordinary requisition was made to the adjacent provinces of Thrace, Bithynia, and Phrygia: but the proprietors, after a wearisome journey and a perilous navigation, received so inadequate a compensation, that they would have chosen the alternative of delivering both the corn and price at the doors of their granaries. These precautions might indicate a tender solicitude for the welfare of the capital; yet Constantinople did not escape the rapacious despotism of Justinian. Till his reign, the streights of the Bosphorus and Hellespont were open to the freedom of trade, and nothing was prohibited except the exportation of arms for the service of the Barbarians. At each of these gates of the city, a prætor was stationed, the minister of Imperial avarice; heavy customs were imposed on the vessels and their merchandize; the oppression was retaliated on the helpless consumer: the poor were afflicted by the artificial scarcity, and exorbitant price of the market; and a people, accustomed to depend on the liberality of their prince, might sometimes complain of the

Taxes.

---

85. One to Scythopolis, capital of the second Palestine, and twelve for the rest of the province. Aleman (p. 59.) honestly produces this fact from a MS. life of St. Sabas, by his disciple Cyril, in the Vatican library, and since published by Cotelerius.

deficiency of water and bread.[86] The *aerial* tribute, without a name, a law, or a definite object, was an annual gift of one hundred and twenty thousand pounds, which the emperor accepted from his Prætorian præfect; and the means of payment were abandoned to the discretion of that powerful magistrate. IV. Even such a tax was less intolerable than the

Monopolies. privilege of monopolies, which checked the fair competition of industry, and, for the sake of a small and dishonest gain, imposed an arbitrary burthen on the wants and luxury of the subject. "As soon (I transcribe the anecdotes) as the exclusive sale of silk was usurped by the Imperial treasurer, a whole people, the manufacturers of Tyre and Berytus, was reduced to extreme misery, and either perished with hunger, or fled to the hostile dominions of Persia." A province might suffer by the decay of its manufactures, but in this example of silk, Procopius has partially overlooked the inestimable and lasting benefit which the empire received from the curiosity of Justinian. His addition of one-seventh to the ordinary price of copper-money may be interpreted with the same candour; and the alteration, which might be wise, appears to have been innocent; since he neither allayed the purity, nor enhanced the value, of the gold coin,[87] the legal measure of public and private payments. V. The ample jurisdiction

Venality. required by the farmers of the revenue to accomplish their engagements, might be placed in an odious light, as if they had purchased from the emperor the lives and fortunes of their fellow-citizens. And a more direct sale of honours and offices was transacted in the palace, with the permission, or at least with the connivance, of Justinian and Theodora. The claims of merit, even those of favour, were disregarded, and it was almost reasonable to expect, that the bold adventurer who had undertaken the trade of a magistrate should find a rich compensation for infamy, labour, danger, the debts which he had contracted, and the heavy interest which he paid. A sense of the disgrace and mischief of this venal practice, at length awakened the slumbering virtue of Justinian; and he attempted, by the sanction of oaths[88] and penalties, to guard the integrity of his government:

86. John Malala (tom. ii. p. 232.) mentions the want of bread, and Zonaras (l. xiv. p. 63.) the leaden pipes, which Justinian or his servants stole from the aqueducts.

87. For an aureus, one-sixth of an ounce of gold, instead of 210, he gave no more than 180 folles, or ounces, of copper. A disproportion of the mint, below the market price,

must have soon produced a scarcity of small money. In England, *twelve* pence in copper would sell for no more than *seven* pence (Smith's Inquiry into the Wealth of Nations, vol. i. p. 49.). For Justinian's gold coin, see Evagrius (l. iv. c. 30.).

88. The oath is conceived in the most formidable words (Novell. viii. tit. 3.). The defaulters

but at the end of a year of perjury, his rigorous edict was suspended, and corruption licentiously abused her triumph over the impotence of the laws. VI. The testament of Eulalius, count of the domestics, declared the emperor his sole heir, on condition, however, that *Testaments.* he should discharge his debts and legacies, allow to his three daughters a decent maintenance, and bestow each of them in marriage, with a portion of ten pounds of gold. But the splendid fortune of Eulalius had been consumed by fire; and the inventory of his goods did not exceed the trifling sum of five hundred and sixty-four pieces of gold. A similar instance, in Grecian history, admonished the emperor of the honourable part pre-scribed for his imitation. He checked the selfish murmurs of the treasury, applauded the confidence of his friend, discharged the legacies and debts, educated the three virgins under the eye of the empress Theodora, and doubled the marriage portion which had satisfied the tenderness of their father.[89] The humanity of a prince (for princes cannot be generous) is entitled to some praise; yet even in this act of virtue we may discover the inveterate custom of supplanting the legal or natural heirs, which Procopius imputes to the reign of Justinian. His charge is supported by eminent names and scandalous examples; neither widows nor orphans were spared; and the art of soliciting or extorting or supposing testaments, was beneficially practised by the agents of the palace. This base and mischievous tyranny invades the security of private life; and the monarch who has indulged an appetite for gain will soon be tempted to anticipate the moment of suc-cession, to interpret wealth as an evidence of guilt, and to proceed, from the claim of inheritance, to the power of confiscation. VII. Among the forms of rapine, a philosopher may be permitted to name the conversion of Pagan or heretical riches to the use of the faithful; but in the time of Justinian, this holy plunder was condemned by the sectaries alone, who became the victims of his orthodox avarice.[90]

Dishonour might be ultimately reflected on the character of Justinian; but much of the guilt, and still more of the profit, was intercepted by the ministers, who were seldom promoted for *The ministers of Justinian.*

---

imprecate on themselves, quicquid habent telorum armamentaria cœli: the part of Judas, the leprosy of Giezi, the tremor of Cain, &c. besides all temporal pains.

89. A similar or more generous act of friend-

ship is related by Lucian of Eudamidas of Corinth (in Toxare, c. 22, 23. tom. ii. p. 530.), and the story has produced an ingenious, though feeble, comedy of Fontenelle.

90. John Malala, tom. ii. p. 101, 102, 103.

their virtues, and not always selected for their talents.[91] The merits of Tribonian the quæstor will hereafter be weighed in the reformation of the Roman law; but the œconomy of the East was subordinate to the Prætorian præfect, and Procopius has justified his anecdotes by the portrait which he exposes in his public history, of the notorious vices of John of Cappadocia.[92] His knowledge was not borrowed from the schools,[93] and his style was scarcely legible; but he excelled in the powers of native genius, to suggest the wisest counsels, and to find expedients in the most desperate situations. The corruption of his heart was equal to the vigour of his understanding. Although he was suspected of magic and Pagan superstition, he appeared insensible to the fear of God or the reproaches of man; and his aspiring fortune was raised on the death of thousands, the poverty of millions, the ruin of cities, and the desolation of provinces. From the dawn of light to the moment of dinner, he assiduously laboured to enrich his master and himself at the expence of the Roman world; the remainder of the day was spent in sensual and obscene pleasures, and the silent hours of the night were interrupted by the perpetual dread of the justice of an assassin. His abilities, perhaps his vices, recommended him to the lasting friendship of Justinian: the emperor yielded with reluctance to the fury of the people; his victory was displayed by the immediate restoration of their enemy; and they felt above ten years, under his oppressive administration, that he was stimulated by revenge, rather than instructed by misfortune. Their murmurs served only to fortify the resolution of Justinian; but the præfect, in the insolence of favour, provoked the resentment of Theodora, disdained a power before which every knee was bent, and attempted to sow the seeds of discord between the emperor and his beloved consort. Even Theodora herself was constrained to dissemble, to wait a favourable moment, and by an artful conspiracy to render John of Cappadocia the accomplice of his own destruction. At a time when Belisarius, unless he had been a hero, must have shewn himself a rebel, his wife Antonina, who enjoyed the secret

John of Cappadocia.

91. One of these, Anatolius, perished in an earthquake – doubtless a judgment! The complaints and clamours of the people in Agathias (l. v. p. 146, 147.) are almost an echo of the anecdote. The aliena pecunia reddenda of Corippus (l. ii. 381, &c.) is not very honourable to Justinian's memory.
92. See the history and character of John of

Cappadocia in Procopius (Persic. l. i. c. 24, 25. l. ii. c. 30. Vandal. l. i. c. 13. Anecdot. c. 2. 17. 22.). The agreement of the history and anecdotes is a mortal wound to the reputation of the præfect.
93. Ου γαρ αλλο ουδεν ες γραμματιστους φοιτων εμαθεν οτι μη γραμματα, και ταυτα κακα κακως γραψαι – a forcible expression.

confidence of the empress, communicated his feigned discontent to Euphemia the daughter of the præfect; the credulous virgin imparted to her father the dangerous project, and John, who might have known the value of oaths and promises, was tempted to accept a nocturnal, and almost treasonable, interview with the wife of Belisarius. An ambuscade of guards and eunuchs had been posted by the command of Theodora; they rushed with drawn swords to seize or to punish the guilty minister: he was saved by the fidelity of his attendants; but instead of appealing to a gracious sovereign, who had privately warned him of his danger, he pusillanimously fled to the sanctuary of the church. The favourite of Justinian was sacrificed to conjugal tenderness or domestic tranquillity; the conversion of a præfect into a priest extinguished his ambitious hopes; but the friendship of the emperor alleviated his disgrace, and he retained in the mild exile of Cyzicus an ample portion of his riches. Such imperfect revenge could not satisfy the unrelenting hatred of Theodora; the murder of his old enemy, the bishop of Cyzicus, afforded a decent pretence; and John of Cappadocia, whose actions had deserved a thousand deaths, was at last condemned for a crime of which he was innocent. A great minister, who had been invested with the honours of consul and patrician, was ignominiously scourged like the vilest of malefactors; a tattered cloak was the sole remnant of his fortunes; he was transported in a bark to the place of his banishment at Antinopolis in Upper Egypt, and the præfect of the East begged his bread through the cities which had trembled at his name. During an exile of seven years, his life was protracted and threatened by the ingenious cruelty of Theodora; and when her death permitted the emperor to recall a servant whom he had abandoned with regret, the ambition of John of Cappadocia was reduced to the humble duties of the sacerdotal profession. His successors convinced the subjects of Justinian, that the arts of oppression might still be improved by experience and industry; the frauds of a Syrian banker were introduced into the administration of the finances; and the example of the præfect was diligently copied by the quæstor, the public and private treasurer, the governors of provinces, and the principal magistrates of the Eastern empire.[94]

---

94. The chronology of Procopius is loose and obscure; but with the aid of Pagi I can discern that John was appointed Prætorian præfect of the East in the year 530; that he was removed in January 532 – restored before June 533 – banished in 541 – and recalled between June 548 and April 1, 549. Aleman (p. 96, 97.) gives the list of his ten successors – a rapid series in a part of a single reign.

His edifices and architects.

V. The *edifices* of Justinian were cemented with the blood and treasure of his people; but those stately structures appeared to announce the prosperity of the empire, and actually displayed the skill of their architects. Both the theory and practice of the arts which depend on mathematical science and mechanical power were cultivated under the patronage of the emperors; the fame of Archimedes was rivalled by Proclus and Anthemius; and if their *miracles* had been related by intelligent spectators, they might now enlarge the speculations, instead of exciting the distrust, of philosophers. A tradition has prevailed, that the Roman fleet was reduced to ashes in the port of Syracuse by the burning-glasses of Archimedes;[95] and it is asserted that a similar expedient was employed by Proclus to destroy the Gothic vessels in the harbour of Constantinople, and to protect his benefactor Anastasius against the bold enterprize of Vitalian.[96] A machine was fixed on the walls of the city, consisting of an hexagon mirror of polished brass, with many smaller and moveable polygons to receive and reflect the rays of the meridian sun; and a consuming flame was darted to the distance, perhaps, of two hundred feet.[97] The truth of these two extraordinary facts is invalidated by the silence of the most authentic historians; and the use of burning-glasses was never adopted in the attack or defence of places.[98] Yet the admirable experiments of a French philosopher[99] have demonstrated the possibility of such a mirror; and, since it is possible, I am more disposed to attribute the art to the greatest mathematicians of antiquity, than to give the merit of the fiction to the

95. This conflagration is hinted by Lucian (in Hippia, c. 2.) and Galen (l. iii. de Temperamentis, tom. i. p. 81. edit. Basil.) in the second century. A thousand years afterwards, it is positively affirmed by Zonaras (l. ix. p. 424.), on the faith of Dion Cassius, by Tzetzes (Chiliad ii. 119, &c.), Eustathius (ad Iliad E. p. 338.), and the scholiast of Lucian. See Fabricius (Bibliot. Græc. l. iii. c. 22. tom. ii. p. 551, 552.), to whom I am more or less indebted for several of these quotations.

96. Zonaras (l. xiv. p. 55.) affirms the fact, without quoting any evidence.

97. Tzetzes describes the artifice of these burning-glasses, which he had read, perhaps with no learned eyes, in a mathematical treatise of Anthemius. That treatise, περι παραδοξων μηχαμηματων, has been lately published,

translated, and illustrated by M. Dupuys, a scholar and a mathematician (Memoires de l'Academie des Inscriptions, tom. xlii. p. 392–451.).

98. In the siege of Syracuse, by the silence of Polybius, Plutarch, Livy; in the siege of Constantinople, by that of Marcellinus and all the contemporaries of the vith century.

99. Without any previous knowledge of Tzetzes or Anthemius, the immortal Buffon imagined and executed a set of burning-glasses, with which he could inflame planks at the distance of 200 feet (Supplement a l'Hist. Naturelle, tom. i. p. 399–483. quarto edition). What miracles would not his genius have performed for the public service, with royal expence, and in the strong sun of Constantinople or Syracuse?

idle fancy of a monk or a sophist. According to another story, Proclus applied sulphur to the destruction of the Gothic fleet;[100] in a modern imagination, the name of sulphur is instantly connected with the suspicion of gun-powder, and that suspicion is propagated by the secret arts of his disciple Anthemius.[101] A citizen of Tralles in Asia had five sons, who were all distinguished in their respective professions by merit and success. Olympius excelled in the knowledge and practice of the Roman jurisprudence. Dioscorus and Alexander became learned physicians; but the skill of the former was exercised for the benefit of his fellow-citizens, while his more ambitious brother acquired wealth and reputation at Rome. The fame of Metrodorus the grammarian, and of Anthemius the mathematician and architect, reached the ears of the emperor Justinian, who invited them to Constantinople; and while the one instructed the rising generation in the schools of eloquence, the other filled the capital and provinces with more lasting monuments of his art. In a trifling dispute relative to the walls or windows of their contiguous houses, he had been vanquished by the eloquence of his neighbour Zeno; but the orator was defeated in his turn by the master of mechanics, whose malicious, though harmless stratagems, are darkly represented by the ignorance of Agathias. In a lower room, Anthemius arranged several vessels or cauldrons of water, each of them covered by the wide bottom of a leathern tube, which rose to a narrow top, and was artificially conveyed among the joists and rafters of the adjacent building. A fire was kindled beneath the cauldron; the steam of the boiling water ascended through the tubes; the house was shaken by the efforts of imprisoned air, and its trembling inhabitants might wonder that the city was unconscious of the earthquake which they had felt. At another time, the friends of Zeno, as they sat at table, were dazzled by the intolerable light which flashed in their eyes from the reflecting mirrors of Anthemius: they were astonished by the noise which he produced from the collision of certain minute and sonorous particles; and the orator declared in tragic style to the senate, that a mere mortal must yield to the power of an antagonist, who shook the earth with the trident of Neptune, and imitated the thunder and lightning of Jove himself. The genius of Anthemius and his colleague Isidore the Milesian, was excited and employed by a prince,

100. John Malala (tom. ii. p. 120–124.) relates the fact; but he seems to confound the names or persons of Proclus and Marinus.

101. Agathias, l. v. p. 149–152. The merit of Anthemius as an architect is loudly praised by Procopius (de Edif. l. i. c. 1.) and Paulus Silentiarius (part i. 134, &c.).

whose taste for architecture had degenerated into a mischievous and costly passion. His favourite architects submitted their designs and difficulties to Justinian, and discreetly confessed how much their laborious meditations were surpassed by the intuitive knowledge or celestial inspiration of an emperor, whose views were always directed to the benefit of his people, the glory of his reign, and the salvation of his soul.[102]

Foundation of the church of St. Sophia.

The principal church, which was dedicated by the founder of Constantinople to saint Sophia, or the eternal wisdom, had been twice destroyed by fire; after the exile of John Chrysostom, and during the *Nika* of the blue and green factions. No sooner did the tumult subside, than the Christian populace deplored their sacrilegious rashness; but they might have rejoiced in the calamity, had they foreseen the glory of the new temple, which at the end of forty days was strenuously undertaken by the piety of Justinian.[103] The ruins were cleared away, a more spacious plan was described, and as it required the consent of some proprietors of ground, they obtained the most exorbitant terms from the eager desires and timorous conscience of the monarch. Anthemius formed the design, and his genius directed the hands of ten thousand workmen, whose payment in pieces of fine silver was never delayed beyond the evening. The emperor himself, clad in a linen tunic, surveyed each day their rapid progress, and encouraged their diligence by his familiarity, his zeal, and his rewards. The new cathedral of St. Sophia was consecrated by the patriarch, five years, eleven months, and ten days from the first founda-

102. See Procopius (de Edificiis, l. i. c. 1, 2. l. ii. c. 3.). He relates a coincidence of dreams, which supposes some fraud in Justinian or his architect. They both saw, in a vision, the same plan for stopping an inundation at Dara. A stone-quarry near Jerusalem was revealed to the emperor (l. v. c. 6.): an angel was tricked into the perpetual custody of St. Sophia (Anonym. de Antiq. C.P. l. iv. p. 70.).

103. Among the crowd of ancients and moderns who have celebrated the edifice of St. Sophia, I shall distinguish and follow, 1. Four original spectators and historians: Procopius (de Edific. l. i. c. 1.), Agathias (l. v. p. 152, 153.), Paul Silentiarius (in a poem of 1026 hexameters, ad calcem Annæ Comnen. Alexiad.), and Evagrius (l. iv. c. 31.). 2. Two legendary Greeks of a later period: George

Codinus (de Origin. C.P. p. 64–74.), and the anonymous writer of Banduri (Imp. Orient, tom. i. l. iv. p. 65–80.). 3. The great Byzantine antiquarian, Ducange (Comment. ad Paul Silentiar. p. 525–598. and C.P. Christ. l. iii. p. 5–78). 4. Two French travellers – the one, Peter Gyllius (de Topograph. C.P. l. ii. c. 3, 4.) in the xvith; the other, Grelot (Voyage de C.P. p. 95–164. Paris, 1680. in 4to): he has given plans, prospects, and inside-views of St. Sophia; and his plans, though on a smaller scale, appear more correct than those of Ducange. I have adopted and reduced the measures of Grelot: but as no Christian can now ascend the dome, the height is borrowed from Evagrius, compared with Gyllius, Greaves, and the Oriental Geographer.

tion; and in the midst of the solemn festival, Justinian exclaimed with devout vanity, "Glory be to God, who hath thought me worthy to accomplish so great a work; I have vanquished thee, O Solomon"[104]! But the pride of the Roman Solomon, before twenty years had elapsed, was humbled by an earthquake, which overthrew the eastern part of the dome. Its splendour was again restored by the perseverance of the same prince; and in the thirty-sixth year of his reign, Justinian celebrated the second dedication of a temple, which remains, after twelve centuries, a stately monument of his fame. The architecture of St. Sophia, which is now converted into the principal mosch, has been imitated by the Turkish sultans, and that venerable pile continues to excite the fond admiration of the Greeks, and the more rational curiosity of European travellers.

Description.

The eye of the spectator is disappointed by an irregular prospect of half-domes and shelving roofs: the western front, the principal approach, is destitute of simplicity and magnificence; and the scale of dimensions has been much surpassed by several of the Latin cathedrals. But the architect who first erected an *aerial* cupola, is entitled to the praise of bold design and skilful execution. The dome of St. Sophia, illuminated by four and twenty windows, is formed with so small a curve, that the depth is equal only to one-sixth of its diameter; the measure of that diameter is one hundred and fifteen feet, and the lofty center, where a crescent has supplanted the cross, rises to the perpendicular height of one hundred and eighty feet above the pavement. The circle which encompasses the dome, lightly reposes on four strong arches, and their weight is firmly supported by four massy piles, whose strength is assisted on the northern and southern sides by four columns of Egyptian granite. A Greek cross, inscribed in a quadrangle, represents the form of the edifice; the exact breadth is two hundred and forty-three feet, and two hundred and sixty-nine may be assigned for the extreme length from the sanctuary in the east to the nine western doors which open into the vestibule, and from thence into the *narthex* or exterior portico. That portico was the humble station of the penitents. The nave or body of the church was filled by the congregation of the faithful; but the two sexes were prudently distinguished, and the upper and lower

---

104. Solomon's temple was surrounded with courts, porticos, &c.; but the proper structure of the house of God was no more (if we take the Egyptian or Hebrew cubit at 22 inches) than 55 feet in height, 36⅔ in breadth, and

110 in length – a small parish church, says Prideaux (Connection, vol. i. p. 144. folio); but few sanctuaries could be valued at four or five millions sterling!

galleries were allotted for the more private devotion of the women. Beyond the northern and southern piles, a balustrade, terminated on either side by the thrones of the emperor and the patriarch, divided the nave from the choir: and the space, as far as the steps of the altar, was occupied by the clergy and singers. The altar itself, a name which insensibly became familiar to Christian ears, was placed in the eastern recess, artificially built in the form of a demi-cylinder; and this sanctuary communicated by several doors with the sacristy, the vestry, the baptistery, and the contiguous buildings, subservient either to the pomp of worship, or the private use of the ecclesiastical ministers. The memory of past calamities inspired Justinian with a wise resolution, that no wood, except for the doors, should be admitted into the new edifice; and the choice of the materials was applied to the strength, the lightness, or the splendour of the respective parts. The solid piles which sustained the cupola were composed of huge blocks of freestone, hewn into squares and triangles, fortified by circles of iron, and firmly cemented by the infusion of lead and quicklime: but the weight of the cupola was diminished by the levity of its substance, which consists either of pumice-stone that floats in the water, or of bricks from the isle of Rhodes, five times less ponderous than the ordinary sort. The whole frame of the edifice was constructed of brick; but those base materials were concealed by a crust of marble; and the inside of St. Sophia, the cupola, the two larger, and the six smaller semi-domes, the walls, the hundred columns, and the pavement, delight even the eyes of Barbarians, with a rich and variegated picture. A poet,[105] who beheld the primitive lustre of St. Sophia, enumerates the colours, the shades, and the spots of ten or

Marbles. twelve marbles, jaspers, and porphyries, which nature had profusely diversified, and which were blended and contrasted as it were by a skilful painter. The triumph of Christ was adorned with the last spoils of Paganism, but the greater part of these costly stones was extracted from the quarries of Asia Minor, the isles and continent of Greece, Egypt, Africa,

---

105. Paul Silentiarius, in dark and poetic language, describes the various stones and marbles that were employed in the edifice of St. Sophia (P. ii. p. 129. 133, &c. &c.): 1. The *Carystian* – pale, with iron veins. 2. The *Phrygian* – of two sorts, both of a rosy hue; the one with a white shade, the other purple, with silver flowers. 3. The *Porphry of Egypt* – with small stars. 4. The *green marble of Laconia.*

5. The *Carian* – from Mount Iassis, with oblique veins, white and red. 6. The *Lydian* – pale, with a red flower. 7. The *African,* or *Mauritanian* – of a gold or saffron hue. 8. The *Celtic* – black, with white veins. 9. The *Bosphoric* – white, with black edges. Besides the *Proconnesian*, which formed the pavement; the *Thessalian, Molossian,* &c. which are less distinctly painted.

and Gaul. Eight columns of porphyry, which Aurelian had placed in the temple of the sun, were offered by the piety of a Roman matron; eight others of green marble were presented by the ambitious zeal of the magistrates of Ephesus: both are admirable by their size and beauty, but every order of architecture disclaims their fantastic capitals. A variety of ornaments and figures was curiously expressed in mosaic; and the images of Christ, of the Virgin, of saints, and of angels, which have been defaced by Turkish fanaticism, were dangerously exposed to the superstition of the Greeks. According to the sanctity of each object, the precious metals were distributed in thin leaves or in solid masses. The balustrade of the choir, the capitals of the pillars, the ornaments of the doors and galleries, were of gilt bronze; the spectator was dazzled by the glittering aspect of the cupola; the sanctuary contained forty thousand pound weight of silver; and the holy vases and vestments of the altar were of the purest gold, enriched with inestimable gems. Before the structure of the church had arisen two cubits above the ground, forty-five thousand two hundred pounds were already *Riches.* consumed; and the whole expence amounted to three hundred and twenty thousand: each reader, according to the measure of his belief, may estimate their value either in gold or silver; but the sum of one million sterling is the result of the lowest computation. A magnificent temple is a laudable monument of national taste and religion, and the enthusiast who entered the dome of St. Sophia, might be tempted to suppose that it was the residence, or even the workmanship of the Deity. Yet how dull is the artifice, how insignificant is the labour, if it be compared with the formation of the vilest insect that crawls upon the surface of the temple!

So minute a description of an edifice which time has respected, may attest the truth, and excuse the relation, of the innumerable *Churches and palaces.* works, both in the capital and provinces, which Justinian constructed on a smaller scale and less durable foundations.[106] In Constantinople alone, and the adjacent suburbs, he dedicated twenty-five churches to the honour of Christ, the Virgin, and the saints: most of these churches were decorated with marble and gold; and their various situation was skilfully chosen in a populous square, or a pleasant grove; on the margin of the

---

106. The six books of the Edifices of Procopius are thus distributed: the *first* is confined to Constantinople; the *second* includes Mesopotamia and Syria; the *third*, Armenia and the Euxine; the *fourth*, Europe; the *fifth*, Asia Minor and Palestine; the *sixth*, Egypt and Africa. Italy is forgot by the emperor or the historian, who published this work of adulation before the date (A.D. 555.) of its final conquest.

sea-shore, or on some lofty eminence which overlooked the continents of Europe and Asia. The church of the Holy Apostles at Constantinople, and that of St. John at Ephesus, appear to have been framed on the same model: their domes aspired to imitate the cupolas of St. Sophia; but the altar was more judiciously placed under the center of the dome, at the junction of four stately porticoes, which more accurately expressed the figure of the Greek cross. The Virgin of Jerusalem might exult in the temple erected by her Imperial votary on a most ungrateful spot, which afforded neither ground nor materials to the architect. A level was formed, by raising part of a deep valley to the height of the mountain. The stones of a neighbouring quarry were hewn into regular forms; each block was fixed on a peculiar carriage drawn by forty of the strongest oxen, and the roads were widened for the passage of such enormous weights. Lebanon furnished her loftiest cedars for the timbers of the church; and the seasonable discovery of a vein of red marble, supplied its beautiful columns, two of which, the supporters of the exterior portico, were esteemed the largest in the world. The pious munificence of the emperor was diffused over the Holy Land; and if reason should condemn the monasteries of both sexes which were built or restored by Justinian, yet charity must applaud the wells which he sunk, and the hospitals which he founded, for the relief of the weary pilgrims. The schismatical temper of Egypt was ill-entitled to the royal bounty; but in Syria and Africa some remedies were applied to the disasters of wars and earthquakes, and both Carthage and Antioch, emerging from their ruins, might revere the name of their gracious benefactor.[107] Almost every saint in the calendar acquired the honours of a temple; almost every city of the empire obtained the solid advantages of bridges, hospitals, and aqueducts; but the severe liberality of the monarch disdained to indulge his subjects in the popular luxury of baths and theatres. While Justinian laboured for the public service, he was not unmindful of his own dignity and ease. The Byzantine palace, which had been damaged by the conflagration, was restored with new magnificence; and some notion may be conceived of the whole edifice, by the vestibule or hall, which, from the doors perhaps, or the roof, was surnamed *chalce*, or the brazen. The dome of a spacious quadrangle was supported by massy pillars; the pavement and walls were

---

107. Justinian once gave forty-five centenaries of gold (180,000*l.*) for the repairs of Antioch after the earthquake (John Malala, tom. ii. p. 146–149.).

incrusted with many-coloured marbles – the emerald green of Laconia, the fiery red, and the white Phrygian stone intersected with veins of a sea-green hue: the mosaic paintings of the dome and sides represented the glories of the African and Italian triumphs. On the Asiatic shore of the Propontis, at a small distance to the east of Chalcedon, the costly palace and gardens of Heræum[108] were prepared for the summer residence of Justinian, and more especially of Theodora. The poets of the age have celebrated the rare alliance of nature and art, the harmony of the nymphs of the groves, the fountains, and the waves; yet the crowd of attendants who followed the court complained of their inconvenient lodgings,[109] and the nymphs were too often alarmed by the famous Porphyrio, a whale of ten cubits in breadth, and thirty in length, who was stranded at the mouth of the river Sangaris, after he had infested more than half a century the seas of Constantinople.[110]

The fortifications of Europe and Asia were multiplied by Justinian; but the repetition of those timid and fruitless precautions exposes to a philosophic eye the debility of the empire.[111] From Belgrade to the Euxine, from the conflux of the Save to the mouth of the Danube, a chain of above fourscore fortified places was extended along the banks of the great river. Single watch-towers were changed into spacious citadels; vacant walls, which the engineers contracted or enlarged according to the nature of the ground, were filled with colonies or garrisons; a strong fortress defended the ruins of Trajan's bridge,[112] and several military stations

Fortifications of Europe.

---

108. For the Heræum, the palace of Theodora, see Gyllius (de Bosphoro Thracio, l. iii. c. xi.), Aleman (Not. ad Anecdot. p. 80, 81. who quotes several epigrams of the Anthology), and Ducange (C.P. Christ. l. iv. c. 13. p. 175, 176.).

109. Compare, in the Edifices (l. i. c. 11.) and in the Anecdotes (c. 8. 15.), the different styles of adulation and malevolence: stript of the paint, or cleansed from the dirt, the object appears to be the same.

110. Procopius, l. viii. 29.; most probably a stranger and wanderer, as the Mediterranean does not breed whales. Balænæ quoque in nostra maria penetrant (Plin. Hist. Natur. ix. 2.). Between the polar circle and the tropic, the cetaceous animals of the ocean grow to

the length of 50, 80, or 100 feet (Hist. des Voyages, tom. xv. p. 289. Pennant's British Zoology, vol. iii. p. 35.).

111. Montesquieu observes (tom. iii. p. 503. Considerations sur la Grandeur et la Decadence des Romains, c. xx.) that Justinian's empire was like France in the time of the Norman inroads – never so weak as when every village was fortified.

112. Procopius affirms (l. iv. c. 6.) that the Danube was stopped by the ruins of the bridge. Had Apollodorus, the architect, left a description of his own work, the fabulous wonders of Dion Cassius (l. lxviii. p. 1129.) would have been corrected by the genuine picture. Trajan's bridge consisted of twenty or twenty-two stone piles, with wooden arches; the

affected to spread beyond the Danube the pride of the Roman name. But that name was divested of its terrors; the Barbarians, in their annual inroads, passed, and contemptuously repassed, before these useless bulwarks, and the inhabitants of the frontier, instead of reposing under the shadow of the general defence, were compelled to guard, with incessant vigilance, their separate habitations. The solitude of ancient cities was replenished; the new foundations of Justinian acquired, perhaps too hastily, the epithets of impregnable and populous; and the auspicious place of his own nativity attracted the grateful reverence of the vainest of princes. Under the name of *Justiniana prima*, the obscure village of Tauresium became the seat of an archbishop and a præfect, whose jurisdiction extended over seven warlike provinces of Illyricum;[113] and the corrupt appellation of *Giustendil* still indicates, about twenty miles to the south of Sophia, the residence of a Turkish sanjak.[114] For the use of the emperor's countrymen, a cathedral, a palace, and an aqueduct, were speedily constructed; the public and private edifices were adapted to the greatness of a royal city; and the strength of the walls resisted, during the life-time of Justinian, the unskilful assaults of the Huns and Sclavonians. Their progress was sometimes retarded, and their hopes of rapine were disappointed, by the innumerable castles, which in the provinces of Dacia, Epirus, Thessaly, Macedonia, and Thrace, appeared to cover the whole face of the country. Six hundred of these forts were built or repaired by the emperor; but it seems reasonable to believe, that the far greater part consisted only of a stone or brick tower, in the midst of a square or circular area, which was surrounded by a wall and ditch, and afforded in a moment of danger some protection to the peasants and cattle of the neighbouring villages.[115] Yet these military works, which exhausted the public treasure, could not remove the just apprehensions of Justinian and his European subjects. The warm baths of Anchialus in Thrace were

---

river is shallow, the current gentle, and the whole interval no more than 443 (Reimar ad Dion. from Marsigli) or 515 *toises* (d'Anville Geographie Ancienne, tom. i. p. 305.).

113. Of the two Dacias, *Mediterranea* and *Ripensis*, Dardania, Prævalitana, the second Mæsia, and the second Macedonia. See Justinian (Novell. xi.), who speaks of his castles beyond the Danube, and of homines semper bellicis sudoribus inhærentes.

114. See d'Anville (Memoires de l'Academie,

&c. tom. xxxi. p. 289, 290.), Rycaut (Present State of the Turkish Empire, p. 97. 316.), Marsigli (Stato Militare del Imperio Ottomano, p. 130.). The sanjak of Giustendil is one of the twenty under the beglerbeg of Rumelia, and his district maintains 48 *zaims* and 588 *timariots*.

115. These fortifications may be compared to the castles in Mingrelia (Chardin, Voyages en Perse, tom. i. p. 60. 131.) – a natural picture.

rendered as safe as they were salutary; but the rich pastures of Thessalonica were foraged by the Scythian cavalry; the delicious vale of Tempe, three hundred miles from the Danube, was continually alarmed by the sound of war;[116] and no unfortified spot, however distant or solitary, could securely enjoy the blessings of peace. The streights of Thermopylæ, which seemed to protect, but which had so often betrayed, the safety of Greece, were diligently strengthened by the labours of Justinian. From the edge of the sea-shore, through the forests and vallies, and as far as the summit of the Thessalian mountains, a strong wall was continued, which occupied every practicable entrance. Instead of an hasty crowd of peasants, a garrison of two thousand soldiers was stationed along the rampart; granaries of corn, and reservoirs of water, were provided for their use; and by a precaution that inspired the cowardice which it foresaw, convenient fortresses were erected for their retreat. The walls of Corinth, overthrown by an earthquake, and the mouldering bulwarks of Athens and Platæa, were carefully restored; the Barbarians were discouraged by the prospect of successive and painful sieges; and the naked cities of Peloponnesus were covered by the fortifications of the isthmus of Corinth. At the extremity of Europe, another peninsula, the Thracian Chersonesus, runs three days journey into the sea, to form, with the adjacent shores of Asia, the streights of the Hellespont. The intervals between eleven populous towns were filled by lofty woods, fair pastures, and arable lands; and the isthmus, of thirty-seven stadia or furlongs, had been fortified by a Spartan general nine hundred years before the reign of Justinian.[117] In an age of freedom and valour, the slightest rampart may prevent a surprise; and Procopius appears insensible of the superiority of ancient times, while he praises the solid construction and double parapet of a wall, whose long arms stretched on either side into the sea; but whose strength was deemed insufficient to guard the Chersonesus, if each city, and particularly Gallipoli and Sestus, had not been secured by their peculiar fortifications. The *long* wall, as it was emphatically styled, was a work as disgraceful in the object, as it was respectable in the execution. The riches of a capital diffuse themselves over the neighbouring country,

116. The valley of Tempe is situate along the river Peneus, between the hills of Ossa and Olympus: it is only five miles long, and in some places no more than 120 feet in breadth. Its verdant beauties are elegantly described by Pliny (Hist. Natur. l. iv. 15.), and more diffusely by Ælian (Hist. Var. l. iii. c. 1.).

117. Xenophon Hellenic. l. iii. c. 2. After a long and tedious conversation with the Byzantine declaimers, how refreshing is the truth, the simplicity, the elegance of an Attic writer!

and the territory of Constantinople, a paradise of nature, was adorned with the luxurious gardens and villas of the senators and opulent citizens. But their wealth served only to attract the bold and rapacious Barbarians; the noblest of the Romans, in the bosom of peaceful indolence, were led away into Scythian captivity, and their sovereign might view from his palace the hostile flames which were insolently spread to the gates of the Imperial city. At the distance only of forty miles, Anastasius was constrained to establish a last frontier; his long wall of sixty miles from the Propontis to the Euxine, proclaimed the impotence of his arms; and as the danger became more imminent, new fortications were added by the indefatigable prudence of Justinian.[118]

Security of Asia, after the conquest of Isauria.   Asia Minor, after the submission of the Isaurians,[119] remained without enemies and without fortifications. Those bold savages, who had disdained to be the subjects of Gallienus, persisted two hundred and thirty years in a life of independence and rapine. The most successful princes respected the strength of the mountains and the despair of the natives; their fierce spirit was sometimes soothed with gifts, and sometimes restrained by terror; and a military count, with three legions, fixed his permanent and ignominious station in the heart of the Roman provinces.[120] But no sooner was the vigilance of power relaxed or diverted, than the light-armed squadrons descended from the hills, and invaded the peaceful plenty of Asia. Although the Isaurians were not remarkable for stature or bravery, want rendered them bold, and experience made them skilful in the exercise of predatory war. They advanced with secrecy and speed to the attack of villages and defenceless towns; their flying parties have sometimes touched the Hellespont, the Euxine, and the gates of Tarsus, Antioch, or Damascus;[121] and the spoil was lodged in their inaccessible mountains, before the Roman troops had received their orders, or the distant province had computed its loss. The guilt of rebellion and robbery excluded them from the rights of national enemies; and the

118. See the long wall in Evagrius (l. iv. c. 38.). The whole article is drawn from the fourth book of the Edifices, except Anchialus (l. iii c. 7.).

119. Turn back to vol. i. p. 293, 294. In the course of this history, I have sometimes mentioned, and much oftener slighted, the hasty inroads of the Isaurians, which were not attended with any consequences.

120. Trebellius Pollio in Hist. August. p. 107. who lived under Diocletian, or Constantine. See likewise Pancirolus ad Notit. Imp. Orient. c. 115. 141. See Cod. Theodos. l. ix. tit. 35. leg. 37. with a copious collective Annotation of Godefroy, tom. iii. p. 256, 257.

121. See the full and wide extent of their inroads in Philostorgius (Hist. Eccles. l. xi. c. 8.), with Godefroy's learned Dissertations.

magistrates were instructed, by an edict, that the trial or punishment of an Isaurian, even on the festival of Easter, was a meritorious act of justice and piety.[122] If the captives were condemned to domestic slavery, they maintained, with their sword or dagger, the private quarrel of their masters; and it was found expedient for the public tranquillity, to prohibit the service of such dangerous retainers. When their countrymen Tarcalissæus or Zeno ascended the throne, he invited a faithful and formidable band of Isaurians, who insulted the court and city, and were rewarded by an annual tribute of five thousand pounds of gold. But the hopes of fortune depopulated the mountains, luxury enervated the hardiness of their minds and bodies, and in proportion as they mixed with mankind, they became less qualified for the enjoyment of poor and solitary freedom. After the death of Zeno, his successor Anastasius suppressed their pensions, exposed their persons to the revenge of the people, banished them from Constantinople, and prepared to sustain a war, which left only the alternative of victory or servitude. A brother of the last emperor usurped the title of Augustus, his cause was powerfully supported by the arms, the treasures, and the magazines, collected by Zeno; and the native Isaurians must have formed the smallest portion of the hundred and fifty thousand Barbarians under his standard, which was sanctified, for the first time, by the presence of a fighting bishop. Their disorderly numbers were vanquished in the plains of Phrygia by the valour and discipline *A.D. 492–498.* of the Goths; but a war of six years almost exhausted the courage of the emperor.[123] The Isaurians retired to their mountains; their fortresses were successively besieged and ruined; their communication with the sea was intercepted; the bravest of their leaders died in arms; the surviving chiefs, before their execution, were dragged in chains through the hippodrome; a colony of their youth was transplanted into Thrace, and the remnant of the people submitted to the Roman government. Yet some generations elapsed before their minds were reduced to the level of slavery. The populous villages of Mount Taurus were filled with horsemen and archers; they resisted the imposition of tributes, but they recruited the armies of

---

122. Cod. Justinian. l. ix. tit. 12. leg. 10. The punishments are severe – a fine of an hundred pounds of gold, degradation, and even death. The public peace might afford a pretence, but Zeno was desirous of monopolizing the valour and service of the Isaurians.

123. The Isaurian war and the triumph of Anastasius are briefly and darkly represented by John Malala (tom. ii. p. 106, 107.), Evagrius (l. iii. c. 35.), Theophanes (p. 118–120.), and the Chronicle of Marcellinus.

Justinian; and his civil magistrates, the proconsul of Cappadocia, the count of Isauria, and the prætors of Lycaonia and Pisidia, were invested with military power to restrain the licentious practice of rapes and assassinations.[124]

Fortifications of the empire, from the Euxine to the Persian frontier.   If we extend our view from the tropic to the mouth of the Tanais, we may observe on one hand, the precautions of Justinian to curb the savages of Æthiopia,[125] and on the other, the long walls which he constructed in Crimæa for the protection of his friendly Goths, a colony of three thousand shepherds and warriors.[126] From that peninsula to Trebizond, the eastern curve of the Euxine was secured by forts, by alliance, or by religion: and the possession of *Lazica*, the Colchos of ancient, the Mingrelia of modern, geography, soon became the object of an important war. Trebizond, in after-times the seat of a romantic empire, was indebted to the liberality of Justinian for a church, an aqueduct, and a castle, whose ditches are hewn in the solid rock. From that maritime city, a frontier-line of five hundred miles may be drawn to the fortress of Circesium, the last Roman station on the Euphrates.[127] Above Trebizond immediately, and five days journey to the south, the country rises into dark forests and craggy mountains, as savage though not so lofty as the Alps and the Pyrenees. In this rigorous climate,[128]

---

124. Fortes ea regio (says Justinian) viros habet, nec in ullo differt ab Isauria, though Procopius (Persic. l. i. c. 18.) marks an essential difference between their military character; yet in former times the Lycaonians and Pisidians had defended their liberty against the great king (Xenophon. Anabasis, l. iii. c. 2.). Justinian introduces some false and ridiculous erudition of the ancient empire of the Pisidians, and of Lycaon, who, after visiting Rome (long before Æneas), gave a name and people to Lycaonia (Novell. 24, 25. 27. 30.).

125. See Procopius, Persic. l. i. c. 19. The altar of national concord, of annual sacrifice and oaths, which Diocletian had erected in the isle of Elephantine, was demolished by Justinian with less policy than zeal.

126. Procopius de Edificiis, l. iii. c. 7. Hist. l. viii. c. 3, 4. These unambitious Goths had refused to follow the standard of Theodoric. As late as the xvth and xvith century, the name and nation might be discovered between Cassa and the streights of Azoph (d'Anville Memoires de l'Academie, tom. xxx. p. 240.). They well deserved the curiosity of Busbequius (p. 321–326.); but seem to have vanished in the more recent account of the Missions du Levant (tom. i.), Tott, Peyssonel, &c.

127. For the geography and architecture of this Armenian border, see the Persian Wars and Edifices (l. ii. c. 4–7. l. iii. c. 2–7.) of Procopius.

128. The country is described by Tournefort (Voyage au Levant, tom. iii. lettre xvii. xviii.). That skilful botanist soon discovered the plant that infects the honey (Plin. xxi. 44, 45.): he observes, that the soldiers of Lucullus might indeed be astonished at the cold, since, even in the plain of Erzerum, snow sometimes falls in June, and the harvest is seldom finished before September. The hills of

where the snows seldom melt, the fruits are tardy and tasteless, even honey is poisonous; the most industrious tillage would be confined to some pleasant vallies; and the pastoral tribes obtained a scanty sustenance from the flesh and milk of their cattle. The *Chalybians*[129] derived their name and temper from the iron quality of the soil; and, since the days of Cyrus, they might produce, under the various appellations of Chaldæans and Zanians, an uninterrupted prescription of war and rapine. Under the reign of Justinian, they acknowledged the God and the emperor of the Romans, and seven fortresses were built in the most accessible passes, to exclude the ambition of the Persian monarch.[130] The principal source of the Euphrates descends from the Chalybian mountains, and seems to flow towards the west and the Euxine; bending to the south-west, the river passes under the walls of Satala and Melitene (which were restored by Justinian as the bulwarks of the lesser Armenia), and gradually approaches the Mediterranean sea; till at length, repelled by Mount Taurus,[131] the Euphrates inclines his long and flexible course to the south-east and the gulf of Persia. Among the Roman cities beyond the Euphrates, we distinguish two recent foundations, which were named from Theodosius, and the relics of the martyrs; and two capitals, Amida and Edessa, which are celebrated in the history of every age. Their strength was proportioned by Justinian to the danger of their situation. A ditch and palisade might be sufficient to resist the artless force of the cavalry of Scythia; but more elaborate works were required to sustain a regular siege against the arms and treasures of the great king. His skilful engineers understood the methods of conducting deep mines, and of raising platforms to the level of the rampart: he shook the

---

Armenia are below the fortieth degree of latitude; but in the mountainous country which I inhabit, it is well known that an ascent of some hours carries the traveller from the climate of Languedoc to that of Norway: and a general theory has been introduced, that, under the line, an elevation of 2400 *toises* is equivalent to the cold of the polar circle (Remond, Observations sur les Voyage de Coxe dans la Suisse, tom. ii. p. 104.).

129. The identity or proximity of the Chalybians, or Chaldæans, may be investigated in Strabo (l. xii. p. 825, 826.), Cellarius (Geograph. Antiq. tom. ii. p. 202–204.), and

Freret (Mem. de l'Academie, tom. iv. p. 594.). Xenophon supposes, in his romance (Cyropæd. l. iii.), the same Barbarians against whom he had fought in his retreat (Anabasis, l. iv.).

130. Procopius, Persic. l. i. c. 15. De Edific. l. iii. c. 6.

131. Ni Taurus obstet in nostra maria venturus (Pomponius Mela, iii. 8.). Pliny, a poet as well as a naturalist (v. 20.), personifies the river and mountain, and describes their combat. See the course of the Tigris and Euphrates, in the excellent treatise of d'Anville.

strongest battlements with his military engines, and sometimes advanced to the assault with a line of moveable turrets on the backs of elephants. In the great cities of the East, the disadvantage of space, perhaps of position, was compensated by the zeal of the people, who seconded the garrison in the defence of their country and religion; and the fabulous promise of the Son of God, that Edessa should never be taken, filled the citizens with valiant confidence, and chilled the besiegers with doubt and dismay.[132] The subordinate towns of Armenia and Mesopotamia were diligently strengthened, and the posts which appeared to have any command of ground or water, were occupied by numerous forts, substantially built of stone, or more hastily erected with the obvious materials of earth and brick. The eye of Justinian investigated every spot; and his cruel precautions might attract the war into some lonely vale, whose peaceful natives, connected by trade and marriage, were ignorant of national discord and the quarrels of princes. Westward of the Euphrates, a sandy desert extends above six hundred miles to the Red Sea. Nature had interposed a vacant solitude between the ambition of two rival empires: the Arabians, till Mahomet arose, were formidable only as robbers; and in the proud security of peace, the fortifications of Syria were neglected on the most vulnerable side.

Death of Perozes, king of Persia.
A.D. 488.

But the national enmity, at least the effects of that enmity, had been suspended by a truce, which continued above four-score years. An ambassador from the emperor Zeno, accompanied the rash and unfortunate Perozes, in his expedition against the Nepthalites or white Huns, whose conquests had been stretched from the Caspian to the heart of India, whose throne was enriched with emeralds,[133] and whose cavalry was supported by a line of two thousand

---

132. Procopius (Persic. l. ii. c. 12.) tells the story with the tone half sceptical, half superstitious, of Herodotus. The promise was not in the primitive lye of Eusebius, but dates at least from the year 400; and a third lye, the *Veronica*, was soon raised on the two former (Evagrius, l. iv. c. 27.). As Edessa *has* been taken, Tillemont *must* disclaim the promise (Mem. Eccles. tom. i. p. 362. 383. 617.).

133. They were purchased from the merchants of Adulis who traded to India (Cosmas, Topograph. Christ. l. xi. p. 339); yet, in the estimate of precious stones, the Scythian emerald was the first, the Bactrian the second, the Æthiopian only the third (Hill's Theophrastus, p. 61, &c. 92.). The production, mines, &c. of emeralds, are involved in darkness; and it is doubtful whether we possess any of the twelve sorts known to the ancients (Goguet, Origine des Loix, &c. part ii. l. ii. c. 2. art. 3.). In this war the Huns got, or at least Perozes lost, the finest pearl in the world, of which Procopius relates a ridiculous fable.

elephants.[134] The Persians were twice circumvented, in a situation which made valour useless and flight impossible; and the double victory of the Huns was atchieved by military stratagem. They dismissed their royal captive after he had submitted to adore the majesty of a Barbarian; and the humiliation was poorly evaded by the casuistical subtilty of the Magi, who instructed Perozes to direct his intention to the rising sun. The indignant successor of Cyrus forgot his danger and his gratitude; he renewed the attack with headstrong fury, and lost both his army and his life.[135] The death of Perozes abandoned Persia to her foreign and domestic enemies; and twelve years of confusion elapsed before his son Cabades or Kobad could embrace any designs of ambition or revenge. The unkind parsimony of Anastasius was the motive or pretence of a Roman war;[136] the Huns and Arabs marched under the Persian standard, and the fortifications of Armenia and Mesopotamia were, *The Persian war, A.D. 502–505.* at that time, in a ruinous or imperfect condition. The emperor returned his thanks to the governor and people of Martyropolis, for the prompt surrender of a city which could not be successfully defended, and the conflagration of Theodosiopolis might justify the conduct of their prudent neighbours. Amida sustained a long and destructive siege: at the end of three months, the loss of fifty thousand of the soldiers of Cabades was not balanced by any prospect of success, and it was in vain that the Magi deduced a flattering prediction from the indecency of the women on the ramparts, who had revealed their most secret charms to the eyes of the assailants. At length, in a silent night, they ascended the most accessible tower, which was guarded only by some monks, oppressed, after the duties of a festival, with sleep and wine. Scaling-ladders were applied at the dawn

---

134. The Indo-Scythæ continued to reign from the time of Augustus (Dionys. Perieget. 1088. with the Commentary of Eustathius, in Hudson, Geograph. Minor. tom. iv.) to that of the elder Justin (Cosmas, Topograph. Christ. l. xi. p. 338, 339.). On their origin and conquests, see d'Anville (sur l'Inde, p. 18. 45, &c. 69. 85. 89.). In the second century they were masters of Larice or Guzerat.

135. See the fate of Phirouz or Perozes, and its consequences, in Procopius (Persic. l. i. c. 3–6), who may be compared with the fragments of Oriental history (d'Herbelot,

Bibliot. Orient. p. 351. and Texeira, History of Persia, translated or abridged by Stevens, l. i. c. 32. p. 132–138.). The chronology is ably ascertained by Asseman (Bibliot. Orient. tom. iii. p. 396–427.).

136. The Persian war, under the reigns of Anastasius and Justin, may be collected from Procopius (Persic. l. i. c. 7, 8, 9.), Theophanes (in Chronograph. p. 124–127.), Evagrius (l. iii. c. 37.), Marcellinus (in Chron. p. 47.), and Josua Stylites (apud Asseman. tom. i. p. 272–281.).

of day; the presence of Cabades, his stern command, and his drawn sword, compelled the Persians to vanquish; and before it was sheathed, fourscore thousand of the inhabitants had expiated the blood of their companions. After the siege of Amida, the war continued three years, and the unhappy frontier tasted the full measure of its calamities. The gold of Anastasius was offered too late, the number of his troops was defeated by the number of their generals; the country was stripped of its inhabitants, and both the living and the dead were abandoned to the wild beasts of the desert. The resistance of Edessa, and the deficiency of spoil, inclined the mind of Cabades to peace: he sold his conquests for an exorbitant price; and the same line, though marked with slaughter and devastation, still separated the two empires. To avert the repetition of the same evils, Anastasius resolved to found a new colony, so strong, that it should defy the power of the Persian, so far advanced towards Assyria, that its stationary troops might defend the province by the menace or operation of offensive war.

Fortifications of Dara. For this purpose, the town of Dara,[137] fourteen miles from Nisibis, and four days journey from the Tigris, was peopled and adorned; the hasty works of Anastasius were improved by the perseverance of Justinian; and without insisting on places less important, the fortifications of Dara may represent the military architecture of the age. The city was surrounded with two walls, and the interval between them, of fifty paces, afforded a retreat to the cattle of the besieged. The inner wall was a monument of strength and beauty: it measured sixty feet from the ground, and the height of the towers was one hundred feet; the loopholes, from whence an enemy might be annoyed with missile weapons, were small, but numerous; the soldiers were planted along the rampart, under the shelter of double galleries, and a third platform, spacious and secure, was raised on the summit of the towers. The exterior wall appears to have been less lofty, but more solid; and each tower was protected by a quadrangular bulwark. A hard rocky soil resisted the tools of the miners, and on the south-east, where the ground was more tractable, their approach was retarded by a new work, which advanced in the shape of an half-moon. The double and treble ditches were filled with a stream of water; and in the management of the river, the most skilful labour was employed to

---

137. The description of Dara is amply and correctly given by Procopius (Persic. l. i. c. 10. l. ii. c. 13. De Edific. l. ii. c. 1, 2, 3. l. iii. c. 5.). See the situation in d'Anville (l'Euphrate et le Tigre, p. 53, 54, 55.), though he seems to double the interval between Dara and Nisibis.

supply the inhabitants, to distress the besiegers, and to prevent the mischiefs of a natural or artificial inundation. Dara continued more than sixty years to fulfil the wishes of its founders, and to provoke the jealousy of the Persians, who incessantly complained, that this impregnable fortress had been constructed in manifest violation of the treaty of peace between the two empires.

Between the Euxine and the Caspian, the countries of Colchos, Iberia, and Albania, are intersected in every direction by the branches of Mount Caucasus; and the two principal *The Caspian or Iberian gates.* *gates*, or passes, from north to south, have been frequently confounded in the geography both of the ancients and moderns. The name of *Caspian* or *Albanian* gates, is properly applied to Derbend,[138] which occupies a short declivity between the mountains and the sea: the city, if we give credit to local tradition, had been founded by the Greeks; and this dangerous entrance was fortified by the kings of Persia, with a mole, double walls, and doors of iron. The *Iberian* gates[139] are formed by a narrow passage of six miles in Mount Caucasus, which opens from the northern side of Iberia or Georgia, into the plain that reaches to the Tanais and the Volga. A fortress, designed by Alexander perhaps, or one of his successors, to command that important pass, had descended by right of conquest or inheritance to a prince of the Huns, who offered it for a moderate price to the emperor: but while Anastasius paused, while he timorously computed the cost and the distance, a more vigilant rival interposed, and Cabades forcibly occupied the streights of Caucasus. The Albanian and Iberian gates excluded the horsemen of Scythia from the shortest and most practicable roads, and the whole front of the mountains was covered by the rampart of Gog and Magog, the long wall which has excited the curiosity of an Arabian caliph[140]

138. For the city and pass of Derbend, see d'Herbelot (Bibliot. Orient. p. 157. 291. 807.), Petis de la Croix (Hist. de Gengiscan, l. iv. c. 9.), Histoire Genealogique des Tatars (tom. i. p. 120.), Olearius (Voyage en Perse, p. 1039–1041.), and Corneille le Bruyn (Voyages, tom. i. p. 146, 147.): his view may be compared with the plan of Olearius, who judges the wall to be of shells and gravel hardened by time.

139. Procopius, though with some confusion, always denominates them Caspian (Persic. l. i.

c. 10.). The pass is now styled Tatar-topa, the Tartar-gates (d'Anville, Geographie Ancienne, tom. ii. p. 119, 120.).

140. The imaginary rampart of Gog and Magog, which was seriously explored and believed by a caliph of the ixth century, appears to be derived from the gates of Mount Caucasus and a vague report of the wall of China (Geograph, Nubiensis, p. 267–270. Memoires de l'Academie, tom. xxxi. p. 210–219.).

and a Russian conqueror.[141] According to a recent description, huge stones seven feet thick, twenty-one feet in length or height, are artificially joined without iron or cement, to compose a wall, which runs above three hundred miles from the shores of Derbend, over the hills, and through the vallies of Daghestan and Georgia. Without a vision, such a work might be undertaken by the policy of Cabades; without a miracle, it might be accomplished by his son, so formidable to the Romans under the name of Chosroes; so dear to the Orientals, under the appellation of Nushirwan. The Persian monarch held in his hand the keys both of peace and war; but he stipulated, in every treaty, that Justinian should contribute to the expence of a common barrier, which equally protected the two empires from the inroads of the Scythians.[142]

VII. Justinian suppressed the schools of Athens and the consulship of Rome, which had given so many sages and heroes to mankind. Both these institutions had long since degenerated from their primitive glory; yet some reproach may be justly inflicted on the avarice and jealousy of a prince, by whose hand such venerable ruins were destroyed.

The schools of Athens. Athens, after her Persian triumphs, adopted the philosophy of Ionia and the rhetoric of Sicily; and these studies became the patrimony of a city, whose inhabitants, about thirty thousand males, condensed, within the period of a single life, the genius of ages and millions. Our sense of the dignity of human nature, is exalted by the simple recollection, that Isocrates[143] was the companion of Plato and Xenophon; that he assisted, perhaps with the historian Thucydides, at the first representations of the Oedipus of Sophocles and the Iphigenia of Euripides; and that his pupils Æschines and Demosthenes contended for the crown of patriotism in the presence of Aristotle, the master of Theophrastus, who taught at Athens with the founders of the Stoic and Epicurean sects.[144] The

---

141. See a learned dissertation of Baier, *de muro Caucaseo*, in Comment. Acad. Petropol. ann. 1726. tom. i. p. 425–463.; but it is destitute of a map or plan. When the czar Peter I. became master of Derbend in the year 1722, the measure of the wall was found to be 3285 Russian *orgygiæ*, or fathom, each of seven feet English; in the whole, somewhat more than four miles in length.

142. See the fortifications and treaties of Chosroes or Nushirwan, in Procopius (Persic. l. i.

c. 16. 22. l. ii.) and d'Herbelot (p. 682.).

143. The life of Isocrates extends from Olymp. lxxxvi. 1. to cx. 3. (ante Christ. 436–338.). See Dionys. Halicarn. tom. ii. p. 149–150. edit. Hudson. Plutarch (sive anonymus), in Vit. X. Oratorum, p. 1538–1543. edit. H. Steph. Phot. cod. cclix. p. 1453.

144. The schools of Athens are copiously though concisely represented in the Fortuna Attica of Meursius (c. viii. p. 59–73. in tom. i. Opp.). For the state and arts of the city, see

ingenuous youth of Attica enjoyed the benefits of their domestic education, which was communicated without envy to the rival cities. Two thousand disciples heard the lessons of Theophrastus;[145] the schools of rhetoric must have been still more populous than those of philosophy; and a rapid succession of students diffused the fame of their teachers, as far as the utmost limits of the Grecian language and name. Those limits were enlarged by the victories of Alexander; the arts of Athens survived her freedom and dominion; and the Greek colonies which the Macedonians planted in Egypt, and scattered over Asia, undertook long and frequent pilgrimages to worship the Muses in their favourite temple on the banks of the Ilissus. The Latin conquerors respectfully listened to the instructions of their subjects and captives; the names of Cicero and Horace were enrolled in the schools of Athens; and after the perfect settlement of the Roman empire, the natives of Italy, of Africa, and of Britain, conversed in the groves of the academy with their fellow-students of the East. The studies of philosophy and eloquence are congenial to a popular state, which encourages the freedom of enquiry, and submits only to the force of persuasion. In the republics of Greece and Rome, the art of speaking was the powerful engine of patriotism or ambition; and the schools of rhetoric poured forth a colony of statesmen and legislators. When the liberty of public debate was suppressed, the orator, in the honourable profession of an advocate, might plead the cause of innocence and justice; he might abuse his talents in the more profitable trade of panegyric; and the same precepts continued to dictate the fanciful declamations of the sophist, and the chaster beauties of historical composition. The systems which professed to unfold the nature of God, of man, and of the universe, entertained the curiosity of the philosophic student; and according to the temper of his mind, he might doubt with the sceptics, or decide with the stoics, sublimely speculate with Plato, or severely argue with Aristotle. The pride of the adverse sects had fixed an unattainable term of moral happiness and perfection: but the race was glorious and salutary; the disciples of Zeno, and even those of Epicurus, were taught both to act and to suffer; and the death of Petronius was not less effectual than that of Seneca, to humble a tyrant by the discovery of his impotence. The light of science could not indeed be confined within

---

the first book of Pausanias, and a small tract of Dicæarchus (in the second volume of Hudson's Geographers), who wrote about

Olymp. cxvii. (Dodwell's Dissertat. sect. 4.) **145**. Diogen. Laert. de Vit. Philosoph. l. v. segm. 37. p. 289.

the walls of Athens. Her incomparable writers address themselves to the human race; the living masters emigrated to Italy and Asia; Berytus, in later times, was devoted to the study of the law; astronomy and physic were cultivated in the musæum of Alexandria; but the Attic schools of rhetoric and philosophy maintained their superior reputation from the Peloponnesian war to the reign of Justinian. Athens, though situate in a barren soil, possessed a pure air, a free navigation, and the monuments of ancient art. That sacred retirement was seldom disturbed by the business of trade or government; and the last of the Athenians were distinguished by their lively wit, the purity of their taste and language, their social manners, and some traces, at least in discourse, of the magnanimity of their fathers. In the suburbs of the city, the *academy* of the Platonists, the *lycæum* of the Peripatetics, the *portico* of the Stoics, and the *garden* of the Epicureans, were planted with trees and decorated with statues; and the philosophers, instead of being immured in a cloyster, delivered their instructions in spacious and pleasant walks, which, at different hours, were consecrated to the exercises of the mind and body. The genius of the founders still lived in those venerable seats; the ambition of succeeding to the masters of human reason, excited a generous emulation; and the merit of the candidates was determined, on each vacancy, by the free voices of an enlightened people. The Athenian professors were paid by their disciples: according to their mutual wants and abilities, the price appears to have varied from a mina to a talent; and Isocrates himself, who derides the avarice of the sophists, required in his school of rhetoric, about thirty pounds from each of his hundred pupils. The wages of industry are just and honourable, yet the same Isocrates shed tears at the first receipt of a stipend; the Stoic might blush when he was hired to preach the contempt of money; and I should be sorry to discover, that Aristotle or Plato so far degenerated from the example of Socrates, as to exchange knowledge for gold. But some property of lands and houses was settled by the permission of the laws, and the legacies of deceased friends, on the philosophic chairs of Athens. Epicurus bequeathed to his disciples the gardens which he had purchased for eighty minæ or two hundred and fifty pounds, with a fund sufficient for their frugal subsistence and monthly festivals;[146] and the

146. See the testament of Epicurus in Diogen. Laert. l. x. segm. 16–20. p. 611, 612. A single epistle (ad Familiares, xiii. 1.) displays the injustice of the Areopagus, the fidelity of the Epicureans, the dextrous politeness of Cicero, and the mixture of contempt and esteem with which the Roman senators considered the philosophy and philosophers of Greece.

patrimony of Plato afforded an annual rent, which, in eight centuries, was gradually encreased from three to one thousand pieces of gold.[147] The schools of Athens were protected by the wisest and most virtuous of the Roman princes. The library which Hadrian founded, was placed in a portico adorned with pictures, statues, and a roof of alabaster, and supported by one hundred columns of Phrygian marble. The public salaries were assigned by the generous spirit of the Antonines; and each professor, of politics, of rhetoric, of the Platonic, the Peripatetic, the Stoic, and the Epicurean philosophy, received an annual stipend of ten thousand drachmæ, or more than three hundred pounds sterling.[148] After the death of Marcus, these liberal donations, and the privileges attached to the *thrones* of science, were abolished and revived, diminished and enlarged: but some vestige of royal bounty may be found under the successors of Constantine; and their arbitrary choice of an unworthy candidate might tempt the philosophers of Athens to regret the days of independence and poverty.[149] It is remarkable, that the impartial favour of the Antonines was bestowed on the four adverse sects of philosophy, which they considered as equally useful or at least as equally innocent. Socrates had formerly been the glory and the reproach of his country; and the first lessons of Epicurus so strangely scandalized the pious ears of the Athenians, that by his exile, and that of his antagonists, they silenced all vain disputes concerning the nature of the gods. But in the ensuing year they recalled the hasty decree, restored the liberty of the schools, and were convinced by the experience of ages, that the moral character of philosophers is not affected by the diversity of their theological speculations.[150]

147. Damascius, in Vit. Isidor. apud Photium, cod. ccxlii. p. 1054.

148. See Lucian (in Eunech. tom. ii. p. 350–359. edit. Reitz), Philostratus (in Vit. Sophist. l. ii. c. 2.), and Dion Cassius, or Xiphilin (l. lxxi. p. 1195.), with their editors Du Soul, Olearius, and Reimar, and, above all, Salmasius (ad Hist. August. p. 72.). A judicious philosopher (Smith's Wealth of Nations, vol. ii. p. 340–374.) prefers the free contributions of the students to a fixed stipend for the professor.

149. Brucker, Hist. Crit. Philosoph. tom. ii. p. 310, &c.

150. The birth of Epicurus is fixed to the year 342 before Christ (Bayle), Olympiad cix. 3.; and he opened his school at Athens, Olymp. cxviii. 3. 306 years before the same æra. This intolerant law (Athenæus, l. xiii. p. 610. Diogen. Laertius, l. v. s. 38. p. 290. Julius Pollux, ix. 5.) was enacted in the same, or the succeeding year (Sigonius, Opp. tom. v. p. 62. Menagius, ad Diogen. Laert. p. 204. Corsini Fasti Attici, tom. iv. p. 67, 68.). Theophrastus, chief of the Peripatetics, and disciple of Aristotle, was involved in the same exile.

They are suppressed by Justinian.

The Gothic arms were less fatal to the schools of Athens than the establishment of a new religion, whose ministers superseded the exercise of reason, resolved every question by an article of faith, and condemned the infidel or sceptic to eternal flames. In many a volume of laborious controversy, they exposed the weakness of the understanding and the corruption of the heart, insulted human nature in the sages of antiquity, and proscribed the spirit of philosophical enquiry, so repugnant to the doctrine, or at least to the temper, of an humble believer. The surviving sect of the Platonists, whom Plato would have blushed to acknowledge, extravagantly mingled a sublime theory with the practice of superstition and magic; and as they remained alone in the midst of a Christian world, they indulged a secret rancour against the government of the church and state, whose severity was still suspended over their heads. About a century after the reign of Julian,[151] Proclus[152]

Proclus.

was permitted to teach in the philosophic chair of the academy, and such was his industry, that he frequently, in the same day, pronounced five lessons, and composed seven hundred lines. His sagacious mind explored the deepest questions of morals and metaphysics, and he ventured to urge eighteen arguments against the Christian doctrine of the creation of the world. But in the intervals of study, he *personally* conversed with Pan, Æsculapius, and Minerva, in whose mysteries he was secretly initiated, and whose prostrate statues he adored; in the devout persuasion that the philosopher, who is a citizen of the universe, should be the priest of its various deities. An eclipse of the sun announced his approaching end; and his life, with that of his scholar Isidore,[153] compiled by two of their most learned disciples, exhibits a deplorable picture of the second childhood of human reason. Yet the golden chain, as it was fondly styled, of the Platonic succession, continued forty-four years from the death of Proclus to the edict

His successors, A.D. 485-529.

151. This is no fanciful æra: the Pagans reckoned their calamities from the reign of their hero. Proclus, whose nativity is marked by his horoscope (A.D. 412, February 8, at C.P.), died 124 years απο Ιουλιανου βασιλεως, A.D. 485 (Marin. in Vitâ Procli, c. 36.). 152. The life of Proclus, by Marinus, was published by Fabricius (Hamburg, 1700, et ad calcem Bibliot. Latin. Lond. 1703). See Suidas

(tom. iii. p. 185, 186.), Fabricius (Bibliot, Græc. l. v. c. 26. p. 449–552.), and Brucker (Hist. Crit. Philosoph. tom. ii. p. 319–326.). 153. The life of Isidore was composed by Damascius (apud Photium, cod. ccxlii. p. 1028–1076.). See the last age of the Pagan philosophers in Brucker (tom. ii. p. 341–351.).

of Justinian,[154] which imposed a perpetual silence on the schools of Athens, and excited the grief and indignation of the few remaining votaries of Grecian science and superstition. Seven friends and philosophers, Diogenes and Hermias, Eulalius and Priscian, Damascius, Isidore, and Simplicius, who dissented from the religion of their sovereign, embraced the resolution of seeking in a foreign land the freedom which was denied in their native country. They had heard, and they credulously believed, that the republic of Plato was realized in the despotic government of Persia, and that a patriot king reigned over the happiest and most virtuous of nations. They were soon astonished by the natural discovery, that Persia resembled the other countries of the globe; that Chosroes, who affected the name of a philosopher, was vain, cruel, and ambitious; that bigotry, and a spirit of intolerance, prevailed among the Magi; that the nobles were haughty, the courtiers servile, and the magistrates unjust; that the guilty sometimes escaped, and that the innocent were often oppressed. The disappointment of the philosophers provoked them to overlook the real virtues of the Persians; and they were scandalized, more deeply perhaps than became their profession, with the plurality of wives and concubines, the incestuous marriages, and the custom of exposing dead bodies to the dogs and vultures, instead of hiding them in the earth, or consuming them with fire. Their repentance was expressed by a precipitate return, and they loudly declared that they had rather die on the borders of the empire, than enjoy the wealth and favour of the Barbarian. From this journey, however, they derived a benefit which reflects the purest lustre on the character of Chosroes. He required, that the seven sages who had visited the court of Persia, should be exempted from the penal laws which Justinian enacted against his Pagan subjects; and this privilege, expressly stipulated in a treaty of peace, was guarded by the vigilance of a powerful mediator.[155] Simplicius and his companions ended their lives in peace and obscurity; and as they left no disciples, they terminate the long list of Grecian philosophers, who may be justly praised, notwithstanding their defects, as the wisest and most virtuous of their contemporaries. The

The last of the philosophers.

154. The suppression of the schools of Athens is recorded by John Malala (tom. ii. p. 187, sur Decio Cos. Sol.), and an anonymous Chronicle in the Vatican library (apud Aleman, p. 106.).

155. Agathias (l. ii. p. 69, 70, 71.) relates this curious story. Chosroes ascended the throne in the year 531, and made his first peace with the Romans in the beginning of 533, a date most compatible with his *young* fame and the *old* age of Isidore (Asseman, Bibliot. Orient. tom. iii. p. 404. Pagi, tom. ii. p. 543. 550.).

writings of Simplicius are now extant. His physical and metaphysical commentaries on Aristotle have passed away with the fashion of the times; but his moral interpretation of Epictetus, is preserved in the library of nations, as a classic book, most excellently adapted to direct the will, to purify the heart, and to confirm the understanding, by a just confidence in the nature both of God and man.

The Roman consulship extinguished by Justinian, A.D. 541.

About the same time that Pythagoras first invented the appellation of philosopher, liberty and the consulship were founded at Rome by the elder Brutus. The revolutions of the consular office, which may be viewed in the successive lights of a substance, a shadow and a name, have been occasionally mentioned in the present history. The first magistrates of the republic had been chosen by the people, to exercise, in the senate and in the camp, the powers of peace and war, which were afterwards translated to the emperors. But the tradition of ancient dignity was long revered by the Romans and Barbarians. A Gothic historian applauds the consulship of Theodoric as the height of all temporal glory and greatness;[156] the king of Italy himself congratulates those annual favourites of fortune, who, without the cares, enjoyed the splendour of the throne; and at the end of a thousand years, two consuls were created by the sovereigns of Rome and Constantinople, for the sole purpose of giving a date to the year, and a festival to the people. But the expences of this festival, in which the wealthy and the vain aspired to surpass their predecessors, insensibly arose to the enormous sum of fourscore thousand pounds; the wisest senators declined an useless honour, which involved the certain ruin of their families; and to this reluctance I should impute the frequent chasms in the last age of the consular *Fasti*. The predecessors of Justinian had assisted from the public treasures the dignity of the less opulent candidates; the avarice of that prince preferred the cheaper and more convenient method of advice and regulation.[157] Seven *processions* or spectacles were the number to which his edict confined the horse and chariot races, the athletic sports, the music, and pantomimes of the theatre, and the hunting of wild beasts; and small pieces of silver were discreetly substituted to the gold medals, which had always excited tumult and drunkenness, when they were scattered with a profuse hand among

156. Cassiodor. Variarum Epist. vi. 1. Jornandes, c. 57. p. 696. edit. Grot. Quod summum bonum primumque in mundo decus edicitur.

157. See the regulations of Justinian (Novell. cv.) dated at Constantinople, July 5, and addressed to Strategius, treasurer of the empire.

the populace. Notwithstanding these precautions, and his own example, the succession of consuls finally ceased in the thirteenth year of Justinian, whose despotic temper might be gratified by the silent extinction of a title which admonished the Romans of their ancient freedom.[158] Yet the annual consulship still lived in the minds of the people; they fondly expected its speedy restoration; they applauded the gracious condescension of successive princes, by whom it was assumed in the first year of their reign; and three centuries elapsed, after the death of Justinian, before that obsolete dignity, which had been suppressed by custom, could be abolished by law.[159] The imperfect mode of distinguishing each year by the name of a magistrate, was usefully supplied by the date of a permanent æra: the creation of the world, according to the septuagint version, was adopted by the Greeks[160] and the Latins, since the age of Charlemagne, have computed their time from the birth of Christ.[161]

158. Procopius, in Anecdot. c. 26. Aleman, p. 106. In the xviii[th] year after the consulship of Basilius, according to the reckoning of Marcellinus, Victor, Marius, &c. the secret history was composed, and, in the eyes of Procopius, the consulship was finally abolished.

159. By Leo, the philosopher (Novell, xciv. A.D. 886–911.). See Pagi (Dissertat. Hypatica, p. 325–362.) and Ducange (Gloss. Græc. p. 1635, 1636.). Even the title was vilified: consulatus codicilli ... vilescunt, says the emperor himself.

160. According to Julius Africanus, &c. the world was created the first of September, 5508 years, three months, and twenty-five days before the birth of Christ (see Pezron, Antiquité des Tems defendüe, p. 20–28.); and this æra has been used by the Greeks, the Oriental Christians, and even by the Russians, till the reign of Peter I. The period, however arbitrary, is clear and convenient. Of the 7296 years which are supposed to elapse since the creation, we shall find 3000 of ignorance and

darkness; 2000 either fabulous or doubtful; 1000 of ancient history, commencing with the Persian empire, and the republics of Rome and Athens; 1000 from the fall of the Roman empire in the west to the discovery of America; and the remaining 296 will almost complete three centuries of the modern state of Europe and mankind. I regret this chronology, so far preferable to our double and perplexed method of counting backwards and forwards the years before and after the Christian æra.

161. The æra of the world has prevailed in the East since the vith general council (A.D. 681). In the West the Christian æra was first invented in the vith century: it was propagated in the viii[th] by the authority and writings of venerable Bede; but it was not till the xth that the use became legal and popular. See l'Art de verifier les Dates, Dissert. Preliminaire, p. iii. xii. Dictionaire Diplomatique, tom. i. p. 329–337: the works of a laborious society of Benedictine monks.

CHAPTER XLI

Conquests of Justinian in the West. – Character and first Campaigns of
Belisarius. – He invades and subdues the Vandal Kingdom of Africa. – His
Triumph. – The Gothic War. – He recovers Sicily, Naples, and Rome. –
Siege of Rome by the Goths. – Their Retreat and Losses. – Surrender of
Ravenna. – Glory of Belisarius. – His domestic Shame and Misfortunes.

Justinian
resolves to
invade Africa,
A.D. 533.

When Justinian ascended the throne, about fifty years after the
fall of the Western empire, the kingdoms of the Goths and
Vandals had obtained a solid, and, as it might seem, a legal
establishment both in Europe and Africa. The titles which
Roman victory had inscribed, were erazed with equal justice by
the sword of the Barbarians; and their successful rapine derived a more
venerable sanction from time, from treaties, and from the oaths of fidelity,
already repeated by a second or third generation of obedient subjects.
Experience and christianity had refuted the superstitious hope, that Rome
was founded by the gods to reign for ever over the nations of the earth.
But the proud claims of perpetual and indefeasible dominion, which her
soldiers could no longer maintain, was firmly asserted by her statesmen and
lawyers, whose opinions have been sometimes revived and propagated in
the modern schools of jurisprudence. After Rome herself had been stripped
of the Imperial purple, the princes of Constantinople assumed the sole and
sacred sceptre of the monarchy; demanded, as their rightful inheritance,
the provinces which had been subdued by the consuls, or possessed by the
Cæsars; and feebly aspired to deliver their faithful subjects of the West from
the usurpation of heretics and Barbarians. The execution of this splendid
design was in some degree reserved for Justinian. During the five first years
of his reign, he reluctantly waged a costly and unprofitable war against the
Persians; till his pride submitted to his ambition, and he purchased, at the
price of four hundred and forty thousand pounds sterling, the benefit of a
precarious truce, which, in the language of both nations, was dignified
with the appellation of the *endless* peace. The safety of the East enabled the
emperor to employ his forces against the Vandals; and the internal state of

Africa afforded an honourable motive, and promised a powerful support, to the Roman arms.[1]

According to the testament of the founder, the African kingdom had lineally descended to Hilderic the eldest of the Vandal princes. A mild disposition inclined the son of a tyrant, the grandson of a conqueror, to prefer the counsels of clemency and peace; and his accession was marked by the salutary edict, *State of the Vandals. Hilderic, A.D. 523–530.* which restored two hundred bishops to their churches, and allowed the free profession of the Athanasian creed.[2] But the Catholics accepted with cold and transient gratitude, a favour so inadequate to their pretensions, and the virtues of Hilderic offended the prejudices of his countrymen. The Arian clergy presumed to insinuate that he had renounced the faith, and the soldiers more loudly complained that he had degenerated from the courage, of his ancestors. His ambassadors were suspected of a secret and disgraceful negociation in the Byzantine court; and his general, the Achilles,[3] as he was named, of the Vandals, lost a battle against the naked and disorderly Moors. The public discontent was exasperated by Gelimer, whose age, descent, and military fame, gave him an apparent title to the succession: he assumed, with the consent *Gelimer, A.D. 530–534.* of the nation, the reins of government; and his unfortunate sovereign sunk without a struggle from the throne to a dungeon, where he was strictly guarded with a faithful counsellor, and his unpopular nephew the Achilles of the Vandals. But the indulgence which Hilderic had shewn to his Catholic subjects had powerfully recommended him to the favour of Justinian, who, for the benefit of his own sect, could acknowledge the use

1. The complete series of the Vandal war is related by Procopius in a regular and elegant narrative (l. i. c. 9–25. l. ii. c. 1–13.); and happy would be my lot, could I always tread in the footsteps of such a guide. From the entire and diligent perusal of the Greek text, I have a right to pronounce that the Latin and French versions of Grotius and Cousin may not be implicitly trusted: yet the president Cousin has been often praised, and Hugo Grotius was the first scholar of a learned age.
2. See Ruinart, Hist. Persecut. Vandal. c. xii. p. 589. His best evidence is drawn from the life of St. Fulgentius, composed by one of his disciples, transcribed in a great measure in

the annals of Baronius, and printed in several great collections (Catalog. Bibliot. Bunavi-ænæ, tom. i. vol. ii. p. 1258.).
3. For what quality of the mind or body? For speed, or beauty, or valour? – In what language did the Vandals read Homer? – Did he speak German? – The Latins had four versions (Fabric. tom. i. l. ii. c. 3. p. 297.): yet, in spite of the praises of Seneca (Consol. c. 26.), they appear to have been more successful in imitating, than in translating, the Greek poets. But the name of Achilles might be famous and popular, even among the illiterate Barbarians.

and justice of religious toleration: their alliance, while the nephew of Justin remained in a private station, was cemented by the mutual exchange of gifts and letters; and the emperor Justinian asserted the cause of royalty and friendship. In two successive embassies, he admonished the usurper to repent of his treason, or to abstain, at least, from any further violence which might provoke the displeasure of God and of the Romans; to reverence the laws of kindred and succession, and to suffer an infirm old man peaceably to end his days, either on the throne of Carthage or in the palace of Constantinople. The passions or even the prudence of Gelimer compelled him to reject these requests, which were urged in the haughty tone of menace and command; and he justified his ambition in a language rarely spoken in the Byzantine court, by alleging the right of a free people to remove or punish their chief magistrate, who had failed in the execution of the kingly office. After this fruitless expostulation, the captive monarch was more rigorously treated, his nephew was deprived of his eyes, and the cruel Vandal, confident in his strength and distance, derided the vain threats and slow preparations of the emperor of the East. Justinian resolved to deliver or revenge his friend, Gelimer to maintain his usurpation: and the war was preceded, according to the practice of civilized nations, by the most solemn protestations, that each party was sincerely desirous of peace.

Debates on the African war. The report of an African war was grateful only to the vain and idle populace of Constantinople, whose poverty exempted them from tribute, and whose cowardice was seldom exposed to military service. But the wiser citizens, who judged of the future by the past, revolved in their memory the immense loss, both of men and money, which the empire had sustained in the expedition of Basiliscus. The troops, which, after five laborious campaigns, had been recalled from the Persian frontier, dreaded the sea, the climate, and the arms of an unknown enemy. The ministers of the finances computed, as far as they might compute, the demands of an African war; the taxes which must be found and levied to supply those insatiate demands; and the danger, lest their own lives, or at least their lucrative employments, should be made responsible for the deficiency of the supply. Inspired by such selfish motives (for we may not suspect him of any zeal for the public good), John of Cappadocia ventured to oppose in full council the inclinations of his master. He confessed, that a victory of such importance could not be too dearly purchased; but he represented in a grave discourse the certain difficulties and the uncertain event. "You undertake," said the præfect, "to besiege Carthage: by land, the distance is not less than one hundred and forty days journey; on the sea, a whole year[4] must elapse before you can receive any intelligence from your fleet. If Africa should be reduced, it cannot be preserved without the additional conquest of Sicily and Italy. Success will impose the obligation of new labours; a single misfortune will attract the Barbarians into the heart of your exhausted empire." Justinian felt the weight of this salutary advice; he was confounded by the unwonted freedom of an obsequious servant; and the design of the war would perhaps have been relinquished, if his courage had not been revived by a voice which silenced the doubts of profane reason. "I have seen a vision," cried an artful or fanatic bishop of the East. "It is the will of heaven, O emperor, that you should not abandon your holy enterprise for the deliverance of the African church. The God of battles will march before your standard, and disperse your enemies, who are the enemies of his Son." The emperor might be tempted, and his counsellors were constrained, to give credit to this seasonable revelation: but they derived more rational hope from the revolt, which the adherents of Hilderic or Athanasius had already excited on the borders of the Vandal monarchy. Pudentius, an African subject, had privately signified his loyal intentions, and a small military aid restored the province of Tripoli to the obedience of the Romans. The government of Sardinia had been entrusted to Godas, a valiant Barbarian: he suspended the payment of tribute, disclaimed his allegiance to the usurper, and gave audience to the emissaries of Justinian, who found him master of that fruitful island, at the head of his guards, and proudly invested with the ensigns of royalty. The forces of the Vandals were diminished by discord and suspicion; the Roman armies were animated by the spirit of Belisarius; one of those heroic names which are familiar to every age and to every nation.

The Africanus of new Rome was born, and perhaps educated, among the Thracian peasants,[5] without any of those advantages which had formed the virtues of the elder and younger Scipio; a noble origin, liberal studies, and the emulation of a free state.

Character and choice of Belisarius.

---

4. *A year* – absurd exaggeration! The conquest of Africa may be dated A.D. 533, September 14: it is celebrated by Justinian in the preface to his Institutes, which were published November 21, of the same year. Including the voyage and return, such a computation might be truly applied to *our* Indian empire.

5. Ὥρμητο δε ὁ Βελισαριος εκ Γερμανιας,

ἡ Θρακωντε και Ιλλυριων μεταξυ κειται (Procop. Vandal. l. i. c. 11.). Aleman (Not. ad Anecdot. p. 5.), an Italian, could easily reject the German vanity of Giphanius and Velserus, who wished to claim the hero; but his Germania, a metropolis of Thrace, I cannot find in any civil or ecclesiastical lists of the provinces and cities.

The silence of a loquacious secretary may be admitted, to prove that the youth of Belisarius could not afford any subject of praise: he served, most assuredly with valour and reputation, among the private guards of Justinian; and when his patron became emperor, the domestic was promoted to military command. After a bold inroad into Persarmenia, in which his glory was shared by a colleague, and his progress was checked by an enemy, Belisarius repaired to the important station of Dara, where he first accepted the service of Procopius, the faithful companion, and diligent historian, of his exploits.[6] The Mirranes of Persia advanced, with forty thousand of her best troops, to raze the fortifications of Dara; and signified the day and the hour on which the citizens should prepare a bath for his refreshment after the toils of victory. He encountered an adversary equal to himself, by the new title of General of the East; his superior in the science of war, but much inferior in the number and quality of his troops, which amounted only to twenty-five thousand Romans and strangers, relaxed in their discipline, and humbled by recent disasters. As the level plain of Dara refused all shelter to stratagem and ambush, Belisarius protected his front with a deep trench, which was prolonged at first in perpendicular, and afterwards in parallel, lines, to cover the wings of cavalry advantageously posted to command the flanks and rear of the enemy. When the Roman centre was shaken, their well-timed and rapid charge decided the conflict: the standard of Persia fell; the *immortals* fled; the infantry threw away their bucklers, and eight thousand of the vanquished were left on the field of battle. In the next campaign, Syria was invaded on the side of the desert; and Belisarius, with twenty thousand men, hastened from Dara to the relief of the province. During the whole summer, the designs of the enemy were baffled by his skilful dispositions: he pressed their retreat, occupied each night their camp of the preceding day, and would have secured a bloodless victory, if he could have resisted the impatience of his own troops. Their valiant promise was faintly supported in the hour of battle; the right wing was exposed by the treacherous or cowardly desertion of the Christian Arabs; the Huns, a veteran band of eight hundred warriors, were oppressed by superior numbers; the flight of the Isaurians was intercepted; but the Roman infantry stood firm on the left; for Belisarius himself, dismounting from his horse, shewed them that

His services in the Persian war, A.D. 529–532.

6. The two first Persian campaigns of Belisarius are fairly and copiously related by his secretary (Persic. l. i. c. 12–18.).

intrepid despair was their only safety. They turned their backs to the Euphrates, and their faces to the enemy: innumerable arrows glanced without effect from the compact and shelving order of their bucklers; an impenetrable line of pikes was opposed to the repeated assaults of the Persian cavalry; and after a resistance of many hours, the remaining troops were skilfully embarked under the shadow of the night. The Persian commander retired with disorder and disgrace, to answer a strict account of the lives of so many soldiers which he had consumed in a barren victory. But the fame of Belisarius was not sullied by a defeat, in which he alone had saved his army from the consequences of their own rashness: the approach of peace relieved him from the guard of the eastern frontier, and his conduct in the sedition of Constantinople amply discharged his obligations to the emperor. When the African war became the topic of popular discourse and secret deliberation, each of the Roman generals was apprehensive, rather than ambitious, of the dangerous honour; but as soon as Justinian had declared his preference of superior merit, their envy was rekindled by the unanimous applause which was given to the choice of Belisarius. The temper of the Byzantine court may encourage a suspicion, that the hero was darkly assisted by the intrigues of his wife, the fair and subtle Antonina, who alternately enjoyed the confidence and incurred the hatred of the empress Theodora. The birth of Antonina was ignoble, she descended from a family of charioteers; and her chastity has been stained with the foulest reproach. Yet she reigned with long and absolute power over the mind of her illustrious husband; and if Antonina disdained the merit of conjugal fidelity, she expressed a manly friendship to Belisarius, whom she accompanied with undaunted resolution in all the hardships and dangers of a military life.[7]

The preparations for the African war were not unworthy of the last contest between Rome and Carthage. The pride and flower of the army consisted of the guards of Belisarius, who, according to the pernicious indulgence of the times, devoted themselves by a particular oath of fidelity to the service of their patron. Their strength and stature, for which they had been curiously selected, the goodness of their horses and armour, and the assiduous practice of all the exercises of war, enabled them to act whatever their courage might prompt;

Preparations for the African war, A.D. 533.

7. See the birth and character of Antonina, in the Anecdotes, c. 1. and the Notes of Alemannus, p. 3.

and their courage was exalted by the social honour of their rank, and the personal ambition of favour and fortune. Four hundred of the bravest of the Heruli marched under the banner of the faithful and active Pharas; their untractable valour was more highly prized than the tame submission of the Greeks and Syrians; and of such importance was it deemed to procure a reinforcement of six hundred Massagetæ, or Huns, that they were allured by fraud and deceit to engage in a naval expedition. Five thousand horse and ten thousand foot were embarked at Constantinople for the conquest of Africa, but the infantry, for the most part levied in Thrace and Isauria, yielded to the more prevailing use and reputation of the cavalry; and the Scythian bow was the weapon on which the armies of Rome were now reduced to place their principal dependence. From a laudable desire to assert the dignity of his theme, Procopius defends the soldiers of his own time against the morose critics, who confined that respectable name to the heavy-armed warriors of antiquity, and maliciously observed, that the word *archer* is introduced by Homer[8] as a term of contempt. "Such contempt might perhaps be due to the naked youths who appeared on foot in the fields of Troy, and, lurking behind a tombstone, or the shield of a friend, drew the bow-string to their breast,[9] and dismissed a feeble and lifeless arrow. But our archers (pursues the historian) are mounted on horses, which they manage with admirable skill; their head and shoulders are protected by a cask or buckler; they wear greaves of iron on their legs, and their bodies are guarded by a coat of mail. On their right side hangs a quiver, a sword on their left, and their hand is accustomed to wield a lance or javelin in closer combat. Their bows are strong and weighty; they shoot in every possible direction, advancing, retreating, to the front, to the rear, or to either flank; and as they are taught to draw the bow-string not to the breast, but to the right ear, firm indeed must be the armour that can resist the rapid violence of their shaft." Five hundred transports, navigated by twenty thousand mariners of Egypt, Cilicia, and Ionia, were collected in the

---

8. See the Preface of Procopius. The enemies of archery might quote the reproaches of Diomede (Iliad *Δ*. 385, &c.) and the permittere vulnera ventis of Lucan (viii. 384.): yet the Romans could not despise the arrows of the Parthians; and in the siege of Troy, Pandarus, Paris, and Teucer, pierced those haughty warriors who insulted them as women or children.

9. Νευρην μεν μαξῳ πελασεν, τοξῳ δε σιδηρον (Iliad *Δ*. 123.). How concise – how just – how beautiful is the whole picture! I see the attitudes of the archer – I hear the twanging of the bow:

Λιγξε βιος, νευηρ δε μεγ᾽ ιαχεν, αλτο δ᾽ οϊσος.

harbour of Constantinople. The smallest of these vessels may be computed at thirty, the largest at five hundred, tons; and the fair average will supply an allowance, liberal, but not profuse, of about one hundred thousand tons,[10] for the reception of thirty-five thousand soldiers and sailors, of five thousand horses, of arms, engines, and military stores, and of a sufficient stock of water and provisions for a voyage, perhaps, of three months. The proud gallies, which in former ages swept the Mediterranean with so many hundred oars, had long since disappeared; and the fleet of Justinian was escorted only by ninety-two light brigantines, covered from the missile weapons of the enemy, and rowed by two thousand of the brave and robust youth of Constantinople. Twenty-two generals are named, most of whom were afterwards distinguished in the wars of Africa and Italy: but the supreme command, both by land and sea was delegated to Belisarius alone, with a boundless power of acting according to his direction as if the emperor himself were present. The separation of the naval and military professions is at once the effect and the cause of the modern improvements in the science of navigation and maritime war.

In the seventh year of the reign of Justinian, and about the time of the summer solstice, the whole fleet of six hundred ships was ranged in martial pomp before the gardens of the palace. The patriarch pronounced his benediction, the emperor signified his last commands, the general's trumpet gave the signal of departure, *Departure of the fleet, A.D. 533, June.* and every heart, according to its fears or wishes, explored with anxious curiosity the omens of misfortune and success. The first halt was made at Perinthus or Heraclea, where Belisarius waited five days to receive some Thracian horses, a military gift of his sovereign. From thence the fleet pursued their course through the midst of the Propontis; but as they struggled to pass the streights of the Hellespont, an unfavourable wind detained them four days at Abydus, where the general exhibited a memorable lesson of firmness and severity. Two of the Huns, who in a drunken quarrel had slain one of their fellow-soldiers, were instantly shewn to the

10. The text appears to allow for the largest vessels 50,000 medimni, or 3000 tons (since the *medimnus* weighed 160 Roman, or 120 averdupois, pounds). I have given a more rational interpretation, by supposing that the Attic style of Procopius conceals the legal and popular *modius*, a sixth part of the *medimnus* (Hooper's Ancient Measures, p. 152, &c.). A contrary, and indeed a stranger mistake, has crept into an oration of Dinarchus (contra Demosthenem, in Reiske Orator. Græc. tom. iv. P. ii. p. 34.). By reducing the *number* of ships from 500 to 50, and translating μεδιμνοι by *mines*, or pounds, Cousin has generously allowed 500 tons for the whole of the Imperial fleet! – Did he never think?

army suspended on a lofty gibbet. The national indignity was resented by their countrymen, who disclaimed the servile laws of the empire, and asserted the free privilege of Scythia, where a small fine was allowed to expiate the hasty sallies of intemperance and anger. Their complaints were specious, their clamours were loud, and the Romans were not averse to the example of disorder and impunity. But the rising sedition was appeased by the authority and eloquence of the general: and he represented to the assembled troops the obligation of justice, the importance of discipline, the rewards of piety and virtue, and the unpardonable guilt of murder, which, in his apprehension, was aggravated rather than excused by the vice of intoxication.[11] In the navigation from the Hellespont to Peloponnesus, which the Greeks, after the siege of Troy, had performed in four days;[12] the fleet of Belisarius was guided in their course by his master-galley, conspicuous in the day by the redness of the sails, and in the night by the torches blazing from the mast-head. It was the duty of the pilots, as they steered between the islands, and turned the capes of Malea and Tænarium, to preserve the just order and regular intervals of such a multitude of ships; as the wind was fair and moderate, their labours were not unsuccessful, and the troops were safely disembarked at Methone on the Messenian coast, to repose themselves for a while after the fatigues of the sea. In this place they experienced how avarice, invested with authority, may sport with the lives of thousands which are bravely exposed for the public service. According to military practice, the bread or biscuit of the Romans was twice prepared in the oven, and a diminution of one-fourth was cheerfully allowed for the loss of weight. To gain this miserable profit, and to save the expence of wood, the præfect John of Cappadocia had given orders, that the flour should be slightly baked by the same fire which warmed the baths of Constantinople; and when the sacks were opened, a soft and mouldy paste was distributed to the army. Such unwholesome food, assisted by the heat of the climate and season, soon produced an epidemical disease, which swept away five hundred soldiers. Their health was restored

---

11. I have read of a Greek legislator, who inflicted a *double* penalty on the crimes committed in a state of intoxication; but it seems agreed that this was rather a political than a moral law.

12. Or even in three days, since they anchored the first evening in the neighbouring isle of Tenedos: the second day they sailed to Lesbos, the third to the promontory of Eubœa, and on the fourth they reached Argos (Homer, Odyss. Γ. 130–183. Wood's Essay on Homer, p. 40–46.). A pirate sailed from the Hellespont to the sea-port of Sparta in three days (Xenophon, Hellen. l. ii. c. 1.).

by the diligence of Belisarius, who provided fresh bread at Methone, and boldly expressed his just and humane indignation: the emperor heard his complaint; the general was praised; but the minister was not punished. From the port of Methone, the pilots steered along the western coast of Peloponnesus, as far as the isle of Zacynthus or Zant, before they undertook the voyage (in their eyes a most arduous voyage) of one hundred leagues over the Ionian sea. As the fleet was surprised by a calm, sixteen days were consumed in the slow navigation; and even the general would have suffered the intolerable hardship of thirst, if the ingenuity of Antonina had not preserved the water in glass-bottles, which she buried deep in the sand in a part of the ship impervious to the rays of the sun. At length the harbour of Caucana,[13] on the southern side of Sicily, afforded a secure and hospitable shelter. The Gothic officers who governed the island in the name of the daughter and grandson of Theodoric, obeyed their imprudent orders, to receive the troops of Justinian like friends and allies: provisions were liberally supplied, the cavalry was remounted,[14] and Procopius soon returned from Syracuse with correct information of the state and designs of the Vandals. His intelligence determined Belisarius to hasten his operations, and his wise impatience was seconded by the winds. The fleet lost sight of Sicily, passed before the isle of Malta, discovered the capes of Africa, ran along the coast with a strong gale from the north-east, and finally cast anchor at the promontory of Caput vada, about five days journey to the south of Carthage.[15]

If Gelimer had been informed of the approach of the enemy, he must have delayed the conquest of Sardinia, for the immediate defence of his person and kingdom. A detachment of five thousand soldiers, and one hundred and twenty gallies, would have joined the remaining forces of the Vandals; and the descendant of Genseric might have surprised and oppressed a fleet of deep-laden transports incapable of action, and of light brigantines that seem only qualified for flight. Belisarius had secretly trembled when he overheard

Belisarius lands on the coast of Africa — September.

---

13. Caucana, near Camarina, is at least 50 miles (350 or 400 stadia) from Syracuse (Cluver, Sicilia Antiqua, p. 191.).
14. Procopius, Gothic. l. i. c. 3. Tibi tollit hinnitum apta quadrigis equa, in the Sicilian pastures of Grosphus (Horat. Carm. ii. 16.). Acragas . . . magnanimûm quondam generator equorum (Virgil. Æneid. iii. 704.).

Thero's horses, whose victories are immortalized by Pindar, were bred in this country.
15. The Caput vada of Procopius (where Justinian afterwards founded a city – de Edific. l. vi. c. 6.) is the promontory of Ammon in Strabo, the Brachodes of Ptolemy, the Capaudia of the moderns, a long narrow slip that runs into the sea (Shaw's Travels, p. 111.).

his soldiers, in the passage, emboldening each other to confess their apprehensions: if they were once on shore, they hoped to maintain the honour
of their arms; but if they should be attacked at sea, they did not blush to
acknowledge that they wanted courage to contend at the same time
with the winds, the waves, and the Barbarians.[16] The knowledge of their
sentiments decided Belisarius to seize the first opportunity of landing them
on the coast of Africa; and he prudently rejected, in a council of war, the
proposal of sailing with the fleet and army into the port of Carthage. Three
months after their departure from Constantinople, the men and horses, the
arms and military stores, were safely disembarked, and five soldiers were
left as a guard on board each of the ships, which were disposed in the form
of a semicircle. The remainder of the troops occupied a camp on the
sea-shore, which they fortified, according to ancient discipline, with a ditch
and rampart; and the discovery of a source of fresh water, while it allayed
the thirst, excited the superstitious confidence, of the Romans. The next
morning, some of the neighbouring gardens were pillaged; and Belisarius,
after chastising the offenders, embraced the slight occasion, but the decisive
moment, of inculcating the maxims of justice, moderation, and genuine
policy. "When I first accepted the commission of subduing Africa, I
depended much less," said the general, "on the numbers, or even the
bravery, of my troops, than upon the friendly disposition of the natives,
and their immortal hatred to the Vandals. You alone can deprive me of
this hope: if you continue to extort by rapine what might be purchased
for a little money, such acts of violence will reconcile these implacable
enemies, and unite them in a just and holy league against the invaders of
their country." These exhortations were enforced by a rigid discipline; of
which the soldiers themselves soon felt and praised the salutary effects. The
inhabitants, instead of deserting their houses, or hiding their corn, supplied
the Romans with a fair and liberal market: the civil officers of the province
continued to exercise their functions in the name of Justinian; and the
clergy, from motives of conscience and interest, assiduously laboured to
promote the cause of a Catholic emperor. The small town of Sullecte,[17]

16. A centurion of Mark Antony expressed,
though in a more manly strain, the same dislike
to the sea and to naval combats (Plutarch in
Antonio, p. 1730. edit. Hen. Steph.).
17. Sullecte is perhaps the Turris Hannibalis,
an old building, now as large as the Tower of

London. The march of Belisarius to Leptis,
Adrumetum, &c. is illustrated by the campaign of Cæsar (Hirtius, de Bello Africano,
with the Analyse of Guichardt), and Shaw's
Travels (p. 105–113.) in the same country.

one day's journey from the camp, had the honour of being foremost to open her gates, and to resume her ancient allegiance: the larger cities of Leptis and Adrumetum imitated the example of loyalty as soon as Belisarius appeared; and he advanced without opposition as far as Grasse, a palace of the Vandal kings, at the distance of fifty miles from Carthage. The weary Romans indulged themselves in the refreshment of shady groves, cool fountains, and delicious fruits; and the preference which Procopius allows to these gardens over any that he had seen, either in the East or West, may be ascribed either to the taste or the fatigue of the historian. In three generations, prosperity and a warm climate had dissolved the hardy virtue of the Vandals, who insensibly became the most luxurious of mankind. In their villas and gardens, which might deserve the Persian name of *paradise*,[18] they enjoyed a cool and elegant repose; and, after the daily use of the bath, the Barbarians were seated at a table profusely spread with the delicacies of the land and sea. Their silken robes, loosely flowing after the fashion of the Medes, were embroidered with gold: love and hunting were the labours of their life, and their vacant hours were amused by pantomimes, chariot races, and the music and dances of the theatre.

In a march of ten or twelve days, the vigilance of Belisarius was constantly awake and active against his unseen enemies, by whom in every place, and at every hour, he might be suddenly attacked. An officer of confidence and merit, John the Armenian, led the vanguard of three hundred horse; six hundred Massagetæ covered at a certain distance the left flank; and the whole fleet, steering along the coast, seldom lost sight of the army, which moved each day about twelve miles, and lodged in the evening in strong camps, or in friendly towns. The near approach of the Romans to Carthage filled the mind of Gelimer with anxiety and terror. He prudently wished to protract the war till his brother, with his veteran troops, should return from the conquest of Sardinia; and he now lamented the rash policy of his ancestors, who, by destroying the fortifications of Africa, had left him only the dangerous resource of risking a battle in the neighbourhood of his capital. The Vandal conquerors, from their original number of fifty thousand, were multiplied, without including their women and children, to one hundred and sixty

Defeats the Vandals in a first battle.

---

18. Παραδεισος καλλιστος ἁπαντων ὡν ἡμεις ισμεν. The paradises, a name and fashion adopted from Persia, may be represented by the royal garden of Ispahan (Voyage d'Olearius, p. 774.). See, in the Greek romances, their most perfect model (Longus, Pastoral. l. iv. p. 99–101. Achilles Tatius, l. i. p. 22, 23.).

thousand fighting men: and such forces, animated with valour and union, might have crushed, at their first landing, the feeble and exhausted bands of the Roman general. But the friends of the captive king were more inclined to accept the invitations, than to resist the progress, of Belisarius; and many a proud Barbarian disguised his aversion to war under the more specious name of his hatred to the usurper. Yet the authority and promises of Gelimer collected a formidable army, and his plans were concerted with some degree of military skill. An order was dispatched to his brother Ammatas, to collect all the forces of Carthage, and to encounter the van of the Roman army at the distance of ten miles from the city: his nephew Gibamund, with two thousand horse, was destined to attack their left, when the monarch himself, who silently followed, should charge their rear, in a situation which excluded them from the aid or even the view of their fleet. But the rashness of Ammatas was fatal to himself and his country. He anticipated the hour of the attack, outstripped his tardy followers, and was pierced with a mortal wound, after he had slain with his own hand twelve of his boldest antagonists. His Vandals fled to Carthage; the highway, almost ten miles, was strewed with dead bodies; and it seemed incredible that such multitudes could be slaughtered by the swords of three hundred Romans. The nephew of Gelimer was defeated after a slight combat by the six hundred Massagetæ: they did not equal the third part of his numbers; but each Scythian was fired by the example of his chief, who gloriously exercised the privilege of his family, by riding foremost and alone to shoot the first arrow against the enemy. In the mean while, Gelimer himself, ignorant of the event, and misguided by the windings of the hills, inadvertently passed the Roman army, and reached the scene of action where Ammatas had fallen. He wept the fate of his brother and of Carthage, charged with irresistible fury the advancing squadrons, and might have pursued, and perhaps decided the victory, if he had not wasted those inestimable moments in the discharge of a vain, though pious, duty to the dead. While his spirit was broken by this mournful office, he heard the trumpet of Belisarius, who, leaving Antonina and his infantry in the camp, pressed forwards with his guards and the remainder of the cavalry to rally his flying troops, and to restore the fortune of the day. Much room could not be found in this disorderly battle for the talents of a general; but the king fled before the hero; and the Vandals, accustomed only to a Moorish enemy, were incapable of withstanding the arms and discipline of the Romans. Gelimer retired with hasty steps towards the desert of Numidia; but he had soon the consolation of learning that his private orders for the execution of Hilderic and his captive friends had been faithfully obeyed. The tyrant's revenge was useful only to his enemies. The death of a lawful prince excited the compassion of his people; his life might have perplexed the victorious Romans; and the lieutenant of Justinian, by a crime of which he was innocent, was relieved from the painful alternative of forfeiting his honour or relinquishing his conquests.

As soon as the tumult had subsided, the several parts of the army informed each other of the accidents of the day; and Belisarius pitched his camp on the field of victory, to which the tenth milestone from Carthage had applied the Latin appellation of *decimus*. From a wise suspicion of the stratagems and resources of the Vandals, he marched the next day in order of battle, halted in the evening before the gates of Carthage, and allowed a night of repose, that he might not, in darkness and disorder, expose the city to the licence of the soldiers, or the soldiers themselves to the secret ambush of the city. But as the fears of Belisarius were the result of calm and intrepid reason, he was soon satisfied that he might confide, without danger, in the peaceful and friendly aspect of the capital. Carthage blazed with innumerable torches, the signals of the public joy; the chain was removed that guarded the entrance of the port; the gates were thrown open, and the people, with acclamations of gratitude, hailed and invited their Roman deliverers. The defeat of the Vandals, and the freedom of Africa, were announced to the city on the eve of St. Cyprian, when the churches were already adorned and illuminated for the festival of the martyr, whom three centuries of superstition had almost raised to a local deity. The Arians, conscious that their reign had expired, resigned the temple to the Catholics, who rescued their saint from profane hands, performed the holy rites, and loudly proclaimed the creed of Athanasius and Justinian. One awful hour reversed the fortunes of the contending parties. The suppliant Vandals, who had so lately indulged the vices of conquerors, sought an humble refuge in the sanctuary of the church; while the merchants of the East were delivered from the deepest dungeon of the palace by their affrighted keeper, who implored the protection of his captives, and shewed them through an aperture in the wall, the sails of the Roman fleet. After their separation from the army, the naval commanders had proceeded with slow caution along the coast, till they reached the Hermæan promontory, and obtained

Reduction of Carthage, A.D. 533, Sept. 15.

the first intelligence of the victory of Belisarius. Faithful to his instructions, they would have cast anchor about twenty miles from Carthage, if the more skilful seamen had not represented the perils of the shore, and the signs of an impending tempest. Still ignorant of the revolution, they declined, however, the rash attempt of forcing the chain of the port; and the adjacent harbour and suburb of Mandracium were insulted only by the rapine of a private officer who disobeyed and deserted his leaders. But the Imperial fleet, advancing with a fair wind, steered through the narrow entrance of the Goletta, and occupied in the deep and capacious lake of Tunis a secure station about five miles from the capital.[19] No sooner was Belisarius informed of their arrival, than he dispatched orders, that the greatest part of the mariners should be immediately landed to join the triumph, and to swell the apparent numbers of the Romans. Before he allowed them to enter the gates of Carthage, he exhorted them, in a discourse worthy of himself and the occasion, not to disgrace the glory of their arms; and to remember that the Vandals had been the tyrants, but that *they* were the deliverers of the Africans, who must now be respected as the voluntary and affectionate subjects of their common sovereign. The Romans marched through the streets in close ranks, prepared for battle if an enemy had appeared; the strict order maintained by the general imprinted on their minds the duty of obedience; and in an age in which custom and impunity almost sanctified the abuse of conquest, the genius of one man repressed the passions of a victorious army. The voice of menace and complaint was silent; the trade of Carthage was not interrupted; while Africa changed her master and her government, the shops continued open and busy; and the soldiers, after sufficient guards had been posted, modestly departed to the houses which were allotted for their reception. Belisarius fixed his residence in the palace; seated himself on the throne of Genseric; accepted and distributed the Barbaric spoil; granted their lives to the suppliant Vandals; and laboured to repair the damage which the suburb of Mandracium had sustained in the preceding night. At supper he entertained his principal officers with the form and magnificence of a royal

19. The neighbourhood of Carthage, the sea, the land, and the rivers, are changed almost as much as the works of man. The isthmus, or neck, of the city is now confounded with the continent: the harbour is a dry plain; and the lake, or stagnum, no more than a morass, with six or seven feet water in the mid-channel. See d'Anville (Geographie Ancienne, tom. iii. p. 82.), Shaw (Travels, p. 77–84.), Marmol (Description de l'Afrique, tom. ii. p. 465.), and Thuanus (lviii. 12. tom. iii. p. 334.).

banquet.[20] The victor was respectfully served by the captive officers of the household; and in the moments of festivity, when the impartial spectators applauded the fortune and merit of Belisarius, his envious flatterers secretly shed their venom on every word and gesture which might alarm the suspicions of a jealous monarch. One day was given to these pompous scenes, which may not be despised as useless if they attracted the popular veneration; but the active mind of Belisarius, which in the pride of victory could suppose a defeat, had already resolved, that the Roman empire in Africa should not depend on the chance of arms, or the favour of the people. The fortifications of Carthage had alone been exempted from the general proscription; but in the reign of ninety-five years they were suffered to decay by the thoughtless and indolent Vandals. A wiser conqueror restored with incredible dispatch the walls and ditches of the city. His liberality encouraged the workmen; the soldiers, the mariners, and the citizens, vied with each other in the salutary labour; and Gelimer, who had feared to trust his person in an open town, beheld with astonishment and despair the rising strength of an impregnable fortress.

That unfortunate monarch, after the loss of his capital, applied himself to collect the remains of an army scattered, rather than destroyed, by the preceding battle; and the hopes of pillage attracted some Moorish bands to the standard of Gelimer. He encamped in the fields of Bulla, four days journey from Carthage; insulted the capital, which he deprived of the use of an aqueduct; proposed an high reward for the head of every Roman; affected to spare *Final defeat of Gelimer and the Vandals, A.D. 533, November.* the persons and property of his African subjects, and secretly negociated with the Arian sectaries and the confederate Huns. Under these circumstances, the conquest of Sardinia served only to aggravate his distress: he reflected with the deepest anguish, that he had wasted, in that useless enterprise, five thousand of his bravest troops; and he read, with grief and shame, the victorious letters of his brother Zano, who expressed a sanguine confidence that the king, after the example of their ancestors, had already chastised the rashness of the Roman invader. "Alas! my brother," replied Gelimer, "Heaven has declared against our unhappy nation. While you have subdued Sardinia, we have lost Africa. No sooner did Belisarius appear with a handful

20. From Delphi, the name of Delphicum was given, both in Greek and Latin, to a tripod; and, by an easy analogy, the same appellation was extended at Rome, Con-stantinople, and Carthage, to the royal ban-queting room (Procopius, Vandal. l. i. c. 21. Ducange, Gloss. Græc. p. 277. Δελφικον, ad Alexiad. p. 412.).

of soldiers, than courage and prosperity deserted the cause of the Vandals. Your nephew Gibamund, your brother Ammatas, have been betrayed to death by the cowardice of their followers. Our horses, our ships, Carthage itself, and all Africa, are in the power of the enemy. Yet the Vandals still prefer an ignominious repose, at the expence of their wives and children, their wealth and liberty. Nothing now remains, except the field of Bulla, and the hope of your valour. Abandon Sardinia; fly to our relief; restore our empire, or perish by our side." On the receipt of this epistle, Zano imparted his grief to the principal Vandals, but the intelligence was prudently concealed from the natives of the island. The troops embarked in one hundred and twenty gallies at the port of Cagliari, cast anchor the third day on the confines of Mauritania, and hastily pursued their march to join the royal standard in the camp of Bulla. Mournful was the interview: the two brothers embraced; they wept in silence; no questions were asked of the Sardinian victory; no enquiries were made of the African misfortunes: they saw before their eyes the whole extent of their calamities; and the absence of their wives and children afforded a melancholy proof, that either death or captivity had been their lot. The languid spirit of the Vandals was at length awakened and united by the entreaties of their king, the example of Zano, and the instant danger which threatened their monarchy and religion. The military strength of the nation advanced to battle; and such was the rapid increase, that before their army reached Tricameron, about twenty miles from Carthage, they might boast, perhaps with some exaggeration, that they surpassed, in a tenfold proportion, the diminutive powers of the Romans. But these powers were under the command of Belisarius; and, as he was conscious of their superior merit, he permitted the Barbarians to surprise him at an unseasonable hour. The Romans were instantly under arms: a rivulet covered their front; the cavalry formed the first line, which Belisarius supported in the center, at the head of five hundred guards; the infantry, at some distance, was posted in the second line; and the vigilance of the general watched the separate station and ambiguous faith of the Massagetæ, who secretly reserved their aid for the conquerors. The historian has inserted, and the reader may easily supply, the speeches[21] of the commanders, who, by arguments the most apposite

---

21. These orations always express the sense of the times, and sometimes of the actors. I have condensed that sense, and thrown away declamation.

to their situation, inculcated the importance of victory and the contempt of life. Zano, with the troops which had followed him to the conquest of Sardinia, was placed in the center; and the throne of Genseric might have stood, if the multitude of Vandals had imitated their intrepid resolution. Casting away their lances and missile weapons, they drew their swords, and expected the charge: the Roman cavalry thrice passed the rivulet; they were thrice repulsed; and the conflict was firmly maintained, till Zano fell, and the standard of Belisarius was displayed. Gelimer retreated to his camp; the Huns joined the pursuit; and the victors despoiled the bodies of the slain. Yet no more than fifty Romans, and eight hundred Vandals, were found on the field of battle; so inconsiderable was the carnage of a day, which extinguished a nation, and transferred the empire of Africa. In the evening, Belisarius led his infantry to the attack of the camp; and the pusillanimous flight of Gelimer exposed the vanity of his recent declarations, that, to the vanquished, death was a relief, life a burthen, and infamy the only object of terror. His departure was secret; but as soon as the Vandals discovered that their king had deserted them, they hastily dispersed, anxious only for their personal safety, and careless of every object that is dear or valuable to mankind. The Romans entered the camp without resistance; and the wildest scenes of disorder were veiled in the darkness and confusion of the night. Every Barbarian who met their swords was inhumanly massacred; their widows and daughters, as rich heirs, or beautiful concubines, were embraced by the licentious soldiers; and avarice itself was almost satiated with the treasures of gold and silver, the accumulated fruits of conquest or œconomy in a long period of prosperity and peace. In this frantic search, the troops even of Belisarius forgot their caution and respect. Intoxicated with lust and rapine, they explored in small parties, or alone, the adjacent fields, the woods, the rocks, and the caverns, that might possibly conceal any desirable prize: laden with booty, they deserted their ranks, and wandered, without a guide, on the high-road to Carthage; and if the flying enemies had dared to return, very few of the conquerors would have escaped. Deeply sensible of the disgrace and danger, Belisarius passed an apprehensive night on the field of victory; at the dawn of day, he planted his standard on a hill, recalled his guards and veterans, and gradually restored the modesty and obedience of the camp. It was equally the concern of the Roman general to subdue the hostile, and to save the prostrate Barbarian: and the suppliant Vandals, who could be found only in churches, were protected by his authority, disarmed, and separately confined, that they might neither disturb the public peace, nor become the victims of popular revenge. After dispatching a light detachment to tread the footsteps of Gelimer, he advanced with his whole army, about ten days march, as far as Hippo Regius, which no longer possessed the relics of St. Augustin.[22] The season, and the certain intelligence that the Vandal had fled to the inaccessible country of the Moors, determined Belisarius to relinquish the vain pursuit, and to fix his winter-quarters at Carthage. From thence he dispatched his principal lieutenant, to inform the emperor, that, in the space of three months, he had atchieved the conquest of Africa.

Conquest of Africa by Belisarius, A.D. 534.

Belisarius spoke the language of truth. The surviving Vandals yielded, without resistance, their arms and their freedom: the neighbourhood of Carthage submitted to his presence; and the more distant provinces were successively subdued by the report of his victory. Tripoli was confirmed in her voluntary allegiance; Sardinia and Corsica surrendered to an officer, who carried, instead of a sword, the head of the valiant Zano; and the isles of Majorca, Minorca, and Yvica, consented to remain an humble appendage of the African kingdom. Cæsarea, a royal city, which in looser geography may be confounded with the modern Algiers, was situate thirty days march to the westward of Carthage: by land, the road was infested by the Moors; but the sea was open, and the Romans were now masters of the sea. An active and discreet tribune sailed as far as the Streights, where he occupied Septem or Ceuta,[23] which rises opposite to Gibraltar on the African coast: that remote place was afterwards adorned and fortified by Justinian; and he seems to have indulged the vain ambition of extending his empire to the columns of Hercules. He received the messengers of victory at the time when he was preparing to publish the pandects of the Roman law; and the

---

22. The relics of St. Augustin were carried by the African bishops to their Sardinian exile (A.D. 500.); and it was believed in the viiith century that Liutprand, king of the Lombards, transported them (A.D. 721.) from Sardinia to Pavia. In the year 1695, the Augustin friars of that city *found* a brick arch, marble coffin, silver case, silk wrapper, bones, blood, &c. and perhaps an inscription of Agostino in Gothic letters. But this useful discovery has been disputed by reason and jealousy (Baronius, Annal. A.D. 725. N° 2–9. Tillemont, Mem. Eccles. tom. xiii. p. 944. Montfaucon,

Diarium Ital. p. 26–30. Muratori, Antiq. Ital. Medii Ævi, tom. v. dissert. lviii. p. 9. who had composed a separate treatise before the decree of the bishop of Pavia, and Pope Benedict XIII.).

23. Τα της πολιτειας προοιμια, is the expression of Procopius (de Edific. l. vi. c. 7.). Ceuta, which has been defaced by the Portuguese, flourished in nobles and palaces, in agriculture and manufactures, under the more prosperous reign of the Arabs (l'Afrique de Marmol, tom. ii. p. 236.).

devout or jealous emperor celebrated the divine goodness, and confessed, in silence, the merit of his successful general.[24] Impatient to abolish the temporal and spiritual tyranny of the Vandals, he proceeded, without delay, to the full establishment of the Catholic church. Her jurisdiction, wealth, and immunities, perhaps the most essential part of episcopal religion, were restored and amplified with a liberal hand; the Arian worship was suppresed; the Donatist meetings were proscribed;[25] and the synod of Carthage, by the voice of two hundred and seventeen bishops,[26] applauded the just measure of pious retaliation. On such an occasion, it may not be presumed, that many orthodox prelates were absent; but the comparative smallness of their number, which in ancient councils had been twice or even thrice multiplied, most clearly indicates the decay both of the church and state. While Justinian approved himself the defender of the faith, he entertained an ambitious hope, that his victorious lieutenant would speedily enlarge the narrow limits of his dominion to the space which they occupied before the invasion of the Moors and Vandals; and Belisarius was instructed to establish five *dukes* or commanders in the convenient stations of Tripoli, Leptis, Cirta, Cæsarea, and Sardinia, and to compute the military force of *palatines* or *borderers* that might be sufficient for the defence of Africa. The kingdom of the Vandals was not unworthy of the presence of a Prætorian præfect; and four consulars, three presidents, were appointed to administer the seven provinces under his civil jurisdiction. The number of their subordinate officers, clerks, messengers, or assistants, was minutely expressed; three hundred and ninety-six for the præfect himself, fifty for each of his vicegerents; and the rigid definition of their fees and salaries was more effectual to confirm the right, than to prevent the abuse. These magistrates might be oppressive, but they were not idle: and the subtle questions of justice and revenue were infinitely propagated under the new government, which professed to revive the freedom and equity of the Roman republic. The conqueror was solicitous to extract a prompt and

24. See the second and third preambles to the Digest, or Pandects, promulgated A.D. 533, December 16. To the titles of *Vandalicus* and *Africanus*, Justinian, or rather Belisarius, had acquired a just claim: *Gothicus* was premature, and *Francicus* false and offensive to a great nation.

25. See the original acts in Baronius (A.D. 535. N° 21–54.). The emperor applauds his own clemency to the heretics, cum sufficiat eis vivere.

26. Dupin (Geograph. Sacra Africana, p.lix. ad Optat. Milev.) observes and bewails this episcopal decay. In the more prosperous age of the church, he had noticed 690 bishoprics; but however minute were the dioceses, it is not probable that they all existed at the same time.

plentiful supply from his African subjects; and he allowed them to claim, even in the third degree, and from the collateral line, the houses and lands of which their families had been unjustly despoiled by the Vandals. After the departure of Belisarius, who acted by an high and special commission, no ordinary provision was made for a master-general of the forces: but the office of Prætorian præfect was intrusted to a soldier; the civil and military powers were united, according to the practice of Justinian, in the chief governor; and the representative of the emperor in Africa as well as in Italy, was soon distinguished by the appellation of Exarch.[27]

Distress and captivity of Gelimer, A.D. 534 – the Spring.   Yet the conquest of Africa was imperfect, till her former sovereign was delivered, either alive or dead, into the hands of the Romans. Doubtful of the event, Gelimer had given secret orders that a part of his treasure should be transported to Spain, where he hoped to find a secure refuge at the court of the king of the Visigoths. But these intentions were disappointed by accident, treachery, and the indefatigable pursuit of his enemies, who intercepted his flight from the sea-shore, and chaced the unfortunate monarch, with some faithful followers, to the inaccessible mountain of Papua,[28] in the inland country of Numidia. He was immediately besieged by Pharas, an officer whose truth and sobriety were the more applauded, as such qualities could be seldom found among the Heruli, the most corrupt of the Barbarian tribes. To his vigilance Belisarius had entrusted this important charge; and, after a bold attempt to scale the mountain, in which he lost an hundred and ten soldiers, Pharas expected, during a winter siege, the operation of distress and famine on the mind of the Vandal king. From the softest habits of pleasure, from the unbounded command of industry and wealth, he was reduced to share the poverty of the Moors,[29] supportable only to themselves by their ignorance of a happier condition. In their rude hovels, of mud and hurdles, which confined the smoke and excluded the light, they promiscuously slept on the ground, perhaps on a sheep-skin,

27. The African laws of Justinian are illustrated by his German biographer (Cod. l. i. tit. 27. Novell. 36, 37. 131. Vit. Justinian. p. 349–377.).

28. Mount Papua is placed by d'Anville (tom. iii. p. 92. and Tabul. Imp. Rom. Occident.) near Hippo Regius and the sea; yet this situation ill agrees with the long pursuit beyond Hippo, and the words of Procopius (l. ii. c. 4.),

εν τοις Νουμιδιας εσχατοις.

29. Shaw (Travels, p. 220.) most accurately represents the manners of the Bedoweens and Kabyles, the last of whom, by their language, are the remnant of the Moors: yet how changed – how civilized are these modern savages! – provisions are plenty among them, and bread is common.

with their wives, their children, and their cattle. Sordid and scanty were their garments; the use of bread and wine was unknown; and their oaten or barley cakes, imperfectly baked in the ashes, were devoured almost in a crude state by the hungry savages. The health of Gelimer must have sunk under these strange and unwonted hardships, from whatsoever cause they had been endured; but his actual misery was embittered by the recollection of past greatness, the daily insolence of his protectors, and the just apprehension, that the light and venal Moors might be tempted to betray the rights of hospitality. The knowledge of his situation dictated the humane and friendly epistle of Pharas. "Like yourself," said the chief of the Heruli, "I am an illiterate Barbarian, but I speak the language of plain sense, and an honest heart. Why will you persist in hopeless obstinacy? Why will you ruin yourself, your family, and nation? The love of freedom and abhorrence of slavery? Alas! my dearest Gelimer, are you not already the worst of slaves, the slave of the vile nation of the Moors? Would it not be preferable to sustain at Constantinople a life of poverty and servitude, rather than to reign the undoubted monarch of the mountain of Papua? Do you think it a disgrace to be the subject of Justinian? Belisarius is his subject; and we ourselves, whose birth is not inferior to your own, are not ashamed of our obedience to the Roman emperor. That generous prince will grant you a rich inheritance of lands, a place in the senate, and the dignity of Patrician: such are his gracious intentions, and you may depend with full assurance on the word of Belisarius. So long as heaven has condemned us to suffer, patience is a virtue; but if we reject the proffered deliverance, it degenerates into blind and stupid despair." "I am not insensible," replied the king of the Vandals, "how kind and rational is your advice. But I cannot persuade myself to become the slave of an unjust enemy, who has deserved my implacable hatred. *Him* I had never injured either by word or deed: yet he has sent against me, I know not from whence, a certain Belisarius, who has cast me headlong from the throne into this abyss of misery. Justinian is a man; he is a prince; does he not dread for himself a similar reverse of fortune? I can write no more: my grief oppresses me. Send me, I beseech you, my dear Pharas, send me, a lyre,[30] a spunge, and a loaf of bread." From the Vandal messenger, Pharas

---

30. By Procopius it is styled a *lyre*; perhaps *harp* would have been more national. The instruments of music are thus distinguished by Venantius Fortunatus:

Romanusque *lyrâ* tibi plaudat, Barbarus *harpâ*.

was informed of the motives of this singular request. It was long since the king of Africa had tasted bread; a defluxion had fallen on his eyes, the effect of fatigue or incessant weeping; and he wished to solace the melancholy hours, by singing to the lyre the sad story of his own misfortunes. The humanity of Pharas was moved; he sent the three extraordinary gifts; but even his humanity prompted him to redouble the vigilance of his guard, that he might sooner compel his prisoner to embrace a resolution advantageous to the Romans, but salutary to himself. The obstinacy of Gelimer at length yielded to reason and necessity; the solemn assurances of safety and honourable treatment were ratified in the emperor's name, by the ambassador of Belisarius; and the king of the Vandals descended from the mountain. The first public interview was in one of the suburbs of Carthage; and when the royal captive accosted his conqueror, he burst into a fit of laughter. The crowd might naturally believe, that extreme grief had deprived Gelimer of his senses; but in this mournful state, unseasonable mirth insinuated to more intelligent observers, that the vain and transitory scenes of human greatness are unworthy of a serious thought.[31]

Return and triumph of Belisarius, A.D. 534. Autumn. Their contempt was soon justified by a new example of a vulgar truth; that flattery adheres to power, and envy to superior merit. The chiefs of the Roman army presumed to think themselves the rivals of an hero. Their private dispatches maliciously affirmed, that the conqueror of Africa, strong in his reputation and the public love, conspired to seat himself on the throne of the Vandals. Justinian listened with too patient an ear; and his silence was the result of jealousy rather than of confidence. An honourable alternative, of remaining in the province, or of returning to the capital, was indeed submitted to the discretion of Belisarius; but he wisely concluded from intercepted letters, and the knowledge of his sovereign's temper, that he must either resign his head, erect his standard, or confound his enemies by his presence and submission. Innocence and courage decided his choice: his guards, captives, and treasures, were diligently embarked; and so prosperous was the navigation, that his arrival at Constantinople preceded any certain account of his departure from the port of Carthage. Such unsuspecting loyalty removed

---

31. Herodotus elegantly describes the strange effects of grief in another royal captive, Psammetichus of Egypt, who wept at the lesser, and was silent at the greatest of his calamities (l. iii. c. 14.). In the interview of Paulus Æmilius and Perses, Belisarius might study his part: but it is probable that he never read either Livy or Plutarch; and it is certain that his generosity did not need a tutor.

the apprehensions of Justinian: envy was silenced and inflamed by the public gratitude; and the third Africanus obtained the honours of a triumph, a ceremony which the city of Constantine had never seen, and which ancient Rome, since the reign of Tiberius, had reserved for the *auspicious* arms of the Cæsars.[32] From the palace of Belisarius, the procession was conducted through the principal streets to the hippodrome; and this memorable day seemed to avenge the injuries of Genseric, and to expiate the shame of the Romans. The wealth of nations was displayed, the trophies of martial or effeminate luxury: rich armour, golden thrones, and the chariots of state which had been used by the Vandal queen; the massy furniture of the royal banquet, the splendour of precious stones, the elegant forms of statues and vases, the more substantial treasure of gold, and the holy vessels of the Jewish temple, which, after their long peregrination, were respectfully deposited in the Christian church of Jerusalem. A long train of the noblest Vandals reluctantly exposed their lofty stature and manly countenance. Gelimer slowly advanced: he was clad in a purple robe, and still maintained the majesty of a king. Not a tear escaped from his eyes, not a sigh was heard; but his pride or piety derived some secret consolation from the words of Solomon,[33] which he repeatedly pronounced, VANITY! VANITY! ALL IS VANITY! Instead of ascending a triumphal car drawn by four horses or elephants, the modest conqueror marched on foot at the head of his brave companions: his prudence might decline an honour too conspicuous for a subject; and his magnanimity might justly disdain what had been so often sullied by the vilest of tyrants. The glorious procession entered the gate of the hippodrome; was saluted by the acclamations of the senate and people; and halted before the throne where Justinian and Theodora were seated to receive the homage of the captive monarch and the victorious hero. They both performed the customary adoration; and falling prostrate on the ground, respectfully touched the footstool of a prince who had not unsheathed his sword, and of a prostitute, who had danced on the theatre: some gentle violence was used to bend the stubborn

---

32. After the title of *imperator* had lost the old military sense, and the Roman *auspices* were abolished by Christianity (see La Bleterie, Mem. de l'Academie, tom. xxi. p. 302−332.), a triumph might be given with less inconsistency to a private general.

33. If the Ecclesiastes be truly a work of Solomon, and not, like Prior's poem, a pious and moral composition of more recent times, in his name, and on the subject of his repentance. The latter is the opinion of the learned and free-spirited Grotius (Opp. Theolog. tom. i. p. 258.): and indeed the Ecclesiastes and Proverbs display a larger compass of thought and experience than seem to belong either to a Jew or a king.

spirit of the grandson of Genseric; and however trained to servitude, the

His sole consulship, A.D. 535, January 1.

genius of Belisarius must have secretly rebelled. He was immediately declared consul for the ensuing year, and the day of his inauguration resembled the pomp of a second triumph: his curule chair was borne aloft on the shoulders of captive Vandals; and the spoils of war, gold cups, and rich girdles, were profusely scattered among the populace.

End of Gelimer and the Vandals.

But the purest reward of Belisarius was in the faithful execution of a treaty for which his honour had been pledged to the king of the Vandals. The religious scruples of Gelimer, who adhered to the Arian heresy, were incompatible with the dignity of senator or patrician: but he received from the emperor an ample estate in the province of Galatia, where the abdicated monarch retired with his family and friends, to a life of peace, of affluence, and perhaps of content.[34] The daughters of Hilderic were entertained with the respectful tenderness due to their age and misfortune; and Justinian and Theodora accepted the honour of educating and enriching the female descendants of the great Theodosius. The bravest of the Vandal youth were distributed into five squadrons of cavalry, which adopted the name of their benefactor, and supported in the Persian wars the glory of their ancestors. But these rare exceptions, the reward of birth or valour, are insufficient to explain the fate of a nation, whose numbers, before a short and bloodless war, amounted to more than six hundred thousand persons. After the exile of their king and nobles, the servile crowd might purchase their safety, by abjuring their character, religion, and language; and their degenerate posterity would be insensibly mingled with the common herd of African subjects. Yet even in the present age, and in the heart of the Moorish tribes, a curious traveller has discovered the white complexion and long flaxen hair of a northern race;[35] and it was formerly believed, that the boldest of the Vandals fled beyond the power, or even the knowledge, of the Romans, to enjoy their solitary freedom on the shores of the

34. In the Belisaire of Marmontel, the king and the conqueror of Africa meet, sup, and converse, without recollecting each other. It is surely a fault of that romance, that not only the hero, but all to whom he had been so conspicuously known, appear to have lost their eyes or their memory.

35. Shaw, p. 59. Yet since Procopius (l. ii.

c. 13.) speaks of a people of mount Atlas, as already distinguished by white bodies and yellow hair, the phænomenon (which is likewise visible in the Andes of Peru, Buffon, tom. iii. p. 504.) may naturally be ascribed to the elevation of the ground and the temperature of the air.

Atlantic ocean.[36] Africa had been their empire, it became their prison; nor could they entertain an hope, or even a wish, of returning to the banks of the Elbe, where their brethren, of a spirit less adventurous, still wandered in their native forests. It was impossible for cowards to surmount the barriers of unknown seas and hostile Barbarians: it was impossible for brave men to expose their nakedness and defeat before the eyes of their countrymen, to describe the kingdoms which they had lost, and to claim a share of the humble inheritance, which, in a happier hour, they had almost unanimously renounced.[37] In the country between the Elbe and the Oder, several populous villages of Lusatia are inhabited by the Vandals: they still preserve their language, their customs, and the purity of their blood; support with some impatience, the Saxon, or Prussian yoke; and serve with secret and voluntary allegiance, the descendant of their ancient kings, who in his garb and present fortune is confounded with the meanest of his vassals.[38] The name and situation of this unhappy people might indicate their descent from one common stock with the conquerors of Africa. But the use of a Sclavonian dialect more clearly represents them as the last remnant of the new colonies, who succeeded to the genuine Vandals, already scattered or destroyed in the age of Procopius.[39]

If Belisarius had been tempted to hesitate in his allegiance, he might have urged, even against the emperor himself, the indispensable duty of saving Africa from an enemy more barbarous than the Vandals. The origin of the Moors is involved in darkness: they were ignorant of the use of letters.[40] Their limits cannot be precisely defined: a boundless continent was open to the Libyan shepherds;

Manners and defeat of the Moors, A.D. 535.

---

36. The geographer of Ravenna (l. iii. c. xi. p. 129, 130, 131. Paris, 1688.) describes the Mauritania *Gaditana* (opposite to Cadiz), ubi gens Vandalorum, a Belisario devicta in Africâ, fugit, et nunquam comparuit.

37. A single voice had protested, and Generic dismissed, without a formal answer, the Vandals of Germany: but those of Africa derided his prudence, and affected to despise the poverty of their forests (Procopius, Vandal. l. i. c. 22.).

38. From the mouth of the great elector (in 1687), Tollius describes the secret royalty and rebellious spirit of the Vandals of Brandenburgh, who could muster five or six thousand

soldiers who had procured some cannon, &c. (Itinerar. Hungar. p. 42. apud Dubos, Hist. de la Monarchie Françoise, tom. i. p. 182, 183.). The veracity, not of the elector, but of Tollius himself, may justly be suspected.

39. Procopius (l. i. c. 22.) was in total darkness – ουδε μνημη τις ουδε ονομα ες εμε σωζεται. Under the reign of Dagobert (A.D. 630.), the Sclavonian tribes of the Sorbi and Venedi already bordered on Thuringia (Mascou, Hist. of the Germans, xv. 3, 4, 5).

40. Sallust represents the Moors as a remnant of the army of Heracles (de Bell. Jugurth. c. 21.), and Procopius (Vandal. l. ii. c. 10.) as the posterity of the Cananæans who fled from

the change of seasons and pastures regulated their motions; and their rude huts and slender furniture were transported with the same ease as their arms, their families, and their cattle, which consisted of sheep, oxen, and camels.[41] During the vigour of the Roman power, they observed a respectful distance from Carthage and the sea-shore; under the feeble reign of the Vandals, they invaded the cities of Numidia, occupied the sea-coast from Tangier to Cæsarea, and pitched their camps, with impunity, in the fertile province of Byzacium. The formidable strength and artful conduct of Belisarius secured the neutrality of the Moorish princes, whose vanity aspired to receive, in the emperor's name, the ensigns of their regal dignity.[42] They were astonished by the rapid event, and trembled in the presence of their conqueror. But his approaching departure soon relieved the apprehensions of a savage and superstitious people; the number of their wives allowed them to disregard the safety of their infant hostages; and when the Roman general hoisted sail in the port of Carthage, he heard the cries, and almost beheld the flames, of the desolated province. Yet he persisted in his resolution; and leaving only a part of his guards to reinforce the feeble garrisons, he entrusted the command of Africa to the eunuch Solomon,[43] who proved himself not unworthy to be the successor of Belisarius. In the first invasion, some detachments, with two officers of merit, were surprised and intercepted; but Solomon speedily assembled his troops, marched from Carthage into the heart of the country, and in two great battles destroyed sixty thousand of the Barbarians. The Moors depended on their multitude, their swiftness, and their inaccessible mountains; and the aspect and smell of their camels are said to have produced some confusion in the Roman cavalry.[44] But as soon as they were commanded to dismount, they derided this contemptible obstacle: as soon as the columns ascended the hills, the

---

the robber Joshua (ληστης). He quotes two columns, with a Phœnician inscription. I believe in the columns – I doubt the inscription – and I reject the pedigree.

41. Virgil (Georgic. iii. 339.) and Pomponius Mela (i. 8.) describe the wandering life of the African shepherds, similar to that of the Arabs and Tartars: and Shaw (p. 222.) is the best commentator on the poet and the geographer.

42. The customary gifts were a sceptre, a crown or cap, a white cloak, a figured tunic and shoes, all adorned with gold and silver;

nor were these precious metals less acceptable in the shape of coin (Procop. Vandal. l. i. c. 25.).

43. See the African government and warfare of Solomon, in Procopius (Vandal. l. ii. c. 10, 11, 12, 13. 19, 20.). He was recalled, and again restored; and his last victory dates in the xiii[th] year of Justinian (A.D. 539.). An accident in his childhood had rendered him an eunuch (l. i. c. 11.): the other Roman generals were amply furnished with beards, πωγονος επιπλαμενοι (l. ii. c. 8.).

44. This natural antipathy of the horse for the

naked and disorderly crowd was dazzled by glittering arms and regular evolutions; and the menace of their female prophets was repeatedly fulfilled, that the Moors should be discomfited by a *beardless* antagonist. The victorious eunuch advanced thirteen days journey from Carthage, to besiege mount Aurasius,[45] the citadel, and at the same time the garden of Numidia. That range of hills, a branch of the great Atlas, contains within a circumference of one hundred and twenty miles, a rare variety of soil and climate; the intermediate vallies and elevated plains abound with rich pastures, perpetual streams, and fruits of a delicious taste and uncommon magnitude. This fair solitude is decorated with the ruins of Lambesa, a Roman city once the seat of a legion, and the residence of forty thousand inhabitants. The Ionic temple of Æsculapius is encompassed with Moorish huts; and the cattle now graze in the midst of an amphitheatre, under the shade of Corinthian columns. A sharp perpendicular rock rises above the level of the mountain, where the African princes deposited their wives and treasure; and a proverb is familiar to the Arabs, that the man may eat fire, who dares to attack the craggy cliffs and inhospitable natives of mount Aurasius. This hardy enterprize was twice attempted by the eunuch Solomon: from the first, he retreated with some disgrace; and in the second, his patience and provisions were almost exhausted; and he must again have retired, if he had not yielded to the impetuous courage of his troops, who audaciously scaled, to the astonishment of the Moors, the mountain, the hostile camp, and the summit of the Geminian rock. A citadel was erected to secure this important conquest, and to remind the Barbarians of their defeat: and as Solomon pursued his march to the west, the long-lost province of Mauritanian Sitifi was again annexed to the Roman empire. The Moorish war continued several years after the departure of Belisarius; but the laurels which he resigned to a faithful lieutenant, may be justly ascribed to his own triumph.

The experience of past faults, which may sometimes correct the mature age of an individual, is seldom profitable to the successive generations of mankind. The nations of antiquity,

Neutrality of the Visigoths.

---

camel, is affirmed by the ancients (Xenophon. Cyropæd. l. vi. p. 438. l. vii. p. 483. 492. edit. Hutchinson. Polyæn. Stratagem. vii. 6. Plin. Hist. Nat. viii. 26. Ælian de Natur. Animal. l. iii. c. 7.); but it is disproved by daily experience, and derided by the best judges, the Orientals (Voyage d'Olearius, p. 553.).

45. Procopius is the first who describes mount Aurasius (Vandal. l. ii. c. 13. De Edific. l. vi. c. 7.). He may be compared with Leo Africanus (dell Africa, parte v. in Ramusio, tom. i. fol. 77. recto.), Marmol (tom. ii. p. 430.), and Shaw (p. 56–59.).

careless of each other's safety, were separately vanquished and enslaved by the Romans. This awful lesson might have instructed the Barbarians of the West to oppose, with timely counsels and confederate arms, the unbounded ambition of Justinian. Yet the same error was repeated, the same consequences were felt, and the Goths, both of Italy and Spain, insensible of their approaching danger, beheld with indifference, and even with joy, the rapid downfal of the Vandals. After the failure of the royal line, Theudes, a valiant and powerful chief, ascended the throne of Spain, which he had formerly administered in the name of Theodoric and his infant grandson. Under his command, the Visigoths besieged the fortress of Ceuta on the African coast: but, while they spent the sabbath-day in peace and devotion, the pious security of their camp was invaded by a sally from the town; and the king himself, with some difficulty and danger, escaped from the hands of a sacrilegious enemy.[46] It was not long before his pride and resentment were gratified by a suppliant embassy from the unfortunate Gelimer, who implored, in his distress, the aid of the Spanish monarch. But instead of sacrificing these unworthy passions to the dictates of generosity and prudence, Theudes amused the ambassadors, till he was secretly informed of the loss of Carthage, and then dismissed them with obscure and contemptuous advice, to seek in their native country a true knowledge of the state of the Vandals.[47] The long continuance of the Italian war delayed the punishment of the Visigoths; and the eyes of Theudes were closed before they tasted the fruits of his mistaken policy. After his death, the sceptre of Spain was disputed by a civil war. The weaker candidate solicited the protection of Justinian, and ambitiously subscribed a treaty of alliance, which deeply wounded the independence and happiness of his country. Several cities, both on the ocean and the Mediterranean, were ceded to the Roman troops, who afterwards refused to evacuate those pledges, as it should seem, either of safety or payment; and as they were fortified by perpetual supplies from Africa, they maintained their impregnable stations, for the mischievous purpose of inflaming the civil and religious factions of the Barbarians. Seventy years elapsed before this painful thorn could be extirpated from the bosom of the monarchy; and as long as the emperors retained any share

Conquests of the Romans in Spain, A.D. 550–620.

---

46. Isidor. Chron. p. 722. edit. Grot. Mariana, Hist. Hispan. l. v. c. 8. p. 173. Yet according to Isidore, the siege of Ceuta, and the death of Theudis, happened, A. Æ. H. 586. A.D. 548. and the place was defended, not by the Vandals, but by the Romans.

47. Procopius, Vandal. l. i. c. 24.

of these remote and useless possessions, their vanity might number Spain in the list of their provinces, and the successors of Alaric in the rank of their vassals.[48]

The error of the Goths who reigned in Italy, was less excusable than that of the Spanish brethren, and their punishment was still more immediate and terrible. From a motive of a private revenge, they enabled their most dangerous enemy to destroy their most valuable ally. A sister of the great Theo-

Belisarius threatens the Ostrogoths of Italy, A.D. 534.

doric had been given in marriage to Thrasimond the African king:[49] on this occasion, the fortress of Lilybæum[50] in Sicily was resigned to the Vandals; and the princess Amalafrida was attended by a martial train of one thousand nobles, and five thousand Gothic soldiers, who signalized their valour in the Moorish wars. Their merit was over-rated by themselves, and perhaps neglected by the Vandals: they viewed the country with envy, and the conquerors with disdain; but their real or fictitious conspiracy was prevented by a massacre; the Goths were oppressed, and the captivity of Amalafrida was soon followed by her secret and suspicious death. The eloquent pen of Cassiodorius was employed to reproach the Vandal court with the cruel violation of every social and public duty; but the vengeance which he threatened in the name of his sovereign, might be derided with impunity, as long as Africa was protected by the sea, and the Goths were destitute of a navy. In the blind impotence of grief and indignation, they joyfully saluted the approach of the Romans, entertained the fleet of Belisarius in the ports of Sicily, and were speedily delighted or alarmed by the surprising intelligence, that their revenge was executed beyond the measure of their hopes, or perhaps of their wishes. To their friendship the emperor was indebted for the kingdom of Africa, and the Goths might reasonably think, that they were entitled to resume the possession of a barren rock, so recently separated as a nuptial gift from the island of Sicily. They were soon undeceived by the haughty mandate of Belisarius, which excited their tardy and unavailing repentance. "The city and promontory

---

48. See the original Chronicle of Isidore, and the vth and vi[th] books of the History of Spain by Mariana. The Romans were finally expelled by Suintila king of the Visigoths (A.D. 621–626.), after their reunion to the Catholic church.

49. See the marriage and fate of Amalafrida in Procopius (Vandal. l. i. c. 8, 9.), and in Cassiodorius (Var. ix. i.) the expostulation of her royal brother. Compare likewise the Chronicle of Victor Tunnunensis.

50. Lilybæum was built by the Carthaginians, Olymp. xcv. 4.; and in the first Punic war, a strong situation, and excellent harbour, rendered that place an important object to both nations.

of Lilybæum," said the Roman general, "belonged to the Vandals, and I claim them by the right of conquest. Your submission may deserve the favour of the emperor; your obstinacy will provoke his displeasure, and must kindle a war, that can terminate only in your utter ruin. If you compel us to take up arms, we shall contend, not to regain the possession of a single city, but to deprive you of all the provinces which you unjustly with-hold from their lawful sovereign." A nation of two hundred thousand soldiers might have smiled at the vain menace of Justinian and his lieutenant: but a spirit of discord and disaffection prevailed in Italy, and the Goths supported, with reluctance, the indignity of a female reign.[51]

Government and death of Amalasontha, queen of Italy.

A.D. 522–534.

The birth of Amalasontha, the regent and queen of Italy,[52] united the two most illustrious families of the Barbarians. Her mother, the sister of Clovis, was descended from the long-haired kings of the *Merovingian* race;[53] and the regal succession of the *Amali* was illustrated in the eleventh generation, by her father, the great Theodoric, whose merit might have ennobled a plebeian origin. The sex of his daughter excluded her from the Gothic throne; but his vigilant tenderness for his family and his people discovered the last heir of the royal line, whose ancestors had taken refuge in Spain; and the fortunate Eutharic was suddenly exalted to the rank of a consul and a prince. He enjoyed only a short time the charms of Amalasontha, and the hopes of the succession; and his widow, after the death of her husband and father, was left the guardian of her son Athalaric, and the kingdom of Italy. At the age of about twenty-eight years, the endowments of her mind and person had attained their perfect maturity. Her beauty, which, in the apprehension of Theodora herself, might have disputed the conquest of an emperor, was animated by manly sense, activity, and resolution. Education and experience had cultivated her talents; her philosophic studies were exempt from vanity; and, though she expressed herself with equal elegance and ease in the Greek, the Latin, and the Gothic tongue, the daughter of Theodoric maintained in her counsels a discreet

---

51. Compare the different passages of Procopius (Vandal. l. ii. c. 5. Gothic. l. i. c. 3.).

52. For the reign and character of Amalasontha, see Procopius (Gothic. l. i. c. 2, 3, 4. and Anecdot. c. 16. with the Notes of Alemannus), Cassiodorius (Var viii, ix. x, and xi. 1.), and Jornandes (de Rebus Geticis, c. 59. and De Successione Regnorum, in

Muratori, tom. i. p. 241.).

53. The marriage of Theodoric with Audefleda, the sister of Clovis, may be placed in the year 495, soon after the conquest of Italy (de Buat, Hist. des Peuples, tom. ix. p. 213.). The nuptials of Eutharic and Amalasontha were celebrated in 515 (Cassiodor. in Chron. p. 453.).

and impenetrable silence. By a faithful imitation of the virtues, she revived the prosperity, of his reign: while she strove, with pious care, to expiate the faults, and to obliterate the darker memory of his declining age. The children of Boethius and Symmachus were restored to their paternal inheritance: her extreme lenity never consented to inflict any corporal or pecuniary penalties on her Roman subjects; and she generously despised the clamours of the Goths, who, at the end of forty years, still considered the people of Italy as their slaves or their enemies. Her salutary measures were directed by the wisdom, and celebrated by the eloquence of Cassiodorius; she solicited and deserved the friendship of the emperor; and the kingdoms of Europe respected, both in peace and war, the majesty of the Gothic throne. But the future happiness of the queen and of Italy depended on the education of her son; who was destined by his birth, to support the different and almost incompatible characters of the chief of a Barbarian camp, and the first magistrate of a civilized nation. From the age of ten years,[54] Athalaric was diligently instructed in the arts and sciences, either useful or ornamental for a Roman prince; and three venerable Goths were chosen to instil the principles of honour and virtue into the mind of their young king. But the pupil who is insensible of the benefits, must abhor the restraints, of education; and the solicitude of the queen, which affection rendered anxious and severe, offended the untractable nature of her son and his subjects. On a solemn festival, when the Goths were assembled in the palace of Ravenna, the royal youth escaped from his mother's apartment, and, with tears of pride and anger, complained of a blow which his stubborn disobedience had provoked her to inflict. The Barbarians resented the indignity which had been offered to their king, accused the regent of conspiring against his life and crown; and imperiously demanded, that the grandson of Theodoric should be rescued from the dastardly discipline of women and pedants, and educated, like a valiant Goth, in the society of his equals, and the glorious ignorance of his ancestors. To this rude clamour, importunately urged as the voice of the nation, Amalasontha was compelled to yield her reason, and the dearest wishes of her heart. The king of Italy was abandoned to wine, to women, and to rustic sports; and the indiscreet contempt of the ungrateful youth, betrayed the mischievous designs of his favourites and her enemies. Encompassed with domestic foes, she entered

---

54. At the death of Theodoric, his grandson Athalaric is described by Procopius as a boy about eight years old – οχτω γεγονως ετη.

Cassiodorius, with authority and reason, adds two years to his age – infantulum adhuc vix decennem.

into a secret negociation with the emperor Justinian; obtained the assurance of a friendly reception, and had actually deposited at Dyrrachium in Epirus, a treasure of forty thousand pounds of gold. Happy would it have been for her fame and safety, if she had calmly retired from barbarous faction, to the peace and splendour of Constantinople. But the mind of Amalasontha was inflamed by ambition and revenge; and while her ships lay at anchor in the port, she waited for the success of a crime which her passions excused or applauded as an act of justice. Three of the most dangerous malecontents had been separately removed, under the pretence of trust and command, to the frontiers of Italy: they were assassinated by her private emissaries; and the blood of these noble Goths rendered the queen-mother absolute in the court of Ravenna, and justly odious to a free people. But if she had lamented the disorders of her son, she soon wept his irreparable loss; and the death of Athalaric, who, at the age of sixteen, was consumed by premature intemperance, left her destitute of any firm support or legal authority. Instead of submitting to the laws of her country, which held as a fundamental maxim, that the succession could never pass from the lance to the distaff, the daughter of Theodoric conceived the impracticable design of sharing, with one of her cousins, the regal title, and of reserving in her own hands the substance of supreme power. He received the proposal with profound respect and affected gratitude; and the eloquent Cassiodorius announced to the senate and the emperor, that Amalasontha and Theodatus had ascended the throne of Italy. His birth (for his mother was the sister of Theodoric) might be considered as an imperfect title; and the choice of Amalasontha was more strongly directed by her contempt of his avarice and pusillanimity, which had deprived him of the love of the Italians, and the esteem of the Barbarians. But Theodatus was exasperated by the contempt which he deserved: her justice had repressed and reproached the oppression which he exercised against his Tuscan neighbours; and the principal Goths, united by common guilt and resentment, conspired to instigate his slow and timid disposition.

Her exile and death, A.D. 535, April 30.

The letters of congratulation were scarcely dispatched before the queen of Italy was imprisoned in a small island of the lake of Bolsena,[55] where, after a short confinement,

---

55. The lake, from the neighbouring towns of Etruria, was styled either Vulsiniensis (now of Bolsena) or Tarquiniensis. It is surrounded with white rocks, and stored with fish and wild fowl. The younger Pliny (Epist. ii. 96.) celebrates two woody islands that floated on its waters: if a fable, how credulous the ancients! – if a fact, how careless the moderns!

she was strangled in the bath, by the order, or with the connivance of the new king, who instructed his turbulent subjects to shed the blood of their sovereigns.

Justinian beheld with joy the dissensions of the Goths; and the mediation of an ally concealed and promoted the ambitious views of the conqueror. His ambassadors, in their public audience, demanded the fortress of Lilybæum, ten Barbarian fugitives, and a just compensation for the pillage of a small town on the Illyrian borders; but they secretly negociated with Theodatus to betray the province of Tuscany, and tempted Amalasontha to extricate herself from danger and perplexity, by a free surrender of the kingdom of Italy. A false and servile epistle was subscribed by the reluctant hand of the captive queen; but the confession of the Roman senators, who were sent to Constantinople, revealed the truth of her deplorable situation; and Justinian, by the voice of a new ambassador, most powerfully interceded for her life and liberty. Yet the secret instructions of the same minister were adapted to serve the cruel jealousy of Theodora, who dreaded the presence and superior charms of a rival: he prompted, with artful and ambiguous hints, the execution of a crime so useful to the Romans;[56] received the intelligence of her death with grief and indignation, and denounced in his master's name, immortal war against the perfidious assassin. In Italy, as well as in Africa, the guilt of an usurper appeared to justify the arms of Justinian; but the forces which he prepared, were insufficient for the subversion of a mighty kingdom, if their feeble numbers had not been multiplied by the name, the spirit, and the conduct of an hero. A chosen troop of guards, who served on horseback, and were armed with lances and bucklers, attended the person of Belisarius: his cavalry was composed of two hundred Huns, three hundred Moors, and four thousand *confederates*, and the infantry consisted only of three thousand Isaurians. Steering the same course as in his former expedition, the Roman consul cast anchor before Catana in Sicily, to survey the strength of the island, and to decide whether he should attempt the conquest, or peaceably pursue his voyage for the African coast. He found a fruitful land and a friendly

Belisarius invades and subdues Sicily, A.D. 535, Dec. 31.

Yet, since Pliny, the islands may have been fixed by new and gradual accessions.

56. Yet Procopius discredits his own evidence (Anecdot. c. 16.), by confessing that in his public history he had not spoken the truth.

See the Epistles from queen Gundelina to the empress Theodora (Var. x. 20, 21. 23. and observe a suspicious word, de illâ personâ, &c.), with the elaborate Commentary of Buat (tom. x. p. 177–185.).

people. Notwithstanding the decay of agriculture, Sicily still supplied the granaries of Rome: the farmers were graciously exempted from the oppression of military quarters; and the Goths, who trusted the defence of the island to the inhabitants, had some reason to complain, that their confidence was ungratefully betrayed. Instead of soliciting and expecting the aid of the king of Italy, they yielded to the first summons a cheerful obedience: and this province, the first fruits of the Punic wars, was again, after a long separation, united to the Roman empire.[57] The Gothic garrison of Palermo, which alone attempted to resist, was reduced after a short siege, by a singular stratagem. Belisarius introduced his ships into the deepest recess of the harbour; their boats were laboriously hoisted with ropes and pullies to the topmast head, and he filled them with archers, who, from that superior station, commanded the ramparts of the city. After this easy, though successful campaign, the conqueror entered Syracuse in triumph, at the head of his victorious bands, distributing gold medals to the people, on the day which so gloriously terminated the year of the consulship. He passed the winter season in the palace of ancient kings, amidst the ruins of a Grecian colony, which once extended to a circumference of two and twenty miles:[58] but in the spring, about the festival of Easter, the prosecution of his designs was interrupted by a dangerous revolt of the African forces. Carthage was saved by the presence of Belisarius, who suddenly landed with a thousand guards. Two thousand soldiers of doubtful faith returned to the standard of their old commander: and he marched, without hesitation, about fifty miles, to seek an enemy, whom he affected to pity and despise. Eight thousand rebels trembled at his approach; they were routed at the first onset, by the dexterity of their master: and this ignoble victory would have restored the peace of Africa, if the conqueror had not been hastily recalled to Sicily, to appease a sedition which was kindled during his absence in his own camp.[59] Disorder and disobedience were the common malady of the times: the genius to command, and the virtue to obey, resided only in the mind of Belisarius.

---

57. For the conquest of Sicily, compare the narrative of Procopius with the complaints of Totila (Gothic. l. i. c. 5. l. iii. c. 16.). The Gothic queen had lately relieved that thankless island (Var. ix. 10, 11.).

58. The ancient magnitude and splendour of the five quarters of Syracuse, are delineated by Cicero (in Verrem, actio ii. l. iv. c. 52, 53.), Strabo (l. vi. p. 415.), and d'Orville Sicula (tom. ii. p. 174–202.). The new city, restored by Augustus, shrunk towards the island.

59. Procopius (Vandal. l. ii. c. 14, 15.) so clearly relates the return of Belisarius into Sicily (p. 146. edit. Hoeschelii), that I am

Although Theodatus descended from a race of heroes, he was ignorant of the art, and averse to the dangers, of war. Although he had studied the writings of Plato and Tully, philosophy was incapable of purifying his mind from the basest passions, avarice and fear. He had purchased a sceptre by ingratitude and murther: at the first menace of an enemy, he degraded his own majesty, and that of a nation, which already disdained their unworthy sovereign. Astonished by the recent example of Gelimer, he saw himself dragged in chains through the streets of Constantinople: the terrors which Belisarius inspired, were heightened by the eloquence of Peter, the Byzantine ambassador; and that bold and subtle advocate persuaded him to sign a treaty, too ignominious to become the foundation of a lasting peace. It was stipulated, that in the acclamations of the Roman people, the name of the emperor should be always proclaimed before that of the Gothic king; and that as often as the statue of Theodatus was erected in brass or marble, the divine image of Justinian should be placed on its right hand. Instead of conferring, the king of Italy was reduced to solicit, the honours of the senate; and the consent of the emperor was made indispensable before he could execute, against a priest or senator, the sentence either of death or confiscation. The feeble monarch resigned the possession of Sicily; offered, as the annual mark of his dependence, a crown of gold, of the weight of three hundred pounds; and promised to supply, at the requisition of his sovereign, three thousand Gothic auxiliaries for the service of the empire. Satisfied with these extraordinary concessions, the successful agent of Justinian hastened his journey to Constantinople; but no sooner had he reached the Alban villa,[60] than he was recalled by the anxiety of Theodatus; and the dialogue which passed between the king and the ambassador deserves to be represented in its original simplicity. "Are you of opinion that the emperor will ratify this treaty? *Perhaps.* If he refuses, what consequence will ensue? *War.* Will such a war be just or reasonable? *Most assuredly: every one should act according to his character.* What is your meaning? *You are a philosopher – Justinian is emperor of the Romans: it*

Reign and weakness of Theodatus, the Gothic king of Italy, A.D. 534, October – A.D. 536, August.

---

astonished at the strange misapprehension and reproaches of a learned critic (Oeuvres de la Mothe le Vayer, tom. vii. p. 162, 163.). 60. The ancient Alba was ruined in the first age of Rome. On the same spot, or at least in the neighbourhood, successively arose, 1. The villa of Pompey, &c. 2. A camp of the Prætorian cohorts. 3. The modern episcopal city of Albanum or Albano (Procop. Goth. l. ii. c. 4. Cluver. Ital. Antiq. tom. ii. p. 914.).

would ill become the disciple of Plato to shed the blood of thousands in his private quarrel: the successor of Augustus should vindicate his rights, and recover by arms the ancient provinces of his empire." This reasoning might not convince, but it was sufficient to alarm and subdue the weakness of Theodatus; and he soon descended to his last offer, that for the poor equivalent of a pension of forty-eight thousand pounds sterling, he would resign the kingdom of the Goths and Italians, and spend the remainder of his days in the innocent pleasures of philosophy and agriculture. Both treaties were entrusted to the hands of the ambassador, on the frail security of an oath not to produce the second till the first had been positively rejected. The event may be easily foreseen: Justinian required and accepted the abdication of the Gothic king. His indefatigable agent returned from Constantinople to Ravenna, with ample instructions; and a fair epistle, which praised the wisdom and generosity of the royal philosopher, granted his pension, with the assurance of such honours as a subject and a Catholic might enjoy; and wisely referred the final execution of the treaty, to the presence and authority of Belisarius. But in the interval of suspense, two Roman generals, who had entered the province of Dalmatia, were defeated and slain by the Gothic troops. From blind and abject despair, Theodatus capriciously rose to groundless and fatal presumption,[61] and dared to receive with menace and contempt, the ambassador of Justinian who claimed his promise, solicited the allegiance of his subjects, and boldly asserted the inviolable privilege of his own character. The march of Belisarius dispelled this visionary pride; and as the first campaign[62] was employed in the reduction of Sicily, the invasion of Italy is applied by Procopius to the second year of the GOTHIC WAR.[63]

61. A Sibylline oracle was ready to pronounce – Africâ captâ *mundus* cum nato peribit; a sentence of portentous ambiguity (Gothic. l. i. c. 7.), which has been published in unknown characters by Opsopæus, an editor of the oracles. The Pere Maltret has promised a commentary; but all his promises have been vain and fruitless.

62. In his chronology, imitated in some degree from Thucydides, Procopius begins each spring the years of Justinian and of the Gothic war; and his first æra coincides with the 1st of April 535, and not 536, according to the

Annals of Baronius (Pagi, Crit. tom. ii. p. 555. who is followed by Muratori and the editors of Sigonius). Yet in some passages we are at a loss to reconcile the dates of Procopius with himself, and with the Chronicle of Marcellinus.

63. The series of the first Gothic war is represented by Procopius (l. i. c. 5–29. l. ii. c. 1– 30. l. iii. c. 1.) till the captivity of Vitiges. With the aid of Sigonius (Opp. tom. i. de Imp. Occident, l. xvii, xviii.) and Muratori (Annali d'Italia, tom. v.), I have gleaned some few additional facts.

After Belisarius had left sufficient garrisons in Palermo and Syracuse, he embarked his troops at Messina, and landed them, without resistance, on the opposite shores of Rhegium. A Gothic prince, who had married the daughter of Theodatus, was stationed with an army to guard the entrance of Italy; but he imitated, without scruple, the example of a sovereign, faithless *Belisarius invades Italy, and reduces Naples, A.D. 537.*
to his public and private duties. The perfidious Ebermor deserted with his followers to the Roman camp, and was dismissed to enjoy the servile honours of the Byzantine court.[64] From Rhegium to Naples, the fleet and army of Belisarius, almost always in view of each other, advanced near three hundred miles along the sea-coast. The people of Bruttium, Lucania, and Campania, who abhorred the name and religion of the Goths, embraced the specious excuse, that their ruined walls were incapable of defence: the soldiers paid a just equivalent for a plentiful market; and curiosity alone interrupted the peaceful occupations of the husbandman or artificer. Naples, which has swelled to a great and populous capital, long cherished the language and manners of a Grecian colony;[65] and the choice of Virgil had ennobled this elegant retreat, which attracted the lovers of repose and study, from the noise, the smoke, and the laborious opulence of Rome.[66] As soon as the place was invested by sea and land, Belisarius gave audience to the deputies of the people, who exhorted him to disregard a conquest unworthy of his arms, to seek the Gothic king in a field of battle, and after his victory, to claim, as the sovereign of Rome, the allegiance of the dependent cities. "When I treat with my enemies," replied the Roman chief, with an haughty smile, "I am more accustomed to give than to receive counsel: but I hold in one hand inevitable ruin, and in the other, peace and freedom, such as Sicily now enjoys." The impatience of delay urged him to grant the most liberal terms; his honour secured their performance: but Naples was divided into two factions; and the Greek democracy was inflamed by their orators, who, with much spirit and some truth,

---

64. Jornandes, de Rebus Geticis, c. 60. p. 702. edit. Grot. and tom. i. p. 221. Muratori, de Success. Regn. p. 241.

65. Nero (says Tacitus, Annal. xv. 35.) Neapolim quasi Græcam urbem delegit. One hundred and fifty years afterwards, in the time of Septimius Severus, the *Hellenism* of the Neapolitans is praised by Philostratus: γενος Ελληνες και αστυκοι, οθεν και τας σπουδας

των λογων Ελληνικοι εισι (Icon. l. i. p. 763. edit. Olear.).

66. The otium of Naples is praised by the Roman poets, by Virgil, Horace, Silius Italicus, and Statius (Cluver. Ital. Ant. l. iv. p. 1149, 1150.). In an elegant epistle (Sylv. l. iii. 5. p. 94–98. edit. Markland), Statius undertakes the difficult task of drawing his wife from the pleasures of Rome to that calm retreat.

represented to the multitude, that the Goths would punish their defection, and that Belisarius himself must esteem their loyalty and valour. Their deliberations, however, were not perfectly free: the city was commanded by eight hundred Barbarians, whose wives and children were detained at Ravenna as the pledge of their fidelity; and even the Jews, who were rich and numerous, resisted, with desperate enthusiasm, the intolerant laws of Justinian. In a much later period, the circumference of Naples[67] measured only two thousand three hundred and sixty-three paces:[68] the fortifications were defended by precipices or the sea; when the aqueducts were intercepted, a supply of water might be drawn from wells and fountains; and the stock of provisions was sufficient to consume the patience of the besiegers. At the end of twenty days, that of Belisarius was almost exhausted, and he had reconciled himself to the disgrace of abandoning the siege, that he might march, before the winter season, against Rome and the Gothic king. But his anxiety was relieved by the bold curiosity of an Isaurian, who explored the dry channel of an aqueduct, and secretly reported, that a passage might be perforated to introduce a file of armed soldiers into the heart of the city. When the work had been silently executed, the humane general risked the discovery of his secret, by a last and fruitless admonition of the impending danger. In the darkness of the night, four hundred Romans entered the aqueduct, raised themselves by a rope, which they fastened to an olive tree, into the house or garden of a solitary matron, sounded their trumpets, surprised the centinels, and gave admittance to their companions, who on all sides scaled the walls, and burst open the gates of the city. Every crime which is punished by social justice, was practised as the rights of war; the Huns were distinguished by cruelty and sacrilege, and Belisarius alone appeared in the streets and churches of Naples, to moderate the calamities which he predicted. "The gold and silver," he repeatedly exclaimed, "are the just rewards of your valour. But spare the inhabitants, they are Christians, they are suppliants, they are now your fellow-subjects. Restore the children to their parents, the wives to their husbands; and shew them by your generosity, of what friends they have

67. This measure was taken by Roger I. after the conquest of Naples (A.D. 1139), which he made the capital of his new kingdom (Giannone, Istoria Civile, tom. ii. p. 169.). That city, the third in Christian Europe, is now at least twelve miles in circumference (Jul. Cæsar. Capaccii Hist. Neapol. l. i. p. 47.), and contains more inhabitants (350,000) in a given space, than any other spot in the known world. 68. Not geometrical, but common, paces or steps, of 22 French inches (d'Anville, Mesures Itineraires, p. 7, 8.): the 2363 do not make an English mile.

obstinately deprived themselves." The city was saved by the virtue and authority of its conqueror;[69] and when the Neapolitans returned to their houses, they found some consolation in the secret enjoyment of their hidden treasures. The Barbarian garrison enlisted in the service of the emperor; Apulia and Calabria, delivered from the odious presence of the Goths, acknowledged his dominion; and the tusks of the Calydonian boar, which were still shewn at Beneventum, are curiously described by the historian of Belisarius.[70]

The faithful soldiers and citizens of Naples had expected their deliverance from a prince, who remained the inactive and almost indifferent spectator of their ruin. Theodatus secured his person within the walls of Rome, while his cavalry advanced forty miles on the Appian way, and encamped in the Pomptine marshes; which, by a canal of nineteen miles in length, had been recently drained and converted into excellent pastures.[71] But the principal forces of the Goths were dispersed in Dalmatia, Venetia, and Gaul; and the feeble mind of their king was confounded by the unsuccessful event of a divination, which seemed to presage the downfal of his empire.[72] The most abject slaves have arraigned the guilt or weakness of an unfortunate master. The character of Theodatus was rigorously scrutinized by a free and idle camp of Barbarians, conscious of their privilege and power: he was declared unworthy of his race, his nation, and his throne; and their general Vitiges, whose valour had been signalized in the Illyrian war, was raised with unanimous applause on the bucklers of his companions. On the first rumour, the abdicated monarch fled from the justice of his country; but he was

Vitiges, king of Italy, A.D. 536, August – A.D. 540.

---

69. Belisarius was reproved by Pope Sylverius for the massacre. He repeopled Naples, and imported colonies of African captives into Sicily, Calabria, and Apulia (Hist. Miscell. l. xvi. in Muratori, tom. i. p. 106, 107).

70. Beneventum was built by Diomede, the nephew of Meleager (Cluver, tom. ii. p. 1195, 1196). The Calydonian hunt is a picture of savage life (Ovid. Metamorph. l. viii.). Thirty or forty heroes were leagued against a hog: the brutes (not the hog) quarrelled with a lady for the head.

71. The *Decennovium* is strangely confounded by Cluverius (tom. ii. p. 1007.) with the river Ufens. It was in truth a canal of nineteen

miles, from Forum Appii to Terracina, on which Horace embarked in the night. The Decennovium which is mentioned by Lucan, Dion Cassius, and Cassiodorius, has been successively ruined, restored, and obliterated (d'Anville, Analyse de l'Italie, p. 185, &c.).

72. A Jew gratified his contempt and hatred for *all* the Christians, by inclosing three bands, each of ten hogs, and discriminated by the names of Goths, Greeks, and Romans. Of the first, almost all were found dead – almost all of the second were alive – of the third, half died and the rest lost their bristles. No unsuitable emblem of the event.

pursued by private revenge. A Goth whom he had injured in his love, overtook Theodatus on the Flaminian way, and regardless of his unmanly cries, slaughtered him, as he lay prostrate on the ground, like a victim (says the historian) at the foot of the altar. The choice of the people is the best and purest title to reign over them: yet such is the prejudice of every age, that Vitiges impatiently wished to return to Ravenna, where he might seize, with the reluctant hand of the daughter of Amalasontha, some faint shadow of hereditary right. A national council was immediately held, and the new monarch reconciled the impatient spirit of the Barbarians, to a measure of disgrace, which the misconduct of his predecessor rendered wise and indispensable. The Goths consented to retreat in the presence of a victorious enemy; to delay till the next spring the operations of offensive war; to summon their scattered forces; to relinquish their distant possessions, and to trust even Rome itself to the faith of its inhabitants. Leuderis, an aged warrior, was left in the capital with four thousand soldiers; a feeble garrison, which might have seconded the zeal, though it was incapable of opposing the wishes, of the Romans. But a momentary enthusiasm of religion and patriotism was kindled in their minds. They furiously exclaimed, that the apostolic throne should no longer be profaned by the triumph or toleration of Arianism; that the tombs of the Cæsars should no longer be trampled by the savages of the north; and without reflecting, that Italy must sink into a province of Constantinople, they fondly hailed the restoration of a Roman emperor as a new æra of freedom and prosperity. The deputies of the pope and clergy, of the senate and people, invited the lieutenant of Justinian to accept their voluntary allegiance, and to enter the city, whose gates would be thrown open for his reception. As soon as Belisarius had fortified his new conquests, Naples and Cumæ, he advanced about twenty miles to the banks of the Vulturnus, contemplated the decayed grandeur of Capua, and halted at the separation of the Latin and Appian ways. The work of the censor, after the incessant use of nine centuries, still preserved its primæval beauty, and not a flaw could be discovered in the large polished stones, of which that solid, though narrow road, was so firmly compacted.[73] Belisarius, however, preferred the Latin way, which, at a distance from the sea and the marshes, skirted in a space of one hundred and twenty miles along the foot of the mountains. His

73. Bergier (Hist. des Grands Chemins des Romains, tom. i. p. 221–228. 440–444.) examines the structure and materials, while d'Anville (Analyse de l'Italie, p. 200–213.) defines the geographical line.

enemies had disappeared; when he made his entrance through
the Asinarian gate, the garrison departed without molestation
along the Flaminian way; and the city, after sixty years servitude,
was delivered from the yoke of the Barbarians. Leuderis alone,
from a motive of pride or discontent, refused to accompany the
fugitives; and the Gothic chief, himself a trophy of the victory, was sent
with the keys of Rome, to the throne of the emperor Justinian.[74]

Belisarius enters Rome, A.D. 536 Dec. 10.

The first days, which coincided with the old Saturnalia, were
devoted to mutual congratulation and the public joy: and the
Catholics prepared to celebrate, without a rival, the approaching
festival of the nativity of Christ. In the familiar conversation of
an hero, the Romans acquired some notion of the virtues which
history ascribed to their ancestors; they were edified by the apparent respect
of Belisarius for the successor of St. Peter, and his rigid discipline secured
in the midst of war the blessings of tranquillity and justice. They applauded
the rapid success of his arms, which over-ran the adjacent country, as far
as Narni, Perusia, and Spoleto; but they trembled, the senate, the clergy,
and the unwarlike people, as soon as they understood, that he had resolved,
and would speedily be reduced, to sustain a siege against the powers of the
Gothic monarchy. The designs of Vitiges were executed, during the winter
season, with diligence and effect. From their rustic habitations, from their
distant garrisons, the Goths assembled at Ravenna for the defence of their
country; and such were their numbers, that after an army had been detached
for the relief of Dalmatia, one hundred and fifty thousand fighting men
marched under the royal standard. According to the degrees of rank or
merit, the Gothic king distributed arms and horses, rich gifts, and liberal
promises: he moved along the Flaminian way, declined the useless sieges
of Perusia and Spoleto, respected the impregnable rock of Narni, and
arrived within two miles of Rome at the foot of the Milvian bridge. The
narrow passage was fortified with a tower, and Belisarius had computed
the value of the twenty days, which must be lost in the construction of
another bridge. But the consternation of the soldiers of the tower, who
either fled or deserted, disappointed his hopes, and betrayed his person into

Siege of Rome by the Goths, A.D. 537, March.

---

74. Of the first recovery of Rome, the *year*
(536) is certain, from the series of events,
rather than from the corrupt, or interpolated,
text of Procopius: the *month* (December) is
ascertained by Evagrius (l. iv. c. 19.); and the
day (the *tenth*) may be admitted on the slight
evidence of Nicephorus Callistus (l. xvii.
c. 13). For this accurate chronology, we are
indebted to the diligence and judgment of
Pagi (tom. ii. p. 559, 560.).

the most imminent danger. At the head of one thousand horse, the Roman general sallied from the Flaminian gate to mark the ground of an advantageous position, and to survey the camp of the Barbarians; but while he still believed them on the other side of the Tyber, he was suddenly encompassed and assaulted by their innumerable squadrons. The fate of Italy depended on his life; and the deserters pointed to the conspicuous horse, a bay,[75] with a white face, which he rode on that memorable day. "Aim at the bay horse," was the universal cry. Every bow was bent, every javelin was directed against that fatal object, and the command was repeated and obeyed by thousands who were ignorant of its real motive. The bolder Barbarians advanced to the more honourable combat of swords and spears; and the praise of an enemy has graced the fall of Visandus, the standard-bearer,[76] who maintained his foremost station, till he was pierced with thirteen wounds, perhaps by the hand of Belisarius himself. The Roman general was strong, active, and dextrous: on every side he discharged his weighty and mortal strokes: his faithful guards imitated his valour, and defended his person; and the Goths, after the loss of a thousand men, fled before the arms of an hero. They were rashly pursued to their camp; and the Romans, oppressed by multitudes, made a gradual, and at length a precipitate retreat to the gates of the city: the gates were shut against the fugitives; and the public terror was encreased, by the report, that Belisarius was slain. His countenance was indeed disfigured by sweat, dust, and blood; his voice was hoarse, his strength was almost exhausted; but his unconquerable spirit still remained; he imparted that spirit to his desponding companions; and their last desperate charge was felt by the flying Barbarians, as if a new army, vigorous and entire, had been poured from the city. The Flaminian

Valour of Belisarius. gate was thrown open to a *real* triumph; but it was not before Belisarius had visited every post, and provided for the public safety, that he could be persuaded by his wife and friends, to taste the needful refreshments of food and sleep. In the more improved state of the

---

75. An horse of a bay or red colour was styled φαλιος by the Greeks, balan by the Barbarians, and spadix by the Romans. Honesti spadices, says Virgil (Georgic. l. iii. 72. with the Observations of Martin and Heyne). Σπαδιξ or βαιον, signifies a branch of the palm-tree, whose name, φοινιξ is synonymous to red (Aulus Gellius, ii. 26.).

76. I interpret βανδαλαριος, not as a proper name, but an office, standard-bearer, from bandum (vexillum), a Barbaric word adopted by the Greeks and Romans (Paul Diacon. l. i. c. 20. p. 760. Grot. Nomina Gothica, p. 575. Ducange, Gloss. Latin. tom. i. p. 539, 540.).

art of war, a general is seldom required, or even permitted to display the personal prowess of a soldier; and the example of Belisarius may be added to the rare examples of Henry IV. of Pyrrhus, and of Alexander.

After this first and unsuccessful trial of their enemies, the whole army of the Goths passed the Tyber, and formed the siege of the city, which continued above a year, till their final departure. *His defence of Rome.* Whatever fancy may conceive, the severe compass of the geographer defines the circumference of Rome within a line of twelve miles and three hundred and forty-five paces; and that circumference, except in the Vatican, has invariably been the same from the triumph of Aurelian, to the peaceful but obscure reign of the modern popes.[77] But in the day of her greatness, the space within her walls was crowded with habitations and inhabitants; and the populous suburbs that stretched along the public roads, were darted like so many rays from one common centre. Adversity swept away these extraneous ornaments, and left naked and desolate, a considerable part even of the seven hills. Yet Rome, in its present state, could send into the field about thirty thousand males of a military age;[78] and, notwithstanding the want of discipline and exercise, the far greater part, enured to the hardships of poverty, might be capable of bearing arms for the defence of their country and religion. The prudence of Belisarius did not neglect this important resource. His soldiers were relieved by the zeal and diligence of the people, who watched while *they* slept, and laboured while *they* reposed: he accepted the voluntary service of the bravest and most indigent of the Roman youth; and the companies of townsmen sometimes represented, in a vacant post, the presence of the troops which had been drawn away to more essential duties. But his just confidence was placed in the veterans who had fought under his banner in the Persian and African wars; and although that gallant band was reduced to five thousand men, he undertook, with such contemptible numbers, to defend a circle of twelve miles, against an army of one hundred and fifty thousand Barbarians. In the walls of

77. M. d'Anville has given, in the Memoires of the Academy for the year 1756 (tom. xxx. p. 198–236.), a plan of Rome on a smaller scale, but far more accurate than that which he delineated in 1738 for Rollin's history. Experience had improved his knowledge; and, instead of Rossi's topography, he used the new and excellent map of Nolli. Pliny's old measure of xiii must be reduced to viii miles. It is easier to alter a text, than to remove hills or buildings.

78. In the year 1709, Labat (Voyages en Italie, tom. iii. p. 218.) reckoned 138,568 Christian souls, besides 8 or 10,000 Jews – without souls? – In the year 1763, the numbers exceeded 160,000.

Rome, which Belisarius constructed or restored, the materials of ancient architecture may be discerned;[79] and the whole fortification was completed, except in a chasm still extant between the Pincian and Flaminian gates, which the prejudices of the Goths and Romans left under the effectual guard of St. Peter the apostle.[80] The battlements or bastions were shaped in sharp angles; a ditch, broad and deep, protected the foot of the rampart; and the archers on the rampart were assisted by military engines; the *balista*, a powerful cross-bow, which darted short but massy arrows; the *onagri*, or wild asses, which, on the principle of a sling, threw stones and bullets of an enormous size.[81] A chain was drawn across the Tyber; the arches of the aqueducts were made impervious, and the mole or sepulchre of Hadrian[82] was converted, for the first time, to the uses of a citadel. That venerable structure which contained the ashes of the Antonines, was a circular turret rising from a quadrangular basis: it was covered with the white marble of Paros, and decorated by the statues of gods and heroes; and the lover of the arts must read with a sigh, that the works of Praxiteles or Lysippus were torn from their lofty pedestals, and hurled into the ditch on the heads of the besiegers.[83] To each of his lieutenants, Belisarius assigned the defence of a gate, with the wise and peremptory instruction, that, whatever might be the alarm, they should steadily adhere to their respective posts, and trust their general for the safety of Rome. The formidable host of the Goths was insufficient to embrace the ample measure of the city: of the fourteen gates, seven only were invested from the Prænestine to the Flaminian way; and Vitiges divided his troops into six camps, each of which was fortified

---

79. The accurate eye of Nardini (Roma Antica, l. i. c. viii. p. 31.) could distinguish the tumultuarie opere di Belisario.

80. The fissure and leaning in the upper part of the wall, which Procopius observed (Goth. l. i. c. 13.), is visible to the present hour (Donat. Roma Vetus, l. i. c. 17. p. 53, 54.).

81. Lipsius (Opp. tom. iii. Poliorcet. l. iii.) was ignorant of this clear and conspicuous passage of Procopius (Goth. l. i. c. 21.). The engine was named οναγρος, the wild ass, a calcitrando (Hen. Steph. Thesaur. Linguæ Græc. tom. ii. p. 1340, 1341. tom. iii. p. 877.). I have seen an ingenious model, contrived and executed by general Melville, which imitates or surpasses the art of antiquity.

82. The description of this mausoleum, or mole, in Procopius (l. i. c. 25.) is the first and best. The height above the walls σχεδον ες λιθου βολην. On Nolli's great plan, the sides measure 260 English feet.

83. Praxiteles excelled in Fauns, and that of Athens was his own master-piece. Rome now contains above thirty of the same character. When the ditch of St. Angelo was cleansed under Urban VIII. the workmen found the sleeping Faun of the Barberini palace; but a leg, a thigh, and the right arm, had been broken from that beautiful statue (Winckelman, Hist. de l'Art, tom. ii. p. 52, 53. tom. iii. p. 265.).

with a ditch and rampart. On the Tuscan side of the river, a seventh encampment was formed in the field or circus of the Vatican, for the important purpose of commanding the Milvian bridge and the course of the Tyber; but they approached with devotion the adjacent church of St. Peter; and the threshold of the holy apostles was respected during the siege by a Christian enemy. In the ages of victory, as often as the senate decreed some distant conquest, the consul denounced hostilities, by unbarring, in solemn pomp, the gates of the temple of Janus.[84] Domestic war now rendered the admonition superfluous, and the ceremony was superseded by the establishment of a new religion. But the brazen temple of Janus was left standing in the forum; of a size sufficient only to contain the statue of the god, five cubits in height, of a human form, but with two faces, directed to the east and west. The double gates were likewise of brass; and a fruitless effort to turn them on their rusty hinges, revealed the scandalous secret, that some Romans were still attached to the superstition of their ancestors.

Eighteen days were employed by the besiegers, to provide all the instruments of attack which antiquity had invented. Fascines were prepared to fill the ditches, scaling-ladders to ascend the walls. The largest trees of the forest supplied the timbers of four battering-rams; their heads were armed with iron; they were suspended by *Repulses a general assault of the Goths.* ropes, and each of them was worked by the labour of fifty men. The lofty wooden turrets moved on wheels or rollers, and formed a spacious platform of the level of the rampart. On the morning of the nineteenth day, a general attack was made from the Prænestine gate to the Vatican: seven Gothic columns, with their military engines, advanced to the assault; and the Romans who lined the ramparts, listened with doubt and anxiety to the cheerful assurances of their commander. As soon as the enemy approached the ditch, Belisarius himself drew the first arrow; and such was his strength and dexterity, that he transfixed the foremost of the Barbarian leaders. A shout of applause and victory was re-echoed along the wall. He drew a second arrow, and the stroke was followed with the same success and the same acclamation. The Roman general then gave the word, that the archers should aim at the teams of oxen; they were instantly covered with mortal

---

84. Procopius has given the best description of the temple of Janus, a national deity of Latium (Heyne, Excurs. v. ad. l. vii. Æneid). It was once a gate in the primitive city of Romulus and Numa (Nardini, p. 13. 256. 329.). Virgil has described the ancient rite, like a poet and an antiquarian.

wounds; the towers which they drew, remained useless and immovable, and a single moment disconcerted the laborious projects of the king of the Goths. After this disappointment, Vitiges still continued, or feigned to continue, the assault of the Salarian gate, that he might divert the attention of his adversary, while his principal forces more strenuously attacked the Prænestine gate and the sepulchre of Hadrian, at the distance of three miles from each other. Near the former, the double walls of the Vivarium[85] were low or broken; the fortifications of the latter were feebly guarded: the vigour of the Goths was excited by the hope of victory and spoil; and if a single post had given way, the Romans, and Rome itself, were irrecoverably lost. This perilous day was the most glorious in the life of Belisarius. Amidst tumult and dismay, the whole plan of the attack and defence was distinctly present to his mind; he observed the changes of each instant, weighed every possible advantage, transported his person to the scenes of danger, and communicated his spirit in calm and decisive orders. The contest was fiercely maintained from the morning to the evening, the Goths were repulsed on all sides, and each Roman might boast, that he had vanquished thirty Barbarians, if the strange disproportion of numbers were not counterbalanced by the merit of one man. Thirty thousand Goths, according to the confession of their own chiefs, perished in this bloody action; and the multitude of the wounded was equal to that of the slain. When they advanced to the assault, their close disorder suffered not a javelin to fall without effect; and as they retired, the populace of the city joined the pursuit, and slaughtered, with impunity, the backs of their flying enemies. Belisarius instantly sallied from the gates; and while

His sallies.

the soldiers chaunted his name and victory, the hostile engines of war were reduced to ashes. Such was the loss and consternation of the Goths, that, from this day, the siege of Rome degenerated into a tedious and indolent blockade; and they were incessantly harassed by the Roman general, who, in frequent skirmishes, destroyed above five thousand of their bravest troops. Their cavalry was unpractised in the use of the bow; their archers served on foot; and this divided force was incapable of contending with their adversaries, whose lances and arrows, at a distance, or at hand, were alike formidable. The consummate skill of Belisarius embraced the favourable opportunities; and as he chose the ground and

---

85. *Vivarium* was an angle in the new wall inclosed for wild beasts (Procopius, Goth. l. i. c. 23.). The spot is still visible in Nardini (l. iv. c. 2. p. 159, 160.) and Nolli's great plan of Rome.

the moment, as he pressed the charge or sounded the retreat,[86] the squadrons which he detached, were seldom unsuccessful. These partial advantages diffused an impatient ardour among the soldiers and people, who began to feel the hardships of a siege, and to disregard the dangers of a general engagement. Each plebeian conceived himself to be an hero, and the infantry, who, since the decay of discipline, were rejected from the line of battle, aspired to the ancient honours of the Roman legion. Belisarius praised the spirit of his troops, condemned their presumption, yielded to their clamours, and prepared the remedies of a defeat, the possibility of which he alone had courage to suspect. In the quarter of the Vatican, the Romans prevailed; and if the irreparable moments had not been wasted in the pillage of the camp, they might have occupied the Milvian bridge, and charged in the rear of the Gothic host. On the other side of the Tyber, Belisarius advanced from the Pincian and Salarian gates. But his army, four thousand soldiers perhaps, was lost in a spacious plain; they were encompassed and oppressed by fresh multitudes, who continually relieved the broken ranks of the Barbarians. The valiant leaders of the infantry were unskilled to conquer; they died: the retreat (an hasty retreat) was covered by the prudence of the general, and the victors started back with affright from the formidable aspect of an armed rampart. The reputation of Belisarius was unsullied by a defeat; and the vain confidence of the Goths was not less serviceable to his designs, than the repentance and modesty of the Roman troops.

From the moment that Belisarius had determined to sustain a siege, his assiduous care provided Rome against the danger of famine, more dreadful than the Gothic arms. An extraordinary *Distress of the city.* supply of corn was imported from Sicily: the harvests of Campania and Tuscany were forcibly swept for the use of the city; and the rights of private property were infringed by the strong plea of the public safety. It might easily be foreseen that the enemy would intercept the aqueducts; and the cessation of the water-mills was the first inconvenience, which was speedily removed by mooring large vessels, and fixing mill-stones, in the current of the river. The stream was soon embarrassed by the trunks of trees, and polluted with dead bodies; yet so effectual were the precautions of the

---

86. For the Roman trumpet and its various notes, consult Lipsius, de Militiâ Romanâ (Opp. tom. iii. l. iv. Dialog. x. p. 125–129.). A mode of distinguishing the *charge* by the horse-trumpet of solid brass, and the *retreat* by the foot-trumpet of leather and light wood, was recommended by Procopius, and adopted by Belisarius (Goth. l. ii. c. 23.).

Roman general, that the waters of the Tyber still continued to give motion to the mills and drink to the inhabitants: the more distant quarters were supplied from domestic wells; and a besieged city might support, without impatience, the privation of her public baths. A large portion of Rome, from the Prænestine gate to the church of St. Paul, was never invested by the Goths; their excursions were restrained by the activity of the Moorish troops: the navigation of the Tyber, and the Latin, Appian, and Ostian ways, were left free and unmolested for the introduction of corn and cattle, or the retreat of the inhabitants, who sought a refuge in Campania or Sicily. Anxious to relieve himself from an useless and devouring multitude, Belisarius issued his peremptory orders for the instant departure of the women, the children, and slaves; required his soldiers to dismiss their male and female attendants, and regulated their allowance, that one moiety should be given in provisions, and the other in money. His foresight was justified by the encrease of the public distress, as soon as the Goths had occupied two important posts in the neighbourhood of Rome. By the loss of the port, or as it is now called, the city of Porto, he was deprived of the country on the right of the Tyber, and the best communication with the sea; and he reflected with grief and anger, that three hundred men, could he have spared such a feeble band, might have defended its impregnable works. Seven miles from the capital, between the Appian and the Latin ways, two principal aqueducts crossing, and again crossing each other, inclosed within their solid and lofty arches a fortified space,[87] where Vitiges established a camp of seven thousand Goths to intercept the convoys of Sicily and Campania. The granaries of Rome were insensibly exhausted, the adjacent country had been wasted with fire and sword; such scanty supplies as might yet be obtained by hasty excursions, were the reward of valour, and the purchase of wealth: the forage of the horses, and the bread of the soldiers, never failed; but in the last months of the siege, the people was exposed to the miseries of scarcity, unwholesome food,[88] and con-

---

87. Procopius (Goth. l. ii. c. 3.) has forgot to name these aqueducts; nor can such a double intersection, at such a distance from Rome, be clearly ascertained from the writings of Frontinus Fabretti and Eschinard, de Aquis and de Agro Romano, or from the local maps of Lameti and Cingolani. Seven or eight miles from the city (50 stadia), on the road to Albano, between the Latin and Appian ways,

I discern the remains of an aqueduct (probably the Septimian), a series (630 paces) of arches twenty-five feet high (ὑψηλῳ εσαγαν).

88. They made sausages, αλλατας, of mule's flesh: unwholesome, if the animals had died of the plague. Otherwise the famous Bologna sausages are said to be made of ass flesh (Voyages de Labat, tom. ii. p. 218.).

tagious disorders. Belisarius saw and pitied their sufferings; but he had foreseen, and he watched the decay of their loyalty, and the progress of their discontent. Adversity had awakened the Romans from the dreams of grandeur and freedom, and taught them the humiliating lesson, that it was of small moment to their real happiness, whether the name of their master was derived from the Gothic or the Latin language. The lieutenant of Justinian listened to their just complaints, but he rejected with disdain the idea of flight or capitulation; repressed their clamorous impatience for battle; amused them with the prospect of sure and speedy relief; and secured himself and the city from the effects of their despair or treachery. Twice in each month he changed the station of the officers to whom the custody of the gates was committed: the various precautions, of patrols, watchwords, lights, and music, were repeatedly employed to discover whatever passed on the ramparts; outguards were posted beyond the ditch, and the trusty vigilance of dogs supplied the more doubtful fidelity of mankind. A letter was intercepted, which assured the king of the Goths, that the Asinarian gate, adjoining to the Lateran church, should be secretly opened to his troops. On the proof or suspicion of treason, several senators were banished, and the pope Sylverius was summoned to attend the representative of his sovereign, at his head-quarters in the Pincian palace.[89] The ecclesiastics who followed their bishop, were detained in the first or second apartment,[90] and he alone was admitted to the presence of Belisarius. The conqueror of *Exile of Pope Sylverius, A.D. 537, Nov. 17.* Rome and Carthage was modestly seated at the feet of Antonina, who reclined on a stately couch: the general was silent, but the voice of reproach and menace issued from the mouth of his imperious wife. Accused by credible witnesses, and the evidence of his own subscription, the successor of St. Peter was despoiled of his pontifical ornaments, clad in the mean habit of a monk, and embarked, without delay, for a distant exile in the East. At the emperor's command, the clergy of Rome proceeded to the

89. The name of the palace, the hill, and the adjoining gate, were all derived from the senator Pincius. Some recent vestiges of temples and churches are now smoothed in the garden of the Minims of the Trinità del Monte (Nardini, l. iv. c. 7. p. 196. Eschinard, p. 209, 210. the old plan of Buffalino, and the great plan of Nolli). Belisarius had fixed his station between the *Pincian* and Salarian gates (Procop. Goth. l. i. c. 15.).

90. From the mention of the primum et secundum velum, it should seem that Belisarius, even in a siege, represented the emperor, and maintained the proud ceremonial of the Byzantine palace.

choice of a new bishop; and after a solemn invocation of the Holy Ghost, elected the deacon Vigilius, who had purchased the papal throne by a bribe of two hundred pounds of gold. The profit, and consequently the guilt of this simony, was imputed to Belisarius: but the hero obeyed the orders of his wife; Antonina served the passions of the empress; and Theodora lavished her treasures, in the vain hope of obtaining a pontiff hostile or indifferent to the council of Chalcedon.[91]

Deliverance of the city.

The epistle of Belisarius to the emperor announced his victory, his danger, and his resolution. "According to your commands, we have entered the dominions of the Goths, and reduced to your obedience, Sicily, Campania, and the city of Rome: but the loss of these conquests will be more disgraceful than their acquisition was glorious. Hitherto we have successfully fought against the multitudes of the Barbarians, but their multitudes may finally prevail. Victory is the gift of Providence, but the reputation of kings and generals depends on the success or the failure of their designs. Permit me to speak with freedom; if you wish that we should live, send us subsistence; if you desire that we should conquer, send us arms, horses, and men. The Romans have received us as friends and deliverers; but in our present distress, *they* will be either betrayed by their confidence, or we shall be oppressed by *their* treachery and hatred. For myself, my life is consecrated to your service: it is yours to reflect, whether my death in this situation will contribute to the glory and prosperity of your reign." Perhaps that reign would have been equally prosperous, if the peaceful master of the East had abstained from the conquest of Africa and Italy: but as Justinian was ambitious of fame, he made some efforts, they were feeble and languid, to support and rescue his victorious general. A reinforcement of sixteen hundred Sclavonians and Huns was led by Martin and Valerian; and as they had reposed during the winter season in the harbours of Greece, the strength of the men and horses was not impaired by the fatigues of a sea-voyage; and they distinguished their valour in the first sally against the besiegers. About the time of the summer solstice, Euthalius landed at Terracina with large sums of money for the payment of the troops: he cautiously proceeded along the Appian way, and this convoy entered Rome through the gate

---

91. Of this act of sacrilege, Procopius (Goth. l. i. c. 25.) is a dry and reluctant witness. The narratives of Liberatus (Breviarium, c. 22.) and Anastasius (de Vit. Pont. p. 39.) are characteristic, but passionate. Hear the execrations of Cardinal Baronius (A.D. 536. N° 123. A.D. 538. N° 4–20.): portentum, facinus omni execratione dignum.

Capena,[92] while Belisarius, on the other side, diverted the attention of
the Goths by a vigorous and successful skirmish. These seasonable aids, the
use and reputation of which were dextrously managed by the Roman
general, revived the courage, or at least the hopes of the soldiers and people.
The historian Procopius was dispatched with an important commission,
to collect the troops and provisions which Campania could furnish, or
Constantinople had sent; and the secretary of Belisarius was soon followed
by Antonina herself,[93] who boldly traversed the posts of the enemy, and
returned with the Oriental succours to the relief of her husband and the
besieged city. A fleet of three thousand Isaurians cast anchor in the bay of
Naples, and afterwards at Ostia. Above two thousand horse, of whom a
part were Thracians, landed at Tarentum; and, after the junction of five
hundred soldiers of Campania, and a train of waggons laden with wine and
flour, they directed their march on the Appian way, from Capua to the
neighbourhood of Rome. The forces that arrived by land and sea, were
united at the mouth of the Tyber. Antonina convened a council of war: it
was resolved to surmount, with sails and oars, the adverse stream of the
river: and the Goths were apprehensive of disturbing, by any rash hostilities,
the negociation to which Belisarius had craftily listened. They credulously
believed, that they saw no more than the vanguard of a fleet and army,
which already covered the Ionian sea and the plains of Campania; and the
illusion was supported by the haughty language of the Roman general,
when he gave audience to the ambassadors of Vitiges. After a specious
discourse to vindicate the justice of his cause, they declared, that, for the
sake of peace, they were disposed to renounce the possession of Sicily.
"The emperor is not less generous," replied his lieutenant, with a disdainful
smile, "in return for a gift which you no longer possess; he presents you
with an ancient province of the empire; he resigns to the Goths the
sovereignty of the British island." Belisarius rejected with equal firmness
and contempt, the offer of a tribute; but he allowed the Gothic ambassadors
to seek their fate from the mouth of Justinian himself; and consented, with
seeming reluctance, to a truce of three months, from the winter solstice to
the equinox of spring. Prudence might not safely trust either the oaths or

92. The old Capena was removed by Aurelian
to, or near, the modern gate of St. Sebastian
(see Nolli's plan). That memorable spot has
been consecrated by the Egerian grove, the
memory of Numa, triumphal arches, the

sepulchres of the Scipios, Metelli, &c.
93. The expression of Procopius has an
invidious cast – τυχην εκ του ασφαλους την
σφισι συμβησομενην καραδοκειν (Goth. l. ii.
c. 4.). Yet he is speaking of a woman.

hostages of the Barbarians, but the conscious superiority of the Roman chief was expressed in the distribution of his troops. As soon as fear or hunger compelled the Goths to evacuate Alba, Porto, and Cen-

Belisarius recovers many cities of Italy.

tumcellæ, their place was instantly supplied; the garrisons of Narni, Spoleto, and Perusia, were reinforced, and the seven camps of the besiegers were gradually encompassed with the calamities of a siege. The prayers and pilgrimage of Datius, bishop of Milan, were not without effect; and he obtained one thousand Thracians and Isaurians, to assist the revolt of Liguria against her Arian tyrant. At the same time, John the Sanguinary,[94] the nephew of Vitalian, was detached with two thousand chosen horse, first to Alba on the Fucine lake, and afterwards to the frontiers of Picenum on the Hadriatic sea. "In that province," said Belisarius, "the Goths have deposited their families and treasures, without a guard or the suspicion of danger. Doubtless, they will violate the truce: let them feel your presence, before they hear of your motions. Spare the Italians; suffer not any fortified places to remain hostile in your rear; and faithfully reserve the spoil for an equal and common partition. It would not be reasonable," he added with a laugh, "that whilst we are toiling to the destruction of the drones, our more fortunate brethren should rifle and enjoy the honey."

The Goths raise the siege of Rome, A.D. 538, March.

The whole nation of the Ostrogoths had been assembled for the attack, and was almost entirely consumed in the siege, of Rome. If any credit be due to an intelligent spectator, one-third at least of their enormous host was destroyed, in frequent and bloody combats under the walls of the city. The bad fame and pernicious qualities of the summer air, might already be imputed to the decay of agriculture and population; and the evils of famine and pestilence were aggravated by their own licentiousness, and the unfriendly disposition of the country. While Vitiges struggled with his fortune; while he hesitated between shame and ruin; his retreat was hastened by domestic alarms. The king of the Goths was informed by trembling messengers, that John the Sanguinary spread the devastations of war from the Appenine to the Hadriatic; that the rich spoils and innumerable captives of Picenum were lodged in the fortifications of Rimini; and that this formidable chief had defeated his uncle, insulted his capital, and seduced, by secret

94. Anastasius (p. 40.) has preserved this epithet of *Sanguinárius*, which might do honour to a tyger.

correspondence, the fidelity of his wife, the imperious daughter of Amala-sontha. Yet, before he retired, Vitiges made a last effort, either to storm or to surprise the city. A secret passage was discovered in one of the aque-ducts; two citizens of the Vatican were tempted by bribes to intoxicate the guards of the Aurelian gate; an attack was meditated on the walls beyond the Tyber, in a place which was not fortified with towers; and the Barbarians advanced, with torches and scaling-ladders, to the assault of the Pincian gate. But every attempt was defeated by the intrepid vigilance of Belisarius and his band of veterans, who, in the most perilous moments, did not regret the absence of their companions; and the Goths, alike destitute of hope and subsistence, clamorously urged their departure, before the truce should expire, and the Roman cavalry should again be united. One year and nine days after the commencement of the siege, an army, so lately strong and triumphant, burnt their tents, and tumultuously repassed the Milvian bridge. They repassed not with impunity: their thronging multi-tudes, oppressed in a narrow passage, were driven headlong into the Tyber, by their own fears and the pursuit of the enemy; and the Roman general, sallying from the Pincian gate, inflicted a severe and disgraceful wound on their retreat. The slow length of a sickly and desponding host was heavily dragged along the Flaminian way; from whence the Barbarians were sometimes compelled to deviate, lest they should encounter the hostile garrisons that guarded the high road to Rimini and Ravenna. Yet so powerful was this flying army, that Vitiges spared ten thousand men for the defence of the cities which he was most solicitous to preserve, and detached his nephew Uraias, with an adequate force, for the chastisement of rebellious Milan. At the head of his principal army, he besieged Rimini, only thirty-three miles distant from the Gothic capital. A feeble rampart, and a shallow ditch, were maintained by the skill and valour of John the Sanguinary, who shared the danger and fatigue of the meanest soldier, and emulated, on a theatre less illustrious, the military virtues of his great commander. The towers and battering engines of the Barbarians were rendered useless; their attacks were repulsed; and the tedious blockade, which reduced the garrison to the last extremity of *Lose Rimini;* hunger, afforded time for the union and march of the Roman forces. A fleet which had surprised Ancona, sailed along the coast of the Hadriatic, to the relief of the besieged city. The eunuch Narses landed in Picenum with two thousand Heruli and five thousand of the bravest troops of the East. The rock of the Appenine was forced; ten thousand veterans moved

round the foot of the mountains, under the command of Belisarius himself;
and a new army, whose encampment blazed with innumerable lights,
appeared to advance along the Flaminian way. Overwhelmed with astonishment and despair, the Goths abandoned the siege of Rimini, their tents,
their standards, and their leaders; and Vitiges, who gave or followed
the example of flight, never halted till he found a shelter within the
walls and morasses of Ravenna.

retire to Ravenna.

To these walls, and to some fortresses destitute of any mutual
support, the Gothic monarchy was now reduced. The provinces
of Italy had embraced the party of the emperor; and his army,
gradually recruited to the number of twenty thousand men, must
have atchieved an easy and rapid conquest, if their invincible
powers had not been weakened by the discord of the Roman chiefs. Before
the end of the siege, an act of blood, ambiguous and indiscreet, sullied the
fair fame of Belisarius. Presidius, a loyal Italian, as he fled from Ravenna
to Rome, was rudely stopped by Constantine, the military governor of
Spoleto, and despoiled, even in a church, of two daggers richly inlaid with
gold and precious stones. As soon as the public danger had subsided,
Presidius complained of the loss and injury: his complaint was heard, but
the order of restitution was disobeyed by the pride and avarice of the
offender. Exasperated by the delay, Presidius boldly arrested the general's
horse as he passed through the forum; and with the spirit of a citizen,
demanded the common benefit of the Roman laws. The honour of
Belisarius was engaged; he summoned a council; claimed the obedience of
his subordinate officer; and was provoked, by an insolent reply, to call
hastily for the presence of his guards. Constantine, viewing their entrance
as the signal of death, drew his sword, and rushed on the general, who
nimbly eluded the stroke, and was protected by his friends; while the
desperate assassin was disarmed, dragged into a neighbouring chamber
and executed, or rather murdered, by the guards, at the arbitrary
command of Belisarius.[95] In this hasty act of violence, the guilt
of Constantine was no longer remembered; the despair and death
of that valiant officer were secretly imputed to the revenge of Antonina;

Jealousy of the Roman generals, A.D. 538.

Death of Constantine.

---

95. This transaction is related in the public history (Goth. l. ii. c. 8.) with candour or caution; in the Anecdotes (c. 7.) with malevolence or freedom; but Marcellinus, or rather his continuator (in Chron.), casts a shade of premeditated assassination over the death of Constantine. He had performed good service at Rome and Spoleto (Procop. Goth. l. i. c. 7. 14.); but Alemannus confounds him with a Constantianus comes stabuli.

and each of his colleagues, conscious of the same rapine, was apprehensive of the same fate. The fear of a common enemy suspended the effects of their envy and discontent; but in the confidence of approaching victory, they instigated a powerful rival to oppose the conqueror of Rome and Africa. From the domestic service of the palace, and the administration of the private revenue, Narses the eunuch was suddenly exalted to the head of an army; and the spirit of an hero, who *The eunuch Narses.* afterwards equalled the merit and glory of Belisarius, served only to perplex the operations of the Gothic war. To his prudent counsels, the relief of Rimini was ascribed by the leaders of the discontented faction, who exhorted Narses to assume an independent and separate command. The epistle of Justinian had indeed enjoined his obedience to the general; but the dangerous exception, "as far as may be advantageous to the public service," reserved some freedom of judgment to the discreet favourite, who had so lately departed from the *sacred* and familiar conversation of his sovereign. In the exercise of this doubtful right, the eunuch perpetually dissented from the opinions of Belisarius; and, after yielding with reluctance to the siege of Urbino, he deserted his colleague in the night, and marched away to the conquest of the Æmilian province. The fierce and formidable bands of the Heruli were attached to the person of Narses;[96] ten thousand Romans and confederates were persuaded to march under his banners; every malecontent embraced the fair opportunity of revenging his private or imaginary wrongs; and the remaining troops of Belisarius were divided and dispersed from the garrisons of Sicily to the shores of the Hadriatic. His skill and perseverance overcame every obstacle: *Firmness and authority of Belisarius.* Urbino was taken, the sieges of Fæsulæ, Orvieto, and Auximum, were undertaken and vigorously prosecuted; and the eunuch Narses was at length recalled to the domestic cares of the palace. All dissensions were healed, and all opposition was subdued by the temperate authority of the Roman general, to whom his enemies could not refuse their esteem; and Belisarius inculcated the salutary lesson, that the forces of the state should compose one body, and be animated by one soul. But in the interval of discord, the Goths were permitted to breathe; an important

---

96. They refused to serve after his departure; sold their captives and cattle to the Goths; and swore never to fight against them. Procopius introduces a curious digression on the manners and adventurers of this wandering nation, a part of whom finally emigrated to Thule or Scandinavia (Goth. l. ii. c. 14, 15.).

season was lost, Milan was destroyed, and the northern provinces of Italy were afflicted by an inundation of the Franks.

Invasion of Italy by the Franks, A.D. 538, 539.

When Justinian first meditated the conquest of Italy, he sent ambassadors to the kings of the Franks, and adjured them, by the common ties of alliance and religion, to join in the holy enterprise against the Arians. The Goths, as their wants were more urgent, employed a more effectual mode of persuasion, and vainly strove, by the gift of lands and money, to purchase the friendship, or at least the neutrality, of a light and perfidious nation.[97] But the arms of Belisarius, and the revolt of the Italians, had no sooner shaken the Gothic monarchy, than Theodebert of Austrasia, the most powerful and warlike of the Merovingian kings, was persuaded to succour their distress by an indirect and seasonable aid. Without expecting the consent of their sovereign, ten thousand Burgundians, his recent subjects, descended from the Alps, and joined the troops which Vitiges had sent to chastise the revolt of Milan. After an obstinate siege, the capital of Liguria was reduced by famine, but no capitulation could be obtained, except for the safe retreat of the Roman garrison. Datius, the orthodox bishop, who had seduced his countrymen to rebellion[98] and ruin, escaped to the luxury and honours of the Byzantine court;[99] but the clergy, perhaps the Arian clergy, were slaughtered at the foot of their own altars by the defenders of the Catholic faith. Three hundred thousand males were *reported* to be slain;[100] the female sex, and the more precious spoil, was resigned to the Burgundians; and the houses, or at least the walls, of Milan were levelled with the ground. The Goths, in their last moments, were revenged by the destruction of a city, second only to Rome in size and opulence, in the splendour of its buildings, or the number of its inhabitants; and Belisarius

Destruction of Milan.

---

97. This national reproach of perfidy (Procop. Goth. l. ii. c. 25.) offends the ear of La Mothe le Vayer (tom. viii. p. 163–165.), who criticises, as if he had not read, the Greek historian.
98. Baronius applauds his treason, and justifies the Catholic bishops – qui ne sub heretico principe degant omnem lapidem movent – an useful caution. The more rational Muratori (Annali d'Italia, tom. v. p. 54.) hints at the guilt of perjury, and blames at least the *imprudence* of Datius.
99. St. Datius was more successful against

devils than against Barbarians. He travelled with a numerous retinue, and occupied at Corinth a large house (Baronius, A.D. 538. Nº 89. A.D. 539. Nº 20.).
100. Μυριαδες τριακοντα (compare Procopius, Goth. l. ii, c. 7. 21.). Yet such population is incredible; and the second or third city of Italy need not repine if we only decimate the numbers of the present text. Both Milan and Genoa revived in less than thirty years (Paul Diacon. de Gestis Langobard. l. ii. c. 38.).

sympathized alone in the fate of his deserted and devoted friends. Encouraged by this successful inroad, Theodebert himself, in the ensuing spring, invaded the plains of Italy with an army of one hundred thousand Barbarians.[101] The king, and some chosen followers, were mounted on horseback, and armed with lances: the infantry, without bows or spears, were satisfied with a shield, a sword, and a double-edged battle-axe, which, in their hands, became a deadly and unerring weapon. Italy trembled at the march of the Franks; and both the Gothic prince and the Roman general, alike ignorant of their designs, solicited, with hope and terror, the friendship of these dangerous allies. Till he had secured the passage of the Po on the bridge of Pavia, the grandson of Clovis dissembled his intentions, which he at length declared, by assaulting, almost at the same instant, the hostile camps of the Romans and Goths. Instead of uniting their arms, they fled with equal precipitation; and the fertile, though desolate provinces of Liguria and Æmilia, were abandoned to a licentious host of Barbarians, whose rage was not mitigated by any thoughts of settlement or conquest. Among the cities which they ruined, Genoa, not yet constructed of marble, is particularly enumerated: and the deaths of thousands, according to the regular practice of war, appear to have excited less horror than some idolatrous sacrifices of women and children, which were performed with impunity in the camp of the most Christian king. If it were not a melancholy truth, that the first and most cruel sufferings must be the lot of the innocent and helpless, history might exult in the misery of the conquerors, who, in the midst of riches, were left destitute of bread or wine, reduced to drink the waters of the Po, and to feed on the flesh of distempered cattle. The dysentery swept away one-third of their army; and the clamours of his subjects, who were impatient to pass the Alps, disposed Theodebert to listen with respect to the mild exhortations of Belisarius. The memory of this inglorious and destructive warfare was perpetuated on the medals of Gaul; and Justinian, without unsheathing his sword, assumed the title of conqueror of the Franks. The Merovingian prince was offended by the vanity of the emperor; he affected to pity the fallen fortunes of the Goths; and his insidious offer of a fœderal union was fortified by the promise or menace of descending from the Alps at the head of five hundred thousand

---

101. Besides Procopius, perhaps too Roman, see the Chronicles of Marius and Marcellinus, Jornandes (in Success. Regn. in Muratori, tom. i. p. 241.). and Gregory of Tours (l. iii.

c. 32. in tom. ii. of the Historians of France). Gregory supposes a defeat of Belisarius, who, in Aimoin (de Gestis Franc. l. ii. c. 23. in tom. iii. p. 59), is slain by the Franks.

men. His plans of conquest were boundless and perhaps chimerical. The king of Austrasia threatened to chastise Justinian, and to march to the gates of Constantinople:[102] he was overthrown and slain[103] by a wild bull,[104] as he hunted in the Belgic or German forests.

Belisarius besieges Ravenna;

As soon as Belisarius was delivered from his foreign and domestic enemies, he seriously applied his forces to the final reduction of Italy. In the siege of Osimo, the general was nearly transpierced with an arrow, if the mortal stroke had not been intercepted by one of his guards, who lost, in that pious office, the use of his hand. The Goths of Osimo, four thousand warriors, with those of Fæsulæ and the Cottian Alps, were among the last who maintained their independence; and their gallant resistance, which almost tired the patience, deserved the esteem, of the conqueror. His prudence refused to subscribe the safe conduct which they asked, to join their brethren of Ravenna; but they saved, by an honourable capitulation, one moiety at least of their wealth, with the free alternative of retiring peaceably to their estates, or enlisting to serve the emperor in his Persian wars. The multitudes which yet adhered to the standard of Vitiges, far surpassed the number of the Roman troops; but neither prayers, nor defiance, nor the extreme danger of his most faithful subjects, could tempt the Gothic king beyond the fortifications of Ravenna. These fortifications were, indeed, impregnable to the assaults of art or violence; and when Belisarius invested the capital, he was soon convinced that famine only could tame the stubborn spirit of the Barbarians. The sea, the land, and the channels of the Po, were guarded by the vigilance of the Roman general; and his morality extended the rights of war to the practice of poisoning the waters,[105] and secretly firing

---

102. Agathias, l. i. p. 14, 15. Could he have seduced or subdued the Gepidæ or Lombards of Pannonia, the Greek historian is confident that he must have been destroyed in Thrace.
103. The king pointed his spear – the bull overturned a tree on his head – he expired the same day. Such is the story of Agathias; but the original historians of France (tom. ii. p. 202. 403. 558. 667.) impute his death to a fever.
104. Without losing myself in a labyrinth of species and names – the aurochs, urus, bisons, bubalus, bonasus, buffalo, &c. (Buffon, Hist. Nat. tom. xi. and Supplement, tom. iii. vi.),

it is certain, that in the sixth century a large wild species of horned cattle was hunted in the great forests of the Vosges in Lorraine, and the Ardennes (Greg. Turon. tom. ii. l. x. c. 10. p. 369.).
105. In the siege of Auximum, he first laboured to demolish an old aqueduct, and then cast into the stream. 1. dead bodies; 2. mischievous herbs; and, 3. quick lime, which is named (says Procopius, l. ii. c. 29.) τιτανος by the ancients; by the moderns ασβεστος. Yet both words are used as synonymous in Galen, Dioscorides, and Lucian (Hen. Steph. Thesaur. Ling. Græc. tom. iii. p. 748.).

the granaries[106] of a besieged city.[107] While he pressed the blockade of Ravenna, he was surprised by the arrival of two ambassadors from Constantinople, with a treaty of peace, which Justinian had imprudently signed, without deigning to consult the author of his victory. By this disgraceful and precarious agreement, Italy and the Gothic treasure were divided, and the provinces beyond the Po were left with the regal title to the successor of Theodoric. The ambassadors were eager to accomplish their salutary commission; the captive Vitiges accepted, with transport, the unexpected offer of a crown; honour was less prevalent among the Goths, than the want and appetite of food; and the Roman chiefs, who murmured at the continuance of the war, professed implicit submission to the commands of the emperor. If Belisarius had possessed only the courage of a soldier, the laurel would have been snatched from his hand by timid and envious counsels; but in this decisive moment, he resolved, with the magnanimity of a statesman, to sustain alone the danger and merit of generous disobedience. Each of his officers gave a written opinion, that the siege of Ravenna was impracticable and hopeless: the general then rejected the treaty of partition, and declared his own resolution of leading Vitiges in chains to the feet of Justinian. The Goths retired with doubt and dismay: this peremptory refusal deprived them of the only signature which they could trust, and filled their minds with a just apprehension, that a sagacious enemy had discovered the full extent of their deplorable state. They compared the fame and fortune of Belisarius with the weakness of their ill-fated king; and the comparison suggested an extraordinary project to which Vitiges, with apparent resignation, was compelled to acquiesce. Partition would ruin the strength, exile would disgrace the honour, of the nation; but they offered their arms, their treasures, and the fortifications of Ravenna, if Belisarius would disclaim the authority of a master, accept the choice of the Goths, and assume, as he had deserved, the kingdom of Italy.

---

106. The Goths suspected Mathasuintha as an accomplice in the mischief, which perhaps was occasioned by accidental lightning.
107. In strict philosophy, a limitation of the rights of war seems to imply nonsense and contradiction. Grotius himself is lost in an idle distinction between the jus naturæ and the jus gentium, between poison and infection. He balances in one scale the passages of Homer (Odyss. A. 259, &c.) and Florus (l. ii. c. 20.

N° 7. ult.); and in the other, the examples of Solon (Pausanias, l. x. c. 37.) and Belisarius. See his great work De Jure Belli et Pacis (l. iii. c. 4. s. 15, 16, 17. and in Barbeyrac's version, tom. ii. p. 257, &c.). Yet I can understand the benefit and validity of an agreement, tacit or express, mutually to abstain from certain modes of hostility. See the Amphictyonic oath in Eschines, de Falsâ Legatione.

If the false lustre of a diadem could have tempted the loyalty of a faithful subject, his prudence must have foreseen the inconstancy of the Barbarians, and his rational ambition would prefer the safe and honourable station of a Roman general. Even the patience and seeming satisfaction with which he entertained a proposal of treason, might be susceptible of a malignant interpretation. But the lieutenant of Justinian was conscious of his own rectitude; he entered into a dark and crooked path, as it might lead to the voluntary submission of the Goths; and his dextrous policy persuaded them that he was disposed to comply with their wishes, without engaging an oath or a promise for the performance of a treaty which he secretly abhorred. The day of the surrender of Ravenna was stipulated by the Gothic ambassadors: a fleet laden with provisions, sailed as a welcome guest into the deepest recess of the harbour: the gates were opened to the fancied king of Italy; and Belisarius, without meeting an enemy, triumphantly marched through the streets of an impregnable city.[108] The Romans were astonished by their success; the multitudes of tall and robust Barbarians were confounded by the image of their own patience; and the masculine females, spitting in the faces of their sons and husbands, most bitterly reproached them for betraying their dominion and freedom to these pygmies of the south, contemptible in their numbers, diminutive in their stature. Before the Goths could recover from the first surprise, and claim the accomplishment of their doubtful hopes, the victor established his power in Ravenna, beyond the danger of repentance and revolt. Vitiges, who perhaps had attempted to escape, was honourably guarded in his palace;[109] the flower of the Gothic youth was selected for the service of the emperor; the remainder of the people was dismissed to their peaceful habitations in the southern provinces; and a colony of Italians was invited to replenish the depopulated city. The

subdues the Gothic kingdom of Italy, A.D. 539, December.

Captivity of Vitiges.

108. Ravenna was taken, not in the year 540, but in the latter end of 539; and Pagi (tom. ii. p. 569.) is rectified by Muratori (Annali d'Italia, tom. v. p. 62.), who proves, from an original act on papyrus (Antiquit. Italiæ Medii Ævi, tom. ii. dissert. xxxii. p. 999–1007. Maffei, Istoria Diplomat. p. 155–160.), that before the 3d of January 540, peace and free correspondence were restored between Ravenna and Faenza.

109. He was seized by John the Sanguinary, but an oath or sacrament was pledged for his safety in the Basilica Julii (Hist. Miscell. l. xvii. in Muratori, tom. i. p. 107.). Anastasius (in Vit. Pont. p. 40.) gives a dark but probable account. Montfaucon is quoted by Mascou (Hist. of the Germans, xii. 21.) for a votive shield representing the captivity of Vitiges, and now in the collection of signor Landi at Rome.

submission of the capital was imitated in the towns and villages of Italy, which had not been subdued, or even visited by the Romans; and the independent Goths who remained in arms at Pavia and Verona, were ambitious only to become the subjects of Belisarius. But his inflexible loyalty rejected, except as the substitute of Justinian, their oaths of allegiance; and he was not offended by the reproach of their deputies, that he rather chose to be a slave than a king.

After the second victory of Belisarius, envy again whispered, Justinian listened, and the hero was recalled. "The
remnant of the Gothic war was no longer worthy of his
presence: a gracious sovereign was impatient to reward his

*Return and glory
of Belisarius,
A.D. 540, &c.*

services, and to consult his wisdom; and he alone was capable of defending the East against the innumerable armies of Persia." Belisarius understood the suspicion, accepted the excuse, embarked at Ravenna his spoils and trophies; and proved, by his ready obedience, that such an abrupt removal from the government of Italy was not less unjust than it might have been indiscreet. The emperor received with honourable courtesy, both Vitiges and his more noble consort: and as the king of the Goths conformed to the Athanasian faith, he obtained, with a rich inheritance of lands in Asia, the rank of senator and patrician.[110] Every spectator admired, without peril, the strength and stature of the young Barbarians: they adored the majesty of the throne, and promised to shed their blood in the service of their benefactor. Justinian deposited in the Byzantine palace the treasures of the Gothic monarchy. A flattering senate was sometimes admitted to gaze on the magnificent spectacle; but it was enviously secluded from the public view; and the conqueror of Italy renounced, without a murmur, perhaps without a sigh, the well-earned honours of a second triumph. His glory was indeed exalted above all external pomp; and the faint and hollow praises of the court were supplied, even in a servile age, by the respect and admiration of his country. Whenever he appeared in the streets and public places of Constantinople, Belisarius attracted and satisfied the eyes of the people. His lofty stature and majestic countenance fulfilled their expect-ations of an hero; the meanest of his fellow-citizens were emboldened by his gentle and gracious demeanour; and the martial train which attended

---

110. Vitiges lived two years at Constantinople, and imperatoris in affectû *convictus* (or con-junctus) rebus excessit humanis. His widow, *Mathasuenta*, the wife and mother of the patricians, the elder and younger Germanus, united the streams of Anician and Amali blood (Jornandes, c. 60. p. 221. in Muratori, tom. i.).

his footsteps, left his person more accessible than in a day of battle. Seven thousand horsemen, matchless for beauty and valour, were maintained in the service, and at the private expence of the general.[111] Their prowess was always conspicuous in single combats, or in the foremost ranks; and both parties confessed, that in the siege of Rome, the guards of Belisarius had alone vanquished the Barbarian host. Their numbers were continually augmented by the bravest and most faithful of the enemy; and his fortunate captives, the Vandals, the Moors, and the Goths, emulated the attachment of his domestic followers. By the union of liberality and justice, he acquired the love of the soldiers, without alienating the affections of the people. The sick and wounded were relieved with medicines and money; and still more efficaciously, by the healing visits and smiles of their commander. The loss of a weapon or an horse was instantly repaired, and each deed of valour was rewarded by the rich and honourable gifts of a bracelet or a collar, which were rendered more precious by the judgment of Belisarius. He was endeared to the husbandmen, by the peace and plenty which they enjoyed under the shadow of his standard. Instead of being injured, the country was enriched by the march of the Roman armies; and such was the rigid discipline of their camp, that not an apple was gathered from the tree, not a path could be traced in the fields of corn. Belisarius was chaste and sober. In the licence of a military life, none could boast that they had seen him intoxicated with wine: the most beautiful captives of Gothic or Vandal race were offered to his embraces; but he turned aside from their charms, and the husband of Antonina was never suspected of violating the laws of conjugal fidelity. The spectator and historian of his exploits has observed, that amidst the perils of war, he was daring without rashness, prudent without fear, slow or rapid according to the exigences of the moment; that in the deepest distress, he was animated by real or apparent hope, but that he was modest and humble in the most prosperous fortune. By these virtues, he equalled or excelled the ancient masters of the military art. Victory, by sea and land, attended his arms. He subdued Africa, Italy, and the adjacent islands, led away captives the successors of Genseric and Theodoric; filled Constantinople with the spoils of their palaces, and in the space of six years recovered half the provinces of the

---

111. Procopius, Goth. l. iii. c. 1. Aimoin, a French monk of the xi[th] century, who had obtained, and has disfigured, some authentic information of Belisarius, mentions, in his name, 12,000 *pueri* or slaves – quos propriis alimus stipendiis – besides 18,000 soldiers (Historians of France, tom. iii. De Gestis Franc, l. ii. c. 6. p. 48.).

Western empire. In his fame and merit, in wealth and power, he remained, without a rival, the first of the Roman subjects: the voice of envy could only magnify his dangerous importance; and the emperor might applaud his own discerning spirit, which had discovered and raised the genius of Belisarius.

It was the custom of the Roman triumphs, that a slave should be placed behind the chariot to remind the conqueror of the instability of fortune, and the infirmities of human nature. *Secret history of his wife Antonina.* Procopius, in his anecdotes, has assumed that servile and ungrateful office. The generous reader may cast away the libel, but the evidence of facts will adhere to his memory; and he will reluctantly confess, that the fame, and even the virtue of Belisarius, were polluted by the lust and cruelty of his wife; and that the hero deserved an appellation which may not drop from the pen of the decent historian. The mother of Antonina[112] was a theatrical prostitute, and both her father and grandfather exercised at Thessalonica and Constantinople, the vile, though lucrative, profession of charioteers. In the various situations of their fortune, she became the companion, the enemy, the servant, and the favourite of the empress Theodora: these loose and ambitious females had been connected by similar pleasures; they were separated by the jealousy of vice, and at length reconciled by the partnership of guilt. Before her marriage with Belisarius, Antonina had one husband and many lovers: Photius, the son of her former nuptials, was of an age to distinguish himself at the siege of Naples; and it was not till the autumn of her age and beauty[113] that she indulged a scandalous attachment to a Thracian youth. Theodosius had been educated in the Eunomian heresy; the African voyage was conse- *Her lover Theodosius.* crated by the baptism and auspicious name of the first soldier who embarked; and the proselyte was adopted into the family of his spiritual parents,[114] Belisarius and Antonina. Before they touched the shores of

112. The diligence of Alemannus could add but little to the four first and most curious chapters of the Anecdotes. Of these strange Anecdotes, a part may be true, because probable – and a part true, because improbable. Procopius must have *known* the former, and the latter he could scarcely *invent*.

113. Procopius insinuates (Anecdot. c. 4.) that, when Belisarius returned to Italy (A.D. 543), Antonina was sixty years of age. A forced, but more polite construction, which refers that date to the moment when he was writing (A.D. 559), would be compatible with the manhood of Photius (Gothic. l. i. c. 10.) in 536.

114. Compare the Vandalic War (l. i. c. 12.) with the Anecdotes (c. 1.) and Alemannus (p. 2, 3.). This mode of baptismal adoption was revived by Leo the philosopher.

Africa, this holy kindred degenerated into sensual love; and as Antonina soon overleaped the bounds of modesty and caution, the Roman general was alone ignorant of his own dishonour. During their residence at Carthage, he surprised the two lovers in a subterraneous chamber, solitary, warm, and almost naked. Anger flashed from his eyes. "With the help of this young man," said the unblushing Antonina, "I was secreting our most precious effects from the knowledge of Justinian." The youth resumed his garments, and the pious husband consented to disbelieve the evidence of his own senses. From this pleasing and perhaps voluntary delusion, Belisarius was awakened at Syracuse, by the officious information of Macedonia: and that female attendant, after requiring an oath for her security, produced two chamberlains, who, like herself, had often beheld the adulteries of Antonina. An hasty flight into Asia saved Theodosius from the justice of an injured husband, who had signified to one of his guards the order of his death; but the tears of Antonina, and her artful seductions, assured the credulous hero of her innocence; and he stooped, against his faith and judgment, to abandon those imprudent friends who had presumed to accuse or doubt the chastity of his wife. The revenge of a guilty woman is implacable and bloody: the unfortunate Macedonia, with the two witnesses, were secretly arrested by the minister of her cruelty; their tongues were cut out, their bodies were hacked into small pieces, and their remains were cast into the sea of Syracuse. A rash, though judicious saying of Constantine; "I would sooner have punished the adultress than the boy," was deeply remembered by Antonina; and two years afterwards, when despair had armed that officer against his general, her sanguinary advice decided and hastened his execution. Even the indignation of Photius was not forgiven by his mother; the exile of her son prepared the recal of her lover; and Theodosius condescended to accept the pressing and humble invitation of the conqueror of Italy. In the absolute direction of his household, and in the important commissions of peace and war,[115] the favourite youth most rapidly acquired a fortune of four hundred thousand pounds sterling: and after their return to Constantinople, the passion of Antonina, at least, continued ardent and unabated. But fear, devotion, and lassitude perhaps, inspired Theodosius with more serious thoughts. He dreaded the busy

---

115. In November 537, Photius arrested the pope (Liberat. Brev. c. 22. Pagi, tom. ii. p. 562.). About the end of 539, Belisarius sent Theodosius – τον τῇ οικίᾳ τῇ αυτου εφεστωτα – on an important and lucrative commission to Ravenna (Goth. l. ii. c. 18.).

scandal of the capital, and the indiscreet fondness of the wife of Belisarius; escaped from her embraces, and retiring to Ephesus, shaved his head, and took refuge in the sanctuary of a monastic life. The despair of the new Ariadne could scarcely have been excused by the death of her husband. She wept, she tore her hair, she filled the palace with her cries; "she had lost the dearest of friends, a tender, a faithful, a laborious friend!" But her warm entreaties, fortified by the prayers of Belisarius, were insufficient to draw the holy monk from the solitude of Ephesus. It was not till the general moved forward for the Persian war, that Theodosius could be tempted to return to Constantinople; and the short interval before the departure of Antonina herself was boldly devoted to love and pleasure.

A philosopher may pity and forgive the infirmities of female nature, from which he receives no real injury; but contemptible is the husband who feels, and yet endures, his own infamy in that of his wife. Antonina pursued her son with implacable *Resentment of Belisarius and her son Photius.* hatred; and the gallant Photius[116] was exposed to her secret persecutions in the camp beyond the Tigris. Enraged by his own wrongs, and by the dishonour of his blood, he cast away in his turn the sentiments of nature, and revealed to Belisarius the turpitude of a woman who had violated all the duties of a mother and a wife. From the surprise and indignation of the Roman general, his former credulity appears to have been sincere: he embraced the knees of the son of Antonina, adjured him to remember his obligations rather than his birth, and confirmed at the altar their holy vows of revenge and mutual defence. The dominion of Antonina was impaired by absence; and when she met her husband, on his return from the Persian confines, Belisarius, in his first and transient emotions, confined her person and threatened her life. Photius was more resolved to punish, and less prompt to pardon: he flew to Ephesus; extorted from a trusty eunuch of his mother the full confession of her guilt; arrested Theodosius and his treasures in the church of St. John the Apostle, and concealed his captives, whose execution was only delayed, in a secure and sequestered fortress of Cilicia. Such a daring outrage against public justice could not pass with impunity; and the cause of Antonina was espoused by the empress, whose

---

116. Theophanes (Chronograph. p. 204.) styles him *Photinus*, the son-in-law of Belisarius; and he is copied by the Historia Miscella and Anastasius.

favour she had deserved by the recent services of the disgrace of a præfect, and the exile and murder of a pope. At the end of the campaign, Belisarius was recalled: he complied, as usual, with the Imperial mandate. His mind was not prepared for rebellion: his obedience, however adverse to the dictates of honour, was consonant to the wishes of his heart; and when he embraced his wife, at the command, and perhaps in the presence, of the empress, the tender husband was disposed to forgive or to be forgiven. The bounty of Theodora reserved for her companion a more precious favour. "I have found," she said, "my dearest patrician, a pearl of inestimable value: it has not yet been viewed by any mortal eye; but the sight and the possession of this jewel are destined for my friend." As soon as the curiosity and impatience of Antonina were kindled, the door of a bedchamber was thrown open, and she beheld her lover, whom the diligence of the eunuchs had discovered in his secret prison. Her silent wonder burst into passionate exclamations of gratitude and joy, and she named Theodora her queen, her benefactress, and her saviour. The monk of Ephesus was nourished in the palace with luxury and ambition; but instead of assuming, as he was promised, the command of the Roman armies, Theodosius expired in the first fatigues of an amorous interview. The grief of Antonina could only be assuaged by the sufferings of her son. A youth of consular rank, and a

Persecution of her son.

sickly constitution, was punished, without a trial, like a malefactor and a slave: yet such was the constancy of his mind, that Photius sustained the tortures of the scourge and the rack, without violating the faith which he had sworn to Belisarius. After this fruitless cruelty, the son of Antonina, while his mother feasted with the empress, was buried in her subterraneous prisons, which admitted not the distinction of night and day. He twice escaped to the most venerable sanctuaries of Constantinople, the churches of St. Sophia and of the Virgin: but his tyrants were insensible of religion as of pity; and the helpless youth, amidst the clamours of the clergy and people, was twice dragged from the altar to the dungeon. His third attempt was more successful. At the end of three years, the prophet Zachariah, or some mortal friend, indicated the means of an escape: he eluded the spies and guards of the empress, reached the holy sepulchre of Jerusalem, embraced the profession of a monk; and the abbot Photius was employed, after the death of Justinian, to reconcile and regulate the churches of Egypt. The son of Antonina suffered all that an enemy can inflict: her patient husband imposed on himself the more exquisite misery of violating his promise and deserting his friend.

In the succeeding campaign, Belisarius was again sent against *Disgrace and*
the Persians: he saved the East, but he offended Theodora, *submission of*
and perhaps the emperor himself. The malady of Justinian had *Belisarius.*
countenanced the rumour of his death; and the Roman general,
on the supposition of that probable event, spoke the free language of a
citizen and a soldier. His colleague Buzes, who concurred in the same
sentiments, lost his rank, his liberty, and his health, by the persecution of
the empress: but the disgrace of Belisarius was alleviated by the dignity
of his own character, and the influence of his wife, who might wish to
humble, but could not desire to ruin the partner of her fortunes. Even his
removal was coloured by the assurance, that the sinking state of Italy would
be retrieved by the single presence of its conqueror. But no sooner had he
returned, alone and defenceless, than an hostile commission was sent to
the East, to seize his treasures and criminate his actions; the guards and
veterans who followed his private banner, were distributed among the
chiefs of the army, and even the eunuchs presumed to cast lots for the
partition of his martial domestics. When he passed with a small and sordid
retinue through the streets of Constantinople, his forlorn appearance
excited the amazement and compassion of the people. Justinian and Theodora received him with cold ingratitude; the servile crowd, with insolence
and contempt; and in the evening he retired with trembling steps to his
deserted palace. An indisposition, feigned or real, had confined Antonina
to her apartment: and she walked disdainfully silent in the adjacent portico,
while Belisarius threw himself on his bed, and expected, in an agony of
grief and terror, the death which he had so often braved under the walls
of Rome. Long after sun-set, a messenger was announced from the empress;
he opened with anxious curiosity the letter which contained the sentence
of his fate. "You cannot be ignorant how much you have deserved my
displeasure. I am not insensible of the services of Antonina. To her merits
and intercession I have granted your life, and permit you to retain a part
of your treasures, which might be justly forfeited to the state. Let your
gratitude, where it is due, be displayed, not in words, but in your future
behaviour." I know not how to believe or to relate the transports with
which the hero is said to have received this ignominious pardon. He fell
prostrate before his wife, he kissed the feet of his saviour, and he devoutly
promised to live the grateful and submissive slave of Antonina. A fine of
one hundred and twenty thousand pounds sterling was levied on the
fortunes of Belisarius; and with the office of count, or master of the royal

stables, he accepted the conduct of the Italian war. At his departure from Constantinople, his friends, and even the public, were persuaded, that as soon as he regained his freedom, he would renounce his dissimulation, and that his wife, Theodora, and perhaps the emperor himself, would be sacrificed to the just revenge of a virtuous rebel. Their hopes were deceived; and the unconquerable patience and loyalty of Belisarius appear either *below* or *above* the character of a MAN.[117]

117. The continuator of the Chronicle of Marcellinus gives, in a few decent words, the substance of the Anecdotes: Belisarius de Oriente evocatus, in offensam periculumque incurrens grave, et invidiæ subjacens rursus remittitur in Italiam (p. 54.).

[CHAPTERS XLII—XLIX]

In these chapters Gibbon's widening vision encompasses a series of nations on the empire's eastern and northern frontiers, while at the same time underlining grievous depopulation at the centre as a result of natural disasters:

I shall conclude this chapter with the comets, the earthquakes, and the plague, which astonished or afflicted the age of Justinian.

I. In the fifth year of his reign, and in the month of September, a comet was seen during twenty days in the western quarter of the heavens, and which shot its rays into the north. Eight years afterwards, while the sun was in Capricorn, another comet appeared to follow in the Sagitary: the size was gradually encreasing; the head was in the east, the tail in the west, and it remained visible above forty days. The nations, who gazed with astonishment, expected wars and calamities from their baleful influence; and these expectations were abundantly fulfilled. The astronomers dissembled their ignorance of the nature of these blazing stars, which they affected to represent as the floating meteors of the air; and few among them embraced the simple notion of Seneca and the Chaldæans, that they are only planets of a longer period and more eccentric motion. Time and science have justified the conjectures and predictions of the Roman sage: the telescope has opened new worlds to the eyes of astronomers; and, in the narrow space of history and fable, one and the same comet is already found to have revisited the earth in *seven* equal revolutions of five hundred and seventy-five years. The *first*, which ascends beyond the Christian æra one thousand seven hundred and sixty-seven years, is coëval with Ogyges the father of Grecian antiquity. And this appearance explains the tradition which Varro has preserved, that under his reign, the planet Venus changed her colour, size, figure, and course; a prodigy, without example either in past or succeeding ages. The *second* visit, in the year eleven hundred and ninety-three, is darkly implied in the fable of Electra the seventh of the Pleiads, who have been reduced to six since the time of the Trojan war. That nymph, the wife of Dardanus, was unable to support the ruin of her country: she abandoned the dances of her sister orbs, fled from the zodiac to the north pole, and obtained, from her dishevelled locks, the name of the *comet*. The *third* period expires in the year six hundred and eighteen, a date that exactly agrees with the tremendous comet of the Sibyll, and perhaps of Pliny, which arose in the West two generations before the reign of Cyrus. The *fourth* apparition, forty-four years before the birth of Christ, is of all others the most splendid and important. After the death of Cæsar, a long-haired star was conspicuous to Rome and to the nations, during the games which were exhibited by young Octavian, in honour of Venus and his uncle. The vulgar opinion, that it conveyed to heaven the divine soul of the dictator, was cherished and consecrated by the piety of a statesman: while his secret superstition referred the comet to the glory of his own times. The *fifth* visit has been already ascribed to the fifth year of Justinian, which coincides with the five hundred and thirty-first of the Christian æra. And it may deserve notice, that in this, as in the preceding instance, the comet was followed, though at a longer interval, by a remarkable paleness of the sun. The *sixth* return, in the year eleven hundred and six, is recorded by the chronicles of Europe and China; and in the first fervour of the Crusades, the Christians and the Mahometans might surmise with equal reason, that it portended the destruction of the Infidels. The *seventh* phæ-nomenon, of one thousand six hundred and eighty, was presented to the eyes of an enlightened age. The philosophy of Bayle dispelled a prejudice which Milton's muse had so recently adorned, that the comet "from its horrid hair shakes pestilence and war." Its road in the heavens was observed with exquisite skill by Flamstead and Cassini; and the mathematical science of Bernoulli, Newton, and Halley, investigated the laws of its revolutions. At the *eighth* period, in the year two thousand three hundred and fifty-five, their calculations may perhaps be verified by the astronomers of some future capital in the Siberian or American wilderness.

II. The near approach of a comet may injure or destroy the globe which we inhabit; but the changes on its surface have been hitherto produced by the action of vulcanos and earthquakes. The nature of the soil may indicate the countries most exposed to these formidable concussions, since they are caused by subterraneous fires, and such fires are kindled by the union and fermentation of iron and sulphur. But their times and effects appear to lie beyond the reach of human curiosity, and the philosopher will discreetly abstain from the prediction of earthquakes, till he has counted the drops of water that silently filtrate on the inflammable mineral, and measured the caverns which encrease by resistance the explosion of the imprisoned air. Without assigning the cause, history will distinguish the periods in which these calamitous events have been rare or frequent, and will observe, that this fever of the earth raged with uncommon violence during the reign of Justinian. Each year is marked by the repetition of earthquakes, of such duration, that Constantinople has been shaken above forty days; of such extent, that the shock has been communicated to the whole surface of the globe, or at least of the Roman empire. An impulsive or vibratory motion was felt: enormous chasms were opened, huge and heavy bodies were discharged into the air, the sea alternately advanced and retreated beyond its ordinary bounds, and a mountain was torn from Libanus, and cast into the waves, where it protected, as a mole, the new harbour of Botrys in Phœnicia. The stroke that agitates an ant-hill, may crush the insect-myriads in the dust; yet truth must extort a confession, that man has industriously laboured for his own destruction. The institution of great cities, which include a nation within the limits of a wall, almost realizes the wish of Caligula, that the Roman people had but one neck. Two hundred and fifty thousand persons are said to have perished in the earthquake of Antioch, whose domestic multitudes were swelled by the conflux of strangers to the festival of the Ascension. The loss of Berytus was of smaller account, but of much greater value. That city, on the coast of Phœnicia, was illustrated by the study of the civil law, which opened the surest road to wealth and dignity: the schools of Berytus were filled with the rising spirits of the age, and many a youth was lost in the earthquake, who might have lived to be the scourge or the guardian of his country. In these disasters, the architect becomes the enemy of mankind. The hut of a savage, or the tent of an Arab, may be thrown down without injury to the inhabitant; and the Peruvians had reason to deride the folly of their Spanish conquerors, who with so much cost and labour erected their own sepulchres. The rich marbles of a patrician are dashed on his own head: a whole people is buried under the ruins of public and private edifices, and the conflagration is kindled and propagated by the innumerable fires which are necessary for the subsistence and manufactures of a great city. Instead of the mutual sympathy which might comfort and assist the distressed, they dreadfully experience the vices and passions which are released from the fear of punishment: the tottering houses are pillaged by intrepid avarice; revenge embraces the moment, and selects the victim; and the earth often swallows the assassin or the ravisher in the consummation of their crimes. Superstition involves the present danger with invisible terrors; and if the image of death may sometimes be subservient to the virtue or repentance of individuals, an affrighted people is more forcibly moved to expect the end of the world, or to deprecate with servile homage the wrath of an avenging Deity.

III. Æthiopia and Egypt have been stigmatised in every age, as the original source and seminary of the plague. In a damp, hot, stagnating air, this African fever is generated from the putrefaction of animal substances, and especially from the swarms of locusts, not less destructive to mankind in their death than in their lives. The fatal disease which depopulated the earth in the time of Justinian and his successors, first appeared in the neighbourhood of Pelusium, between the Serbonian bog and the eastern channel of the Nile. From thence, tracing as it were a double path, it spread to the East, over Syria, Persia, and the Indies, and penetrated to the West, along the coast of Africa, and over the continent of Europe. In the spring of the second year, Constantinople, during three or four months, was visited by the pestilence: and Procopius, who observed its progress and symptoms with the eyes of a physician, has emulated the skill and diligence of Thucydides in the description of the plague of Athens. The infection was sometimes announced by the visions of a distempered fancy, and the victim despaired as soon as he had heard the menace and felt the stroke of an invisible spectre. But the greater number, in their beds, in the streets, in their usual occupation, were surprised by a slight fever; so slight indeed, that neither the pulse nor the colour of the patient gave any signs of the approaching danger. The same, the next, or the succeeding day, it was declared by the swelling of the glands, particularly those of the groin, of the arm-pits, and under the ear; and when these bubos or tumours were opened, they were found to contain a *coal*, or black substance, of the size of a lentil. If they came to a just swelling and suppuration, the patient was saved by this kind and natural discharge of the morbid humour. But if they continued hard and dry, a mortification quickly ensued, and the fifth day was commonly the term of his life. The fever was often accompanied with lethargy or delirium; the bodies of the sick were covered with black pustules or carbuncles, the symptoms of immediate death; and in the constitutions too feeble to produce an eruption, the vomiting of blood was followed by a mortification of the bowels. To pregnant women the plague was generally mortal: yet one infant was drawn alive from his dead mother, and three mothers survived the loss of their infected fœtus. Youth was the most perilous season; and the female sex was less susceptible than the male: but every rank and profession was attacked with indiscriminate rage, and many of those who escaped were deprived of the use of their speech, without being secure from a return of the disorder. The physicians of Constantinople were zealous and skilful: but their art was baffled by the various symptoms and pertinacious vehemence of the disease: the same remedies were productive of contrary effects, and the event capriciously disappointed their prognostics of death or recovery. The order of funerals, and the right of sepulchres, were confounded; those who were left without friends or servants, lay unburied in the streets or in their desolate houses; and a magistrate was authorised to collect the promiscuous heaps of dead bodies, to transport them by land or water, and to inter them in deep pits beyond the precincts of the city. Their own danger, and the prospect of public distress, awakened some remorse in the minds of the most vicious of mankind: the confidence of health again revived their passions and habits; but philosophy must disdain the observation of Procopius, that the lives of such men were guarded by the peculiar favour of fortune or providence. He forgot, or perhaps he secretly recollected, that the plague had touched the person of Justinian himself: but the abstemious diet of the emperor may suggest, as in the case of Socrates, a more rational and honourable cause for his recovery. During his sickness, the public consternation was expressed in the habits of the citizens; and their idleness and despondence occasioned a general scarcity in the capital of the East.

Contagion is the inseparable symptom of the plague; which, by mutual respiration, is transfused from the infected persons to the lungs and stomach of those who approach them. While philosophers believe and tremble, it is singular, that the existence of a real danger should have been denied by a people most prone to vain and imaginary terror. Yet the fellow-citizens of Procopius were satisfied, by some short and partial experience, that the infection could not be gained by the closest conversation; and this persuasion might support the assiduity of friends or physicians in the care of the sick, whom inhuman prudence would have condemned to solitude and despair. But the fatal security, like the predestination of the Turks, must have aided the progress of the contagion; and those salutary precautions to which Europe is indebted for her safety, were unknown to the government of Justinian. No restraints were imposed on the free and frequent intercourse of the Roman provinces: from Persia to France, the nations were mingled and infected by wars and emigrations; and the pestilential odour which lurks for years in a bale of cotton, was imported, by the abuse of trade, into the most distant regions. The mode of its propagation is explained by the remark of Procopius himself, that it always spread from the sea-coast to the inland country: the most sequestered islands and mountains were successively visited; the places which had escaped the fury of its first passage, were alone exposed to the contagion of the ensuing year. The winds might diffuse that subtle venom; but unless the atmosphere be previously disposed for its reception, the plague would soon expire in the cold or temperate climates of the earth. Such was the universal corruption of the air, that the pestilence which burst forth in the fifteenth year of Justinian was not checked or alleviated by any difference of the seasons. In time, its first malignity was abated and dispersed; the disease alternately languished and revived; but it was not till the end of a calamitous period of fifty-two years, that mankind recovered their health, or the air resumed its pure and salubrious quality. No facts have been preserved to sustain an account, or even a conjecture, of the numbers that perished in this extraordinary mortality. I only find, that during three months, five, and at length ten, thousand persons died each day at Constantinople; that many cities of the East were left vacant, and that in several districts of Italy the harvest and the vintage withered on the ground. The triple scourge of war, pestilence, and famine, afflicted the subjects of Justinian, and his reign is disgraced by a visible decrease of the human species, which has never been repaired in some of the fairest countries of the globe. (*DF*, ii. 770–77)

Chapters on Roman law (chapter XLIV), and on the doctrine of the Incarnation (chapter XLVII), interrupt and relieve the onward press of narrative, which might otherwise threaten to become the inexplicable vision of succession which Coleridge thought it was: 'When I read a chapter in Gibbon . . . figures come and go, I know not how or why.'[1] But Gibbon is already reaching forward to the next main focus of his history. The shortcomings of Byzantium required a change of plan:

I have now deduced from Trajan to Constantine, from Constantine to Heraclius, the regular series of the Roman emperors; and faithfully exposed the prosperous and adverse fortunes of their reigns. Five centuries of the decline and fall of the empire have already elapsed; but a period of more than eight hundred years still separates me from the term of my labours,

1. S. T. Coleridge, *Table Talk and Omniana* (Oxford, 1917), p. 293.

the taking of Constantinople by the Turks. Should I persevere in the same course, should I observe the same measure, a prolix and slender thread would be spun through many a volume, nor would the patient reader find an adequate reward of instruction or amusement. At every step, as we sink deeper in the decline and fall of the Eastern empire, the annals of each succeeding reign would impose a more ungrateful and melancholy task. These annals must continue to repeat a tedious and uniform tale of weakness and misery; the natural connection of causes and events would be broken by frequent and hasty transitions, and a minute accumulation of circumstances must destroy the light and effect of those general pictures which compose the use and ornament of a remote history. From the time of Heraclius, the Byzantine theatre is contracted and darkened: the line of empire, which had been defined by the laws of Justinian and the arms of Belisarius, recedes on all sides from our view: the Roman name, the proper subject of our enquiries, is reduced to a narrow corner of Europe, to the lonely suburbs of Constantinople; and the fate of the Greek empire has been compared to that of the Rhine, which loses itself in the sands, before its waters can mingle with the ocean. The scale of dominion is diminished to our view by the distance of time and place: nor is the loss of external splendour compensated by the nobler gifts of virtue and genius. In the last moments of her decay, Constantinople was doubtless more opulent and populous than Athens at her most flourishing æra, when a scanty sum of six thousand talents, or twelve hundred thousand pounds sterling, was possessed by twenty-one thousand male citizens of an adult age. But each of these citizens was a freeman, who dared to assert the liberty of his thoughts, words, and actions; whose person and property were guarded by equal law; and who exercised his independent vote in the government of the republic. Their numbers seem to be multiplied by the strong and various discriminations of character: under the shield of freedom, on the wings of emulation and vanity, each Athenian aspired to the level of the national dignity: from this commanding eminence, some chosen spirits soared beyond the reach of a vulgar eye; and the chances of superior merit in a great and populous kingdom, as they are proved by experience, would excuse the computation of imaginary millions. The territories of Athens, Sparta, and their allies, do not exceed a moderate province of France or England: but after the trophies of Salamis and Platæa, they expand in our fancy to the gigantic size of Asia, which had been trampled under the feet of the victorious Greeks. But the subjects of the Byzantine empire, who assume and dishonour the names both of Greeks and Romans, present a dead uniformity of abject vices, which are neither softened by the weakness of humanity, nor animated by the vigour of memorable crimes. The freemen of antiquity might repeat with generous enthusiasm the sentence of Homer, "that on the first day of his servitude, the captive is deprived of one half of his manly virtue." But the poet had only seen the effects of civil or domestic slavery, nor could he foretell that the second moiety of manhood must be annihilated by the spiritual despotism, which shackles, not only the actions, but even the thoughts of the prostrate votary. By this double yoke, the Greeks were oppressed under the successors of Heraclius; the tyrant, a law of eternal justice, was degraded by the vices of his subjects; and on the throne, in the camp, in the schools, we search, perhaps with fruitless diligence, the names and characters that may deserve to be rescued from oblivion. Nor are the defects of the subject compensated by the skill and variety of the painters. Of a space of eight hundred years, the four first centuries are overspread with a cloud interrupted by some faint and broken rays of historic light: in the lives of the emperors, from Maurice to Alexius, Basil the Macedonian has alone been the theme of a separate work; and the absence, or loss, or imperfection of contemporary evidence, must be poorly supplied by the doubtful authority of more recent compilers. The four last centuries are exempt from the reproach of penury: and with the Comnenian family, the historic muse of Constantinople again revives, but her apparel is gaudy, her motions are without elegance or grace. A succession of priests, or courtiers, treads in each other's footsteps in the same path of servitude and superstition: their views are narrow, their judgment is feeble or corrupt; and we close the volume of copious barrenness, still ignorant of the causes of events, the characters of the actors, and the manners of the times, which they celebrate or deplore. The observation which has been applied to a man, may be extended to a whole people, that the energy of the sword is communicated to the pen; and it will be found by experience, that the tone of history will rise or fall with the spirit of the age.

From these considerations, I should have abandoned without regret the Greek slaves and their servile historians, had I not reflected that the fate of the Byzantine monarchy is *passively* connected with the most splendid and important revolutions which have changed the state of the world. The space of the lost provinces was immediately replenished with new colonies and rising kingdoms: the active virtues of peace and war deserted from the vanquished to the victorious nations; and it is in their origin and conquests, in their religion and government, that we must explore the causes and effects of the decline and fall of the Eastern empire. Nor will this scope of narrative, the riches and variety of these materials, be incompatible with the unity of design and composition. As, in his daily prayers, the Musulman of Fez or Delhi still turns his face towards the temple of Mecca, the historian's eye shall be always fixed on the city of Constantinople. The excursive line may embrace the wilds of Arabia and Tartary, but the circle will be ultimately reduced to the decreasing limit of the Roman monarchy.

On this principle I shall now establish the plan of the two last volumes of the present work. The first chapter will contain, in a regular series, the emperors who reigned at Constantinople during a period of six hundred years, from the days of Heraclius to the Latin conquest: a rapid abstract, which may be supported by a *general* appeal to the order and text of the original historians. In this introduction, I shall confine myself to the revolutions of the throne, the succession of families, the personal characters of the Greek princes, the mode of their life and death, the maxims and influence of their domestic government, and the tendency of their reign to accelerate or suspend the downfal of the Eastern empire. Such a chronological review will serve to illustrate the various argument of the subsequent chapters; and each circumstance of the eventful story of the Barbarians will adapt itself in a proper place to the Byzantine annals. The internal state of the empire, and the dangerous heresy of the Paulicians, which shook the East and enlightened the West, will be the subject of two separate chapters; but these enquiries must be postponed till our farther progress shall have opened the view of the world in the ninth and tenth centuries of the Christian æra. After this foundation of Byzantine history, the following nations will pass before our eyes, and each will occupy the space to which it may be entitled by greatness or merit, or the degree of connection with the Roman world and the present age. I. The FRANKS; a general appellation which includes all the Barbarians of France, Italy, and Germany, who were united by the sword and sceptre of Charlemagne. The persecution of images and their votaries, separated Rome and Italy from the Byzantine throne, and prepared the restoration of the Roman empire in the West. II. The ARABS or SARACENS. Three ample chapters will be devoted to this curious and interesting object. In the first, after a picture of the country and its inhabitants, I shall investigate the character of Mahomet; the character, religion, and success of the prophet. In the second I shall lead the Arabs to the conquest of Syria, Egypt, and Africa, the provinces of the Roman empire; nor can I check their victorious career till they have overthrown the monarchies of Persia and Spain. In the third I shall enquire how Constantinople and Europe were saved by the luxury and arts, the division and decay, of the empire of the caliphs. A single chapter will include, III. The BULGARIANS, IV. HUNGARIANS, and, V. RUSSIANS, who assaulted by sea or by land the provinces and the capital; but the last of these, so important in their present greatness, will excite some curiosity in their origin and infancy. VI. The NORMANS; or rather the private adventurers of that warlike people, who founded a powerful kingdom in Apulia and Sicily, shook the throne of Constantinople, displayed the trophies of chivalry, and almost realized the wonders of romance. VII. The LATINS; the subjects of the pope, the nations of the West, who enlisted under the banner of the cross for the recovery or relief of the holy sepulchre. The Greek emperors were terrified and preserved by the myriads of pilgrims who marched to Jerusalem with Godfrey of Bouillon and the peers of Christendom. The second and third crusades trod in the footsteps of the first: Asia and Europe were mingled in a sacred war of two hundred years; and the Christian powers were bravely resisted, and finally expelled, by Saladin and the Mamalukes of Egypt. In these memorable crusades, a fleet and army of French and Venetians were diverted from Syria to the Thracian Bosphorus: they assaulted the capital, they subverted the Greek monarchy: and a dynasty of Latin princes was seated near threescore years on the throne of Constantine. VIII. The GREEKS themselves, during this period of captivity and exile, must be considered as a foreign nation; the enemies, and again the sovereigns, of Constantinople. Misfortune had rekindled a spark of national virtue; and the Imperial series may be continued with some dignity from their restoration to the Turkish conquest. IX. The MOGULS and TARTARS. By the arms of Zingis and his descendants, the globe was shaken from China to Poland and Greece: the sultans were overthrown: the caliphs fell, and the Cæsars trembled on their throne. The victories of Timour suspended above fifty years the final ruin of the Byzantine empire. X. I have already noticed the first appearance of the TURKS, and the names of the fathers, of *Seljuk* and *Othman*, discriminate the two successive dynasties of the nation, which emerged in the eleventh century from the Scythian wilderness. The former established a potent and splendid kingdom from the banks of the Oxus to Antioch and Nice; and the first crusade was provoked by the violation of Jerusalem and the danger of Constantinople. From an humble origin, the *Ottomans* arose, the scourge and terror of Christendom. Constantinople was besieged and taken by Mahomet II. and his triumph annihilates the remnant, the image, the title, of the Roman empire in the East. The schism of the Greeks will be connected with their last calamities, and the restoration of learning in the Western world. I shall return from the captivity of the new, to the ruins of ancient ROME: and the venerable name, the interesting theme, will shed a ray of glory on the conclusion of my labours. (*DF*, iii. 23–7)

A comparison of antique strength and more recent debility in the West, between Augustus and the emperor Charles IV, creates another of those vivid evocations of historical change of which Gibbon was so fond:

If we annihilate the interval of time and space between Augustus and Charles, strong and striking will be the contrast between the two Cæsars; the Bohemian, who concealed his weakness under the mask of ostentation, and the Roman, who disguised his strength under the semblance of modesty. At the head of his victorious legions, in his reign over the sea and land, from the Nile and Euphrates to the Atlantic ocean, Augustus professed himself the servant of the state and the equal of his fellow-citizens. The conqueror of Rome and her provinces assumed the popular and legal form of a censor, a consul, and a tribune. His will was the law of mankind, but in the declaration of his laws he borrowed the voice of the senate and people; and, from their decrees, their master accepted and renewed his temporary commission to administer the republic. In his dress, his domestics, his titles, in all the offices of social life, Augustus maintained the character of a private Roman; and his most artful flatterers respected the secret of his absolute and perpetual monarchy. (*DF*, iii. 149–50)

It also sets the scene for an explosion of energy in the East, with the advent of Mahomet, the latest in the series of charismatic religious leaders to capture Gibbon's historical imagination.

CHAPTER L

Description of Arabia and its Inhabitants. – Birth, Character, and Doctrine of
Mahomet. – He preaches at Mecca. – Flies to Medina. – Propagates his
Religion by the Sword. – Voluntary or reluctant Submission of the Arabs. –
His Death and Successors. – The Claims and Fortunes of Ali and his
Descendants.

After pursuing above six hundred years the fleeting Cæsars of Constantinople and Germany, I now descend, in the reign of Heraclius, on the
eastern borders of the Greek monarchy. While the state was exhausted by
the Persian war, and the church was distracted by the Nestorian and
Monophysite sects, Mahomet, with the sword in one hand and the Koran
in the other, erected his throne on the ruins of Christianity and of Rome.
The genius of the Arabian prophet, the manners of his nation, and the
spirit of his religion, involve the causes of the decline and fall of the Eastern
empire; and our eyes are curiously intent on one of the most memorable
revolutions, which have impressed a new and lasting character on the
nations of the globe.[1]

Description
of Arabia.
In the vacant space between Persia, Syria, Egypt, and Æthiopia,
the Arabian peninsula[2] may be conceived as a triangle of spacious

1. As in this and the following chapter I shall
display much Arabic learning, I must profess
my total ignorance of the Oriental tongues,
and my gratitude to the learned interpreters,
who have transfused their science into the
Latin, French, and English languages. Their
collections, versions, and histories, I shall
occasionally notice.
2. The geographers of Arabia may be divided
into three classes: 1. The *Greeks* and *Latins*,
whose progressive knowledge may be traced
in Agatharcides (de Mari Rubro, in Hudson,
Geograph. Minor. tom. i.), Diodorus Siculus
(tom. i. l. ii. p. 159–167. l. iii. p. 211–216.

edit. Wesseling), Strabo (l. xvi. p. 1112–1114.
from Eratosthenes, p. 1122–1132. from Artemidorus), Dionysius (Periegesis, 927–969.),
Pliny (Hist. Natur. v. 12. vi. 32.), and Ptolemy
(Descript. et Tabulæ Urbium, in Hudson,
tom. iii.). 2. The *Arabic writers*, who have
treated the subject with the zeal of patriotism
or devotion: the extracts of Pocock (Specimen
Hist. Arabum, p. 125–128.) from the Geography of the Sherif al Edrissi, render us still more
dissatisfied with the version or abridgment
(p. 24–27. 44–56. 108, &c. p. 119, &c.) which
the Maronites have published under the
absurd title of Geographia Nubiensis (Paris,

but irregular dimensions. From the northern point of Beles[3] on the Euphrates, a line of fifteen hundred miles is terminated by the streights of
Babelmandel and the land of frankincense. About half this length may be
allowed for the middle breadth, from east to west, from Bassora to Suez,
from the Persian Gulf to the Red Sea.[4] The sides of the triangle are gradually enlarged, and the southern basis presents a front of a thousand miles to
the Indian ocean. The entire surface of the peninsula exceeds in a fourfold
proportion that of Germany or France; but the far greater part
has been justly stigmatised with the epithets of the *stony* and the
sandy. Even the wilds of Tartary are decked, by the hand of
nature, with lofty trees and luxuriant herbage; and the lonesome traveller
derives a sort of comfort and society from the presence of vegetable life.
But in the dreary waste of Arabia, a boundless level of sand is intersected
by sharp and naked mountains; and the face of the desert, without shade
or shelter, is scorched by the direct and intense rays of a tropical sun. Instead
of refreshing breezes, the winds, particularly from the south-west, diffuse
a noxious and even deadly vapour; the hillocks of sand which they alternately
raise and scatter, are compared to the billows of the ocean, and whole
caravans, whole armies, have been lost and buried in the whirlwind. The
common benefits of water are an object of desire and contest; and such is
the scarcity of wood, that some art is requisite to preserve and propagate
the element of fire. Arabia is destitute of navigable rivers, which fertilize
the soil, and convey its produce to the adjacent regions: the torrents that
fall from the hills are imbibed by the thirsty earth: the rare and hardy plants,

The soil and climate.

1619); but the Latin and French translators,
Greaves (in Hudson, tom. iii.) and Galland
(Voyage de la Palestine par La Roque, p. 265–
346.), have opened to us the Arabia of Abulfeda, the most copious and correct account
of the peninsula, which may be enriched,
however, from the Bibliotheque Orientale of
d'Herbelot, p. 120. et alibi passim. 3. The
European travellers; among whom Shaw
(p. 438–455.) and Niebuhr (Description,
1773. Voyages, tom. i. 1776) deserve an honourable distinction: Busching (Geographie
par Berenger, tom. viii. p. 416–510.) has compiled with judgment; and d'Anville's Maps
(Orbis Veteribus Notus, and 1ʳᵉ Partie de
l'Asie) should lie before the reader, with his

Geographie Ancienne, tom. ii. p. 208–231.
3. Abulfed. Descript. Arabiæ, p. 1. D'Anville,
l'Euphrate et le Tigre, p. 19, 20. It was in this
place, the paradise or garden of a satrap, that
Xenophon and the Greeks first passed the
Euphrates (Anabasis, l. i. c. 10. p. 29. edit.
Wells).
4. Reland has proved, with much superfluous
learning, 1. That our Red Sea (the Arabian
Gulf) is no more than a part of the *Mare
Rubrum*, the $E\varrho\upsilon\theta\varrho\alpha\ \theta\alpha\lambda\alpha\sigma\sigma\eta$ of the ancients,
which was extended to the indefinite space
of the Indian ocean. 2. That the synonymous
words $\varepsilon\varrho\upsilon\theta\varrho\sigma\varsigma, \alpha\iota\theta\iota\sigma\psi\varsigma$, allude to the colour
of the blacks or negroes (Dissert. Miscell. tom.
i. p. 59–117.).

the tamarind or the acacia, that strike their roots into the clefts of the rocks, are nourished by the dews of the night: a scanty supply of rain is collected in cisterns and aqueducts: the wells and springs are the secret treasure of the desert; and the pilgrim of Mecca,[5] after many a dry and sultry march, is disgusted by the taste of the waters, which have rolled over a bed of sulphur or salt. Such is the general and genuine picture of the climate of Arabia. The experience of evil enhances the value of any local or partial enjoyments. A shady grove, a green pasture, a stream of fresh water, are sufficient to attract a colony of sedentary Arabs to the fortunate spots which can afford food and refreshment to themselves and their cattle, and which encourage their industry in the cultivation of the palm-tree and the vine. The high lands that border on the Indian ocean are distinguished by their superior plenty of wood and water: the air is more temperate, the fruits are more delicious, the animals and the human race more numerous; the fertility of the soil invites and rewards the toil of the husbandman; and the peculiar gifts of frankincense[6] and coffee have attracted in different ages the merchants of the world. If it be compared with the rest of the peninsula, this sequestered region may truly deserve the appellation of the *happy*; and the splendid colouring of fancy and fiction has been suggested by contrast and countenanced by distance. It was for this earthly paradise that nature had reserved her choicest favours and her most curious work- manship: the incompatible blessings of luxury and innocence were ascribed to the natives: the soil was impregnated with gold[7] and gems, and both the land and sea were taught to exhale the odours of aromatic sweets. This division of the *sandy*, and *stony*, and the *happy*, so familiar to the Greeks and Latins, is unknown to the Arabians themselves; and it is singular enough, that a country, whose language and inhabitants have ever been the same,

Division of the sandy, the stony, and the happy, Arabia.

---

5. In the thirty days, or stations, between Cairo and Mecca, there are fifteen destitute of good water. See the route of the Hadjees, in Shaw's Travels, p. 477.

6. The aromatics, especially the *thus* or frank-incense, of Arabia, occupy the xii[th] book of Pliny. Our great poet (Paradise Lost, l. iv.) introduces, in a simile, the spicy odours that are blown by the north-east wind from the Sabæan coast:

—— Many a league,

Pleas'd with the grateful scent, old Ocean smiles.

(Plin. Hist. Natur. xii. 42.)

7. Agatharcides affirms, that lumps of pure gold were found, from the size of an olive to that of a nut; that iron was twice, and silver ten times, the value of gold (de Mari Rubro, p. 60.). These real or imaginary treasures are vanished; and no gold mines are at present known in Arabia (Niebuhr, Description, p. 124.).

should scarcely retain a vestige of its ancient geography. The maritime districts of *Bahrein* and *Oman* are opposite to the realm of Persia. The kingdom of *Yemen* displays the limits, or at least the situation, of Arabia Fœlix: the name of *Neged* is extended over the inland space; and the birth of Mahomet has illustrated the province of *Hejaz* along the coast of the Red Sea.[8]

The measure of population is regulated by the means of subsistence; and the inhabitants of this vast peninsula might be out-numbered by the subjects of a fertile and industrious province. Along the shores of the Persian gulf, of the ocean, *Manners of the Bedoweens, or pastoral Arabs.* and even of the Red Sea, the *Icthyophagi*,[9] or fish-eaters, continued to wander in quest of their precarious food. In this primitive and abject state, which ill deserves the name of society, the human brute, without arts or laws, almost without sense or language, is poorly distinguished from the rest of the animal creation. Generations and ages might roll away in silent oblivion, and the helpless savage was restrained from multiplying his race, by the wants and pursuits which confined his existence to the narrow margin of the sea-coast. But in an early period of antiquity the great body of the Arabs had emerged from this scene of misery; and as the naked wilderness could not maintain a people of hunters, they rose at once to the more secure and plentiful condition of the pastoral life. The same life is uniformly pursued by the roving tribes of the desert, and in the portrait of the modern *Bedoweens*, we may trace the features of their ancestors,[10] who, in the age of Moses or Mahomet, dwelt under similar tents, and conducted their horses, and camels, and sheep, to the same springs and the same pastures. Our toil is lessened, and our wealth is encreased, by our

---

8. Consult, peruse, and study, the Specimen Historia Arabum of Pocock! (Oxon. 1650, in 4to). The thirty pages of text and version are extracted from the Dynasties of Gregory Abulpharagius, which Pocock afterwards translated (Oxon. 1663, in 4to): the three hundred and fifty-eight notes form a classic and original work on the Arabian antiquities.

9. Arrian remarks the Icthyophagi of the coast of Hejaz (Periplus Maris Erythræi, p. 12.) and beyond Aden (p. 15.). It seems probable that the shores of the Red Sea (in the largest sense) were occupied by these savages in the time, perhaps, of Cyrus; but I can hardly believe

that any cannibals were left among the savages in the reign of Justinian (Procop. de Bell. Persic. l. i. c. 19.).

10. See the Specimen Historiæ. Arabum of Pocock, p. 2. 5. 86, &c. The journey of M. d'Arvieux, in 1664, to the camp of the emir of Mount Carmel (Voyage de la Palestine, Amsterdam, 1718), exhibits a pleasing and original picture of the life of the Bedoweens, which may be illustrated from Niebuhr (Description de l'Arabie, p. 327–344.) and Volney (tom. i. p. 343–385.), the last and most judicious of our Syrian travellers.

dominion over the useful animals; and the Arabian shepherd had acquired the absolute possession of a faithful friend and a laborious slave.[11] Arabia, in the opinion of the naturalist, is the genuine and original country of the *horse*; the climate most propitious, not indeed to the size, but to the spirit and swiftness, of that generous animal. The merit of the Barb, the Spanish, and the English breed, is derived from a mixture of Arabian blood:[12] the Bedoweens preserve, with superstitious care, the honours and the memory of the purest race: the males are sold at a high price, but the females are seldom alienated: and the birth of a noble foal was esteemed, among the tribes, as a subject of joy and mutual congratulation. These horses are educated in the tents, among the children of the Arabs, with a tender familiarity, which trains them in the habits of gentleness and attachment. They are accustomed only to walk and to gallop: their sensations are not blunted by the incessant abuse of the spur and the whip: their powers are reserved for the moments of flight and pursuit; but no sooner do they feel the touch of the hand or the stirrup, than they dart away with the swiftness of the wind; and if their friend be dismounted in the rapid career, they instantly stop till he has recovered his seat. In the sands of Afric and Arabia, the *camel* is a sacred and precious gift. That strong and patient beast of burthen can perform, without eating or drinking, a journey of several days; and a reservoir of fresh water is preserved in a large bag, a fifth stomach of the animal, whose body is imprinted with the marks of servitude: the larger breed is capable of transporting a weight of a thousand pounds; and the dromedary, of a lighter and more active frame, outstrips the fleetest courser in the race. Alive or dead, almost every part of the camel is serviceable to man: her milk is plentiful and nutritious: the young and tender flesh has the taste of veal:[13] a valuable salt is extracted from the urine: the dung supplies the

The horse.

The camel.

---

11. Read (it is no unpleasing task) the incomparable articles of the *Horse* and the *Camel*, in the Natural History of M. de Buffon.

12. For the Arabian horses, see d'Arvieux (p. 159–173.) and Niebuhr (p. 142–144.). At the end of the xiii[th] century, the horses of Neged were esteemed sure-footed, those of Yemen strong and serviceable, those of Hejaz most noble. The horses of Europe, the tenth and last class, were generally despised, as having too much body and too little spirit (d'Herbelot, Bibliot. Orient. p. 339.): their strength was requisite to bear the weight of the knight and his armour.

13. Qui carnibus camelorum vesci solent odii tenaces sunt, was the opinion of an Arabian physician (Pocock, Specimen, p. 88.). Mahomet himself, who was fond of milk, prefers the cow, and does not even mention the camel; but the diet of Mecca and Medina was already more luxurious (Gagnier, Vie de Mahomet, tom. iii. p. 404.).

deficiency of fuel; and the long hair, which falls each year and is renewed, is coarsely manufactured into the garments, the furniture, and the tents, of the Bedoweens. In the rainy seasons they consume the rare and insufficient herbage of the desert: during the heats of summer and the scarcity of winter, they remove their encampments to the sea-coast, the hills of Yemen, or [ne]ighbourhood of the Euphrates, and have often extorted the dangerous [licen]ce of visiting the banks of the Nile, and the villages of Syria and [Pales]tine. The life of a wandering Arab is a life of danger and distress; and [thou]gh sometimes, by rapine or exchange, he may appropriate the fruits [of in]dustry, a private citizen in Europe is in the possession of more solid [and] pleasing luxury than the proudest emir, who marches in the field at [the h]ead of ten thousand horse.

[Y]et an essential difference may be found between the [nomad]s of Scythia and the Arabian tribes, since many of the [latte]r were collected into towns, and employed in the labours of trade [and] agriculture. A part of their time and industry was still devoted to the management of their cattle: they mingled, in peace and war, with their brethren of the desert; and the Bedoweens derived from their useful intercourse, some supply of their wants, and some rudiments of art and knowledge. Among the forty-two cities of Arabia,[14] enumerated by Abulfeda, the most ancient and populous were situate in the *happy* Yemen: the towers of Saana,[15] and the marvellous reservoir of Merab,[16] were constructed by the kings of the Homerites; but their profane lustre was eclipsed by the prophetic glories of MEDINA[17] and

Cities of Arabia:

14. Yet Marcian of Heraclea (in Periplo, p. 16. in tom. i. Hudson, Minor Geograph.) reckons one hundred and sixty-four towns in Arabia Fœlix. The size of the towns might be small – the faith of the writer might be large.

15. It is compared by Abulfeda (in Hudson, tom. iii. p. 54) to Damascus, and is still the residence of the Imam of Yemen (Voyages de Niebuhr, tom. i. p. 331–342.). Saana is twenty-four parasangs from Dafar (Abulfeda, p. 51.), and sixty-eight from Aden (p. 53.).

16. Pocock, Specimen, p. 57. Geograph. Nubiensis, p. 52. Meriaba, or Merab, six miles in circumference, was destroyed by the legions of Augustus (Plin. Hist. Nat. vi. 32.),

and had not revived in the xiv[th] century (Abulfed. Descript. Arab. p. 58.).

17. The name of *city*, *Medina*, was appropriated, κατ' εξοχην, to Yatreb (the Iatrippa of the Greeks), the seat of the prophet. The distances from Medina are reckoned by Abulfeda in stations, or days journey of a caravan (p. 15.): to Bahrein, xv; to Bassora, xviii; to Cufah, xx; to Damascus or Palestine, xx; to Cairo, xxv; to Mecca, x; from Mecca to Saana (p. 52.) or Aden, xxx; to Cairo, xxxi days, or 412 hours (Shaw's Travels, p. 477.); which, according to the estimate of d'Anville (Mesures Itineraires, p. 99.), allows about twenty-five English miles for a day's journey. From

Mecca; MECCA,[18] near the Red Sea, and at the distance from each other of two hundred and seventy miles. The last of these holy places was known to the Greeks under the name of Macoraba; and the termination of the word is expressive of its greatness, which has not indeed, in the most flourishing period, exceeded the size and populousness of Marseilles. Some latent motive, perhaps of superstition, must have impelled the founders, in the choice of a most unpromising situation. They erected their habitations of mud or stone, in a plain about two miles long and one mile broad, at the foot of three barren mountains: the soil is a rock; the water even of the holy well of Zemzem is bitter or brackish; the pastures are remote from the city; and grapes are transported above seventy miles from the gardens of Tayef. The fame and spirit of the Koreishites, who reigned in Mecca, were conspicuous among the Arabian tribes; but their ungrateful soil refused the labours of agriculture, and their position was

her trade. favourable to the enterprises of trade. By the sea-port of Gedda, at the distance only of forty miles, they maintained an easy correspondence with Abyssinia; and that Christian kingdom afforded the first refuge to the disciples of Mahomet. The treasures of Africa were conveyed over the peninsula to Gerrha or Katif, in the province of Bahrein, a city built, as it is said, of rock-salt, by the Chaldean exiles:[19] and from thence, with the native pearls of the Persian Gulf, they were floated on rafts to the mouth of the Euphrates. Mecca is placed almost at an equal distance, a month's journey, between Yemen on the right, and Syria on the left hand. The former was the winter, the latter the summer station of her caravans; and their seasonable arrival relieved the ships of India from the tedious and troublesome navigation of the Red Sea. In the markets of Saana and Merab, in the harbours of Oman and Aden, the camels of the Koreishites were laden with a precious cargo of aromatics; a

---

the land of frankincense (Hadramaut, in Yemen, between Aden and Cape Fartasch) to Gaza, in Syria, Pliny (Hist. Nat. xii. 32.) computes lxv mansions of camels. These measures may assist fancy and elucidate facts.

18. Our notions of Mecca must be drawn from the Arabians (d'Herbelot, Bibliotheque Orientale, p. 368–371. Pocock, Specimen, p. 125–128. Abulfeda, p. 11–40.). As no unbeliever is permitted to enter the city, our travellers are silent; and the short hints of Thevenot (Voyages du Levant, part i. p. 490.) are taken from the suspicious mouth of an African renegado. Some Persians counted 6000 houses (Chardin, tom. iv. p. 167.).

19. Strabo, l. xvi. p. 1110. See one of these salt houses near Bassora, in d'Herbelot, Bibliot. Orient. p. 6.

supply of corn and manufactures was purchased in the fairs of Bostra and Damascus; the lucrative exchange diffused plenty and riches in the streets of Mecca; and the noblest of her sons united the love of arms with the profession of merchandise.[20]

The perpetual independence of the Arabs has been the theme of praise among strangers and natives; and the arts of controversy transform this singular event into a prophecy and a miracle, in favour of the posterity of Ismael.[21] Some exceptions, that can neither be dissembled nor eluded, render this mode of reasoning as indiscreet as it is superfluous: the kingdom of Yemen has been successively subdued by the Abyssinians, the Persians, the sultans of Egypt,[22] and the Turks:[23] the holy cities of Mecca and Medina have repeatedly bowed under a Scythian tyrant; and the Roman province of Arabia[24] embraced the peculiar wilderness in which Ismael and his sons must have pitched their tents in the face of their brethren. Yet these exceptions are temporary or local; the body of the nation has escaped the yoke of the most powerful monarchies: the arms of Sesostris and Cyrus, of Pompey and Trajan, could

National independence of the Arabs.

20. Mirum dictû ex innumeris populis pars æqua in *commerciis* aut in latrociniis degit (Plin. Hist. Nat. vi. 32.). See Sale's Koran. Surat cvi. p. 503. Pocock, Specimen, p. 2. D'Herbelot, Bibliot. Orient. p. 361. Prideaux's Life of Mahomet, p. 5. Gagnier, Vie de Mahomet, tom. i. p. 72. 120. 126, &c.

21. A nameless doctor (Universal Hist. vol. xx. octavo edition) has formally *demonstrated* the truth of Christianity by the independence of the Arabs. A critic, besides the exceptions of fact, might dispute the meaning of the text (Genes. xvi. 12.), the extent of the application, and the foundation of the pedigree.

22. It was subdued, A.D. 1173, by a brother of the great Saladin, who founded a dynasty of Curds or Ayoubites (Guignes, Hist. des Huns, tom. i. p. 425. D'Herbelot, p. 477.).

23. By the lieutenant of Soliman I. (A.D. 1538) and Selim II. (1568). See Cantemir's Hist. of the Othman empire, p. 201. 221. The Pasha, who resided at Saana, commanded twenty-one Beys, but no revenue was ever remitted to the Porte (Marsigli, Stato Militare

dell' Imperio Ottomanno, p. 124.), and the Turks were expelled about the year 1630 (Niebuhr, p. 167, 168.).

24. Of the Roman province, under the name of Arabia and the third Palestine, the principal cities were Bostra and Petra, which dated their æra from the year 105, when they were subdued by Palma a lieutenant of Trajan (Dion Cassius, l. lxviii.). Petra was the capital of the Nabathæans; whose name is derived from the eldest of the sons of Ismael (Genes. xxv. 12, &c. with the Commentaries of Jerom, Le Clerc, and Calmet). Justinian relinquished a palm country of ten days journey to the south of Ælah (Procop. de Bell. Persis. l. i. c. 19.), and the Romans maintained a centurion and a custom-house (Arrian in Periplo Maris Erythræi, p. 11. in Hudson, tom. i.), at a place (λευκη κωμη, Pagus Albus Hawara) in the territory of Medina (d'Anville Memoire sur l'Egypte, p. 243.). These real possessions, and some naval inroads of Trajan (Peripl. p. 14, 15.), are magnified by history and medals into the Roman conquest of Arabia.

never atchieve the conquest of Arabia; the present sovereign of the Turks[25] may exercise a shadow of jurisdiction, but his pride is reduced to solicit the friendship of a people, whom it is dangerous to provoke and fruitless to attack. The obvious causes of their freedom are inscribed on the character and country of the Arabs. Many ages before Mahomet,[26] their intrepid valour had been severely felt by their neighbours in offensive and defensive war. The patient and active virtues of a soldier are insensibly nursed in the habits and discipline of a pastoral life. The care of the sheep and camels is abandoned to the women of the tribe; but the martial youth under the banner of the emir, is ever on horseback, and in the field, to practise the exercise of the bow, the javelin, and the scymetar. The long memory of their independence is the firmest pledge of its perpetuity, and succeeding generations are animated to prove their descent and to maintain their inheritance. Their domestic feuds are suspended on the approach of a common enemy; and in their last hostilities against the Turks, the caravan of Mecca was attacked and pillaged by fourscore thousand of the confederates. When they advance to battle, the hope of victory is in the front; in the rear, the assurance of a retreat. Their horses and camels, who in eight or ten days can perform a march of four or five hundred miles, disappear before the conqueror; the secret waters of the desert elude his search; and his victorious troops are consumed with thirst, hunger, and fatigue, in the pursuit of an invisible foe, who scorns his efforts, and safely reposes in the heart of the burning solitude. The arms and deserts of the Bedoweens are not only the safeguards of their own freedom, but the barriers also of the happy Arabia, whose inhabitants, remote from war, are enervated by the luxury of the soil and climate. The legions of Augustus melted away in disease and lassitude;[27] and it is only by a naval power that the reduction of Yemen has been successfully attempted. When Mahomet erected his holy

25. Niebuhr (Description de l'Arabie, p. 302, 303. 329–331.) affords the most recent and authentic intelligence of the Turkish empire in Arabia.

26. Diodorus Siculus (tom. ii. l. xix. p. 390–393. edit. Wesseling) has clearly exposed the freedom of the Nabathæan Arabs, who resisted the arms of Antigonus and his son.

27. Strabo, l. xvi. p. 1127–1129. Plin. Hist. Natur. vi. 32. Ælius Gallus landed near Medina, and marched near a thousand miles into the part of Yemen between Mareb and the Ocean. The non ante devictis Sabeæ regibus (Od. i. 29.), and the intacti Arabum thesauri (Od. iii. 24.) of Horace, attest the virgin purity of Arabia.

standard,[28] that kingdom was a province of the Persian empire; yet seven princes of the Homerites still reigned in the mountains; and the vicegerent of Chosroes was tempted to forget his distant country and his unfortunate master. The historians of the age of Justinian represent the state of the independent Arabs, who were divided by interest or affection in the long quarrel of the East: the tribe of *Gassan* was allowed to encamp on the Syrian territory: the princes of *Hira* were permitted to form a city about forty miles to the southward of the ruins of Babylon. Their service in the field was speedy and vigorous; but their friendship was venal, their faith inconstant, their enmity capricious: it was an easier task to excite than to disarm these roving Barbarians; and, in the familiar intercourse of war, they learned to see, and to despise, the splendid weakness both of Rome and of Persia. From Mecca to the Euphrates, the Arabian tribes[29] were confounded by the Greeks and Latins, under the general appellation of SARACENS,[30] a name which every Christian mouth has been taught to pronounce with terror and abhorrence.

The slaves of domestic tyranny may vainly exult in their national independence; but the Arab is personally free; and he enjoys, in some degree, the benefits of society, without forfeiting the prerogatives of nature. In every tribe, superstition, or grati-

Their domestic freedom and character.

tude, or fortune, has exalted a particular family above the heads of their equals. The dignities of sheich and emir invariably descend in this chosen race; but the order of succession is loose and precarious; and the most

---

28. See the imperfect history of Yemen in Pocock, Specimen. p. 55–66. of Hira, p. 66–74. of Gassan, p. 75–78, as far as it could be known or preserved in the time of ignorance.

29. The Σαρακηνικα φυλα, μυριαδες ταυτα, και πο πλειστον αυτων ερημονομοι, και αδεσποτοι, are described by Menander (Excerpt. Legation. p. 149.), Procopius (de Bell. Persic. l. i. c. 17. 19. l. ii. c. 10.); and, in the most lively colours, by Ammianus Marcellinus (l. xiv. c. 4.), who had spoken of them as early as the reign of Marcus.

30. The name which, used by Ptolemy and Pliny in a more confined, sense, has been derived, ridiculously, from *Sarah*, the wife of Abraham,

obscurely from the village of *Saraka* (μετα Ναβαταιους. Stephan. de Urbibus), more plausibly from the Arabic words, which signify a *thievish* character, or *Oriental* situation, (Hottinger, Hist. Oriental. l. i. c. i. p. 7, 8. Pocock, Specimen, p. 33–35. Asseman. Bibliot. Orient. tom. iv. p. 567.). Yet the last and most popular of these etymologies, is refuted by Ptolemy (Arabia, p. 2. 18. in Hudson, tom. iv.), who expressly remarks the western and southern position of the Saracens, then an obscure tribe on the borders of Egypt. The appellation cannot therefore allude to any *national* character; and, since it was imposed by strangers, it must be found, not in the Arabic, but in a foreign language.

worthy or aged of the noble kinsmen are preferred to the simple, though important, office of composing disputes by their advice, and guiding valour by their example. Even a female of sense and spirit has been permitted to command the countrymen of Zenobia.[31] The momentary junction of several tribes produces an army: their more lasting union constitutes a nation; and the supreme chief, the emir of emirs, whose banner is displayed at their head, may deserve, in the eyes of strangers, the honours of the kingly name. If the Arabian princes abuse their power, they are quickly punished by the desertion of their subjects, who had been accustomed to a mild and parental jurisdiction. Their spirit is free, their steps are unconfined, the desert is open, and the tribes and families are held together by a mutual and voluntary compact. The softer natives of Yemen supported the pomp and majesty of a monarch; but if he could not leave his palace without endangering his life,[32] the active powers of government must have been devolved on his nobles and magistrates. The cities of Mecca and Medina present, in the heart of Asia, the form, or rather the substance, of a commonwealth. The grandfather of Mahomet, and his lineal ancestors, appear in foreign and domestic transactions as the princes of their country; but they reigned, like Pericles at Athens, or the Medici at Florence, by the opinion of their wisdom and integrity; their influence was divided with their patrimony; and the sceptre was transferred from the uncles of the prophet to a younger branch of the tribe of Koreish. On solemn occasions they convened the assembly of the people; and, since mankind must be either compelled or persuaded to obey, the use and reputation of oratory among the ancient Arabs is the clearest evidence of public freedom.[33] But their simple freedom was of a very different cast from the nice and artificial machinery of the Greek and Roman republics, in which each member possessed an undivided share of the civil and political rights of the

---

31. Saraceni . . . mulieres aiunt in eos regnare (Expositio totius Mundi, p. 3. in Hudson, tom. iii.). The reign of Mavia is famous in ecclesiastical story. Pocock, Specimen, p. 69. 83.

32. *Μη εξειναι εκ των βασιλειων*, is the report of Agatharades (de Mari Rubro, p. 63, 64. in Hudson, tom. i.), Diodorus Siculus (tom. i. l. iii. c. 47. p. 215.), and Strabo (l. xvi. p. 1124.). But I much suspect that this is one of the popular tales, or extraordinary accidents,

which the credulity of travellers so often transforms into a fact, a custom, and a law.

33. Non gloriabantur antiquitus Arabes, nisi gladio, hospite, et *eloquentiâ* (Sephadius, apud Pocock, Specimen, p. 161, 162.). This gift of speech they shared only with the Persians; and the sententious Arabs would probably have disdained the simple and sublime logic of Demosthenes.

community. In the more simple state of the Arabs, the nation is free, because each of her sons disdains a base submission to the will of a master. His breast is fortified with the austere virtues of courage, patience, and sobriety: the love of independence prompts him to exercise the habits of self-command; and the fear of dishonour guards him from the meaner apprehension of pain, of danger, and of death. The gravity and firmness of the mind is conspicuous in his outward demeanor: his speech is slow, weighty, and concise, he is seldom provoked to laughter, his only gesture is that of stroking his beard, the venerable symbol of manhood; and the sense of his own importance teaches him to accost his equals without levity, and his superiors without awe.[34] The liberty of the Saracens survived their conquests: the first caliphs indulged the bold and familiar language of their subjects: they ascended the pulpit to persuade and edify the congregation; nor was it before the seat of empire was removed to the Tigris, that the Abbassides adopted the proud and pompous ceremonial of the Persian and Byzantine courts.

In the study of nations and men, we may observe the causes that render them hostile or friendly to each other, that tend to narrow or enlarge, to mollify or exasperate, the social character. *Civil wars and private revenge.* The separation of the Arabs from the rest of mankind, has accustomed them to confound the ideas of stranger and enemy; and the poverty of the land has introduced a maxim of jurisprudence, which they believe and practise to the present hour. They pretend, that in the division of the earth the rich and fertile climates were assigned to the other branches of the human family; and that the posterity of the outlaw Ismael might recover, by fraud or force, the portion of inheritance of which he had been unjustly deprived. According to the remark of Pliny, the Arabian tribes are equally addicted to theft and merchandise: the caravans that traverse the desert are ransomed or pillaged; and their neighbours, since the remote times of Job and Sesostris,[35] have been the victims of their rapacious spirit. If a Bedoween discovers from afar a solitary traveller, he

---

34. I must remind the reader that d'Arvieux, d'Herbelot, and Niebuhr, represent, in the most lively colours, the manners and government of the Arabs, which are illustrated by many incidental passages in the life of Mahomet.

35. Observe the first chapter of Job, and the long wall of 1500 stadia, which Sesostris built from Pelusium to Heliopolis (Diodor. Sicul. tom. i. l. i. p. 67.). Under the name of *Hycsos*, the shepherd-kings, they had formerly subdued Egypt (Marsham, Canon. Chron. p. 98–163, &c.).

rides furiously against him, crying, with a loud voice, "Undress thyself, thy aunt (*my wife*) is without a garment." A ready submission entitles him to mercy; resistance will provoke the aggressor, and his own blood must expiate the blood which he presumes to shed in legitimate defence. A single robber, or a few associates, are branded with their genuine name; but the exploits of a numerous band assume the character of lawful and honourable war. The temper of a people, thus armed against mankind, was doubly inflamed by the domestic licence of rapine, murder, and revenge. In the constitution of Europe, the right of peace and war is now confined to a small, and the actual exercise to a much smaller, list of respectable potentates; but each Arab, with impunity and renown, might point his javelin against the life of his countryman. The union of the nation consisted only in a vague resemblance of language and manners; and in each community, the jurisdiction of the magistrate was mute and impotent. Of the time of ignorance which preceded Mahomet, seventeen hundred battles[36] are recorded by tradition: hostility was embittered with the rancour of civil faction; and the recital, in prose or verse, of an obsolete feud was sufficient to rekindle the same passions among the descendents of the hostile tribes. In private life, every man, at least every family, was the judge and avenger of its own cause. The nice sensibility of honour, which weighs the insult rather than the injury, sheds its deadly venom on the quarrels of the Arabs: the honour of their women, and of their *beards*, is most easily wounded; an indecent action, a contemptuous word, can be expiated only by the blood of the offender; and such is their patient inveteracy, that they expect whole months and years the opportunity of revenge. A fine or compensation for murder is familiar to the Barbarians of every age: but in Arabia the kinsmen of the dead are at liberty to accept the atonement, or to exercise with their own hands the law of retaliation. The refined malice of the Arabs refuses even the head of the murderer, substitutes an innocent to the guilty person, and transfers the penalty to the best and most considerable of the race by whom they have been injured. If he falls by their hands, they are exposed in their turn to the danger of reprisals, the interest and principal of the bloody debt are accumulated; the individuals

---

36. Or, according to another account, 1200 (d'Herbelot, Bibliotheque Orientale, p. 75.): the two historians who wrote of the *Ayam al Arab*, the battles of the Arabs, lived in the ix[th] and x[th] century. The famous war of Dahes and Gabrah was occasioned by two horses, lasted forty years, and ended in a proverb (Pocock, Specimen, p. 48.).

of either family lead a life of malice and suspicion, and fifty years may sometimes elapse before the account of vengeance be finally settled.[37] This sanguinary spirit, ignorant of pity or forgiveness, has been moderated, however, by the maxims of honour, which require in every private encounter some decent equality of age and strength, of numbers and weapons. An annual festival of two, perhaps of four, months, was observed by the Arabs before the time of Mahomet, during which their *Annual truce.* swords were religiously sheathed both in foreign and domestic hostility; and this partial truce is more strongly expressive of the habits of anarchy and warfare.[38]

But the spirit of rapine and revenge was attempered by the milder influence of trade and literature. The solitary peninsula is encompassed by the most civilized nations of the ancient world: the merchant is the friend of mankind; and the annual caravans *Their social qualifications and virtues.* imported the first seeds of knowledge and politeness into the cities, and even the camps of the desert. Whatever may be the pedigree of the Arabs, their language is derived from the same original stock with the Hebrew, the Syriac, and the Chaldæan tongues; the independence of the tribes was marked by their peculiar dialects;[39] but each, after their own, allowed a just preference to the pure and perspicuous idiom of Mecca. In Arabia as well as in Greece, the perfection of language outstripped the refinement of manners; and her speech could diversify the fourscore names of honey, the two hundred of a serpent, the five hundred of a lion, the thousand of a sword, at a time when this copious dictionary was entrusted to the memory of an illiterate people. The monuments of the Homerites were inscribed with an obsolete and mysterious character; but the Cufic letters,

---

37. The modern theory and practice of the Arabs in the revenge of murder, are described by Niebuhr (Description, p. 26–31.). The harsher features of antiquity may be traced in the Koran, c. 2. p. 20. c. 17. p. 230. with Sale's Observations.

38. Procopius (de Bell. Persic. l. i. c. 16.) places the *two* holy months about the summer solstice. The Arabians consecrate *four* months of the year – the first, seventh, eleventh, and twelfth; and pretend, that in a long series of ages the truce was infringed only four or six times (Sale's Preliminary Discourse,

p. 147–150. and Notes on the ix[th] chapter of the Koran, p. 154, &c. Casiri, Bibliot. Hispano-Arabica, tom. ii. p. 20, 21.).

39. Arrian, in the second century, remarks (in Periplo Maris Erythræi, p. 12.) the partial or total difference of the dialects of the Arabs. Their language and letters are copiously treated by Pocock (Specimen, p. 150–154.), Casiri (Bibliot. Hispano-Arabica, tom. i. p. 1. 83. 292. tom. ii. p. 25, &c.), and Niebuhr (Description de l'Arabie, p. 72–86). I pass slightly; I am not fond of repeating words like a parrot.

the ground-work of the present alphabet, were invented on the banks of the Euphrates; and the recent invention was taught at Mecca by a stranger who settled in that city after the birth of Mahomet. The arts of grammar, of metre, and of rhetoric, were unknown to the freeborn eloquence of the Arabians; but their penetration was sharp, their fancy luxuriant, their wit strong and sententious,[40] and their more elaborate compositions were addressed with energy and effect to the minds of their hearers. The genius and merit of a rising poet was celebrated by the applause of his own and the kindred tribes. A solemn banquet was prepared, and a chorus of women, striking their tymbals, and displaying the pomp of their nuptials, sung in the presence of their sons and husbands the felicity of their native tribe; that a champion had now appeared to vindicate their rights; that a herald had raised his voice to immortalise their renown. The distant or hostile tribes resorted to an annual fair which was abolished by the fanaticism of the first Moslems; a national assembly that must have contributed to refine and harmonise the Barbarians. Thirty days were employed in the exchange, not only of corn and wine, but of eloquence and poetry. The prize was disputed by the generous emulation of the bards; the victorious performance was deposited in the archives of princes and emirs; and we may read in our own language, the seven original poems which were inscribed in letters of gold, and suspended in the temple of Mecca.[41] The Arabian poets were the historians and moralists of the age; and if they sympathised with the prejudices, they inspired and crowned the virtues, of their countrymen. The indissoluble union of generosity and valour was the darling theme of their song; and when they pointed their keenest satire against a despicable race, they affirmed, in the bitterness of reproach, that the men knew not how to give, nor the women

Love of poetry.

---

40. A familiar tale in Voltaire's Zadig (le Chien et le Cheval) is related, to prove the natural sagacity of the Arabs (d'Herbelot, Bibliot. Orient. p. 120, 121. Gagnier, Vie de Mahomet, tom. i. p. 37–46.); but d'Arvieux, or rather La Roque (Voyage de Palestine, p. 92.), denies the boasted superiority of the Bedoweens. The one hundred and sixty-nine sentences of Ali (translated by Ockley, London, 1718) afford a just and favourable specimen of Arabian wit.

41. Pocock (Specimen, p. 158–161.) and Casiri (Bibliot. Hispano-Arabica, tom. i. p. 48. 84, &c. 119. tom. ii. p. 17, &c.) speak of the Arabian poets before Mahomet: the seven poems of the Caaba have been published in English by Sir William Jones; but his honourable mission to India has deprived us of his own notes, far more interesting than the obscure and obsolete text.

to deny.[42] The same hospitality, which was practised by Abraham and celebrated by Homèr, is still renewed in the camps of the Arabs. The ferocious Bedoweens, the terror of the desert, embrace, *Examples of generosity.* without enquiry or hesitation, the stranger who dares to confide in their honour and to enter their tent. His treatment is kind and respectful: he shares the wealth or the poverty of his host; and, after a needful repose, he is dismissed on his way, with thanks, with blessings, and perhaps with gifts. The heart and hand are more largely expanded by the wants of a brother or a friend; but the heroic acts that could deserve the public applause, must have surpassed the narrow measure of discretion and experience. A dispute had arisen, who, among the citizens of Mecca, was entitled to the prize of generosity; and a successive application was made to the three who were deemed most worthy of the trial. Abdallah, the son of Abbas, had undertaken a distant journey, and his foot was in the stirrup when he heard the voice of a suppliant, "O son of the uncle of the apostle of God, I am a traveller and in distress." He instantly dismounted to present the pilgrim with his camel, her rich caparison, and a purse of four thousand pieces of gold, excepting only the sword, either for its intrinsic value, or as the gift of an honoured kinsman. The servant of Kais informed the second suppliant that his master was asleep; but he immediately added, "Here is a purse of seven thousand pieces of gold (it is all we have in the house), and here is an order, that will entitle you to a camel and a slave;" the master, as soon as he awoke, praised and enfranchised his faithful steward, with a gentle reproof, that by respecting his slumbers he had stinted his bounty. The third of these heroes, the blind Arabah, at the hour of prayer, was supporting his steps on the shoulders of two slaves. "Alas!" he replied, "my coffers are empty! but these you may sell; if you refuse, I renounce them." At these words, pushing away the youths, he groped along the wall with his staff. The character of Hatem is the perfect model of Arabian virtue;[43] he was brave and liberal, an eloquent poet and a successful robber: forty camels were roasted at his hospitable feasts; and at the prayer of a suppliant enemy, he restored both the captives and the spoil.

---

42. Sale's Preliminary Discourse, p. 29, 30.
43. D'Herbelot, Bibliot. Orient. p. 458. Gagnier, Vie de Mahomet, tom. iii. p. 118. Caab and Hesnus (Pocock, Specimen, p. 43. 46. 48.) were likewise conspicuous for their liberality; and the latter is elegantly praised by an Arabian poet: "Videbis eum cum accesseris exultantem, ac si dares illi quod ab illo petis."

The freedom of his countrymen disdained the laws of justice: they proudly indulged the spontaneous impulse of pity and benevolence.

Ancient idolatry.   The religion of the Arabs,[44] as well as of the Indians, consisted in the worship of the sun, the moon, and the fixed stars, a primitive and specious mode of superstition. The bright luminaries of the sky display the visible image of a Deity: their number and distance convey to a philosophic, or even a vulgar, eye, the idea of boundless space: the character of eternity is marked on these solid globes, that seem incapable of corruption or decay: the regularity of their motions may be ascribed to a principle of reason or instinct; and their real or imaginary influence encourages the vain belief that the earth and its inhabitants are the object of their peculiar care. The science of astronomy was cultivated at Babylon; but the school of the Arabs was a clear firmament and a naked plain. In their nocturnal marches, they steered by the guidance of the stars: their names, and order, and daily station, were familiar to the curiosity and devotion of the Bedoween; and he was taught by experience to divide in twenty-eight parts, the zodiac of the moon, and to bless the constellations who refreshed, with salutary rains, the thirst of the desert. The reign of the heavenly orbs could not be extended beyond the visible sphere; and some metaphysical powers were necessary to sustain the transmigration of souls and the resurrection of bodies: a camel was left to perish on the grave, that he might serve his master in another life; and the invocation of departed spirits implies that they were still endowed with consciousness and power. I am ignorant, and I am careless, of the blind mythology of the Barbarians; of the local deities, of the stars, the air, and the earth, of their sex or titles, their attributes or subordination. Each tribe, each family, each independent warrior, created and changed the rites and the object of his fantastic worship; but the nation, in every age, has bowed to the religion, as well as to the language, of Mecca. The genuine antiquity of the CAABA ascends beyond the Christian æra: in describing the coast of the Red Sea, the Greek historian Diodorus[45] has remarked, between the Thamudites and the Sabæans, a famous

The Caaba, or temple of Mecca.

44. Whatever can now be known of the idolatry of the ancient Arabians, may be found in Pocock (Specimen, p. 89–136. 163, 164.). His profound erudition is more clearly and concisely interpreted by Sale (Preliminary Discourse, p. 14–24.); and Assemanni (Bibliot. Orient. tom. iv. p. 580–590.) has added some valuable remarks.

45. Ιερον αγιωτατον ιδρυται τιμωμενον υπο παντων Αραβων περιττοτερον (Diodor.

temple, whose superior sanctity was revered by *all* the Arabians: the linen or silken veil, which is annually renewed by the Turkish emperor, was first offered by a pious king of the Homerites, who reigned seven hundred years before the time of Mahomet.[46] A tent or a cavern might suffice for the worship of the savages, but an edifice of stone and clay has been erected in its place; and the art and power of the monarchs of the East have been confined to the simplicity of the original model.[47] A spacious portico incloses the quadrangle of the Caaba; a square chapel, twenty-four cubits long, twenty-three broad, and twenty-seven high: a door and a window admit the light; the double roof is supported by three pillars of wood; a spout (now of gold) discharges the rain-water, and the well Zemzem is protected by a dome from accidental pollution. The tribe of Koreish, by fraud or force, had acquired the custody of the Caaba: the sacerdotal office devolved through four lineal descents to the grandfather of Mahomet; and the family of the Hashemites, from whence he sprung, was the most respectable and sacred in the eyes of their country.[48] The precincts of Mecca enjoyed the rights of sanctuary; and, in the last month of each year, the city and the temple were crowded with a long train of pilgrims, who presented their vows and offerings in the house of God. The same rites, which are now accomplished by the faithful Musulman, were invented and practised by the superstition of the idolaters. At an awful distance they

---

Sicul. tom. i. l. iii. p. 211.). The character and position are so correctly apposite, that I am surprised how this curious passage should have been read without notice or application. Yet this famous temple had been overlooked by Agatharcides (de Mari Rubro, p. 58. in Hudson, tom. i.), whom Diodorus copies in the rest of the description. Was the Sicilian more knowing than the Egyptian? Or was the Caaba built between the years of Rome 650 and 746, the dates of their respective histories? (Dodwell, in Dissert. ad tom. i. Hudson, p. 72. Fabricius, Bibliot. Græc. tom. ii. p. 770.)

46. Pocock, Specimen, p. 60, 61. From the death of Mahomet we ascend to 68, from his birth to 129, years, before the Christian æra. The veil or curtain, which is now of silk and

gold, was no more than a piece of Egyptian linen (Abulfeda, in Vit. Mohammed. c. 6. p. 14.).

47. The original plan of the Caaba (which is servilely copied in Sale, the Universal History, &c.) was a Turkish draught, which Reland (de Religione Mohammedicâ, p. 113–123.) has corrected and explained from the best authorities. For the description and legend of the Caaba, consult Pocock (Specimen, p. 115–122.), the Bibliotheque Orientale of d'Herbelot (*Caaba, Hagier, Zemzem, &c.*), and Sale (Preliminary Discourse, p. 114–122.).

48. Cosa, the fifth ancestor of Mahomet, must have usurped the Caaba A.D. 440; but the story is differently told by Jannabi (Gagnier, Vie de Mahomet, tom. i. p. 65–69.) and by Abulfeda (in Vit. Moham. c. 6. p. 13.).

cast away their garments: seven times, with hasty steps, they encircled the
Caaba, and kissed the black stone: seven times they visited and adored
the adjacent mountains: seven times they threw stones into the valley of
Mina; and the pilgrimage was atchieved, as at the present hour, by a sacrifice of sheep and camels, and the burial of their hair and nails in the consecrated ground. Each tribe either found or introduced in the Caaba their
domestic worship: the temple was adorned, or defiled, with three hundred
and sixty idols of men, eagles, lions, and antelopes; and most conspicuous
was the statue of Hebal, of red agate, holding in his hand seven arrows,
without heads or feathers, the instruments and symbols of profane
divination. But this statue was a monument of Syrian arts: the devotion
of the ruder ages was content with a pillar or a tablet; and the rocks of
the desert were hewn into gods or altars, in imitation of the black stone[49]

Sacrifices and rites. of Mecca, which is deeply tainted with the reproach of an idolatrous
origin. From Japan to Peru, the use of sacrifice has universally
prevailed; and the votary has expressed his gratitude, or fear, by
destroying or consuming, in honour of the gods, the dearest and most
precious of their gifts. The life of a man[50] is the most precious oblation to
deprecate a public calamity: the altars of Phœnicia and Egypt, of Rome
and Carthage, have been polluted with human gore: the cruel practice
was long preserved among the Arabs; in the third century, a boy was
annually sacrificed by the tribe of the Dumatians;[51] and a royal captive
was piously slaughtered by the prince of the Saracens, the ally and soldier
of the emperor Justinian.[52] A parent who drags his son to the altar, exhibits

49. In the second century, Maximus of Tyre
attributes to the Arabs the worship of a stone
– Αραβιοι σεβουσι μεν, οντινα δε ουκ οιδα,
το δε αγαλμα ειδον; λιθος ην τετραγωνος
(dissert. viii. tom. i. p. 142. edit. Reiske); and
the reproach is furiously re-echoed by the
Christians (Clemens Alex. in Protreptico,
p. 40. Arnobius contra Gentes, l. vi. p. 246.).
Yet these stones were no other than the
βαιτυλα of Syria and Greece, so renowned in
sacred and profane antiquity (Euseb. Præp.
Evangel. l. i. p. 37. Marsham, Canon. Chron.
p. 54–56.).

50. The two horrid subjects of Ανδροθυσια
and Παιδοθυσια, are accurately discussed by
the learned Sir John Marsham (Canon.

Chron. p. 76–78. 301–304.). Sanchoniatho
derives the Phœnician sacrifices from the
example of Chronus; but we are ignorant
whether Chronus lived before or after Abraham, or indeed whether he lived at all.

51. Κατ' ετος εκαστον παιδα εθυον, is the
reproach of Porphyry; but he likewise imputes to the Roman the same barbarous
custom, which, A.U.C. 657, had been finally
abolished. Dumætha, Daumat al Gendal, is
noticed by Ptolemy (Tabul. p. 37. Arabia,
p. 9–29.) and Abulfeda (p. 57.); and may be
found in d'Anville's maps, in the mid-desert
between Chaibar and Tadmor.

52. Procopius (de Bell. Persico, l. i. c. 28.),
Evagrius (l. vi. c. 21.), and Pocock (Specimen,

the most painful and sublime effort of fanaticism: the deed, or the intention, was sanctified by the example of saints and heroes; and the father of Mahomet himself was devoted by a rash vow, and hardly ransomed for the equivalent of an hundred camels. In the time of ignorance, the Arabs, like the Jews and Egyptians, abstained from the taste of swine's flesh;[53] they circumcised[54] their children at the age of puberty: the same customs, without the censure or the precept of the Koran, have been silently transmitted to their posterity and proselytes. It has been sagaciously conjectured, that the artful legislator indulged the stubborn prejudices of his countrymen. It is more simple to believe that he adhered to the habits and opinions of his youth, without foreseeing that a practice congenial to the climate of Mecca, might become useless or inconvenient on the banks of the Danube or the Volga.

Arabia was free: the adjacent kingdoms were shaken by the storms of conquest and tyranny, and the persecuted sects fled to the happy land where they might profess what they thought, *Introduction of the Sabians.* and practice what they professed. The religions of the Sabians and Magians, of the Jews and Christians, were disseminated from the Persian Gulf to the Red Sea. In a remote period of antiquity, Sabianism was diffused over Asia by the science of the Chaldæans[55] and the arms of the Assyrians. From the observations of two thousand years, the priests and astronomers of Babylon[56] deduced the eternal laws of nature and providence. They adored

---

p. 72. 86.), attest the human sacrifices of the Arabs in the vi[th] century. The danger and escape of Abdallah, is a tradition rather than a fact (Gagnier, Vie de Mahomet, tom. i. p. 82–84.).

53. Suillis carnibus abstinent, says Solinus (Polyhistor. c. 33.), who copies Pliny (l. viii. c. 68.) in the strange supposition, that hogs cannot live in Arabia. The Egyptians were actuated by a natural and superstitious horror for that unclean beast (Marsham, Canon. p. 205.). The old Arabians likewise practised, *post coitum,* the rite of ablution (Herodot. l. i. c. 80.), which is sanctified by the Mahometan law (Reland, p. 75, &c. Chardin, or rather the *Mollah* of Shaw Abbas, tom. iv. p. 71, &c.).

54. The Mahometan doctors are not fond of the subject; yet they hold circumcision necessary to salvation, and even pretend that Mahomet was miraculously born without a foreskin (Pocock, Specimen, p. 319, 320. Sale's Preliminary Discourse, p. 106, 107.).

55. Diodorus Siculus (tom. i. l. ii. p. 142–145.) has cast on their religion the curious but superficial glance of a Greek. Their astronomy would be far more valuable: they had looked through the telescope of reason, since they could doubt whether the sun were in the number of the planets or of the fixed stars.

56. Simplicius (who quotes Porphyry), de Cœlo, l. ii. com. xlvi. p. 123. lin. 18. apud Marsham, Canon. Chron. p. 474. who doubts the fact, because it is adverse to his systems.

the seven gods or angels who directed the course of the seven planets, and shed their irresistible influence on the earth. The attributes of the seven planets, with the twelve signs of the zodiac, and the twenty-four constellations of the northern and southern hemisphere, were represented by images and talismans; the seven days of the week were dedicated to their respective deities; the Sabians prayed thrice each day; and the temple of the moon at Haran was the term of their pilgrimage.[57] But the flexible genius of their faith was always ready either to teach or to learn: in the tradition of the creation, the deluge, and the patriarchs, they held a singular agreement with their Jewish captives; they appealed to the secret books of Adam, Seth, and Enoch; and a slight infusion of the gospel has transformed the last remnant of the Polytheists into the Christians of St. John, in the territory of Bassora.[58] The altars of Babylon were overturned by the

The Magians. Magians; but the injuries of the Sabians were revenged by the sword of Alexander; Persia groaned above five hundred years under a foreign yoke; and the purest disciples of Zoroaster escaped from the contagion of idolatry, and breathed with their adversaries the freedom of the desert.[59] Seven hundred years before the death of

The Jews. Mahomet, the Jews were settled in Arabia: and a far greater multitude was expelled from the holy land in the wars of Titus and Hadrian. The industrious exiles aspired to liberty and power: they erected synagogues in the cities and castles in the wilderness, and their Gentile converts were confounded with the children of Israel, whom they re-

The Christians. sembled in the outward mark of circumcision. The Christian missionaries were still more active and successful: the Catholics

---

The earliest date of the Chaldean observations is the year 2234 before Christ. After the conquest of Babylon by Alexander, they were communicated, at the request of Aristotle, to the astronomer Hipparchus. What a moment in the annals of science!

57. Pocock (Specimen, p. 138–146.), Hottinger (Hist. Oriental. p. 162–203.), Hyde (de Religione Vet. Persarum, p. 124. 128, &c.), d'Herbelot (*Sabi*, p. 725, 726.), and Sale (Preliminary Discourse, p. 14, 15.), rather excite than gratify our curiosity; and the last of these writers confounds Sabianism with the primitive religion of the Arabs.

58. D'Anville (l'Euphrate et le Tigre, p. 130–147.) will fix the position of these ambiguous Christians; Assemannus (Bibliot. Oriental. tom. iv. p. 607–614.) may explain their tenets. But it is a slippery task to ascertain the creed of an ignorant people, afraid and ashamed to disclose their secret traditions.

59. The Magi were fixed in the province of Bahrein (Gagnier, Vie de Mahomet, tom. iii. p. 114.), and mingled with the old Arabians (Pocock, Specimen, p. 146–150.).

asserted their universal reign; the sects whom they oppressed successively retired beyond the limits of the Roman empire; the Marcionites and Manichæans dispersed their *phantastic* opinions and apocryphal gospels; the churches of Yemen, and the princes of Hira and Gassan, were instructed in a purer creed by the Jacobite and Nestorian bishops.[60] The liberty of choice was presented to the tribes: each Arab was free to elect or to compose his private religion: and the rude superstition of his house was mingled with the sublime theology of saints and philosophers. A fundamental article of faith was inculcated by the consent of the learned strangers; the existence of one supreme God, who is exalted above the powers of heaven and earth, but who has often revealed himself to mankind by the ministry of his angels and prophets, and whose grace or justice has interrupted, by seasonable miracles, the order of nature. The most rational of the Arabs acknowledged his power, though they neglected his worship;[61] and it was habit rather than conviction that still attached them to the relics of idolatry. The Jews and Christians were the people of the *book*; the bible was already translated into the Arabic language,[62] and the volume of the old testament was accepted by the concord of these implacable enemies. In the story of the Hebrew patriarchs, the Arabs were pleased to discover the fathers of their nation. They applauded the birth and promises of Ismael; revered the faith and virtue of Abraham; traced his pedigree and their own to the creation of the first man, and imbibed with equal credulity, the prodigies of the holy text, and the dreams and traditions of the Jewish rabbis.

---

60. The state of the Jews and Christians in Arabia, is described by Pocock from Sharestani, &c. (Specimen, p. 60. 134, &c.), Hottinger (Hist. Orient. p. 212–238), d'Herbelot (Bibliot. Orient. p. 474–476.), Basnage (Hist. des Juifs, tom. vii. p. 185. tom. viii. p. 280.), and Sale (Preliminary Discourse, p. 22, &c. 33, &c.).

61. In their offerings it was a maxim to defraud God for the profit of the idol, not a more potent, but a more irritable patron (Pocock, Specimen, p. 108, 109.).

62. Our versions now extant, whether Jewish or Christian, appear more recent than the Koran; but the existence of a prior translation may be fairly inferred, 1. From the perpetual practice of the synagogue, of expounding the Hebrew lesson by a paraphrase in the vulgar tongue of the country. 2. From the analogy of the Armenian, Persian, Æthiopic versions, expressly quoted by the fathers of the fifth century, who assert that the Scriptures were translated into *all* the Barbaric languages (Walton, Prolegomena ad Biblia Polyglot. p. 34. 93–97.). Simon, Hist. Critique du V. et du N. Testament, tom. i. p. 180, 181, 282–286. 293. 305, 306. tom. iv. p. 206.).

*Birth and
education of
Mahomet,
A.D. 569–609.*
    The base and plebeian origin of Mahomet is an unskilful
calumny of the Christians,[63] who exalt instead of degrading
the merit of their adversary. His descent from Ismael was a
national privilege or fable; but if the first steps of the pedigree[64]
are dark and doubtful, he could produce many generations of
pure and genuine nobility: he sprung from the tribe of Koreish and the
family of Hashem, the most illustrious of the Arabs, the princes of Mecca,
and the hereditary guardians of the Caaba. The grandfather of Mahomet
was Abdol Motalleb, the son of Hashem, a wealthy and generous citizen,
who relieved the distress of famine with the supplies of commerce. Mecca,
which had been fed by the liberality of the father, was saved by the courage
of the son. The kingdom of Yemen was subject to the Christian princes
of Abyssinia; their vassal Abrahah was provoked by an insult to avenge the
honour of the cross; and the holy city was invested by a train of elephants
and an army of Africans. A treaty was proposed; and in the first audience,
the grandfather of Mahomet demanded the restitution of his cattle. "And
why," said Abrahah, "do you not rather implore my clemency in favour
of your temple, which I have threatened to destroy?" "Because," replied
the intrepid chief, "the cattle is my own; the Caaba belongs to the gods,
and *they* will defend their house from injury and sacrilege." The want of
provisions, or the valour of the Koreish, compelled the Abyssinians to a
disgraceful retreat; their discomfiture has been adorned with a miraculous
flight of birds, who showered down stones on the heads of the infidels;
and the deliverance was long commemorated by the æra of the
elephant.[65] The glory of Abdol Motalleb was crowned with domestic happiness, his life was prolonged to the age of one hundred

*Deliverance
of Mecca.*

---

63. In eo conveniunt omnes, ut plebeio
vilique genere ortum, &c. (Hottinger, Hist.
Orient. p. 136.). Yet Theophanes, the most
ancient of the Greeks, and the father of many
a lie, confesses that Mahomet was of the race
of Ismael, εκ μιας γενικωτατης φυλης
(Chronograph. p. 277.).

64. Abulfeda (in Vit. Mohammed. c. 1, 2.)
and Gagnier (Vie de Mahomet, p. 25–97.)
describe the popular and approved genealogy
of the prophet. At Mecca, I would not dispute
its authenticity; at Lausanne, I will venture to
observe, 1. *That* from Ismael to Mahomet, a
period of 2500 years, they reckon thirty,

instead of seventy-five, generations. 2. *That*
the modern Bedoweens are ignorant of their
history and careless of their pedigree (Voyage
de d'Arvieux, p. 100. 103.).

65. The seed of this history, or fable, is contained in the cv[th] chapter of the Koran; and
Gagnier (in Præfat. ad Vit. Moham. p. 18,
&c.) has translated the historical narrative of
Abulfeda, which may be illustrated from
d'Herbelot. (Bibliot. Orientale, p. 12.), and
Pocock (Specimen, p. 64.). Prideaux (Life of
Mahomet, p. 48.) calls it a lie of the coinage
of Mahomet; but Sale (Koran, p. 501–503.),
who is half a Musulman, attacks the inconsist-

and ten years, and he became the father of six daughters and thirteen sons. His best beloved Abdallah was the most beautiful and modest of the Arabian youth; and in the first night, when he consummated his marriage with Amina, of the noble race of the Zahrites, two hundred virgins are said to have expired of jealousy and despair. Mahomet, or more properly Mohammed, the only son of Abdallah and Amina, was born at Mecca, four years after the death of Justinian, and two months after the defeat of the Abyssinians,[66] whose victory would have introduced into the Caaba the religion of the Christians. In his early infancy, he was deprived of his father, his mother, and his grandfather; his uncles were strong and numerous; and in the division of the inheritance, the orphan's share was reduced to five camels and an Æthiopian maid-servant. At home and abroad, in peace and war, Abu Taleb, the most respectable of his uncles, was the guide and guardian of his youth; in his twenty-fifth year, he entered into the service of Cadijah, a rich and noble widow of Mecca, who soon rewarded his fidelity with the gift of her hand and fortune. The marriage-contract, in the simple style of antiquity, recites the mutual love of Mahomet and Cadijah; describes him as the most accomplished of the tribe of Koreish; and stipulates a dowry of twelve ounces of gold and twenty camels, which was supplied by the liberality of his uncle.[67] By this alliance, the son of Abdallah was restored to the station of his ancestors; and the judicious

---

ent faith of the Doctor for believing the miracles of the Delphic Apollo. Maracci (Alcoran, tom. i. part ii. p. 14. tom. ii. p. 823.) ascribes the miracle to the devil, and extorts from the Mahometans the confession, that God would not have defended against the Christians the idols of the Caaba.

66. The safest æras of Abulfeda (in Vit. c. i. p. 2.), of Alexander, or the Greeks, 882, of Bocht Naser, or Nabonasser, 1316, equally lead us to the year 569. The old Arabian calendar is too dark and uncertain to support the Benedictines (Art de verifier les Dates, p. 15.), who from the day of the month and week deduce a new mode of calculation, and remove the birth of Mahomet to the year of Christ 570, the 10th of November. Yet this date would agree with the year 882 of the Greeks, which is assigned by Elmacin (Hist. Saracen. p. 5.) and Abulpharagius (Dynast.

p. 101. and Errata Pocock's version). While we refine our chronology, it is possible that the illiterate prophet was ignorant of his own age.

67. I copy the honourable testimony of Abu Taleb to his family and nephew. Laus Dei, qui nos a stirpe Abrahami et femine Ismaelis constituit, et nobis regionem sacram dedit, et nos judices hominibus statuit. Porro Mohammed filius Abdollahi nepotis mei *(nepos meus)* quo cum ex æquo librabitur e Koraishidis quispiam cui non præpondera-turus est, bonitate et excellantiâ, et intellectû et gloria et acumine etsi opum inops fuerit (et certe opes umbra transiens sunt et depositum quod reddi debet), desiderio Chadijæ filiæ Chowailedi tenetur, et illa vicissim ipsius, quicquid autem dotis vice petieritis, ego in me suscipiam (Pocock, Specimen, e septimâ parte libri Ebn Hamduni).

matron was content with his domestic virtues, till, in the fortieth year of his age,[68] he assumed the title of a prophet, and proclaimed the religion of the Koran.

Qualifications of the prophet. According to the tradition of his companions, Mahomet[69] was distinguished by the beauty of his person, an outward gift which is seldom despised, except by those to whom it has been refused. Before he spoke, the orator engaged on his side the affections of a public or private audience. They applauded his commanding presence, his majestic aspect, his piercing eye, his gracious smile, his flowing beard, his countenance that painted every sensation of the soul, and his gestures that enforced each expression of the tongue. In the familiar offices of life he scrupulously adhered to the grave and ceremonious politeness of his country: his respectful attention to the rich and powerful was dignified by his condescension and affability to the poorest citizens of Mecca: the frankness of his manner concealed the artifice of his views; and the habits of courtesy were imputed to personal friendship or universal benevolence. His memory was capacious and retentive, his wit easy and social, his imagination sublime, his judgment clear, rapid, and decisive. He possessed the courage both of thought and action; and, although his designs might gradually expand with his success, the first idea which he entertained of his divine mission bears the stamp of an original and superior genius. The son of Abdallah was educated in the bosom of the noblest race, in the use of the purest dialect of Arabia; and the fluency of his speech was corrected and enhanced by the practice of discreet and seasonable silence. With these powers of eloquence, Mahomet was an illiterate Barbarian: his youth had never been instructed in the arts of reading and writing;[70] the common

68. The private life of Mahomet, from his birth to his mission, is preserved by Abulfeda (in Vit. c. 3–7.), and the Arabian writers of genuine or apocryphal note, who are alleged by Hottinger (Hist. Orient. p. 204–211.), Maracci (tom. i. p. 10–14.), and Gagnier (Vie de Mahomet, tom. i. p. 97–134.).

69. Abulfeda, in Vit. c. lxv, lxvi. Gagnier, Vie de Mahomet, tom. iii. p. 272–289.; the best traditions of the person and conversation of the prophet are derived from Ayesha, Ali and Abu Horaira (Gagnier, tom. ii. p. 267. Ockley's Hist. of the Saracens, vol. ii. p. 149.),

surnamed the father of a cat, who died in the year 59 of the Hegira.

70. Those who believe that Mahomet could read or write, are incapable of reading what is written, with another pen, in the Surats, or chapters of the Koran vii. xxix. xcvi. These texts, and the traditions of the Sonna, are admitted, without doubt, by Abulfeda (in Vit. c. vii.), Gagnier (Not. ad Abulfed. p. 15.), Pocock (Specimen, p. 151.), Reland (de Religione Mohammedicâ, p. 236.), and Sale (Preliminary Discourse, p. 42.). Mr. White, almost alone, denies the ignorance, to accuse the

ignorance exempted him from shame or reproach, but he was reduced to a narrow circle of existence, and deprived of those faithful mirrors, which reflect to our mind the minds of sages and heroes. Yet the book of nature and of man was open to his view; and some fancy has been indulged in the political and philosophical observations which are ascribed to the Arabian *traveller*.[71] He compares the nations and the religions of the earth; discovers the weakness of the Persian and Roman monarchies; beholds, with pity and indignation, the degeneracy of the times; and resolves to unite, under one God and one king, the invincible spirit and primitive virtues of the Arabs. Our more accurate enquiry will suggest, that instead of visiting the courts, the camps, the temples of the East, the two journies of Mahomet into Syria were confined to the fairs of Bostra and Damascus: that he was only thirteen years of age when he accompanied the caravan of his uncle, and that his duty compelled him to return as soon as he had disposed of the merchandise of Cadijah. In these hasty and superficial excursions, the eye of genius might discern some objects invisible to his grosser companions; some seeds of knowledge might be cast upon a fruitful soil; but his ignorance of the Syriac language must have checked his curiosity; and I cannot perceive, in the life or writings of Mahomet, that his prospect was far extended beyond the limits of the Arabian world. From every region of that solitary world, the pilgrims of Mecca were annually assembled, by the calls of devotion and commerce: in the free concourse of multitudes, a simple citizen, in his native tongue, might study the political state and character of the tribes, the theory and practice of the Jews and Christians. Some useful strangers might be tempted, or forced, to implore the rights of hospitality; and the enemies of Mahomet have named the Jew,

---

imposture, of the prophet. His arguments are far from satisfactory. Two short trading journies to the fairs of Syria, were surely not sufficient to infuse a science so rare among the citizens of Mecca: it was not in the cool deliberate act of a treaty, that Mahomet would have dropt the mask; nor can any conclusion be drawn from the words of disease and delirium. The *lettered* youth, before he aspired to the prophetic character, must have often exercised, in private life, the arts of reading and writing; and his first converts, of his own family, would have been the first to detect

and upbraid his scandalous hypocrisy (White's Sermons, p. 203. 204. Notes, p. xxxvi–xxxviii.).

71. The Count de Boulainvilliers (Vie de Mahomed, p. 202–228.) leads his Arabian pupil, like the Telemachus of Fenelon, or the Cyrus of Ramsay. His journey to the court of Persia is probably a fiction; nor can I trace the origin of his exclamation, "Les Grecs sont pourtant des hommes." The two Syrian journies are expressed by almost all the Arabian writers, both Mahometans and Christians (Gagnier ad Abulfed. p. 10.).

the Persian, and the Syrian monk, whom they accuse of lending their secret aid to the composition of the Koran.[72] Conversation enriches the understanding, but solitude is the school of genius; and the uniformity of a work denotes the hand of a single artist. From his earliest youth, Mahomet was addicted to religious contemplation: each year, during the month of Ramadan, he withdrew from the world, and from the arms of Cadijah: in the cave of Hera, three miles from Mecca,[73] he consulted the spirit of fraud or enthusiasm, whose abode is not in the heavens, but in the mind of the prophet. The faith which, under the name of *Islam*, he preached to his family and nation, is compounded of an eternal truth, and a necessary fiction, THAT THERE IS ONLY ONE GOD, AND THAT MAHOMET IS THE APOSTLE OF GOD.

One God.   It is the boast of the Jewish apologists, that while the learned nations of antiquity were deluded by the fables of polytheism, their simple ancestors of Palestine preserved the knowledge and worship of the true God. The moral attributes of Jehovah may not easily be reconciled with the standard of *human* virtue: his metaphysical qualities are darkly expressed; but each page of the Pentateuch and the Prophets is an evidence of his power: the unity of his name is inscribed on the first table of the law; and his sanctuary was never defiled by any visible image of the invisible essence. After the ruin of the temple, the faith of the Hebrew exiles was purified, fixed, and enlightened, by the spiritual devotion of the synagogue; and the authority of Mahomet will not justify his perpetual reproach, that the Jews of Mecca or Medina adored Ezra as the son of God.[74] But the children of Israel had ceased to be a people; and the religions of the world were guilty, at least in the eyes of the prophet, of giving sons, or daughters, or companions, to the supreme God. In the rude idolatry of the Arabs, the crime is manifest and audacious: the Sabians are poorly excused by the

---

72. I am not at leisure to pursue the fables or conjectures which name the strangers accused or suspected by the infidels of Mecca (Koran, c. 16, p. 223. c. 35. p. 297. with Sale's Remarks. Prideaux's Life of Mahomet, p. 22–27. Gagnier, Not. ad Abulfed. p. 11. 74. Maracci, tom. ii. p. 400.). Even Prideaux has observed, that the transaction must have been secret, and that the scene lay in the heart of Arabia.

73. Abulfeda in Vit. c. 7. p. 15. Gagnier, tom.

i. p. 133. 135. The situation of mount Hera is remarked by Abulfeda (Geograph. Arab. p. 4.). Yet Mahomet had never read of the cave of Egeria, ubi nocturnæ Numa constituebat amicæ, of the Idæan mount, where Minos conversed with Jove, &c.

74. Koran, c. 9. p. 153. Al Beidawi, and the other commentators quoted by Sale, adhere to the charge; but I do not understand that it is coloured by the most obscure or absurd tradition of the Talmudists.

pre-eminence of the first planet, or intelligence, in their cœlestial hierarchy; and in the Magian system the conflict of the two principles betrays the imperfection of the conqueror. The Christians of the seventh century had insensibly relapsed into a semblance of paganism: their public and private vows were addressed to the relics and images that disgraced the temples of the East: the throne of the Almighty was darkened by a cloud of martyrs, and saints, and angels, the objects of popular veneration; and the Collyridian heretics, who flourished in the fruitful soil of Arabia, invested the Virgin Mary with the name and honours of a goddess.[75] The mysteries of the Trinity and Incarnation *appear* to contradict the principle of the divine unity. In their obvious sense, they introduce three equal deities, and transform the man Jesus into the substance of the son of God:[76] an orthodox commentary will satisfy only a believing mind: intemperate curiosity and zeal had torn the veil of the sanctuary; and each of the Oriental sects was eager to confess that all, except themselves, deserved the reproach of idolatry and polytheism. The creed of Mahomet is free from suspicion or ambiguity; and the Koran is a glorious testimony to the unity of God. The prophet of Mecca rejected the worship of idols and men, of stars and planets, on the rational principle that whatever rises must set, that whatever is born must die, that whatever is corruptible must decay and perish.[77] In the Author of the universe, his rational enthusiasm confessed and adored an infinite and eternal being, without form or place, without issue or similitude, present to our most secret thoughts, existing by the necessity of his own nature, and deriving from himself all moral and intellectual perfection. These sublime truths, thus announced in the language of the

75. Hottinger, Hist. Orient. p. 225–228. The Collyridian heresy was carried from Thrace to Arabia by some women, and the name was borrowed from the κολλυρις, or cake, which they offered to the goddess. This example, that of Beryllus bishop of Bostra (Euseb. Hist. Eccles. l. vi. c. 33.), and several others, may excuse the reproach, Arabia hæreseωη ferax.

76. The three gods in the Koran, (c. 4. p. 81. c. 5. p. 92.) are obviously directed against our Catholic mystery: but the Arabic commentators understand them of the Father, the Son, and the Virgin Mary, an heretical Trinity, maintained, as it is said, by some Barbarians

at the council of Nice (Eutych. Annal. tom. i. p. 440.). But the existence of the *Marianites* is denied by the candid Beausobre (Hist. de Manicheisme, tom. i. p. 532.): and he derives the mistake from the word *Rouah*, the Holy Ghost, which in some Oriental tongues is of the feminine gender, and is figuratively styled the mother of Christ in the gospel of the Nazarenes.

77. This train of thought is philosophically exemplified in the character of Abraham, who opposed in Chaldæa the first introduction of idolatry (Koran, c. 6. p. 106. d'Herbelot, Bibliot. Orient. p. 13.).

prophet,[78] are firmly held by his disciples, and defined with metaphysical precision by the interpreters of the Koran. A philosophic theist might subscribe the popular creed of the Mahometans;[79] a creed too sublime perhaps for our present faculties. What object remains for the fancy, or even the understanding, when we have abstracted from the unknown substance all ideas of time and space, of motion and matter, of sensation and reflection? The first principle of reason and revelation was confirmed by the voice of Mahomet: his proselytes, from India to Morocco, are distinguished by the name of *Unitarians*; and the danger of idolatry has been prevented by the interdiction of images. The doctrine of eternal decrees and absolute predestination is strictly embraced by the Mahometans; and they struggle with the common difficulties, *how* to reconcile the prescience of God with the freedom and responsibility of man; *how* to explain the permission of evil under the reign of infinite power and infinite goodness.

Mahomet, the apostle of God, and the last of the prophets.

The God of nature has written his existence on all his works, and his law in the heart of man. To restore the knowledge of the one and the practice of the other, has been the real or pretended aim of the prophets of every age: the liberality of Mahomet allowed to his predecessors the same credit which he claimed for himself; and the chain of inspiration was prolonged from the fall of Adam to the promulgation of the Koran.[80] During that period, some rays of prophetic light had been imparted to one hundred and twenty-four thousand of the elect, discriminated by their respective measure of virtue and grace; three hundred and thirteen apostles were sent with a special commission to recal their country from idolatry and vice; one hundred and four volumes have been dictated by the holy spirit; and six legislators of transcendent brightness have announced to mankind the six successive revelations of various rites, but of one immutable religion. The authority and station of Adam, Noah, Abraham, Moses, Christ, and Mahomet, rise

78. See the Koran, particularly the second (p. 30.), the fifty-seventh (p. 437.), the fifty-eighth (p. 441.) chapter, which proclaim the omnipotence of the Creator.

79. The most orthodox creeds are translated by Pocock (Specimen, p. 274. 284–292.), Ockley (Hist. of the Saracens, vol. ii. p. lxxxii–xcv.), Reland (de Religion. Moham. l. i. p. 7–13.), and Chardin (Voyages en Perse, tom. iv. p. 4–28.). The great truth, that God

is without similitude, is foolishly criticised by Maracci (Alcoran, tom. i. part iii. p. 87–94.), because he made man after his own image.

80. Reland, de Relig. Moham. l. i. p. 17–47. Sale's Preliminary Discourse, p. 73–76. Voyage de Chardin, tom. iv. p. 28–37. and 37–47. for the Persian addition, "Ali is the vicar of God!" Yet the precise number of prophets is not an article of faith.

in just gradation above each other; but whosoever hates or rejects any one of the prophets, is numbered with the infidels. The writings of the patriarchs were extant only in the apocryphal copies of the Greeks and Syrians:[81] the conduct of Adam had not entitled him to the gratitude or respect of his children; the seven precepts of Noah were observed by an inferior and imperfect class of the proselytes of the synagogue;[82] and the memory of Abraham was obscurely revered by the Sabians in his native land of Chaldæa: of the myriads of prophets, Moses and Christ alone lived and reigned; and the remnant of the inspired writings was comprised in the books of the Old and the New Testament. The miraculous story of Moses is consecrated and embellished in the Koran;[83] and the captive Jews enjoy the secret revenge of imposing their own belief on the nations whose recent creeds they deride. For the author of Christianity, the Mahometans are taught by the prophet to entertain an high and mysterious reverence.[84] "Verily, Christ Jesus, the son of Mary, is the apostle of God, and his word, which he conveyed unto Mary, and a Spirit proceeding from him: honourable in this world, and in the world to come; and one of those who approach near to the presence of God."[85] The wonders of the genuine and apocryphal gospels[86] are profusely heaped on his head; and the Latin church has not disdained to borrow from the Koran the immaculate conception[87] of his virgin mother. Yet Jesus was a mere mortal; and, at the day of judgment, his testimony will serve to condemn both the Jews, who

Moses.

Jesus.

---

81. For the apocryphal books of Adam, see Fabricius, Codex Pseudepigraphus V. T. p. 27–29.; of Seth, p. 154–157.; of Enoch, p. 160–219. But the book of Enoch is consecrated, in some measure, by the quotation of the apostle St. Jude; and a long legendary fragment is alleged by Syncellus and Scaliger.

82. The seven precepts of Noah are explained by Marsham (Canon. Chronicus, p. 154–180.), who adopts, on this occasion, the learning and credulity of Selden.

83. The articles of *Adam, Noah, Abraham, Moses*, &c. in the Bibliotheque of d'Herbelot, are gaily bedecked with the fanciful legends of the Mahometans, who have built on the ground-work of Scripture and the Talmud.

84. Koran, c. 7. p. 128, &c. c. 10. p. 173, &c. D'Herbelot, p. 647, &c.

85. Koran, c. 3. p. 40. c. 4. p. 80. D'Herbelot, p. 399, &c.

86. See the gospel of St. Thomas, or of the Infancy, in the Codex Apocryphus N. T. of Fabricius, who collects the various testimonies concerning it (p. 128–158.). It was published in Greek by Cotelier, and in Arabic by Sike, who thinks our present copy more recent than Mahomet. Yet his quotations agree with the original about the speech of Christ in his cradle, his living birds of clay, &c. (*Sike*, c. 1. p. 168, 169. c. 36. p. 198, 199. c. 46. p. 206. *Cotelier*, c. 2. p. 160, 161.).

87. It is darkly hinted in the Koran (c. 3. p. 39.), and more clearly explained by the tradition of the Sonnites (Sale's Note, and Maracci, tom. ii. p. 112.). In the xii[th] century, the immaculate conception was condemned

reject him as a prophet, and the Christians, who adore him as the Son of God. The malice of his enemies aspersed his reputation, and conspired against his life; but their intention only was guilty, a phantom or a criminal was substituted on the cross, and the innocent saint was translated to the seventh heaven.[88] During six hundred years the gospel was the way of truth and salvation; but the Christians insensibly forgot both the laws and the example of their founder; and Mahomet was instructed by the Gnostics to accuse the church, as well as the synagogue, of corrupting the integrity of the sacred text.[89] The piety of Moses and of Christ rejoiced in the assurance of a future prophet, more illustrious than themselves: the evangelic promise of the *Paraclete*, or Holy Ghost, was prefigured in the name, and accomplished in the person, of Mahomet,[90] the greatest and the last of the apostles of God.

The Koran.   The communication of ideas requires a similitude of thought and language: the discourse of a philosopher would vibrate without effect on the ear of a peasant; yet how minute is the distance of *their* understandings, if it be compared with the contact of an infinite and a finite mind, with the word of God expressed by the tongue or the pen of a mortal? The inspiration of the Hebrew prophets, of the apostles and evangelists of Christ, might not be incompatible with the exercise of their reason and memory; and the diversity of their genius is strongly marked in

---

by St. Bernard as a presumptuous novelty (Fra Paolo, Istoria del Concilio di Trento, l. ii.).
88. See the Koran, c. 3. v. 53. and c. 4. v. 156. of Maracci's edition. Deus est præstantissimus dolose agentium (an odd praise) . . . nec crucifixerunt eum, sed objecta est eis similitudo: an expression that may suit with the system of the Docetes; but the commentators believe (Maracci, tom. ii. p. 113–115. 173. Sale, p. 42. 43. 79.), that another man, a friend or an enemy, was crucified in the likeness of Jesus; a fable which they had read in the gospel of St. Barnabas, and which had been started as early as the time of Irenæus, by some Ebionite heretics (Beausobre, Hist. du Manicheisme, tom. ii. p. 25. Mosheim de Reb. Christ. p. 353.).
89. This charge is obscurely urged in the Koran (c. 3. p. 45.): but neither Mahomet,

nor his followers, are sufficiently versed in languages and criticism to give any weight or colour to their suspicions. Yet the Arians and Nestorians could relate some stories, and the illiterate prophet might listen to the bold assertions of the Manichæans. See Beausobre, tom. i. p. 291–305.
90. Among the prophecies of the Old and New Testament, which are perverted by the fraud or ignorance of the Musulmans, they apply to the prophet the promise of the *Paraclete*, or Comforter, which had been already usurped by the Montanists and Manichæans (Beausobre, Hist. Critique du Manicheisme, tom. i. p. 263, &c.); and the easy change of letters, περικλυτος for παρακλητος, affords the etymology of the name of Mohammed (Maracci, tom. i. part i. p. 15–28.).

the style and composition of the books of the Old and New Testament. But Mahomet was content with a character, more humble, yet more sublime, of a simple editor: the substance of the Koran,[91] according to himself or his disciples, is uncreated and eternal; subsisting in the essence of the Deity, and inscribed with a pen of light on the table of his everlasting decrees. A paper copy in a volume of silk and gems, was brought down to the lowest heaven by the angel Gabriel, who, under the Jewish œconomy, had indeed been dispatched on the most important errands; and this trusty messenger successively revealed the chapters and verses to the Arabian prophet. Instead of a perpetual and perfect measure of the divine will, the fragments of the Koran were produced at the discretion of Mahomet; each revelation is suited to the emergencies of his policy or passion; and all contradiction is removed by the saving maxim, that any text of scripture is abrogated or modified by any subsequent passage. The word of God, and of the apostle, was diligently recorded by his disciples on palm-leaves and the shoulder-bones of mutton; and the pages, without order or connection, were cast into a domestic chest in the custody of one of his wives. Two years after the death of Mahomet, the sacred volume was collected and published by his friend and successor Abubeker: the work was revised by the caliph Othman, in the thirtieth year of the Hegira; and the various editions of the Koran assert the same miraculous privilege of an uniform and incorruptible text. In the spirit of enthusiasm or vanity, the prophet rests the truth of his mission on the merit of his book, audaciously challenges both men and angels to imitate the beauties of a single page, and presumes to assert that God alone could dictate this incomparable performance.[92] This argument is most powerfully addressed to a devout Arabian, whose mind is attuned to faith and rapture, whose ear is delighted by the music of sounds, and whose ignorance is incapable of comparing the productions of human genius.[93] The harmony and copiousness of style will not reach, in a version, the European infidel: he will peruse with impatience the endless incoherent rhapsody of fable, and precept, and declamation, which seldom excites a sentiment or an idea, which

---

91. For the Koran, see d'Herbelot, p. 85–88. Maracci, tom. i. in Vit. Mohammed. p. 32–45. Sale, Preliminary Discourse, p. 56–70.

92. Koran, c. 17. v. 89. In Sale, p. 235, 236. In Maracci, p. 410.

93. Yet a sect of Arabians was persuaded, that it might be equalled or surpassed by an human pen (Pocock, Specimen, p. 221, &c.); and Maracci (the polemic is too hard for the translator) derides the rhyming affectation of the most applauded passage (tom. i. part ii. p. 69–75.).

sometimes crawls in the dust, and is sometimes lost in the clouds. The divine attributes exalt the fancy of the Arabian missionary; but his loftiest strains must yield to the sublime simplicity of the book of Job, composed in a remote age, in the same country and in the same language.[94] If the composition of the Koran exceed the faculties of a man, to what superior intelligence should we ascribe the Iliad of Homer or the Philippics of Demosthenes? In all religions, the life of the founder supplies the silence of his written revelation: the sayings of Mahomet were so many lessons of truth; his actions so many examples of virtue; and the public and private memorials were preserved by his wives and companions. At the end of two hundred years, the *Sonna* or oral law was fixed and consecrated by the labours of Al Bochari, who discriminated seven thousand two hundred and seventy-five genuine traditions, from a mass of three hundred thousand reports, of a more doubtful or spurious character. Each day the pious author prayed in the temple of Mecca, and performed his ablutions with the water of Zemzem: the pages were successively deposited on the pulpit, and the sepulchre of the apostle; and the work has been approved by the four orthodox sects of the Sonnites.[95]

Miracles.   The mission of the ancient prophets, of Moses and of Jesus, had been confirmed by many splendid prodigies; and Mahomet was repeatedly urged, by the inhabitants of Mecca and Medina, to produce a similar evidence of his divine legation; to call down from heaven the angel or the volume of his revelation, to create a garden in the desert, or to kindle a conflagration in the unbelieving city. As often as he is pressed by the demands of the Koreish, he involves himself in the obscure boast of vision and prophecy, appeals to the internal proofs of his doctrine, and shields himself behind the providence of God, who refuses those signs and wonders that would depreciate the merit of faith and aggravate the guilt of infidelity. But the modest or angry tone of his apologies betrays his weakness and vexation; and these passages of scandal establish, beyond suspicion, the integrity of the Koran.[96] The votaries of Mahomet are more

---

94. Colloquia (whether real or fabulous) in media Arabia atque ab Arabibus habita (Lowth, de Poesi Hebræorum Prælect. xxxii, xxxiii, xxxiv. with his German editor Michaelis, Epimetron iv.). Yet Michaelis (p. 671–673.) has detected many Egyptian images, the elephantiasis, papyrus, Nile, crocodile, &c. The language is ambiguously styled, *Arabico-Hebræa*. The resemblance of the sister dialects was much more visible in their childhood than in their mature age (Michaelis, p. 682. Schultens, in Præfat. Job).

95. Al Bochari died A.H. 224. See d'Herbelot, p. 208. 416. 827. Gagnier, Not. ad Abulfed. c. 19. p. 33.

96. See more remarkably, Koran, c. 2. 6. 12.

assured than himself of his miraculous gifts, and their confidence and credulity encrease as they are farther removed from the time and place of his spiritual exploits. They believe or affirm that trees went forth to meet him; that he was saluted by stones; that water gushed from his fingers; that he fed the hungry, cured the sick, and raised the dead; that a beam groaned to him; that a camel complained to him; that a shoulder of mutton informed him of its being poisoned; and that both animate and inanimate nature were equally subject to the apostle of God.[97] His dream of a nocturnal journey is seriously described as a real and corporeal transaction. A mysterious animal, the Borak, conveyed him from the temple of Mecca to that of Jerusalem: with his companion Gabriel, he successively ascended the seven heavens, and received and repaid the salutations of the patriarchs, the prophets, and the angels, in their respective mansions. Beyond the seventh heaven, Mahomet alone was permitted to proceed; he passed the veil of unity, approached within two bow-shots of the throne, and felt a cold that pierced him to the heart, when his shoulder was touched by the hand of God. After this familiar though important conversation, he again descended to Jerusalem, remounted the Borak, returned to Mecca, and performed in the tenth part of a night the journey of many thousand years.[98] According to another legend, the apostle confounded in a national assembly the malicious challenge of the Koreish. His resistless word split asunder the orb of the moon: the obedient planet stooped from her station in the sky, accomplished the seven revolutions round the Caaba, saluted Mahomet in the

13. 17. Prideaux (Life of Mahomet, p. 18, 19.) has confounded the impostor. Maracci, with a more learned apparatus, has shewn that the passages which deny his miracles are clear and positive (Alcoran, tom. i. part ii. p. 7–12.), and those which seem to assert them, are ambiguous and insufficient (p. 12–22.).

97. See the Specimen Hist. Arabum, the text of Abulpharagius, p. 17. the notes of Pocock, p. 187–190. D'Herbelot Bibliotheque Orientale, p. 76, 77. Voyages de Chardin, tom. iv. p. 200–203. Maracci (Alcoran, tom. i. p. 22–64.) has most laboriously collected and confuted the miracles and prophecies of Mahomet, which, according to some writers, amount to three thousand.

98. The nocturnal journey is circumstantially related by Abulfeda (in Vit. Mohammed. c. 19. p. 33.), who wishes to think it a vision; by Prideaux (p. 31–40.), who aggravates the absurdities; and by Gagnier (tom. i. p. 252–343.), who declares, from the zealous Al Jannabi, that to deny this journey, is to disbelieve the Koran. Yet the Koran, without naming either heaven, or Jerusalem, or Mecca, has only dropt a mysterious hint: Laus illi qui transtulit servum suum ab oratorio Haram ad oratorium remotissimum (Koran, c. 17. v. 1. in Maracci, tom. ii. p. 407.; for Sale's version is more licentious). A slender basis for the aërial structure of tradition.

Arabian tongue, and suddenly contracting her dimensions, entered at the collar, and issued forth through the sleeve, of his shirt.[99] The vulgar are amused with these marvellous tales; but the gravest of the Musulman doctors imitate the modesty of their master, and indulge a latitude of faith or interpretation.[100] They might speciously allege, that in preaching the religion, it was needless to violate the harmony, of nature; that a creed unclouded with mystery may be excused from miracles; and that the sword of Mahomet was not less potent than the rod of Moses.

Precepts of Mahomet – prayer, fasting, alms.   The polytheist is oppressed and distracted by the variety of superstition: a thousand rites of Egyptian origin were interwoven with the essence of the Mosaic law; and the spirit of the gospel had evaporated in the pageantry of the church. The prophet of Mecca was tempted by prejudice, or policy, or patriotism, to sanctify the rites of the Arabians, and the custom of visiting the holy stone of the Caaba. But the precepts of Mahomet himself inculcate a more simple and rational piety: prayer, fasting, and alms, are the religious duties of a Musulman; and he is encouraged to hope, that prayer will carry him half way to God, fasting will bring him to the door of his palace, and alms will gain him admittance.[101] I. According to the

99. In the prophetic style, which uses the present or past for the future, Mahomet had said: Appropinquavit hora et scissa est luna (Koran, c. 54. v. 1. in Maracci, tom. ii. p. 688.). This figure of rhetoric has been converted into a fact, which is said to be attested by the most respectable eye-witnesses (Maracci, tom. ii. p. 690.). The festival is still celebrated by the Persians (Chardin, tom. iv. p. 201.); and the legend is tediously spun out by Gagnier (Vie de Mahomet, tom. i.p. 183–234.) on the faith, as it should seem, of the credulous Al Jannabi. Yet a Mahometan doctor has arraigned the credit of the principal witness (apud Pocock, Specimen, p. 187.); the best interpreters are content with the simple sense of the Koran (Al Beidawi, apud Hottinger, Hist. Orient. l. ii. p. 302); and the silence of Abulfeda is worthy of a prince and a philosopher.

100. Abulpharagius, in Specimen Hist. Arab. p. 17.; and his scepticism is justified in the notes of Pocock, p. 190–194. from the purest authorities.

101. The most authentic account of these precepts, pilgrimage, prayer, fasting, alms, and ablutions, is extracted from the Persian and Arabian theologians by Maracci (Prodrom. part iv. p. 9–24.). Reland in his excellent treatise de Religione Mohammedicâ, Utrecht, 1717, p. 67–123.); and Chardin (Voyages en Perse, tom. iv. p. 47–195.). Maracci is a partial accuser; but the jeweller, Chardin, had the eyes of a philosopher; and Reland, a judicious student, had travelled over the East in his closet at Utrecht. The xiv[th] letter of Tournefort (Voyage du Levant, tom. ii. p. 325–360. in octavo) describes what he had seen of the religion of the Turks.

tradition of the nocturnal journey, the apostle, in his personal conference with the Deity, was commanded to impose on his disciples the daily obligation of fifty prayers. By the advice of Moses, he applied for an alleviation of this intolerable burthen; the number was gradually reduced to five; without any dispensation of business or pleasure, or time or place: the devotion of the faithful is repeated at day-break, at noon, in the afternoon, in the evening, and at the first watch of the night; and, in the present decay of religious fervour, our travellers are edified by the profound humility and attention of the Turks and Persians. Cleanliness is the key of prayer: the frequent lustration of the hands, the face, and the body, which was practised of old by the Arabs, is solemnly enjoined by the Koran; and a permission is formally granted to supply with sand the scarcity of water. The words and attitudes of supplication, as it is performed either sitting, or standing, or prostrate on the ground, are prescribed by custom or authority, but the prayer is poured forth in short and fervent ejaculations; the measure of zeal is not exhausted by a tedious liturgy; and each Musulman, for his own person, is invested with the character of a priest. Among the theists, who reject the use of images, it has been found necessary to restrain the wanderings of the fancy, by directing the eye and the thought towards a *kebla*, or visible point of the horizon. The prophet was at first inclined to gratify the Jews by the choice of Jerusalem; but he soon returned to a more natural partiality; and five times every day the eyes of the nations at Astracan, at Fez, at Delhi, are devoutly turned to the holy temple of Mecca. Yet every spot for the service of God is equally pure: the Mahometans indifferently pray in their chamber or in the street. As a distinction from the Jews and Christians, the Friday in each week is set apart for the useful institution of public worship: the people is assembled in the mosch and the imam: some respectable elder ascends the pulpit, to begin the prayer and pronounce the sermon. But the Mahometan religion is destitute of priesthood or sacrifice; and the independent spirit of fanaticism looks down with contempt on the ministers and the slaves of superstition. II. The voluntary[102] penance of the ascetics, the torment and glory of their lives, was odious to a prophet who censured in his companions a

---

102. Mahomet (Sale's Koran, c. 9. p. 153.) reproaches the Christians with taking their priests and monks for their lords, besides God. Yet Maracci (Prodromus, part iii. p. 69, 70.) excuses the worship, especially of the pope, and quotes, from the Koran itself, the case of Eblis, or Satan, who was cast from heaven for refusing to adore Adam.

rash vow of abstaining from flesh, and women, and sleep; and firmly declared, that he would suffer no monks in his religion.[103] Yet he instituted, in each year, a fast of thirty days; and strenuously recommended the observance, as a discipline which purifies the soul and subdues the body, as a salutary exercise of obedience to the will of God and his apostle. During the month of Ramadan, from the rising to the setting of the sun, the Musulman abstains from eating, and drinking, and women, and baths, and perfumes; from all nourishment that can restore his strength, from all pleasure that can gratify his senses. In the revolution of the lunar year, the Ramadan coincides by turns with the winter cold and the summer heat; and the patient martyr, without assuaging his thirst with a drop of water, must expect the close of a tedious and sultry day. The interdiction of wine, peculiar to some orders of priests or hermits, is converted by Mahomet alone into a positive and general law;[104] and a considerable portion of the globe has abjured, at his command, the use of that salutary, though dangerous, liquor. These painful restraints are, doubtless, infringed by the libertine and eluded by the hypocrite; but the legislator, by whom they are enacted, cannot surely be accused of alluring his proselytes by the indulgence of their sensual appetites. III. The charity of the Mahometans descends to the animal creation; and the Koran repeatedly inculcates, not as a merit, but as a strict and indispensable duty, the relief of the indigent and unfortunate. Mahomet, perhaps, is the only lawgiver who has defined the precise measure of charity: the standard may vary with the degree and nature of property, as it consists either in money, in corn or cattle, in fruits or merchandise; but the Musulman does not accomplish the law, unless he bestows a *tenth* of his revenue; and if his conscience accuses him of fraud or extortion, the tenth, under the idea of restitution, is enlarged to a *fifth*.[105] Benevolence is

---

103. Koran, c. 5. p. 94. and Sale's note, which refers to the authority of Jallaloddin and Al Beidawi. D'Herbelot declares, that Mahomet condemned *la vie religieuse*; and that the first swarms of fakirs, dervises, &c. did not appear till after the year 300 of the Hegira (Bibliot. Orient. p. 292. 718.).

104. See the double prohibition (Koran, c. 2. p. 25. c. 5. p. 94.); the one in the style of a legislator, the other in that of a fanatic. The public and private motives of Mahomet are investigated by Prideaux (Life of Mahomet,

p. 62–64.); and Sale (Preliminary Discourse, p. 124.).

105. The jealousy of Maracci (Prodromus, part iv. p. 33.) prompts him to enumerate the more liberal alms of the Catholics of Rome. Fifteen great hospitals are open to many thousand patients and pilgrims, fifteen hundred maidens are annually portioned, fifty-six charity schools are founded for both sexes, one hundred and twenty confraternities relieve the wants of their brethren, &c. The benevolence of London is still more extensive;

the foundation of justice, since we are forbid to injure those whom we are bound to assist. A prophet may reveal the secrets of heaven and of futurity; but in his moral precepts he can only repeat the lessons of our own hearts.

The two articles of belief, and the four practical duties of Islam, are guarded by rewards and punishments; and the faith of *Resurrection.* the Musulman is devoutly fixed on the event of the judgment and the last day. The prophet has not presumed to determine the moment of that awful catastrophe, though he darkly announces the signs, both in heaven and earth, which will precede the universal dissolution, when life shall be destroyed, and the order of creation shall be confounded in the primitive chaos. At the blast of the trumpet, new worlds will start into being; angels, genii, and men, will arise from the dead, and the human soul will again be united to the body. The doctrine of the resurrection was first entertained by the Egyptians;[106] and their mummies were embalmed, their pyramids were constructed, to preserve the ancient mansion of the soul, during a period of three thousand years. But the attempt is partial and unavailing; and it is with a more philosophic spirit that Mahomet relies on the omnipotence of the Creator, whose word can reanimate the breathless clay, and collect the innumerable atoms, that no longer retain their form or substance.[107] The intermediate state of the soul it is hard to decide; and those who most firmly believe her immaterial nature are at a loss to understand how she can think or act without the agency of the organs of sense.

The re-union of the soul and body will be followed by the final judgment of mankind; and, in his copy of the Magian picture, the *Hell and* prophet has too faithfully represented the forms of proceeding, and *paradise.* even the slow and successive operations of an earthly tribunal. By his intolerant adversaries he is upbraided for extending, even to themselves,

---

but I am afraid that much more is to be ascribed to the humanity, than to the religion, of the people.

106. See Herodotus (l. ii. c. 123.) and our learned countryman Sir John Marsham (Canon. Chronicus, p. 46.). The Ἀδης of the same writer (p. 254–274.) is an elaborate sketch of the infernal regions, as they were

painted by the fancy of the Egyptians and Greeks, of the poets and philosophers of antiquity.

107. The Koran (c. 2. p. 259, &c.; of Sale, p. 32.; of Maracci, p. 97.) relates an ingenious miracle, which satisfied the curiosity, and confirmed the faith, of Abraham.

the hope of salvation, for asserting the blackest heresy, that every man who believes in God, and accomplishes good works, may expect in the last day a favourable sentence. Such rational indifference is ill adapted to the character of a fanatic; nor is it probable that a messenger from heaven should depreciate the value and necessity of his own revelation. In the idiom of the Koran,[108] the belief of God is inseparable from that of Mahomet: the good works are those which he has enjoined; and the two qualifications imply the profession of Islam, to which all nations and all sects are equally invited. Their spiritual blindness, though excused by ignorance and crowned with virtue, will be scourged with everlasting torments; and the tears which Mahomet shed over the tomb of his mother, for whom he was forbidden to pray, display a striking contrast of humanity and enthusiasm.[109] The doom of the infidels is common: the measure of their guilt and punishment is determined by the degree of evidence which they have rejected, by the magnitude of the errors which they have entertained: the eternal mansions of the Christians, the Jews, the Sabians, the Magians, and the idolaters, are sunk below each other in the abyss; and the lowest hell is reserved for the faithless hypocrites who have assumed the mask of religion. After the greater part of mankind has been condemned for their opinions, the true believers only will be judged by their actions. The good and evil of each Musulman will be accurately weighed in a real or allegorical balance, and a singular mode of compensation will be allowed for the payment of injuries: the aggressor will refund an equivalent of his own good actions, for the benefit of the person whom he has wronged; and if he should be destitute of any moral property, the weight of his sins will be loaded with an adequate share of the demerits of the sufferer. According as the shares of guilt or virtue shall preponderate, the sentence will be pronounced, and all, without distinction, will pass over the sharp and perilous bridge of the abyss; but the innocent, treading in the footsteps of Mahomet, will gloriously enter the gates of paradise, while the guilty

---

108. The candid Reland has demonstrated, that Mahomet damns all unbelievers (de Religion. Moham. p. 128–142.), that devils will not be finally saved (p. 196–199.); that paradise will not *solely* consist of corporeal delights (p. 199–205.); and that women's souls are immortal (p. 205–209.).

109. Al Beidawi, apud Sale, Koran, c. 9. p. 164.

The refusal to pray for an unbelieving kindred, is justified, according to Mahomet, by the duty of a prophet, and the example of Abraham, who reprobated his own father as an enemy of God. Yet Abraham (he adds, c. 9. v. 116. Maracci, tom. ii. p. 317.) fuit sane pius, mitis.

will fall into the first and mildest of the seven hells. The term of expiation will vary from nine hundred to seven thousand years; but the prophet has judiciously promised, that *all* his disciples, whatever may be their sins, shall be saved, by their own faith and his intercession, from eternal damnation. It is not surprising that superstition should act most powerfully on the fears of her votaries, since the human fancy can paint with more energy the misery than the bliss of a future life. With the two simple elements of darkness and fire, we create a sensation of pain, which may be aggravated to an infinite degree by the idea of endless duration. But the same idea operates with an opposite effect on the continuity of pleasure; and too much of our present enjoyments is obtained from the relief or the comparison of evil. It is natural enough that an Arabian prophet should dwell with rapture on the groves, the fountains, and the rivers, of paradise; but instead of inspiring the blessed inhabitants with a liberal taste for harmony and science, conversation and friendship, he idly celebrates the pearls and diamonds, the robes of silk, palaces of marble, dishes of gold, rich wines, artificial dainties, numerous attendants, and the whole train of sensual and costly luxury, which becomes insipid to the owner, even in the short period of this mortal life. Seventy-two *Houris*, or black-eyed girls, of resplendent beauty, blooming youth, virgin purity, and exquisite sensibility, will be created for the use of the meanest believer; a moment of pleasure will be prolonged to a thousand years, and his faculties will be encreased an hundred fold, to render him worthy of his felicity. Notwithstanding a vulgar prejudice, the gates of heaven will be open to both sexes; but Mahomet has not specified the male companions of the female elect, lest he should either alarm the jealousy of their former husbands, or disturb their felicity, by the suspicion of an everlasting marriage. This image of a carnal paradise has provoked the indignation, perhaps the envy, of the monks: they declaim against the impure religion of Mahomet; and his modest apologists are driven to the poor excuse of figures and allegories. But the sounder and more consistent party adhere, without shame, to the literal interpretation of the Koran: useless would be the resurrection of the body, unless it were restored to the possession and exercise of its worthiest faculties; and the union of sensual and intellectual enjoyment is requisite to complete the happiness of the double animal, the perfect man. Yet the joys of the Mahometan paradise will not be confined to the indulgence of luxury and appetite; and the prophet has expressly declared, that all meaner happiness will be forgotten and despised by the saints and martyrs, who shall be admitted to the beatitude of the divine vision.[110]

Mahomet
preaches at
Mecca,
A.D. 609.

The first and most arduous conquests of Mahomet[111] were those of his wife, his servant, his pupil, and his friend;[112] since he presented himself as a prophet to those who were most conversant with his infirmities as a man. Yet Cadijah believed the words, and cherished the glory, of her husband; the obsequious and affectionate Zeid was tempted by the prospect of freedom; the illustrious Ali, the son of Abu Taleb, embraced the sentiments of his cousin with the spirit of a youthful hero; and the wealth, the moderation, the veracity of Abubeker, confirmed the religion of the prophet whom he was destined to succeed.

110. For the day of judgment, hell, paradise, &c. consult the Koran (c. 2. v. 25. c. 56. 78, &c.); with Maracci's virulent, but learned, refutation (in his notes, and in the Prodromus, part iv. p. 78. 120. 122, &c.); d'Herbelot, Bibliotheque Orientale, p. 368. 375. Reland, p. 47–61.); and Sale (p. 76–103.). The original ideas of the Magi are darkly and doubtfully explored by their apologist Dr. Hyde (Hist. Religionis Persarum, c. 33. p. 402–412. Oxon. 1760). In the article of Mahomet, Bayle has shewn how indifferently wit and philosophy supply the absence of genuine information.

111. Before I enter on the history of the prophet, it is incumbent on me to produce my evidence. The Latin, French, and English versions of the Koran, are preceded by historical discourses, and the three translators, Maracci (tom. i. p. 10–32.), Savary (tom. i. p. 1–248.), and Sale (Preliminary Discourse, p. 33–56.), had accurately studied the language and character of their author. Two professed lives of Mahomet have been composed by Dr. Prideaux (Life of Mahomet, seventh edition, London, 1718, in octavo) and the count de Boulainvilliers (Vie de Mahomet, Londres, 1730, in octavo); but the adverse wish of finding an impostor or an hero, has too often corrupted the learning of the doctor and the ingenuity of the count. The article in d'Herbelot (Bibliot. Orient.

p. 598–603.), is chiefly drawn from Novairi and Mircond; but the best and most authentic of our guides is M. Gagnier, a Frenchman by birth, and professor at Oxford of the Oriental tongues. In two elaborate works (Ismael Abulfeda de Vita et Rebus gestis Mohammedis, &c. Latine vertit, Praefatione et Notis illustravit Johannes Gagnier, Oxon. 1723, in folio. La Vie de Mahomet traduite et compilée de l'Alcoran, des Traditions authentiques de la Sonna et des meilleurs Auteurs Arabes; Amsterdam, 1748, 3 vols. in 12mo) he has interpreted, illustrated, and supplied the Arabic text of Abulfeda and Al Jannabi; the first, an enlightened prince, who reigned at Hamah, in Syria, A.D. 1310–1332 (see Gagnier Praefat. ad Abulfed.); the second, a credulous doctor, who visited Mecca A.D. 1556 (d'Herbelot, p. 397. Gagnier, tom. iii. p. 209, 210.). These are my general vouchers, and the inquisitive reader may follow the order of time, and the division of chapters. Yet I must observe, that both Abulfeda and Al Jannabi are modern historians, and that they cannot appeal to any writers of the first century of the Hegira.

112. After the Greeks, Prideaux (p. 8.) discloses the secret doubts of the wife of Mahomet. As if he had been a privy counsellor of the prophet, Boulainvilliers (p. 272, &c.) unfolds the sublime and patriotic views of Cadijah and the first disciples.

By his persuasion, ten of the most respectable citizens of Mecca were introduced to the private lessons of Islam; they yielded to the voice of reason and enthusiasm; they repeated the fundamental creed; "there is but one God, and Mahomet is the apostle of God;" and their faith, even in this life, was rewarded with riches and honours, with the command of armies and the government of kingdoms. Three years were silently employed in the conversion of fourteen proselytes, the first fruits of his mission; but in the fourth year he assumed the prophetic office, and resolving to impart to his family the light of divine truth, he prepared a banquet, a lamb, as it is said, and a bowl of milk, for the entertainment of forty guests of the race of Hashem. "Friends and kinsmen," said Mahomet to the assembly, "I offer you, and I alone can offer, the most precious of gifts, the treasures of this world and of the world to come. God has commanded me to call you to his service. Who among you will support my burthen? Who among you will be my companion and my vizir?"[113] No answer was returned, till the silence of astonishment, and doubt, and contempt, was at length broken by the impatient courage of Ali, a youth in the fourteenth year of his age. "O prophet, I am the man: whosoever rises against thee, I will dash out his teeth, tear out his eyes, break his legs, rip up his belly. O prophet, I will be thy vizir over them." Mahomet accepted his offer with transport, and Abu Taleb was ironically exhorted to respect the superior dignity of his son. In a more serious tone, the father of Ali advised his nephew to relinquish his impracticable design. "Spare your remonstrances," replied the intrepid fanatic to his uncle and benefactor; "if they should place the sun on my right-hand and the moon on my left, they should not divert me from my course." He persevered ten years in the exercise of his mission; and the religion which has overspread the East and the West, advanced with a slow and painful progress within the walls of Mecca. Yet Mahomet enjoyed the satisfaction of beholding the encrease of his infant congregation of Unitarians, who revered him as a prophet, and to whom he seasonably dispensed the spiritual nourishment of the Koran. The number of proselytes may be esteemed by the absence of eighty-three men and eighteen women, who retired to Æthiopia in the seventh year of his mission: and his party was fortified by the timely conversion of his uncle

---

113. *Vezirus, portitor, bajulus, onus ferens*; and this plebeian name was transferred by an apt metaphor to the pillars of the state (Gagnier, Not. ad Abulfed. p. 19.). I endeavour to preserve the Arabian idiom, as far as I can feel it myself, in a Latin or French translation.

Hamza, and of the fierce and inflexible Omar, who signalised in the cause of Islam the same zeal which he had exerted for its destruction. Nor was the charity of Mahomet confined to the tribe of Koreish or the precincts of Mecca: on solemn festivals, in the days of pilgrimage, he frequented the Caaba, accosted the strangers of every tribe, and urged, both in private converse and public discourse, the belief and worship of a sole Deity. Conscious of his reason and of his weakness, he asserted the liberty of conscience, and disclaimed the use of religious violence:[114] but he called the Arabs to repentance, and conjured them to remember the ancient idolaters of Ad and Thamud, whom the divine justice had swept away from the face of the earth.[115]

Is opposed by the Koreish, A.D. 613–622. The people of Mecca was hardened in their unbelief by superstition and envy. The elders of the city, the uncles of the prophet, affected to despise the presumption of an orphan, the reformer of his country: the pious orations of Mahomet in the Caaba were answered by the clamours of Abu Taleb. "Citizens and pilgrims, listen not to the tempter, hearken not to his impious novelties. Stand fast in the worship of Al Lâta and Al Uzzah." Yet the son of Abdallah was ever dear to the aged chief; and he protected the fame and person of his nephew against the assaults of the Koreishites, who had long been jealous of the pre-eminence of the family of Hashem. Their malice was coloured with the pretence of religion: in the age of Job, the crime of impiety was punished by the Arabian magistrate;[116] and Mahomet was guilty of deserting and denying the national deities. But so loose was the policy of Mecca, that the leaders of the Koreish, instead of accusing a criminal, were compelled to employ the measures of persuasion or violence. They repeatedly addressed Abu Taleb in the style of reproach

114. The passages of the Koran in behalf of toleration, are strong and numerous: c. 2. v. 257. c. 16. 129. c. 17. 54. c. 45. 15. c. 50. 39. c. 88. 21, &c. with the notes of Maracci and Sale. This character alone may generally decide the doubts of the learned, whether a chapter was revealed at Mecca or Medina.
115. See the Koran (passim, and especially c. 7. p. 123, 124, &c.), and the tradition of the Arabs (Pocock, Specimen, p. 35–37.). The caverns of the tribe of Thamud, fit for men of the ordinary stature, were shewn in the midway between Medina and Damascus

(Abulfed. Arabiæ Descript. p. 43, 44.), and may be probably ascribed to the Troglodytes of the primitive world (Michaelis, ad Lowth de Poesi Hebræor. p. 131–134. Recherches sur les Egyptiens, tom. ii. p. 48, &c.).
116. In the time of Job, the crime of impiety was punished by the Arabian magistrate (c. 31. v. 26, 27, 28.). I blush for a respectable prelate (de Poesi Hebræorum, p. 650, 651. edit. Michaelis; and letter of a late professor in the university of Oxford, p. 15–53.), who justifies and applauds this patriarchal inquisition.

and menace. "Thy nephew reviles our religion; he accuses our wise forefathers of ignorance and folly; silence him quickly, lest he kindle tumult and discord in the city. If he persevere, we shall draw our swords against him and his adherents, and thou wilt be responsible for the blood of thy fellow-citizens." The weight and moderation of Abu Taleb eluded the violence of religious faction; the most helpless or timid of the disciples retired to Æthiopia, and the prophet withdrew himself to various places of strength in the town and country. As he was still supported by his family, the rest of the tribe of Koreish engaged themselves to renounce all intercourse with the children of Hashem, neither to buy nor sell, neither to marry nor to give in marriage, but to pursue them with implacable enmity, till they should deliver the person of Mahomet to the justice of the gods. The decree was suspended in the Caaba before the eyes of the nation; the messengers of the Koreish pursued the Musulman exiles in the heart of Africa: they besieged the prophet and his most faithful followers, intercepted their water, and inflamed their mutual animosity by the retaliation of injuries and insults. A doubtful truce restored the appearances of concord; till the death of Abu Taleb abandoned Mahomet to the power of his enemies, at the moment when he was deprived of his domestic comforts by the loss of his faithful and generous Cadijah. Abu Sophian, the chief of the branch of Ommiyah, succeeded to the principality of the republic of Mecca. A zealous votary of the idols, a mortal foe of the line of Hashem, he convened an assembly of the Koreishites and their allies, to decide the fate of the apostle. His imprisonment might provoke the despair of his enthusiasm; and the exile of an eloquent and popular fanatic would diffuse the mischief through the provinces of Arabia. His death was resolved; and they agreed that a sword from each tribe should be buried in his heart, to divide the guilt of his blood and baffle the vengeance of the Hashemites. An angel or a spy revealed their conspiracy; and flight was the only resource of Mahomet.[117] At the dead of night, accompanied by his friend Abubeker, he silently escaped from his house: the assassins watched at the door; but they were deceived by the figure of Ali, who reposed on the bed, and was covered with the green vestment of the apostle. The Koreish respected the piety of the heroic youth; but some verses of Ali, which are still extant, exhibit an interesting picture of

and driven from Mecca, A.D. 622.

117. D'Herbelot, Bibliot. Orient. p. 445. He quotes a particular history of the flight of Mahomet.

his anxiety, his tenderness, and his religious confidence. Three days Mahomet and his companion were concealed in the cave of Thor, at the distance of a league from Mecca; and in the close of each evening, they received from the son and daughter of Abubeker, a secret supply of intelligence and food. The diligence of the Koreish explored every haunt in the neighbourhood of the city, they arrived at the entrance of the cavern; but the providential deceit of a spider's web and a pigeon's nest, is supposed to convince them that the place was solitary and inviolate. "We are only two," said the trembling Abubeker. "There is a third," replied the prophet; "it is God himself." No sooner was the pursuit abated, than the two fugitives issued from the rock, and mounted their camels: on the road to Medina, they were overtaken by the emissaries of the Koreish; they redeemed themselves with prayers and promises from their hands. In this eventful moment, the lance of an Arab might have changed the history of the world. The flight of the prophet from Mecca to Medina has fixed the memorable æra of the *Hegira*,[118] which, at the end of twelve centuries, still discriminates the lunar years of the Mahometan nations.[119]

Received as prince of Medina, A.D. 622. The religion of the Koran might have perished in its cradle, had not Medina embraced with faith and reverence the holy outcasts of Mecca. Medina, or the *city*, known under the name of Yathreb, before it was sanctified by the throne of the prophet, was divided between the tribes of the Charegites and the Awsites, whose hereditary feud was rekindled by the slightest provocations: two colonies of Jews, who boasted a sacerdotal race, were their humble allies, and without converting the Arabs, they introduced the taste of science and religion, which distinguished Medina as the city of the book. Some of her noblest citizens, in a pilgrimage to the Caaba, were converted by the preaching of Mahomet; on their return they diffused the belief of God and his prophet, and the new alliance was ratified by their deputies in two secret and nocturnal interviews on a hill in the suburbs of Mecca. In the

118. The *Hegira* was instituted by Omar, the second caliph, in imitation of the æra of the martyrs of the Christians (d'Herbelot, p. 444.); and properly commenced sixty-eight days before the flight of Mahomet, with the first of Moharren, or first day of that Arabian year, which coincides with Friday July 16th, A.D. 622 (Abulfeda, Vit. Moham. c. 22, 23. p. 45-

50.; and Greaves's edition of Ullug Beig's Epochæ Arabum, &c. c. 1. p. 8. 10, &c.).
119. Mahomet's life, from his mission to the Hegira, may be found in Abulfeda (p. 14-45.) and Gagnier (tom. i. p. 134-251. 342-383.). The legend from p. 187-234. is vouched by Al Jannabi, and disdained by Abulfeda.

first, ten Charegites and two Awsites united in faith and love, protested in
the name of their wives, their children, and their absent brethren, that they
would for ever profess the creed, and observe the precepts, of the Koran.
The second was a political association, the first vital spark of the empire of
the Saracens.[120] Seventy-three men and two women of Medina held a
solemn conference with Mahomet, his kinsmen, and his disciples; and
pledged themselves to each other by a mutual oath of fidelity. They
promised in the name of the city, that if he should be banished, they would
receive him as a confederate, obey him as a leader, and defend him to the
last extremity, like their wives and children. "But if you are recalled by
your country," they asked with a flattering anxiety, "will you not abandon
your new allies?" "All things," replied Mahomet with a smile, "are now
common between us; your blood is as my blood, your ruin as my ruin.
We are bound to each other by the ties of honour and interest. I am your
friend, and the enemy of your foes." "But if we are killed in your service,
what," exclaimed the deputies of Medina, "will be our reward?" "PARA-
DISE," replied the prophet. "Stretch forth thy hand." He stretched it forth,
and they reiterated the oath of allegiance and fidelity. Their treaty was
ratified by the people, who unanimously embraced the profession of Islam;
they rejoiced in the exile of the apostle, but they trembled for his safety,
and impatiently expected his arrival. After a perilous and rapid journey
along the sea-coast, he halted at Koba, two miles from the city, and made
his public entry into Medina, sixteen days after his flight from Mecca.
Five hundred of the citizens advanced to meet him; he was hailed with
acclamations of loyalty and devotion; Mahomet was mounted on a she-
camel, an umbrella shaded his head, and a turban was unfurled before him
to supply the deficiency of a standard. His bravest disciples, who had been
scattered by the storm, assembled round his person: and the equal, though
various, merit of the Moslems was distinguished by the names of *Mohagerians*
and *Ansars*, the fugitives of Mecca, and the auxiliaries of Medina. To
eradicate the seeds of jealousy, Mahomet judiciously coupled his principal
followers with the rights and obligations of brethren, and when Ali found
himself without a peer, the prophet tenderly declared, that *he* would be
the companion and brother of the noble youth. The expedient was crowned

120. The triple inauguration of Mahomet is
described by Abulfeda (p. 30. 33. 40. 86.) and
Gagnier (tom. i. p. 342, &c. 349, &c. tom. ii.
p. 223, &c.).

with success; the holy fraternity was respected in peace and war, and the two parties vied with each other in a generous emulation of courage and fidelity. Once only the concord was slightly ruffled by an accidental quarrel; a patriot of Medina arraigned the insolence of the strangers, but the hint of their expulsion was heard with abhorrence, and his own son most eagerly offered to lay at the apostle's feet the head of his father.

His regal dignity, A.D. 622– 632.   From his establishment at Medina, Mahomet assumed the exercise of the regal and sacerdotal office; and it was impious to appeal from a judge whose decrees were inspired by the divine wisdom. A small portion of ground, the patrimony of two orphans, was acquired by gift or purchase;[121] on that chosen spot, he built an house and a mosch more venerable in their rude simplicity than the palaces and temples of the Assyrian caliphs. His seal of gold, or silver, was inscribed with the apostolic title; when he prayed and preached in the weekly assembly, he leaned against the trunk of a palm-tree; and it was long before he indulged himself in the use of a chair or pulpit of rough timber.[122] After a reign of six years, fifteen hundred Moslems, in arms and in the field, renewed their oath of allegiance; and their chief repeated the assurance of protection till the death of the last member, or the final dissolution of the party. It was in the same camp that the deputy of Mecca was astonished by the attention of the faithful to the words and looks of the prophet, by the eagerness with which they collected his spittle, an hair that dropt on the ground, the refuse water of his lustrations, as if they participated in some degree of the prophetic virtue. "I have seen," said he, "the Chosroes of Persia and the Cæsar of Rome, but never did I behold a king among his subjects like Mahomet among his companions." The devout fervour of enthusiasm acts with more energy and truth than the cold and formal servility of courts.

---

121. Prideaux (Life of Mahomet, p. 44.) reviles the wickedness of the impostor, who despoiled two poor orphans, the sons of a carpenter; a reproach which he drew from the Disputatio contra Saracenos, composed in Arabic before the year 1130; but the honest Gagnier (ad Abulfed. p. 53.) has shewn that they were deceived by the word *Al Nagjar,* which signifies, in this place, not an obscure trade, but a noble tribe of Arabs. The desolate state of the ground is described by Abulfeda;

and his worthy interpreter has proved, from Al Bochari, the offer of a price; from Al Jannabi, the fair purchase; and from Ahmed Ben Joseph, the payment of the money by the generous Abubeker. On these grounds the prophet must be honourably acquitted.

122. Al Jannabi (apud Gagnier, tom. ii. p. 246. 324.) describes the seal and pulpit, as two venerable relics of the apostle of God; and the portrait of his court is taken from Abulfeda (c. 44. p. 85.).

In the state of nature every man has a right to defend, by force *He declares* of arms, his person and his possessions; to repel, or even to prevent, *war against* the violence of his enemies, and to extend his hostilities to a *the infidels.* reasonable measure of satisfaction and retaliation. In the free society of the Arabs, the duties of subject and citizen imposed a feeble restraint; and Mahomet, in the exercise of a peaceful and benevolent mission, had been despoiled and banished by the injustice of his countrymen. The choice of an independent people had exalted the fugitive of Mecca to the rank of a sovereign; and he was invested with the just prerogative of forming alliances, and of waging offensive or defensive war. The imperfection of human rights was supplied and armed by the plenitude of divine power: the prophet of Medina assumed, in his new revelations, a fiercer and more sanguinary tone, which proves that his former moderation was the effect of weakness:[123] the means of persuasion had been tried, the season of forbearance was elapsed, and he was now commanded to propagate his religion by the sword, to destroy the monuments of idolatry, and, without regarding the sanctity of days or months, to pursue the unbelieving nations of the earth. The same bloody precepts, so repeatedly inculcated in the Koran, are ascribed by the author to the Pentateuch and the Gospel. But the mild tenor of the evangelic style may explain an ambiguous text, that Jesus did not bring peace on the earth, but a sword: his patient and humble virtues should not be confounded with the intolerant zeal of princes and bishops, who have disgraced the name of his disciples. In the prosecution of religious war, Mahomet might appeal with more propriety to the example of Moses, of the judges and the kings of Israel. The military laws of the Hebrews are still more rigid than those of the Arabian legislator.[124] The Lord of hosts marched in person before the Jews: if a city resisted their summons, the males, without distinction, were put to the sword: the seven nations of Canaan were devoted to destruction; and neither repentance nor conversion could shield them from the inevitable doom, that no creature within their precincts should be left alive. The fair option of

---

123. The viii[th] and ix[th] chapters of the Koran are the loudest and most vehement; and Maracci (Prodromus, part iv. p. 59—64.) has inveighed with more justice than discretion against the double-dealing of the impostor.
124. The xth and xx[th] chapters of Deuteronomy, with the practical comments of Joshua, David, &c. are read with more awe than satisfaction by the pious Christians of the present age. But the bishops, as well as the rabbis of former times, have beat the drum-ecclesiastic with pleasure and success (Sale's Preliminary Discourse, p. 142, 143.).

friendship, or submission, or battle, was proposed to the enemies of Mahomet. If they professed the creed of Islam, they were admitted to all the temporal and spiritual benefits of his primitive disciples, and marched under the same banner to extend the religion which they had embraced. The clemency of the prophet was decided by his interest, yet he seldom trampled on a prostrate enemy; and he seems to promise, that, on the payment of a tribute, the least guilty of his unbelieving subjects might be indulged in their worship, or at least in their imperfect faith. In the first months of his reign, he practised the lessons of holy warfare, and displayed his white banner before the gates of Medina: the martial apostle fought in person at nine battles or sieges;[125] and fifty enterprises of war were atchieved in ten years by himself or his lieutenants. The Arab continued to unite the professions of a merchant and a robber; and his petty excursions for the defence or the attack of a caravan insensibly prepared his troops for the conquest of Arabia. The distribution of the spoil was regulated by a divine law:[126] the whole was faithfully collected in one common mass: a fifth of the gold and silver, the prisoners and cattle, the moveables and immoveables, was reserved by the prophet for pious and charitable uses; the remainder was shared in adequate portions by the soldiers who had obtained the victory or guarded the camp: the rewards of the slain devolved to their widows and orphans; and the encrease of cavalry was encouraged by the allotment of a double share to the horse and to the man. From all sides the roving Arabs were allured to the standard of religion and plunder: the apostle sanctified the licence of embracing the female captives as their wives or concubines; and the enjoyment of wealth and beauty was a feeble type of the joys of paradise prepared for the valiant martyrs of the faith. "The sword," says Mahomet, "is the key of heaven and of hell: a drop of blood shed in the cause of God, a night spent in arms, is of more avail than two months of fasting or prayer: whosoever falls in battle, his sins are forgiven: at the day of judgment his wounds shall be resplendent as vermillion and odoriferous as musk; and the loss of his limbs shall be

---

125. Abulfeda, in Vit. Moham. p. 156. The private arsenal of the apostle consisted of nine swords, three lances, seven pikes or half-pikes, a quiver and three bows, seven cuirasses, three shields, and two helmets (Gagnier, tom. iii. p. 328–334.), with a large white standard, a black banner (p. 335.), twenty horses (p. 322.),

&c. Two of his martial sayings are recorded by tradition (Gagnier, tom. ii. p. 88. 337.).
126. The whole subject de jure belli Mohammedanorum, is exhausted in a separate dissertation by the learned Reland (Dissertationes Miscellaneæ, tom. iii. Dissert. x. p. 3–53.).

supplied by the wings of angels and cherubim." The intrepid souls of the Arabs were fired with enthusiasm: the picture of the invisible world was strongly painted on their imagination; and the death which they had always despised became an object of hope and desire. The Koran inculcates, in the most absolute sense, the tenets of fate and predestination, which would extinguish both industry and virtue, if the actions of man were governed by his speculative belief. Yet their influence in every age has exalted the courage of the Saracens and Turks. The first companions of Mahomet advanced to battle with a fearless confidence: there is no danger where there is no chance: they were ordained to perish in their beds; or they were safe and invulnerable amidst the darts of the enemy.[127]

Perhaps the Koreish would have been content with the flight of Mahomet, had they not been provoked and alarmed by the vengeance of an enemy, who could intercept their Syrian trade as it passed and repassed through the territory of Medina. Abu Sophian himself, with only thirty or forty followers, conducted a wealthy caravan of a thousand camels: the fortune or dexterity of his march escaped the vigilance of Mahomet; but the chief of the Koreish was informed that the holy robbers were placed in ambush to await his return. He dispatched a messenger to his brethren of Mecca, and they were roused, by the fear of losing their merchandise and their provisions, unless they hastened to his relief with the military force of the city. The sacred band of Mahomet was formed of three hundred and thirteen Moslems, of whom seventy-seven were fugitives, and the rest auxiliaries: they mounted by turns a train of seventy camels (the camels of Yathreb were formidable in war); but such was the poverty of his first disciples, that only two could appear on horseback in the field.[128] In the fertile and famous vale of

His defensive wars against the Koreish of Mecca.

---

127. The doctrine of absolute predestination, on which few religions can reproach each other, is sternly exposed in the Koran (c. 3. p. 52, 53. c. 4. p. 70, &c. with the notes of Sale, and c. 17. p. 413. with those of Maracci). Reland (de Relig. Mohamm. p. 61–64.) and Sale (Prelim. Discourse, p. 103.) represent the opinions of the doctors, and our modern travellers the confidence, the fading confidence, of the Turks.

128. Al Jannabi (apud Gagnier, tom. ii. p. 9.)

allows him seventy or eighty horse; and on two other occasions prior to the battle of Ohud, he enlists a body of thirty (p. 10.), and of 500 (p. 66.) troopers. Yet the Musulmans, in the field of Ohud, had no more than two horses, according to the better sense of Abulfeda (in Vit. Mohamm. p. xxxi. p. 65.). In the *stony* province, the camels were numerous; but the horse appears to have been less common than in the *Happy* or the *Desert* Arabia.

Beder,[129] three stations from Medina, he was informed by his scouts of the caravan that approached on one side; of the Koreish, one hundred horse, eight hundred and fifty foot, who advanced on the other. After a short debate, he sacrificed the prospect of wealth to the pursuit of glory and revenge; and a slight intrenchment was formed, to cover his troops, and a stream of fresh water that glided through the valley. "O God," he ex-

Battle of Beder, A.D. 623.

claimed as the numbers of the Koreish descended from the hills, "O God, if these are destroyed, by whom wilt thou be worshipped on the earth? – Courage, my children, close your ranks; discharge your arrows, and the day is your own." At these words he placed himself, with Abubeker, on a throne or pulpit,[130] and instantly demanded the succour of Gabriel and three thousand angels. His eye was fixed on the field of battle: the Musulmans fainted and were pressed: in that decisive moment the prophet started from his throne, mounted his horse, and cast a handful of sand into the air; "Let their faces be covered with confusion." Both armies heard the thunder of his voice: their fancy beheld the angelic warriors:[131] the Koreish trembled and fled: seventy of the bravest were slain; and seventy captives adorned the first victory of the faithful. The dead bodies of the Koreish were despoiled and insulted: two of the most obnoxious prisoners were punished with death; and the ransom of the others, four thousand drams of silver, compensated in some degree the escape of the caravan. But it was in vain that the camels of Abu Sophian

---

129. Bedder Houneene, twenty miles from Medina, and forty from Mecca, is on the high road of the caravan of Egypt; and the pilgrims annually commemorate the prophet's victory by illuminations, rockets, &c. Shaw's Travels, p. 477.

130. The place to which Mahomet retired during the action is styled by Gagnier (in Abulfeda, c. 27. p. 58. Vie de Mahomet, tom. ii. p. 30. 33.), *Umbraculum, une loge de bois avec une porte.* The same Arabic word is rendered by Reiske (Annales Moslemici Abulfedæ, p. 23.) by *Solium, Suggestus editior*; and the difference is of the utmost moment for the honour both of the interpreter and of the hero. I am sorry to observe the pride and acrimony with which Reiske chastises his fellow-labourer. Sæpe sic vertit, ut integræ

paginæ nequeant nisi unâ liturâ corrigi: Arabice non satis callebat et carebat judicio critico. J. J. Reiske, Prodidagmata ad Hagji Chalisæ Tabulas, p. 228. ad calcem Abulfedæ Syriæ Tabulæ; Lipsiæ, 1766, in 4º.

131. The loose expressions of the Koran (c. 3. p. 124, 125. c. 8. p. 9.) allow the commentators to fluctuate between the numbers of 1000, 3000, or 9000 angels; and the smallest of these might suffice for the slaughter of seventy of the Koreish (Maracci, Alcoran, tom. ii. p. 131.). Yet the same scholiasts confess, that this angelic band was not visible to any mortal eye (Maracci, p. 297.). They refine on the words (c. 8. 16.), "not thou, but God, &c." (d'Herbelot, Bibliot. Orientale, p. 600, 601.).

explored a new road through the desert and along the Euphrates: they were overtaken by the diligence of the Musulmans; and wealthy must have been the prize, if twenty thousand drams could be set apart for the fifth of the apostle. The resentment of the public and private loss stimulated Abu Sophian to collect a body of three thousand men, seven hundred of whom were armed with cuirasses, and two hundred were mounted on horseback: three thousand camels attended his march; and his wife Henda, with fifteen matrons of Mecca, incessantly sounded their timbrels to animate the troops, and to magnify the greatness of Hobal, the most popular deity of the Caaba. The standard of God and Mahomet was upheld by nine hundred and fifty believers: the *of Ohud, A.D. 623.* disproportion of numbers was not more alarming than in the field of Beder; and their presumption of victory prevailed against the divine and human sense of the apostle. The second battle was fought on mount Ohud, six miles to the north of Medina:[132] the Koreish advanced in the form of a crescent; and the right wing of cavalry was led by Caled, the fiercest and most successful of the Arabian warriors. The troops of Mahomet were skilfully posted on the declivity of the hill; and their rear was guarded by a detachment of fifty archers. The weight of their charge impelled and broke the centre of the idolaters; but in the pursuit they lost the advantage of their ground: the archers deserted their station: the Musulmans were tempted by the spoil, disobeyed their general, and disordered their ranks. The intrepid Caled, wheeling his cavalry on their flank and rear, exclaimed, with a loud voice, that Mahomet was slain. He was indeed wounded in the face with a javelin: two of his teeth were shattered with a stone; yet, in the midst of tumult and dismay, he reproached the infidels with the murder of a prophet; and blessed the friendly hand that staunched his blood, and conveyed him to a place of safety. Seventy martyrs died for the sins of the people: they fell said the apostle, in pairs, each brother embracing his lifeless companion:[133] their bodies were mangled by the inhuman females of Mecca; and the wife of Abu Sophian tasted the entrails of Hamza, the uncle of Mahomet. They might applaud their superstition and satiate their fury; but the Musulmans soon rallied in the field, and the

132. Geograph. Nubiensis, p. 47.
133. In the iii[d] chapter of the Koran (p. 50–53. with Sale's notes), the prophet alleges some poor excuses for the defeat of Ohud.

Koreish wanted strength or courage to undertake the siege of Medina. It

*The nations,
or the ditch,
A.D. 625.*

was attacked the ensuing year by an army of ten thousand enemies; and this third expedition is variously named from the *nations*, which marched under the banner of Abu Sophian, from the *ditch* which was drawn before the city, and a camp of three thousand Musulmans. The prudence of Mahomet, declined a general engagement: the valour of Ali was signalized in single combat; and the war was protracted twenty days, till the final separation of the confederates. A tempest of wind, rain, and hail, overturned their tents: their private quarrels were fomented by an insidious adversary; and the Koreish, deserted by their allies, no longer hoped to subvert the throne, or to check the conquests, of their invincible exile.[134]

*Mahomet
subdues the
Jews of Arabia,
A.D. 623–627.*

The choice of Jerusalem for the first kebla of prayer, discovers the early propensity of Mahomet in favour of the Jews; and happy would it have been for their temporal interest, had they recognised, in the Arabian prophet, the hope of Israel and the promised Messiah. Their obstinacy converted his friendship into implacable hatred, with which he pursued that unfortunate people to the last moment of his life: and in the double character of an apostle and a conqueror, his persecution was extended to both worlds.[135] The Kainoka dwelt at Medina under the protection of the city; he seized the occasion of an accidental tumult, and summoned them to embrace his religion, or contend with him in battle. "Alas," replied the trembling Jews, "we are ignorant of the use of arms, but we persevere in the faith and worship of our fathers; why wilt thou reduce us to the necessity of a just defence?" The unequal conflict was terminated in fifteen days; and it was with extreme reluctance that Mahomet yielded to the importunity of his allies, and consented to spare the lives of the captives. But their riches were confiscated, their arms became more effectual in the hands of the Musulmans; and a wretched colony of seven hundred exiles was driven with their wives and children to implore a refuge on the confines of Syria. The Nadhirites were more guilty, since they conspired in a friendly interview

134. For the detail of the three Koreish wars, of Beder, of Ohud, and of the ditch, peruse Abulfeda (p. 56–61. 64–69. 73–77.), Gagnier (tom. ii. p. 23–45. 70–96. 120–139.), with the proper articles of d'Herbelot, and the abridgments of Elmacin (Hist. Saracen. p. 6,

7.) and Abulpharagius (Dynast. p. 102.).
135. The wars of Mahomet against the Jewish tribes, of Kainoka, the Nadhirites, Koraidha, and Chaibar, are related by Abulfeda (p. 61. 71. 77. 87, &c.) and Gagnier (tom. ii. p. 61–65. 107–112. 139–148. 268–294.).

to assassinate the prophet. He besieged their castle three miles from Medina, but their resolute defence obtained an honourable capitulation; and the garrison, sounding their trumpets and beating their drums, was permitted to depart with the honours of war. The Jews had excited and joined the war of the Koreish: no sooner had the *nations* retired from the *ditch*, than Mahomet, without laying aside his armour, marched on the same day to extirpate the hostile race of the children of Koraidha. After a resistance of twenty-five days, they surrendered at discretion. They trusted to the intercession of their old allies of Medina: they could not be ignorant that fanaticism obliterates the feelings of humanity. A venerable elder, to whose judgment they appealed, pronounced the sentence of their death: seven hundred Jews were dragged in chains to the market-place of the city: they descended alive into the grave prepared for their execution and burial; and the apostle beheld with an inflexible eye the slaughter of his helpless enemies. Their sheep and camels were inherited by the Musul-mans: three hundred cuirasses, five hundred pikes, a thousand lances, composed the most useful portion of the spoil. Six days journey to the north-east of Medina, the ancient and wealthy town of Chaibar was the seat of the Jewish power in Arabia; the territory, a fertile spot in the desert, was covered with plantations and cattle, and protected by eight castles, some of which were esteemed of impregnable strength. The forces of Mahomet consisted of two hundred horse and fourteen hundred foot: in the succession of eight regular and painful sieges they were exposed to danger, and fatigue, and hunger; and the most undaunted chiefs despaired of the event. The apostle revived their faith and courage by the example of Ali, on whom he bestowed the surname of the Lion of God: perhaps we may believe that an Hebrew champion of gigantic stature was cloven to the chest by his irresistible scymetar; but we cannot praise the modesty of romance, which represents him as tearing from its hinges the gate of a fortress, and wielding the ponderous buckler in his left-hand.[136] After the reduction of the castles, the town of Chaibar submitted to the yoke. The chief of the tribe was tortured, in the presence of Mahomet, to force a confession of his hidden treasure: the industry of the shepherds and husbandmen was rewarded with a precarious toleration: they were

---

136. Abu Rafe, the servant of Mahomet, is said to affirm, that he himself, and seven other men, afterwards tried, without success, to move the same gate from the ground (Abul-feda, p. 90.). Abu Rafe was an eye-witness, but who will witness for Abu Rafe?

permitted, so long as it should please the conqueror, to improve their patrimony, in equal shares, for *his* emolument and their own. Under the reign of Omar, the Jews of Chaibar were transplanted to Syria; and the caliph alleged the injunction of his dying master, that one and the true religion should be professed in his native land of Arabia.[137]

Submission of Mecca, A.D. 629.

Five times each day the eyes of Mahomet were turned towards Mecca,[138] and he was urged by the most sacred and powerful motives to revisit, as a conqueror, the city and the temple from whence he had been driven as an exile. The Caaba was present to his waking and sleeping fancy: an idle dream was translated into vision and prophecy; he unfurled the holy banner; and a rash promise of success too hastily dropped from the lips of the apostle. His march from Medina to Mecca, displayed the peaceful and solemn pomp of a pilgrimage: seventy camels chosen and bedecked for sacrifice, preceded the van; the sacred territory was respected, and the captives were dismissed without ransom to proclaim his clemency and devotion. But no sooner did Mahomet descend into the plain, within a day's journey of the city, than he exclaimed, "they have clothed themselves with the skins of tygers;" the numbers and resolution of the Koreish opposed his progress; and the roving Arabs of the desert might desert or betray a leader whom they had followed for the hopes of spoil. The intrepid fanatic sunk into a cool and cautious politician: he waved in the treaty his title of apostle of God, concluded with the Koreish and their allies a truce of ten years, engaged to restore the fugitives of Mecca who should embrace his religion, and stipulated only, for the ensuing year, the humble privilege of entering the city as a friend, and of remaining three days to accomplish the rites of the pilgrimage. A cloud of shame and sorrow hung on the retreat of the Musulmans, and their disappointment might justly accuse the failure of a prophet who had so often appealed to the evidence of success. The faith and hope of the pilgrims were rekindled by the prospect of Mecca: their swords were sheathed; seven times in the footsteps of the apostle they encompassed the Caaba:

137. The banishment of the Jews is attested by Elmacin (Hist. Saracen. p. 9.) and the great Al Zabari (Gagnier, tom. ii. p. 285.). Yet Niebuhr (Description de l'Arabie, p. 324.) believes, that the Jewish religion, and Kareite sect, are still professed by the tribe of Chaibar; and that in the plunder of the caravans, the disciples of Moses are the confederates of those of Mahomet.

138. The successive steps of the reduction of Mecca are related by Abulfeda (p. 84–87. 97–100. 102–111.) and Gagnier (tom. ii. p. 209–245. 309–322. tom. iii. p. 1–58.), Elmacin (Hist. Saracen. p. 8, 9, 10.), Abulpharagius (Dynast. p. 103.).

the Koreish had retired to the hills, and Mahomet, after the customary sacrifice, evacuated the city on the fourth day. The people was edified by his devotion; the hostile chiefs were awed or divided, or seduced; and both Caled and Amrou, the future conquerors of Syria and Egypt, most seasonably deserted the sinking cause of idolatry. The power of Mahomet was encreased by the submission of the Arabian tribes; ten thousand soldiers were assembled for the conquest of Mecca, and the idolaters, the weaker party, were easily convicted of violating the truce. Enthusiasm and discipline impelled the march and preserved the secret, till the blaze of ten thousand fires proclaimed to the astonished Koreish, the design, the approach, and the irresistible force of the enemy. The haughty Abu Sophian presented the keys of the city, admired the variety of arms and ensigns that passed before him in review; observed that the son of Abdallah had acquired a mighty kingdom, and confessed, under the scymetar of Omar, that he was the apostle of the true God. The return of Marius and Sylla was stained with the blood of the Romans: the revenge of Mahomet was stimulated by religious zeal, and his injured followers were eager to execute or to prevent the order of a massacre. Instead of indulging their passions and his own,[139] the victorious exile forgave the guilt, and united the factions, of Mecca. His troops, in three divisions, marched into the city: eight and twenty of the inhabitants were slain by the sword of Caled; eleven men and six women were proscribed by the sentence of Mahomet; but he blamed the cruelty of his lieutenant; and several of the most obnoxious victims were indebted for their lives to his clemency or contempt. The chiefs of the Koreish were prostrate at his feet. "What mercy can you expect from the man whom you have wronged?" "We confide in the generosity of our kinsman." "And you shall not confide in vain: begone! you are safe, you are free." The people of Mecca deserved their pardon by the profession of Islam; and after an exile of seven years, the fugitive missionary was inthroned as the prince and prophet of his native country.[140] But the three hundred and sixty idols of the Caaba were ignominiously

139. After the conquest of Mecca, the Mahomet of Voltaire imagines and perpetrates the most horrid crimes. The poet confesses, that he is not supported by the truth of history, and can only allege, que celui qui fait la guerre à sa patrie au nom de Dieu, est capable de tout (Oeuvres de Voltaire, tom. xv. p. 282.). The maxim is neither charitable nor philosophic; and some reverence is surely due to the fame of heroes and the religion of nations. I am informed that a Turkish ambassador at Paris was much scandalized at the representation of this tragedy.

140. The Mahometan doctors still dispute, whether Mecca was reduced by force or consent (Abulfeda, p. 107, et Gagnier ad locum);

broken: the house of God was purified and adorned; as an example to future times, the apostle again fulfilled the duties of a pilgrim; and a perpetual law was enacted that no unbeliever should dare to set his foot on the territory of the holy city.[141]

Conquest of Arabia, A.D. 629–632. The conquest of Mecca determined the faith and obedience of the Arabian tribes;[142] who, according to the vicissitudes of fortune, had obeyed or disregarded the eloquence or the arms of the prophet. Indifference for rites and opinions still marks the character of the Bedoweens; and they might accept, as loosely as they hold, the doctrine of the Koran. Yet an obstinate remnant still adhered to the religion and liberty of their ancestors, and the war of Honain derived a proper appellation from the *idols*, whom Mahomet had vowed to destroy, and whom the confederates of Tayef had sworn to defend.[143] Four thousand pagans advanced with secrecy and speed to surprise the conqueror; they pitied and despised the supine negligence of the Koreish, but they depended on the wishes, and perhaps the aid, of a people who had so lately renounced their gods, and bowed beneath the yoke of their enemy. The banners of Medina and Mecca were displayed by the prophet; a crowd of Bedoweens encreased the strength or numbers of the army, and twelve thousand Musulmans entertained a rash and sinful presumption of their invincible strength. They descended without precaution into the valley of Honain: the heights had been occupied by the archers and slingers of the confederates; their numbers were oppressed, their discipline was confounded, their courage was appalled, and the Koreish smiled at their impending destruction. The prophet, on his white mule, was encompassed by the enemies; he attempted to rush against their spears in search of a

---

and this verbal controversy is of as much moment, as our own about William the *Conqueror*.

141. In excluding the Christians from the peninsula of Arabia, the province of Hejaz, or the navigation of the Red Sea, Chardin (Voyages en Perse, tom. iv. p. 166.) and Reland (Dissert. Miscell. tom. iii. p. 51.) are more rigid than the Musulmans themselves. The Christians are received without scruple into the ports of Mocha, and even of Gedda, and it is only the city and precincts of Mecca that are inaccessible to the profane (Niebuhr,

Description de l'Arabie, p. 308, 309. Voyage en Arabie, tom. i. p. 205. 248, &c.).

142. Abulfeda, p. 112–115. Gagnier, tom. iii. p. 67–88. D'Herbelot, MOHAMMED.

143. The siege of Tayef, division of the spoil, &c. are related by Abulfeda (p. 117–123.); and Gagnier, (tom. iii. p. 88–111.). It is Al Jannabi who mentions the engines and engineers of the tribe of Daws. The fertile spot of Tayef was supposed to be a piece of the land of Syria detached and dropped in the general deluge.

glorious death: ten of his faithful companions interposed their weapons and their breasts; three of these fell dead at his feet: "O my brethren," he repeatedly cried with sorrow and indignation, "I am the son of Abdallah, I am the apostle of truth! O man stand fast in the faith! O God send down thy succour!" His uncle Abbas, who, like the heroes of Homer, excelled in the loudness of his voice, made the valley resound with the recital of the gifts and promises of God: the flying Moslems returned from all sides to the holy standard; and Mahomet observed with pleasure, that the furnace was again rekindled: his conduct and example restored the battle, and he animated his victorious troops to inflict a merciless revenge on the authors of their shame. From the field of Honain, he marched without delay to the siege of Tayef, sixty miles to the south-east of Mecca, a fortress of strength, whose fertile lands produce the fruits of Syria in the midst of the Arabian desert. A friendly tribe, instructed (I know not how) in the art of sieges, supplied him with a train of battering rams and military engines, with a body of five hundred artificers. But it was in vain that he offered freedom to the slaves of Tayef; that he violated his own laws by the extirpation of the fruit-trees; that the ground was opened by the miners; that the breach was assaulted by the troops. After a siege of twenty days, the prophet sounded a retreat, but he retreated with a song of devout triumph, and affected to pray for the repentance and safety of the unbelieving city. The spoil of this fortunate expedition amounted to six thousand captives, twenty-four thousand camels, forty thousand sheep, and four thousand ounces of silver: a tribe who had fought at Honain, redeemed their prisoners by the sacrifice of their idols; but Mahomet compensated the loss, by resigning to the soldiers his fifth of the plunder, and wished for their sake, that he possessed as many head of cattle as there were trees in the province of Tehama. Instead of chastising the disaffection of the Koreish, he endeavoured to cut out their tongues (his own expression), and to secure their attachment by a superior measure of liberality: Abu Sophian alone was presented with three hundred camels and twenty ounces of silver; and Mecca was sincerely converted to the profitable religion of the Koran. The *fugitives* and *auxiliaries* complained, that they who had borne the burthen were neglected in the season of victory. "Alas," replied their artful leader, "suffer me to conciliate these recent enemies, these doubtful proselytes, by the gift of some perishable goods. To your guard I entrust my life and fortunes. You are the companions of my exile, of my kingdom, of my paradise." He was followed by the deputies of Tayef, who

dreaded the repetition of a siege. "Grant us, O apostle of God! a truce of
three years, with the toleration of our ancient worship." "Not a month,
not an hour." "Excuse us at least from the obligation of prayer." "Without
prayer religion is of no avail." They submitted in silence; their temples
were demolished, and the same sentence of destruction was executed on
all the idols of Arabia. His lieutenants, on the shores of the Red Sea, the
Ocean, and the Gulf of Persia, were saluted by the acclamations of a faithful
people; and the ambassadors who knelt before the throne of Medina, were
as numerous (says the Arabian proverb) as the dates that fall from the
maturity of a palm-tree. The nation submitted to the God and the sceptre
of Mahomet: the opprobrious name of tribute was abolished: the spontaneous or reluctant oblations of alms and tithes were applied to the service
of religion: and one hundred and fourteen thousand Moslems accompanied
the last pilgrimage of the apostle.[144]

First war of
the Mahometans
against the
Roman empire,
A.D. 629, 630.

When Heraclius returned in triumph from the Persian
war, he entertained, at Emesa, one of the ambassadors of
Mahomet, who invited the princes and nations of the earth
to the profession of Islam. On this foundation the zeal of the
Arabians has supposed the secret conversion of the Christian
emperor: the vanity of the Greeks has feigned a personal visit
of the prince of Medina, who accepted from the royal bounty a rich
domain, and a secure retreat, in the province of Syria.[145] But the friendship of Heraclius and Mahomet was of short continuance: the new
religion had inflamed rather than assuaged the rapacious spirit of the
Saracens; and the murder of an envoy afforded a decent pretence for
invading, with three thousand soldiers, the territory of Palestine, that
extends to the eastward of the Jordan. The holy banner was entrusted to
Zeid; and such was the discipline or enthusiasm of the rising sect, that the
noblest chiefs served, without reluctance, under the slave of the prophet.
On the event of his decease, Jaafar and Abdallah were successively substituted to the command; and if the three should perish in the war, the troops
were authorised to elect their general. The three leaders were slain in the

---

144. The last conquests and pilgrimage of
Mahomet are contained in Abulfeda (p. 121–
133.), Gagnier (tom. iii. p. 119–219.), Elmacin (p. 10, 11.), Abulpharagius (p. 103.). The
ixth of the Hegira was styled the Year of
Embassies (Gagnier, Not. ad Abulfed. p. 121.).

145. Compare the bigotted Al Jannabi (apud
Gagnier, tom. ii. p. 232–255.) with the no
less bigotted Greeks, Theophanes (p. 276–
278.), Zonaras (tom. ii. l. xiv. p. 86.), and
Cedrenus (p. 421.).

battle of Muta,[146] the first military action which tried the valour of the Moslems against a foreign enemy. Zeid fell, like a soldier, in the foremost ranks: the death of Jaafar was heroic and memorable; he lost his right-hand; he shifted the standard to his left; the left was severed from his body; he embraced the standard with his bleeding stumps, till he was transfixed to the ground with fifty honourable wounds. "Advance," cried Abdallah, who stepped into the vacant place, "advance with confidence; either victory or paradise is our own." The lance of a Roman decided the alternative; but the falling standard was rescued by Caled, the proselyte of Mecca: nine swords were broken in his hand; and his valour withstood and repulsed the superior numbers of the Christians. In the nocturnal council of the camp he was chosen to command: his skilful evolutions of the ensuing day secured either the victory or the retreat of the Saracens; and Caled is renowned among his brethren and his enemies by the glorious appellation of the *Sword of God*. In the pulpit, Mahomet described, with prophetic rapture, the crowns of the blessed martyrs; but in private he betrayed the feelings of human nature: he was surprised as he wept over the daughter of Zeid: "What do I see?" said the astonished votary. "You see," replied the apostle, "a friend, who is deploring the loss of his most faithful friend." After the conquest of Mecca the sovereign of Arabia affected to prevent the hostile preparations of Heraclius; and solemnly proclaimed war against the Romans, without attempting to disguise the hardships and dangers of the enterprise.[147] The Moslems were discouraged: they alleged the want of money, or horses, or provisions: the season of harvest, and the intolerable heat of the summer: "Hell is much hotter," said the indignant prophet. He disdained to compel their service; but on his return he admonished the most guilty, by an excommunication of fifty days. Their desertion enhanced the merit of Abubeker, Othman, and the faithful companions who devoted their lives and fortunes; and Mahomet displayed his banner at the head of ten thousand horse and twenty thousand foot. Painful indeed was the distress of the march: lassitude and thirst were aggravated by the scorching and pestilential winds of the desert: ten men

---

146. For the battle of Muta, and its consequences, see Abulfeda (p. 100–102.) and Gagnier (tom. ii. p. 327–343.). Καλεδος (says Theophanes) ὁν λεγουσι μαχαιραν του Θεου.

147. The expedition of Tabuc is recorded by our ordinary historians, Abulfeda (Vit. Moham. p. 123–127.) and Gagnier (Vie de Mahomet, tom. iii. p. 147–163.); but we have the advantage of appealing to the original evidence of the Koran (c. 9. p. 154. 165.), with Sale's learned and rational notes.

rode by turns on the same camel; and they were reduced to the shameful necessity of drinking the water from the belly of that useful animal. In the mid-way, ten days journey from Medina and Damascus, they reposed near the grove and fountain of Tabuc. Beyond that place, Mahomet declined the prosecution of the war; he declared himself satisfied with the peaceful intentions, he was more probably daunted by the martial array, of the emperor of the East. But the active and intrepid Caled spread around the terror of his name; and the prophet received the submission of the tribes and cities, from the Euphrates to Ailah, at the head of the Red Sea. To his Christian subjects, Mahomet readily granted the security of their persons, the freedom of their trade, the property of their goods, and the toleration of their worship.[148] The weakness of their Arabian brethren had restrained them from opposing his ambition; the disciples of Jesus were endeared to the enemy of the Jews; and it was the interest of a conqueror to propose a fair capitulation to the most powerful religion of the earth.

Death of Mahomet, A.D. 632, June 7.   Till the age of sixty-three years, the strength of Mahomet was equal to the temporal and spiritual fatigues of his mission. His epileptic fits, an absurd calumny of the Greeks, would be an object of pity rather than abhorrence;[149] but he seriously believed that he was poisoned at Chaibar by the revenge of a Jewish female.[150]

148. The *Diploma securitatis Ailensibus*, is attested by Ahmed Ben Joseph, and the author *Libri Splendorum* (Gagnier, Not. ad Abulfedam, p. 125.); but Abulfeda himself, as well as Elmacin (Hist. Saracen. p. 11.), though he owns Mahomet's regard for the Christians (p. 13.), only mention peace and tribute. In the year 1630, Sionita published at Paris the text and version of Mahomet's patent in favour of the Christians; which was admitted and reprobated by the opposite taste of Salmasius and Grotius (Bayle, MAHOMET. Rem. AA.). Hottinger doubts of its authenticity (Hist. Orient. p. 237.); Renaudot urges the consent of the Mahometans (Hist. Patriarch. Alex. p. 169.); but Mosheim (Hist. Eccles. p. 244.) shews the futility of their opinion, and inclines to believe it spurious. Yet Abulpharagius quotes the impostor's treaty with the Nestorian patriarch (Asseman. Bibliot. Orient. tom. ii. p. 418.); but Abulpharagius was primate of the Jacobites.

149. The epilepsy, or falling-sickness, of Mahomet, is asserted by Theophanes, Zonaras, and the rest of the Greeks; and is greedily swallowed by the gross bigotry of Hottinger (Hist. Orient. p. 10, 11.), Prideaux (Life of Mahomet, p. 12.), and Maracci (tom. ii.), Alcoran (p. 762, 763.). The titles *(the wrapped-up, the covered)* of two chapters of the Koran (73, 74.), can hardly be strained to such an interpretation; the silence, the ignorance of the Mahometan commentators, is more conclusive than the most peremptory denial; and the charitable side is espoused by Ockley (Hist. of the Saracens, tom. i. p. 301.), Gagnier (ad Abulfeda, p. 9. Vie de Mahomet. tom. i. p. 118.), and Sale (Koran. p. 469–474.).

150. This poison (more ignominious since it was offered as a test of his prophetic knowledge) is frankly confessed by his zealous votaries, Abulfeda (p. 92.), and Al Jannabi (apud Gagnier, tom. ii. p. 286–288.).

During four years, the health of the prophet declined; his infirmities encreased; but his mortal disease was a fever of fourteen days, which deprived him by intervals of the use of reason. As soon as he was conscious of his danger, he edified his brethren by the humility of his virtue or penitence. "If there be any man," said the apostle from the pulpit, "whom I have unjustly scourged, I submit my own back to the lash of retaliation. Have I aspersed the reputation of a Musulman? let him proclaim *my* faults in the face of the congregation. Has any one been despoiled of his goods? the little that I possess shall compensate the principal and the interest of the debt." "Yes," replied a voice from the crowd, "I am entitled to three drams of silver." Mahomet heard the complaint, satisfied the demand, and thanked his creditor for accusing him in this world rather than at the day of judgment. He beheld with temperate firmness the approach of death; enfranchised his slaves (seventeen men, as they are named, and eleven women); minutely directed the order of his funeral, and moderated the lamentations of his weeping friends, on whom he bestowed the benediction of peace. Till the third day before his death, he regularly performed the function of public prayer: the choice of Abubeker to supply his place, appeared to mark that ancient and faithful friend as his successor in the sacerdotal and regal office; but he prudently declined the risk and envy of a more explicit nomination. At a moment when his faculties were visibly impaired, he called for pen and ink, to write, or, more properly, to dictate, a divine book, the sum and accomplishment of all his revelations: a dispute arose in the chamber, whether he should be allowed to supersede the authority of the Koran; and the prophet was forced to reprove the indecent vehemence of his disciples. If the slightest credit may be afforded to the traditions of his wives and companions, he maintained, in the bosom of his family, and to the last moments of his life, the dignity of an apostle and the faith of an enthusiast; described the visits of Gabriel, who bade an everlasting farewel to the earth, and expressed his lively confidence, not only of the mercy, but of the favour, of the Supreme Being. In a familiar discourse he had mentioned his special prerogative, that the angel of death was not allowed to take his soul till he had respectfully asked the permission of the prophet. The request was granted; and Mahomet immediately fell into the agony of his dissolution: his head was reclined on the lap of Ayesha, the best beloved of all his wives; he fainted with the violence of pain; recovering his spirits, he raised his eyes towards the roof of the house, and, with a steady look, though a faultering voice, uttered the last broken, though articulate, words: "O God! . . . pardon my sins . . . Yes, . . . I come, . . . among my fellow-citizens on high:" and thus peaceably expired on a carpet spread upon the floor. An expedition for the conquest of Syria was stopped by this mournful event: the army halted at the gates of Medina; the chiefs were assembled round their dying master. The city, more especially the house, of the prophet was a scene of clamorous sorrow or silent despair: fanaticism alone could suggest a ray of hope and consolation. "How can he be dead, our witness, our intercessor, our mediator, with God? By God he is not dead; like Moses and Jesus he is wrapt in a holy trance, and speedily will he return to his faithful people." The evidence of sense was disregarded; and Omar, unsheathing his scymetar, threatened to strike off the heads of the infidels, who should dare to affirm that the prophet was no more. The tumult was appeased by the weight and moderation of Abubeker. "Is it Mahomet," said he to Omar and the multitude, "or the God of Mahomet, whom you worship. The God of Mahomet liveth for ever, but the apostle was a mortal like ourselves, and according to his own prediction, he has experienced the common fate of mortality." He was piously interred by the hands of his nearest kinsman, on the same spot on which he expired;[151] Medina has been sanctified by the death and burial of Mahomet, and the innumerable pilgrims of Mecca often turn aside from the way, to bow, in voluntary devotion,[152] before the simple tomb of the prophet.[153]

His character.   At the conclusion of the life of Mahomet, it may perhaps be expected, that I should balance his faults and virtues, that I should

151. The Greeks and Latins have invented and propagated the vulgar and ridiculous story, that Mahomet's iron tomb is suspended in the air at *Mecca* (σημα μετεωριζομενον. Laonicus Chalcocondyles de Rebus Turcicis, l. iii. p. 66.), by the action of equal and potent loadstones (Dictionaire de Bayle, MAHOMET, Rem. EE. FF.). Without any philosophical enquiries, it may suffice, that, 1. The prophet was not buried at Mecca; and, 2. That his tomb at Medina, which has been visited by millions, is placed on the ground (Reland de Relig. Moham. l. ii. c. 19. p. 209–211.), Gagnier (Vie de Mahomet, tom. iii. p. 263–268.).

152. Al Jannabi enumerates (Vie de Mahomet. tom. iii. p. 372–391.) the multifarious duties

of a pilgrim who visits the tombs of the prophet and his companions; and the learned casuist decides, that this act of devotion is nearest in obligation and merit to a divine precept. The doctors are divided which, of Mecca or Medina, be the most excellent (p. 391–394.).

153. The last sickness, death, and burial of Mahomet, are described by Abulfeda and Gagnier (Vit. Moham. p. 133–142. Vie de Mahomet, tom. iii. p. 220–271.). The most private and interesting circumstances were originally received from Ayesha, Ali, the sons of Abbas, &c.; and as they dwelt at Medina, and survived the prophet many years, they might repeat the pious tale to a second or third generation of pilgrims.

decide whether the title of enthusiast or impostor more properly belongs to that extraordinary man. Had I been intimately conversant with the son of Abdallah, the task would still be difficult, and the success uncertain: at the distance of twelve centuries, I darkly contemplate his shade through a cloud of religious incense; and could I truly delineate the portrait of an hour, the fleeting resemblance would not equally apply to the solitary of mount Hera, to the preacher of Mecca, and to the conqueror of Arabia. The author of a mighty revolution appears to have been endowed with a pious and contemplative disposition: so soon as marriage had raised him above the pressure of want, he avoided the paths of ambition and avarice; and till the age of forty, he lived with innocence, and would have died without a name. The unity of God is an idea most congenial to nature and reason; and a slight conversation with the Jews and Christians would teach him to despise and detest the idolatry of Mecca. It was the duty of a man and a citizen to impart the doctrine of salvation, to rescue his country from the dominion of sin and error. The energy of a mind incessantly bent on the same object, would convert a general obligation into a particular call; the warm suggestions of the understanding or the fancy, would be felt as the inspirations of heaven; the labour of thought would expire in rapture and vision; and the inward sensation, the invisible monitor, would be described with the form and attributes of an angel of God.[154] From enthusiasm to imposture, the step is perilous and slippery: the dæmon of Socrates[155] affords a memorable instance, how a wise man may deceive himself, how a good man may deceive others, how the conscience may slumber in a mixed and middle state between self-illusion and voluntary fraud. Charity

154. The Christians, rashly enough, have assigned to Mahomet a tame pigeon, that seemed to descend from heaven and whisper in his ear. As this pretended miracle is urged by Grotius (de Veritate Religionis Christianæ), his Arabic translator, the learned Pocock, enquired of him the names of his authors; and Grotius confessed, that it is unknown to the Mahometans themselves. Lest it should provoke their indignation and laughter, the pious *lie* is suppressed in the Arabic version; but it has maintained an edifying place in the numerous editions of the Latin text (Pocock, Specimen Hist. Arabum, p. 186, 187. Reland, de Religion. Moham. l. ii. c. 39. p. 259–262.).

155. *Εμοι δε τουτο εστιν εκ παιδος αρξαμενον, φωνη τις γιγνομενη η όταν γενηται αει αποτρεπει με τουτου ό αν μελλω πραττειν, προτρεπει δε ουποτε* (Plato, in Apolog. Socrat. c. 19. p. 121, 122. edit. Fischer). The familiar examples, which Socrates urges in his Dialogue with Theages (Platon. Opera, tom. i. p. 128, 129. edit. Hen. Stephan), are beyond the reach of human foresight; and the divine inspiration (the *Δαιμονιον*) of the philosopher, is clearly taught in the Memorabilia of Xenophon. The ideas of the most rational Platonists are expressed by Cicero (de Divinat. i. 54.) and in the xiv[th] and xv[th] Dissertations of Maximus of Tyre (p. 153–172. edit. Davis).

may believe that the original motives of Mahomet were those of pure and genuine benevolence; but a human missionary is incapable of cherishing the obstinate unbelievers who reject his claims, despise his arguments, and persecute his life; he might forgive his personal adversaries, he may lawfully hate the enemies of God; the stern passions of pride and revenge were kindled in the bosom of Mahomet, and he sighed, like the prophet of Niniveh, for the destruction of the rebels whom he had condemned. The injustice of Mecca, and the choice of Medina, transformed the citizen into a prince, the humble preacher into the leader of armies; but his sword was consecrated by the example of the saints; and the same God who afflicts a sinful world with pestilence and earthquakes, might inspire for their conversion or chastisement the valour of his servants. In the exercise of political government, he was compelled to abate of the stern rigour of fanaticism, to comply in some measure with the prejudices and passions of his followers, and to employ even the vices of mankind as the instruments of their salvation. The use of fraud and perfidy, of cruelty and injustice, were often subservient to the propagation of the faith; and Mahomet commanded or approved the assassination of the Jews and idolaters who had escaped from the field of battle. By the repetition of such acts, the character of Mahomet must have been gradually stained; and the influence of such pernicious habits would be poorly compensated by the practice of the personal and social virtues which are necessary to maintain the reputation of a prophet among his sectaries and friends. Of his last years, ambition was the ruling passion; and a politician will suspect, that he secretly smiled (the victorious impostor!) at the enthusiasm of his youth and the credulity of his proselytes.[156] A philosopher will observe, that *their* credulity and *his* success, would tend more strongly to fortify the assurance of his divine mission, that his interest and religion were inseparably connected, and that his conscience would be soothed by the persuasion, that he alone was absolved by the Deity from the obligation of positive and moral laws. If he retained any vestige of his native innocence, the sins of Mahomet may be allowed as an evidence of his sincerity. In the support of truth, the arts of fraud and fiction may be deemed less criminal; and he would have started at the foulness of the means, had he not been satisfied of the importance and justice of the end. Even in a conqueror or a priest, I can surprise a

---

156. In some passage of his voluminous writings, Voltaire compares the prophet, in his old age, to a fakir: "qui detache la chaine de son cou pour en donner sur les oreilles à ses confreres."

word or action of unaffected humanity; and the decree of Mahomet, that, in the sale of captives, the mothers should never be separated from their children, may suspend or moderate the censure of the historian.[157]

The good sense of Mahomet[158] despised the pomp of royalty: the apostle of God submitted to the menial offices of the family: he kindled the fire, swept the floor, milked the ewes, and mended with his own hands his shoes and his woollen garment. Disdaining the penance and merit of an hermit, he observed without effort or vanity, the abstemious diet of an Arab and a soldier. On solemn occasions he feasted his companions with rustic and hospitable plenty; but in his domestic life, many weeks would elapse without a fire being kindled on the hearth of the prophet. The interdiction of wine was confirmed by his example; his hunger was appeased with a sparing allowance of barley-bread; he delighted in the taste of milk and honey: but his ordinary food consisted of dates and water. Perfumes and women were the two sensual enjoyments which his nature required and his religion did not forbid: and Mahomet affirmed, that the fervour of his devotion was encreased by these innocent pleasures. The heat of the climate inflames the blood of the Arabs; and their libidinous complexion has been noticed by the writers of antiquity.[159] Their incontinence was regulated by the civil and religious laws of the Koran: their incestuous alliances were blamed, the boundless licence of polygamy was reduced to four legitimate wives or concubines; their rights, both of bed and of dowry, were equitably determined; the freedom of divorce was discouraged, adultery was condemned as a capital offence, and fornication, in either sex, was punished with an hundred stripes.[160] Such were the calm and rational precepts of the legislator: but in

Private life of Mahomet.

157. Gagnier relates, with the same impartial pen, this humane law of the prophet, and the murders of Caab, and Sophian, which he prompted and approved (Vie de Mahomet, tom. ii. p. 69. 97. 208.).

158. For the domestic life of Mahomet, consult Gagnier, and the corresponding chapters of Abulfeda; for his diet (tom. iii. p. 285–288); his children (p. 189. 289.); his wives (p. 290–303.); his marriage with Zeineb (tom. ii. p. 152–160.); his amour with Mary (p. 303–309); the false accusation of Ayesha (p. 186–199.). The most original evidence of the three last transactions, is contained in the xxiv[th],

xxxiii[d], and lxvi[th] chapters of the Koran, with Sale's Commentary. Prideaux (Life of Mahomet, p. 80–90.) and Maracci (Prodrom. Alcoran, part iv. p. 49–59.) have maliciously exaggerated the frailties of Mahomet.

159. Incredibile est quo ardore apud eos in Venerem uterque solvitur sexus (Ammian. Marcellin. l. xiv. c. 4.).

160. Sale (Preliminary Discourse, p. 133–137.) has recapitulated the laws of marriage, divorce, &c.; and the curious reader of Selden's Uxor Hebraica will recognize many Jewish ordinances.

his private conduct, Mahomet indulged the appetites of a man, and abused the claims of a prophet. A special revelation dispensed him from the laws which he had imposed on his nation; the female sex, without reserve, was abandoned to his desires; and this singular prerogative excited the envy, rather than the scandal, the veneration, rather than the envy, of the devout Musulmans. If we remember the seven hundred wives and three hundred concubines of the wise Solomon, we shall applaud the modesty *His wives,* of the Arabian who espoused no more than seventeen or fifteen wives; eleven are enumerated who occupied at Medina their separate apartments round the house of the apostle, and enjoyed in their turns the favour of his conjugal society. What is singular enough, they were all widows, excepting only Ayesha, the daughter of Abubeker. *She* was doubtless a virgin, since Mahomet consummated his nuptials (such is the premature ripeness of the climate) when she was only nine years of age. The youth, the beauty, the spirit of Ayesha, gave her a superior ascendant: she was beloved and trusted by the prophet; and, after his death, the daughter of Abubeker was long revered as the mother of the faithful. Her behaviour had been ambiguous and indiscreet: in a nocturnal march, she was accidentally left behind; and in the morning Ayesha returned to the camp with a man. The temper of Mahomet was inclined to jealousy; but a divine revelation assured him of her innocence: he chastised her accusers, and published a law of domestic peace, that no woman should be condemned unless four male witnesses had seen her in the act of adultery.[161] In his adventures with Zeineb, the wife of Zeid, and with Mary, an Egyptian captive, the amorous prophet forgot the interest of his reputation. At the house of Zeid, his freedman and adopted son, he beheld, in a loose undress, the beauty of Zeineb, and burst forth into an ejaculation of devotion and desire. The servile, or grateful, freedman understood the hint, and yielded without hesitation to the love of his benefactor. But as the filial relation had excited some doubt and scandal, the angel Gabriel descended from heaven to ratify the deed, to annul the adoption, and gently to reprove the apostle for distrusting the indulgence of his God. One of his wives, Hafna, the daughter of Omar, surprised him on her own bed, in the embraces of his Egyptian captive: she promised secrecy and forgiveness: he swore that

---

161. In a memorable case, the caliph Omar decided that all presumptive evidence was of no avail; and that all the four witnesses must have actually seen stylum in pyxide (Abulfedæ Annales Moslemici, p. 71. vers. Reiske).

he would renounce the possession of Mary. Both parties forgot their engagements; and Gabriel again descended with a chapter of the Koran, to absolve him from his oath, and to exhort him freely to enjoy his captives and concubines, without listening to the clamours of his wives. In a solitary retreat of thirty days, he laboured, alone with Mary, to fulfil the commands of the angel. When his love and revenge were satiated, he summoned to his presence his eleven wives, reproached their disobedience and indiscretion, and threatened them with a sentence of divorce, both in this world and in the next: a dreadful sentence, since those who had ascended the bed of the prophet were for ever excluded from the hope of a second marriage. Perhaps the incontinence of Mahomet may be palliated by the tradition of his natural or preternatural gifts:[162] he united the manly virtue of thirty of the children of Adam; and the apostle might rival the thirteenth labour[163] of the Grecian Hercules.[164] A more serious and decent excuse may be drawn from his fidelity to Cadijah. During the twenty-four years of their marriage, her youthful husband abstained from the right of polygamy, and the pride or tenderness of the venerable matron was never insulted by the society of a rival. After her death, he placed her in the rank of the four perfect women, with the sister of Moses, the mother of Jesus, and Fatima, the best beloved of his daughters. "Was she not old?" said Ayesha, with the insolence of a blooming beauty; "has not God given you a better in her place?" "No, by God," said Mahomet, with an effusion of honest gratitude, "there never can be a better! She believed in me, when men despised me: she relieved my wants, when I was poor and persecuted by the world."[165]

---

162. Sibi robur ad generationem, quantum triginta viri habent, inesse jactaret: ita ut unicâ hora posset undecim fœminis *satisfacere*, ut ex Arabum libris refert S^{tus} Petrus Paschasius, c. 2. (Maracci, Prodromus Alcoran, p. iv. p. 55. See likewise Observations de Belon, l. iii. c. 10. fol. 179. recto). Al Jannabi (Gagnier, tom. iii. p. 287.) records his own testimony, that he surpassed all men in conjugal vigour; and Abulfeda mentions the exclamation of Ali, who washed his body after his death, "O propheta, certe penis tuus cœlum versus erectus est" (in Vit. Mohammed. p. 140.).

163. I borrow the style of a father of the church, εναθλευων 'Ηρακλης τρισκαιδεκα-

τον αθλον (Greg. Nazianzen, Orat. iii. p. 108.).

164. The common and most glorious legend includes, in a single night, the fifty victories of Hercules over the virgin daughters of Thestius (Diodor. Sicul. tom. i. l. iv. p. 274. Pausanias, l. ix. p. 763. Statius Sylv. l. i. eleg. iii. v. 42.). But Athenæus allows seven nights (Deipnosophist. l. xiii. p. 556.), and Apollodorus fifty, for this arduous atchievement of Hercules, who was then no more than eighteen years of age (Bibliot. l. ii. c. 4. p. 111. cum notis Heyne, part i. p. 332.).

165. Abulfeda in Vit. Moham. p. 12, 13, 16, 17. cum notis Gagnier.

and children.   In the largest indulgence of polygamy, the founder of a religion and empire might aspire to multiply the chances of a numerous posterity and a lineal succession. The hopes of Mahomet were fatally disappointed. The virgin Ayesha, and his ten widows of mature age and approved fertility, were barren in his potent embraces. The four sons of Cadijah died in their infancy. Mary, his Egyptian concubine, was endeared to him by the birth of Ibrahim. At the end of fifteen months the prophet wept over his grave; but he sustained with firmness the raillery of his enemies, and checked the adulation or credulity of the Moslems, by the assurance that an eclipse of the sun was *not* occasioned by the death of the infant. Cadijah had likewise given him four daughters, who were married to the most faithful of his disciples: the three eldest died before their father; but Fatima, who possessed his confidence and love, became the wife of her cousin Ali, and the mother of an illustrious progeny. The merit and misfortunes of Ali and his descendants will lead me to anticipate, in this place, the series of the Saracen caliphs, a title which describes the commanders of the faithful as the vicars and successors of the apostle of God.[166]

Character of Ali.   The birth, the alliance, the character of Ali, which exalted him above the rest of his countrymen, might justify his claim to the vacant throne of Arabia. The son of Abu Taleb was, in his own right, the chief of the family of Hashem, and the hereditary prince or guardian of the city and temple of Mecca. The light of prophecy was extinct; but the husband of Fatima might expect the inheritance and blessing of her father: the Arabs had sometimes been patient of a female reign; and the two grandsons of the prophet had often been fondled in his lap, and shewn in his pulpit, as the hope of his age, and the chief of the youth of paradise. The first of the true believers might aspire to march before them in this world and in the next; and if some were of a graver and more rigid cast, the zeal and virtue of Ali were never outstripped by any recent proselyte. He united the qualifications of a poet, a soldier, and

---

166. This outline of the Arabian history is drawn from the Bibliotheque Orientale of d'Herbelot (under the names of *Aboubecre, Omar, Othman, Ali,* &c.); from the Annals of Abulfeda, Abulpharagius, and Elmacin (under the proper years of the *Hegira*) and especially from Ockley's History of the Saracens (vol. i. p. 1–10. 115–122. 229. 249. 363–372. 378–391. and almost the whole of the second volume). Yet we should weigh with caution the traditions of the hostile sects; a stream which becomes still more muddy as it flows farther from the source. Sir John Chardin has too faithfully copied the fables and errors of the modern Persians (Voyages, tom. ii. p. 235–250, &c.).

a saint: his wisdom still breathes in a collection of moral and religious sayings;[167] and every antagonist, in the combats of the tongue or of the sword, was subdued by his eloquence and valour. From the first hour of his mission, to the last rites of his funeral, the apostle was never forsaken by a generous friend, whom he delighted to name his brother, his vice-gerent, and the faithful Aaron of a second Moses. The son of Abu Taleb was afterwards reproached for neglecting to secure his interest by a solemn declaration of his right, which would have silenced all competition, and sealed his succession by the decrees of heaven. But the unsuspecting hero confided in himself: the jealousy of empire, and perhaps the fear of opposition, might suspend the resolutions of Mahomet; and the bed of sickness was besieged by the artful Ayesha, the daughter of Abubeker, and the enemy of Ali.

The silence and death of the prophet restored the liberty of the people; and his companions convened an assembly to deliberate on the choice of his successor. The hereditary claim and lofty spirit of Ali, were offensive to an aristocracy of elders, desirous of bestowing and resuming the sceptre by a free and frequent election: the Koreish could never be reconciled to the proud pre-eminence of the line of Hashem; the ancient discord of the tribes was rekindled; the *fugitives* of Mecca and the *auxiliaries* of Medina asserted their respective merits, and the rash proposal of chusing two independent caliphs would have crushed in their infancy the religion and empire of the Saracens. The tumult was appeased by the disinterested resolution of Omar, who, suddenly renouncing his own pretensions, stretched forth his hand, and declared himself the first subject of the mild and venerable Abubeker. The urgency of the moment, and the acquiescence of the people, might excuse this illegal and precipitate measure; but Omar himself confessed from the pulpit, that if any Musulman should hereafter presume to anticipate the suffrage of his brethren, both the elector and the elected would be worthy of death.[168] After the simple inauguration of Abubeker, he was obeyed in

Reign of Abubeker; A.D. 632, June 7.

---

167. Ockley (at the end of his second volume) has given an English version of 169 sentences, which he ascribes, with some hesitation, to Ali, the son of Abu Taleb. His preface is coloured by the enthusiasm of a translator: yet these sentences delineate a characteristic, though dark, picture of human life.
168. Ockley (Hist. of the Saracens, vol. i. p. 5,

6.) from an Arabian MS. represents Ayesha as adverse to the substitution of her father in the place of the apostle. This fact, so improbable in itself, is unnoticed by Abulfeda, Al Jannabi, and Al Bochari, the last of whom quotes the tradition of Ayesha herself (Vit. Mohammed, p. 136. Vie de Mahomet, tom. iii. p. 236.).

Medina, Mecca, and the provinces of Arabia; the Hashemites alone declined the oath of fidelity; and their chief, in his own house, maintained, above six months, a sullen and independent reserve; without listening to the threats of Omar, who attempted to consume with fire the habitation of the daughter of the apostle. The death of Fatima, and the decline of his party, subdued the indignant spirit of Ali: he condescended to salute the commander of the faithful, accepted his excuse of the necessity of preventing their common enemies, and wisely rejected his courteous offer of abdicating the government of the Arabians. After a reign of two years, the aged caliph was summoned by the angel of death. In his testament, with the tacit approbation of the companions, he bequeathed the sceptre to the firm and intrepid virtue of Omar. "I have no occasion," said the modest candidate, "for the place." "But the place has occasion for you," replied Abubeker; who expired with a fervent prayer, that the God of Mahomet would ratify his choice, and direct the Musulmans in the way of concord and obedience. The prayer was not ineffectual, since Ali himself, in a life of privacy and prayer, professed to revere the superior worth and dignity of his rival; who comforted him for the loss of empire, by the most flattering marks of confidence and esteem. In the twelfth year of his reign, Omar received a mortal wound from the hand of an assassin: he rejected with equal impartiality the names of his son and of Ali, refused to load his conscience with the sins of his successor, and devolved on six of the most respectable companions, the arduous task of electing a commander of the faithful. On this occasion, Ali was again blamed by his friends[169] for submitting his right to the judgment of men, for recognizing their jurisdiction by accepting a place among the six electors. He might have obtained their suffrage, had he deigned to promise a strict and servile conformity, not only to the Koran and tradition, but likewise to the determinations of two *seniors*.[170] With these limitations, Othman, the secretary of Mahomet, accepted the government; nor was it till after the third caliph,

of Omar;
A.D. 634,
July 24.

of Othman,
A.D. 644,
November 6.

---

169. Particularly by his friend and cousin Abdallah, the son of Abbas, who died A.D. 687, with the title of grand doctor of the Moslems. In Abulfeda he recapitulated the important occasions in which Ali had neglected his salutary advice (p. 76. vers. Reiske); and concludes (p. 85.), O princeps fidelium,

absque controversia tu quidem vere fortis es, at inops boni consilii, et rerum gerendarum parum callens.

170. I suspect that the two seniors (Abulpharagius, p. 115. Ockley, tom. i. p. 371.) may signify not two actual counsellors, but his two predecessors, Abubeker and Omar.

twenty-four years after the death of the prophet, that Ali was invested, by the popular choice, with the regal and sacerdotal office. The manners of the Arabians retained their primitive simplicity, and the son of Abu Taleb despised the pomp and vanity of this world. At the hour of prayer, he repaired to the mosch of Medina, clothed in a thin cotton gown, a coarse turban on his head, his slippers in one hand, and his bow in the other, instead of a walking staff. The companions of the prophet and the chiefs of the tribes saluted their new sovereign, and gave him their right hands as a sign of fealty and allegiance.

The mischiefs that flow from the contests of ambition are usually confined to the times and countries in which they have been agitated. But the religious discord of the friends and enemies of Ali has been renewed in every age of the Hegira, and is still *Discord of the Turks and Persians.* maintained in the immortal hatred of the Persians and Turks.[171] The former, who are branded with the appellation of *Shiites* or sectaries, have enriched the Mahometan creed with a new article of faith; and if Mahomet be the apostle, his companion Ali is the vicar, of God. In their private converse, in their public worship, they bitterly execrate the three usurpers who intercepted his indefeasible right to the dignity of Imam and Caliph; and the name of Omar expresses in their tongue the perfect accomplishment of wickedness and impiety.[172] The *Sonnites*, who are supported by the general consent and orthodox tradition of the Musulmans, entertain a more impartial, or at least a more decent opinion. They respect the memory of Abubeker, Omar, Othman, and Ali, the holy and legitimate successors of the prophet. But they assign the last and most humble place to the husband of Fatima, in the persuasion that the order of succession was determined by the degrees of sanctity.[173] An historian who balances the four caliphs with a hand unshaken by superstition, will calmly pronounce, that their

---

171. The schism of the Persians is explained by all our travellers of the last century, especially in the ii^d and ivth volume of their master, Chardin. Niebuhr, though of inferior merit, has the advantage of writing so late as the year 1764 (Voyages en Arabie, &c. tom. ii. p. 208−233.), since the ineffectual attempt of Nadir Shah to change the religion of the nation (see his Persian History translated into French by Sir William Jones, tom. ii. p. 5. 6. 47, 48. 144−155.).

172. Omar is the name of the devil; his murderer is a saint. When the Persians shoot with the bow, they frequently cry, "May this arrow go to the heart of Omar!" (Voyages de Chardin, tom. ii. p. 239, 240. 259, &c.).

173. This gradation of merit is distinctly marked in a creed illustrated by Reland (de Relig. Mohamm. l. i. p. 37.); and a Sonnite argument inserted by Ockley (Hist. of the Saracens, tom. ii. p. 230.). The practice of cursing the memory of Ali was abolished,

manners were alike pure and exemplary; that their zeal was fervent, and probably sincere; and that, in the midst of riches and power, their lives were devoted to the practice of moral and religious duties. But the public virtues of Abubeker and Omar, the prudence of the first, the severity of the second, maintained the peace and prosperity of their reigns. The feeble temper and declining age of Othman were incapable of sustaining the weight of conquest and empire. He chose, and he was deceived; he trusted, and he was betrayed: the most deserving of the faithful became useless or hostile to his government, and his lavish bounty was productive only of ingratitude and discontent. The spirit of discord went forth in the provinces, their deputies assembled at Medina, and the Charegites, the desperate fanatics who disclaimed the yoke of subordination and reason, were confounded among the free-born Arabs, who demanded the redress of their wrongs and the punishment of their oppressors. From Cufa, from Bassora, from Egypt, from the tribes of the desert, they rose in arms, encamped about a league from Medina, and dispatched an haughty mandate to their sovereign, requiring him to execute justice, or to descend from the throne. His repentance began to disarm and disperse the insurgents; but their fury was rekindled by the arts of his enemies; and the forgery of a perfidious secretary was contrived to blast his reputation and precipitate his fall. The caliph had lost the only guard of his predecessors, the esteem and confidence of the Moslems; during a siege of six weeks his water and provisions were intercepted, and the feeble gates of the palace were protected only by the scruples of the more timorous rebels. Forsaken by those who had abused his simplicity, the helpless and venerable caliph expected the approach of death: the brother of Ayesha marched at the head of the assassins; and Othman, with the Koran in his lap, was pierced with a multitude of wounds. A tumultuous anarchy of five days was appeased by the inauguration of Ali; his refusal would have provoked a general massacre. In this painful situation he supported the becoming pride of the chief of the Hashemites; declared that he had rather serve than reign; rebuked the presumption of the strangers; and required the formal, if not the voluntary, assent of the chiefs of the

Death of Othman, A.D. 655, June 18.

---

after forty years, by the Ommiades themselves (d'Herbelot, p. 690.); and there are few among the Turks who presume to revile him as an infidel (Voyages de Chardin, tom. iv. p. 46.).

nation. He has never been accused of prompting the assassin of Omar, though Persia indiscreetly celebrates the festival of that holy martyr. The quarrel between Othman and his subjects was assuaged by the early mediation of Ali; and Hassan, the eldest of his sons, was insulted and wounded in the defence of the caliph. Yet it is doubtful whether the father of Hassan was strenuous and sincere in his opposition to the rebels; and it is certain that he enjoyed the benefit of their crime. The temptation was indeed of such magnitude as might stagger and corrupt the most obdurate virtue. The ambitious candidate no longer aspired to the barren sceptre of Arabia: the Saracens had been victorious in the East and West; and the wealthy kingdoms of Persia, Syria, and Egypt, were the patrimony of the commander of the faithful.

A life of prayer and contemplation had not chilled the martial activity of Ali; but in a mature age, after a long experience of mankind, he still betrayed in his conduct the rashness and *Reign of Ali, A.D. 655–660.* indiscretion of youth. In the first days of his reign, he neglected to secure, either by gifts or fetters, the doubtful allegiance of Telha and Zobeir, two of the most powerful of the Arabian chiefs. They escaped from Medina to Mecca, and from thence to Bassora; erected the standard of revolt; and usurped the government of Irak, or Assyria, which they had vainly so-licited as the reward of their services. The mask of patriotism is allowed to cover the most glaring inconsistencies; and the enemies, perhaps the assassins, of Othman now demanded vengeance for his blood. They were accompanied in their flight by Ayesha, the widow of the prophet, who cherished, to the last hour of her life, an implacable hatred against the husband and the posterity of Fatima. The most reasonable Moslems were scandalised, that the mother of the faithful should expose in a camp her person and character; but the superstitious crowd was confident that her presence would sanctify the justice, and assure the success, of their cause. At the head of twenty thousand of his loyal Arabs, and nine thousand valiant auxiliaries of Cufa, the caliph encountered and defeated the superior numbers of the rebels under the walls of Bassora. Their leaders, Telha and Zobeir, were slain in the first battle that stained with civil blood the arms of the Moslems. After passing through the ranks to animate the troops, Ayesha had chosen her post amidst the dangers of the field. In the heat of the action, seventy men, who held the bridle of her camel, were suc-cessively killed or wounded; and the cage or litter in which she sat, was stuck with javelins and darts like the quills of a porcupine. The venerable captive sustained with firmness the reproaches of the conqueror, and was speedily dismissed to her proper station, at the tomb of Mahomet, with the respect and tenderness that was still due to the widow of the apostle. After this victory, which was styled the Day of the Camel, Ali marched against a more formidable adversary; against Moawiyah, the son of Abu Sophian, who had assumed the title of caliph, and whose claim was supported by the forces of Syria and the interest of the house of Ommiyah. From the passage of Thapsacus, the plain of Siffin[174] extends along the western bank of the Euphrates. On this spacious and level theatre, the two competitors waged a desultory war of one hundred and ten days. In the course of ninety actions or skirmishes, the loss of Ali was estimated at twenty-five, that of Moawiyah at forty-five, thousand soldiers; and the list of the slain was dignified with the names of five and twenty veterans who had fought at Beder under the standard of Mahomet. In this sanguinary contest, the lawful caliph displayed a superior character of valour and humanity. His troops were strictly enjoined to await the first onset of the enemy, to spare their flying brethren, and to respect the bodies of the dead, and the chastity of the female captives. He generously proposed to save the blood of the Moslems by a single combat; but his trembling rival declined the challenge as a sentence of inevitable death. The ranks of the Syrians were broken by the charge of a hero who was mounted on a pyebald horse, and wielded with irresistible force his ponderous and two-edged sword. As often as he smote a rebel, he shouted the Allah Acbar, "God is victorious;" and in the tumult of a nocturnal battle, he was heard to repeat four hundred times that tremendous exclamation. The prince of Damascus already meditated his flight, but the certain victory was snatched from the grasp of Ali by the disobedience and enthusiasm of his troops. Their conscience was awed by the solemn appeal to the books of the Koran which Moawiyah exposed on the foremost lances; and Ali was compelled to yield to a disgraceful truce and an insidious compromise. He retreated with sorrow and indignation to Cufa; his party was discouraged; the distant provinces of Persia, of Yemen, and of Egypt, were subdued or seduced by his crafty rival; and the stroke of fanaticism which was aimed against the three chiefs of the nation, was fatal only to the cousin of Mahomet. In the temple of

174. The plain of Siffin is determined by d'Anville (l'Euphrate et le Tigre, p. 29.) to be the Campus Barbaricus of Procopius.

Mecca, three Charegites or enthusiasts discoursed of the disorders of the church and state: they soon agreed, that the deaths of Ali, of Moawiyah, and of his friend Amrou, the viceroy of Egypt, would restore the peace and unity of religion. Each of the assassins chose his victim, poisoned his dagger, devoted his life, and secretly repaired to the scene of action. Their resolution was equally desperate: but the first mistook the person of Amrou, and stabbed the deputy who occupied his seat; the prince of Damascus was dangerously hurt by the second; the lawful caliph, in the mosch of Cufa, received a mortal wound from the hand of the third. He expired in the sixty-third year of his age, and mercifully recommended to his children, that they would dispatch the murderer by a single stroke. The sepulchre of Ali[175] was concealed from the tyrants of the house of Ommiyah;[176] but in the fourth age of the Hegira, a tomb, a temple, a city, arose near the ruins of Cufa.[177] Many thousands of the Shiites repose in holy ground at the feet of the vicar of God; and the desert is vivified by the numerous and annual visits of the Persians, who esteem their devotion not less meritorious than the pilgrimage of Mecca.

The persecutors of Mahomet usurped the inheritance of his children; and the champions of idolatry became the supreme heads of his religion and empire. The opposition of Abu Sophian had been fierce and obstinate; his conversion was tardy and reluctant; his new faith was fortified by necessity and interest; *Reign of Moawiyah, A.D. 655, or 661–680.* he served, he fought, perhaps he believed; and the sins of the time of ignorance were expiated by the recent merits of the family of Ommiyah. Moawiyah, the son of Abu Sophian, and of the cruel Henda, was dignified in his early youth with the office or title of secretary of the prophet: the judgment of Omar entrusted him with the government of Syria; and he administered that important province above forty years either in a

---

175. Abulfeda, a moderate Sonnite, relates the different opinions concerning the burial of Ali, but adopts the sepulchre of Cufa, hodie famâ numeroque religiose frequentantium celebratum. This number is reckoned by Niebuhr to amount annually to 2000 of the dead, and 5000 of the living (tom. ii. p. 208, 209.).
176. All the tyrants of Persia, from Adhad el Dowlat (A.D. 977, d'Herbelot, p. 58, 59. 95.) to Nadir Shah (A.D. 1743, Hist. de Nadir Shah, tom. ii. p. 155.), have enriched the

tomb of Ali with the spoils of the people. The dome is copper, with a bright and massy gilding, which glitters to the sun at the distance of many a mile.
177. The city of Meshed Ali, five or six miles from the ruins of Cufa, and one hundred and twenty to the south of Bagdad, is of the size and form of the modern Jerusalem. Meshed Hosein, larger and more populous, is at the distance of thirty miles.

subordinate or supreme rank. Without renouncing the fame of valour and liberality, he affected the reputation of humanity and moderation: a grateful people was attached to their benefactor; and the victorious Moslems were enriched with the spoils of Cyprus and Rhodes. The sacred duty of pursuing the assassins of Othman was the engine and pretence of his ambition. The bloody shirt of the martyr was exposed in the mosch of Damascus: the emir deplored the fate of his injured kinsman; and sixty thousand Syrians were engaged in his service by an oath of fidelity and revenge. Amrou, the conqueror of Egypt, himself an army, was the first who saluted the new monarch, and divulged the dangerous secret, that the Arabian caliphs might be created elsewhere than in the city of the prophet.[178] The policy of Moawiyah eluded the valour of his rival; and, after the death of Ali, he negociated the abdication of his son Hassan, whose mind was either above or below the government of the world, and who retired without a sigh from the palace of Cufa to an humble cell near the tomb of his grandfather. The aspiring wishes of the caliph were finally crowned by the important change of an elective to an hereditary kingdom. Some murmurs of freedom or fanaticism attested the reluctance of the Arabs, and four citizens of Medina refused the oath of fidelity; but the designs of Moawiyah were conducted with vigour and address; and his son Yezid, a feeble and dissolute youth, was proclaimed as the commander of the faithful and the successor of the apostle of God.

Death of Hosein, A.D. 680, October 10.

A familiar story is related of the benevolence of one of the sons of Ali. In serving at table, a slave had inadvertently dropt a dish of scalding broth on his master: the heedless wretch fell prostrate, to deprecate his punishment, and repeated a verse of the Koran: "Paradise is for those who command their anger:" – "I am not angry:" – "and for those who pardon offences:" – "I pardon your offence:" – "and for those who return good for evil:" – "I give you your liberty, and four hundred pieces of silver." With an equal measure of piety, Hosein, the younger brother of Hassan, inherited a remnant of his father's spirit, and served with honour against the Christians in the siege of Constantinople. The primogeniture of the line of Hashem, and the holy character of grandson of the apostle, had centered in his person, and he was at liberty

178. I borrow, on this occasion, the strong sense and expression of Tacitus (Hist. i. 4.): Evulgato imperii arcano posse imperatorem alibi quam Romæ fieri.

to prosecute his claim against Yezid the tyrant of Damascus, whose vices he despised, and whose title he had never deigned to acknowledge. A list was secretly transmitted from Cufa to Medina, of one hundred and forty thousand Moslems, who professed their attachment to his cause, and who were eager to draw their swords so soon as he should appear on the banks of the Euphrates. Against the advice of his wisest friends, he resolved to trust his person and family in the hands of a perfidious people. He traversed the desert of Arabia with a timorous retinue of women and children; but as he approached the confines of Irak, he was alarmed by the solitary or hostile face of the country, and suspected either the defection or ruin of his party. His fears were just; Obeidollah, the governor of Cufa, had extinguished the first sparks of an insurrection; and Hosein, in the plain of Kerbela, was encompassed by a body of five thousand horse, who intercepted his communication with the city and the river. He might still have escaped to a fortress in the desert, that had defied the power of Cæsar and Chosroes, and confided in the fidelity of the tribe of Tai, which would have armed ten thousand warriors in his defence. In a conference with the chief of the enemy, he proposed the option of three honourable conditions; that he should be allowed to return to Medina, or be stationed in a frontier garrison against the Turks, or safely conducted to the presence of Yezid. But the commands of the caliph, or his lieutenant, were stern and absolute; and Hosein was informed that he must either submit as a captive and a criminal to the commander of the faithful, or expect the consequences of his rebellion. "Do you think," replied he, "to terrify me with death?" And, during the short respite of a night, he prepared with calm and solemn resignation to encounter his fate. He checked the lamentations of his sister Fatima, who deplored the impending ruin of his house. "Our trust," said Hosein, "is in God alone. All things, both in heaven and earth, must perish and return to their Creator. My brother, my father, my mother, were better than me; and every Musulman has an example in the prophet." He pressed his friends to consult their safety by a timely flight: they unanimously refused to desert or survive their beloved master; and their courage was fortified by a fervent prayer and the assurance of paradise. On the morning of the fatal day, he mounted on horseback, with his sword in one hand and the Koran in the other: his generous band of martyrs consisted only of thirty-two horse and forty foot; but their flanks and rear were secured by the tent-ropes, and by a deep trench which they had filled with lighted faggots, according to the practice of the Arabs. The enemy advanced with reluctance; and one of their chiefs deserted, with thirty followers, to claim the partnership of inevitable death. In every close onset, or single combat, the despair of the Fatimites was invincible; but the surrounding multitudes galled them from a distance with a cloud of arrows, and the horses and men were successively slain: a truce was allowed on both sides for the hour of prayer; and the battle at length expired by the death of the last of the companions of Hosein. Alone, weary, and wounded, he seated himself at the door of his tent. As he tasted a drop of water, he was pierced in the mouth with a dart; and his son and nephew, two beautiful youths, were killed in his arms. He lifted his hands to heaven, they were full of blood, and he uttered a funeral prayer for the living and the dead. In a transport of despair his sister issued from the tent, and adjured the general of the Cufians, that he would not suffer Hosein to be murdered before his eyes: a tear trickled down his venerable beard; and the boldest of his soldiers fell back on every side as the dying hero threw himself among them. The remorseless Shamer, a name detested by the faithful, reproached their cowardice; and the grandson of Mahomet was slain with three and thirty strokes of lances and swords. After they had trampled on his body, they carried his head to the castle of Cufa, and the inhuman Obeidollah struck him on the mouth with a cane: "Alas!" exclaimed an aged Musulman, "on these lips have I seen the lips of the apostle of God!" In a distant age and climate the tragic scene of the death of Hosein will awaken the sympathy of the coldest reader.[179] On the annual festival of his martyrdom, in the devout pilgrimage to his sepulchre, his Persian votaries abandon their souls to the religious frenzy of sorrow and indignation.[180]

Posterity of Mahomet and Ali.
    When the sisters and children of Ali were brought in chains to the throne of Damascus, the caliph was advised to extirpate the enmity of a popular and hostile race, whom he had injured beyond the hope of reconciliation. But Yezid preferred the counsels of mercy; and the mourning family was honourably dismissed to mingle their

---

179. I have abridged the interesting narrative of Ockley (tom. ii. p. 170–231.). It is long and minute; but the pathetic, almost always, consists in the detail of little circumstances.

180. Niebuhr the Dane (Voyages en Arabie, &c. tom. ii. p. 208, &c.) is perhaps the only European traveller who has dared to visit Meshed Ali and Meshed Hosein. The two sepulchres are in the hands of the Turks, who tolerate and tax the devotion of the Persian heretics. The festival of the death of Hosein is amply described by Sir John Chardin, a traveller whom I have often praised.

tears with their kindred at Medina. The glory of martyrdom superseded the right of primogeniture; and the twelve IMAMS,[181] or pontiffs, of the Persian creed are Ali, Hassan, Hosein, and the lineal descendants of Hosein to the ninth generation. Without arms, or treasures, or subjects, they successively enjoyed the veneration of the people, and provoked the jealousy of the reigning caliphs: their tombs at Mecca or Medina, on the banks of the Euphrates, or in the province of Chorasan, are still visited by the devotion of their sect. Their names were often the pretence of sedition and civil war; but these royal saints despised the pomp of the world, submitted to the will of God and the injustice of man, and devoted their innocent lives to the study and practice of religion. The twelfth and last of the Imams, conspicuous by the title of *Mahadi*, or the Guide, surpassed the solitude and sanctity of his predecessors. He concealed himself in a cavern near Bagdad: the time and place of his death are unknown; and his votaries pretend, that he still lives, and will appear before the day of judgment to overthrow the tyranny of Dejal, or the Antichrist.[182] In the lapse of two or three centuries the posterity of Abbas, the uncle of Mahomet, had multiplied to the number of thirty-three thousand:[183] the race of Ali might be equally prolific; the meanest individual was above the first and greatest of princes; and the most eminent were supposed to excel the perfection of angels. But their adverse fortune, and the wide extent of the Musulman empire, allowed an ample scope for every bold and artful impostor, who claimed affinity with the holy seed: the sceptre of the Almohades in Spain and Afric, of the Fatimites in Egypt and Syria,[184] of the Sultans of Yemen, and of the Sophis of

181. The general article of *Imam*, in d'Herbelot's Bibliotheque, will indicate the succession; and the lives of the *twelve* are given under their respective names.

182. The name of *Antichrist* may seem ridiculous, but the Mahometans have liberally borrowed the fables of every religion (Sale's Preliminary Discourse, p. 80. 82.). In the royal stable of Ispahan, two horses were always kept saddled, one for the Mahadi himself, the other for his lieutenant, Jesus the son of Mary.

183. In the year of the Hegira 200 (A.D. 815). See d'Herbelot, p. 546.

184. D'Herbelot, p. 342. The enemies of the Fatimites disgraced them by a Jewish origin. Yet they accurately deduced their genealogy from Jaafar, the sixth Imam; and the impartial Abulfeda allows (Annal. Moslem. p. 230.) that they were owned by many, qui absque controversiâ genuini sunt Alidarum, homine propaginum suæ gentis exacte callentes. He quotes some lines from the celebrated *Scherif or Rahdi*, Egone humilitatem induam in terris hostium? (I suspect him to be an Edrissite of Sicily) cum in Ægypto sit Chalifa de gente Alii, quocum ego communem habeo patrem et vindicem.

Persia,[185] has been consecrated by this vague and ambiguous title. Under their reigns it might be dangerous to dispute the legitimacy of their birth; and one of the Fatimite caliphs silenced an indiscreet question, by drawing his scymetar: "This," said Moez, "is my pedigree; and these," casting an handful of gold to his soldiers, "and these are my kindred and my children." In the various conditions of princes, or doctors, or nobles, or merchants, or beggars, a swarm of the genuine or fictitious descendants of Mahomet and Ali is honoured with the appellation of sheiks, or sherifs, or emirs. In the Ottoman empire, they are distinguished by a green turban, receive a stipend from the treasury, are judged only by their chief, and, however debased by fortune or character, still assert the proud pre-eminence of their birth. A family of three hundred persons, the pure and orthodox branch of the caliph Hassan, is preserved without taint or suspicion in the holy cities of Mecca and Medina, and still retains, after the revolutions of twelve centuries, the custody of the temple and the sovereignty of their native land. The fame and merit of Mahomet would ennoble a plebeian race, and the ancient blood of the Koreish transcends the recent majesty of the kings of the earth.[186]

Success of Mahomet. The talents of Mahomet are entitled to our applause, but his success has perhaps too strongly attracted our admiration. Are we surprised that a multitude of proselytes should embrace the doctrine and the passions of an eloquent fanatic? In the heresies of the church, the same seduction has been tried and repeated from the time of the apostles to that of the reformers. Does it seem incredible that a private citizen should grasp the sword and the sceptre, subdue his native country, and erect a monarchy by his victorious arms? In the moving picture of the dynasties of the East, an hundred fortunate usurpers have arisen from a baser origin, surmounted more formidable obstacles, and filled a larger scope of empire and conquest. Mahomet was alike instructed to preach and to fight, and the union of these opposite qualities, while it enhanced

185. The kings of Persia of the last dynasty are descended from Sheik Sefi, a saint of the xiv[th] century, and through him from Moussa Cassem, the son of Hosein, the son of Ali (Olearius, p. 957. Chardin, tom. iii. p. 288.). But I cannot trace the intermediate degrees in any genuine or fabulous pedigree. If they were truly Fatimites, they might draw their origin from the princes of Mazanderan, who reigned in the ix[th] century (d'Herbelot, p. 96.).

186. The present state of the family of Mahomet and Ali is most accurately described by Demetrius Cantemir (Hist. of the Othman Empire, p. 94.); and Niebuhr (Description de l'Arabie, p. 9–16. 317, &c.). It is much to be lamented, that the Danish traveller was unable to purchase the chronicles of Arabia.

his merit, contributed to his success: the operation of force and persuasion, of enthusiasm and fear, continually acted on each other, till every barrier yielded to their irresistible power. His voice invited the Arabs to freedom and victory, to arms and rapine, to the indulgence of their darling passions in this world and the other; the restraints which he imposed were requisite to establish the credit of the prophet, and to exercise the obedience of the people; and the only objection to his success, was his rational creed of the unity and perfections of God. It is not the propagation but the permanency of his religion that deserves *Permanency* our wonder: the same pure and perfect impression which he *of his religion.* engraved at Mecca and Medina, is preserved, after the revolutions of twelve centuries, by the Indian, the African, and the Turkish proselytes of the Koran. If the Christian apostles, St. Peter or St. Paul, could return to the Vatican, they might possibly enquire the name of the Deity who is worshipped with such mysterious rites in that magnificent temple: at Oxford or Geneva, they would experience less surprise; but it might still be incumbent on them to peruse the catechism of the church, and to study the orthodox commentators on their own writings and the words of their master. But the Turkish dome of St. Sophia, with an encrease of splendór and size, represents the humble tabernacle erected at Medina by the hands of Mahomet. The Mahometans have uniformly withstood the temptation of reducing the object of their faith and devotion to a level with the senses and imagination of man. "I believe in one God, and Mahomet the apostle of God," is the simple and invariable profession of Islam. The intellectual image of the Deity has never been degraded by any visible idol; the honours of the prophet have never transgressed the measure of human virtue; and his living precepts have restrained the gratitude of his disciples within the bounds of reason and religion. The votaries of Ali have indeed consecrated the memory of their hero, his wife, and his children, and some of the Persian doctors pretend that the divine essence was incarnate in the person of the Imams; but their superstition is universally condemned by the Sonnites; and their impiety has afforded a seasonable warning against the worship of saints and martyrs. The metaphysical questions on the attributes of God, and the liberty of man, have been agitated in the schools of the Mahometans, as well as in those of the Christians; but among the former they have never engaged the passions of the people or disturbed the tranquillity of the state. The cause of this important difference may be found in the separation or union of the regal and sacerdotal characters. It was the interest of the caliphs, the successors of the prophet and commanders of the faithful, to repress and discourage all religious innovations: the order, the discipline, the temporal and spiritual ambition of the clergy, are unknown to the Moslems; and the sages of the law are the guides of their conscience and the oracles of their faith. From the Atlantic to the Ganges, the Koran is acknowledged as the fundamental code, not only of theology but of civil and criminal jurisprudence; and the laws which regulate the actions and the property of mankind, are guarded by the infallible and immutable sanction of the will of God. This religious servitude is attended with some practical disadvantage; the illiterate legislator had been often misled by his own prejudices and those of his country; and the institutions of the Arabian desert may be ill-adapted to the wealth and numbers of Ispahan and Constantinople. On these occasions, the Cadhi respectfully places on his head the holy volume, and substitutes a dextrous interpretation more apposite to the principles of equity, and the manners and policy of the times.

His merit towards his country. His beneficial or pernicious influence on the public happiness is the last consideration in the character of Mahomet. The most bitter or most bigotted of his Christian or Jewish foes, will surely allow that he assumed a false commission to inculcate a salutary doctrine, less perfect only than their own. He piously supposed, as the basis of his religion, the truth and sanctity of *their* prior revelations, the virtues and miracles of their founders. The idols of Arabia were broken before the throne of God; the blood of human victims was expiated by prayer, and fasting, and alms, the laudable or innocent arts of devotion; and his rewards and punishments of a future life were painted by the images most congenial to an ignorant and carnal generation. Mahomet was perhaps incapable of dictating a moral and political system for the use of his countrymen: but he breathed among the faithful a spirit of charity and friendship, recommended the practice of the social virtues, and checked, by his laws and precepts, the thirst of revenge and the oppression of widows and orphans. The hostile tribes were united in faith and obedience, and the valour which had been idly spent in domestic quarrels, was vigorously directed against a foreign enemy. Had the impulse been less powerful, Arabia, free at home, and formidable abroad, might have flourished under a succession of her native monarchs. Her sovereignty was lost by the extent and rapidity of conquest. The colonies of the nation were scattered over the East and West, and their blood was mingled with the blood of their converts and captives. After the reign of three caliphs, the throne was transported from Medina to the valley of Damascus and the banks of the Tigris; the holy cities were violated by impious war; Arabia was ruled by the rod of a subject, perhaps of a stranger; and the Bedoweens of the desert, awakening from their dream of dominion, resumed their old and solitary independence.[187]

187. The writers of the Modern Universal History (vol. i. and ii.) have compiled, in 850 folio pages, the life of Mahomet and the annals of the caliphs. They enjoyed the advantage of reading, and sometimes correcting, the Arabic texts; yet, notwithstanding their high-sounding boasts, I cannot find, after the conclusion of my work, that they have afforded me much (if any) additional information. The dull mass is not quickened by a spark of philosophy or taste: and the compilers indulge the criticism of acrimonious bigotry against Boulainvilliers, Sale, Gagnier, and all who have treated Mahomet with favour, or even justice.

[CHAPTERS LI–LIII]

After Mahomet's death the empire of his successors, the caliphs, appears to display the same sequence of apparent prosperity yielding to eventual collapse as had overtaken the Roman empire in the West:

We should vainly seek the indissoluble union and easy obedience that pervaded the government of Augustus and the Antonines; but the progress of the Mahometan religion diffused over this ample space a general resemblance of manners and opinions. The language and laws of the Koran were studied with equal devotion at Samarcand and Seville: the Moor and the Indian embraced as countrymen and brothers in the pilgrimage of Mecca; and the Arabian language was adopted as the popular idiom in all the provinces to the westward of the Tigris. (*DF*, iii. 322)

But the inconveniences which broad and absolute dominion brings in its wake are as inevitable on the banks of the Tigris as the banks of the Tiber. Military despotism cannot survive without the artificial support of mercenary troops, and mercenary troops – in the case of the caliphs, Turks 'who in four years created, deposed, and murdered three commanders of the faithful' – are prepared to entertain only shallow loyalties:

As often as the Turks were inflamed by fear, or rage, or avarice, these caliphs were dragged by the feet, exposed naked to the scorching sun, beaten with iron clubs, and compelled to purchase, by the abdication of their dignity, a short reprieve of inevitable fate. At length, however, the fury of the tempest was spent or diverted: the Abbassides returned to the less turbulent residence of Bagdad; the insolence of the Turks was curbed with a firmer and more skilful hand, and their numbers were divided and destroyed in foreign warfare. But the nations of the East had been taught to trample on the successors of the prophet; and the blessings of domestic peace were obtained by the relaxation of strength and discipline. So uniform are the mischiefs of military despotism, that I seem to repeat the story of the prætorians of Rome. (*DF*, iii. 366)

However, such moments are unusual and isolated in *The Decline and Fall* as a whole (because Gibbon does not in general subscribe to a cyclical view of human history), and in the final three volumes in particular, where his historical sensibility is becoming increasingly attuned to the strands of filiation which connect the remote to the recent past in relationships of development, rather than repetition. His most remarkable essay in this vein is chapter LIV, on the obscure Byzantine sect of the Paulicians. From this apparently unpromising material Gibbon develops a startling analysis of the origins of the religious culture of northern Europe in his own day.

CHAPTER LIV

Origin and Doctrine of the Paulicians. — Their Persecution by the Greek
Emperors. — Revolt in Armenia, &c. — Transplantation into Thrace. —
Propagation in the West. — The Seeds, Character, and Consequences of the
Reformation.

Supine
superstition of
the Greek
church.

In the profession of Christianity, the variety of national characters may be clearly distinguished. The natives of Syria and Egypt abandoned their lives to lazy and contemplative devotion: Rome again aspired to the dominion of the world; and the wit of the lively and loquacious Greeks was consumed in the disputes of metaphysical theology. The incomprehensible mysteries of the Trinity and Incarnation, instead of commanding their silent submission, were agitated in vehement and subtle controversies, which enlarged their faith at the expence perhaps of their charity and reason. From the council of Nice to the end of the seventh century, the peace and unity of the church was invaded by these spiritual wars; and so deeply did they affect the decline and fall of the empire, that the historian has too often been compelled to attend the synods, to explore the creeds, and to enumerate the sects, of this busy period of ecclesiastical annals. From the beginning of the eighth century to the last ages of the Byzantine empire the sound of controversy was seldom heard: curiosity was exhausted, zeal was fatigued; and, in the decrees of six councils, the articles of the Catholic faith had been irrevocably defined. The spirit of dispute, however vain and pernicious, requires some energy and exercise of the mental faculties; and the prostrate Greeks were content to fast, to pray, and to believe, in blind obedience to the patriarch and his clergy. During a long dream of superstition, the Virgin and the Saints, their visions and miracles, their relics and images, were preached by the monks and worshipped by the people; and the appellation of people might be extended without injustice to the first ranks of civil society. At an unseasonable moment, the Isaurian emperors attempted somewhat rudely to awaken their subjects: under their influence, reason might obtain some proselytes, a far greater number was swayed by interest or fear; but the

Eastern world embraced or deplored their visible deities, and the restoration of images was celebrated as the feast of orthodoxy. In this passive and unanimous state the ecclesiastical rulers were relieved from the toil, or deprived of the pleasure, of persecution. The Pagans had disappeared; the Jews were silent and obscure; the disputes with the Latins were rare and remote hostilities against a national enemy; and the sects of Egypt and Syria enjoyed a free toleration, under the shadow of the Arabian caliphs. About the middle of the seventh century, a branch of Manichæans was selected as the victims of spiritual tyranny: their patience was at length exasperated to despair and rebellion; and their exile has scattered over the West the seeds of reformation. These important events will justify some enquiry into the doctrine and story of the PAULICIANS;[1] and, as they cannot plead for themselves, our candid criticism will magnify the *good*, and abate or suspect the *evil*, that is reported by their adversaries.

The Gnostics, who had distracted the infancy, were oppressed by the greatness and authority, of the church. Instead of emulating or surpassing the wealth, learning, and numbers, of the Catholics, their obscure remnant was driven from the capitals of the East and West, and confined to the villages and mountains along the borders of the Euphrates. Some vestige of the Marcionites may be detected in the fifth century;[2] but the numerous sects were finally lost in the odious name of the Manichæans; and these heretics, who presumed to reconcile the doctrines of Zoroaster and Christ, were pursued by the two religions with equal and unrelenting hatred. Under the grandson of Heraclius, in the neighbourhood of Samosata, more famous for the birth of Lucian than for the title of a Syrian kingdom, a reformer arose, esteemed by the *Paulicians* as the chosen messenger of truth. In his humble dwelling of Mananalis, Constantine entertained a deacon, who returned from Syrian captivity, and received the inestimable gift of

Origin of the Paulicians, or disciples of St. Paul, A.D. 660, &c.

---

1. The errors and virtues of the Paulicians are weighed, with his usual judgment and candour, by the learned Mosheim (Hist. Ecclesiast. seculum ix. p. 311, &c.). He draws his original intelligence from Photius (contra Manichæos, l. i.) and Peter Siculus (Hist. Manichæorum). The first of these accounts has not fallen into my hands; the second, which Mosheim prefers, I have read in a Latin version inserted in the Maxima Bibliotheca

Patrum (tom. xvi. p. 754–764.), from the edition of the Jesuit Raderus (Ingolstadii, 1604, in 4º).

2. In the time of Theodoret, the diocese of Cyrrhus, in Syria, contained eight hundred villages. Of these, two were inhabited by Arians and Eunomians, and eight by *Marcionites*, whom the laborious bishop reconciled to the Catholic church (Dupin, Bibliot. Ecclesiastique, tom. iv. p. 81, 82.).

the New Testament, which was already concealed from the vulgar by the prudence of the Greek, and perhaps of the Gnostic, clergy.[3] These books became the measure of his studies and the rule of his faith; and the Catholics, who dispute his interpretation, acknowledge that his text was genuine and sincere. But he attached himself with peculiar devotion to the writings and character of St. Paul: the name of the Paulicians is derived by their enemies from some unknown and domestic teacher; but I am confident that they gloried in their affinity to the apostle of the Gentiles. His disciples, Titus, Timothy, Sylvanus, Tychichus, were represented by Constantine and his fellow-labourers: the names of the apostolic churches were applied to the congregations which they assembled in Armenia and Cappadocia; and this innocent allegory revived the example and memory of the first

Their bible.   ages. In the gospel, and the epistles of St. Paul, his faithful follower investigated the creed of primitive Christianity; and, whatever might be the success, a protestant reader will applaud the spirit, of the enquiry. But if the scriptures of the Paulicians were pure, they were not perfect. Their founders rejected the two epistles of St. Peter,[4] the apostle of the circumcision, whose dispute with their favourite for the observance of the law could not easily be forgiven.[5] They agreed with their Gnostic brethren in the universal contempt for the Old Testament, the books of Moses and the prophets, which have been consecrated by the decrees of the Catholic church. With equal boldness, and doubtless with more reason, Constantine, the new Sylvanus, disclaimed the visions, which, in so many bulky and splendid volumes, had been published by the Oriental sects;[6]

---

3. Nobis profanis ista (*sacra Evangelia*) legere non licet sed sacerdotibus duntaxat; was the first scruple of a Catholic when he was advised to read the Bible (Petr. Sicul. p. 761.).

4. In rejecting the *second* epistle of St. Peter, the Paulicians are justified by some of the most respectable of the ancients and moderns (see Wetstein ad loc. Simon, Hist. Critique du Nouveau Testament, c. 17.). They likewise overlooked the Apocalypse (Petr. Sicul. p. 756.); but as such neglect is not imputed as a crime, the Greeks of the ix[th] century must have been careless of the credit and honour of the Revelations.

5. This contention, which has not escaped the malice of Porphyry, supposes some error

and passion in one or both of the apostles. By Chrysostom, Jerom, and Erasmus, it is represented as a sham quarrel, a pious fraud, for the benefit of the Gentiles and the correction of the Jews (Middleton's Works, vol. ii. p. 1–20.).

6. Those who are curious of this heterodox library, may consult the researches of Beausobre (Hist. Critique du Manicheisme, tom. i. p. 305–437.). Even in Africa, St. Austin could describe the Manichæan books, tam multi, tam grandes, tam pretiosi codices (contra Faust. xiii. 14.); but he adds, without pity, Incendite omnes illas membranas: and his advice has been rigorously followed.

the fabulous productions of the Hebrew patriarchs and the sages of the East; the spurious gospels, epistles, and acts, which in the first age had overwhelmed the orthodox code; the theology of Manes, and the authors of the kindred heresies; and the thirty generations, or æons, which had been created by the fruitful fancy of Valentine. The Paulicians sincerely condemned the memory and opinions of the Manichæan sect, and complained of the injustice which impressed that invidious name on the simple votaries of St. Paul and of Christ.

Of the ecclesiastical chain, many links had been broken by the Paulician reformers; and their liberty was enlarged, as they reduced the number of masters, at whose voice profane reason must bow to mystery and miracle. The early separation of the *The simplicity of their belief and worship.* Gnostics had preceded the establishment of the Catholic worship; and against the gradual innovations of discipline and doctrine, they were as strongly guarded by habit and aversion, as by the silence of St. Paul and the evangelists. The objects which had been transformed by the magic of superstition, appeared to the eyes of the Paulicians in their genuine and naked colours. An image made without hands, was the common workmanship of a mortal artist, to whose skill alone the wood and canvas must be indebted for their merit or value. The miraculous relics were an heap of bones and ashes, destitute of life or virtue, or of any relation, perhaps, with the person to whom they were ascribed. The true and vivifying cross was a piece of sound or rotten timber; the body and blood of Christ, a loaf of bread and a cup of wine, the gifts of nature and the symbols of grace. The mother of God was degraded from her celestial honours and immaculate virginity; and the saints and angels were no longer solicited to exercise the laborious office, of mediation in heaven, and ministry upon earth. In the practice, or at least in the theory of the sacraments, the Paulicians were inclined to abolish all visible objects of worship, and the words of the gospel were, in their judgment, the baptism and communion of the faithful. They indulged a convenient latitude for the interpretation of scripture; and as often as they were pressed by the literal sense, they could escape to the intricate mazes of figure and allegory. Their utmost diligence must have been employed to dissolve the connection between the old and the new testament; since they adored the latter as the oracles of God, and abhorred the former, as the fabulous and absurd invention of men or dæmons. We cannot be surprised, that they should have found in the gospel, the orthodox mystery of the trinity: but instead of confessing the human nature and substantial sufferings of Christ, they amused their fancy with a celestial body that passed through the virgin like water through a pipe; with a phantastic crucifixion, that eluded the vain and impotent malice of the Jews. A creed thus simple and spiritual was not adapted to the genius of the times;[7]

They hold the two principles of the Magians and Manichæans.

and the rational Christian who might have been contented with the light yoke and easy burthen of Jesus and his apostles, was justly offended, that the Paulicians should dare to violate the unity of God, the first article of natural and revealed religion. Their belief and their trust was in the Father, of Christ, of the human soul, and of the invisible world. But they likewise held the eternity of matter; a stubborn and rebellious substance, the origin of a second principle, of an active being, who has created this visible world, and exercises his temporal reign till the final consummation of death and sin.[8] The appearances of moral and physical evil had established the two principles in the ancient philosophy and religion of the East; from whence this doctrine was transfused to the various swarms of the Gnostics. A thousand shades may be devised in the nature and character of *Ahriman*, from a rival god to a subordinate dæmon, from passion and frailty to pure and perfect malevolence: but, in spite of our efforts, the goodness, and the power, of Ormusd are placed at the opposite extremities of the line; and every step that approaches the one must recede in equal proportion from the other.[9]

The establishment of the Paulicians in Armenia, Pontus, &c.

The apostolic labours of Constantine-Sylvanus, soon multiplied the number of his disciples, the secret recompence of spiritual ambition. The remnant of the Gnostic sects, and especially the Manichæans of Armenia, were united under his standard; many Catholics were converted or seduced by his arguments; and he preached with success in the regions of Pontus[10] and Cappadocia, which had long since imbibed the religion of Zoroaster. The

---

7. The six capital errors of the Paulicians are defined by Peter Siculus (p. 756.) with much prejudice and passion.

8. Primum illorum axioma est, duo rerum esse principia; Deum malum et Deum bonum aliumque hujus mundi conditorem et principem, et alium futuri ævi (Petr. Sicul. p. 756.).

9. Two learned critics, Beausobre (Hist. Critique du Manicheisme, l. i. iv, v, vi.) and

Mosheim (Institut. Hist. Eccles. and de Rebus Christianis ante Constantinum, sec. i, ii, iii.), have laboured to explore and discriminate the various systems of the Gnostics on the subject of the two principles.

10. The countries between the Euphrates and the Halys, were possessed above 350 years by the Medes (Herodot. l. i. c. 103.) and Persians; and the kings of Pontus were of the royal race

Paulician teachers were distinguished only by their scriptural names, by the modest title of fellow-pilgrims, by the austerity of their lives, their zeal or knowledge, and the credit of some extraordinary gifts of the holy spirit. But they were incapable of desiring, or at least of obtaining, the wealth and honours of the Catholic prelacy: such anti-christian pride they bitterly censured; and even the rank of elders or presbyters was condemned as an institution of the Jewish synagogue. The new sect was loosely spread over the provinces of Asia Minor to the westward of the Euphrates; six of their principal congregations represented the churches to which St. Paul had addressed his epistles; and their founder chose his residence in the neighbourhood of Colonia,[11] in the same district of Pontus which had been celebrated by the altars of Bellona[12] and the miracles of Gregory.[13] After a mission of twenty-seven years, Sylvanus, who had retired from the tolerating government of the Arabs, fell a sacrifice to Roman persecution. The laws of the pious emperors, which seldom touched the lives of less odious heretics, proscribed without mercy or disguise the tenets, the books, and the persons of the Montanists and Manichæans: the books were delivered to the flames; and all who should presume to secrete such writings, or to profess such opinions, were devoted to an ignominious death.[14] A Greek minister, armed with legal and military powers, appeared at Colonia to strike the shepherd, and

Persecution of the Greek emperors.

---

of the Achæmenides (Salust. Fragment. l. iii. with the French supplement and notes of the president de Brosses).

11. Most probably founded by Pompey after the conquest of Pontus. This Colonia, on the Lycus above Neo-Cæsarea, is named by the Turks Coulei-hisar, or Chonac, a populous town in a strong country (d'Anville, Geographie Ancienne, tom. ii. p. 34. Tournefort, Voyage du Levant, tom. iii. lettre xxi. p. 293.).

12. The temple of Bellona at Comana in Pontus, was a powerful and wealthy foundation, and the high priest was respected as the second person in the kingdom. As the sacerdotal office had been occupied by his mother's family, Strabo (l. xii. p. 809. 835. 836, 837.) dwells with peculiar complacency on the temple, the worship, and festival, which was twice celebrated every year. But the Bellona of Pontus had the features and

character of the goddess, not of war, but of love.

13. Gregory, bishop of Neo-Cæsarea (A.D. 240–265), surnamed Thaumaturgus, or the Wonder-worker. An hundred years afterwards, the history or romance of his life was composed by Gregory of Nyssa, his namesake and countryman, the brother of the great St. Basil.

14. Hoc cæterum ad sua egregia facinora, divini atque orthodoxi Imperatores addiderunt, ut Manichæos Montanosque capitali puniri sententiâ juberent, eorumque libros, quocunque in loco inventi essent, flammis tradi; quòd siquis uspiam eosdem occultasse deprehenderetur, hunc eundem mortis pœnæ addici, ejusque bona in fiscum inferri (Petr. Sicul. p. 759.). What more could bigotry and persecution desire?

to reclaim, if possible, the lost sheep. By a refinement of cruelty, Simeon placed the unfortunate Sylvanus before a line of his disciples, who were commanded, as the price of their pardon and the proof of their repentance, to massacre their spiritual father. They turned aside from the impious office; the stones dropt from their filial hands, and of the whole number, only one executioner could be found, a new David, as he is styled by the Catholics, who boldly overthrew the giant of heresy. This apostate, Justus was his name, again deceived and betrayed his unsuspecting brethren, and a new conformity to the acts of St. Paul may be found in the conversion of Simeon: like the apostle, he embraced the doctrine which he had been sent to persecute, renounced his honours and fortunes, and acquired among the Paulicians the fame of a missionary and a martyr. They were not ambitious of martyrdom,[15] but in a calamitous period of one hundred and fifty years, their patience sustained whatever zeal could inflict: and power was insufficient to eradicate the obstinate vegetation of fanaticism and reason. From the blood and ashes of the first victims, a succession of teachers and congregations repeatedly arose: amidst their foreign hostilities, they found leisure for domestic quarrels: they preached, they disputed, they suffered; and the virtues, the apparent virtues, of Sergius, in a pilgrimage of thirty-three years, are reluctantly confessed by the orthodox historians.[16] The native cruelty of Justinian the second was stimulated by a pious cause, and he vainly hoped to extinguish in a single conflagration the name and memory of the Paulicians. By their primitive simplicity, their abhorrence of popular superstition, the Iconoclast princes might have been reconciled to some erroneous doctrines; but they themselves were exposed to the calumnies of the monks, and they chose to be the tyrants, lest they should be accused as the accomplices, of the Manichæans. Such a reproach has sullied the clemency of Nicephorus, who relaxed in their favour the severity of the penal statutes, nor will his character sustain the honour of a more liberal motive. The feeble Michael the first, the rigid Leo the Armenian, were foremost in the race of persecution;

---

15. It should seem, that the Paulicians allowed themselves some latitude of equivocation and mental reservation: till the Catholics discovered the pressing questions, which reduced them to the alternative of apostacy or martyrdom (Petr. Sicul. p. 760.).

16. The persecution is told by Petrus Siculus

(p. 579–763.) with satisfaction and pleasantry. Justus *justa* persolvit. Simeon was not τιτος but κητος (the pronunciation of the two vowels must have been nearly the same), a great whale that drowned the mariners who mistook him for an island. See likewise Cedrenus (p. 432–435.).

but the prize must doubtless be adjudged to the sanguinary devotion of Theodora, who restored the images to the Oriental church. Her inquisitors explored the cities and mountains of the lesser Asia, and the flatterers of the empress have affirmed that, in a short reign, one hundred thousand Paulicians were extirpated by the sword, the gibbet, or the flames. Her guilt or merit has perhaps been stretched beyond the measure of truth: but if the account be allowed, it must be presumed that many simple Iconoclasts were punished under a more odious name; and that some who were driven from the church, unwillingly took refuge in the bosom of heresy.

The most furious and desperate of rebels are the sectaries of a religion long persecuted, and at length provoked. In an holy cause they are no longer susceptible of fear or remorse: the justice of their arms hardens them against the feelings of humanity; and they revenge their fathers wrongs on the children of their tyrants. *Revolt of the Paulicians, A.D. 845–880.* Such have been the Hussites of Bohemia and the Calvinists of France, and such, in the ninth century, were the Paulicians of Armenia and the adjacent provinces.[17] They were first awakened to the massacre of a governor and bishop, who exercised the Imperial mandate of converting or destroying the heretics; and the deepest recesses of mount Argæus protected their independence and revenge. A more dangerous and consuming flame was kindled by the persecution of Theodora, and the revolt of Carbeas, a valiant Paulician, who commanded the guards of the general of the East. His father had been impaled by the Catholic inquisitors; and religion, or at least nature, might justify his desertion and revenge. Five thousand of his brethren were united by the same motives; they renounced the allegiance of anti-christian Rome; a Saracen emir introduced Carbeas to the caliph; and the commander of the faithful extended his sceptre to the implacable enemy of the Greeks. In the mountains between Siwas and Trebizond he founded or fortified the city of Tephrice,[18] *They fortify Tephrice,* which is still occupied by a fierce and licentious people, and the neighbouring hills were covered with the Paulician fugitives, who now

---

17. Petrus Siculus (p. 763, 764.), the continuator of Theophanes (l. iv. c. 4. p. 103, 104.), Cedrenus (p. 541, 542. 545.), and Zonaras (tom. ii. l. xvi. p. 156.), describe the revolt and exploits of Carbeas and his Paulicians.
18. Otter (Voyage en Turquie et en Perse,

tom. ii.) is probably the only Frank who has visited the independent Barbarians of Tephrice, now Divrigni, from whom he fortunately escaped in the train of a Turkish officer.

reconciled the use of the Bible and the sword. During more than thirty years, Asia was afflicted by the calamities of foreign and domestic war: in their hostile inroads the disciples of St. Paul were joined with those of Mahomet; and the peaceful Christians, the aged parent and tender virgin, who were delivered into barbarous servitude, might justly accuse the intolerant spirit of their sovereign. So urgent was the mischief, so intolerable the shame, that even the dissolute Michael, the son of Theodora, was compelled to march in person against the Paulicians: he was defeated under the walls of Samosata; and the Roman emperor fled before the heretics whom his mother had condemned to the flames. The Saracens fought under the same banners, but the victory was ascribed to Carbeas; and the captive generals, with more than an hundred tribunes, were either released by his avarice, or tortured by his fanaticism. The valour and ambition of Chrysocheir,[19] his successor, embraced a wider circle of rapine and revenge. In alliance with his faithful Moslems, he boldly penetrated into the heart of Asia; the troops of the frontier and the palace were repeatedly overthrown; the edicts of persecution were answered by the

and pillage Asia Minor. pillage of Nice and Nicomedia, of Ancyra and Ephesus; nor could the apostle St. John protect from violation his city and sepulchre. The cathedral of Ephesus was turned into a stable for mules and horses; and the Paulicians vied with the Saracens in their contempt and abhorrence of images and relics. It is not unpleasing to observe the triumph of rebellion over the same despotism which has disdained the prayers of an injured people. The emperor Basil, the Macedonian, was reduced to sue for peace, to offer a ransom for the captives, and to request, in the language of moderation and charity, that Chrysocheir would spare his fellow-christians, and content himself with a royal donative of gold and silver and silk garments. "If the emperor," replied the insolent fanatic, "be desirous of peace, let him abdicate the East, and reign without molestation in the West. If he refuse, the servants of the Lord will precipitate him from the throne." The reluctant Basil suspended the treaty, accepted the defiance, and led his army into the land of heresy, which he wasted with fire and sword. The open country of the Paulicians was exposed to the same

---

19. In the history of Chrysocheir, Genesius (Chron. p. 67–70. edit. Venet.) has exposed the nakedness of the empire. Constantine Porphyrogenitus (in Vit. Basil. c. 37–43. p. 166–171.) has displayed the glory of his grandfather. Cedrenus (p. 570–573.) is without their passions or their knowledge.

calamities which they had inflicted; but when he had explored the strength of Tephrice, the multitude of the Barbarians, and the ample magazines of arms and provisions, he desisted with a sigh from the hopeless siege. On his return to Constantinople he laboured, by the foundation of convents and churches, to secure the aid of his celestial patrons, of Michael the archangel and the prophet Elijah; and it was his daily prayer that he might live to transpierce, with three arrows, the head of his impious adversary. Beyond his expectations, the wish was accomplished: after a successful inroad, Chrysocheir was surprised and slain in his retreat; and the rebel's head was triumphantly presented at the foot of the throne. On the reception of this welcome trophy, Basil instantly called for his bow, discharged three arrows with unerring aim, and accepted the applause of the court, who hailed the victory of the royal archer. With Chrysocheir, the glory of the Paulicians faded and withered;[20] on the second expedition of the emperor, the impregnable Tephrice was deserted by the heretics, who sued for mercy or escaped to the borders. The city was ruined, but the spirit of independence survived in the mountains: the Paulicians defended, above a century, their religion and liberty, infested the Roman limits, and maintained their perpetual alliance with the enemies of the empire and the gospel.

Their decline.

About the middle of the eighth century, Constantine, surnamed Copronymus by the worshippers of images, had made an expedition into Armenia, and found, in the cities of Melitene and Theodosiopolis, a great number of Paulicians, his kindred heretics. As a favour or punishment, he transplanted them from the banks of the Euphrates to Constantinople and Thrace; and by this emigration their doctrine was introduced and diffused in Europe.[21] If the sectaries of the metropolis were soon mingled with the promiscuous mass, those of the country struck a deep root in a foreign soil. The Paulicians of Thrace resisted the storms of persecution, maintained a secret correspondence with their Armenian brethren, and gave aid and comfort to their preachers, who solicited, not without success, the infant faith of the Bulgarians.[22] In the tenth century, they were restored and multiplied

Their transplantation from Armenia to Thrace.

20. Συναπεμαρανθη πασα ἡ ανθουσα της Τεφρικης ευανδια. How elegant is the Greek tongue, even in the mouth of Cedrenus!

21. Copronymus transported his συγγενεις, heretics; and thus επλατυνθη ἡ αιρεσις

Παυλικιανον, says Cedrenus (p. 463.), who has copied the annals of Theophanes.

22. Petrus Siculus, who resided nine months at Tephrice (A.D. 870) for the ransom of captives (p. 764.), was informed of their

by a more powerful colony, which John Zimisces[23] transported from the Chalybian hills to the vallies of mount Hæmus. The Oriental clergy, who would have preferred the destruction, impatiently sighed for the absence, of the Manichæans: the warlike emperor had felt and esteemed their valour; their attachment to the Saracens was pregnant with mischief but, on the side of the Danube, against the Barbarians of Scythia, their service might be useful, and their loss would be desirable. Their exile in a distant land was softened by a free toleration: the Paulicians held the city of Philippopolis and the keys of Thrace; the Catholics were their subjects; the Jacobite emigrants their associates: they occupied a line of villages and castles in Macedonia and Epirus; and many native Bulgarians were associated to the communion of arms and heresy. As long as they were awed by power and treated with moderation, their voluntary bands were distinguished in the armies of the empire; and the courage of these *dogs*, ever greedy of war, ever thirsty of human blood, is noticed with astonishment, and almost with reproach, by the pusillanimous Greeks. The same spirit rendered them arrogant and contumacious: they were easily provoked by caprice or injury; and their privileges were often violated by the faithless bigotry of the government and clergy. In the midst of the Norman war, two thousand five hundred Manichæans deserted the standard of Alexius Comnenus,[24] and retired to their native homes. He dissembled till the moment of revenge; invited the chiefs to a friendly conference; and punished the innocent and guilty by imprisonment, confiscation, and baptism. In an interval of peace, the emperor undertook the pious office of reconciling them to the church and state: his winter-quarters were fixed at Philippopolis; and the thirteenth apostle, as he is styled by his pious daughter, consumed whole days and nights in theological controversy. His arguments were fortified, their obstinacy was melted, by the honours and rewards which he bestowed on the most eminent proselytes; and a new city, surrounded with gardens, enriched with immunities, and dignified with his own name, was founded by Alexius, for the residence of his vulgar converts. The important station of

---

intended mission, and addressed his preservative, the Historia Manichæorum, to the new archbishop of the Bulgarians (p. 754.).

23. The colony of Paulicians and Jacobites, transplanted by John Zimisces (A.D. 970.) from Armenia to Thrace, is mentioned by Zonaras (tom. ii. l. xvii. p. 209.) and Anna

Comnena (Alexiad, l. xiv. p. 450, &c.).

24. The Alexiad of Anna Comnena (l. v. p. 131. l. vi. p. 154, 155. l. xiv. p. 450–457. with the annotations of Ducange) records the transactions of her apostolic father with the Manichæans, whose abominable heresy she was desirous of refuting.

Philippopolis was wrested from their hands; the contumacious leaders were secured in a dungeon, or banished from their country; and their lives were spared by the prudence, rather than the mercy, of an emperor, at whose command a poor and solitary heretic was burnt alive before the church of St. Sophia.[25] But the proud hope of eradicating the prejudices of a nation was speedily overturned by the invincible zeal of the Paulicians, who ceased to dissemble or refused to obey. After the departure and death of Alexius, they soon resumed their civil and religious laws. In the beginning of the thirteenth century, their pope or primate (a manifest corruption) resided on the confines of Bulgaria, Croatia, and Dalmatia, and governed, by his vicars, the filial congregations of Italy and France.[26] From that æra, a minute scrutiny might prolong and perpetuate the chain of tradition. At the end of the last age, the sect or colony still inhabited the vallies of mount Hæmus, where their ignorance and poverty were more frequently tormented by the Greek clergy than by the Turkish government. The modern Paulicians have lost all memory of their origin; and their religion is disgraced by the worship of the cross, and the practice of bloody sacrifice, which some captives have imported from the wilds of Tartary.[27]

In the West, the first teachers of the Manichæan theology had been repulsed by the people or suppressed by the prince. The favour and success of the Paulicians in the eleventh and twelfth centuries must be imputed to the strong, though secret, discontent which armed the most pious Christians against the church of Rome. Her avarice was oppressive, her despotism odious: less degenerate perhaps than the Greeks in the worship of saints and images, her innovations were more rapid and scandalous: she had rigorously defined and imposed the doctrine of transubstantiation: the lives of the Latin clergy were more corrupt, and the Eastern bishops might pass for the successors of the apostles, if they were compared with the lordly prelates, who wielded by turns the crosier, the sceptre, and the sword. Three different roads might introduce the Paulicians into the heart of Europe. After the conversion of Hungary, the pilgrims who visited Jerusalem might safely

Their introduction into Italy and France.

25. Basil, a monk, and the author of the Bogomiles, a sect of Gnostics, who soon vanished (Anna Comnena, Alexiad, l. xv. p. 486–494. Mosheim, Hist. Ecclesiastica, p. 420.).

26. Matt. Paris, Hist. Major. p. 267. This passage of our English historian is alleged by

Ducange in an excellent note on Villehardouin (N° 208.), who found the Paulicians at Philippopolis the friends of the Bulgarians.

27. See Marsigli, Stato Militare dell' Impero Ottomano, p. 24.

follow the course of the Danube: in their journey and return they passed through Philippopolis; and the sectaries, disguising their name and heresy, might accompany the French or German caravans to their respective countries. The trade and dominion of Venice pervaded the coast of the Adriatic, and the hospitable republic opened her bosom to foreigners of every climate and religion. Under the Byzantine standard, the Paulicians were often transported to the Greek provinces of Italy and Sicily; in peace and war they freely conversed with strangers and natives, and their opinions were silently propagated in Rome, Milan, and the kingdoms beyond the Alps.[28] It was soon discovered, that many thousand Catholics of every rank, and of either sex, had embraced the Manichæan heresy; and the flames which consumed twelve canons of Orleans, was the first act and signal of persecution. The Bulgarians,[29] a name so innocent in its origin, so odious in its application, spread their branches over the face of Europe. United in common hatred of idolatry and Rome, they were connected by a form of episcopal and presbyterian government; their various sects were discriminated by some fainter or darker shades of theology; but they generally agreed in the two principles, the contempt of the old testament, and the denial of the body of Christ, either on the cross or in the Eucharist. A confession of simple worship and blameless manners is extorted from their enemies; and so high was their standard of perfection, that the encreasing congregations were divided into two classes of disciples, of those who practised, and of those who aspired. It was in the country of the Albigeois,[30]

---

28. The introduction of the Paulicians into Italy and France, is amply discussed by Muratori (Antiquitat. Italiæ medii Ævi, tom. v. dissert. lx. p. 81–152.), and Mosheim (p. 379–382. 419–422.). Yet both have overlooked a curious passage of William the Appulian, who clearly describes them in a battle between the Greeks and Normans, A.D. 1040 (in Muratori, Script. Rerum Ital. tom. v. p. 256.).

> Cum Græcis aderant, quidem quos
>   pessimus error,
> Fecerat amentes, et ab ipso nomen
>   habebant.

But he is so ignorant of their doctrine as to make them a kind of Sabellians or Patripassians.

29. Bulgari, Boulgres, Bougres, a national appellation, has been applied by the French as a term of reproach to usurers and unnatural sinners. The Paterini, or Patelini, has been made to signify a smooth and flattering hypocrite, such as l'Avocat Patelin of that original and pleasant farce (Ducange, Gloss. Latinitat. medii et infimi Ævi). The Manichæans were likewise named Cathari, or the pure, by corruption, Gazari, &c.

30. Of the laws, crusade, and persecution against the Albigeois, a just, though general idea, is expressed by Mosheim (p. 477–481.). The detail may be found in the ecclesiastical historians, ancient and modern, Catholics and Protestants; and among these Fleury is the most impartial and moderate.

in the southern provinces of France, that the Paulicians were most deeply implanted; and the same vicissitudes of martyrdom and revenge which had been displayed in the neighbourhood of the Euphrates, were repeated in the thirteenth century on the banks of the Rhône. The laws of the Eastern emperors were revived by Frederic the second. The insurgents of Tephrice were represented by the barons and cities of Languedoc: Pope Innocent III. surpassed the sanguinary fame of Theodora. It was in cruelty alone that her soldiers could equal the heroes of the Crusades, and the cruelty of her priests was far excelled by the founders of the inquisition;[31] an office more adapted to confirm, than to refute, the belief of an evil principle. The visible assemblies of the Paulicians, or Albigeois, were extirpated by fire and sword; and the bleeding remnant escaped by flight, concealment, or catholic conformity. But the invincible spirit which they had kindled still lived and breathed in the Western world. In the state, in the church, and even in the cloister, a latent succession was preserved of the disciples of St. Paul; who protested against the tyranny of Rome, embraced the bible as the rule of faith, and purified their creed from all the visions of the Gnostic theology. The struggles of Wickliff in England, of Huss in Bohemia, were premature and ineffectual; but the names of Zuinglius, Luther, and Calvin, are pronounced with gratitude as the deliverers of nations.

Persecution of the Albigeois, A.D. 1200, &c.

A philosopher, who calculates the degree of their merit and the value of their reformation, will prudently ask from what articles of faith, *above* or *against* our reason, they have enfranchised the Christians; for such enfranchisement is doubtless a benefit so far as it may be compatible with truth and piety. After a fair discussion we shall rather be surprised by the timidity, than scandalised by the freedom, of our first reformers.[32] With the Jews, they adopted the belief and defence of all the Hebrew scriptures, with all their prodigies, from the garden of Eden to the visions of the prophet Daniel; and they were bound,

Character and consequences of the reformation.

---

31. The Acts (Liber Sententiarum) of the Inquisition of Tholouse (A.D. 1307–1323) have been published by Limborch (Amstelodami, 1692), with a previous History of the Inquisition in General. They deserved a more learned and critical editor. As we must not calumniate even Satan, or the Holy Office, I will observe, that of a list of criminals which fills nineteen folio pages, only fifteen men and four women were delivered to the secular arm.

32. The opinions and proceedings of the reformers are exposed in the second part of the general history of Mosheim: but the balance, which he has held with so clear an eye, and so steady an hand, begins to incline in favour of his Lutheran brethren.

like the Catholics, to justify against the Jews the abolition of a divine law. In the great mysteries of the Trinity and Incarnation the reformers were severely orthodox: they freely adopted the theology of the four, or the six first councils; and with the Athanasian creed, they pronounced the eternal damnation of all who did not believe the Catholic faith. Transubstantiation, the invisible change of the bread and wine into the body and blood of Christ, is a tenet that may defy the power of argument and pleasantry; but instead of consulting the evidence of their senses, of their sight, their feeling, and their taste, the first protestants were entangled in their own scruples, and awed by the words of Jesus in the institution of the sacrament. Luther maintained a *corporeal*, and Calvin a *real*, presence of Christ in the eucharist; and the opinion of Zuinglius, that it is no more than a spiritual communion, a simple memorial, has slowly prevailed in the reformed churches.[33] But the loss of one mystery was amply compensated by the stupendous doctrines of original sin, redemption, faith, grace, and predestination, which have been strained from the epistles of St. Paul. These subtle questions had most assuredly been prepared by the fathers and schoolmen; but the final improvement and popular use may be attributed to the first reformers, who enforced them as the absolute and essential terms of salvation. Hitherto the weight of supernatural belief inclines against the Protestants; and many a sober Christian would rather admit that a wafer is God, than that God is a cruel and capricious tyrant.

Yet the services of Luther and his rivals are solid and important; and the philosopher must own his obligations to these fearless enthusiasts.[34] I. By their hands the lofty fabric of superstition, from the abuse of indulgences to the intercession of the Virgin, has been levelled with the ground. Myriads of both sexes of the monastic profession were restored to the liberty and labours of social life. An hierarchy of saints and angels, of imperfect and subordinate deities, were stripped of their temporal power, and reduced to the enjoyment of celestial happiness: their images and relics were banished from the church; and the credulity of the people was no longer nourished with the daily repetition of miracles and visions. The imitation of Paganism

33. Under Edward VI. our reformation was more bold and perfect: but in the fundamental articles of the church of England, a strong and explicit declaration against the real presence was obliterated in the original copy, to please the people, or the Lutherans, or Queen Elizabeth (Burnet's History of the Reformation, vol. ii. p. 82. 128. 302.).

34. "Had it not been for such men as Luther and myself," said the fanatic Whiston to Halley the philosopher, "you would now be kneeling before an image of St. Winifred."

was supplied by a pure and spiritual worship of prayer and thanksgiving, the most worthy of man, the least unworthy of the Deity. It only remains to observe, whether such sublime simplicity be consistent with popular devotion; whether the vulgar, in the absence of all visible objects, will not be inflamed by enthusiasm, or insensibly subside in languor and indifference. II. The chain of authority was broken, which restrains the bigot from thinking as he pleases, and the slave from speaking as he thinks: the popes, fathers, and councils, were no longer the supreme and infallible judges of the world; and each Christian was taught to acknowledge no law but the scriptures, no interpreter but his own conscience. This freedom however was the consequence, rather than the design, of the reformation. The patriot reformers were ambitious of succeeding the tyrants whom they had dethroned. They imposed with equal rigour their creeds and confessions; they asserted the right of the magistrate to punish heretics with death. The pious or personal animosity of Calvin proscribed in Servetus[35] the guilt of his own rebellion;[36] and the flames of Smithfield, in which he was afterwards consumed, had been kindled for the Anabaptists by the zeal of Cranmer.[37] The nature of the tyger was the same, but he was gradually deprived of his teeth and fangs. A spiritual and temporal kingdom was possessed by the Roman pontiff: the Protestant doctors were subjects of an humble rank, without revenue or jurisdiction. *His* decrees were consecrated by the antiquity of the Catholic church: *their* arguments and disputes were submitted to the people; and their appeal to private judgment was accepted beyond their wishes, by curiosity and enthusiasm. Since the days of Luther and Calvin, a secret reformation has been silently working

35. The article of *Servet* in the Dictionaire Critique of Chauffepié, is the best account which I have seen of this shameful transaction. See likewise the Abbé d'Artigny, Nouveaux Memoires d'Histoire, &c. tom. ii. p. 55-154.
36. I am more deeply scandalised at the single execution of Servetus, than at the hecatombs which have blazed in the Auto da Fès of Spain and Portugal. 1. The zeal of Calvin seems to have been envenomed by personal malice, and perhaps envy. He accused his adversary before their common enemies, the judges of Vienna, and betrayed, for his destruction, the sacred trust of a private correspondence. 2. The deed of cruelty was not varnished by the

pretence of danger to the church or state. In his passage through Geneva, Servetus was an harmless stranger, who neither preached, nor printed, nor made proselytes. 3. A Catholic inquisitor yields the same obedience which he requires, but Calvin violated the golden rule of doing as he would be done by; a rule which I read in a moral treatise of Isocrates (in Nicocle, tom. i. p. 93. edit. Battie), four hundred years before the publication of the gospel. Ἅ πασχοντες ὑφ' ἑτερων ὀργιζεσθε, ταυτα τοις αλλοις μη ποιειτε.
37. See Burnet, vol. ii. p. 84-86. The sense and humanity of the young king were oppressed by the authority of the primate.

in the bosom of the reformed churches; many weeds of prejudice were eradicated; and the disciples of Erasmus[38] diffused a spirit of freedom and moderation. The liberty of conscience has been claimed as a common benefit, an inalienable right:[39] the free governments of Holland[40] and England[41] introduced the practice of toleration; and the narrow allowance of the laws has been enlarged by the prudence and humanity of the times. In the exercise, the mind has understood the limits, of its powers, and the words and shadows that might amuse the child can no longer satisfy his manly reason. The volumes of controversy are overspread with cobwebs: the doctrine of a Protestant church is far removed from the knowledge or belief of its private members; and the forms of orthodoxy, the articles of faith, are subscribed with a sigh or a smile by the modern clergy. Yet the friends of Christianity are alarmed at the boundless impulse of enquiry and scepticism. The predictions of the Catholics are accomplished: the web of mystery is unravelled by the Arminians, Arians, and Socinians, whose numbers must not be computed from their separate congregations. And the pillars of revelation are shaken by those men who preserve the name without the substance of religion, who indulge the licence without the temper of philosophy.[42]

38. Erasmus may be considered as the father of rational theology. After a slumber of an hundred years, it was revived by the Arminians of Holland, Grotius, Limborch, and Le Clerc: in England by Chillingworth, the latitudinarians of Cambridge (Burnet, Hist. of own Times, vol. i. p. 261–268. octavo edition), Tillotson, Clarke, Hoadley, &c.

39. I am sorry to observe, that the three writers of the last age, by whom the rights of toleration have been so nobly defended, Bayle, Leibnitz, and Locke, are all laymen and philosophers.

40. See the excellent chapter of Sir William Temple on the religion of the United Provinces. I am not satisfied with Grotius (de Rebus Belgicis, Annal. l. i. p. 13, 14. edit. in 12mo), who approves the Imperial laws of persecution, and only condemns the bloody tribunal of the inquisition.

41. Sir William Blackstone (Commentaries, vol. iv. p. 53, 54.) explains the law of England as it was fixed at the Revolution. The exceptions of Papists, and of those who deny the Trinity, would still leave a tolerable scope for persecution, if the national spirit were not more effectual than an hundred statutes.

42. I shall recommend to public animadversion two passages in Dr. Priestley, which betray the ultimate tendency of his opinions. At the first of these (Hist. of the Corruptions of Christianity, vol. i. p. 275, 276.), the priest; at the second (vol. ii. p. 484.), the magistrate, may tremble!

[CHAPTER LV–LXVII]

In the final stretches of *The Decline and Fall* the most momentous phenomenon Gibbon addresses is the Crusades, which were well adapted to engage his intelligence for a multitude of reasons: their sheer scale, the clash of cultures they display, the opportunities for reflecting on the psychology of religious belief they offer. Gibbon's judgement on the significance of the Crusades shows his powers of historical comprehension, his humanity, and the security of his judgement in the relative attribution of significance:

In the profession of Christianity, in the cultivation of a fertile land, the northern conquerors of the Roman empire insensibly mingled with the provincials, and rekindled the embers of the arts of antiquity. Their settlements about the age of Charlemagne had acquired some degree of order and stability, when they were overwhelmed by new swarms of invaders, the Normans, Saracens, and Hungarians, who replunged the western countries of Europe into their former state of anarchy and barbarism. About the eleventh century, the second tempest had subsided by the expulsion or conversion of the enemies of Christendom: the tide of civilization, which had so long ebbed, began to flow with a steady and accelerated course; and a fairer prospect was opened to the hopes and efforts of the rising generations. Great was the increase, and rapid the progress, during the two hundred years of the crusades; and some philosophers have applauded the propitious influence of these holy wars, which appear to me to have checked rather than forwarded the maturity of Europe. The lives and labours of millions, which were buried in the East, would have been more profitably employed in the improvement of their native country: the accumulated stock of industry and wealth would have overflowed in navigation and trade; and the Latins would have been enriched and enlightened by a pure and friendly correspondence with the climates of the East. In one respect I can indeed perceive the accidental operation of the crusades, not so much in producing a benefit as in removing an evil. The larger portion of the inhabitants of Europe was chained to the soil, without freedom, or property, or knowledge; and the two orders of ecclesiastics and nobles, whose numbers were comparatively small, alone deserved the name of citizens and men. This oppressive system was supported by the arts of the clergy and the swords of the barons. The authority of the priests operated in the darker ages as a salutary antidote: they prevented the total extinction of letters, mitigated the fierceness of the times, sheltered the poor and defenceless, and preserved or revived the peace and order of civil society. But the independence, rapine, and discord, of the feudal lords were unmixed with any semblance of good; and every hope of industry and improvement was crushed by the iron weight of the martial aristocracy. Among the causes that undermined that Gothic edifice, a conspicuous place must be allowed to the crusades. The estates of the barons were dissipated, and their race was often extinguished, in these costly and perilous expeditions. Their poverty extorted from their pride those charters of freedom which unlocked the fetters of the slave, secured the farm of the peasant and the shop of the artificer, and gradually restored a substance and a soul to the most numerous and useful part of the community. The conflagration which destroyed the tall and barren trees of the forest gave air and scope to the vegetation of the smaller and nutritive plants of the soil. (*DF*, iii. 727–8)

Whatever their benign unintended consequences in the West, the Crusades achieved nothing durable in the East. They were unable to hinder the rise of the Turks, which Gibbon traces – relying on some of the most advanced historical research of his own day and extending his vision now to China – to the collapse of Mogul power. The siege of Constantinople by the Turks, which gave the *coup de grâce* to Byzantium, is a great set-piece of description, and one whose emotional and intellectual impact on the reader is deepened by the resonant echoes it sets up back down the sixty-seven chapters and five volumes of narrative to which it gives the period.

CHAPTER LXVIII

*Reign and Character of Mahomet the Second. – Siege, Assault, and final
Conquest, of Constantinople by the Turks. – Death of Constantine
Palæologus. – Servitude of the Greeks. – Extinction of the Roman Empire in
the East. – Consternation of Europe. – Conquests and Death of Mahomet the
Second.*

The siege of Constantinople by the Turks attracts our first attention to the person and character of the great destroyer. Mahomet the second[1] was the son of the second Amurath; and though his mother has been decorated with the titles of Christian and princess, she is more probably confounded with the numerous concubines who peopled from every climate the haram of the sultan. His first education and sentiments were those of a devout Musulman; and as often as he conversed with an infidel, he purified his hands and face by the legal rites of ablution. Age and empire appear to have relaxed this narrow bigotry: his aspiring genius disdained to acknowledge a power above his own; and in his looser hours he presumed (it is said) to brand the prophet of Mecca as a robber and impostor. Yet the sultan persevered in a decent reverence for the doctrine and discipline of the Koran:[2] his private indiscretion must have been sacred from the vulgar ear; and we should suspect the credulity of strangers and sectaries, so prone to believe that a mind which is hardened against truth, must be armed with superior contempt for absurdity and error. Under the tuition of the most skilful masters, Mahomet advanced with an early and rapid progress in the paths of knowledge; and besides his native tongue, it

Character of Mahomet II.

---

1. For the character of Mahomet II. it is dangerous to trust either the Turks or the Christians. The most moderate picture appears to be drawn by Phranza (l. i. c. 33.), whose resentment had cooled in age and solitude; see likewise Spondanus (A.D. 1451, Nº 11.) and the continuator of Fleury (tom. xxii. p. 552.), the *Elogia* of Paulus Jovius (l. iii.

p. 164–166.), and the Dictionaire de Bayle (tom. iii. p. 272–279.).
2. Cantemir (p. 115), and the moschs which he founded, attest his public regard for religion. Mahomet freely disputed with the patriarch Gennadius on the two religions (Spond. A.D. 1453, Nº 22.).

is affirmed that he spoke or understood five languages,[3] the Arabic, the Persian, the Chaldæan or Hebrew, the Latin, and the Greek. The Persian might indeed contribute to his amusement, and the Arabic to his edification; and such studies are familiar to the Oriental youth. In the intercourse of the Greeks and Turks, a conqueror might wish to converse with the people over whom he was ambitious to reign: his own praises in Latin poetry[4] or prose[5] might find a passage to the royal ear; but what use or merit could recommend to the statesman or the scholar the uncouth dialect of his Hebrew slaves? The history and geography of the world were familiar to his memory: the lives of the heroes of the East, perhaps of the West,[6] excited his emulation: his skill in astrology is excused by the folly of the times, and supposes some rudiments of mathematical science; and a profane taste for the arts is betrayed in his liberal invitation and reward of the painters of Italy.[7] But the influence of religion and learning were employed without effect on his savage and licentious nature. I will not transcribe, nor do I firmly believe, the stories of his fourteen pages, whose bellies were ripped open in search of a stolen melon; or of the beauteous slave, whose head he severed from her body, to convince the Janizaries that their master was not the votary of love. His sobriety is attested by the silence of the Turkish annals, which accuse three, and three only, of the Ottoman line of the vice of drunkenness.[8] But it cannot be denied that his

3. Quinque linguas præter suam noverat; Græcam, Latinam, Chaldaicam, Persicam. The Latin translator of Phranza has dropt the Arabic, which the Koran must recommend to every Musulman.

4. Philelphus, by a Latin ode, requested and obtained the liberty of his wife's mother and sisters from the conqueror of Constantinople. It was delivered into the sultan's hands by the envoys of the duke of Milan. Philelphus himself was suspected of a design of retiring to Constantinople; yet the orator often sounded the trumpet of holy war (see his Life by M. Lancelot, in the Memoires de l'Academie des Inscriptions, tom. x. p. 718. 724, &c.).

5. Robert Valturio published at Verona, in 1483, his xii books de Re Militari, in which he first mentions the use of bombs. By his patron Sigismond Malatesta, prince of Rimini, it had been addressed with a Latin epistle to Mahomet II.

6. According to Phranza, he assiduously studied the lives and actions of Alexander, Augustus, Constantine, and Theodosius. I have read somewhere, that Plutarch's Lives were translated by his orders into the Turkish language. If the sultan himself understood Greek, it must have been for the benefit of his subjects. Yet these lives are a school of freedom as well as of valour.

7. The famous Gentile Bellino, whom he had invited from Venice, was dismissed with a chain and collar of gold, and a purse of 3000 ducats. With Voltaire, I laugh at the foolish story of a slave purposely beheaded, to instruct the painter in the action of the muscles.

8. These Imperial drunkards were Soliman I. Selim II. and Amurath IV. (Cantemir, p. 61.). The sophis of Persia can produce a more regular succession; and in the last age, our

passions were at once furious and inexorable; that in the palace, as in the field, a torrent of blood was split on the slightest provocation; and that the noblest of the captive youth were often dishonoured by his unnatural lust. In the Albanian war, he studied the lessons, and soon surpassed the example, of his father; and the conquest of two empires, twelve kingdoms, and two hundred cities, a vain and flattering account, is ascribed to his invincible sword. He was doubtless a soldier, and possibly a general; Constantinople has sealed his glory; but if we compare the means, the obstacles, and the atchievements, Mahomet the second must blush to sustain a parallel with Alexander or Timour. Under his command, the Ottoman forces were always more numerous than their enemies; yet their progress was bounded by the Euphrates and the Adriatic; and his arms were checked by Huniades and Scanderbeg, by the Rhodian knights and by the Persian king.

In the reign of Amurath, he twice tasted of royalty, and twice descended from the throne: his tender age was incapable of opposing his father's restoration, but never could he forgive the vizirs who had recommended that salutary measure. His nuptials were celebrated with the daughter of a Turkman emir; and, after a festival of two months, he departed from Adrianople *His reign, A.D. 1451, February 9 – A.D. 1481, July 2.* with his bride, to reside in the government of Magnesia. Before the end of six weeks, he was recalled by a sudden message from the divan, which announced the decease of Amurath, and the mutinous spirit of the Janizaries. His speed and vigour commanded their obedience: he passed the Hellespont with a chosen guard; and at the distance of a mile from Adrianople, the vizirs and emirs, the imams and cadhis, the soldiers and the people, fell prostrate before the new sultan. They affected to weep, they affected to rejoice; he ascended the throne at the age of twenty-one years, and removed the cause of sedition by the death, the inevitable death, of his infant brothers.[9] The ambassadors of Europe and Asia soon appeared to congratulate his accession and solicit his friendship; and to all he spoke the language of moderation and peace. The confidence of the

---

European travellers were the witnesses and companions of their revels.

9. Calapin, one of these royal infants, was saved from his cruel brother, and baptised at Rome under the name of Callistus Othomannus. The emperor Frederic III. presented him with an estate in Austria, where he ended his life; and Cuspinian, who in his youth conversed with the aged prince at Vienna, applauds his piety and wisdom (de Cæsaribus, p. 672, 673).

Greek emperor was revived by the solemn oaths and fair assurances, with
which he sealed the ratification of the treaty: and a rich domain on
the banks of the Strymon was assigned for the annual payment of three
hundred thousand aspers, the pension of an Ottoman prince, who was
detained at his request in the Byzantine court. Yet the neighbours of
Mahomet might tremble at the severity with which a youthful monarch
reformed the pomp of his father's household: the expences of luxury were
applied to those of ambition, and an useless train of seven thousand falconers
was either dismissed from his service or enlisted in his troops. In the first
summer of his reign, he visited with an army the Asiatic provinces; but
after humbling the pride, Mahomet accepted the submission, of the Cara-
manian, that he might not be diverted by the smallest obstacle from the
execution of his great design.[10]

*Hostile
intentions of
Mahomet,
A.D. 1451.*
The Mahometan, and more especially the Turkish casuists,
have pronounced that no promise can bind the faithful against
the interest and duty of their religion; and that the sultan may
abrogate his own treaties and those of his predecessors. The
justice and magnanimity of Amurath had scorned this immoral
privilege; but his son, though the proudest of men, could stoop from
ambition to the basest arts of dissimulation and deceit. Peace was on his
lips, while war was in his heart: he incessantly sighed for the possession of
Constantinople; and the Greeks, by their own indiscretion, afforded the

10. See the accession of Mahomet II. in Ducas
(c. 33.), Phranza (l. i. c. 33. l. iii. c. 2.),
Chalcocondyles (l. vii. p. 199), and Cantemir
(p. 96.).

11. Before I enter on the siege of Constantinople I shall observe, that except the short
hints of Cantemir and Leunclavius, I have not
been able to obtain any Turkish account of
this conquest: such an account as we possess
of the siege of Rhodes by Soliman II.
(Memoires de l'Academie des Inscriptions,
tom. xxvi. p. 723–769.). I must therefore
depend on the Greeks, whose prejudices, in
some degree, are subdued by their distress.
Our standard texts are those of Ducas (c. 34–
42.), Phranza (l. iii. c. 7–20.), Chalcocondyles
(l. viii. p. 201–214.), and Leonardus Chiensis
(Historia C.P. a Turco expugnatæ. Norimberghæ, 1544, in 4to, 20 leaves). The last of

these narratives is the earliest in date, since it
was composed in the isle of Chios, the 16th
of August 1453, only seventy-nine days after
the loss of the city, and in the first confusion
of ideas and passions. Some hints may be
added from an epistle of cardinal Isidore (in
Farragine Rerum Turcicarum, ad calcem
Chalcocondyl. Clauseri, Basil, 1556) to pope
Nicholas V. and a tract of Theodosius
Zygomala, which he addressed in the year
1581 to Martin Crusius (Turco-Græcia, l. i.
p. 74–98. Basil, 1584). The various facts and
materials are briefly, though critically,
reviewed by Spondanus (A.D. 1453, Nᵒ 1–
27.). The hearsay relations of Monstrelet and
the distant Latins, I shall take leave to disregard.

first pretence of the fatal rupture.[11] Instead of labouring to be forgotten, their ambassadors pursued his camp, to demand the payment, and even the encrease, of their annual stipend: the divan was importuned by their complaints, and the vizir, a secret friend of the Christians, was constrained to deliver the sense of his brethren. "Ye foolish and miserable Romans," said Calil, "we know your devices, and ye are ignorant of your own danger! the scrupulous Amurath is no more; his throne is occupied by a young conqueror, whom no laws can bind and no obstacles can resist: and if you escape from his hands, give praise to the divine clemency, which yet delays the chastisement of your sins. Why do ye seek to affright us by vain and indirect menaces? Release the fugitive Orchan, crown him sultan of Romania; call the Hungarians from beyond the Danube; arm against us the nations of the West: and be assured, that you will only provoke and precipitate your ruin." But, if the fears of the ambassadors were alarmed by the stern language of the vizir, they were soothed by the courteous audience and friendly speeches of the Ottoman prince; and Mahomet assured them that on his return to Adrianople he would redress the griev-ances, and consult the true interest, of the Greeks. No sooner had he repassed the Hellespont than he issued a mandate to suppress their pension, and to expel their officers from the banks of the Strymon: in this measure he betrayed an hostile mind; and the second order announced, and in some degree commenced, the siege of Constantinople. In the narrow pass of the Bosphorus, an Asiatic fortress had formerly been raised by his grand-father: in the opposite situation, on the European side, he resolved to erect a more formidable castle; and a thousand masons were commanded to assemble in the spring on a spot named Asomaton, about five miles from the Greek metropolis.[12] Persuasion is the resource of the feeble; and the feeble can seldom persuade: the ambassadors of the emperor attempted, without success, to divert Mahomet from the execution of his design. They represented, that his grandfather had solicited the permission of Manuel to build a castle on his own territories; but that this double fortification, which would command the streight, could only tend to violate the alliance of the nations; to intercept the Latins who traded in the Black Sea, and perhaps

12. The situation of the fortress, and the top-ography of the Bosphorus, are best learned from Peter Gyllius (de Bosphoro Thracio, l. ii. c. 13), Leunclavius (Pandect. p. 445.), and Tournefort (Voyage dans le Levant, tom. ii. lettre xv. p. 413, 444.); but I must regret the map or plan which Tournefort sent to the French minister of the marine. The reader may turn back to vol. ii. ch. 17. of this History.

to annihilate the subsistence of the city. "I form no enterprise," replied the perfidious sultan, "against the city; but the empire of Constantinople is measured by her walls. Have you forgot the distress to which my father was reduced, when you formed a league with the Hungarians; when they invaded our country by land, and the Hellespont was occupied by the French gallies? Amurath was compelled to force the passage of the Bosphorus; and your strength was not equal to your malevolence. I was then a child at Adrianople; the Moslems trembled; and for a while the *Gabours*[13] insulted our disgrace. But when my father had triumphed in the field of Warna, he vowed to erect a fort on the western shore, and that vow it is my duty to accomplish. Have ye the right, have ye the power, to control my actions on my own ground? For that ground *is* my own: as far as the shores of the Bosphorus, Asia is inhabited by the Turks, and Europe is deserted by the Romans. Return, and inform your king that the present Ottoman is far different from his predecessors; that *his* resolutions surpass *their* wishes; and that *he* performs more than *they* could resolve. Return in safety – but the next who delivers a similar message may expect to be flayed alive." After this declaration, Constantine, the first of the Greeks in spirit as in rank,[14] had determined to unsheathe the sword, and to resist the approach and establishment of the Turks on the Bosphorus. He was disarmed by the advice of his civil and ecclesiastical ministers, who recommended a system less generous, and even less prudent, than his own, to approve their patience and long-suffering, to brand the Ottoman with the name and guilt of an aggressor, and to depend on chance and time for their own safety and the destruction of a fort which could not long be maintained in the neighbourhood of a great and populous city. Amidst hope and fear, the fears of the wise and the hopes of the credulous, the winter rolled away; the proper business of each man, and each hour, was postponed; and the Greeks shut their eyes against the impending

---

13. The opprobrious name which the Turks bestow on the Infidels, is expressed $K\alpha\beta o\nu\varrho$ by Ducas, and *Giaour* by Leunclavius and the moderns. The former term is derived by Ducange (Gloss. Græc. tom. i. p. 530) from $K\alpha\beta o\nu\varrho o\nu$ in vulgar Greek, a tortoise, as denoting a retrograde motion from the faith. But, alas! *Gabour* is no more than *Gheber*, which was transferred from the Persian to the Turkish language, from the worshippers of

fire to those of the crucifix (d'Herbelot, Bibliot. Orient. p. 375.).

14. Phranza does justice to his master's sense and courage. Calliditatem hominis non ignorans Imperator prior arma movere constituit, and stigmatises the folly of the cum sacri tum profani proceres, which he had heard, amentes spe vanâ pasci. Ducas was not a privycounsellor.

danger, till the arrival of the spring and the sultan decided the assurance of their ruin.

Of a master who never forgives, the orders are seldom disobeyed. On the twenty-sixth of March, the appointed spot of Asomaton was covered with an active swarm of Turkish artificers; and the materials by sea and land, were diligently transported from Europe and Asia.[15] The lime had been burnt in Cataphrygia; the timber was cut down in the woods of Heraclea and Nicomedia; and the stones were dug from the Anatolian quarries. Each of the thousand masons was assisted by two workmen; and a measure of two cubits was marked for their daily task. The fortress[16] was built in a triangular form; each angle was flanked by a strong and massy tower; one on the declivity of the hill, two along the sea-shore: a thickness of twenty-two feet was assigned for the walls, thirty for the towers; and the whole building was covered with a solid platform of lead. Mahomet himself pressed and directed the work with indefatigable ardour: his three vizirs claimed the honour of finishing their respective towers; the zeal of the cadhis emulated that of the Janizaries; the meanest labour was ennobled by the service of God and the sultan; and the diligence of the multitude was quickened by the eye of a despot, whose smile was the hope of fortune, and whose frown was the messenger of death. The Greek emperor beheld with terror the irresistible progress of the work; and vainly strove, by flattery and gifts, to assuage an implacable foe, who sought, and secretly fomented, the slightest occasion of a quarrel. Such occasions must soon and inevitably be found. The ruins of stately churches, and even the marble columns which had been consecrated to St. Michael the archangel, were employed without scruple by the profane and rapacious Moslems; and some Christians, who presumed to oppose the removal, received from their hands the crown of martyrdom. Constantine had solicited a Turkish guard to protect the fields and harvests of his subjects: the guard was fixed; but their first order was to allow free pasture

He builds a fortress on the Bosphorus, A.D. 1452, March.

---

15. Instead of this clear and consistent account, the Turkish Annals (Cantemir, p. 97.) revived the foolish tale of the ox's hide, and Dido's stratagem in the foundation of Carthage. These annals (unless we are swayed by an antichristian prejudice) are far less valuable than the Greek historians.

16. In the dimensions of this fortress, the old castle of Europe, Phranza does not exactly agree with Chalcocondyles, whose description has been verified on the spot by his editor Leunclavius.

to the mules and horses of the camp, and to defend their brethren if they should be molested by the natives. The retinue of an Ottoman chief had left their horses to pass the night among the ripe corn: the damage was felt; the insult was resented; and several of both nations were slain in a tumultuous conflict. Mahomet listened with joy to the complaint; and a detachment was commanded to exterminate the guilty village: the guilty had fled; but forty innocent and unsuspecting reapers were massacred by the soldiers. Till this provocation, Constantinople had been open to the visits of commerce and curiosity: on the first alarm, the gates were shut; but the emperor, still anxious for peace, released on the third day his Turkish captives;[17] and expressed, in a last message, the firm resignation of a Christian and a soldier. "Since neither oaths, nor treaty, nor submission, can secure peace, pursue," said he to Mahomet, "your impious warfare. My trust is in God alone: if it should please him to mollify your heart, I shall rejoice in the happy change; if he delivers the city into your hands, I submit without a murmur to his holy will. But until the Judge of the earth shall pronounce between us, it is my duty to live and die in the defence of my people." The sultan's answer was hostile and decisive: his fortifications were completed; and before his departure for Adrianople, he stationed a vigilant Aga and four hundred Janizaries, to levy a tribute of the ships of every nation that should pass within the reach of their cannon. A Venetian vessel, refusing obedience to the new lords of the Bosphorus, was sunk with a single bullet. The master and thirty sailors escaped in the boat; but they were dragged in chains to the *porte:* the chief was impaled; his companions were beheaded; and the historian Ducas[18] beheld, at Demotica, their bodies exposed to the wild beasts. The siege of Constantinople was deferred till the ensuing spring; but an Ottoman army marched into the Morea to divert the force of the brothers of Constantine. At this æra of calamity, one of these princes, the despot Thomas, was blessed or afflicted with the birth of a son; "the last heir," says the plaintive Phranza, "of the last spark of the Roman empire".[19]

The Turkish war, June;

September 1;

A.D. 1453, January 17.

---

17. Among these were some pages of Mahomet so conscious of his inexorable rigour, that they begged to lose their heads in the city unless they could return before sun-set.

18. Ducas, c. 35. Phranza (l. iii. c. 3.), who had sailed in his vessel, commemorates the Venetian pilot as a martyr.

19. Auctum est Palæologorum genus, et Imperii successor, parvæque Romanorum scintillæ hæres natus, Andreas, &c. (Phranza, l. iii. c. 7.) The strong expression was inspired by his feelings.

The Greeks and the Turks passed an anxious and sleepless winter: the former were kept awake by their fears, the latter by their hopes; both by the preparations of defence and attack; and the two emperors, who had the most to lose or to gain, were the most deeply affected by the national sentiment. In Mahomet, that sentiment was inflamed by the ardour of his youth and temper: he amused his leisure with building at Adrianople[20] the lofty palace of Jehan Numa (the watch-tower

Preparations for the siege of Constantinople, A.D. 1452, September – A.D. 1453, April.

of the world); but his serious thoughts were irrevocably bent on the conquest of the city of Cæsar. At the dead of night, about the second watch, he started from his bed, and commanded the instant attendance of his prime vizir. The message, the hour, the prince, and his own situation, alarmed the guilty conscience of Calil Basha; who had possessed the confidence, and advised the restoration, of Amurath. On the accession of the son, the vizir was confirmed in his office and the appearances of favour; but the veteran statesman was not insensible that he trod on a thin and slippery ice, which might break under his footsteps, and plunge him in the abyss. His friendship for the Christians, which might be innocent under the late reign, had stigmatised him with the name of Gabour Ortachi, or foster-brother of the infidels;[21] and his avarice entertained a venal and treasonable correspondence, which was detected and punished after the conclusion of the war. On receiving the royal mandate, he embraced, perhaps for the last time, his wife and children; filled a cup with pieces of gold, hastened to the palace, adored the sultan, and offered, according to the Oriental custom, the slight tribute of his duty and gratitude.[22] "It is not my wish," said Mahomet, "to resume my gifts, but rather to heap and multiply them on thy head. In my turn I ask a present far more valuable and important; – Constantinople." As soon as the vizir had recovered from his surprise, "the same God," said he, "who has already given thee so large a portion of the Roman empire, will not deny the remnant, and the capital.

---

20. Cantemir, p. 97, 98. The sultan was either doubtful of his conquest, or ignorant of the superior merits of Constantinople. A city or a kingdom may sometimes be ruined by the Imperial fortune of their sovereign.

21. Συντροφος, by the president Cousin, is translated *pere* nourricier, most correctly indeed from the Latin version; but in his haste, he has overlooked the note by which Ismael

Boillaud (ad Ducam, c. 35) acknowledges and rectifies his own error.

22. The Oriental custom of never appearing without gifts before a sovereign or a superior, is of high antiquity, and seems analogous with the idea of sacrifice, still more ancient and universal. See the examples of such Persian gifts, Ælian, Hist. Var. l. i. c. 31, 32, 33.

His providence, and thy power, assure thy success; and myself, with the rest of thy faithful slaves, will sacrifice our lives and fortunes." "Lala,"[23] (or preceptor), continued the sultan, "do you see this pillow? all the night, in my agitation, I have pulled it on one side and the other; I have risen from my bed, again have I lain down; yet sleep has not visited these weary eyes. Beware of the gold and silver of the Romans: in arms we are superior; and with the aid of God, and the prayers of the prophet, we shall speedily become masters of Constantinople." To sound the disposition of his soldiers, he often wandered through the streets alone and in disguise: and it was fatal to discover the sultan, when he wished to escape from the vulgar eye. His hours were spent in delineating the plan of the hostile city: in debating with his generals and engineers, on what spot he should erect his batteries; on which side he should assault the walls; where he should spring his mines; to what place he should apply his scaling-ladders: and the exercises of the day repeated and proved the lucubrations of the night.

The great cannon of Mahomet. Among the implements of destruction, he studied with peculiar care the recent and tremendous discovery of the Latins; and his artillery surpassed whatever had yet appeared in the world. A founder of cannon, a Dane or Hungarian, who had been almost starved in the Greek service, deserted to the Moslems, and was liberally entertained by the Turkish sultan. Mahomet was satisfied with the answer to his first question, which he eagerly pressed on the artist. "Am I able to cast a cannon capable of throwing a ball or stone of sufficient size to batter the walls of Constantinople? I am not ignorant of their strength, but were they more solid than those of Babylon, I could oppose an engine of superior power: the position and management of that engine must be left to your engineers." On this assurance, a foundery was established at Adrianople: the metal was prepared; and at the end of three months, Urban produced a piece of brass ordnance of stupendous, and almost incredible, magnitude; a measure of twelve palms is assigned to the bore; and the stone bullet weighed above six hundred pounds.[24] A vacant place before the new

---

23. The *Lala* of the Turks (Cantemir, p. 34.), and the *Tata* of the Greeks (Ducas, c. 35.), are derived from the natural language of children; and it may be observed, that all such primitive words which denote their parents, are the simple repetition of one syllable, composed of a labial or dental consonant and an open

vowel (des Brosses, Mechanisme des Langues, tom. i. p. 231–247.).

24. The Attic talent weighed about sixty minæ, or averdupois pounds (see Hooper on Ancient Weights, Measures, &c.): but among the modern Greeks, that classic appellation was extended to a weight of one hundred, or

palace was chosen for the first experiment; but, to prevent the sudden and mischievous effects of astonishment and fear, a proclamation was issued, that the cannon would be discharged the ensuing day. The explosion was felt or heard in a circuit of an hundred furlongs: the ball, by the force of gunpowder, was driven above a mile; and on the spot where it fell, it buried itself a fathom deep in the ground. For the conveyance of this destructive engine, a frame or carriage of thirty waggons was linked together and drawn along by a team of sixty oxen: two hundred men on both sides were stationed to poise and support the rolling weight; two hundred and fifty workmen marched before to smooth the way and repair the bridges; and near two months were employed in a laborious journey of one hundred and fifty miles. A lively philosopher[25] derides on this occasion the credulity of the Greeks, and observes, with much reason, that we should always distrust the exaggerations of a vanquished people. He calculates, that a ball, even of two hundred pounds, would require a charge of one hundred and fifty pounds of powder; and that the stroke would be feeble and impotent, since not a fifteenth part of the mass could be inflamed at the same moment. A stranger as I am to the art of destruction, I can discern that the modern improvements of artillery prefer the number of pieces to the weight of metal; the quickness of the fire to the sound, or even the consequence, of a single explosion. Yet I dare not reject the positive and unanimous evidence of contemporary writers; nor can it seem improbable, that the first artists, in their rude and ambitious efforts, should have transgressed the standard of moderation. A Turkish cannon, more enormous than that of Mahomet, still guards the entrance of the Dardanelles; and if the use be inconvenient, it has been found on a late trial that the effect was far from contemptible. A stone bullet of *eleven* hundred pounds weight was once discharged with three hundred and thirty pounds of powder; at the distance of six hundred yards it shivered into three rocky fragments, traversed the streight, and, leaving the waters in a foam, again rose and bounded against the opposite hill.[26]

---

one hundred and twenty-five pounds (Ducange, ταλαντον). Leonardus Chiensis measured the ball or stone of the *second* cannon: Lapidem, qui palmis undecim ex meis ambibat in gyro.

25. See Voltaire (Hist. Generale, c. xci. p. 294,

295.). He was ambitious of universal monarchy; and the poet frequently aspires to the name and style of an astronomer, a chymist, &c.

26. The Baron de Tott (tom. iii. p. 85–89.), who fortified the Dardanelles against the

Mahomet II.
forms the siege of
Constantinople,
A.D. 1453,
April 6.

While Mahomet threatened the capital of the East, the Greek emperor implored with fervent prayers the assistance of earth and heaven. But the invisible powers were deaf to his supplications; and Christendom beheld with indifference the fall of Constantinople, while she derived at least some promise of supply from the jealous and temporal policy of the sultan of Egypt. Some states were too weak, and others too remote; by some the danger was considered as imaginary, by others as inevitable: the Western princes were involved in their endless and domestic quarrels; and the Roman pontiff was exasperated by the falsehood or obstinacy of the Greeks. Instead of employing in their favour the arms and treasures of Italy, Nicholas the fifth had foretold their approaching ruin; and his honour was engaged in the accomplishment of his prophecy. Perhaps he was softened by the last extremity of their distress; but his compassion was tardy; his efforts were faint and unavailing; and Constantinople had fallen, before the squadrons of Genoa and Venice could sail from their harbours.[27] Even the princes of the Morea and of the Greek islands affected a cold neutrality: the Genoese colony of Galata negociated a private treaty; and the sultan indulged them in the delusive hope, that by his clemency they might survive the ruin of the empire. A plebeian crowd, and some Byzantine nobles, basely withdrew from the danger of their country; and the avarice of the rich denied the emperor, and reserved for the Turks, the secret treasures which might have raised in their defence whole armies of mercenaries.[28] The indigent and solitary prince prepared however to sustain his formidable adversary; but if his courage were equal to the peril, his strength was

---

Russians, describes in a lively, and even comic, strain his own prowess, and the consternation of the Turks. But that adventurous traveller does not possess the art of gaining our confidence.

27. Non audivit, indignum ducens, says the honest Antoninus; but as the Roman court was afterwards grieved and ashamed, we find the more courtly expression of Platina, in animo fuisse pontifici juvare Græcos, and the positive assertion of Æneas Sylvius, structam classem, &c. (Spond. A.D. 1453, Nᵒ 3.).

28. Antonin. in Proem. – Epist. Cardinal. Isidor. apud Spondanum; and Dr. Johnson, in the tragedy of Irene, has happily seized this characteristic circumstance:

> The groaning Greeks dig up the golden caverns,
> The accumulated wealth of hoarding ages;
> That wealth which, granted to their weeping prince,
> Had rang'd embattled nations at their gates.

inadequate to the contest. In the beginning of the spring, the Turkish vanguard swept the towns and villages as far as the gates of Constantinople: submission was spared and protected; whatever presumed to resist was exterminated with fire and sword. The Greek places on the Black Sea, Mesembria, Acheloum, and Bizon, surrendered on the first summons; Selybria alone deserved the honours of a siege or blockade; and the bold inhabitants, while they were invested by land, launched their boats, pillaged the opposite coast of Cyzicus, and sold their captives in the public market. But on the approach of Mahomet himself all was silent and prostrate: he first halted at the distance of five miles; and from thence advancing in battle array, planted before the gate of St. Romanus the Imperial standard; and, on the sixth day of April, formed the memorable siege of Constantinople.

The troops of Asia and Europe extended on the right and left from the Propontis to the harbour: the Janizaries in the front were stationed before the sultan's tent; the Ottoman line was covered *Forces of the Turks;* by a deep intrenchment; and a subordinate army inclosed the suburb of Galata, and watched the doubtful faith of the Genoese. The inquisitive Philelphus, who resided in Greece about thirty years before the siege, is confident, that all the Turkish forces, of any name or value, could not exceed the number of sixty thousand horse and twenty thousand foot; and he upbraids the pusillanimity of the nations, who had tamely yielded to an handful of Barbarians. Such indeed might be the regular establishment of the *Capiculi*,[29] the troops of the Porte, who marched with the prince, and were paid from his royal treasury. But the bashaws, in their respective governments, maintained or levied a provincial militia; many lands were held by a military tenure; many volunteers were attracted by the hope of spoil; and the sound of the holy trumpet invited a swarm of hungry and fearless fanatics, who might contribute at least to multiply the terrors, and in a first attack to blunt the swords, of the Christians. The whole mass of the Turkish powers is magnified by Ducas, Chalcocondyles, and Leonard of Chios, to the amount of three or four hundred thousand men; but Phranza was a less remote and more accurate judge; and his precise definition of two hundred and fifty-eight thousand does not exceed

---

29. The palatine troops are styled *Capiculi*, the provincials, *Seratculi:* and most of the names and institutions of the Turkish militia existed before the *Canon Nameh* of Soliman II. from which, and his own experience, count Marsigli has composed his military state of the Ottoman empire.

the measure of experience and probability.[30] The navy of the besiegers was less formidable: the Propontis was overspread with three hundred and twenty sail; but of these no more than eighteen could be rated as gallies of war; and the far greater part must be degraded to the condition of storeships and transports, which poured into the camp fresh supplies of men, ammunition, and provisions. In her last decay, Constanti-

of the Greeks.

nople was still peopled with more than an hundred thousand inhabitants, but these numbers are found in the accounts, not of war, but of captivity, and they mostly consisted of mechanics, of priests, of women, and of men devoid of that spirit which even women have sometimes exerted for the common safety. I can suppose, I could almost excuse, the reluctance of subjects to serve on a distant frontier, at the will of a tyrant; but the man who dares not expose his life in the defence of his children and his property has lost in society the first and most active energies of nature. By the emperor's command, a particular enquiry had been made through the streets and houses, how many of the citizens, or even of the monks, were able and willing to bear arms for their country. The lists were entrusted to Phranza;[31] and, after a diligent addition, he informed his master, with grief and surprise, that the national defence was reduced to four thousand nine hundred and seventy *Romans*. Between Constantine and his faithful minister, this comfortless secret was preserved; and a sufficient proportion of shields, cross-bows, and muskets, was distributed from the arsenal to the city bands. They derived some accession from a body of two thousand strangers, under the command of John Justiniani, a noble Genoese; a liberal donative was advanced to these auxiliaries; and a princely re-compense, the isle of Lemnos, was promised to the valour and victory of their chief. A strong chain was drawn across the mouth of the harbour: it was supported by some Greek and Italian vessels of war and merchandise; and the ships of every Christian nation, that successively arrived from Candia and the Black Sea, were detained for the public service. Against

---

30. The observation of Philelphus is approved by Cuspinian in the year 1508 (de Cæsaribus, in Epilog. de Militiâ Turcicâ, p. 697.). Marsigli proves, that the effective armies of the Turks are much less numerous than they appear. In the army that besieged Constantinople, Leonardus Chiensis reckons no more than 15,000 Janizaries.

31. Ego, eidem (Imp.) tabellas extribui non absque dolore et mœstitia, mansitque apud nos duos aliis occultus numerus (Phranza, l. iii. c. 8.). With some indulgence for national prejudices, we cannot desire a more authentic witness, not only of public facts, but of private counsels.

the powers of the Ottoman empire, a city of the extent of thirteen, perhaps of sixteen, miles was defended by a scanty garrison of seven or eight thousand soldiers. Europe and Asia were open to the besiegers; but the strength and provisions of the Greeks must sustain a daily decrease; nor could they indulge the expectation of any foreign succour or supply.

The primitive Romans would have drawn their swords in the resolution of death or conquest. The primitive Christians might have embraced each other, and awaited in patience and charity the stroke of martyrdom. But the Greeks of Constantinople were animated only by the spirit of religion, and that *False union of the two churches, A.D. 1452, Dec. 12.* spirit was productive only of animosity and discord. Before his death, the emperor John Palæologus had renounced the unpopular measure of an union with the Latins; nor was the idea revived, till the distress of his brother Constantine imposed a last trial of flattery and dissimulation.[32] With the demand of temporal aid, his ambassadors were instructed to mingle the assurance of spiritual obedience: his neglect of the church was excused by the urgent cares of the state; and his orthodox wishes solicited the presence of a Roman legate. The Vatican had been too often deluded; yet the signs of repentance could not decently be overlooked; a legate was more easily granted than an army; and about six months before the final destruction, the cardinal Isidore of Russia appeared in that character with a retinue of priests and soldiers. The emperor saluted him as a friend and father; respectfully listened to his public and private sermons; and with the most obsequious of the clergy and laymen subscribed the act of union, as it had been ratified in the council of Florence. On the twelfth of December, the two nations, in the church of St. Sophia, joined in the communion of sacrifice and prayer; and the names of the two pontiffs were solemnly commemorated; the names of Nicholas the fifth, the vicar of Christ, and of the patriarch Gregory who had been driven into exile by a rebellious people.

But the dress and language of the Latin priest who officiated at the altar, were an object of scandal; and it was observed with horror, that he consecrated a cake or wafer of *unleavened* bread, and poured cold water into the cup of the sacrament. A national *Obstinacy and fanaticism of the Greeks.*

32. In Spondanus, the narrative of the union is not only partial, but imperfect. The bishop of Pamiers died in 1642, and the history of Ducas, which represents these scenes (c. 36, 37.) with such truth and spirit, was not printed till the year 1649.

historian acknowledges with a blush, that none of his countrymen, not the emperor himself, were sincere in this occasional conformity.[33] Their hasty and unconditional submission was palliated by a promise of future revisal; but the best, or the worst, of their excuses was the confession of their own perjury. When they were pressed by the reproaches of their honest brethren, "Have patience," they whispered, "have patience till God shall have delivered the city from the great dragon who seeks to devour us. You shall then perceive whether we are truly reconciled with the Azymites." But patience is not the attribute of zeal; nor can the arts of a court be adapted to the freedom and violence of popular enthusiasm. From the dome of St. Sophia, the inhabitants of either sex, and of every degree, rushed in crowds to the cell of the monk Gennadius,[34] to consult the oracle of the church. The holy man was invisible; entranced, as it should seem, in deep meditation, or divine rapture; but he had exposed on the door of his cell, a speaking tablet; and they successively withdrew after reading these tremendous words: "O miserable Romans, why will ye abandon the truth; and why, instead of confiding in God, will ye put your trust in the Italians? In losing your faith, you will lose your city. Have mercy on me, O Lord! I protest in thy presence, that I am innocent of the crime. O miserable Romans, consider, pause, and repent. At the same moment that you renounce the religion of your fathers, by embracing impiety, you submit to a foreign servitude." According to the advice of Gennadius, the religious virgins, as pure as angels and as proud as dæmons, rejected the act of union, and abjured all communion with the present and future associates of the Latins; and their example was applauded and imitated by the greatest part of the clergy and people. From the monastery, the devout Greeks dispersed themselves in the taverns; drank confusion to the slaves of the pope; emptied their glasses in honour of the image of the holy Virgin; and besought her to defend against Mahomet, the city which she had formerly saved from Chosroes and the Chagan. In the double

33. Phranza, one of the conforming Greeks, acknowledges that the measure was adopted only propter spem auxilii; he affirms with pleasure, that those who refused to perform their devotions in St. Sophia, extra culpam et in pace essent (l. iii. c. 20.).

34. His primitive and secular name was George Scholarius, which he changed for that of Gennadius, either when he became a monk or a patriarch. His defence, at Florence, of the same union which he so furiously attacked at Constantinople, has tempted Leo Allatius (Diatrib. de Georgiis, in Fabric. Bibliot. Græc. tom. x. p. 760–786.) to divide him into two men; but Renaudot (p. 343–384.) has restored the identity of his person and the duplicity of his character.

intoxication of zeal and wine, they valiantly exclaimed, "What occasion have we for succour, or union, or Latins? far from us be the worship of the Azymites!" During the winter that preceded the Turkish conquest, the nation was distracted by this epidemical frenzy; and the season of Lent, the approach of Easter, instead of breathing charity and love, served only to fortify the obstinacy and influence of the zealots. The confessors scrutinised and alarmed the conscience of their votaries, and a rigorous penance was imposed on those, who had received the communion from a priest, who had given an express or tacit consent to the union. His service at the altar propagated the infection to the mute and simple spectators of the ceremony: they forfeited, by the impure spectacle, the virtue of the sacerdotal character; nor was it lawful, even in danger of sudden death, to invoke the assistance of their prayers or absolution. No sooner had the church of St. Sophia been polluted by the Latin sacrifice, than it was deserted as a Jewish synagogue, or an heathen temple, by the clergy and people: and a vast and gloomy silence prevailed in that venerable dome, which had so often smoked with a cloud of incense, blazed with innumerable lights, and resounded with the voice of prayer and thanksgiving. The Latins were the most odious of heretics and infidels; and the first minister of the empire, the great duke, was heard to declare, that he had rather behold in Constantinople the turban of Mahomet, than the pope's tiara or a cardinal's hat.[35] A sentiment so unworthy of Christians and patriots, was familiar and fatal to the Greeks: the emperor was deprived of the affection and support of his subjects; and their native cowardice was sanctified by resignation to the divine decree, or the visionary hope of a miraculous deliverance.

Of the triangle which composes the figure of Constantinople, the two sides along the sea were made inaccessible to an enemy; the Propontis by nature, and the harbour by art. Between the two waters, the basis of the triangle, the land side was protected by a double wall, and a deep ditch of the depth of one hundred feet. Against this line of fortification, which Phranza, an eye-witness, prolongs to the measure of six miles,[36] the Ottomans directed their principal attack; and the emperor, after

Siege of Constantinople by Mahomet II. A.D. 1453, April 6– May 29.

---

35. Θακιολιον, καλυπτρα, may be fairly translated a cardinal's hat. The difference of the Greek and Latin habits embittered the schism.

36. We are obliged to reduce the Greek miles to the smallest measure which is preserved in the wersts of Russia, of 547 French *toises*, and of 104⅖ to a degree. The six miles of Phranza do not exceed four English miles (d'Anville, Mesures Itineraires, p. 61. 123, &c.).

distributing the service and command of the most perilous stations, undertook the defence of the external wall. In the first days of the siege, the
Greek soldiers descended into the ditch, or sallied into the field; but they
soon discovered, that, in the proportion of their numbers, one Christian
was of more value than twenty Turks: and, after these bold preludes, they
were prudently content to maintain the rampart with their missile weapons.
Nor should this prudence be accused of pusillanimity. The nation was
indeed pusillanimous and base; but the last Constantine deserves the
name of an hero: his noble band of volunteers was inspired with Roman
virtue; and the foreign auxiliaries supported the honour of the Western
chivalry. Their incessant vollies of lances and arrows were accompanied
with the smoke, the sound, and the fire, of their musketry and cannon.
Their small arms discharged at the same time either five, or even ten, balls
of lead, of the size of a walnut; and, according to the closeness of the
ranks and the force of the powder, several breast-plates and bodies were
transpierced by the same shot. But the Turkish approaches were soon sunk
in trenches, or covered with ruins. Each day added to the science of the
Christians; but their inadequate stock of gunpowder was wasted in the
operations of each day. Their ordnance was not powerful, either in size or
number; and if they possessed some heavy cannon, they feared to plant
them on the walls, lest the aged structure should be shaken and overthrown by the explosion.[37] The same destructive secret had been revealed
to the Moslems; by whom it was employed with the superior energy of
zeal, riches, and despotism. The great cannon of Mahomet has been
separately noticed; an important and visible object in the history of the
times: but that enormous engine was flanked by two fellows almost of
equal magnitude:[38] the long order of the Turkish artillery was pointed
against the walls; fourteen batteries thundered at once on the most accessible places; and of one of these it is ambiguously expressed, that it was
mounted with one hundred and thirty guns, or that it discharged one
hundred and thirty bullets. Yet, in the power and activity of the sultan, we

37. At indies doctiores nostri facti paravere
contra hostes machinamenta, quæ tamen
avare dabantur. Pulvis erat nitri modica
exigua; tela modica; bombardæ, si aderant
incommoditate loci primum hostes offendere
maceriebus alveisque tectos non poterant.
Nam siquæ magnæ erant, ne murus con-
cuteretur noster, quiescebant. This passage
of Leonardus Chiensis is curious and
important.

38. According to Chalcocondyles and
Phranza, the great cannon burst; an accident
which, according to Ducas, was prevented by
the artist's skill. It is evident that they do not
speak of the same gun.

may discern the infancy of the new science. Under a master who counted the moments, the great cannon could be loaded and fired no more than seven times in one day.[39] The heated metal unfortunately burst; several workmen were destroyed; and the skill of an artist was admired who bethought himself of preventing the danger and the accident, by pouring oil, after each explosion, into the mouth of the cannon.

The first random shots were productive of more sound than effect; and it was by the advice of a Christian, that the engineers were taught to level their aim against the two opposite sides of the salient angles of a bastion. However imperfect, the weight and repetition of the fire made some impression on the walls; and the Turks, pushing their approaches to the edge of the ditch, attempted to fill the enormous chasm, and to build a road to the assault.[40] Innumerable fascines, and hogsheads, and trunks of trees, were heaped on each other; and such was the impetuosity of the throng, that the foremost and the weakest were pushed headlong down the precipice, and instantly buried under the accumulated mass. To fill the ditch, was the toil of the besiegers; to clear away the rubbish, was the safety of the besieged; and, after a long and bloody conflict, the web that had been woven in the day was still unravelled in the night. The next resource of Mahomet was the practice of mines; but the soil was rocky; in every attempt he was stopped and undermined by the Christian engineers; nor had the art been yet invented of replenishing those subterraneous passages with gunpowder, and blowing whole towers and cities into the air.[41] A circumstance that distinguishes the siege of Constantinople, is the re-union of the ancient and modern artillery. The cannon were intermingled with the mechanical engines for casting stones and darts; the bullet and the battering-ram were directed against the same walls; nor had the discovery of gunpowder

Attack and defence.

39. Near an hundred years after the siege of Constantinople, the French and English fleets in the Channel were proud of firing 300 shot in an engagement of two hours (Memoires de Martin du Bellay, l. x. in the Collection Generale, tom. xxi. p. 239.).

40. I have selected some curious facts, without striving to emulate the bloody and obstinate eloquence of the abbé de Vertot, in his prolix descriptions of the sieges of Rhodes, Malta, &c. But that agreeable historian had a turn

for romance, and as he wrote to please the order, he has adopted the same spirit of enthusiasm and chivalry.

41. The first theory of mines with gunpowder appears in 1480, in a MS. of George of Sienna (Tiraboschi, tom. vi. P. i. p. 324.). They were first practised at Sarzanella, in 1487; but the honour and improvement in 1503 is ascribed to Peter of Navarre, who used them with success in the wars of Italy (Hist. de la Ligue de Cambray, tom. ii. p. 93–97.).

superseded the use of the liquid and unextinguishable fire. A wooden turret of the largest size was advanced on rollers: this portable magazine of ammunition and fascines was protected by a threefold covering of bulls hides; incessant vollies were securely discharged from the loop-holes; in the front, three doors were contrived for the alternate sally and retreat of the soldiers and workmen. They ascended by a stair-case to the upper platform; and, as high as the level of that platform, a scaling-ladder could be raised by pullies to form a bridge and grapple with the adverse rampart. By these various arts of annoyance, some as new as they were pernicious to the Greeks, the tower of St. Romanus was at length overturned: after a severe struggle, the Turks were repulsed from the breach and interrupted by darkness; but they trusted, that with the return of light they should renew the attack with fresh vigour and decisive success. Of this pause of action, this interval of hope, each moment was improved by the activity of the emperor and Justiniani, who passed the night on the spot, and urged the labours which involved the safety of the church and city. At the dawn of day, the impatient sultan perceived, with astonishment and grief, that his wooden turret had been reduced to ashes: the ditch was cleared and restored; and the tower of St. Romanus was again strong and entire. He deplored the failure of his design; and uttered a profane exclamation, that the word of the thirty-seven thousand prophets should not have compelled him to believe that such a work, in so short a time, could have been accomplished by the infidels.

Succour and victory of four ships. The generosity of the Christian princes was cold and tardy; but in the first apprehension of a siege, Constantine had negociated, in the isles of the Archipelago, the Morea, and Sicily, the most indispensable supplies. As early as the beginning of April, five[42] great ships, equipped for merchandise and war, would have sailed from the harbour of Chios, had not the wind blown obstinately from the north.[43] One of these ships bore the Imperial flag; the remaining four belonged to the Genoese; and they were laden with wheat and barley, with

---

42. It is singular that the Greeks should not agree in the number of these illustrious vessels; the *five* of Ducas, the *four* of Phranza and Leonardus, and the *two* of Chalcocondyles, must be extended to the smaller, or confined to the larger, size. Voltaire, in giving one of these ships to Frederic III. confounds the emperors of the East and West.

43. In bold defiance, or rather in gross ignorance, of language and geography, the president Cousin detains them at Chios with a south, and wafts them to Constantinople with a north, wind.

wine, oil, and vegetables, and, above all, with soldiers and mariners, for the service of the capital. After a tedious delay, a gentle breeze, and, on the second day, a strong gale from the south, carried them through the Hellespont and the Propontis: but the city was already invested by sea and land; and the Turkish fleet, at the entrance of the Bosphorus, was stretched from shore to shore, in the form of a crescent, to intercept, or at least to repel, these bold auxiliaries. The reader who has present to his mind the geographical picture of Constantinople, will conceive and admire the greatness of the spectacle. The five Christian ships continued to advance with joyful shouts, and a full press, both of sails and oars, against an hostile fleet of three hundred vessels; and the rampart, the camp, the coasts of Europe and Asia, were lined with innumerable spectators, who anxiously awaited the event of this momentous succour. At the first view that event could not appear doubtful; the superiority of the Moslems was beyond all measure or account; and, in a calm, their numbers and valour must inevitably have prevailed. But their hasty and imperfect navy had been created, not by the genius of the people, but by the will of the sultan: in the height of their prosperity, the Turks have acknowledged, that if God had given them the earth, he had left the sea to the infidels;[44] and a series of defeats, a rapid progress of decay, has established the truth of their modest confession. Except eighteen gallies of some force, the rest of their fleet consisted of open boats, rudely constructed and awkwardly managed, crowded with troops, and destitute of cannon; and, since courage arises in a great measure from the consciousness of strength, the bravest of the Janizaries might tremble on a new element. In the Christian squadron, five stout and lofty ships were guided by skilful pilots, and manned with the veterans of Italy and Greece, long practised in the arts and perils of the sea. Their weight was directed to sink or scatter the weak obstacles that impeded their passage: their artillery swept the waters: their liquid fire was poured on the heads of the adversaries, who, with the design of boarding, presumed to approach them; and the winds and waves are always on the side of the ablest navigators. In this conflict, the Imperial vessel, which had been almost overpowered, was rescued by the Genoese; but the Turks, in a distant and a closer attack, were twice repulsed with

44. The perpetual decay and weakness of the Turkish navy, may be observed in Rycaut (State of the Ottoman Empire, p. 372–378.), Thevenot (Voyages, P.i. p. 229–242.), and Tott (Memoires, tom iii.); the last of whom is always solicitous to amuse and amaze his reader.

considerable loss. Mahomet himself sat on horseback on the beach, to encourage their valour by his voice and presence, by the promise of reward, and by fear, more potent than the fear of the enemy. The passions of his soul, and even the gestures of his body,[45] seemed to imitate the actions of the combatants; and, as if he had been the lord of nature, he spurred his horse with a fearless and impotent effort into the sea. His loud reproaches, and the clamours of the camp, urged the Ottomans to a third attack, more fatal and bloody than the two former; and I must repeat, though I cannot credit, the evidence of Phranza, who affirms, from their own mouth, that they lost above twelve thousand men in the slaughter of the day. They fled in disorder to the shores of Europe and Asia, while the Christian squadron, triumphant and unhurt, steered along the Bosphorus, and securely anchored within the chain of the harbour. In the confidence of victory, they boasted that the whole Turkish power must have yielded to their arms; but the admiral, or captain bashaw, found some consolation for a painful wound in his eye, by representing that accident as the cause of his defeat. Baltha Ogli was a renegade of the race of the Bulgarian princes: his military character was tainted with the unpopular vice of avarice; and under the despotism of the prince or people, misfortune is a sufficient evidence of guilt. His rank and services were annihilated by the displeasure of Mahomet. In the royal presence, the captain bashaw was extended on the ground by four slaves, and received one hundred strokes with a golden rod:[46] his death had been pronounced; and he adored the clemency of the sultan, who was satisfied with the milder punishment of confiscation and exile. The introduction of this supply revived the hopes of the Greeks, and accused the supineness of their western allies. Amidst the deserts of Anatolia and the rocks of Palestine, the millions of the crusades had buried themselves in a voluntary and inevitable grave; but the situation of the Imperial city was strong against her enemies, and accessible to her friends; and a rational and moderate armament of the maritime states might have saved the relics of the Roman name, and maintained a Christian fortress in the heart of the Ottoman empire. Yet this was the sole and feeble

---

45. I must confess, that I have before my eyes the living picture which Thucydides (l. vii. c. 71.) has drawn of the passions and gestures of the Athenians in a naval engagement in the great harbour of Syracuse.

46. According to the exaggeration or corrupt text of Ducas (c. 38.), this golden bar was of the enormous and incredible weight of 500 libræ, or pounds. Bouillaud's reading of 500 drachms, or five pounds, is sufficient to exercise the arm of Mahomet, and bruise the back of his admiral.

attempt for the deliverance of Constantinople: the more distant powers were insensible of its danger; and the ambassador of Hungary, or at least of Huniades, resided in the Turkish camp, to remove the fears, and to direct the operations, of the sultan.[47]

It was difficult for the Greeks to penetrate the secret of the divan; yet the Greeks are persuaded, that a resistance, so obstinate and surprising, had fatigued the perseverance of Mahomet. He began to meditate a retreat, and the siege would

Mahomet transports his navy over land.

have been speedily raised if the ambition and jealousy of the second vizir had not opposed the perfidious advice of Calil Bashaw, who still maintained a secret correspondence with the Byzantine court. The reduction of the city appeared to be hopeless, unless a double attack could be made from the harbour as well as from the land; but the harbour was inaccessible: an impenetrable chain was now defended by eight large ships, more than twenty of a smaller size, with several gallies and sloops; and, instead of forcing this barrier, the Turks might apprehend a naval sally, and a second encounter in the open sea. In this perplexity, the genius of Mahomet conceived and executed a plan of a bold and marvellous cast, of transporting by land his lighter vessels and military stores from the Bosphorus into the higher part of the harbour. The distance is about ten miles; the ground is uneven, and was overspread with thickets; and, as the road must be opened behind the suburb of Galata, their free passage or total destruction must depend on the option of the Genoese. But these selfish merchants were ambitious of the favour of being the last devoured; and the deficiency of art was supplied by the strength of obedient myriads. A level way was covered with a broad platform of strong and solid planks; and to render them more slippery and smooth, they were anointed with the fat of sheep and oxen. Fourscore light gallies and brigantines of fifty and thirty oars, were disembarked on the Bosphorus shore; arranged successively on rollers; and drawn forwards by the power of men and pullies. Two guides or pilots were stationed at the helm, and the prow, of each vessel; the sails were unfurled to the winds; and the labour was cheered by song and acclamation. In the course of a single night, this Turkish fleet painfully climbed the hill, steered over the plain, and was launched from the declivity into the shallow waters of the harbour, far above the

---

47. Ducas, who confesses himself ill informed of the affairs of Hungary, assigns a motive of superstition, a fatal belief that Constantinople would be the term of the Turkish conquests. See Phranza (l. iii. c. 20.) and Spondanus.

molestation of the deeper vessels of the Greeks. The real importance of this operation was magnified by the consternation and confidence which it inspired: but the notorious, unquestionable, fact was displayed before the eyes, and is recorded by the pens, of the two nations.[48] A similar stratagem had been repeatedly practised by the ancients;[49] the Ottoman gallies (I must again repeat) should be considered as large boats; and, if we compare the magnitude and the distance, the obstacles and the means, the boasted miracle[50] has perhaps been equalled by the industry of our own times.[51] As soon as Mahomet had occupied the upper harbour with a fleet and army; he constructed, in the narrowest part, a bridge, or rather mole, of fifty cubits in breadth and one hundred in length: it was formed of casks and hogsheads; joined with rafters, linked with iron, and covered with a solid floor. On this floating battery, he planted one of his largest cannon, while the fourscore gallies, with troops and scaling-ladders, approached the most accessible side, which had formerly been stormed by the Latin conquerors. The indolence of the Christians has been accused for not destroying these unfinished works; but their fire, by a superior fire was controlled and silenced; nor were they wanting in a nocturnal attempt to burn the vessels as well as the bridge of the sultan. His vigilance prevented their approach; their foremost galliots were sunk or taken; forty youths, the bravest of Italy and Greece, were inhumanly massacred at his command; nor could the emperor's grief be assuaged by the just though cruel retaliation, of exposing from the walls the heads of two hundred and sixty Musulman captives. After a siege of forty days, the fate of Constantinople could no longer be averted. The diminutive garrison was exhausted by a double attack: the fortifications, which had stood for ages against hostile violence, were dismantled on all sides by the Ottoman cannon: many breaches were opened; and near the gate of

Distress of the city.

---

48. The unanimous testimony of the four Greeks is confirmed by Cantemir (p. 96.) from the Turkish annals: but I could wish to contract the distance of *ten* miles, and to prolong the term of *one* night.

49. Phranza relates two examples of a similar transportation over the six miles of the Isthmus of Corinth; the one fabulous, of Augustus after the battle of Actium; the other true, of Nicetas, a Greek general in the xth century. To these he might have added a bold enter-

prise of Hannibal, to introduce his vessels into the harbour of Tarentum (Polybius, l. viii. p. 749 edit. Gronov.).

50. A Greek of Candia, who had served the Venetians in a similar undertaking (Spond. A.D. 1438, N° 37.), might possibly be the adviser and agent of Mahomet.

51. I particularly allude to our own embarkations on the lakes of Canada in the years 1776 and 1777, so great in the labour, so fruitless in the event.

St. Romanus, four towers had been levelled with the ground. For the payment of his feeble and mutinous troops, Constantine was compelled to despoil the churches with the promise of a fourfold restitution; and his sacrilege offered a new reproach to the enemies of the union. A spirit of discord impaired the remnant of the Christian strength: the Genoese and Venetian auxiliaries asserted the pre-eminence of their respective service; and Justiniani and the great duke, whose ambition was not extinguished by the common danger, accused each other of treachery and cowardice.

During the siege of Constantinople, the words of peace and capitulation had been sometimes pronounced; and several embassies had passed between the camp and the city.[52] The Greek emperor was humbled by adversity; and would have yielded to any terms compatible with religion and royalty.

Preparations of the Turks for the general assault, May 26.

The Turkish sultan was desirous of sparing the blood of his soldiers; still more desirous of securing for his own use the Byzantine treasures; and he accomplished a sacred duty in presenting to the *Gabours*, the choice of circumcision, of tribute, or of death. The avarice of Mahomet might have been satisfied with an annual sum of one hundred thousand ducats: but his ambition grasped the capital of the East: to the prince he offered a rich equivalent, to the people a free toleration, or a safe departure: but after some fruitless treaty, he declared his resolution of finding either a throne, or a grave, under the walls of Constantinople. A sense of honour, and the fear of universal reproach, forbade Palæologus to resign the city into the hands of the Ottomans; and he determined to abide the last extremities of war. Several days were employed by the sultan in the preparations of the assault; and a respite was granted by his favourite science of astrology, which had fixed on the twenty-ninth of May, as the fortunate and fatal hour. On the evening of the twenty-seventh, he issued his final orders; assembled in his presence the military chiefs; and dispersed his heralds through the camp to proclaim the duty, and the motives, of the perilous enterprise. Fear is the first principle of a despotic government; and his menaces were expressed in the Oriental style, that the fugitives and deserters, had they the wings of a bird,[53] should not escape from his inexorable

---

52. Chalcocondyles and Ducas differ in the time and circumstances of the negociation; and as it was neither glorious nor salutary, the faithful Phranza spares his prince even the thought of a surrender.

53. These wings (Chalcocondyles, l. viii. p. 208.) are no more than an Oriental figure: but in the tragedy of Irene, Mahomet's passion soars above sense and reason:

justice. The greatest part of his bashaws and Janizaries were the offspring of Christian parents; but the glories of the Turkish name were perpetuated by successive adoption; and in the gradual change of individuals, the spirit of a legion, a regiment, or an *oda*, is kept alive by imitation and discipline. In this holy warfare, the Moslems were exhorted to purify their minds with prayer, their bodies with seven ablutions; and to abstain from food till the close of the ensuing day. A crowd of dervishes visited the tents to instil the desire of martyrdom, and the assurance of spending an immortal youth amidst the rivers and gardens of paradise, and in the embraces of the black-eyed virgins. Yet Mahomet principally trusted to the efficacy of temporal and visible rewards. A double pay was promised to the victorious troops; "The city and the buildings," said Mahomet, "are mine; but I resign to your valour the captives and the spoil, the treasures of gold and beauty: be rich and be happy. Many are the provinces of my empire: the intrepid soldier who first ascends the walls of Constantinople, shall be rewarded with the government of the fairest and most wealthy; and my gratitude shall accumulate his honours and fortunes above the measure of his own hopes." Such various and potent motives diffused among the Turks a general ardour, regardless of life and impatient for action: the camp re-echoed with the Moslem shouts of, "God is God, there is but one God, and Mahomet is the apostle of God;"[54] and the sea and land, from Galata to the seven towers, were illuminated by the blaze of their nocturnal fires.

Should the fierce North, upon his frozen wings,
Bear him aloft above the wondering clouds,
And seat him in the Pleiads golden chariot –
Thence should my fury drag him down to tortures.

Besides the extravagance of the rant, I must observe, 1. That the operation of the winds must be confined to the *lower* region of the air. 2. That the name, etymology, and fable of the Pleiads are purely Greek (Scholiast ad Homer. Σ 686. Eudocia in Ioniâ, p. 339. Apollodor. l. iii. c. 10. Heine, p. 229. Not. 682.), and had no affinity with the astronomy of the East (Hyde ad Ulugbeg, Tabul. in Syntagma Dissert. tom. i. p. 40. 42. Goguet, Origine des Arts, &c. tom. vi. p. 73–78. Gebelin, Hist. du Calendrier, p. 73.), which Mahomet had studied. 3. The golden chariot does not exist either in science or fiction; but I much fear that Dr. Johnson has confounded the Pleiads with the great bear or waggon, the zodiac with a northern constellation:

Αρκτον θ’ ήν και άμαξαν επικλησιν καλεουσι.

54. Phranza quarrels with these Moslem acclamations, not for the name of God, but for that of the prophet: the pious zeal of Voltaire is excessive, and even ridiculous.

Far different was the state of the Christians; who, with loud and impotent complaints, deplored the guilt, or the punishment, of their sins. The celestial image of the Virgin had been exposed in solemn procession; but their divine patroness was

Last farewel of the emperor and the Greeks.

deaf to their entreaties; they accused the obstinacy of the emperor for refusing a timely surrender; anticipated the horrors of their fate; and sighed for the repose and security of Turkish servitude. The noblest of the Greeks, and the bravest of the allies, were summoned to the palace, to prepare them, on the evening of the twenty-eighth, for the duties and dangers of the general assault. The last speech of Palæologus was the funeral oration of the Roman empire:[55] he promised, he conjured, and he vainly attempted to infuse the hope which was extinguished in his own mind. In this world all was comfortless and gloomy; and neither the gospel nor the church have proposed any conspicuous recompense to the heroes who fall in the service of their country. But the example of their prince, and the confinement of a siege, had armed these warriors with the courage of despair; and the pathetic scene is described by the feelings of the historian Phranza, who was himself present at this mournful assembly. They wept, they embraced; regardless of their families and fortunes, they devoted their lives; and each commander, departing to his station, maintained all night a vigilant and anxious watch on the rampart. The emperor, and some faithful companions, entered the dome of St. Sophia, which in a few hours was to be converted into a mosch; and devoutly received, with tears and prayers, the sacrament of the holy communion. He reposed some moments in the palace, which resounded with cries and lamentations; solicited the pardon of all whom he might have injured;[56] and mounted on horseback to visit the guards, and explore the motions of the enemy. The distress and fall of the last Constantine are more glorious than the long prosperity of the Byzantine Cæsars.

---

55. I am afraid that this discourse was composed by Phranza himself: and it smells so grossly of the sermon and the convent, that I almost doubt whether it was pronounced by Constantine. Leonardus assigns him another speech, in which he addresses himself more respectfully to the Latin auxiliaries.

56. This abasement, which devotion has sometimes extorted from dying princes, is an improvement of the gospel doctrine of the forgiveness of injuries: it is more easy to forgive 490 times, than once to ask pardon of an inferior.

In the confusion of darkness an assailant may sometimes succeed; but in this great and general attack, the military judgment and astrological knowledge of Mahomet advised him to expect the morning, the memorable twenty-ninth of May, in the fourteen hundred and fifty-third year of the Christian æra. The preceding night had been strenuously employed: the troops, the cannon, and the fascines, were advanced to the edge of the ditch, which in many parts presented a smooth and level passage to the breach; and his fourscore gallies almost touched with the prows and their scaling-ladders, the less defensible walls of the harbour. Under pain of death, silence was enjoined: but the physical laws of motion and sound are not obedient to discipline or fear; each individual might suppress his voice and measure his footsteps; but the march and labour of thousands must inevitably produce a strange confusion of dissonant clamours, which reached the ears of the watchmen of the towers. At day-break, without the customary signal of the morning gun, the Turks assaulted the city by sea and land; and the similitude of a twined or twisted thread had been applied to the closeness and continuity of their line of attack.[57] The foremost ranks consisted, of the refuse of the host, a voluntary crowd who fought without order or command; of the feebleness of age or childhood, of peasants and vagrants, and of all who had joined the camp in the blind hope of plunder and martyrdom. The common impulse drove them onwards to the wall: the most audacious to climb were instantly precipitated; and not a dart, not a bullet, of the Christians, was idly wasted on the accumulated throng. But their strength and ammunition were exhausted in this laborious defence: the ditch was filled with the bodies of the slain; they supported the footsteps of their companions; and of this devoted vanguard, the death was more serviceable than the life. Under their respective bashaws and sanjaks, the troops of Anatolia and Romania were successively led to the charge: their progress was various and doubtful; but, after a conflict of two hours, the Greeks still maintained, and improved, their advantage; and the voice of the emperor was heard, encouraging his soldiers to atchieve, by a last effort, the deliverance of their country. In that fatal moment, the Janizaries arose, fresh, vigorous, and invincible. The sultan himself on horseback, with an iron mace in his hand, was the spectator and judge of their valour: he was surrounded by ten thousand of his

---

57. Besides the 10,000 guards, and the sailors and the marines, Ducas numbers in this general assault 250,000 Turks both horse and foot.

domestic troops, whom he reserved for the decisive occasions; and the tide of battle was directed and impelled by his voice and eye. His numerous ministers of justice were posted behind the line, to urge, to restrain, and to punish; and if danger was in the front, shame and inevitable death were in the rear, of the fugitives. The cries of fear and of pain were drowned in the martial music of drums, trumpets, and attaballs; and experience has proved, that the mechanical operation of sounds, by quickening the circulation of the blood and spirits, will act on the human machine more forcibly than the eloquence of reason and honour. From the lines, the gallies, and the bridge, the Ottoman artillery thundered on all sides; and the camp and city, the Greeks and the Turks, were involved in a cloud of smoke, which could only be dispelled by the final deliverance or destruction of the Roman empire. The single combats of the heroes of history or fable, amuse our fancy and engage our affections: the skilful evolutions of war may inform the mind, and improve a necessary, though pernicious, science. But in the uniform and odious pictures of a general assault, all is blood, and horror, and confusion; nor shall I strive, at the distance of three centuries and a thousand miles, to delineate a scene, of which there could be no spectators, and of which the actors themselves were incapable of forming any just or adequate idea.

The immediate loss of Constantinople may be ascribed to the bullet, or arrow, which pierced the gauntlet of John Justiniani. The sight of his blood, and the exquisite pain, appalled the courage of the chief, whose arms and counsels were the firmest rampart of the city. As he withdrew from his station in quest of a surgeon, his flight was perceived and stopped by the indefatigable emperor. "Your wound," exclaimed Palæologus, "is slight; the danger is pressing; your presence is necessary; and whither will you retire?" "I will retire," said the trembling Genoese, "by the same road which God has opened to the Turks;" and at these words he hastily passed through one of the breaches of the inner wall. By this pusillanimous act, he stained the honours of a military life; and the few days which he survived in Galata, or the isle of Chios, were embittered by his own and the public reproach.[58] His example was imitated by the greatest part of the Latin

---

58. In the severe censure of the flight of Justiniani, Phranza expresses his own feelings, and those of the public. For some private reasons, he is treated with more lenity and respect by Ducas; but the words of Leonardus Chiensis express his strong and recent indignation, gloriæ salutis suique oblitus. In the whole series of their Eastern policy, his countrymen, the Genoese, were always suspected, and often guilty.

auxiliaries, and the defence began to slacken when the attack was pressed with redoubled vigour. The number of the Ottomans was fifty, perhaps an hundred, times superior to that of the Christians: the double walls were reduced by the cannon to an heap of ruins: in a circuit of several miles, some places must be found more easy of access, or more feebly guarded; and if the besiegers could penetrate in a single point, the whole city was irrecoverably lost. The first who deserved the sultan's reward was Hassan the Janizary, of gigantic stature and strength. With his scymetar in one hand and his buckler in the other, he ascended the outward fortification: of the thirty Janizaries, who were emulous of his valour, eighteen perished in the bold adventure. Hassan and his twelve companions had reached the summit; the giant was precipitated from the rampart; he rose on one knee, and was again oppressed by a shower of darts and stones. But his success had proved that the atchievement was possible: the walls and towers were instantly covered with a swarm of Turks; and the Greeks, now driven from the vantage ground, were overwhelmed by encreasing multitudes. Amidst these multitudes, the emperor,[59] who accomplished all the duties of a general and a soldier, was long seen, and finally lost. The nobles, who fought round his person, sustained till their last breath the honourable names of Palæologus and Cantacuzene: his mournful exclamation was heard, "Cannot there be found a Christian to cut off my head?"[60] and his last fear was that of falling alive into the hands of the infidels.[61]

Death of the emperor Constantine Palæologus. The prudent despair of Constantine cast away the purple: amidst the tumult he fell by an unknown hand, and his body was buried under a mountain of the slain. After his death, resistance and order were no more: the Greeks fled towards the city; and many were

---

59. Ducas kills him with two blows of Turkish soldiers; Chalcocondyles wounds him in the shoulder, and then tramples him in the gate. The grief of Phranza carrying him among the enemy, escapes from the precise image of his death; but we may, without flattery, apply these noble lines of Dryden:

As to Sebastian, let them search the field;
And where they find a mountain of the slain;
Send one to climb, and looking down beneath,

There they will find him at his manly length,
With his face up to heaven, in that red monument
Which his good sword had digged.

60. Spondanus (A.D. 1453, Nº 10.), who has hopes of his salvation, wishes to absolve this demand from the guilt of suicide.

61. Leonardus Chiensis very properly observes, that the Turks, had they known the emperor, would have laboured to save and secure a captive so acceptable to the sultan.

pressed and stifled in the narrow pass of the gate of St. Romanus. The victorious Turks rushed through the breaches of the inner wall; and as they advanced into the streets, they were soon joined by their brethren, who had forced the gate Phenar on the side of the harbour.[62] In the first heat of the pursuit, about two thousand Christians were put to the sword; but avarice soon prevailed over cruelty; and the victors acknowledged, that they should immediately have given quarter if the valour of the emperor and his chosen bands had not prepared them for a similar opposition in every part of the capital. It was thus, after a siege of fifty-three days, that Constantinople, which had defied the power of Chosroes, the Chagan, and the caliphs, was irretrievably subdued by the arms of Mahomet the second. Her empire only had been subverted by the Latins: her religion was trampled in the dust by the Moslem conquerors.[63]

Loss of the city and empire.

The tidings of misfortune fly with a rapid wing; yet such was the extent of Constantinople, that the more distant quarters might prolong some moments the happy ignorance of their ruin.[64] But in the general consternation, in the feelings of selfish or social anxiety, in the tumult and thunder of the assault, a *sleepless* night and morning must have elapsed; nor can I believe that many Grecian ladies were awakened by the Janizaries from a sound and tranquil slumber. On the assurance of the public calamity, the houses and convents were instantly deserted, and the trembling inhabitants flocked together in the streets, like an herd of timid animals; as if accumulated weakness could be productive of strength, or in the vain hope, that amid the crowd, each individual might be safe and invisible. From every part of the capital, they flowed into the church of St. Sophia: in the space of an hour, the sanctuary, the choir, the nave, the upper and lower galleries, were filled with the multitudes of fathers and husbands, of women and children, of priests, monks, and religious virgins: the doors were barred on

The Turks enter and pillage Constantinople.

---

62. Cantemir, p. 96. The Christian ships in the mouth of the harbour, had flanked and retarded this naval attack.

63. Chalcocondyles most absurdly supposes, that Constantinople was sacked by the Asiatics in revenge for the ancient calamities of Troy; and the grammarians of the xv^th century are happy to melt down the uncouth appellation of Turks, into the more classical name of *Teucri*.

64. When Cyrus surprised Babylon during the celebration of a festival, so vast was the city, and so careless were the inhabitants, that much time elapsed before the distant quarters knew that they were captives. Herodotus (l. i. c. 191.), and Usher (Annal, p. 78.), who has quoted from the prophet Jeremiah a passage of similar import.

the inside, and they sought protection from the sacred dome, which they had so lately abhorred as a profane and polluted edifice. Their confidence was founded on the prophecy of an enthusiast or impostor; that one day the Turks would enter Constantinople, and pursue the Romans as far as the column of Constantine in the square before St. Sophia: but that this would be the term of their calamities: that an angel would descend from heaven, with a sword in his hand, and would deliver the empire, with that celestial weapon, to a poor man seated at the foot of the column. "Take this sword," would he say, "and avenge the people of the Lord." At these animating words, the Turks would instantly fly, and the victorious Romans would drive them from the West, and from all Anatolia, as far as the frontiers of Persia. It is on this occasion, that Ducas, with some fancy and much truth, upbraids the discord and obstinacy of the Greeks. "Had that angel appeared," exclaims the historian, "had he offered to exterminate your foes if you would consent to the union of the church, even then, in that fatal moment, you would have rejected your safety or have deceived your God."[65]

Captivity of the Greeks. While they expected the descent of the tardy angel, the doors were broken with axes; and as the Turks encountered no resistance, their bloodless hands were employed in selecting and securing the multitude of their prisoners. Youth, beauty, and the appearance of wealth, attracted their choice; and the right of property was decided among themselves by a prior seizure, by personal strength, and by the authority of command. In the space of an hour, the male captives were bound with cords, the females with their veils and girdles. The senators were linked with their slaves; the prelates, with the porters, of the church; and young men of a plebeian class, with noble maids, whose faces had been invisible to the sun and their nearest kindred. In this common captivity, the ranks of society were confounded; the ties of nature were cut asunder; and the inexorable soldier was careless of the father's groans, the tears of the mother, and the lamentations of the children. The loudest in their wailings were the nuns, who were torn from the altar with naked bosoms, outstretched hands, and dishevelled hair: and we should piously believe that few could be tempted to prefer the vigils of the haram to those of the

65. This lively description is extracted from Ducas (c. 39.), who two years afterwards was sent ambassador from the prince of Lesbos to the sultan (c. 44.). Till Lesbos was subdued in 1463 (Phranza, l. iii. c. 27.), that island must have been full of the fugitives of Constantinople, who delighted to repeat, perhaps to adorn, the tale of their misery.

monastery. Of these unfortunate Greeks, of these domestic animals, whole strings were rudely driven through the streets; and as the conquerors were eager to return for more prey, their trembling pace was quickened with menaces and blows. At the same hour, a similar rapine was exercised in all the churches and monasteries, in all the palaces and habitations of the capital; nor could any place, however sacred or sequestered, protect the persons or the property of the Greeks. Above sixty thousand of this devoted people were transported from the city to the camp and fleet; exchanged or sold according to the caprice or interest of their masters, and dispersed in remote servitude through the provinces of the Ottoman empire. Among these we may notice some remarkable characters. The historian Phranza, first chamberlain and principal secretary, was involved with his family in the common lot. After suffering four months the hardships of slavery, he recovered his freedom; in the ensuing winter he ventured to Adrianople, and ransomed his wife from the *mir bashi* or master of the horse; but his two children, in the flower of youth and beauty, had been seized for the use of Mahomet himself. The daughter of Phranza died in the seraglio, perhaps a virgin: his son, in the fifteenth year of his age, preferred death to infamy, and was stabbed by the hand of the royal lover.[66] A deed thus inhuman, cannot surely be expiated by the taste and liberality with which he released a Grecian matron, and her two daughters, on receiving a Latin ode from Philelphus, who had chosen a wife in that noble family.[67] The pride or cruelty of Mahomet would have been most sensibly gratified by the capture of a Roman legate; but the dexterity of cardinal Isidore eluded the search, and he escaped from Galata in a plebeian habit.[68] The chain and entrance of the outward harbour was still occupied by the Italian ships of merchandise and war. They had signalised their valour in

---

66. See Phranza, l. iii. c. 20, 21. His expressions are positive: Ameras suâ manû jugulavit . . . volebat enim eo turpiter et nefarie abuti. Me miserum et infelicem. Yet he could only learn from report, the bloody or impure scenes that were acted in the dark recesses of the seraglio.

67. See Tiraboschi (tom. vi. P. i. p. 290.) and Lancelot (Mem. de l'Academie des Inscriptions, tom. x. p. 718.). I should be curious to learn how he could praise the public enemy, whom he so often reviles as

the most corrupt and inhuman of tyrants.

68. The Commentaries of Pius II. suppose, that he craftily placed his cardinal's hat on the head of a corpse which was cut off and exposed in triumph, while the legate himself was bought and delivered, as a captive of no value. The great Belgic Chronicle adorns his escape with new adventures, which he suppressed (says Spondanus, A.D. 1453, N° 15.) in his own letters, lest he should lose the merit and reward of suffering for Christ.

the siege; they embraced the moment of retreat, while the Turkish mariners were dissipated in the pillage of the city. When they hoisted sail, the beach was covered with a suppliant and lamentable crowd: but the means of transportation were scanty: the Venetians and Genoese selected their countrymen; and, notwithstanding the fairest promises of the sultan, the inhabitants of Galata evacuated their houses, and embarked with their most precious effects.

Amount of the spoil. In the fall and the sack of great cities, an historian is condemned to repeat the tale of uniform calamity: the same effects must be produced by the same passions; and when those passions may be indulged without control, small, alas! is the difference between civilized and savage man. Amidst the vague exclamations of bigotry and hatred, the Turks are not accused of a wanton or immoderate effusion of Christian blood: but according to their maxims (the maxims of antiquity), the lives of the vanquished were forfeited; and the legitimate reward of the con- queror was derived from the service, the sale, or the ransom, of his cap- tives of both sexes.[69] The wealth of Constantinople had been granted by the sultan to his victorious troops: and the rapine of an hour is more productive than the industry of years. But as no regular division was attempted of the spoil, the respective shares were not determined by merit; and the rewards of valour were stolen away by the followers of the camp, who had declined the toil and danger of the battle. The narrative of their depredations could not afford either amusement or instruction: the total amount, in the last poverty of the empire, has been valued at four millions of ducats;[70] and of this sum, a small part was the property of the Venetians, the Genoese, the Florentines, and the merchants of Ancona. Of these foreigners, the stock was improved in quick and perpetual circu- lation: but the riches of the Greeks were displayed in the idle ostentation of palaces and wardrobes, or deeply buried in treasures of ingots and old coin, lest it should be demanded at their hands for the defence of their country. The profanation and plunder of the monasteries and churches, excited the most tragic complaints. The dome of St. Sophia itself, the

69. Busbequius expatiates with pleasure and applause on the rights of war, and the use of slavery, among the ancients and the Turks (de Legat. Turcicâ, epist. iii. p. 161.).

70. This sum is specified in a marginal note of Leunclavius (Chalcocondyles, l. viii.

p. 211), but in the distribution to Venice, Genoa, Florence, and Ancona, of 50, 20, 20, and 15,000 ducats, I suspect that a figure has been dropt. Even with the restitution, the foreign property would scarcely exceed one- fourth.

earthly heaven, the second firmament, the vehicle of the cherubim, the throne of the glory of God,[71] was despoiled of the oblations of ages; and the gold and silver, the pearls and jewels, the vases and sacerdotal ornaments, were most wickedly converted to the service of mankind. After the divine images had been stripped of all that could be valuable to a profane eye, the canvass, or the wood, was torn, or broken, or burnt, or trod under foot, or applied, in the stables or the kitchen, to the vilest uses. The example of sacrilege was imitated however from the Latin conquerors of Constantinople; and the treatment which Christ, the Virgin, and the saints, had sustained from the guilty Catholic, might be inflicted by the zealous Musulman on the monuments of idolatry. Perhaps, instead of joining the public clamour, a philosopher will observe, that in the decline of the arts, the workmanship could not be more valuable than the work, and that a fresh supply of visions and miracles would speedily be renewed by the craft of the priest and the credulity of the people. He will more seriously deplore the loss of the Byzantine libraries, which were destroyed or scattered in the general confusion: one hundred and twenty thousand manuscripts are said to have disappeared;[72] ten volumes might be purchased for a single ducat; and the same ignominious price, too high perhaps for a shelf of theology, included the whole works of Aristotle and Homer, the noblest productions of the science and literature of ancient Greece. We may reflect with pleasure, that an inestimable portion of our classic treasures was safely deposited in Italy; and that the mechanics of a German town had invented an art which derides the havock of time and barbarism.

From the first hour[73] of the memorable twenty-ninth of May, disorder and rapine prevailed in Constantinople, till the eighth hour of the same day; when the sultan himself passed in triumph through the gate of St. Romanus. He was attended by his vizirs, bashaws, and guards, each of whom (says a Byzantine historian) was robust as Hercules, dextrous as Apollo, and equal in battle to any ten of the race of ordinary mortals. The conqueror[74] gazed with satisfaction and wonder on the strange though splendid appearance of the

Mahomet II. visits the city, St. Sophia, the palace, &c.

---

71. See the enthusiastic praises and lamentations of Phranza (l. iii. c. 17.).

72. See Ducas (c. 43.), and an epistle, July 15th, 1453, from Laurus Quirinus to pope Nicholas V. (Hody de Græcis, p. 192. from a MS. in the Cotton library).

73. The Julian Calendar, which reckons the days and hours from midnight, was used at Constantinople. But Ducas seems to understand the natural hours from sunrise.

74. See the Turkish Annals, p. 329. and the Pandects of Leunclavius, p. 448.

domes and palaces, so dissimilar from the style of Oriental architecture. In the hippodrome, or *atmeidan*, his eye was attracted by the twisted column of the three serpents; and, as a trial of his strength, he shattered with his iron mace or battle-axe the under jaw of one of these monsters,[75] which in the eyes of the Turks were the idols or talismans of the city. At the principal door of St. Sophia, he alighted from his horse, and entered the dome: and such was his jealous regard for that monument of his glory, that on observing a zealous Musulman in the act of breaking the marble pavement, he admonished him with his scymetar, that, if the spoil and captives were granted to the soldiers, the public and private buildings had been reserved for the prince. By his command, the metropolis of the Eastern church was transformed into a mosch: the rich and portable instruments of superstition had been removed; the crosses were thrown down; and the walls, which were covered with images and mosaics, were washed and purified, and restored to a state of naked simplicity. On the same day, or on the ensuing Friday, the *muezin* or crier ascended the most lofty turret, and proclaimed the *ezan*, or public invitation in the name of God and his prophet; the imam preached; and Mahomet the second performed the *namaz* of prayer and thanksgiving on the great altar, where the Christian mysteries had so lately been celebrated before the last of the Cæsars.[76] From St. Sophia he proceeded to the august, but desolate, mansion of an hundred successors of the great Constantine; but which in a few hours had been stripped of the pomp of royalty. A melancholy reflection on the vicissitudes of human greatness, forced itself on his mind; and he repeated an elegant distich of Persian poetry: "The spider has wove his web in the Imperial palace; and the owl hath sung her watch-song on the towers of Afrasiab."[77]

His behaviour to the Greeks. Yet his mind was not satisfied, nor did the victory seem complete, till he was informed of the fate of Constantine; whether he had escaped, or been made prisoner, or had fallen in the battle. Two Janizaries claimed the honour and reward of his death:

---

75. I have had occasion (vol. i. p. 597.) to mention this curious relic of Græcian antiquity.

76. We are obliged to Cantemir (p. 102.) for the Turkish account of the conversion of St. Sophia, so bitterly deplored by Phranza and Ducas. It is amusing enough to observe, in what opposite lights the same object appears to a Musulman and a Christian eye.

77. This distich, which Cantemir gives in the original, derives new beauties from the application. It was thus that Scipio repeated, in the sack of Carthage, the famous prophecy of Homer. The same generous feeling carried the mind of the conqueror to the past or the future.

the body, under an heap of slain, was discovered by the golden eagles embroidered on his shoes: the Greeks acknowledged with tears the head of their late emperor; and, after exposing the bloody trophy,[78] Mahomet bestowed on his rival the honours of a decent funeral. After his decease, Lucas Notaras, great duke,[79] and first minister of the empire, was the most important prisoner. When he offered his person and his treasures at the foot of the throne, "And why," said the indignant sultan, "did you not employ these treasures in the defence of your prince and country?" "They were yours," answered the slave, "God had reserved them for your hands." "If he reserved them for me," replied the despot, "how have you presumed to with-hold them so long by a fruitless and fatal resistance?" The great duke alleged the obstinacy of the strangers, and some secret encouragement from the Turkish vizir; and from this perilous interview, he was at length dismissed with the assurance of pardon and protection. Mahomet condescended to visit his wife, a venerable princess oppressed with sickness and grief; and his consolation for her misfortunes was in the most tender strain of humanity and filial reverence. A similar clemency was extended to the principal officers of state, of whom several were ransomed at his expence; and during some days he declared himself the friend and father of the vanquished people. But the scene was soon changed; and before his departure, the hippodrome streamed with the blood of his noblest captives. His perfidious cruelty is execrated by the Christians: they adorn with the colours of heroic martyrdom the execution of the great duke and his two sons; and his death is ascribed to the generous refusal of delivering his children to the tyrant's lust. Yet a Byzantine historian has dropt an unguarded word of conspiracy, deliverance, and Italian succour: such treason may be glorious; but the rebel who bravely ventures, has justly forfeited, his life; nor should we blame a conqueror for destroying the enemies whom he can no longer trust. On the eighteenth of June, the victorious sultan returned to Adrianople; and smiled at the base and hollow embassies of the Christian princes, who viewed their approaching ruin in the fall of the Eastern empire.

---

78. I cannot believe with Ducas (see Spondanus, A.D. 1453, Nº 13.), that Mahomet sent round Persia, Arabia, &c. the head of the Greek emperor: he would surely content himself with a trophy less inhuman.

79. Phranza was the personal enemy of the Greek duke; nor could time, or death, or his own retreat to a monastery, extort a feeling of sympathy or forgiveness. Ducas is inclined to praise and pity the martyr; Chalcocondyles is neuter, but we are indebted to him for the hint of the Greek conspiracy.

He repeoples and adorns Constantinople.

Constantinople had been left naked and desolate, without a prince or a people. But she could not be despoiled of the incomparable situation which marks her for the metropolis of a great empire; and the genius of the place will ever triumph over the accidents of time and fortune. Boursa and Adrianople, the ancient seats of the Ottomans, sunk into provincial towns; and Mahomet the second established his own residence, and that of his successors, on the same commanding spot which had been chosen by Constantine.[80] The fortifications of Galata, which might afford a shelter to the Latins, were prudently destroyed; but the damage of the Turkish cannon was soon repaired; and before the month of August, great quantities of lime had been burnt for the restoration of the walls of the capital. As the entire property of the soil and buildings, whether public or private, or profane or sacred, was now transferred to the conqueror, he first separated a space of eight furlongs from the point of the triangle for the establishment of his seraglio or palace. It is here, in the bosom of luxury, that the *grand signor* (as he has been emphatically named by the Italians) appears to reign over Europe and Asia; but his person on the shores of the Bosphorus may not always be secure from the insults of an hostile navy. In the new character of a mosch, the cathedral of St. Sophia was endowed with an ample revenue, crowned with lofty minarets, and surrounded with groves and fountains, for the devotion and refreshment of the Moslems. The same model was imitated in the *jami* or royal moschs; and the first of these was built, by Mahomet himself, on the ruins of the church of the holy apostles and the tombs of the Greek emperors. On the third day after the conquest, the grave of Abu Ayub or Job, who had fallen in the first siege of the Arabs, was revealed in a vision; and it is before the sepulchre of the martyr, that the new sultans are girded with the sword of empire.[81] Constantinople no longer appertains to the Roman historian; nor shall I enumerate the civil and religious edifices that were profaned or erected by

---

80. For the restitution of Constantinople and the Turkish foundations, see Cantemir (p. 102–109.), Ducas (c. 42.), with Thevenot, Tournefort, and the rest of our modern travellers. From a gigantic picture of the greatness, population, &c. of Constantinople and the Ottoman empire (Abregé de l'Histoire Ottomane, tom. i. p. 16–21.), we may learn, that in the year 1586, the Moslems were less numerous in the capital than the Christians, or even the Jews.

81. The *Turbé*, or sepulchral monument of Abou Ayub, is described and engraved in the Tableau General de l'Empire Ottoman (Paris, 1787, in large folio), a work of less use, perhaps, than magnificence (tom. i. p. 305, 306.).

its Turkish masters: the population was speedily renewed; and before the end of September, five thousand families of Anatolia and Romania had obeyed the royal mandate, which enjoined them, under pain of death, to occupy their new habitations in the capital. The throne of Mahomet was guarded by the numbers and fidelity of his Moslem subjects: but his rational policy aspired to collect the remnant of the Greeks; and they returned in crowds, as soon as they were assured of their lives, their liberties, and the free exercise of their religion. In the election and investiture of a patriarch, the ceremonial of the Byzantine court was revived and imitated. With a mixture of satisfaction and horror, they beheld the sultan on his throne; who delivered into the hands of Gennadius the crosier or pastoral staff, the symbol of his ecclesiastical office; who conducted the patriarch to the gate of the seraglio, presented him with an horse richly caparisoned, and directed the vizirs and bashaws to lead him to the palace which had been allotted for his residence.[82] The churches of Constantinople were shared between the two religions: their limits were marked; and, till it was infringed by Selim the grandson of Mahomet, the Greeks[83] enjoyed above sixty years the benefit of this equal partition. Encouraged by the ministers of the divan, who wished to elude the fanaticism of the sultan, the Christian advocates presumed to allege that this division had been an act, not of generosity, but of justice; not a concession, but a compact; and that if one half of the city had been taken by storm, the other moiety had surrendered on the faith of a sacred capitulation. The original grant had indeed been consumed by fire: but the loss was supplied by the testimony of three aged Janizaries who remembered the transaction; and their venal oaths are of more weight in the opinion of Cantemir, than the positive and unanimous consent of the history of the times.[84]

---

82. Phranza (l. iii. c. 19.) relates the ceremony, which has possibly been adorned in the Greek reports to each other, and to the Latins. The fact is confirmed by Emanuel Malaxus, who wrote, in vulgar Greek, the History of the Patriarchs after the taking of Constantinople, inserted in the Turco-Græcia of Crusius (l. v. p. 106–184.). But the most patient reader will not believe that Mahomet adopted the Catholic form, "Sancta Trinitas quæ mihi donavit imperium te in patriarcham novæ Romæ deligit."

83. From the Turco-Græcia of Crusius, &c. Spondanus (A.D. 1453, N° 21. 1458, N° 16.) describes the slavery and domestic quarrels of the Greek church. The patriarch who succeeded Gennadius, threw himself in despair into a well.

84. Cantemir (p. 101–105.) insists on the unanimous consent of the Turkish historians, ancient as well as modern, and argues, that they would not have violated the truth to diminish their national glory, since it is esteemed more honourable to take a city by

Extinction of the Imperial families of Comnenus and Palæologus.   The remaining fragments of the Greek kingdom in Europe and Asia I shall abandon to the Turkish arms; but the final extinction of the two last dynasties[85] which have reigned in Constantinople, should terminate the decline and fall of the Roman empire in the East. The despots of the Morea, Demetrius and Thomas,[86] the two surviving brothers of the name of PALÆOLOGUS, were astonished by the death of the emperor Constantine, and the ruin of the monarchy. Hopeless of defence, they prepared with the noble Greeks who adhered to their fortune, to seek a refuge in Italy, beyond the reach of the Ottoman thunder. Their first apprehensions were dispelled by the victorious sultan, who contented himself with a tribute of twelve thousand ducats; and while his ambition explored the continent and the islands in search of prey, he indulged the Morea in a respite of seven years. But this respite was a period of grief, discord, and misery. The *hexamilion*, the rampart of the Isthmus, so often raised and so often subverted, could not long be defended by three hundred Italian archers: the keys of Corinth were seized by the Turks: they returned from their summer excursions with a train of captives and spoil; and the complaints of the injured Greeks were heard with indifference and disdain. The Albanians, a vagrant tribe of shepherds and robbers, filled the peninsula with rapine and murder: the two despots implored the dangerous and humiliating aid of a neighbouring bashaw; and when he had quelled the revolt, his lessons inculcated the rule of their future conduct. Neither the ties of blood, nor the oaths which they repeatedly pledged in the communion and before the altar, nor the stronger pressure of necessity, could reconcile or suspend their domestic quarrels. They ravaged each other's patrimony with fire and sword: the alms and succours of the West were consumed in civil hostility; and their

---

force than by composition. But, 1. I doubt this consent, since he quotes no particular historian, and the Turkish Annals of Leunclavius affirm, without exception, that Mahomet took Constantinople *per vim* (p. 329.). 2. The same argument may be turned in favour of the Greeks of the times, who would not have forgotten this honourable and salutary treaty. Voltaire, as usual, prefers the Turks to the Christians.

85. For the genealogy and fall of the Comneni of Trebizond, see Ducange (Fam. Byzant.

p. 195.); for the last Palæologi, the same accurate antiquarian (p. 244. 247. 248.). The Palæologi of Montferrat were not extinct till the next century; but they had forgotten their Greek origin and kindred.

86. In the worthless story of the disputes and misfortunes of the two brothers, Phranza (l. iii. c. 21–30.) is too partial on the side of Thomas; Ducas (c. 44, 45.) is too brief, and Chalcocondyles (l. viii, ix, x.) too diffuse and digressive.

power was only exerted in savage and arbitrary executions. The distress and revenge of the weaker rival invoked their supreme lord; and, in the season of maturity and revenge, Mahomet declared himself the friend of Demetrius, and marched into the Morea with an irresistible force. When he had taken possession of Sparta, "You are too weak," said the sultan, "to control this turbulent province: I will take your daughter to my bed; and you shall pass the remainder of your life in security and honour." Demetrius sighed and obeyed; surrendered his daughter and his castles; followed to Adrianople his sovereign and son; and received for his own maintenance, and that of his followers, a city in Thrace, and the adjacent isles of Imbros, Lemnos, and Samothrace. He was joined the next year by a companion of misfortune, the last of the COMNENIAN race, who, after the taking of Constantinople by the Latins, had founded a new empire on the coast of the Black Sea.[87] In the progress of his Anatolian conquests, Mahomet invested with a fleet and army the capital of David, who presumed to style himself emperor of Trebizond;[88] and the negociation was comprised in a short and peremptory question, "Will you secure your life and treasures by resigning your kingdom? or had you rather forfeit your kingdom, your treasures, and your life?" The feeble Comnenus was subdued by his own fears, and the example of a Musulman neighbour, the prince of Sinope,[89] who, on a similar summons, had yielded a fortified city with four hundred cannon and ten or twelve thousand soldiers. The capitulation of Trebizond was faithfully performed; and the emperor, with his family, was transported to a castle in Romania: but on a slight suspicion of corresponding with the Persian king, David, and the whole Comnenian race, were sacrificed to the jealousy or avarice of the conqueror. Nor could the

Loss of the Morea, A.D. 1460;

of Trebizond, A.D. 1461.

---

87. See the loss or conquest of Trebizond in Chalcocondyles (l. ix. p. 263–266.), Ducas (c. 45), Phranza (l. iii. c. 27.), and Cantemir (p. 107.).

88. Though Tournefort (tom. iii. lettre xvii. p. 179.) speaks of Trebizond as mal peuplée, Peyssonel, the latest and most accurate observer, can find 100,000 inhabitants (Commerce de la Mer Noire, tom. ii. p. 72. and for the province, p. 53–90.). Its prosperity and trade are perpetually disturbed by the factious quarrels of two *odas* of Janizaries, in

one of which 30,000 Lazi are commonly enrolled (Memoires de Tott, tom. iii. p. 16, 17.).

89. Ismael Beg, prince of Sinope or Sinople, was possessed (chiefly from his copper mines) of a revenue of 200,000 ducats (Chalcocond. l. ix. p. 258, 259.). Peyssonel (Commerce de la Mer Noire, tom. ii. p. 100.) ascribes to the modern city 60,000 inhabitants. This account seems enormous: yet it is by trading with a people that we become acquainted with their wealth and numbers.

name of father long protect the unfortunate Demetrius from exile and confiscation; his abject submission moved the pity and contempt of the sultan; his followers were transplanted to Constantinople; and his poverty was alleviated by a pension of fifty thousand aspers, till a monastic habit and a tardy death released Palæologus from an earthly master. It is not easy to pronounce whether the servitude of Demetrius, or the exile of his brother Thomas,[90] be the most inglorious. On the conquest of the Morea, the despot escaped to Corfu, and from thence to Italy, with some naked adherents: his name, his sufferings, and the head of the apostle St. Andrew, entitled him to the hospitality of the Vatican; and his misery was prolonged by a pension of six thousand ducats from the pope and cardinals. His two sons, Andrew and Manuel, were educated in Italy; but the eldest, contemptible to his enemies and burthensome to his friends, was degraded by the baseness of his life and marriage. A title was his sole inheritance; and that inheritance he successively sold to the kings of France and Arragon.[91] During his transient prosperity, Charles the eighth was ambitious of joining the empire of the East with the kingdom of Naples: in a public festival, he assumed the appellation and the purple of *Augustus*: the Greeks rejoiced, and the Ottoman already trembled, at the approach of the French chivalry.[92] Manuel Palæologus, the second son, was tempted to revisit his native country: his return might be grateful, and could not be dangerous, to the Porte: he was maintained at Constantinople in safety and ease; and an honourable train of Christians and Moslems attended him to the grave. If there be some animals of so generous a nature that they refuse to propagate in a domestic state, the last of the Imperial race must be ascribed to an inferior kind: he accepted from the sultan's liberality two beautiful females; and his surviving son was lost in the habit and religion of a Turkish slave.

90. Spondanus (from Gobelin Comment. Pii II. l. v.) relates the arrival and reception of the despot Thomas at Rome (A.D. 1461, N° 3.).
91. By an act dated A.D. 1494, Sept. 6. and lately transmitted from the archives of the Capitol to the royal library of Paris, the despot Andrew Palæologus, reserving the Morea, and stipulating some private advantages, conveys to Charles VIII. king of France the empires of Constantinople and Trebizond (Spondanus, A.D. 1495, N° 2.). M. de Foncemagne (Mem. de l'Academie des Inscriptions, tom. xvii. p. 539–578.) has bestowed a dissertation on this national title, of which he had obtained a copy from Rome.
92. See Philippe de Comines (l. vii. c. 14.), who reckons with pleasure the number of Greeks who were prepared to rise, 60 miles of an easy navigation, eighteen days journey from Valona to Constantinople, &c. On this occasion the Turkish empire was saved by the policy of Venice.

The importance of Constantinople was felt and magnified in its loss: the pontificate of Nicholas the fifth, however peaceful and prosperous, was dishonoured by the fall of the Eastern empire; and the grief and terror of the Latins revived, or seemed

Grief and terror of Europe, A.D. 1453.

to revive, the old enthusiasm of the crusades. In one of the most distant countries of the West, Philip duke of Burgundy entertained, at Lisle in Flanders, an assembly of his nobles; and the pompous pageants of the feast were skilfully adapted to their fancy and feelings.[93] In the midst of the banquet, a gigantic Saracen entered the hall, leading a fictitious elephant, with a castle on his back: a matron in a mourning robe, the symbol of religion, was seen to issue from the castle; she deplored her oppression, and accused the slowness of her champions: the principal herald of the golden fleece advanced, bearing on his fist a live pheasant, which, according to the rites of chivalry, he presented to the duke. At this extraordinary summons, Philip, a wise and aged prince, engaged his person and powers in the holy war against the Turks; his example was imitated by the barons and knights of the assembly; they swore to God, the Virgin, the ladies, and the *pheasant*; and their particular vows were not less extravagant than the general sanction of their oath. But the performance was made to depend on some future and foreign contingency; and, during twelve years, till the last hour of his life, the duke of Burgundy might be scrupulously, and perhaps sincerely, on the eve of his departure. Had every breast glowed with the same ardour; had the union of the Christians corresponded with their bravery; had every country, from Sweden[94] to Naples, supplied a just proportion of cavalry and infantry, of men and money, it is indeed probable that Constantinople would have been delivered, and that the Turks might have been chased beyond the Hellespont or the Euphrates. But the secretary of the emperor, who composed every epistle, and attended every meeting, Æneas Sylvius,[95] a statesman and orator, describes from his own

---

93. See the original feast in Olivier de la Marche (Memoires, P. i. c. 29, 30.), with the abstract and observations of M. de S.te Palaye (Memoires sur la Chevalerie, tom. i. P. iii. p. 182–185.). The peacock and the pheasant were distinguished as royal birds.

94. It was found by an actual enumeration, that Sweden, Gothland, and Finland, contained 1,800,000 fighting men, and consequently were far more populous than at present.

95. In the year 1454 Spondanus has given, from Æneas Sylvius, a view of the state of Europe, enriched with his own observations. That valuable annalist, and the Italian Muratori, will continue the series of events from the year 1453 to 1481, the end of Mahomet's life, and of this chapter.

experience the repugnant state and spirit of Christendom. "It is a body," says he, "without an head; a republic without laws or magistrates. The pope and the emperor may shine as lofty titles, as splendid images; but *they* are unable to command, and none are willing to obey: every state has a separate prince, and every prince has a separate interest. What eloquence could unite so many discordant and hostile powers under the same standard? Could they be assembled in arms, who would dare to assume the office of general? What order could be maintained? – what military discipline? Who would undertake to feed such an enormous multitude? Who would understand their various languages, or direct their stranger and incompatible manners? What mortal could reconcile the English with the French, Genoa with Arragon, the Germans with the natives of Hungary and Bohemia? If a small number enlisted in the holy war, they must be overthrown by the infidels; if many, by their own weight and confusion." Yet the same Æneas, when he was raised to the papal throne, under the name of Pius the second, devoted his life to the prosecution of the Turkish war. In the council of Mantua he excited some sparks of a false or feeble enthusiasm; but when the pontiff appeared at Ancona to embark in person with the troops, engagements vanished in excuses; a precise day was adjourned to an indefinite term; and his effective army consisted of some German pilgrims, whom he was obliged to disband with indulgences and alms. Regardless of futurity, his successors and the powers of Italy were involved in the schemes of present and domestic ambition; and the distance or proximity of each object determined, in their eyes, its apparent magnitude. A more enlarged view of their interest would have taught them to maintain a defensive and naval war against the common enemy; and the support of Scanderbeg and his brave Albanians, might have prevented the subsequent invasion of the kingdom of Naples. The siege and sack of Otranto by the Turks, diffused a general consternation; and pope Sixtus was preparing to fly beyond the Alps, when the storm was instantly dispelled by the death of Mahomet the second, in the fifty-first year of his age.[96] His lofty genius aspired to the conquest of Italy: he

Death of Mahomet II. A.D. 1481, May 3, or July 2.

---

96. Besides the two annalists, the reader may consult Giannone (Istoria Civile, tom. iii. p. 449–455.) for the Turkish invasion of the kingdom of Naples. For the reign and conquests of Mahomet II. I have occasionally used the Memorie Istoriche de Monarchi Ottomanni di Giovanni Sagredo (Venezia, 1677, in 4⁰). In peace and war, the Turks have ever engaged the attention of the republic of Venice. All her dispatches and archives

was possessed of a strong city and a capacious harbour; and the same reign might have been decorated with the trophies of the NEW and the ANCIENT ROME.[97]

---

were open to a procurator of St. Mark, and Sagredo is not contemptible either in sense or style. Yet he too bitterly hates the infidels; he is ignorant of their language and manners; and his narrative, which allows only seventy pages to Mahomet II. (p. 69–140.), becomes more copious and authentic as he approaches the years 1640 and 1644, the term of the historic labours of John Sagredo.

97. As I am now taking an everlasting farewell of the Greek empire, I shall briefly mention the great collection of Byzantine writers, whose names and testimonies have been successively repeated in this work. The Greek presses of Aldus and the Italians, were confined to the classics of a better age; and the first rude editions of Procopius, Agathias,

Cedrenus, Zonaras, &c. were published by the learned diligence of the Germans. The whole Byzantine series (xxxvi volumes in folio) has gradually issued (A.D. 1648, &c.) from the royal press of the Louvre, with some collateral aid from Rome and Leipsic; but the Venetian edition (A.D. 1729), though cheaper and more copious, is not less inferior in correctness than in magnificence to that of Paris. The merits of the French editors are various; but the value of Anna Comnena, Cinnamus, Villehardouin, &c. is enhanced by the historical notes of Charles du Fresne du Cange. His supplemental works, the Greek Glossary, the Constantinopolis Christiana, the Familiæ Byzantinæ, diffuse a steady light over the darkness of the Lower Empire.

[CHAPTERS LXIX—LXX]

Once Constantinople has fallen, we enter the coda of *The Decline and Fall*: three chapters which match and complete the opening three chapters of general analysis. Gibbon's theme in these chapters is the revival of ancient culture:

In the busy age of the crusades, some sparks of curiosity and reason were rekindled in the Western world: the heresy of Bulgaria, the Paulician sect, was successfully transplanted into the soil of Italy and France; the Gnostic visions were mingled with the simplicity of the gospel; and the enemies of the clergy reconciled their passions with their conscience, the desire of freedom with the profession of piety. (*DF*, iii. 987)

But Gibbon understands very well that a perfect and full recovery of the past is a practical and theoretical impossibility. This is what Cola di Rienzi, the Roman demagogue, fails to grasp:

the Roman hero was fast declining from the meridian of fame and power; and the people, who had gazed with astonishment on the ascending meteor, began to mark the irregularity of its course, and the vicissitudes of light and obscurity. More eloquent than judicious, more enterprising than resolute, the faculties of Rienzi were not balanced by cool and commanding reason: he magnified in a tenfold proportion the objects of hope and fear; and prudence, which could not have erected, did not presume to fortify, his throne. In the blaze of prosperity, his virtues were insensibly tinctured with the adjacent vices; justice with cruelty, liberality with profusion, and the desire of fame with puerile and ostentatious vanity. He might have learned, that the ancient tribunes, so strong and sacred in the public opinion, were not distinguished in style, habit, or appearance, from an ordinary plebeian; and that as often as they visited the city on foot, a single *viator*, or beadle, attended the exercise of their office. The Gracchi would have frowned or smiled, could they have read the sonorous titles and epithets of their successor, "NICHOLAS, SEVERE AND MERCIFUL; DELIVERER OF

738

ROME; DEFENDER OF ITALY; FRIEND OF MANKIND, AND OF LIBERTY, PEACE, AND JUSTICE; TRIBUNE AUGUST:" his theatrical pageants had prepared the revolution; but Rienzi abused, in luxury and pride, the political maxim of speaking to the eyes, as well as the understanding, of the multitude. From nature he had received the gift of an handsome person, till it was swelled and disfigured by intemperance; and his propensity to laughter was corrected in the magistrate by the affectation of gravity and sternness. He was cloathed, at least on public occasions, in a party-coloured robe of velvet or sattin, lined with fur, and embroidered with gold: the rod of justice, which he carried in his hand, was a sceptre of polished steel, crowned with a globe and cross of gold, and enclosing a small fragment of the true and holy wood. In his civil and religious processions through the city, he rode on a white steed, the symbol of royalty: the great banner of the republic, a sun with a circle of stars, a dove with an olive branch, was displayed over his head; a shower of gold and silver was scattered among the populace; fifty guards with halberds encompassed his person; a troop of horse preceded his march; and their tymbals and trumpets were of massy silver.

The ambition of the honours of chivalry betrayed the meanness of his birth, and degraded the importance of his office; and the equestrian tribune was not less odious to the nobles, whom he adopted, than to the plebeians, whom he deserted. All that yet remained of treasure, or luxury, or art, was exhausted on that solemn day. Rienzi led the procession from the Capitol to the Lateran; the tediousness of the way was relieved with decorations and games; the ecclesiastical, civil, and military orders marched under their various banners; the Roman ladies attended his wife; and the ambassadors of Italy might loudly applaud, or secretly deride, the novelty of the pomp. In the evening, when they had reached the church and palace of Constantine, he thanked and dismissed the numerous assembly, with an invitation to the festival of the ensuing day. From the hands of a venerable knight he received the order of the Holy Ghost; the purification of the bath was a previous ceremony; but in no step of his life did Rienzi excite such scandal and censure as by the prophane use of the porphyry vase, in which Constantine (a foolish legend) had been healed of his leprosy by pope Sylvester. With equal presumption the tribune watched or reposed within the consecrated precincts of the baptistery; and the failure of his state-bed was interpreted as an omen of his approaching downfal. At the hour of worship he shewed himself to the returning crowds in a majestic attitude, with a robe of purple, his sword, and gilt spurs; but the holy rites were soon interrupted by his levity and insolence. Rising from his throne, and advancing towards the congregation, he proclaimed in a loud voice: "We summon to our tribunal pope Clement; and command him to reside in his diocese of Rome: we also summon the sacred college of cardinals. We again summon the two pretenders, Charles of Bohemia and Lewis of Bavaria, who style themselves emperors: we likewise summon all the electors of Germany, to inform us on what pretence they have usurped the inalienable right of the Roman people, the ancient and lawful sovereigns of the empire." Unsheathing his maiden-sword, he thrice brandished it to the three parts of the world, and thrice repeated the extravagant declaration, "And this too is mine!" The pope's vicar, the bishop of Orvieto, attempted to check this career of folly; but his feeble protest was silenced by martial music; and instead of withdrawing from the assembly, he consented to dine with his brother tribune, at a table which had hitherto been reserved for the supreme pontiff. A banquet, such as the Cæsars had given, was prepared for the Romans. The apartments, porticoes, and courts, of the Lateran were spread with innumerable tables for either sex, and every condition; a stream of wine flowed from the nostrils of Constantine's brazen horse; no complaint, except of the scarcity of water, could be heard; and the licentiousness of the multitude was curbed by discipline and fear. A subsequent day was appointed for the coronation of Rienzi; seven crowns of different leaves or metals were successively placed on his head by the most eminent of the Roman clergy; they represented the seven gifts of the Holy Ghost; and he still professed to imitate the example of the ancient tribunes. These extraordinary spectacles might deceive or flatter the people; and their own vanity was gratified in the vanity of their leader. But in his private life he soon deviated from the strict rule of frugality and abstinence; and the plebeians, who were awed by the splendour of the nobles, were provoked by the luxury of their equal. His wife, his son, his uncle (a barber in name and profession), exposed the contrast of vulgar manners and princely expence; and without acquiring the majesty, Rienzi degenerated into the vices, of a king. (*DF*, iii. 1031–4)

Cola is guilty of an historical, as well as a political, blunder. In the final chapter of the history Gibbon gives shape to the insight, never better embodied than in his own work, that historical imagination is the only true restoration.

CHAPTER LXXI

Prospect of the Ruins of Rome in the Fifteenth Century. – Four Causes of Decay and Destruction. – Example of the Coliseum. – Renovation of the City. – Conclusion of the whole Work.

In the last days of pope Eugenius the fourth, two of his servants, the learned Poggius[1] and a friend, ascended the Capitoline hill; reposed themselves among the ruins of columns and temples; and viewed from that commanding spot the wide and various prospect of desolation.[2] The place and the object gave ample scope for moralising on the vicissitudes of fortune, which spares neither man nor the proudest of his works, which buries empires and cities in a common grave; and it was agreed, that in proportion to her former greatness, the fall of Rome was the more awful and deplorable. "Her primæval state, such as she might appear in a remote age, when Evander entertained the stranger of Troy,[3] has been delineated by the fancy of Virgil. This Tarpeian rock was then a savage and solitary thicket: in the time of the poet, it was crowned with the golden roofs of a temple; the temple is overthrown, the gold has been pillaged, the wheel of fortune has accomplished her revolution, and the sacred ground is again disfigured with thorns and brambles. The hill of the Capitol, on which we sit, was formerly the head of the Roman empire, the citadel of the earth, the terror of kings; illustrated by the footsteps of so many triumphs, enriched with the spoils and tributes of so many nations. This spectacle of the world, how is it fallen! how changed! how defaced! the path of victory is obliterated by vines, and the benches of the senators are concealed by a dunghill. Cast

View and discourse of Poggius from the Capitoline hill, A.D. 1430.

1. I have already (not. 50, 51. on chap. 65.) mentioned the age, character, and writings of Poggius; and particularly noticed the date of this elegant moral lecture on the varieties of fortune.
2. Consedimus in ipsis Tarpeiæ arcis ruinis, pone ingens portæ cujusdam, ut puto, templi, marmoreum limen, plurimasque passim con-

fractas columnas, unde magnâ ex parte prospectus urbis patet (p. 5.).
3. Æneid viii. 97–369. This ancient picture, so artfully introduced, and so exquisitely finished, must have been highly interesting to an inhabitant of Rome; and our early studies allow us to sympathise in the feelings of a Roman.

your eyes on the Palatine hill, and seek among the shapeless and enormous fragments, the marble theatre, the obelisks, the colossal statues, the porticoes of Nero's palace: survey the other hills of the city, the vacant space is interrupted only by ruins and gardens. The forum of the Roman people, where they assembled to enact their laws and elect their magistrates, is now enclosed for the cultivation of pot-herbs, or thrown open for the reception of swine and buffaloes. The public and private edifices, that were founded for eternity, lie prostrate, naked, and broken, like the limbs of a mighty giant; and the ruin is the more visible, from the stupendous relics that have survived the injuries of time and fortune."[4]

His description of the ruins.

These relics are minutely described by Poggius, one of the first who raised his eyes from the monuments of legendary, to those of classic, superstition.[5] 1. Besides a bridge, an arch, a sepulchre, and the pyramid of Cestius, he could discern, of the age of the republic, a double row of vaults in the salt-office of the Capitol, which were inscribed with the name and munificence of Catulus. 2. Eleven temples were visible in some degree, from the perfect form of the Pantheon, to the three arches and a marble column of the temple of peace, which Vespasian erected after the civil wars and the Jewish triumph. 3. Of the number, which he rashly defines, of seven *thermæ* or public baths, none were sufficiently entire to represent the use and distribution of the several parts; but those of Diocletian and Antoninus Caracalla still retained the titles of the founders, and astonished the curious spectator, who, in observing their solidity and extent, the variety of marbles, the size and multitude of the columns, compared the labour and expence with the use and importance. Of the baths of Constantine, of Alexander, of Domitian, or rather of Titus, some vestige might yet be found. 4. The triumphal arches of Titus, Severus, and Constantine, were entire, both the structure and the inscriptions; a falling fragment was honoured with the name of Trajan; and two arches, then extant, in the Flaminian way, have been ascribed to the baser memory of Faustina and Gallienus. 5. After the wonder of the Coliseum, Poggius might have overlooked a small amphitheatre of brick, most probably for the use of the prætorian camp: the theatres of Marcellus and Pompey were occupied in a great measure by public and private

4. Capitolium adeo . . . immutatum ut vineæ in senatorum subsellia successerint, stercorum ac purgamentorum receptaculum factum. Respice ad Palatinum montem . . . vasta rud-

era . . . cæteros colles perlustra omnia vacua ædificiis, ruinis vineisque oppleta conspicies (Poggius de Varietat. Fortunæ, p. 21.).
5. See Poggius, p. 8–22.

buildings; and in the Circus, Agonalis and Maximus, little more than the situation and the form could be investigated. 6. The columns of Trajan and Antonine were still erect; but the Egyptian obelisks were broken or buried. A people of gods and heroes, the workmanship of art, was reduced to one equestrian figure of gilt brass, and to five marble statues, of which the most conspicuous were the two horses of Phidias and Praxiteles. 7. The two mausoleums or sepulchres of Augustus and Hadrian could not totally be lost; but the former was only visible as a mound of earth; and the latter, the castle of St. Angelo, had acquired the name and appearance of a modern fortress. With the addition of some separate and nameless columns, such were the remains of the ancient city: for the marks of a more recent structure might be detected in the walls, which formed a circumference of ten miles, included three hundred and seventy-nine turrets, and opened into the country by thirteen gates.

This melancholy picture was drawn above nine hundred years after the fall of the Western empire, and even of the Gothic kingdom of Italy. A long period of distress and anarchy, in which *Gradual decay of Rome.* empire, and arts, and riches, had migrated from the banks of the Tyber, was incapable of restoring or adorning the city; and, as all that is human must retrograde if it do not advance, every successive age must have hastened the ruin of the works of antiquity. To measure the progress of decay, and to ascertain at each æra the state of each edifice, would be an endless and a useless labour, and I shall content myself with two observations which will introduce a short enquiry into the general causes and effects. 1. Two hundred years before the eloquent complaint of Poggius, an anonymous writer composed a description of Rome.[6] His ignorance may repeat the same objects under strange and fabulous names. Yet this barbarous topographer had eyes and ears, he could observe the visible remains, he could listen to the tradition of the people, and he distinctly enumerates seven theatres, eleven baths, twelve arches, and eighteen palaces, of which many had disappeared before the time of Poggius. It is apparent, that many

---

6. Liber de Mirabilibus Romæ, ex Registro Nicolai Cardinalis de Arragoniâ, in Bibliothecâ St. Isidori Armario IV. Nº 69. This treatise, with some short but pertinent notes, has been published by Montfaucon (Diarium Italicum, p. 283–301.), who thus delivers his own critical opinion: Scriptor xiiiᵐⁱ circiter sæculi, ut ibidem notatur; antiquariæ rei imperitus, et, ut ab illo ævo, nugis et anilibus fabellis refertus: sed, quia monumenta quæ iis temporibus Romæ supererant pro modulo recenset, non parum inde lucis mutuabitur qui Romanis antiquitatibus indagandis operam navabit (p. 283.)

stately monuments of antiquity survived till a late period,[7] and that the principles of destruction acted with vigorous and encreasing energy in the thirteenth and fourteenth centuries. 2. The same reflection must be applied to the three last ages; and we should vainly seek the Septizonium of Severus,[8] which is celebrated by Petrarch and the antiquarians of the sixteenth century. While the Roman edifices were still entire, the first blows, however weighty and impetuous, were resisted by the solidity of the mass and the harmony of parts; but the slightest touch would precipitate the fragments of arches and columns, that already nodded to their fall.

Four causes of destruction:

After a diligent enquiry, I can discern four principal causes of the ruin of Rome, which continued to operate in a period of more than a thousand years. I. The injuries of time and nature. II. The hostile attacks of the Barbarians and Christians. III. The use and abuse of the materials. And, IV. The domestic quarrels of the Romans.

I. The injuries of nature;

I. The art of man is able to construct monuments far more permanent than the narrow span of his own existence: yet these monuments, like himself, are perishable and frail; and in the boundless annals of time, his life and his labours must equally be measured as a fleeting moment. Of a simple and solid edifice, it is not easy however to circumscribe the duration. As the wonders of ancient days, the pyramids[9] attracted the curiosity of the ancients: an hundred generations, the leaves of autumn,[10] have dropt into the grave; and after the fall of the Pharaohs and Ptolemies, the Cæsars and caliphs, the same pyramids stand erect and unshaken above the floods of the Nile. A complex figure of various and minute parts is more accessible to injury and decay; and the silent lapse of time is often accelerated by hurricanes and earthquakes, by fires and inundations. The air and earth have doubtless been shaken; and the lofty turrets of Rome have tottered from their

hurricanes and earthquakes;

7. The Pere Mabillon (Analecta, tom. iv. p. 502.) has published an anonymous pilgrim of the ix[th] century, who, in his visit round the churches and holy places of Rome, touches on several buildings, especially porticoes, which had disappeared before the xiii[th] century.

8. On the Septizonium, see the Memoires sur Petrarque (tom. i. p. 325.), Donatus (p. 338.), and Nardini (p. 117. 414.).

9. The age of the pyramids is remote and

unknown, since Diodorus Siculus (tom. i. l. i. c. 44. p. 72.) is unable to decide whether they were constructed 1000, or 3400, years before the clxxx[th] Olympiad. Sir John Marsham's contracted scale of the Egyptian dynasties would fix them about 2000 years before Christ (Canon. Chronicus, p. 47.).

10. See the speech of Glaucus in the Iliad (Z. 146.). This natural but melancholy image is familiar to Homer.

foundations: but the seven hills do not appear to be placed on the great cavities of the globe; nor has the city, in any age, been exposed to the convulsions of nature, which, in the climate of Antioch, Lisbon, or Lima, have crumbled in a few moments the works of ages into dust.

Fire is the most powerful agent of life and death: the rapid mischief may be kindled and propagated by the industry or negligence of mankind; and every period of the Roman annals is marked by the repetition of similar calamities. A memorable conflagration, the guilt or misfortune of Nero's reign, continued, though with unequal fury, either six, or nine days.[11] Innumerable buildings, crowded in close and crooked streets, supplied perpetual fewel for the flames; and when they ceased, four only of the fourteen regions were left entire; three were totally destroyed, and seven were deformed by the relics of smoking and lacerated edifices.[12] In the full meridian of empire, the metropolis arose with fresh beauty from her ashes; yet the memory of the old deplored their irreparable losses, the arts of Greece, the trophies of victory, the monuments of primitive or fabulous antiquity. In the days of distress and anarchy, every wound is mortal, every fall irretrievable; nor can the damage be restored either by the public care of government or the activity of private interest. Yet two causes may be alleged, which render the calamity of fire more destructive to a flourishing than a decayed city. 1. The more combustible materials of brick, timber, and metals, are first melted or consumed; but the flames may play without injury or effect on the naked walls, and massy arches, that have been despoiled of their ornaments. 2. It is among the common and plebeian habitations, that a mischievous spark is most easily blown to a conflagration; but as soon as they are devoured, the greater edifices which have resisted or escaped, are left as so many islands in a state of solitude and safety. From her situation, Rome is exposed to the danger of frequent

fires;

11. The learning and criticism of M. des Vignoles (Histoire Critique de la Republique des Lettres, tom. viii, p. 74–118. ix. p. 172–187.) dates the fire of Rome from A.D. 64, July 19, and the subsequent persecution of the Christians from November 15, of the same year.

12. Quippe in regiones quatuordecim Roma dividitur, quarum quatuor integræ manebant, tres solo tenus dejectæ: septem reliquis pauca tectorum vestigia supererant, lacera et semiusta. Among the old relics that were irreparably lost, Tacitus enumerates the temple of the moon of Servius Tullius; the fane and altar consecrated by Evander præsenti Herculi; the temple of Jupiter Stator, a vow of Romulus; the palace of Numa; the temple of Vesta cum Penatibus populi Romani. He then deplores the opes tot victoriis quæsitæ et Græcarum artium decora . . . multa quæ seniores meminerant, quæ reparari nequibant (Annal. xv. 40, 41.).

inundations. inundations. Without excepting the Tyber, the rivers that descend from either side of the Apennine have a short and irregular course: a shallow stream in the summer heats; an impetuous torrent, when it is swelled in the spring or winter, by the fall of rain, and the melting of the snows. When the current is repelled from the sea by adverse winds, when the ordinary bed is inadequate to the weight of waters, they rise above the banks, and overspread, without limits or control, the plains and cities of the adjacent country. Soon after the triumph of the first Punic war, the Tyber was encreased by unusual rains; and the inundation, surpassing all former measure of time and place, destroyed all the buildings that were situate below the hills of Rome. According to the variety of ground, the same mischief was produced by different means; and the edifices were either swept away by the sudden impulse, or dissolved and undermined by the long continuance, of the flood.[13] Under the reign of Augustus, the same calamity was renewed: the lawless river overturned the palaces and temples on its banks;[14] and, after the labours of the emperor in cleansing and widening the bed that was incumbered with ruins,[15] the vigilance of his successors was exercised by similar dangers and designs. The project of diverting into new channels the Tyber itself, or some of the dependent streams, was long opposed by superstition and local interests;[16] nor did the use compensate the toil and cost of the tardy and imperfect execution. The

13. A.U.C. 507, repentina subversio ipsius Romæ prævenit triumphum Romanorum . . . diversæ ignium aquarumque clades pene absumsere urbem. Nam Tiberis insolitis auctus imbribus et ultra opinionem, vel diurnitate vel magnitudine redundans, *omnia* Romæ ædificia in plano posita delevit. Diversæ qualitates locorum ad unam convenere perniciem: quoniam et quæ segnior inundatio tenuit madefacta dissolvit, et quæ cursus torrentis invenit impulsa dejecit (Orosius, Hist. l. iv. c. 11. p. 244. edit. Havercamp). Yet we may observe, that it is the plan and study of the Christian apologist, to magnify the calamities of the pagan world.

14.
Vidimus flavum Tiberim, retortis
Littore Etrusco violenter undis
Ire dejectum monumenta Regis
Templaque Vestæ.

(Horat. Carm. I. 2.)

If the palace of Numa, and temple of Vesta, were thrown down in Horace's time, what was consumed of those buildings by Nero's fire could hardly deserve the epithets of vetustissima or incorrupta.

15. Ad coercendas inundationes alveum Tiberis laxavit, ac repurgavit, completum olim ruderibus, et ædificiorum prolapsionibus coarctatum (Suetonius in Augusto, c. 30.).

16. Tacitus (Annal. i. 79.) reports the petitions of the different towns of Italy to the senate against the measure; and we may applaud the progress of reason. On a similar occasion, local interests would undoubtedly be consulted: but an English house of commons would reject with contempt the arguments of superstition, "that nature had assigned to the rivers their proper course, &c."

servitude of rivers is the noblest and most important victory which man has obtained over the licentiousness of nature;[17] and if such were the ravages of the Tyber under a firm and active government, what could oppose, or who can enumerate, the injuries of the city after the fall of the Western empire? A remedy was at length produced by the evil itself: the accumulation of rubbish and the earth, that has been washed down from the hills, is supposed to have elevated the plain of Rome, fourteen or fifteen feet, perhaps, above the ancient level;[18] and the modern city is less accessible to the attacks of the river.[19]

II. The crowd of writers of every nation, who impute the destruction of the Roman monuments to the Goths and the Christians, have neglected to enquire how far they were animated by an hostile principle, and how far they possessed the means and the leisure to satiate their enmity. In the preceding

II. The hostile attacks of the Barbarians and Christians.

volumes of this History, I have described the triumph of barbarism and religion; and I can only resume, in a few words, their real or imaginary connection with the ruin of ancient Rome. Our fancy may create, or adopt, a pleasing romance, that the Goths and Vandals sallied from Scandinavia, ardent to avenge the flight of Odin,[20] to break the chains, and to chastise the oppressors, of mankind; that they wished to burn the records of classic literature, and to found their national architecture on the broken members of the Tuscan and Corinthian orders. But in simple truth, the northern conquerors were neither sufficiently savage, nor sufficiently refined, to entertain such aspiring ideas of destruction and revenge. The shepherds of Scythia and Germany had been educated in the armies of the empire, whose discipline they acquired, and whose weakness they invaded: with the familiar use of the Latin tongue, they had learned to reverence

17. See the Epoques de la Nature of the eloquent and philosophic Buffon. His picture of Guyana in South America, is that of a new and savage land, in which the waters are abandoned to themselves, without being regulated by human industry (p. 212. 561. quarto edition).
18. In his Travels in Italy, Mr. Addison (his works, vol. ii. p. 98. Baskerville's edition) has observed this curious and unquestionable fact.
19. Yet in modern times, the Tyber has sometimes damaged the city; and in the years 1530,

1557, 1598, the Annals of Muratori record three mischievous and memorable inundations (tom. xiv. p. 268. 429. tom. xv. p. 99, &c.).
20. I take this opportunity of declaring, that in the course of twelve years I have forgotten, or renounced, the flight of Odin from Azoph to Sweden, which I never very seriously believed (vol. i. p. 257.). The Goths are apparently Germans: but all beyond Cæsar and Tacitus, is darkness or fable, in the antiquities of Germany.

the name and titles of Rome; and, though incapable of emulating, they were more inclined to admire, than to abolish, the arts and studies of a brighter period. In the transient possession of a rich and unresisting capital, the soldiers of Alaric and Genseric were stimulated by the passions of a victorious army; amidst the wanton indulgence of lust or cruelty, portable wealth was the object of their search; nor could they derive either pride or pleasure from the unprofitable reflection, that they had battered to the ground the works of the consuls and Cæsars. Their moments were indeed precious; the Goths evacuated Rome on the sixth,[21] the Vandals on the fifteenth, day;[22] and, though it be far more difficult to build than to destroy, their hasty assault would have made a slight impression on the solid piles of antiquity. We may remember, that both Alaric and Genseric affected to spare the buildings of the city; that they subsisted in strength and beauty under the auspicious government of Theodoric;[23] and that the momentary resentment of Totila[24] was disarmed by his own temper and the advice of his friends and enemies. From these innocent Barbarians, the reproach may be transferred to the Catholics of Rome. The statues, altars, and houses, of the dæmons were an abomination in their eyes; and in the absolute command of the city, they might labour with zeal and perseverance to eraze the idolatry of their ancestors. The demolition of the temples in the East[25] affords to *them* an example of conduct, and to *us* an argument of belief; and it is probable, that a portion of guilt or merit may be imputed with justice to the Roman proselytes. Yet their abhorrence was confined to the monuments of heathen superstition; and the civil structures that were dedicated to the business or pleasure of society might be preserved without injury or scandal. The change of religion was accomplished, not by a popular tumult, but by the decrees of the emperors, of the senate, and of time. Of the Christian hierarchy, the bishops of Rome were commonly the most prudent and least fanatic: nor can any positive charge be opposed to the meritorious act of saving and converting the majestic structure of the Pantheon.[26]

---

21. History of the Decline, &c. vol. ii. p. 209.

22. —— vol. ii. p. 360.

23. —— vol. ii. p. 542–544.

24. —— vol. ii. p. 744.

25. History of the Decline, &c. vol. ii. c. xxviii. p. 79–81.

26. Eodem tempore petiit a Phocate principe templum, quod appellatur *Pantheon*, in quo fecit ecclesiam Sanctæ Mariæ semper Virginis, et omnium martyrum; in quâ ecclesiæ princeps multa bona obtulit (Anastasius vel potius Liber Pontificalis in Bonifacio IV. in Muratori, Script. Rerum Italicarum, tom. iii. P. i. p. 135.). According to the anonymous

III. The value of any object that supplies the wants or pleasures of mankind, is compounded of its substance and its form, of the materials and the manufacture. Its price must depend on the number of persons by whom it may be acquired and used; on the extent of the market; and consequently on the ease or difficulty of remote exportation, according to the nature of the commodity, its local situation, and the temporary circumstances of the world. The Barbarian conquerors of Rome usurped in a moment the toil and treasure of successive ages; but, except the luxuries of immediate consumption, they must view without desire all that could not be removed from the city in the Gothic waggons or the fleet of the Vandals.[27] Gold and silver were the first objects of their avarice; as in every country, and in the smallest compass, they represent the most ample command of the industry and possessions of mankind. A vase or a statue of those precious metals might tempt the vanity of some Barbarian chief; but the grosser multitude, regardless of the form, was tenacious only of the substance; and the melted ingots might be readily divided and stamped into the current coin of the empire. The less active or less fortunate robbers were reduced to the baser plunder of brass, lead, iron, and copper: whatever had escaped the Goths and Vandals was pillaged by the Greek tyrants; and the emperor Constans, in his rapacious visit, stripped the bronze tiles from the roof of the Pantheon.[28] The edifices of Rome might be considered as a vast and various mine; the first labour of extracting the materials was already performed; the metals were purified and cast; the marbles were hewn and polished; and after foreign and domestic rapine had been satiated, the remains of the city, could a purchaser have been found, were still venal. The monuments of antiquity had been left naked of their precious ornaments, but the

III. The use and abuse of the materials.

---

writer in Montfaucon, the Pantheon had been vowed by Agrippa to Cybele and Neptune, and was dedicated by Boniface IV. on the calends of November to the Virgin, quæ est mater omnium sanctorum (p. 297, 298.).

27. Flaminius Vacca (apud Montfaucon, p. 155, 156. His Memoir is likewise printed, pp. 21. at the end of the Roma Antica of Nardini), and several Romans, doctrinâ graves, were persuaded that the Goths buried their treasures at Rome, and bequeathed the secret marks filiis nepotibusque. He relates

some anecdotes to prove, that in his own time, these places were visited and rifled by the Transalpine pilgrims, the heirs of the Gothic conquerors.

28. Omnia quæ erant in ære ad ornatum civitatis deposuit: sed et ecclesiam B. Mariæ ad martyres quæ de tegulis æreis cooperta discooperuit (Anast. in Vitalian. p. 141.). The base and sacrilegious Greek had not even the poor pretence of plundering an heathen temple; the Pantheon was already a Catholic church.

Romans would demolish with their own hands the arches and walls, if the hope of profit could surpass the cost of the labour and exportation. If Charlemagne had fixed in Italy the seat of the Western empire, his genius would have aspired to restore, rather than to violate, the works of the Cæsars: but policy confined the French monarch to the forests of Germany; his taste could be gratified only by destruction; and the new palace of Aix la Chapelle was decorated with the marbles of Ravenna[29] and Rome.[30] Five hundred years after Charlemagne, a king of Sicily, Robert, the wisest and most liberal sovereign of the age, was supplied with the same materials by the easy navigation of the Tyber and the sea; and Petrarch sighs an indignant complaint, that the ancient capital of the world should adorn from her own bowels the slothful luxury of Naples.[31] But these examples of plunder or purchase were rare in the darker ages; and the Romans, alone and unenvied, might have applied to their private or public use the remaining structures of antiquity, if in their present form and situation they had not been useless in a great measure to the city and its inhabitants. The walls still described the old circumference, but the city had descended from the

---

29. For the spoils of Ravenna (musiva atque marmora) see the original grant of pope Adrian I. to Charlemagne (Codex Carolin. epist. lxvii. in Muratori, Script. Ital. tom. iii. P. ii. p. 223.).

30. I shall quote the authentic testimony of the Saxon poet (A.D. 887–899), de Rebus gestis Caroli magni, l. v. 437–440. in the Historians of France (tom. v. p. 180.):

Ad quæ marmoreas præstabat ROMA columnas,
Quasdam præcipuas pulchra Ravenna dedit
De tam longinquâ poterit regione vetustas.
Illius ornatum Francia ferre tibi.

And I shall add, from the Chronicle of Sigebert (Historians of France, tom. v. p. 378.), extruxit etiam Aquisgrani basilicam plurimæ pulchritudinis, ad cujus structuram a ROMA et Ravenna columnas et marmora devehi fecit.

31. I cannot refuse to transcribe a long passage of Petrarch (Opp. p. 536, 537. in Epistolâ hortatoria ad Nicolaum Laurentium); it is so

strong and full to the point: Nec pudor aut pietas continuit quominus impii spoliata Dei templa, occupatas arces, opes publicas regiones urbis, atque honores magistratûum inter se divisos; (habeant?) quam unâ in re, turbulenti ac seditiosi homines et totius reliquæ vitæ consiliis et rationibus discordes, inhumani fœderis stupendâ societate convenerant, in pontes et mœnia atque immeritos lapides desævirent. Denique post vi vel senio collapsa palatia, quæ quondam ingentes tenuerunt viri, post diruptos arcus triumphales (unde majores horum forsitan corruerunt), de ipsius vetustatis ac propriæ impietatis fragminibus vilem questûm turpi mercimonio captare non puduit. Itaque nunc, heu dolor! heu scelus indignum! de vestris marmoreis columnis, de liminibus templorum (ad quæ nuper ex orbe toto concursus devotissimus fiebat), de imaginibus sepulchrorum sub quibus patrum vestrorum venerabilis civis (cinis?) erat, ut reliquas sileam, desidiosa Neapolis adornatur. Sic paullatim ruinæ ipsæ deficiunt. Yet king Robert was the friend of Petrarch.

---

seven hills into the Campus Martius; and some of the noblest monuments which had braved the injuries of time were left in a desert, far remote from the habitations of mankind. The palaces of the senators were no longer adapted to the manners or fortunes of their indigent successors: the use of baths[32] and porticoes was forgotten: in the sixth century, the games of the theatre, amphitheatre, and circus, had been interrupted: some temples were devoted to the prevailing worship; but the Christian churches preferred the holy figure of the cross; and fashion, or reason, had distributed after a peculiar model the cells and offices of the cloyster. Under the ecclesiastical reign, the number of these pious foundations was enormously multiplied; and the city was crowded with forty monasteries of men, twenty of women, and sixty chapters and colleges of canons and priests,[33] who aggravated, instead of relieving, the depopulation of the tenth century. But if the forms of ancient architecture were disregarded by a people insensible of their use and beauty, the plentiful materials were applied to every call of necessity or superstition; till the fairest columns of the Ionic and Corinthian orders, the richest marbles of Paros and Numidia, were degraded, perhaps to the support of a convent or a stable. The daily havock which is perpetrated by the Turks in the cities of Greece and Asia, may afford a melancholy example; and in the gradual destruction of the monuments of Rome, Sixtus the fifth may alone be excused for employing the stones of the Septizonium in the glorious edifice of St Peter's.[34] A fragment, a ruin, howsoever mangled or profaned, may be viewed with pleasure and regret; but the greater part of the marble was deprived of substance, as well as of place and proportion; it was burnt to lime for the purpose of cement. Since the arrival of Poggius, the temple of Concord,[35] and many capital

---

32. Yet Charlemagne washed and swam at Aix la Chapelle with a hundred of his courtiers (Eginhart, c. 22. p. 108, 109.), and Muratori describes as late as the year 814, the public baths which were built at Spoleto in Italy (Annali, tom. vi. p. 416.).

33. See the Annals of Italy, A.D. 988. For this and the preceding fact, Muratori himself is indebted to the Benedictine history of Pére Mabillon.

34. Vita di Sisto Quinto, da Gregorio Leti, tom. iii. p. 50.

35. Porticus ædis Concordiæ, quam cum primum ad urbem accessi vidi fere integram opere marmoreo admodum specioso: Romani postmodum ad calcem ædem totam et porticûs partem disjectis columnis sunt demoliti (p. 12.). The temple of Concord was therefore *not* destroyed by a sedition in the xiii[th] century, as I have read in a MS. treatise del' Governo civile di Rome, lent me formerly at Rome, and ascribed (I believe falsely) to the celebrated Gravina. Poggius likewise affirms, that the sepulchre of Cæcilia Metella was burnt for lime (p. 19, 20.).

structures, had vanished from his eyes; and an epigram of the same age expresses a just and pious fear, that the continuance of this practice would finally annihilate all the monuments of antiquity.[36] The smallness of their numbers was the sole check on the demands and depredations of the Romans. The imagination of Petrarch might create the presence of a mighty people;[37] and I hesitate to believe, that, even in the fourteenth century, they could be reduced to a contemptible list of thirty-three thousand inhabitants. From that period to the reign of Leo the tenth, if they multiplied to the amount of eighty-five thousand,[38] the encrease of citizens was in some degree pernicious to the ancient city.

IV. The domestic quarrels of the Romans.
        IV. I have reserved for the last, the most potent and forcible cause of destruction, the domestic hostilities of the Romans themselves. Under the dominion of the Greek and French emperors, the peace of the city was disturbed by accidental, though frequent, seditions: it is from the decline of the latter, from the beginning of the tenth century, that we may date the licentiousness of private war, which violated with impunity the laws of the Code and the Gospel; without respecting the majesty of the absent sovereign, or the presence and person of the vicar of Christ. In a dark period of five hundred years, Rome was perpetually afflicted by the sanguinary quarrels of the nobles and the people, the Guelphs and Ghibelines, the Colonna and Ursini; and if much has escaped the knowledge, and much is unworthy of the notice, of history, I have exposed in the two preceding chapters, the causes and effects of the public disorders. At such a time, when every quarrel was decided by the sword; and none could trust their lives or properties to the impotence of law; the powerful citizens were armed for safety or offence, against the domestic enemies, whom they feared or hated. Except Venice alone, the same dangers and designs were common to all the free republics of Italy; and the nobles usurped the prerogative of fortifying their houses,

---

36. Composed by Æneas Sylvius, afterwards pope Pius II. and published by Mabillon from a MS. of the queen of Sweden (Musæum Italicum, tom. i. p. 97.).

> Oblectat me, Roma, tuas spectare ruinas;
>   Ex cujus lapsû gloria prisca patet.
> Sed tuus hic populus muris defossa vetustis
>   *Calcis in obsequium* marmora dura' coquit

> Impia tercentum si sic gens egerit annos
>   Nullum hinc indicium nobilitatis erit.

37. Vagabamur pariter in illâ urbe tam magnâ; quæ, cum propter spatium vacua videretur, populum habet immensum (Opp. p. 605. Epist. Familiares, ii. 14.).

38. These states of the population of Rome at different periods, are derived from an ingenious treatise of the physician Lancisi, de Romani Cœli Qualitatibus (p. 122.).

and erecting strong towers[39] that were capable of resisting a sudden attack. The cities were filled with these hostile edifices; and the example of Lucca, which contained three hundred towers; her law, which confined their height to the measure of fourscore feet, may be extended with suitable latitude to the more opulent and populous states. The first step of the senator Brancaleone in the establishment of peace and justice, was to demolish (as we have already seen) one hundred and forty of the towers of Rome; and, in the last days of anarchy and discord, as late as the reign of Martin the fifth, forty-four still stood in one of the thirteen or fourteen regions of the city. To this mischievous purpose, the remains of antiquity were most readily adapted: the temples and arches afforded a broad and solid basis for the new structures of brick and stone; and we can name the modern turrets that were raised on the triumphal monuments of Julius Cæsar, Titus, and the Antonines.[40] With some slight alterations, a theatre, an amphitheatre, a mausoleum, was transformed into a strong and spacious citadel. I need not repeat, that the mole of Adrian has assumed the title and form of the castle of St. Angelo;[41] the Septizonium of Severus was capable of standing against a royal army;[42] the sepulchre of Metella has sunk under its outworks;[43] the theatres of Pompey and Marcellus were occupied by the Savelli and Ursini families;[44] and the rough fortress has

39. All the facts that relate to the towers at Rome, and in other free cities of Italy, may be found in the laborious and entertaining compilation of Muratori, Antiquitates Italiæ medii Ævi, dissertat. xxvi. (tom. ii. p. 493– 496. of the Latin, tom. i. p. 446. of the Italian work).

40. As for instance, Templum Jani nunc dicitur, turris Centii Frangapanis; et sane Jano impositæ turris lateritiæ conspicua hodieque vestigia supersunt (Montfaucon Diarium Italicum, p. 186). The anonymous writer (p. 285.) enumerates, arcus Titi, turris Cartularia; Arcus Julii Cæsaris et Senatorum, turres de Bratis; arcus Antonini, turris de Cosectis, &c.

41. Hadriani molem ... magna ex parte Romanorum injuria ... disturbavit: quod certe funditus evertissent, si eorum manibus pervia, absumptis grandibus saxis, reliqua moles exstitisset (Poggius de Varietate Fortunæ, p. 12.).

42. Against the emperor Henry IV. (Muratori, Annali d'Italia, tom. ix. p. 147.).

43. I must copy an important passage of Montfaucon: Turris ingens rotunda ... Cæciliæ Metallæ ... sepulchrum erat, cujus muri tam solidi, ut spatium perquam minimum intus vacuum supersit: et Torre di Bove dicitur, a boum capitibus muro inscriptis. Huic sequiori ævo, tempore intestinorum bellorum, ceu urbecula adjuncta fuit, cujus mœnia et turres etiamnum visuntur; ita ut sepulchrum Metellæ quasi arx oppiduli fuerit. Ferventibus in urbe partibus, cum Ursini atque Columnenses mutuis cladibus perniciem inferrent civitati, in utriusve partis ditionem cederet magni momenti erat (p. 142.).

44. See the testimonies of Donatus, Nardini, and Montfaucon. In the Savelli palace, the remains of the theatre of Marcellus are still great and conspicuous.

been gradually softened to the splendour and elegance of an Italian palace. Even the churches were encompassed with arms and bulwarks, and the military engines on the roof of St. Peter's were the terror of the Vatican and the scandal of the Christian world. Whatever is fortified will be attacked; and whatever is attacked may be destroyed. Could the Romans have wrested from the popes the castle of St. Angelo, they had resolved by a public decree to annihilate that monument of servitude. Every building of defence was exposed to a siege; and in every siege the arts and engines of destruction were laboriously employed. After the death of Nicholas the fourth, Rome, without a sovereign or a senate, was abandoned six months to the fury of civil war. "The houses," says a cardinal and poet of the times,[45] "were crushed by the weight and velocity of enormous stones;[46] the walls were perforated by the strokes of the battering-ram; the towers were involved in fire and smoke; and the assailants were stimulated by rapine and revenge." The work was consummated by the tyranny of the laws; and the factions of Italy alternately exercised a blind and thoughtless vengeance on their adversaries, whose houses and castles they razed to the ground.[47] In comparing the *days* of foreign, with the *ages* of domestic, hostility, we must pronounce, that the latter have been far more ruinous to the city, and our opinion is confirmed by the evidence of Petrarch. "Behold," says the laureat, "the relics of Rome, the image of her pristine greatness! neither time nor the Barbarian can boast the merit of this stupendous destruction: it was perpetrated by her own citizens, by the most illustrious of her sons; and your ancestors (he writes to a noble Annibaldi) have done with the battering-ram, what the Punic hero could not accom-

---

45. James cardinal of St. George, ad velum aureum, in his metrical Life of Pope Celestin V. (Muratori, Script. Ital. tom. i. P. iii. p. 621. l. i. c. 1. ver. 132, &c.)

> Hoc dixisse sat est, Romam caruisse
>   Senatû
> Mensibus exactis heu sex; belloque
>   vocatum (*vocatos*)
> In scelus, in socios fraternaque vulnera
>   patres:
> Tormentis jecisse viros immania saxa;
> Perfodisse domus trabibus, fecisse ruinas
> Ignibus; incensas turres, obscurataque
>   fumo
> Lumina vicino, quo sit spoliata supellex.

46. Muratori (Dissertazione sopra le Antiquitá Italiane, tom. i. p. 427–431.) finds, that stone bullets of two or three hundred pounds weight were not uncommon; and they are sometimes computed at xii or xviii *cantari* of Genoa, each *cantaro* weighing 150 pounds.

47. The vi[th] law of the Visconti prohibits this common and mischievous practice; and strictly enjoins, that the houses of banished citizens should be preserved pro communi utilitate (Gualvaneus de la Flamma, in Muratori, Script. Rerum Italicarum, tom. xii. p. 1041.).

plish with the sword."[48] The influence of the two last principles of decay must in some degree be multiplied by each other; since the houses and towers, which were subverted by civil war, required a new and perpetual supply from the monuments of antiquity.

These general observations may be separately applied to the amphitheatre of Titus, which has obtained the name of the COLISEUM,[49] either from its magnitude or from Nero's colossal statue: an edifice, had it been left to time and nature, which might perhaps have claimed an eternal duration. The curious antiquaries, who have computed the numbers and seats, are disposed to believe that above the upper row of stone steps, the amphitheatre was encircled and elevated with several stages of wooden galleries, which were repeatedly consumed by fire, and restored by the emperors. Whatever was precious, or portable, or profane, the statues of gods and heroes, and the costly ornaments of sculpture, which were cast in brass, or overspread with leaves of silver and gold, became the first prey of conquest or fanaticism, of the avarice of the Barbarians or the Christians. In the massy stones of the Coliseum, many holes are discerned; and the two most probable conjectures represent the various accidents of its decay. These stones were connected by solid links of brass or iron, nor had the eye of rapine overlooked the value of the baser metals:[50] the vacant space was converted into a fair or

The Coliseum or amphitheatre of Titus.

---

48. Petrarch thus addresses his friend who, with shame and tears, had shewn him the mœnia, laceræ specimen miserabile Romæ, and declared his own intention of restoring them (Carmina Latina, l. ii. epist. Paulo Annibalensi, xii. p. 97, 98.):

Nec te parva manet servatis fama ruinis
Quanta quod integræ fuit olim gloria
 Romæ
Reliquiæ testantur adhuc; quas longior
 ætas
Frangere non valuit; non vis aut ira
 cruenti
Hostis, ab egregiis franguntur civibus
 heu! heu!
——Quod *ille* nequivit (*Hannibal*)
Perficit hic aries. ——

49. The fourth part of the Verona Illustrata of the Marquis Maffei, professedly treats of amphitheatres, particularly those of Rome and Verona, of their dimensions, wooden galleries, &c. It is from magnitude that he derives the name of *Colosseum*, or *Coliseum*: since the same appellation was applied to the amphitheatre of Capua, without the aid of a colossal statue; since that of Nero was erected in the court *(in atrio)* of his palace, and not in the Coliseum (P. iv. p. 15–19. l. i. c. 4.).

50. Joseph Maria Suarés, a learned bishop, and the author of an history of Præneste, has composed a separate dissertation on the seven or eight probable causes of these holes, which has been since reprinted in the Roman Thesaurus of Sallengre. Montfaucon (Diarium, p. 233.) pronounces the rapine of the Barbarians to be the unam germanamque causam foraminum.

market; the artisans of the Coliseum are mentioned in an ancient survey; and the chasms were perforated or enlarged to receive the poles that supported the shops or tents of the mechanic trades.[51] Reduced to its naked majesty, the Flavian amphitheatre was contemplated with awe and admiration by the pilgrims of the North; and their rude enthusiasm broke forth in a sublime proverbial expression, which is recorded in the eighth century, in the fragments of the venerable Bede: "As long as the Coliseum stands, Rome shall stand; when the Coliseum falls, Rome will fall; when Rome falls, the world will fall."[52] In the modern system of war, a situation commanded by three hills would not be chosen for a fortress; but the strength of the walls and arches could resist the engines of assault; a numerous garrison might be lodged in the enclosure; and while one faction occupied the Vatican and the Capitol, the other was intrenched in the Lateran and the Coliseum.[53]

Games of Rome.   The abolition at Rome of the ancient games must be understood with some latitude; and the carnival sports, of the Testacean mount and the Circus Agonalis,[54] were regulated by the law[55] or custom of the city. The senator presided with dignity and pomp to adjudge and distribute the prizes, the gold ring, or the *pallium*,[56] as it was styled, of cloth or silk. A tribute on the Jews supplied the annual

51. Donatus, Roma Vetus et Nova, p. 285.

52. Quamdiu stabit Colyseus, stabit et Roma; quando cadet Colyseus, cadet Roma; quando cadet Roma, cadet et mundus (Beda in Excerptis seu Collectaneis apud Ducange Glossar. med. et infimæ Latinitatis, tom. ii. p. 407. edit. Basil). This saying must be ascribed to the Anglo-Saxon pilgrims who visited Rome before the year 735, the æra of Bede's death; for I do not believe that our venerable monk ever passed the sea.

53. I cannot recover in Muratori's original Lives of the Popes (Script. Rerum Italicarum, tom. iii. P. i.) the passage that attests this hostile partition, which must be applied to the end of the xi[th] or the beginning of the xii[th] century.

54. Although the structure of the Circus Agonalis be destroyed, it still retains its form and name (Agona, Nagona, Navona): and the

interior space affords a sufficient level for the purpose of racing. But the Monte Testaceo, that strange pile of broken pottery, seems only adapted for the annual practice of hurling from top to bottom some waggon-loads of live hogs for the diversion of the populace (Statuta Urbis Romæ, p. 186.).

55. See the Statuta Urbis Romæ, l. iii. c. 87, 88, 89. p. 185, 186. I have already given an idea of this municipal code. The races of Nagona and Monte Testaceo are likewise mentioned in the Diary of Peter Antonius from 1404 to 1417 (Muratori, Script. Rerum Italicarum, tom. xxiv. p. 1124.).

56. The *Pallium*, which Menage so foolishly derives from *Palmarium*, is an easy extension of the idea and the words, from the robe or cloak, to the materials, and from thence to their application as a prize (Muratori, dissert. xxxiii.).

expence;[57] and the races, on foot, on horseback, or in chariots, were ennobled by a tilt and tournament of seventy-two of the Roman youth. In the year one thousand three hundred and thirty-two, a bull-feast, after the fashion of the Moors and Spaniards, was celebrated in the Coliseum itself; and the living manners are painted in a diary of the times.[58] A convenient order of benches was restored; and a general proclamation, as far as Rimini and Ravenna, invited the nobles to exercise their skill and courage in this perilous adventure. The Roman ladies were marshalled in three squadrons, and seated in three balconies, which on this day, the third of September, were lined with scarlet cloth. The fair Jacova di Rovere led the matrons from beyond the Tyber, a pure and native race, who still represent the features and character of antiquity. The remainder of the city was divided as usual between the Colonna and Ursini: the two factions were proud of the number and beauty of their female bands: the charms of Savella Ursini are mentioned with praise; and the Colonna regretted the absence of the youngest of their house, who had sprained her ancle in the garden of Nero's tower. The lots of the champions were drawn by an old and respectable citizen; and they descended into the *arena*, or pit, to encounter the wild-bulls, on foot as it should seem, with a single spear. Amidst the crowd, our annalist has selected the names, colours, and devices, of twenty of the most conspicuous knights. Several of the names are the most illustrious of Rome, and the ecclesiastical state; Malatesta, Polenta, della Valle, Cafarello, Savelli, Capoccio, Conti, Annibaldi, Altieri, Corsi; the colours were adapted to their taste and situation; the devices are expressive of hope or despair, and breathe the spirit of gallantry and arms. "I am alone, like the youngest of the Horatii," the confidence of an intrepid stranger: "I live disconsolate," a weeping widower: "I burn under the ashes," a discreet lover: "I adore Lavinia, or Lucretia," the ambiguous declaration of a modern passion: "My faith is as pure," the motto of a white livery: "Who is stronger than myself?" of a

A bull-feast in the Coliseum, A.D. 1332, September 3.

57. For these expences, the Jews of Rome paid each year 1130 florins, of which the odd thirty represented the pieces of silver for which Judas had betrayed his master to their ancestors. There was a foot-race of Jewish, as well as of Christian youths (Statuta Urbis, ibidem).

58. This extraordinary bull-feast in the Coliseum, is described from tradition, rather than memory, by Ludovico Buonconte Monaldesco, in the most ancient fragments of Roman annals (Muratori, Script. Rerum Italicarum, tom. xii. p. 535, 536.): and however fanciful they may seem, they are deeply marked with the colours of truth and nature.

lion's hide: "If I am drowned in blood, what a pleasant death," the wish of ferocious courage. The pride or prudence of the Ursini restrained them from the field, which was occupied by three of their hereditary rivals, whose inscriptions denoted the lofty greatness of the Colonna name: "Though sad, I am strong:" "Strong as I am great:" "If I fall," addressing himself to the spectators, "you fall with me:" – intimating (says the contemporary writer) that while the other families were the subjects of the Vatican, they alone were the supporters of the Capitol. The combats of the amphitheatre were dangerous and bloody. Every champion successively encountered a wild bull; and the victory may be ascribed to the quadrupedes, since no more than eleven were left on the field, with the loss of nine wounded and eighteen killed on the side of their adversaries. Some of the noblest families might mourn, but the pomp of the funerals, in the churches of St. John Lateran and St. Maria Maggiore, afforded a second holiday to the people. Doubtless it was not in such conflicts that the blood of the Romans should have been shed; yet in blaming their rashness, we are compelled to applaud their gallantry; and the noble volunteers, who display their magnificence, and risk their lives, under the balconies of the fair, excite a more generous sympathy than the thousands of captives and malefactors who were reluctantly dragged to the scene of slaughter.[59].

Injuries,   This use of the amphitheatre was a rare, perhaps a singular, festival: the demand for the materials was a daily and continual want, which the citizens could gratify without restraint or remorse. In the fourteenth century, a scandalous act of concord secured to both factions the privilege of extracting stones from the free and common quarry of the Coliseum;[60] and Poggius laments that the greater part of these stones had been burnt to lime by the folly of the Romans.[61] To check this abuse, and to prevent the nocturnal crimes that might be perpetrated in the vast and gloomy recess, Eugenius the fourth surrounded it with a wall; and, by a charter long extant, granted both the ground and edifice to the monks of an

---

59. Muratori has given a separate dissertation (the xxix[th]) to the games of the Italians in the middle ages.

60. In a concise but instructive memoir, the abbé Barthelemy (Memoires de l'Academie des Inscriptions, tom. xxviii. p. 585.) has mentioned this agreement of the factions of the xiv[th] century, de Tiburtino faciendo in the

Coliseum, from an original act in the archives of Rome.

61. Coliseum . . . ob stultitiam Romanorum *majori ex parte* ad calcem deletum, says the indignant Poggius (p. 17.): but his expression, too strong for the present age, must be very tenderly applied to the xv[th] century.

adjacent convent.[62] After his death, the wall was overthrown in a tumult of the people; and had they themselves respected the noblest monument of their fathers, they might have justified the resolve that it should never be degraded to private property. The inside was damaged; but in the middle of the sixteenth century, an æra of taste and learning, the exterior circumference of one thousand six hundred and twelve feet was still entire and inviolate; a triple elevation of fourscore arches, which rose to the height of one hundred and eight feet. Of the present ruin, the nephews of Paul the third are the guilty agents; and every traveller who views the Farnese palace may curse the sacrilege and luxury of these upstart princes.[63] A similar reproach is applied to the Barberini; and the repetition of injury might be dreaded from every reign, till the Coliseum was placed under the safeguard of religion, by the most liberal of the pontiffs, Benedict the fourteenth, who consecrated a spot which persecution and fable had stained with the blood of so many Christian martyrs.[64]

and consecration of the Coliseum.

When Petrarch first gratified his eyes with a view of those monuments, whose scattered fragments so far surpass the most eloquent descriptions, he was astonished at the supine indifference[65] of the Romans themselves;[66] he was humbled rather than elated by the discovery, that, except his friend Rienzi and one of the Colonna, a stranger of the Rhône was more conversant with these

Ignorance and barbarism of the Romans.

---

62. Of the Olivetan monks, Montfaucon (p. 142.) affirms this fact from the memorials of Flaminius Vacca (N° 72.). They still hoped, on some future occasion, to revive and vindicate their grant.

63. After measuring the priscus amphitheatri gyrus. Montfaucon (p. 142.) only adds, that it was entire under Paul III.; tacendo clamat. Muratori (Annali d'Italia, tom. xiv. p. 371.) more freely reports the guilt of the Farnese pope, and the indignation of the Roman people. Against the nephews of Urban VIII. I have no other evidence than the vulgar saying, "Quod non fecerunt Barbari, fecere Barbarini," which was perhaps suggested by the resemblance of the words.

64. As an antiquarian and a priest, Montfaucon thus deprecates the ruin of the Coliseum: Quôd si non suopte merito atque

pulchritudine dignum fuisset quod improbas arceret manus, indigna res utique in locum tot martyrum cruore sacrum tantopere sævitum esse.

65. Yet the Statutes of Rome (l. iii. c. 81. p. 182.) impose a fine of 500 *aurei* on whosoever shall demolish any ancient edifice, ne ruinis civitas deformetur, et ut antiqua ædificia decorem urbis perpetuo representent.

66. In his first visit to Rome (A.D. 1337. See Memoires sur Petrarque, tom. i. p. 322, &c.), Petrarch is struck mute miraculo , rerum tantarum, et stuporis mole obrutus . . . Præsentia vero, mirum dictû, nihil imminuit: vere major fuit Roma majoresque sunt reliquiae quam rebar. Jam non orbem ab hâc urbe domitum, sed tam sero domitum, miror (Opp. p. 605. Familiares, ii. 14. Joanni Columnæ).

antiquities than the nobles and natives of the metropolis.[67] The ignorance and credulity of the Romans are elaborately displayed in the old survey of the city which was composed about the beginning of the thirteenth century; and, without dwelling on the manifold errors of name and place, the legend of the Capitol[68] may provoke a smile of contempt and indignation. "The Capitol," says the anonymous writer, "is so named as being the head of the world; where the consuls and senators formerly resided for the government of the city and the globe. The strong and lofty walls were covered with glass and gold, and crowned with a roof of the richest and most curious carving. Below the citadel stood a palace, of gold for the greatest part, decorated with precious stones, and whose value might be esteemed at one third of the world itself. The statues of all the provinces were arranged in order, each with a small bell suspended from its neck; and such was the contrivance of art or magic,[69] that if the province rebelled against Rome, the statue turned round to that quarter of the heavens, the bell rang, the prophet of the Capitol reported the prodigy, and the senate was admonished of the impending danger." A second example of less importance, though of equal absurdity, may be drawn from the two marble horses, led by two naked youths, which have since been transported from the baths of Constantine to the Quirinal hill. The groundless application of the names of Phidias and Praxiteles may perhaps be excused; but these Grecian sculptors should not have been removed above four hundred years from the age of Pericles to that of Tiberius: they should not have been transformed into two philosophers or magicians, whose nakedness was the symbol of truth and knowledge, who revealed to the emperor his most

67. He excepts and praises the *rare* knowledge of John Colonna. Qui enim hodie magis ignari rerum Romanarum, quam Romani cives? Invitus dico nusquam minus Roma cognoscitur quam Romæ.

68. After the description of the Capitol, he adds, statuæ erant quot sunt mundi provinciæ; et habebat quælibet tintinnabulum ad collum. Et erant ita per magicam artem dispositæ, ut quando aliqua regio Romano Imperio rebellis erat, statim imago illius provinciæ vertebat se contra illam; unde tintinnabulum resonabat quod pendebat ad collum; tuncque vates Capitolii qui erant custodes senatui, &c. He mentions an example of the Saxons and Suevi,

who, after they rebelled: tintinnabulum sonuit; sacerdos qui erat in speculo in hebdomadâ senatoribus nuntiavit: Agrippa marched back and reduced the — Persians (Anonym. in Montfaucon, p. 297, 298.).

69. The same writer affirms, that Virgil captus a Romanis invisibiliter exiit, ivitque Neapolim. A Roman magician, in the xi[th] century, is introduced by William of Malmsbury (de Gestis Regum Anglorum, l. ii. p. 86.); and in the time of Flaminius Vacca (N° 81. 103.) it was the vulgar belief that the strangers (the *Goths*) invoked the dæmons for the discovery of hidden treasures.

secret actions; and, after refusing all pecuniary recompense, solicited the honour of leaving this eternal monument of themselves.[70] Thus awake to the power of magic, the Romans were insensible to the beauties of art: no more than five statues were visible to the eyes of Poggius; and of the multitudes which chance or design had buried under the ruins, the resurrection was fortunately delayed till a safer and more enlightened age.[71] The Nile, which now adorns the Vatican, had been explored by some labourers in digging a vineyard near the temple, or convent, of the Minerva; but the impatient proprietor, who was tormented by some visits of curiosity, restored the unprofitable marble to its former grave.[72] The discovery of a statue of Pompey, ten feet in length, was the occasion of a law-suit. It had been found under a partition-wall: the equitable judge had pronounced, that the head should be separated from the body to satisfy the claims of the contiguous owners; and the sentence would have been executed, if the intercession of a cardinal, and the liberality of a pope, had not rescued the Roman hero from the hands of his barbarous countrymen.[73]

But the clouds of barbarism were gradually dispelled; and the peaceful authority of Martin the fifth and his successors, restored the ornaments of the city as well as the order of the ecclesiastical state. The improvements of Rome, since the fifteenth century, have not been the spontaneous produce of freedom and industry. The first and most natural root of a great city, is the labour and populousness of the adjacent country, which supplies the materials of subsistence, of manufactures, and of foreign trade. But the greater part of the Campagna of Rome is reduced to a dreary and desolate wilderness: the overgrown estates of the princes and the clergy are cultivated by the lazy

Restoration and ornaments of the city, A.D. 1420, &c.

---

70. Anonym. p. 289. Montfaucon (p. 191.) justly observes, that if Alexander be represented, these statues cannot be the work of Phidias (Olympiad lxxxiii.) or Praxiteles (Olympiad civ.), who lived before that conqueror (Plin. Hist. Natur. xxxiv. 19.).

71. William of Malmsbury (l. ii. p. 86, 87.) relates a marvellous discovery (A.D. 1046) of Pallus, the son of Evander, who had been slain by Turnus; the perpetual light in his sepulchre, a Latin epitaph, the corpse, yet entire, of a young giant, the enormous wound in his breast (pectus perforat ingens), &c. If this fable rests on the slightest foundation, we may pity the bodies, as well as the statues, that were exposed to the air in a barbarous age.

72. Prope porticum Minervæ, statua est recubantis, cujus caput integrâ effigie, tantæ magnitudinis, ut signa omnia excedat. Quidam ad plantandos arbores scrobes faciens detexit. Ad hoc visendum cum plures in dies magis concurrerent, strepitum adeuntium fastidiumque pertæsus, horti patronus congestâ humo texit (Poggius de Varietate Fortunæ, p. 12.).

73. See the Memorials of Flaminius Vacca, N° 57. p. 11, 12. at the end of the Roma Antica of Nardini (1704, in 4°).

hands of indigent and hopeless vassals; and the scanty harvests are confined or exported for the benefit of a monopoly. A second and more artificial cause of the growth of a metropolis, is the residence of a monarch, the expence of a luxurious court, and the tributes of dependent provinces. Those provinces and tributes had been lost in the fall of the empire: and if some streams of the silver of Peru and the gold of Brasil have been attracted by the Vatican; the revenues of the cardinals, the fees of office, the oblations of pilgrims and clients, and the remnant of ecclesiastical taxes, afford a poor and precarious supply, which maintains however the idleness of the court and city. The population of Rome, far below the measure of the great capitals of Europe, does not exceed one hundred and seventy thousand inhabitants;[74] and within the spacious inclosure of the walls, the largest portion of the seven hills is overspread with vineyards and ruins. The beauty and splendour of the modern city may be ascribed to the abuses of the government, to the influence of superstition. Each reign (the exceptions are rare) has been marked by the rapid elevation of a new family, enriched by the childless pontiff at the expence of the church and country. The palaces of these fortunate nephews are the most costly monuments of elegance and servitude; the perfect arts of architecture, painting, and sculpture, have been prostituted in their service, and their galleries and gardens are decorated with the most precious works of antiquity, which taste or vanity has prompted them to collect. The ecclesiastical revenues were more decently employed by the popes themselves in the pomp of the Catholic worship; but it is superfluous to enumerate their pious foundations of altars, chapels, and churches, since these lesser stars are eclipsed by the sun of the Vatican, by the dome of St. Peter, the most glorious structure that ever has been applied to the use of religion. The fame of Julius the second, Leo the tenth, and Sixtus the fifth, is accompanied by the superior merit of Bramante and Fontana, of Raphael and Michael-Angelo: and the same munificence which had been displayed in palaces and temples, was directed with equal zeal to revive and emulate the labours of antiquity. Prostrate obelisks were raised from the ground, and erected in the most conspicuous places; of the eleven aqueducts of the Cæsars and consuls, three were restored; the artificial rivers were conducted over a long series of old, or

74. In the year 1709, the inhabitants of Rome (without including eight or ten thousand Jews) amounted to 138,568 souls (Labat, Voyages en Espagne et en Italie, tom. iii. p. 217, 218.). In 1740 they had increased to 146,080; and in 1765, I left them, without the Jews, 161,899. I am ignorant whether they have since continued in a progressive state.

of new, arches, to discharge into marble basins a flood of salubrious and refreshing waters: and the spectator, impatient to ascend the steps of St. Peter's, is detained by a column of Egyptian granite, which rises between two lofty and perpetual fountains, to the height of one hundred and twenty feet. The map, the description, the monuments of ancient Rome, have been elucidated by the diligence of the antiquarian and the student:[75] and the footsteps of heroes, the relics, not of superstition, but of empire, are devoutly visited by a new race of pilgrims from the remote, and once savage, countries of the North.

★

Of these pilgrims, and of every reader, the attention will be excited by an history of the decline and fall of the Roman empire; the greatest, perhaps, and most awful scene, in the history of mankind. *Final conclusion.*
The various causes and progressive effects are connected with many of the events most interesting in human annals: the artful policy of the Cæsars, who long maintained the name and image of a free republic; the disorders of military despotism; the rise, establishment, and sects of Christianity; the foundation of Constantinople; the division of the monarchy; the invasion and settlements of the Barbarians of Germany and Scythia; the institutions of the civil law; the character and religion of Mahomet; the temporal sovereignty of the popes; the restoration and decay of the Western empire of Charlemagne; the crusades of the Latins in the East; the conquests of the Saracens and Turks; the ruin of the Greek empire; the state and revolutions of Rome in the middle age. The historian may applaud the importance and variety of his subject; but, while he is conscious of his own

75. The Pere Montfaucon distributes his own observations into twenty days, he should have styled them weeks, or months, of his visits to the different parts of the city (Diarium Italicum, c. 8–20. p. 104–301.). That learned Benedictine reviews the topographers of ancient Rome; the first efforts of Blondus, Fulvius, Martianus, and Faunus, the superior labours of Pyrrhus Ligorius, had his learning been equal to his labours; the writings of Onuphrius Panvinius, qui omnes obscuravit, and the recent but imperfect books of Donatus and Nardini. Yet Montfaucon still sighs for a more complete plan and description of the old city, which must be attained by the three following methods: 1. The measurement of the space and intervals of the ruins. 2. The study of inscriptions, and the places where they were found. 3. The investigation of all the acts, charters, diaries of the middle ages, which name any spot or building of Rome. The laborious work, such as Montfaucon desired, must be promoted by princely or public munificence: but the great modern plan of Nolli (A.D. 1748) would furnish a solid and accurate basis for the ancient topography of Rome.

imperfections, he must often accuse the deficiency of his materials. It was among the ruins of the Capitol, that I first conceived the idea of a work which has amused and exercised near twenty years of my life, and which, however inadequate to my own wishes, I finally deliver to the curiosity and candour of the Public.

LAUSANNE,
June 27, 1787.

BIOGRAPHICA

The purpose of this *Biographica* is to provide succinct information about all but the most fleeting or minor proper names of actual persons (but not mythological figures) referred to in the text and notes. Further information can often be found in standard works of reference such as the *Dictionary of National Biography*, the *Oxford Companion to Classical Literature*, or *Paulys Real-Encyclopädie des classischen Altertumswissenschaft*. In the case of Gibbon's authorities, works by that author which were contained in Gibbon's library are also listed.

A

Abubeker (*c.*573–634); adviser and successor to Mahomet; initiator of the caliphate.

Abulfeda, more accurately Abu al-Fida (1273–1331); Ayoubite prince of Hamah; geographer and historian; Gibbon owned his *Annales Moslemici Latinos ex Arabicis fecit J. J. Reiske* (Leipzig, 1774), *Annales Muslemici, Opera J. J. Reiskii*, 3 vols (Copenhagen, 1789–91), *Chorasmide et Mawaralnahræ* (London, 1650), *De Vita et Rebus Gestis Mohammedis. Latine vertit J. Gagnier* (Oxford, 1723), *Descriptio Ægypti. Latine vertit J. D. Michaelis* (Göttingen, 1776), *Opus Geographicum. Latinum fecit J. Reiske*, 2 vols (Hamburg, 1770, 1771), and *Tabula Syriæ Arabicé edidit, Latiné vertit J. B. Kochler* (Leipzig, 1766).

Abulpharagius, Gregory, or Bar Hebraeus (1226–86); Jacobite primate of the East; author of *De Rebus Gestis Richardi, Angliæ Regis, in Palæstina: Excerpta ex Chronico Syriaco* (Oxford,

1780), *Historia Compendiosa Dynastiarum, edita ab E. Pocockio* (Oxford, 1663) and *Specimen Historiæ Arabum, sive de Origine et Moribus Arabum, Opera E. Pocockii* (Oxford, 1650).

Addison, Joseph (1672–1719); essayist, poet, dramatist and politician; Gibbon owned his *Works*, 4 vols (Birmingham, 1761), *De la religion chrétienne*, 3 vols (Geneva, 1771), *The Freeholder* (London, 1761) and *The Spectator*, 8 vols (London, n.d.).

Ædesius (d. 355); Greek neoplatonic philosopher.

Ælian, or Claudianus Ælianus (*c.*170–*c.*235); Roman author and rhetorician; Gibbon owned two editions of his *De Natura Animalium* (2 vols, London, 1744; Leipzig, 1784), *Varia Historia* (Leyden, 1731) and *Varia Historia et Fragmenta*, 2 vols (Leipzig, 1780).

Ælianus Tacticus (*fl.* 2nd century AD); Greek military writer.

Æneas Sylvius (1405–64); Italian humanist and politician; writer on history and geography; as Pope Pius II he tried to unite Christendom in a Crusade against the Turks.

Æschines Socraticus (390–314 BC); Greek orator; Gibbon owned three editions of his *Dialogi Tres* (Amsterdam, 1711, 1740; Leipzig, 1766).

Ætius Flavius (d. 454); Roman general and dominant chief minister of Valentinian III.

Agatharcides, or Agatharchides; geographer of Arabia; author of *De Mari Rubro*.

Agathias (c.536–82); Byzantine poet and historian; author of *De Imperio et Rebus Gestis Iustiniarii Imperatoris*.

Agricola, Gnæus Julius (40–93); Roman general; celebrated by his son-in-law Tacitus.

Agrippa, Herod, more fully, Marcus Julius Agrippa (10 BC–AD 44); king of Judæa.

Agrippa, Marcus Vipsanius (63–12 BC); deputy and military commander of Augustus.

Alaric (c.370–410); chief of the Visigoths; leader of the army that sacked Rome in 410.

Alexander Severus (208–35); emperor.

Alexander the Great (356–323 BC); king of Macedonia; conqueror of the Persian empire; legendary military commander.

Alexius Comnenus (1081–1118); Alexius I; Byzantine emperor.

Algardi, Alessandro (1595–1654); Baroque Italian sculptor.

Al Jannabi; Arabian historian.

Allatius, Leo, or Leone Allacci (1586–1669); Italian editor of Byzantine texts.

Amalasontha (498–535); daughter of Theodoric the Great; queen and regent of the Ostrogoths.

Ambrose (c.339–97); st; bp of Milan.

Amelot de la Houssaie, Abraham Nicolas (1634–1706); historian, writer, diplomat; Gibbon owned his *Histoire du gouvernement de Venise*, 3 vols (Amsterdam, 1714).

Ammianus Marcellinus (c.330–395); soldier and historian; Gibbon owned three editions of his *Rerum Gestarum Libri* (Augsburg, 1533; Leyden 1693; Leipzig, 1773).

Amurath II (1404–51); Ottoman sultan.

Amurath IV (1612–40); Ottoman sultan.

Anastasius (?430–518); Byzantine emperor.

Anna Comnena (1083–1148); daughter of Alexius I; author of the *Alexiad*, a history of the life and times of her father.

Antinous (c.110–130); favourite and catamite of the emperor Hadrian.

Antonina; wife of Belisarius.

Antoninus, Marcus Aurelius (121–80); emperor and Stoic philosopher.

Antoninus Pius (86–161); emperor.

Antony, Marc (c.82–30 BC); Marcus Antonius; Roman general and triumvir.

Antony, Melissa (fl. 11th century); Byzantine monk and formulator of ascetic practice and discipline.

Anville, Jean Baptiste Bourguignon d' (1697–1782); geographer; Gibbon owned his *Analyse de la carte, intitulée, Les Côtes de la Grèce, et l'Archipel* (Paris, 1757), *Analyse géographique de l'Italie* (Paris, 1744), *Antiquité géographique de l'Inde, et de plusieurs autres contrées de la haute Asie* (Paris, 1755), *Atlas ancien et moderne* (n.p., n.d.), *Dissertation sur l'étendue de l'ancienne Jérusalem et de son temple* (Paris, 1747), *Éclaircissemens géographiques sur l'ancienne Gaule* (Paris, 1741), *Éclaircissemens géographiques sur la carte de l'Inde* (Paris, 1753), *L'Empire de Russie, son origine, et ses acroissemens* (Paris, 1772), *L'Empire turc consideré dans son établissement et dans ses accroissemens successifs* (Paris, 1772), *États formés en Europe après la chute de l'empire romain en Occident* (Paris, 1771), two editions of

Géographie ancienne abrégée (Paris, 1768, 1769), *Mémoire sur la Chine* (Paris, 1776), *Mémoire sur la mer Caspienne* (Paris, 1777), *Mémoires sur l'Égypte ancienne et moderne* (Paris, 1766), *Notice de l'ancienne Gaule tirée des monumens romains* (Paris, 1760), *Traité des mesures itinéraires* (Paris, 1769), and *Twelve Maps of Antient Geography* (London, 1757).

Apollinaris the Younger (*c*.310–*c*.390); heretical bp of Laodicea.

Appian of Alexandria (*fl*. 2nd century AD); historian; Gibbon owned his *Historia delle guerre esterni . . . de Romani*, 2 vols (Verona, 1730), *Romanarum Historiarum*, 2 vols (Amsterdam, 1670), and *Romanarum Historiarum quæ Supersunt*, 3 vols (Leipzig, 1785).

Apuleius, Lucius (*c*.124–*c*.170); Platonic philosopher and rhetorician; author of *The Golden Ass*; Gibbon owned his *Metamorphoses Libri XI* (Gouda, 1650) and *Opera*, 2 vols (Paris, 1688).

Arbuthnot, John (1667–1735); mathematician and physician; member of the Scriblerus Club; Gibbon owned his *Tables of Coins, Weights and Measures* (London, 1727).

Arcadius II (*c*.377–408); Byzantine emperor; father of Theodosius II.

Archimedes (*c*.290–212 BC); Greek mathematician, inventor and engineer.

Aristides (*fl*. 2nd century AD); early Christian apologist; Gibbon owned his *Opera Omnia*, ed. S. Jebb, 2 vols (Oxford, 1722 and 1730).

Aristotle (384–322 BC); philosopher; Gibbon owned the *Andronici Rhodii Ethicorum Nicomacheorum Paraphrasis* (Cambridge, 1769), *Ars Rhetoricæ Libri III* (Frankfort, 1584), *De Physica Auscultatione* (Frankfort, 1577), *De Poetica* (Oxford, 1780), *Ethicorum . . . Libri Decem* (Frankfort, 1577), *Ethicorum Nicomacheorum* (Oxford, 1716), *Histoire des animaux*, tr. M. Camus, 2 vols (Paris, 1783), *Liber de*

Mirabilibus Auscultationibus (Göttingen, 1786), *Opera Omnia*, 2 vols (Paris, 1619), *La Poëtique*, tr. M. Dacier (Paris, 1692), *La Rhétorique*, tr. M. Cassandre (Amsterdam, 1698), and *A Treatise on Government*, tr. W. Ellis (London, 1776).

Arnobius the elder (*fl*. 4th century AD); Christian apologist; Gibbon owned his *Adversus Gentes Libri VII* (Leyden, 1651).

Arrian, Flavius Arrianus (*fl*. 2nd century AD); biographer of Alexander the Great; follower of Epictetus; Gibbon owned his *Ars Tactica* (Amsterdam, 1683), *De Expeditione Alexandri Magni* (Amsterdam, 1668) and *Expeditionis Alexandri Libri Septem et Historia Indica* (Leyden, 1704).

Artaxerxes II (*fl*. late 5th and early 4th centuries BC); king of Persia.

Artemidorus of Daldia (*fl*. 2nd century AD); author of *De Somniorum Interpretatione*; Gibbon owned the *Artemidori & Achmeti Oneirocritica* (Paris, 1603).

Artigny, Antoine Gachet d' (1704–78); author of the *Nouveaux Mémoires d'histoire, de Critique, et de littérature*, 7 vols (Paris, 1749–56).

Arvieux, Chevalier Laurent d' (1635–1702); Gibbon owned his *Mémoires*, 6 vols (Paris, 1735) and *Voyage dans la Palestine* (Amsterdam, 1718).

Assemanus, Joseph Simon, or Giuseppe Simonio Assemani (1687–1768); Italian librarian and antiquarian; Gibbon owned his *Bibliotheca Orientalis Clementino-Vaticana*, 3 vols (Rome, 1719–28).

Athanasius (*c*.293–373); st; theologian; ecclesiastical statesman; defender of Christian orthodoxy against Arianism.

Athenæus (*fl. c*.AD 200); Greek grammarian and author of the *Deipnosophistai* ('The Gastronomers'); Gibbon owned his *Deipnosophistarum Libri Quindecim* (Lyons, 1657).

*Atticus, Titus Pomponius*NM (109–32 BC); friend of Cicero; philosopher and man of letters, none of whose writings have survived.

Attila (d. 453); king of the Huns.

Aubigné, Théodore Agrippa d' (1552–1630); Gibbon owned his *Histoire universelle*, 3 vols (1616–20), and *Mémoires écrits par lui-même*, 2 vols (Amsterdam, 1731).

Augustine (354–430); st; major theologian of the early Western church; Gibbon owned his *De Civitate Dei* (Venice, 1732).

Augustus, Cæsar (63 BC–AD 14); first *princeps*; transformer of the Roman republic into an autocracy.

Aurelianus, Lucius Domitius (c.215–275); emperor.

Aurelius Victor, Sextus (c.320–389); historian; author of *De Cæsaribus*, abbreviated as *Aurelii Victoris Historiæ Abbreviatæ*; Gibbon owned his *Historiæ Romanæ Breviarum* (Utrecht, 1696).

Ausonius, Decimus Magnus (c.310–395); poet; Gibbon owned two editions of his *Opera* (Amsterdam, 1671; Paris, 1752).

Austin (d. 604); st; also known as Augustine; founder of the Christian church in southern England.

B

Balbinus, Decimus Caelius Calvinus; emperor with Pupienus Maximus in 238.

Banduri, Anselme (1671–1743); antiquarian and clergyman; editor of *Imperium Orientale, sive, Antiquitates Constantinopolitanæ*.

Barbeyrac, Jean (1674–1744); lawyer and historian; author of *Histoire des anciens traités* (Amsterdam, 1739); Gibbon owned his *Traité de la morale des pères de l'église* (Amsterdam, 1728).

Bardesanes (c.154–c.222); Syrian Gnostic and theologian.

Baronius, Cæsar (1538–1607); cardinal; Gibbon owned his *Annales Ecclesiastici*, 12 vols (Cologne, 1622–7).

Barthélemy, Jean Jacques, abbé de (1716–95); numismatist and antiquarian.

Basil I (c.826–886); Byzantine emperor; formulated the Greek legal code.

Basil the Great (c.329–379); st; bp of Cæsarea; defender of orthodoxy against Arianism.

Basnage, Henri, sieur de Beauval (1656–1710); lawyer; Gibbon owned his *Histoire des Juifs*, 15 vols (The Hague, 1716).

Bayer, Gottlieb Siegfried (1694–1738); German orientalist; Gibbon owned his *Historia Osrhoena et Edessena* (St Petersburg, 1734) and *Historia Regni Græcorum Bactriani* (St Petersburg, 1738).

Bayle, Pierre (1647–1706); *philosophe*, controversialist and intellectual; Gibbon owned his *Analyse raisonnée de Bayle, ou abregé de ses ouvrages*, 8 vols (London, 1755–70), *Critique générale de l'histoire du calvinisme de Mr Maimbourg* ('Villefranche', 1683), *Dictionnaire historique et critique*, 4 vols (Amsterdam, 1740), *Nouvelles de la république de lettres*, 8 vols (Amsterdam, 1685–7), *Nouvelles lettres*, 2 vols (The Hague, 1739), *Œuvres Diverses*, 4 vols (The Hague, 1727–31), and *Pensées diverses, à l'occasion de comète qui parut au mois de Décembre 1680*, 2 vols (Rotterdam, 1683).

Beau, Jean Baptiste le (1602–70); antiquarian and writer on the Roman legion.

Beaufort, Louis de (c.1720–95); antiquarian and pyrrhonist historian; Gibbon owned his *Dissertation sur l'incertitude des cinq premiers siècles de l'histoire romaine* (The Hague, 1750) and *La République romaine*, 2 vols (The Hague, 1766).

Beausobre, Isaac de (1659–1738); theologian and historian; Gibbon owned his *Histoire critique de Manichée et du manichéisme*, 2 vols (Amsterdam, 1734, 1739).

Bede, *The Venerable* (673–735); st; theologian and historian; Gibbon owned his *Historiæ Ecclesiasticæ Gentis Anglorum Libri Quinque* (Cambridge, 1722).

Belisarius (c. 505–565); Byzantine general and statesman.

Bellini, Gentile (1429–1507); Venetian painter.

Bentley, Richard (1662–1742); classical scholar; master of Trinity College, Cambridge; Gibbon owned his *A Dissertation upon the Epistles of Phalaris* (London, 1699) and two editions of *Remarks Upon a Late Discourse of Free-Thinking* (London, 1713; Cambridge, 1743).

Bergier, Nicolas (1557–1623); historian and lawyer; Gibbon owned his *Histoire des grands chemins de l'empire romain*, 2 vols (Brussels, 1736).

Bernard of Clairvaux (1090–1153); st; Cistercian monk and mystic.

Bernier, François (fl. 1610); historian and clergyman; Gibbon owned his *Voyages*, 2 vols (Amsterdam, 1723, 1724).

Bèze, Théodore de, or Beza (1519–1605); Protestant nobleman, scholar, poet and theologian.

Bingham, Joseph (1668–1723); Fellow of University College, Oxford; clergyman and historian; author of *Christian Antiquities*; Gibbon owned his *Works*, 2 vols (London, 1726).

Blackstone, Sir William (1723–80); jurist and legal historian; Gibbon owned two editions of his *Commentaries on the Laws of England*, 4 vols (Oxford, 1773; London, 1774), *Law Tracts*, 2 vols (Oxford, 1762), and *Tracts Chiefly Relating to the Antiquities and Laws of England* (Oxford, 1771).

Blétérie, Jean Philippe René de la (1696–1772); Jansenist abbé; Gibbon owned his *Histoire de l'empereur Jovien*, 2 vols (n.p., 1748), and *Vie de l'empereur Julien* (Paris, 1746).

Blondel, David (1591–1655); Protestant theologian; successor to Vossius at Amsterdam; Gibbon owned his *Apologia pro Sententia Hieronymi de Episcopis et Presbyteris* (Amsterdam, 1646), *De la primauté en l'église* (Geneva, 1641) and *Des sybilles celebrées tant par l'antiquité que par les saincts pères* (Charenton, 1649).

Boadicea (d. AD 60); queen of the Iceni; led an initially successful rebellion against Roman rule in Britain.

Boethius, *Anicius Manlius Severinus* (c. 470–524); scholar, statesman and Christian philosopher; author of *De Consolatione Philosophiæ*; Gibbon owned his *Consolationis Philosophiæ Libros Quinque* (Paris, 1695).

Bonamy, Pierre Nicolas (1694–1770); man of letters; student of ancient literature.

Bossuet, Jacques-Bénigne (1627–1704); bp of Meaux; French divine; Gibbon owned two editions of his *Discours sur l'histoire universelle* (Paris, 1732; 2 vols, Lyons, 1782), two editions of its English translation as *An Universal History* (4 vols, London, 1736; 21 vols, London, 1747), *Exposition de la doctrine de l'église catholique sur les matières de controverse* (Paris, 1680), *Histoire des variations des églises protestantes*, 4 vols (Paris, 1718–30) and two editions of *Recueil des oraisons funèbres* (Paris, 1754, 1761).

Boulainvilliers, Henri de (1658–1722); man of letters, historian and occultist; Gibbon owned his *Mémoires historiques sur l'état de la France*, 3 vols ('London', 1727–8), and *La Vie de Mahomed* ('London', 1730).

Boze, Claude Gros de (1680–1753); numismatist, antiquarian and librarian.

Bramante, Donato (1444–1514); architect;oﬂ* initiator of the high Renaissance style of building.

Brosses, Charles de (1709–77); historian and editor of Sallust; Gibbon owned his *Histoire des navigations aux terres Australes*, 2 vols (Paris, 1756), and *Traité de la formation mécaniques des langues*, 4 vols (Paris, 1765).

Brotier, Gabriel (1723–89); Jesuit; editor of Pliny and Tacitus.

Brucker, Johann Jacob (1696–1770); historian of philosophy; Gibbon owned his *Historia Critica Philosophiæ*, 6 vols (Leipzig, 1767).

Brutus, Lucius Junius (fl. late 6th century BC); founder of the Roman republic.

Brutus, Marcus Junius (85–42 BC); Roman statesman and soldier; one of the conspirators who assassinated Cæsar in 44 BC.

Bruyn, Corneille le, or Cornelis de Bruin (1624–1719); traveller; Gibbon owned his *Voyage au Levant* (Paris, 1714) and *Voyages par la Moscovie, en Perse, et aux Indes Orientales*, 2 vols (Amsterdam, 1718).

Buchanan, George (1506–82); Scottish humanist and educator; Gibbon owned his *Opera*, 2 vols (Edinburgh, 1715).

Buffon, Georges Louis Le Clerc, comte de (1707–88); naturalist; Gibbon owned his *Collection complette des œuvres*, 45 vols (Paris, 1769–85), and *Histoire naturelle, générale et particulière*, 35 vols (Paris, 1749–88).

Burigny, Jean Lévesque de (1692–1785); historian and theologian; Gibbon owned his *Vie d'Érasme*, 2 vols (Paris, 1757), and *Vie de Grotius*, 2 vols (Paris, 1752).

Burnet, Gilbert (1643–1715); bp of Salisbury; Whig historian; Gibbon owned his *History of His Own Time*, 4 vols (London, 1753), *The History of the Reformation of the Church of Eng-*land, 3 vols (London, 1679–1753), and *Travels* (London, 1737).

Burnet, Thomas (1635?–1715); master of the Charterhouse and clergyman; Gibbon owned his *De Statu Mortuorum et Resurgentium Liber* (London, 1727) and *The Sacred Theory of the Earth*, 2 vols (London, 1759).

Busbequius, Augerius Gislenius, or Augier Ghislain de Busbecq (1522–92); Flemish diplomat and man of letters; source of valuable information on Turkish life and history; Gibbon owned two editions of his *Opera* (Amsterdam, 1632; Leyden, 1633).

Büsching, Anton Friedrich (1724–93); German geographer and educator; Gibbon owned his *Caractère de Frédéric II., roi de Prusse*, 2 vols (Berne, 1788), *Géographie, ornée d'un précis de l'histoire de chaque état par M. Bérenger*, 12 vols (Lausanne, 1776–82), and *A New System of Geography*, 6 vols (London, 1762).

C

Cæsar, Gaius Julius (?100–44 BC); Roman soldier and statesman; Gibbon owned two editions of his *C. Julii Cæsaris et A. Hirtii de Rebus a C. J. Cæsare Gestis Commentarii* (London, 1716 and 1736), *C. Julii Cæsaris et A. Hirtii quæ Exstant Omnia* (Cambridge, 1727), *The Commentaries*, tr. E. Edmonds (London, 1695), *De Bellis Gallico et Civili Pompejano*, 2 vols (Leyden, 1737), and *Omnia quæ Extant* (Leyden, 1593).

Caligula, or Gaius Cæsar Germanicus (AD 12–41); Roman emperor and tyrant.

Calmet, Augustin (1672–1757); theologian and historian; Gibbon owned his *Dissertations qui peuvent servir de prolégomènes de l'écriture sainte*, 3 vols (Paris, 1720), and *Histoire ecclésiastique et civile de la Lorraine* (Nancy, 1728).

Calvin, Jean (1509–64); theologian and ecclesiastical statesman; pre-eminent Protestant reformer; Gibbon owned his *Institutio Christianæ Religionis* (Geneva, 1559).

Camden, William, or Cambden (1551–1623); historian; Gibbon owned his *Anglica, Hibernica, Normannica, Cambrica a Veteribus Scripta* (Frankfort, 1603) and *Britannia* (London, 1607), tr. E. Gibson, 2 vols (London, 1753).

Camillus, Marcus Furius (d. 365 BC); Roman soldier and statesman; second founder of the city.

Cantemir, Demetrius, or Dmitry Kantemir (1673–1723); prince of Moldavia; statesman, scientist and historian; author of the *History of the Othman Empire*.

Caracalla (188–217); Roman emperor and tyrant.

Caractacus (*fl*. late 1st century AD); king of the Trinovantes; organized British resistance to the invading Romans.

Casaubon, Isaac (1559–1614); classical scholar and theologian.

Casiri, Miguel (1710–91); librarian of the Escurial; Gibbon owned his *Bibliotheca Arabica-Hispana Escurialensis*, 2 vols (Madrid, 1760, 1770).

Cassiodorus, or, erroneously, Cassiodorius (*c*.480–575); statesman and historian of Theodoric the Great and the Ostrogoths; Gibbon owned his *Opera* (Paris, 1589).

Cassius Dio Cocceianus, or Dio Cassio (*c*.150–235); Roman administrator and historian; Gibbon owned his *Historiæ Romanæ quæ Supersunt*, 2 vols (Hamburg, 1750, 1752).

Catiline, Lucius Sergius Catilina (*c*.108–62 BC); Roman aristocrat; failed in an attempt to overthrow the republic, being anticipated and defeated by Cicero.

Cato the Elder (234–149 BC); Roman statesman and orator.

Cato the Younger (95–46 BC); Roman statesman and defender of the republic against Cæsar; of legendary moral integrity.

Catullus, Gaius Valerius (84–54 BC); Roman poet; Gibbon owned *Catullus, et in eum Isaaci Vossii Observationes* (London, 1684) and *Catullus, Tibullus, et Propertius* (Paris, 1754).

Cave, William (1637–1713); Anglican divine; Gibbon owned his *Primitive Christianity*, 2 vols (London, 1673), and *Scriptorum Ecclesiasticorum Historia Literaria* (Geneva, 1720).

Cecrops; traditionally the first king of Attica in ancient Greece.

Cedrenus; 11th-century Byzantine historian.

Cellarius, Christopherus (1638–1707); historian; Gibbon owned his *Historia Nova, hoc est XVI. et XVII. Sæculorum* (Halle, 1696) and *Notitia Orbis Antiqui*, 2 vols (Cambridge and Amsterdam, 1703, 1706).

Celsus, Aulus Cornelius (*fl*. 1st century AD); medical writer.

Censorinus (*fl*. early 3rd century AD); Gibbon owned his *Liber de Die Natali* (Leyden, 1767).

Chais, Charles (1701–85); French minister at The Hague; Gibbon owned his *Lettres historiques et dogmatiques sur les jubilés et les indulgences*, 3 vols (The Hague, 1751).

Chalcocondyles, Laonicus (*c*.1423–?1490); Athenian; historian of Byzantium.

Chandler, Richard (1738–1810); travel writer; Gibbon owned his *Travels in Asia Minor* (Oxford, 1775) and *Travels in Greece* (Oxford, 1776).

Chardin, Jean (1643–1713); French traveller to the Levant and India; Gibbon owned his *Voyages en Perse*, 4 vols (Amsterdam, 1735).

Charlemagne (*c*.742–814); king of the Franks and of the Lombards; emperor of the West, 800–814.

Chauffepié, Jacques Georges de (1702–86);

Protestant clergyman; Gibbon owned his *Nouveau dictionnaire historique et critique*, 4 vols (Amsterdam, 1750–56).

Cherefeddin Ali, or Sherefeddin; more accurately, Sharāf al-Din (d. 1454); Persian historian; Gibbon owned his *Histoire de Timur Bec, traduite par Pétis de la Croix*, 4 vols (Paris, 1722), and *The History of Timur-Bec*, 2 vols (London, 1723).

Chillingworth, William (1602–44); theologian; Gibbon owned his *Religion of Protestants a Safe Way to Salvation* (London, 1674) and *Works* (London, 1674).

Chosroes I (d. 579); Persian ruler.

Chosroes II (d. 628); Persian ruler.

Chrysostom, John (347–407); st; early church father; abp of Constantinople.

Cicero, Marcus Tullius (106–43 BC); Roman statesman, scholar, lawyer and man of letters; Gibbon owned his *Cato; or, an Essay on Old Age*, tr. W. Melmoth (London, 1773), *De Natura Deorum* (Cambridge, 1718), three editions of *De Officiis* (London, 1651; 2 vols, Amsterdam, 1688; Brunswick, 1783), *Entretiens sur la nature des dieux*, tr. D'Olivet, 2 vols (Paris, 1749), *The Epistles to M. Brutus, and of Brutus to Cicero*, tr. C. Middleton (London, 1743), three editions of *Epistolæ ad Familiares* (2 vols, Amsterdam, 1676, 1677; Amsterdam, 1684; 2 vols, Amsterdam, 1693), *Letters to Several of his Friends*, tr. W. Melmoth, 3 vols (London, 1753), *Lettres à Atticus*, 6 vols (Amsterdam, 1741), three editions of his *Opera* (Amsterdam, 1699; 9 vols, Paris, 1740–42; 14 vols, Paris, 1768), two editions of his *Opera Omnia* (21 vols, Glasgow, 1748–9; 7 vols, Halle, 1773–6), *Orationes*, 3 vols (Amsterdam, 1695–9), *Orationes Quædam Selectæ* (London, 1722) and

Tusculanes, tr. Bouhier and D'Olivet, 3 vols (Paris, 1746–7).

Cimon (*c*.510–451 BC); Athenian statesman and general.

Cinna (*fl.* 1st century BC); Roman poet.

Cinna, Lucius Cornelius (d. 84 BC); leader of the Marian party in Rome against Sulla.

Clarke, Samuel (1675–1729); latitudinarian divine; author of *The Scripture-Doctrine of the Trinity* (1712) and commentator on Homer.

Claudianus, Claudius (*c*.370–*c*.404); last great poet of the classical tradition; protégé of Stilicho, the Roman general.

Claudius (10 BC–AD 54); Roman emperor; extended Roman rule in North Africa and Britain.

Clemens, Titus Flavius (*c*.150–*c*.215); Clement of Alexandria; st.

Clodion (d. 447); king of the Franks; defeated by Ætius at Helena.

Cluverius, Philippus, or Cluvier (1580–1623); geographer and historian; Gibbon owned his *Germaniæ Antiquæ Libri Tres* (Leyden, 1616) and *Italia Antiqua*, 2 vols (Leyden, 1624).

Cola di Rienzi (1313–54); Italian demagogue who tried to restore the ancient greatness of Rome.

Columella, Lucius Junius Moderatus (*fl.* 1st century AD); soldier and agriculturalist; author of *De Re Rustica*.

Comines, Philippe de (1445–1509); historian; Gibbon owned his *Mémoires* (Leyden, 1648; 4 vols, London and Paris, 1747).

Commodus (161–92); Roman emperor and tyrant.

Constans, Flavius Julius (*c*.323–350); Roman emperor; vigorous opponent of Arianism.

Constantine Copronymus, otherwise known as Constantine V (718–75); Byzantine emperor; waged vigorous campaigns against the Arabs and the Bulgars.

Constantine Palæologus (1404–53); the last Byzantine emperor, killed defending Constantinople against the Turks.

Constantine Porphyrogenitus (905–59); Byzantine emperor; author of the valuable treatise *De Administrando Imperio*.

Constantine the Great (*c*.280–337); Roman emperor; established Christianity as the religion of the empire.

Constantius II (317–61); Roman emperor.

Corbulo, Gnæus Domitius (d. 67 AD); Roman general under Nero; forced to commit suicide.

Corneille, Pierre (1606–84); French playwright; Gibbon owned his *Chefs-d'œuvre* (Oxford, 1746) and two editions of his *Théâtre*, ed. Voltaire (12 vols, Amsterdam, 1764; 10 vols, n.p., 1776).

Correggio, properly, Antonio Allegri (1494–1534); painter, who exerted great influence on Baroque and Rococo artists.

Cousin, Louis (1627–1707); historian, and editor of and commentator on Greek literature; Gibbon owned his *Histoire de Constantinople*, 8 vols (Paris, 1684), and *Histoire de l'empire d'Occident*, 2 vols (Paris, 1684).

Cranmer, Thomas (1489–1556); first Protestant abp of Canterbury; drew up the Book of Common Prayer.

Crassus, Marcus Licinius (115–53 BC); Roman politician and soldier; killed in Parthia at the battle of Carrhae.

Crusius, Martin, or Martinus Crusius (1526–1607); German Greek scholar; author of *Turco Græcia Libri Octo* (Basle, 1584).

Curtius Rufus, Quintus (*fl.* 1st century AD); historian and biographer; author of a life of Alexander the Great; Gibbon owned three editions of his *De Rebus Gestis Alexandri Magni* (Strasburg, 1670; London, 1716; Delft and Leyden, 1724).

Cuspinian, Joannes (1473–1529); German diplomat and educator; author of *De Cæsaribus*.

Cyprian, more fully, Thasius Caecilius Cyprianus (*c*.200–258); st; bp of Carthage; leader of the church in Africa; Gibbon owned two editions of his *Opera* (Cologne, 1617; Amsterdam, 1700).

Cyril of Alexandria (*c*.375–444); st; opponent of Nestorianism.

Cyrus II, or Cyrus the Great (*c*.590–*c*.529 BC); founder of the Achaemenid empire.

D

Dampier, William (1651–1715); traveller and author of various collections of voyages.

Decebalus (d. AD 106); king of the Dacians.

Decius, Gaius Messius Quintus Trajanus (*c*.201–251); Roman emperor; organizer of the first Roman persecution of the Christians.

Demosthenes (d. 413 BC); Athenian general and strategist in the Peloponnesian War against Sparta.

Demosthenes (384–322 BC); Athenian statesman and orator; Gibbon owned his *All the Orations*, tr. T. Leland (London, 1771), *Demosthenis et Æschinis Opera*, 2 vols (Cambridge, 1744), *Œuvres Complettes*, tr. Auger, 4 vols (Paris, 1777), *Opera* (Paris, 1570), *Oratio Adversus Leptinem* (Halle, 1789), and *Philippiques*, tr. D'Olivet (Paris, 1744).

Dicæarchus (*fl. c*.320 BC); Greek peripatetic philosopher.

Diocletian, Gaius Aurelius Valerius Diocletianus; (245–316); Roman emperor and architect of a new system of imperial administration.

Diodorus Siculus (*fl.* 1st century BC); Greek historian; Gibbon owned two editions of his *Bibliothecæ Historicæ Libri XV* (Basle, 1559; 2 vols, Amsterdam, 1746) and two editions of *Histoire Universelle* (4 vols, Amsterdam, 1743; 7 vols, Paris, 1758).

Diogenes (d. 320 BC); Greek Cynic philosopher, emphasizing self-sufficiency and the rejection of the inessential.

Diogenes Lærtius (*fl.* 3rd century AD); historian of Greek philosophy; Gibbon owned two editions of his *De Vitis . . . Clarorum Philosophorum* (2 vols, Amsterdam, 1692; Leipzig, 1759).

Dionysius of Halicarnassus (*fl. c.*20 BC); Greek historian and teacher of rhetoric; Gibbon owned his *De Antiquis Oratoribus* (Oxford, 1781), *Delle cose antiche della città di Roma*, 2 vols (Verona, 1738), *De Structura Orationis* (London, 1728), *Opera*, 6 vols (Leipzig, 1774–7) and *Works*, ed. J. Hudson, 2 vols (Oxford, 1704).

Dionysius the Areopagite (*fl.* 1st century AD); later, forged Christian writings of a neoplatonic nature were mistakenly attributed to him.

Dodwell, Henry (1641–1711); scholar and theologian; non-juror; Gibbon owned his *De Veteribus Græcorum Romanorumque Cyclis* (Oxford, 1701–2) and *Prælectiones Academicæ in Schola Historices Camdeniana* (Oxford, 1692).

Domitian, Cæsar Domitianus Augustus (51–96); Roman emperor and tyrant.

Donati, Alessandro, or Donatus (1584–1640); antiquarian and poet; author of the *Roma Antiqua et Nova* (properly, *Roma vetus ac recens*), of which Gibbon owned two editions (Rome, 1639, 1738).

Dubos, Jean Baptiste (1670–1742); historian and critic; Gibbon owned his *Histoire critique de l'établissement de la Monarchie française dans les Gaules*, 2 vols (Paris, 1742), *Histoire de la Ligue faite à Cambray*, 2 vols (Paris, 1709), and two editions of *Réflexions critiques sur la poésie et sur la peinture* (Paris, 1755; 3 vols, Paris, 1770).

Du Buat-Nançay, Louis Gabriel, comte (1732–87); Gibbon owned his *Histoire des anciens peuples de l'Europe*, 12 vols (Paris, 1772).

Ducange, Charles du Fresne, seigneur (1610–88); oriental scholar and philologist; Gibbon owned his *Glossarium ad Scriptores Mediæ et Infimæ Græcitatis*, 2 vols (Leyden, 1688), and *Glossarium ad Scriptores Mediæ et Infimæ Latinitatis*, 6 vols (Basle, 1762).

Ducas, Michael (*fl.* 15th century); Byzantine historian.

Dupin, Louis Ellies (1657–1719); theologian; Gibbon owned his *Nouvelle bibliothèque des auteurs ecclésiastiques*, 19 vols (Paris, Mons, Amsterdam, 1690–1715).

E

Edward VI (1537–1553); king of England.

Elagabalus, or Heliogabalus (204–22); Roman emperor and degenerate.

Elizabeth I (1533–1603); queen of England.

Elmacin, Georgius; historian of the Saracens; author of *Historia Saracenica . . . operâ et studio Thomæ Erpinii* (Lugd. Batavorum, 1625).

Epictetus (*c.*55–*c.*135); philosopher of Stoic persuasions; Gibbon owned the *Epicteti quæ Supersunt Dissertationes*, 2 vols (London, 1741).

Epicurus (341–270 BC); Greek philosopher.

Erasmus, Desiderius (*c.*1466–1536); humanist; Gibbon owned his *Adag-*

iorum Chiliades (Geneva, 1606), *The Apophthegms of the Ancients*, 2 vols (London, 1753), *Colloquia* (Leyden, 1729), *Epistolarum Opus* (Basle, 1558), *Epistolarum D. Erasmi Libri XXXI* (London, 1642), *Epistolæ Selectiores* (Basle, 1719) and *Opera*, 10 vols (Leyden, 1703–6).

Eratosthenes of Cyrene (*c*.276–*c*.194 BC); Greek scientist, astronomer and poet; the first man to calculate the circumference of the earth.

Euclid (*fl. c*.300 BC); the greatest mathematician of antiquity; Gibbon owned his *Elements of Geometry*, tr. E. Stone (London, 1752), *The English Euclid* (Oxford, 1705) and *Euclidis quæ Supersunt Omnia* (Oxford, 1703).

Eugenius IV, or Gabriele Condulmer (*c*.1383–1447); pope.

Eunapius (*c*.345–*c*.420); Greek rhetorician and historiographer; Gibbon owned his *De Vitis Philosophorum et Sophistarum* (Antwerp, 1568).

Euripides (*c*.484–406 BC); Athenian tragic dramatist; Gibbon owned the *Euripidis quæ Extant Omnia* (Cambridge, 1694), *Quæ Extant Omnia*, 4 vols (Oxford, 1778), *Tragædia Hippolytus* (Leyden, 1767–8), *Tragædiæ Quatuor* (Strasburg, 1780) and *Tragædiæ XIX* (Antwerp, 1771).

Eusebius (d. *c*.342); bp of Nicomedia; one of the main advocates of Arianism.

Eusebius of Cæsarea (*fl*. 4th century AD); bp of Cæsarea; historian and polemicist; Gibbon owned the *Eusebii . . . quæ Extant Historiæ Ecclesiasticæ*, 3 vols (Cambridge, 1720), *Histoire de l'église*, tr. M. Cousin (Paris, 1686), *Præparatio Evangelica*, 2 vols (Cologne, 1688), and *Thesaurus Temporum* (Amsterdam, 1658).

Eustathius (d. *c*.337); bp of Antioch; adversary of the Arians and the Council of Nicæa; Gibbon owned his *Commentarii in Homeri Iliadem*, 3 vols (Florence, 1730–35), and

Παρεκβολαι, 4 vols (Rome, 1542–51).

Eutropius (*fl*. late 4th century AD); Roman historian; accompanied Julian the Apostate on his Persian campaign; Gibbon owned his *Breviarium Historiæ Romanæ* (Leyden, 1729).

Eutyches, or Eutichius (*c*.375–454); archimandrite of the Eastern church; Gibbon owned his *Contextio Gemmarum, sive Annales*, 2 vols (Oxford, 1654 and 1656).

Evagrius Ponticus (346–99); Christian mystic.

Evodius (*fl*. 1st century AD); bp of Uzalis; martyr.

F

Fabretti, Raffaello (1620–1700); scholar and antiquarian; Gibbon owned his *De Aquis et Aquæductibus Veteris Romæ* (Rome, 1680).

Fabricius, Johann Albert (1668–1736); scholar and philologist; Gibbon owned his *Bibliotheca Græca*, 14 vols (Hamburg, 1705–28), *Bibliotheca Latina*, 2 vols (Leipzig, 1773–4), *Bibliotheca Latina Mediæ et Infimæ Ætatis*, 6 vols (Padua, 1754), *Codex Apocryphus Novi Testamenti*, 3 vols (Hamburg, 1719), *Codex Pseudepigraphus Veteris Testamenti*, 2 vols (Hamburg, 1722, 1723) and *Imp. Cæs. Augusti Temporum Notatio, Genus, et Scriptorum Fragmenta* (Hamburg, 1727).

Fénelon, François de Salignac de la Mothe (1651–1715); abp of Cambrai; theologian and man of letters; Gibbon owned his *Les aventures de Télémaque*, 2 vols (Lausanne, 1781), and *Œuvres philosophiques* (Amsterdam, 1721).

Fleury, Claude (1640–1723); ecclesiastical historian and clergyman; Gibbon owned his *Discours sur l'histoire ecclésiastique* (Paris, 1764, 1771), *Histoire*

ecclésiastique, 21 vols (Brussels, 1713–26), *Institution au droit ecclésiastique*, 2 vols (Paris, 1767), and *Les Mœurs des Israélites et des Chrétiens* (Paris, 1712).

Florus, Publius Annius (*fl.* late 1st and early 2nd centuries AD); poet and Roman historian; Gibbon owned three editions of his *Epitome Rerum Romanarum* (2 vols, Amsterdam, 1702; Amsterdam, 1736; Paris, 1776).

Folard, Jean Charles, Chevalier de (1669–1752); French soldier and military theorist.

Foncemagne, Étienne Lauréault de (1694–1779); historian of the Franks.

Fontana, Domenico (1543–1607); architect.

Fortis, Alberto (1741–1803); geographer and naturalist; Gibbon owned his *Viaggio in Dalmazia*, 2 vols (Venice, 1774).

Freret, Nicolas (1688–1749); scholar and *érudit*; Gibbon owned his *Défense de la chronologie, fondée sur les monumens de l'histoire ancienne, contre le système de M. Newton* (Paris, 1758) and *Examen critique des apologistes de la religion chrétienne* (London, 1767).

Fulgentius (*c.*467–533); st; bp of Ruspe; defender of doctrinal orthodoxy against Arianism and semi-Pelagianism.

G

Gagnier, John (1670–1740); orientalist; editor of *Ismael Abulfeda de Vita et Rebus Gestis Mohammedis* (Oxford, 1723); Gibbon owned his *La Vie de Mahomet*, 2 vols (Amsterdam, 1748).

Galba (3 BC–AD 69); Roman emperor.

Gale, Thomas (1635?–1702); British antiquary; editor of *Antoninus's Itinerary in Britain*; editor of Gildas and Nennius; Gibbon owned his *Historiæ Poeticæ Scriptores Antiqui Græci et Latini* (Paris, 1675), his edition of the *Iter Britanniarum* (London, 1709), *Opuscula Mythologica Physica et Ethica* (Amsterdam, 1688) and *Rerum Anglicarum Scriptorum Veterum*, 3 vols (Oxford, 1684–91).

Galen of Pergamum (*c.*129–*c.*199); Greek physician; founder of experimental physiology.

Galerius (d. 311); Roman emperor, notorious for his persecution of the Christians.

Galland, Antoine (1646–1715); orientalist.

Gallienus, Publius Licinius Egnatius (218–68); Roman emperor.

Gallus, Flavius Claudius Constantius (*c.*325–354); Cæsar under Constantius II.

Gaubil, Antoine (1689–1759); Jesuit; historian and orientalist; editor and translator of the *Histoire de la dynastie des Mongous* (Paris, 1739).

Gébelin, Antoine Court de (1728–84); historian and *érudit*; author of the *Histoire du calendrier* and the *Monde primitif analysé et comparé avec le monde moderne*, 9 vols (Paris, 1773–82).

Geddes, Michael (1650?–1713); ecclesiastical historian; Gibbon owned his *The Church-history of Æthiopia* (London, 1696), *The Council of Trent no Free Assembly* (London, 1714), *The History of the Church of Malabar* (London, 1694), *Miscellaneous Tracts*, 3 vols (London, 1730), and *Several Tracts against Popery* (London, 1715).

Gedoyn, Nicolas (1667–1744); translator and man of letters; Gibbon owned his translation of *Pausanias, ou voyage historique de la Grèce*, 2 vols (Paris, 1731).

Gelimer (*fl.* early 6th century AD); last of the Vandal kings of North Africa.

Gellius, Aulus (*fl.* 2nd century AD); Latin author of the *Noctes Atticæ*, a miscellaneous anthology of classical literature; Gibbon owned his *Noctes Atticæ* (Amsterdam, 1651) and *Noc-*

tium Atticarum Libri XX (Leyden, 1706).

Gennadius, George Scholarius (*c*.1405–*c*.1473); the first Patriarch of Constantinople under Turkish rule.

Genseric (d. 477); king of the Vandals; sacked Rome in 455.

George of Cappadocia (d. 361); bp of Alexandria; extreme Arian.

Germanicus (15 BC–19 AD); Cæsar; Roman general.

Geta, Publius Septimius (189–212); Roman emperor.

Giannone, Pietro (1676–1748); historian; Gibbon owned his *Istoria Civile del Regno di Napoli*, 4 vols (The Hague, 1753), and *Opere posthume in difesa della sua storia civile del regno di Napoli* (Lausanne, 1760).

Godefroy, Jacques, or Gothofredus (1587–1652); historian and jurist; editor of the *Theodosian Code*, of Libanius, and of Philostorgius; Gibbon owned his edition of the *Codex Theodosianus*, 4 vols (Lyons, 1665).

Goguet, Antoine Yves (1716–58); lawyer and historian; Gibbon owned his (together with A. C. Fugère) *De l'origine des loix, des arts et des sciences, et de leur progrès chez les anciens peuples*, 6 vols (Paris, 1758).

Gordianus I (*c*.157–238); Roman emperor.

Gordianus II (d. 238); Roman emperor.

Gordianus III (225–44); Roman emperor.

Gratian (359–83); Roman emperor.

Greaves, John (1602–52); mathematician and natural philosopher; Gibbon owned his *Miscellaneous Works*, 2 vols (London, 1737).

Gregory Nazianzen (*c*.330–*c*.389); st; defender of doctrinal orthodoxy against Arianism; Gibbon owned a French translation of his *Discours contre Julien* (Lyons, 1735).

Gregory of Nyssa (*c*.335–*c*.394); st; philosophical theologian and mystic;

defender of the orthodox doctrine of the Trinity.

Gregory of Tours, Georgius Florentius (*c*.538–*c*.594); st; historian of the Franks.

Gregory Thaumaturgus (*c*.213–*c*.270); st; upholder of orthodoxy in disputes over the Trinity.

Gronovius, Johannes Fredericus (1611–71); scholar and antiquarian; Gibbon owned his *De Sestertiis* (Leyden, 1671).

Grotius, Hugo (1583–1645); Dutch jurist and historian; Gibbon owned his *Annales et Historiæ de Rebus Belgicis* (Amsterdam, 1657, 1658), *De Jure Belli ac Pacis* (Amsterdam, 1689), *Le Droit de la guerre et de la paix* (Basle, 1746), *De Veritate Religionis Christianæ* (The Hague, 1729), *Epistolæ* (Amsterdam, 1687), *Excerpta Tragœdiis et Comœdiis Græcis* (Paris, 1626), *Historia Gothorum, Vandalorum et Langobardorum* (Amsterdam, 1655), *Opera Omnia Theologica*, 3 vols (Amsterdam, 1679), and *Poemata* (Leyden, 1617).

Gruter, Jan (1560–1624); scholar and antiquarian; Gibbon owned his *Inscriptiones Antiquæ Totius Orbis Romani*, 4 vols (Amsterdam, 1707).

Guignes, Joseph de (1721–1800); ethnologist and historian; Gibbon owned his *Histoire générale des Huns, des Turcs, des Mongols, et des autres peuples tartares occidentaux*, 4 vols published as 5 vols (Paris, 1756–8).

Guischardt, Carl Gottlieb, or Guichardt, or Guischard, or 'Quintus Icilius' (1724–75); military historian; Gibbon owned his *Mémoires critiques et historiques sur plusieurs points d'antiquités militaires*, 4 vols (Berlin, 1774), and *Mémoires militaires sur les Grecs et les Romains*, 2 vols (Lyons, 1760).

Gyllius, Peter, more accurately, Pierre Gilles (1490–1555); naturalist; Gibbon owned his *De Bosporo Thracio* (Lyons, 1561).

H

Hadrian, Publius Ælius Hadrianus (76–138); Roman emperor.

Hakluyt, Richard (1552–1616); geographer and traveller; Gibbon owned his *The Principal Nauigations, Voyages, Traffiques and Discoueries of the English Nation*, 3 vols (London, 1599–1600).

Halley, Edmond (1656–1742); astronomer.

Hannibal (247–c.183 BC); Carthaginian general; led the Carthaginian armies against Rome during the Second Punic War (218–201 BC).

Hardouin, Jean (1646–1729); Jesuit; pyrrhonist; editor of Pliny and Themistius.

Harte, Walter (1709–74); academic and man of letters; Gibbon owned two editions of his *Essays on Husbandry* (Bath, 1764; 2 vols, London, 1770) and his *History of the Life of Gustavus Adolphus*, 2 vols (London, 1759).

Hauteville, John de, or Hanville (*fl.* 1184); monk and poet.

Havercamp, Sigebertus (1684–1742); classical scholar; editor of Eutropius, Censorinus, Orosius and Josephus; Gibbon owned his *Sylloge Scriptorum*, 2 vols (Leyden, 1736).

Heineccius, Johann Christian, or Heinecke (1681–1741); legal historian; Gibbon owned his *Antiquitatum Romanarum Jurisprudentiam Illustrantium Syntagma*, 2 vols (Utrecht, 1745), *Elementa Juris Civilis Secundum Ordinem Institutorum* (Leyden, 1751), *Elementa Juris Civilis Secundum Ordinem Pandectarum*, 2 vols (Utrecht, 1772), and *Historia Juris Civilis Romani ac Germanici* (Leyden, 1740).

Helvidius Priscus (d. *c.* AD 70–79); Roman Stoic and defender of the rights of the senate against the pretensions of the *princeps*.

Heraclius (c.575–641); Eastern Roman emperor.

Herbelot de Molainville, Barthélemy d' (1625–95); orientalist; Gibbon owned his *Bibliothèque orientale* (Paris, 1697).

Herodes Atticus (c.101–177); orator and writer.

Herodotus (c.484–c.430 BC); Greek historian; Gibbon owned his *Historia*, 3 vols (Glasgow, 1761), and *Historiarum Libri IX* (Amsterdam, 1763).

Herod the Great (73–4 BC); king of Judæa.

Heylin, Peter, or Heylyn (1600–62); author of a *History of St. George* and the *Life of Archbishop Laud*; Gibbon owned his *Cosmography* (London, 1682).

Heyne, Christian Gottlob (1729–1812); classical scholar; Gibbon owned his *Opuscula Academica*, 3 vols (Göttingen, 1785–8).

Hirtius, Aulus (c.90–43 BC); Roman soldier and writer.

Hoadly, Benjamin (1676–1761); successively bp of Bangor, Hereford, Salisbury and Winchester; Whig controversialist and latitudinarian; Gibbon owned his *An Account of the State of the Roman Catholick Religion* (London, 1715).

Hody, Humphrey (1659–1707); divine and scholar; Gibbon owned his *De Græcis Illustribus Linguæ Græcæ Literarumque Humaniorum Instauratoribus* (London, 1742).

Hoeschelius, David, of Augsburgh (1556–1617); educator and printer of the *editio princeps* of Procopius.

Homer (*fl.* 8th or 9th century BC); epic poet; Gibbon owned the *Homeri quæ Extant Omnia* (Geneva, 1606), *Hymnus in Cererem* (Leyden, 1788), *L'Iliad*, tr. Bitaubé, 2 vols (Paris, 1764), *Ilias et Odyssea*, 2 vols (Cambridge, 1711), *Index Vocabulorum*

(Oxford, 1780), Ὀδύσσεια, 2 vols (Strasburg, 1525), *Opera Omnia*, 5 vols (Leipzig, 1759–64), three editions of his *Works* (2 vols, London, 1740, 1754; 4 vols, Glasgow, 1756–8; 4 vols, Oxford, 1780, 1782), and two editions of the *Works*, tr. Pope and Parnell (11 vols, London, 1760; 9 vols, London, 1771).

Honorius, Flavius (384–423); Roman emperor in the West.

Hooker, Richard (1554?–1600); theologian and writer on church government; Gibbon owned his *Works* (London, 1723).

Hooper, George (1640–1727); bp of Bath and Wells; antiquarian; Gibbon owned his *An Inquiry into the State of the Ancient Measures* (London, 1721).

Horace, more fully, Quintus Horatius Flaccus (65–8 BC); lyric poet and satirist; Gibbon owned his *Eclogæ* (Leipzig, 1772), two editions of *Epistolæ ad Pisones* (2 vols, Cambridge, 1757; tr. G. Colman, London, 1783), seven editions of his *Opera* (Frankfort, 1596; Paris, 1604; Antwerp, 1608; Amsterdam, 1728; 8 vols, Amsterdam, 1735; Amsterdam, 1743; Dublin, 1745), *Poésies,* tr. Sanadon, 2 vols (Paris, 1728), and Philip Francis's *Poetical Translation of the Works of Horace,* 4 vols (London, 1749, 1750).

Hormisdas (d. 523); st; re-united the Eastern and Western churches.

Horsley, John (1685–1732); antiquary; Gibbon owned his *Britannia Romana* (London, 1732).

Hottinger, Johann Heinrich (1620–67); orientalist; Gibbon owned two editions of his *Historia Orientalis* (Zurich, 1651; Heidelberg, 1658) and *Promtuarium sive Bibliotheca Orientalis* (Heidelberg, 1658).

Hudson, John (1662–1719); classical scholar; Gibbon owned his *Geogra-*

phiæ Veteris Scriptores Græci Minores, 4 vols (Oxford, 1698–1712).

Hume, David (1711–76); philosopher; Gibbon owned his *Dialogues Concerning Natural Religion* (London, 1779), three editions of *Essays and Treatises on Several Subjects* (4 vols, London, 1760; 2 vols, London, 1768; 2 vols, London, 1777) and two editions of *The History of England,* 8 vols (London, 1770, 1778).

Huniades, John (1407–1456); Hungarian general; leading Christian commander against the Turks.

Huss, Jan (1372–1415); Czech religious reformer; convicted of heresy at the Council of Constance and burnt at the stake.

Hutchinson, Thomas (1698–1769); historian and classical scholar; editor of Xenophon; Gibbon owned his *Collection of Original Papers Relative to the History of the Colony of Massachusetts Bay* (Boston, 1769) and *History of the Colony of Massachusetts Bay,* 2 vols (London, 1765, 1768).

Hyde, Thomas (1636–1703); orientalist; Gibbon owned his *Syntagma Dissertationum* (Oxford, 1767) and *Veterum Persarum et Parthorum et Medorum Religionis Historia* (Oxford, 1760).

I

Iamblichus (*c.*250–*c.*330); Syrian philosopher; Gibbon owned his *De Mysteriis Ægyptiorum* (Oxford, 1768) and *De Vita Pythagorica* (Amsterdam, 1707).

Innocent III (1160–1216); pope; presided over the Fourth Crusade and the Albigensian Crusade.

Irenæus (*c.*120–*c.*200); st; bp of Lugdunum; author of *Adversus Hæreses,* opposing Gnosticism.

Isidore of Seville (*c.*560–636); st; abp of Seville, theologian.

Isocrates (436–338 BC); Athenian orator, rhetorician and teacher; Gibbon owned his *Opera Omnia*, 3 vols (Paris, 1782), and *Orationes Septem et Epistolæ* (Cambridge, 1729).

J

Jebb, Samuel (?1694–1772); physician and scholar; non-juror; editor of Aristides; Gibbon owned his edition of Aristides' *Opera Omnia*, 2 vols (Oxford, 1722, 1730).

Jerome, Eusebius Hieronymus (*c*.347–*c*.419); st; translator and monastic leader; Gibbon owned an edition of the *Epistolæ Selectæ* (Paris, 1666).

John Palæologus VII (1360–1410); Byzantine emperor.

John Palæologus VIII (1390–1448); Byzantine emperor.

Johnson, Samuel (1709–84); poet, essayist, critic and lexicographer; Gibbon owned his *A Dictionary of the English Language*, 2 vols (London, 1755), two editions of *The Idler*, 2 vols (London, 1761, 1783), *A Journey to the Western Islands of Scotland* (London, 1775), *Letters to and from the late Samuel Johnson*, 2 vols (London, 1788), *Political Tracts* (London, 1776), *The Prince of Abissinia* (London, 1759), two editions of *The Rambler* (4 vols, London, 1752; London, 1784), *Taxation no Tyranny* (London, 1775) and *The Works of the English Poets*, 68 vols (London, 1779–81).

Jones, Sir William (1746–94); orientalist; Gibbon owned his *An Essay on the Law of Bailments* (London, 1781), *Poems, consisting chiefly of Translations from the Asiatic Languages* (Oxford, 1772) and *Poeseos Asiaticæ Commentatiorum Libri Sex* (London, 1774); translator of the *History of Nader Shah*.

Jornandes, properly, Jordanes (*fl*. mid 6th century AD); historian of the Goths; author of *De Rebus Geticis*.

Jortin, John (1698–1770); historian and divine; Gibbon owned his *The Life of Erasmus*, 2 vols (London, 1758, 1760), *Remarks on Ecclesiastical History*, 2 vols (London, 1767), and *Tracts*, 2 vols (London, 1790).

Joseph of Arimathea (*fl*. *c*.AD 30); st; secret disciple of Jesus.

Josephus, Flavius (*c*.37–*c*.100); Jewish priest, scholar and historian; Gibbon owned his *Decreta Romana* (Leyden, 1712), *The Genuine Works of Josephus*, tr. William Whiston (London, 1737), and *Opera Omnia*, 2 vols (Amsterdam, 1726).

Jovian, or Flavius Jovianus (*c*.331–364); Roman emperor.

Julian the Apostate (*c*.331–363); Roman emperor; inveterate enemy of Christianity; Gibbon owned his *Cæsares* (Erlangen, 1785), *Les Césars* (Paris, 1683) and *Opera*, 3 vols (Leipzig, 1696).

Julius II (1443–1513); pope; patron of the fine arts.

Justin I (*c*.450–527); Byzantine emperor.

Justin Martyr (*c*.100–*c*.165); st; theologian.

Justinian I (483–565); Byzantine emperor; Gibbon owned the *Justiniani Institutiones* (Leyden, 1753).

Justinian II (*c*.669–711); Byzantine emperor.

Juvenal, Decimus Junius Juvenalis (*c*.55–*c*.127); Roman satirist; Gibbon owned two editions of his *Satires*, tr. John Dryden (London, 1693, 1713), and four editions of *Satyræ* (Amsterdam, 1684; Leyden, 1695, 1709; Birmingham, 1761).

K

Kæmpfer, Engelbert (1651–1716); orientalist; Gibbon owned his *Amœnitatum Exoticarum Politico-Physico-Medicarum Fasciculi V* (Lemgo, 1712) and *The History of Japan*, 2 vols (London, 1728).

Kuster, Ludolph (1670–1716); classical scholar; editor of Suidas.

L

Labat, Jean Baptiste (1663–1738); traveller; Gibbon owned his *Nouvelle Relation de l'Afrique occidentale*, 5 vols (Paris, 1728), *Voyage aux isles françoises de l'Amerique* (The Hague, 1724), *Voyage du Chevalier Des Marchais en Guinée*, 4 vols (Amsterdam, 1731), and *Voyages en Espagne et en Italie*, 8 vols (Amsterdam, 1731).

Labb, Philippe, or Labbe (1607–67); theologian and historian; editor of the *Notitia Dignitatum Imperii Romani*.

La Croze, Mathurin Veyssière de (1661–1739); orientalist and historian; Gibbon owned his *Histoire du Christianisme des Indes*, 2 vols (The Hague, 1758), *Histoire du Christianisme d'Éthiopie et d'Arménie* (The Hague, 1739) and *Thesauri Epistolici Lacroziani*, 3 vols (Leipzig, 1742–46).

Lactantius (*c.*240–*c.*320); Christian apologist; Gibbon owned his *De Mortibus Persecutorum* (Utrecht, 1663), and three editions of his *Opera* (Leyden, 1660; Antwerp, 1660; 2 vols, Paris, 1748).

La Mothe le Vayer, François de (1588–1672); writer and *philosophe*; Gibbon owned his *Œuvres*, 14 vols (Dresden, 1756–9).

Lancelot, Claude (1615–95); grammarian; biographer of Francis Philelphus; Gibbon owned his *Le Jardin de racines grecques mises en vers français* (Paris, 1741) and *Nouvelle Méthode pour apprendre facilement la langue grecque* [The Grammar of Port Royal] (Paris, 1754).

Lancisi, Giovanni Maria (1654–1720); physician; Gibbon owned his *Dissertatio de Nativis deque Adventitiis Romani Cœli Qualitatibus* (Rome, 1711).

Lardner, Nathaniel (1684–1768); nonconformist divine; biblical and patristic scholar; Gibbon owned his *The Credibility of the Gospel History*, 17 vols (London, 1741–62), and *A Large Collection of Ancient Jewish and Heathen Testimonies to the Truth of the Christian Religion*, 4 vols (London, 1764–7).

La Roque, Jean de (1661–1745); traveller; Gibbon owned his *Voyage de l'Arabie heureuse* (Amsterdam, 1716) and *Voyage de Syrie et du Mont-Liban* (Amsterdam, 1723).

Le Clerc, Jean (1657–1736); Arminian scholar; Gibbon owned two editions of his *Ars Critica*, 2 vols (Amsterdam, 1697; 1730), *Bibliothèque ancienne et moderne*, 29 vols (The Hague, 1726–30), *Bibliothèque choisie*, 28 vols (Amsterdam, 1718), *Bibliothèque universelle et historique*, 26 vols (Amsterdam, 1700–13), *Harmonia Evangelica* (Amsterdam, 1699), *Historia Ecclesiastica Duorum Primorum a Christo Nato Sæculorum* (Amsterdam, 1716) and *Parrhasiana, ou pensées diverses*, 2 vols (Amsterdam, 1699, 1701).

Le Comte, Louis Daniel (1655–1729); orientalist; editor of *Mémoires sur la Chine*, 2 vols (Paris, 1696); Gibbon owned his *Memoirs and Observations Made in a Late Journey through the Empire of China* (London, 1699).

Leibnitz, Gottfried Wilhelm von, or Leibniz (1646–1716); philosopher, mathematician and political adviser;

Gibbon owned two editions of his *Essais de Théodicée*, 2 vols (Lausanne, 1709, 1760), *Esprit de Leibnitz*, 2 vols (Lyons, 1772), and *Origines Guelficæ*, 5 vols (Hanover, 1750–80).

Leo X (1475–1521); pope.

Leo the Armenian (d. 820); Byzantine emperor; iconoclast.

Leonard of Chios, or Leonardus Chiensis (*fl.* 15th century); author of *Historia C.P. a Turco Expugnatæ* (Norimberghæ, 1544).

Leunclavius, Joannes; historian and orientalist; Gibbon owned his *Historiæ Musulmanæ Turcorum Libri XVIII* (Frankfort, 1591).

Libanius (314–93); sophist and rhetorician; Gibbon owned his *Epistolæ* (Amsterdam, 1738), *Orationes et Declamationes* (Altenburg, 1784) and *Præludia Oratoria LXXII*, 2 vols (Paris, 1606, 1627).

Limborch, Philippus van (1633–1712); scholar and theologian; Gibbon owned his *De Veritate Religionis Christianæ* (Gouda, 1687) and *Historia Inquisitionis* (Amsterdam, 1692).

Lindenbrogius, Friedrich, or Lindenbrog (1573–1648); classical scholar; editor of Ammianus Marcellinus.

Lipsius, Justus, or Joest Lips (1547–1606); scholar and political theorist; Gibbon owned his *Opera*, 4 vols (Antwerp, 1637).

Livia Drusilla (58 BC–29 AD); wife of Augustus.

Livy, Titus Livius (*c.*59 BC–AD 17); Roman historian; Gibbon owned his *Historiarum quod Exstat*, 10 vols (Amsterdam, 1710), *Historiarum Libri qui Supersunt Omnes*, 7 vols (Amsterdam, Leyden, 1738–46), and *Historiarum Libri XCI* (Rome, 1773).

Locke, John (1632–1704); philosopher and political theorist; Gibbon owned two editions of his *Works* (3 vols, London, 1759; 4 vols, London, 1777).

Longinus, Dionysius (*fl.* 1st century AD); deemed to be the author of the critical treatise *On the Sublime*; Gibbon owned two editions of *De Sublimitate Commentarius* (Utrecht, 1694; London, 1743), *On the Sublime*, tr. William Smith (London, 1770), and *Quæ Supersunt* (Oxford, 1778).

Longuerue, Louis Dufour de (1652–1733); historian and érudit; Gibbon owned his *Description historique et géographique de la France ancienne et moderne*, 2 vols (Paris, 1722), and *Longueruana*, 2 vols (Berlin, 1754).

Lowth, Robert (1710–87); bp of London; Gibbon owned his *De Sacra Poesi Hebræorum Prælectiones* (Oxford, 1775), *A Letter to the Author of 'The Divine Legation of Moses Demonstrated'* (London, 1766), *The Life of William of Wykeham* (London, 1758) and *A Short Introduction to English Grammar* (London, 1784).

Lucan, Marius Annæus Lucanus (39–65); Roman epic poet; author of the *Pharsalia*; Gibbon owned his *La Pharsale*, tr. Marmontel (Paris, 1766), and *Pharsalia* (Leyden, 1728).

Lucian (120–*c.*180); Greek rhetorician and satirist; Gibbon owned his *Lucien*, tr. Perrot (Amsterdam, 1722), *Opera*, 3 vols (Amsterdam, 1743), and *Quomodo Historia Conscribenda Sit* (Oxford, 1776).

Lucullus, Lucius Licinius (*c.*117–*c.*58 BC); Roman general; opponent of Mithridates, king of Pontus; extravagantly wealthy, his name became a byword for luxury.

Ludewig, Johann Peter von (1668–1743); historian and jurist; Gibbon owned his *Vita Justiniani M. atque Theodoræ Augustorum nec non Triboniani Jurisprudentiæ Justinianæ Proscenium* (Halle, 1731).

Luther, Martin (*c.*1483–1546); religious reformer.

M

Mabillon, Jean (1632–1707); monastic scholar, antiquarian and historian; founder of the science of diplomatic (i.e. the study of the documentary sources of history); Gibbon owned the *Ouvrages posthumes de J. Mabillon et de Thierry Ruinart*, 3 vols (Paris, 1724), and *Traité des Études Monastiques*, 2 vols (Paris, 1692).

Macpherson, John (1710–65); scholar and historian; Gibbon owned his *Critical Dissertations on the Origin, Antiquities, Language, Government, Manners and Religion of the Ancient Caledonians* (London, 1768).

Macrobius, Ambrosius Theodosius (*fl. c.* AD 400); Latin grammarian and philosopher; Gibbon owned two editions of his *Opera* (Leyden, 1670; London, 1694).

Mæcenas, Gaius (*c.*70–8 BC); Roman statesman; counsellor to Augustus; notable patron of poetry.

Maffei, Francesco Scipione, marchesi (1675–1755); dramatist, architect and scholar; Gibbon owned his *Della scienza chiamata cavalleresca* (Trento, 1717), *Istoria diplomatica* (Mantua, 1727), *Osservazioni letterarie che possono servir di continuazione al giornal de' letterati d'Italia*, 6 vols (Verona, 1737–40), and *Verona illustrata*, 2 vols (Verona, 1731, 1732).

Mahomet (*c.*569–632); religious leader; founder of Islam.

Maimonides, Moses (1135–1204); Jewish philosopher, jurist and physician; Gibbon owned the *Porta Mosis*, 2 vols (Oxford, 1654, 1655).

Malatesta, Sigismondo Pandolfo (1417–68); feudal lord of Rimini; patron of the arts.

Malmesbury, William of (d. *c.*1143); historian.

Maltret, Claude, or Maltretus (1621–74); Hellenist; Jesuit; editor of Procopius.

Mamæa, Julia (d. 235); mother of the Roman emperor Severus Alexander.

Mamertinus, Claudius (*fl. c.*360); Roman official; author of panegyric on Julian the Apostate.

Marcian (396–457); Eastern Roman emperor.

Mariana, Juan de (1536–1624); Jesuit; historian; Gibbon owned his *Historiæ de Rebus Hispanicis*, 4 vols (The Hague, 1733).

Marius, Gaius (*c.*157–86 BC); Roman general and politician; consul on seven separate occasions.

Marracci, Lodovico (1612–1700); orientalist and historian; translator of the Koran into Latin.

Marsham, Sir John (1602–85); chronologist; Gibbon owned two editions of his *Canon Chronicus* (London, 1672; Frankfort, 1696).

Marsigli, Luigi Fernando, count (1658–1730); soldier and writer; Gibbon owned his *Stato militare dell'imperio ottomano* (The Hague, 1732).

Martial, Marcus Valerius Martialis (*c.*38–*c.*103); Roman poet and epigrammatist; Gibbon owned his *Epigrammatum Libros XV* (Paris, 1680).

Martin (316–97); st; bp of Tours; father of Western monasticism.

Martin V (1368–1431); pope; asserter of papal supremacy.

Mascou, Johann Jacob, or Mascow, or Mascov (1689–1761); jurist and historian; Gibbon owned his *History of the Ancient Germans*, 2 vols (London, 1738).

Maximin (d. 238); the first man to rise from the ranks to become Roman emperor.

Mela, Pomponius (*fl.* AD 43); Latin geographer; author of *De Situ Orbis*, or *De Chorographia*; Gibbon owned his *Libri Tres de Situ Orbis* (Frankfort, 1700).

Memnon; ally of the Trojans against the

Greeks at the siege of Troy; killed by Achilles.

Menander (*c.*342–*c.*292 BC); Athenian comic dramatist; Gibbon owned the *Menandri et Philemonis Reliquiæ* (Amsterdam, 1709).

Menander (*fl.* later 6th century AD); Byzantine historian.

Menelaus; king of Sparta; husband of Helen and brother of Agamemnon.

Messange, or Messance (*fl.* 1765–85); Gibbon owned his *Recherches sur la population des généralités d'Auvergne, de Lyon, de Rouen* (Paris, 1766).

Meursius, Joannes (1579–1639); Greek scholar; editor of Constantine Porphyrogenitus; Gibbon owned his *Ceramicus Geminus* (Utrecht, 1663), *Creta, Cyprus, Rhodus* (Amsterdam, 1765), *Græcia Ludibunda, siue de Ludis Græcorum Liber* (Leyden, 1625), *Miscellanea Laconica* (Amsterdam, 1661), *Opera Omnia*, 12 vols (Florence, 1741–63), and *Regnum Atticum* (Amsterdam, 1633).

Mezeriac, Claude Gaspar Bachet, sieur de, or Méziriac (1581–1638); poet and classical scholar.

Michael I (d. *c.*843); Byzantine emperor.

Michael-Angelo, or Michelangelo (1475–1564); sculptor, painter, architect and poet.

Michaelis, Johann David (1717–91); orientalist and theologian; Gibbon owned his edition of Abulfeda's *Descriptio Ægypti* (Göttingen, 1776).

Middleton, Conyers (1683–1750); polemicist and divine; Gibbon owned his *The History of the Life of M. T. Cicero*, 3 vols (London, 1741), *Miscellaneous Works*, 4 vols (London, 1752), and *The Origin of Printing* [with Supplement by Bowyer and Nichols] (London, 1776–81).

Miltiades (d. 314); st; pope.

Miltiades the Elder (*fl.* 6th century BC); Athenian statesman.

Miltiades the Younger (*c.*554–*c.*489 BC);

Athenian general; victor at the battle of Marathon.

Milton, John (1608–74); Gibbon owned two editions of his *Poetical Works* (2 vols, London, 1753; 3 vols, London, 1761), and his *Works, Historical, Political and Miscellaneous*, 2 vols (London, 1753).

Minos; legendary ruler of Crete.

Mircond, or Mirchond, or Mirkhond; more correctly, Mir Khwand (1433–98); Persian historian; Gibbon owned his *Historia Priorum Regum Persarum* (Vienna, 1782), *The History of Persia*, tr. J. Stevens (London, 1715), and *Relaciones de Pedro Teixeira del origen, descendencia y succession de los reyes de Persia* (Amberes, 1610).

Mithridates (d. 63 BC); king of Pontus; implacable enemy of Roman power in Asia Minor.

Moawiyah (*c.*602–680); a successor to Mahomet as leader of Islam.

Monaldesco, Ludovico Buonconte (1327–1442); Italian historian.

Mongault, Nicholas Hubert de (1674–1746); editor of Cicero's letters to Atticus.

Monstrelet, Enguerrand de (*c.*1390–1453); chronicler.

Montesquieu, Charles de Sécondat, baron de la Brède et de (1689–1755); *philosophe* and historian; Gibbon owned his *Considérations sur les causes de la grandeur des romains, et de leur décadence* (Paris, 1755), *Lettres* (London, 1767), two editions of his *Œuvres*, 3 vols (Amsterdam and Leipzig, 1758; London, 1772), and his *Œuvres posthumes* (Lausanne, 1784).

Montfaucon, Bernard de (1655–1741); *érudit*; Gibbon owned his *L'Antiquité expliquée et représentée*, 10 vols (Paris, 1719–24), *Diarium Italicum* (Paris, 1702) and *Les Monumens de la monarchie françoise*, 5 vols (Paris, 1729–33).

More, Sir Thomas (1478–1535); politician, historian, man of letters, theological polemicist; Gibbon owned his *De Optimo Reipublicæ Statu, deque Nova Insula Utopia Libri II* (Glasgow, 1750).

Moses of Chorene (*fl.* 5th century AD); father of Armenian literature; author of a *History of Armenia*; Gibbon owned his *Historiæ Armeniacæ Libri III* (London, 1736).

Mosheim, Johann Lorenz von (1694–1755); ecclesiastical historian; Gibbon owned his *De Rebus Christianorum ante Constantinum Magnum Commentarii* (Helmstadt, 1753), *Dissertationum ad Historiam Ecclesiasticam Pertinentium Volumen Primum et Alterum*, 2 vols (Altona and Lubeck, 1767), two editions of *An Ecclesiastical History* (2 vols, London, 1765; 6 vols, London, 1782), and *Institutionum Historiæ Ecclesiasticæ Libri Quatuor* (Helmstadt, 1764).

Moyle, Walter (1672–1721); Whig political writer; Gibbon owned his *Works*, 3 vols (London, 1726–7).

Muratori, Lodovico Antonio (1672–1750); antiquarian; Gibbon owned his *Annali d'Italia*, 18 vols (Milan, 1753–6), *Antiquitates Italicæ Medii Aevi*, 6 vols (Milan, 1738–42), *Delle Antichità Estensi ed Italiane*, 2 vols (Modena, 1717–40), *Dissertazioni sopra le Antichità Italiane*, 3 vols (Milan, 1751), and *Novus Thesaurus Veterum Inscriptionum*, 4 vols (Milan, 1739–42).

N

Nardini, Famiano (d. 1661); historian; Gibbon owned his *Roma Antica* (Rome, 1704).

Narses (*c.*480–574); Byzantine general under Justinian I.

Nepos, Cornelius (100–*c.*25 BC); Roman historian and friend of Cicero; Gib-

bon owned his *Vitæ Excellentium Imperatorum* (Amsterdam, 1707).

Nero Claudius Cæsar Drusus Germanicus (37–68); Roman emperor and tyrant.

Nerva Cæsar Augustus (*c.*30–98); Roman emperor.

Nestor, king of Pylos; counsellor to the Greeks at the siege of Troy.

Newton, Sir Isaac (1642–1727); mathematician and chronologist; Gibbon owned his *The Chronology of Ancient Kingdoms Amended* (London, 1728) and *Opticks* (London, 1704).

Nicetas (*c.*1000–*c.*1080); Byzantine mystic, theologian and polemicist.

Nicholas IV (1227–92); pope.

Nicholas V (d. 1333); pope.

Niebuhr, Carsten (1733–1815); German explorer and scientist; Gibbon owned his *Description de l'Arabie* (Copenhagen, 1773) and *Voyage en Arabie*, 2 vols (Amsterdam, 1776, 1780).

Nolli, Giovanni Battista (*fl.* 1759); cartographer of modern Rome.

Noodt, Gerard (1647–1725); Dutch scholar of Roman law.

Numa Pompilius (*fl. c.*700 BC); second king of Rome.

O

Ockley, Simon (1678–1720); orientalist; Gibbon owned his *The Conquest of Syria, Persia, and Ægypt, by the Saracens* (i.e. *The History of the Saracens*), 2 vols (London, 1708, 1718).

Omar (*c.*586–644); adviser to Mahomet; second caliph.

Oricellarius, Bernardus, or Rucellai (1449–1514); philosopher, historian and ambassador; Gibbon owned a manuscript copy of his *Descriptio Urbis Romæ*.

Origen (*c.*185–*c.*254); theologian and biblical scholar; Gibbon owned his

Contra Celsum (Cambridge, 1677) and *Traité contre Celse* (Amsterdam, 1700).

Orosius, Paulus (*fl.* 414–17); theologian; defender of orthodoxy; historian; Gibbon owned his *Adversus Paganos Historiarum Libri Septem* (Leyden, 1738).

'*Ossian*'; the pseudonym under which James Macpherson published his 'translations' of spurious Gaelic poetry; Gibbon owned *The Works of Ossian* (London, 1765).

Otho Cæsar Augustus, Marcus (32–69); Roman emperor.

Otter, Jean (1707–48); orientalist; Gibbon owned his *Voyage en Turquie et en Perse*, 2 vols (Paris, 1748).

Ovid, Publius Ovidius Naso (43 BC–AD 17); Roman poet; banished by Augustus in AD 8 for alleged immorality; Gibbon owned the *Commentaires sur les Épistres d'Ovide*, 2 vols (The Hague, 1716), *Metamorphoseon Libri XV* (London, 1778), *Opera Omnia*, 4 vols (Amsterdam, 1727), and *Opera quæ Supersunt*, 3 vols (Paris, 1762).

P

Pachomius (*c*.290–346); st; founder of cenobitic monasticism.

Pagi, Antoine (1624–95); chronologist; Gibbon owned his *Critica Historico-Chronologica in Universos Annales Ecclesiasticos Baronii*, 4 vols (Antwerp, 1727), and *Dissertatio Hypatica, seu de Consulibus Cæsareis* (Lyons, 1682).

Paris, Matthew (d. 1259); historian; Gibbon owned his *Historia Major* (London, 1684).

Paul the Deacon, or Paulus Diaconus, or Paul Warnefrid (*c*.720–*c*.799); historian of the Lombards; author of *De Gestis Langobardorum*.

Pausanias (*fl.* 143–76); Greek traveller

and geographer; Gibbon owned his *Græciæ Descriptio* (Leipzig, 1696) and *Pausanias, ou voyage historique de la Grèce*, tr. Gedoyn, 2 vols (Paris, 1731).

Pearson, John (1613–86); bp of Chester; author of the *Vindiciæ Epistolarum s. Ignatii* (Cambridge, 1672); Gibbon owned his *Opera Posthuma Chronologica* (London, 1687, 1688).

Pelloutier, Simon (1694–1757); historian; Gibbon owned his *Histoire des Celtes*, 8 vols (Paris, 1769–71).

Penelope; wife of Odysseus, king of Ithaca.

Pennant, Thomas (1726–98); traveller and naturalist; Gibbon owned his *Arctic Zoology*, 2 vols (London, 1784, 1787), *British Zoology*, 4 vols (London, 1768, 1770), *A History of Quadrupeds*, 2 vols (London, 1781), *The Journey to Snowdon* (London, 1781), *Some Account of London* (London, 1791), *Synopsis of Quadrupeds* (Chester, 1771), *A Tour in Scotland*, 3 vols (London, 1776), and *A Tour in Wales* (London, 1778).

Pericles (*c*.495–429 BC); Athenian statesman; constructor of the Parthenon.

Perron, Jacques Davy du (1556–1618); abp of Sens; cardinal.

Persius Flaccus, Aulus (34–62); Roman satirist.

Persona, Cristoforo (1416–1484); monk; classical scholar; early Latin translator of Procopius.

Petavius, Denis, or Petau (1583–1652); *érudit*; Jesuit; translator and editor of Julian the Apostate, Synesius, Cicero and St Nicephorus, patriarch of Constantinople; Gibbon owned his *De Doctrina Temporum*, 3 vols (Antwerp, 1703).

Petit de la Croix, François, the elder, or Pétis de la Croix (1622–95); orientalist; Gibbon owned two editions of his *Histoire du grand Genghizcan* (Paris, 1710; tr. London, 1722), to which he commonly referred as the *Vie de Gengiscan*.

Petrarch, Francesco, or Petrarca (1304–74); scholar, poet and humanist; Gibbon owned his *Epistolarum Familiarium Libri XIV* (Lyons, 1601), *Le Rime* (Modena, 1711) and *Opera* (Basle, 1581).

Petronius Arbiter, Gaius (d. AD 66); author of the *Satyricon*, a portrait of Roman life in the 1st century AD; Gibbon owned his *Satyricon Quæ Supersunt* (Utrecht, 1709).

Peysonnel, Claude Charles de (1700–57); historian and ethnologist; Gibbon owned his *Examen du livre intitulé Considérations sur la guerre actuelle des Turcs, par M. Volney* (Amsterdam, 1788) and *Observations historiques et géographiques sur les peuples barbares qui ont habité les bords du Danube et du Pont-Euxin* (Paris, 1765).

Phidias (*fl. c.*490–430 BC); Athenian sculptor.

Philip III (1396–1467); duke of Burgundy.

Philip of Macedon (382–336 BC); king of Macedonia; father of Alexander the Great.

Philippus, Marcus Julius, commonly known as Philip (the Arab) (d. 249); Roman emperor.

Philo Judæus (*c.*15 BC–*c.*AD 45); Greek-speaking Jewish philosopher; Gibbon owned his *Opera*, 2 vols (London, 1742).

Philostorgius (*c.*368–*c.*433); Byzantine historian; Gibbon owned his *Ecclesiasticæ Historiæ Libri XII* (Geneva, 1643).

Philostratus, Flavius (*c.*170–*c.*245); Greek philosopher; author of the *Lives of the Sophists*; Gibbon owned his *Philostratorum quæ Supersunt Omnia* (Leipzig, 1709).

Photius (*c.*820–*c.*891); patriarch of Constantinople and historian; Gibbon owned his *Epistolæ* (London, 1651), *Librorum quos Legit Photius* (Augsburg, 1601), *Myriobiblon* (Rouen, 1653) and *Nomocanon* (Paris, 1615).

Phranza, George, or Phranzes (*fl.* 15th century); Byzantine historian.

Pignoria, Lorenzo (1571–1631); Jesuit; man of letters and historian; Gibbon owned his *De Servis Commentarius* (Padua, 1656).

Pindar (*c.*518–*c.*438 BC); Greek lyric poet; Gibbon owned his *Carmina*, 2 vols (Göttingen, 1773, 1774), *Odes*, tr. G. West, 2 vols (London, 1753), and *Olympia, Nemea, Pythia, Isthmia* (Oxford, 1697).

Plato (*c.*428–*c.*348 BC); ancient Greek philosopher; Gibbon owned his *De Rebus Divinis Dialogi Selecti* (Cambridge, 1683), *De Republica Libri X*, 2 vols (Cambridge, 1713), *Dialogi Tres* (Oxford, 1771), *Dialogi Quatuor*, 2 vols (Leipzig, 1783), *Dialogi V* (Oxford, 1765), *Dialogues*, tr. Floyer Sydenham, 4 vols (London, 1767–80), *Euthydemus et Gorgias* (Oxford, 1784), *Les Œuvres traduites*, 2 vols (Amsterdam, 1700), *Opera*, 3 vols (Geneva, 1578), *Parmenides* (Oxford, 1728) and *The Republic*, tr. H. Spens (Glasgow, 1763).

Pliny the Elder, C. Plinius Secundus (23–79); author of the *Natural History*; Gibbon owned two editions of his *Historiæ Naturalis Libri XXXVII* (3 vols, Paris, 1723; 6 vols, Paris, 1779) and his *Histoire Naturelle*, 12 vols (Paris, 1771–82).

Pliny the Younger, C. Plinius Cæcilius Secundus (61–113); author of the *Epistles*; Gibbon owned his *An Address of Thanks to a Good Prince, Presented in the Panegyrick of Pliny upon Trajan* (London, 1686), *C. Plinii Panegyricus* (Amsterdam, 1653), *Epistolæ et Panegyricus* (Leyden, 1653), *Epistolarum Libri Decem* (Amsterdam, 1734), *The Letters of Pliny the Consul*, tr. W. Melmoth, 2 vols (London, 1770), and *Panegyricus Cæsari imp. Nervæ Trajano Aug. Dictus* (Nuremberg, 1746).

Plotinus (205–70); neoplatonic philosopher.

Plutarch (*c.*46–*c.*119); biographer, philosopher and man of letters; Gibbon owned two editions of his *Apophthegmata* (Geneva, 1568; London, 1741), *De Iside et Osiride* (Cambridge, 1744), *Liber de Sera Numinis Vindicta* (Leyden, 1772), *Liber Quomodo Juveni Audienda Sint Poemata* (Glasgow, 1753), *Les Œuvres morales et meslées,* tr. Amyot, 7 vols (Paris, 1574), *Opera,* 2 vols (Frankfort, 1599), *Les Vies des hommes illustres,* tr. Amyot, 6 vols (Paris, 1567), and *Vitæ Parallelæ,* 5 vols (London, 1723–9).

Pocock, Edward (1604–91); orientalist; editor of *Annales Eutychii,* 2 vols (Oxford, 1656), and of Abulpharagius' *Historia Compendiosa Dynastiarum* (Oxford, 1663), which Gibbon owned.

Pocock, Richard (1704–65); bp of Meath; Gibbon owned his *A Description of the East,* 2 vols (London, 1743, 1745).

Poggius, or Poggio Bracciolini (1380–1459); Italian humanist; Gibbon owned his *Historiæ de Varietate Fortunæ Libri Quatuor* (Paris, 1723).

Pollio, Trebellius (*fl.* 290–300); one of the compilers of the *Historia Augusta;* Gibbon owned the *Historiæ Augustæ Scriptores Sex* (Paris, 1620).

Polybius (*c.*200–*c.*118 BC); Greek historian who composed a history of the rise of the Roman Republic; Gibbon owned his *General History,* tr. Hampton, 4 vols (London, 1772, 1773), *Histoire,* tr. Thuillier, 7 vols (Amsterdam, 1753, 1759), three editions of *Historiarum Libri* (Paris, 1609; 3 vols, Amsterdam, 1670; 5 vols, Leipzig, 1789–92) and *Polybii . . . Excerpta* (Paris, 1634).

Pompey the Great (106–48 BC); Gnæus Pompeius Magnus; Roman statesman and general.

Pope, Alexander (1688–1744); poet, editor and translator; Gibbon owned his *Poetical Works,* 3 vols (Glasgow, 1785), *Works,* 9 vols (London, 1770), and *Works, with the Notes of Mr. Warburton,* 9 vols (London, 1751).

Porphyry (*c.*234–*c.*305); Greek neoplatonic philosopher; biographer of Plotinus.

Praxiteles (*fl.* 370–330 BC); greatest of ancient Greek sculptors.

Prideaux, Humphrey (1648–1724); orientalist; Gibbon owned two editions of his *The Old and New Testament Connected in the History of the Jews* (London, 1718, 1749) and *The True Nature of Imposture Fully Displayed in the Life of Mahomet* (London, 1718).

Priestley, Joseph (1733–1804); theologian and scientist; Gibbon owned his *Disquisitions Relating to Matter and Spirit,* 2 vols (Birmingham, 1782), *A Free Discussion of the Doctrines of Materialism and Philosophical Necessity, in a Correspondence between Dr. Price and Dr. Priestley* (London, 1778), *An History of the Corruptions of Christianity,* 2 vols (Birmingham, 1782), *Letters to a Philosophical Unbeliever. Part II, Containing a State of the Evidence of Revealed Religion, with Animadversions on the Two Last Chapters of the First Volume of Mr. Gibbon's History* (Birmingham, 1787) and *The Rudiments of English Grammar* (London, 1768).

Priscus of Panium (*fl.* 5th century AD); historian and rhetorician.

Proclus (*c.*410–485); last of the major neoplatonic philosophers.

Procopius of Cæsarea (*fl.* early 6th century AD); historian of Byzantium; Gibbon owned his *Arcana Historia* (Leyden, 1623) and *Historiarum Libri VIII* (Augsburg, 1607).

Prosper-Tyro, or Prosper of Aquitaine (c.390–463); st; historian of France.

Prudentius Clemens, Aurelius (348–c.405); Christian Latin poet; author of the Psychomachia; Gibbon owned two editions of his Opera (Amsterdam, 1667; Parma, 1788).

Ptolemy, Claudius Ptolemæus (fl. 127–145); astronomer, geographer and mathematician; posited that the earth was at the centre of the universe.

Pulcheria (399–453); Roman empress; regent for Theodosius II, her younger brother.

Pythagoras (c.580–c.500 BC); Greek philosopher and mathematician.

Q

Quintilian (c.35–c.96); Latin educator and rhetorician; author of the Institutio Oratoria; Gibbon owned his Institutionum Oratoriarum Libri Duodecim, 2 vols (Leyden, 1665), and Opera, 2 vols (Leyden, 1720).

R

Raderus, Matthæus, or Rader (1561–1634); Jesuit; German classical scholar; editor of Petrus Siculus, Historia de Vana Manichæorum Hæresi (Ingolstadt, 1604).

Ramusio, Giovanni Battista (1485–1557); humanist and geographer; Gibbon owned his Navigationi et viaggi, 3 vols (Venice, 1550–56).

Raphael, Raffaello Sanzio (1483–1520); painter and architect of the Italian High Renaissance.

Raynal, Guillaume Thomas F. (1713–96); historian and philosophe; Gibbon owned two editions of his Histoire Philosophique et Politique des . . . Deux Indes (7 vols, The Hague, 1774; 4 vols, Geneva, 1780).

Reitz, Johann Frederik (1695–1778); classical scholar; editor of Lucian.

Reland, Adrian (1676–1718); orientalist; author of De Religione Mohammedicâ (Utrecht, 1717); Gibbon owned his De Spoliis Templi Hierosolymitani in Arcu Titiano (Utrecht, 1716), Dissertationum Miscellanearum Pars Prima (–Tertia), 3 vols (Utrecht, 1706–8), and Palæstina ex Monumentis Veteribus Illustrata, 2 vols (Utrecht, 1714).

Renaudot, Eusèbe (1646–1720); historian and orientalist; Gibbon owned his Anciennes relations des Indes et de la Chine (Paris, 1718), Ancient Accounts of India and China, by two Mahommedan Travellers (London, 1733) and Historia Patriarcharum Alexandrinorum Jacobitarum (Paris, 1713).

Richard of Cirencester (d.1401?); monk and chronicler; author of De Sitû Britanniæ.

Romulus; legendary founder of Rome.

Rufinus, Tyrannius (c.345–c.410); priest, writer and theologian; translator of Greek texts into Latin.

Ruinart, Thierry (1657–1709); editor of Gregory of Tours; Gibbon owned his Acta Primorum Martyrum (Amsterdam, 1713) and Historia Persecutionis Vandalicæ (Paris, 1694).

Rycaut, Sir Paul (1628–1700); traveller and author; Gibbon owned his The History of the Present State of the Ottoman Empire (London, 1675).

S

Sabas (439–532); st; Palestinian monk; defender of orthodox doctrines concerning the nature of Christ.

Sagredo, Giovanni (1551–1614); traveller and writer; Gibbon owned his Memorie istoriche de' monarchi ottomanni (Venice, 1677).

Ste Palaye, Jean Baptiste de la Curne de

(1697–1781); historian; author of *Mémoires sur l'ancienne chevalerie*.

Sale, George (1697–1736); orientalist; Persian scholar; editor of the Koran.

Sallust, Gaius Sallustius Crispus (*c*.86–*c*.35 BC); Roman historian; Gibbon owned his *La Congiuratione di Catilina* (Naples, 1760), *Histoire de la république romaine*, 3 vols (Dijon, 1777) and four editions of his *Opera* (Cambridge, 1710; 2 vols, Amsterdam, 1742; Glasgow, 1751; Birmingham, 1773).

Sallust; præfect of Julian the Apostate in Gaul.

Sallust; præfect of Julian the Apostate in the East; recall Gibbon's admonition, in n. 60 to ch. XXII, that 'the two Sallusts, the præfect of Gaul, and the præfect of the East, must be carefully distinguished' – an instruction it is easier to applaud than to follow.

Salmasius, Claudius, or Claude de Saumaise (1588–1653); classical scholar and *érudit*.

Salvian of Marseilles (*c*.390–*c*.484); theologian; Gibbon owned his *De Gubernatione Dei* (Paris, 1608).

Sandys, George (1578–1644); poet and traveller; Gibbon owned his *Travels* (London, 1673).

Sapor I (d. AD 272); Persian king; captured the emperor Valerian at Edessa in 260.

Sapor II (309–79); Persian king against whom Julian the Apostate mounted the Persian expedition in which he lost his life.

Sappho (*fl. c*.610–590 BC); female Greek lyric poet.

Sarpi, Paolo (1552–1623); historian; Gibbon owned his *Histoire du Concile de Trente*, 2 vols (London, 1736), *Istoria del Concilio Tridentino*, 2 vols (London, 1757), and *Opere*, 6 vols (Helmstatt, 1761–5).

Schultens, Albert (1686–1756); Dutch orientalist and linguist.

Scipio Æmilianus (184–129 BC); Roman general and statesman; destroyer of Carthage at the end of the Third Punic War (149–146 BC).

Scipio Africanus (236–184 BC); Roman general and statesman; defeated Hannibal at the battle of Zama (202 BC).

Selden, John (1584–1654); jurist; Gibbon owned his *The Historie of Tithes* (London, 1618) and *Opera Omnia*, 3 vols (London, 1726).

Seneca, Lucius Annæus (4 BC–AD 65); Roman philosopher, statesman and dramatist; Gibbon owned his *L. A. Senecæ ... Singulares Sententiæ* (Leyden, 1727), *Les Œuvres de Sénèque*, tr. La Grange, 7 vols (Paris, 1778, 1779), two editions of his *Opera* (Antwerp, 1632; 3 vols, Leyden, 1649), *Syntagma Tragœdiæ Latinæ*, 2 vols (Antwerp, 1593), and *Tragœdiæ* (Delft, 1728).

Servetus, Michael, or Miguel Serveto (?1511–53); Spanish physician and theologian; condemned and executed as an heretic.

Servius Tullius (*fl.* 578–534 BC); sixth king of Rome.

Severini, Joannes (1716–89); antiquarian; Gibbon owned his *Pannonia Veterum Monumentis Illustrata* (Leipzig, 1770).

Severus, Septimius (146–211); Roman emperor, who converted the principate into a military monarchy.

Shaw, Thomas (1694–1751); traveller and explorer; Gibbon owned his *Travels, or Observations Relating to Several Parts of Barbary and the Levant* (London, 1757).

Siculus, Peter; author of the *Historia de Vana Manichæorum Hæresi*, ed. Matthæus Rader (Ingolstadt, 1604).

Sidonius, C. Sollius Modestus Apollinaris (*c*.430–*c*.479); poet; bp of Clermont; Gibbon owned two editions of his *Opera* (Paris, 1599, 1652).

Simon, Richard (1638–1712); biblical scholar; Gibbon owned his *Bibliothèque critique: ou recueil de diverses pièces critiques, publiées par Mr. de Sainjore*, 4 vols (Basle, 1709–10), *Histoire critique des principaux commentateurs du nouveau Testament* (Rotterdam, 1693), *Histoire critique des versions du nouveau Testament* (Rotterdam, 1689), *Histoire critique du vieux Testament* (Amsterdam, 1685) and *Réponse au livre [by J. le Clerc] intitulé Sentimens de quelques théologiens de Hollande sur l'histoire critique du vieux Testament* (Amsterdam, '1621').

Sixtus V (1520–90); pope.

Smith, Adam (1723–90); political economist and moral philosopher; Gibbon owned his *An Inquiry into the Nature and Causes of the Wealth of Nations*, 2 vols (London, 1776), and two editions of *The Theory of Moral Sentiments* (London, 1767, 1790).

Socrates (*c.*470–399 BC); Athenian philosopher.

Socrates Scholasticus (*c.*380–*c.*450); Byzantine church historian.

Solinus, Caius Julius; Gibbon owned his *Cl. Salmasii Plinianæ Exercitationes in C. Julii Solini Polyhistora. Item C. J. Solini Polyhistor Emendatus*, 2 vols (Utrecht, 1688, 1689), *Polyhistor* (Leipzig, 1777).

Sophocles (*c.*496–406 BC); Athenian tragic dramatist; Gibbon owned *Antigone et Trachiniæ* (Oxford, 1708), *Œdipe*, tr. Boivin (Paris, 1729), *The Tragedies*, tr. T. Francklin (London, 1778), *Tragédies*, tr. Dacier (Paris, 1693), *Tragédies*, tr. Dupuis (Paris, 1761), and three editions of his *Tragœdiæ* (Geneva, 1568; Leyden, 1593; Strasburg, 1786).

Sozomen (*c.*400–*c.*450); lawyer and church historian.

Spanheim, Ezechiel (1629–1710); classical scholar and *érudit*; editor of Julian the Apostate; Gibbon owned his *Dissert-ationes de Præstantia et Usu Numismatum Antiquorum*, 2 vols (London, Amsterdam, 1717), *In Callimachi Hymnos Observationes* (Utrecht, 1697) and *Orbis Romanus* (London, 1703).

Spartacus (d. 71 BC); Thracian gladiator; leader of a slave uprising against Roman power in Italy.

Spelman, Edward (d. 1767); translator of Xenophon; Gibbon owned his translation of *The Expedition of Cyrus* (London, 1749).

Spence, Joseph (1699–1768); anecdotalist and man of letters; Gibbon owned his *An Essay on Mr. Pope's Odyssey* (London, 1747) and *Polymetis* (London, 1755).

Sponde, Henri de, or Spondanus (1568–1643); bp of Pamiers; church historian; author of *Ecclesiastical Annals*.

Stephanus, Henricus, or Henri Étienne (1528–98); classical scholar; editor of the *Anthologia Græca*, and of Plutarch.

Stephanus, Robertus, or Robert Estienne (1503–59); classical scholar and author of *Thesaurus Linguæ Latinæ*.

Strabo (?64 BC–AD ?23); Greek geographer and historian; Gibbon owned his *Rerum Geographicarum Libri XVII*, 2 vols (Amsterdam, 1707).

Stukeley, William (1687–1765); antiquarian; Gibbon owned his *The Medallic History of M. A. Valerius Carausius, Emperor in Brittain*, 2 vols (London, 1757, 1759).

Suarés, Joseph Maria; bp; Gibbon owned his *Prænestes Antiquæ Libri Duo* (Rome, 1655).

Suetonius Tranquillus, Gaius (*c.*69–*c.*122); Roman biographer and antiquarian; Gibbon owned four editions of his *Historiæ* (Amsterdam, 1697; Utrecht, 1708; 2 vols, Amsterdam, 1736; Leipzig, 1775).

Suidas (*fl. c.*1000); Byzantine lexicographer; Gibbon owned his *Lexicon*, 3 vols (Cambridge, 1705).

Sulla, Lucius Cornelius (138–78 BC); Roman statesman and dictator.

Sulpicius Severus (*c.*363–*c.*420); early Christian ascetic; biographer of Martin of Tours.

Symmachus, Quintus Aurelius Nemmius (d. 524); Roman senator; friend of Boethius; Gibbon owned two editions of his *Epistolæ* (Paris, 1604; Naples, 1617).

T

Tacitus, Gaius Cornelius (*c.*56–*c.*120); Roman historian; admired by Gibbon as a model of the philosophic historian; Gibbon owned four editions of his *Opera* (Antwerp, 1627; 2 vols, Leyden, 1686, 1687; 2 vols, Utrecht, 1721; 4 vols, Paris, 1771), *Tibère, ou les six premiers livres des Annales*, tr. La Bléterie, 3 vols (Paris, 1768), *Traduction de Quelques Ouvrages de Tacite*, tr. La Bléterie, 2 vols (Paris, 1755), and his *Works*, tr. T. Gordon, 2 vols (London, 1728, 1731).

Tavernier, Jean Baptiste, or Taberna (1622–86); theologian; Gibbon owned his *Six voyages en Turquie, en Perse et aux Indes*, 2 vols (Paris, 1692), and *Recueil de plusieurs relations et traitez* (Paris, 1692).

Temple, Sir William (1628–99); statesman and man of letters; Gibbon owned two editions of his *Works* (2 vols, London, 1721; 4 vols, London, 1770).

Templeman, Thomas; Gibbon owned his *A New Survey of the Globe* (London, 1729).

Tertullian, Quintus Septimius Florens Tertullianus (*c.*155–post 220); early Christian theologian and polemicist; Gibbon owned his *Apologeticus*

(Leyden, 1718) and *Opera* (Paris, 1689).

Theodora (*c.*500–548); Byzantine empress; wife of Justinian I.

Theodoric (*c.*454–526); king of the Ostrogoths.

Theodosius (347–95); Roman emperor; suppressor of paganism and Arianism.

Theodotus of Ancyra (d. *c.*446); bp of Ancyra; theologian; opponent of Nestorianism.

Theophanes (*c.*752–*c.*818); st; the Confessor; monk, theologian and chronicler; author of *Chronographia*, ed. J. Goar (Paris, 1648).

Theophilus (*fl.* early 5th century AD); st; abp of Alexandria; active in the destruction of pagan temples.

Theophrastus (*c.*372–*c.*287 BC); Greek philosopher; pupil of Aristotle; Gibbon owned two editions of *Les Caractères de Théophraste et de La Bruyère* (2 vols, Amsterdam, 1743; 2 vols, Paris, 1775), three editions of *Characteres* (Cambridge, 1712; Coburg, 1763; Oxford, 1754), and *Theophrastus's History of Stones*, tr. John Hill (London, 1746).

Thevenot, Jean de (1633–67); traveller; Gibbon owned his *Travels into the Levant* (London, 1687) and *Voyages tant en Europe qu'en Asie et en Afrique*, 5 vols (Paris, 1689).

Thrasea Pætus, Publius Clodius (d. AD 66); Roman senator; opponent of Nero.

Thucydides (*fl.* late 5th century BC); Greek historian of the Peloponnesian War between Athens and Sparta; Gibbon owned two editions of *De Bello Peloponnesiaco* (Amsterdam, 1731; 8 vols, Glasgow, 1759).

Tiberius, Cæsar Augustus (42 BC–AD 37); Roman emperor; in his last years, of tyrannical tendencies.

Tibullus, Albius (*c.*55–*c.*19 BC); Roman poet; Gibbon owned his *A. Tibulli* *quæ Exstant* (Amsterdam, 1708) and *Carmina* (Leipzig, 1777).

Tillemont, Louis Sébastien le Nain de (1637–98); ecclesiastical historian; Gibbon owned two editions of his *Histoire des empereurs* (5 vols, Brussels, 1707; 6 vols, Paris, 1720–38) and *Mémoires pour servir à l'histoire ecclési-astique des six premiers siècles*, 10 vols (Brussels, 1706).

Tillotson, John (1630–94); abp of Canterbury; latitudinarian; Gibbon owned his *Works*, 10 vols (Dublin, 1739).

Timour (1336–1405); Turkic conqueror in Asia Minor and the near East; in English commonly called Tamerlane.

Tiraboschi, Girolamo (1731–94); historian of Italian literature; Gibbon owned his *Histoire de la littérature d'Italie*, 5 vols (Berne, 1784), and *Storia della letteratura italiana*, 10 vols (Modena, 1786–90).

Titus Vespasianus Augustus (39–81); Roman emperor; conqueror of Jerusalem.

Totila (d. 552); king of the Ostrogoths.

Tott, François de (1733–93); diplomat and soldier; Gibbon owned his *Mémoires sur les Turcs et les Tartares* (Amsterdam, 1784).

Tournefort, Joseph Pitton de (1656–1708); traveller; Gibbon owned his *Relation d'un voyage du Levant*, 3 vols (Lyons, 1717).

Trajan (53–117); the first Roman emperor to be born outside Italy.

Tzetzes, Joannes (*fl.* 12th century); monk, historian, scholar and poet; author of *Chiliads*.

U

Ulysses; king of Ithaca; most cunning of the Greek leaders at the siege of Troy.

Usher, James, or Ussher (1581–1656); abp of Armagh; historian and chronologist; Gibbon owned his *Annales Veteris et Novi Testamenti* (Geneva, 1722) and *Britannicarum Ecclesiarum Antiquitates* (London, 1687).

V

Vacca, Flaminius (*c.*1538–*c.*1592); sculptor and antiquarian.

Valentinian I (321–75); Roman emperor.

Valentinian II (371–92); Roman emperor.

Valentinian III (419–55); Roman emperor.

Valerian, Publius Licinius Valerianus (d. 260); Roman emperor.

Valerius Maximus (*fl. c.*AD 20); Roman historian and moralist.

Valle, Pietro Della (1586–1652); traveller; Gibbon owned his *Viaggi, divisi in tre parti*, 4 vols (Rome, 1650–63).

Valturio, Roberto (*fl.*1473–83); minister and counsellor; author of *De Re Militari Libri XII* (Verona, 1483).

Vandale, Jacob, or Jacob van Dalen, or Jacob Cornelisz (1608–63); theologian.

Varro, Marcus Terentius (116–27 BC); scholar and satirist; Gibbon owned his *Opera* (Geneva, 1581).

Varus, Publius Quintilius (d. AD 9); Roman general; lost three legions in a calamitous defeat at the hands of an army of confederated German tribes.

Vegetius Renatus, Flavius (*fl.* 4th century AD); Roman military expert; Gibbon owned his *Institutions militaires* (Paris, 1643).

Velleius Paterculus (*c.*19 BC–AD 30); Roman soldier and historian; Gibbon owned four editions of his *Historiæ Romanæ* (Paris, 1620, 1719, 1777; 2 vols, Leyden, 1779).

Vespasian, Titus Flavius Vespasianus (9–79); Roman emperor.

Vignoles, Alphonse des (1649–1744); *éru-dit*; author of *Histoire critique de la république des lettres* (1712–15).

Virgil, Publius Virgilius Maro (70–19 BC); greatest Roman poet; author of the *Æneid*; Gibbon owned his *Bucolica, Georgica et Æneis* (Glasgow, 1758), *Bucolicorum Eclogæ Decem* (London, 1749), *Georgicorum Libri Quatuor* (London, 1741), two editions of *Les Géorgiques*, tr. J. Delille (Paris, 1771, 1780), *La Quarta Egloga* (Rome, 1758), three editions of his *Opera* (2 vols, Leeuwarden, 1717; 4 vols, Leipzig, 1767–75, 1788), *Les Poésies*, 4 vols (Paris, 1729), and two editions of his *Works* (tr. John Dryden, 3 vols, London, 1721; tr. C. Pitt and J. Warton, 4 vols, London, 1753).

Vitellius, Aulus (15–69); Roman emperor.

Volaterra, Raphael de, or Volaterranus, Raphael Maffeius (d. 1522); early Latin translator of Homer, Procopius and St Basil.

Voltaire, François Marie Arouet de (1694–1778); *philosophe*; man of letters; Gibbon owned two editions of his *Collection complette des œuvres* (30 vols, Geneva, 1768–77; 57 vols, Lausanne, 1780–81), *History of the War of 1741* (London, 1756), *Mémoires écrits par lui-même* (Amsterdam, 1785) and *Le Siècle de Louis XIV* (London, 1752).

Vossius, Gerardus Joannes (1577–1649); classical scholar, critic, linguist and theologian; Gibbon owned his *De Historicis Græcis* (Leyden, 1651), *De Historicis Latinis* (Leyden, 1651), *De Septuaginta Interpretibus* (The Hague, 1661–3), *De Studiorum Ratione Opuscula* (Utrecht, 1651), *Etymologicon Linguæ Latinæ* (Leyden, 1664), and *Opera*, 6 vols (Amsterdam, 1701).

W

Walton, Brian (1600?–1661); bp of Chester; biblical scholar; author of *The Considerator Considered: or, A Brief View of Certain Considerations upon the Biblia Polyglotta, the Prolegomena and Appendix therof* (London, 1659).

Warburton, William (1698–1779); bp of Gloucester; scholar and controversialist; Gibbon owned his *The Alliance between Church and State* (London, 1736), *The Divine Legation of Moses Demonstrated*, 5 vols (London, 1765), *The Doctrine of Grace*, 2 vols (London, 1763), *Julian* (London, 1751) and *Tracts* (London, 1789).

Warton, Thomas (1728–90); poet, classical scholar and historian of English poetry; Gibbon owned his *History of English Poetry*, 3 vols (London, 1774–81), *Life of Sir Thomas Pope* (London, 1772) and *Observations on the Fairy Queen of Spenser*, 2 vols (London, 1762).

Wesselingius, Petrus, or Wesseling (1692–1764); librarian and legal scholar; editor of Diodorus Siculus; Gibbon owned his *Vetera Romanorum Itineraria* (Amsterdam, 1735).

West, Gilbert (1703–56); translator of Pindar; author of *Dissertation on the Olympic Games*; Gibbon owned his translation of Pindar's *Odes*, 2 vols (London, 1753).

Wetstein, Johann Jacob (1693–1754); German professor of theology.

Whiston, William (1667–1752); divine; Lucasian professor of mathematics; natural scientist; Boyle lecturer 1707; of suspected Arian persuasions; Gibbon owned two editions of his *Memoirs* (London, 1773, 1787).

Whitaker, John (1735–1808); historian; Gibbon owned his *Genuine History of the Britons Asserted* (London, 1772), *History of Manchester*, 2 vols (London, 1771, 1775), and *Mary Queen of Scots Vindicated*, 3 vols (London, 1787–8).

White, Joseph (1745–1814); orientalist; Bampton lecturer; editor (with Major Davy) of Tamerlane's *Institutes* (Oxford, 1783); Gibbon owned his *Sermons Preached Before the University of Oxford* (London, 1785).

Wickliff, John, or Wycliffe (c.1330–1384); English theologian, philosopher and religious reformer.

Winckelman, Johann Joachim (1717–68); historian of art; Gibbon owned his *Histoire de l'art chez les anciens*, 2 vols (Amsterdam, 1766), *Histoire de l'art de l'antiquité*, 3 vols (Leipzig, 1781), and *Lettre sur les découvertes d'Herculanum* (Dresden, 1764).

Wolf, Johann Christoph, or Wolfius (1683–1739); translator and editor of the letters of Libanius; Gibbon owned his *Anecdota Græca*, 4 vols (Hamburg, 1722–4) and *Mulierum Græcarum quæ Oratione Prosa Usæ Sunt Fragmenta et Elogia* (Hamburg, 1735).

Wood, Robert (?1717–1771); traveller and politician; Gibbon owned his *An Essay on the Original Genius and Writings of Homer* (London, 1775) and *The Ruins of Balbec* (London, 1757).

X

Xenophon (431–c.350 BC); Greek historian; author of the *Anabasis*; Gibbon owned two editions of his *De*

Cyri Expeditione (Oxford, 1735; Glasgow, 1764), three editions of *De Cyri Institutione* (2 vols, Oxford, 1727; 4 vols, Glasgow, 1767; Leipzig, 1784), *The Expedition of Cyrus*, tr. E. Spelman (London, 1749), *Historia Græca* (Leipzig, 1778), the *History of Greece* (Glasgow, 1762), *Memorabilium Socratis Dictorum Libri IV* (Leipzig, 1755), *Œconomicus* (Leipzig, 1749), *Opera*, 5 vols (Oxford, 1700–3), and *Opuscula Politica* (Leipzig, 1778).

Z

Zeno (d. 491); Eastern Roman emperor.

Zenobia, Septimia (d. c.274); queen of the Roman colony of Palmyra.

Zeno of Citium (c.335–c.263 BC); Greek Stoic philosopher.

Zeno of Elea (c.495–c.430 BC); Greek philosopher and mathematician.

Zingis Khan (c.1155–1227); Mongolian warlord and ruler, whose dominion extended from China to the Adriatic.

Zonaras (fl. 11th century); Byzantine historian; Gibbon owned his *Compendium Historiarum* (Basle, 1557) and *Historia*, tr. M. Emilio (Venice, 1560).

Zoroaster (c.628–c.551 BC); religious reformer and founder of Zoroastrianism.

Zwingli, Ulrich, or Zuinglius (1484–1531); Swiss religious reformer.

READ MORE IN PENGUIN

In every corner of the world, on every subject under the sun, Penguin represents quality and variety – the very best in publishing today.

For complete information about books available from Penguin – including Puffins, Penguin Classics and Arkana – and how to order them, write to us at the appropriate address below. Please note that for copyright reasons the selection of books varies from country to country.

In the United Kingdom: Please write to *Dept. EP, Penguin Books Ltd, Bath Road, Harmondsworth, West Drayton, Middlesex UB7 0DA*

In the United States: Please write to *Consumer Services, Penguin Putnam Inc., 405 Murray Hill Parkway, East Rutherford, New Jersey 07073-2136.* VISA and MasterCard holders call 1-800-631-8571 to order Penguin titles

In Canada: Please write to *Penguin Books Canada Ltd, 10 Alcorn Avenue, Suite 300, Toronto, Ontario M4V 3B2*

In Australia: Please write to *Penguin Books Australia Ltd, 487 Maroondah Highway, Ringwood, Victoria 3134*

In New Zealand: Please write to *Penguin Books (NZ) Ltd, Private Bag 102902, North Shore Mail Centre, Auckland 10*

In India: Please write to *Penguin Books India Pvt Ltd, 11 Community Centre, Panchsheel Park, New Delhi 110017*

In the Netherlands: Please write to *Penguin Books Netherlands bv, Postbus 3507, NL-1001 AH Amsterdam*

In Germany: Please write to *Penguin Books Deutschland GmbH, Metzlerstrasse 26, 60594 Frankfurt am Main*

In Spain: Please write to *Penguin Books S. A., Bravo Murillo 19, 1°B, 28015 Madrid*

In Italy: Please write to *Penguin Italia s.r.l., Via Vittorio Emanuele 45la, 20094 Corsico, Milano*

In France: Please write to *Penguin France, 12, Rue Prosper Ferradou, 31700 Blagnac*

In Japan: Please write to *Penguin Books Japan Ltd, Iidabashi KM-Bldg, 2-23-9 Koraku, Bunkyo-Ku, Tokyo 112-0004*

In South Africa: Please write to *Penguin Books South Africa (Pty) Ltd, P.O. Box 751093, Gardenview, 2047 Johannesburg*

READ MORE IN PENGUIN

A CHOICE OF CLASSICS

READ MORE IN PENGUIN

A CHOICE OF CLASSICS

Hesiod/Theognis	**Theogony/Works and Days/Elegies**
Hippocrates	**Hippocratic Writings**
Homer	**The Iliad**
	The Odyssey
Horace	**Complete Odes and Epodes**
Horace/Persius	**Satires and Epistles**
Juvenal	**The Sixteen Satires**
Livy	**The Early History of Rome**
	Rome and Italy
	Rome and the Mediterranean
	The War with Hannibal
Lucretius	**On the Nature of the Universe**
Martial	**Epigrams**
	Martial in English
Ovid	**The Erotic Poems**
	Heroides
	Metamorphoses
	The Poems of Exile
Pausanias	**Guide to Greece (in two volumes)**
Petronius/Seneca	**The Satyricon/The Apocolocyntosis**
Pindar	**The Odes**
Plato	**Early Socratic Dialogues**
	Gorgias
	The Last Days of Socrates (Euthyphro/ The Apology/Crito/Phaedo)
	The Laws
	Phaedrus and Letters VII and VIII
	Philebus
	Protagoras/Meno
	The Republic
	The Symposium
	Theaetetus
	Timaeus/Critias
Plautus	**The Pot of Gold and Other Plays**
	The Rope and Other Plays

READ MORE IN PENGUIN

A CHOICE OF CLASSICS

Pliny	**The Letters of the Younger Pliny**
Pliny the Elder	**Natural History**
Plotinus	**The Enneads**
Plutarch	**The Age of Alexander (Nine Greek Lives)**
	Essays
	The Fall of the Roman Republic (Six Lives)
	The Makers of Rome (Nine Lives)
	Plutarch on Sparta
	The Rise and Fall of Athens (Nine Greek Lives)
Polybius	**The Rise of the Roman Empire**
Procopius	**The Secret History**
Propertius	**The Poems**
Quintus Curtius Rufus	**The History of Alexander**
Sallust	**The Jugurthine War/The Conspiracy of Cataline**
Seneca	**Dialogues and Letters**
	Four Tragedies/Octavia
	Letters from a Stoic
	Seneca in English
Sophocles	**Electra/Women of Trachis/Philoctetes/Ajax**
	The Theban Plays
Suetonius	**The Twelve Caesars**
Tacitus	**The Agricola/The Germania**
	The Annals of Imperial Rome
	The Histories
Terence	**The Comedies (The Girl from Andros/The Self-Tormentor/The Eunuch/Phormio/ The Mother-in-Law/The Brothers)**
Thucydides	**History of the Peloponnesian War**
Virgil	**The Aeneid**
	The Eclogues
	The Georgics
Xenophon	**Conversations of Socrates**
	Hiero the Tyrant
	A History of My Times
	The Persian Expedition

READ MORE IN PENGUIN

A CHOICE OF CLASSICS

READ MORE IN PENGUIN

A CHOICE OF CLASSICS

Oliver Goldsmith	**The Vicar of Wakefield**
Gray/Churchill/Cowper	**Selected Poems**
William Hazlitt	**Selected Writings**
George Herbert	**The Complete English Poems**
Thomas Hobbes	**Leviathan**
Samuel Johnson	**Gabriel's Ladder**
	History of Rasselas, Prince of Abissinia
	Selected Writings
Samuel Johnson/ James Boswell	**A Journey to the Western Islands of Scotland and The Journal of a Tour of the Hebrides**
Matthew Lewis	**The Monk**
John Locke	**An Essay Concerning Human Understanding**
Andrew Marvell	**Complete Poems**
Thomas Middleton	**Five Plays**
John Milton	**Complete Poems**
	Paradise Lost
Samuel Richardson	**Clarissa**
	Pamela
Earl of Rochester	**Complete Works**
Richard Brinsley Sheridan	**The School for Scandal and Other Plays**
Sir Philip Sidney	**Arcadia**
Christopher Smart	**Selected Poems**
Adam Smith	**The Wealth of Nations (Books I–III)**
Tobias Smollett	**Humphrey Clinker**
	Roderick Random
Edmund Spenser	**The Faerie Queene**
Laurence Sterne	**The Life and Opinions of Tristram Shandy**
	A Sentimental Journey Through France and Italy
Jonathan Swift	**Complete Poems**
	Gulliver's Travels
Thomas Traherne	**Selected Poems and Prose**
Henry Vaughan	**Complete Poems**

READ MORE IN PENGUIN

READ MORE IN PENGUIN

A CHOICE OF CLASSICS

Charles Dickens	**American Notes for General Circulation**
	Barnaby Rudge
	Bleak House
	The Christmas Books (in two volumes)
	David Copperfield
	Dombey and Son
	Great Expectations
	Hard Times
	Little Dorrit
	Martin Chuzzlewit
	The Mystery of Edwin Drood
	Nicholas Nickleby
	The Old Curiosity Shop
	Oliver Twist
	Our Mutual Friend
	The Pickwick Papers
	Pictures from Italy
	Selected Journalism 1850–1870
	Selected Short Fiction
	Sketches by Boz
	A Tale of Two Cities
George Eliot	**Adam Bede**
	Daniel Deronda
	Felix Holt
	Middlemarch
	The Mill on the Floss
	Romola
	Scenes of Clerical Life
	Silas Marner
Fanny Fern	**Ruth Hall**
Elizabeth Gaskell	**Cranford/Cousin Phillis**
	The Life of Charlotte Brontë
	Mary Barton
	North and South
	Ruth
	Sylvia's Lovers
	Wives and Daughters

READ MORE IN PENGUIN

A CHOICE OF CLASSICS

Edward Gibbon	**The Decline and Fall of the Roman Empire** (in three volumes)
	Memoirs of My Life
George Gissing	**New Grub Street**
	The Odd Women
William Godwin	**Caleb Williams**
	Concerning Political Justice
Thomas Hardy	**Desperate Remedies**
	The Distracted Preacher and Other Tales
	Far from the Madding Crowd
	Jude the Obscure
	The Hand of Ethelberta
	A Laodicean
	The Mayor of Casterbridge
	A Pair of Blue Eyes
	The Return of the Native
	Selected Poems
	Tess of the d'Urbervilles
	The Trumpet-Major
	Two on a Tower
	Under the Greenwood Tree
	The Well-Beloved
	The Woodlanders
George Lyell	**Principles of Geology**
Lord Macaulay	**The History of England**
Henry Mayhew	**London Labour and the London Poor**
George Meredith	**The Egoist**
	The Ordeal of Richard Feverel
John Stuart Mill	**The Autobiography**
	On Liberty
	Principles of Political Economy
William Morris	**News from Nowhere and Other Writings**
John Henry Newman	**Apologia Pro Vita Sua**
Margaret Oliphant	**Miss Marjoribanks**
Robert Owen	**A New View of Society and Other Writings**
Walter Pater	**Marius the Epicurean**
John Ruskin	**Unto This Last and Other Writings**

READ MORE IN PENGUIN

A CHOICE OF CLASSICS

Walter Scott	**The Antiquary**
	Heart of Mid-Lothian
	Ivanhoe
	Kenilworth
	The Tale of Old Mortality
	Rob Roy
	Waverley
Robert Louis Stevenson	**Kidnapped**
	Dr Jekyll and Mr Hyde and Other Stories
	In the South Seas
	The Master of Ballantrae
	Selected Poems
	Weir of Hermiston
William Makepeace Thackeray	**The History of Henry Esmond**
	The History of Pendennis
	The Newcomes
	Vanity Fair
Anthony Trollope	**Barchester Towers**
	Can You Forgive Her?
	Doctor Thorne
	The Eustace Diamonds
	Framley Parsonage
	He Knew He Was Right
	The Last Chronicle of Barset
	Phineas Finn
	The Prime Minister
	The Small House at Allington
	The Warden
	The Way We Live Now
Oscar Wilde	**Complete Short Fiction**
Mary Wollstonecraft	**A Vindication of the Rights of Woman**
	Mary and **Maria** (includes Mary Shelley's **Matilda**)
Dorothy and William Wordsworth	**Home at Grasmere**